Multilingual glossary of language testing terms

STUDIES IN LANGUAGE TESTING ...6
Series editor: Michael Milanovic

Also in this series:

An investigation into the comparability of two tests of English as a Foreign Language: The Cambridge–TOEFL comparability study
Lyle F. Bachman, F. Davidson, K. Ryan, I–C Choi

Test taker characteristics and performance: A structural modelling approach
Antony John Kunnan

Performance Testing, cognition and assessment: Selected papers from the 15th Language Testing Research Colloquium, Cambridge and Arnhem
Michael Milanovic, Nick Saville

The development of IELTS: A study of the effect of background knowledge on reading comprehension
Caroline M. Clapham

Verbal protocol analysis in language testing research: A handbook
Alison Green

Multilingual glossary of language testing terms

Prepared by ALTE members

ebmi

CAMBRIDGE
UNIVERSITY PRESS

Published by the Press Syndicate of the University of Cambridge
The Pitt Building, Trumpington Street, Cambridge CB2 1RP, UK
40 West 20th Street, New York, NY 10011–4211, USA
10 Stamford Road, Oakleigh, Melbourne 3166, Australia

First published 1998

Printed in Great Britain at the University Press, Cambridge, UK.

British Library cataloguing in publication data

University of Cambridge Local Examinations Syndicate
Multilingual glossary of language testing terms.

Prepared by ALTE Members

1. Education. Assessment 2. Education. Tests. Setting

ISBN 0 521–650992 hard cover
0 521–658772 paperback
0 521–658241 CD-ROM

Contents

Series Editor's note

Since the Association of Language Testers in Europe was set up in 1990, the members have been meeting twice a year to plan and develop projects which will be of benefit to people involved in foreign language testing, and those in industries which use their services. Members of ALTE are engaged in a long-term project, the final aim of which is to establish a framework of critical levels of foreign language performance, which will make it possible to compare and equate qualifications gained in different states of the European Union.

Work on the initial phases of this project produced a number of documents - *European Language Examinations, The ALTE Code of Practice* and *The ALTE Framework* (now combined into one single document - *The ALTE Handbook).*

It became clear at an early stage in this work that, with members speaking at least ten first languages and having to discuss aspects of language testing together, it was vital to have an equivalent terminology related to assessment and language testing in all the languages. In conducting the business of ALTE, we have to be sure that we are able to use technical and semi-technical terms with precision, and that terms in different languages which appear to mean the same as one another really do. Initial work on this multilingual glossary was based on a CITO in-house glossary, which proved of great value as a starting point.

It was particularly important that a terminology of language testing terms should be established for the less commonly used and taught languages of the European Union, several of which are represented in ALTE, in order to help language testing to become better established and developed in these languages. It was in the less widely spoken languages that a vocabulary of testing and assessment was least well-established, and in some cases it was not clear whether many terms existed at all. Inevitably, it is in the most commonly used and taught languages that the vocabulary of language testing and assessment is most highly developed, and that most of the literature has been produced. A multilingual glossary has a particularly significant role to play in encouraging the development of language testing in less widely taught languages by establishing terms which may be new alongside their well-known equivalents in the commonly-used languages.

The idea of producing a multilingual glossary of assessment and language testing terms has thus grown out of the needs experienced by members of ALTE while engaged in work on their framework project. Such a glossary will be of great use, not only to members of ALTE, but to the many others working in the context of European languages who are involved in language testing and assessment. The glossary also exists as a CD and work is in progress to add Finnish, Norwegian, Swedish and Greek.

Volume 7 in this series is the Dictionary of Language Testing. This is not multilingual, but will serve as a useful reference document to the Glossary.

Acknowledgements

The overall co-ordination of the work carried out on the Glossary by the ALTE partners and by staff at UCLES was provided by Michael Milanovic and Nick Saville.

The text layout and editing was carried out by Isabelle Salenbier and Paulo Pinto da Cunha.

We would also like to thank the following people for their collaboration:

Catalan:

Núria Jornet i Saló and Lluís Ràfols i Ràfols from the Departament de Cultura of the Direcció General de Política Lingüística, Generalitat de Catalunya.

Danish:

John E. Andersen, Peter Villads Vedel and Lars Skov from the Danish Language Testing Consortium.

The translation was carried out by Hans Henrik Sorgenfrey from the Departament of Youth and Adult Education, Ministry of Education.

Dutch:

John H. A. L. de Jong, Marie-Christine Sprengers, José van Zuijlen, Inge Hermsen, Hoetjes, Geer Furtjes and Marion Feddema from CITO, The Netherlands.

English:

Chris Banks, Neil Jones, Rosalie Kerr and Simon Beeston, from UCLES.

Additional checking and proof reading was provided by Marianne Hirtzel.

Comments on earlier drafts were also made by Antony Kunnan, Lyle Bachman, Fred Davidson and Caroline Clapham.

French:

Gilles Breton from the Alliance Française (Paris) and Christine Tagliante from the Centre International d'Études Pédagogiques.

German:

Dr. Sibylle Bolton from the Goethe-Institut, Jens U. Schmidt from the Bundesinstitut für Berufsbildung who translated most of the testing terms into German and Uwe Richter from the Anglia Polytechnic University, Cambridge.

Irish:
Colm Breatnach from the Terminology Committee, Department of Education, and Eoghan Mac Aogáin, Siuán Ní Mhaonaigh and Dónall Ó Baoill from ITÉ/The Linguistics Institute of Ireland.

Italian:
Giuliana Grego Bolli from the Assessment and Certification Unit of the Università per Stranieri di Perugia, who prepared the Italian version of this Glossary.

Further support was received from Paola Bianchi De Vecchi, Rector of the University, and Anna Ciliberti.

Portuguese:
José Pascoal, from the Departamento de Língua e Cultura Portuguesa (DLCP) da Universidade de Lisboa (UL), who prepared the Portuguese version of this Glossary.

Further support was received from João Malaca Casteleiro, President of the DLCP da UL.

Spanish:
Clara de Vega from Cursos Internacionales de la Universidad de Salamanca, who prepared the Spanish version of this Glossary.

Contributions to the drafting of the Glossary in Spanish were received from José Luis Rodríguez Diéguez and Esperanza Herrera García from the Departamento de Didáctica, Organización y Métodos de Investigación of the Universidad de Salamanca.

Further comments were received from José J. Gómez Asencio, Juan Eguiluz, Alberto Buitrago, Juan Miguel Prieto, Juan Felipe García Santos, Javier de Santiago, Jesús Fernandez and Charles Stansfield.

Introduction

About ALTE

Introduction

The Association of Language Testers in Europe (ALTE) is an association of institutions within Europe, each of which produces examinations and certification for language learners. Each member provides examinations of the language which is spoken as a mother tongue in their own country or region.

The concept of ALTE was initially formed by the universities of Cambridge and Salamanca late in 1989, and at the first meeting of the association in 1990 there were eight founder members. Since then membership has grown so that there are now 18 full institutional members, representing 15 European languages. A number of associate members are in the process of joining.

Members

The current members of ALTE, and the languages in which they specialize, are as follows:

Alliance Française	*French*
Centre de Langues Luxembourg (CLL)	*Luxembourgish*
CITO	*Dutch*
Danish Language Testing Consortium	*Danish*
Deutscher Volkshochschul-Verband (DVV)	*German*
Goethe-Institut	*German*
Generalitat de Catalunya (Direcció General de Política Lingüística)	*Catalan*
Institiúid Teangeolaíochta Éireann (ITÉ)	*Irish*
Instituto Cervantes	*Spanish*
Universidad de Salamanca	*Spanish*
Universidade de Lisboa	*Portuguese*
Università per Stranieri, Perugia	*Italian*
Certificaat Nederlands als Vreemde Taal (CNaVT) (Université Catholique de Louvain and Dutch Language Union)	*Dutch*

University of Athens	*Greek*
Universitetet i Bergen	*Norwegian*
University of Cambridge Local Examinations Syndicate (UCLES)	*English*
Jyväskylän yliopisto	*Finnish*
Stockholms Universitet	*Swedish*

With the breaking down of international barriers between European states and increasing opportunities for the members of the workforce to move from one country to another, the need for transferability of qualifications is clear.

Employers and employees alike need to know what language qualifications gained in various countries mean – what the holder of a given certificate can actually be expected to be able to do – and how to make meaningful comparisons between qualifications gained in different states of the European Union. Employers need to know which particular language qualification it is realistic to demand when advertising a post, and employees have an interest in being able to rate their own present level of expertise and future training needs. Since 1990 the members of ALTE have been working together to devise a means of describing and comparing their examinations.

Objectives

The principal objectives of ALTE are:

- to establish common levels of proficiency in order to promote the transnational recognition of certification in Europe;

- to establish common standards for all stages of the language-testing process: that is, for test development, task and item writing, test administration, marking and grading, reporting of test results, test analysis and reporting of findings;

- to collaborate on joint projects and in the exchange of ideas and know-how.

The first of these objectives is particularly relevant to the needs of the workforce. The goal of establishing common levels of proficiency is being pursued by means of a long-term 'ALTE Framework Project'. The first stage of this project was achieved in 1991 with the publication of a document describing the general language examinations offered by all ALTE members. All the examinations included were described using the same format, and details given of recognition as educational or workplace qualifications, the relative importance attached to different skills, the testing focus of each paper, and the number and types of questions used. With the expansion of the membership of ALTE, this document has been fully revised and updated.

As for the second of ALTE's objectives, in making comparisons between qualifications in different languages it is important not only to establish the framework of levels on which the examinations can be placed, but to agree on the standards to which they are produced. The members of ALTE have jointly developed a Code of Practice which specifies a set of principles to which all members adhere.

The ALTE Framework

In developing a framework of levels for the comparison of language tests, ALTE members have drawn heavily on the work of the Council of Europe and, in recent years, ALTE as an association has been able to make its own contributions to a number of Council of Europe projects, including the development of Vantage Level and work on the Common European Framework of Reference for Language Learning and Teaching.

Specification of Objectives: Waystage and Threshold

The ALTE Framework comprises five main levels. The first two have been defined respectively as Waystage User and Threshold User, terms taken from the work of the Council of Europe. In 1971 the Council recognized the importance of dividing the task of learning a language into smaller units, each of which could be credited separately, and also the necessity of basing curricula on learners' needs rather than on language structures, as had previously been common practice. One of the major outcomes of this work is the Threshold Level specification (van Ek, 1975) which proposed a model for the description of language ability based on the principle that language teaching should provide learners with the means of meeting their personal communicative needs. A lower level specification was also produced, under the name Waystage Level. In 1991 revised and updated versions of both documents appeared as Threshold Level 1990 and Waystage Level 1990 (by J. A. van Ek and J. L. M. Trim, published by Council of Europe Press). These documents are now also available from Cambridge University Press (ISBNs 0-521-56707-6 and 0-521-56706-8).

Many of the members of ALTE also offer examinations at Level 3 and there was therefore considerable interest among ALTE members when the Council of Europe expressed an interest in producing a Level 3 description beyond Threshold. In 1995, ALTE agreed to co-sponsor the development of this level description, known as Vantage Level.

The development work, carried out by Trim and van Ek in 1996, adhered to the existing model set for their earlier descriptions in order to maintain a coherent progression for the audience, and in general they set out to provide an objective 'as far above Threshold as Waystage is below it'.

On publication of this volume, Vantage Level is still in its piloting phase and as such has not yet been fully incorporated into the ALTE Framework in the same way as Waystage and Threshold. Nevertheless some aspects are clearly relevant to the definition of Level 3 in the ALTE Framework.

Vantage Level provides language users with an objective which takes them beyond the stage where they have acquired the minimal means needed to transact the business of everyday life and to make social contact with those they meet in another country. In linguistic terms, they will have at their disposal an expanded range of grammar and vocabulary as well as greater control of discourse and conversational strategies and greater socio-cultural awareness. This allows them to be more flexible in dealing with the unexpected and with the normal complexities of daily living, including use of their foreign language in the workplace or for study purposes.

The ALTE Framework of Language Examinations includes the examinations provided by ALTE members at each of the five levels. All five ALTE levels are characterized in the summaries given below and for Levels One and Two reference is made to Waystage and Threshold. In general, the brief descriptions are divided into what the candidates can do receptively and what they can do in terms of production and interaction.

Examples, rather than full descriptions, of what users at each level can do are given.

ALTE Level One – Waystage User

Examinations provided by ALTE members at Level One are influenced by the Council of Europe's 'Waystage 90' specification. At this level, users are acquiring a general basic ability to communicate in a limited number of the most familiar situations in which language is used in everyday life. Users at this level need to be able to understand the main points of simple texts, many of which are of the kind needed for survival when travelling or going about in public in a foreign country. At this level, they are using language for survival and to gain basic points of information.

Productive skills

Speaking

In social and travel contexts, users at this level can ask for goods in shops where goods are on display, and order a meal in a restaurant if dishes are either displayed or illustrated on the menu. They can book a hotel room (face-to-face) and ask simple questions of a host family. In a post office or bank, they can ask for basic services, and they can indicate the nature of a medical problem to a doctor, although they would probably need to supplement their explanation with gestures. On a guided tour they can understand simple information given in a predictable situation, but their ability to follow up with questions and requests for further information is very limited.

In the workplace they can state simple requirements within their own job area and pass on simple messages.

If studying, they can ask simple questions, for example to check instructions or ask for information, but cannot understand more than a very brief answer.

Writing

In social and travel contexts, users at this level can write a simple fax or letter, for example, to book a hotel room, and can fill in a form to register at a hotel or join a bank. They can write a brief factual note or a simple 'thank-you' letter.

In the workplace, also, they can write a message or request to a colleague of a simple routine type. They can note down instructions and requests such as clients' orders and delivery dates.

If studying, they can note down times, dates and places from classroom boards or notice boards.

Receptive skills

Reading

In social and travel contexts, 'Waystage' users can read such things as road signs, store guides and simple written directions, price labels, names on product labels, common names of food on a standard sort of menu, bills, hotel signs, basic information from adverts for accommodation, signs in banks and post offices and on cash machines and notices related to use of the emergency services.

In the workplace, they can identify standard letters such as orders and enquiries, and derive basic information from factual texts within their own area of expertise. They can understand short, standard notices (e.g. 'No Smoking').

If studying, they can get basic information such as class times from notices, and make some limited use of sources of information such as computers and bilingual dictionaries. At this level users are unlikely to be able to study an academic subject through the medium of a foreign language, and are most likely to be studying the language itself.

Listening

In social and travel contexts, users at this level can understand such things as simple house rules such as meal-times and location of rooms, prices in shops, simple questions and instructions from a doctor, the cost and terms of renting a flat, simple directions on how to get to places and routine questions asked at immigration.

In the workplace, they can understand simple instructions and receive a simple phone message in a familiar and predictable context.

If studying, they can follow a very simple presentation or demonstration, as long as it is illustrated with diagrams and examples, and in a familiar field of study. They can understand basic instructions about class times and dates and details about when assignments are to be carried out.

ALTE Level Two – Threshold User

Examinations provided by ALTE members at Level Two are influenced by the Council of Europe's 'Threshold 90' specification. At this level users should be able to cope linguistically in a range of everyday situations which require a largely predictable use of language. Much of what learners at this level can do involves a better understanding of the types of texts from which 'Waystage' users can derive only the most basic points of information. Understanding at Level 2 differs in that it goes beyond merely being able to pick out facts and may involve opinions, attitudes, moods and wishes.

Several of the examinations provided by members of ALTE at Level 2 are used as measures of language ability for official or institutional purposes, such as entry to courses of study and as part of degree courses.

Productive skills

Speaking

In social and travel contexts, users at this level can buy goods in counter service shops, and order a meal in a restaurant, asking questions about the dishes on the menu and the services (such as use of credit cards) available. They can book a hotel room over the phone, and deal with most situations likely to arise while staying in a hotel. They can deal with a small number of routine situations in a bank, and ask questions about post office services. They can make a medical appointment over the phone, and give a simple explanation of a problem to a doctor, dentist or pharmacist. As tourists, they can get standard information from a Tourist Information office, and understand the main points of a guided tour, asking some simple questions for further information.

In the workplace, they can exchange opinions with colleagues as long as the topic is predictable, pass on messages and offer advice to clients within their own area of expertise.

If studying, they can ask simple questions, for example, for clarification, and take a limited part in a seminar or tutorial.

Writing

In social and travel contexts, users at this level can write short notes and messages and simple personal letters of a narrative or descriptive type, such as 'thank-you' letters and postcards.

In the workplace, they can write a short note of request and record a routine order. They can make notes during a meeting for their own purposes, and write a straightforward routine letter, although this will need to be checked by a colleague.

If studying, they can write down some information at a lecture, provided extra time is given for this. They can take notes from written sources, though these may well contain inaccuracies. They can write a simple narrative, but not an academic essay.

Receptive skills

Reading

In social and travel contexts, 'Threshold' users can understand most of the language on an ordinary menu, routine letters and forms, adverts and brochures related to hotels or other forms of accommodation. They can understand most labels on everyday medical and food products, and follow simple instructions for use of medicines and cooking instructions found on food packaging. As a general point, they can distinguish between personal and promotional mail from institutions such as banks, and get the general meaning of simple articles in newspapers or leaflets produced by post offices and banks.

In the workplace, they can read and act on standard letters which fall within their own work area. If given enough time, they can understand a report on a familiar topic. Instructions and product descriptions are also within the range of understanding at this level, provided that the language is simple and the subject matter predictable.

If studying, reading speed for longer texts is likely to be slow. They can understand a graphic presentation of a familiar topic, as long as not much text is involved. They can extract information from a textbook or article if it is presented in simplified form or if they are given plenty of time and they can make use of support materials such as dictionaries.

Listening

In social and travel contexts, users at this level can cope well enough to take part in a routine conversation on predictable topics to deal with most situations which might arise during a stay in a hotel. They can understand the general outline of a guided tour, the general meaning of a TV broadcast, and a simple phone message, but in each case the topic must be predictable and familiar.

In the workplace, users can take a routine order and deal with a predictable request from a visitor, for example, a request for a taxi to be called. They can take part in exchanges of opinions on familiar, predictable matters.

If studying, users at this level can understand some parts of a lecture and take a limited part in a seminar or tutorial, but only if allowances are made for the presence of non-native speakers. They can understand instructions on classes or assignments given by a teacher or lecturer.

ALTE Level Three – Independent User

Level Three may be referred to as an intermediate stage of proficiency. Users at this level are expected to be able to handle the main structures of the language with some confidence, demonstrate knowledge of a wide range of vocabulary and use appropriate communicative strategies in a variety of social situations. Their understanding of spoken language and written texts should go beyond being able to pick out items of factual information, and they should be able to distinguish between main and subsidiary points and between the general topic of a text and specific detail. They should be able to produce written texts of various types, showing the ability to develop an argument as well as describe or recount events. This level of ability allows the user a certain degree of independence when called upon to use the language in a variety of contexts. At this level the user has developed a greater flexibility and an ability to deal with the unexpected and to rely less on fixed patterns of language and short utterances. There is also a developing awareness of register and the conventions of politeness and degrees of formality as they are expressed through language.

Examinations at ALTE Level Three are frequently used as proof that the learner can do office work or take a non-academic course of study in the language being learned, e.g. in the country where the language is spoken. Learners at this level can be assumed to have sufficient expertise in the language for it to be of use in clerical, secretarial and managerial posts, and in some industries, such as tourism, in particular.

Productive skills

Speaking

In social and travel contexts, users at this level can deal with most situations that may arise in shops, restaurants, and hotels; for example, they can ask for a refund or for faulty goods to be replaced, and express pleasure or displeasure at the service given. Similarly, routine situations at the doctor's, in a bank or post office or at an airport or station can all be handled. In social conversation they can talk about a range of topics and express opinions to a limited extent. As tourists they can ask for further explanations about information given on a guided tour. They themselves can show visitors around, describe a place and answer questions about it.

In the workplace, users at this level can give detailed information and state detailed requirements within a familiar topic area, and can take some limited part in a meeting. They can take and pass on messages, although there may be difficulties if these are complex, and can carry out simple negotiations, for example on prices and conditions of delivery.

If studying, users at this level can ask questions during a lecture or presentation on a familiar or predictable topic, although this may be done with some difficulty. They can also give a short, simple presentation on a familiar topic. They can take part in a seminar or tutorial, again with some difficulty.

Writing

In social and travel contexts, users at this level can write most kinds of letters connected with accommodation, and can also write personal letters on a limited range of predictable topics.

In the workplace, users can produce a range of written documents but may need to have these checked by a native speaker if accuracy and register are important. They can produce texts which describe and give detailed information, e.g. about a product or service, as long as it is within a familiar area of work and they can write requests, also within a predictable range. They can take and pass on messages, but may have difficulty if these are lengthy or complex. They can take dictation if the pace is fairly slow, and there are opportunities for checking.

If studying, users at this level can make notes in lectures and seminars which are of some limited use for revision purposes, but may find this difficult unless extra time is given. They can also make notes from written sources, although key points may be missed, and they may not be sufficiently selective. They can write an essay which shows some ability to communicate, or an account of an experiment which demonstrates basic understanding of the work done.

Receptive skills

Reading

In social and travel contexts, users at this level can read texts which are longer than the very brief signs, notices, etc. which are characteristic of what can be handled at the two lower levels. They can go beyond routine letters and the most basic newspaper and magazine articles, and have developed reading skills related to factual topics in which they have a special interest or to their own tastes in fiction. In everyday, practical situations, such as eating out, shopping and using services such as banks, they can read competently enough to deal with anything which does not involve some kind of specialized language (such as legal terms in a tenancy agreement).

In the workplace, they can deal with routine letters and understand the general meaning of a fair range of non-routine correspondence, although complex situations and the use of non-standard language would cause problems. They can handle short reports or articles on predictable topics, and grasp the general meaning of a report or article on a less familiar topic, but misunderstanding is likely where information is not clearly expressed. Instructions and product descriptions within the learner's own area of work can be understood, but only the general meaning of more theoretical material (e.g. technical reports) can be understood without access to support such as dictionaries, even when it is within the learner's area of expertise.

At this level, users are likely to have enough language ability to cope with some non-academic training courses which are conducted in the language being learnt. Users at this level can follow a lecture, presentation or demonstration on a familiar topic or where the context is well known, but are likely to have difficulty in following abstract argumentation. They can read simple textbooks and articles, but cannot read quickly enough to cope with an academic course.

Listening

In social and travel contexts, users at this level can cope with casual conversation on a fairly wide range of familiar, predictable topics, such as personal experiences, work and current events. They can understand routine medical advice. They can understand most of a TV programme because of the visual support provided, and grasp the main points of a radio programme. On a guided tour they have the understanding required in order to ask and answer questions.

In the workplace, they can follow presentations or demonstrations of a factual nature if they relate to a visible, physical object such as a product.

If studying, they can understand the general meaning of a lecture, as long as the topic is predictable.

ALTE Level Four – Competent User

At this level, users are expected to be able to use the structures of a language with ease and fluency. They are aware of the relationship between the language and the culture it exists in, and of the significance of register. This means that to some extent they are able to adapt their language use to a variety of social situations, and express opinions and take part in discussions and arguments in a culturally acceptable way. Users at this level can develop their own interests in reading both factual and fictional texts. They can also produce a variety of types of texts and utterances, such as letters of varying degrees of formality. They can use language in a creative and flexible way, with the ability to respond appropriately to unforeseen as well as predictable situations, producing quite long and complex utterances.

The written and spoken texts encountered in most common everyday situations can be dealt with at a level below that reached by the Level Four User, but some of the more difficult situations connected with renting accommodation demand this level of language. Users at this level can enjoy a wide range of social contacts.

Examinations at Level Four may be used as proof of the level of language necessary to work at a managerial or professional level or follow a course of academic study at university level.

Productive skills

Speaking

In social and travel contexts, users at this level are beyond the stage of having any problems in dealing with many of the routine situations of everyday life, such as those which arise in shops, restaurants, banks and hotels. They can take part in lengthy casual conversations, and discuss abstract or cultural topics fluently and with a good range of expression. Nuances of meaning and opinion are not beyond their grasp, but there may be difficulties when talking about sensitive or complex issues. With this degree of competence, they can handle the requirements of entertaining socially, or of being entertained as a guest. Users at this level are able to participate quite actively in and enjoy a foreign culture.

In the workplace, they can argue a point persuasively, and ask questions which go outside their own immediate area of responsibility or expertise. They can contribute effectively to meetings and seminars within their own area of work, and give a presentation or demonstration. Users at this level can use the telephone for most business purposes.

If studying, users at this level can give a clear presentation on a familiar topic, but may have difficulty developing or explaining complex points, or answering unpredictable questions. In a seminar or tutorial, they can present and, to some extent, justify their opinions, but may not be able to handle probing or hostile questioning.

Writing

In social and travel contexts, users at this level can write personal letters, only encountering difficulties where very complex issues arise, and they can produce some of the more formal types of letters, such as a letter to a newspaper.

In the workplace, they can deal with routine requests for goods and services, but may need help to deal with a situation which demands tact or delicacy. They can take dictation and make notes, provided that very complex, delicate or abstract matters are not being dealt with. They can write letters of many familiar types, such as enquiry, complaint, request and application.

If studying, users at this level can take notes in a lecture or seminar which will be useful for later writing or revision. They can make notes from written sources and write an essay, although errors of grammar and vocabulary, as well as style, may occur. Similarly, an account of an experiment may be written fairly adequately, but occasional errors may occur, and conclusions may not be adequately supported.

Receptive skills

Reading

In social and travel contexts, users at this level can understand magazine and newspaper articles, although complex plots, arguments and humour may present difficulties.

In the workplace, they can understand instructions, articles and reports, as long as, in most of these cases, the topic area is within the learner's own field, and no particularly complex concepts and arguments or unusual vocabulary are involved.

If studying, reading related to the user's own subject area presents problems only when abstract or metaphorical language and cultural allusions are frequent. However, the user still has difficulty getting through the amount of reading required on an academic course, and may not be able to cope with postgraduate study.

Listening

In social and travel contexts, Level Four users can cope with everyday life up to the level of being able to understand details of accommodation arrangements such as tenancy agreements. They have sufficient competence in comprehension to cope with being entertained or entertaining socially, and taking part in a variety of casual conversations. They can understand a great deal of what is available on TV and radio and in plays and films, but complex plots and detailed arguments will escape them.

In the workplace they can understand most of what takes place in meetings and seminars within their own area of work. They can follow arguments unless they are very complex or abstract.

If studying, users at this level can follow much of what is said in a lecture, demonstration or presentation, seminar or tutorial, although unfamiliar accents, cultural allusions and jokes, unfamiliar or complex subject matter and colloquial language may cause difficulties.

ALTE Level Five – Good User

At this level the learner is approaching the linguistic competence of an educated native speaker, and is able to use the language in a range of culturally appropriate ways. Users at this level are able to improve their use of the language by extending their vocabulary and refining their usage and command of style and register rather than by learning about new areas of grammar. Their level of competence gives them access to the press and other media, and to areas of the culture such as drama, film and literature.

Success in examinations at this level may be seen as proof that the learner is able to cope with high level academic work. Such examinations frequently have some cultural or academic content, often in the form of an optional component.

Productive skills

Speaking

In social and travel contexts, a Level Five user can cope with ease with the language use situations of everyday life, including conversations on a variety of topics and in a variety of contexts. Lapses in understanding or appropriacy of language use which occur are likely to be minor, and users at this level have the strategies for repairing misunderstandings. They can also handle phone conversations with people they know on a variety of topics.

In the workplace, they can argue a case effectively, justifying demands and specifying needs clearly. They can handle a wide range of non-routine as well as routine situations arising out of dealings with colleagues and outside contacts. In meetings they can participate fully in discussions and arguments. If unknown terms are used, they can check them or compensate for lack of knowledge in the same way a native speaker would.

If studying, users at this level can give a presentation or demonstration, handling questions or criticisms appropriately, although a complex, theoretical matter may prove difficult to explain. They can take an active part in seminars and tutorials, arguing and expressing disagreement without giving offence.

Writing

In the social and travel context, all normal uses of writing are available at a level below this.

In the workplace, learners at this level can handle a wide range of non-routine as well as routine situations arising out of dealings with colleagues and outside contacts. They can take dictation on all matters likely to arise in their area of expertise, but may need to use a dictionary to check spellings, just as a native speaker would. In meetings, they can make full and accurate notes while continuing to follow discussions and arguments and participate in them. Correspondence, even of a specialist type, can be understood at this level, and the learner can write any type of letter demanded by the area of work. They can write reports without taking much longer than a native speaker, and without the risk of more than occasional, minor errors, and can write a set of instructions with little risk of error, even when complex or sensitive issues are involved.

If studying, users at this level can make useful notes from text, and write essays with only the occasional error in grammar or vocabulary. They can write accounts of experiments with sensitivity to the conventions of presentation and style.

Receptive skills

Reading

In social and travel contexts, users at this level can cope with all areas of the media with little risk of misunderstanding.

In the workplace, they can deal with correspondence, even where specialist areas of knowledge are involved. Reports and articles are also fully accessible, with the possibility of difficulties only where very complex or technical points are being made.

If studying, they can use written sources of information effectively. In dealing with texts, reading speed is still slow for a postgraduate level of study, and culturally remote references in the material may interfere with understanding. Sources of information can be accessed, the usefulness of materials assessed and dictionaries used effectively.

Listening

In social and travel contexts, users at this level can cope with most of what is available in the media.

In the workplace, such learners can follow presentations, demonstrations, with difficulties only where complex theoretical information, of a kind which might also present difficulties to a native speaker, is given.

If studying, they can cope with lectures, presentations and demonstrations, although jokes and allusions and unfamiliar accents could cause difficulties.

Other ALTE Projects

Besides establishing the ALTE Framework, ALTE members have also worked on a number of other projects which relate to the three principal objectives mentioned earlier. The projects, several of which received funding from the European Commission under the Lingua Project, are listed below with a brief explanation.

The Content Analysis Checklists Project

This Project relates to the description of test content, and the development of an instrument to allow for a systematic comparison of examination materials across various languages. The instrument has been designed to offer two levels of description:

i. a brief checklist which permits rapid assessment of the salient features of a test;

ii. a more detailed checklist which allows for the specific description of materials within components of a test battery or for test tasks used for various purposes.

The Item-writer Guidelines Project

This project set out to produce a guide for materials writers who are employed in the production of test materials. These guidelines have been translated into many of the ALTE languages and can be used as the basis of a taught course or can be adapted as self-access materials. The areas covered include: Models of Language Ability; The Test Production Process; Item Types; and Issues in Marking and Scoring.

Competency-based Proficiency Scales

This project concerns the development of competency-based proficiency scales, or 'can-do' statements, which have been written and grouped at the five levels in the ALTE Framework. These 'can-do' statements, as the term suggests, are a series of statements which define what a language learner can reasonably be expected to do in typical situations (to carry out particular activities in specific environments) at the different levels of competence. They cover the range from post-beginner (Level 1) to advanced (Level 5) and have been grouped according to three contextual categories of language use (which broadly speaking relate to the domains of the Common European Framework, which is described below):

- Social and Tourist (public and personal domains)
- The Workplace (the occupational domain)
- Study (the educational domain)

Each of these categories is sub-divided into areas of concern which relate to situated language use with reference to the necessary skills (speaking, listening, reading, writing). The project is an attempt to address the important question of communication between the stakeholders in the testing process (test takers, teachers, employers etc.), and focuses in particular on the interpretation of test results by non-specialists.

The Council of Europe: a Common European Framework of Reference for Language Learning and Teaching

The Council of Europe's *Common European Framework of Reference for Language Learning and Teaching* project was one of the main components in Phase 2 of the more extensive project, *Language Learning for European Citizenship* (1989–1996).

ALTE members were involved in various stages of the development work of the Common European Framework and in particular ALTE was commissioned by the Council of Europe to prepare a supplementary document intended for people involved in language test development. This document is entitled 'User's Guide for Examiners'. The work to produce this User's Guide was able to draw extensively on work completed for The Item-writer Guidelines Project.

Certain aspects of the Common Framework have already had an influence on the way ALTE members describe their examinations. In particular this relates to the specification of domains and communicative activities. In this view of communication, the language user's communicative competence is activated through various language activities which are themselves contextualised within domains. These domains are broadly classified as fourfold: personal, public, occupational and educational and the communicative activities are sub-divided into those which are productive, receptive, interactive and mediating.

- Production includes speaking activities as diverse as addressing audiences and singing, while examples of written production include creative writing as well as filling in forms and questionnaires.
- Receptive activities concern listening and reading, including specific purposes for these activities, listening or reading for gist, for specific

information, for detailed understanding, etc.

- Interactive activities may be spoken or written. For speaking, these range from formal discussion, debate and interviews to informal conversations and verbal exchanges. For writing they include the exchange of correspondence by memos, faxes, letters and e-mail.
- Mediating activities include translation, interpretation, summarizing and paraphrasing in order to facilitate communication between others.

This work is consistent with the ALTE projects to develop competency-based proficiency scales and ALTE's attempts to describe examinations in terms of what language users at each level 'can do'. This is reflected in the descriptions given earlier.

1 Català: Glossari multilingüe de termes d'avaluació de llengua

1 acord de qualificadors Vegeu les definicions d'acord interqualificador i acord intraqualificador.

CA:1, DA:307, DE:56, EN:312, ES:10, FR:1, GA:70, IT:84, NE:36, PO:1.

2 acord interqualificador Grau de concordança entre dos avaluadors o més en la mateixa mostra d'actuació. Té especial rellevància en l'avaluació d'habilitats d'expressió oral i expressió escrita en proves que requereixen opinions subjectives dels examinadors.

CA:2, DA:31, DE:159, EN:181, ES:11, FR:2, GA:68, IT:84, NE:185, PO:2.

3 acord intraqualificador Grau de concordança entre dues avaluacions de la mateixa mostra d'actuació fetes en diferents moments pel mateix avaluador. Té especial rellevància en l'avaluació d'habilitats d'expressió oral i expressió escrita en proves que requereixen opinions subjectives dels examinadors.

CA:3, DA:33, DE:163, EN:185, ES:12, FR:3, GA:69, IT:90, NE:190, PO:3.

4 acreditació Atorgament de reconeixement d'un examen, generalment per part d'una institució oficial com ara un organisme governamental, un organisme avaluador, etc.

CA:4, DA:10, DE:8, EN:5, ES:1, FR:4, GA:92, IT:303, NE:3, PO:325.

5 actuació Acte de produir una llengua parlada o escrita. L'actuació, en termes de la llengua produïda realment, sovint es distingeix de la competència, que és el coneixement subjacent d'una llengua.
Compareu: competència.
Vegeu: prova d'actuació.
Més informació: Bachman, 1990, pàg. 52–108.

CA:5, DA:282, DE:283, EN:277, ES:9, FR:297, GA:141, IT:267, NE:286, PO:304.

6 administració Data o període en què té lloc una prova. Algunes proves tenen una data fixada d'administració alguns cops l'any, mentre que d'altres poden ser administrades a petició dels usuaris.

CA:6, DA:403, DE:308, EN:8, ES:77, FR:7, GA:288, IT:331, NE:10, PO:23.

7 adquisició lingüística Procés mitjançant el qual s'adquireix la capacitat en una primera o una segona llengua. En el cas d'una segona llengua, de vegades s'estableix una distinció entre adquisició (i.e. per exposició natural) i aprenentatge (i.e. mitjançant estudi conscient).

CA:7, DA:356, DE:367, EN:204, ES:14, FR:5, GA:349, IT:22, NE:380, PO:24.

8 ajustament Grau de concordança entre les prediccions d'un model i els resultats observats. Es poden calcular diferents índexs d'ajustament. En la teoria de resposta d'ítem, l'anàlisi d'ajustament mostra fins a quin punt l'ítem estimat i els paràmetres personals (per exemple, dificultat i capacitat) prediuen les puntuacions d'una persona en una prova: un ajustament estadístic d'ítems pot ser vist com a anàleg a l'índex de discriminació en l'estadística clàssica.
Vegeu: teoria de resposta d'ítem (TRI).

CA:8, DA:99, DE:248, EN:145, ES:15, FR:6, GA:268, IT:107, NE:135, PO:5.

9 alfa (coeficient alfa) Estimació de fiabilitat que mesura la consistència interna d'una prova. Els valors van de 0 a 1. Sovint s'utilitza per a proves amb escales de valoració i no per a proves amb ítems dicotòmics, encara que es pot fer servir en tots dos tipus de prova. S'anomena també coeficient alfa de Cronbach.
Compareu: Kuder-Richardson.
Vegeu: consistència interna.
Més informació: Henning, 1987, pàg. 84.

CA:9, DA:11, DE:10, EN:10, ES:16, FR:8, GA:10, IT:10, NE:12, PO:6.

10 alfa de Cronbach Vegeu la definició d'alfa (coeficient alfa).

CA:10, DA:54, DE:70, EN:84, ES:17, FR:9, GA:11, IT:11, NE:89, PO:7.

11 àmbit Àrea definida de contingut i/o capacitat que s'avalua en una tasca específica o en una part d'un examen.
Més informació: Bachman, 1990, pàg. 244–246.
CA:11, DA:83, DE:238, EN:119, ES:119, FR:113, GA:137, IT:332, NE:113, PO:129.

12 amplitud Diferència entre el valor màxim i el valor mínim que adopta una variable.
Més informació: Hatch i Lazaraton, 1991, pàg. 169–170.
CA:12, DA:431, DE:431, EN:308, ES:260, FR:241, GA:285, IT:233, NE:311, PO:12.

13 anàlisi d'ítems Descripció de l'actuació de cada ítem d'una prova, generalment usant índexs estadístics clàssics com ara facilitat i discriminació. En aquesta anàlisi s'utilitza software del tipus MicroCAT Iteman.
Vegeu: discriminació, índex de facilitat.
CA:13, DA:161, DE:167, EN:190, ES:25, FR:17, GA:13, IT:12, NE:198, PO:16.

14 anàlisi de covariància Vegeu la definició d'ANCOVA.
CA:14, DA:200, DE:193, EN:12, ES:20, FR:14, GA:16, IT:18, NE:85, PO:13.

15 anàlisi de la prova Anàlisi que es fa després que les proves hagin estat utilitzades amb examinands, sovint amb mètodes estadístics i informàtics. L'objectiu pot ser investigar l'actuació dels examinands o el funcionament de la mateixa prova.
CA:15, DA:389, DE:390, EN:396, ES:22, FR:16, GA:14, IT:17, NE:389, PO:18.

16 anàlisi de necessitats Mètode per determinar les necessitats lingüístiques (en termes d'habilitats, tasques, vocabulari, etc.) d'un grup concret d'aprenents abans de dissenyar un curs per a ells.
CA:16, DA:35, DE:45, EN:246, ES:21, FR:11, GA:19, IT:13, NE:31, PO:17.

17 anàlisi de variància Vegeu la definició d'ANOVA.
CA:17, DA:430, DE:430, EN:13, ES:23/425, FR:15, GA:15, IT:19, NE:418, PO:14.

18 anàlisi del contingut Mitjà per descriure i analitzar el contingut del material d'una prova. Aquesta anàlisi és necessària a fi de garantir que el contingut de la prova en compleix les especificacions. És essencial en establir la validesa de contingut i de constructe.
CA:18, DA:133, DE:153, EN:72, ES:19, FR:12, GA:12, IT:15, NE:178, PO:15.

19 anàlisi del discurs Tipus d'anàlisi centrada en l'estructura i la funció de diverses classes de text oral o escrit.
CA:19, DA:76, DE:86, EN:107, ES:24, FR:13, GA:17, IT:16, NE: 104, PO:19.

20 anàlisi factorial Procediment matemàtic utilitzat per identificar els trets, les capacitats o els factors que expliquen la variància d'una prova a partir de la matriu de correlacions entre els seus ítems. Un grup de variables que estan molt intercorrelacionades constitueix un factor. Un investigador pot iniciar una anàlisi factorial de manera exploratòria, a fi de formular hipòtesis, o de manera confirmatòria, examinant determinades hipòtesis.
Més informació: Bachman, 1990, pàg. 262; Crocker i Algina, 1986, pàg. 232.
CA:20, DA:96, DE:115, EN:142, ES:26, FR:18, GA:18, IT:14, NE:133, PO:20.

21 ANCOVA Tipus d'anàlisi de variància que permet restar estadísticament l'efecte de variables confoses (les que encobreixen els efectes d'altres variables).
Vegeu: ANOVA.
Més informació: Hatch i Lazaraton, 1991, pàg. 387.
CA:21, DA:14, DE:13, EN:17, ES:27, FR:19, GA:20, IT:20, NE:16, PO:21.

22 ANOVA Anàlisi de la significació estadística de les diferències entre les puntuacions mitjanes de dos o més grups amb relació a una o més variables o factors. S'examina la variabilitat de les puntuacions dins del grup i també entre les mitjanes dels grups.
Més informació: Hatch i Lazaraton, 1991, pàg. 308–312.
CA:22, DA:19, DE:20, EN:18, ES:28, FR:20, GA:21, IT:21, NE:19, PO:22.

23 aprovat Puntuació mínima que ha d'assolir un examinand a fi de passar una prova o examen.
Compareu: puntuació de tall.
CA:23, DA:36, DE:52, EN:273, ES:30, FR:277, GA:278, IT:288 NE:341, PO:282.

24 arrodoniment Procés de reduir la precisió d'un nombre disminuint-ne la quantitat de xifres significatives. Per exemple, 564.8 es podria arrodonir per sobre en 565 o per sota en 560. L'escala d'arrodoniment depèn de la precisió requerida.
CA:24, DA:245, DE:331, EN:335, ES:363, FR:22, GA:354, IT:24, NE:11, PO:25.

25 asimetria Característica d'una

distribució en què el pic de la corba està a la dreta del centre (asimetria negativa) o a l'esquerra del centre (asimetria positiva).

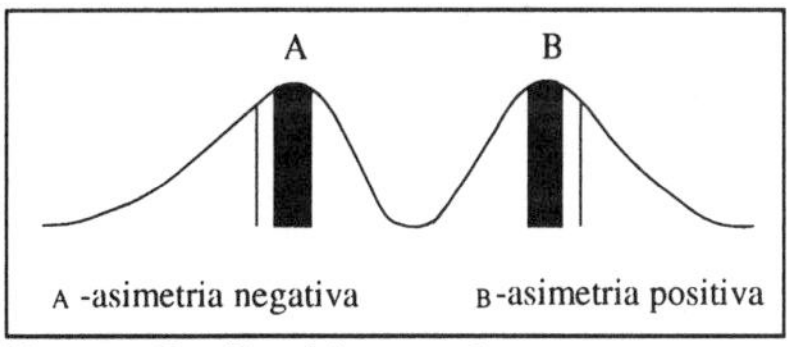

Vegeu: distribució normal.
Més informació: Hatch i Lazaraton, 1991, pàg. 165.
CA:25, DA:343, DE:337, EN:366, ES:31, FR:109, GA:323, IT:25, NE:330, PO:120.

26 assaig Fase en el desenvolupament de les tasques d'una prova que té per objectiu determinar si la prova funciona de la manera prevista. Sovint s'utilitza en tasques de correcció subjectiva, com ara preguntes de redacció, que s'administren a una població limitada.
Compareu: experimentació.
CA:26, DA:301, DE:104, EN:418, ES:135, FR:160, GA:436, IT:336, NE:303, PO:185.

27 autenticitat Com a característica d'una prova, grau en què les tasques d'una prova reflecteixen l'ús de la llengua en una situació real.
Més informació: Bachman, 1990, pàg. 300–303.
CA:27, DA:21, DE:42, EN:24, ES:33, FR:24, GA:115, IT:35, NE:23, PO:26.

28 autenticitat interaccional Consideració de l'autenticitat com una característica de la interacció que té lloc entre qui fa la prova i la tasca de la prova a fi de produir una resposta adequada.
Compareu: autenticitat situacional.
Vegeu: autenticitat.
Més informació: Bachman, 1990, pàg. 315–323.
CA:28, DA:146, DE:157, EN:177, ES:34, FR:25, GA:116, IT:36, NE:183, PO:27.

29 autenticitat situacional Grau en què una prova pot ser considerada versemblant en relació amb el món real, amb situacions reals d'ús de la llengua.
Compareu: autenticitat interaccional, enfocament basat en situacions reals.
Vegeu: autenticitat.
Més informació: Bachman, 1990, capítol 8.
CA:29, DA:336, DE:351, EN:365, ES:35, FR:26, GA:117, IT:37, NE:340, PO:28.

30 autoavaluació Procés en què un estudiant avalua el seu nivell de capacitat, fent una prova que pot ser autoadministrada o mitjançant algun altre recurs com, per exemple, un qüestionari o una llista de control.
CA:30, DA:331, DE:345, EN:354, ES:36, FR:27, GA:142, IT:38, NE:334, PO:29.

31 avaluació a) En proves de llengua, mesura i judici d'un o de més aspectes de la proficiència lingüística mitjançant algun tipus de prova o procediment.
Més informació: Bachman, 1990, pàg. 50.
CA:31, DA:, DE:54, EN:21, ES:180, FR:165, GA:228, IT:418, NE:39, PO:36.

b) Recopilació d'informació amb la intenció d'utilitzar-la com a base de presa de decisions. En proves de llengua, l'avaluació pot centrar-se en l'eficàcia o impacte d'un programa d'ensenyament, un examen o un projecte.
CA:31, DA:93, DE:106, EN:132, ES:180, FR:166, GA:235, IT:413, NE:126, PO:30.

32 avaluació formativa a) Prova que té lloc durant un curs o programa d'ensenyament, i no al final. Els resultats poden permetre al professor donar atenció compensatòria en una fase inicial o canviar l'èmfasi d'un curs si és necessari. Els resultats poden ajudar un estudiant a identificar i focalitzar els seus punts febles.
Compareu: avaluació sumatòria.
CA:32, DA:225, DE:213, EN:147, ES:184, FR:168, GA:232, IT:422, NE:137, PO:32.

b) Avaluació contínua durant un procés. Aquest tipus d'avaluació permet adaptar i millorar el procés. Pot fer referència a un programa d'ensenyament.
Compareu: avaluació sumatòria.
CA:32, DA:226, DE:46, EN:148, ES:184, FR:168, GA:236, IT:414, NE:136, PO:32.

33 avaluació global Mètode de puntuació que pot ser utilitzat en proves d'expressió escrita i expressió oral. L'avaluador dóna una única puntuació segons la impressió general que provoca la producció de l'examinand, sense repartir en diferents puntuacions els diversos aspectes de l'ús de la llengua.
Compareu: puntuació analítica, correcció segons la impressió (correcció segons la impressió general).
CA:33, DA:124, DE:137, EN:155, ES:427, FR:169, GA:231, IT:186, NE:161, PO:33.

34 avaluació sumatòria a) Prova que té lloc en acabar un curs o programa d'ensenyament.
Compareu: avaluació formativa.

CA:34, DA:267, DE:4, EN:390, ES:186, FR:172, GA:233, IT:423, NE:375, PO:36.

b) Avaluació d'un procés que té lloc després d'haver–lo completat. Pot fer referència a un programa d'ensenyament.
Compareu: avaluació formativa.

CA:34, DA:266, DE:3, EN:391, ES:186, FR:172, GA:238, IT:415, NE:374, PO:36.

35 avaluador Persona que assigna una puntuació a l'actuació d'un examinand en una prova, tot utilitzant un judici subjectiu per fer-ho. Els avaluadors normalment estan qualificats en l'àmbit pertinent i han de passar un procés de capacitació i estandardització. En les proves orals, els rols d'avaluador i interlocutor es diferencien de vegades. S'anomena també examinador o qualificador.
Compareu: interlocutor, corrector.

CA:35, DA:32, DE:55, EN:22, ES:46, FR:174, GA:234, IT:165, NE:33, PO:182.

36 banc d'ítems Mètode de gestió dels ítems d'una prova que comporta emmagatzemar informació sobre els ítems per poder elaborar proves de contingut i dificultat coneguts. Normalment s'utilitza una base de dades informàtica i es basa en la teoria del tret latent, que proposa que els ítems es poden relacionar entre si mitjançant una escala de dificultat comuna.
Més informació: Henning, 1987, capítol 9.

CA:36, DA:155, DE:28, EN:191, ES:37, FR:28, GA:40, IT:111, NE:199, PO:37.

37 banda En el sentit més ampli, part d'una escala. En una prova basada en ítems cobreix una varietat de puntuacions que es pot presentar com una qualificació o com una puntuació de banda. En una escala de valoració dissenyada per avaluar un tret específic o una capacitat, com ara l'expressió oral o l'expressió escrita, una banda normalment representa una actuació concreta en un nivell particular.

CA:37, DA:339, DE:44, EN:29, ES:38, FR:200, GA:41, IT:39 NE:28, PO:210.

38 bateria Sèrie de proves o subproves relacionades que fan aportacions independents (per exemple, per avaluar diferents habilitats), però que es poden combinar per produir una puntuació total.

CA:38, DA:28, DE:393, EN:32, ES:40, FR:30, GA:64, IT:41, NE:30, PO:38.

39 bateria de proves Vegeu la definició de bateria.

CA:39, DA:390, DE:406, EN:397, ES:41, FR:31, GA:63, IT:42, NE:390, PO:39.

40 biaix Distribució sistemàtica de l'error de mesura. Una prova o un ítem es poden considerar esbiaixats si un sector concret de la població d'examinands resulta privilegiat o desafavorit per alguna característica de la prova o l'ítem no rellevant per a allò que es vol mesurar. Les fonts de biaix poden estar relacionades amb el sexe, l'edat, la cultura, etc.
Més informació: Bachman, 1990, pàg. 271–279; Crocker i Algina, 1986, capítols 12 i 16.

CA:40, DA:344, DE:383, EN:33, ES:384, FR:32, GA:208, IT:160, NE:46, PO:40.

41 biaix cultural Una prova amb biaix cultural afavoreix o perjudica els examinands amb un antecedent cultural determinat.
Vegeu: biaix.

CA:41, DA:207, DE:201, EN:85, ES:385, FR:33, GA:209, IT:161, NE:90, PO:41.

42 buit d'informació Tècnica d'ensenyament i d'elaboració de proves d'una llengua que simula una comunicació real construint situacions en què els estudiants no comparteixen la mateixa informació i, per tant, han de comunicar-se amb tots els altres a fi de completar una tasca. Normalment s'utilitza per practicar o avaluar les habilitats d'expressió oral i expressió escrita.

CA:42, DA:140, DE:151, EN:172, ES:411, FR:213, GA:43, IT:424, NE:176, PO:223.

43 calibrar En la teoria de resposta d'ítem, calcular la dificultat d'una sèrie d'ítems d'una prova.
Vegeu: calibratge.

CA:43, DA:163, DE:93, EN:39, ES:43, FR:40, GA:48, IT:43, NE:206, PO:47.

44 calibratge Procés de determinar l'escala d'una prova o proves. El calibratge pot implicar ítems àncora de diferents proves en una escala de dificultat comuna (l'escala theta). Quan s'elabora una prova amb ítems calibrats, les puntuacions en la prova indiquen la capacitat de l'examinand i.e. la seva localització en l'escala theta.

CA:44, DA:164, DE:94, EN:40, ES:42, FR:35, GA:49, IT:44, NE:205, PO:42.

45 candidat Vegeu la definició d'examinand.

CA:45, DA:165, DE:302, EN:41, ES:48, FR:41, GA:178, IT:49, NE:207, PO:48.

46 capacitat Tret mental o facultat per fer alguna cosa.
Compareu: competència, proficiència.
Més informació: Bachman, 1990, pàg. 16 i 19.

CA:46, DA:2, DE:113, EN:2, ES:49, FR:42, GA:96, IT:1A, NE:411, PO:49.

47 capacitat lingüística Coneixements o habilitats que defineixen conjuntament la capacitat d'un individu per utilitzar una llengua per a una varietat de propòsits comunicatius.
Més informació: Bachman, 1990, pàg. 3–4.
CA:47, DA:354, DE:368, EN:203, ES:50, FR:43, GA:97, IT:4, NE:379, PO:50.

48 característiques del mètode de prova Característiques definitòries de diferents mètodes de prova. Poden incloure entorn, rúbrica, tipus de llengua de les instruccions, format, etc.
Més informació: Bachman, 1990, capítol 5.
CA:48, DA:397, DE:403, EN:402, ES:51, FR:46, GA:401, IT:50, NE:398, PO:54.

49 categoria a) Divisió d'una escala categòrica; per exemple, "sexe" té les categories "home" i "dona".

b) En una prova, es diu que una escala de valoració amb cinc punts, per exemple, té cinc categories de resposta.
CA:49, DA:169, DE:176, EN:43, ES:52, FR:48, GA:50, IT:51, NE:52, PO:55.

50 certificat Document que exposa que una persona identificada ha fet una prova o una part d'una prova i ha assolit una qualificació determinada, normalment almenys un aprovat.
Compareu: diploma.
CA:50, DA:38, DE:448, EN:47, ES:53, FR:50, GA:386, IT:52, NE:56, PO:56.

51 clau Opció correcta en un ítem d'elecció múltiple.
Compareu: distractor.
Vegeu: ítem d'elecció múltiple.
CA:51, DA:256, DE:339, EN:198, ES:54, FR:329, GA:133, DE:339, IT:53, NE:342, PO:335.

52 clau de respostes Vegeu la definició de model de correcció.
CA:52, DA:256, DE:339, EN:198, ES:54, FR:329, GA:133, DE:339, IT:53, NE:342, PO:335.

53 coeficient Índex numèric utilitzat com a mesura d'una propietat o una característica.
Vegeu: alfa (coeficient alfa), coeficient de correlació.
CA:53, DA:175, DE:178, EN:53, ES:55, FR:54, GA:73, IT:57, NE:62, PO:69.

54 coeficient alfa Vegeu la definició d'alfa.
CA:54, DA:176, DE:179, EN:54, ES:56, FR:55, GA:74, IT:58, NE:63, PO:70.

55 coeficient de correlació Índex estadístic que expressa quantitativament el grau de relació entre dues variables. Varia de -1 a +1. Les variables més correlacionades estan representades per un coeficient de correlació que s'acosta a +1.
Més informació: Guilford i Frutcher, 1981, pàg. 86–88.
CA:55, DA:197, DE:191, EN:79, ES:57, FR:56, GA:75, IT:60, NE:82, PO:71.

56 coeficient de correlació biserial (*rbis*) Coeficient de correlació usat quan una variable és contínua i l'altra és dicotomitzada artificialment. La correlació biserial dóna una estimació del que hauria estat la correlació si la variable dicotomitzada s'hagués deixat com a variable contínua. Normalment, l'estimació és alta. El valor de *rbis* és almenys un 25 % superior al de la correlació biserial puntual (*rbp*). Un avantatge de *rbis* és que es manté força estable a través de mostres de diferent nivell de capacitat.
Compareu: coeficient de correlació biserial puntual.
Vegeu: discriminació.
Més informació: Crocker i Algina, 1986, pàg. 317–318; Guilford i Fruchter, 1981, pàg. 304–311.
CA:56, DA:40, DE:60, EN:35, ES:85, FR:86, GA:79, IT:96, NE:48, PO:101.

57 coeficient de correlació biserial puntual (*rbp*) Correlació entre una variable dicotòmica i una variable contínua. Un avantatge de *rbp* respecte al coeficient de correlació biserial (*rbis*) és que pot ser utilitzada adequadament quan la capacitat subjacent no està distribuïda normalment.
Compareu: coeficient de correlació biserial.
CA:57, DA:41, DE:311, EN:283, ES:86, FR:57, GA:80, IT:97, NE:309, PO:102.

58 coeficient de correlació de Spearman Coeficient de correlació no paramètric que mesura el grau d'associació entre dues variables ordinals.
Vegeu: coeficient de correlació ordinal de Spearman.
CA:58, DA:351, DE:361, EN:373, ES:87, FR:60, GA:83, IT:99, NE:347, PO:73.

59 coeficient de correlació lineal de Pearson Coeficient de correlació que resulta de dividir la covariància de dues variables pel producte de les seves

desviacions estàndard.
Vegeu: coeficient de correlació.
Més informació: Hatch i Lazaraton, 1991, pàg. 427–431; Guilford i Fruchter, 1981, pàg. 81.
CA:59, DA:279, DE:298, EN:274, ES:90, FR:87, GA:84, IT:98, NE:283, PO:104.

60 coeficient de correlació ordinal de Spearman Vegeu la definició de coeficient de correlació de Spearman.
CA:60, DA:304, DE:315, EN:309, ES:89, FR:59, GA:82, IT:100, NE:312, PO:72.

61 coeficient de fiabilitat Índex estadístic que indica la fiabilitat d'una escala, una prova o una altra mesura. Els valors d'aquest coeficient estan entre 0 i 1. Els coeficients de fiabilitat normalment són correlacions entre dues administracions, versions o meitats de la mateixa prova. L'estimació de fiabilitat pot basar-se en l'administració repetida d'una prova (que hauria de produir resultats similars) o, si no es pot fer, en alguna forma de mesura de consistència interna. De vegades s'anomena índex de fiabilitat.
Vegeu: consistència interna, fiabilitat, fiabilitat per test-retest.
CA:61, DA:313, DE:323, EN:328, ES:58, FR:61, GA:77, IT:59, NE:44, PO:74.

62 coeficient fi Coeficient de correlació utilitzat per mostrar el grau de la relació entre dues variables binàries; per exemple, les puntuacions en dos ítems d'una prova valorats com a correcte o incorrecte.
Vegeu: coeficient de correlació.
Més informació: Guilford i Fruchter, 1981, pàg. 316–318; Crocker i Algina, 1986, pàg. 92–94.
CA:62, DA:284, DE:286, EN:279, ES:59, FR:58, GA:76, IT:61, NE:288, PO:75.

63 coincidència tot-part Efecte que es presenta, per exemple, quan les puntuacions en una subprova estan correlacionades amb les puntuacions de tota la prova. Com que les puntuacions de la subprova estan incloses en les puntuacions totals de la prova, la correlació és exagerada. Hi ha tècniques per corregir la coincidència tot-part.
Més informació: Henning, 1987, pàg. 69.
CA:63, DA:62, DE:282, EN:271, ES:387, FR:51, GA:283, IT:146, NE:276, PO:331.

64 competència Coneixement o capacitat per fer alguna cosa. S'utilitza en lingüística per referir-se al coneixement que una persona té del sistema lingüístic i a la capacitat per crear i entendre frases, incloent-hi frases que no ha escoltat mai abans, en oposició a actuació, que és la manifestació de la competència com a llengua en ús. La distinció s'origina en el treball de Chomsky.
Compareu: actuació.
Més informació: Bachman, 1990, pàg. 52 i 108.
CA:64, DA:180, DE:183, EN:59, ES:60, FR:62, GA:191, IT:62, NE:67, PO:76.

65 competència comunicativa Capacitat per utilitzar una llengua de manera adequada en una varietat de situacions i entorns.
Més informació: Bachman, 1990, pàg. 16 i 68.
CA:65, DA:179, DE:182, EN:58, ES:61, FR:63, GA:195, IT:63, NE:66, PO:77.

66 competència discursiva Capacitat d'entendre i produir un discurs. En alguns models de competència lingüística, la competència discursiva es distingeix com un component del model.
Més informació: Bachman, 1990, capítol 4.
CA:66, DA:78, DE:87, EN:108, ES:62, FR:64, GA:196, IT:64, NE:105, PO:78.

67 competència gramatical En un model de capacitat lingüística comunicativa, la competència gramatical és el component que regeix les regles de funcionament del sistema lingüístic: morfologia, sintaxi, vocabulari, fonologia i ortografia.
Més informació: Bachman, 1990, pàg. 84–88.
CA:67, DA:119, DE:138, EN:158, ES:63, FR:65, GA:193, IT:65, NE:162, PO:79.

68 competència lingüística Vegeu la definició de competència.
CA:68, DA:217, DE:224, EN:214, ES:64, FR:67, GA:198, IT:66, NE:231, PO:80.

69 competència pragmàtica Categoria possible en models de capacitat lingüística comunicativa que inclou la capacitat de produir actes de parla i el coneixement de les convencions sociolingüístiques.
Més informació: Bachman, 1990, pàg. 42.
CA:69, DA:294, DE:295, EN:290, ES:66, FR:69, GA:194, IT:68, NE:297, PO:83.

70 competència sociolingüística Categoria possible en models de capacitat lingüística comunicativa que inclou la capacitat d'adaptar el discurs a entorns i a situacions concrets d'acord amb les normes socials.
Més informació: Bachman, 1990, pàg. 42.

CA:70, DA:347, DE:358, EN:369, ES:67, FR:70, GA:197, IT:69, NE:345, PO:84.

71 competència unitària Teoria lingüística, promoguda concretament per Oller, que postula l'existència d'una única competència subjacent a totes les habilitats lingüístiques.

CA:71, DA:91, DE:423, EN:428, ES:68, FR:71, GA:192, IT:70, NE:408, PO:85.

72 compleció gramatical Tipus d'ítem en què només es dóna la meitat d'una oració. La tasca de l'examinand consisteix a completar l'oració, proporcionant els mots adequats (possiblement amb la lectura d'un text) o triant-los entre diverses opcions donades.

CA:72, DA:382, DE:332, EN:357, ES:69, FR:298, GA:93, IT:80, NE:442, PO:86.

73 component Part d'un examen, sovint presentada com una prova separada, amb el seu propi full d'instruccions i límit de temps. Els components sovint es basen en habilitats i tenen títols com ara comprensió oral o composició. S'anomena també subprova.

CA:73, DA:181, DE:306, EN:61, ES:29, FR:72, GA:85, IT:81, NE:128, PO:87.

74 composició discursiva Tasca escrita en què l'examinand ha de dissertar sobre un tema, respecte al qual és possible mantenir diversos punts de vista o argumentar en suport d'opinions personals.
Vegeu: redacció.

CA:74, DA:77, DE:342, EN:113, ES:70, FR:74, GA:52, IT:83, NE:42, PO:89.

75 coneixement previ Coneixement d'un examinand sobre un tema o un contingut cultural en una prova determinada, que pot afectar la manera com l'examinand s'enfronti a l'estímul. Té una rellevància particular en proves de llengua per a propòsits específics.
Més informació: Bachman, 1990, pàg. 273.

CA:75, DA:26, DE:144, EN:27, ES:73, FR:77, GA:134, IT:85, NE:4, PO:91.

76 coneixement sociocultural Coneixement del món relacionat amb la manera com una societat actua en una cultura concreta. És rellevant per a la conducta adequada i l'ús de la llengua en contextos culturals específics.
Compareu: competència sociolingüística.

CA:76, DA:346, DE:357, EN:368, ES:72, FR:341, GA:135, IT:86, NE:344, PO:90.

77 consistència interna Característica d'una prova que representa el grau en què les puntuacions dels examinands en cada ítem de la prova són coherents amb la puntuació total. Es considera una mesura de la fiabilitat de la prova, per a la qual cosa s'usa el coeficient de consistència interna; es poden calcular diversos índexs com, per exemple, KR-20 o alfa.
Vegeu: alfa (coeficient alfa), Kuder-Richardson, fiabilitat.
Més informació: Bachman, 1990, pàg. 172.

CA:77, DA:147, DE:155, EN:180, ES:74, FR:186, GA:87, IT:87, NE:186, PO:93.

78 constructe Capacitat hipotetitzada o tret mental que no es pot mesurar o observar directament; per exemple, en proves de llengua la capacitat de comprensió oral. Les proves de llengua intenten mesurar els diferents constructes subjacents a la capacitat lingüística. A més de la capacitat lingüística, altres constructes rellevants són la motivació, l'actitud i l'aculturació.
Més informació: Hatch i Lazaraton, 1991, pàg. 15.

CA:78, DA:184, DE:185, EN:68, ES:76, FR:80, GA:394, IT:108, NE:72, PO:94.

79 corba característica d'ítem (CCI) En la teoria de resposta d'ítem, una corba característica d'ítem mostra com la probabilitat de respondre correctament un ítem es relaciona amb el tret de capacitat subjacent a l'actuació en els ítems de la prova.
Més informació: Crocker i Algina, 1986, pàg. 340–342.

CA:79, DA:157, DE:168, EN:192, ES:95, FR:90, GA:94, IT:115, NE:196, PO:109.

80 correcció Assignació d'una nota a les respostes d'un examinand en una prova. Pot comportar un judici professional o l'aplicació d'un model de correcció que inclogui totes les respostes acceptables.

CA:80, DA:289, DE:40, EN:222, ES:47, FR:265, GA:218, IT:29, NE:83, PO:57.

81 correcció d'examinador Mètode de correcció aplicat per correctors que han de tenir un nivell de perícia i capacitació especial a fi d'exercir un judici subjectiu. Les proves d'expressió oral i expressió escrita extenses es corregeixen habitualment d'aquesta manera.
Compareu: correcció mecànica.

CA:81, DA:29, DE:107, EN:136, ES:81, FR:272, GA:223, IT:30, NE:131, PO:67.

82 correcció de l'atzar Mètode per disminuir l'obtenció de punts que resulta d'encertar la resposta per atzar en proves construïdes amb ítems de selecció.

Més informació: Ebel i Frisbie, 1986, pàg. 215–218.

CA:82, DA:193, DE:317/450, EN:77, ES:80, FR:83, GA:54, IT:103, NE:77, PO:98.

83 correcció de Spearman-Brown Mètode estadístic d'estimació de la fiabilitat d'una prova en el cas que s'allargui o s'escurci afegint o eliminant ítems. Pot ser utilitzat per predir el nombre d'ítems necessari per tal de satisfer una fiabilitat especificada.

Més informació: Crocker i Algina, 1986, pàg. 118–119.

CA:83, DA:349, DE:359, EN:371, ES:207, FR:197, GA:147, IT:180, NE:350, PO:203.

84 correcció doble Mètode d'avaluar en què dues persones valoren separadament l'actuació d'un examinand en una prova.

Vegeu: correcció múltiple.

CA:84, DA:82, DE:91, EN:121, ES:118, FR:114, GA:221, IT:104, NE:116, PO:61.

85 correcció informatitzada Diverses maneres de fer servir sistemes informàtics per minimitzar els errors en la correcció de proves objectives. Per exemple, es pot escannejar informació mitjançant una màquina de lectura òptica i produir dades que poden ser utilitzades per proporcionar puntuacions i anàlisis.

CA:85, DA:53, DE:69, EN:65, ES:82, FR:273, GA:222, IT:28, NE:69, PO:66.

86 correcció mecànica Mètode de correcció en què els correctors no necessiten exercitar una perícia especial o un judici subjectiu. Corregeixen seguint un model de correcció que especifica totes les respostes acceptables de cada ítem de la prova.

Compareu: correcció d'examinador.

CA:86, DA:23, DE:231, EN:51, ES:78, FR:274, GA:219, IT:31, NE:25, PO:62.

87 correcció múltiple Mètode per augmentar la fiabilitat de valoració de proves d'expressió escrita extensa, en què necessàriament hi ha algun grau de subjectivitat. Consisteix a fer corregir cada resposta d'aquest tipus per separat a més d'un avaluador.

Més informació: Weir, 1988, pàg. 65–66.

CA:87, DA:274, DE:233, EN:240, ES:45, FR:271, GA:183, IT:105, NE:241, PO:63.

88 correcció per atenuació Estimació del coeficient de validesa de criteri que s'obtindria en el cas hipotètic que tant la prova com el criteri fossin totalment fiables.

Més informació: Guilford i Fruchter, 1981, pàg. 450–453; Hatch i Lazaraton, 1990, pàg. 444–445.

CA:88, DA:194, DE:243, EN:76, ES:79, FR:82, GA:53, IT:106, NE:78, PO:99.

89 correcció segons la impressió (correcció segons la impressió general) Mètode de puntuació que pot ser utilitzat en proves d'ús productiu de llengua, i.e. expressió escrita o expressió oral. L'avaluador fa una valoració de cada resposta de l'examinand, sense intentar analitzar cada tret discret de la tasca.

Compareu: puntuació analítica, avaluació global.

CA:89, DA:116, DE:133, EN:168, ES:429, FR:270, GA:220, IT:33, NE:172, PO:68.

90 corrector Persona que assigna una puntuació a les respostes d'un examinand en una prova escrita. Pot comportar la utilització d'un judici expert o, en el cas d'una correcció mecànica, l'aplicació relativament no qualificada d'un model de correcció.

Vegeu: avaluador.

CA:90, DA:288, DE:39, EN:221, ES:83, FR:81, GA:225, IT:102, NE:80, PO:182.

91 correlació Relació entre dues mesures o més, referida al grau en què tendeixen a variar en el mateix sentit. Per exemple, si els examinands tendeixen a assolir un nivell similar en dues proves diferents, hi ha una correlació positiva entre les dues sèries de puntuacions.

Compareu: covariància.

Vegeu: coeficient de correlació de Spearman, coeficient de correlació lineal de Pearson.

Més informació: Guilford i Fruchter, 1981, capítol 6; Bachman, 1990, pàg. 259–260.

CA:91, DA:196, DE:190, EN:78, ES:84, FR:85, GA:78, IT:95, NE:81, PO:100.

92 correlació fi Vegeu la definició de coeficient fi.

CA:92, DA:285, DE:287, EN:280, ES:88, FR:88, GA:81, IT:101, NE:289, PO:103.

93 covariància Mesura de la variància conjunta de dues o més variables. Per exemple, la longitud d'una oració i la dificultat lèxica són característiques d'un text de comprensió lectora que tendirien a estar relacionades, i.e. covariar. S'ha de tenir en consideració la covariància quan es prediu una variable a partir d'unes altres; per exemple, quan es prediu la dificultat d'un text de comprensió lectora a partir de la longitud de les frases i la dificultat lèxica.

Vegeu: variància.

CA:93, DA:199, DE:192, EN:80, ES:91, FR:92, GA:71, IT:112, NE:84, PO:106.

94 currículum Descripció global dels objectius, contingut, organització, mètodes i avaluació d'un curs.
Compareu: programa.
CA:94, DA:55, DE:71, EN:87, ES:93, FR:93, GA:99, IT:113, NE:220, PO:107.

95 curtosi Grau de convexitat o aplatament de la corba de distribució respecte a la distribució normal. Les dades que formen una corba plana mostren una distribució platicúrtica, mentre que les dades que formen una corba convexa mostren una distribució leptocúrtica.

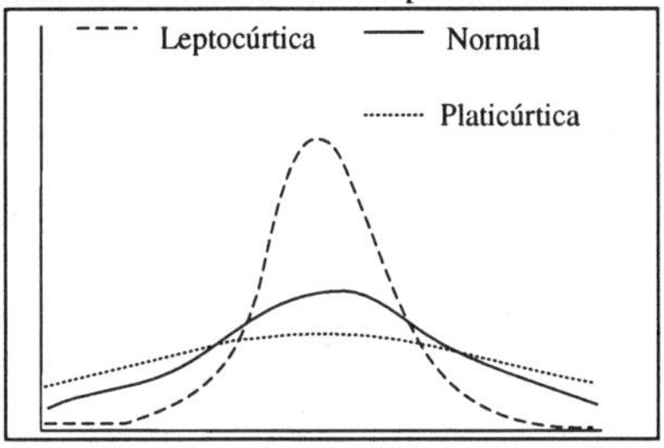

Vegeu: distribució normal.
CA:95, DA:412, DE:108, EN:202, ES:94, FR:428, GA:100, IT:114, NE:213, PO:108.

96 d d'Ebel Vegeu la definició d'índex D.
CA:96, DA:85, DE:92, EN:122, ES:96, FR:94, GA:101, IT:116, NE:117, PO:111.

97 descriptor Descripció breu que acompanya una banda en una escala de valoració i que defineix el grau de competència o el tipus d'actuació esperat per un examinand que assoleix aquesta puntuació determinada.
CA:97, DA:64, DE:76, EN:96, ES:98, FR:97, GA:437, IT:118, NE:96, PO:113.

98 descriptor d'escala Vegeu la definició de descriptor.
CA:98, DA:338, DE:353, EN:344, ES:99, FR:96, GA:438, IT:119, NE:327, PO:112.

99 desenvolupament d'oracions Tipus d'ítem en què es dóna un estímul en forma de sèrie de mots lèxics, però en què no hi ha les preposicions, els verbs auxiliars, els articles, etc. La tasca de l'examinand consisteix a afegir els mots que hi falten de tal manera que es desenvolupi una oració gramatical completa.
CA:99, DA:380, DE:333, EN:358, ES:18, FR:175, GA:148, IT:166, NE:441, PO:184.

100 destinatari de la prova Vegeu la definició d'examinand.
CA:100, DA:402, DE:407, EN:406, ES:190, FR:351, GA:110, IT:49, NE:395, PO:183.

101 desviació estàndard Mesura de la dispersió d'un conjunt d'observacions amb relació a la mitjana aritmètica. És igual a l'arrel quadrada de la variància. En una distribució normal el 68 % de la mostra està dins d'una desviació estàndard de la mitjana i el 95 % dins de dues desviacions estàndard de la mitjana.

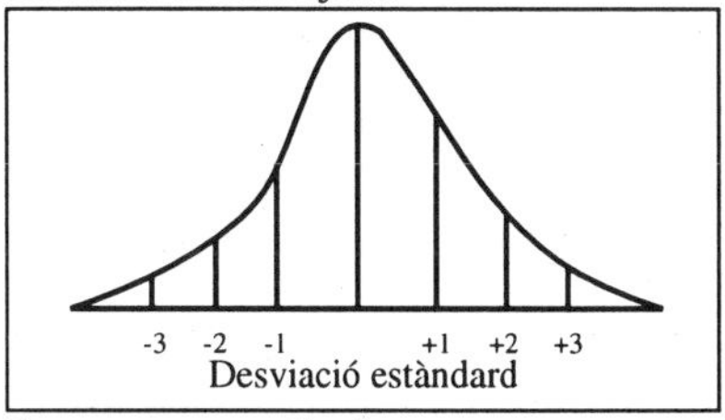

Compareu: amplitud.
Vegeu: variància.
Més informació: Ebel i Frisbie, 1991, pàg. 61–62; Crocker i Algina, 1986, pàg. 21–22.
CA:101, DA:362, DE:372, EN:379, ES:103, FR:98, GA:113, IT:122, NE:360, PO:114.

102 diagrama de barres Mètode per mostrar distribucions de freqüència de variables categòriques en forma gràfica.

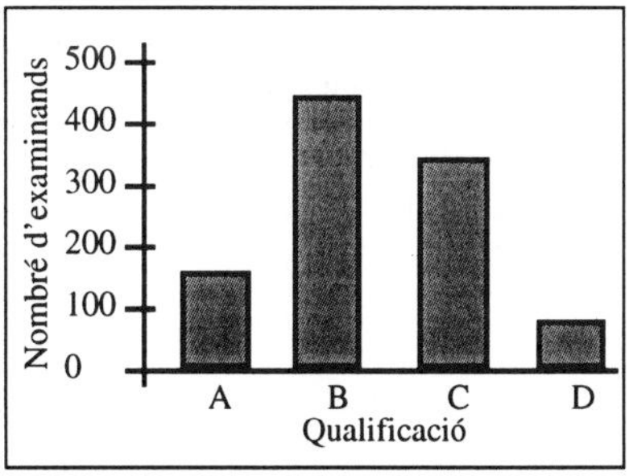

Compareu: histograma.
Més informació: Hatch i Lazaraton, 1991, pàg. 147.
CA:102, DA:383, DE:335, EN:31, ES:104, FR:201, GA:42, IT:123, NE:357, PO:211.

103 dictat Tipus de prova en què l'examinand ha d'escoltar un text i escriure les paraules que sent. Els criteris per corregir els dictats varien segons el propòsit de la prova; poden incloure ortografia i puntuació.
CA:103, DA:68, DE:79, EN:99, ES:105, FR:99, GA:109, IT:121, NE:99, PO:125.

104 diploma Document que exposa que una persona identificada ha fet un examen o una part d'un examen i ha assolit una qualificació determinada, normalment almenys un aprovat. Sovint s'interpreta com un nivell de qualificació superior a un certificat.
Compareu: certificat.
CA:104, DA:69, DE:80, EN:103, ES:106, FR:100, GA:118, IT:124, NE:101, PO:115.

105 discriminació Poder d'un ítem per discriminar entre examinands bons i dolents. S'usen diversos índexs de discriminació. Alguns (per exemple, el biserial o el biserial puntual) es basen en una correlació entre la puntuació d'un ítem i un criteri, com ara la puntuació total en la prova o alguna mesura externa de competència. Altres es basen en la diferència en la dificultat dels ítems per a grups de baixa capacitat i alta capacitat. En la teoria de resposta d'ítem, els models de paràmetre 2 i 3 consideren la discriminació d'un ítem com el paràmetre A.
Vegeu: coeficient de correlació biserial, coeficient de correlació biserial puntual, teoria de resposta d'ítem (TRI).
Més informació: Crocker i Algina, 1986, pàg. 313–320; Ebel i Frisbie, 1991, pàg. 231–232.
CA:105, DA:74, DE:416, EN:112, ES:107, FR:102, GA:180, IT:126, NE:109, PO:116.

106 discurs Text oral o escrit, vist com un acte lingüístic comunicatiu.
CA:106, DA:75, DE:85, EN:106, ES:108, FR:101, GA:119, IT:125, NE:103, PO:117.

107 dispersió Desviació d'un conjunt de valors respecte a un valor central, generalment la mitjana aritmètica.
Vegeu: desviació estàndard, variància, amplitud.
CA:107, DA:353, DE:385, EN:114, ES:110, FR:103, GA:357, IT:127, NE:356, PO:118.

108 disseny multitret-multimètode Disseny experimental que utilitza una matriu de correlació per examinar la validesa convergent i discriminant d'un constructe. La matriu conté correlacions entre dos o més constructes (trets) mesurats de dues o més maneres diferents (mètodes). L'anàlisi hauria de mostrar, per exemple, que la correlació entre mesures de la capacitat de comprensió oral obtingudes per mètodes diferents és més alta que la correlació entre mesures d'habilitats diferents obtingudes pel mateix mètode de prova.
Més informació: Bachman, 1990, pàg. 263–265.
CA:108, DA:238, DE:252, EN:243, ES:109, FR:299, GA:111, IT:277, NE:254, PO:305.

109 dissenyador d'una prova Persona implicada en el procés de desenvolupar una prova nova.
CA:109, DA:405, DE:395, EN:399, ES:133, FR:145, GA:149, IT:149, NE:399, PO:141.

110 distractor Cada opció incorrecta en un ítem d'elecció múltiple.
Compareu: clau.
Vegeu: ítem d'elecció múltiple.
Més informació: Ebel i Frisbie, 1986, pàg. 176–185.
CA:110, DA:79, DE:88, EN:115, ES:111, FR:104, GA:348, IT:129, NE:8, PO:126.

111 distribució Vegeu la definició de distribució de freqüències.

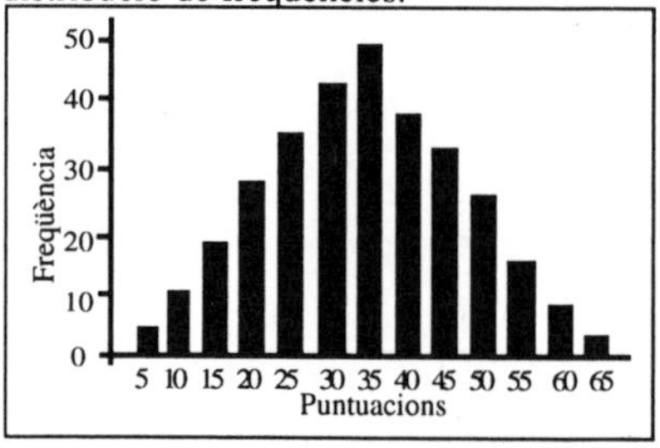

Vegeu: distribució normal, asimetria.
Més informació: Hatch i Lazaraton, 1991, pàg. 159–178.
CA:111, DA:103, DE:434, EN:117, ES:112, FR:105, GA:103, IT:130, NE:110, PO:119.

112 distribució bimodal Distribució amb dues modes o pics, que poden indicar que hi ha dos grups diferents en la mateixa mostra.

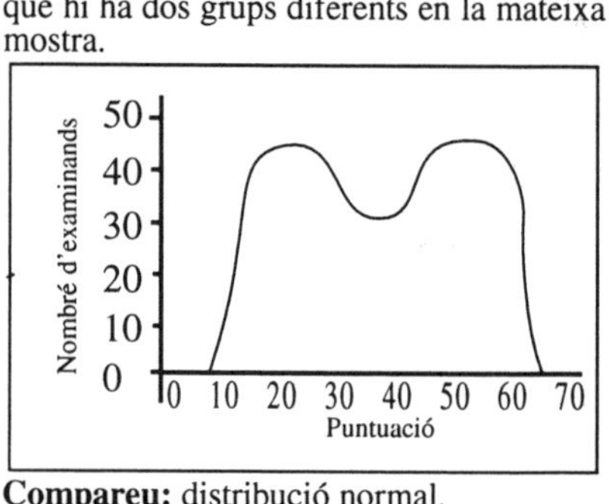

Compareu: distribució normal.
Vegeu: moda.

Més informació: Hatch i Lazaraton, 1991, pàg. 165–166.
CA:112, DA:39, DE:59, EN:34, ES:113, FR:106, GA:104, IT:131, NE:47, PO:121.

113 distribució de freqüències Tabulació que mostra la freqüència dels valors o d'intervals de valors d'una variable, o de la combinació de diverses variables.
CA:113, DA:107, DE:142, EN:149, ES:114, FR:107, GA:106, IT:132, NE:138, PO:122.

114 distribució de Gauss Vegeu la definició de distribució normal.
CA:114, DA:114, DE:129, EN:152, ES:115, FR:91, GA:105, IT:133, NE:140, PO:110.

115 distribució normal Distribució de freqüències en forma de campana, en què la mitjana, la moda i la mediana es troben totes en el mateix punt; té una representació gràfica simètrica respecte a la seva mitjana aritmètica, amb cues asimptòtiques a l'eix de la variables i amb una desviació estàndard un punt per sobre i per sota de la mitjana. S'anomena també distribució de Gauss.
Compareu: distribució bimodal.
Més informació: Hatch i Lazaraton, 1991, pàg. 164.
CA:115, DA:252, DE:265, EN:252, ES:116, FR:108, GA:107, IT:134, NE:262, PO:123.

116 distribució truncada Tipus de distribució de freqüències característic d'una mostra que té una amplitud més reduïda que la població de què prové perquè els alumnes amb les puntuacions més altes i més baixes no són presents en la mostra. Un exemple d'aquest tipus de distribució podria ser un grup d'estudiants admesos en un curs després de passar la prova d'accés.
CA:116, DA:376, DE:1, EN:421, ES:117, FR:110, GA:108, IT:135, NE:343, PO:124.

117 efecte d'aurèola Tendència dels avaluadors d'exàmens de correcció subjectiva a deixar-se influir per l'actuació d'un examinand en certes tasques d'una prova i, en conseqüència, a donar una puntuació massa alta o massa baixa en una altra tasca.
Vegeu: efectes del qualificador.
CA:117, DA:118, DE:141, EN:161, ES:127, FR:137, GA:170, IT:139, NE:164, PO:133.

118 efecte de contaminació Efecte del qualificador que es produeix quan assigna una puntuació sobre la base d'un factor diferent del que s'està avaluant. Un exemple en podria ser augmentar la puntuació d'un examinand en una prova escrita perquè té bona lletra.
Vegeu: efectes del qualificador.
CA:118, DA:9, DE:226, EN:71, ES:122, FR:136, GA:174, IT:141, NE:74, PO:132.

119 efecte de la pràctica Efecte sobre les puntuacions en una prova d'examinands familiaritzats amb el tipus de tasca o els ítems que s'hi utilitzen.
CA:119, DA:443, DE:419, EN:289, ES:123, FR:138, GA:169, IT:140, NE:298, PO:131.

120 efecte de la seqüència Efecte del qualificador sobre les valoracions originat per l'ordre amb què es fan.
Vegeu: efectes del qualificador.
CA:120, DA:329, DE:292, EN:360, ES:125, FR:142, GA:172, IT:148, NE:337, PO:136.

121 efecte del mètode Efecte en les puntuacions d'una prova produït pel mètode de prova utilitzat i no per la capacitat de l'examinand.
CA:121, DA:229, DE:242, EN:233, ES:126, FR:139, GA:171, IT:142, NE:244, PO:134.

122 efecte llindar Efecte límit que resulta del fet que una prova esdevingui massa difícil per a un grup determinat d'examinands, de manera que totes les puntuacions s'agrupen al capdavall de la distribució.
Vegeu: efectes límit.
CA:122, DA:42, DE:61/121, EN:146, ES:128, FR:141, GA:175, IT:144, NE:49, PO:130.

123 efecte sostre Efecte límit que resulta del fet que una prova sigui massa fàcil per a un grup particular d'examinands; de manera que totes les puntuacions s'agrupen al capdamunt de la distribució.
Vegeu: efectes límit.
CA:123, DA:219, DE:63/73, EN:44, ES:129, FR:140, GA:173, IT:145, NE:292, PO:137.

124 efectes del qualificador Font d'error en una avaluació, resultat de certes tendències dels avaluadors com ara la rigorositat o la indulgència, o un prejudici a favor de certs tipus d'examinand, que afecten les puntuacions donades als examinands d'una prova. En són exemples l'efecte de contaminació, l'efecte d'aurèola i l'efecte de la seqüència.

CA:124, DA:34, DE:425, EN:313, ES:130, FR:144, GA:176, IT:143, NE:35, PO:138.

125 efectes límit Efectes d'una prova massa fàcil o massa difícil per a un grup particular d'examinands. Les puntuacions tendeixen a acumular-se al capdamunt de la distribució (efecte sostre) o al capdavall (efecte llindar).
Vegeu: efecte llindar, efecte sostre.
CA:125, DA:120, DE:139, EN:36, ES:131, FR:143, GA:177, IT:138, NE:163, PO:139.

126 elaboració d'una prova Procés de seleccionar ítems o tasques i manera de presentar-los en una prova. Aquest procés sovint està precedit per l'experimentació o l'assaig de materials. Per a l'elaboració d'una prova, els ítems i les tasques es poden seleccionar a partir d'un banc de materials.
CA:126, DA:394, DE:397, EN:398, ES:75, FR:146, GA:393, IT:110, NE:392, PO:140.

127 elaborador Persona que dissenya i elabora una prova.
CA:127, DA:392, DE:400, EN:361, ES:92, FR:145, GA:121, IT:149, NE:391, PO:141.

128 element d'avaluació Focus d'un ítem o punt concret sobre el qual un ítem intenta elicitar el coneixement que en té l'examinand.
CA:128, DA:399, DE:309, EN:409, ES:289, FR:300, GA:281, IT:293, NE:384, PO:307.

129 enfocament basat en situacions reals En proves de llengua, enfocament que considera que les proves haurien d'incloure tipus de tasca tan semblants a activitats de la vida real com fos possible. Per exemple, en un enfocament d'aquest tipus, el contingut d'un text dissenyat per avaluar si els examinands poden afrontar un curs acadèmic en una llengua estrangera hauria de basar-se en una anàlisi de necessitats lingüístiques i en les activitats lingüístiques habituals d'aquest curs.
Vegeu: autenticitat.
Més informació: Bachman, 1990, pàg. 301–328.
CA:129, DA:433, DE:320, EN:322, ES:134, FR:345, GA:98, IT:23, NE:226, PO:349.

130 entrevista de proficiència oral semidirecta/simulada Prova de competència oral en què un magnetòfon proporciona l'estímul i la resposta de l'examinand s'enregistra per qualificar-la més tard. En la bibliografia en anglès sobre avaluació de llengua es fa servir la sigla SOPI (Semi-Direct/ Simulated Oral Proficiency Interview).
Vegeu: prova semidirecta.
CA:130, DA:348, DE:356, EN:370, ES:137, FR:392, GA:356, IT:93, NE:346, PO:144.

131 entrevista oral Les habilitats d'expressió oral sovint es proven mitjançant una entrevista oral, que pot variar des d'una conversa completament lliure entre examinand(s) i avaluador(s) fins a una sèrie de tasques orals completament estructurades.
CA:131, DA:150, DE:305, EN:263, ES:136, FR:148, GA:1, IT:92, NE:355, PO:143.

132 equiparació d'equipercentils Mètode per equiparar les puntuacions directes de proves segons el qual es considera que les puntuacions estan equiparades si corresponen al mateix rang de percentil en un grup d'examinands.
CA:132, DA:440, DE:24, EN:127, ES:140, FR:36, GA:88, IT:150, NE:121, PO:43.

133 equiparació horitzontal Procés de posar les puntuacions de dues proves d'aproximadament la mateixa dificultat en una única escala, amb el propòsit d'aplicar els mateixos estàndards tant en una prova com en l'altra.
Compareu: equiparació vertical.
CA:133, DA:128, DE:149, EN:166, ES:141, FR:37, GA:89, IT:152, NE:170, PO:44.

134 equiparació lineal Procediment d'equiparació en què s'equipara la puntuació obtinguda en una prova a la puntuació obtinguda en una segona prova. Les puntuacions equivalents en totes dues proves tenen el mateix nombre de desviacions estàndard per sobre o per sota de la puntuació mitjana de la prova en què apareixen.
Vegeu: regressió.
Més informació: Crocker i Algina, 1986, pàg. 457–461.
CA:134, DA:216, DE:17, EN:212, ES:142, FR:38, GA:91, IT:151, NE:229, PO:45.

135 equiparació vertical Procés de col·locar les puntuacions de dues proves de diferent grau de dificultat en la mateixa escala.
Més informació: Crocker i Algina, 1986, pàg. 473–477.
CA:135, DA:432, DE:435, EN:434, ES:143, FR:39, GA:90, IT:153, NE:419, PO:46.

136 error En la teoria clàssica de mesura de la puntuació vertadera, una puntuació observada en una prova està constituïda per dos components: una puntuació vertadera que reflecteix la capacitat de la persona i una puntuació errònia que reflecteix la influència de tots els altres factors no relacionats amb la capacitat que s'ha de provar. S'espera que l'error sigui aleatori, i.e. no sistemàtic. Addicionalment, hi poden haver factors en una prova que afectin regularment l'actuació d'alguns individus i ocasionin un error sistemàtic o biaix de la prova.
Compareu: biaix.
Més informació: Bachman, 1990, pàg. 167.
CA:136, DA:98, DE:116, EN:129, ES:144, FR:151, GA:122, IT:154, NE:124, PO:146.

137 error aleatori Vegeu la definició d'error.
CA:137, DA:408, DE:449, EN:306, ES:145, FR:152, GA:128, IT:156, NE:310, PO:147.

138 error de mesura Vegeu la definició d'error estàndard de mesura.
CA:138, DA:240/241, DE:239/240, EN:130/231, ES:146, FR:153, GA:130/123, IT:159, NE:243/242, PO:149.

139 error de mostreig En recerca, error introduït en una anàlisi estadística a causa de la selecció d'una mostra específica utilitzada en l'estudi (per exemple, si la mostra no és representativa de la població).
Vegeu: població.
CA:139, DA:372, DE:381, EN:341, ES:147, FR:158, GA:129, IT:155, NE:370, PO:148.

140 error de primera espècie Error que es comet quan, com a resultat d'un contrast d'hipòtesis, es rebutja la hipòtesi nul·la quan és certa. S'anomena també error de tipus I.
Compareu: error de segona espècie.
Vegeu: hipòtesi nul·la.
Més informació: Hatch i Lazaraton, 1991, pàg. 224.
CA:140, DA:417, DE:9/117, EN:425, ES:150, FR:154, GA:126, IT:157, NE:405, PO:150.

141 error de segona espècie Error que es comet quan, com a resultat d'un contrast d'hipòtesis, s'accepta la hipòtesi nul·la quan es falsa. S'anomena també error de tipus II.
Compareu: error de primera espècie.
Vegeu: hipòtesi nul·la.
Més informació: Hatch i Lazaraton, 1991, pàg. 224.
CA:141, DA:418, DE:118, EN:426, ES:151, FR:155, GA:127, IT:158, NE:406, PO:151.

142 error estàndard d'estimació Mesura de l'exactitud de la predicció d'una variable a partir d'una altra, per exemple en una regressió lineal. Proporciona intervals de confiança per a puntuacions de criteri.
Vegeu: interval de confiança.
Més informació: Hatch i Lazaraton, 1991, pàg. 477–479.
CA:142, DA:361, DE:375, EN:380, ES:148, FR:156, GA:124, IT:163, NE:363, PO:152.

143 error estàndard de mesura En la teoria clàssica de la prova, l'error estàndard de mesura (*Se*) és una indicació de la imprecisió d'una mesura. La magnitud de l'error estàndard de mesura depèn de la fiabilitat (*r*) i la desviació estàndard de les puntuacions de la prova. La fórmula per calcular *Se:*

$$Se = Sx\sqrt{(1-r)}$$

Per exemple, si un examinand amb una puntuació vertadera de T en una prova i un error estàndard de mesura de *Se* fa la prova reiteradament, aleshores el 68 % de les vegades la puntuació observada estarà en l'amplitud T ± *Se* i el 95 % de les vegades en l'amplitud T ± 2*Se*.
Més informació: Crocker i Algina, 1986, pàg. 122–124.
CA:143, DA:364, DE:374, EN:381, ES:149, FR:157, GA:125, IT:12, NE:362, PO:153.

144 escala Sèrie de nombres o categories per mesurar alguna cosa. Es diferencien quatre tipus d'escala de mesura: nominal, ordinal, d'interval i de raó.
Més informació: Crocker i Algina, 1986, pàg. 46–49.
CA:144, DA:337, DE:352, EN:343, ES:152, FR:121, GA:308, IT:314, NE:326, PO:154.

145 escala absoluta Escala amb un punt zero real, per exemple una escala per mesurar la longitud. El punt zero absolut no es pot definir en proves de llengua; per tant, aquest tipus d'escala no hi és aplicable.
Compareu: escala d'interval, escala nominal, escala ordinal.
CA:145, DA:4, DE:433, EN:4, ES:153, FR:122, GA:112, IT:317, NE:2, PO:155.

146 escala categòrica Escala usada per a variables categòriques com són el sexe, la primera llengua, l'ocupació, etc.
Compareu: escala d'interval, escala nominal, escala ordinal, escala de raó.
CA:146, DA:170, DE:175, EN:42, ES:154, FR:123, GA:310, IT:318, NE:53, PO:156.

147 escala comuna Mètode per expressar puntuacions de dues proves o més en una mateixa escala, amb el propòsit de permetre una comparació directa dels resultats. Les puntuacions de dues proves o més es poden expressar en una escala comuna si les puntuacions directes han estat transformades mitjançant un procediment estadístic, per exemple l'equiparació de proves.
Més informació: Bachman, 1990, pàg. 340–344.
CA:147, DA:110, DE:131, EN:57, ES:156, FR:125, GA:86, IT:320, NE:148, PO:158.

148 escala d'interval Escala de mesura en què la distància entre dues unitats de mesura adjacents és la mateixa, però en què no hi ha un punt zero real.
Compareu: escala categòrica, escala nominal, escala ordinal, escala de raó.
Més informació: Crocker i Algina, 1986, pàg. 48.
CA:148, DA:149, DE:161, EN:184, ES:158, FR:126, GA:315, IT:315, NE:188, PO:162.

149 escala d'intervals iguals Vegeu la definició d'escala d'interval.
CA:149, DA:213, DE:161, EN:125, ES:159, FR:127, GA:316, IT:316, NE:145, PO:161.

150 escala de capacitat En la teoria de resposta d'ítem, escala d'intervals iguals en què es pot situar la capacitat d'una persona i la dificultat de les tasques d'una prova. S'anomena també escala theta.
Més informació: Bachman, 1990, pàg. 345.
CA:150, DA:3, DE:114, EN:3, ES:157, FR:128, GA:313, IT:322, NE:413, PO:159.

151 escala de centil Escala ordinal que està dividida en 100 unitats o centils. Per exemple, si se li dóna a algú un valor de centil 95, significa que en una mostra típica de 100 aquesta persona podria estar classificada per sobre d'uns altres 95. S'anomena també escala de percentil.
Més informació: Crocker i Algina, 1986, pàg. 439–442; Guilford i Fruchter, 1981, pàg. 38–41.
CA:151, DA:46, DE:300, EN:46, ES:155, FR:124, GA:311, IT:319, NE:54, PO:157.

152 escala de likert Tipus d'escala utilitzat en qüestionaris per mesurar actituds o opinions. Es demana que es respongui una sèrie d'enunciats triant la resposta entre, aproximadament, cinc possibilitats del tipus "totalment d'acord", "d'acord", "no ho sé", "en desacord", "totalment en desacord".
CA:152, DA:214, DE:222, EN:211, ES:163, FR:129, GA:317, IT:325, NE:228, PO:163.

153 escala de raó Escala de mesura que diferencia valors distints, hi estableix un ordre, permet determinar la distància entre aquests valors i té un origen natural o zero real.
Compareu: escala categòrica, escala d'interval, escala ordinal.
Més informació: Crocker i Algina, 1986, pàg. 48–49.
CA:153, DA:210, DE:433, EN:317, ES:160, FR:131, GA:312, IT:324, NE:314, PO:164.

154 escala de valoració Escala que consisteix en diverses categories ordenades utilitzades per fer judicis subjectius. En proves de llengua, les escales de valoració per avaluar una actuació estan acompanyades habitualment de descriptors que n'aclareixen la interpretació.
Compareu: escala de likert.
Vegeu: descriptor.
CA:154, DA:172, DE:58, EN:315, ES:161, FR:130, GA:319, IT:323, NE:40, PO:160.

155 escala delta Escala normalitzada amb una mitjana aritmètica de 13 i una desviació estàndard de 4.
CA:155, DA:60, DE:75, EN:93, ES:162, FR:132, GA:314, IT:321, NE:94, PO:165.

156 escala nominal Escala de mesura que diferencia valors distints però que no hi estableix un ordre. S'utilitza amb variables categòriques (com són el sexe o la primera llengua) i l'interès se centra en la freqüència d'ocurrència.
Compareu: escala d'interval, escala ordinal, escala de raó.
Més informació: Hatch i Lazaraton, 1991, pàg. 55–56.
CA:156, DA:249, DE:262, EN:248, ES:164, FR:133, GA:309, IT:326, NE:260, PO:166.

157 escala ordinal Escala de mesura que diferencia valors distints i que hi estableix un ordre, sense indicar la distància relativa entre ells.
Compareu: escala categòrica, escala

d'interval, escala nominal, escala de raó.
Més informació: Hatch i Lazaraton, 1991, pàg. 56–57.
CA:157, DA:271, DE:275, EN:265, ES:165, FR:134, GA:318, IT:327, NE:275, PO:167.

158 escala theta
Vegeu: escala de capacitat.
CA:158, DA:407, DE:413, EN:413, ES:166, FR:128, GA:320, IT:328, NE:385, PO:168.

159 escalonament Procés de produir escales de mesura. En proves de llengua, comporta associar números amb l'actuació dels examinands per tal de reflectir nivells creixents de coneixement o capacitat. L'escalonament pot implicar modificar una sèrie de puntuacions a fi de produir una escala per a un propòsit donat; per exemple, presentar els resultats d'una prova d'una manera estandarditzada o equiparar una versió d'una prova amb una altra.
Vegeu: escala, escala de capacitat, escala de centil, escala comuna, escala d'interval, escala nominal, escala ordinal, escala de raó, escala de valoració, formes equiparades, equiparació lineal.
CA:159, DA:341, DE:355, EN:346, ES:167, FR:135, GA:321, IT:109, NE:329, PO:169.

160 escànner Vegeu la definició de màquina de lectura òptica.
CA:160, DA:327, DE:336, EN:347, ES:168, FR:342, GA:322, IT:226, NE:325, PO:346.

161 especificacions de la prova Conjunt detallat de documentació que s'elabora normalment durant el procés de disseny d'una prova nova o de revisió d'una ja existent. Les especificacions donen detalls sobre el disseny, el contingut, el nivell, el tipus de tasca i d'ítems utilitzats, la població objectiu, l'ús de la prova, etc., i sovint inclouen materials de mostra.
CA:161, DA:401, DE:394, EN:404, ES:169, FR:346, GA:355, IT:120, NE:400, PO:171.

162 estabilitat Aspecte de la fiabilitat en què l'estimació es basa en el mètode test-retest. Es relaciona amb l'estabilitat de les puntuacions al llarg del temps.
Vegeu: fiabilitat, fiabilitat per test-retest.
CA:162, DA:359, DE:371, EN:378, ES:170, FR:79, GA:65, IT:337, NE:358, PO:173.

163 estadístic Quantitat que conté informació expressada en forma numèrica. Estrictament, un estadístic és una propietat del grup mostra, en contrast amb paràmetre, que és una propietat de la població. Els estadístics s'escriuen generalment en caràcters llatins i els paràmetres, en grecs. Per exemple, la desviació estàndard d'una mostra s'escriu *s* o *SD*, mentre que la població s'escriu σ.
Compareu: paràmetre.
Vegeu: població, mostra.
CA:163, DA:368, DE:379, EN:385, ES:174, FR:348, GA:363, IT:117, NE:367, PO:174.

164 estadística Ciència que recull, classifica, analitza i interpreta dades relatives a un conjunt d'elements.
CA:164, DA:369, DE:378, EN:386, ES:171, FR:348, GA:362, IT:339, NE:366, PO:175.

165 estadística descriptiva Estadística utilitzada per descriure una sèrie de dades en terme de quantitats, amplitud, valors centrals, correlacions amb altres dades, etc. Es distingeix entre estadística descriptiva i estadística inferencial o mostral.
Compareu: estadística inferencial.
CA:165, DA:63, DE:51, EN:95, ES:172, FR:349, GA:365, IT:340, NE:95, PO:176.

166 estadística inferencial Estadística que va més enllà de la informació proporcionada per l'estadística descriptiva. Permet fer inferències sobre la probabilitat que una sèrie de dades pugui representar una població més àmplia que la de la mostra.
Compareu: estadística descriptiva.
CA:166, DA:139, DE:338, EN:171, ES:173, FR:350, GA:364, IT:341, NE:175, PO:177.

167 estandardització Procés que permet garantir que els avaluadors compleixen un procediment establert i apliquen els barems de puntuació de la manera adequada.
Vegeu: avaluador.
CA:167, DA:363, DE:373, EN:383, ES:175, NE:361, FR:162, GA:45, IT:338, PO:295.

168 estimació pel mètode de dues meitats de Spearman-Brown Vegeu la definició de fiabilitat pel mètode de dues meitats.
CA:168, DA:350, DE:360, EN:372, ES:177, FR:161, GA:228, IT:342, NE:349, PO:178.

169 estímul Material que es proporciona a l'examinand en una tasca d'una prova perquè l'utilitzi a fi de produir una resposta adequada. En una prova de comprensió oral, per exemple, pot tenir la forma d'un text enregistrat i acompanyat d'alguns ítems escrits.

CA:169, DA:142, DE:408, EN:174, ES:228, FR:147, GA:199, IT:199, NE:180, PO:254.

170 estudi pilot Estudi preliminar mitjançant el qual els investigadors o els dissenyadors d'una prova experimenten les seves idees amb un nombre limitat de subjectes, a fi de localitzar problemes abans de fer un assaig, programa o producte a escala real.
Vegeu: assaig, experimentació.

CA:170, DA:286, DE:288, EN:281, ES:179, FR:163, GA:361, IT:344, NE:290, PO:180.

171 examen Procediment per avaluar la competència o els coneixements d'una persona mitjançant l'administració de tasques orals i/o escrites. L'obtenció d'un certificat, l'admissió en una institució educativa o en un programa d'estudi, etc. poden dependre del resultat. S'anomena també prova.
Més informació: Bachman, 1990, pàg. 50.

CA:171, DA:86, DE:303, EN:133, ES:188, FR:173, GA:347, IT:164, NE:127, PO:181.

172 examinador Vegeu la definició d'avaluador.

CA:172, DA:89, DE:301, EN:135, ES:189, FR:174, GA:346, IT:165, NE:130, PO:182.

173 examinand Persona que fa un examen. S'anomena també candidat.

CA:173, DA:87, DE:307, EN:134, ES:190, FR:351, GA:345, IT:49, NE:129, PO:183.

174 experimentació Fase en el desenvolupament dels materials d'un examen en què els ítems es proven amb mostres representatives de la població objectiu, a fi de determinar-ne la dificultat. Seguint l'anàlisi estadística, els ítems considerats satisfactoris poder ser utilitzats en proves autèntiques.
Compareu: assaig.

CA:174, DA:105, DE:436, EN:293, ES:191, FR:307, GA:289, IT:273, NE:302, PO:311.

175 facetes del mètode de prova Vegeu la definició de característiques del mètode de prova.

CA:175, DA:396, DE:402, EN:403, ES:193, FR:176, GA:163, IT:50, NE:397, PO:186.

176 factor G En la teoria de la intel·ligència, "factor general" hipotetitzat subjacent a totes les habilitats cognitives. John Oller va popularitzar aquesta noció durant la dècada dels setanta com a evidència d'una competència unitària subjacent a la competència lingüística.
Més informació: Oller, 1979, pàg. 426–458; Bachman, 1990, pàg. 6.

CA:176, DA:113, DE:127, EN:153, ES:194, FR:177, GA:136, IT:170, NE:139, PO:187.

177 factors afectius Factors de tipus no cognitiu relacionats amb les variables emocionals, preferències i actituds dels destinataris d'una prova.
Compareu: factors cognitius.
Més informació: Ebel i Frisbie, 1991, pàg. 52.

CA:177, DA:6, DE:7, EN:9, ES:195, FR:178, GA:399, IT:172, NE:6, PO:188.

178 factors cognitius Factors del procés d'aprenentatge o del procés d'examinar-se que es relacionen amb l'estructura i el model de coneixement de l'aprenent.
Compareu: factors afectius.
Més informació: Ebel i Frisbie, 1991, pàg. 52.

CA:178, DA:177, DE:180, EN:55, ES:196, FR:179, GA:398, IT:171, NE:65, PO:189.

179 familiaritat amb la prova Coneixement sobre el format d'una prova o experiència a fer una prova que permet als examinands resoldre la prova per sobre del seu nivell real de capacitat.

CA:179, DA:406, DE:396, EN:408, ES:197, FR:314, GA:161, IT:167, NE:401, PO:191.

180 fiabilitat Consistència o estabilitat de les mesures d'una prova. Una prova és més fiable com menys error aleatori té. Una prova que tingui un error sistemàtic, per exemple un biaix amb relació a un grup determinat, pot ser fiable però no vàlida.
Compareu: validesa.
Vegeu: KR-20 (fórmula 20 de Kuder-Richardson), alfa (coeficient alfa), fiabilitat pel mètode de dues meitats, fiabilitat per test-retest.
Més informació: Bachman, 1990, pàg. 24; Crocker i Algina, 1986, capítol 6.

CA:180, DA:312, DE:322/453, EN:327, ES:198, FR:183, GA:200, IT:6, NE:43, PO:193.

181 fiabilitat interqualificador Estimació de la fiabilitat d'una prova que es basa en el grau en què diferents avaluadors concorden en l'avaluació de l'actuació dels examinands.
Vegeu: acord interqualificador, fiabilitat.
CA:181, DA:145, DE:158, EN:182, ES:199, FR:185, GA:201, IT:8, NE:184, PO:195.

182 fiabilitat intraqualificador Estimació de la fiabilitat d'una valoració que es basa en el grau en què el mateix avaluador puntua la mateixa actuació de manera similar en diferents ocasions.
Vegeu: acord intraqualificador, fiabilitat.
CA:182, DA:151, DE:162, EN:186, ES:200, FR:187, GA:202, IT:89, NE:189, PO:196.

183 fiabilitat pel mètode de dues meitats Mesura de consistència interna de fiabilitat. L'estimació es basa en una correlació entre les puntuacions de les dues meitats d'una prova que es consideren dues proves alternes. La divisió en dues meitats es pot fer de diverses maneres; per exemple: primera meitat, segona meitat, o posant els ítems parells en una meitat i els ítems senars en l'altra.
Vegeu: fiabilitat.
Més informació: Ebel i Frisbie, 1991, pàg. 82–83; Crocker i Algina, 1986, pàg. 136–138.
CA:183, DA:259, DE:364/398, EN:377, ES:201, FR:184, GA:203, IT:7, NE:353, PO:194.

184 fiabilitat per test-retest Estimació de la fiabilitat obtinguda administrant la mateixa prova als mateixos examinands en les mateixes condicions, i correlacionant les puntuacions en totes dues sessions. Es relaciona amb l'estabilitat de les puntuacions i també s'utilitza adequadament quan l'estimació de la consistència interna no és possible.
Compareu: consistència interna.
Vegeu: fiabilitat, estabilitat.
CA:184, DA:318, DE:409/325, EN:410, ES:202, FR:188, GA:204, IT:9, NE:383, PO:197.

185 formes alternes Vegeu la definició de formes equivalents.
CA:185, DA:12, DE:11, EN:11, ES:203, NE:13, FR:193, GA:146, IT:176, PO:199.

186 formes equiparades Diferents formes d'una prova, les distribucions de puntuació de les quals han estat transformades per poder ser utilitzades en una mateixa escala.
Més informació: Crocker i Algina, 1986, capítol 20.
CA:186, DA:442, DE:16/14, EN:126, ES:204, FR:194, GA:145, IT:177 NE:141, PO:200.

187 formes equivalents Les diferents versions d'una mateixa prova es consideren equivalents entre elles pel fet que es basen en les mateixes especifica-cions i mesuren la mateixa competència. Per complir els requisits estrictes d'equiva-lència segons la teoria clàssica de la prova, les diferents formes d'una prova han de tenir la mateixa mitjana de dificultat, variància i covariància quan s'administren a les mateixes persones. L'equivalència és molt difícil d'aconseguir a la pràctica. S'anomenen també formes alternatives o formes paral·leles.
Compareu: formes equiparades.
Més informació: Crocker i Algina, 1986, pàg. 132.
CA:187, DA:441, DE:25, EN:128 ES:205, FR:195, GA:143, IT:178, NE:122, PO:201.

188 formes paral·leles Vegeu la definició de formes equivalents.
CA:188, DA:275, DE:278, EN:268, ES:206, FR:196, GA:144, IT:179, NE:279, PO:202.

189 freqüència cumulativa Suma de les freqüències d'una variable fins al valor que es considera.
Més informació: Guilford i Fruchter, 1981, pàg. 35–36.
CA:189, DA:208, DE:202, EN:86, ES:208, FR:198, GA:239, IT:181, NE:91, PO:204.

190 freqüència de mots Recompte de la quantitat de vegades que un mot concret o un tipus de mot apareix en un text. En proves de llengua, pot ser útil quan les proves s'elaboren d'acord amb una especificació lèxica concreta.
CA:190, DA:270, DE:143, EN:440, ES:362, FR:75, GA:67, IT:256, NE:436, PO:95.

191 full de resposta Paper en què un examinand anota les respostes.
Compareu: màquina de lectura òptica.
CA:191, DA:261/37, DE:341/22, EN:350/220, ES:219, FR:343/181, GA:343/152, IT:174/175, NE:20/218, PO:170/198.

192 funció ítem-informació En la teoria de resposta d'ítem, índex de la quantitat d'informació que proporciona un ítem o una prova sobre una persona donat un nivell de capacitat; depèn de la

discriminació de l'ítem i de fins a quin punt es correspon amb el nivell.
Compareu: funció prova-informació.
CA:192, DA:156, DE:169, EN:193, ES:212, FR:190, GA:138, IT:184, NE:197, PO:206.

193 funció ítem-resposta En la teoria de resposta d'ítem, funció matemàtica que relaciona la probabilitat d'èxit en un ítem amb la capacitat del tret mesurat per l'ítem. S'anomena també funció característica de l'ítem.
CA:193, DA:158, DE:172, EN:194, ES:210, FR:189, GA:140, IT:183, NE:200, PO:205.

194 funció prova-informació En la teoria de resposta d'ítem, índex de la quantitat d'informació que proporciona una prova sobre una persona en un nivell de capacitat determinat. És la suma de les funcions ítem-informació.
Compareu: funció ítem-informació.
Més informació: Crocker i Algina, 1986, pàg. 369–371.
CA:194, DA:388, DE:399, EN:400, ES:211, FR:191, GA:139, IT:185, NE:394, PO:207.

195 funcionament diferencial d'ítems (FDI) El fet que la dificultat relativa d'un ítem depèn d'alguna característica del grup al qual s'administra, com és, per exemple, la primera llengua o el sexe.
Vegeu: biaix.
CA:195, DA:66, DE:78, EN:100, ES:209, FR:192, GA:114, IT:182, NE:100, PO:208.

196 grup de referència Mostra feta a partir d'una població clarament definida d'examinands que serveix de norma per a una prova.
Vegeu: norma.
CA:196, DA:309, DE:267, EN:324, ES:213, FR:202, GA:166, IT:189, NE:316, PO:212.

197 grup norma Habitualment, grup gran d'individus representatiu de les persones per a les quals s'ha dissenyat una prova. L'actuació del grup norma s'utilitza en la interpretació d'una prova referida a la norma. S'anomena també grup de referència.
Vegeu: prova referida a la norma.
CA:197, DA:254, DE:266, EN:251, ES:214, FR:203, GA:264, IT:190, NE:265, PO:213.

198 guia de l'interlocutor Indicació escrita sobre el llenguatge que hauria d'utilitzar un interlocutor per conduir una prova d'expressió oral. El propòsit és estandarditzar el llenguatge que escolten tots els examinands per fer la prova més imparcial i més fiable.
CA:198, DA:324, DE:438, EN:179, ES:215, FR:34, GA:151, IT:128, NE:156, PO:321.

199 habilitat Capacitat per fer alguna cosa. En proves de llengua es distingeixen quatre habilitats: comprensió lectora, expressió escrita, expressió oral i comprensió oral.
Vegeu: competència.
CA:199, DA:111, DE:119, EN:367, ES:100, FR:340, GA:325, IT:1, NE:413, PO:51.

200 habilitats d'ordre inferior Capacitats poc complexes hipotetitzades que es demanen als examinands en proves de llengua; per exemple, el reconeixement de mots o lletres.
Compareu: habilitats d'ordre superior.
CA:200, DA:27, DE:424, EN:219, ES:101, FR:44, GA:327, IT:2, NE:409, PO:52.

201 habilitats d'ordre superior Capacitats complexes hipotetitzades, com ara la deducció i la síntesi.
Compareu: habilitats d'ordre inferior.
CA:201, DA:130, DE:418, EN:162, ES:102, FR:45, GA:326, IT:3, NE:410, PO:53.

202 hipòtesi nul·la Hipòtesi que planteja que dues variables o més no estan relacionades. Per exemple, la suposició que no hi ha diferència en l'actuació en una prova entre els membres de grups de primera llengua diferent és una hipòtesi nul·la.
Més informació: Hatch i Lazaraton, 1991, pàg. 24; Guilford i Fruchter, 1981, pàg. 146–147.
CA:202, DA:255, DE:271, EN:255, ES:217, FR:206, GA:167, IT:206, NE:266, PO:214.

203 histograma Representació gràfica de la distribució de freqüències en què el nombre de casos per classe de freqüència es presenta amb una barra vertical.

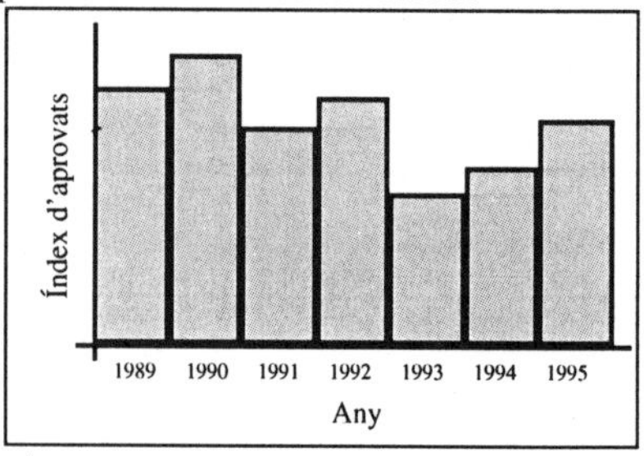

Compareu: diagrama de barres.
CA:203, DA:125, DE:145, EN:163, ES:218, FR:204, GA:168, IT:207, NE:167, PO:215.

204 homogeneïtat Característica d'una prova o subprova per mitjà de la qual els ítems mesuren la mateixa competència, o característica d'un grup per mitjà de la qual els individus comparteixen les mateixes propietats. L'índex de fiabilitat expressa el grau d'homogeneïtat.
CA:204, DA:127, DE:148, EN:165, ES:221, FR:205, GA:22, IT:257, NE:169, PO:216.

205 impacte Efecte creat per una prova, tant en termes d'influència en el procés pedagògic en general com en termes dels individus afectats pels resultats de la prova.
Vegeu: repercussió.
CA:205, DA:303, DE:444, EN:167, ES:222, FR:207, GA:391, IT:191, NE:171, PO:217.

206 índex D Índex de discriminació per als ítems d'una prova. Sovint es fa servir per a escales petites de proves d'aula perquè es pot calcular a mà. A partir de la puntuació total d'una prova, se selecciona un grup superior i un grup inferior, de manera que en cada un hi hagi entre el 10% i el 33% dels examinands. Per a puntuacions distribuïdes normalment, és òptim utilitzar el 27% en cada grup. Es compten les respostes a cada ítem dels examinands de la prova i en els ítems que discriminen bé el grup superior puntuarà més alt que el grup inferior. La fórmula següent dóna l'índex de discriminació de l'ítem:

$$D = p_{gs} - p_{gi}$$

on p_{gs} és la fracció de la puntuació del grup superior que dóna l'ítem correcte i on p_{gi} és la fracció de la puntuació del grup inferior que dóna l'ítem correcte. En general, els ítems amb un índex de 0.3 o similar es consideren que discriminen bé.
CA:206, DA:59/246, DE:72/257, EN:91/247, ES:97/223, FR:115/208, GA:102/186, IT:194, NE:92/256, PO:111/218.

207 índex de dificultat En la teoria clàssica de la prova, la dificultat d'un ítem és la proporció (p) d'examinands que el responen correctament. Això significa que l'índex de dificultat de l'ítem depèn de la mostra i canvia d'acord amb el nivell de capacitat dels examinands de la mostra.
Compareu: índex de facilitat, valor-p.
CA:207, DA:378, DE:343, EN:101, ES:224, FR:209, GA:187, IT:196, NE:249, PO:219.

208 índex de dificultat mitjana d'ítem (*p* mitjana) Proporció mitjana de respostes correctes de tots els ítems d'una escala d'ítems puntuats dicotòmicament. Per exemple, una *p* mitjana de 0.5 indica que l'índex de facilitat mitjana per a la prova és de 0.5.
Vegeu: puntuació dicotòmica.
CA:208, DA:132, DE:246, EN:228, ES:227, FR:212, GA:190, IT:195 NE:150, PO:222.

209 índex de facilitat Proporció de respostes correctes d'un ítem, expressada en una escala de 0 a 1. De vegades s'expressa com a percentatge. S'anomena també valor de facilitat o valor *p*.
Compareu: índex de dificultat.
CA:209, DA:191, DE:208, EN:141, ES:225, FR:210, GA:188, IT:197, NE:146, PO:220.

210 índex de legibilitat Mesura de la complexitat gramatical i lèxica que s'utilitza per avaluar el grau en què els lectors trobaran comprensible un text. Alguns exemples d'índexs de legibilitat són l'índex Gunning's Fog i l'escala de legibilitat de Flesch.
CA:210, DA:222, DE:219, EN:320, ES:226, FR:211, GA:189, IT:198, NE:223, PO:221.

211 instruccions Directrius generals facilitades als examinands d'una prova (per exemple, a l'anvers del full de resposta) que donen informació sobre aspectes com ara la durada de la prova, el nombre de tasques que cal respondre i on s'han d'anotar les respostes.
Compareu: rúbrica.
CA:211, DA:143, DE:391, EN:175, ES:230, FR:214, GA:402, IT:208, NE:181, PO:225.

212 intercepció Y En una regressió lineal, el punt en què la línia de regressió s'encreua amb l'eix *y* (vertical).
Vegeu: regressió lineal.
CA:212, DA:438, DE:146, EN:441, ES:231, FR:215, GA:181, IT:200, NE:438, PO:226.

213 interlocutor En proves d'expressió oral, examinador que explica les tasques, fa preguntes i, en general, interactua amb l'examinand o els examinands. L'interlocutor també pot fer la valoració dels examinands i assignar-los una puntuació, o això ho pot fer un segon

examinador, que observa però no interactua amb els examinands.
Compareu: avaluador.
CA:213, DA:325, DE:125, EN:178, ES:138, FR:216, GA:72, IT:201, NE:155, PO:227.

214 interval Diferència entre dos punts en una escala.
CA:214, DA:148, DE:160, EN:183, ES:232, FR:218, GA:131, IT:203, NE:187, PO:228.

215 interval de confiança Interval de puntuacions d'una variable, dins el qual es considera que les diferències entre aquestes són estadísticament irrellevants. El grau de probabilitat normalment es defineix en nivells de confiança del 95 % o el 99 %.
CA:215, DA:182, DE:184, EN:67, ES:233, FR:219, GA:132, IT:204, NE:45, PO:229.

216 invariància En la teoria de resposta d'ítem, pressupòsit que la dificultat d'un ítem i les mesures de discriminació són característiques inherents que no depenen de la capacitat dels examinands, i així mateix que les mesures de capacitat no depenen dels ítems concrets utilitzats.
CA:216, DA:152, DE:164, EN:187, ES:234, FR:220, GA:120, IT:205, NE:191, PO:230.

217 ítem Cada element d'una prova al qual s'assigna un o més punts. En són exemples un buit en una prova de compleció, una pregunta d'elecció múltiple amb tres o quatre opcions, una oració que s'ha de transformar gramaticalment o una pregunta en què s'espera com a resposta una oració llarga.
Compareu: tasca.
CA:217, DA:154, DE:166, EN:189, ES:235, FR:221, GA:240, IT:209, NE:195, PO:231.

218 ítem àncora Ítem que s'inclou en dues proves o més. Els ítems àncora tenen característiques conegudes i formen una secció d'una nova versió d'una prova a fi de proporcionar informació sobre aquesta prova i els examinands que l'han feta; per exemple, per calibrar una nova prova en una escala de mesura.
Compareu: prova d'ancoratge.
Vegeu: calibratge.
CA:218, DA:16, DE:18, EN:15, ES:237, FR:225, GA:241, IT:212, NE:17, PO:232.

219 ítem basat en el text Ítem basat en un fragment d'un discurs; per exemple, ítems d'elecció múltiple basats en un text de comprensió lectora.
CA:219, DA:387, DE:412, EN:412, ES:236, FR:226, GA:254, IT:213, NE:269, PO:233.

220 ítem d'elecció múltiple Tipus d'ítem d'una prova que consisteix en una pregunta o oració incompleta (nucli), amb una tria de respostes o maneres de completar l'oració (opcions). La tasca de l'examinand consisteix a triar l'opció correcta (clau) entre una sèrie de tres, quatre o cinc possibilitats, sense implicar cap producció lingüística. Per aquesta raó, els ítems d'elecció múltiple s'utilitzen normalment en proves de comprensió lectora i comprensió oral. Poden ser discrets o basats en el text.
Vegeu: ítem discret, ítem basat en el text.
CA:220, DA:236, DE:249/234, EN:238, ES:244, FR:222, GA:247, IT:211, NE:252, PO:236.

221 ítem d'enllaç Vegeu la definició d'ítem àncora.
CA:221, DA:218, DE:432, EN:215, ES:239, FR:231, GA:250, IT:214, NE:232, PO:244.

222 ítem d'escala Ítem que es puntua mitjançant una escala.
Vegeu: puntuació graduada.
CA:222, DA:342, DE:27, EN:342, ES:248, FR:230, GA:252, IT:220, NE:328, PO:242.

223 ítem d'omplir buits Tipus d'ítem en què l'examinand ha d'escriure alguna cosa (lletres, números, mots solts, locucions, oracions o paràgrafs) en els espais buits d'un text. La resposta pot ser proporcionada per l'examinand o seleccionada entre una sèrie d'opcions.
CA:223, DA:138, DE:229, EN:151, ES:241, FR:317, GA:249, IT:78, NE:192, PO:235.

224 ítem d'omplir buits d'elecció múltiple Tipus d'ítem d'una prova en què la tasca de l'examinand consisteix a seleccionar, entre una sèrie d'opcions, el mot o sintagma correcte per situar-lo en un espai d'un text determinat.
Vegeu: ítem d'omplir buits.
CA:224, DA:237, DE:250, EN:239, ES:242, FR:386, GA:215, IT:79, NE:251, PO:390.

225 ítem de punt discret Ítem discret que avalua un punt específic, per exemple d'estructura o vocabulari, i que no està vinculat a cap altre ítem. Robert Lado va popularitzar les proves de llengua de punt discret a la dècada dels seixanta.

Compareu: ítem integratiu/tasca integrativa.
Vegeu: ítem discret.
CA:225, DA:72, DE:82, EN:110, ES:247 FR:229, GA:251, IT:210, NE:107, PO:240.

226 ítem de completar Tipus d'ítem en què l'examinand ha de completar una oració o una frase, normalment escrivint alguns mots o proporcionant detalls com ara horaris i números de telèfon.
CA:226, DA:421, DE:102, EN:60, ES:238, FR:223, GA:243, IT:215, NE:193, PO:234.

227 ítem de formació de mots Tipus d'ítem en què l'examinand ha de produir una forma d'una paraula basada en una altra forma del mateix mot donat com a estímul. Exemple: Aquesta mena de feina requereix una .... del vocabulari tècnic. (comprendre)
CA:227, DA:269, DE:445, EN:439, ES:231, FR:227, GA:244, IT:216, NE:437, PO:237 .

228 ítem de resposta curta ítem obert en què l'examinand ha de formular una resposta escrita utilitzant un mot o un sintagma.
CA:228, DA:198, DE:205, EN:362, ES:243, FR:224, GA:246, IT:311, NE:209, PO:238.

229 ítem de transformació Vegeu la definició de transformació gramatical.
CA:229, DA:413, DE:420, EN:416, ES:245, FR:403, GA:242, IT:217, NE:402, PO:239.

230 ítem discret Ítem autònom. No està vinculat a un text, a altres ítems ni a cap material suplementari. Un exemple d'un ítem usat d'aquesta manera és el d'elecció múltiple.
Compareu: ítem basat en el text.
CA:230, DA:71, DE:421, EN:109, ES:246, FR:228, GA:253, IT:219, NE:106, PO:241.

231 ítem integratiu / tasca integrativa S'utilitza per referir-se a ítems o tasques que requereixen més d'una habilitat o subhabilitat per completar-los. En són exemples els ítems en una prova de compleció, una entrevista oral, llegir una carta i escriure'n la resposta.
Compareu: ítem de punt discret.
CA:231, DA:144, DE:156, EN:176, ES:249, FR:316, GA:248, IT:221, NE:182, PO:245.

232 ítem vertader/fals Tipus d'ítem de resposta seleccionada en què l'examinand ha d'indicar si una sèrie d'enunciats són certs o falsos en relació amb un text.
CA:232, DA:326, DE:326, EN:419, ES:250, FR:429, GA:245, IT:218, NE:426, PO:243.

233 joc de rol Tipus de tasca utilitzat de vegades en proves d'expressió oral en què els examinands han d'imaginar-se ells mateixos en una situació específica o adoptar uns rols específics.
CA:233, DA:320, DE:329, EN:334, ES:251, FR:232, GA:294, IT:202, NE:323, PO:345.

234 KR-20 (fórmula 20 de Kuder-Richardson) Vegeu la definició de Kuder-Richardson.
CA:234, DA:201, DE:194, EN:199, ES:252, FR:233, GA:205, IT:222, NE:210, PO:246.

235 KR-21 (fórmula 21 de Kuder-Richardson) Vegeu la definició de Kuder-Richardson.
CA:235, DA:202, DE:195, EN:200 ES:253, FR:234, GA:206, IT:223, NE:211, PO:247.

236 Kuder-Richardson Dues mesures de consistència interna desenvolupades per Kuder i Richardson i utilitzades per a l'estimació de la fiabilitat d'una prova. KR-21 requereix menys informació i es calcula més fàcilment, però en general dóna una estimació inferior a KR-20.
Compareu: alfa (coeficient alfa).
Vegeu: consistència interna.
Més informació: Henning, 1987, pàg. 84.
CA:236, DA:206, DE:200, EN:201, ES:254, FR:235, GA:207, IT:224, NE:212, PO:248.

237 lèxic Terme utilitzat per referir-se al vocabulari.
CA:237, DA:212, DE:221, EN:210, ES:257, FR:238, GA:213, IT:225, NE:227, PO:250.

238 llengua per a propòsits específics Ensenyament o avaluació de llengua utilitzada per a una activitat o professió concreta, com per exemple anglès per a control del trànsit aeri o espanyol comercial.
CA:238, DA:95, DE:111, EN:205, ES:256, FR:236, GA:385, IT:227, NE:378, PO:251.

239 llibret d'examen S'utilitza de vegades per denominar el document en què es presenta una prova.
CA:239, DA:263, DE:123, EN:304, ES:220, FR:180, GA:271, IT:169, NE:425, PO:145.

240 llista de comprovació Llista de preguntes o punts que s'ha de contestar o emplenar. Sovint s'utilitza com a eina d'observació o anàlisi de proves de llengua.
CA:240, DA:48, DE:64, EN:48, ES:258, FR:239, GA:351, IT:228, NE:58, PO:252.

241 lògit Unitat de mesura en una escala d'interval de tret latent, derivada de la transformació logarítmica natural de la ràtio entre la possibilitat d'èxit i la possibilitat de fracàs. La diferència en lògits entre la capacitat d'una persona i la dificultat de l'ítem és la probabilitat logarítmica d'algú d'encertar l'ítem.
Més informació: Henning, 1987, pàg. 118–126.
CA:241, DA:220, DE:227, EN:218, ES:259, FR:240, GA:216, IT:232, NE:234, PO:253.

242 màquina de lectura òptica Aparell electrònic utilitzat per escannejar informació directament del full de resposta. Els examinands o els examinadors poden marcar les respostes dels ítems o de les tasques en un full i l'ordinador llegeix directament aquesta informació. S'anomena també escànner.
CA:242, DA:268, DE:274, EN:261, ES:255, FR:237, GA:214, IT:226, NE:274, PO:249.

243 marca del distractor Freqüència amb què se selecciona cada distractor en un ítem d'elecció múltiple. La marca posa de manifest l'atractiu de cada distractor.
CA:243, DA:80, DE:89, EN:116, ES:71, FR:301, GA:384, IT:88, NE:9, PO:96.

244 mediana Mesura de tendència central, igual al valor de la variable que divideix una distribució de freqüències o de probabilitat en dues parts iguals: la meitat per sobre i la meitat per sota de la mediana.
Vegeu: mesura de tendència central.
Compareu: moda.
Més informació: Hatch i Lazaraton, 1991, pàg. 161.
CA:244, DA:228, DE:232, EN:232, ES:263, FR:242, GA:3, IT:235, NE:239, PO:256.

245 mesura Generalment, procés d'esbrinar una quantitat comparant-la amb una unitat fixada, per exemple utilitzant un regle per mesurar la longitud. En ciències socials, la mesura sovint fa referència a la quantificació de característiques de les persones, com ara la proficiència lingüística.
Més informació: Bachman, 1990, capítol 2.
CA:245, DA:242, DE:241, EN:230, ES:264, FR:243, GA:395, IT:238, NE:245, PO:257.

246 mesura de tendència central Paràmetre que redueix les dades obtingudes referents a una variable a un valor central que s'utilitza com a representació i resum del conjunt de valors de la variable. Les tres mesures de tendència central usades habitualment són la mitjana, la mediana i la moda.
Més informació: Henning, 1987, pàg. 39–40; Guilford i Fruchter, 1981, capítol 4; Hatch i Lazaraton, 1991, pàg. 159–164.
CA:246, DA:47, DE:447, EN:45, ES:391, FR:358, GA:62, IT:348, NE:55, PO:356.

247 mesura independent de la mostra En recerca, interpretació de conclusions que no és dependent de la mostra que s'utilitza en una investigació concreta.
Vegeu: mostra.
CA:247, DA:373, DE:382, EN:339, ES:265, FR:244, GA:396, IT:239, NE:371, PO:258.

248 mètode de prova La capacitat lingüística pot ser avaluada utilitzant una varietat de mètodes: elecció múltiple, compleció, composició, entrevista oral, etc. S'ha observat que el mètode de prova interactua amb la capacitat en la mesura de l'actuació de l'examinand.
Vegeu: característiques del mètode de prova.
Més informació: Bachman, 1990, pàg. 77.
CA:248, DA:395, DE:401, EN:401, ES:266, FR:245, GA:257, IT:236, NE:396, PO:259.

249 mètode del gràfic delta Mètode per considerar el funcionament diferencial d'ítems. S'utilitza per identificar ítems que exageren o minimitzen diferències en actuacions de grup i es basa en les dificultats clàssiques dels ítems (valors-*p*). Els valors-*p* es transformen en puntuacions *z* normalitzades i aquests valors es marquen per parelles en un gràfic per mostrar la dificultat relativa dels ítems per als dos grups en qüestió.
Vegeu: funcionament diferencial d'ítems (FDI).
Més informació: Crocker i Algina, 1986, pàg. 388–390.
CA:249, DA:61, DE:74, EN:92, ES:267, FR:246, GA:256, IT:237, NE:93, PO:260.

250 mitjana aritmètica Mesura de tendència central d'un conjunt de valors d'una variable, que resulta de la suma

d'aquests valors dividida pel seu nombre.
Compareu: mediana, moda.
Vegeu: mesura de tendència central.
Més informació: Hatch i Lazaraton, 1991, pàg. 161–163.
CA:250, DA:231, DE:244, EN:227, ES:261, FR:257, GA:226, IT:234, NE:151, PO:255.

251 mitjana quadràtica Mesura de tendència central d'un conjunt de valors d'una variable, que resulta de l'arrel quadrada de la mitjana aritmètica dels quadrats dels valors de les observacions de la variable.
Vegeu: ANOVA.
CA:251, DA:230, DE:245, EN:229, ES:262, FR:47, GA:227, IT:295, NE:149, PO:319.

252 moda Mesura de tendència central igual al valor més freqüent d'una variable respecte als valors que l'envolten.

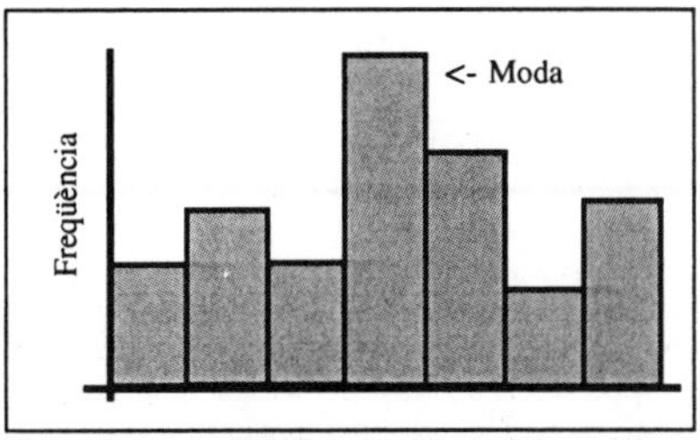

Compareu: distribució bimodal, mitjana aritmètica, mediana.
Vegeu: mesura de tendència central.
Més informació: Hatch i Lazaraton, 1991, pàg. 160–161.
CA:252, DA:232, DE:247, EN:235, ES:268, FR:247, GA:255, IT:240, NE:248, PO:261.

253 model cognitiu Teoria sobre la manera en què s'estructuren els coneixements d'una persona, en el sentit tant de conceptes com de processos. És important en proves de llengua perquè, com a teoria, pot tenir un efecte en l'elecció del mètode de prova o del contingut de la prova.
CA:253, DA:178, DE:181, EN:56, ES:269, FR:250, GA:297, IT:243, NE:64, PO:262.

254 model d'escala de valoració Extensió del model de Rasch simple que tracta dades d'escala; per exemple, puntuacions de l'expressió oral.
Compareu: model de Rasch.
Vegeu: model de crèdit parcial.
Més informació: Wright, B. D. i Masters, G. N., 1982, Rating Scale Analysis, Chicago, MESA Press.
CA:254, DA:173, DE:236, EN:316, ES:272, FR:251, GA:303, IT:246, NE:41, PO:263.

255 model d'un paràmetre En la teoria de resposta d'ítem, model de mesura que opera amb una única escala que representa dificultat (de tasques) i capacitat (de persones), i no considera les variables de discriminació d'ítem ni l'atzar.
Compareu: model de Rasch.
CA:255, DA:92, DE:99, EN:259, ES:273, FR:249, GA:296, IT:242, NE:118, PO:265.

256 model de correcció Llista de totes les respostes acceptables dels ítems d'una prova. Un model de correcció fa possible que el corrector assigni acuradament una puntuació a una prova.
CA:256, DA:319, DE:228, EN:223, ES:301, FR:29, GA:324, IT:329, NE:79, PO:172.

257 model de crèdit parcial En la teoria de resposta d'ítem, model per tractar les dades d'escala. Podria ser un model adequat per utilitzar en l'anàlisi de les respostes en ítems de compleció gramatical, en què s'usa una escala, per exemple 1, 2 o 3, per puntuar ítems, o en una entrevista oral en què es fan servir diverses escales per puntuar l'actuació.
Compareu: model d'escala de valoració, model de Rasch multifaceta.
Vegeu: model de Rasch.
Més informació: Wright i Masters, 1982, pàg. 40–48.
CA:257, DA:278, DE:281, EN:272, ES:270, FR:253, GA:301, IT:244, NE:282, PO:267.

258 model de dos paràmetres En la teoria de resposta d'ítem, model que té en compte el paràmetre de discriminació d'un ítem a més del paràmetre capacitat/dificultat.
Compareu: model d'un paràmetre, model de Rasch.
Vegeu: teoria de resposta d'ítem.
CA:258, DA:411, DE:454, EN:424, ES:271, FR:248, GA:298, IT:241, NE:404, PO:264.

259 model de Rasch Model matemàtic, també anomenat model logístic simple, que planteja una relació entre la probabilitat que una persona completi una tasca i la diferència entre la capacitat de la persona i la dificultat de la tasca. Matemàticament és equivalent al model d'un paràmetre en la teoria de resposta

d'ítem. El model de Rasch s'utilitza de diverses maneres, per exemple per manipular respostes d'escala o explicar les facetes múltiples que donen compte de la "dificultat" d'una tasca.
Vegeu: teoria de resposta d'ítem, model de crèdit parcial, model d'escala de valoració, model de Rasch multifaceta.
Més informació: Henning, 1987, pàg. 117–125.
CA:259, DA:305, DE:316, EN:310, ES:275, FR:252, GA:302, IT:248, NE:313, PO:266.

260 model de Rasch multifaceta Ampliació del model de Rasch, que permet que les probabilitats de resposta siguin modelades sobre la base d'una combinació additiva de facetes. Per exemple, l'actuació en una tasca escrita pot ser modelada per reflectir la dificultat de la tasca més la severitat del qualificador. El model de Rasch multifaceta ha estat implementat pel programa FACETS, entre d'altres.
Vegeu: model de Rasch.
Més informació: Linacre, J. M., 1989, Many-Facet Rasch Measurement, Chicago, MESA Press.
CA:260, DA:235, DE:289, EN:220, ES:276, FR:254, GA:300, IT:249, NE:236, PO:268.

261 model de resposta Bon exemple de la resposta esperada en una tasca oberta que proporciona el redactor de l'ítem i que pot ser utilitzat en el desenvolupament d'un model de correcció per guiar els correctors.
CA:261, DA:233, DE:253, EN:236, ES:376, FR:333, GA:156, IT:245, NE:21, PO:340.

262 model probabilístic Model en què les relacions causals (com ara dificultat d'ítem i capacitat de l'examinand en l'actuació en una prova) s'expliquen en termes de grau de probabilitat. El model de Rasch n'és un exemple.
CA:262, DA:295, DE:297, EN:294, ES:274, FR:255, GA:299, IT:247, NE:430, PO:269.

263 moderació a) Part del procés de preparació d'ítems o tasques per fer servir en una prova. En aquesta fase un grup d'experts (per exemple, redactors de proves i professors) examina de manera crítica els materials i decideix si finalment són acceptats per ser utilitzats (possiblement amb alguna revisió o correcció).

b) En el procés de valoració, ajustament fet per un supervisor a les notes ja assignades per un avaluador.
Compareu: revisió.
CA:263, DA:410, DE:31, EN:237, ES:277, FR:256, GA:260, IT:250, NE:247, PO:270.

264 mostra Selecció d'un subconjunt d'elements d'una població. Es poden distingir diversos tipus de mostra: mostra aleatòria, mostra estratificada, etc.
Més informació: Crocker i Algina, 1986, pàg. 432–438; Guilford i Fruchter, 1981, pàg. 44–45.
CA:264, DA:371, DE:380, EN:337, ES:278, FR:116, GA:304, IT:46, NE:369, PO:8.

265 mostra aleatòria Mostra probabilística en la qual tots els subconjunts d'elements de grandària *n* de la població tenen la mateixa probabilitat de ser seleccionats.
Vegeu: mostra.
Més informació: Crocker i Algina, 1986, pàg. 433–438; Guilford i Fruchter, 1981, pàg. 120.
CA:265, DA:409, DE:451, EN:307, ES:279, FR:117, GA:305, IT:47, NE:120, PO:9.

266 mostra estratificada Mostra d'una població objecte d'estudi que primer se subdivideix en un nombre de subpoblacions (capes, rangs, estrats) de cada una de les quals s'agafa una mostra.
Vegeu: mostra.
Més informació: Guilford i Fruchter, 1981, pàg. 122–123.
CA:266, DA:375, DE:134, EN:388, ES:280, FR:119, GA:306, IT:48, NE:157, PO:11.

267 mostreig Selecció d'una mostra.
Vegeu: mostra.
CA:267, DA:374, DE:384, EN:340, ES:281, FR:120, GA:307, IT:45, NE:368, PO:313.

268 mostres d'examen Mostra de les respostes d'un examinand que representa un ventall divers de la capacitat objecte d'avaluació. S'utilitza en l'estandardització d'avaluadors.
CA:268, DA:370, DE:254, EN:338, ES:132, FR:118, GA:344, IT:330, NE:420, PO:10.

269 *N, n* *N* s'utilitza sovint per representar el nombre de casos d'un estudi o d'individus d'una població, mentre que *n* sovint representa el nombre d'una mostra o subgrup. Per exemple: "La prova es va passar a enginyers superiors ($N = 600$) el 10

% dels quals eren dones (*n* = 60)".
CA:269, DA:248, DE:256, EN:244, ES:282, FR:258, GA:261, IT:251, NE:259, PO:271.

270 nivell Grau de proficiència exigit a un estudiant per ser en una classe determinada o grau de proficiència representat per una prova concreta. Hi ha diferents nivells: elemental, intermedi, avançat, etc.
CA:270, DA:247, DE:260, EN:209, ES:283, FR:259, GA:210, IT:229, NE:258, PO:272.

271 nivell inicial Especificació d'un nivell bàsic de competència en llengua estrangera publicat inicialment pel Consell d'Europa el 1977 per a l'anglès i revisat el 1990. Amb relació al nivell llindar, estableix un objectiu menys exigent i es considera que té aproximadament la meitat de continguts d'aprenentatge.
Compareu: nivell llindar.
CA:271, DA:437, DE:443, EN:436, ES:284, FR:261, GA:211, IT:231, NE:433, PO:274.

272 nivell llindar Especificació en termes funcionals d'un nivell elemental de competència en llengua estrangera, publicat pel Consell d'Europa el 1976 i actualitzat el 1990. Des d'aleshores se n'han fet versions per a diferents llengües europees.
CA:272, DA:419, DE:414, EN:414, ES:285, FR:262, GA:212, IT:230, NE:386, PO:275.

273 norma Estàndard d'actuació. En una prova estandarditzada la norma es determina enregistrant les puntuacions d'un grup gran. La norma o estàndards basats en l'actuació d'aquest grup s'utilitzen per valorar l'actuació de grups posteriors d'examinands d'un tipus similar.
Vegeu: grup norma, prova referida a la norma.
CA:273, DA:250, DE:263, EN:250, ES:286, FR:264, GA:262, IT:252, NE:261, PO:278.

274 normalització Canvi de puntuacions per transformar la distribució en una distribució normal. Habitualment comportarà la utilització d'escalonament d'equipercentils.
Compareu: puntuació estàndard.
CA:274, DA:253, DE:264, EN:253, ES:287, FR:263, GA:263, IT:253, NE:263, PO:279.

275 nota La puntuació aconseguida en una prova es pot presentar a l'examinand com una nota; per exemple, en una escala d'A a E, A és la nota més alta assolible, B és un notable, C és un aprovat, i D i E són qualificacions suspeses.
Compareu: puntuació.
CA:275, DA:167, DE:270, EN:156, ES:288, FR:259, GA:164, IT:188, NE:426, PO:272.

276 nucli de l'ítem Part d'un estímul escrit, habitualment una oració incompleta per a la compleció de la qual cal proporcionar o seleccionar alguna opció.
Compareu: clau, opcions.
Vegeu: ítem d'elecció múltiple.
CA:276, DA:360, DE:29, EN:387, ES:139, FR:10, GA:160, IT:346, NE:359, PO:224.

277 objectiu d'aprenentatge Objectiu o resultat desitjat d'una activitat pedagògica.
CA:277, DA:136, DE:215, EN:208, ES:290, FR:289, GA:360, IT:255, NE:217, PO:292.

278 objectius Coneixement, competència i actituds que s'han establert com a propòsits d'un curs de qualsevol tipus.
CA:278, DA:244, DE:216, EN:256, ES:291, FR:288, GA:359, IT:254, NE:112, PO:293.

279 opcions Varietat de possibilitats en un ítem d'elecció múltiple o una tasca de relació entre les quals se n'ha de seleccionar la correcta.
CA:279, DA:425, DE:38, EN:262, ES:292, FR:290, GA:293, IT:258, NE:14, PO:294.

280 paràmetre Característica numèrica d'una mostra o d'una població; per exemple, la desviació estàndard d'una població.
Compareu: estadístic.
CA:280, DA:276, DE:279, EN:269, ES:293, FR:291, GA:272, IT:259, NE:280, PO:296.

281 paràmetre A Paràmetre de la teoria de resposta d'ítem que està relacionat amb la discriminació d'un ítem.
Vegeu: teoria de resposta d'ítem (TRI).
Més informació: Bachman, 1990, pàg. 204.
CA:281, DA:1, DE:84, EN:1, ES:294, FR:292, GA:273, IT:260, NE:1, PO:297.

282 paràmetre B Paràmetre de la teoria de resposta d'ítem que està relacionat amb el grau de dificultat d'un ítem.
Vegeu: teoria de resposta d'ítem (TRI).
Més informació: Bachman, 1990, pàg. 204.
CA:282, DA:24, DE:170, EN:26, ES:295,

FR:293, GA:274, IT:261, NE:26, PO:298.

283 paràmetre C Paràmetre de la teoria de resposta d'ítem que està relacionat amb l'atzar.
Vegeu: teoria de resposta d'ítem (TRI).
Més informació: Bachman, 1990, pàg. 204.
CA:283, DA:44, DE:318, EN:37, ES:296, FR:294, GA:275, IT:262, NE:50, PO:299.

284 paràmetre d'atzar Vegeu la definició de paràmetre C.
CA:284, DA:122, DE:319, EN:159, ES:297, FR:295, GA:277, IT:263, NE:160, PO:301.

285 paràmetre de dificultat Vegeu la definició de paràmetre B.
CA:285, DA:379, DE:344, EN:102, ES:298, FR:296, GA:276, IT:264, NE:250, PO:300.

286 parlant nadiu Parlant d'una llengua adquirida com a primera llengua.
CA:286, DA:234, DE:255, EN:245, ES:216, FR:217, GA:47, IT:265, NE:255, PO:190.

287 percentil Els 99 punts d'una escala que divideixen una distribució de freqüència en 100 grups d'igual magnitud. El ciquantè (P50) s'anomena mediana. Els quartils divideixen la distribució en quatre grups iguals.
Més informació: Hatch i Lazaraton, 1991, pàg. 187–188.
CA:287, DA:280, DE:285, EN:275, ES:299, FR:49, GA:279, IT:266, NE:284, PO:302.

288 perfil Manera de presentar els resultats d'una prova desglossats en els diversos components de la prova, de forma que l'examinand o altres usuaris de la prova poden identificar les àrees de punts forts i punts febles.
CA:288, DA:297, DE:404, EN:297, ES:300, FR:312, GA:282, IT:395, NE:307, PO:303.

289 població Conjunt finit o infinit d'elements; per exemple, tots els examinands possibles que fan un examen. En estadística, s'anomena també univers de puntuacions.
Compareu: mostra.
CA:289, DA:292, DE:290, EN:285, ES:302, FR:303, GA:280, IT:269, NE:294, PO:308.

290 ponderació Assignació d'un nombre diferent de punts màxims en un ítem, tasca o component d'una prova a fi de canviar-ne la contribució relativa amb relació a les altres parts de la mateixa prova. Per exemple, si es dóna una puntuació doble en tots els ítems de la primera tasca d'una prova, la primera tasca obtindrà una proporció més gran de la puntuació total que les altres tasques.
Més informació: Ebel i Frisbie, 1991, pàg. 214–216.
CA:290, DA:435, DE:136, EN:438, ES:303, FR:302, GA:439, IT:268, NE:434, PO:306.

291 pregunta S'utilitza de vegades per denominar una tasca o un ítem d'una prova.
Vegeu: ítem, tasca.
CA:291, DA:357, DE:122, EN:303, ES:304, FR:315, GA:55, IT:136, NE:423, PO:323.

292 pregunta oberta Tipus d'ítem o tasca en una prova escrita que implica que l'examinand doni una resposta, en comptes de seleccionar-ne una. El propòsit d'aquest tipus d'ítem és provocar una resposta relativament espontània, que pot variar en extensió des de pocs mots fins a una redacció extensa. El model de correcció té en compte, per tant, una varietat de respostes acceptables.
CA:292, DA:444, DE:273, EN:260, ES:305, FR:318, GA:56, IT:137, NE:273, PO:324.

293 procediments d'elicitació Tècnica per produir una resposta d'un examinand en una prova. Normalment s'utilitza en el context d'una resposta oral en una prova d'expressió oral.
Més informació: Hughes, 1989, pàg. 104–110.
CA:293, DA:8, DE:212, EN:123, ES:310, FR:307, GA:162, IT:276, NE:320, PO:314.

294 procediments no paramètrics Procediments estadístics que s'usen quan les dades subjectes a anàlisi no tenen una distribució normal i no es poden mesurar amb escales d'interval o de raó; n'és un exemple el khi quadrat.
Compareu: procediments paramètrics.
Més informació: Hatch i Lazaraton, pàg. 237–239.
CA:294, DA:131, DE:259, EN:249, ES:308, FR:309, GA:258, IT:274, NE:257, PO:315.

295 procediments paramètrics Procediments estadístics que s'apliquen quan les dades estan distribuïdes normalment i es mesuren en escales d'interval o de raó. A la pràctica, els procediments paramètrics s'utilitzen quan hi ha prou casos per

aproximar les dades a la distribució normal.
Compareu: procediments no paramètrics.
Més informació: Hatch i Lazaraton, 1991, pàg. 237–238.
CA:295, DA:277, DE:280, EN:270, ES:309, FR:310, GA:259, IT:275, NE:281, PO:316.

296 proficiència Coneixement d'una llengua i grau d'habilitat en utilitzar-la.
Compareu: capacitat, competència.
Més informació: Bachman, 1990, pàg. 16.
CA:296, DA:296, DE:47, EN:295, ES:120, FR:260, GA:265, IT:62, NE:305, PO:273.

297 proficiència lingüística Grau de capacitat o d'habilitat amb què una persona pot fer servir una llengua, és a dir, fins a quin punt una persona pot entendre, llegir, parlar i escriure una llengua. El terme s'utilitza sovint com a sinòmin de capacitat lingüística.
Més informació: Bachman, 1990, pàg. 16.
CA:297, DA:355, DE:365, EN:206, ES:121, FR:66, GA:267, IT:66, NE:215, PO:81.

298 proficiència oral Proficiència en l'expressió oral en una llengua.
CA:298, DA:239, DE:370, EN:264, ES:65, FR:68, GA:266, IT:67, NE:354, PO:82.

299 programa Document detallat que inventaria totes les àrees cobertes en un programa concret d'estudi i l'ordre en què es presenten els continguts.
Compareu: currículum.
CA:299, DA:224, DE:207, EN:392, ES:310, FR:352, GA:352, IT:335, NE:225, PO:318.

300 prova Procediment per avaluar aspectes específics de la proficiència o del coneixement.

a) Grup de components que constitueixen conjuntament un procediment d'avaluació; s'usa com a sinònim d'examen.

b) Tasca individual o component per avaluar una àrea d'habilitat o de coneixement; per exemple, expressió oral o expressió escrita. En aquest sentit, una prova pot formar part també d'un examen complet com a component (per exemple, prova d'expressió oral) o com una tasca individual (per exemple, prova de compleció).

c) Procediment d'avaluació que és relativament breu i fàcil d'administrar, sovint dissenyat i administrat per una institució (per exemple, una prova de progrés) o usada com a part d'un progama de recerca o amb finalitats de validació (per exemple, una prova d'ancoratge).
Compareu: examen.
Vegeu: prova d'ancoratge, prova de compleció, prova de progrés.
Més informació: Bachman 1990 pàg.50.
CA:300, DA:300, DE:389, EN:395, ES:311, FR:359, GA:403, IT:353, NE:388, PO:361.

301 prova a mida Adaptació de proves existents per satisfer els requeri-ments d'un grup concret d'usuaris o destinataris d'una prova.
CA:301, DA:404, DE:410, EN:405, ES:13, FR:395, GA:370, IT:5, NE:382, PO:4.

302 prova adaptativa Tipus de prova en què els ítems es presenten a l'examinand mentre fa la prova segons els encerts i errors que va comentent en els ítems anteriors. La selecció es fa d'acord amb una estimació de la capacitat que demostra l'examinand. Sovint s'utilitza per referir-se a la prova administrada per ordinador, encara que una entrevista oral també pot ser una prova adaptativa.
Vegeu: prova adaptativa per ordinador
Més informació: Bachman, 1990, pàg. 151; Henning, 1987, pàg. 136.
CA:302, DA:102, DE:6, EN:7, ES:312, FR:361, GA:429, IT:356, NE:5, PO:363.

303 prova adaptativa per ordinador Mètode de prova administrat per mitjà de l'ordinador en què es presenta el contingut de la prova a l'examinand considerant contínuament la capacitat que aquest demostra durant el procés d'examen; adapta el nivell de dificultat dels ítems a la capacitat estimada.
Vegeu: prova per ordinador.
CA:303, DA:51, DE:67, EN:63, ES:181, FR:362, GA:379, IT:386, NE:68, PO:364.

304 prova C Tipus de tasca d'omplir buits en què se suprimeix la segona meitat de determinades paraules. La freqüència de supressió pot ser com a màxim de cada dos mots. L'examinand ha de completar les paraules incompletes.
Compareu: prova de compleció.
Més informació: Weir, 1990, pàg. 49.
CA:304, DA:45, DE:62, EN:38, ES:314, FR:394, GA:408, IT:384, NE:51, PO:366.

305 prova d'accés Prova utilitzada per determinar si un examinand és admès en una institució determinada o en un curs.
Compareu: prova de col·locació.
CA:305, DA:5, DE:346, EN:124, ES:319, FR:369, GA:422, IT:364, NE:387, PO:377.

306 prova d'actuació Procediment de prova que requereix que l'examinand produeixi una mostra de llengua, escrita o oral (per exemple, redaccions o entrevistes orals). Aquests procediments sovint estan dissenyats per reproduir l'actuació lingüística en contextos reals.
Més informació: Bachman, 1990, pàg. 304–305.
CA:306, DA:283, DE:284, EN:278, ES:318, FR:380, GA:416, IT:367, NE:287, PO:381.

307 prova d'ancoratge Prova amb característiques de mesura conegudes que s'administra conjuntament amb una altra prova. L'actuació en una prova d'ancoratge proporciona informació sobre l'altra prova i sobre els examinands que les han fetes totes dues.
Compareu: ítem àncora.
CA:307, DA:17, DE:19, EN:16, ES:320, FR:367, GA:404, IT:357, NE:18, PO:365.

308 prova d'aptitud Prova dissenyada per predir o mesurar les possibilitats d'èxit d'un examinand en una àrea determinada d'aprenentatge, per exemple en l'aprenentatge d'una llengua estrangera o en un curs concret.
Més informació: Henning, 1987, pàg. 6; Ebel i Frisbie, 1991, pàg. 339.
CA:308, DA:18, DE:96, EN:20, ES:322, FR:368, GA:421, IT:358, NE:22, PO:370.

309 prova d'assoliment Prova dissenyada per mesurar el grau d'aprenentatge assolit per un examinand amb relació a un curs determinat, llibre de text, etc., i.e. una prova dependent del currículum. S'anomena també prova de rendiment.
CA:309, DA:366, DE:369, EN:6, ES:321, FR:374, GA:419, IT:368, NE:301, PO:374.

310 prova de capacitat Prova que dóna prou temps perquè quasi tots els examinands l'acabin, però que conté alguns ítems o tasques amb un grau de dificultat que fa impossible que la majoria d'examinands facin tots els ítems correctament.
Compareu: prova de rapidesa.
CA:310, DA:299, DE:261/293, EN:288, ES:329, FR:379, GA:413, IT:360, NE:296, PO:371.

311 prova de col·locació Prova administrada a fi de col·locar els estudiants en un grup o classe amb un nivell adequat al seu grau de coneixements i capacitat.
CA:311, DA:137, DE:101, EN:282, ES:323, FR:377, GA:434, IT:365, NE:291, PO:372.

312 prova de competència mínima Prova que estableix els requisits específics d'un nivell mínim de competència en un àmbit concret d'ús de llengua. Un examinand que demostra aquest nivell de competència passa la prova.
CA:312, DA:398, DE:304, EN:234, ES:183, FR:167, GA:378, IT:388, NE:246, PO:31.

313 prova de compleció Tipus de tasca d'omplir buits en què se suprimeixen mots sencers d'un text. En una prova de compleció tradicional, la supressió és cada *x* mots. Altres tasques d'omplir buits on se suprimeixen frases curtes d'un text o on l'autor dels ítems tria els mots que han de ser suprimits s'anomenen habitualment proves de compleció, com per exemple la prova de compleció racional. Els examinands poden haver de proporcionar els mots desapareguts (prova de compleció oberta) o bé triar entre una sèrie d'opcions (prova de compleció d'elecció múltiple o tancada). La correcció de proves de compleció pot ser per "mot exacte" (només es considera resposta correcta el mot suprimit en el text original) o per "mot acceptable" (es dóna als correctors una llista de respostes acceptables).
Compareu: prova C, ítem d'omplir buits.
Més informació: Weir, 1990, pàg. 46–48; Oller, 1979, capítol 12.
CA:313, DA:50, DE:66, EN:52, ES:315, FR:370, GA:410, IT:362, NE:61, PO:378.

314 prova de compleció racional Vegeu la definició de prova de compleció.
CA:314, DA:308, DE:230, EN:318, ES:316, FR:371, GA:60, IT:56, NE:315, PO:367.

315 prova de comprensió oral Prova de comprensió de llengua oral que normalment s'administra mitjançant un magnetòfon o un vídeo.
CA:315, DA:221, DE:147, EN:216, ES:324, FR:372, GA:411, IT:361, NE:235, PO:373.

316 prova de detecció Prova, habitualment curta i fàcil d'administrar, utilitzada per identificar els examinands que poden ser admesos en un curs o els examinands per a un examen.
Compareu: prova de col·locació.
CA:316, DA:424, DE:98, EN:349, ES:332, FR:375, GA:432, IT:370, NE:332, PO:375.

317 prova de diagnòstic Prova utilitzada per descobrir els punts forts i els punts febles específics d'un aprenent. Els resultats poden servir per prendre decisions en la formació, l'aprenentatge o l'ensenya-

ment futurs.
CA:317, DA:65, DE:77, EN:97, ES:325, FR:383, GA:414, IT:373, NE:97, PO:386.

318 prova de llengua per a propòsits específics Prova dissenyada per mesurar la capacitat d'un examinand per actuar en un context professional o acadèmic específic. En conseqüència, el contingut de la prova es dissenya sobre la base d'una anàlisi de les tasques lingüístiques que els examinands necessitaran per enfrontar-se amb la situació d'ús lingüístic objecte d'avaluació.
CA:318, DA:243, DE:112, EN:375, ES:328, FR:393, GA:431, IT:378, NE:351, PO:393.

319 prova de proficiència Prova que mesura una capacitat general o habilitat, sense fer referència a cap curs específic o conjunt de materials.
CA:319, DA:112, DE:120, EN:296, ES:326, FR:378, GA:428, IT:363, NE:306, PO:379.

320 prova de progrés Prova administrada durant un curs a fi de valorar l'aprenentatge d'algun o alguns aspectes.
CA:320, DA:108, DE:214, EN:298, ES:330, FR:381, GA:418, IT:369, NE:422, PO:382.

321 prova de rapidesa Prova amb un límit de temps per completar-la. Els examinands més lents assoleixen una puntuació més baixa perquè no arriben a les últimes preguntes. Normalment, en una prova de rapidesa la dificultat de les preguntes s'ha establert de manera que els examinands en general les podrien respondre correctament si no hi hagués restricció de temps. S'anomena també prova de velocitat.
Compareu: prova de capacitat.
CA:321, DA:129, DE:340/363, EN:376, ES:334, FR:363, GA:424, IT:372, NE:352, PO:385.

322 prova de rendiment Vegeu la definició de prova d'assoliment.
CA:322, DA:20, DE:203, EN:23, ES:331, FR:366, GA:419, IT:368, NE:421, PO:374.

323 prova de selecció Vegeu la definició de prova d'accés.
CA:323, DA:330, DE:36, EN:353, ES:332, FR:382, GA:430, IT:370, NE:333, PO:383.

324 prova de significació Prova per determinar la significació estadística.
Vegeu: significació.
CA:324, DA:334, DE:350, EN:364, ES:333, FR:373, GA:435, IT:371, NE:339, PO:384.

325 prova dependent del currículum Prova vinculada estretament a un programa concret, que té un rol determinat en el procés pedagògic.
Compareu: prova independent del currículum.
Vegeu: prova d'assoliment.
CA:325, DA:56, DE:217, EN:88, ES:313, FR:365, GA:406, IT:374, NE:221, PO:380.

326 prova directa Prova que mesura les habilitats productives d'expressió oral i expressió escrita, en què l'actuació de l'habilitat es mesura directament. Un exemple n'és una prova de capacitat d'expressió escrita en què l'examinand ha d'escriure una carta.
Compareu: prova indirecta.
Més informació: Hughes, 1989, pàg. 14–16.
CA:326, DA:70, DE:81, EN:104, ES:335, FR:384, GA:415, IT:375, NE:102, PO:387.

327 prova final Prova o un altre tipus de mesura administrat al final d'un curs. El contrast dels resultats amb els resultats d'una prova administrada a l'inici del curs proporciona evidències sobre l'eficàcia del curs.
Compareu: prova preliminar.
CA:327, DA:345, DE:5, EN:287, ES:336, FR:305, GA:179, IT:271, NE:295, PO:310.

328 prova independent del currículum Prova que no està vinculada a un programa o un curs determinat.
Compareu: prova dependent del currículum.
Vegeu: prova de proficiència.
CA:328, DA:57, DE:218, EN:89, ES:339, FR:387, GA:405, IT:376, NE:222, PO:388.

329 prova indirecta (tasca) Prova o tasca que intenta mesurar les capacitats subjacents a una habilitat lingüística i no l'actuació en l'habilitat. Un exemple n'és una prova de capacitat d'expressió escrita en què l'examinand ha de corregir les estructures utilitzades incorrectament en un text.
Compareu: prova directa.
Més informació: Hughes, 1989, pàg. 14–16.
CA:329, DA:135, DE:150, EN:170, ES:337, FR:385, GA:420, IT:354, NE:173, PO:389.

330 prova khi quadrat Procediment estadístic no paramètric que compara els valors de respostes observades i esperades a fi d'indicar si la diferència és estadís-

ticament significativa, prenent com a punt de referència les respostes esperades.
Vegeu: procediments no paramètrics.
Més informació: Hatch i Lazaraton, 1991, pàg. 393–415.
CA:330, DA:49, DE:65, EN:49, ES:396, FR:149, GA:409, IT:359, NE:59, PO:395.

331 prova objectiva Prova que pot ser puntuada aplicant un model de correcció, sense la necessitat de formular una opinió experta o un judici subjectiu sobre la tasca.
CA:331, DA:257, DE:272, EN:257, ES:341, FR:389, GA:427, IT:377, NE:267, PO:392.

332 prova per ordinador Mètode de prova en què es presenten els ítems als examinands mitjançant ordinador. Les respostes també es poden donar per mitjà de l'ordinador.
CA:332, DA:52, DE:68, EN:64, ES:182, FR:171, GA:380, IT:387, NE:70, PO:35.

333 prova preliminar Prova administrada abans de l'inici d'un curs. Els resultats de la prova preliminar poden ser contrastats amb els resultats obtinguts en una altra prova al final del curs a fi d'avaluar l'eficàcia del curs.
Compareu: prova final.
CA:333, DA:104, DE:440, EN:292, ES:338, FR:306, GA:290, IT:272, NE:299, PO:312.

334 prova psicomètrica Prova de trets psicològics, com són personalitat, intel·ligència, aptitud i competència lingüística, que fa suposicions específiques sobre la naturalesa de la capacitat provada, per exemple si està distribuïda unidimensionalment o normalment.
Més informació: Bachman, 1990, pàg. 73–74.
CA:334, DA:302, DE:310, EN:301, ES:397, FR:390, GA:433, IT:379, NE:308, PO:394.

335 prova referida a l'àmbit Prova en què els resultats s'interpreten respecte a l'àmbit d'un contingut específic o una capacitat.
Compareu: prova referida al criteri, prova referida a la norma.
CA:335, DA:84, DE:50, EN:120, ES:342, FR:391, GA:417, IT:382, NE:114, PO:368.

336 prova referida a la norma Prova en què les puntuacions s'interpreten respecte a la mitjana estàndard d'un grup determinat, comparable a la dels individus que fan la prova. El terme tendeix a ser utilitzat en proves la interpretació de les quals se centra a ordenar els individus amb relació al grup norma o entre ells mateixos.
Compareu: prova referida al criteri.
CA:336, DA:251, DE:268, EN:254, ES:340, FR:388, GA:426, IT:381, NE:264, PO:391.

337 prova referida al criteri Prova en què l'actuació de l'examinand s'interpreta respecte a uns criteris predeterminats. Es fa èmfasi en l'assoliment d'objectius més que no pas a ordenar els examinands dins del grup d'acord amb les seves puntuacions.
Compareu: prova referida a la norma, prova referida a l'àmbit.
CA:337, DA:203, DE:196, EN:81, ES:317, FR:364, GA:412, IT:380, NE:86, PO:369.

338 prova referida al domini Prova dissenyada per establir si un estudiant ha assolit un camp ben definit d'habilitats o coneixement.
CA:338, DA:227, DE:204, EN:225, ES:327, FR:376, GA:425, IT:366, NE:237, PO:376.

339 prova semidirecta Prova que intenta avaluar l'actuació lingüística substituint algun aspecte de la participació de l'examinador; per exemple, una prova d'expressió oral que utilitza un magnetòfon per proporcionar l'estímul sense un entrevistador. Un exemple de prova semidirecta és la SOPI (Semi–Direct Oral Proficiency Interview o entrevista de competència oral semidirecta).
Compareu: prova directa.
CA:339, DA:332, DE:347, EN:356, ES:343, FR:392, GA:423, IT:383, NE:336, PO:396.

340 prova *t* de Student Prova estadística utilitzada per determinar si hi ha cap diferència significativa entre les mitjanes de dues mostres.
CA:340, DA:385, DE:387, EN:423, ES:398, FR:150, GA:368, IT:385, NE:377, PO:397.

341 prova/ítem vigent Prova disponible per utilitzar i que, per aquesta raó, s'ha de mantenir en condicions de seguretat.
CA:341, DA:101, DE:225, EN:217, ES:344, FR:360, GA:407, IT:355, NE:233, PO:362.

342 puntuació a) Nombre total de punts que algú assoleix en una prova, abans de l'escalonament (puntuació directa) o després (puntuació escalonada).

b) Assignació de valors numèrics a actuacions observades.

c) Nombre total de punts possibles per a un ítem, subprova o prova.
Compareu: mesura.

CA:342, DA:287/328, DE:312/313, EN:224/348, ES:44/345, FR:275/287, GA:224/328, IT:278/292, NE:60/331, PO:105/280.

343 puntuació analítica Mètode de puntuació que es pot utilitzar en proves d'ús productiu de llengua, com són expressió oral i expressió escrita. L'avaluador fa una valoració amb l'ajut d'una llista de punts específics. Per exemple, en una prova d'expressió escrita l'escala analítica pot centrar-se en la gramàtica, el vocabulari o l'ús de connectors.
Compareu: avaliació global, correcció segons la impressió (correcció segons la impressió general).
Més informació: Ebel i Frisbie, 1991, pàg. 195.

CA:343, DA:13, DE:12, EN:14, ES:426, FR:266, GA:340, IT:27, NE:15, PO:58.

344 puntuació d'estanina Procediment per agrupar les puntuacions d'una prova en nou grups, basat en la distribució normal. Tant en el grup superior com en l'inferior hi ha el 4 % dels examinands. El percentatge d'examinands en cada un dels grups està il·lustrat en el gràfic següent.

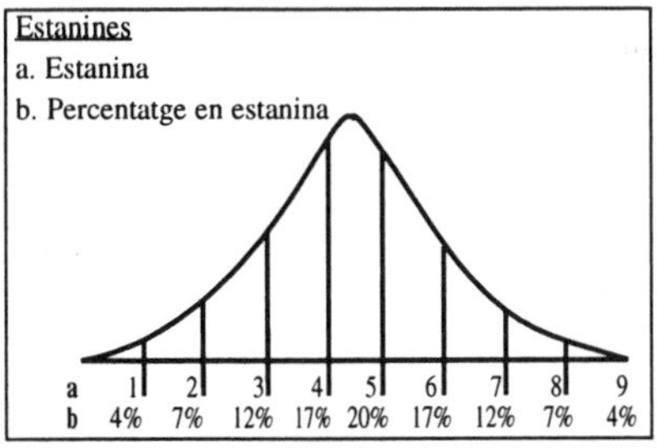

Més informació: Crocker i Algina, 1986, pàg. 446–447.

CA:344, DA:367, DE:377, EN:384, ES:176, FR:282, GA:332, IT:279, NE:365, PO:284.

345 puntuació d'ítem En l'anàlisi d'ítems, suma de les respostes correctes d'un ítem concret.

CA:345, DA:160, DE:171, EN:196, ES:346, FR:267, GA:336, IT:281, NE:202, PO:60.

346 puntuació de banda Part d'una escala que es refereix a l'abast específic d'una capacitat.

CA:346, DA:258, DE:210, EN:30, ES:39, FR:269, GA:330, IT:40, NE:29, PO:65.

347 puntuació dicotòmica Puntuació basada en dues categories, com per exemple vertader/fals, aprovat/suspès o sí/no.

CA:347, DA:67, DE:455, EN:98, ES:347, FR:268, GA:341, IT:32, NE:98, PO:59.

348 puntuació directa Puntuació d'una prova que no ha estat transformada, ponderada o reescalonada.
Vegeu: puntuació.

CA:348, DA:321, DE:328, EN:319, ES:348, FR:276, GA:329, IT:282, NE:324, PO:281.

349 puntuació escalonada Puntuació produïda com a resultat d'un escalonament.
Vegeu: escalonament.

CA:349, DA:340, DE:354, EN:345, ES:349, FR:278, GA:337, IT:286, NE:153, PO:283.

350 puntuació estàndard Puntuació transformada linealment a partir d'un grup de puntuacions. La mitjana i la desviació estàndard estan situades en qualsevol valor que necessiti l'usuari. Són exemples de puntuacions estàndard la puntuació *z* i la puntuació *t*.
Compareu: puntuació *t*, puntuació *z*, puntuació d'estanina.
Més informació: Ebel i Frisbie, 1991, pàg. 67–68.

CA:350, DA:365, DE:376, EN:382, ES:350, FR:281, GA:333, IT:287, NE:364, PO:291.

351 puntuació graduada Puntuació d'un ítem en què s'utilitza una escala d'almenys tres punts. Per exemple, la resposta a una pregunta pot tenir assignats 0, 1 o 2 punts, tres distincions. Les preguntes obertes sovint es puntuen de manera graduada. S'anomena també puntuació d'escala.
Compareu: puntuació dicotòmica.

CA:351, DA:291, DE:237, EN:284, ES:353, FR:89, GA:342, IT:34, NE:293, PO:64.

352 puntuació millorada Diferència entre la puntuació assolida en una prova abans d'iniciar un curs i la puntuació assolida en la mateixa prova o en una de semblant al final del curs. La puntuació millorada indica el progrés durant el curs.

CA:352, DA:290, DE:211, EN:150, ES:32, FR:199, GA:44, IT:192, NE:434, PO:209.

353 puntuació observada Puntuació obtinguda per un examinand. La teoria clàssica de la prova considera que està formada per la puntuació vertadera i l'error.
Vegeu: error, puntuació vertadera.
CA:353, DA:183, DE:49, EN:258, ES:352, FR:279, GA:331, IT:283, NE:429, PO:285.

354 puntuació ponderada d'una prova Puntuació atorgada a un examinand en una prova després d'aplicar-hi la ponderació.
Vegeu: ponderació.
CA:354, DA:434, DE:135, EN:437, ES:354, FR:280, GA:339, IT:284, NE:159, PO:286.

355 puntuació *t* Extensió de la puntuació *z*. Elimina els decimals i els signes negatius. La puntuació *t* és igual a deu vegades la puntuació *z* més 50. La distribució té una mitjana de 50 i una desviació estàndard de 10.
Vegeu: puntuació *z*.
Més informació: Ebel i Frisbie, 1991, pàg. 68.
CA:355, DA:384, DE:388, EN:422, ES:355, FR:283, GA:367, IT:289, NE:376, PO:287.

356 puntuació transformada Puntuació directa que ha estat transformada matemàticament. Pot servir per a propòsits d'escalonament o de ponderació.
Més informació: Ebel i Frisbie, 1991, pàg. 64–70.
CA:356, DA:414, DE:415, EN:417, ES:356, FR:284, GA:334, IT:290, NE:158, PO:288.

357 puntuació vertadera Puntuació que podria obtenir un examinand si no hi hagués un error de mesura en el moment de la prova o de la puntuació. És un concepte fonamental en la teoria clàssica de la prova.
CA:357, DA:415, DE:441, EN:420, ES:357, FR:285, GA:335, IT:285, NE:431, PO:289.

358 puntuació *z* Ocurrència habitual de la puntuació estàndard amb una mitjana de 0 i una desviació estàndard d'1. És la puntuació estàndard usada amb més freqüència; es calcula amb la fórmula següent:

$$z = (X - \bar{X}) \div Sx$$

on:

z és la puntuació z,
X és la puntuació de la prova,
$\bar{X}$ és la puntuació mitjana de la prova i
Sx és la desviació estàndard de les puntuacions de la prova.

Compareu: puntuació *t*.
Vegeu: puntuació estàndard.
Més informació: Ebel i Frisbie, 1991, pàg. 68.
CA:358, DA:439, DE:446, EN:442, ES:358, FR:286, GA:441, IT:291, NE:439, PO:290.

359 puntuació de tall Puntuació mínima que ha d'assolir un examinand a fi de tenir una qualificació en una prova o un examen. En proves referides al domini, puntuació en una prova que s'estima que és el nivell requerit a fi de ser considerat mínimament competent o tenir el nivell de domini.
Compareu: aprovat.
Vegeu: prova referida al domini, prova de competència mínima.
Més informació: Bachman, 1990, pàg. 214–115; Crocker i Algina, pàg. 421–428.
CA:359, DA:58, DE:199, EN:90, ES:351, FR:277, GA:338, IT:280, NE:57, PO:282.

360 qualificació Distinció posterior a un curs reconegut de capacitació o a una prova que faculta una persona per dur a terme una activitat o feina concreta. Un certificat de proficiència lingüística pot ser considerat una qualificació per a determinats propòsits.
Compareu: certificat, diploma.
CA:360, DA:209, DE:314, EN:302, ES:405, FR:313, GA:46, IT:294, NE:214, PO:322.

361 qualificador Vegeu la definició d'avaluador.
CA:361, DA:306, DE:100, EN:311, ES:187, FR:164, GA:287, IT:102, NE:34, PO:182.

362 qualificar Procés de convertir les puntuacions d'una prova o correccions en una nota.
CA:362, DA:168, DE:48, EN:157, ES:47, FR:52, GA:165, IT:94, NE:427, PO:277.

363 rang de percentil Nombre o puntuació que indica el rang que mostra el percentatge situat per sota d'aquesta puntuació. Si un examinand té en una prova un rang de percentil de 60, significa que el 60 % de tots els examinands han assolit una puntuació igual o inferior a aquesta.
CA:363, DA:281, DE:299, EN:276, ES:359, FR:53, GA:284, IT:55, NE:285, PO:276.

364 ràtio F En anàlisi de variància, ràtio calculada que indica si les diferències entre les mitjanes d'uns grups són estadísticament significatives; per exemple, si

un grup ho ha fet considerablement millor que un altre en una prova de llengua.
Vegeu: formes alternes.
Més informació: Hatch i Lazaraton, 1991, pàg. 315–317.
CA:364, DA:94, DE:109, EN:139, ES:368, FR:319, GA:66, IT:296, NE:132, PO:332.

365 reconeixement Acceptació formal per una institució d'una qualificació concreta per a un propòsit específic, per exemple l'admissió a un curs de postgrau.
CA:365, DA:15, DE:269, EN:323, ES:361, FR:321, GA:9, IT:303, NE:123, PO:325.

366 redacció Tasca que implica l'examinand en la producció d'un text escrit extens. Els tipus de text que es fan en una tasca de redacció inclouen narracions d'esdeveniments i discussions de temes en què es poden considerar diferents opinions. També poden incloure altres tipus com ara informes, cartes informals i formals.
CA:366, DA:109/262, DE:32/33, EN:62/131, ES:192/306, FR:73/159, GA:7/51, IT:82/313, NE:125/372, PO:88/142.

367 reescalonament Vegeu la definició d'escalonament.
CA:367, DA:314, DE:258, EN:330, ES:389, FR:320, GA:29, IT:304, NE:166, PO:326.

368 registre Varietat de la llengua associada a l'ús i determinada pel tema, el grau de formalitat, el canal de comunicació i la intenció.
CA:368, DA:310, DE:366, EN:325, ES:364, FR:323, GA:291, IT:297, NE:317, PO:327.

369 regressió Tècnica per predir el valor més probable d'una variable (la variable dependent) a partir de valors coneguts d'una altra variable o més (variables independents).
Més informació: Hatch i Lazaraton, 1991, pàg. 467–480; Guilford i Fruchter, 1981, pàg. 346–361.
CA:369, DA:311, DE:321, EN:326, ES:365, FR:324, GA:4, IT:298, NE:318, PO:328.

370 regressió lineal Tècnica de regressió que suposa una relació lineal entre les variables dependent i independent.
CA:370, DA:215, DE:223, EN:213, ES:366, FR:325, GA:5, IT:299, NE:230, PO:329.

371 regressió múltiple Regressió entre una variable dependent i més d'una variable explicativa. Per exemple, amb la dificultat d'una tasca com a variable dependent, es podrien investigar els efectes del tipus de tasca, la dificultat lèxica, etc.
Vegeu: variable independent, regressió.
Més informació: Hatch i Lazaraton, 1991, pàg. 480–486.
CA:371, DA:117, DE:251, EN:242, ES:367, FR:326, GA:182, IT:300, NE:240, PO:330.

372 repercussió Impacte d'una prova en l'ensenyament. Els professors poden sentir-se influenciats pels coneixements que els seus alumnes tenen d'una prova determinada a la qual es volen presentar, i adapten la metodologia i el contingut de les lliçons per tal de reflectir les demandes de la prova. El resultat pot ser positiu o negatiu. S'anomena també efecte de rebot.
Vegeu: impacte.
CA:372, DA:25/436, DE:43/442, EN:28/435, ES:124/369, FR:95/322, GA:95, IT:147, NE:27/432, PO:135.

373 reproducció Possibilitat de repetir les conclusions d'un treball de recerca més d'una vegada, de manera que augmenti la confiança en els resultats.
CA:373, DA:189, DE:324, EN:329, ES:370, FR:335, GA:185, IT:301, NE:165, PO:333.

374 resposta Conducta de l'examinand provocada per l'estímul d'una prova; per exemple, la resposta donada a un ítem d'elecció múltiple o la feina produïda en una prova d'expressió escrita.
Compareu: estímul, suport.
CA:374, DA:315, DE:21, EN:331, ES:371, FR:327, GA:153, IT:305, NE:319, PO:334.

375 resposta certa Resposta comptada com a correcta en la puntuació d'una prova.
CA:375, DA:190, DE:327, EN:333, ES:373, FR:331, GA:155, IT:307, NE:204, PO:337.

376 resposta elaborada Tipus de resposta escrita d'un ítem d'una prova que implica producció activa i no tan sols triar entre una sèrie d'opcions.
Compareu: resposta seleccionada.
Vegeu: resposta.
CA:376, DA:185, DE:126, EN:70, ES:372, FR:330, GA:154, IT:309, NE:272, PO:336.

377 resposta esperada Resposta o respostes que l'autor d'un ítem o una tasca es proposa obtenir.
CA:377, DA:106, DE:105, EN:137, ES:374, FR:328, GA:157, IT:306, NE:32, PO:338.

378 resposta extensa Tipus de resposta d'un ítem o una tasca en què s'espera que l'examinand produeixi, en comptes que seleccioni, una resposta que sigui més llarga que una frase o dues.
Compareu: ítem de resposta curta.
CA:378, DA:423, DE:35, EN:138, ES:375, FR:332, GA:159, IT:308, NE:407, PO:339.

379 resposta seleccionada Tipus de resposta d'una prova que implica triar entre un nombre d'alternatives en comptes de proporcionar una resposta.
Compareu: resposta elaborada.
Vegeu: resposta.
CA:379, DA:422, DE:37, EN:352, ES:377, FR:334, GA:158, IT:310, NE:154, PO:341.

380 resultat Qualificació d'una prova presentada al destinatari o a l'usuari de la prova.
CA:380, DA:317, DE:103, EN:332, ES:378, FR:336, GA:397, IT:312, NE:322, PO:342.

381 retroalimentació Comentaris de gent implicada en el procés d'avaluació (examen, administració, etc.) que proporcionen una base per avaluar aquest procés. La retroalimentació es pot obtenir informalment o utilitzant qüestionaris dissenyats amb aquesta finalitat.
CA:381, DA:97, DE:330, EN:144, ES:379, FR:337, GA:6, IT:173, NE:134, PO:192.

382 revisió Fase en el cicle d'elaboració d'una prova en què els elaboradors de la prova valoren els materials fets pels redactors i decideixen quins han de ser rebutjats perquè no satisfan les especificacions de la prova i quins han de passar a la fase de correcció.
Compareu: moderació.
CA:382, DA:400, DE:405, EN:433 ES:383, FR:338, GA:184, IT:91, NE:115, PO:343.

383 ro de Spearman Vegeu la definició de coeficient de correlació de Spearman.
CA:383, DA:352, DE:362, EN:374, ES:380, FR:339, GA:292, IT:302, NE:348, PO:344.

384 rúbrica Instruccions donades als examinands per guiar les seves respostes en una tasca concreta d'una prova.
Compareu: instruccions.
CA:384, DA:264, DE:23, EN:336, ES:229, FR:78, GA:295, IT:193, NE:219, PO:92.

385 secció Manera de denominar un component d'una prova, com per exemple secció de comprensió lectora o secció de comprensió oral.
CA:385, DA:393, DE:277, EN:267, ES:381, FR:182, GA:270, IT:168, NE:278, PO:87.

386 seguiment del curs Tècnica d'avaluació qualitativa del procés d'ensenyament–aprenentatge. El professor duu a terme un seguiment continu del procés d'ensenyament–aprenentatge, elaborant-ne dossiers descriptius.
CA:386, DA:293, DE:291, EN:286, ES:185, FR:304, GA:237, IT:270, NE:37, PO:309.

387 seguretat Aspecte de la gestió de l'administració d'una prova que té per objectiu prevenir la revelació del contingut dels materials de la prova durant el seu període de vigència.
CA:387, DA:335, DE:348, EN:351, ES:382, FR:344, GA:353, IT:333, NE:142, PO:347.

388 significació Qualitat d'aquells resultats dels quals es té prou seguretat que no són deguts a l'atzar sinó a factors específics.
Vegeu: error de primera espècie, error de segona espècie, hipòtesi nul·la.
Més informació: Guilford i Fruchter, 1981, pàg. 208–210.
CA:388, DA:333, DE:349, EN:363, ES:386, FR:76, GA:366, IT:334, NE:338, PO:348.

389 subprova Vegeu la definició de component.
CA:389, DA:377, DE:386, EN:389, ES:388, FR:346, GA:150, IT:345, NE:373, PO:350.

390 suport En proves d'expressió oral o escrita, materials gràfics o textos dissenyats per provocar la resposta de l'examinand.
CA:390, DA:316, DE:437 EN:299, ES:178, FR:95, GA:358, IT:343, NE:321, PO:179.

391 tasca Combinació de rúbrica, estímul i resposta; per exemple, un text de comprensió lectora amb diversos ítems d'elecció múltiple que es responen a partir d'un únic enunciat.
CA:391, DA:260, DE:26, EN:393, ES:2, FR:354, GA:371, IT:71, NE:270, PO:352.

392 tasca d'expressió escrita dirigida Vegeu la definició de tasca d'expressió escrita guiada.
CA:392, DA:43, DE:15, EN:105, ES:6, FR:356, GA:376, IT:77, NE:144, PO:355.

393 tasca d'expressió escrita guiada Tasca que implica l'examinand en la producció d'un text escrit, on la informació gràfica o textual, com ara il·lustracions, cartes, postals i instruccions, s'utilitza per controlar i estandarditzar la resposta esperada.
Compareu: redacció.
CA:393, DA:121, DE:130, EN:160, ES:5, FR:311, GA:377, IT:76, NE:143, PO:317.

394 tasca de comprensió lectora Tipus de tasca que generalment consisteix en un text de comprensió lectora o textos i ítems dels tipus següents: elecció múltiple, preguntes de resposta curta, compleció/omplir buits, transferència d'informació, etc.
CA:394, DA:223, DE:220, EN:321, ES:3, FR:357, GA:373, IT:74, NE:224, PO:351.

395 tasca de correcció Tasca d'una prova que implica detectar els errors d'un tipus específic, per exemple ortografia o estructura, en un text. Part de la tasca també pot consistir a corregir els errors i proporcionar les formes correctes.
CA:395, DA:195, DE:189, EN:300, ES:4, FR:84, GA:374, IT:75, NE:304, PO:97.

396 tasca de relació múltiple Tasca d'una prova en què es presenten una sèrie de preguntes o ítems gramaticals de compleció, generalment basats en un text llegit. Les respostes es proporcionen en forma d'una filera de mots o sintagmes, cada un dels quals es pot utilitzar un nombre il·limitat de vegades. L'avantatge rau en el fet que les opcions no s'eliminen a mesura que l'examinand completa els ítems (com en altres tipus de tasca de relació), de tal manera que la tasca no resulta progressivament més fàcil.
Vegeu: tasca de relacionar.
CA:396, DA:100, DE:235, EN:241, ES:8, FR:355, GA:372, IT:72, NE:253, PO:354.

397 tasca de relacionar Tasca d'una prova que implica unir elements de dues llistes separades. Un tipus de tasca de relacionar consisteix a seleccionar el sintagma correcte per completar cada oració d'una sèrie d'oracions incompletes. Un tipus utilitzat en proves de comprensió lectora implica triar festes o llibres d'una llista per adaptar-los a una persona els requisits concrets de la qual s'han descrit.
CA:397, DA:322, DE:452, EN:226, ES:7, FR:21, GA:375, IT:73, NE:238, PO:353.

398 taula de contingència Taula de freqüències classificada segons dues sèries o més de valors de variables categòriques. Per exemple:

	Domini	No Domini
Mètode A	35	5
Mètode B	20	20

Vegeu: prova khi quadrat.
CA:398, DA:187, DE:187, EN:74, ES:390, FR:353, GA:369, IT:347, NE:75, PO:320.

399 teoria clàssica de la prova Teoria de mesura que consisteix en una sèrie de pressupòsits sobre les relacions entre les puntuacions reals o observades d'una prova i els factors que les afecten, que generalment s'anomenen error. S'anomena també teoria de la puntuació vertadera.
Compareu: teoria de resposta d'ítem (TRI).
Més informació: Bachman, 1990, pàg. 166–187.
CA:399, DA:174, DE:177, EN:50, ES:392, FR:397, GA:387, IT:349, NE:208, PO:357.

400 teoria de la generalització Model estadístic per investigar els efectes relatius de diferents fonts de variància en les puntuacions d'una prova.
Més informació: Bachman, 1990, pàg. 7; Crocker i Algina, 1986, capítol 8.
CA:400, DA:115, DE:132, EN:154, ES:393, FR:399, GA:388, IT:351, NE:152, PO:359.

401 teoria de resposta d'ítem (TRI) Grup de models matemàtics que relacionen l'actuació d'un individu en una prova amb el nivell de capacitat d'aquest individu. Aquests models es basen en la teoria bàsica que l'actuació esperada d'un individu en una pregunta d'una prova, o ítem, és una funció tant del nivell de dificultat de l'ítem com del nivell de capacitat de l'individu.
Més informació: Henning, 1987, capítol 8; Crocker i Algina, 1986, capítol 15.
CA:401, DA:159, DE:173/296, EN:195, ES:394, FR:400, GA:389, IT:352, NE:201, PO:360.

402 teoria del tret latent Vegeu la definició de teoria de resposta d'ítem.
CA:402, DA:211, DE:206, EN:207, ES:395, FR:398, GA:390, IT:350, NE:216, PO:358.

403 text Fragment d'un discurs relacionat, escrit o oral, utilitzat com a base d'un conjunt d'ítems d'una prova.
CA:403, DA:386, DE:411, EN:411, ES:399, FR:396, GA:381, IT:389, NE:381, PO:398.

404 text autèntic Text utilitzat en una prova que consisteix en un material originalment elaborat amb un propòsit diferent al d'una prova de llengua i no produït especialment per a la prova.
Compareu: text semiautèntic.
CA:404, DA:22, DE:41, EN:25, ES:401, FR:111, GA:382, IT:390, NE:24, PO:127.

405 text semiautèntic Text procedent d'una font real que ha estat revisat per utilitzar-lo en una prova, per exemple per adaptar el vocabulari i/o la gramàtica al nivell dels examinands.
Vegeu: text autèntic.
CA:405, DA:123, DE:140, EN:355, ES:400, FR:112, GA:383, IT:391, NE:335, PO:128.

406 tipus d'ítem Els ítems d'una prova es coneixen amb noms que tendeixen a descriure'n la forma; per exemple, ítem d'elecció múltiple, ítem de transformació gramatical, ítem de resposta curta, prova de compleció oberta, etc.
CA:406, DA:162, DE:174, EN:197 ES:405, FR:405, GA:58, IT:392, NE:203, PO:399.

407 tipus de pregunta Vegeu les definicions de tipus d'ítem i tipus de tasca.
CA:407, DA:358, DE:124, EN:305, ES:404, FR:406, GA:57, IT:394, NE:424, PO:400.

408 tipus de tasca Les tasques es designen amb noms que tendeixen a ser descriptius d'allò que avaluen i de la forma que tenen; per exemple, tasca de comprensió lectora d'elecció múltiple, tasca d'expressió escrita guiada, etc.
CA:408, DA:265, DE:30, EN:394, ES:402, FR:407, GA:59, IT:393, NE:271, PO:401.

409 transferència d'informació Tècnica d'elaboració de proves que implica agafar la informació donada d'una manera determinada i presentar-la de forma diferent. Exemples de tasques com aquesta són agafar informació d'un text i utilitzar-la per retolar un diagrama o rescriure una nota informal com un anunci formal.
Més informació: Hughes, 1989, pàg. 84, 124–125 i 138.
CA:409, DA:141, DE:152, EN:173, ES:406, FR:402, GA:8, IT:396, NE:177, PO:404.

410 transformació gramatical Tipus d'ítem en què es dóna com a suport una oració completa, seguida per un o dos mots d'una segona oració que expressa el contingut de la primera en una forma gramatical diferent. Per exemple, la primera oració pot ser en veu activa i la tasca de l'examinand consisteix a presentar el mateix contingut en forma passiva.
CA:410, DA:381, DE:334, EN:359, ES:407, FR:404, GA:61, IT:397, NE:440, PO:405.

411 tret Característica física o psicològica d'una persona (per exemple, la capacitat lingüística) o l'escala de mesura elaborada per descriure-la.
CA:411, DA:416, DE:95, EN:415, ES:360, FR:23, GA:400, IT:26, NE:403, PO:403.

412 TRI Vegeu la definició de teoria de resposta d'ítem.
CA:412, DA:153, DE:165, EN:188, ES:408, FR:401, GA:392, IT:352, NE:194, PO:402.

413 unidimensionalitat Noció d'una dimensió única, que és una assumpció necessària per elaborar una escala per mesurar trets psicològics, per exemple utilitzant models de la teoria de resposta d'ítem actual. La unidimensionalitat és una propietat de l'instrument de mesura i no dels processos psicològics subjacents.
Més informació: Crocker i Algina, 1986, pàg. 343.
CA:413, DA:90, DE:97, EN:427, ES:409, FR:408, GA:23, IT:398, NE:119, PO:406.

414 usuari de la prova Persona o institució (per exemple, un professor o una empresa) que utilitza els resultats d'una prova a fi de prendre una decisió respecte al destinatari de la prova.
CA:414, DA:391, DE:392, EN:407, ES:410, FR:409, GA:440, IT:399, NE:393, PO:407.

415 validació Procés de recopilació d'evidències per donar suport a les inferències fetes a partir de les puntuacions d'una prova. El que es valida són les inferències fetes amb relació als usos específics d'una prova, no la prova mateixa.
Vegeu: validesa.
CA:415, DA:426, DE:426, EN:429, ES:412, FR:412, GA:39, IT:400, NE:414, PO:408.

416 validesa Grau en què les puntuacions d'una prova permeten fer inferències adequades, significatives i útils, donats els propòsits d'una prova. S'identifiquen diferents aspectes de la validesa, com ara validesa del contingut, de criteri i de constructe; aquests aspectes proporcionen diferents tipus d'evidència per jutjar la validesa total d'una prova per a un

propòsit donat.
Vegeu: validesa concurrent, validesa de constructe, validesa de criteri, validesa del contingut, validesa convergent, validesa discriminant, validesa aparent, validesa predictiva.
Més informació: Bachman, 1990, pàg. 25 i 236–237.
CA:416, DA:427, DE:427, EN:430, ES:413, FR:413, GA:30, IT:401, NE:415, PO:409.

417 validesa aparent Grau en què una prova sembla, als examinands o als qui la seleccionen per a ells, una mesura acceptable de la capacitat que volen avaluar. És un judici més subjectiu que un que es basi en una anàlisi objectiva de la prova, i sovint es considera que la validesa aparent no és una veritable forma de validesa. De vegades s'anomena atractiu de la prova.
Vegeu: validesa.
Més informació: Bachman, 1990, pàg. 285–289.
CA:417, DA:272, DE:110/34, EN:140, ES:414, FR:414 GA:2, IT:402, NE:174, PO:410.

418 validesa concurrent Grau de correlació entre les puntuacions d'una prova i algun criteri extern reconegut que mesura la mateixa àrea de coneixement o habilitat.
Vegeu: validesa de criteri.
Més informació: Bachman, 1990, pàg. 248–250.
CA:418, DA:323, DE:417, EN:66, ES:415, FR:415, GA:33, IT:403, NE:71, PO:411.

419 validesa convergent Es diu que una prova té validesa convergent si hi ha una correlació alta entre les puntuacions assolides i les assolides en una prova amb un mètode diferent que mesuri el mateix constructe. Es pot considerar un aspecte de la validesa de constructe.
Compareu: validesa discriminant.
Vegeu: validesa de constructe.
Més informació: Guilford i Fruchter, 1981, pàg. 436–437.
CA:419, DA:188, DE:188, EN:75, ES:416, FR:416, GA:32, IT:404, NE:76, PO:412.

420 validesa de constructe Es diu que una prova té validesa de constructe si les puntuacions es poden presentar com a reflex d'una teoria sobre la naturalesa d'un constructe o la seva relació amb altres constructes. Es podria predir, per exemple, que dues proves vàlides de comprensió oral classificarien els aprenents de la mateixa manera, però cada una tindria una relació més feble amb les puntuacions d'una prova de competència gramatical.
Vegeu: validesa, especificacions de la prova.
Més informació: Ebel i Frisbie, 1991, pàg. 108; Hatch i Lazaraton, 1991, pàg. 37–38.
CA:420, DA:186, DE:186, EN:69, ES:418, FR:418, GA:37, IT:406, NE:73, PO:414.

421 validesa de criteri Es diu que una prova té validesa de criteri si es pot demostrar una relació entre les puntuacions de la prova i algun criteri extern reconegut com a mesura de la mateixa capacitat. La informació sobre la relació amb el criteri s'utilitza també per determinar fins a quin punt una prova prediu la conducta futura.
Vegeu: validesa concurrent, validesa predictiva.
Més informació: Bachman, 1990, pàg. 248–250.
CA:421, DA:204, DE:197, EN:82, ES:417, FR:417, GA:34, IT:407, NE:87, PO:413.

422 validesa del contingut Es diu que una prova té validesa del contingut si els ítems o les tasques de què es compon constitueixen una mostra representativa dels ítems o les tasques de l'àrea de coneixement o capacitat que s'ha de provar. Sovint estan relacionats amb un programa o curs.
Vegeu: validesa, especificacions de la prova.
Més informació: Bachman, 1990, pàg. 244–247.
CA:422, DA:134, DE:154, EN:73, ES:419, FR:419, GA:31, IT:405, NE:179, PO:415.

423 validesa discriminant Es diu que una prova té validesa discriminant si la seva correlació amb proves que mesuren un tret diferent és inferior a la correlació amb proves que mesuren el mateix tret, independentment del mètode de prova. Es pot considerar un aspecte de la validesa de constructe.
Compareu: validesa convergent.
Vegeu: validesa de constructe.
Més informació: Crocker i Algina, 1986, pàg. 23; Guilford i Fruchter, 1981, pàg. 436–437.
CA:423, DA:73, DE:83, EN:111, ES:420, FR:420, GA:36, IT:408, NE:108, PO:416.

424 validesa divergent Vegeu la definició de validesa discriminant.
CA:424, DA:81, DE:90, EN:118, ES:421, FR:421, GA:35, IT:409, NE:111, PO:417.

425 validesa predictiva Indicació de la manera com una prova prediu l'actuació

futura en l'habilitat pertinent.
Compareu: validesa de criteri.
Més informació: Guilford i Fruchter, 1987, pàg. 437–438.

CA:425, DA:298, DE:294/439, EN:291, ES:422, FR:422, GA:38, IT:410, NE:300, PO:418.

426 valor de facilitat Vegeu la definició d'índex de facilitat.

CA:426, DA:192, DE:209, EN:143, ES:423, FR:410, GA:217, IT:411, NE:147, PO:419.

427 valor-*p* Vegeu la definició d'índex de facilitat.

CA:427, DA:273, DE:276, EN:266, ES:424, FR:411, GA:269, IT:412, NE:277, PO:420.

428 valoració a) El fet d'assignar valors numèrics a actuacions en una prova mitjançant un judici.

b) Puntuació atorgada com a resulat del procès de valoració.

CA:428, DA:171, DE:57, EN:314, ES:425, FR:265, GA:286, IT:54, NE:38, PO:57.

429 valoració holística Vegeu la definició de valoració global.

CA:429, DA:126, DE:128, EN:164, ES:428, FR:170, GA:230, IT:187, NE:168, PO:34.

430 variable a) Nom donat a una sèrie d'observacions sobre un element; aquest element pot ser un ítem d'una prova, el sexe, l'edat o la puntuació de la prova.

b) Element, en un disseny experimental o anàlisi estadística, que pot donar una sèrie de valors. Per exemple, les variables d'interès en un context de proves de llengua poden incloure la dificultat dels ítems d'una prova, el sexe i l'edat dels destinataris de la prova, etc.

CA:430, DA:428, DE:428, EN:431, ES:430, FR:423, GA:25, IT:416, NE:416, PO:422.

431 variable de criteri En recerca, variable dependent.
Vegeu: variable dependent.

CA:431, DA:205, DE:198, EN:83, ES:431, FR:424, GA:26, IT:417, NE:88, PO:423.

432 variable dependent Variable sota investigació en un treball de recerca. Per exemple, les puntuacions en una prova (la variable independent) poden ser utilitzades per predir l'èxit en el lloc de treball (la variable dependent).
Compareu: variable independent.
Vegeu: variable.
Més informació: Hatch i Lazaraton, 1991, pàg. 63.

CA:432, DA:7, DE:2, EN:94, ES:432, FR:425, GA:28, IT:418, NE:7, PO:424.

433 variable independent En recerca, variable que es considera relacionada amb la variable dependent o que la pot influir. Per exemple, les puntuacions en una prova (la variable independent) poden ser utilizades per predir l'èxit en el lloc de treball (la variable dependent).
Compareu: variable dependent
Vegeu: variable.
Més informació: Hatch i Lazaraton, 1991, pàg. 64.

CA:433, DA:420, DE:422, EN:169, ES:433, FR:426, GA:27, IT:419, NE:268, PO:425.

434 variància Mesura de la dispersió d'una variable respecte a la seva mitjana aritmètica. La variància és més gran com més puntuacions individuals diferents hi ha a partir de la mitjana.

CA:434, DA:429, DE:429, EN:432, ES:434, FR:427, GA:24, IT:420, NE:417, PO:421.

2 Dansk: Et flersprogsglosar af sprogprøvningsudtryk

1 a-parameter Parameter som ifølge item-responsteorien vedrører diskrimineringsevne af et item.
Se: item-responsteori (IRT) .
Øvrig litteratur: Bachman, 1990, p. 204.
CA:281, DA:1, DE:84, EN:1, ES:294, FR:292, GA:273, IT:260, NE:1, PO:297.

2 abilitet Mental egenskab, kapacitet eller evne til at udføre et eller andet.
Sammenlign: kompetens, færdighed.
Øvrig litteratur: Bachman, 1990, p. 16, p. 19.
CA:46, DA:2, DE:113, EN:2, ES:49, FR:42, GA:96, IT:1A, NE:411, PO:49.

3 abilitetsskala I item-responsteorien en skala med lige intervaller til identificering af personers sprogevne og forskellige testopgavers sværhedsgrad. Kaldes også theta-skala.
Øvrig litteratur: Bachman, 1990, p. 345.
CA:150, DA:3, DE:114, EN:3, ES:157, FR:128, GA:313, IT:322, NE:413, PO:159.

4 absolut skala Skala med et virkeligt nulpunkt, f.eks en skala til længdemåling. Eftersom det absolutte nulpunkt ikke kan defineres i sprogtestning, anvendes denne skalatype ikke.
Sammenlign: intervalskala, nominalskala, ordinalskala.
CA:145, DA:4, DE:433, EN:4, ES:153, FR:122, GA:112, IT:317, NE:2, PO:155.

5 adgangsprøve Test som anvendes til at afgøre, hvorvidt en deltager skal have adgang til en bestemt uddannelsesinstitution eller uddannelsesforløb.
Sammenlign: indplaceringsprøve.
CA:306, DA:5, DE:346, EN:124, ES:319, FR:369, GA:422, IT:364, NE:387, PO:377.

6 affektive faktorer Faktorer af ikke-kognitiv art som vedrører test-deltagernes emotionelle variabler, præferencer og holdninger.
Sammenlign: kognitive faktorer.
Øvrig litteratur: Ebel og Frisbie, 1991, p. 52.
CA:177, DA:6, DE:7, EN:9, ES:195, FR:178, GA:399, IT:172, NE:6, PO:188.

7 afhængig variabel Variabel som er genstand for forskningsmæssig undersøgelse. For eksempel kan point fra en test (den uafhængige variabel) benyttes til at forudsige succes på arbejdspladsen (den afhængige variabel).
Sammenlign: uafhængig variabel.
Se: variabel.
Øvrig litteratur: Hatch og Lazaraton, 1991, p. 63.
CA:432, DA:7, DE:2, EN:94, ES:432, FR:425, GA:28, IT:418, NE:7, PO:424.

8 aflokkelsesmetoder Spørgeteknik som aflokker testdeltageren et svar. Anvendes normalt inden for rammerne af en mundtlig sprogfærdighedstest.
Øvrig litteratur: Hughes, 1989, pp. 104–110.
CA:293, DA:8, DE:212, EN:123, ES:307, FR:308, GA:162, IT:276, NE:320, PO:314.

9 afsmitningseffekt Virkning som opstår når bedømmeren tildeler point på grundlag af andre faktorer end det, der skal testes. F.eks. tildeling af højere point for en skriftlig test på grundlag af håndskriftens udseende.
CA:118, DA:9, DE:226, EN:71, ES:122, FR:136, GA:174, IT:141, NE:74, PO:132.

10 akkreditering Anerkendelse af en test, sædvanligvis af en officiel instans såsom et ministerium, en institution, opgavekommission etc.
CA:4, DA:10, DE:8, EN:5, ES:1, FR:4, GA:92, IT:303, NE:3, PO:325.

11 alfa (alfakoefficient) Reliabilitetsvurdering til måling af testens interne sammenhæng. Skalaen går fra 0 til 1. Benyttes ofte til test med pointskala i modsætning til test med dikotomisk bedømte items, selvom den kan benyttes til begge. Kaldes også koefficient alfa.
Sammenlign: Kuder-Richardson.
Se: intern konsekvens.

Øvrig litteratur: Henning, 1987, p. 84.
CA:9, DA:11, DE:10, EN:10, ES:16, FR:8, GA:10, IT:10, NE:12, PO:6.

12 alternative udgaver Se under ækvivalente udgaver.
CA:185, DA:12, DE:11, EN:11, ES:203, NE:13, FR:193, GA:146, IT:176, PO:199.

13 analytisk bedømmelse (scoring) Bedømmelsesmetode som kan benyttes ved testning af produktiv sprogbrug, som f.eks. tale og skriftlig produktion. Bedømmeren foretager en bedømmelse ved hjælp af en liste med en række specifikke punkter. I en skrivetest, for eksempel, kan den analytiske skala fokusere på grammatik, sammenhængsmarkering, ordforråd etc.
Sammenlign: helhedsbedømmelse, generel (impressionistisk) bedømmelse.
Øvrig litteratur: Ebel og Frisbie, 1991, p. 195.
CA:343, DA:13, DE:12, EN:14, ES:426, FR:266, GA:340, IT:27, NE:15, PO:58.

14 ANCOVA En form for variansanalyse som gør det muligt at kontrollere for effekten af forvirrende variabler (de variabler, som ændres sammen med interessevariablen).
Se: ANOVA.
Øvrig litteratur: Hatch og Lazaraton, 1991, p. 387.
CA:21, DA:14, DE:13, EN:17, ES:27, FR:19, GA:20, IT:20, NE:16, PO:21.

15 anerkendelse Institutions formelle accept af en bestemt kvalifikation til et bestemt formål, f.eks. adgang til et videregående studium.
CA:365, DA:15, DE:269, EN:323, ES:361, FR:321, GA:9, IT:303, NE:123, PO:325.

16 anker-item Item som indgår i to eller flere test. Anker-items har kendte egenskaber og udgør et afsnit af en ny testversion med det formål at fremskaffe oplysninger om testen og deltagerne, f.eks. for at kalibrere en ny test i forhold til en klassificeringsskala.
Sammenlign: ankertest.
Se: kalibrering.
CA:218, DA:16, DE:18, EN:15, ES:237, FR:225, GA:241, IT:212, NE:17, PO:232.

17 anker-test Test med kendte måleegenskaber, som gives i forbindelse med en anden test. Udførelse af ankertesten giver oplysninger om den anden test og de deltagere, som har gennemført begge.
Sammenlign: anker-item.
CA:307, DA:17, DE:19, EN:16, ES:320, FR:367, GA:404, IT:357, NE:18, PO:365.

18 anlægstest (aptitude test) Test som er beregnet til at måle en deltagers succespotentiale inden for et bestemt område, f.eks. i et bestemt studieforløb eller for at lære et fremmedsprog.
Øvrig litteratur: Henning, 1987, p. 6; Ebel og Frisbie, 1991, p. 339.
CA:308, DA:18, DE:96, EN:20, ES:322, FR:368, GA:421, IT:358, NE:22, PO:370.

19 ANOVA Statistisk teknik som benyttes til at teste den nulhypotese, at forskellige gruppegennemsnit er ens. Variabiliteten af observationer inden for hver gruppe undersøges ligesom variabiliteten i gruppegennemsnit.
Øvrig litteratur: Hatch og Lazaraton, 1991, pp. 308–312.
CA:22, DA:19, DE:20, EN:18, ES:28, FR:20, GA:21, IT:21, NE:19, PO:22.

20 attainment test Se under standpunktstest (achievement test).
CA:322, DA:20, DE:203, EN:23, ES:331, FR:366, GA:419, IT:368, NE:421, PO:374.

21 autenticitet Den udstrækning i hvilken en test afspejler sproget uden for testsituationen.
Øvrig litteratur: Bachman, 1990, pp. 300–303.
CA:27, DA:21, DE:42, EN:24, ES:33, FR:24, GA:115, IT:35, NE:23, PO:26.

22 autentisk tekst Tekst benyttet i en test bestående af materialer, der oprindelig ikke er blevet fremstillet til sprogtestning og som ikke er specialfremstillet til testen.
Sammenlign: halvautentisk test.
CA:404, DA:22, DE:41, EN:25, ES:401, FR:111, GA:382, IT:390, NE:24, PO:127.

23 automatisk bedømmelse Bedømmelsesmetode hvor bedømmeren ikke behøver at være i besiddelse af nogen specialviden eller foretage subjektive afgørelser. Bedømmelsen foregår ved at følge et retteskema, som angiver samtlige acceptable svar på hver enkelt test-item.
Sammenlign: bedømmelse ved eksaminator.
CA:86, DA:23, DE:231, EN:51, ES:78, FR:274, GA:219, IT:31, NE:25, PO:62.

24 b-parameter Parameter som ifølge item-responsteorien vedrører et items sværhedsgrad.
Se: item-responsteori (IRT) .
Øvrig litteratur: Bachman, 1990, p. 204.
CA:282, DA:24, DE:170, EN:26, ES:295, FR:293, GA:274, IT:261, NE:26, PO:298.

25 backwash Virkningen af en test på

klasseundervisningen. Hvis en lærer er vidende om, at nogle elever planlægger at tage en bestemt test, kan det få indflydelse på tilrettelæggelsen af undervisningen, således at metoder og indhold indrettes efter testens krav. Resultatet kan være positivt eller negativt. Kaldes også washback.
Se: påvirkning.
CA:372, DA:25, DE:43, EN:28, ES:369, FR:322, GA:95, IT:147, NE:27, PO:135.

26 baggrundsviden Deltagerens viden om det emne eller kulturelle indhold af en test, som har betydning for behandlingen af input. Af særlig relevans for fagsprogstestning (LSP = Language for Specific Purposes).
Øvrig litteratur: Bachman, 1990, p. 273.
CA:75, DA:26, DE:144, EN:27, ES:73, FR:77, GA:134, IT:85, NE:4, PO:91.

27 basale færdigheder Hypotetiske, mindre komplekse færdigheder, som kræves af deltagere i sprogtest, f.eks. genkendelse af ord eller bogstaver.
CA:200, DA:27, DE:424, EN:219, ES:101, FR:44, GA:327, IT:2, NE:409, PO:52.

28 batteri Se under testbatteri.
CA:38, DA:28, DE:393, EN:32, ES:40, FR:30, GA:64, IT:41, NE:30, PO:38.

29 bedømmelse ved censor Bedømmelsesmetode, hvor den der udfører bedømmelsen skal være i besiddelse af specialviden og uddannelse for at kunne foretage subjektive bedømmelser. Testning af mundtlig sprogfærdighed og længere skriftlige fremstillinger bedømmes normalt på denne måde.
Sammenlign: automatisk bedømmelse.
CA:81, DA:29, DE:107, EN:136, ES:81, FR:272, GA:223, IT:30, NE:131, PO:67.

30 bedømmelse (assessment) I sprogtestning: måling af et eller flere aspekter af sprogfærdighed ved hjælp af en test eller anden fremgangsmåde.
Øvrig litteratur: Bachman, 1990, p. 50.
CA:31, DA:30, DE:54, EN:21, ES:180, FR:165, GA:229, IT:421, NE:39, PO:30.

31 bedømmer (censor)-enighed Graden af enighed imellem to eller flere bedømmere (censorer) af samme præstationer. Dette har især relevans for bedømmelse af tale- og skrivefærdighed i test, hvor bedømmerne afkræves en subjektiv vurdering.
CA:2, DA:31, DE:159, EN:181, ES:11, FR:2, GA:68, IT:84, NE:185, PO:2.

32 bedømmer (censor) Person som tildeler point for resultatet af en test på grundlag af subjektive kriterier. Bedømmere (censorer) vil normalt være kvalificerede inden for det relevante område, og vil skulle gennemgå en trænings- og tilpasningsproces. I mundtlig testning skelnes til tider imellem censorens og eksaminatorens roller.
Sammenlign: samtalepartner, marker.
CA:35, DA:32, DE:55, EN:22, ES:46, FR:174, GA:234, IT:165, NE:33, PO:182.

33 bedømmer (censor)-konstans Graden af overensstemmelse imellem to bedømmelser af samme præstationer, foretaget på forskellige tidspunkter. Dette har især relevans for bedømmelse af mundtlig og skriftlig sprogfærdighed i test, hvor bedømmerne afkræves en subjektiv vurdering.
CA:3, DA:33, DE:163, EN:185, ES:12, FR:3, GA:69, IT:90, NE:190, PO:3.

34 bedømmereffekt Kilde til fejlagtig bedømmelse. Skyldes individuelle tendenser blandt bedømmerne, f.eks. strenghed eller mildhed, eller fordomme, som kommer bestemte deltagertyper tilgode, og som påvirker de samlede point. Som eksempler på denne effekt kan nævnes: afsmitningseffekt, glorieeffekt, sekvenseffekt.
CA:124, DA:34, DE:425, EN:313, ES:130, FR:144, GA:176, IT:143, NE:35, PO:138.

35 behovsanalyse Metode til at fastslå en bestemt gruppe lørneres sprogbehov (defineret som færdigheder, opgaver, ordforråd etc.), før udarbejdelsen af et kursusforløb.
CA:16, DA:35, DE:45, EN:246, ES:21, FR:11, GA:19, IT:13, NE:31, PO:17.

36 bestået Den minimumskarakter som en deltager skal opnå for at bestå en test eller eksamen.
Sammenlign: cut-off score.
CA:23, DA:36, DE:52, EN:273, ES:30, FR:277, GA:278, IT:288 NE:341, PO:282.

37 besvarelsesark Papir hvorpå deltageren noterer sine svar.
Sammenlign: optisk svarlæser
CA:191, DA:37, DE:22, EN:19, ES:219, FR:181, GA:152, IT:174, NE:20, PO:198.

38 bevis Dokument som angiver, at en navngivet person har bestået en test eller en del af en test og har opnået en bestemt karakter, normalt minimum 'bestået'.
Sammenlign: diplom.
CA:50, DA:38, DE:448, EN:47, ES:53, FR:50, GA:386, IT:52, NE:56, PO:56.

39 bimodal fordeling Statistisk fordeling med to toppe, som antyder, at der er to forskellige grupper inden for samme stikprøve.

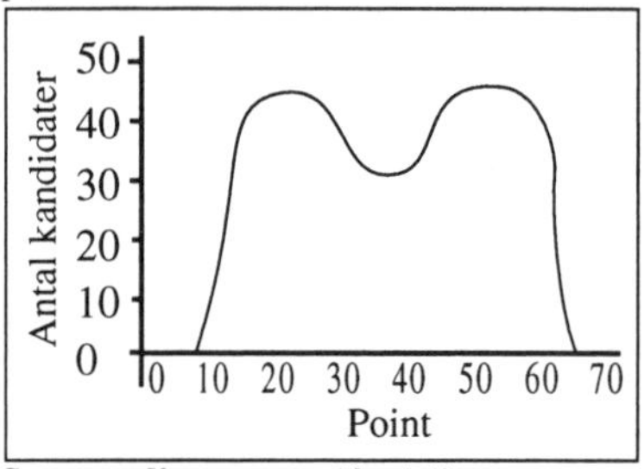

Sammenlign: normalfordeling.
Se: modalværdi.
Øvrig litteratur: Hatch og Lazaraton, 1991, pp. 165–166.

CA:112, DA:39, DE:59, EN:34, ES:113, FR:106, GA:104, IT:131, NE:47, PO:121.

40 biseriel korrelation Indeks for item-diskriminering af dikotomiske items, skrives rbis; korrelationen imellem et kriterium (normalt den samlede test-score) og den færdighed, som ligger til grund for de rigtige og forkerte besvarelser af det pågældende item. Værdien af r_{bis} er mindst 25% højere for den biserielle korrelationskoefficient (r_{pbi}). En fordel ved r_{bis} er at den forbliver rimelig stabil henover stikprøver fra forskellige færdighedsniveauer.
Sammenlign: biserielt korrelationspunkt.
Se: diskriminering.
Øvrig litteratur: Crocker og Algina, 1986, pp. 317–318; Guilford og Fruchter, 1981, pp. 304–311.

CA:56, DA:40, DE:60, EN:35, ES:85, FR:86, GA:79, IT:96, NE:48, PO:101.

41 biserielt korrelationspunkt Itemdiskriminationsindeks for dikotomiske items, skrives r_{pbi}; korrelationen imellem et kriterium (sædvanligvis samlede point for en test) og responsen på det pågældende item. Fordelen ved r_{pbi} frem for den biserielle korrelation (r_{bis}) er, at den kan anvendes med held, når den tilgrundliggende færdighed ikke er normalt fordelt.
Sammenlign: biseriel korrelation.

CA:57, DA:41, DE:311, EN:283, ES:86, FR:57, GA:80, IT:97, NE:309, PO:102.

42 bundeffekt Grænseeffekt som er et resultat af, at en test er for svær for en bestemt deltagergruppe, sådan at deres point grupperer sig i bunden af fordelingen.
Se: grænseeffekt.

CA:122, DA:42, DE:61/121, EN:146, ES:128, FR:141, GA:175, IT:144, NE:49, PO:130.

43 bunden skriftlig fremstilling Se under guidet skriftlig opgave.

CA:392, DA:43, DE:15, EN:105, ES:6, FR:356, GA:376, IT:77, NE:144, PO:355.

44 c-parameter Parameter som ifølge item-responsteorien vedrører det at gætte.
Se: item-responsteori (IRT) .
Øvrig litteratur: Bachman, 1990, p. 204.

CA:283, DA:44, DE:318, EN:37, ES:296, FR:294, GA:275, IT:262, NE:50, PO:299.

45 c-test Udfyldningstest hvor sidste halvdel af visse ord er udeladt. Udeladelsesfrekvensen kan være så høj som hvert andet ord. Deltagerens opgave består i at fuldende de påbegyndte ord.
Sammenlign: cloze test.
Øvrig litteratur: Weir, 1990, p. 49.

CA:304, DA:45, DE:62, EN:38, ES:314, FR:394, GA:408, IT:384, NE:51, PO:366.

46 centilskala Ordinalskala som er opdelt i 100 enheder eller centiler. Hvis en person opnår centilværdien 95, betyder det, at vedkommende ud af en stikprøve på 100 placerer sig over 95 andre. Også kaldet percentilskala.
Øvrig litteratur: Crocker og Algina, 1986, pp. 439–442; Guilford og Fruchter, 1981, pp. 38–41.

CA:151, DA:46, DE:300, EN:46, ES:155, FR:124, GA:311, IT:319, NE:54, PO:157.

47 centraltendens Metode til lokalisering omkring hvilken værdi en fordeling samler sig. Tre almindeligt anvendte mål for centraltendens er middeltal, meridianværdi og typeværdi.
Øvrig litteratur: Henning, 1987, pp. 39–40; Guilford og Fruchter, 1981, kapitel 4; Hatch og Lazaraton, 1991, pp. 159–164.

CA:246, DA:47, DE:447, EN:45, ES:391, FR:358, GA:62, IT:348, NE:55, PO:356.

48 checkliste Liste med spørgsmål eller punkter, som skal besvares eller behandles. Benyttes ofte i forbindelse med sprogtestning, som et redskab til observation eller analyse.

CA:240, DA:48, DE:64, EN:48, ES:258, FR:239, GA:351, IT:228, NE:58, PO:252.

49 chi-kvadrattest Statistisk metode til sammenligning af værdierne fra konstaterede og forventede svar med henblik på angivelse af, hvorvidt forskellen imellem dem er statistisk signifikant på grundlag af de forventede svar. Der er tale om en ikke-parametrisk metode.

Se: ikke-parametriske metoder.
Øvrig litteratur: Hatch og Lazaraton, 1991, pp. 393–415.
CA:330, DA:49, DE:65, EN:49, ES:396, FR:149, GA:409, IT:359, NE:59, PO:395.

50 cloze test (udfyldningstest) Udfyldningsopgave hvor hele ord er udeladt fra en tekst. I en traditionel cloze test udelades ord med faste mellemrum. Også andre udfyldningsopgaver, hvor korte sætninger udelades fra teksten, eller hvor itemforfatteren vælger de ord, der skal udelades, omtales som cloze test, f.eks. rationel cloze. I nogle tilfælde vil kandidaten skulle indføje manglende ord (åben cloze), eller vælge blandt en række muligheder (multiple-choice eller banked cloze). Bedømmelse af en open cloze kan enten være i form af rigtige ord (kun det ord, som blev slettet fra den oprindelige tekst accepteres som det korrekte svar) eller acceptable ord (en liste over acceptable svar udleveres til bedømmeren).
Sammenlign: c-test, udfyldnings-item.
Øvrig litteratur: Weir, 1990, p. 46–48; Oller, 1979, kapitel 12.
CA:313, DA:50, DE:66, EN:52, ES:315, FR:370, GA:410, IT:362, NE:61, PO:378.

51 computer-baseret flexibel test Computer-baseret testning som gør det muligt løbende at tilpasse sværhedgraden af de forskellige items til deltagerens færdighedsniveau på grundlag af de afgivne svar.
Se: computer-baseret testning (bedømmelse).
CA:303, DA:51, DE:67, EN:63, ES:181, FR:362, GA:379, IT:386, NE:68, PO:364.

52 computer-baseret testning (bedømmelse) Testningsmetode hvor en computer præsenterer deltagerne for de forskellige items. Svarene kan ligeledes foretages via computeren.
CA:332, DA:52, DE:68, EN:64, ES:182, FR:171, GA:380, IT:387, NE:70, PO:35.

53 computerbedømmelse (scoring) Forskellige anvendelser af computersystemer til reduktion af fejlprocenten i bedømmelsen af objektive test. F.eks. ved at scanne oplysninger fra en besvarelse med optisk scanner og på det grundlag fremstille data, som kan anvendes til pointgivning og analyser.
CA:85, DA:53, DE:69, EN:65, ES:82, FR:273, GA:222, IT:28, NE:69, PO:66.

54 Cronbachs alfa Se under alfa (alfakoefficient).
CA:10, DA:54, DE:70, EN:84, ES:17, FR:9, GA:11, IT:11, NE:89, PO:7.

55 curriculum Overordnet beskrivelse af målsætninger, indhold, tilrettelæggelse, metoder og evaluering af et kursus.
Sammenlign: pensum.
CA:94, DA:55, DE:71, EN:87, ES:93, FR:93, GA:99, IT:113, NE:220, PO:107.

56 curriculum-afhængig test Test som er tæt knyttet til et bestemt pensum og som spiller en særlig rolle i uddannelsesforløbet.
Sammenlign: curriculum-uafhængig test.
Se: færdighedstest.
CA:325, DA:56, DE:217, EN:88, ES:313, FR:365, GA:406, IT:374, NE:221, PO:380.

57 curriculum-uafhængig test Test som ikke er knyttet til nogen bestemt undervisningsplan eller studieforløb.
Sammenlign: curriculum-afhængig test.
Se: færdighedstest.
CA:328, DA:57, DE:218, EN:89, ES:339, FR:387, GA:405, IT:376, NE:222, PO:388.

58 cut-off score (beståelseskarakter/point) De minimumspoint som deltageren skal opnå for at få en given karakter i en test eller eksamen. I kompetence-testning er der tale om det pointtal, som vurderes at repræsentere et mindstemål af kompetence eller beherskelse.
Se: kompetence-test, testning af minimumskompetence.
Sammenlign: bestået.
Øvrig litteratur: Bachman, 1990, pp. 214–215; Crocker og Algina, 1986, pp. 421–428.
CA:359, DA:58, DE:199, EN:90, ES:351, FR:277, GA:338, IT:280, NE:57, PO:282.

59 d-indeks Indeks for diskrimineringen af testitems. Benyttes ofte til mindre test i klassen, fordi det kan udregnes i hånden. På grundlag af et samlet pointtal udvælges en øvre og en nedre gruppe, således at mellem 10% og 33% af deltagerne befinder sig i hver gruppe. For normalt fordelte point er det optimalt at benytte 27% i hver gruppe. Testdeltagernes svar på hvert enkelt item inden for grupperne optælles, og for items med god diskriminationsevne vil den øvre gruppe score højere end bundgruppen. Følgende formel opstilles for itemdiskriminationsindekset:

$$D = p_U - p_L$$

hvor p_U repræsenterer den del af den øvre gruppe, som besvarer det pågældende item korrekt, og hvor p_L er den del af den nedregruppe, som besvarer det pågældende item korrekt. Generelt betragtes items med et indeks på 0,3 eller derover som velegnede til at diskriminere.

CA:206, DA:59, DE:72, EN:91, ES:223, FR:208, GA:186, IT:194, NE:92, PO:218.

60 delta-skala Normaliseret skala med et gennemsnit på 13 og en standardafvigelse på 4.

CA:155, DA:60, DE:75, EN:93, ES:162, FR:132, GA:314, IT:321, NE:94, PO:165.

61 deltaplot-metoden Metode til vurdering af differentiel item-funktion. Den benyttes til at identificere items, som overdriver eller minimiserer forskelle på forskellige gruppers præstationer og som er baseret på klassiske item-vanskeligheder (a-værdier). A-værdierne konverteres til normaliserede *z*-point og disse værdier plottes parvis ind på en graf for at vise den relative vanskelighed af items for de pågældende to grupper.
Se: differentiel item-funktion.
Øvrig litteratur: Crocker og Algina, 1986, pp. 388–390.

CA:249, DA:61, DE:74, EN:92, ES:267, FR:246, GA:256, IT:237, NE:93, PO:260.

62 delvis overlapning Resultat af f.eks. korrellering af point for en deltest med de samlede testpoint. Eftersom pointene for deltesten er omfattet af de samlede point, overdrives korrelationen. Det er teknisk muligt at korrigere for delvis overlapning.
Øvrig litteratur: Henning, 1987, p. 69.

CA:63, DA:62, DE:282, EN:271, ES:387, FR:51, GA:283, IT:146, NE:276, PO:331.

63 deskriptiv statistik Statistik der anvendes til at beskrive et datasæt udtrykt i kvanta, spredning, gennemsnitsværdier, korrelationer med andre data etc. Der skelnes imellem deskriptiv statistik og stikprøveudvælgelse eller inferensstatistik.
Sammenlign: inferensstatistik.

CA:165, DA:63, DE:51, EN:95, ES:172, FR:349, GA:365, IT:340, NE:95, PO:176.

64 deskriptor Kort beskrivelse tilknyttet en kategori på en bedømmelsesskala, som opsummerer den færdighedsgrad eller præstationstype, som kræves for at få tilstrækkeligt med point til at havne i den pågældende kategori.

CA:97, DA:64, DE:76, EN:96, ES:98, FR:97, GA:437, IT:118, NE:96, PO:113.

65 diagnostisk test Test som anvendes til at finde en lørners stærke eller svage sider. Resultaterne kan bruges til at træffe afgørelser om fremtidig træning eller undervisning.

CA:317, DA:65, DE:77, EN:97, ES:325, FR:383, GA:414, IT:373, NE:97, PO:386.

66 differentiel item-funktion Den kendsgerning, at den relative sværhedsgrad for et item afhænger af visse træk ved deltagergruppen, f.eks. modersmål eller køn.
Se: forudindtagethed.

CA:195, DA:66, DE:78, EN:100, ES:209, FR:192, GA:114, IT:182, NE:100, PO:208.

67 dikotomisk bedømmelse Bedømmelse baseret på to kategorier, f.eks. rigtig/forkert, bestået/ikke-bestået, ja/nej.

CA:347, DA:67, DE:455, EN:98, ES:347, FR:268, GA:341, IT:32, NE:98, PO:59.

68 diktat Testopgave hvor deltageren lytter til en tekst og derefter nedskriver de ord han/hun hører. Bedømmelseskriterierne kan svinge noget. Afhængig af formålet med testen kan der f.eks. være tale om stavning eller tegnsætning.

CA:103, DA:68, DE:79, EN:99, ES:105, FR:99, GA:109, IT:121, NE:99, PO:125.

69 diplom Dokument som angiver, at en navngiven person har bestået en test eller en del af en test og har opnået en bestemt karakter, normalt mindst et 'bestået'. Anses ofte for at dokumentere en højere grad af kvalifikation end et bevis.
Sammenlign: bevis.

CA:104, DA:69, DE:80, EN:103, ES:106, FR:100, GA:118, IT:124, NE:101, PO:115.

70 direkte test Test som måler produktive tale- og skrivefærdigheder, hvor det er selve udførelsen af færdigheden, som måles direkte. For eksempel en test af skriftlig sprogfærdighed, hvor deltageren bliver bedt om at skrive et brev.
Sammenlign: indirekte test.
Øvrig litteratur: Hughes, 1989, pp. 14–16.

CA:326, DA:70, DE:81, EN:104, ES:335, FR:384, GA:415, IT:375, NE:102, PO:387.

71 diskret item Uafhængigt item som ikke er knyttet til en tekst, andre items eller supplerende materiale. Et eksempel på en itemtype, som bruges på denne måde er flervalgsopgaver (multiple-choice).

CA:230, DA:71, DE:421, EN:109, ES:246, FR:228, GA:253, IT:219, NE:106, PO:241.

72 diskret-point item Diskret item som tester et specifikt aspekt af f.eks struktur eller ordforråd, og som ikke er knyttet til andre items. I 1960erne var bl.a. Robert Lado medvirkende til at gøre diskret-point sprogtestning populært.
Sammenlign: integrativt item/opgave.
Se: diskret item.

CA:225, DA:72, DE:82, EN:110, ES:247 FR:229, GA:251, IT:210, NE:107, PO:240.

73 diskriminant validitet En test siges at udvise diskriminant validitet, hvis dens korrelation med en test af en anden egenskab er lavere end korrelationen med en test af samme egenskab, uanset testningsmetode. Kan betragtes som et aspekt af begrebsvaliditet.
Se: begrebsvaliditet.
Sammenlign: samstemmende validitet.
Øvrig litteratur: Crocker og Algina, 1986, p. 23; Guilford og Fruchter, 1981, pp. 436–437.
CA:423, DA:73, DE:83, EN:111, ES:420, FR:420, GA:36, IT:408, NE:108, PO:416.

74 diskrimination Et items evne til at diskriminere imellem svagere og stærkere kandidater. Der benyttes forskellige diskriminationsindekser. Nogle af disse (f.eks. biserielt korrelationspunkt, biseriel) baseres på korrelationen imellem et items pointtal og et kriterium, som f.eks. de samlede point for en test eller et eksternt færdighedsmål. Andre baseres på forskellen på et items sværhedsgrad for den øvre og den nedre gruppe. Inden for item-responsteorien har 2. og 3. parametermodel item-diskrimination som A-parameter.
Se: biseriel korrelation, biserielt korrelationpunkt, item-responsteori (IRT) .
Øvrig litteratur: Crocker og Algina, 1986, pp. 313–320, Ebel og Frisbie, 1991, pp. 231–232.
CA:105, DA:74, DE:416, EN:112, ES:107, FR:102, GA:180, IT:126, NE:109, PO:116.

75 diskurs Talt eller skreven tekst, set som en kommunikativ handling.
CA:106, DA:75, DE:85, EN:106, ES:108, FR:101, GA:119, IT:125, NE:103, PO:117.

76 diskursanalyse Analyseform som fokuserer på strukturen og funktionen af forskellige slags talte eller skrevne tekster.
CA:19, DA:76, DE:86, EN:107, ES:24, FR:13, GA:17, IT:16, NE: 104, PO:19.

77 diskursiv opgave Skriftlig opgave hvor kandidaten diskuterer et emne, hvorom der kan være mange opfattelser, eller argumenterer for sine egne synspunkter.
Se: fri skriftlig fremstilling.
CA:74, DA:77, DE:342, EN:113, ES:70, FR:74, GA:52, IT:83, NE:42, PO:89.

78 diskurskompetens Evnen til at forstå og producere diskurs. I visse modeller for sprogkompetens anerkendes begrebet diskurskompetens som en komponent.
Øvrig litteratur: Bachman, 1990, kapitel 4.
CA:66, DA:78, DE:87, EN:108, ES:62, FR:64, GA:196, IT:64, NE:105, PO:78.

79 distraktor Fejlagtigt alternativ i et multiple-choice item.
Sammenlign: nøglesvar.
Se: multiple-choice item.
Øvrig litteratur: Ebel og Frisbie, 1986, pp. 176–185.
CA:110, DA:79, DE:88, EN:115, ES:111, FR:104, GA:348, IT:129, NE:8, PO:126.

80 distraktorfrekvens Den hyppighed hvormed hver enkelt distraktor i et multiple-choice item vælges. Frekvensen afslører hvor populær distraktoren er.
CA:243, DA:80, DE:89, EN:116, ES:71, FR:301, GA:384, IT:88, NE:9, PO:96.

81 divergent validitet Se under diskriminant validitet.
CA:424, DA:81, DE:90, EN:118, ES:421, FR:421, GA:35, IT:409, NE:111, PO:417.

82 dobbeltbedømmelse Bedømmelsesmetode hvor to personer foretager en uafhængig bedømmelse af en deltagers besvarelse.
Se: multipel bedømmelse.
CA:84, DA:82, DE:91, EN:121, ES:118, FR:114, GA:221, IT:104, NE:116, PO:61.

83 domæne Det afgrænsede indholds og/eller færdighedsområde, som testes ved hjælp af en specifik opgave eller eksamenskomponent.
Øvrig litteratur: Bachman 1990, pp. 244–246.
CA:11, DA:83, DE:238, EN:119, ES:119, FR:113, GA:137, IT:332, NE:113, PO:129.

84 domæne-relateret test Test hvis resultater fortolkes i relation til et specifikt indholds- eller færdighedsdomæne.
Sammenlign: kriterie-relateret test, normrelateret test.
CA:335, DA:84, DE:50, EN:120, ES:342, FR:391, GA:417, IT:382, NE:114, PO:368.

85 Ebel's d Se under D-indeks.
CA:96, DA:85, DE:92, EN:122, ES:96, FR:94, GA:101, IT:116, NE:117, PO:111.

86 eksamen Metode til at teste en persons færdighed eller viden ved hjælp af mundtlige og/eller skriftlige opgaver. Opnåelsen af en formel kvalifikation (f.eks. et bevis), adgang til en uddannelsesinstitution eller -forløb etc. kan afhænge af resultatet.
Sammenlign: test.
Øvrig litteratur: Bachman, 1990, p. 50.
CA:171, DA:86, DE:303, EN:133, ES:188,

FR:173, GA:347, IT:164, NE:127, PO:181.

87 eksaminand Se under kandidat.

CA:173, DA:87, DE:307, EN:134, ES:190, FR:351, GA:345, IT:49, NE:129, PO:183.

88 eksaminator Den bedømmer af en mundtlig sprogfærdighedstest, som forklarer opgaverne, stiller spørgsmålene og i det hele taget sørger for samspillet med deltager. Samtalepartneren kan også foretage bedømmelsen af deltageren og tildele point, eller også kan dette gøres af en anden bedømmer, som observerer men ikke indgår i samspillet med deltageren.
Sammenlign: bedømmer (censor).

CA:35, DA:88, DE:55, EN:22, ES:46, FR:174, GA:234, IT:165, NE:33, PO:182.

89 eksaminator Se under bedømmer (censor).

CA:172, DA:89, DE:301, EN:135, ES:189, FR:174, GA:346, IT:165, NE:130, PO:182.

90 endimensionalitet Forestillingen om en enkelt dimension, som er en nødvendig antagelse for at kunne konstruere en skala til måling af psykologiske træk, f.eks. anvendelse af eksisterende item-respons modeller. Endimensionalitet er en egenskab ved måleinstrumentet, ikke ved de tilgrundliggende psykologiske processer.
Øvrig litteratur: Crocker og Algina, 1986, p. 343.

CA:413, DA:90, DE:97, EN:427, ES:410, FR:408, GA:23, IT:398, NE:119, PO:406.

91 enhedskompetens Sprogteori, især fremført af Oller, som postulerer eksistensen af en enkelt kompetens, som ligger til grund for samtlige sprogfærdigheder.

CA:71, DA:91, DE:423, EN:428, ES:68, FR:71, GA:192, IT:70, NE:408, PO:85.

92 enkeltparameter-model I itemresponsteorien en model, som fungerer med en enkelt skala, repræsenterende sværhedsgrad (opgaver) og færdighed (personer), og som ikke tager variabel itemdiskrimination eller gæt i betragtning.
Sammenlign: Rasch-model.

CA:255, DA:92, DE:99, EN:259, ES:273, FR:249, GA:296, IT:242, NE:118, PO:265.

93 evaluering Indsamling af oplysninger med det formål at benytte dem som grundlag for en beslutning. Inden for sprogtestning kan evalueringen fokusere på effektiviteten eller virkningen af et undervisningsforløb, eksamen eller projekt.

CA:31, DA:93, DE:106, EN:132, ES:180, FR:166, GA:235, IT:413, NE:126, PO:30.

94 F-ratio Den beregnede ratio, som angiver hvorvidt forskelle mellem forskellige gruppers gennemsnit er statistisk signifikante. F.eks. hvorvidt en gruppe har klaret sig signifikant bedre end en anden i en sprogtest.
Se: alternative udgaver.
Øvrig litteratur: Hatch og Lazaraton, 1991, pp. 315–317.

CA:364, DA:94, DE:109, EN:139, ES:368, FR:319, GA:66, IT:296, NE:132, PO:332.

95 fagsprog (LSP) Sprogundervisning eller -testning, som fokuserer på den del af sproget, som benyttes til en bestemt aktivitet eller profession. F.eks.: engelsk for flyveledere, kommercielt spansk.

CA:238, DA:95, DE:111, EN:205, ES:256, FR:236, GA:385, IT:227, NE:378, PO:251.

96 faktoranalyse Statistisk metode som gør det muligt for en forsker at reducere et stort antal variabler til et mindre antal ved at påvise mønstre i værdiudsvingene for et antal variabler. En gruppe variabler, som udviser høj grad af interkorrelation, udgør en faktor. Faktoranalyser kan iværksættes i undersøgelsesøjemed, eller til brug for formuleringen af en hypotese, eller for at få bekræftet/undersøgt bestemte hypoteser.
Øvrig litteratur: Bachman, 1990, p. 262; Crocker og Algina, 1986, p. 232.

CA:20, DA:96, DE:115, EN:142, ES:26, FR:18, GA:18, IT:14, NE:133, PO:20.

97 feedback Kommentarer fra de personer, som er involveret i testprocessen (deltagere, administratorer etc.) og som udgør grundlaget for en evaluering af den pågældende proces. Feedback kan indsamles uformelt eller ved hjælp af særligt udformede spørgeskemaer.

CA:381, DA:97, DE:330, EN:144, ES:379, FR:337, GA:6, IT:173, NE:134, PO:192.

98 fejlscore I klassisk true-score teori består det konstaterede pointtal for en test af to komponenter: true-scoren, som afspejler deltagerens abilitet, og fejl-scoren, som repræsenterer påvirkning fra alle øvrige faktorer, som ikke har relation til den abilitet, som testes. Fejlscore forventes at være tilfældig, dvs. usystematisk. Desuden kan en test indeholde faktorer, som regelmæssigt påvirker visse personers præstation og dermed forårsager systematisk fejlscore eller skævvægtning (bias).
Sammenlign: forudindtagethed.
Øvrig litteratur: Bachman, 1990, p. 167.

CA:136, DA:98, DE:116, EN:129, ES:144, FR:151, GA:122, IT:154, NE:124, PO:146.

99 fit (model-tilpasning) Graden af overensstemmelse imellem forudsigelser for en model og det konstaterede resultat.

Det er muligt at beregne forskellige fit-indeks. Inden for Item Response-teorien viser fit-analyser, hvor godt de skønnede item- og personparametre (f.eks. sværhedsgrad og abilitet) er i stand til at forudsige deltagernes point. Et items fit-statistik kan ses som analogt til dets diskriminationsindeks inden for klassisk teststatistik.
Se: item-responsteori (IRT) .
CA:8, DA:99, DE:248, EN:145, ES:15, FR:6, GA:268, IT:107, NE:135, PO:5.

100 flergangssammenstillingsopgave Testopgave med et antal spørgsmål eller sætningsudfyldninger, almindeligvis baseret på en læsetekst. Svarene gives i form af en ord- eller sætningsbank, som kan benyttes ubegrænset. Fordelen er, at valgmulighederne ikke mindskes i takt med, at deltageren arbejder sig igennem de forskellige items (som tilfældet er med andre typer matchopgaver) med det resultat, at opgaven ikke bliver gradvist lettere.
Se: matchopgave.
CA:396, DA:100, DE:235, EN:241, ES:8, FR:355, GA:372, IT:72, NE:253, PO:354.

101 flergangstest Test som løbende kan anvendes og som derfor skal opbevares sikkert.
CA:341, DA:101, DE:225, EN:217, ES:344, FR:360, GA:407, IT:355, NE:233, PO:362.

102 flexibel test (adaptive test) Test hvor de forskellige items vælges undervejs på baggrund af deres sværhedsgrad som reaktion på en vurdering af deltagerens sprogevne. Ofte foregår testen ved hjælp af computer, men en flexibel test kan også bestå af et interview.
Se: computer-baseret flexibel test.
Øvrig litteratur: Bachman, 1990, p. 151; Henning, 1987, p. 136.
CA:302, DA:102, DE:6, EN:7, ES:312, FR:361, GA:429, IT:356, NE:5, PO:363.

103 fordeling Test-data Det antal gange et bestemt pointtal opnås af kandidaterne. Dette illustreres ofte med et histogram.

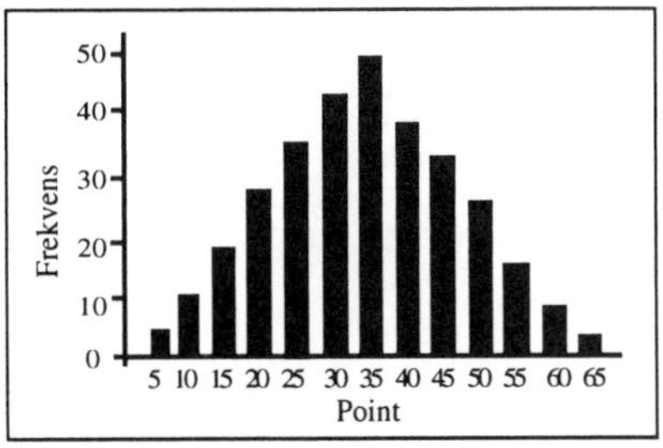

Se: normal fordeling, skæv fordeling.

Øvrig litteratur: Hatch og Lazaraton, 1991, pp. 159–178.
CA:111, DA:103, DE:434, EN:117, ES:112, FR:105, GA:103, IT:130, NE:110, PO:119.

104 forprøve Test som gives før starten på et kursusforløb. Resultatet af fortesten kan sammenlignes med de resultater, som opnås ved en anden test i slutningen af forløbet, hvilket muliggør evaluering af kursets effektivitet.
CA:333, DA:104, DE:440, EN:292, ES:338, FR:306, GA:290, IT:272, NE:299, PO:312.

105 forprøvning Stadiumudviklingen af testmateriale, hvor de forskellige items afprøves på repræsentative stikprøver fra målpopulationen med henblik på at fastslå sværhedsgraden. Efter statistisk analyse kan de items, som betragtes som tilfredsstillende, benyttes i en levende test.
Sammenlign: prøvekørsel.
CA:174, DA:105, DE:436, EN:293, ES:191, FR:307, GA:289, IT:273, NE:302, PO:311.

106 forventet respons Den respons som item-forfatteren ønsker at afæske deltageren.
CA:377, DA:106, DE:105, EN:137, ES:374, FR:328, GA:157, IT:306, NE:32, PO:338.

107 frekvensfordeling Se under fordeling.
CA:113, DA:107, DE:142, EN:149, ES:114, FR:107, GA:106, IT:132, NE:138, PO:122.

108 fremskridtstest Test som anvendes undervejs i et kursusforløb for at bedømme, hvorvidt der er sket fremskridt.
CA:320, DA:108, DE:214, EN:298, ES:330, FR:381, GA:418, IT:369, NE:422, PO:382.

109 fri skriftlig fremstilling Opgavetype hvor deltageren skal producere en længere skriftlig fremstilling. De teksttyper, som produceres under denne overskrift, omfatter fortællende fremstillinger af begivenheder og diskussioner af emner, hvorom der kan være flere forskellige opfattelser. Der kan også være tale om rapporter samt uformelle og formelle breve. Omtales også som essay eller essay-opgave.
CA:366, DA:109, DE:32, EN:62, ES:192, FR:73, GA:51, IT:82, NE:372, PO:88.

110 fællesskala Angivelse af pointene fra to eller flere test på samme skala med

det formål at opnå en direkte sammenligning af resultaterne. Point fra to eller flere test kan angives på en fællesskala, hvis de rå resultater er blevet udsat for statistisk transformation, f.eks. testækvivalering.
Øvrig litteratur: Bachman, 1990, pp. 340–344.
CA:147, DA:110, DE:131, EN:57, ES:156, FR:125, GA:86, IT:320, NE:148, PO:158.

111 færdighed Evne til at udføre et eller andet. Inden for sprogtestning skelnes ofte imellem fire færdigheder: læse, skrive, tale og lytte.
Se: kompetens.
CA:199, DA:111, DE:119, EN:367, ES:100, FR:340, GA:325, IT:1B, NE:413, PO:51.

112 færdighedstest Test som måler generel abilitet eller færdighed uden reference til noget specifikt kursusforløb eller materialesæt.
CA:319, DA:112, DE:120, EN:296, ES:326, FR:378, GA:428, IT:363, NE:306, PO:379.

113 G-faktor Intelligensteori. Hypotetisk 'generel' faktor, som ligger til grund for alle kognitive færdigheder. Denne forestilling blev i 1970erne udbredt af John Oller som bevis for en enhedskompetens, som skulle ligge til grund for sprogfærdighed.
Øvrig litteratur: Oller, 1979, pp. 426–458; Bachman, 1990, p. 6.
CA:176, DA:113, DE:127, EN:153, ES:195, FR:177, GA:136, IT:170, NE:139, PO:187.

114 Gauss–fordeling Se under normalfordeling.
CA:114, DA:114, DE:129, EN:152, ES:115, FR:91, GA:105, IT:133, NE:140, PO:110.

115 generaliserbarhedsteori Statistisk metode til undersøgelse af den relative betydning af forskellige årsager til varians i testresultater.
Øvrig litteratur: Bachman, 1990, p. 7; Crocker og Algina, 1986, kapitel 8.
CA:400, DA:115, DE:132, EN:154, ES:393, FR:399, GA:388, IT:351, NE:152, PO:359.

116 generel (impressionistisk) bedømmelse Scoringsmetode som kan anvendes ved testning af produktiv sprogbrug, dvs. skrive og tale. Censoren foretager en bedømmelse af hver besvarelse uden forsøg på at adskille opgavens diskrete træk.
Sammenlign: analytisk bedømmelse (scoring), helhedsbedømmelse.
CA:89, DA:116, DE:133, EN:168, ES:429, FR:270, GA:220, IT:33, NE:172, PO:68.

117 gentagen regression Statistisk teknik som anvendes til at fastslå de lineære virkninger af flere uafhængige variabler. F.eks. er det muligt med opgavesværhedsgraden som afhængig variabel at undersøge virkningerne af opgavetype, leksikalsk vanskelighed, etc.
Se: uafhængig variabel, regression.
Øvrig litteratur: Hatch og Lazaraton, 1991, pp. 480–486.
CA:371, DA:117, DE:251, EN:242, ES:367, FR:326, GA:182, IT:300, NE:240, PO:330.

118 glorieeffekt Tendens hos censorer, som medvirker til subjektiv bedømmelse, til at lade sig influere af deltagerens præstation i visse test–opgaver og følgelig tildeler for høj eller lav score for en anden test.
Se: bedømmereffekt.
CA:117, DA:118, DE:141, EN:161, ES:127, FR:137, GA:170, IT:139, NE:164, PO:133.

119 grammatisk kompetens I en model for kommunikativ sprogfærdighed er grammatisk kompetens den komponent, som vedrører viden om sådanne aspekter af sprogbrug som morfologi, syntaks, ordforråd, fonologi og grafologi.
Øvrig litteratur: Bachman, 1990, pp. 84–88.
CA:67, DA:119, DE:138, EN:158, ES:63, FR:65, GA:193, IT:65, NE:162, PO:79.

120 grænseeffekt Virkningen af, at en test er for nem eller for svær for en bestemt deltagergruppe. Karaktererne viser tendens til at samle sig enten i toppen af fordelingen (loftseffekten) eller i bunden (bundeffekten).
Se: bundeffekt, loftseffekt.
CA:125, DA:120, DE:139, EN:36, ES:131, FR:143, GA:177, IT:138, NE:163, PO:139.

121 guidet skriftlig opgave Opgave hvor deltageren producerer en skreven tekst og hvor grafiske eller tekstmæssige oplysninger, såsom billeder, breve, postkort og instrukser, benyttes til at kontrollere og standardisere den forventede respons.
Sammenlign: fri skriftlig fremstilling, opgaveformulering.
CA:393, DA:121, DE:130, EN:160, ES:5, FR:311, GA:377, IT:76, NE:143, PO:317.

122 gætteparameter Se under c–parameter.

CA:284, DA:122, DE:319, EN:159, ES:297, FR:295, GA:277, IT:263, NE:160, PO:301.

123 halvautentisk tekst Autentisk test som er blevet redigeret til testformål, f.eks. ved tilpasning af ordforråd og/eller grammatik til deltagernes niveau.
Se: autentisk tekst.
CA:405, DA:123, DE:140, EN:355, ES:400, FR:112, GA:383, IT:391, NE:335, PO:128.

124 helhedsbedømmelse Scoringsmetode som kan anvendes i test af skriftlig og mundtlig sprogfærdighed. Censoren giver point på baggrund af det generelle sproglige indtryk snarere end en række point for forskellige aspekter af sprogbrug.
Sammenlign: analytisk bedømmelse (scoring), generel bedømmelse.
CA:33, DA:124, DE:137, EN:155, ES:427, FR:169, GA:231, IT:186, NE:161, PO:33.

125 histogram Grafisk fremstilling af frekvensfordeling, hvor antallet af tilfælde pr. frekvensgruppe vises i form af en lodret søjle.

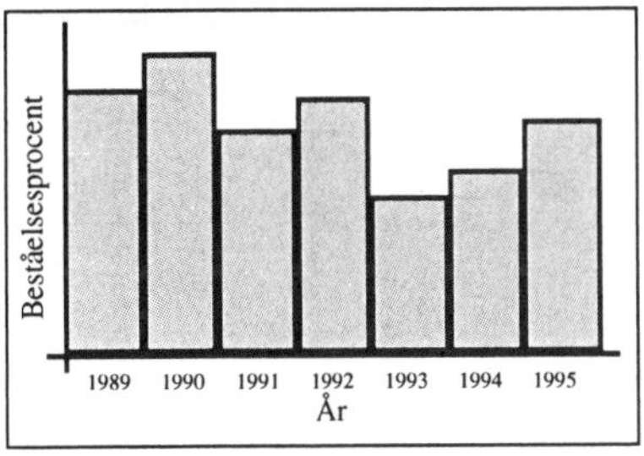

Sammenlign: søjlediagram.
CA:203, DA:125, DE:145, EN:163, ES:218, FR:204, GA:168, IT:207, NE:167, PO:215.

126 holistisk bedømmelse Se under helhedsbedømmelse.
CA:429, DA:126, DE:128, EN:164, ES:428, FR:170, GA:230, IT:187, NE:168, PO:34.

127 homogenitet Træk ved en test eller deltest, hvor de forskellige items måler samme kompetens, eller ved en gruppe, hvor de enkelte personer har samme karakteristika. Homogenitets-graden udtrykkes ved hjælp af reliabilitetsindekset.
CA:204, DA:127, DE:148, EN:165, ES:221, FR:205, GA:22, IT:257, NE:169, PO:216.

128 horisontal ækvivalering Placering af pointtal fra to test af nogenlunde samme sværhedsgrad på én skala med det formål at anvende identiske normer i begge test.
Sammenlign: vertikal ækvivalering.
Se: kalibrering.
CA:133, DA:128, DE:149, EN:166, ES:141, FR:37, GA:89, IT:152, NE:170, PO:44.

129 hurtighedstest Tidsbegrænset test. Langsommere deltagere vil opnå færre point, fordi de ikke når at besvare de sidste spørgsmål. Spørgsmålene i en hurtighedstest er normalt af en sådan karakter, at deltagerne ville kunne besvare dem korrekt, hvis ikke det havde været for den tidsmæssige begrænsning.
Sammenlign: præstationstest.
CA:321, DA:129, DE:340/363, EN:376, ES:334, FR:363, GA:424, IT:372, NE:352, PO:385.

130 højere-rangerende færdigheder Hypotetiske, komplekse færdigheder, såsom følgeslutninger og opsummering.
Sammenlign: basale færdigheder.
CA:201, DA:130, DE:418, EN:162, ES:102, FR:45, GA:326, IT:3, NE:410, PO:53.

131 ikke-parametriske metoder Statistiske metoder som ikke forudsætter, at data kommer fra en særlig type fordeling, eller hvor data ikke er baseret på en intervalskala. Chi-kvadrat er et kendt eksempel.
Sammenlign: parametriske metoder.
Øvrig litteratur: Hatch og Lazaraton, 1991, pp. 237–239.
CA:294, DA:131, DE:259, EN:249, ES:308, FR:309, GA:258, IT:274, NE:257, PO:315.

132 indeks for middel-sværhedsgrad (middel-a) Den gennemsnitlige andel af korrekte svar hen over samtlige items på en skala med dikotomisk bedømte items. For eksempel viser et middel-a på 0,5, at testens middel-korrekthedsindeks er 0,5.
Se: dikotomisk bedømmelse.
CA:208, DA:132, DE:246, EN:228, ES:227, FR:212, GA:190, IT:195 NE:150, PO:222.

133 indholdsanalyse Metode til beskrivelse og analyse af et testmateriale. Analysen er nødvendig til sikring af, at testindholdet svarer til specifikationerne, og er afgørende for at kunne fastslå indholds- og begrebsvaliditet.
CA:18, DA:133, DE:153, EN:72, ES:19, FR:12, GA:12, IT:15, NE:178, PO:15.

134 indholdsvaliditet En test siges at have indholdsvaliditet, hvis indholdet af items eller opgaver udgør et repræsentativt udsnit for det videns- eller færdighedsområde, som skal testes. Indholdsvaliditet vurderes ofte i relation til et pensum eller kursusforløb.
Se: validitet, testspecifikationer.
Øvrig litteratur: Bachman, 1990, pp. 244–247.
CA:422, DA:134, DE:154, EN:73, ES:419, FR:419, GA:31, IT:405, NE:179, PO:415.

135 indirekte test (opgave) Test eller opgave som forsøger at måle de færdigheder, som ligger til grund for en sprogfærdighed snarere end en testning af færdigheden selv. Et eksempel på dette er testning af skrivefærdighed ved at bede deltageren markere de strukturer i en tekst, som er anvendt ukorrekt.
Sammenlign: direkte test.
Øvrig litteratur: Hughes, 1989, pp. 14–16.
CA:329, DA:135, DE:150, EN:170, ES:337, FR:385, GA:420, IT:354, NE:173, PO:389.

136 indlæringsmål Målsætningen eller det ønskede resultat af et undervisningsforløb.
CA:277, DA:136, DE:215, EN:208, ES:290, FR:289, GA:360, IT:255, NE:217, PO:292.

137 indplaceringsprøve Test som har til formål at indplacere elever i en gruppe eller klasse på et niveau, som svarer til deres viden og færdigheder.
CA:311, DA:137, DE:101, EN:282, ES:323, FR:377, GA:434, IT:365, NE:291, PO:372.

138 indsætnings-item Item som kræver at deltageren indsætter en eller anden form for skriftligt materiale- bogstaver, tal, enkeltord, ordforbindelser, sætninger eller afsnit - i et hul i en tekst. Svaret kan enten leveres af deltageren eller vælges blandt en række muligheder.
CA:223, DA:138, DE:229, EN:151, ES:241, FR:317, GA:249, IT:78, NE:192, PO:235.

139 inferensstatistik Statistik som går ud over de oplysninger, der er tilvejebragt gennem deskriptiv statistik og som muliggør følgeslutninger om, i hvor høj grad et enkelt datasæt måtte være repræsentativt for en større gruppe.
Sammenlign: deskriptiv statistik.
CA:166, DA:139, DE:338, EN:171, ES:173, FR:350, GA:364, IT:341, NE:175, PO:177.

140 informationskløft (information gap) Teknik til sprogundervisning og testning, som stimulerer ægte kommunikation ved at opstille situationer, hvor lærere og elever ikke er i besiddelse af samme oplysninger og derfor har behov for at kommunikere med hinanden for at fuldende en opgave. Benyttes normalt til træning og testning af tale- og skrivefærdigheder.
CA:42, DA:140, DE:151, EN:172, ES:411, FR:213, GA:43, IT:424, NE:176, PO:223.

141 informationsoverførsel Testningsteknik som indebærer at oplysninger, som er modtaget i en bestemt form, viderebringes i en anden form. Eksempelvis: udvælgelse af oplysninger fra en tekst, som anvendes til rubricering af et diagram; omskrivning af en uformel skrivelse, så den fremstår som en formel bekendtgørelse.
Øvrig litteratur: Hughes, 1989, pp. 84, 124–125, 138.
CA:409, DA:141, DE:152, EN:173, ES:406, FR:402, GA:8, IT:396, NE:177, PO:404.

142 input Materiale som indgår i en testopgave med det formål at sætte deltageren i stand til at frembringe en passende respons. I en lyttetest kan f.eks. indgå en indspillet tekst tilknyttet et antal skrevne items.
CA:169, DA:142, DE:408, EN:174, ES:228, FR:147, GA:199, IT:199, NE:180, PO:254.

143 instrukser Generelle anvisninger til deltageren, f.eks. på opgavehæftets forside, vedr. testens varighed, antallet af opgaver og om hvor svarene skal placeres.
CA:211, DA:143, DE:391, EN:175, ES:230, FR:214, GA:402, IT:208, NE:181, PO:225.

144 integrativt item/opgave Benyttes til at referere til items eller opgaver, hvor løsningen kræver mere end én færdighed eller 'delfærdighed'. F.eks. items i en cloze test, et mundtligt interview, læsning og skriftlig besvarelse af et brev.
Sammenlign: diskret-point item.
CA:231, DA:144, DE:156, EN:176, ES:249, FR:316, GA:248, IT:221, NE:182, PO:245.

145 inter-reliabilitet Vurdering af en tests reliabilitet baseret på graden af enighed imellem forskellige bedømmere (censorer) om deltagernes præstationer.
Se: bedømmer (censor)-enighed, reliabilitet.

CA:181, DA:145, DE:158, EN:182, ES:199, FR:185, GA:201, IT:8, NE:184, PO:195.

146 interaktional autenticitet Opfattelse af autenticitet i sprogtestning som en egenskab af den interaktion, som skal finde sted imellem kandidaten og testopgaven for at frembringe en passende respons.
Sammenlign: autenticitet.

CA:28, DA:146, DE:157, EN:177, ES:34, FR:25, GA:116, IT:36, NE:183, PO:27.

147 intern konsekvens Graden af overensstemmelse imellem deltagernes point for forskellige testitems med de samlede point. Vurderinger af den interne konsekvens kan anvendes som indeks for testens reliabilitet. Der er muligt at beregne forskellige indekser, f.eks. KR20, alfa.
Se: alfa (alfakoefficient), Kuder-Richardson, reliabilitet.
Øvrig litteratur: Bachman, 1990, p. 172.

CA:77, DA:147, DE:155, EN:180, ES:74, FR:186, GA:87, IT:87, NE:186, PO:93.

148 interval Afstanden imellem to punkter på en skala.

CA:214, DA:148, DE:160, EN:183, ES:232, FR:218, GA:131, IT:203, NE:187, PO:228.

149 intervalskala Skala på hvilken afstanden mellem de forskellige skalaværdier er lige store, men hvor der ikke er noget absolut nulpunkt.
Sammenlign: kategorisk skala, nominalskala, ordinalskala, kvotientskala.
Øvrig litteratur: Crocker og Algina, 1986, p. 48.

CA:148, DA:149, DE:161, EN:184, ES:158, FR:126, GA:315, IT:315, NE:188, PO:162.

150 interview Talefærdighed testes ofte ved hjælp af et interview, som kan tage form af en fuldstændig fri samtale imellem deltagere og bedømmere eller som en nøje struktureret serie taleopgaver.

CA:131, DA:150, DE:305, EN:263, ES:136, FR:148, GA:1, IT:92, NE:355, PO:143.

151 intra-reliabilitet Vurdering af reliabiliteten af bedømmelser baseret på den udstrækning i hvilken samme præstation bedømmes ens ved forskellige lejligheder af samme bedømmer.
Se: bedømmer (censor)-konstans, reliabilitet.

CA:182, DA:151, DE:162, EN:186, ES:200, FR:187, GA:202, IT:89, NE:189, PO:196.

152 invarians Inden for IRT, den vigtige antagelse, at et items sværhedsgrad og evne til at diskriminere er iboende træk, som ikke er afhængige af deltagernes færdighed, og at færdighedsmål på tilsvarende vis er uafhængige af det enkelte item.

CA:216, DA:152, DE:164, EN:187, ES:234, FR:220, GA:120, IT:205, NE:191, PO:230.

153 IRT Se under item-responsteori (IRT) .

CA:412, DA:153, DE:165, EN:188, ES:408, FR:401, GA:392, IT:352, NE:194, PO:402.

154 item Element i en tekst, som bedømmes separat. For eksempel: en udfyldning i en cloze test; et multiple-choice spørgsmål med tre eller fire valgmuligheder; en sætning, som skal udsættes for grammatiske ændringer; et spørgsmål, hvortil der forventes et svar af sætningslængde.
Sammenlign: opgave.

CA:217, DA:154, DE:166, EN:189, ES:235, FR:221, GA:240, IT:209, NE:195, PO:231.

155 item-bank Metode til at holde styr på test-items, som indebærer lagring af items til konstruktion af test med kendt indhold og sværhedsgrad. Metoden anvender normalt computer-baserede databaser og baseres på teorien om latente træk, hvilket indebærer, at items kan relateres til hinanden ved hjælp af en fælles sværhedsskala.
Øvrig litteratur: Henning, 1987, kapitel 9.

CA:36, DA:155, DE:28, EN:191, ES:37, FR:28, GA:40, IT:111, NE:199, PO:37.

156 item-informationsfunktion (IRT). Indeks over hvor mange oplysninger et item eller en test giver om en person på et givent færdighedsniveau, hvilket afhænger af det pågældende items diskrimination og af hvor godt det er afpasset niveauet.
Sammenlign: test-informationsfunktion.

CA:192, DA:156, DE:169, EN:193, ES:212, FR:190, GA:138, IT:184, NE:197, PO:206.

157 item-karakteristisk kurve (IKK) I item-responsteorien viser en IKK, hvordan sandsynligheden for at besvare et item korrekt står i forhold til det latente abilitetstræk, som ligger til grund for besvarelsen.
Øvrig litteratur: Crocker og Algina, 1986, pp. 340–342.

CA:79, DA:157, DE:168, EN:192, ES:95, FR:90, GA:94, IT:115, NE:196, PO:109.

158 item-responsfunktion (IRT).

Matematisk funktion, som sætter sandsynligheden for rigtig besvarelse af et item i forhold til færdigheden i den egenskab, som skal måles af det pågældende item. Også kaldet item-karakteristisk funktion.

CA:193, DA:158, DE:172, EN:194, ES:210, FR:189, GA:140, IT:183, NE:200, PO:205.

159 item-responsteori (IRT) Gruppe af matematiske modeller til relatering af individuelle testpræstationer til individuelle færdighedsniveauer. Disse modeller er baseret på den grundlæggende teori, at en persons forventede besvarelse af et bestemt testspørgsmål, eller item, er en funktion af både det pågældende items sværhedsgrad og personens færdighedsniveau.

Øvrig litteratur: Henning, 1987, kapitel 8; Crocker og Algina, 1986, kapitel 15.

CA:401, DA:159, DE:173/296, EN:195, ES:394, FR:400, GA:389, IT:352, NE:201, PO:360.

160 item-score I item-analyse summen af korrekte svar på et givent item.

CA:345, DA:160, DE:171, EN:196, ES:346, FR:267, GA:336, IT:281, NE:202, PO:60.

161 itemanalyse Beskrivelse af de enkelte items præstationer, sædvanligvis ved hjælp af klassiske statistiske indekser såsom korrekthed og diskrimination. Der anvendes software, f.eks. MicroCat Iteman, til denne analyse.

Se: diskrimination, korrekthedsindeks.

CA:13, DA:161, DE:167, EN:190, ES:25, FR:17, GA:13, IT:12, NE:198, PO:16.

162 itemtype Testitems udstyres ofte med beskrivende navne. F.eks. multiple-choice, sætningstransformation, kort-svar, open cloze.

CA:406, DA:162, DE:174, EN:197 ES:405, FR:405, GA:58, IT:392, NE:203, PO:399.

163 kalibrere Ifølge item-responsteorien at forudsige vanskeligheden af et sæt test-items.

Se: theta-skala.

CA:43, DA:163, DE:93, EN:39, ES:43, FR:40, GA:48, IT:43, NE:206, PO:47.

164 kalibrering Fastsættelsen af en sværhedsskala for en eller flere test. Kalibreringen kan omfatte forankringen af items fra forskellige test til en fælles sværhedsskala (theta-skalaen). Når en test konstrueres ud fra kalibrerede items, vil pointene angive deltagernes færdighed, dvs. deres placering på theta-skalaen.

CA:44, DA:164, DE:94, EN:40, ES:42, FR:35, GA:49, IT:44, NE:205, PO:42.

165 kandidat Person som går op til en eksamen/test. Også kaldet eksaminand.

CA:45, DA:165, DE:302, EN:41, ES:48, FR:41, GA:178, IT:49, NE:207, PO:48.

166 karakter Samlede point som kan opnås for et item, en test eller deltest, eller det antal point, som en deltager opnår for sin besvarelse af et item, en test eller deltest.

CA:342, DA:166, DE:313, EN:224, ES:44, FR:287, GA:224, IT:292, NE:60, PO:105.

167 karakter Deltageren kan få tildelt sine testpoint i form af en karakter, f.eks. på en skala fra A til E, hvor A er højeste karakter, B er over middel, C bestået og D og E er dumpekarakterer.

Sammenlign: point.

CA:275, DA:167, DE:270, EN:156, ES:288, FR:259, GA:164, IT:188, NE:426, PO:272.

168 karaktergivning Konverteringen af scores eller point til karakterer.

CA:362, DA:168, DE:48, EN:157, ES:47, FR:52, GA:165, IT:94, NE:427, PO:277.

169 kategori a) Inddeling af en kategorisk skala, f.eks. kan 'køn' inddeles i kategorierne maskulinum og feminimum.

b) Inden for testning siges en klassificeringsskala med f. eks. fem pointinddelinger at have fem svar-kategorier.

CA:49, DA:169, DE:176, EN:43, ES:52, FR:48, GA:50, IT:51, NE:52, PO:55.

170 kategorisk skala Skala som anvendes til kategoriske variabler såsom køn, modersmål, erhverv.

Sammenlign: intervalskala, nominalskala, ordinalskala, kvotientskala.

CA:146, DA:170, DE:175, EN:42, ES:154, FR:123, GA:310, IT:318, NE:53, PO:156.

171 klassificering a) Tildeling af point for en testpræstation på baggrund af bedømmelsesprocessen.

b) De point, som opnås på baggrund af klassificeringsprocessen.

CA:428, DA:171, DE:57, EN:314, ES:425, FR:265, GA:286, IT:54, NE:38, PO:57.

172 klassificeringsskala (rating scale) Skala som består af adskillige rangordnede kategorier, der anvendes til at foretage subjektive skøn. Inden for sprogtestning ledsages klassiferingsskalaer til bedømmelse af præstationer typisk af områdedeskriptorer, som tydeliggør tolk-

ningen.
Sammenlign: likertskala.
Se: deskriptor.
CA:154, DA:172, DE:58, EN:315, ES:161, FR:130, GA:319, IT:323, NE:40, PO:160.

173 klassificeringsskalamodel Udvidelse af den simple Rasch-model til håndtering af skalære data, som er udledt af f.eks. klassificering af mundtlige præstationer.
Sammenlign: Rasch-model.
Se: partial-credit modellen.
Øvrig litteratur: Wright, B.D. og Masters G.N., 1982, Rating Scale Analysis, Chicago, MESA Press.
CA:254, DA:173, DE:236, EN:316, ES:272, FR:251, GA:303, IT:246, NE:41, PO:263.

174 klassisk testteori Måleteori bestående af et sæt antagelser om forholdet imellem faktiske eller konstaterede point og de faktorer, som påvirker de pågældende resultater og som normalt kaldes fejl. Også kaldet 'true-score' teori.
Sammenlign: item-responsteori (IRT) .
Øvrig litteratur: Bachman, 1990, pp. 166–187.
CA:399, DA:174, DE:177, EN:50, ES:392, FR:397, GA:387, IT:349, NE:208, PO:357.

175 koefficient Numerisk indeks som anvendes som mål for en egenskab eller karakteristik.
Se: alfa (alfakoefficient), korrellationskoefficient.
CA:53, DA:175, DE:178, EN:53, ES:55, FR:54, GA:73, IT:57, NE:62, PO:69.

176 koefficient alfa Se under alfa (alfakoefficient).
CA:54, DA:176, DE:179, EN:54, ES:56, FR:55, GA:74, IT:58, NE:63, PO:70.

177 kognitive faktorer Faktorer i lærings- eller testningsprocessen, som vedrører lørnerens vidensmønstre (scripts).
Sammenlign: affektive faktorer.
Øvrig litteratur: Ebel og Frisbie, 1991, p. 52.
CA:178, DA:177, DE:180, EN:55, ES:196, FR:179, GA:398, IT:171, NE:65, PO:189.

178 kognitiv model Teori om hvordan en persons viden, forstået som begreber og processer, struktureres. Dette er vigtigt i sprogtestning, eftersom en sådan teori kan have indflydelse på valget af testmetode eller testindhold.
CA:253, DA:178, DE:181, EN:56, ES:269, FR:250, GA:297, IT:243, NE:64, PO:262.

179 kommunikativ kompetens Evnen til at anvende sproget hensigtsmæssigt i forskellige situationer og sammenhænge.
Øvrig litteratur: Bachman, 1990, p. 16, p. 68.
CA:65, DA:179, DE:182, EN:58, ES:61, FR:63, GA:195, IT:63, NE:66, PO:77.

180 kompetens Viden eller evne til at udføre noget. Benyttes inden for lingvistikken til at angive en grundlæggende færdighed, modsat performans, som er manifestationen af kompetens i sprogbrug. Denne skelnen har sin oprindelse i Chomskys teori.
Sammenlign: performans.
Øvrig litteratur: Bachman, 1990, pp. 52 og 108.
CA:64, DA:180, DE:183, EN:59, ES:60, FR:62, GA:191, IT:62, NE:67, PO:76.

181 komponent Del af eksamination, ofte præsenteret som en separat test med eget instruktionshæfte og tidsfrist. Komponenter er ofte færdighedsbaserede og har overskrifter såsom 'Lytteforståelse' eller 'Fri skriftlig fremstilling'. Kaldes også deltest.
CA:73, DA:181, DE:306, EN:61, ES:29, FR:72, GA:85, IT:81, NE:128, PO:87.

182 konfidensinterval Det område omkring en anslået værdi, hvor den virkelige værdi sandsynligvis vil komme til at ligge. Sandsynlighedsgraden defineres normalt med konfidensintervaller på 95% eller 99%.
CA:215, DA:182, DE:184, EN:67, ES:233, FR:219, GA:132, IT:204, NE:45, PO:229.

183 konstaterede point De point som en deltager har opnået. Ifølge klassisk testteori er disse sammensat af true-score og fejl.
Se: fejlscore, true-score.
CA:353, DA:183, DE:49, EN:258, ES:352, FR:279, GA:331, IT:283, NE:429, PO:285.

184 konstruct Hypotetisk abilitet eller mental egenskab, som ikke nødvendigvis kan konstateres eller måles direkte. I sprogtestning kan det f.eks. være lytteevne. Sprogtest forsøger at måle de forskellige konstrukter, som ligger til grund for vores sprogfærdighed. Ud over sprog-færdigheden selv, udgør motivation, indstilling og kulturel tilpasning alle relevante konstrukter.
Øvrig litteratur: Hatch og Lazaraton, 1991, p. 15.
CA:78, DA:184, DE:185, EN:68, ES:76,

FR:80, GA:394, IT:108, NE:72, PO:94.

185 konstrueret svar Skriftlig besvarelse af et item, hvor deltageren, i stedet for blot at vælge imellem en række muligheder, selv producerer svaret.
Sammenlign: udvalgt svar.
Se: respons.
CA:376, DA:185, DE:126, EN:70, ES:372, FR:330, GA:154, IT:309, NE:272, PO:336.

186 konstruktvaliditet En test anses at udvise konstruktvaliditet, såfremt de opnåede point kan påvises at afspejle en teori om en konstrukts beskaffenhed eller dets forhold til andre konstrukter. Det vil f.eks. kunne forudsiges, at to valide lytteforståelses-test klassificerer lørnere på samme måde, men begge vil udvise svagere relation til resultaterne af en grammatiktest.
Se: validitet, testspecifikationer.
Øvrig litteratur: Ebel og Frisbie, 1991, p. 108; Hatch og Lazaraton, 1991, pp. 37–38.
CA:420, DA:186, DE:186, EN:69, ES:418, FR:418, GA:37, IT:406, NE:73, PO:414.

187 kontingenstabel Tabel over frekvenser, som klassificeres i henhold til to eller flere sæt kategoriske variabler, f. eks.:

	Beherskelse	Ikke–Beherskelse
Metode A	35	5
Metode B	20	20

Se: chi-kvadrattest.
CA:398, DA:187, DE:187, EN:74, ES:390, FR:353, GA:369, IT:347, NE:75, PO:320.

188 konvergerende validitet En test siges at udvise konvergerende validitet, når der er høj grad af korrelation imellem de opnåede point og resultaterne fra en anden test, som måler samme konstrukt (uanset metode). Kan betragtes som et aspekt af konstruktvaliditet.
Sammenlign: diskriminant validitet.
Se: konstruktvaliditet.
Øvrig litteratur: Guilford og Fruchter, 1981, pp. 436–437.
CA:419, DA:188, DE:188, EN:75, ES:416, FR:416, GA:32, IT:404, NE:76, PO:412.

189 kopierbarhed Muligheden for at gentage forskningsresultater ved flere lejligheder, hvorved resultaterne opnår større troværdighed.
CA:373, DA:189, DE:324, EN:329, ES:370, FR:335, GA:185, IT:301, NE:165, PO:333.

190 korrekt svar Den respons som betragtes som korrekt ved bedømmelsen af en test.
CA:375, DA:190, DE:327, EN:333, ES:373, FR:331, GA:155, IT:307, NE:204, PO:337.

191 korrekthedsindex Andelen af korrekte besvarelser af et item, udtrykt på en skala fra 0 til 1. Udtrykkes også som en procent. Kaldes også korrekthedsværdi eller a-værdi.
Sammenlign: sværhedsindeks.
CA:209, DA:191, DE:208, EN:141, ES:225, FR:210, GA:188, IT:197, NE:146, PO:220.

192 korrekthedsværdi Se under korrekthedsindeks.
CA:426, DA:192, DE:209, EN:143, ES:423, FR:410, GA:217, IT:411, NE:147, PO:419.

193 korrektion for gætteri Metode til at reducere pointgevinsten ved at gætte det korrekte svar i test, som består af objektive items.
Øvrig litteratur: Ebel og Frisbie, 1986, pp. 215–218.
CA:82, DA:193, DE:317/450, EN:77, ES:80, FR:83, GA:54, IT:103, NE:77, PO:98.

194 korrektion for dæmpning Metode til at anslå korrelationen imellem to eller flere variabler, hvis der ikke er nogen forskel på variablerne med hensyn til reliabilitet.
Øvrig litteratur: Guilford og Fruchter, 1981, pp. 450–453; Hatch og Lazaraton, 1990, pp. 444–445.
CA:88, DA:194, DE:243, EN:76, ES:79, FR:82, GA:53, IT:106, NE:78, PO:99.

195 korrekturlæsningsopgave Testopgave som indebærer kontrol af en tekst for nærmere angivne fejltyper, f.eks. stavefejl eller strukturelle fejl. En del af opgaven kan også bestå i markering af fejl og indføjelse af rettelser.
CA:395, DA:195, DE:189, EN:300, ES:4, FR:84, GA:374, IT:75, NE:304, PO:97.

196 korrelation Forholdet imellem to eller flere målinger, for så vidt angår deres tendens til at ændre sig ensartet. Hvis f.eks. deltagerne viser tendens til at opnå nogenlunde samme klassificering i to forskellige test, vil der være en positiv korrelation imellem de to pointsæt.
Sammenlign: kovarians.
Se: rangkorrelation, Pearsons produktmomentkorrelation.
Øvrig litteratur: Guilford og Fruchter,

1981, kapitel 6; Bachman, 1990, pp. 259–260.

CA:91, DA:196, DE:190, EN:78, ES:84, FR:85, GA:78, IT:95, NE:81, PO:100.

197 korrelationskoefficient Indeks som viser i hvilken grad to eller flere variabler korrelerer. Variationen går fra -1 til +1. Høj grad af korrelation imellem variabler gengives med en korrelationskoefficient, som nærmer sig + eller -1.
Øvrig litteratur: Guilford og Fruchter, 1981, pp. 86–88.

CA:55, DA:197, DE:191, EN:79, ES:57, FR:56, GA:75, IT:60, NE:82, PO:71.

198 kortsvars-item Åbent item som kræver, at deltageren formulerer et skriftligt svar indeholdende et bestemt ord eller ordforbindelse.

CA:228, DA:198, DE:205, EN:362, ES:243, FR:224, GA:246, IT:311, NE:209, PO:238.

199 kovarians Fælles varians for to eller flere variabler. For eksempel repræsenterer sætningslængde og leksikalsk sværhedsgrad træk ved en læsetest, som har tendens til at hænge sammen, dvs. til fælles varians. Kovarians tages i betragtning, når en variabel forudsiges på grundlag af andre, f. eks. når man forudsiger vanskeligheden af en læsetekst på grundlag af sætningslængden og den leksikalske sværhedsgrad.
Se: varians.

CA:93, DA:199, DE:192, EN:80, ES:91, FR:92, GA:71, IT:112, NE:84, PO:106.

200 kovariansanalyse Se under ANCOVA.

CA:14, DA:200, DE:193, EN:12, ES:20, FR:14, GA:16, IT:18, NE:85, PO:13.

201 KR-20 (Kuder-Richardson formel 20) Se under Kuder-Richardson.

CA:234, DA:201, DE:194, EN:199, ES:252, FR:233, GA:205, IT:222, NE:210, PO:246.

202 KR-21 (Kuder-Richardson formel 21) Se under Kuder-Richardson.

CA:235, DA:202, DE:195, EN:200 ES:253, FR:234, GA:206, IT:223, NE:211, PO:247.

203 kriterie-relateret test Test hvori deltagerens præstation fortolkes i relation til forudbestemte kriterier. Til at afspejle deltagernes indbyrdes rangplacering fokuseres i højere grad på opfyldelse af målsætninger end på point.
Sammenlign: norm-relateret test, domænerelateret test.

CA:337, DA:203, DE:196, EN:81, ES:317, FR:364, GA:412, IT:380, NE:86, PO:369.

204 kriterie-relateret validitet En test siges at udvise kriterie-relateret validitet, hvis det er muligt at påvise et forhold imellem de opnåede point og eksterne kriterier, som anses for at være et mål for samme færdighed. Oplysninger om kriterie-relation benyttes også til at afgøre, i hvor høj grad en test er i stand til at forudsige fremtidig adfærd.
Se: samstemmende validitet, prædiktiv validitet.
Øvrig litteratur: Bachman, 1990, pp. 248–250.

CA:421, DA:204, DE:197, EN:82, ES:417, FR:417, GA:34, IT:407, NE:87, PO:413.

205 kriterievariabel Andet udtryk for afhængig variabel.
Se: afhængig variabel.

CA:431, DA:205, DE:198, EN:83, ES:431, FR:424, GA:26, IT:417, NE:88, PO:423.

206 Kuder-Richardson To mål for intern konsekvens, udviklet af Kuder og Richardson som benyttes til at vurdere en tests reliabilitet. KR-21 kræver færre oplysninger og er nemmere at beregne, men giver almindeligvis et lavere skøn end KR-20.
Sammenlign: alfa (alfakoefficient).
Se: intern konsekvens.
Øvrig litteratur: Henning, 1987, p. 84.

CA:236, DA:206, DE:200, EN:201, ES:254, FR:235, GA:207, IT:224, NE:212, PO:248.

207 kulturel skævvægtning (bias) Test med kulturel forudindtagethed til fordel eller ulempe for deltagere med en bestemt kulturel baggrund.
Se: skævvægtning (bias).

CA:41, DA:207, DE:201, EN:85, ES:385, FR:33, GA:209, IT:161, NE:90, PO:41.

208 kumulativ frekvens Metode til fremstilling af deltagerfordeling ved at tælle antallet af deltagere i hver pointkategori, som har opnået point i den pågældende kategori samt i alle lavere kategorier.
Øvrig litteratur: Guilford og Fruchter, 1981, pp. 35–36.

CA:189, DA:208, DE:202, EN:86, ES:208, FR:198, GA:239, IT:181, NE:91, PO:204.

209 kvalifikation Belønning som tildeles efter et anerkendt kursusforløb eller efter en test, som kvalificerer til at udføre en bestemt aktivitet eller arbejde. Et bevis for sprogfærdighed kan betragtes som en kvalifikation til visse formål.

Sammenlign: bevis, diplom.
CA:360, DA:209, DE:314, EN:302, ES:405, FR:313, GA:46, IT:294, NE:214, PO:322.

210 kvotientskala Skala hvorpå der er et virkeligt nulpunkt og hvor afstanden imellem to tilstødende punkter er den samme i hele skalaens udstrækning. For eksempel højde. En person, som er 2 m høj er dobbelt så høj, som en, der er 1 m høj.
Sammenlign: kategorisk skala, intervalskala, ordinalskala.
Øvrig litteratur: Crocker og Algina, 1986, pp. 48–49.
CA:153, DA:210, DE:433, EN:317, ES:160, FR:131, GA:312, IT:324, NE:314, PO:164.

211 latente træk Se under itemresponsteori.
CA:402, DA:211, DE:206, EN:207, ES:395, FR:398, GA:390, IT:350, NE:216, PO:358.

212 lexis Begreb som henviser til ordforråd.
CA:237, DA:212, DE:221, EN:210, ES:257, FR:238, GA:213, IT:225, NE:227, PO:250.

213 lige intervalskala Se under intervalskala.
CA:149, DA:213, DE:161, EN:125, ES:159, FR:127, GA:316, IT:316, NE:145, PO:161.

214 likertskala Skalatype som anvendes i spørgeskemaer til at måle holdninger og meninger. Folk bliver bedt om at reagere på en række udsagn ved at vælge en af ca. fem mulige svar, såsom meget enig, enig, ved ikke, uenig, meget uenig.
CA:152, DA:214, DE:222, EN:211, ES:163, FR:129, GA:317, IT:325, NE:228, PO:163.

215 lineær regression Regressionsteknik som forudsætter et lineært forhold imellem de afhængige og uafhængige variabler.
CA:370, DA:215, DE:223, EN:213, ES:366, FR:325, GA:5, IT:299, NE:230, PO:329.

216 lineær ækvivalering Ækvivaleringsmetode hvor point fra en test ækvivaleres med point fra en anden test. De ækvivalente point fra de to test vil være samme antal standardafvigelser over eller under gennemsnitresultatet for den test, hvori de forekommer.
Se: kalibrering, regression.
Øvrig litteratur: Crocker og Algina, 1986, pp. 457–461.
CA:134, DA:216, DE:17, EN:212, ES:142, FR:38, GA:91, IT:151, NE:229, PO:45.

217 lingvistisk kompetens Se under kompetens.
CA:68, DA:217, DE:224, EN:214, ES:64, FR:67, GA:198, IT:66, NE:231, PO:80.

218 link item Se under ankeritem.
CA:221, DA:218, DE:432, EN:215, ES:239, FR:231, GA:250, IT:214, NE:232, PO:244.

219 loftseffekt Grænseeffekt som fremkommer, hvis en test er for nem for en bestemt gruppe deltagere, således at alle gruppens point samler sig i den øverste ende af fordelingen.
Se: grænseeffekt.
CA:123, DA:219, DE:63/73, EN:44, ES:129, FR:140, GA:173, IT:145, NE:292, PO:137.

220 logit Item-responsteori. Måleenhed som er afledt af den naturlige logaritme af forholdet imellem chancen for succes og risikoen for fiasko, dvs. logaritmiske odds. Forskellen i logits imellem en persons abilitet og et items sværhedsgrad er personens logit odds for at besvare det pågældende item korrekt.
Øvrig litteratur: Henning, 1987, pp. 118–126.
CA:241, DA:220, DE:227, EN:218, ES:259, FR:240, GA:216, IT:232, NE:234, PO:253.

221 lytte-forståelsestest Testning af forståelsen af talt sprog. Gives normalt ved hjælp af båndoptager eller video.
CA:315, DA:221, DE:147, EN:216, ES:324, FR:372, GA:411, IT:361, NE:235, PO:373.

222 læsbarhedsindeks Mål for grammatisk og leksikalsk kompleksitet, som benyttes til at bedømme i hvilken udstrækning læsere vil finde en tekst forståelig. Eksempler på læselighedsindekser er Gunning's Fog indekset og Flesch læselighedsskalaen.
CA:210, DA:222, DE:219, EN:320, ES:226, FR:211, GA:189, IT:198, NE:223, PO:221.

223 læseforståelsesopgave Opgavetype som almindeligvis består af en læsetekst eller tekster samt items af følgende typer: multiple-choice, kortsvarsspørgsmål, cloze/udfyldning, informationsoverførsel etc.

CA:394, DA:223, DE:220, EN:321, ES:3, FR:357, GA:373, IT:74, NE:224, PO:351.

224 læseplan Dokument indeholdende detaljerede beskrivelser af alle de områder, som dækkes af et bestemt studieforløb, samt den rækkefølge i hvilken indholdet præsenteres.

CA:299, DA:224, DE:207, EN:392, ES:310, FR:352, GA:352, IT:335, NE:225, PO:318.

225 løbende bedømmelse Testning som finder sted under, snarere end i slutningen af, et kursus eller undervisningsforløb. Resultaterne kan sætte læreren i stand til at iværksætte hjælpeforanstaltninger på et tidligt stadium eller om nødvendigt foretage ændringer i forløbet. Resultaterne kan også hjælpe eleverne til at identificere og fokusere på deres svagheder.
Sammenlign: opsummerende bedømmelse.

CA:32, DA:225, DE:213, EN:147, ES:184, FR:168, GA:232, IT:422, NE:137, PO:32.

226 løbende evaluering Kontinuær evaluering af en proces, som muliggør tilpasninger og forbedringer undervejs, f.eks. af et undervisningsforløb.
Sammenlign: opsummerende evaluering.

CA:32, DA:226, DE:46, EN:148, ES:184, FR:168, GA:236, IT:414, NE:136, PO:32.

227 mastery-test Test som er designet til at vise, om en elev har opnået tilstrækkelig beherskelse af et klart afgrænset færdigheds- eller vidensområde.

CA:338, DA:227, DE:204, EN:225, ES:327, FR:376, GA:425, IT:366, NE:237, PO:376.

228 median Det pointtal, som befinder sig i centrum af fordelingen af et sæt rangordnede point. Den ene halvdel af pointene ligger over medianen og den anden halvdel under.
Se: centraltendens.
Sammenlign: middelværdi, modalværdi.
Øvrig litteratur: Hatch og Lazaraton, 1991, p. 161.

CA:244, DA:228, DE:232, EN:232, ES:263, FR:242, GA:3, IT:235, NE:239, PO:256.

229 metode-effekt Pointpåvirkning som snarere skyldes den anvendte testningsmetode end deltagernes færdigheder.

CA:121, DA:229, DE:242, EN:233, ES:126, FR:139, GA:171, IT:142, NE:244, PO:134.

230 middelkvadrat Navnet på variansen i variansanalyse (ANOVA).
Se: ANOVA.

CA:251, DA:230, DE:245, EN:229, ES:262, FR:47, GA:227, IT:295, NE:149, PO:319.

231 middelværdi Mål for centraltendens. Kaldes ofte gennemsnittet. Middelværdien for testpoint fremkommer ved at lægge samtlige resultater sammen og derefter dividere med antal point.
Sammenlign: median, modalværdi.
Se: centraltendens.
Øvrig litteratur: Hatch og Lazaraton, 1991, pp. 161–163.

CA:250, DA:231, DE:244, EN:227, ES:261, FR:257, GA:226, IT:234, NE:151, PO:255.

232 modalværdi Det punkt i fordelingen af et sæt point, hvor disse optræder oftest, det højeste punkt på fordelingskurven.

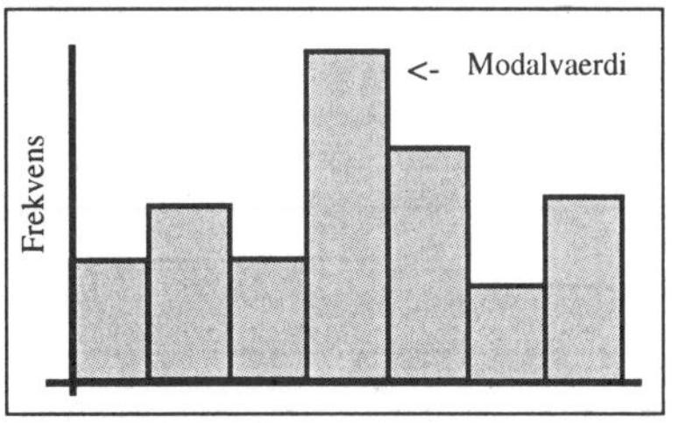

Sammenlign: bimodal fordeling, middelværdi, median.
Se: centraltendens.
Øvrig litteratur: Hatch og Lazaraton, 1991, pp. 160–161.

CA:252, DA:232, DE:247, EN:235, ES:268, FR:247, GA:255, IT:240, NE:248, PO:261.

233 modelsvar Godt eksempel på det svar, som forventes på en åben opgave, som er stillet af item-forfatteren og som kan anvendes til at udarbejde et retteskema, som vejledning for bedømmerne.

CA:261, DA:233, DE:253, EN:236, ES:376, FR:333, GA:156, IT:245, NE:21, PO:340.

234 modersmåls-talende (Native Speaker) Person som taler et sprog som sit førstesprog (modersmål).

CA:286, DA:234, DE:255, EN:245, ES:216, FR:217, GA:47, IT:265, NE:255, PO:190.

235 multi-facetteret Rasch-model Udvidelse af Rasch-modellen, som gør det muligt at forme responssandsynligheder på

grundlag af en additiv kombination af facetter. For eksempel kan udførelse af en skriveopgave udformes, så den afspejler både opgavens sværhedsgrad og bedømmerens strenghed. Den multi-facetterede Rasch-model er bl.a. blevet implementeret i programmet FACETS.
Se: Rasch-model.
Øvrig litteratur: Linacre, J.M., 1989, Many-Facet Rasch Measurement, Chicago, MESA Press.
CA:260, DA:235, DE:289, EN:220, ES:276, FR:254, GA:300, IT:249, NE:236, PO:268.

236 multiple-choice item Test-item som består af et spørgsmål eller en ufuldstændig sætning (stamme) med et udvalg af mulige svar eller måder at fuldende sætningen på (valg). Deltagerens opgave består i at træffe det korrekte valg (vælge den rigtige svarmulighed) ud fra de tre eller fire muligheder, og der er ikke tale om selvstændig sprogproduktion. Derfor anvendes multiple-choice items normalt i læse- eller lyttetest. Der kan være tale om diskrete eller tekstbaserede items.
Se: diskret item, tekst-baseret item.
CA:220, DA:236, DE:249/234, EN:238, ES:244, FR:222, GA:247, IT:211, NE:252, PO:236.

237 multiple-choice udfyldning Testopgave i hvilken deltageren blandt et antal valgmuligheder skal vælge det korrekte ord eller den rigtige ordforbindelse, som derefter indsættes på den tomme plads i teksten.
Se: indsætnings-item.
CA:224, DA:237, DE:250, EN:239, ES:242, FR:386, GA:215, IT:79, NE:251, PO:390.

238 multitræk-multimetode Eksperimentel konstruktion som anvendes til validering af constructs, hvorved et sæt formodet særskilte træk måles af hver enkelt af et formodet sæt særskilte metoder. Analyser bør vise, at eksempelvis mål for lyttefærdighed, som er opnået ved forskellige metoder, har en højere grad af indbyrdes korrelation end mål for forskellige færdigheder, som er opnået ved samme testningsmetode.
Øvrig litteratur: Bachman, 1990, pp. 263–265.
CA:108, DA:238, DE:252, EN:243, ES:109, FR:299, GA:111, IT:277, NE:254, PO:305.

239 mundtlig sprogfærdighed Færdighed i at tale et sprog.
CA:298, DA:239, DE:370, EN:264, ES:65, FR:68, GA:266, IT:67, NE:354, PO:82.

240 målefejl Se under standard målefejl.
CA:138, DA:240, DE:239, EN:130, ES:146, FR:153, GA:130, IT:159, NE:243, PO:149.

241 målefejl Se under fejl.
CA:138, DA:241, DE:240, EN:231, ES:146, FR:153, GA:123, IT:159, NE:242, PO:149.

242 måling Almindeligvis det at finde frem til mængden af et eller andet ved at sammenligne med en fast enhed, f.eks. at benytte en lineal til længdemåling. Inden henviser måling ofte til kvantificeringen af personers færdigheder, f.eks. sprogfærdighed.
Øvrig litteratur: Bachman, 1990, kapitel 2.
CA:245, DA:242, DE:241, EN:230, ES:264, FR:243, GA:395, IT:238, NE:245, PO:257.

243 målrettet test (specific purpose test) Test som er konstrueret til at måle en deltagers evne til at fungere inden for en nærmere bestemt faglig eller akademisk sammenhæng. Indholdet af testen baseres på en analyse af de sproglige opgaver, som deltageren vil få behov for at klare i målsprogssituationen.
CA:318, DA:243, DE:112, EN:375, ES:328, FR:393, GA:431, IT:378, NE:351, PO:393.

244 målsætninger Den viden og kompetens og de holdninger, som er de erklærede mål for et uddannelsesforløb.
CA:278, DA:244, DE:216, EN:256, ES:291, FR:288, GA:359, IT:254, NE:112, PO:293.

245 nedrunding Reduktion af en præcis talstørrelse ved at mindske antallet af signifikante tal. For eksempel kan 564,8 rundes op til 565 eller ned til 560. Omfanget af nedrundingen afhænger af behovet for præcision.
CA:24, DA:245, DE:331, EN:335, ES:363, FR:22, GA:354, IT:24, NE:11, PO:25.

246 net D Se unde D-indeks.
CA:206, DA:246, DE:257, EN:247, ES:97, FR:115, GA:102, IT:194, NE:256, PO:111.

247 niveau Nødvendige færdighedsgrad for at kunne forblive i en given klasse eller bestå en given test. Defineres ofte ved en række niveauer, som almindeligvis kaldes niveau for begyndere, øvede og viderekomne etc.
CA:270, DA:247, DE:260, EN:209,

ES:45/283, FR:259, GA:210, IT:229, NE:258, PO:272.

248 ***N, n*** Antal. Stort *N* henviser ofte til gennemsnitsantal tilfælde i en undersøgelse eller til enkeltindivider ud af en større gruppe. Lille *n* henviser ofte til antallet i en stikprøve eller undergruppe. F.eks. Testen blev taget af civilingeniører ($N = 600$), hvoraf 10% var kvinder ($n = 60$).

CA:269, DA:248, DE:256, EN:244, ES:282, FR:258, GA:261, IT:251, NE:259, PO:271.

249 nominalskala Skala som anvendes med kategoriske variabler, såsom køn eller førstesprog. Variablerne vil enten være til stede eller ikke til stede, og der fokuseres på hyppigheden af forekomsten. Også kaldet kategorisk skala.
Sammenlign: parametriske metoder.
Øvrig litteratur: Hatch og Lazaraton, 1991, pp. 237–239.

CA:156, DA:249, DE:262, EN:248, ES:164, FR:133, GA:309, IT:326, NE:260, PO:166.

250 norm Præstationsstandard. I en standardiseret test, fastslås normen ved at registrere point fra en større gruppe. Normen eller de præstations-baserede standarder for den pågældende gruppe, anvendes til at bedømme en tilsvarende deltagergruppes præstationer.
Se: normgruppe, norm-relateret test.

CA:273, DA:250, DE:263, EN:250, ES:286, FR:264, GA:262, IT:252, NE:261, PO:278.

251 norm-relateret test Test hvor opnåede point fortolkes i relation til en given gruppes præstationer. Denne skal være sammenlignelig med deltagerne. Betegnelsen anvendes normalt om test, hvor tolkningen fokuserer på en rangordning af de pågældende i forhold til normgruppen eller til hinanden.
Sammenlign: kriterie-relateret test.

CA:336, DA:251, DE:268, EN:254, ES:340, FR:388, GA:426, IT:381, NE:264, PO:391.

252 normalfordeling Matematisk fordeling som er den grundlæggende forudsætning for adskillige statistiske metoder. Fordelingen er en symmetrisk klokkeform, og middelværdien, medianen og modalværdien optræder alle på samme punkt. Der eksisterer en hel familie af fordelinger, afhængig af middelværdien, standardafvigelsen og antallet af observationer. Også kaldet Gauss-fordeling.
Sammenlign: bimodal fordeling.
Øvrig litteratur: Hatch og Lazaraton, 1991, p. 164.

CA:115, DA:252, DE:265, EN:252, ES:116, FR:108, GA:107, IT:134, NE:262, PO:123.

253 normalisering ændring af point så fordelingen ændres til en normalfordeling. Dette vil typisk medføre anvendelsen af ækvipercentil skalering.
Sammenlign: standardpoint (standardscore).

CA:274, DA:253, DE:264, EN:253, ES:287, FR:263, GA:263, IT:253, NE:263, PO:279.

254 normgruppe Typisk en stor gruppe individer, som er repræsentative for de mennesker, som testen er designet til. Normgruppens præstation benyttes til tolkningen af en norm-relateret test. Kaldes også referencegruppe.
Se: norm-relateret test.

CA:197, DA:254, DE:266, EN:251, ES:214, FR:203, GA:264, IT:190, NE:265, PO:213.

255 nulhypotese Hypotese ifølge hvilken to eller flere variabler ikke er forbundne. F.eks. er det en nulhypotese at antage, at der ikke er nogen forskel på testpræstationerne for medlemmerne af to særskilte modersmålsgrupper, en nulhypotese.
Øvrig litteratur: Hatch og Lazaraton, 1991, p. 24; Guilford og Fruchter, 1981, pp. 146–147.

CA:202, DA:255, DE:271, EN:255, ES:217, FR:206, GA:167, IT:206, NE:266, PO:214.

256 nøglesvar a) Det korrekte svar på et multiple-choice item.

b) Oftere: et sæt bestående af samtlige korrekte eller acceptable svar på test-items.
Sammenlign: distraktor, retteskema
Se: multiple-choice item.

CA:51/52, DA:256, DE:339, EN:198, ES:54, FR:329, GA:133, DE:339, IT:53, NE:342, PO:335.

257 objektiv test Test som kan bedømmes ved hjælp af et retteskema uden behov for ekspertviden eller subjektive bedømmelser.

CA:331, DA:257, DE:272, EN:257, ES:341, FR:389, GA:427, IT:377, NE:267, PO:392.

258 områdebedømmelse Del af skala som henviser til et nærmere bestemt færdighedsområde.

CA:346, DA:258, DE:210, EN:30, ES:39, FR:269, GA:330, IT:40, NE:29, PO:65.

259 opdelingsmetoden Metode til beregning af en tests pålidelighed. Vurderingen baseres på en korrelation imellem de opnåede point for to halve test, som betragtes som alternativer til hinanden. Opdelingen kan foretages på en række forskellige måder, f.eks. første halvdel, anden halvdel, eller ved at placere items med lige numre i den ene halvdel og items med ulige numre i den anden.
Se: reliabilitet.
Øvrig litteratur: Ebel og Frisbie, 1991, pp. 82–83; Crocker og Algina, 1986, pp. 136–138.

CA:183, DA:259, DE:364/398, EN:377, ES:201, FR:184, GA:203, IT:7, NE:353, PO:194.

260 opgave Kombination af opgaveinstruks, input og respons. F.eks. en læsetekst med et antal multiple-choice items, som alle kan besvares med henvisning til en enkelt opgaveinstruks.

CA:391, DA:260, DE:26, EN:393, ES:2, FR:354, GA:371, IT:71, NE:270, PO:352.

261 opgavebesvarelse Det papir som indeholder deltagerens svar på en test. Benyttes især til åbne opgavetyper.

CA:191, DA:261, DE:341, EN:350, ES:219, FR:343, GA:343, IT:175, NE:218, PO:170.

262 opgaveformulering Se under fri skriftlig fremstilling.

CA:366, DA:262, DE:33, EN:131, ES:306, FR:159, GA:7, IT:313, NE:125, PO:142.

263 opgavehæfte Bruges til tider om det ark eller hæfte, som indeholder testen.

CA:239, DA:263, DE:123, EN:304, ES:220, FR:180, GA:271, IT:169, NE:425, PO:145.

264 opgaveinstruks Instrukser til deltageren vedrørende en bestemt testopgave.
Sammenlign: instrukser.

CA:384, DA:264, DE:23, EN:336, ES:229, FR:78, GA:295, IT:193, NE:219, PO:92.

265 opgavetype Der er en tendens til, at opgaver udstyres med deskriptive navne, som angiver formål og udformning. F.eks. multiple-choice læseforståelse, bunden skrivetest etc.

CA:408, DA:265, DE:30, EN:394, ES:402, FR:407, GA:59, IT:393, NE:271, PO:401.

266 opsummerende evaluering Evaluering af en proces som finder sted efter dens gennemførelse. Kan benyttes i forbindelse med et undervisningsforløb.
Sammenlign: løbende evaluering.

CA:34, DA:266, DE:3, EN:391, ES:186, FR:172, GA:238, IT:415, NE:374, PO:36.

267 opsummerende bedømmelse Testning som finder sted i slutningen af et kursus eller undervisningsforløb.
Sammenlign: løbende bedømmelse.

CA:34, DA:267, DE:4, EN:390, ES:186, FR:172, GA:233, IT:423, NE:375, PO:36.

268 optisk svarlæser Elektronisk anordning som benyttes til at scanne oplysninger direkte fra retteskemaet eller de indleverede besvarelser. Deltagere eller bedømmere kan anføre svarene på de forskellige items eller opgaver, og disse oplysninger kan læses direkte ind i en computer. Også kaldet scanner.

CA:242, DA:268, DE:274, EN:261, ES:255, FR:237, GA:214, IT:226, NE:274, PO:249.

269 orddannelses-item Itemtype hvor deltageren skal danne en form af et ord pågrundlag af input-ordet. Eksempel: Dette arbejde kræver............... af de relevante fagtermer (beherske).

CA:227, DA:269, DE:445, EN:439, ES:231, FR:227, GA:244, IT:216, NE:437, PO:237 .

270 ordfrekvens-tæller Optælling af hvor ofte bestemte ord eller ordtyper optræder i en tekst. Inden for sprogtestning kan det være nyttigt i forbindelse med konstruktion af tester ifølge bestemte leksikalske specifikationer.

CA:190, DA:270, DE:143, EN:440, ES:362, FR:75, GA:67, IT:256, NE:436, PO:95.

271 ordinalskala Måleskala som rangordner deltagerne uden at angive deres relative indbyrdes afstand.
Sammenlign: kategorisk skala, intervalskala, nominalskala, kvotientskala.
Øvrig litteratur: Hatch og Lazaraton, 1991, pp. 56–57.

CA:157, DA:271, DE:275, EN:265, ES:165, FR:134, GA:318, IT:327, NE:275, PO:167.

272 overflade-validitet Den udstrækning i hvilken en test forekommer deltagerne, eller dem, der har udvalgt testen, at være acceptabel til at måle den pågældende abilitet. Der er tale om en subjektiv vurdering snarere end en, der baseres på objektive analyser af testen, og umiddelbar validitet anses ofte for ikke at være en rigtig form for validitet. Omtales ind imellem som test

appeal.
Se: validitet.
Øvrig litteratur: Bachman, 1990, pp. 285–289.
CA:417, DA:272, DE:110/34, EN:140, ES:414, FR:414 GA:2, IT:402, NE:174, PO:410.

273 *p*-værdi Se under sværhedsindeks.
CA:427, DA:273, DE:276, EN:266, ES:424, FR:411, GA:269, IT:412, NE:277, PO:420.

274 parallel-bedømmelse Metode til at forbedre pålideligheden ved bedømmelsen af længere skriftlige fremstillinger, som nødvendigvis i nogen grad må være subjektiv ved at sikre, at hver enkelt deltagersvar rettes uafhængigt af mere end en bedømmer.
Øvrig litteratur: Weir, 1988, pp. 65–66.
CA:87, DA:274, DE:233, EN:240, ES:45, FR:271, GA:183, IT:105, NE:241, PO:63.

275 parallelle former Se under ækvivalente former.
CA:188, DA:275, DE:278, EN:268, ES:206, FR:196, GA:144, IT:179, NE:279, PO:202.

276 parameter Kendetegn for en population (gruppe), f.eks. den pågældende populations standardafvigelse.
Sammenlign: statistik.
CA:280, DA:276, DE:279, EN:269, ES:293, FR:291, GA:272, IT:259, NE:280, PO:296.

277 parametriske metoder Statistiske metoder som forudsætter, at data er normalt fordelt og målt på interval- eller kvotientskalaer. I praksis anvendes parametriske metoder, når der er tilstrækkeligt med materiale til, at data kan tilnærmes normalfordelingen.
Sammenlign: ikke-parametriske metoder.
Øvrig litteratur: Hatch og Lazaraton, 1991, pp. 237–238.
CA:295, DA:277, DE:280, EN:270, ES:309, FR:310, GA:259, IT:275, NE:281, PO:316.

278 partial-credit modellen I itemresponsteorien en model til at håndtere skalære data. Denne model vil være velegnet til at analysere responsen i sætningsudfyldnings-items, hvor der anvendes en skala, f.eks. 1, 2 eller 3, til bedømmelsen, eller i forbindelse med et interview, hvor der anvendes flere forskellige skalaer til at score præstationen.
Sammenlign: klassificeringsskalamodel.
Se: Rasch-modellen.
Øvrig Litteratur: Wright og Masters, 1982, pp. 40–48.
CA:257, DA:278, DE:281, EN:272, ES:270, FR:253, GA:301, IT:244, NE:282, PO:267.

279 Pearsons produkt-momentkorrelation Korrelationskoefficient som passende anvendes med variabler, der er målt på interval- eller kvotientskalaer.
Se: korellationskoefficient.
Øvrig litteratur: Hatch og Lazaraton, 1991, pp. 437–441; Guilford og Fruchter, 1981, p. 81.
CA:59, DA:279, DE:298, EN:274, ES:90, FR:87, GA:84, IT:98, NE:283, PO:104.

280 percentil De 99 skalapoint som inddeler en frekvensfordeling i 100 grupper af ens størrelse. Den halvtredssindstyvende percentil (P50) kaldes medianen. Kvartiler inddeler fordelingen i fire lige store grupper.
Øvrig litteratur: Hatch og Lazaraton, 1991, pp. 187–188.
CA:287, DA:280, DE:285, EN:275, ES:299, FR:49, GA:279, IT:266, NE:284, PO:302.

281 percentil rangplacering Tal eller point som angiver rangplacering ved at vise den procentdel, som befinder sig under det pågældende pointtal. Hvis en deltager i en test har en percentil rangplacering på 60, er det ensbetydende med, at 60% af alle deltagere har opnået samme eller lavere resultat.
CA:363, DA:281, DE:299, EN:276, ES:359, FR:53, GA:284, IT:55, NE:285, PO:276.

282 performans Sprogproduktion ved at tale eller skrive. Performans i form af det sprog, som mennesker faktisk frembringer, kontrasteres ofte med kompetens, som er den grundlæggende viden om et sprog.
Sammenlign: kompetens.
Se: performans-test.
Øvrig litteratur: Bachman, 1990, pp. 52 og 108.
CA:5, DA:282, DE:283, EN:277, ES:9, FR:297, GA:141, IT:267, NE:286, PO:304.

283 performans-test Testmetode som kræver, at deltagerne giver prøver på sprog, enten skriftligt eller mundtligt (f.eks. essays og interviews). Sådanne metoder er ofte konstrueret med henblik på at kopiere performans uden for testmæssige sammenhænge.
Øvrig litteratur: Bachman, 1990, pp. 304–305.
CA:306, DA:283, DE:284, EN:278,

ES:318, FR:380, GA:416, IT:367, NE:287, PO:381.

284 phi-koefficient Korrelations-koefficient som anvendes til at vise det stærke forhold imellem to tætte variabler, f.eks. point for to testitems, som har opnået bedømmelsen rigtig eller forkert.
Se: korrelationskoefficient.
Øvrig litteratur: Guilford og Fruchter, 1981, pp. 316–318; Crocker og Algina, 1986, pp. 92–94.
CA:62, DA:284, DE:286, EN:279, ES:59, FR:58, GA:76, IT:61, NE:288, PO:75.

285 phi-korrelation Se under phi-koefficient.
CA:92, DA:285, DE:287, EN:280, ES:88, FR:88, GA:81, IT:101, NE:289, PO:103.

286 pilotundersøgelse Foreløbig undersøgelse hvorved forskere eller testudviklere kan afprøve deres ideer på et begrænset antal deltagere for at identificere problemerne før man iværksætter en prøvekørsel, et program eller et produkt i fuldt omfang.
Se: prøvekørsel, forprøvning.
CA:170, DA:286, DE:288, EN:281, ES:179, FR:163, GA:361, IT:344, NE:290, PO:180.

287 point Det samlede pointantal, der kan opnås for et prøveelement, en delprøve eller prøve eller det antal point tildelt for kandidatens svar på et prøveelement, en delprøve eller prøve.
CA:342, DA:287, DE:313, EN:224, ES:44, FR:287, GA:224, IT:292, NE:60, PO:105.

288 pointgiver Person som giver point for en besvarelse af en skriftlig test. Dette kan gøres på grundlag af en faglig vurdering eller, hvor der er tale om administrativ bedømmelse, ved anvendelse af et retteskema, hvilket ikke i samme grad kræver faglig indsigt.
Se: bedømmer (censor).
CA:90, DA:288, DE:39, EN:221, ES:83, FR:81, GA:225, IT:102, NE:80, PO:182.

289 pointgivning Tildeling af point for en opgavebesvarelse. Dette kan gøres på grundlag af en faglig vurdering eller ved hjælp af et retteskema, som angiver samtlige acceptable svar.
CA:80, DA:289, DE:40, EN:222, ES:47, FR:265, GA:218, IT:29, NE:83, PO:57.

290 pointtilvækst Positiv forskel mellem resultatet af test, som gives før starten af et kursusforløb, og resultatet af samme eller tilsvarende test efter afslutningen af forløbet. En pointtilvækst tyder på fremskridt i løbet af kurset.
CA:352, DA:290, DE:211, EN:150, ES:32, FR:199, GA:44, IT:192, NE:434, PO:209.

291 polytom bedømmelse Polytom (også kaldet 'polykotomisk') bedømmelse betyder bedømmelse af et item ved hjælp af en skala med mindst tre punkter. For eksempel kan svaret på et spørgsmål tildeles enten 0, 1 eller 2. Åbne spørgsmål bedømmes ofte polytomt. Kaldes også skalær bedømmelse.
Sammenlign: Dikotomisk bedømmelse.
CA:351, DA:291, DE:237, EN:284, ES:353, FR:89, GA:342, IT:34, NE:293, PO:64.

292 population Fuldstændigt sæt værdier, dvs. alle mulige deltagere i en test. Inden for statistik ofte benævnt scoringsunivers.
Sammenlign: Stikprøve.
CA:289, DA:292, DE:290, EN:285, ES:302, FR:303, GA:280, IT:269, NE:294, PO:308.

293 porteføljebedømmelse Bedømmelsesteknik som indebærer, at deltageren indsamler eksempler på sit arbejde inden for en periode og præsenterer dem som bevis for sine færdigheder.
CA:386, DA:293, DE:291, EN:286, ES:185, FR:304, GA:237, IT:270, NE:37, PO:309.

294 pragmatisk kompetens Mulig kategori i kommunikativ sprogfærdig-hedsmodel. Omfatter evnen til at udføre talehandlinger samt viden om sociolingvistiske konventioner.
Øvrig litteratur: Bachman, 1990, p. 42.
CA:69, DA:294, DE:295, EN:290, ES:66, FR:69, GA:194, IT:68, NE:297, PO:83.

295 probabilistisk model Model i hvilken tilfældige forbindelser (så som item-sværhed og deltagerabilitet ved udførelsen af en test) forklares, udtrykt ved graden af sandsynlighed. Rasch-modellen er et eksempel på en probabilistisk model.
CA:262, DA:295, DE:297, EN:294, ES:274, FR:255, GA:299, IT:247, NE:430, PO:269.

296 proficiency (sprogfærdighed) Kendskab til et sprog og evnen til at anvende det.
Sammenlign: abilitet, kompetens.
Øvrig litteratur: Bachman, 1990, p. 16.
CA:296, DA:296, DE:47, EN:295, ES:120, FR:260, GA:265, IT:62, NE:305, PO:273.

297 profilering Præsentation af testresultater opløst i de forskellige testkomponenter, således at deltagerne eller andre brugere af testen kan identificere stærke og svage sider.

CA:288, DA:297, DE:404, EN:297, ES:300, FR:312, GA:282, IT:395, NE:307, PO:303.

298 prædiktiv validitet Indikation af en tests velegnethed til at forudsige fremtidige præstationer med den relevante færdighed.
Sammenlign: kriterie-relateret validitet.
Øvrig litteratur: Guilford og Fruchter, 1987, pp. 437–438.

CA:425, DA:298, DE:294/439, EN:291, ES:422, FR:422, GA:38, IT:410, NE:300, PO:418.

299 præstationstest Test som giver alle deltagere tilstrækkeligt med tid til at gøre den færdig, men som indeholder visse opgaver eller items af en sådan sværhedsgrad, at flertallet af deltagerne sandsynligvis ikke vil besvare dem korrekt.
Sammenlign: hurtighedstest.

CA:310, DA:299, DE:261/293, EN:288, ES:329, FR:379, GA:413, IT:360, NE:296, PO:371.

300 prøve En procedure til prøvning af specifikke elementer af færdigheder eller viden: a) et sæt delemner, som tilsammen danner en bedømmelsprocedure, ofte brugt i samme betydning som eksamen; b) en opgave eller et delemne til prøvning af en færdighed eller viden, f. eks. talefærdighed eller skrivefærdighed. I denne betydning kan en prøve udgøre en del af en komplet eksamen som delemne (f. eks. den mundtlige prøve) eller som en enkelt opgave (f. eks. en cloze test); c) en bedømmelsesprocedure af relative kort varighed, som er forholdsvis nem at administrere og ofte er produceret og administreret inden for en institution (f. eks. en fremtidstest) eller brugt som del af et forskningsprogram eller i en valideringsproces (f. eks. ankertest).
Sammenlign: eksamen
Øvrig litteratur: Bachman, 1990, p. 50.

CA:300, DA:300, DE:389, EN:395, ES:311, FR:359, GA:403, IT:353, NE:388, PO:361.

301 prøvekørsel Stadium i testudviklingen. Testen afprøves for at sikre, at den fungerer som planlagt. Anvendes også med subjektivt bedømte opgaver, f.eks. essays, som gives til en begrænset population.
Sammenlign: forprøvning.

CA:26, DA:301, DE:104, EN:418, ES:135, FR:160, GA:436, IT:336, NE:303, PO:185.

302 psykometrisk test Test af psykologiske træk, såsom personlighed, intelligens, lærenemhed og sprogfærdighed, som opstiller specifikke antagelser om arten af den testede abilitet, dvs. at den er endimensional og normalt fordelt.
Øvrig litteratur: Bachman, 1990, p. 73–74.

CA:334, DA:302, DE:310, EN:301, ES:397, FR:390, GA:433, IT:379, NE:308, PO:394.

303 påvirkning Den effekt som skabes af en test, både med hensyn til indflydelse på de generelle uddannelsesmæssige processer og med hensyn til de personer, som påvirkes af testresultaterne.
Se: backwash, washback.

CA:205, DA:303, DE:444, EN:167, ES:222, FR:207, GA:391, IT:191, NE:171, PO:217.

304 rangkorrelation Korrelation som er baseret ikke på variablernes absolutte værdier, men på deres relative rangordning.
Øvrig litteratur: Guilford og Fruchter, 1981, pp. 294–296.

CA:60, DA:304, DE:315, EN:309, ES:89, FR:59, GA:82, IT:100, NE:312, PO:72.

305 Rasch-model Matematisk model, også kendt som den simple logistiske model, som postulerer et forhold imellem sandsynligheden for, at en person løser en opgave, og forskellen mellem personens abilitet og opgavens sværhedsgrad. Matematisk ækvivalent til item-responsteoriens enkeltparameter-model. Raschmodellen er blevet udvidet på forskellige måder, f.eks. til at håndtere skalære svar, eller multiple facetter, som forklarer en opgaves vanskelighed.
Se: item-responsteori (IRT) , partial-credit modellen, klassificeringsskalamodel, multi-facetteret Rasch-model.
Øvrig litteratur: Henning, 1987, pp. 117–125.

CA:259, DA:305, DE:316, EN:310, ES:275, FR:252, GA:302, IT:248, NE:313, PO:266.

306 rater (opgaveretter) Se under bedømmer (censor).

CA:361, DA:306, DE:100, EN:311, ES:187, FR:164, GA:287, IT:102, NE:34, PO:182.

307 rater agreement (bedømmeroverensstemmelse) Se under inter-reliabilitet og intra-reliabilitet.

CA:1, DA:307, DE:56, EN:312, ES:10, FR:1, GA:70, IT:84, NE:36, PO:1.

308 rationel cloze Se under cloze test.
CA:314, DA:308, DE:230, EN:318, ES:316, FR:371, GA:60, IT:56, NE:315, PO:367.

309 referencegruppe Stikprøve fra en klartdefineret deltagerpopulation, som har sat normer for testen.
Se: norm.
CA:196, DA:309, DE:267, EN:324, ES:213, FR:202, GA:166, IT:189, NE:316, PO:212.

310 register Særlig variation af talt eller skrevet sprog, som er karakteristisk for en bestemt aktivitet eller en bestemt grad af formalitet.
CA:368, DA:310, DE:366, EN:325, ES:364, FR:323, GA:291, IT:297, NE:317, PO:327.

311 regression Teknik som anvendes til at forudsige den mest sandsynlige værdi af en variabel (den afhængige variabel) ud fra kendte værdier af en eller flere andre variabler (uafhængige variabler).
Øvrig litteratur: Hatch og Lazaraton, 1991, pp. 467–480; Guilford og Fruchter, 1981, p. 346–361.
CA:369, DA:311, DE:321, EN:326, ES:365, FR:324, GA:4, IT:298, NE:318, PO:328.

312 reliabilitet Konsekvens eller stabilitet af måleresultater. Jo mere pålidelig en test er, des færre tilfældige fejl vil den indeholde. En test, som indeholder systematiske fejl, f.eks. forudindtagethed imod en bestemt gruppe, kan være pålidelige, men ikke valide.
Se: KR-20, alfa (alfakoefficient), opdelingsmetoden, retestreliabilitet.
Øvrig litteratur: Bachman, 1990, p. 24; Crocker og Algina, 1986, kapitel 6.
CA:180, DA:312, DE:322/453, EN:327, ES:198, FR:183, GA:200, IT:6, NE:43, PO:193.

313 reliabilitetskoefficient Mål for reliabilitet, gående fra 0 til 1. Reliabilitetsskøn kan baseres på gentagne forsøg med en test (hvor resultaterne bør være sammenlignelige), eller, hvor dette ikke er praktisk muligt, på et eller andet mål for intern konsekvens. Kaldes også reliabilitetsindeks.
Se: intern konsekvens, reliabilitet, retestreliabilitet.
CA:61, DA:313, DE:323, EN:328, ES:58, FR:61, GA:77, IT:59, NE:44, PO:74.

314 reskalering Se under skalering.
CA:367, DA:314, DE:258, EN:330, ES:389, FR:320, GA:29, IT:304, NE:166, PO:326.

315 respons Den adfærd, som testinput aflokker deltageren. For eksempel valg af multiple-choice item eller resultatet af en skrivetest.
Sammenlign: input, responsfremkalder.
CA:374, DA:315, DE:21, EN:331, ES:371, FR:327, GA:153, IT:305, NE:319, PO:334.

316 responsfremkalder Grafisk materiale eller tekster som anvendes i mundtlige eller skriftlige test med det formål af aflokke deltageren en respons.
CA:390, DA:316, DE:437 EN:299, ES:178, FR:95, GA:358, IT:343, NE:321, PO:179.

317 resultat Det udfald af en test som indberettes til en testdeltager elle-bruger.
CA:380, DA:317, DE:103, EN:332, ES:378, FR:336, GA:397, IT:312, NE:322, PO:342.

318 retestreliabilitet Mål for reliabilitet, som opnås ved at give samme test til samme deltagere under samme forhold to gange og derefter korrelere de opnåede point. Formålet er at sikre pointstabiliteten over en længere periode. Anvendes også i de tilfælde, hvor det ikke er muligt at foretage vurderinger af intern konsekvens.
Sammenlign: intern konsekvens.
Se: reliabilitet, stabilitet.
CA:184, DA:318, DE:409/325, EN:410, ES:202, FR:188, GA:204, IT:9, NE:383, PO:197.

319 retteskema Liste over samtlige acceptable svar på et testitem. Retteskemaet giver mulighed for nøjagtig tildeling af point for en test.
CA: 52/256, DA:319, DE:228, EN:223, ES:301, FR:29, GA:324, IT:329, NE:79, PO:172.

320 rollespil Opgavetype som ind imellem anvendes ved testning af mundtlig sprogfærdighed, hvor deltagerne foregiver at befinde sig i en nærmere angivet situation eller påtager sig specifikke roller.
CA:233, DA:320, DE:329, EN:334, ES:251, FR:232, GA:294, IT:202, NE:323, PO:345.

321 råscore (råpoint) Point som ikke er blevet statistisk manipuleret gennem transformation, vægtning eller skalatransformation.
Se: score (point).
CA:348, DA:321, DE:328, EN:319, ES:348, FR:276, GA:329, IT:282, NE:324, PO:281.

322 sammenstillingsopgave Opgavetype som indebærer sammenstilling af elementer fra to separate lister. En type match-test består af at vælge de korrekte ordforbindelser til fuldendelse af en række ufuldendte sætninger. I en anden type, som anvendes i testning af læseforståelse, vælges et eller andet fra en liste, f.eks. en ferie eller en bog, som passer til den beskrevne persons særlige behov.

CA:397, DA:322, DE:452, EN:226, ES:7, FR:21, GA:375, IT:73, NE:238, PO:353.

323 samstemmende validitet En test anses at udvise samstemmende validitet, såfremt de opnåede point udviser høj grad af korrelation med et anerkendt eksternt kriterium, som måler samme videns- eller færdighedsområde.
Se: kriterie-relateret validitet.
Øvrig litteratur: Bachman, 1990, pp. 248–250.

CA:418, DA:323, DE:417, EN:66, ES:415, FR:415, GA:33, IT:403, NE:71, PO:411.

324 samtaleramme Drejebog over den sprogbrug, som en samtalepartner bør anvende under en mundtlig sprogfærdighedstest. Formålet er en sproglig standardisering, så testen bliver mere retfærdig og pålidelig for samtlige deltagere.

CA:198, DA:324, DE:438, EN:179, ES:215, FR:34, GA:151, IT:128, NE:156, PO:321.

325 samtalepartner I en mundtlig prøve er det eksaminatoren, som forklarer opgaverne, stiller spørgsmålene og generelt indgår i dialog med kandidaten/erne. Eksaminatoren kan også bedømme kandidaten/erne og give point, ellers kan point gives af en anden bedømmer, som observerer, men som ikke indgår i dialog med kandidaten/erne.
Sammenlign: bedømmer (censor).

CA:213, DA:325, DE:125, EN:178, ES:138, FR:216, GA:72, IT:201, NE:155, PO:227.

326 sandt/falsk item Itemtype som kræver, at deltageren angiver, hvorvidt en række udtalelser er sande eller falske i relation til en tekst.

CA:232, DA:326, DE:326, EN:419, ES:250, FR:429, GA:245, IT:218, NE:426, PO:243.

327 scanner Se under optisk svarlæser.

CA:160, DA:327, DE:336, EN:347, ES:168, FR:342, GA:322, IT:226, NE:325, PO:346.

328 score (point) a) Det samlede antal point, som opnås i en test, enten før skalering (råpoint) eller efter (skalerede point).

b) Tildeling af numeriske værdier til konstaterede præstationer.
Sammenlign: måling.

CA:342, DA:328, DE:312, , EN:348, ES:345, FR:275, GA:328, IT:278, NE:331, PO:280.

329 sekvenseffekt Bedømmereffekt som skyldes den rækkefølge, i hvilken bedømmelserne foretages.
Se: bedømmereffekt.

CA:120, DA:329, DE:292, EN:360, ES:125, FR:142, GA:172, IT:148, NE:337, PO:136.

330 selektionsprøve Se under adgangsprøve.

CA:323, DA:330, DE:36, EN:353, ES:332, FR:382, GA:430, IT:370, NE:333, PO:383.

331 selvevaluering Vurdering af egne færdigheder, enten ved hjælp af en test, som man selv administrerer, eller ved hjælp af f.eks. et spørgeskema eller en checkliste.

CA:30, DA:331, DE:345, EN:354, ES:36, FR:27, GA:142, IT:38, NE:334, PO:29.

332 semi-direkte test Test som benyttes til bedømmelse af sproglig performans ved hjælp af andet input end det, som leveres i form af et decideret interview. F.eks. anvendelse af båndoptager i en mundtlig sprogfærdighedstest. Den såkaldte SOPI (Semi-Direct Oral Proficiency Interview) er et eksempel på denne testtype.
Sammenlign: direkte test.

CA:339, DA:332, DE:347, EN:356, ES:343, FR:392, GA:423, IT:383, NE:336, PO:396.

333 signifikans Statistisk begreb som angiver, hvorvidt et resultat skyldes tilfældigheder.
Se: type-1 fejl, type-2 fejl, nulhypotese.
Øvrig litteratur: Guilford og Fruchter, 1981, p. 208–210.

CA:388, DA:333, DE:349, EN:363, ES:386, FR:76, GA:366, IT:334, NE:338, PO:348.

334 signifikanstest Test af statistisk signifikans.
Se: signifikans.

CA:324, DA:334, DE:350, EN:364, ES:333, FR:373, GA:435, IT:371, NE:339, PO:384.

335 sikkerhed Forholdsregler der har til formål at forhindre afsløring af indholdet, så længe testen er i brug.

CA:387, DA:335, DE:348, EN:351, ES:382, FR:344, GA:353, IT:333, NE:142, PO:347.

336 situationel autenticitet Den udstrækning i hvilken en test kan betragtes som autentisk i relation til virkeligheden eller ikke testrelaterede sprogbrugssituationer.
Sammenlign: interaktional autenticitet, virkelighedstro metode.
Se: autenticitet.
Øvrig litteratur: Bachman, 1990, kapitel 8.
CA:29, DA:336, DE:351, EN:365, ES:35, FR:26, GA:117, IT:37, NE:340, PO:28.

337 skala Tal- eller kategorisæt til at måle et eller andet. Der skelnes imellem fire måleskalaer - nominal-, ordinal-, interval- og kvotient-.
Øvrig litteratur: Crocker og Algina, 1986, pp. 46–49.
CA:144, DA:337, DE:352, EN:343, ES:152, FR:121, GA:308, IT:314, NE:326, PO:154.

338 skaladeskriptor Se under deskriptor.
CA:98, DA:338, DE:353, EN:344, ES:99, FR:96, GA:438, IT:119, NE:327, PO:112.

339 skalaområde (bånd) I bredeste forstand en del af en skala. I en item-baseret test dækker begrebet en række resultater, som kan indberettes i form af en karakter eller en områdebedømmelse. I en klassificeringsskala, som er beregnet til at bedømme et særligt træk eller en særlig færdighed, som f.eks. at tale eller skrive, repræsenterer et skalaområde normalt et bestemt niveau.
CA:37, DA:339, DE:44, EN:29, ES:38, FR:200, GA:41, IT:39 NE:28, PO:210.

340 skalerede point Point, som er fremkommet ved hjælp af skalering.
Se: skalering.
CA:349, DA:340, DE:354, EN:345, ES:349, FR:278, GA:337, IT:286, NE:153, PO:283.

341 skalering Udarbejdelsen af skalaer til målebrug. Inden for sprogtestning indebærer dette at tilknytte tal til deltagerpræstationer for at kunne afspejle stigende videns- eller færdighedsniveauer. Skalering kan indebære modificering af et pointsæt til fremstilling af en skala til et specifikt formål - for eksempel standardiseret indberetning af testresultater - eller til ækvivalering af en testudgave med en anden.
Se: skala, abilitetsskala, centilskala, fællesskala, intervalskala, nominalskala, ordinalskala, kvotientskala, klassificeringsskala (rating-scale), ækvivalerede udgaver, lineær ækvivalering.
CA:159, DA:341, DE:355, EN:346, ES:167, FR:135, GA:321, IT:109, NE:329, PO:169.

342 skalært item Item som bedømmes ved hjælp af en skala.
Se: polytom bedømmelse.
CA:222, DA:342, DE:27, EN:342, ES:248, FR:230, GA:252, IT:220, NE:328, PO:242.

343 skævhed Statistisk fordeling hvor toppen af kurven befinder sig enten til højre for centrum (negativ skævhed) eller til venstre for centrum (positiv skævhed).

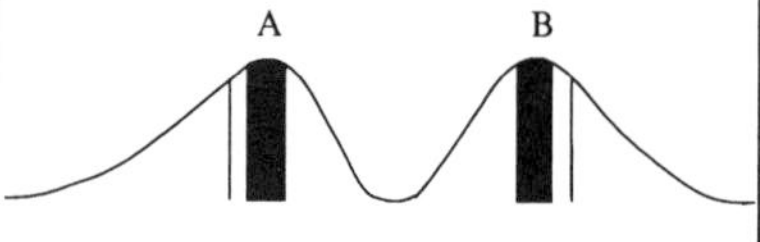

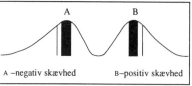

A –negativ skævhed B–positiv skævhed

Se:normalfordeling.
Øvrig litteratur: Hatch og Lazaraton, 1991, p. 165.
CA:25, DA:343, DE:337, EN:366, ES:31, FR:109, GA:323, IT:25, NE:330, PO:120.

344 skævvægtning (bias) Test eller et item kan betragtes som skævvægtning, såfremt et bestemt segment af deltagergruppen vil få særlige fordele eller ulemper på grund af et eller andet træk ved testen eller itemet, som ikke har relevans for det, der skal måles. Skævvægtningen kan være i forhold til køn, alder, kultur etc.
Øvrig litteratur: Bachman, 1990, pp. 271–279; Crocker og Algina, 1986, kap. 12 og 16.
CA:40, DA:344, DE:383, EN:33, ES:384, FR:32, GA:208, IT:160, NE:46, PO:40.

345 sluttest Test eller anden form for måling, som benyttes i slutningen af et kursus. Ved sammenligning med resultaterne fra en test i begyndelsen af kurset opnås bevis for kursets effektivitet.
Sammenlign: forprøve.
CA:327, DA:345, DE:5, EN:287, ES:336, FR:305, GA:179, IT:271, NE:295, PO:310.

346 sociokulturel viden Viden om samfundets funktion inden for en bestemt kultur. Har betydning for valg af hensigtsmæssig adfærd og sprogbrug i specifikke kulturelle sammenhænge.
Sammenlign: sociolingvistisk kompetens.
CA:76, DA:346, DE:357, EN:368, ES:72,

FR:341, GA:135, IT:86, NE:344, PO:90.

347 sociolingvistisk kompetens Kategori som benyttes i modeller for kommunikativ sprogfærdighed. Omfatter evnen til at tilpasse talesprog til bestemte miljøer og situationer i overensstemmelse med sociale normer.
Øvrig litteratur: Bachman, 1990, p. 42.
CA:70, DA:347, DE:358, EN:369, ES:67, FR:70, GA:197, IT:69, NE:345, PO:84.

348 SOPI (Semi-Direct Oral Proficiency Interview) Mundtlig sprogfærdighedstest, hvor input leveres af en båndoptagelse, og hvor deltagerens respons optages med henblik på efterfølgende bedømmelse.
Se: semi-direkte test.
CA:130, DA:348, DE:356, EN:370, ES:137, FR:392, GA:356, IT:93, NE:346, PO:144.

349 Spearman-Brown formel Statistisk metode til vurdering af testreliabilitet i tilfælde af forlængelse eller forkortelse ved tilførsel eller fjernelse af items. Kan benyttes til at forudsige det nødvendige antal items til dækning af en nærmere angivet reliabilitet.
Øvrig litteratur: Crocker og Algina, 1986, pp. 118–119.
CA:83, DA:349, DE:359, EN:371, ES:207, FR:197, GA:147, IT:180, NE:350, PO:203.

350 Spearman-Browns halveringsmetode Se under opdelingsmetoden.
CA:168, DA:350, DE:360, EN:372, ES:177, FR:161, GA:228, IT:342, NE:349, PO:178.

351 Spearmans rangkorrelation Rangkorrelation som anvendes til små stikprøver, dvs. stikprøver på mindre end 30.
Se: rangkorrelation.
CA:58, DA:351, DE:361, EN:373, ES:87, FR:60, GA:83, IT:99, NE:347, PO:73.

352 Spearmans rho Se under Spearmans rangkorrelation.
CA:383, DA:352, DE:362, EN:374, ES:380, FR:339, GA:292, IT:302, NE:348, PO:344.

353 spredning Variationen i point for en deltagergruppe. Hvis spredningen er stor, vil pointene være meget spredte, og hvis den er lille, vil de ligge mere samlet.
Se: standardafvigelse, varians, variationsbrede.
CA:107, DA:353, DE:385, EN:114, ES:110, FR:103, GA:357, IT:127, NE:356, PO:118.

354 sprogabilitet Kompetenser som tilsammen definerer en persons evne til at anvende sproget til flere forskellige kommunikative formål.
Øvrig litteratur: Bachman, 1990, pp. 3–4.
CA:47, DA:354, DE:368, EN:203, ES:50, FR:43, GA:97, IT:4, NE:379, PO:50.

355 sprogfærdighed Beherskelse af et sprog. Benyttes ofte synonymt med sprogabilitet.
Øvrig litteratur: Bachman, 1990, p. 16.
CA:297, DA:355, DE:365, EN:206, ES:121, FR:66, GA:267, IT:66, NE:215, PO:81.

356 sprogtilegnelse Proces hvorved man tilegner sig færdighed på et førsteeller andetsprog. I forbindelse med andetsprog skelnes ofte imellem tilegnelse (dvs. ved naturlig udsættelse for sproget) og indlæring (dvs. gennem en bevidst proces).
CA:7, DA:356, DE:367, EN:204, ES:14, FR:5, GA:349, IT:22, NE:380, PO:24.

357 spørgsmål Benyttes til tider synonymt med testopgave eller item.
Se: item, opgave.
CA:291, DA:357, DE:122, EN:303, ES:304, FR:315, GA:55, IT:136, NE:423, PO:323.

358 spørgsmålstype Se under itemtype, opgavetype.
CA:407, DA:358, DE:124, EN:305, ES:404, FR:406, GA:57, IT:394, NE:424, PO:400.

359 stabilitet Reliabilitetsaspekt hvor vurderingen baseres på retestmetoden. Vedrører stabiliteten af point henover et tidsinterval.
Se: reliabilitet, retestreliabilitet.
CA:162, DA:359, DE:371, EN:378, ES:170, FR:79, GA:65, IT:337, NE:358, PO:173.

360 stamme Del af skriftlig responsfremkalder. Sædvanligvis en ufuldendt sætning, som skal fuldendes ved at træffe et valg eller producere et svar.
Sammenlign: nøglesvar, valgmulighed.
Se: multiple-choice item.
CA:276, DA:360, DE:29, EN:387, ES:139, FR:10, GA:160, IT:346, NE:359, PO:224.

361 standard estimatfejl Mål for nøjagtigheden af at forudsige en variabel på grundlag af en anden, f.eks. i lineær regression. Opstiller konfidensintervaller for kriterielaterede point.
Se: konfidensinterval.
Øvrig litteratur: Hatch og Lazaraton, 1991, pp. 477–479.
CA:142, DA:361, DE:375, EN:380, ES:148, FR:156, GA:124, IT:163, NE:363, PO:152.

362 standardafvigelse Mål for spredningen i et sæt observationer omkring gennemsnittet. Er lig med kvadratroden af variansen. I en normalfordeling ligger 68% af stikprøven inden for standardafvigelsen fra gennemsnittet og 95% ligger inden for to standardafvigelser fra gennemsnittet.

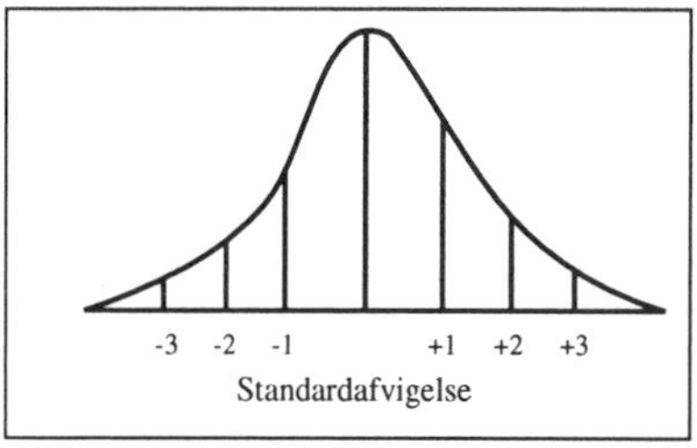

Sammenlign: variationsbredde.
Se: varians.
Øvrig litteratur: Ebel og Frisbie, 1991, pp. 61–62; Crocker og Algina, 1986, pp. 21–22.
CA:101, DA:362, DE:372, EN:379, ES:103, FR:98, GA:113, IT:122, NE:360, PO:114.

363 standardisering Sikring af ensartethed i anvendelsen af aftalte procedurer og karakterskalaer.
Se: bedømmer (censor).
CA:167, DA:363, DE:373, EN:383, ES:175, NE:361, FR:162, GA:45, IT:338, PO:295.

364 standardmålefejl I klassisk truescore testteori er standardmålefejlen (*Se*) en indikation for et måleresultats manglende præcision. Størrelsen af standardmålefejlen afhænger af realiabiliteten (*r*) og standardafvigelsen for testpointene (*Sx*). Formlen for beregning af *Se* er:

$$Se = Sx\sqrt{(1-r)}.$$

For eksempel, hvis en deltager med en truescore på T og en standardmålefejl på *Se* gentagne gange deltager i en test, vil de konstaterede point i 68% af tilfældene ligge inden for området T±*Se* og i 95% af tilfældene indenfor området T±2*Se*.
Øvrig litteratur: Crocker og Algina, 1986, pp. 122–124.
CA:143, DA:364, DE:374, EN:381, ES:149, FR:157, GA:125, IT:12, NE:362, PO:153.

365 standardpoint (standardscore) Lineært transformerede point fra et pointsæt. Gennemsnit og standardafvigelse sættes til de værdier, som brugeren har behov for. Som eksempler på standardpoint kan nævnes -*z* og *t*-point.
CA:350, DA:365, DE:376, EN:382, ES:350, FR:281, GA:333, IT:287, NE:364, PO:291.

366 standpunktstest (achievement test) Test som er udviklet til at måle det standpunkt, som deltageren har opnået i relation til et specifikt kursus, lærebog etc., dvs. en curriculum-afhængig test. Kaldes også på engelsk attainment test.
CA:309, DA:366, DE:369, EN:6, ES:321, FR:374, GA:419, IT:368, NE:301, PO:374.

367 staninescore Metode til inddeling af testpoint i ni grupper på grundlag af normalfordelingen. Både den højeste og den laveste gruppe repræsenterer 4% af deltagerne. Den procentvise fordeling af deltagere på alle grupper illustreres grafisk nedenfor.

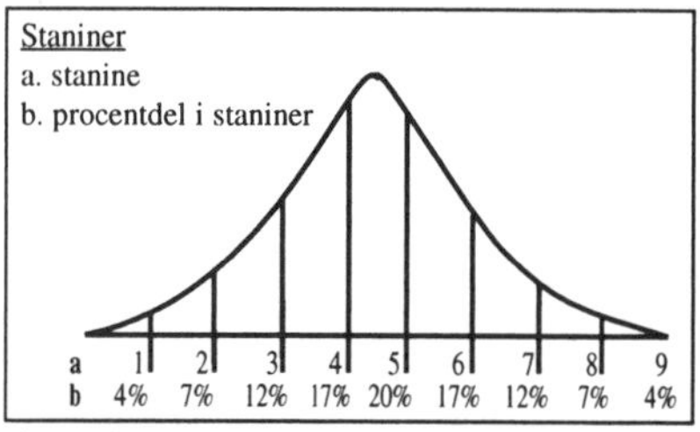

Øvrig litteratur: Crocker og Algina, 1986, pp. 446–447.
CA:344, DA:367, DE:377, EN:384, ES:176, FR:282, GA:332, IT:279, NE:365, PO:284.

368 statistik Præsentation af forskellige oplysninger i numerisk form. Strengt taget er en statistik en egenskab ved en stikprøve-gruppe, i modsætning til et parameter, som er en egenskab ved en population. Statistiske oplysninger skrives normalt med romerske bogstaver, hvorimod parametre skrives med græske. For eksempel skrives standardafvigelsen for en stikprøve s eller SA, hvorimod tegnet σ anvendes for en population.
Sammenlign: parameter.
Se: population, stikprøve.
CA:163, DA:368, DE:379, EN:385, ES:174, FR:348, GA:363, IT:117, NE:367, PO:174.

369 statistik Videnskabelig bearbejdning og fortolkning af numeriske data.
CA:164, DA:369, DE:378, EN:386, ES:171, FR:348, GA:362, IT:339, NE:366, PO:175.

370 stikprøve af resultater Stikprøve af deltagerrespons, som repræsenterer et

færdighedsniveau. Benyttes til standardisering af bedømmelse.
CA:268, DA:370, DE:254, EN:338, ES:132, FR:118, GA:344, IT:330, NE:420, PO:10.

371 stikprøve Udsnit af en population. Der skelnes imellem forskellige typer stikprøver, f.eks. tilfældig stikprøve, stratificeret stikprøve etc.
Øvrig litteratur: Crocker og Algina, 1986, pp. 432–438; Guilford og Fruchter, 1981, pp. 44–45.
CA:264, DA:371, DE:380, EN:337, ES:278, FR:116, GA:304, IT:46, NE:369, PO:8.

372 stikprøvefejl Fejl i statistisk analyse, som skyldes valget af den specifikke stikprøve, som blev anvendt i undersøgelsen (f.eks. hvis stikprøven ikke er repræsentativ for populationen).
Se: population.
CA:139, DA:372, DE:381, EN:341, ES:147, FR:158, GA:129, IT:155, NE:370, PO:148.

373 stikprøvefri måling Anvendes i forskningssammenhænge om resultattolkning, som er uafhængig af en stikprøve, som er blevet anvendt i en specifik undersøgelse.
Se: stikprøve.
CA:247, DA:373, DE:382, EN:339, ES:265, FR:244, GA:396, IT:239, NE:371, PO:258.

374 stikprøveudvælgelse Udvælgelse af stikprøve.
Se: stikprøve.
CA:267, DA:374, DE:384, EN:340, ES:281, FR:120, GA:307, IT:45, NE:368, PO:313.

375 stratificeret stikprøve Stikprøve af en population, som først inddeles i et antal sub-populationer (lag, rangplaceringer, strata), hvorefter der udtages en stikprøve fra hver.
Se: stikprøve.
Øvrig litteratur: Guilford og Fruchter, 1981, pp. 122–123.
CA:266, DA:375, DE:134, EN:388, ES:280, FR:119, GA:306, IT:48, NE:157, PO:11.

376 stump fordeling Frekvensfordeling som er karakteristisk for en stikprøve med en smallere variationsbredde and den population, hvorfra den er taget, fordi elever med høje eller lave point ikke er medtaget i stikprøven. En sådan stikprøve kunne være en gruppe elever, som optages på et kursus efter at have bestået en adgangsprøve.
CA:116, DA:376, DE:1, EN:421, ES:117, FR:110, GA:108, IT:135, NE:343, PO:124.

377 subtest Se under komponent.
CA:389, DA:377, DE:386, EN:389, ES:388, FR:346, GA:150, IT:345, NE:373, PO:350.

378 sværhedsindeks I klassisk testteori repræsenterer et items sværhedsgrad den andel (a) af deltagerne, som svarer rigtigt. Dette betyder, at sværhedsindekset for det enkelte item er gruppeafhængigt og vil skifte i overensstemmelse med deltagernes færdighed.
Sammenlign: korrekthedsindeks.
CA:207, DA:378, DE:343, EN:101, ES:224, FR:209, GA:187, IT:196, NE:249, PO:219.

379 sværhedsparameter Se under B-parameter.
CA:285, DA:379, DE:344, EN:102, ES:298, FR:296, GA:276, IT:264, NE:250, PO:300.

380 sætningsrekonstruktion Itemtype som giver stikord i form af en række indholdsord, men udelader præpositioner, hjælpeverber, artikler etc. Deltagerens opgave består i at tilføje de manglende ord, hvorved de oprindelige stikord udvides til en fuldstændig grammatisk sætning.
CA:99, DA:380, DE:333, EN:358, ES:18, FR:175, GA:148, IT:166, NE:441, PO:184.

381 sætningstransformation Itemtype hvor en fuldstændig sætning fungerer som stikord. Denne følges af de første par ord fra en anden sætning, som udtrykker indholdet af den første sætning, men i en anden grammatisk udformning. F. eks. kan den første sætning være aktiv, hvorefter deltageren har til opgave at gengive den i passiv form.
CA:410, DA:381, DE:334, EN:359, ES:407, FR:404, GA:61, IT:397, NE:440, PO:405.

382 sætningsudfyldelse Itemtype hvor kun halvdelen af en sætning gives som input. Deltagerens opgave består i at fuldende sætningen, enten ved at indsætte passende ord (eventuelt baseret på en læst tekst) eller ved at vælge blandt en række mulige svar.
CA:72, DA:382, DE:332, EN:357, ES:69, FR:298, GA:93, IT:80, NE:442, PO:86.

383 søjlediagram Grafisk fremstilling af forekomsten af forskellige variabler.

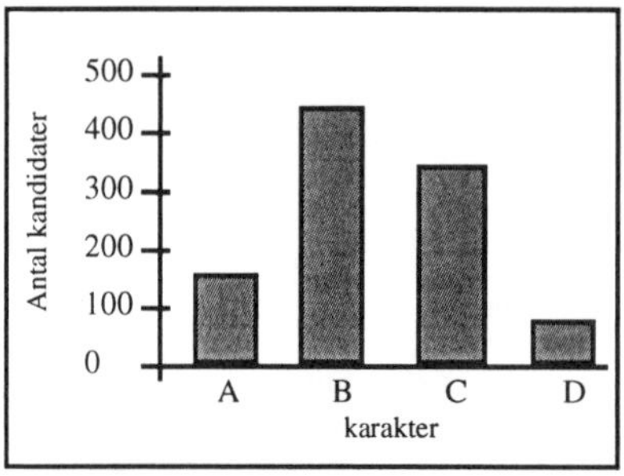

Sammenlign: histogram.
Øvrig litteratur: Hatch og Lazaraton, 1991, p. 147.
CA:102, DA:383, DE:335, EN:31, ES:104, FR:201, GA:42, IT:123, NE:357, PO:211.

384 *t*-point Udvidelse af *z*-point. Fjerner decimalpladser og minustegn. *t*-point er lig ti gange *z*-point plus 50. Fordelingen har et gennemsnit på 50 og en standardafvigelse på 10.
Se: *z*-score.
Øvrig litteratur: Ebel og Frisbie, 1991, p. 68.
CA:355, DA:384, DE:388, EN:422, ES:355, FR:283, GA:367, IT:289, NE:376, PO:287.

385 *t*-test Statistisk test som anvendes til at fastslå eksistensen af signifikante forskelle imellem gennemsnit for to stikprøver.
CA:340, DA:385, DE:387, EN:423, ES:398, FR:150, GA:368, IT:385, NE:377, PO:397.

386 tekst Sammenhængende diskurs, skreven eller talt, som anvendes som grundlag for en række items.
CA:403, DA:386, DE:411, EN:411, ES:399, FR:396, GA:381, IT:389, NE:381, PO:398.

387 tekst-baseret item Item som er baseret på sammenhængende diskurs, f.eks. multiple-choice items baseret på en læseforståelsestekst.
CA:219, DA:387, DE:412, EN:412, ES:236, FR:226, GA:254, IT:213, NE:269, PO:233.

388 test-informationsfunktion (IRT) Et indeks for den mængde information en test er i stand til at frembringe om personer på et givent færdighedsniveau. Summen af item-informationsfunktioner.
Sammenlign: item-informationsfunktion.
Øvrig litteratur: Crocker og Algina, 1986, pp. 369–371.
CA:194, DA:388, DE:399, EN:400, ES:211, FR:191, GA:139, IT:185, NE:394, PO:207.

389 testanalyse Analyse af test efter anvendelse. Ofte ved hjælp af statistik og computer. Formålet kan være at undersøge deltagernes præstationer eller selve testen.
CA:15, DA:389, DE:390, EN:396, ES:22, FR:16, GA:14, IT:17, NE:389, PO:18.

390 testbatteri Et sæt forbundne test eller deltest, som leverer uafhængige bidrag (f.eks. ved at teste forskellige færdigheder), men som kan kombineres til at give et samlet pointtal.
CA:39, DA:390, DE:406, EN:397, ES:41, FR:31, GA:63, IT:42, NE:390, PO:39.

391 testbruger Person eller institution (f.eks. lærer eller arbejdsgiver), som anvender testresultater som beslutningsgrundlag vedrørende testtageren.
CA:414, DA:391, DE:392, EN:407, ES:410, FR:409, GA:440, IT:399, NE:393, PO:407.

392 testforfatter Person som skriver og konstruerer en test.
CA:127, DA:392, DE:400, EN:361, ES:92, FR:145, GA:121, IT:149, NE:391, PO:141.

393 testkomponent (paper) Selvstændig komponent (opgaveark) som udgør en del af en test, f.eks. læsekomponent, lyttekomponent.
CA:385, DA:393, DE:277, EN:267, ES:381, FR:182, GA:270, IT:168, NE:278, PO:87.

394 testkonstruktion Udvælgelse af items eller opgaver m.h.p. at kombinere dem til en test. Forud for denne proces foregår ofte en forprøvning eller prøvekørsel af materialerne. Items og opgaver vælges ofte fra en materialebank.
CA:126, DA:394, DE:397, EN:398, ES:75, FR:146, GA:393, IT:110, NE:392, PO:140.

395 testmetode Sprogfærdighed kan testes ved hjælp af en lang række metoder, såsom multiple-choice, cloze, stilskrivning, interview, etc. Man har konstateret et samspil imellem testmetode og abilitet ved målingen af præstationer.
Se: testmetodetræk.
Øvrig litteratur: Bachman, 1990, p. 77.
CA:248, DA:395, DE:401, EN:401, ES:266, FR:245, GA:257, IT:236, NE:396, PO:259.

396 testmetodefacetter Se under

testmetodetræk.
CA:175, DA:396, DE:402, EN:403, ES:193, FR:176, GA:163, IT:50, NE:397, PO:186.

397 testmetodetræk Karakteristiske træk ved forskellige testmetoder. F.eks. miljø, opgaveinstruks, instruktionssprog, format etc.
Øvrig litteratur: Bachman, 1990, kapitel 5.
CA:48, DA:397, DE:403, EN:402, ES:51, FR:46, GA:401, IT:50, NE:398, PO:54.

398 testning af minimumskompetence Testningsmetode som opstiller specifikke krav til minimumskompetence inden for et nærmere bestemt sprogbrugsområde. En deltager, som er i stand til at opfylde dette kompetenceniveau, vil bestå testen.
CA:312, DA:398, DE:304, EN:234, ES:183, FR:167, GA:378, IT:388, NE:246, PO:31.

399 testpunkt Fokus for et item. Det særlige vidensområde, som deltageren testes i.
CA:128, DA:399, DE:309, EN:409, ES:289, FR:300, GA:281, IT:293, NE:384, PO:307.

400 testredaktion Stadium i testproduktionen, hvor testkonstruktørerne vurderer materiale, som er bestilt hos itemforfattere, og beslutter hvad der skal afvises, fordi det ikke opfylder testens specifikationer, og hvad der skal tages med til den endelige redigering.
Sammenlign: tilpasning.
CA:382, DA:400, DE:405, EN:433 ES:383, FR:338, GA:184, IT:91, NE:115, PO:343.

401 testspecifikationer Detaljeret dokumentationsmateriale, som normalt udarbejdes under konstruktionen af en ny test eller i forbindelse med revisionen af en eksisterende test. Specifikationerne vedrører design, indhold, niveau, anvendte opgave- og itemtyper, målpopulation, anvendelse af testen etc. Eksempelmateriale vedlægges ofte.
CA:161, DA:401, DE:394, EN:404, ES:169, FR:346, GA:355, IT:120, NE:400, PO:171.

402 testtager Se under kandidat.
CA:100, DA:402, DE:407, EN:406, ES:190, FR:351, GA:110, IT:49, NE:395, PO:183.

403 testtermin Den dato eller periode hvor testen foregår. Mange test foregår på en fast dato flere gange om året, hvorimod andre gives efter behov.
CA:6, DA:403, DE:308, EN:8, ES:77, FR:7, GA:288, IT:331, NE:10, PO:23.

404 testtilpasning Tilpasning af en eksisterende test til en bestemt gruppes formål.
CA:301, DA:404, DE:410, EN:405, ES:13, FR:395, GA:370, IT:5, NE:382, PO:4.

405 testudvikler Person som er involveret i udviklingen af en ny test.
CA:109, DA:405, DE:395, EN:399, ES:133, FR:145, GA:149, IT:149, NE:399, PO:141.

406 testvant Erfaringer med testformen eller med selve det at tage en test. Sætter deltageren i stand til at levere en præstation, som ligger over det reelle færdighedsniveau.
CA:179, DA:406, DE:396, EN:408, ES:197, FR:314, GA:161, IT:167, NE:401, PO:191.

407 theta skala Refererer til abilitetsskala.
CA:158, DA:407, DE:413, EN:413, ES:166, FR:128, GA:320, IT:328, NE:385, PO:168.

408 tilfældig fejl Se under fejlscore.
CA:137, DA:408, DE:449, EN:306, ES:145, FR:152, GA:128, IT:156, NE:310, PO:147,

409 tilfældig stikprøve En samling elementer, som er udtaget tilfældigt fra en population, som er genstand for undersøgelse, sådan at alle elementer i den pågældende population har en ligelig chance for at blive udvalgt til undersøgelse.
Se: stikprøve.
Øvrig litteratur: Crocker og Algina, 1986, pp. 433–438; Guilford og Fruchter, 1981, p. 120.
CA:265, DA:409, DE:451, EN:307, ES:279, FR:117, GA:305, IT:47, NE:120, PO:9.

410 tilpasning a) Del af processen med at forberede items eller opgaver til brug i en test. På dette stadium undersøges materialer kritisk af et antal eksperter (så som testforfattere og lærere), som beslutter om de er egnede til formålet (måske efter redigering eller omskrivning).

b) I bedømmelsesprocessen, justering af en bedømmers point ved hjælp af en moderator.
Sammenlign: testredaktion.
CA:263, DA:410, DE:31, EN:237, ES:277,

FR:256, GA:260, IT:250, NE:247, PO:270.

411 toparameter-model Model inden for item-responsteorien, som inddrager et item-diskrimineringsparameter i tilgift til abilitets-/sværhedsparametre.
Sammenlign: enkeltparameter-model, Rasch-model.
Se: item-responsteori (IRT) .
CA:258, DA:411, DE:454, EN:424, ES:271, FR:248, GA:298, IT:241, NE:404, PO:264.

412 topstejlhed Den udstrækning i hvilken en fordeling er mere spids eller flad end normalkurven. Data, som er spredt ud på en flad kurve, udviser platykurtisk fordeling, hvorimod data, som danner en meget spids kurve, udviser leptokurtisk fordeling.

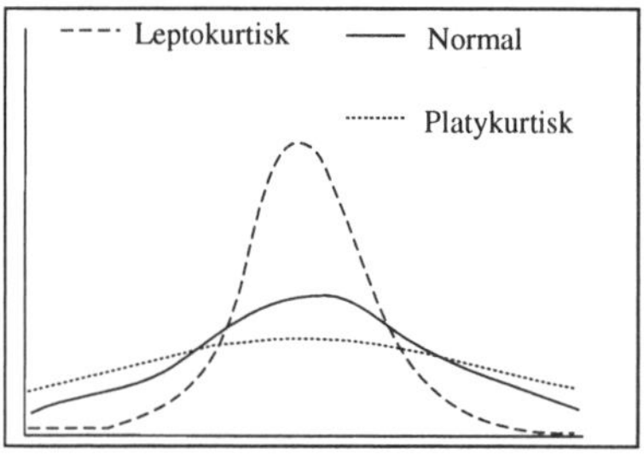

Se: normal fordeling.
CA:95, DA:412, DE:108, EN:202, ES:94, FR:428, GA:100, IT:114, NE:213, PO:108.

413 transformationsitem Se under sætningstransformation.
CA:229, DA:413, DE:420, EN:416, ES:245, FR:403, GA:242, IT:217, NE:402, PO:239.

414 transformerede point Matematisk transformerede råpoint. Anvendes til f.eks. skalering eller vægtning.
Øvrig litteratur: Ebel og Frisbie, 1991, pp. 64–70.
CA:356, DA:414, DE:415, EN:417, ES:356, FR:284, GA:334, IT:290, NE:158, PO:288.

415 true-score Point som en deltager ville opnå, hvis der ikke optrådte målefejl på testnings- eller scoringstidspunktet. Fundamentalt begreb i klassisk testteori.
CA:357, DA:415, DE:441, EN:420, ES:357, FR:285, GA:335, IT:285, NE:431, PO:289.

416 træk Personers fysiske eller psykiske karakteristika (såsom sprogfærdighed), eller en måleskala, som er konstrueret til at beskrive disse.
CA:411, DA:416, DE:95, EN:415, ES:360, FR:23, GA:400, IT:26, NE:403, PO:403.

417 type-1 fejl Statistik. Fejlagtig afvisning af nul-hypotesen, hvor denne faktisk er sand.
Sammenlign: type-2 fejl.
Se: nulhypotese.
Øvrig litteratur: Hatch og Lazaraton, 1991, p. 224.
CA:140, DA:417, DE:9/117, EN:425, ES:150, FR:154, GA:126, IT:157, NE:405, PO:150.

418 type-2 fejl Statistik. Fejlagtig accept af nul-hypotesen, hvor denne faktisk er falsk.
Sammenlign: type-1 fejl.
Se: nulhypotese.
Øvrig litteratur: Hatch og Lazaraton, 1991, p. 224.
CA:141, DA:418, DE:118, EN:426, ES:151, FR:155, GA:127, IT:158, NE:406, PO:151.

419 tærskelniveau (threshold level) Indflydelsesrig, funktionel specifikation af grundlæggende fremmedsprogsfærdighed. Udgivet af Europarådet i 1976 for engelsk og opdateret i 1990. Efterfølgende er tilsvarende udgaver blevet udarbejdet for en række europæiske sprog.
CA:272, DA:419, DE:414, EN:414, ES:285, FR:262, GA:212, IT:230, NE:386, PO:275.

420 uafhængig variabel I forskningssammenhæng en variabel, som menes at være forbundet med eller have indflydelse på den afhængige variabel. For eksempel kan point fra en test (den uafhængige variabel) benyttes til at forudsige succes på arbejdspladsen (den afhængige variabel).
Sammenlign: afhængig variabel.
Se: variabel.
Øvrig litteratur: Hatch og Lazaraton, 1991, p. 64.
CA:433, DA:420, DE:422, EN:169, ES:433, FR:426, GA:27, IT:419, NE:268, PO:425.

421 udfyldnings-item Itemtype som kræver, at deltageren udfylder en sætning eller ordforbindelse, normalt ved at indføje et antal ord eller ved at tilføje enkeltheder, såsom tidspunkter og telefonnumre.
CA:226, DA:421, DE:102, EN:60, ES:238, FR:223, GA:243, IT:215, NE:193, PO:234.

422 udvalgt svar Itemrespons som indebærer valg blandt en række alternativer, i stedet for individuel konstruktion af et

svar.
CA:379, DA:422, DE:37, EN:352, ES:377, FR:334, GA:158, IT:310, NE:154, PO:341.

423 udvidet respons Respons på et item, hvor deltageren forventes at producere (modsat vælge) et svar, som fylder mere end en eller to sætninger.
Sammenlign: kortsvars-item.
CA:378, DA:423, DE:35, EN:138, ES:375, FR:332, GA:159, IT:308, NE:407, PO:339.

424 udvælgelsestest (screening test) Test, sædvanligvis kort og enkel at anvende, som benyttes til at udvælge de deltagere, som kan blive optaget på et kursus eller få adgang til en eksamen.
Sammenlign: indplaceringsprøve.
CA:316, DA:424, DE:98, EN:349, ES:332, FR:375, GA:432, IT:370, NE:332, PO:375.

425 valgmuligheder Udvalget af mulige svar i et multiple-choice item eller sammenstillingsopgave, blandt hvilke det korrekte svar skal vælges.
CA:279, DA:425, DE:38, EN:262, ES:292, FR:290, GA:293, IT:258, NE:14, PO:294.

426 validering Indsamling af bevismateriale til støtte for slutninger, som er draget på basis af testresultater. Det er slutningerne vedrørende specifikke anvendelser af en test, som valideres, ikke selve testen.
Se: validitet.
CA:415, DA:426, DE:426, EN:429, ES:412, FR:412, GA:39, IT:400, NE:414, PO:408.

427 validitet Den udstrækning i hvilken testresultater gør det muligt at drage slutninger, som er hensigtsmæssige, meningsfulde og anvendelige, ud fra testens formål. Det er muligt at skelne imellem forskellige validitetsaspekter, f.eks. indholds-, kriterierelateret- og begrebsvaliditet. Disse udgør forskellige former for beviser, som kan anvendes til bedømmelse af den generelle validitet af en test til et bestemt formål.
Se: samstemmende validitet, kosntruktvaliditet, kriterie-relateret validitet, indholdsvaliditet, konvergerende validitet, diskriminant validitet, overfladevaliditet, prædiktiv validitet.
Øvrig litteratur: Bachman, 1990, pp. 25, 236–237.
CA:416, DA:427, DE:427, EN:430, ES:413, FR:413, GA:30, IT:401, NE:415, PO:409.

428 variabel a) Betegnelse for en serie observationer på et enkelt item, hvor det pågældende item kan være et testitem, køn, alder eller testpoint.
b) Et element i eksperimentelt design eller statistisk analyse, som kan antage en række værdier. F.eks. kan interessevariabler i en sprogtestningssammenhæng omfatte itemsværhed, deltagernes køn og alder etc.
CA:430, DA:428, DE:428, EN:431, ES:430, FR:423, GA:25, IT:416, NE:416, PO:422.

429 varians Mål for spredningen af et sæt point. Jo større varians, des længere vil individuelle resultater befinde sig fra gennemsnittet.
CA:434, DA:429, DE:429, EN:432, ES:434, FR:427, GA:24, IT:420, NE:417, PO:421.

430 variansanalyse Se under ANOVA.
CA:17, DA:430, DE:430, EN:13, ES:23, FR:15, GA:15, IT:19, NE:418, PO:14.

431 variationsbredde Mål for spredningen af observationer. Variationsbredden er afstanden mellem højeste og laveste score.
Øvrig litteratur: Hatch og Lazaraton, 1991, pp. 169–170.
CA:12, DA:431, DE:431, EN:308, ES:260, FR:241, GA:285, IT:233, NE:311, PO:12.

432 vertikal ækvivalering Placering af to test af forskellig sværhedsgrad på samme skala.
Øvrig litteratur: Crocker og Algina, 1986, pp. 437–477.
CA:135, DA:432, DE:435, EN:434, ES:143, FR:39, GA:90, IT:153, NE:419, PO:46.

433 virkelighedstro metode I sprogtestning det synspunkt, at test bør indeholde opgavetyper, som så vidt muligt ligner aktiviteter, man kunne komme ud for i virkeligheden. Med denne metode vil, f.eks. indholdet af en test, som er konstrueret til at bedømme, om deltagerne kan klare et sprogkursus på akademisk niveau, være baseret på en behovsanalyse af det sprog og de sproglige aktiviteter, som typisk findes på det pågældende kursus.
Se: autenticitet.
Øvrig litteratur: Bachman, 1990, pp. 301–328.
CA:129, DA:433, DE:320, EN:322, ES:134, FR:345, GA:98, IT:23, NE:226, PO:349.

434 vægtet testscore Point som tildeles for en test efter vægtning.
Se: vægtning.
CA:354, DA:434, DE:135, EN:437,

ES:354, FR:280, GA:339, IT:284, NE:159, PO:286.

435 vægtning Tildeling af et ændret antal maksimumpoint for et testitem, -opgave eller -komponent for at ændre dets relative bidrag i forhold til andre dele af samme test. Hvis man f.eks. giver dobbeltpoint for alle items i Opgave I, vil den pågældende opgave repræsentere en større andel af det samlede pointtal end de øvrige opgaver.
Øvrig litteratur: Ebel og Frisbie, 1991, pp. 214–216.
CA:290, DA:435, DE:136, EN:438, ES:3034, FR:302, GA:439, IT:268, NE:434, PO:306.

436 washback Se under backwash.
CA:372, DA:436, DE:442, EN:435, ES:124, FR:322, GA:95, IT:147, NE:432, PO:135.

437 Waystage-niveau Specifikation af elementært niveau for fremmedsprogsfærdighed. Først offentliggjort af Europarådet i 1977 for engelsk og revideret i 1990. Opstiller mindre krævende mål end tærskelniveau, eftersom det anslås at kræve ca. halv så stor indlæringsbelastning som tærskelniveau.
Sammenlign: tærskelniveau (Threshold level).
CA:271, DA:437, DE:443, EN:436, ES:284, FR:261, GA:211, IT:231, NE:433, PO:274.

438 y-opsnapper Punkt i lineær regression hvor regressionslinien krydser y-aksen (vertikale akse).
Se: lineær regression.
CA:212, DA:438, DE:146, EN:441, ES:231, FR:215, GA:181, IT:200, NE:438, PO:226.

439 *z*-score Almindeligt forekommende standardscore med et gennemsnit på 0 og en standard afvigelse på 1. Formlen for beregning af *z*-score er:

$$z = (X - \overline{X}) \div Sx$$

Hvor z = z-score
X = testscore
$\overline{X}$ = gennemsnitlig testscore
Sx= standardafvigelse af testscores
Sammenlign: *t*-point.
Se: standardpoint (standardscore).
Øvrig litteratur: Ebel og Frisbie, 1991, p. 68.
CA:358, DA:439, DE:446, EN:442, ES:358, FR:286, GA:441, IT:291, NE:439, PO:290.

440 ækvipercentil ækvivalering Metode til ækvivalering af råpoint fra en test, hvorved pointtallene anses for at være ækvivalerede, hvis de svarer til samme percentile rangplacering i en deltagergruppe.
CA:132, DA:440, DE:24, EN:127, ES:140, FR:36, GA:88, IT:150, NE:121, PO:43.

441 ækvivalente udgaver Også kendt som parallelle eller alternative udgaver. Forskellige versioner af samme test, som anses for at være ækvivalente i og med, at de er baseret på samme specifikationer og måler samme kompetens. For at overholde de stramme krav til ækvivalens i henhold til klassisk testteori skal forskellige udgaver af en test have samme gennemsnitlige sværhedsgrad, varians og kovarians, når den gives til de samme personer. Det er meget vanskeligt at opnå ækvivalens i praksis. Også kaldet alternative eller parallelle udgaver.
Sammenlign: ækvivalerede udgaver.
Øvrig litteratur: Crocker og Algina, 1986, p. 132.
CA:187, DA:441, DE:25, EN:128 ES:205, FR:195, GA:143, IT:178, NE:122, PO:201.

442 ækvivalerede udgaver Forskellige versioner af en test, hvor pointfordelingerne er blevet transformeret, så de kan anvendes alternativt.
Øvrig litteratur: Crocker og Algina, 1986, kapitel 20.
CA:186, DA:442, DE:16/14, EN:126, ES:204, FR:194, GA:145, IT:177 NE:141, PO:200.

443 øvethedseffekt Påvirkning af point på grund af deltagernes kendskab til de anvendte opgavetyper eller items.
CA:119, DA:443, DE:419, EN:289, ES:123, FR:138, GA:169, IT:140, NE:298, PO:131.

444 åbent spørgsmål Item- eller opgavetype i en skriftlig test, som forudsætter, at deltageren selv producerer et svar, i stedet for at vælge et. Formålet med denne itemtype er at aflokke et relativt utvungent svar, som kan svinge i omfang fra nogle få ord til en større fremstilling. Retteskemaet giver derfor mulighed for en række acceptable svar.
CA:292, DA:444, DE:273, EN:260, ES:305, FR:318, GA:56, IT:137, NE:273, PO:324.

3 Deutsch: Ein mehrsprachiges Glosar mit Begriffen für Sprachtests

1 abgeschnittene Verteilung Typ einer Häufigkeitsverteilung, der sich ergibt, wenn das erfaßte Merkmal in einer Stichprobe weniger stark streut als in der Population, aus der die Stichprobe gezogen wurde, weil Personen mit besonders hoher oder besonders niedriger Merkmalsausprägung fehlen. Solch eine Stichprobe könnte sich beispielsweise ergeben, wenn sie nur diejenigen Studenten umfaßt, die den Eingangstest eines Kurses bestanden haben.

CA:116, DA:376, DE:1, EN:421, ES:117, FR:110, GA:108, IT:135, NE:343, PO:124.

2 abhängige Variable Die in einer Untersuchung zu prüfende Variable. Beispielsweise können die Testergebnisse (unabhängige Variable) verwendet werden, um den Erfolg an einem Arbeitsplatz (abhängige Variable) vorherzusagen.
Vergleiche: unabhängige Variable.
Siehe: Variable.
Literatur: Hatch & Lazarton 1991, S. 63; Bortz 1993, S.7–8.

CA:432, DA:7, DE:2, EN:94, ES:432, FR:425, GA:28, IT:418, NE:7, PO:424.

3 abschließende Evaluation Evaluation eines Prozesses nach dessen Abschluß. Bei diesem Prozeß kann es sich um ein Kursprogramm handeln.
Vergleiche: begleitende Evaluation.

CA:34, DA:266, DE:3, EN:391, ES:186, FR:172, GA:238, IT:415, NE:374, PO:36.

4 Abschlußprüfung Test am Ende eines Kurses oder Lehrganges.
Vergleiche: Lernerfolgskontrolle.

CA:34, DA:267, DE:4, EN:390, ES:186, FR:172, GA:233, IT:423, NE:375, PO:36.

5 Abschlußtest Test oder andere Meßmethode, die am Ende eines Kurses eingesetzt wird. Vergleicht man die Ergebnisse mit denen, die ein Test am Anfang des Kurses erbrachte, so ergibt sich ein Hinweis auf die Effektivität des Kurses.
Vergleiche: Vortest.

CA:327, DA:345, DE:5, EN:287, ES:336, FR:305, GA:179, IT:271, NE:295, PO:310.

6 adaptiver Test Eine Testform, bei der die Einzelaufgaben während des Tests in Abhängigkeit von ihrer Schwierigkeit und der geschätzten Fähigkeit eines Prüflings ausgewählt werden. Oftmals als Begriff für computergestützte Tests verwendet, obwohl auch ein mündlicher Test ein adaptiver Test sein kann.
Siehe: computergestütztes, adaptives Testen.
Literatur: Bachman 1990, S.151; Henning 1987, S.136; Jäger & Petermann 1992, S.164–166.

CA:302, DA:102, DE:6, EN:7, ES:312, FR:361, GA:429, IT:356, NE:5, PO:363.

7 affektive Faktoren Nichtkognitive Faktoren, die sich auf emotionale Variablen, Vorlieben und Einstellungen des Testteilnehmers beziehen.
Vergleiche: kognitive Faktoren.
Literatur: Ebel & Frisbie 1991, S.52.

CA:177, DA:6, DE:7, EN:9, ES:195, FR:178, GA:399, IT:172, NE:6, PO:188.

8 Akkreditierung Die Gewährung einer Anerkennung für eine Prüfung, üblicherweise ausgesprochen von einer offiziellen Stelle wie eine Regierungsinstitution oder ein Prüfungsausschuß.

CA:4, DA:10, DE:8, EN:5, ES:1, FR:4, GA:92, IT:303, NE:3, PO:325.

9 Alpha-Fehler Vergleiche Definition von Fehler erster Art.

CA:140, DA:417, DE:9, EN:425, ES:150, FR:154, GA:126, IT:157, NE:405, PO:150.

10 Alpha-Koeffizient Eine Reliabilitätsschätzung über die Messung der inneren Konsistenz eines Tests. Der Wert von Alpha reicht von 0 bis 1. Er wird stärker für Einstufungsskalen verwendet als für Tests mit dichotomen Aufgaben, auch wenn er für beide Testarten verwendet werden kann.
Vergleiche: Kuder-Richardson.
Siehe: innere Konsistenz.

Literatur: Henning 1987, S.83–84; Lienert & Raatz 1994, S. 192.

CA:9, DA:11, DE:10, EN:10, ES:16, FR:8, GA:10, IT:10, NE:12, PO:6.

11 Alternativform Vergleiche Definition von äquivalente Formen.

CA:185, DA:12, DE:11, EN:11, ES:203, NE:13, FR:193, GA:146, IT:176, PO:199.

12 analytische Bewertung Eine Bewertungsmethode, die bei Sprachtests verwendet werden kann, in denen es um produktive Sprachverwendung geht, beispielsweise beim Sprechen und Schreiben. Der Beurteiler nimmt eine Einschätzung mit Hilfe einer Liste spezifischer Punkte vor. So kann beispielsweise bei einem Schreibtest die analytische Skala einen Schwerpunkt setzen bei Grammatik, Wortschatz oder der Benutzung von Satzverbindungen.
Vergleiche: globale Bewertung, Gesamteindruck.
Literatur: Ebel & Frisbie 1991, S.195; Weir 1990, S. 63.

CA:343, DA:13, DE:12, EN:14, ES:426, FR:266, GA:340, IT:27, NE:15, PO:58.

13 ANCOVA Ein Typ der Varianzanalyse, der eine Kontrolle der Effekte konfundierender Variablen erlaubt (Variablen, die sich in Abhängigkeit von der interessierenden Variable verändern).
Siehe: Varianzanalyse.
Literatur: Hatch & Lazarton 1991, S.387; Bortz 1993, S.332–356.

CA:21, DA:14, DE:13, EN:17, ES:27, FR:19, GA:20, IT:20, NE:16, PO:21.

14 angeglichene Testformen Verschiedene Testformen, deren Punktwertverteilungen so transformiert wurden, daß sie austauschbar sind.
Literatur: Crocker & Algina 1986, Kap. 20; Lienert & Raatz 1994, S.308–310.

CA:186, DA:442, DE:14, EN:126, ES:204, FR:194, GA:145, IT:177 NE:141, PO:200.

15 angeleitete Schreibaufgabe Vergleiche Definition von gelenkte Schreibaufgabe.

CA:392, DA:43, DE:15, EN:105, ES:6, FR:356, GA:376, IT:77, NE:144, PO:355.

16 Angleichung Methoden zur Anpassung nicht-äquivalenter Parallelformen.
Siehe: Angeglichene Testformen, Angleichung durch lineare Transformation, horizontale Angleichung, Äquiperzentil-Methode.

CA:186, DA:442, DE:16, EN:126, ES:204, FR:194, GA:145, IT:177 NE:141, PO:200.

17 Angleichung durch lineare Transformation Ein Ansatz zur Parallelisierung, bei dem einem bestimmten Wert bei einem Test ein Wert eines anderen Tests gleichgestellt wird. Die jeweils äquivalenten Werte der beiden Tests liegen bezogen auf die Standardabweichung gleich weit vom arithmetischen Mittel ihres Tests entfernt.
Siehe: Angleichung.
Literatur: Crocker & Algina, 1986, S.457–461; Lienert & Raatz, 1994, S. 309.

CA:134, DA:216, DE:17, EN:212, ES:142, FR:38, GA:91, IT:151, NE:229, PO:45.

18 Ankeraufgabe Eine Aufgabe, die in zwei oder mehr Tests enthalten ist. Ankeraufgaben haben bekannte Eigenschaften oder Kennwerte und bilden einen Teil einer neuen Testversion. Dadurch sind Informationen über die neue Version verfügbar und über die Prüflinge, die sie bearbeiteten. Mit Hilfe von Ankeraufgaben, deren statistische Werte festliegen, können andere Aufgaben eines neuen Test auf einer gemeinsamen Schwierigkeitsskala lokalisiert (d.h. geeicht) werden.
Vergleiche: Ankertest.
Siehe: Eichung.

CA:218, DA:16, DE:18, EN:15, ES:237, FR:225, GA:241, IT:212, NE:17, PO:232.

19 Ankertest Ein Test mit bekannten Meßeigenschaften, der zusammen mit einem anderen Test eingesetzt wird. Die mit dem Ankertest erfaßten Leistungen liefern Informationen über den anderen Test und über die Prüflinge, die beide Tests bearbeiteten.
Vergleiche: Ankeraufgabe.

CA:307, DA:17, DE:19, EN:16, ES:320, FR:367, GA:404, IT:357, NE:18, PO:365.

20 ANOVA Eine statistische Methode zur Prüfung der Nullhypothese, daß verschiedene Gruppenmittelwerte gleich sind. Die Streuung der Punktwerte in jeder Gruppe wird geprüft, ebenso wie die Streuung der Gruppenmittelwerte.
Literatur: Hatch & Lazarton 1991, S. 308–312; Bortz 1993, S. 223–331.

CA:22, DA:19, DE:20, EN:18, ES:28, FR:20, GA:21, IT:21, NE:19, PO:22.

21 Antwort Durch einen Test verursachtes Verhalten eines Prüflings. Beispielsweise die Antwort bei einer Multiple-Choice-Aufgabe oder das Ergebnis eines schriftlich zu bearbeitenden Tests.
Vergleiche: Testvorgabe, Vorgaben.

CA:374, DA:315, DE:21, EN:331, ES:371, FR:327, GA:153, IT:305, NE:319, PO:334.

22 Antwortbogen Das Formular, auf dem ein Prüfling seine Lösungen aufschreibt oder markiert.
Vergleiche: optischer Belegleser.
CA:191, DA:37, DE:22, EN:19, ES:219, FR:181, GA:152, IT:174, NE:20, PO:198.

23 Anweisung Instruktionen, die einem Prüfling gegeben werden, um seine Antworten bei einer bestimmten Testaufgabe zu lenken.
Vergleiche: Aufgabe.
CA:384, DA:264, DE:23, EN:336, ES:229, FR:78, GA:295, IT:193, NE:219, PO:92.

24 Äquiperzentil-Methode Methode zur Angleichung der Rohwerte zweier Tests, wobei sie als äquivalent angesehen werden, wenn in der gleichen Personengruppe die Prozentränge miteinander übereinstimmen.
Literatur: Lienert & Raatz 1994, S. 310–312.
CA:132, DA:440, DE:24, EN:127, ES:140, FR:36, GA:88, IT:150, NE:121, PO:43.

25 äquivalente Formen Auch bekannt als parallele oder alternative Formen. Verschiedene Versionen desselben Tests werden als parallel oder äquivalent angesehen, weil sie in der gleichen Weise spezifiziert sind und das gleiche Merkmal messen. Um die strengen Äquivalenzbedingungen der klassischen Testtheorie zu erfüllen, müssen die verschiedenen Formen beim Einsatz bei der gleichen Personenstichprobe die gleiche mittlere Schwierigkeit, Varianz und Kovarianz mit einem konkurrenten Kriterium aufweisen. In der Praxis ist es sehr schwer, echte Parallelformen zu entwickeln.
Vergleiche: angeglichene Testformen.
Literatur: Crocker & Algina 1986, S.132; Lienert & Raatz 1994, S.297–315.
CA:187, DA:441, DE:25, EN:128 ES:205, FR:195, GA:143, IT:178, NE:122, PO:201.

26 Aufgabe Kombination aus allgemeiner Anweisung, Aufgabenstellung und Beantwortung, z.B. ein Lesetext mit mehreren Multiple-Choice-Fragen, die alle nach der gleichen allgemeinen Anweisung beantwortet werden können.
CA:391, DA:260, DE:26, EN:393, ES:2, FR:354, GA:371, IT:71, NE:270, PO:352.

27 Aufgabe mit mehrstufiger Bewertung Lösungen werden mit mehr als einem Punkt (0=falsch, 1=richtig) bewertet, je nach dem Grad ihrer Korrektheit. Vor allem in Tests zum schriftlichen bzw. mündlichen Ausdruck.
Siehe: mehrstufige Punktevergabe.
CA:222, DA:342, DE:27, EN:342, ES:248, FR:230, GA:252, IT:220, NE:328, PO:242.

28 Aufgabenbanken Ansatz zur Verwaltung von Testaufgaben, der die Speicherung von Informationen über die Aufgaben umfaßt, so daß es möglich ist, Tests mit beliebig festlegbarem Inhalt und wählbarer Schwierigkeit zu konstruieren. Normalerweise wird eine computergestützte Datenbank verwendet und auf der Grundlage probabilistischer Testmodelle gearbeitet, wodurch die Aufgaben auf einer gemeinsamen Schwierigkeitsskala lokalisiert werden können.
Literatur: Henning 1987, Kap. 9.
CA:36, DA:155, DE:28, EN:191, ES:37, FR:28, GA:40, IT:111, NE:199, PO:37.

29 Aufgabenstamm Teil einer schriftlichen Aufgabenstellung, meist ein unvollständiger Satz, der vervollständigt werden muß durch Eintragung der Ergänzung oder Auswahl einer von mehreren Möglichkeiten.
Vergleiche: Schlüsselantwort, Auswahlantwort.
CA:276, DA:360, DE:29, EN:387, ES:139, FR:10, GA:160, IT:346, NE:359, PO:224.

30 Aufgabentyp Aufgaben werden mit Bezeichnungen versehen, durch die beschrieben wird, was damit geprüft wird und in welcher Form dies geschieht, z.B. Multiple-Choice-Leseverständnistest, Schreiben nach Leitpunkten.
CA:408, DA:265, DE:30, EN:394, ES:402, FR:407, GA:59, IT:393, NE:271, PO:401.

31 Aufgabenvorrevision Teil des Prozesses der Aufgabenentwicklung für einen Test. In diesem Stadium wird das vorgelegte Aufgabenmaterial kritisch von einer Anzahl von Personen geprüft, die dann darüber entscheiden, ob die Aufgaben für den Einsatz geeignet sind (eventuell nach einer Überarbeitung) oder ob auf sie ganz verzichtet werden sollte.
Vergleiche: Testredaktion.
CA:263, DA:410, DE:31, EN:237, ES:277, FR:256, GA:260, IT:250, NE:247, PO:270.

32 Aufsatz Aufgabe, bei der vom Prüfling die Erstellung eines ausführlichen geschriebenen Textes verlangt wird. Übliche Aufgaben sind das Erzählen eines Ereignisses oder die Diskussion von Themen, wobei unterschiedliche Sichtweisen zu berücksichtigen sind.
CA:366, DA:109, DE:32, EN:62, ES:192, FR:73, GA:51, IT:82, NE:372, PO:88.

33 Aufsatz-Aufgabe Vergleiche Defi-

nition von Aufsatz.
CA:366, DA:262, DE:33, EN:131, ES:306, FR:159, GA:7, IT:313, NE:125, PO:142.

34 Augenscheinvalidität Vergleiche Definition von Face-Validität.
CA:417, DA:272, DE:34, EN:140, ES:414, FR:414 GA:2, IT:402, NE:174, PO:410.

35 ausführliche Antwort Antwortform einer Aufgabe, bei der vom Prüfling erwartet wird, daß er eine längere Antwort als einen oder zwei Sätze produziert (im Gegensatz zur Auswahl einer vorgegebenen Lösung).
Vergleiche: Kurzantwort-Aufgabe.
CA:378, DA:423, DE:35, EN:138, ES:375, FR:332, GA:159, IT:308, NE:407, PO:339.

36 Auslesetest Vergleiche Definition von Selektionstest.
CA:323, DA:330, DE:36, EN:353, ES:332, FR:382, GA:430, IT:370, NE:333, PO:383.

37 Auswahlantwort Art der Reaktion bei einer Testaufgabe, die darin besteht, daß aus einer Anzahl von Alternativen ausgewählt wird und nicht die Antwort frei zu ergänzen ist.
Vergleiche: freie Antwort.
Siehe: Antwort.
CA:379, DA:422, DE:37, EN:352, ES:377, FR:334, GA:158, IT:310, NE:154, PO:341.

38 Auswahlmöglichkeiten Die verschiedenen Möglichkeiten bei Multiple-Choice-Aufgaben oder Zuordnungsaufgaben, von denen die richtige ausgewählt werden muß.
CA:279, DA:425, DE:38, EN:262, ES:292, FR:290, GA:293, IT:258, NE:14, PO:294.

39 Auswerter Eine Person, die den schriftlichen Antworten eines Prüflings einen Zahlenwert zuordnet. Dies kann sowohl eine Experteneinschätzung beinhalten als auch bei mechanischer Auswertung die weitgehend schematische Verwendung eines Lösungsschlüssels.
Vergleiche: Bewerter.
CA:90, DA:288, DE:39, EN:221, ES:83, FR:81, GA:225, IT:102, NE:80, PO:182.

40 Auswertung Zuordnung eines Wertes zu den Antworten in einem Test. Dies bezieht sich sowohl auf Expertenbeurteilung als auch die Verwendung eines Lösungsschlüssels, in dem alle akzeptablen Antworten aufgelistet sind.
CA:80, DA:289, DE:40, EN:222, ES:47, FR:265, GA:218, IT:29, NE:83, PO:57.

41 authentischer Text In einem Test verwendeter Text, der aus Material besteht, das ursprünglich für andere Zwecke geschrieben wurde als für einen Sprachtest.
Vergleiche: halbauthentischer Text.
CA:404, DA:22, DE:41, EN:25, ES:401, FR:111, GA:382, IT:390, NE:24, PO:127.

42 Authentizität Zur Charakterisierung eines Tests bezeichnet der Begriff das Ausmaß, in dem der Test Sprachbenutzung außerhalb einer Testsituation widerspiegelt.
Literatur: Bachman 1990, S.300–303.
CA:27, DA:21, DE:42, EN:24, ES:33, FR:24, GA:115, IT:35, NE:23, PO:26.

43 Backwash (Wechselwirkung) Die Auswirkung eines Tests auf die Unterrichtsgestaltung. Lehrer können dadurch beeinflußt sein, daß ihre Schüler die Teilnahme an einem bestimmten Test planen, und passen deshalb ihre Unterrichtsmethode und die Themen den Anforderungen des Tests an. Das kann positive oder negative Auswirkungen haben. Auch der Begriff 'Washback' ist gebräuchlich.
Siehe: Wirkung.
CA:372, DA:25, DE:43, EN:28, ES:369, FR:322, GA:95, IT:147, NE:27, PO:135.

44 Bandbreite Im weitesten Sinne Teil einer Skala. In einem aufgabenbezogenen Test bezeichnet Bandbreite einen Wertebereich der Skala, dem man einen bestimmten Punktwert oder eine Note zuordnet. In Einschätzungsskalen zur Erfassung bestimmter Eigenschaften oder Fähigkeiten bezeichnet die Bandbreite ein bestimmtes Leistungsniveau.
CA:37, DA:339, DE:44, EN:29, ES:38, FR:200, GA:41, IT:39 NE:28, PO:210.

45 Bedarfsanalyse Möglichkeit zur Ermittlung der Anforderungen oder Bedürfnisse (in Form von Fertigkeiten, Aufgaben, Wortschatz usw.) einer bestimmten Lernergruppe zum Zweck der Festlegung für sie geeigneter Kursinhalte.
CA:16, DA:35, DE:45, EN:246, ES:21, FR:11, GA:19, IT:13, NE:31, PO:17.

46 begleitende Evaluation Fortlaufende Evaluierung eines Prozesses, wodurch eine ständige Anpassung und Verbesserung dieses Prozesses gewährleistet ist. Sie kann sich auf ein Unterrichtsprogramm beziehen.
Vergleiche: abschließende Evaluation.
CA:32, DA:226, DE:46, EN:148, ES:184, FR:168, GA:236, IT:414, NE:136, PO:32.

47 Beherrschung Kenntnis einer Sprache und Fertigkeit bei ihrer Anwendung sowohl in schriftlicher als auch mündlicher Form.
Vergleiche: Fähigkeit, Kompetenz.

Literatur: Bachman 1990, S.16.
CA:296, DA:296, DE:47, EN:295, ES:120, FR:260, GA:265, IT:62, NE:305, PO:273.

48 Benotung Prozeß der Umrechnung von Test- oder Punktwerten in Noten.

CA:362, DA:168, DE:48, EN:157, ES:47, FR:52, GA:165, IT:94, NE:427, PO:277.

49 Beobachtungswert Von dem Prüfling erzielter Punktwert. In der klassischen Testtheorie geht man davon aus, daß sich dieser aus wahrem Wert und Fehler zusammensetzt.
Siehe: Fehler, wahrer Wert.

CA:353, DA:183, DE:49, EN:258, ES:352, FR:279, GA:331, IT:283, NE:429, PO:285.

50 bereichsspezifischer Test Test, dessen Ergebnisse vor dem Hintergrund eines bestimmten Inhalts- oder Fähigkeitsbereichs interpretiert werden.
Vergleiche: kriteriumsorientierter Test, normorientierter Test.

CA:335, DA:84, DE:50, EN:120, ES:342, FR:391, GA:417, IT:382, NE:114, PO:368.

51 beschreibende (deskriptive) Statistik Statistiken, die zur Beschreibung von Datensätzen in Form etwa von Mengen, Streuungen, Durchschnittswerten oder Korrelationen mit anderen Daten verwendet werden. Unterschieden wird zwischen beschreibender und schließender Statistik.
Vergleiche: schließende Statistik (Inferenzstatistik).

CA:165, DA:63, DE:51, EN:95, ES:172, FR:349, GA:365, IT:340, NE:95, PO:176.

52 Bestehensgrenze Minimaler Punktwert, den ein Prüfling erreichen muß, um den Test oder die Prüfung zu bestehen.
Vergleiche: kritischer Wert (cut-off).

CA:23, DA:36, DE:52, EN:273, ES:30, FR:277, GA:278, IT:288 NE:341, PO:282.

53 Beta-Fehler Vergleiche Definition von Fehler zweiter Art.

CA:141, DA:418, DE:53, EN:426, ES:151, FR:155, GA:127, IT:158, NE:406, PO:151.

54 Beurteilung Bei Sprachtests die Messung eines oder mehrerer Aspekte der Sprachbeherrschung mit einer bestimmten Methode oder Prozedur.
Literatur: Bachman 1990, S.50.

CA:31, DA:30, DE:54, EN:21, ES:180, FR:165, GA:229, IT:421, NE:39, PO:30.

55 Bewerter Eine Person, die der Leistung eines Prüflings in einem Test einen bestimmten Punktwert zuweist, wobei eine subjektive Bewertung erforderlich ist. Bewerter sind normalerweise im entsprechenden Tätigkeitsbereich qualifiziert und müssen sich einem Trainingsprozeß unterziehen sowie bestimmten Standardisierungen unterwerfen. Bei mündlichen Prüfungen haben Bewerter und Fragesteller, auch bezeichnet als Prüfer, etwas unterschiedliche Funktionen.
Vergleiche: Fragesteller.

CA:35, DA:32, DE:55, EN:22, ES:46, FR:174, GA:234, IT:165, NE:33, PO:182.

56 Bewerter-Übereinstimmung Vergleiche Definition von Interrater-Übereinstimmung, Intrarater-Übereinstimmung.

CA:1, DA:307, DE:56, EN:312, ES:10, FR:1, GA:70, IT:84, NE:36, PO:1.

57 Bewertung a) Prozeß der Zuweisung eines Punktwerts zu einer erbrachten Testleistung durch subjektive Beurteilung.

b) Der bei der Bewertung vergebene Punktwert.

CA:428, DA:171, DE:57, EN:314, ES:425, FR:265, GA:286, IT:54, NE:38, PO:57.

58 Bewertungsanleitung Aus mehreren rangmäßig abgestuften Kategorien bestehende Skala, die für die subjektive Bewertung des freien schriftlichen und mündlichen Ausdrucks verwendet wird. Bei Sprachtests werden die Skalen üblicherweise mit Leistungsbeschreibungen versehen, wodurch die Interpretation klarer wird.
Vergleiche: Likert-Skala.
Siehe: Deskriptor.

CA:154, DA:172, DE:58, EN:315, ES:161, FR:130, GA:319, IT:323, NE:40, PO:160.

59 bimodale Verteilung Eine zweigipflige Häufigkeitsverteilung, die vermuten läßt, daß innerhalb einer Stichprobe zwei verschiedene Gruppen enthalten sind.

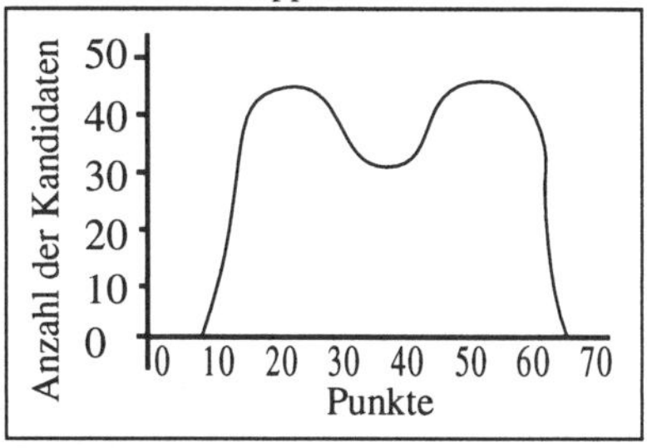

Vergleiche: Normalverteilung.
Siehe: Modalwert.
Literatur: Hatch & Lazarton 1991, S. 165–166; Lienert & Raatz 1994, 152–153; Bortz 1993, S. 34–37.

CA:112, DA:39, DE:59, EN:34, ES:113, FR:106, GA:104, IT:131, NE:47, PO:121.

60 biseriale Korrelation Ein Kennwert für die Diskriminationsfähigkeit einer dichotomen Aufgabe (d.h. die Aufgabe wird mit 0 und 1 Punkt bewertet), normalerweise mit r_{bis} bezeichnet. Korrelation zwischen einem Kriterium (normalerweise der Gesamttestwert) und der Fähigkeit, die einer richtig-falsch-Antwort bei einer Aufgabe zugrundeliegt. Der Wert von r_{bis} liegt um etwa 25% über dem Wert der punktbiserialen Korrelation (r_{pbi}). Ein Vorteil von r_{bis} ist seine relative Stabilität über Personenstichproben unterschiedlichen Fähigkeitsniveaus hinweg.
Vergleiche: punkt-biseriale Korrelation.
Siehe: Trennschärfe.
Literatur: Crocker & Algina 1986, S.317–318; Guilford & Fruchter 304–311; Bortz 1993, S. 208–209.

CA:56, DA:40, DE:60, EN:35, ES:85, FR:86, GA:79, IT:96, NE:48, PO:101.

61 Bodeneffekt Vergleiche Definition von Floor-Effekt.

CA:122, DA:42, DE:61, EN:146, ES:130, FR:141, GA:175, IT:144, NE:49, PO:130.

62 C-Test Eine bestimmte Form eines Lückentests, bei dem die zweite Hälfte bestimmter Wörter weggelassen wurde. Im Extrem kann die zweite Hälfte jedes zweiten Wortes weggelassen sein. Die Aufgabe des Prüflings besteht darin, die Lücken zu füllen.
Siehe: Cloze-Test.
Literatur: Weir 1990, S.49; Grotjahn, 1992.

CA:304, DA:45, DE:62, EN:38, ES:314, FR:394, GA:408, IT:384, NE:51, PO:366.

63 Ceiling-Effekt Ein Grenzeffekt, der sich ergibt, wenn ein Test für eine bestimmte Personengruppe zu leicht ist, so daß alle Testwerte am oberen Rand der Verteilung liegen.
Siehe: Grenzeffekte, Floor-Effekt.

CA:123, DA:219, DE:63, EN:44, ES:129, FR:140, GA:173, IT:145, NE:292, PO:137.

64 Checkliste Liste von Fragen oder Aspekten, die beantwortet oder abgedeckt sein sollten. Wird bei Sprachprüfungen als Beobachtungs- oder Analysemittel verwendet.

CA:240, DA:48, DE:64, EN:48, ES:258, FR:239, GA:351, IT:228, NE:58, PO:252.

65 Chi-Quadrat-Test Statistisches Verfahren zum Vergleich von beobachteten und erwarteten Werten zur Prüfung, ob die Differenz zwischen ihnen signifikant ist. Es handelt sich dabei um ein nicht-parametrisches Verfahren.
Siehe: nicht-parametrische Verfahren.
Literatur: Hatch & Lazarton 1991, S.393–415; Bortz 1993, 153–63.

CA:330, DA:49, DE:65, EN:49, ES:396, FR:149, GA:409, IT:359, NE:59, PO:395.

66 Cloze-Test Lückentest, in dem ganze Wörter weggelassen werden. Im herkömmlichen Cloze wird jedes n-te Wort weggelassen. Andere Lückentests, in denen kurze Satzteile weggelassen werden oder in denen der Testautor die wegzulassenden Wörter auswählt, werden auch als Cloze-Tests bezeichnet, z.B. ‘rationaler Cloze’. Prüflinge müssen entweder die Lücken frei ergänzen (offener Cloze-Test) oder aus mehreren Möglichkeiten auswählen (Multiple-Choice-Cloze-Test oder Lückentest mit Schüttelkasten). Die Bewertung des offenen Cloze-Tests kann entweder das exakt richtige Wort fordern (nur das tatsächlich im Originaltext enthaltene Wort wird als richtig bewertet) oder ein akzeptables Wort (Auswerter arbeiten mit einer Liste zulässiger Antworten).
Vergleiche: C-Test, Lückenaufgabe.
Literatur: Weir 1990, S.46–48; Oller 1979, Kap. 12.

CA:313, DA:50, DE:66, EN:52, ES:315, FR:370, GA:410, IT:362, NE:61, PO:378.

67 computergestütztes, adaptives Testen Methode des computergestützten Testens, bei der der Schwierigkeitsgrad der vorgelegten Aufgaben in Abhängigkeit von den Antworten eines Prüflings an sein Fähigkeitsniveau angepaßt werden kann.
Siehe: computergestütztes Testen (computergestützte Beurteilung).

CA:303, DA:51, DE:67, EN:63, ES:181, FR:362, GA:379, IT:386, NE:68, PO:364.

68 computergestütztesTesten (computergestützte Beurteilung) Test- oder Prüfungsmethode, bei der die Aufgaben vom Computer vorgegeben und u.U. auch per Computereingabe zu beantworten sind.
Siehe: adaptiver Test.

CA:332, DA:52, DE:68, EN:64, ES:182, FR:171, GA:380, IT:387, NE:70, PO:35.

69 computerlesbare Markierung Es gibt unterschiedliche Vorgehensweisen, um bei objektiven Tests durch den Einsatz eines Computersystems Auswertungsfehler zu minimieren. Ein optischer Belegleser kann beispielsweise die Markierungen eines Prüflings von seinem Antwortbogen ab-lesen und dadurch Daten für die Berechnung eines Gesamt-Punktwerts oder für

weitergehende Analysen bereitstellen.
CA:85, DA:53, DE:69, EN:65, ES:82, FR:273, GA:222, IT:28, NE:69, PO:66.

70 Cronbachs Alpha Vergleiche Definition von Alpha-Koeffizient.
CA:10, DA:54, DE:70, EN:84, ES:17, FR:9, GA:11, IT:11, NE:89, PO:7.

71 Curriculum Eine umfassende Beschreibung von Zielen, Inhalt, Organisation, Methoden und Bewertung eines Lehrgangs oder Unterrichts.
Siehe: Lehrplan.
CA:94, DA:55, DE:71, EN:87, ES:93, FR:93, GA:99, IT:113, NE:220, PO:107.

72 D-Index Trennschärfe-Index für Testaufgaben. Wird meist bei kleinen im Klassenverband durchgeführten Tests verwendet, da er sich mit der Hand berechnen läßt. In Abhängigkeit vom Gesamtpunktwert werden zwei Gruppen von Personen mit guten und schlechten Leistungen so zusammengestellt, daß sich in jeder der beiden Gruppen zwischen 10% und 33% der Testteilnehmer befinden. Bei normalverteilten Testwerten ist es am besten, wenn sich 27% in jeder der beiden Gruppen befinden. Für beide Gruppen wird die Anzahl richtiger Lösungen berechnet. Gut diskriminierende Aufgaben sind dadurch gekennzeichnet, daß die Gruppe mit den insgesamt guten Leistungen eine höhere Zahl richtiger Lösungen aufweist als die Gruppe mit den schlechten Leistungen. Der D-Index wird nach folgender Formel berechnet:

$$D = R_{sup} - R_{inf}$$

wobei Rsup die Anzahl der richtigen Lösungen in der besseren Gruppe und Rinf die Anzahl der richtigen Lösungen in der schlechteren Gruppe bezeichnet. Im allgemeinen werden Aufgaben als trennscharf betrachtet, wenn sich ein Index von 0,3 oder höher ergibt.
Literatur: Lienert & Raatz 1994, S. 95.
CA:206, DA:59, DE:72, EN:91, ES:223, FR:208, GA:186, IT:194, NE:92, PO:218.

73 Deckeneffekt Vergleiche Definition von Ceiling-Effekt.
CA:123, DA:219, DE:73, EN:44, ES:129, FR:140, GA:173, IT:145, NE:292, PO:137.

74 Delta-Plot-Methode Eine Methode zur Prüfung, ob Aufgaben in verschiedenen Personenstichproben eine unterschiedliche Funktion haben. Sie wird verwendet, um Aufgaben zu identifizieren, die Unterschiede in gruppenspezifischen Leistungen überhöht oder zu gering darstellen. Sie basiert auf klassischen Aufgabenschwierigkeiten (*p*-Werte). Die *p*-Werte werden in normalisierte *z*-Werte transformiert und dann paarweise grafisch dargestellt, um so die Schwierigkeiten in den beiden vorliegenden Personengruppen vergleichen zu können.
Siehe: Differential Item Functioning.
Literatur: Crocker & Algina 1986, S.388–390.
CA:249, DA:61, DE:74, EN:92, ES:267, FR:246, GA:256, IT:237, NE:93, PO:260.

75 Delta-Skala Eine normalisierte Skala mit Mittelwert 13 und Standardabweichung 4.
CA:155, DA:60, DE:75, EN:93, ES:162, FR:132, GA:314, IT:321, NE:94, PO:165.

76 Deskriptor Eine kurze Beschreibung, die einem Wertebereich auf einer Bewertungsskala beigefügt wird und das Leistungsniveau derjenigen Personen kennzeichnet, die den entsprechenden Punktwert erzielten.
CA:97, DA:64, DE:76, EN:96, ES:98, FR:97, GA:437, IT:118, NE:96, PO:113.

77 diagnostischer Test Test, der zur Entdeckung der spezifischen Stärken oder Schwächen eines Lernenden eingesetzt wird. Das Ergebnis wird herangezogen, um Entscheidungen über den künftigen Unterricht, Lehr- und Lernablauf zu treffen.
CA:317, DA:65, DE:77, EN:97, ES:325, FR:383, GA:414, IT:373, NE:97, PO:386.

78 Differential Item Functioning Die Tatsache, daß die relative Schwierigkeit einer Aufgabe abhängt von bestimmten Merkmalen der Gruppe, die diese Aufgabe zu bearbeiten hatte, wie Muttersprache oder Geschlecht.
Siehe: Stichprobenverzerrung.
CA:195, DA:66, DE:78, EN:100, ES:209, FR:192, GA:114, IT:182, NE:100, PO:208.

79 Diktat Testaufgabe, bei der der Prüfling einen Text hören und die gehörten Worte niederschreiben muß. Die Auswertungskriterien können je nach Testzweck unterschiedlich sein und umfassen meistens Rechtschreibung und Zeichensetzung.
CA:103, DA:68, DE:79, EN:99, ES:105, FR:99, GA:109, IT:121, NE:99, PO:125.

80 Diplom Dokument, das für eine bestimmte Person die Teilnahme an einer Prüfung oder an einem Teil einer Prüfung und die erreichte Note bzw. mindestens das Bestehen der Prüfung bestätigt. Diplome werden oft als höhere Qualifikationsnachweise betrachtet als Zertifikate.

Vergleiche: Zertifikat.
CA:104, DA:69, DE:80, EN:103, ES:106, FR:100, GA:118, IT:124, NE:101, PO:115.

81 direktes Prüfverfahren Test, der produktive Fertigkeiten beim Sprechen oder Schreiben mißt. Dabei wird unmittelbar bei der Ausübung der Fertigkeit gemessen. Ein Beispiel für die Prüfung der Schreibfähigkeit ist die Anforderung an den Prüfling, einen Brief zu schreiben.
Vergleiche: Indirektes Prüfverfahren.
Literatur: Hughes 1989, S.14–16.
CA:326, DA:70, DE:81, EN:104, ES:335, FR:384, GA:415, IT:375, NE:102, PO:387.

82 Discrete-Point-Item Eine Einzelaufgabe. Prüft einen spezifischen Punkt wie Struktur oder Wortschatz unabhängig von allen anderen Aufgaben. Discrete-Point Sprachtests wurden in den 60er Jahren z.B. durch Robert Lado entwickelt.
Vergleiche: integrierte Aufgabe.
Siehe: unabhängige (diskrete) Aufgabe.
CA:225, DA:72, DE:82, EN:110, ES:247 FR:229, GA:251, IT:210, NE:107, PO:240.

83 diskriminante Validität Einem Test wird diskriminante Validität zugesprochen, wenn er niedriger mit Tests für andere Merkmale korreliert als mit Tests, die das gleiche Merkmal möglicherweise mit einer anderen Methode messen. Dies wird als Aspekt der Konstruktvalidität angesehen.
Siehe: Konstruktvalidität, konvergente Validität.
Literatur: Crocker & Algina 1986, S.23; Guilford & Fruchter 1981, S. 436–437; Lienert & Raatz 1994, S. 227.
CA:423, DA:73, DE:83, EN:111, ES:420, FR:420, GA:36, IT:408, NE:108, PO:416.

84 Diskriminationsparameter Parameter probabilistischer Testmodelle, der sich darauf bezieht, wie gut eine Aufgabe zwischen verschiedenen Personen zu unterscheiden gestattet (auch als A-Parameter der Item-Response-Theorie bezeichnet).
Vergleiche: probabilistische Testmodelle.
Literatur: Bachman 1990, S.204; Jäger & Petermann 1992 S. 323; Kubinger 1989, S.39.
CA:281, DA:1, DE:84, EN:1, ES:294, FR:292, GA:273, IT:260, NE:1, PO:297.

85 Diskurs Gesprochener oder geschriebener Text, der als kommunikatives Sprachhandeln betrachtet wird.
CA:106, DA:75, DE:85, EN:106, ES:108, FR:101, GA:119, IT:125, NE:103, PO:117.

86 Diskursanalyse Analysemethode, die sich auf Struktur und Funktion verschiedener Arten gesprochener oder geschriebener Texte bezieht.
CA:19, DA:76, DE:86, EN:107, ES:24, FR:13, GA:17, IT:16, NE: 104, PO:19.

87 Diskursfähigkeit Die Fähigkeit, Texte zu verstehen bzw. zu produzieren. In einigen Modellen über sprachliche Kompetenz wird diese als eine Komponente betrachtet.
Literatur: Bachman 1990, Kap. 4.
CA:66, DA:78, DE:87, EN:108, ES:62, FR:64, GA:196, IT:64, NE:105, PO:78.

88 Distraktor Jede falsche Auswahlantwort in einer Multiple-Choice-Aufgabe.
Vergleiche: Schlüsselantwort.
Siehe: Multiple-Choice-Aufgabe.
Literatur: Ebel & Frisbie 1986, S.176–185, Lienert & Raatz 1994, S.101–104.
CA:110, DA:79, DE:88, EN:115, ES:111, FR:104, GA:348, IT:129, NE:8, PO:126.

89 Distraktorenanalyse Häufigkeit der Wahl jedes Distraktors einer Multiple-Choice-Aufgabe. Die Analyse zeigt die Beliebtheit jedes Distraktors an.
CA:243, DA:80, DE:89, EN:116, ES:71, FR:301, GA:384, IT:88, NE:9, PO:96.

90 divergente Validität Vergleiche Definition von diskriminante Validität.
CA:424, DA:81, DE:90, EN:118, ES:421, FR:421, GA:35, IT:409, NE:111, PO:417.

91 Doppelbewertung Beurteilungsmethode, bei der zwei Bewerter eine Testleistung unabhängig voneinander bewerten.
Siehe: Mehrfach-Bewertung.
CA:84, DA:82, DE:91, EN:121, ES:118, FR:114, GA:221, IT:104, NE:116, PO:61.

92 Ebels D Vergleiche Definition von D-Index.
CA:96, DA:85, DE:92, EN:122, ES:96, FR:94, GA:101, IT:116, NE:117, PO:111.

93 eichen In probabilistischen Testmodellen Schätzung der Schwierigkeit eines Aufgabensatzes.
Siehe: Eichung.
CA:43, DA:163, DE:93, EN:39, ES:43, FR:40, GA:48, IT:43, NE:206, PO:47.

94 Eichung Der Prozeß der Skalenbestimmung eines Tests. Eichung kann auf Ankeraufgaben aus unterschiedlichen Tests basieren mit dem Ziel, eine gemeinsame Schwierigkeitsskala (die Theta-Skala) zu bilden. Wenn ein Test aus geeichten Aufgaben konstruiert wird, sind die Punktwerte des Tests direkter Ausdruck der Fähigkeit

des Prüflings, ausgedrückt durch die Lokalisierung der Person auf der Theta-Skala.
CA:44, DA:164, DE:94, EN:40, ES:42, FR:35, GA:49, IT:44, NE:205, PO:42.

95 Eigenschaft Physisches oder psychisches Merkmal einer Person (wie sprachliche Fähigkeit).
CA:411, DA:416, DE:95, EN:415, ES:360, FR:23, GA:400, IT:26, NE:403, PO:403.

96 Eignungstest Test, der entwickelt wurde, um die Erfolgsaussichten einer Person auf einem bestimmten Lerngebiet vorherzusagen oder zu messen, z.B. Erfolgsaussichten beim Sprachenlernen oder einem bestimmten Lehrgang.
Literatur: Henning 1987, S.6; Ebel & Frisbie 1991, S.339; Fisseni 1990, S.192–194.
CA:308, DA:18, DE:96, EN:20, ES:322, FR:368, GA:421, IT:358, NE:22, PO:370.

97 Eindimensionalität Die Annahme nur einer einzigen Merkmalsdimension, was eine notwendige Annahme darstellt, wenn ein Meßinstrument zur Erfassung psychologischer Eigenschaften etwa über probabilistische Testmodelle konstruiert werden soll. Eindimensionalität ist ein Merkmal des Meßinstruments, nicht des dahinterstehenden psychologischen Prozesses, der auch komplex sein kann.
Literatur: Crocker & Algina 1986 S.343.
CA:413, DA:90, DE:97, EN:427, ES:410, FR:408, GA:23, IT:398, NE:119, PO:406.

98 Eingangstest Kurzer und schnell durchzuführender Test zur Identifikation derjenigen Personen, die zur Teilnahme an einem Kurs oder einer Prüfung zugelassen werden können.
Vergleiche: Einstufungstest.
CA:316, DA:424, DE:98, EN:349, ES:332, FR:375, GA:432, IT:370, NE:332, PO:375.

99 einparametrisches Modell In probabilistischen Testmodellen ein Modell, das auf einer Skala Schwierigkeit (der Aufgaben) und Fähigkeit (der Personen) abbildet und nicht von variablen Trennschärfen und Rateparametern ausgeht. Dies entspricht dem Rasch-Modell.
Vergleiche: Rasch-Modell.
CA:255, DA:92, DE:99, EN:259, ES:273, FR:249, GA:296, IT:242, NE:118, PO:265.

100 Einschätzung Vergleiche Definition von Bewerter.
CA:361, DA:306, DE:100, EN:311, ES:187, FR:164, GA:287, IT:102, NE:34, PO:182.

101 Einstufungstest Test, der durchgeführt wird, um Schüler oder Studenten der Gruppe oder Klasse zuzuordnen, die ihnen hinsichtlich ihres Kenntnis- oder Fähigkeitsniveaus am besten entspricht.
Literatur: Fisseni 1990, S.250–255.
CA:311, DA:137, DE:101, EN:282, ES:323, FR:377, GA:434, IT:365, NE:291, PO:372.

102 Ergänzungsaufgabe Aufgabentyp, bei dem der Prüfling einen Satz oder Ausdruck zu ergänzen hat. Üblicherweise müssen einige Wörter oder Einzelheiten wie Zeiten oder Telefonnummern eingesetzt werden.
CA:226, DA:421, DE:102, EN:60, ES:238, FR:223, GA:243, IT:215, NE:193, PO:234.

103 Ergebnis Resultat einer Prüfung oder eines Tests, wie es dem Prüfling mitgeteilt wird.
CA:380, DA:317, DE:103, EN:332, ES:378, FR:336, GA:397, IT:312, NE:322, PO:342.

104 Erprobung Stadium der Entwicklung von Testaufgaben, in dem geprüft wird, ob der Test in der erwarteten Weise funktioniert. Es handelt sich dabei oft um freie Aufgaben, wie z.B. Aufsatz, die von einer eingeschränkten Stichprobe gelöst werden.
CA:26, DA:301, DE:104, EN:418, ES:135, FR:160, GA:436, IT:336, NE:303, PO:185.

105 erwartete Antwort Antwort oder Antworten, die der Autor einer Aufgabe zu erreichen hofft.
CA:377, DA:106, DE:105, EN:137, ES:374, FR:328, GA:157, IT:306, NE:32, PO:338.

106 Evaluation Systematische Informationssammlung als Grundlage für eine Entscheidungsfindung. Bei Sprachprüfungen kann sich die Evaluation auf die Effektivität oder Auswirkungen eines Lernprogramms, einer Prüfung oder eines Projekts beziehen.
CA:31, DA:93, DE:106, EN:132, ES:180, FR:166, GA:235, IT:413, NE:126, PO:30.

107 Expertenbewertung Beurteilungsmethode, die von Bewertern durchgeführt wird, die über ein besonderes Fachwissen verfügen und besonders ausgebildet wurden, um subjektive Bewertungen vornehmen zu können. Tests zur Prüfung der Sprech- und Schreibfertigkeit werden üblicherweise von solchen Bewertern beurteilt.
Vergleiche: mechanische Auswertung.
CA:81, DA:29, DE:107, EN:136, ES:81, FR:272, GA:223, IT:30, NE:131, PO:67.

108 Exzeß Kennwert für das Ausmaß, in dem eine Verteilung flacher oder spitzer als eine Normalverteilung ist. Daten, die sich in einer flachen Kurve verteilen, bezeichnet man als breitgipflige Verteilung, während Daten, die zu einer sehr spitzen Verteilung führen, eine schmalgipflige Verteilung ergeben.

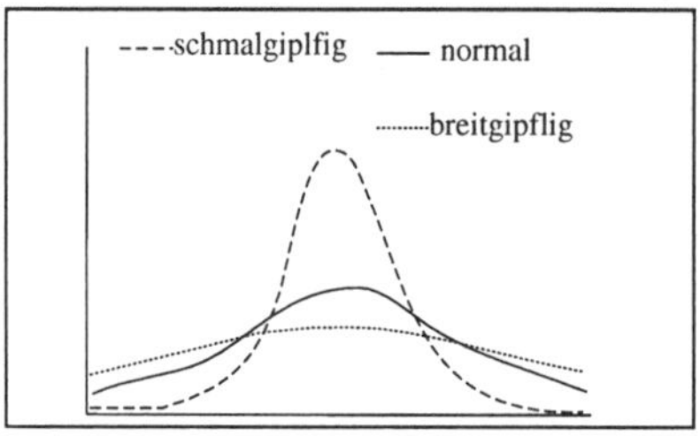

Siehe: Normalverteilung.
Literatur: Bortz 1993, S.45–46.
CA:95, DA:412, DE:108, EN:202, ES:94, FR:428, GA:100, IT:114, NE:213, PO:108.

109 F-Wert In der Varianzanalyse der Wert, der anzeigt, ob der Unterschied zwischen verschiedenen Gruppenmittelwerten statistisch signifikant ist; beispielsweise ob sich Gruppen mit unterschiedlicher Vorbildung hinsichtlich ihrer Leistungen bei einem Sprachtest signifikant voneinander unterscheiden.
Literatur: Hatch & Lazarton 1991, S.315–317; Bortz 1993, S.233.
CA:364, DA:94, DE:109, EN:139, ES:368, FR:319, GA:66, IT:296, NE:132, PO:332.

110 Face-Validität Ausmaß, in dem ein Test für die Prüflinge oder diejenigen, die den Test für eine Prüfung auswählen, als angemessene Meßmethode für die intendierte Fähigkeit erscheint. Es handelt sich dabei um eine subjektive Einschätzung und nicht um das Ergebnis einer objektiven Analyse des Tests, weshalb Face-Validität oftmals nicht als echte Form der Validität betrachtet wird. (Wird auch als Augenschein-Validität bezeichnet).
Siehe: Validität.
Literatur: Bachman 1990, S.285–289.
CA:417, DA:272, DE:110, EN:140, ES:414, FR:414 GA:2, IT:402, NE:174, PO:410.

111 Fachsprachen Sprachunterricht oder Sprachprüfungen, die sich auf die Verwendung der Sprache in einem speziellen Tätigkeits- oder Berufsbereich konzentrieren, z.B. Englisch für Fluglotsen, Spanisch für Kaufleute.
CA:238, DA:95, DE:111, EN:205, ES:256, FR:236, GA:385, IT:227, NE:378, PO:251.

112 fachsprachliche Prüfung Test zur Messung der Fähigkeiten eines Prüflings, bestimmte berufliche oder akademische Situationen zu bewältigen. Dementsprechend ist der Test inhaltlich gestaltet, wobei die Grundlage eine Analyse der sprachlichen Anforderungen darstellt, denen eine Person sprachlich in entsprechenden Situationen gewachsen sein muß.
CA:318, DA:243, DE:112, EN:375, ES:328, FR:393, GA:431, IT:378, NE:351, PO:393.

113 Fähigkeit Eine geistige Eigenschaft oder Kapazität oder Kraft, um etwas zu tun.
Vergleiche: Kompetenz, Fertigkeit.
Literatur: Bachman 1990, S.16, S.19.
CA:46, DA:2, DE:113, EN:2, ES:49, FR:42, GA:96, IT:1A, NE:411, PO:49.

114 Fähigkeitsskala In probabilistischen Testmodellen eine Skala mit gleich großen Intervallen, in der sowohl die Fähigkeit von Personen als auch die Schwierigkeit von Tests lokalisiert werden kann. Wird auch als Theta-Skala bezeichnet.
Literatur: Bachman 1990, S.345; Jäger & Petermann 1992, S. 323.
CA:150, DA:3, DE:114, EN:3, ES:157, FR:128, GA:313, IT:322, NE:413, PO:159.

115 Faktorenanalyse Statistische Technik, die dem Forscher erlaubt, eine große Variablenanzahl auf eine geringere Zahl von Variablen (Faktoren) zu reduzieren, wobei Muster der Variation in den Werten der verschiedenen Variablen ermittelt werden. Eine Gruppe untereinander hoch korrelierender Variablen bilden einen Faktor. Ein Forscher kann die Faktorenanalyse zur Formulierung von Hypothesen exploratorisch einsetzen oder zur Prüfung spezieller Hypothesen auch konfirmatorisch.
Literatur: Bachman 1990, S.262; Crocker & Algina 1986, S.232; Bortz 1993, S.472–521.
CA:20, DA:96, DE:115, EN:142, ES:26, FR:18, GA:18, IT:14, NE:133, PO:20.

116 Fehler In der klassischen Testtheorie wird davon ausgegangen, daß ein beobachteter Meßwert aus zwei Komponenten besteht: ein wahrer Wert, in dem sich die Fähigkeit einer Person ausdrückt, und ein Fehlerwert, der alle Einflüsse auf den Beobachtungswert widerspiegelt, die nichts mit der eigentlich zu messenden Fähigkeit zu tun haben. Der Fehler wird als zufällig bzw. unsystematisch angesehen. Zusätzlich

können in einem Test Faktoren enthalten sein, die regelmäßig die Leistungen bestimmter Personen beeinflussen, was zu einem systematischen Fehler bzw. einer Stichprobenverzerrung (Bias) führt.
Vergleiche: Stichprobenverzerrung.
Literatur: Bachman 1990, S.167; Jäger & Petermann 1992, S. 310–313.
CA:136, DA:98, DE:116, EN:129, ES:144, FR:151, GA:122, IT:154, NE:124, PO:146.

117 Fehler erster Art In der Statistik die Zurückweisung der Nullhypothese, obwohl sie tatsächlich wahr ist.
Vergleiche: Fehler zweiter Art.
Siehe: Nullhypothese.
Literatur: Hatch & Lazarton 1991, S.224; Bortz 1993; S.107–110.
CA:140, DA:417, DE:117, EN:425, ES:151, FR:154, GA:126, IT:157, NE:405, PO:150.

118 Fehler zweiter Art In der Statistik die Annahme der Nullhypothese, obwohl sie tatsächlich falsch ist.
Vergleiche: Fehler erster Art.
Siehe: Nullhypothese.
Literatur: Hatch & Lazarton 1991, S.224; Bortz 1993; S.107–110.
CA:141, DA:418, DE:118, EN:426, ES:150, FR:155, GA:128, IT:158, NE:406, PO:151.

119 Fertigkeit Fähigkeit, etwas zu tun. Bei Sprachtests wird oft zwischen den vier Fertigkeiten Lesen, Schreiben, Sprechen und Hören unterschieden.
Siehe: Kompetenz.
CA:199, DA:111, DE:119, EN:367, ES:100, FR:340, GA:325, IT:1B, NE:413, PO:51.

120 Feststellungsprüfung Test zur Messung einer sprachlichen Fähigkeit oder Fertigkeit, ohne Bezug zu einem bestimmten Kurs oder Lernmaterial.
CA:319, DA:112, DE:120, EN:296, ES:326, FR:378, GA:428, IT:363, NE:306, PO:379.

121 Floor-Effekt Ein Grenzeffekt, der sich ergibt, wenn ein Test für eine bestimmte Personengruppe zu schwierig ist, so daß alle Testwerte am unteren Rand der Verteilung liegen.
Siehe: Grenzeffekte, Ceiling-Effekt.
CA:122, DA:42, DE:121, EN:146, ES:128, FR:141, GA:175, IT:144, NE:49, PO:130.

122 Frage Mitunter analog zum Begriff Prüfungs- oder Testaufgabe gebraucht.
Siehe: Aufgabe, Item.
CA:291, DA:357, DE:122, EN:303, ES:304, FR:315, GA:55, IT:136, NE:423, PO:323.

123 Fragebogen/Fragenheft Bezeichnung eines Papiers oder Hefts, das die Testaufgaben oder Fragen enthält.
CA:239, DA:263, DE:123, EN:304, ES:220, FR:180, GA:271, IT:169, NE:425, PO:145.

124 Fragentyp Vergleiche Definition von Itemtyp, Aufgabentyp.
CA:407, DA:358, DE:124, EN:305, ES:404, FR:406, GA:57, IT:394, NE:424, PO:400.

125 Fragesteller In mündlichen Prüfungen der Prüfer, der die Aufgaben erklärt, Fragen stellt und generell mündlich mit den Prüflingen interagiert. Mitunter nimmt er auch Bewertungen vor und vergibt Punkte, häufig übernimmt dies jedoch ein zweiter Prüfer, der nur beobachtet, ohne aber mit den Prüflingen zu interagieren.
Vergleiche: Bewerter.
CA:213, DA:325, DE:125, EN:178, ES:138, FR:216, GA:72, IT:201, NE:155, PO:227.

126 freie Antwort Form der schriftlichen Beantwortung einer Testaufgabe, bei der eine aktive Produktion und nicht ein bloßes Auswählen aus mehreren Vorgaben erforderlich ist.
Vergleiche: Auswahlantwort.
Siehe: Antwort.
CA:376, DA:185, DE:126, EN:70, ES:372, FR:330, GA:154, IT:309, NE:272, PO:336.

127 G-Faktor Der in einigen Intelligenztheorien angenommene 'Generalfaktor', von dem angenommen wird, daß er allen kognitiven Leistungen zugrunde liegt. John Oller übernahm den Begriff in den 70er Jahren für die Testtheorie als Annahme einer einheitlichen Kompetenz, die allen vier sprachlichen Fertigkeiten zugrunde liegt.
Literatur: Oller 1979, S.426–458; Bachman 1990, S.6; Bortz 1993, S. 475.
CA:176, DA:113, DE:127, EN:153, ES:195, FR:177, GA:136, IT:170, NE:139, PO:187.

128 ganzheitliche Beurteilung Vergleiche Definition von globale Bewertung.
CA:429, DA:126, DE:128, EN:164, ES:428, FR:170, GA:230, IT:187, NE:168, PO:34.

129 Gaußverteilung Vergleiche Definition von Normalverteilung.
CA:114, DA:114, DE:129, EN:152,

ES:115, FR:91, GA:105, IT:133, NE:140, PO:110.

130 gelenkte Schreibaufgabe Aufgabe, bei der ein schriftlicher Text zu verfassen ist, dessen Erstellung durch grafische oder schriftliche Informationen wie Bilder, Briefe, Postkarten oder Anweisungen geleitet und standardisiert wird.
Vergleiche: Aufsatz.

CA:393, DA:121, DE:130, EN:160, ES:5, FR:311, GA:377, IT:76, NE:143, PO:317.

131 gemeinsame Skala Methode, um die Ergebnisse von zwei oder mehr Tests auf einer gemeinsamen Skala zu lokalisieren, um einen direkten Vergleich der Testergebnisse zu ermöglichen. Die Ergebnisse von zwei oder mehr Tests können auf einer gemeinsamen Skala lokalisiert werden, wenn die Rohwerte durch eine statistische Prozedur transformiert wurden, die sogenannte Angleichung von Tests.
Vergleiche: Angleichung.
Literatur: Bachman 1990, S.340–344.

CA:147, DA:110, DE:131, EN:57, ES:156, FR:125, GA:86, IT:320, NE:148, PO:158.

132 Generalisierbarkeitstheorie Statistisches Modell zur Prüfung der relativen Effekte unterschiedlicher Varianzquellen von Testwerten. Die Generalisierbarkeitstheorie fordert, daß für die Messung eines Konstrukts ein Universum zulässiger Beobachtungen definiert wird.
Literatur: Bachman 1990, S. 7; Crocker & Algina 1986, Kap. 8; Fisseni 1990, S.67–69.

CA:400, DA:115, DE:132, EN:154, ES:393, FR:399, GA:388, IT:351, NE:152, PO:359.

133 Gesamteindruck Bewertungsmethode, die vor allem bei Tests für produktiven Sprachgebrauch, z.B. Schreib- und Sprechtests, verwendet wird. Der Bewerter nimmt eine Bewertung der Antworten jedes Prüflings vor, ohne dabei zu versuchen, die Antwort in unabhängige Teilkomponenten zu zerlegen.
Vergleiche: analytische Bewertung, globale Bewertung.

CA:89, DA:116, DE:133, EN:168, ES:429, FR:270, GA:220, IT:33, NE:172, PO:68.

134 geschichtete Stichprobe Stichprobe aus einer Population, wobei die Population zunächst in eine Anzahl von Teilpopulationen (Schichten, Ränge) aufgeteilt wird, aus denen man jeweils eine Stichprobe zieht.
Siehe: Stichprobe.
Literatur: Guilford & Fruchter 1981, S.122–123; Bortz 1984, S.284–298.

CA:266, DA:375, DE:134, EN:388, ES:280, FR:119, GA:306, IT:48, NE:157, PO:11.

135 gewichteter Testwert Punktwert, den ein Prüfling in einem Test erreicht, nachdem eine Gewichtung vorgenommen wurde.
Siehe: Gewichtung.

CA:354, DA:434, DE:135, EN:437, ES:354, FR:280, GA:339, IT:284, NE:159, PO:286.

136 Gewichtung Zuweisung unterschiedlicher maximal erreichbarer Punktwerte zu einem Testitem, einer Aufgabe oder einer Prüfungskomponente mit dem Ziel, den relativen Beitrag dieses Teils im Verhältnis zu den anderen Teilen am Zustandekommen eines Gesamtwertes zu verändern. Wenn beispielsweise für alle Items von Aufgabe 1 die doppelte Punktzahl vergeben wird, erhält Aufgabe 1 ein größeres Gewicht am Gesamtwert als die übrigen Aufgaben.
Literatur: Ebel & Frisbie 1991, S.214–216.

CA:290, DA:435, DE:136, EN:438, ES:303, FR:302, GA:439, IT:268, NE:434, PO:306.

137 globale Bewertung Bewertungsmethode für Sprech- und Schreibtests. Der Bewerter vergibt eine generelle Note oder Punktzahl entsprechend seinem Gesamteindruck über die Sprachverwendung und nicht eine Anzahl unabhängiger Bewertungen von Teilaspekten des Sprachgebrauchs.
Vergleiche: analytische Bewertung, Gesamteindruck.

CA:33, DA:124, DE:137, EN:155, ES:427, FR:169, GA:231, IT:186, NE:161, PO:33.

138 grammatikalische Kompetenz Innerhalb eines Modells der Kommunikationsfähigkeit ist grammatikalische Kompetenz diejenige Komponente, die sich auf Aspekte des Sprachgebrauchs wie Morphologie, Syntax, Wortschatz, Phonologie und Orthographie bezieht.
Literatur: Bachman 1990, S.84–88.

CA:67, DA:119, DE:138, EN:158, ES:63, FR:65, GA:193, IT:65, NE:162, PO:79.

139 Grenzeffekte Effekte,wenn ein Test für eine bestimmte Gruppe von Prüflingen zu leicht oder schwierig ist. Die größten Wertehäufigkeiten finden sich am oberen (Ceiling-Effekt) oder unteren (Floor-Effekt) Ende der Häufigkeitsverteilung.
Siehe: Ceiling-Effekt, Floor-Effekt.
Literatur: Lienert & Raatz 1994, S.155.

CA:125, DA:120, DE:139, EN:36, ES:131, FR:143, GA:177, IT:138, NE:163, PO:139.

140 halbauthentischer Text Aus einer alltäglichen Quelle übernommener Text, der für die Verwendung in einem Test überarbeitet worden ist, z.B. durch eine Anpassung des erforderlichen Wortschatzes und der Grammatik an das Niveau der Prüflinge.
Siehe: authentischer Text.
CA:405, DA:123, DE:140, EN:355, ES:400, FR:112, GA:383, IT:391, NE:335, PO:128.

141 Halo-Effekt (Hof-Effekt) Urteilsfehler bei subjektiven Bewertungen, wobei die Ausführung einer Aufgabe durch einen Prüfling die Beurteilung einer anderen Aufgabe beeinflußt, wodurch letztere zu gut oder zu schlecht beurteilt wird.
Siehe: Urteilsfehler.
CA:117, DA:118, DE:141, EN:161, ES:127, FR:137, GA:170, IT:139, NE:164, PO:133.

142 Häufigkeitsverteilung Vergleiche Definition von Verteilung.
CA:113, DA:107, DE:142, EN:149, ES:114, FR:107, GA:106, IT:132, NE:138, PO:122.

143 Häufigkeitszählung Feststellung, wie häufig ein bestimmtes Wort oder eine bestimmte Wortart in einem Text vorkommt. Bei Sprachprüfungen kann dies nützlich sein, um Tests zu entwickeln, die einen bestimmten lexikalischen Bereich erfassen sollen.
CA:190, DA:270, DE:143, EN:440, ES:362, FR:75, GA:67, IT:256, NE:436, PO:95.

144 Hintergrundwissen Das Wissen eines Prüflings über Thema oder kulturellen Inhalt innerhalb eines bestimmten Tests, was den Umgang mit dem Test beeinflussen kann. Das ist von besonderer Bedeutung für Tests in bestimmten Fachsprachen.
Literatur: Bachman 1990, S. 273.
CA:75, DA:26, DE:144, EN:27, ES:73, FR:77, GA:134, IT:85, NE:4, PO:91.

145 Histogramm Grafische Darstellung einer Häufigkeitsverteilung, bei der die Fallzahl pro Häufigkeitsklasse als vertikaler Balken dargestellt wird.

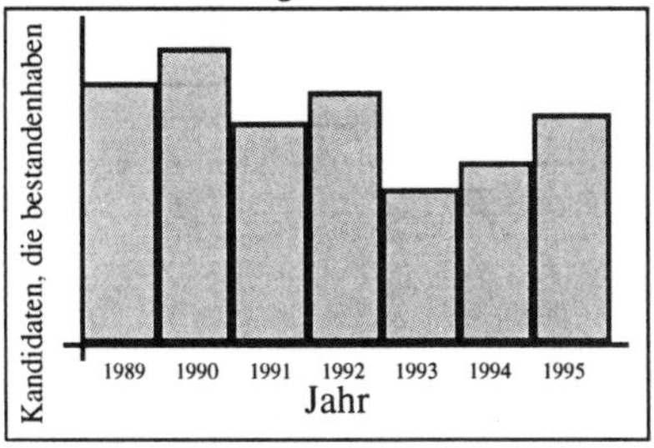

Vergleiche: Säulendiagramm.
CA:203, DA:125, DE:145, EN:163, ES:218, FR:204, GA:168, IT:207, NE:167, PO:215.

146 Höhenlage In der linearen Regression der Punkt, an dem die Regressionsgerade die vertikale y-Achse schneidet.
Siehe: lineare Regression.
CA:212, DA:438, DE:146, EN:441, ES:231, FR:215, GA:181, IT:200, NE:438, PO:226.

147 Hörverständnistest Ein Test zur Prüfung des Verständnisses gesprochener Sprache, der meist unter Einsatz eines Tonbandgeräts oder Videorecorders durchgeführt wird.
CA:315, DA:221, DE:147, EN:216, ES:324, FR:372, GA:411, IT:361, NE:235, PO:373.

148 Homogenität Merkmal eines Tests oder Subtests, bei dem die Aufgaben die gleiche Fähigkeit messen, oder einer Gruppe, deren Mitglieder über eine gemeinsame Eigenschaft verfügen. Der Reliabilitätsindex gibt Hinweise auf den Grad der Homogenität.
CA:204, DA:127, DE:148, EN:165, ES:221, FR:205, GA:22, IT:257, NE:169, PO:216.

149 horizontale Angleichung Testwerte aus zwei Tests mit etwa gleicher Schwierigkeit werden auf einer Skala lokalisiert, damit die gleichen Standards für beide Tests gelten können.
Vergleiche: vertikale Angleichung.
Siehe: angeglichene Testformen.
CA:133, DA:128, DE:149, EN:166, ES:141, FR:37, GA:89, IT:152, NE:170, PO:44.

150 indirektes Prüfverfahren (indirekte Aufgabe) Test oder Testelement, von dem angenommen wird, daß damit nicht die sprachlichen Fertigkeiten selbst, sondern die hinter der Sprachbeherrschung stehenden Fähigkeiten gemessen werden können. Ein Beispiel wäre die Erfassung der Schreibfähigkeit dadurch, daß ein Prüfling aufgefordert wird, fehlerhafte Teile eines Textes anzustreichen.
Vergleiche: direktes Prüfverfahren.
Literatur: Hughes 1989, S.14–16.
CA:329, DA:135, DE:150, EN:170, ES:337, FR:385, GA:420, IT:354, NE:173, PO:389.

151 Informationslücke Eine Sprachlehr- und Sprachtestmethode, bei der echte Gesprächssituationen simuliert werden, wobei eine Situation in der Weise geschaffen wird, daß die Schüler nicht über die gleichen Informationen verfügen und damit untereinander kommunizieren müssen, um die Aufgabe zu erfüllen. Wird normalerweise eingesetzt, um Schreib- und Sprechfertigkeiten zu üben und zu prüfen.

CA:42, DA:140, DE:151, EN:172, ES:411, FR:213, GA:43, IT:424, NE:176, PO:223.

152 Informationstransfer Prüfmethode, bei der die Aufgabe darin besteht, Information in einer bestimmten Weise aufzunehmen und sie in einer anderen weiterzugeben. Beispiele: Informationen aus einem Text sollen verwendet werden, um eine Zeichnung zu beschriften, oder eine Notiz soll in eine offizielle Ankündigung umgeschrieben werden.
Literatur: Hughes 1989, S.84, 124–125, 138.

CA:409, DA:141, DE:152, EN:173, ES:406, FR:402, GA:8, IT:396, NE:177, PO:404.

153 Inhaltsanalyse Methode zur Beschreibung und Analyse des Inhalts von Testmaterialien. Diese Analyse ist notwendig, um sicherzustellen, daß der Inhalt eines Tests seiner Meßintention entspricht. Es ist notwendig für die Feststellung von Inhalts- und Konstruktvalidität.

CA:18, DA:133, DE:153, EN:72, ES:19, FR:12, GA:12, IT:15, NE:178, PO:15.

154 Inhaltsvalidität Einem Test wird Inhaltsvalidität zugesprochen, wenn die Aufgaben, aus denen er besteht, eine repräsentative Stichprobe aller Aufgaben darstellen, die beim zu prüfenden Kenntnisbereich oder der intendierten Fähigkeit vorkommen.
Siehe: Validität, Testbeschreibung.
Literatur: Bachman 1990, S.244–247; Lienert & Raatz 1994, S. 224–225.

CA:422, DA:134, DE:154, EN:73, ES:419, FR:419, GA:31, IT:405, NE:179, PO:415.

155 innere Konsistenz Merkmal eines Tests, der die Homogenität der Aufgaben vor dem Hintergrund ihrer Interkorrelationen bzw. der Korrelationen einzelner Aufgaben mit dem Gesamtwert beschreibt. Daraus läßt sich indirekt auch ableiten, wie hoch die Punktwerte eines Prüflings bei einer Einzelaufgabe mit dem Gesamtwert übereinstimmen. Innere Konsistenzen können zur Reliabilitätsschätzung dienen. Unterschiedliche Indizes können berechnet werden, z.B. KR-20, Alpha.
Siehe: Alpha-Koeffizient, Kuder-Richardson, Reliabilität (Zuverlässigkeit).
Literatur: Bachman 1990, S.172; Lienert & Raatz 1994, S.191–200.

CA:77, DA:147, DE:155, EN:180, ES:74, FR:186, GA:87, IT:87, NE:186, PO:93.

156 integrierte Aufgabe Bezeichnung von Aufgaben, zu deren Bewältigung mehr als eine Fertigkeit oder Teilfertigkeit benötigt wird. Beispiele sind Aufgaben in einem Cloze-Test, ein Prüfungsgespräch, das Lesen und Beantworten eines Briefes.
Vergleiche: Discrete-Point-Item.

CA:231, DA:144, DE:156, EN:176, ES:249, FR:316, GA:248, IT:221, NE:182, PO:245.

157 Interaktionsauthentizität Eine Sichtweise der Authentizität von Sprachprüfungen, bei der die Authentizität als Eigenschaft einer Interaktion gesehen wird, die zwischen Prüfling und Aufgabe stattfindet, um eine angemessene Antwort zu produzieren.
Vergleiche: Situationsauthentizität.
Siehe: Authentizität.
Literatur: Bachman 1990, S.315–323.

CA:28, DA:146, DE:157, EN:177, ES:34, FR:25, GA:116, IT:36, NE:183, PO:27.

158 Interrater-Reliabilität Eigentlich ein Maß für die Beurteilung der Auswertungsobjektivität, das im Zusammenhang mit subjektiven Bewertungen als Reliabilitätsschätzung bezeichnet wird. Es basiert auf dem Ausmaß, in dem verschiedene Bewerter in ihrer Bewertung von Prüfungsleistungen übereinstimmen.
Siehe: Interrater-Übereinstimmung, Reliabilität (Zuverlässigkeit), objektiver Test.

CA:181, DA:145, DE:158, EN:182, ES:199, FR:185, GA:201, IT:8, NE:184, PO:195.

159 Interrater-Übereinstimmung Ausmaß der Übereinstimmung zwischen zwei oder mehr durch unterschiedliche Bewerter vorgenommenen Bewertungen der gleichen Stichprobe von Testleistungen. Das ist besonders wichtig bei schriftlichen oder mündlichen Fertigkeiten, bei denen eine subjektive Bewertung durch Prüfer notwendig ist.

CA:2, DA:31, DE:159, EN:181, ES:11, FR:2, GA:68, IT:84, NE:185, PO:2.

160 Intervall Der Abstand zweier Punkte auf einer Skala.

CA:214, DA:148, DE:160, EN:183, ES:232, FR:218, GA:131, IT:203, NE:187, PO:228.

161 Intervallskala Meßskala, bei der der Abstand zwischen jedem Paar neben-

einanderliegender Meßwerte gleich groß ist, bei der es allerdings keinen echten Nullpunkt gibt.
Vergleiche: Nominalskala, Ordinalskala, Verhältnisskala.
Literatur: Bortz 1993, S.25.
CA:148/149, DA:149/213, DE:161, EN:125/184, ES:158/159, FR:126/127, GA:315/316, IT:315/316, NE:145/188, PO:161/162.

162 Intrarater-Reliabilität Eigentlich ein Maß für die Beurteilung der Auswertungsobjektivität, das im Zusammenhang mit subjektiven Bewertungen als Reliabilitätsschätzung bezeichnet wird. Es basiert auf einer Beurteilung, wie stark die Bewertung einer Testleistung durch den gleichen Bewerter zu verschiedenen Zeitpunkten übereinstimmt.
Siehe: Interrater-Übereinstimmung, Reliabilität (Zuverlässigkeit), objektiver Test.
CA:182, DA:151, DE:162, EN:186, ES:200, FR:187, GA:202, IT:89, NE:189, PO:196.

163 Intrarater-Übereinstimmung Ausmaß der Übereinstimmung zwischen zwei vom gleichen Bewerter zu unterschiedlichen Zeitpunkten vorgenommenen Bewertungen der gleichen Stichprobe von Testleistungen. Das ist besonders wichtig bei schriftlichen oder mündlichen Fertigkeiten, bei denen eine subjektive Bewertung durch Prüfer notwendig ist.
CA:3, DA:33, DE:163, EN:185, ES:12, FR:3, GA:69, IT:90, NE:190, PO:3.

164 Invarianz In probabilistischen Testmodellen die Grundannahme, nach der Aufgabenschwierigkeit und Trennschärfe grundlegende Merkmale sind, die nicht vom Fähigkeitsniveau der Personen abhängen; desgleichen die Annahme, daß Fähigkeitsmessungen davon unabhängig sind, welche Aufgaben zur Bearbeitung vorgelegt werden.
CA:216, DA:152, DE:164, EN:187, ES:234, FR:220, GA:120, IT:205, NE:191, PO:230.

165 IRT Vergleiche Definition von probabilistische Testmodelle.
CA:412, DA:153, DE:165, EN:188, ES:408, FR:401, GA:392, IT:352, NE:194, PO:402.

166 Item Jedes Einzelelement eines Tests, das getrennt bewertet wird. Beispiele sind: Lücken in einem Cloze-Test, Multiple-Choice-Frage mit drei oder vier Auswahlantworten, ein Satz, der grammatikalisch umzuformulieren ist, eine Frage, auf die ein Satz als Antwort erwartet wird.
Vergleiche: Aufgabe.
CA:217, DA:154, DE:166, EN:189, ES:235, FR:221, GA:240, IT:209, NE:195, PO:231.

167 Itemanalyse Analyse der Lösungen einzelner Testaufgaben, wobei üblicherweise die klassischen statistischen Kennwerte Schwierigkeit und Trennschärfe verwendet werden. Software wie MicroCAT Iteman oder SPSS RELIABILITY wird dafür benutzt.
Siehe: Trennschärfe, Schwierigkeitsindex.
CA:13, DA:161, DE:167, EN:190, ES:25, FR:17, GA:13, IT:12, NE:198, PO:16.

168 Item-Charakteristik-Kurve (ICK) In probabilistischen Testmodellen zeigt die ICK an, wie die Wahrscheinlichkeit der richtigen Beantwortung einer Aufgabe in Beziehung steht zur latenten Fähigkeit, die der Lösung aller Aufgaben des Tests zugrunde liegt.
Literatur: Crocker & Algina 1986, S.340–342; Fisseni 1990, S.135–138; Fischer 1983, S.606–609.
CA:79, DA:157, DE:168, EN:192, ES:95, FR:90, GA:94, IT:115, NE:196, PO:109.

169 Item-Informationsfunktion In probabilistischen Testmodellen ein Kennwert über die Informationsmenge, die eine Aufgabe über Personen eines bestimmten Fähigkeitsniveaus bereitstellt und die Anpassung an dieses Niveau. Dies ist abhängig von der Trennschärfe der Aufgabe und der Qualität der Anpassung an das Niveau.
Vergleiche: Test-Informationsfunktion.
Literatur: Fischer 1983, S.606–609.
CA:192, DA:156, DE:169, EN:193, ES:212, FR:190, GA:138, IT:184, NE:197, PO:206.

170 Itemparameter Parameter probabilistischer Testmodelle, der den Schwierigkeitsgrad einer Aufgabe beschreibt (auch als B-Parameter in der Item-Response-Theorie bezeichnet).
Siehe: probabilistische Testmodelle.
Literatur: Bachman 1990, S.204; Fisseni 1990, S.116; Fischer 1983, S.613–615.
CA:282, DA:24, DE:170, EN:26, ES:295, FR:293, GA:274, IT:261, NE:26, PO:298.

171 Item-Punktzahl In der Itemanalyse die Anzahl richtiger Antworten in einer bestimmten Aufgabe.
CA:345, DA:160, DE:171, EN:196, ES:346, FR:267, GA:336, IT:281, NE:202, PO:60.

172 Item-Response-Funktion In

probabilistischen Testmodellen eine mathematische Funktion, die die Beziehung zwischen der Erfolgswahrscheinlichkeit der Lösung einer Aufgabe und dem Fähigkeitsniveau der mit dieser Aufgabe gemessenen Fähigkeit herstellt. Auch bekannt unter dem Begriff Item-Charakteristik-Funktion.

CA:193, DA:158, DE:172, EN:194, ES:210, FR:189, GA:140, IT:183, NE:200, PO:205.

173 Item-Response-Theorie Vergleiche Definition von probabilistische Testmodelle.

CA:401, DA:159, DE:173, EN:195, ES:394, FR:400, GA:389, IT:352, NE:201, PO:360.

174 Itemtyp Testitems werden oftmals mit Bezeichnungen versehen, durch die ihre Form beschrieben wird. Beispiele sind: Multiple-Choice-Item, Satzergänzung, Kurzantwort, offener Cloze-Test.

CA:406, DA:162, DE:174, EN:197 ES:405, FR:405, GA:58, IT:392, NE:203, PO:399.

175 Kategorialskala Skala für kategoriale Daten wie Geschlecht, Muttersprache, Beruf.
Vergleiche: Intervallskala, Nominalskala, Ordinalskala, Verhältnisskala.

CA:146, DA:170, DE:175, EN:42, ES:154, FR:123, GA:310, IT:318, NE:53, PO:156.

176 Kategorie a) Klassen einer Nominalskala, z.B. hat die Nominalskala Geschlecht die Klassen männlich und weiblich.

b) Bei der Bewertung mündlicher und schriftlicher Leistungen hat z.B. eine fünfstufige Bewertungsanleitung fünf Antwortkategorien.

CA:49, DA:169, DE:176, EN:43, ES:52, FR:48, GA:50, IT:51, NE:52, PO:55.

177 klassische Testtheorie Meßtheorie, die auf verschiedenen Annahmen über die Beziehungen zwischen beobachteten und wahren Testwerten und die diese Testwerte beeinflussenden Faktoren, normalerweise den sogenannten Meßfehlern, beruht.
Vergleiche: probabilistische Testmodelle.
Literatur: Bachman 1990, S.166–187; Jäger & Petermann 1992, S. 310–316.

CA:399, DA:174, DE:177, EN:50, ES:392, FR:397, GA:387, IT:349, NE:208, PO:357.

178 Koeffizient Zahlenwert, der zur Messung einer Eigenschaft oder Charakteristik herangezogen wird.
Siehe: Alpha-Koeffizient, Korrelations-Koeffizient.

CA:53, DA:175, DE:178, EN:53, ES:55, FR:54, GA:73, IT:57, NE:62, PO:69.

179 Koeffizient-Alpha Vergleiche Definition von Alpha-Koeffizient.

CA:54, DA:176, DE:179, EN:54, ES:56, FR:55, GA:74, IT:58, NE:63, PO:70.

180 kognitive Faktoren Faktoren im Lern- oder Prüfungsprozeß, die sich auf den Lernprozeß und das Wissensmuster des Lernenden beziehen.
Vergleiche: affektive Faktoren.
Literatur: Ebel & Frisbie 1991, S.52.

CA:178, DA:177, DE:180, EN:55, ES:196, FR:179, GA:398, IT:171, NE:65, PO:189.

181 kognitives Modell Theorie über die Struktur der Kenntnisse einer Person, sowohl im Hinblick auf die Begriffsstruktur als auch auf die beteiligten Prozesse. Dies ist für Sprachprüfungen wichtig, da eine derartige Theorie Auswirkungen auf Testmethode und -inhalt haben kann.

CA:253, DA:178, DE:181, EN:56, ES:269, FR:250, GA:297, IT:243, NE:64, PO:262.

182 Kommunikationsfähigkeit Fähigkeit, eine Sprache in verschiedensten Situationen und in unterschiedlichsten Umgebungen angemessen verwenden zu können.
Literatur: Bachman 1990, S.16 und 68.

CA:65, DA:179, DE:182, EN:58, ES:61, FR:63, GA:195, IT:63, NE:66, PO:77.

183 Kompetenz Wissen oder Fähigkeit, um etwas zu tun. In der Linguistik bezeichnet Kompetenz eine zugrundeliegende Fähigkeit im Gegensatz zur beobachtbaren Performanz, die sich in der Sprachverwendung als Ausdruck der Kompetenz niederschlägt. Diese Unterscheidung stammt aus den Arbeiten von Chomsky.
Vergleiche: Performanz.
Literatur: Bachman 1990, S.52 und 108.

CA:64, DA:180, DE:183, EN:59, ES:60, FR:62, GA:191, IT:62, NE:67, PO:76.

184 Konfidenzintervall Der Bereich um den beobachteten Wert, in dem der wahre Testwert mit vorgegebener Wahrscheinlichkeit liegt. Üblicherweise werden Wahrscheinlichkeitsniveaus von 95% oder 99% verwendet.

CA:215, DA:182, DE:184, EN:67, ES:233, FR:219, GA:132, IT:204, NE:45, PO:229.

185 Konstrukt Eine angenommene Fähigkeit oder geistige Eigenschaft, die nicht unbedingt direkt gemessen oder beobachtet werden kann, z.B. bei Sprachprüfungen das Hörverstehen. Mit Sprachtests wird versucht, die verschiedenen Konstrukte zu erfassen, die der Sprachfähigkeit zugrunde

liegen. Zusätzlich zur Sprachfähigkeit sind Motivation, Einstellungen und kulturelle Anpassung wichtige Konstrukte.
Literatur: Hatch & Lazarton 1991, S.15; Dorsch 1994, S.400.

CA:78, DA:184, DE:185, EN:68, ES:76, FR:80, GA:394, IT:108, NE:72, PO:94.

186 Konstruktvalidität Einem Test wird Konstruktvalidität zugeschrieben, wenn seine Ergebnisse bzw. seine Beziehungen zu anderen Konstrukten einer Theorie über die zugrundeliegenden Konstrukte entsprechen. Es könnte beispielsweise vorhergesagt werden, daß sich Lernende durch zwei valide Tests zur Erfassung des Hörverständnisses in eine ähnliche Rangreihe bringen lassen, während für beide eine sehr viel geringere Übereinstimmung mit den Werten eines Tests für grammatikalische Kenntnisse besteht.
Siehe: Validität, Testbeschreibung.
Literatur: Ebel & Frisbie 191, S.108; Hatch & Lazarton 1991, S.37–38; Lienert & Raatz 1994, S. 226–227.

CA:420, DA:186, DE:186, EN:69, ES:418, FR:418, GA:37, IT:406, NE:73, PO:414.

187 Kontingenztafel Eine Häufigkeitstafel, klassifiziert nach zwei oder mehr Sätzen kategorialer Variablen, z.B.:

	Beherrschung	Keine Beherrschung
Methode A	35	5
Methode B	20	20

Siehe: Chi-Quadrat-Test.
Literatur: Bortz 1993, S.157; Bortz, Lienert & Boehnke 1990, S.102–196.

CA:398, DA:187, DE:187, EN:74, ES:390, FR:353, GA:369, IT:347, NE:75, PO:320.

188 konvergente Validität Einem Test wird konvergente Validität zugeschrieben, wenn sich eine hohe Korrelation zwischen seinen Testwerten und den Werten eines anderen Tests ergibt, der unabhängig von der Methode das gleiche Konstrukt mißt. Wird als Teilaspekt der Konstruktvalidität angesehen.
Vergleiche: diskriminante Validität.
Siehe: Konstruktvalidität.
Literatur: Guilford & Fruchter 1981, S.436–437; Lienert & Raatz 1994, S.227.

CA:419, DA:188, DE:188, EN:75, ES:416, FR:416, GA:32, IT:404, NE:76, PO:412.

189 Korrekturlesen Testaufgabe, bei der ein Text nach bestimmten Fehlern durchgesehen werden muß, z.B. Rechtschreibungs- oder Grammatikfehler. Die Aufgabe kann auch darin bestehen, Fehler anzustreichen und zu korrigieren.

CA:395, DA:195, DE:189, EN:300, ES:4, FR:84, GA:374, IT:75, NE:304, PO:97.

190 Korrelation Die Beziehung zwischen zwei oder mehr Messungen, wobei geprüft wird, in welchem Ausmaß diese in der gleichen Weise variieren. Wenn beispielsweise Prüflinge meist ähnliche Bewertungen bei zwei verschiedenen Tests erhalten, so ergibt sich eine positive Korrelation zwischen den Werten der beiden Tests.
Vergleiche: Kovarianz.
Siehe: Rangkorrelation, Produkt-Moment-Korrelation nach Pearson (Pearson's *r*).
Literatur: Guilford & Fruchter 1981, Kap. 6; Bachman 1990, S.259–260; Bortz 1993, S. 187–191.

CA:91, DA:196, DE:190, EN:78, ES:84, FR:85, GA:78, IT:95, NE:81, PO:100.

191 Korrelationskoeffizient Ein Kennwert, der die Höhe der Korrelation zwischen zwei oder mehr Variablen ausdrückt. Er variiert zwischen -1 und + 1. Eine hohe Korrelation wird durch einen Wert nahe + oder - 1 ausgedrückt.
Literatur: Guilford & Fruchter 1981, S. 86–88; Bortz 1993, S. 187–191.

CA:55, DA:197, DE:191, EN:79, ES:57, FR:56, GA:75, IT:60, NE:82, PO:71.

192 Kovarianz Gemeinsame Varianz von zwei oder mehr Variablen. Satzlänge und lexikalische Schwierigkeit sind beispielsweise Merkmale eines Lesetextes, die meist zusammenhängen, also kovariieren. Kovarianz muß vorliegen, wenn man eine Variable durch andere vorhersagen will, also im Beispiel, wenn man die Schwierigkeit eines Lesetextes aus Satzlänge und lexikalischer Schwierigkeit vorhersagen will.
Siehe: Varianz.

CA:93, DA:199, DE:192, EN:80, ES:91, FR:92, GA:71, IT:112, NE:84, PO:106.

193 Kovarianzanalyse Vergleiche Definition von Analyse der Kovarianz.

CA:14, DA:200, DE:193, EN:12, ES:20, FR:14, GA:16, IT:18, NE:85, PO:13.

194 KR-20 (Kuder-Richardson Formel 20) Vergleiche Definition von Kuder-Richardson.

CA:234, DA:201, DE:194, EN:199, ES:252, FR:233, GA:205, IT:222, NE:210, PO:246.

195 KR-21 (Kuder-Richardson Formel 21) Vergleiche Definition von

Kuder-Richardson.
CA:235, DA:202, DE:195, EN:200 ES:253, FR:234, GA:206, IT:223, NE:211, PO:247.

196 kriteriumsorientierter Test Test, in dem die Leistung eines Prüflings im Verhältnis zu einem zuvor definierten Kriterium interpretiert wird. Es wird vor allem geprüft, ob ein bestimmtes Ziel erreicht wurde und nicht, welchen Rangplatz ein Prüfling innerhalb einer Gruppe einnimmt.
Vergleiche: normorientierter Test, bereichsspezifischer Test.
Literatur: Fisseni 1990, S.103–115.
CA:337, DA:203, DE:196, EN:81, ES:317, FR:364, GA:412, IT:380, NE:86, PO:369.

197 Kriteriumsvalidität Einem Test wird Kriteriumsvalidität zugeschrieben, wenn eine Beziehung zwischen den Testwerten und externen Kriterien vorliegt, von denen man annimmt, daß sie die gleiche Fähigkeit kennzeichnen. Information über Beziehungen zu Kriterien wird verwendet, um zu entscheiden, wie gut ein Test künftiges Verhalten vorhersagen kann.
Siehe: Übereinstimmungsvalidität, Vorhersagevalidität.
Literatur: Bachman 1990, S.248–250; Lienert & Raatz 1994, S. 223–224.
CA:421, DA:204, DE:197, EN:82, ES:417, FR:417, GA:34, IT:407, NE:87, PO:413.

198 Kriteriumsvariable Anderer Ausdruck für abhängige Variable in einem Untersuchungsdesign.
Siehe: abhängige Variable.
CA:431, DA:205, DE:198, EN:83, ES:431, FR:424, GA:26, IT:417, NE:88, PO:423.

199 kritischer Wert (cut-off) Der Punktwert, den ein Prüfling mindestens erreichen muß, um eine bestimmte Note in einer Prüfung oder einem Test zu erzielen. Bei Prüfungen der Testwert, der als Mindestanforderung angesehen wird, um jemandem Minimalkompetenz oder ein bestimmtes Niveau der Beherrschung zuzuschreiben.
Siehe: lernzielorientierter Test, Prüfung der Mindestanforderungen.
Vergleiche: Bestehensgrenze.
Literatur: Bachman 1990, S.214–215, Crocker & Algina 1986, S.421–428.
CA:359, DA:58, DE:199, EN:90, ES:351, FR:277, GA:338, IT:280, NE:57, PO:282.

200 Kuder-Richardson Zwei Koeffizienten für innere Konsistenz zur Schätzung der Reliabilität eines Tests. KR-21 benötigt weniger Informationen und ist einfacher zu berechnen, führt jedoch normalerweise zu einer niedrigeren Schätzung als KR-20.
Vergleiche: Alpha-Koeffizient.
Siehe: innere Konsistenz.
Literatur: Henning 1987, S.84; Lienert & Raatz 1994, S.192–200.
CA:236, DA:206, DE:200, EN:201, ES:254, FR:235, GA:207, IT:224, NE:212, PO:248.

201 kulturspezifische Stichprobenverzerrung Ein Test mit kultureller Stichprobenverzerrung (Bias) begünstigt oder benachteiligt Prüflinge mit spezifischem kulturellem Hintergrund.
Siehe: Stichprobenverzerrung.
CA:41, DA:207, DE:201, EN:85, ES:385, FR:33, GA:209, IT:161, NE:90, PO:41.

202 kumulierte Häufigkeitsverteilung Darstellungsweise für die Verteilung von Prüfungsleistungen, wobei für jeden Punktwert die Anzahl der Prüflinge bestimmt wird, die diesen Wert und alle darunter liegenden Werte erzielten.
Literatur: Guilford & Fruchter 1981, S.35–36; Bortz, 1993, S.30–31.
CA:189, DA:208, DE:202, EN:86, ES:208, FR:198, GA:239, IT:181, NE:91, PO:204.

203 Kursabschlußprüfung Vergleiche Definition von Sprachstandstest.
CA:322, DA:20, DE:203, EN:23, ES:331, FR:366, GA:419, IT:368, NE:421, PO:374.

204 kursbezogener Kenntnistest Test zur Prüfung, ob ein Student einen genau definierten Kenntnis- oder Fertigkeitsbereich beherrscht.
CA:338, DA:227, DE:204, EN:225, ES:327, FR:376, GA:425, IT:366, NE:237, PO:376.

205 Kurzantwort-Aufgabe Offene Aufgabenstellung, bei der der Prüfling eine schriftliche Antwort in Form eines Wortes oder einer kurzen Formulierung schreiben muß.
CA:228, DA:198, DE:205, EN:362, ES:243, FR:224, GA:246, IT:311, NE:209, PO:238.

206 Latent-Trait-Theorie Vergleiche Definition von probabilistische Testmodelle.
CA:402, DA:211, DE:206, EN:207, ES:395, FR:398, GA:390, IT:350, NE:216, PO:358.

207 Lehrplan Ein detailliertes Dokument, in dem alle Bereiche aufgelistet sind, die in einem Lernprogramm behandelt werden, sowie die Reihenfolge, in der der Stoff

vermittelt wird.
Vergleiche: Curriculum.

CA:299, DA:224, DE:207, EN:392, ES:310, FR:352, GA:352, IT:335, NE:225, PO:318.

208 Leichtigkeitsindex Anteil richtiger Antworten bei einer Aufgabe, ausgedrückt auf einer von 0 bis 1 reichenden Skala. Mitunter auch in Prozentwerten ausgedrückt.
Vergleiche: Schwierigkeitsindex.

CA:209, DA:191, DE:208, EN:141, ES:225, FR:210, GA:188, IT:197, NE:146, PO:220.

209 Leichtigkeitswert Vergleiche Definition von Leichtigkeitsindex.

CA:426, DA:192, DE:209, EN:143, ES:423, FR:410, GA:217, IT:411, NE:147, PO:419.

210 Leistungsstufe Teil einer Skala, die sich auf einen bestimmten Fähigkeitsbereich und ein bestimmtes Leistungsniveau bezieht.

CA:346, DA:258, DE:210, EN:30, ES:39, FR:269, GA:330, IT:40, NE:29, PO:65.

211 Leistungszuwachs Differenz zwischen einem Testergebnis, das vor Beginn eines Unterrichtsabschnitts erzielt wurde, und dem Ergebnis, das danach bei dem gleichen oder einem ähnlichen Test erreicht wurde. Der Zuwachs zeigt den kursbedingten Lernfortschritt an.

CA:352, DA:290, DE:211, EN:150, ES:32, FR:199, GA:44, IT:192, NE:434, PO:209.

212 Lenkungsverfahren Im Englischen Oberbegriff für alle Prüfverfahren, die eine sprachliche Reaktion beim Prüfling hervorrufen. Besonders gebräuchlich zur Bezeichnung von Aufgabentypen in der mündlichen Prüfung, wie z.B. Einsatz von Bildern oder Rollenspiel.
Literatur: Hughes 1989, S.104–110.

CA:293, DA:8, DE:212, EN:123, ES:307, FR:308, GA:162, IT:276, NE:320, PO:314.

213 Lernerfolgskontrolle Prüfen, das im Verlauf einer Unterrichtseinheit oder eines Lernprogramms vorgenommen wird und nicht am Ende. Das Ergebnis soll dem Lehrer ermöglichen, frühzeitig Förderunterricht zu erteilen oder, wenn nötig, die Kursgestaltung zu verändern. Dem Lerner soll es ermöglichen, seine Stärken und Schwächen zu erkennen.
Vergleiche: Abschlußprüfung.

CA:32, DA:225, DE:213, EN:147, ES:184, FR:168, GA:232, IT:422, NE:137, PO:32.

214 Lernfortschrittstest Test, der im Verlauf eines Kurses oder Lehrganges durchgeführt wird, um den bis zu diesem Zeitpunkt erreichten Lernstand festzustellen.

CA:320, DA:108, DE:214, EN:298, ES:330, FR:381, GA:418, IT:369, NE:422, PO:382.

215 Lerninhalt Vergleiche Definition von Lernziele.

CA:277, DA:136, DE:215, EN:208, ES:290, FR:289, GA:360, IT:255, NE:217, PO:292.

216 Lernziele Kenntnisse, Kompetenzen oder Einstellungen, die als Ziel irgendeiner pädagogischen Maßnahme festgelegt werden.

CA:278, DA:244, DE:216, EN:256, ES:291, FR:288, GA:359, IT:254, NE:112, PO:293.

217 lernzielorientierter Test Test, der in engem Zusammenhang zu einem bestimmten Lehrplan steht und eine bestimmte Funktion im Unterrichtsablauf einnimmt.
Vergleiche: lernzielunabhängiger Test.
Siehe: Sprachstandstest.

CA:325, DA:56, DE:217, EN:88, ES:313, FR:365, GA:406, IT:374, NE:221, PO:380.

218 lernzielunabhängiger Test Test, der nicht in Verbindung mit einem bestimmten Lehrplan oder Kurs steht.
Siehe: Feststellungsprüfung.

CA:328, DA:57, DE:218, EN:89, ES:339, FR:387, GA:405, IT:376, NE:222, PO:388.

219 Lesbarkeitsindex Maß für die grammatikalische oder lexikalische Komplexität, womit eingeschätzt wird, wie verständlich ein Leser einen Text empfinden wird. Beispiele für Lesbarkeitsindizes sind Gunnings Fog-Index und Fleschs Readability-Skala.

CA:210, DA:222, DE:219, EN:320, ES:226, FR:211, GA:189, IT:198, NE:223, PO:221.

220 Leseverständnisaufgabe Aufgabentyp, der im allgemeinen aus einem oder mehreren Lesetexten besteht und darauf bezogene Fragen der folgenden Art: Multiple-Choice, Kurzantwort-Fragen, Lückenaufgaben, Informationstransfer usw.

CA:394, DA:223, DE:220, EN:321, ES:3, FR:357, GA:373, IT:74, NE:224, PO:351.

221 Lexis Gleichbedeutend mit Wortschatz.

CA:237, DA:212, DE:221, EN:210,

ES:257, FR:238, GA:213, IT:225, NE:227, PO:250.

222 Likert-Skala Skalentyp, der in Fragebogen zur Messung von Einstellungen oder Meinungen verwendet wird. So kann etwa gefordert werden, bei einer Reihe von Aussagen aus zumeist fünf Alternativen auszuwählen wie 'stimme vollständig zu', 'stimme weitgehend zu', 'weiß ich nicht', 'lehne ich weitgehend ab', 'lehne ich vollständig ab'.
Literatur: Bortz 1984, S.152.

CA:152, DA:214, DE:222, EN:211, ES:163, FR:129, GA:317, IT:325, NE:228, PO:163.

223 lineare Regression Eine regressionsanalytische Technik, bei der angenommen wird, daß eine lineare Beziehung zwischen abhängiger und unabhängiger Variable besteht.
Literatur: Bortz 1993, S.167–175.

CA:370, DA:215, DE:223, EN:213, ES:366, FR:325, GA:5, IT:299, NE:230, PO:329.

224 linguistische Kompetenz Vergleiche Definition von Kompetenz.

CA:68, DA:217, DE:224, EN:214, ES:64, FR:67, GA:198, IT:66, NE:231, PO:80.

225 Live Test (Item) Der Begriff bezeichnet Tests oder Testaufgaben, die sich aktuell im Einsatz befinden und deshalb geheim gehalten werden müssen.

CA:341, DA:101, DE:225, EN:217, ES:344, FR:360, GA:407, IT:355, NE:233, PO:362.

226 logischer Fehler Urteilsfehler, der auftritt, wenn der Bewerter aufgrund anderer als der zu messenden Faktoren einen Punktwert vergibt. Ein Beispiel wäre die Erhöhung eines Punktwerts bei einem Schreibtest aufgrund einer schönen Handschrift.
Siehe: Urteilsfehler.
Literatur: Bortz 1984, S.127.

CA:118, DA:9, DE:226, EN:71, ES:122, FR:136, GA:174, IT:141, NE:74, PO:132.

227 Logit Eine Maßeinheit in probabilistischen Testmodellen, abgeleitet aus dem natürlichen Logarithmus des Verhältnisses von Erfolgs- zu Mißerfolgswahrscheinlichkeit. Die in Logits ausgedrückte Differenz zwischen der Fähigkeit einer Person und der Schwierigkeit einer Aufgabe ist die für diese Person geltende Wahrscheinlichkeit für die erfolgreiche Lösung dieser Aufgabe.
Literatur: Henning 1987, S.118–126.

CA:241, DA:220, DE:227, EN:218, ES:259, FR:240, GA:216, IT:232, NE:234, PO:253.

228 Lösungsschlüssel Eine Liste der akzeptablen Antworten auf die in einer Prüfung oder in einem Test gestellten Fragen. Ein Lösungsschlüssel ermöglicht einem Auswerter die genaue Zuweisung von Punktwerten zu einem Test.

CA: 52/256, DA:319, DE:228, EN:223, ES:301, FR:29, GA:324, IT:329, NE:79, PO:172.

229 Lückenaufgabe Jede Aufgabe, bei der vom Prüfling verlangt wird, daß er schriftlich in eine Leerstelle innerhalb eines Textes etwas einzusetzen hat, wobei es sich um Buchstaben, Ziffern, einzelne Wörter, Satzteile, ganze Sätze oder Textabschnitte handeln kann. Es kann sowohl die freie Ergänzung der Antwort als auch die Auswahl der richtigen Lösung aus mehreren Alternativen gefordert sein.

CA:223, DA:138, DE:229, EN:151, ES:241, FR:317, GA:249, IT:78, NE:192, PO:235.

230 Lückentest Vergleiche Definition von Cloze-Test, C-Test.

CA:314, DA:308, DE:230, EN:318, ES:316, FR:371, GA:60, IT:56, NE:315, PO:367.

231 mechanische Auswertung Bewertungsmethode, bei der die Bewerter über kein besonderes Fachwissen und subjektives Urteilsvermögen verfügen müssen. Sie bewerten nach einem Bewertungsschema, in dem alle zulässigen Antworten für jede Aufgabe des Tests festgelegt sind.
Vergleiche: Expertenbewertung.

CA:86, DA:23, DE:231, EN:51, ES:78, FR:274, GA:219, IT:31, NE:25, PO:62.

232 Median Der Wert im Zentrum einer Verteilung bei nach Rängen geordneten Daten. Die Hälfte der Werte sind oberhalb, die andere Hälfte unterhalb des Medians.
Siehe: zentrale Tendenz (Messung der).
Vergleiche: Mittelwert, Modalwert.
Literatur: Hatch & Lazarton 1991, S.161; Bortz 1993, S. 38.

CA:244, DA:228, DE:232, EN:232, ES:263, FR:242, GA:3, IT:235, NE:239, PO:256.

233 Mehrfach-Bewertung Methode zur Erhöhung der Reliabilität der Testbewertung bei Tests mit freien Antworten, bei denen die Bewertung im gewissen Umfang subjektiv ist. Dies wird dadurch erreicht, daß jede Antwort unabhängig von mehr als

einem Bewerter beurteilt wird.
Literatur: Weir 1988, S.65–66.
CA:87, DA:274, DE:233, EN:240, ES:45, FR:271, GA:183, IT:105, NE:241, PO:63.

234 Mehrfach-Wahlaufgabe Vergleiche Definition von Multiple-Choice-Aufgabe.
CA:220, DA:236, DE:234, EN:238, ES:244, FR:222, GA:247, IT:211, NE:252, PO:236.

235 Mehrfach-Zuordnungsaufgabe Testtyp, der aus einer Anzahl von Fragen oder Satzvervollständigungsaufgaben besteht, im allgemeinen auf einem Lesetext basierend. Die Antworten werden als Schüttelkasten, d.h. in Form einer Sammlung von Worten oder Textpassagen vorgegeben, die beliebig oft verwendet werden können. Der Vorteil besteht darin, daß die Antwortmöglichkeiten nicht reduziert werden, während der Prüfling den Test bearbeitet (was bei anderen Zuordnungsaufgaben der Fall ist), wodurch der Test nicht zunehmend leichter wird.
Siehe: Zuordnungsaufgaben.
CA:396, DA:100, DE:235, EN:241, ES:8, FR:355, GA:372, IT:72, NE:253, PO:354.

236 mehrkategoriales eindimensionales Rasch-Modell Erweiterung des einfachen Rasch-Modells zur Einbeziehung von Testaufgaben, die mit einem mehrstufigen Punktsystem bewertet werden, beispielsweise bei der Beurteilung mündlicher Leistungen.
Vergleiche: Rasch-Modell.
Siehe: Partial-Credit Modell.
Literatur: Wright, B.D. & Masters, G.N. 1982, Rating scale analysis. Chicago, MESA Press; Kubinger 1989, S.54–55.
CA:254, DA:173, DE:236, EN:316, ES:272, FR:251, GA:303, IT:246, NE:41, PO:263.

237 mehrstufige Punktevergabe Mehrstufige Punktevergabe bedeutet, daß eine Antwort nach mehr als zwei Punktstufen (d.h. richtig oder falsch) bewertet wird. Beispielsweise kann für die Antwort auf eine Frage 0, 1 oder 2 Punkte vergeben werden (drei Stufen). Offene Fragen werden oft mehrstufig bewertet.
Vergleiche: zweistufige Bewertung.
CA:351, DA:291, DE:237, EN:284, ES:353, FR:89, GA:342, IT:34, NE:293, PO:64.

238 Merkmalsbereich Der festgelegte Inhalts- oder Fähigkeitsbereich, der durch eine bestimmte Aufgabe oder Prüfungskomponente geprüft werden soll.
Literatur: Bachman 1990, S.244–246.
CA:11, DA:83, DE:238, EN:119, ES:119, FR:113, GA:137, IT:332, NE:113, PO:129.

239 Meßfehler Vergleiche Definition von Standardmeßfehler.
CA:138, DA:240, DE:239, EN:130, ES:146, FR:153, GA:130, IT:159, NE:243, PO:149.

240 Meßfehler Vergleiche Definition von Fehler.
CA:138, DA:241, DE:240, EN:231, ES:146, FR:153, GA:123, IT:159, NE:242, PO:149.

241 Messung Allgemein der Prozeß, die Menge von irgend etwas zu bestimmen durch Vergleich mit einer festgelegten Maßeinheit. In den Sozialwissenschaften bezieht sich Messung auf die Quantifizierung von Personenmerkmalen wie beispielsweise Fremdsprachenbeherrschung.
Literatur: Bachman 1990, Kap. 2, Bortz 1984, S.42–45.
CA:245, DA:242, DE:241, EN:230, ES:264, FR:243, GA:395, IT:238, NE:245, PO:257.

242 Methodeneffekt Ein sich auf die Testwerte auswirkender Effekt, der durch die Testmethode bedingt ist und nicht durch die Fähigkeit des Prüflings.
CA:121, DA:229, DE:242, EN:233, ES:126, FR:139, GA:171, IT:142, NE:244, PO:134.

243 Minderungskorrektur Methode, mit der geschätzt wird, wie hoch die Korrelation zwischen zwei oder mehr Variablen wäre, wenn diese eine perfekte Reliabilität von 1,0 hätten.
Literatur: Guilford & Fruchter 1981, S. 450–453; Hatch & Lazarton 1990, S.444–445; Lienert & Raatz 1994, S. 257–259.
CA:88, DA:194, DE:243, EN:76, ES:79, FR:82, GA:53, IT:106, NE:78, PO:99.

244 Mittelwert Ein Koeffizient für zentrale Tendenz, oftmals auch als Durchschnitt bezeichnet. Der Mittelwert einer Testdurchführung wird errechnet, indem alle Testwerte addiert und durch die Anzahl der Testwerte geteilt werden.
Siehe: Median, Modalwert.
Vergleiche: zentrale Tendenz (Messung der).
Literatur: Hatch & Lazarton 1991, S.161–163; Bortz 1993, S.38–39.
CA:250, DA:231, DE:244, EN:227, ES:261, FR:257, GA:226, IT:234, NE:151, PO:255.

245 mittlere Quadratsumme Bezeichnung für die Varianz in der Varianzanalyse, im Deutschen meist nur als Varianz bezeichnet.
Siehe: Varianzanalyse.
CA:251, DA:230, DE:245, EN:229, ES:262, FR:47, GA:227, IT:295, NE:149, PO:319.

246 mittlere Schwierigkeit Durchschnittlicher Anteil richtiger Antworten über alle Aufgaben einer Skala dichotomer Aufgaben. Eine mittlere Schwierigkeit von 0,5 entspricht einer mittleren Leichtigkeit ebenfalls von 0,5.
Siehe: zweistufige Bewertung.
CA:208, DA:132, DE:246, EN:228, ES:227, FR:212, GA:190, IT:195 NE:150, PO:222.

247 Modalwert Der höchste Punkt in einer Häufigkeitsverteilung von Punktwerten, somit der Punkt in der Verteilung, der die von den Kandidaten am häufigsten erreichte Punktzahl anzeigt.

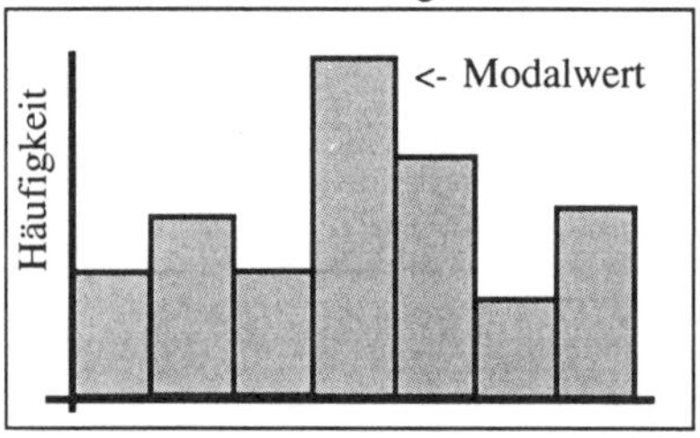

Vergleiche: bimodale Verteilung, Mittelwert, Median.
Siehe: zentrale Tendenz (Messung der).
Literatur: Hatch & Lazarton 1991, S.160–161; Bortz 1993, S.37.
CA:252, DA:232, DE:247, EN:235, ES:268, FR:247, GA:255, IT:240, NE:248, PO:261.

248 Modellanpassung Grad der Übereinstimmung zwischen einer Vorsage aus einem mathematischen Modell und den tatsächlichen Ergebnissen. Im Deutschen wird dafür auch der englische Begriff "fit" gebraucht. Unterschiedliche Indizes können berechnet werden. In probabilistischen Testmodellen zeigt die Analyse der Anpassung, wie gut die geschätzten Aufgaben- und Personenparameter (z.B. Schwierigkeit und Fähigkeit) die beim Test erzielten, persönlichen Testwerte vorherzusagen gestatten. Der Anpassungsindex einer Aufgabe kann als Entsprechung des Trennschärfekoeffizienten bei der klassischen Teststatistik angesehen werden.
Siehe: probabilistische Testmodelle.
CA:8, DA:99, DE:248, EN:145, ES:15, FR:6, GA:268, IT:107, NE:135, PO:5.

249 Multiple-Choice-Aufgabe Aufgabentyp, der aus einer Frage besteht oder einem unvollständigen Satz (Aufgabenstamm) und einer Auswahl von Antworten oder von Möglichkeiten zur Vervollständigung des vorgegebenen Satzes (Optionen). Der Prüfling muß die richtige Antwort (Schlüsselantwort) aus drei, vier oder fünf Möglichkeiten auswählen. Damit ist es nicht notwendig, sprachlich zu antworten. Deshalb werden Multiple-Choice-Aufgaben vorwiegend in Lese- und Hörverständnistests verwendet. Sie können diskret oder textbezogen sein.
Siehe: unabhängige (diskrete) Aufgabe, textbezogene (textgebundene) Aufgabe.
CA:220, DA:236, DE:249, EN:238, ES:244, FR:222, GA:247, IT:211, NE:252, PO:236.

250 Multiple-Choice-Lückentest Aufgabentyp, bei dem der Prüfling zur Vervollständigung einer Textlücke die richtige Lösung aus einer Reihe von vorgegebenen Wörtern auszuwählen hat.
Siehe: Lückenaufgabe.
CA:224, DA:237, DE:250, EN:239, ES:242, FR:386, GA:215, IT:79, NE:251, PO:390.

251 multiple Regression Statistische Technik zur Ermittlung linearer Beziehungen zwischen mehreren unabhängigen Variablen und einer abhängigen Variablen. So könnte beispielsweise für die Aufgabenschwierigkeit als abhängige Variable die Beziehung zum Aufgabentyp, zur lexikalischen Schwierigkeit usw. untersucht werden.
Siehe: unabhängige Variable, Regression.
Literatur: Hatch & Lazarton 1991, S.480–486; Bortz 1993, S.415–419.
CA:371, DA:117, DE:251, EN:242, ES:367, FR:326, GA:182, IT:300, NE:240, PO:330.

252 Multitrait-Multimethod-Validierung Experimentelles Untersuchungsdesign für die Konstruktvalidierung, wobei eine Anzahl unabhängiger Eigenschaften jeweils mit einer Anzahl als unabhängig angenommener Meßmethoden erfaßt wird. Die Analyse soll beispielsweise zeigen, daß mehrere Messungen des Hörverständnisses mit verschiedenen Methoden untereinander höher korrelieren als die Messung verschiedener Fähigkeiten mit der gleichen Meßmethode.
Siehe: Konstruktvalidität.
Literatur: Bachman 1990, S.263–265; Fis-

seni 1990, S.88–91.
CA:108, DA:238, DE:252, EN:243, ES:109, FR:299, GA:111, IT:277, NE:254, PO:305.

253 Musterantwort Die erwartete Antwort auf eine offene Frage, die vom Testautor bereitgestellt wird und bei der Entwicklung eines Lösungsschlüssels verwendet werden kann, um die Auswerter anzuleiten.
CA:261, DA:233, DE:253, EN:236, ES:376, FR:333, GA:156, IT:245, NE:21, PO:340.

254 Musterkorrektur Auswahl an schriftlichen Arbeiten, durch die ein bestimmtes Fähigkeitsniveau charakterisiert wird. Sie wird verwendet, um die Bewertung zu standardisieren. Die Arbeiten werden von erfahrenen Bewertern korrigiert.
CA:268, DA:370, DE:254, EN:338, ES:132, FR:118, GA:344, IT:330, NE:420, PO:10.

255 Muttersprachler Sprecher einer Sprache, die er als erste Sprache lernte.
CA:286, DA:234, DE:255, EN:245, ES:216, FR:217, GA:47, IT:265, NE:255, PO:190.

256 *N, n* Abkürzung für Anzahl (number). Als Großbuchstabe bezeichnet *N* normalerweise die Anzahl von Fällen in einer Untersuchung oder die Anzahl von Personen in einer Population (Grundgesamtheit), dagegen drückt der Kleinbuchstabe *n* oftmals die Anzahl in einer Stichprobe oder Untergruppe aus. Beispiel: 'Der Test wurde von Diplomingenieuren bearbeitet (N=600), wovon 10% weiblich waren (n=60)'.
CA:269, DA:248, DE:256, EN:244, ES:282, FR:258, GA:261, IT:251, NE:259, PO:271.

257 net D Vergleiche Definition von D-Index.
CA:206, DA:246, DE:257, EN:247, ES:97, FR:115, GA:102, IT:194, NE:256, PO:111.

258 Neuskalierung Vergleiche Definition von Skalierung.
CA:367, DA:314, DE:258, EN:330, ES:389, FR:320, GA:29, IT:304, NE:166, PO:326.

259 nicht-parametrische Verfahren Statistische Techniken, bei denen nicht vorausgesetzt wird, daß die Daten einem bestimmten Verteilungstyp entsprechen bzw. die Daten nicht intervallskaliert sind. Ein bekanntes Beispiel ist der Chi-Quadrat-Test.
Vergleiche: parametrische Verfahren.
Literatur: Hatch & Lazarton 1991, S.237–239; Bortz, Lienert & Boehnke 1990, S.79–86.
CA:294, DA:131, DE:259, EN:249, ES:308, FR:309, GA:258, IT:274, NE:257, PO:315.

260 Niveau Das Ausmaß der Beherrschung, das notwendig ist, damit ein Schüler oder Student in eine bestimmte Klasse oder einen bestimmten Kurs kommt bzw. eine bestimmte Prüfung bewältigen kann, wird oftmals durch verschiedene Niveaustufen ausgedrückt. Diese werden oft z.B. als 'Grundstufe', 'Mittelstufe', 'Fortgeschrittene' benannt.
CA:270, DA:247, DE:260, EN:209, ES:283, FR:259, GA:210, IT:229, NE:258, PO:272.

261 Niveautest Test, bei dem für fast alle Teilnehmer ausreichend Zeit für die Beendigung aller Aufgaben zur Verfügung steht, der jedoch so schwierige Aufgaben enthält, daß es unwahrscheinlich ist, daß die meisten Personen alle Aufgaben richtig bearbeiten.
Vergleiche: Schnelligkeitstest.
CA:310, DA:299, DE:261, EN:288, ES:329, FR:379, GA:413, IT:360, NE:296, PO:371.

262 Nominalskala Skala für Kategorialdaten wie Geschlecht oder Muttersprache. Eine Variablenausprägung ist entweder vorhanden oder nicht vorhanden, wobei in der Regel die Auftretenshäufigkeit interessiert. Auch bekannt unter dem Begriff Kategorialskala.
Vergleiche: Intervallskala, Ordinalskala, Verhältnisskala.
Literatur: Hatch & Lazarton 1991, S.55–56; Bortz 1993, S.20.
CA:156, DA:249, DE:262, EN:248, ES:164, FR:133, GA:309, IT:326, NE:260, PO:166.

263 Norm Standard einer Leistung. In standardisierten Testverfahren wird die Norm durch die Ergebnisse einer großen Gruppe von Testteilnehmern festgelegt. Die auf den Ergebnissen dieser Gruppe basierenden Normen oder Standards werden zur Beurteilung der Testleistungen weiterer vergleichbarer Personengruppen herangezogen.
Siehe: Normierungsstichprobe, Normorientierter Test.
Literatur: Lienert & Raatz 1994, S.272–296; Fisseni 1990, S.91–100.
CA:273, DA:250, DE:263, EN:250,

ES:286, FR:264, GA:262, IT:252, NE:261, PO:278.

264 Normalisierung Veränderung von Punktwerten in der Weise, daß die Verteilung der Punktwerte in eine Normalverteilung transformiert wird. Üblicherweise wird die Prozentrang-Methode (Flächentransformation) verwendet.
Vergleiche: Standardwert.
Literatur: Lienert & Raatz, 1994, S.287–288.
CA:274, DA:253, DE:264, EN:253, ES:287, FR:263, GA:263, IT:253, NE:263, PO:279.

265 Normalverteilung Mathematische Verteilung, die als Grundannahme vieler statistischer Verfahren dient. Die Verteilung ist eine symmetrische Glockenkurve, bei der Mittelwert, Median und Modalwert an einem Punkt zusammenfallen. In Abhängigkeit von Mittelwert, Standardabweichung und Anzahl von Beobachtungen ergibt sich eine Familie von Verteilungen. Auch bekannt unter dem Begriff GaußVerteilung.
Vergleiche: bimodale Verteilung.
Literatur: Hatch & Lazarton 1991, S.164; Bortz 1993, S.42–47, 72–78.
CA:115, DA:252, DE:265, EN:252, ES:116, FR:108, GA:107, IT:134, NE:262, PO:123.

266 Normierungsstichprobe Normalerweise eine große Gruppe von Personen, die repräsentativ sind für diejenigen Personen, für die ein Test entwickelt wurde. Die Testbearbeitungen bzw. Testleistungen der Normierungsstichprobe werden für die Interpretation normorientierter Tests benötigt. Im Deutschen auch bezeichnet als Referenzstichprobe.
Siehe: normorientierter Test.
CA:197, DA:254, DE:266, EN:251, ES:214, FR:203, GA:264, IT:190, NE:265, PO:213.

267 Normierungsstichprobe Stichprobe einer genau definierten Population von Prüflingen, an der ein Test normiert wurde.
Siehe: Norm.
CA:196, DA:309, DE:267, EN:324, ES:213, FR:202, GA:166, IT:189, NE:316, PO:212.

268 normorientierter Test Test, bei dem die individuellen Testwerte in Beziehung zur Bearbeitung dieses Tests durch eine vergleichbare Gruppe von Personen interpretiert werden. Der Begriff wird zunehmend für Tests verwendet, deren Interpretation darauf gerichtet ist, Personen in Bezug zur Normgruppe oder untereinander in eine Rangfolge zu bringen.
Vergleiche: kriteriumsorientierter Test.
CA:336, DA:251, DE:268, EN:254, ES:340, FR:388, GA:426, IT:381, NE:264, PO:391.

269 Nostrifikation Die formale Anerkennung einer ausländischen Qualifikation für einen bestimmten Zweck durch eine Institution, z.B. Zulassung zu einem weiterführenden Studiengang.
CA:365, DA:15, DE:269, EN:323, ES:361, FR:321, GA:9, IT:303, NE:123, PO:325.

270 Note Ein Testwert kann auf einer Notenskala dargestellt werden, die beispielsweise von 1 bis 6 reicht, wobei 1 die beste Note ist, 2 mit guten, 3 mit befriedigenden, 4 mit ausreichenden Leistungen bestanden sowie 5 und 6 durchgefallen bedeuten.
Vergleiche: Punkte.
CA:275, DA:167, DE:270, EN:156, ES:288, FR:259, GA:164, IT:188, NE:426, PO:272.

271 Nullhypothese Eine Hypothese, unter der angenommen wird, daß zwischen zwei oder mehr Variablen keine Beziehung besteht. So ist zum Beispiel die Annahme, daß zwischen zwei Gruppen von Personen mit unterschiedlicher Muttersprache kein Unterschied in der Bearbeitung eines Tests besteht, eine Nullhypothese. Eine Nullhypothese kann nicht bestätigt werden, sondern lediglich verworfen oder nicht verworfen.
Literatur: Hatch & Lazarton 1991, S.24; Guilford & Fruchter 1981, S.146–147; Bortz 1993, S.106–107.
CA:202, DA:255, DE:271, EN:255, ES:217, FR:206, GA:167, IT:206, NE:266, PO:214.

272 objektiver Test Test, der mit einem Lösungsschlüssel ausgewertet werden kann, ohne daß die Meinung von Experten oder eine subjektive Beurteilung in die Auswertung einfließt.
CA:331, DA:257, DE:272, EN:257, ES:341, FR:389, GA:427, IT:377, NE:267, PO:392.

273 offene Frage Aufgabentyp in einem schriftlichen Test, bei dem der Prüfling eine Antwort ergänzen muß und diese nicht aus mehreren vorgegebenen auswählen kann. Diese Art von Aufgaben soll zu möglichst freien Antworten führen, deren Umfang zwischen einzelnen Wörtern und einem kompletten Aufsatz liegen kann. Der Lösungsschlüssel sieht deshalb eine

Reihe akzeptabler Antworten vor.
CA:292, DA:444, DE:273, EN:260, ES:305, FR:318, GA:56, IT:137, NE:273, PO:324.

274 optischer Belegleser Ein elektronisches Gerät, das Informationen direkt von einem Antwortbogen abliest. Test- oder Prüfungsteilnehmer können ihre Antworten auf einem Antwortbogen ankreuzen. Diese Informationen werden dann direkt in den Computer eingelesen. Wird auch als Scanner bezeichnet.
CA:242, DA:268, DE:274, EN:261, ES:255, FR:237, GA:214, IT:226, NE:274, PO:249.

275 Ordinalskala Meßskala, bei der die Prüflinge in eine Rangfolge gebracht werden, ohne daß dabei die Größe des Abstands gekennzeichnet wird.
Vergleiche: Nominalskala, Intervallskala, Verhältnisskala.
Literatur: Hatch & Lazarton 1991, S.56–57; Bortz 1993, S.20–21, 25.
CA:157, DA:271, DE:275, EN:265, ES:165, FR:134, GA:318, IT:327, NE:275, PO:167.

276 *p*-Wert Vergleiche Definition von Schwierigkeitsindex.
CA:427, DA:273, DE:276, EN:266, ES:424, FR:411, GA:269, IT:412, NE:277, PO:420.

277 Paper Im Englischen oftmals Bezeichnung eines Prüfungsteils.
CA:385, DA:393, DE:277, EN:267, ES:381, FR:182, GA:270, IT:168, NE:278, PO:87.

278 Parallelformen Vergleiche Definition von äquivalente Formen.
CA:188, DA:275, DE:278, EN:268, ES:206, FR:196, GA:144, IT:179, NE:279, PO:202.

279 Parameter Merkmal einer Population, beispielsweise die Standardabweichung einer Population.
Vergleiche: statistischer Kennwert.
CA:280, DA:276, DE:279, EN:269, ES:293, FR:291, GA:272, IT:259, NE:280, PO:296.

280 parametrische Verfahren Statistische Verfahren, bei denen davon ausgegangen wird, daß die Daten normalverteilt sind und auf Intervall- oder Verhältnisskalenniveau gemessen wurden. In der Praxis werden parametrische Verfahren meist schon dann verwendet, wenn sich eine Normalverteilung der Daten durch eine ausreichend große Stichprobe annähern läßt.
Vergleiche: nicht-parametrische Verfahren.
Literatur: Hatch & Lazarton 1991, 237–238; Bortz, Lienert & Boehnke 1990, S.79–86.
CA:295, DA:277, DE:280, EN:270, ES:309, FR:310, GA:259, IT:275, NE:281, PO:316.

281 Partial-Credit-Modell Ein probabilistisches Testmodell zur Verarbeitung mehrstufiger Daten. Jede mehrstufige Aufgabe eines Tests wird so abgebildet, daß jedem möglichen Testwert ein gesonderter Schwierigkeitswert zugeordnet ist. Die Verwendung dieses Modells bietet sich beispielsweise an für die Analyse einer Anzahl von Satzergänzungsaufgaben oder kurzen freien Antworten, z.B. die Benotung einer Aufgabe mit 1, 2 oder 3 Punkten, je nachdem, wie korrekt die Aufgabe gelöst wurde.
Vergleiche: mehrkategoriales eindimensionales Rasch-Modell, polytomes Rasch-Modell.
Siehe: Rasch-Modell.
Literatur: Wright & Masters 1982, S.40–48; Kubinger 1989, S.54–55.
CA:257, DA:278, DE:281, EN:272, ES:270, FR:253, GA:301, IT:244, NE:282, PO:267.

282 Part-Whole-Überschneidung Effekt, der beispielsweise auftritt, wenn die Werte eines Subtests mit den Gesamttestwerten korreliert werden. Dadurch, daß die Subtestwerte im Gesamttestwert enthalten sind, wird die Korrelation überhöht. Es existieren Korrekturmethoden für die Part-Whole Überschneidung.
Literatur: Henning 1987, S.69; Lienert & Raatz ,1994, S.96–97.
CA:63, DA:62, DE:282, EN:271, ES:387, FR:51, GA:283, IT:146, NE:276, PO:331.

283 Performanz Produktion von Sprache durch Sprechen oder Schreiben. Performanz im Sinne von Anwendung der Sprache wird oftmals sprachlicher Kompetenz gegenübergestellt, die sich auf die einer Sprache zugrundeliegenden Fähigkeiten bezieht.
Vergleiche: Kompetenz.
Siehe: Performanz-Test.
Literatur: Bachman 1990, S.51, 108.
CA:5, DA:282, DE:283, EN:277, ES:9, FR:297, GA:141, IT:267, NE:286, PO:304.

284 Performanz-Test Ein Test- oder Prüfverfahren, bei dem sich der Prüfling sprachlich in schriftlicher oder mündlicher Form äußern muß (z.B. Brief, Gespräch).

Solche Verfahren werden entwickelt, um authentische Verwendungssituationen der Fremdsprache widerzuspiegeln.
Literatur: Bachman 1990, S.304–305.

CA:306, DA:283, DE:284, EN:278, ES:318, FR:380, GA:416, IT:367, NE:287, PO:381.

285 Perzentil Die 99 Skalenpunkte, die sich bei der Aufteilung einer Häufigkeitsverteilung in 100 Gruppen gleicher Größe ergeben. Der 50. Perzentil (P50) wird Median genannt. Quartile teilen die Verteilung in vier gleiche Gruppen.
Literatur: Hatch & Lazarton 1991, S.187–188; Bortz 1993, S.40–41.

CA:287, DA:280, DE:285, EN:275, ES:299, FR:49, GA:279, IT:266, NE:284, PO:302.

286 Phi-Koeffizient Korrelationskoeffizient, der verwendet wird, um die Enge des Zusammenhangs zwischen zwei binären Variablen darzustellen, beispielsweise zwischen zwei Testaufgaben, die nur nach richtig oder falsch bewertet werden.
Siehe: Korrelationskoeffizient.
Literatur: Guilford & Fruchter 1981, S.316–318; Crocker & Algina 1986, S.92–94; Bortz 1993, S.210–211.

CA:62, DA:284, DE:286, EN:279, ES:59, FR:58, GA:76, IT:61, NE:288, PO:75.

287 Phi-Korrelation Vergleiche Definition von Phi-Koeffizient.

CA:92, DA:285, DE:287, EN:280, ES:88, FR:88, GA:81, IT:101, NE:289, PO:103.

288 Pilotstudie Eine Vorstudie, durch die der Forscher oder Testentwickler seine Ideen an einer begrenzten Personenstichprobe erprobt zu dem Zweck, Probleme zu erkennen, bevor eine Erprobung mit einer großen Stichprobe oder ein Programm durchgeführt bzw. ein Produkt auf den Markt gebracht wird.
Siehe: Erprobung, Vorerprobung.

CA:170, DA:286, DE:288, EN:281, ES:178, FR:163, GA:361, IT:344, NE:290, PO:180.

289 polytomes Rasch-Modell Eine Erweiterung des Rasch-Modells, die die Abbildung von Antwortwahrscheinlichkeiten auf der Grundlage der Kombination zusätzlicher Parameter gestattet. So kann die Bearbeitung einer schriftlichen Aufgabe so abgebildet werden, daß sich darin zusätzlich zur Aufgabenschwierigkeit auch die Strenge des Bewerters abbildet. Das mehrparametrische Rasch-Modell kann beispielsweise mit dem Programm FACETS gerechnet werden.
Siehe: Rasch-Modell.
Literatur: Linacre, J.M. 1989, Many-Facet Rasch Measurement, Chicago, MESA Press; Fischer 1983, S.665–675; Kubinger 1989, S.45–51.

CA:260, DA:235, DE:289, EN:220, ES:276, FR:254, GA:300, IT:249, NE:236, PO:268.

290 Population Ein vollständiger Satz von Werten, beispielsweise alle möglichen Prüflinge einer Prüfung. In der Statistik wird auch der Begriff Grundgesamtheit verwendet.
Vergleiche: Stichprobe.

CA:289, DA:292, DE:290, EN:285, ES:302, FR:303, GA:280, IT:269, NE:294, PO:308.

291 Portfolio-Beurteilung Beurteilungstechnik, bei der der Prüfling über eine gewisse Zeit Proben seiner Arbeiten sammelt und diese dann als Beleg seiner Befähigung vorlegt.

CA:386, DA:293, DE:291, EN:286, ES:185, FR:304, GA:237, IT:270, NE:37, PO:309.

292 Positionseffekt (serialer Effekt) Urteilsfehler, der sich aus der Reihenfolge ergibt, in der Bewertungen vorgenommen werden.
Siehe: Urteilsfehler.

CA:120, DA:329, DE:292, EN:360, ES:125, FR:142, GA:172, IT:148, NE:337, PO:136.

293 Power-Test Vergleiche Definition von Niveautest.

CA:311, DA:299, DE:293, EN:288, ES:329, FR:379, GA:413, IT:360, NE:296, PO:371.

294 prädiktive Validität Hinweis darauf, wie gut ein Test künftige Leistungen bezogen auf die relevante Fertigkeit vorherzusagen gestattet. Im Deutschen auch: Vorhersagevalidität.
Vergleiche: Kriteriumsvalidität.
Literatur: Guilford & Fruchter 1987, S.437–438; Lienert & Raatz 1994, S. 223–224; Fisseni 1990, S.80–81.

CA:425, DA:298, DE:294, EN:291, ES:422, FR:422, GA:38, IT:410, NE:300, PO:418.

295 pragmatische Kompetenz Mögliche Kategorie in einem Modell sprachlicher Fähigkeiten:Sie beinhaltet die Fähigkeit zur Durchführung bestimmter sprachlicher Handlungen und die Kenntnis soziolinguistischer Konventionen.
Literatur: Bachman 1990, S.42.

CA:69, DA:294, DE:295, EN:290, ES:66, FR:69, GA:194, IT:68, NE:297, PO:83.

296 probabilistische Testmodelle Eine Gruppe mathematischer Modelle zur Herstellung von Beziehungen zwischen individuellen Testleistungen und dem Fähigkeitsniveau einer Person. Diese Modelle basieren auf der grundlegenden theoretischen Annahme, wonach der zu erwartende Erfolg bei der Bearbeitung einer Aufgabe eine Funktion sowohl des Schwierigkeitsgrades der Aufgabe als auch des individuellen Fähigkeitsniveaus der jeweiligen Person ist. Die Modelle werden auch unter dem Begriff Item-Response-Theorie zusammengefaßt.
Literatur: Henning 1987, Kap. 8; Fisseni 1990, S.116–142.

CA:401, DA:159, DE:296, EN:195, ES:394, FR:400, GA:389, IT:352, NE:201, PO:360.

297 probabilistisches Modell Modell, in dem Kausalbeziehungen (wie zwischen Aufgabenschwierigkeit und Fähigkeit eines Probanden bei der Bearbeitung des Tests) erklärt werden durch Wahrscheinlichkeitsaussagen. Das Rasch-Modell ist ein Beispiel für probabilistische Modelle.

CA:262, DA:295, DE:297, EN:294, ES:274, FR:255, GA:299, IT:247, NE:430, PO:269.

298 Produkt-Moment-Korrelation nach Pearson (Pearsons *r*) Korrelationskoeffizient, der für Variablen geeignet ist, die auf Intervall- oder Verhältnisskalenniveau gemessen wurden.
Siehe: Korrelationskoeffizient.
Literatur: Hatch & Lazarton 1991, S.427–431; Guilford & Fruchter 1981, S.81; Bortz 1993, S.189–191.

CA:59, DA:279, DE:298, EN:274, ES:90, FR:87, GA:84, IT:98, NE:283, PO:104.

299 Prozentrang Zahl oder Punktwert, der den Rangplatz eines Individuums dadurch ausdrückt, daß der Prozentsatz von Personen mit niedrigeren Punktwerten angegeben wird. Wenn ein Prüfling einen Prozentrang von 60 hat, bedeutet dies, daß 60% aller Prüflinge den gleichen oder einen niedrigeren Punktwert erzielten.
Literatur: Lienert & Raatz 1994, S.287–288.

CA:363, DA:281, DE:299, EN:276, ES:359, FR:53, GA:284, IT:55, NE:285, PO:276.

300 Prozentrangskala Ordinalskala, die in 100 Einheiten oder Centile unterteilt ist. Wenn jemand den Prozentrang von 95 erhält, bedeutet dies, daß diese Person in einer repräsentativen Stichprobe von 100 Personen besser abschneidet als 95 dieser Personen. Auch als Perzentilskala bezeichnet.
Literatur: Crocker & Algina 1986, S.439–442; Guilford & Fruchter 1981 S. 38–41; Lienert & Raatz 1994, S. 287.

CA:151, DA:46, DE:300, EN:46, ES:155, FR:124, GA:311, IT:319, NE:54, PO:157.

301 Prüfer Vergleiche Definition von Bewerter.

CA:172, DA:89, DE:301, EN:135, ES:189, FR:174, GA:346, IT:165, NE:130, PO:182.

302 Prüfling Teilnehmer an einer Prüfung oder einem Test. Auch als Testteilnehmer oder Prüfungskandidat bezeichnet.

CA:45, DA:165, DE:302, EN:41, ES:48, FR:41, GA:178, IT:49, NE:207, PO:48.

303 Prüfung Prozedur zur Feststellung der Leistungsfähigkeit oder des Kenntnisstandes von Personen durch mündliche und/oder schriftliche Aufgaben. Das Erreichen einer Qualifikation (z.B. durch ein Abschlußzeugnis oder ein Zertifikat bestätigt) oder der Zugang zu einer Ausbildung oder einem Studium etc. kann von dem Ergebnis abhängen.
Vergleiche: Test, Testbatterie.
Literatur: Bachman 1990, S.50.

CA:171, DA:86, DE:303, EN:133, ES:188, FR:173, GA:347, IT:164, NE:127, PO:181.

304 Prüfung der Mindestanforderungen Testmethode, bei der spezifische Anforderungen hinsichtlich eines Minimalniveaus der Kompetenz in einem bestimmten Bereich der Sprachverwendung gestellt werden. Ein Prüfling, der dieses Kompetenzniveau zeigen kann, besteht den Test.

CA:312, DA:398, DE:304, EN:234, ES:183, FR:167, GA:378, IT:388, NE:246, PO:31.

305 Prüfungsgespräch Methode zur Überprüfung der Sprechfertigkeit, die von einem völlig freien Gespräch zwischen Prüfling(en) und Prüfer(n) bis zu einer vollstrukturierten Serie sprachlicher Aufgaben reichen kann.

CA:131, DA:150, DE:305, EN:263, ES:136, FR:148, GA:1, IT:92, NE:355, PO:143.

306 Prüfungsteil Teil einer Prüfung, der oft als unabhängiger Test vorgegeben wird, mit eigenem Anweisungsheft und eigener Zeitbegrenzung. Prüfungsteile beziehen sich oft auf spezielle Einzelfertigkeiten und sind überschrieben mit Titeln wie 'Hörverständnis' oder 'Aufsatz'.

CA:73, DA:181, DE:306, EN:61, ES:29, FR:72, GA:85, IT:81, NE:128, PO:87.

307 Prüfungsteilnehmer Vergleiche Definition von Prüfling.

CA:173, DA:87, DE:307, EN:134, ES:190, FR:351, GA:345, IT:49, NE:129, PO:183.

308 Prüfungstermin Datum oder Zeitraum, an oder in dem eine Prüfung stattfindet. Viele Prüfungen werden zu bestimmten, festgelegten Terminen mehrfach im Jahr durchgeführt, während andere nach Bedarf angeboten werden.

CA:6, DA:403, DE:308, EN:8, ES:77, FR:7, GA:288, IT:331, NE:10, PO:23.

309 Prüfungsziel der spezielle Aspekt, der mit dem Item bzw. einer Aufgabe überprüft werden soll.

CA:128, DA:399, DE:309, EN:409, ES:289, FR:300, GA:281, IT:293, NE:384, PO:307.

310 psychometrischer Test Test für psychologische Merkmale wie Persönlichkeit, Intelligenz, Eignung und Sprachbeherrschung, wobei bestimmte Annahmen über die Art der geprüften Eigenschaften gemacht werden, wie etwa, daß sie eindimensional und normalverteilt sind.
Literatur: Bachman 1990, S.73–74.

CA:334, DA:302, DE:310, EN:301, ES:397, FR:390, GA:433, IT:379, NE:308, PO:394.

311 Punkt-biseriale Korrelation Kennwert für die Diskriminationsfähigkeit zweistufiger Aufgaben, normalerweise mit r_{pbi} bezeichnet; Korrelation zwischen einem Kriterium (normalerweise dem Gesamttestwert) und der Antwort auf die einzelne Aufgabe. Vorteil von r_{pbi} gegenüber der biserialen Korrelation r_{bis} besteht darin, daß er auch verwendet werden kann, wenn die zugrundeliegende Fähigkeit nicht normalverteilt ist.
Vergleiche: biseriale Korrelation.
Literatur: Bortz 1993, S.207–208.

CA:57, DA:41, DE:311, EN:283, ES:86, FR:57, GA:80, IT:97, NE:309, PO:102.

312 Punkte a) Gesamtzahl der von jemandem erzielten Punktwerte in einem Test, entweder vor der Skalierung (Rohwert) oder danach (skalierter Wert).

b) Zuweisung von Zahlenwerten zu einer beobachteten Leistung.
Vergleiche: Messung.

CA:342, DA:328, DE:312, EN:348, ES:345, FR:275, GA:328, IT:278, NE:331, PO:280.

313 Punktwert Die Gesamtzahl der erreichbaren Punkte bei einer Aufgabe oder die Punktzahl, die ein Prüfling bei einer Aufgabe, einem Subtest oder Test erzielt hat.

CA:342, DA:287, DE:313, EN:224, ES:44, FR:287, GA:224, IT:292, NE:60, PO:105.

314 Qualifikation Bestätigung der Absolvierung eines anerkannten Kurses oder des erfolgreichen Ablegens einer Prüfung, was eine Person berechtigt, eine bestimmte Tätigkeit oder einen bestimmten Beruf auszuüben. Ein Zertifikat über die Beherrschung einer Sprache kann als Qualifikation für bestimmte Zwecke angesehen werden.
Vergleiche: Zertifikat, Diplom.

CA:360, DA:209, DE:314, EN:302, ES:405, FR:313, GA:46, IT:294, NE:214, PO:322.

315 Rangkorrelation Nicht auf den absoluten Variablenwerten basierende Korrelation, sondern auf der Rangfolge der Werte.
Literatur: Guilford & Fruchter 1981, S.294–296; Bortz 1993, S.214–215.

CA:60, DA:304, DE:315, EN:309, ES:89, FR:59, GA:82, IT:100, NE:312, PO:72.

316 Rasch-Modell Mathematisches Modell, auch als einfaches logistisches Modell bezeichnet, das eine Beziehung zwischen der Wahrscheinlichkeit, daß eine Person eine Aufgabe löst, und der Differenz zwischen der Fähigkeit dieser Person und der Schwierigkeit der Aufgabe annimmt. Mathematisch entspricht das Rasch-Modell dem einparametrischen Modell der Item-Response-Theorie. Das Rasch-Modell wurde in vielerlei Hinsicht erweitert, z.B. zur Einbeziehung von Lösungen, die mit einem mehrstufigen Punktesystem bewertet werden, oder zur Berücksichtigung mehrerer für die Schwierigkeit einer Aufgabe verantwortlicher Aspekte.
Siehe: probabilistische Testmodelle, Partial-Credit-Modell, mehrkategoriales einparametrisches Rasch-Modell, polytomes Rasch-Modell.
Literatur: Henning 1987, S.117–125; Fischer 1983, S.606–637; Fisseni 1990, S.116–142; Kubinger 1989 , S.21–45.

CA:259, DA:305, DE:316, EN:310, ES:275, FR:252, GA:302, IT:248, NE:313, PO:266.

317 Ratekorrektur Methode, um bei objektiven Tests die Begünstigung auszugleichen, die Personen haben, die versuchen, die richtige Antwort zu erraten.
Literatur: Ebel & Frisbie 1986, S.

215–218; Lienert & Raatz 1994, S. 68–69.
CA:82, DA:193, DE:317, EN:77, ES:80, FR:83, GA:54, IT:103, NE:77, PO:98.

318 Rateparameter Parameter probabilistischer Testmodelle, der sich auf die Ratewahrscheinlichkeit bezieht.
Siehe: probabilistische Testmodelle.
Literatur: Bachman 1990, S.204; Jäger & Petermann 1992, S. 324.
CA:283, DA:44, DE:318, EN:37, ES:296, FR:294, GA:275, IT:262, NE:50, PO:299.

319 Rateparameter Auch als C-Parameter bezeichnet in der Item-Response-Theorie.
CA:284, DA:122, DE:319, EN:159, ES:297, FR:295, GA:277, IT:263, NE:160, PO:301.

320 Realitätsnähe Sichtweise im Bereich von Sprachprüfungen, wonach Sprachtests solche Aufgabentypen einbeziehen sollten, die möglichst gut Alltagssituationen entsprechen. Bei der Forderung nach Realitätsnähe würde beispielsweise der Inhalt eines Tests für die Beurteilung, ob eine Person einem akademischen Sprachkurs gewachsen ist, auf einer Bedarfsanalyse und den in diesem Kurs üblicherweise vorkommenden sprachlichen Aktivitäten basieren.
Siehe: Authentizität.
Literatur: Bachman 1990, S.301–328.
CA:129, DA:433, DE:320, EN:322, ES:134, FR:345, GA:98, IT:23, NE:226, PO:349.

321 Regression Statistische Technik zur Vorhersage des wahrscheinlichsten Wertes einer Variablen (abhängige Variable) durch die bekannten Werte einer oder mehrerer anderer Variablen (unabhängige Variablen).
Literatur: Hatch & Lazarton 1991, S.467–480; Guilford & Fruchter 1981, S.346–361; Bortz 1993, S.168–181.
CA:369, DA:311, DE:321, EN:326, ES:365, FR:324, GA:4, IT:298, NE:318, PO:328.

322 Reliabilität (Zuverlässigkeit) Konsistenz oder Stabilität der mit einem Test vorgenommenen Messungen. Je reliabler ein Test ist, desto geringer ist der enthaltene Meßfehler. Ein Test, der einen systematischen Fehler enthält, z.B. eine bestimmte Personengruppe begünstigt oder benachteiligt, kann reliabel sein, nicht aber valide.
Vergleiche: Validität.
Siehe: KR-20 (Kuder-Richardson Formel 20), Alpha-Koeffizient, Split-Half-Reliabilität.
Literatur: Bachman 1990, S.24; Crocker & Algina 1986, Kap. 6; Lienert & Raatz 1994, S.9–10, 173–219.
CA:180, DA:312, DE:322, EN:327, ES:198, FR:183, GA:200, IT:6, NE:43, PO:193.

323 Reliabilitätskoeffizient Maß für Reliabilität mit Werten zwischen 0 und 1. Schätzungen der Reliabilität können auf der wiederholten Anwendung des Tests basieren (die zu ähnlichen Ergebnissen führen sollte) oder, wenn dies nicht möglich ist, auf einem Maß für innere Konsistenz. Wird mitunter auch als Reliabilitätsindex bezeichnet.
Siehe: innere Konsistenz, Reliabilität (Zuverlässigkeit), Testwiederholungsmethode.
CA:61, DA:313, DE:323, EN:328, ES:58, FR:61, GA:77, IT:59, NE:44, PO:74.

324 Replizierbarkeit Möglichkeit, bestimmte Forschungsergebnisse wiederholt bei verschiedenen Gelegenheiten zu erzielen, wodurch sich das Vertrauen in die Richtigkeit der Ergebnisse erhöht.
CA:373, DA:189, DE:324, EN:329, ES:370, FR:335, GA:185, IT:301, NE:165, PO:333.

325 Retest-Methode Vergleiche Definition von Testwiederholungsmethode.
CA:184, DA:318, DE:325, EN:410, ES:202, FR:188, GA:204, IT:9, NE:383, PO:197.

326 richtig-falsch-Aufgabe Art einer Auswahlantwort-Aufgabe, bei der der Prüfling vor dem Hintergrund eines vorgegebenen Textes für eine Anzahl von Aussagen entscheiden muß, ob er diese für richtig oder falsch hält.
CA:232, DA:326, DE:326, EN:419, ES:250, FR:429, GA:245, IT:218, NE:426, PO:243.

327 richtige Antwort Diejenige Reaktion auf eine Testaufgabe, die bei der Auswertung als korrekt bewertet wird.
CA:375, DA:190, DE:327, EN:333, ES:373, FR:331, GA:155, IT:307, NE:204, PO:337.

328 Rohwert Testwert, der noch nicht statistisch durch eine Transformation, Gewichtung oder Skalierung verändert wurde.
Siehe: Punkte.
CA:348, DA:321, DE:328, EN:319, ES:348, FR:276, GA:329, IT:282, NE:324, PO:281.

329 Rollenspiel Aufgabentyp, der mitunter bei der Prüfung der Sprechfähigkeit eingesetzt wird. Dabei müssen sich die Prüflinge vorstellen, daß sie sich in einer bestimmten Situation befinden und dabei bestimmte Rollen übernehmen.

CA:233, DA:320, DE:329, EN:334, ES:251, FR:232, GA:294, IT:202, NE:323, PO:345.

330 Rückmeldung Kommentare von in den Testprozeß eingebundenen Personen (Prüflinge, Prüfer, Auswerter etc.), die als eine Grundlage für die Evaluierung dieses Prozesses dienen. Rückmeldungen können informell gesammelt oder durch Einsatz eines für diesen Zweck konstruierten Fragebogens erfaßt werden.

CA:381, DA:97, DE:330, EN:144, ES:379, FR:337, GA:6, IT:173, NE:134, PO:192.

331 Rundung Verringerung der Genauigkeit einer Zahl durch Verringerung der Anzahl angegebener Ziffern. So kann beispielsweise die Zahl 564,8 zu 565 oder 560 gerundet werden, je nach notwendiger Genauigkeit; entsprechend kann 1273 zu 1270, 1300 oder 1000 gerundet werden.

CA:24, DA:245, DE:331, EN:335, ES:363, FR:22, GA:354, IT:24, NE:11, PO:25.

332 Satzergänzung Aufgabentyp, bei dem unvollständige Sätze vorgegeben sind. Der Prüfling muß die Sätze vervollständigen, indem er entweder passende Wörter ergänzt (die möglicherweise auf dem vorangegangenen Studium eines Textes basieren) oder aus verschiedenen Ergänzungsmöglichkeiten eine auswählt.

CA:72, DA:382, DE:332, EN:357, ES:69, FR:298, GA:93, IT:80, NE:442, PO:86.

333 Satzerweiterung Aufgabentyp, bei dem eine Reihe von Wörtern vorgegeben ist, Präpositionen, Hilfswörter, Artikel usw. jedoch fehlen. Der Prüfling muß die fehlenden Wörter ergänzen und mit den vorgegebenen Wörtern einen grammatikalisch vollständigen Satz bilden.

CA:99, DA:380, DE:333, EN:358, ES:18, FR:175, GA:148, IT:166, NE:441, PO:184.

334 Satzumformung Aufgabentyp, bei dem ein vollständiger Satz vorgegeben wird, gefolgt von einem oder zwei Wörtern eines zweiten Satzes, mit dem der gleiche Inhalt ausgedrückt werden soll wie im ersten Satz, dies jedoch in einer anderen grammatikalischen Form. So kann der erste Satz beispielsweise aktiv sein und die Aufgabe des Prüflings darin bestehen, den gleichen Inhalt in passiver Form auszudrücken.

CA:410, DA:381, DE:334, EN:359, ES:407, FR:404, GA:61, IT:397, NE:440, PO:405.

335 Säulendiagramm Grafische Darstellungsform für Häufigkeitsverteilungen von Variablen.

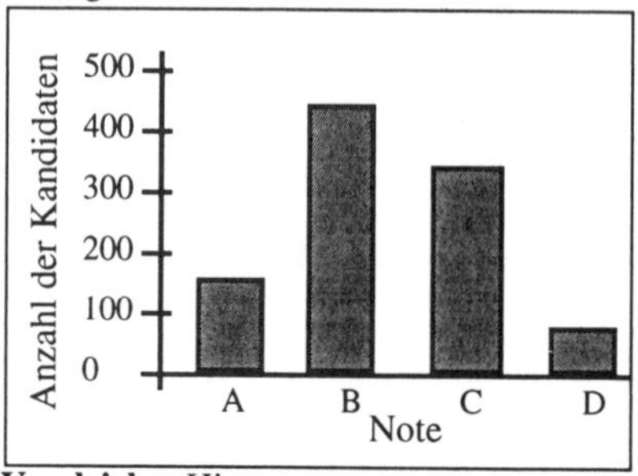

Vergleiche: Histogramm

Literatur: Hatch & Lazarton 1991, S.147; Bortz 1993, S. 31–34.

CA:102, DA:383, DE:335, EN:31, ES:104, FR:201, GA:42, IT:123, NE:357, PO:211.

336 Scanner Vergleiche Definition von optischer Belegleser.

CA:160, DA:327, DE:336, EN:347, ES:168, FR:342, GA:322, IT:226, NE:325, PO:346.

337 Schiefe Kennzeichen einer Häufigkeitsverteilung in Hinblick darauf, ob die Spitze der Kurve entweder rechts vom Zentrum liegt (negative Schiefe) oder links davon (positive Schiefe).

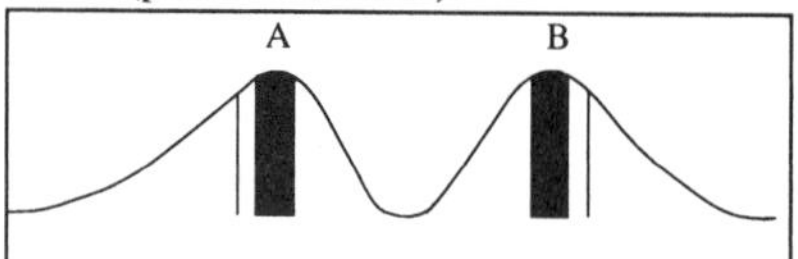

A -negative Schiefe B -positive Schiefe

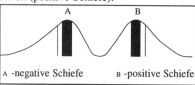

Siehe: Normalverteilung.

Literatur: Hatch & Lazarton 1991, S.165; Bortz 1993, S. 45–46.

CA:25, DA:343, DE:337, EN:366, ES:31, FR:109, GA:323, IT:25, NE:330, PO:120.

338 schließende Statistik (Inferenzstatistik) Statistische Methoden, die über von der beschreibenden Statistik bereitgestellte Informationen hinausgehen. Sie gestatten Vorhersagen darüber, wie repräsentativ ein einzelner Datensatz bei vorgegebener Wahrscheinlichkeit für eine größere Population ist, aus der dieser Datensatz eine Stichprobe darstellt.

Vergleiche: beschreibende (deskriptive) Statistik.

CA:166, DA:139, DE:338, EN:171,

ES:173, FR:350, GA:364, IT:341, NE:175, PO:177.

339 Schlüsselantwort a) die richtige Antwort bei einer Multiple-Choice-Aufgabe (Mehrfachwahlaufgabe).

b) eine Liste aller möglichen bzw. richtigen Antworten in einem Test.
Vergleiche: Distraktor.
Siehe: Multiple-Choice-Aufgabe, Lösungsschlüssel.

CA:51/52, DA:256, DE:339, EN:198, ES:54, FR:329, GA:133, DE:339, IT:53, NE:342, PO:335.

340 Schnelligkeitstest Test mit einer zeitlichen Begrenzung für die Bearbeitung. Langsamere Prüflinge erzielen in der Regel niedrigere Punktwerte, da sie nicht genügend Zeit für die Bearbeitung der letzten Fragen haben. Oftmals ist der Schwierigkeitsgrad der Aufgaben von zeitbegrenzten Tests so, daß der Prüfling alle Aufgaben richtig beantworten würde, bestünde nicht die zeitliche Begrenzung. Wird auch als Speeded-Test bezeichnet.
Vergleiche: Niveautest.

CA:321, DA:129, DE:340, EN:376, ES:334, FR:363, GA:424, IT:372, NE:352, PO:385.

341 schriftliche Arbeit Papier, das die Antworten eines Prüflings bei einer Prüfung enthält, besonders bei Aufgabentypen mit offener Beantwortung.

CA:191, DA:261, DE:341, EN:350, ES:219, FR:343, GA:343, IT:175, NE:218, PO:170.

342 schriftliche Stellungnahme Schriftliche Aufgabe, in der der Prüfling ein Thema diskutiert, zu dem man unterschiedliche Meinungen haben kann, oder bei dem man im Sinne der persönlichen Auffassung argumentieren soll.
Siehe: Aufsatz.

CA:74, DA:77, DE:342, EN:113, ES:70, FR:74, GA:52, IT:83, NE:42, PO:89.

343 Schwierigkeitsindex In der klassischen Testtheorie ist die Schwierigkeit einer Aufgabe der Anteil (Prozentsatz, p) der Prüflinge, der die Aufgabe richtig bearbeitete. Das bedeutet, daß der Schwierigkeitsindex der Aufgabe stichprobenabhängig ist und je nach Fähigkeitsniveau der Prüflinge variiert.
Vergleiche: Leichtigkeitsindex, *p*-Wert.
Literatur: Lienert & Raatz 1994, S. 73–78.

CA:207, DA:378, DE:343, EN:101, ES:224, FR:209, GA:187, IT:196, NE:249, PO:219.

344 Schwierigkeitsparameter Parameter der Item-Response-Theorie, der sich auf den Schwierigkeitsgrad einer Testaufgabe bezieht (auch B-Parameter genannt).

CA:285, DA:379, DE:344, EN:102, ES:298, FR:296, GA:276, IT:264, NE:250, PO:300.

345 Selbsteinstufung Prozeß, bei dem der Student sein eigenes Fähigkeitsniveau selbst beurteilt mit Hilfe entweder eines selbst auswertbaren Tests oder eines anderen Instruments, wie z.B. einem Fragebogen oder einer Checkliste.

CA:30, DA:331, DE:345, EN:354, ES:36, FR:27, GA:142, IT:38, NE:334, PO:29.

346 Selektionstest Test, der für die Entscheidung eingesetzt wird, ob ein Bewerber Zugang zu einer Institution oder einem Studium erhält.
Vergleiche: Einstufungstest.
Literatur: Fisseni 1990, S. 250–255.

CA:305, DA:5, DE:346, EN:124, ES:319, FR:369, GA:422, IT:364, NE:387, PO:377.

347 semi-direktes Prüfverfahren Test zur Erfassung sprachlicher Leistungsfähigkeit, wobei ein Anteil des persönlichen Einsatzes ersetzt ist, z.B. kann in einem Test zur Prüfung der Sprechfertigkeit anstelle eines Prüfers ein Tonband zur Vorgabe der Fragen und Aufgaben verwendet werden. Beispiel für ein semi-direktes Prüfverfahren ist das SOPI (Semi-Direct Oral Proficiency Interview).
Vergleiche: direktes Prüfverfahren.

CA:339, DA:332, DE:347, EN:356, ES:343, FR:392, GA:423, IT:383, NE:336, PO:396.

348 Sicherheit Bereich der Testadministration, der das Bekanntwerden des Inhalts der Testmaterialien verhindert, solange der Test regelmäßig eingesetzt wird.

CA:387, DA:335, DE:348, EN:351, ES:382, FR:344, GA:353, IT:333, NE:142, PO:347.

349 Signifikanz Statistischer Begriff, durch den ausgedrückt wird, ob ein Untersuchungsergebnis als zufällig anzusehen ist oder nicht.
Siehe: Fehler erster Art, Fehler zweiter Art, Nullhypothese.
Literatur: Guilford & Fruchter 1981, S.208–210; Bortz 1993, S.12, 108–112.

CA:388, DA:333, DE:349, EN:363, ES:386, FR:76, GA:366, IT:334, NE:338, PO:348.

350 Signifikanztest Test auf statis-

tische Signifikanz.
Siehe: Signifikanz.
CA:324, DA:334, DE:350, EN:364, ES:333, FR:373, GA:435, IT:371, NE:339, PO:384.

351 Situationsauthentizität Ausmaß, in dem ein Test als realitätsnah im Hinblick auf Alltagssituation anzusehen ist, also auf Situationen, in denen Sprache außerhalb einer Testsituation verwendet wird.
Vergleiche: Interaktionsauthentizität, Realitätsnähe.
Siehe: Authentizität.
Literatur: Bachman 1990, Kap. 8.
CA:29, DA:336, DE:351, EN:365, ES:35, FR:26, GA:117, IT:37, NE:340, PO:28.

352 Skala Satz von Zahlen oder Kategorien, die verwendet werden, um etwas zu messen. Man unterscheidet vier Skalenarten: Nominal-, Ordinal-, Intervall- und Verhältnisskala.
Literatur: Crocker & Algina 1986, S.46–49; Bortz, 1993 S.20–26.
CA:144, DA:337, DE:352, EN:343, ES:152, FR:121, GA:308, IT:314, NE:326, PO:154.

353 Skalendeskriptor Vergleiche Definition von Deskriptor.
CA:98, DA:338, DE:353, EN:344, ES:99, FR:96, GA:438, IT:119, NE:327, PO:112.

354 skalierter Wert Durch Skalierung erzielter Wert.
Siehe: Skalierung.
CA:349, DA:340, DE:354, EN:345, ES:349, FR:278, GA:337, IT:286, NE:153, PO:283.

355 Skalierung Prozeß der Entwicklung von Meßskalen. Bei Sprachprüfungen werden den Leistungen der Prüflinge Zahlen zugewiesen, um den jeweiligen Kenntnisstand oder das Fähigkeitsniveau zu charakterisieren. Skalierung kann auch die Modifikation eines Satzes von Zahlenwerten beinhalten, um eine Skala für einen ganz bestimmten Zweck zu erhalten, beispielsweise, um die Ergebnisse in standardisierter Form darzustellen oder um eine Testform an eine andere anzugleichen.
Siehe: Skala, Fähigkeitsskala, Prozentrangskala, gemeinsame Skala, Intervallskala, Nominalskala, Ordinalskala, Verhältnisskala, Bewertungsanleitung, angeglichene Testformen, Angleichung durch lineare Transformation.
CA:159, DA:341, DE:355, EN:346, ES:167, FR:135, GA:321, IT:109, NE:329, PO:169.

356 SOPI (Semi-Direct/Simulated Oral Proficiency Interview) Test für mündliche Sprachbeherrschung, bei dem von einem Tonband Instruktionen und Fragen vorgegeben werden und die Antworten des Prüflings aufgezeichnet werden, um diese zu einem späteren Zeitpunkt zu bewerten.
Vergleiche: semi-direktes Prüfverfahren.
CA:130, DA:348, DE:356, EN:370, ES:137, FR:392, GA:356, IT:93, NE:346, PO:144.

357 soziokulturelles Wissen Kenntnisse der Welt, die sich darauf beziehen, wie die Gesellschaft in einer bestimmten Kultur funktioniert. Dies ist wichtig, um sich in speziellen kulturellen Situationen angemessen zu verhalten und sprachlich auszudrücken.
Vergleiche: soziolinguistische Kompetenz.
CA:76, DA:346, DE:357, EN:368, ES:72, FR:341, GA:135, IT:86, NE:344, PO:90.

358 soziolinguistische Kompetenz Kategorie in Modellen sprachlichkommunikativer Fähigkeiten:Sie beinhaltet die Fähigkeit, sich sprachlich an bestimmte Rahmenbedingungen oder Situationen gemäß geltender sozialer Normen anzupassen.
Literatur: Bachman 1990, S.42.
CA:70, DA:347, DE:358, EN:369, ES:67, FR:70, GA:197, IT:69, NE:345, PO:84.

359 Spearman-Brown-Formel Statistische Methode zur Schätzung der Reliabilität eines Tests bei einer Verlängerung oder Verkürzung durch Hinzufügen oder Weglassen von Items. Die Formel kann verwendet werden, um die erforderliche Itemanzahl eines Tests zu schätzen, der eine bestimmte Reliabilität aufweisen soll.
Literatur: Crocker & Algina 1968, S.118–119; Lienert & Raatz 1994, S.100.
CA:83, DA:349, DE:359, EN:371, ES:207, FR:197, GA:147, IT:180, NE:350, PO:203.

360 Spearman-Brown-Halbierungskoeffizient Vergleiche Definition von Testhalbierungsmethode.
CA:168, DA:350, DE:360, EN:372, ES:177, FR:161, GA:228, IT:342, NE:349, PO:178.

361 Spearmans Rangkorrelation Form der Rangkorrelation für kleine Stichprobenumfänge (n<30).
Siehe: Rangkorrelation.
Literatur: Bortz, Lienert & Boehnke 1990, 414–422, 580.
CA:58, DA:351, DE:361, EN:373, ES:87,

FR:60, GA:83, IT:99, NE:347, PO:73.

362 Spearmans rho Vergleiche Definition von Spearmans Rangkorrelation.

CA:383, DA:352, DE:362, EN:374, ES:380, FR:339, GA:292, IT:302, NE:348, PO:344.

363 Speeded-Test Ein Test mit festgesetzter, relativ kurzer Bearbeitungszeit. Kandidaten, die die Aufgaben langsamer lösen, erhalten weniger Punkte, weil sie nicht bis zum Ende des Tests kommen. Im allgemeinen ist der Schwierigkeitsgrad der Aufgaben so, daß die Kandidaten die Aufgaben lösen könnten, wenn sie mehr Zeit hätten. Im Deutschen wird ein Speeded-Test oft auch als zeitbegrenzter Test bezeichnet.

CA:322, DA:129, DE:363, EN:376, ES:334, FR:363, GA:424, IT:372, NE:352, PO:385.

364 Split-Half-Reliabilität Vergleiche Definition von Testhalbierungsmethode.

CA:183, DA:259, DE:364, EN:377, ES:201, FR:184, GA:203, IT:7, NE:353, PO:194.

365 Sprachbeherrschung Kenntnis einer Sprache. Begriff wird oftmals synonym mit 'Sprachliche Fähigkeit' verwendet.
Literatur: Bachman 1990, S.16.

CA:297, DA:355, DE:365, EN:206, ES:121, FR:66, GA:267, IT:66, NE:215, PO:81.

366 Sprachebene Klar abgegrenzte Merkmale der gesprochenen oder geschriebenen Sprache bezogen auf ein bestimmtes Handlungsfeld oder einen bestimmten Grad an Förmlichkeit.

CA:368, DA:310, DE:366, EN:325, ES:364, FR:323, GA:291, IT:297, NE:317, PO:327.

367 Spracherwerb Der Prozeß, in dem die erste oder zweite Sprache erworben wird. Bei der zweiten Sprache wird mitunter zwischen Erwerb (z.B. durch natürlichen Umgang) und Erlernen (z.B. durch gezieltes Studium) unterschieden.

CA:7, DA:356, DE:367, EN:204, ES:14, FR:5, GA:349, IT:22, NE:380, PO:24.

368 sprachliche Fähigkeit Diejenigen Kompetenzen, die zusammengenommen die Möglichkeiten einer Person definieren, sprachlich eine Vielzahl kommunikativer Situationen zu bewältigen.
Literatur: Bachman 1990, S.3–4.

CA:47, DA:354, DE:368, EN:203, ES:50, FR:43, GA:97, IT:4, NE:379, PO:50.

369 Sprachstandstest Ein Test zur Messung der in einem bestimmten Lehrgang oder durch ein Lehrbuch erworbenen Kenntnisse. Auch bezeichnet als Kursabschlußprüfung.

CA:309, DA:366, DE:369, EN:6, ES:321, FR:374, GA:419, IT:368, NE:301, PO:374.

370 Sprechfertigkeit Kompetenz beim Sprechen einer Sprache.

CA:298, DA:239, DE:370, EN:264, ES:65, FR:68, GA:266, IT:67, NE:354, PO:82.

371 Stabilität Reliabilitätsaspekt, wobei die Reliabilitätsschätzung auf der Testwiederholungsmethode basiert. Er bezieht sich darauf, wie unveränderlich Testwerte über die Zeit sind.
Siehe: Reliabilität (Zuverlässigkeit), Testwiederholungsmethode.

CA:162, DA:359, DE:371, EN:378, ES:170, FR:79, GA:65, IT:337, NE:358, PO:173.

372 Standardabweichung Maß für die Streuung von Beobachtungen um den arithmetischen Mittelwert herum. Die Standardabweichung ist die Quadratwurzel der Varianz. Bei Vorliegen einer Normalverteilung liegen 68% der Fälle der Stichprobe innerhalb von einer Standardabweichung und 95% innerhalb von zwei Standardabweichungen links und rechts vom Mittelwert.

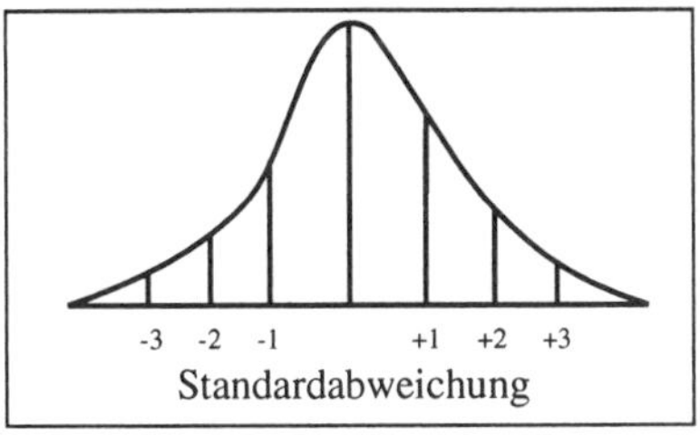

Vergleiche: Variationsbreite.
Siehe: Varianz.
Literatur: Ebel & Frisbie 1991, S.61–62; Crocker & Algina 1986, S.21–22; Bortz 1993, S.41–44.

CA:101, DA:362, DE:372, EN:379, ES:103, FR:98, GA:113, IT:122, NE:360, PO:114.

373 Standardisierung Prozeß, durch den sichergestellt werden soll, daß Bewerter sich an einer vereinbarten Vorgehensweise orientieren und Bewertungsanleitungen (Beurteilungsskalen) in geeigneter Weise verwenden.
Siehe: Bewerter.

CA:167, DA:363, DE:373, EN:383, ES:175, NE:361, FR:162, GA:45, IT:338, PO:295.

374 Standardmeßfehler In der klassischen Testtheorie, in der von wahren Werten und Meßfehlern ausgegangen wird, ist der Standardmeßfehler (*Se*) ein Indikator für die Ungenauigkeit einer Messung. Die Höhe des Standardmeßfehlers hängt von der Reliabilität (*r*) und der Standardabweichung der Testwerte (*Sx*) ab. Die Berechnungsformel ist

$$Se=Sx\sqrt{(1-r)}$$

Wenn also z.B. ein Prüfling mit einem wahren Testwert von T bei einem Test mit Standardmeßfehler von *Se* wiederholt einen Test bearbeitet, wird in 68% der Fälle der beobachtete Testwert im Bereich T±*Se* liegen und in 95% der Fälle im Bereich T±2*Se*.
Literatur: Crocker & Algina 1986, S.122–124; Lienert & Raatz 1994, S.364–368.

CA:143, DA:364, DE:374, EN:381, ES:149, FR:157, GA:125, IT:12, NE:362, PO:153.

375 Standardschätzfehler Maß für die Genauigkeit der Vorhersage einer Variablen aus einer anderen, beispielsweise bei der linearen Regression. Daraus ergeben sich Konfidenzintervalle für die Kriterienwerte.
Siehe: Konfidenzintervall.
Literatur: Hatch & Lazarton 1991, S.477–479; Bortz 1993, S.176–178.

CA:142, DA:361, DE:375, EN:380, ES:148, FR:156, GA:124, IT:163, NE:363, PO:152.

376 Standardwert Linear transformierter Wert aus einer Gruppe von Werten. Mittelwert und Standardabweichung werden je nach Bedarf des Nutzers festgesetzt. Beispiele für Standardwerte sind *z*- und *t*-Werte.
Vergleiche: *t*-Wert, *z*-Wert, Stanine-Wert.
Literatur: Ebel & Frisbie 1991, S.67–68; Lienert & Raatz 1994, S.284–287.

CA:350, DA:365, DE:376, EN:382, ES:350, FR:281, GA:333, IT:287, NE:364, PO:291.

377 Stanine-Wert Methode zur Aufteilung von Testwerten in neun Gruppen gemäß Normalverteilung. Die Personen werden prozentual so aufgeteilt, wie in der folgenden Abbildung dargestellt, wobei jeweils 4% in die oberste bzw. unterste Gruppe fallen:

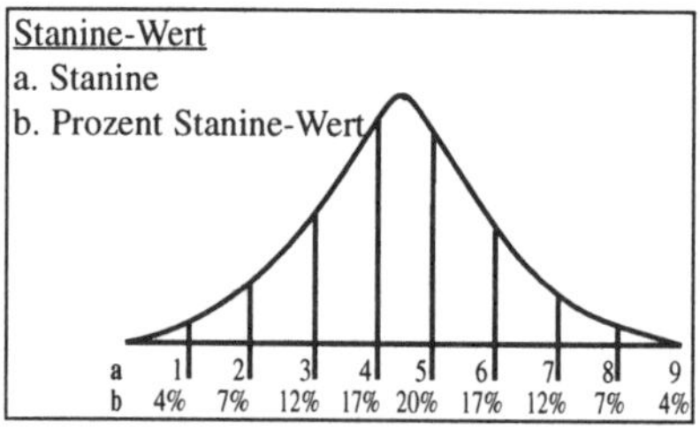

Literatur: Crocker & Algina 1986, S.446–447; Lienert & Raatz 1994, S.285.

CA:344, DA:367, DE:377, EN:384, ES:176, FR:282, GA:332, IT:279, NE:365, PO:284.

378 Statistik Wissenschaft von der Behandlung und Interpretation numerischer Daten.

CA:164, DA:369, DE:378, EN:386, ES:171, FR:348, GA:362, IT:339, NE:366, PO:175.

379 statistischer Kennwert Mengenangabe, durch die eine Information in Form einer Zahl ausgedrückt wird. Streng genommen stellt eine Statistik das Kennzeichen einer Stichprobe dar, während man Eigenschaften einer Population als Parameter bezeichnet. Statistiken werden generell mit römischen Buchstaben, Parameter mit griechischen bezeichnet. Beispielsweise wird die Standardabweichung einer Stichprobe mit s oder SD abgekürzt, während man sie bei einer Population als σ (Sigma) bezeichnet.
Vergleiche: Parameter.
Siehe: Population, Stichprobe.

CA:163, DA:368, DE:379, EN:385, ES:174, FR:348, GA:363, IT:117, NE:367, PO:174.

380 Stichprobe Auswahl eines Teils der Elemente einer Population. Man kann unterschiedliche Arten von Stichproben unterscheiden, z.B. Zufallsstichprobe, geschichtete Stichprobe.
Literatur: Crocker & Algina 1986, S.432–438; Guilford & Fruchter 1981, S.44–45; Bortz 1993, S.84–86.

CA:264, DA:371, DE:380, EN:337, ES:278, FR:116, GA:304, IT:46, NE:369, PO:8.

381 Stichprobenfehler In der Forschung der Fehler in einer statistischen Analyse, der durch die Auswahl einer bestimmten Untersuchungsstichprobe bedingt ist (z.B. dadurch, daß die Stichprobe nicht repräsentativ für die Population ist).
Siehe: Population.

CA:139, DA:372, DE:381, EN:341, ES:147, FR:158, GA:129, IT:155, NE:370, PO:148.

382 stichprobenunabhängige Messung In der Forschung die Interpretation von Ergebnissen, die nicht abhängig von der Stichprobe einer bestimmten Untersuchung sind.
Siehe: Stichprobe.

CA:247, DA:373, DE:382, EN:339, ES:265, FR:244, GA:396, IT:239, NE:371, PO:258.

383 Stichprobenverzerrung Man kann bei einem Test oder einer Aufgabe von Stichprobenverzerrung (Bias) sprechen, wenn ein bestimmter Anteil der Prüflingspopulation begünstigt oder benachteiligt ist durch bestimmte Merkmale des Tests oder der Aufgabe, die nicht Gegenstand dessen sind, was gemessen werden soll. Die Stichprobe kann bezüglich Geschlecht oder Alter, kultureller Besonderheiten etc. verzerrt sein.
Literatur: Bachman 1990, S. 271–279 Crocker & Algina 1986, Kap. 12 & 16; Bortz 1993, S. 85.

CA:40, DA:344, DE:383, EN:33, ES:384, FR:32, GA:208, IT:160, NE:46, PO:40.

384 Stichprobenziehung Auswahl einer Stichprobe.
Siehe: Stichprobe.

CA:267, DA:374, DE:384, EN:340, ES:281, FR:120, GA:307, IT:45, NE:368, PO:313.

385 Streuung Ausmaß an Variation oder Spannweite von Punktwerten in einem Datensatz. Die Streuung ist groß, wenn sich die Werte über einen weiten Bereich verteilen, sie ist gering, wenn die Werte sich auf einem engen Bereich konzentrieren.
Siehe: Standardabweichung, Varianz, Variationsbreite.
Literatur: Bortz 1993, S.40.

CA:107, DA:353, DE:385, EN:114, ES:110, FR:103, GA:357, IT:127, NE:356, PO:118.

386 Subtest Vergleiche Definition von Prüfungsteil.

CA:389, DA:377, DE:386, EN:389, ES:388, FR:346, GA:150, IT:345, NE:373, PO:350.

387 T-Test Statistischer Test, mit dem entschieden werden kann, ob ein signifikanter Unterschied zwischen den Mittelwerten zweier Stichproben besteht.
Literatur: Bortz 1993, S.130–137.

CA:340, DA:385, DE:387, EN:423, ES:398, FR:150, GA:368, IT:385, NE:377, PO:397.

388 *t*-Wert Umwandlung eines *z*-Wertes, bei der Dezimalstellen und negative Vorzeichen entfallen. Der *t*-Wert ergibt sich durch Multiplikation des *z*-Wertes mit 10 und Addition von 50. Die Häufigkeitsverteilung von *t*-Werten hat einen Mittelwert von 50 und eine Standardabweichung von 10.
Siehe: *z*-Wert.
Literatur: Ebel & Frisbie 1991, S.68; Lienert & Raatz 1994, S.285.

CA:355, DA:384, DE:388, EN:422, ES:355, FR:283, GA:367, IT:289, NE:376, PO:287.

389 Test Prozedur zur Feststellung der fremdsprachlichen Leistungsfähigkeit.

a) Vergleiche Definition von Prüfung.

b) Ein Prüfungsteil, der eine bestimmte Fähigkeit bzw. Fertigkeit oder bestimmte Kenntnisse überprüft, z.B. Tests zum Schreiben, Sprechen etc.

c) Informelles Prüfungsverfahren, z.B. Klassentest, Lernfortschrittstest.
Vergleiche: Prüfung.
Siehe: C-Test, Cloze-Test, Ankertest.
Literatur: Bachman 1990, S.50.

CA:300, DA:300, DE:389, EN:395, ES:311, FR:359, GA:403, IT:353, NE:388, PO:361.

390 Testanalyse Analyse eines Tests, nachdem er von Kandidaten bearbeitet wurde, oftmals unter Einbeziehung statistischer und computergestützter Methoden. Ziel kann die Untersuchung des Verhaltens der Kandidaten oder die Brauchbarkeit des Tests selbst sein.

CA:15, DA:389, DE:390, EN:396, ES:22, FR:16, GA:14, IT:17, NE:389, PO:18.

391 Testanweisung Allgemeine Hinweise, die dem Testteilnehmer gegeben werden, beispielsweise auf dem Deckblatt des Antwortbogens oder Aufgabenheftes. Sie umfassen Informationen etwa über Testdauer, Aufgabenanzahl und Art der Lösungseintragung.
Vergleiche: Anweisung.

CA:211, DA:143, DE:391, EN:175, ES:230, FR:214, GA:402, IT:208, NE:181, PO:225.

392 Testanwender Person oder Institution (z.B. Lehrer oder Arbeitgeber), die die Testergebnisse verwendet, um Entscheidungen über den Testteilnehmer zu treffen oder um ihn zu beraten.

CA:414, DA:391, DE:392, EN:407, ES:410, FR:409, GA:440, IT:399, NE:393, PO:407.

393 Testbatterie Eine Serie zusammenhängender Tests oder Subtests, die unabhängige Anteile (z.B. verschiedene Teilfertigkeiten) erfassen, sich aber auch zu einem Gesamtwert zusammenfassen lassen.

CA:38, DA:28, DE:393, EN:32, ES:40, FR:30, GA:64, IT:41, NE:30, PO:38.

394 Testbeschreibung Detaillierte Dokumentation, die üblicherweise beim Entwurf eines neuen Tests oder bei der Revision eines vorhandenen erstellt wird. Die Beschreibung umfaßt Einzelheiten des Entwurfs, Inhalts, Niveaus, der Aufgabenstellung und der Aufgabentypen, der Zielpopulation, der Testanwendung usw., wobei oftmals Beispielaufgaben eingeschlossen sind.

CA:161, DA:401, DE:394, EN:404, ES:169, FR:346, GA:355, IT:120, NE:400, PO:171.

395 Testentwickler Jemand, der sich mit dem Entwurf und der Entwicklung neuer Tests beschäftigt.

CA:109, DA:405, DE:395, EN:399, ES:133, FR:145, GA:149, IT:149, NE:399, PO:141.

396 Testerfahrung Vertrautheit mit einer bestimmten Testform oder Erfahrung mit Tests, was dazu führt, daß der Kandidat bessere Leistungen erbringt, als von seinem Fähigkeitsniveau her zu erwarten wäre.

CA:179, DA:406, DE:396, EN:408, ES:197, FR:314, GA:161, IT:167, NE:401, PO:191.

397 Testerstellung Prozeß der Auswahl von Texten, das Schreiben der Aufgaben und die Zusammenstellung zu einem Test. Dem geht oftmals ein Vortest oder eine Erprobung von Aufgabenmaterialien voraus. Aufgaben können auch aus Aufgabenbanken entnommen werden.

CA:126, DA:394, DE:397, EN:398, ES:75, FR:146, GA:393, IT:110, NE:392, PO:140.

398 Testhalbierungsmethode Maß für innere Konsistenz zur Schätzung der Reliabilität. Die Schätzung basiert auf einer Korrelation zwischen zwei Hälften eines Tests, die wie zwei Paralleltests behandelt werden. Die Teilung kann mit unterschiedlichen Methoden vorgenommen werden, z.B. erste und zweite Hälfte oder Aufteilung nach gerader oder ungerader Aufgabennummer.

Siehe: Reliabilität (Zuverlässigkeit).

Literatur: Ebel & Frisbie 1991, S.82–83; Crocker & Algina 1986, S.136–138; Lienert & Raatz 1994, S. 183–191.

CA:183, DA:259, DE:398, EN:377, ES:201, FR:184, GA:203, IT:7, NE:353, PO:194.

399 Test-Informationsfunktion Bei probabilistischen Testmodellen ein Kennwert, der angibt, wie viele Informationen ein Test über Personen eines bestimmten Fähigkeitsniveaus liefert. Er stellt die Summe der Item-Informationsfunktionen dar.

Vergleiche: Item-Informationsfunktion.

Literatur: Crocker & Algina 1986, S.369–371.

CA:194, DA:388, DE:399, EN:400, ES:211, FR:191, GA:139, IT:185, NE:394, PO:207.

400 Testkonstrukteur Person, die Prüfungen oder Testaufgaben schreibt.

CA:127, DA:392, DE:400, EN:361, ES:92, FR:145, GA:121, IT:149, NE:391, PO:141.

401 Testmethode Sprachliche Fähigkeiten können mit einer Vielzahl unterschiedlicher Methoden geprüft werden, z.B. Multiple-Choice, Lückentest, Aufsatz, Prüfungsgespräch. Dabei wurde festgestellt, daß die Methode einen Einfluß auf die Messung der Fähigkeitsausprägung haben kann.

Literatur: Bachman 1990, S.77; Lienert & Raatz 1994, S.18–28.

CA:248, DA:395, DE:401, EN:401, ES:266, FR:245, GA:257, IT:236, NE:396, PO:259.

402 Testmethoden-Facetten Vergleiche Definition von Testmethoden-Merkmale.

CA:175, DA:396, DE:402, EN:403, ES:193, FR:176, GA:163, IT:50, NE:397, PO:186.

403 Testmethoden-Merkmale Die bestimmenden Eigenschaften unterschiedlicher Testmethoden. Sie können sich auf Rahmenbedingungen, Aufgabenanweisung, Sprache der Instruktion, Aufgabenstellung, Aufgabenformat usw. beziehen.

Literatur: Bachman, 1990, Kap.5; Lienert & Raatz, 1994, S.18–28.

CA:48, DA:397, DE:403, EN:402, ES:51, FR:46, GA:401, IT:50, NE:398, PO:54.

404 Testprofil Darstellung von Testergebnissen, aufgeteilt auf die einzelnen Testkomponenten, wodurch der Prüfling oder Testanwender einzelne Stärken oder Schwächen erkennen kann.

CA:288, DA:297, DE:404, EN:297, ES:300, FR:312, GA:282, IT:395, NE:307, PO:303.

405 Testredaktion Stadium der Testentwicklung, in dem die Testentwickler vorerprobte, erarbeitete Materialien erhalten und entscheiden, welche Aufgaben aufgenommen, welche verworfen und welche zu einer weiteren Überarbeitung gegeben werden können.
Vergleiche: Aufgabenvorrevision.

CA:382, DA:400, DE:405, EN:433 ES:383, FR:338, GA:184, IT:91, NE:115, PO:343.

406 Testserie Vergleiche Definition von Testbatterie.

CA:39, DA:390, DE:406, EN:397, ES:41, FR:31, GA:63, IT:42, NE:390, PO:39.

407 Testteilnehmer Vergleiche Definition von Prüfling.

CA:100, DA:402, DE:407, EN:406, ES:190, FR:351, GA:110, IT:49, NE:395, PO:183.

408 Testvorgabe Material in einer Testaufgabe, das dem Prüfling vorgegeben wird, damit dieser in angemessener Weise darauf antwortet. Z.B. kann in einem Hörverständnistest die Vorgabe in einem auf Band aufgenommenen Text bestehen und einigen dazugehörigen schriftlichen Aufgaben.

CA:169, DA:142, DE:408, EN:174, ES:228, FR:147, GA:199, IT:199, NE:180, PO:254.

409 Testwiederholungsmethode Schätzmethode für Reliabilität, bei der der Test zweifach bei den gleichen Testteilnehmern und unter gleichen Bedingungen durchgeführt wird und eine Korrelation zwischen den Testwerten der beiden Termine berechnet wird. Ihre Verwendung ist vor allem dann angezeigt, wenn eine Berechnung der inneren Konsistenz nicht möglich ist. Nach Auffassung zahlreicher Fachleute ist die Wiederholungsmethode geeigneter für die Reliabilitätsschätzung als die Berechnung der inneren Konsistenz. Die Anwendbarkeit der Wiederholungsmethode ist allerdings eingeschränkt aufgrund der Wiederholungseffekte.
Vergleiche: innere Konsistenz.
Siehe: Reliabilität (Zuverlässigkeit), Stabilität.
Literatur: Lienert & Raatz 1994, S.180–181.

CA:184, DA:318, DE:409, EN:410, ES:202, FR:188, GA:204, IT:9, NE:383, PO:197.

410 Testzuschnitt Anpassung eines vorhandenen Tests nach den Bedürfnissen einer bestimmten Gruppe von Testanwendern oder Testteilnehmern.

CA:301, DA:404, DE:410, EN:405, ES:13, FR:395, GA:370, IT:5, NE:382, PO:4.

411 Text Teil einer zusammenhängenden geschriebenen oder gesprochenen Äußerung, die als Grundlage für eine Anzahl von Testaufgaben dient.

CA:403, DA:386, DE:411, EN:411, ES:399, FR:396, GA:381, IT:389, NE:381, PO:398.

412 textbezogene (textgebundene) Aufgabe Item, das auf einem Teil eines zusammenhängenden Textes basiert, z.B. Multiple-Choice-Aufgabe, die sich auf einen Leseverständnis-Text bezieht.

CA:219, DA:387, DE:412, EN:412, ES:2367, FR:226, GA:254, IT:213, NE:269, PO:233.

413 Theta Skala Vergleiche Definition von Fähigkeitsskala.

CA:158, DA:407, DE:413, EN:413, ES:166, FR:128, GA:320, IT:328, NE:385, PO:168.

414 Threshold Level Einflußreiche Beschreibung des Grundstufenniveaus von Fremdsprachenbeherrschung in funktionalen Begriffen, 1976 vom Europarat für Englisch veröffentlicht, 1990 aktualisiert. Inzwischen liegen weitere Versionen für andere europäische Sprachen vor.

CA:272, DA:419, DE:414, EN:414, ES:285, FR:262, GA:212, IT:230, NE:386, PO:275.

415 transformierter Punktwert Rohwert, der mathematisch transformiert wurde. Dies kann geschehen zum Zweck der Skalierung oder Gewichtung.
Literatur: Ebel & Frisbie 1991, S.64–70.

CA:356, DA:414, DE:415, EN:417, ES:356, FR:284, GA:334, IT:290, NE:158, PO:288.

416 Trennschärfe Die Fähigkeit einer Aufgabe, zwischen besseren und schlechteren Kandidaten zu unterscheiden. Es gibt unterschiedliche Kennwerte dafür. Einige (Punkt-biseriale und biseriale) basieren auf Korrelationen zwischen dem Punktwert der Aufgabe und einem Kriterium wie dem Gesamtwert des Tests oder einer externen Messung der Leistungsfähigkeit. Andere basieren auf den Unterschieden der Aufgabenschwierigkeiten für Gruppen mit gering oder hoch leistungsfähigen Kandidaten. In probabilistischen Testmodellen werden in

den zwei- und dreiparametrischen Modellen Trennschärfen als A-Parameter geschätzt.
Siehe: biseriale Korrelation, Punkt-biseriale Korrelation, probabilistische Testmodelle.
Literatur: Crocker & Algina 1986, S.313–320; Ebel & Frisbie 1991, S. 231–232; Lienert & Raatz 1994, S. 103–108.
CA:105, DA:74, DE:416, EN:112, ES:107, FR:102, GA:180, IT:126, NE:109, PO:116.

417 Übereinstimmungsvalidität Einem Test wird Übereinstimmungsvalidität zugeschrieben, wenn er hoch mit anerkannten externen Kriterien korreliert, die den gleichen Kenntnisbereich oder die gleiche Fähigkeit messen.
Siehe: Kriteriumsvalidität.
Literatur: Bachman 1990, S.248–250; Lienert & Raatz 1994, S. 220–224.
CA:418, DA:323, DE:417, EN:66, ES:415, FR:415, GA:33, IT:403, NE:71, PO:411.

418 übergeordnete Fähigkeiten Vermutete komplexe Fähigkeiten wie schlußfolgerndes Denken oder Zusammenfassen.
Vergleiche: untergeordnete Fähigkeiten.
CA:201, DA:130, DE:418, EN:162, ES:102, FR:45, GA:326, IT:3, NE:410, PO:53.

419 Übungseffekt Auswirkung auf die Testwerte bei Prüflingen, denen der Aufgabentyp oder sogar die konkreten Aufgaben des Tests bereits vertraut sind.
CA:119, DA:443, DE:419, EN:289, ES:123, FR:138, GA:169, IT:140, NE:298, PO:131.

420 Umformungsaufgabe Vergleiche Definition von Satzumformung.
CA:229, DA:413, DE:420, EN:416, ES:245, FR:403, GA:242, IT:217, NE:402, PO:239.

421 unabhängige (diskrete) Aufgabe Eine eigenständige Aufgabe. Sie ist nicht mit einem Text, anderen Aufgaben oder ergänzendem Material verbunden. Multiple-Choice-Aufgaben zu Wortschatz bzw. grammatikalischen Strukturen sind Beispiele für einen derartigen Aufgabentyp.
Vergleiche: textbezogene (textgebundene) Aufgaben.
CA:230, DA:71, DE:421, EN:109, ES:246, FR:228, GA:253, IT:219, NE:106, PO:241.

422 unabhängige Variable Die Variable, von der in einer Untersuchung angenommen wird, daß sie die abhängige Variable beeinflußt bzw. mit ihr in Beziehung steht. Beispielsweise können die Testergebnisse (unabhängige Variable) verwendet werden, um den Erfolg an einem Arbeitsplatz (abhängige Variable) vorherzusagen.
Vergleiche: abhängige Variable.
Siehe: Variable.
Literatur: Hatch & Lazarton 1991, S.64; Bortz 1993, S.7–8.
CA:433, DA:420, DE:422, EN:169, ES:433, FR:426, GA:27, IT:419, NE:268, PO:425.

423 Unitary Competence Sprachtheorie vor allem von Oller (z.B. 1983) aufgestellt, worin von der Existenz einer einzelnen Fähigkeit ausgegangen wird, die allen sprachlichen Fertigkeiten zugrunde liegt (auch: Generelle Sprachbeherrschung).
CA:71, DA:91, DE:423, EN:428, ES:68, FR:71, GA:192, IT:70, NE:408, PO:85.

424 untergeordnete Fähigkeiten Vermutete weniger komplexe Fähigkeiten, so wie Wort- oder Buchstabenerkennung, die von Prüflingen in einem Sprachtest benötigt werden.
Vergleiche: übergeordnete Fähigkeiten.
CA:200, DA:27, DE:424, EN:219, ES:101, FR:44, GA:327, IT:2, NE:409, PO:52.

425 Urteilsfehler Fehlerquelle bei der Beurteilung als Ergebnis bestimmter Verhaltenstendenzen der Bewerter bei der Vergabe von Punktwerten, wie z.B. durchgehend zu gute bzw. zu strenge Bewertung. Weitere Beispiele sind logischer Fehler, Halo-Effekt und Positionseffekt.
Literatur: Bortz 1984, S.126–128; Fisseni 1990, S.155–157.
CA:124, DA:34, DE:425, EN:313, ES:130, FR:144, GA:176, IT:143, NE:35, PO:138.

426 Validierung Prozeß der Sammlung von Belegen für die Richtigkeit von aus den Testwerten gezogenen Schlußfolgerungen. Validiert werden die Schlußfolgerungen in besonderen Anwendungssituationen und nicht der Test selbst.
Siehe: Validität.
CA:415, DA:426, DE:426, EN:429, ES:412, FR:412, GA:39, IT:400, NE:414, PO:408.

427 Validität Ausmaß, in dem Testwerte angemessene, sinnvolle und nützliche Schlußfolgerungen gemäß Meßintention des Tests zulassen. Unterschiedliche Aspekte der Validität werden unterschieden, vor allem Inhalts-, Kriteriums- und Konstruktvalidität, die verschiedene Arten von Hinweisen zur Beurteilung der generellen Validität

eines Tests für einen bestimmten Anwendungszweck ergeben.
Siehe: Übereinstimmungsvalidität, Konstruktvalidität, Kriteriumsvalidität, Inhaltsvalidität, konvergente Validität, diskriminante Validität, Face-Validität, prädiktive Validität.
Literatur: Bachman 1990, S.25, 236–237; Lienert & Raatz 1994, S. 10, 220–271.

CA:416, DA:427, DE:427, EN:430, ES:413, FR:413, GA:30, IT:401, NE:415, PO:409.

428 Variable a) Bezeichnung für eine Serie von Beobachtungen bei einer einzelnen Aufgabe, wobei es sich um eine Testaufgabe, Angabe von Geschlecht oder Alter oder um einen Testwert handeln kann.

b) Element in einer experimentellen Anordnung oder bei einer statistischen Analyse, das unterschiedliche Werte annehmen kann. So beziehen beispielsweise Interessenvariablen im Rahmen von Sprachprüfungen die Schwierigkeit der Testaufgabe, Geschlecht, Alter der Testteilnehmer etc. ein.

CA:430, DA:428, DE:428, EN:431, ES:430, FR:423, GA:25, IT:416, NE:416, PO:422.

429 Varianz Maß für die Streuung einer Anzahl von Punktwerten. Je größer die Varianz, desto stärker weichen die individuellen Werte vom Mittelwert ab.
Literatur: Bortz 1993, S.41–44.

CA:434, DA:429, DE:429, EN:432, ES:434, FR:427, GA:24, IT:420, NE:417, PO:421.

430 Varianzanalyse Vergleiche Definition von Analyse der Varianz.

CA:17, DA:430, DE:430, EN:13, ES:23, FR:15, GA:15, IT:19, NE:418, PO:14.

431 Variationsbreite Maß für die Verteilung von Beobachtungswerten. Die Variationsbreite ist die Differenz zwischen dem höchsten und niedrigsten beobachteten Wert.
Literatur: Hatch & Lazarton 1991, S.169–170; Bortz 1993, S.40.

CA:12, DA:431, DE:431, EN:308, ES:260, FR:241, GA:285, IT:233, NE:311, PO:12.

432 Verbindungsaufgabe Vergleiche Definition von Ankeraufgabe.

CA:221, DA:218, DE:432, EN:215, ES:239, FR:231, GA:250, IT:214, NE:232, PO:244.

433 Verhältnisskala Eine Skala mit echtem Nullpunkt, z.B. eine Skala zur Messung von Längen. Der Abstand zwischen zwei nebeneinanderliegenden Punkten ist für den gesamten Skalenbereich gleich groß, z.B. Körpergröße. Eine Person, die 2m groß ist, ist doppelt so groß wie eine Person von 1m Größe.
Vergleiche: Intervallskala, Nominalskala, Ordinalskala.
Literatur: Crocker & Algina 1986, S.48–49; Bortz 1993, S.23–26.

CA:145/153, DA:4/210, DE:433, EN:4/317, ES:153/160, FR:122/131, GA:112/312, IT:317/324, NE:2/314, PO:155/164.

434 Verteilung Bei Testdaten die Anzahl des Auftretens aller von Prüflingen erreichten Punktwerte. Das Ergebnis wird oftmals in Form eines Histogramms grafisch dargestellt.

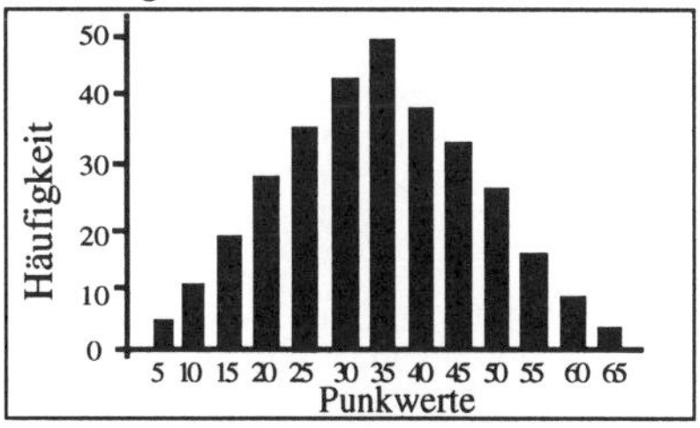

Siehe: Normalverteilung, Schiefe.
Literatur: Hatch & Lazarton, 1991, S.159–178; Bortz , 1993, S. 33–35.

CA:111, DA:103, DE:434, EN:117, ES:112, FR:105, GA:103, IT:130, NE:110, PO:119.

435 vertikale Angleichung Prozeß der Lokalisierung von Punktwerten zweier Tests mit unterschiedlicher Schwierigkeit auf der gleichen Skala.
Siehe: Angleichung.
Literatur: Crocker & Algina 1986, S.473–477.

CA:135, DA:432, DE:435, EN:434, ES:143, FR:39, GA:90, IT:153, NE:419, PO:46.

436 Vorerprobung Stadium im Prozeß der Testentwicklung, in dem Aufgaben an einer repräsentativen Stichprobe aus der Zielpopulation erprobt werden, um die Schwierigkeit der Aufgaben zu ermitteln. Nach der Durchführung statistischer Analysen kann entschieden werden, welche Aufgaben in den endgültigen Test übernommen werden.
Vergleiche: Erprobung.

CA:174, DA:105, DE:436, EN:293, ES:191, FR:307, GA:289, IT:273, NE:302, PO:311.

437 Vorgaben Bezeichnet alle Materialien (grafisches Material oder Texte), die in Tests zum Sprechen oder Schreiben eingesetzt werden, um einen Prüfling zu schriftlichen oder mündlichen Äußerungen anzuregen.

CA:390, DA:316, DE:437 EN:299, ES:178, FR:95, GA:358, IT:343, NE:321, PO:179.

438 vorgegebene Fragen Eine Auflistung der möglichen Fragen, die ein Prüfer bei der Durchführung eines Sprechtests benutzen soll. Damit sollen die allen Prüflingen vorgegebenen sprachlichen Äußerungen standardisiert werden, wodurch die Prüfung gerechter und zuverlässiger (reliabler) werden soll.

CA:198, DA:324, DE:438, EN:179, ES:215, FR:34, GA:151, IT:128, NE:156, PO:321.

439 Vorhersagevalidität Vergleiche Definition von prädiktive Validität.

CA:425, DA:298, DE:439, EN:291, ES:422, FR:422, GA:38, IT:410, NE:300, PO:418.

440 Vortest Test, der vor Beginn eines Kurses oder Lehrganges durchgeführt wird. Vergleicht man die Ergebnisse mit denen, die ein Test am Ende des Kurses erbrachte, so ergibt sich ein Hinweis auf die Effektivität des Kurses.
Vergleiche: Abschlußtest.

CA:333, DA:104, DE:440, EN:292, ES:338, FR:306, GA:290, IT:272, NE:299, PO:312.

441 wahrer Wert Punktwert, den ein Prüfling erzielen würde, wenn kein Meßfehler zum Zeitpunkt der Prüfungsdurchführung oder -bewertung vorhanden wäre. Grundlegendes Konzept der klassischen Testtheorie.

CA:357, DA:415, DE:441, EN:420, ES:357, FR:285, GA:335, IT:285, NE:431, PO:289.

442 Washback Vergleiche Definition von Backwash.

CA:372, DA:436, DE:442, EN:435, ES:124, FR:322, GA:95, IT:147, NE:432, PO:135.

443 Waystage Level Beschreibung eines Grundstufenniveaus von Fremdsprachenbeherrschung, 1977 vom Europarat für Englisch veröffentlicht, 1990 aktualisiert. Die Anforderungen sind geringer als beim Threshhold Level, der Lernumfang wird als annähernd halb so hoch eingeschätzt.
Vergleiche: Threshold Level.

CA:271, DA:437, DE:443, EN:436, ES:284, FR:261, GA:211, IT:231, NE:433, PO:274.

444 Wirkung Effekt einer Prüfung sowohl in Hinsicht auf den allgemeinen Ausbildungsprozeß als auch in bezug auf den Einfluß, den die Prüfungsergebnisse auf die einzelnen Personen haben.
Siehe: Backwash, Washback.

CA:205, DA:303, DE:444, EN:167, ES:222, FR:207, GA:391, IT:191, NE:171, PO:217.

445 Wortbildungs-Aufgabe Aufgabentyp, bei dem der Prüfling ein vorgegebenes Wort in eine andere Form bringen muß. Beispiel: Diese Art der Arbeit erfordert ein ...... des technischen Vokabulars. (verstehen).

CA:227, DA:269, DE:445, EN:439, ES:231, FR:227, GA:244, IT:216, NE:437, PO:237 .

446 *z*-Wert Meist verwendete Form des Standardwertes mit einem Mittelwert von 0 und einer Standardabweichung von 1. Die Berechnungsformel lautet:

$$z = (X-\bar{X}) \div Sx$$

Wobei:

z = z-Wert
X = Testwert
$\bar{X}$ = arithmetisches Mittel der Testwerte
Sx = Standardabweichung der Testwerte sind.

Siehe: Standardwert.
Vergleiche: *t*-Wert.
Literatur: Ebel & Frisbie 1991, S.68; Lienert & Raatz 1994, S. 284.

CA:358, DA:439, DE:446, EN:442, ES:358, FR:286, GA:441, IT:291, NE:439, PO:290.

447 zentrale Tendenz (Messung der) Die Ermittlung des Mittelpunkts oder des statistischen Durchschnitts einer Verteilung. Üblich sind drei Koeffizienten für die zentrale Tendenz: arithmetischer Mittelwert, Median und Modalwert.
Literatur: Henning 1987, S.39–40; Guilford & Fruchter 1981, Kap. 4; Hatch & Lazarton 1991, S.159–164; Bortz 1993 S.36–40.

CA:246, DA:47, DE:447, EN:45, ES:391, FR:358, GA:62, IT:348, NE:55, PO:356.

448 Zertifikat Dokument, das für eine bestimmte Person die Teilnahme an einer Prüfung und die erreichte Note, zumindest das Bestehen der Prüfung, bestätigt.
Vergleiche: Diplom.

CA:50, DA:38, DE:448, EN:47, ES:53, FR:50, GA:386, IT:52, NE:56, PO:56.

449 Zufallsfehler Vergleiche Definition von Fehler.

CA:137, DA:408, DE:449, EN:306, ES:145, FR:152, GA:128, IT:156, NE:310, PO:147,

450 Zufallskorrektur Vergleiche Definition von Ratekorrektur.

CA:82, DA:193, DE:450, EN:77, ES:80, FR:83, GA:54, IT:103, NE:77, PO:98.

451 Zufallsstichprobe Auswahl von Elementen, die ohne gezielte Selektion aus der Untersuchungspopulation getroffen wurde, so daß jedes Element der Population die gleiche Chance hatte, für die Untersuchung ausgewählt zu werden.
Siehe: Stichprobe.
Literatur: Crocker & Algina 1986, S.433–438; Guilford & Fruchter 1981, S.120; Bortz 1993, S.84–85.

CA:265, DA:409, DE:451, EN:307, ES:279, FR:117, GA:305, IT:47, NE:120, PO:9.

452 Zuordnungsaufgabe Aufgabentyp, der eine Zuordnung der Elemente zweier getrennter Listen fordert. Eine Art von Zuordnungsaufgabe besteht darin, daß der richtige Begriff zur Vervollständigung eines Satzes auszuwählen ist. Ein Aufgabentyp in einem Leseverständnistest könnte darin bestehen, daß aus einer Liste etwas wie eine Freizeitbeschäftigung oder ein Buch auszuwählen ist, um zu einer Person zu passen, deren spezielle Bedürfnisse beschrieben sind.

CA:397, DA:322, DE:452, EN:226, ES:7, FR:21, GA:375, IT:73, NE:238, PO:353.

453 Zuverlässigkeit Vergleiche Definition von Reliabilität.

CA:180, DA:312, DE:453, EN:327, ES:198, FR:183, GA:200, IT:6, NE:43, PO:193.

454 zweiparametrisches Modell Bei probabilistischen Testmodellen ein Modell, bei dem außer dem Fähigkeits-/ Schwierigkeitsparameter auch die Aufgabentrennschärfe berücksichtigt wird.
Vergleiche: einparametrisches Modell, Rasch-Modell.
Siehe: probabilistische Testmodelle.

CA:258, DA:411, DE:454, EN:424, ES:271, FR:248, GA:298, IT:241, NE:404, PO:264.

455 zweistufige Bewertung Bewertung auf der Basis nur zweier sich ausschließender Kategorien wie richtig/ falsch, bestanden/nicht bestanden, ja/nein.

CA:347, DA:67, DE:455, EN:98, ES:347, FR:268, GA:341, IT:32, NE:98, PO:59.

4 English: Glossary of language testing terms

1 a-parameter The parameter from item-response theory which relates to the discrimination of an item.
See: item-response theory (IRT).
Further reading: Bachman 1990, p.204.
CA:281, DA:1, DE:84, EN:1, ES:294, FR:292, GA:273, IT:260, NE:1, PO:297.

2 ability A mental trait or the capacity or power to do something.
Compare: competence, proficiency.
Further reading: Bachman 1990, p. 16, p. 19.
CA:46, DA:2, DE:113, EN:2, ES:49, FR:42, GA:96, IT:1A, NE:411, PO:49.

3 ability scale In item response theory, an equal interval scale upon which the ability of persons and the difficulty of test tasks can be located. Also referred to as the theta scale.
Further reading: Bachman 1990, p.345.
CA:150, DA:3, DE:114, EN:3, ES:157, FR:128, GA:313, IT:322, NE:413, PO:159.

4 absolute scale A scale with a true zero point, e.g. a scale for measuring length. The absolute zero point cannot be defined in language testing, so this kind of scale is not applicable.
Compare: interval scale, nominal scale, ordinal scale.
CA:145, DA:4, DE:433, EN:4, ES:153, FR:122, GA:112, IT:317, NE:2, PO:155.

5 accreditation The granting of recognition of a test, usually by an official body such as a government department, examinations board, etc.
CA:4, DA:10, DE:8, EN:5, ES:1, FR:4, GA:92, IT:303, NE:3, PO:325.

6 achievement test A test designed to measure the extent of learning achieved by a candidate in relation to a particular course of instruction, textbook, etc., i.e. a curriculum-dependent test. Also referred to as attainment test.
CA:309, DA:366, DE:369, EN:6, ES:321, FR:374, GA:419, IT:368, NE:301, PO:374.

7 adaptive test A form of testing in which items are selected during the test on the basis of their difficulty, in response to an estimate of the ability of the candidate. Often used to refer to a computer administered test, although an oral interview may also be an adaptive test.
See: computer adaptive testing.
Further reading: Bachman 1990, p.151; Henning 1987, p. 136.
CA:302, DA:102, DE:6, EN:7, ES:312, FR:361, GA:429, IT:356, NE:5, PO:363.

8 administration The date or period during which a test takes place. Many tests have a fixed date of administration several times a year, while others may be administered on demand.
CA:6, DA:403, DE:308, EN:8, ES:77, FR:7, GA:288, IT:331, NE:10, PO:23.

9 affective factors Factors of a non-cognitive nature which relate to the emotional variables, preferences and attitudes of test takers.
Compare: cognitive factors.
Further reading: Ebel and Frisbie 1991, p.52.
CA:177, DA:6, DE:7, EN:9, ES:195, FR:178, GA:399, IT:172, NE:6, PO:188.

10 alpha (alpha coefficient) A reliability estimate, measuring the internal consistency of a test. It ranges in value from 0 to 1. It is often used for tests with rating scales as opposed to tests with dichotomous items, although it may be used for both. Also referred to as coefficient alpha.
Compare: Kuder-Richardson.
See: internal consistency.
Further reading: Henning 1987, p 84.
CA:9, DA:11, DE:10, EN:10, ES:16, FR:8, GA:10, IT:10, NE:12, PO:6.

11 alternate forms Refer to definition for equivalent forms.

CA:185, DA:12, DE:11, EN:11, ES:203, FR:193, GA:146, IT:176, NE:13, PO:199.

12 analysis of covariance Refer to definition for ANCOVA.

CA:14, DA:200, DE:193, EN:12, ES:20, FR:14, GA:16, IT:18, NE:85, PO:13.

13 analysis of variance Refer to definition for ANOVA.

CA:17, DA:430, DE:430, EN:13, ES:23, FR:15, GA:15, IT:19, NE:418, PO:14.

14 analytic scoring A method of scoring which can be used in tests of productive language use, such as speaking and writing. The assessor makes an assessment with the aid of a list of specific points. For example, in a test of writing the analytic scale may include a focus on grammar, vocabulary, use of linking devices, etc.
Compare: global assessment, impression marking (general impression marking).
Further reading: Ebel and Frisbie 1991, p. 195.

CA:343, DA:13, DE:12, EN:14, ES:426, FR:266, GA:340, IT:27, NE:15, PO:58.

15 anchor item An item which is included in two or more tests. Anchor items have known characteristics, and form one section of a new version of a test in order to provide information about that test and the candidates who have taken it, e.g. to calibrate a new test to a measurement scale.
Compare: anchor test.
See: calibration.

CA:218, DA:16, DE:18, EN:15, ES:237, FR:225, GA:241, IT:212, NE:17, PO:232.

16 anchor test A test with known measurement characteristics, which is administered in association with another test. Performance on the anchor test provides information about the other test and about the candidates who have taken both of them.
Compare: anchor item.

CA:307, DA:17, DE:19, EN:16, ES:320, FR:367, GA:404, IT:357, NE:18, PO:365.

17 ANCOVA A type of analysis of variance which allows the effect of confounding variables (those which may change with the variable of interest) to be controlled for.
See: ANOVA.
Further reading: Hatch and Lazaraton 1991, p. 387.

CA:21, DA:14, DE:13, EN:17, ES:27, FR:19, GA:20, IT:20, NE:16, PO:21.

18 ANOVA A statistical technique used to test the null hypothesis that several population means are equal. The variability of the observations within each group is examined, as well as the variability between the group means.
Further reading: Hatch and Lazaraton 1991, pp. 308–312.

CA:22, DA:19, DE:20, EN:18, ES:28, FR:20, GA:21, IT:21, NE:19, PO:22.

19 answer sheet The paper on which a candidate records his/her responses.
Compare: optical mark reader (OMR).

CA:191, DA:37, DE:22, EN:19, ES:219, FR:181, GA:152, IT:174, NE:20, PO:198.

20 aptitude test A test designed to predict or measure a candidate's potential for success within a particular area of learning, e.g. in learning a foreign language, or on a specific course of study.
Further reading: Henning 1987, p.6; Ebel and Frisbie 1991, p. 339.

CA:308, DA:18, DE:96, EN:20, ES:322, FR:368, GA:421, IT:358, NE:22, PO:370.

21 assessment In language testing, the measurement of one or more aspects of language proficiency, by means of some form of test or procedure.
Further reading: Bachman 1990, p.50.

CA:31, DA:30, DE:54, EN:21, ES:180, FR:165, GA:229, IT:421, NE:39, PO:30.

22 assessor Someone who assigns a score to a candidate's performance in a test, using subjective judgement to do so. Assessors are normally qualified in the relevant field, and are required to undergo a process of training and standardization. In oral testing the roles of assessor and interlocutor are sometimes distinguished. Also referred to as examiner or rater.
Compare: interlocutor, marker.

CA:35, DA:32, DE:55, EN:22, ES:46, FR:174, GA:234, IT:165, NE:33, PO:182.

23 attainment test Refer to definition for achievement test.

CA:322, DA:20, DE:203, EN:23, ES:331, FR:366, GA:419, IT:368, NE:421, PO:374.

24 authenticity As a characteristic of tests, the extent to which test tasks reflect language use in a non-test situation.
Further reading: Bachman 1990, pp. 300–303.

CA:27, DA:21, DE:42, EN:24, ES:33, FR:24, GA:115, IT:35, NE:23, PO:26.

25 authentic text Text used in a test which consists of materials originally produced for a non-language testing purpose, and not specially produced for the test.
Compare: semi-authentic text.

CA:404, DA:22, DE:41, EN:25, ES:401, FR:111, GA:382, IT:390, NE:24, PO:127.

26 b-parameter The parameter from item-response theory which relates to the degree of difficulty of an item.
See: item-response theory (IRT).
Further reading: Bachman 1990, p. 204.
CA:282, DA:24, DE:170, EN:26, ES:295, FR:293, GA:274, IT:261, NE:26, PO:298.

27 background knowledge A candidate's knowledge of topic or cultural content within a particular test, which may affect the way input is dealt with. This is of particular relevance in tests of Language for Specific Purposes.
Further reading: Bachman 1990, p. 273.
CA:75, DA:26, DE:144, EN:27, ES:73, FR:77, GA:134, IT:85, NE:4, PO:91.

28 backwash The impact of a test on classroom teaching. Teachers may be influenced by the knowledge that their students are planning to take a certain test, and adapt their methodology and the content of lessons to reflect the demands of the test. The result may be positive or negative. Also referred to as washback.
See: impact.
CA:372, DA:25, DE:43, EN:28, ES:369, FR:322, GA:95, IT:147, NE:27, PO:135.

29 band In its broadest sense, part of a scale. In an item-based test this covers a range of scores which may be reported as a grade or a band score. In a rating scale designed to assess a specific trait or ability such as speaking or writing, a band normally represents a particular level.
CA:37, DA:339, DE:44, EN:29, ES:38, FR:200, GA:41, IT:39, NE:28, PO:210.

30 band score Part of a scale, referring to a specific range of ability.
CA:346, DA:258, DE:210, EN:30, ES:39, FR:269, GA:330, IT:40, NE:29, PO:65.

31 bar graph (chart) A way of showing frequency distributions of variables in graphic form.

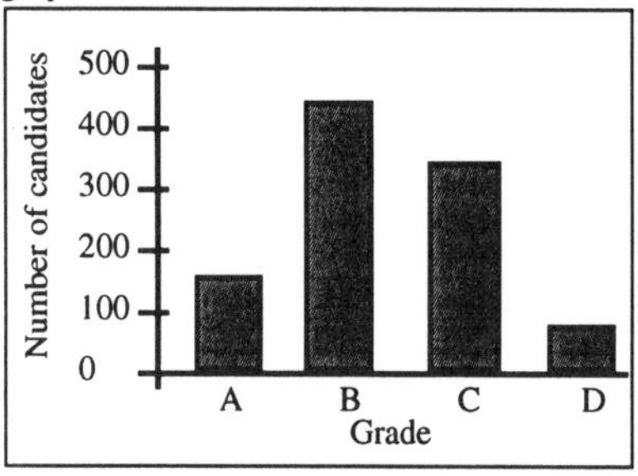

Compare: histogram.
Further reading: Hatch and Lazaraton 1991, p. 147.
CA:102, DA:383, DE:335, EN:31, ES:104, FR:201, GA:42, IT:123, NE:357, PO:211.

32 battery A set of related tests or subtests which make independent contributions (e.g. by testing different skills) but may be combined to produce a total score.
CA:38, DA:28, DE:393, EN:32, ES:40, FR:30, GA:64, IT:41, NE:30, PO:38.

33 bias A test or item can be considered to be biased if one particular section of the candidate population is advantaged or disadvantaged by some feature of the test or item which is not relevant to what is being measured. Sources of bias may be connected with gender, age, culture, etc.
Further reading: Bachman, 1990 pp. 271–279; Crocker and Algina 1986, Chapters 12 and 16.
CA:40, DA:344, DE:383, EN:33, ES:384, FR:32, GA:208, IT:160, NE:46, PO:40.

34 bimodal distribution A distribution with two modes or peaks, which may suggest that there are two different groups within the same sample.

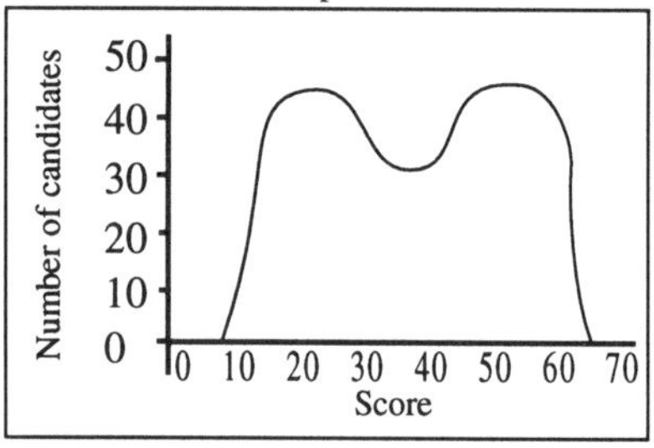

Compare: normal distribution.
See: mode.
Further reading: Hatch and Lazaraton 1991, pp. 165–166.
CA:112, DA:39, DE:59, EN:34, ES:113, FR:106, GA:104, IT:131, NE:47, PO:121.

35 biserial correlation An index of item discrimination for dichotomous items, written r_{bis}; the correlation between a criterion (usually total test score) and the ability underlying the right-wrong response to the item. The value of r_{bis} is at least 25% higher than for the point biserial (r_{pbi}). An advantage of r_{bis} is that it is fairly stable across samples of differing ability level.
Compare: point biserial correlation.
See: discrimination.
Further reading: Crocker and Algina 1986, pp. 317–318; Guilford and Fruchter 1981,

pp. 304–311.
CA:56, DA:40, DE:60, EN:35, ES:85, FR:86, GA:79, IT:96, NE:48, PO:101.

36 boundary effects The effects of a test's being too easy or too difficult for a particular group of candidates. Scores tend to accumulate at the top of the distribution (ceiling effect) or at the bottom (floor effect).
See: ceiling effect, floor effect.

CA:125, DA:120, DE:139, EN:36, ES:131, FR:143, GA:177, IT:138, NE:163, PO:139.

37 c-parameter The parameter from item-response theory which relates to guessing.
See: item-response theory (IRT).
Further reading: Bachman 1990, p. 204.

CA:283, DA:44, DE:318, EN:37, ES:296, FR:294, GA:275, IT:262, NE:50, PO:299.

38 c-test A type of gap-filling task in which the second half of certain words is deleted. The frequency of deletion can be as high as every second word. The candidate's task is to complete the partially deleted words.
Compare: cloze test.
Further reading: Weir 1990, p. 49.

CA:304, DA:45, DE:62, EN:38, ES:314, FR:394, GA:408, IT:384, NE:51, PO:366.

39 calibrate In item response theory, to estimate the difficulty of a set of test items.
See: theta scale.

CA:43, DA:163, DE:93, EN:39, ES:43, FR:40, GA:48, IT:43, NE:206, PO:47.

40 calibration The process of determining the scale of a test or tests. Calibration may involve anchoring items from different tests to a common difficulty scale (the theta scale). When a test is constructed from calibrated items then scores on the test indicate the candidates' ability, i.e. their location on the theta scale.

CA:44, DA:164, DE:94, EN:40, ES:42, FR:35, GA:49, IT:44, NE:205, PO:42.

41 candidate A test/examination taker. Also referred to as examinee.

CA:45, DA:165, DE:302, EN:41, ES:48, FR:41, GA:178, IT:49, NE:207, PO:48.

42 categorical scale A scale used for categorical variables such as gender, first language, occupation.
Compare: interval scale, nominal scale, ordinal scale, ratio scale.

CA:146, DA:170, DE:175, EN:42, ES:154, FR:123, GA:310, IT:318, NE:53, PO:156.

43 category a) A division of a categorical scale, e.g. gender has the categories male and female.

b) In testing, a rating scale with, for instance, five points, is said to have five response categories.

CA:49, DA:169, DE:176, EN:43, ES:52, FR:48, GA:50, IT:51, NE:52, PO:55.

44 ceiling effect A boundary effect which results from a test's being too easy for a particular group of candidates, so that their scores all group at the top of the distribution.
See: boundary effects.

CA:123, DA:219, DE:63/73, EN:44, ES:129, FR:140, GA:173, IT:145, NE:292, PO:137.

45 central tendency (measure of) A way of locating the mid-point or statistical average of a distribution. Three commonly used measures of central tendency are the mean, median and mode.
Further reading: Henning 1987, pp. 39–40; Guilford and Fruchter 1981, Chapter 4; Hatch and Lazaraton 1991, pp. 159–164.

CA:246, DA:47, DE:447, EN:45, ES:391, FR:358, GA:62, IT:348, NE:55, PO:356.

46 centile scale An ordinal scale which is divided into 100 units or centiles. If someone is given a centile value of 95 it means that in a typical sample of 100 that person would be ranked above 95 others. Also referred to as a percentile scale.
Further reading: Crocker and Algina 1986, pp. 439–442; Guilford and Fruchter 1981, pp. 38–41.

CA:151, DA:46, DE:300, EN:46, ES:155, FR:124, GA:311, IT:319, NE:54, PO:157.

47 certificate A document stating that a named person has taken a test or component of a test and has achieved a particular grade, usually at least a pass.
Compare: diploma.

CA:50, DA:38, DE:448, EN:47, ES:53, FR:50, GA:386, IT:52, NE:56, PO:56.

48 checklist A list of questions or points to be answered or covered. Often used in language testing as a tool of observation or analysis.

CA:240, DA:48, DE:64, EN:48, ES:258, FR:239, GA:351, IT:228, NE:58, PO:252.

49 chi-square test A statistical procedure which compares the values from observed and expected responses in order to indicate whether the difference between them is significant statistically, given the

expected responses. It is a non-parametric procedure.
See: non-parametric procedure.
Further reading: Hatch and Lazaraton 1991, pp. 393–415.
CA:330, DA:49, DE:65, EN:49, ES:396, FR:149, GA:409, IT:359, NE:59, PO:395.

50 classical test theory A measurement theory which consists of a set of assumptions about the relationships between actual or observed test scores and the factors that affect these scores, which are generally referred to as error. It is also referred to as true score theory.
Compare: item-response theory (IRT).
Further reading: Bachman 1990, pp. 166–187.
CA:399, DA:174, DE:177, EN:50, ES:392, FR:397, GA:387, IT:349, NE:208, PO:357.

51 clerical marking A method of marking in which markers do not need to exercise any special expertise or subjective judgement. They mark by following a mark scheme which specifies all acceptable responses to each test item.
Compare: examiner marking.
CA:86, DA:23, DE:231, EN:51, ES:78, FR:274, GA:219, IT:31, NE:25, PO:62.

52 cloze test A type of gap-filling task in which whole words are deleted from a text. In a traditional cloze, deletion is every nth word. Other gap-filling tasks where short phrases are deleted from a text, or where the item writer chooses the words to be deleted are commonly referred to as cloze tests, for example 'rational cloze'. Candidates may have to supply the missing words (open cloze), or choose from a set of options (multiple choice or banked cloze). Marking of open cloze may be either 'exact word' (only the word deleted from the original text is taken as the correct response) or 'acceptable word' (a list of acceptable responses is given to markers).
Compare: c-test, gap-filling item.
Further reading: Weir 1990, p. 46–48; Oller 1979, Chapter 12.
CA:313, DA:50, DE:66, EN:52, ES:315, FR:370, GA:410, IT:362, NE:61, PO:378.

53 coefficient A numerical index used as a measure of a property or characteristic.
See: alpha (alpha coefficient), correlation coefficient.
CA:53, DA:175, DE:178, EN:53, ES:55, FR:54, GA:73, IT:57, NE:62, PO:69.

54 coefficient alpha Refer to definition for alpha (alpha coefficient).
CA:54, DA:176, DE:179, EN:54, ES:56, FR:55, GA:74, IT:58, NE:63, PO:70.

55 cognitive factors Factors in the learning or testing process which relate to the learner's schemata and patterns of knowledge.
Compare: affective factors.
Further reading: Ebel and Frisbie 1991, p.52.
CA:178, DA:177, DE:180, EN:55, ES:196, FR:179, GA:398, IT:171, NE:65, PO:189.

56 cognitive model A theory concerning the way in which a person's knowledge, in the sense of both concepts and processes, is structured. This is important in language testing because such a theory may have an effect on choice of test method or test content.
CA:253, DA:178, DE:181, EN:56, ES:269, FR:250, GA:297, IT:243, NE:64, PO:262.

57 common scale A way of expressing scores of two or more tests on the same scale to allow a direct comparison of results of these tests. The scores of two or more tests can be expressed on a common scale if the raw scores have been transformed through a statistical procedure, e.g. test equating.
Further reading: Bachman 1990, pp. 340–344.
CA:147, DA:110, DE:131, EN:57, ES:156, FR:125, GA:86, IT:320, NE:148, PO:158.

58 communicative competence The ability to use language appropriately in a variety of situations and settings.
Further reading: Bachman 1990, p. 16, 68.
CA:65, DA:179, DE:182, EN:58, ES:61, FR:63, GA:195, IT:63, NE:66, PO:77.

59 competence The knowledge or ability to do something. Used in linguistics to refer to an underlying ability, as contrasted with performance, which is the manifestation of competence as language in use. This distinction originates in the work of Chomsky.
Compare: ability, performance.
Further reading: Bachman 1990, pp. 52, 108.
CA:64, DA:180, DE:183, EN:59, ES:60, FR:62, GA:191, IT:62, NE:67, PO:76.

60 completion item An item type in which the candidate has to complete a sentence or phrase, usually by writing in several words or supplying details such as times and telephone numbers.
CA:226, DA:421, DE:102, EN:60, ES:238, FR:223, GA:243, IT:215, NE:193, PO:234.

61 component Part of an examination, often presented as a separate test, with its own instructions booklet and time limit. Components are often skills-based, and have titles such as Listening Comprehension or Composition. Also referred to as subtest.

CA:73, DA:181, DE:306, EN:61, ES:29, FR:72, GA:85, IT:81, NE:128, PO:87.

62 composition A task which involves the candidate in the production of an extended written text. The text types to be produced in composition tasks include narrative accounts of events and discussions of topics on which various opinions may be held. They may also include such types as reports, informal and formal letters. Also referred to as an essay or essay question.

CA:366, DA:109, DE:32, EN:62, ES:192, FR:73, GA:51, IT:82, NE:372, PO:88.

63 computer-adaptive testing A method of computer-based testing in which it is possible for the level of difficulty of the items presented to the candidate to be adapted to the candidate's ability, estimated from the responses given.
See: computer-based testing (assessment).

CA:303, DA:51, DE:67, EN:63, ES:181, FR:362, GA:379, IT:386, NE:68, PO:364.

64 computer-based testing (assessment) A method of testing in which items are presented to candidates on a computer. Responses, too, may be made via the computer.

CA:332, DA:52, DE:68, EN:64, ES:182, FR:171, GA:380, IT:387, NE:70, PO:35.

65 computerized marking (scoring) Various ways of using computer systems to minimize error in the marking of objective tests. For example, this can be done by scanning information from the candidate's mark sheet by means of an optical mark reader, and producing data which can be used to provide scores or analyses.

CA:85, DA:53, DE:69, EN:65, ES:82, FR:273, GA:222, IT:28, NE:69, PO:66.

66 concurrent validity A test is said to have concurrent validity if the scores it gives correlate highly with a recognized external criterion which measures the same area of knowledge or ability.
See: criterion-related validity.
Further reading: Bachman 1990, pp. 248–250.

CA:418, DA:323, DE:417, EN:66, ES:415, FR:415, GA:33, IT:403, NE:71, PO:411.

67 confidence interval The range around the estimate of a value within which the true value is likely to fall. The degree of likelihood is usually defined at confidence levels of 95% or 99%.

CA:215, DA:182, DE:184, EN:67, ES:233, FR:219, GA:132, IT:204, NE:45, PO:229.

68 construct A hypothesized ability or mental trait which cannot necessarily be directly observed or measured, for example, in language testing, listening ability. Language tests attempt to measure the different constructs which underlie language ability. In addition to language ability itself, motivation, attitude and acculturation are all relevant constructs.
Further reading: Hatch and Lazaraton 1991, p.15.

CA:78, DA:184, DE:185, EN:68, ES:76, FR:80, GA:394, IT:108, NE:72, PO:94.

69 construct validity A test is said to have construct validity if scores can be shown to reflect a theory about the nature of a construct or its relation to other constructs. It could be predicted, for example, that two valid tests of listening comprehension would rank learners in the same way, but each would have a weaker relationship with scores on a test of grammatical competence.
See: test specifications, validity.
Further reading: Ebel and Frisbie 1991, p.108; Hatch and Lazaraton 1991, pp. 37–38.

CA:420, DA:186, DE:186, EN:69, ES:418, FR:418, GA:37, IT:406, NE:73, PO:414.

70 constructed response A form of written response to a test item that involves active production, rather than just choosing from a number of options.
Compare: selected response.
See: response.

CA:376, DA:185, DE:126, EN:70, ES:372, FR:330, GA:154, IT:309, NE:272, PO:336.

71 contamination effect A rater effect which occurs when a rater assigns a score on the basis of a factor other than that being tested. An example would be raising a candidate's score on a writing test because he or she has neat handwriting.
See: rater effects.

CA:118, DA:9, DE:226, EN:71, ES:122, FR:136, GA:174, IT:141, NE:74, PO:132.

72 content analysis A means of describing and analysing the content of test materials. This analysis is necessary in order to ensure that the content of the test meets its specification. It is essential in establishing content and construct validity.

CA:18, DA:133, DE:153, EN:72, ES:19, FR:12, GA:12, IT:15, NE:178, PO:15.

73 content validity A test is said to have content validity if the items or tasks of which it is made up constitute a representative sample of items or tasks for the area of knowledge or ability to be tested. These are often related to a syllabus or course.
See: test specifications, validity.
Further reading: Bachman 1990, pp. 244–247.

CA:422, DA:134, DE:154, EN:73, ES:419, FR:419, GA:31, IT:405, NE:179, PO:415.

74 contingency table A table of frequencies classified according to two or more sets of values of categorical variables, e.g. :

	Mastery	Non-Mastery
Method A	35	5
Method B	20	20

See: chi-square test.

CA:398, DA:187, DE:187, EN:74, ES:390, FR:353, GA:369, IT:347, NE:75, PO:320.

75 convergent validity A test is said to have convergent validity when there is a high correlation between scores achieved in it and those achieved in a different test measuring the same construct (irrespective of method). This can be considered an aspect of construct validity.
Compare: discriminant validity.
See: construct validity.
Further reading: Guilford and Fruchter 1981, pp. 436–437.

CA:419, DA:188, DE:188, EN:75, ES:416, FR:416, GA:32, IT:404, NE:76, PO:412.

76 correction for attenuation A method of estimating the correlation between two or more variables if there is no difference in reliability between the variables.
Further reading: Guilford and Fruchter 1981, pp. 450–453; Hatch and Lazaraton 1990, pp. 444–445.

CA:88, DA:194, DE:243, EN:76, ES:79, FR:82, GA:53, IT:106, NE:78, PO:99.

77 correction for guessing A way of reducing the gain in marks resulting from guessing the correct response in tests made up of objective items.
Further reading: Ebel and Frisbie 1986, pp. 215–218.

CA:82, DA:193, DE:317/450, EN:77, ES:80, FR:83, GA:54, IT:103, NE:77, PO:98.

78 correlation The relationship between two or more measures, with regard to the extent to which they tend to vary in the same way. If, for example, candidates tend to achieve similar ranking on two different tests, there is a positive correlation between the two sets of scores.
Compare: covariance.
See: Pearson's product-moment correlation (Pearson's *r*), rank order correlation.
Further reading: Guilford and Fruchter 1981, Chapter 6; Bachman 1990, pp. 259–260.

CA:91, DA:196, DE:190, EN:78, ES:84, FR:85, GA:78, IT:95, NE:81, PO:100.

79 correlation coefficient An index showing the extent to which two or more variables are correlated. It varies from -1 to +1. Highly correlated variables are represented by a correlation coefficient approaching + or -1.
Further reading: Guilford and Fruchter 1981, pp. 86–88.

CA:55, DA:197, DE:191, EN:79, ES:57, FR:56, GA:75, IT:60, NE:82, PO:71.

80 covariance The joint variance of two or more variables. For example, sentence length and lexical difficulty are features of a reading text which will tend to be related, i.e. to covary. Covariance must be considered when predicting one variable from others, for example, when predicting the difficulty of a reading text from sentence length and lexical difficulty.
See: variance.

CA:93, DA:199, DE:192, EN:80, ES:91, FR:92, GA:71, IT:112, NE:84, PO:106.

81 criterion-referenced test A test in which the candidate's performance is interpreted in relation to predetermined criteria. Emphasis is on attainment of objectives rather than on candidates' scores as a reflection of their ranking within the group.
Compare: domain-referenced test, norm-referenced test.

CA:337, DA:203, DE:196, EN:81, ES:317, FR:364, GA:412, IT:380, NE:86, PO:369.

82 criterion-related validity A test is said to have criterion-related validity if a relationship can be demonstrated between test scores and some external criterion which is believed to be a measure of the same ability. Information on criterion-relatedness is also used in determining how well a test predicts future behaviour.
See: concurrent validity, predictive validity.
Further reading: Bachman 1990, pp. 248–250.

CA:421, DA:204, DE:197, EN:82, ES:417, FR:417, GA:34, IT:407, NE:87, PO:413.

83 criterion variable In research

design, another term for dependent variable.
See: dependent variable.

CA:431, DA:205, DE:198, EN:83, ES:431, FR:424, GA:26, IT:417, NE:88, PO:423.

84 Cronbach's alpha Refer to definition for alpha (alpha coefficient).

CA:10, DA:54, DE:70, EN:84, ES:17, FR:9, GA:11, IT:11, NE:89, PO:7.

85 cultural bias A test with cultural bias advantages or disadvantages candidates of particular cultural backgrounds.
See: bias.

CA:41, DA:207, DE:201, EN:85, ES:385, FR:33, GA:209, IT:161, NE:90, PO:41.

86 cumulative frequency A way of presenting the distribution of candidates by counting for each score class the number of candidates who have obtained a score in that class and all classes below it.
Further reading: Guilford and Fruchter 1981, pp. 35–36.

CA:189, DA:208, DE:202, EN:86, ES:208, FR:198, GA:239, IT:181, NE:91, PO:204.

87 curriculum An overall description of the aims, content, organization, methods and evaluation of an educational course.
Compare: syllabus.

CA:94, DA:55, DE:71, EN:87, ES:93, FR:93, GA:99, IT:113, NE:220, PO:107.

88 curriculum-dependent test A test which is closely linked to a particular syllabus, and plays a particular role in educational processes.
Compare: curriculum-independent test.
See: achievement test.

CA:325, DA:56, DE:217, EN:88, ES:313, FR:365, GA:406, IT:374, NE:221, PO:380.

89 curriculum-independent test A test which is not linked to any particular syllabus or course of study.
Compare: curriculum-dependent test.
See: proficiency test.

CA:328, DA:57, DE:218, EN:89, ES:339, FR:387, GA:405, IT:376, NE:222, PO:388.

90 cut-off score The minimum score a candidate has to achieve in order to get a given grade in a test or an examination. In mastery testing, the score on a test which is considered to be the level required in order to be considered minimally competent or at 'mastery' level.
See: mastery test, minimum competency testing.
Compare: pass mark.
Further reading: Bachman 1990, pp. 214–215; Crocker and Algina pp. 421–428.

CA:359, DA:58, DE:199, EN:90, ES:351, FR:277, GA:338, IT:280, NE:57, PO:282.

91 d-index An index of discrimination for test items. Often used for small-scale classroom tests, as it can be calculated by hand. Based on total test score, an upper and a lower group are selected, so that between 10% and 33% of test takers are in each. For normally distributed scores, it is optimal to use 27% in each group. The responses to each item by test takers in each group are counted and, for items which discriminate well, the top group will score more highly than the bottom group. The following formula gives the item discrimination index :

$$D = p_U - p_L$$

where p_U is the fraction of the upper scoring group getting the item correct and where p_L is the fraction of the lower scoring group getting the item correct. In general, items with an index of 0.3 or above are considered to be discriminating well.

CA:206, DA:59, DE:72, EN:91, ES:223, FR:208, GA:186, IT:194, NE:92, PO:218.

92 delta plot method A way of looking at differential item functioning. It is used to identify items which exaggerate or minimize differences in group performances, and is based on classical item difficulties (*p*-values). The *p*-values are converted to normalized *z* scores and these values are plotted in pairs on a graph to show the relative difficulty of items for the two groups in question.
See: differential item functioning (DIF).
Further reading: Crocker and Algina 1986, pp. 388–390.

CA:249, DA:61, DE:74, EN:92, ES:267, FR:246, GA:256, IT:237, NE:93, PO:260.

93 delta scale A normalized scale with a mean of 13 and a standard deviation of 4.

CA:155, DA:60, DE:75, EN:93, ES:162, FR:132, GA:314, IT:321, NE:94, PO:165.

94 dependent variable The variable under investigation in a piece of research. For example, scores on a test (the independent variable) may be used to predict success in the workplace (the dependent variable).
Compare: independent variable.
See: variable.
Further reading: Hatch and Lazaraton 1991, p. 63.

CA:432, DA:7, DE:2, EN:94, ES:432, FR:425, GA:28, IT:418, NE:7, PO:424.

95 descriptive statistics The statistics used to describe a set of data in terms of quantities, spread, average values, correlations with other data, etc. A distinction is made between descriptive statistics and sampling or inferential statistics.
Compare: inferential statistics.

CA:165, DA:63, DE:51, EN:95, ES:172, FR:349, GA:365, IT:340, NE:95, PO:176.

96 descriptor A brief description accompanying a band on a rating scale, which summarizes the degree of proficiency or type of performance expected for a candidate to achieve that particular score.

CA:97, DA:64, DE:76, EN:96, ES:98, FR:97, GA:437, IT:118, NE:96, PO:113.

97 diagnostic test A test which is used for the purpose of discovering a learner's specific strengths or weaknesses. The results may be used in making decisions on future training, learning or teaching.

CA:317, DA:65, DE:77, EN:97, ES:325, FR:383, GA:414, IT:373, NE:97, PO:386.

98 dichotomous scoring Scoring based on two categories, e.g. right/wrong, pass/fail, yes/no.

CA:347, DA:67, DE:455, EN:98, ES:347, FR:268, GA:341, IT:32, NE:98, PO:59.

99 dictation A type of test task in which the candidate is required to listen to a text and write down the words which are heard. Criteria for marking dictations vary, depending on the purpose of the test; they may include spelling and punctuation.

CA:103, DA:68, DE:79, EN:99, ES:105, FR:99, GA:109, IT:121, NE:99, PO:125.

100 differential item functioning (DIF) The fact that the relative difficulty of an item is dependent on some characteristic of the group to which it has been administered, such as first language or gender.
See: bias.

CA:195, DA:66, DE:78, EN:100, ES:209, FR:192, GA:114, IT:182, NE:100, PO:208.

101 difficulty index In classical test theory, the difficulty of an item is the proportion (p) of candidates responding to it correctly. This means that the difficulty index of the item is sample-dependent, and changes according to the ability level of the candidates.
Compare: facility index, *p*-value.

CA:207, DA:378, DE:343, EN:101, ES:224, FR:209, GA:187, IT:196, NE:249, PO:219.

102 difficulty parameter Refer to definition for b-parameter.

CA:285, DA:379, DE:344, EN:102, ES:298, FR:296, GA:276, IT:264, NE:250, PO:300.

103 diploma A document stating that a named person has taken an examination or component of an examination and has achieved a particular grade, usually at least a pass. Often interpreted as being a higher level qualification than a certificate.
Compare: certificate.

CA:104, DA:69, DE:80, EN:103, ES:106, FR:100, GA:118, IT:124, NE:101, PO:115.

104 direct test A test which measures the productive skills of speaking or writing, in which performance of the skill itself is directly measured. An example is testing writing ability by requiring a candidate to write a letter.
Compare: indirect test.
Further reading: Hughes 1989, pp. 14–16.

CA:326, DA:70, DE:81, EN:104, ES:335, FR:384, GA:415, IT:375, NE:102, PO:387.

105 directed writing task Refer to definition for guided writing task.

CA:392, DA:43, DE:15, EN:105, ES:6, FR:356, GA:376, IT:77, NE:144, PO:355.

106 discourse Spoken or written text, viewed as a communicative language act.

CA:106, DA:75, DE:85, EN:106, ES:108, FR:101, GA:119, IT:125, NE:103, PO:117.

107 discourse analysis This type of analysis focuses on the structure and function of various kinds of spoken or written text.

CA:19, DA:76, DE:86, EN:107, ES:24, FR:13, GA:17, IT:16, NE: 104, PO:19.

108 discourse competence The ability to understand and produce discourse. In some models of language competence, discourse competence is distinguished as a component.
Further reading: Bachman 1990, Chapter 4.

CA:66, DA:78, DE:87, EN:108, ES:62, FR:64, GA:196, IT:64, NE:105, PO:78.

109 discrete item A self-contained item. It is not linked to a text, other items or any supplementary material. An example of an item type used in this way is multiple choice.
Compare: text-based item.

CA:230, DA:71, DE:421, EN:109, ES:246, FR:228, GA:253, IT:219, NE:106, PO:241.

110 discrete-point item A discrete

item testing one specific point of e.g. structure or vocabulary, and not linked to any other items. Discrete-point language testing was made popular in the 1960s e.g. by Robert Lado.
Compare: integrative item/task.
See: discrete item.
CA:225, DA:72, DE:82, EN:110, ES:247 FR:229, GA:251, IT:210, NE:107, PO:240.

111 discriminant validity A test is said to have discriminant validity if the correlation it has with tests of a different trait is lower than correlation with tests of the same trait, irrespective of testing method. This can be considered an aspect of construct validity.
See: construct validity.
Compare: convergent validity.
Further reading: Crocker and Algina 1986, p. 23; Guilford and Fruchter 1981, pp. 436–437.
CA:423, DA:73, DE:83, EN:111, ES:420, FR:420, GA:36, IT:408, NE:108, PO:416.

112 discrimination The power of an item to discriminate between weaker and stronger candidates. Various indices of discrimination are used. Some (e.g. point-biserial, biserial) are based on a correlation between the score on the item and a criterion, such as total score on the test or some external measure of proficiency. Others are based on the difference in the item's difficulty for low and high ability groups. In item response theory the 2- and 3- parameter models estimate item discrimination as the a-parameter.
See: biserial correlation, item-response theory (IRT), point-biserial correlation.
Further reading: Crocker and Algina 1986, pp. 313–320; Ebel and Frisbie 1991, pp. 231–232.
CA:105, DA:74, DE:416, EN:112, ES:107, FR:102, GA:180, IT:126, NE:109, PO:116.

113 discursive composition A writing task in which the candidate has to discuss a topic on which various views can be held, or argue in support of personal opinions.
See: composition.
CA:74, DA:77, DE:342, EN:113, ES:70, FR:74, GA:52, IT:83, NE:42, PO:89.

114 dispersion The amount of variation or spread in a set of candidates' scores. If the dispersion is large, the scores are widely scattered, and if it is small they are clustered together.
See: range, standard deviation, variance.
CA:107, DA:353, DE:385, EN:114, ES:110, FR:103, GA:357, IT:127, NE:356, PO:118.

115 distractor Each incorrect option in a multiple choice item.
Compare: key response.
See: multiple choice item.
Further reading: Ebel and Frisbie 1986, pp. 176–185.
CA:110, DA:79, DE:88, EN:115, ES:111, FR:104, GA:348, IT:129, NE:8, PO:126.

116 distractor tally The frequency with which each distractor in a multiple choice item is chosen. The tally reveals how popular each distractor is.
CA:243, DA:80, DE:89, EN:116, ES:71, FR:301, GA:384, IT:88, NE:9, PO:96.

117 distribution In test data, the number of occurrences of each score achieved by candidates. This is often shown in the form of a histogram.

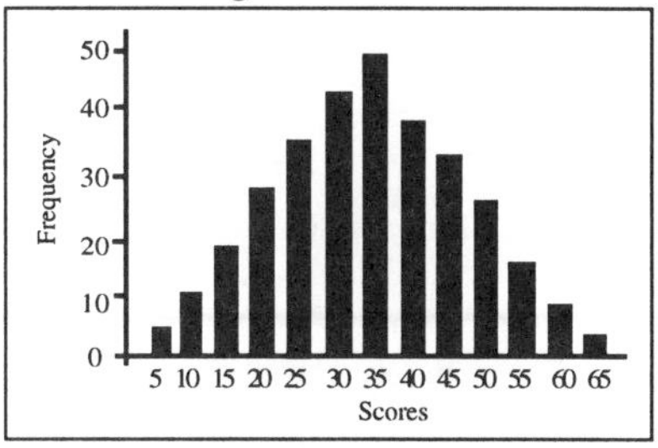

See: normal distribution, skew.
Further reading: Hatch and Lazaraton 1991, pp. 159–178.
CA:111, DA:103, DE:434, EN:117, ES:112, FR:105, GA:103, IT:130, NE:110, PO:119.

118 divergent validity Refer to definition for discriminant validity.
CA:424, DA:81, DE:90, EN:118, ES:421, FR:421, GA:35, IT:409, NE:111, PO:417.

119 domain The defined area of content and/or ability which is to be tested by a specific task or component of an examination.
Further reading: Bachman 1990, pp. 244–246.
CA:11, DA:83, DE:238, EN:119, ES:119, FR:113, GA:137, IT:332, NE:113, PO:129.

120 domain-referenced test A test in which the results are interpreted with respect to a specific content or ability domain.
Compare: criterion-referenced test, norm-referenced test.
CA:335, DA:84, DE:50, EN:120, ES:342, FR:391, GA:417, IT:382, NE:114, PO:368.

121 double marking A method of

assessing performance in which two individuals independently assess candidate performance on a test.
See: multiple marking.
CA:84, DA:82, DE:91, EN:121, ES:118, FR:114, GA:221, IT:104, NE:116, PO:61.

122 Ebel's d Refer to definition for d-index.
CA:96, DA:85, DE:92, EN:122, ES:96, FR:94, GA:101, IT:116, NE:117, PO:111.

123 elicitation procedures A technique for producing a response from a candidate in a test. Normally used in the context of an oral response in a test of spoken language.
Further reading: Hughes 1989, pp. 104–110.
CA:293, DA:8, DE:212, EN:123, ES:307, FR:308, GA:162, IT:276, NE:320, PO:314.

124 entrance test A test used for determining whether or not a candidate gains admission to a particular institution or course of study.
Compare: placement test.
CA:305, DA:5, DE:346, EN:124, ES:319, FR:369, GA:422, IT:364, NE:387, PO:377.

125 equal interval scale Refer to definition for interval scale.
CA:149, DA:213, DE:161, EN:125, ES:159, FR:127, GA:316, IT:316, NE:145, PO:161.

126 equated forms Different forms of a test the score distributions of which have been transformed so that they can be used interchangeably.
Further reading: Crocker and Algina 1986, Chapter 20.
CA:186, DA:442, DE:16/14, EN:126, ES:204, FR:194, GA:145, IT:177 NE:141, PO:200.

127 equipercentile equating A method of equating the raw scores of tests whereby scores are considered to be equated if they correspond to the same percentile rank in a group of candidates.
CA:132, DA:440, DE:24, EN:127, ES:140, FR:36, GA:88, IT:150, NE:121, PO:43.

128 equivalent forms Different versions of the same test, which are regarded as equivalent to each other in that they are based on the same specifications and measure the same competence. To meet the strict requirements of equivalence under classical test theory, different forms of a test must have the same mean difficulty, variance and covariance, when administered to the same persons. Equivalence is very difficult to achieve in practice. Also referred to as alternate forms or parallel forms.
Compare: equated forms.
Further reading: Crocker and Algina 1986, p. 132.
CA:187, DA:441, DE:25, EN:128 ES:205, FR:195, GA:143, IT:178, NE:122, PO:201.

129 error In classical true score measurement theory, an observed score on a test is made up of two components: a true score reflecting the person's ability, and an error score, which reflects the influence of all other factors unrelated to the ability being tested. Error is expected to be random, i.e.unsystematic. Additionally, there may be factors in a test which regularly affect the performance of some individuals, causing systematic error, or test bias.
Compare: bias.
Further reading: Bachman 1990, p. 167.
CA:136, DA:98, DE:116, EN:129, ES:144, FR:151, GA:122, IT:154, NE:124, PO:146.

130 error of measurement Refer to definition for standard error of measurement.
CA:138, DA:240, DE:239, EN:130, ES:146, FR:153, GA:130, IT:159, NE:243, PO:149.

131 essay question Refer to definition for composition.
CA:366, DA:262, DE:33, EN:131, ES:306, FR:159, GA:7, IT:313, NE:125, PO:142.

132 evaluation Gathering information with the intention of using it as a basis for decision-making. In language testing, evaluation may focus on the effectiveness or impact of a programme of instruction, examination, or project.
CA:31, DA:93, DE:106, EN:132, ES:180, FR:166, GA:235, IT:413, NE:126, PO:30.

133 examination A procedure for testing the proficiency or knowledge of individuals by the administration of oral and/or written tasks. The attainment of a qualification (for example, a certificate), admittance to an educational institution or programme of study, etc. may depend on the result.
Compare: test.
Further reading: Bachman 1990, p.50.
CA:171, DA:86, DE:303, EN:133, ES:188, FR:173, GA:347, IT:164, NE:127, PO:181.

134 examinee Refer to definition for candidate.
CA:173, DA:87, DE:307, EN:134, ES:190,

FR:351, GA:345, IT:49, NE:129, PO:183.

135 examiner Refer to definition for assessor.

CA:172, DA:89, DE:301, EN:135, ES:189, FR:174, GA:346, IT:165, NE:130, PO:182.

136 examiner marking A method of marking done by markers who need to have some degree of special expertise and training in order to exercise subjective judgement. Tests of speaking and extended writing are usually marked in this way.
Compare: clerical marking.

CA:81, DA:29, DE:107, EN:136, ES:81, FR:272, GA:223, IT:30, NE:131, PO:67.

137 expected response The response or responses which the writer of an item or task aims to elicit.

CA:377, DA:106, DE:105, EN:137, ES:374, FR:328, GA:157, IT:306, NE:32, PO:338.

138 extended response A form of response to an item or task in which the candidate is expected to produce (as opposed to select) a response which is longer than one or two sentences.
Compare: short answer item.

CA:378, DA:423, DE:35, EN:138, ES:375, FR:332, GA:159, IT:308, NE:407, PO:339.

139 F-ratio In analysis of variance, the ratio computed which indicates whether differences between the means of groups are significant statistically; for example, whether one group has done signficantly better than another on a language test.
See: alternate forms.
Further reading: Hatch and Lazaraton 1991, pp. 315–317.

CA:364, DA:94, DE:109, EN:139, ES:368, FR:319, GA:66, IT:296, NE:132, PO:332.

140 face validity The extent to which a test appears to candidates, or those choosing it on behalf of candidates, to be an acceptable measure of the ability they wish to measure. This is a subjective judgement rather than one based on any objective analysis of the test, and face validity is often considered not to be a true form of validity. It is sometimes referred to as 'test appeal'.
See: validity.
Further reading: Bachman 1990, pp. 285–289.

CA:417, DA:272, DE:110/34, EN:140, ES:414, FR:414 GA:2, IT:402, NE:174, PO:410.

141 facility index The proportion of correct responses to an item, expressed on a scale of 0 to 1. It is also sometimes expressed as a percentage. Also referred to as facility value or *p*-value.
Compare: difficulty index.

CA:209, DA:191, DE:208, EN:141, ES:225, FR:210, GA:188, IT:197, NE:146, PO:220.

142 factor analysis A statistical technique which allows a researcher to reduce a large number of variables to a smaller number, by finding patterns among the variations in the values of several variables. A cluster of variables which are highly intercorrelated form a factor. A researcher may begin factor analysis in the exploratory mode, in order to formulate hypotheses, or in confirmatory mode, examining specific hypotheses.
Further reading: Bachman 1990, p. 262; Crocker and Algina 1986, p. 232.

CA:20, DA:96, DE:115, EN:142, ES:26, FR:18, GA:18, IT:14, NE:133, PO:20.

143 facility value Refer to definition for facility index.

CA:426, DA:192, DE:209, EN:143, ES:423, FR:410, GA:217, IT:411, NE:147, PO:419.

144 feedback Comments of people involved in the testing process (examinees, administrators, etc.) which provide a basis for evaluating that process. Feedback may be gathered informally, or using specially-designed questionnaires.

CA:381, DA:97, DE:330, EN:144, ES:379, FR:337, GA:6, IT:173, NE:134, PO:192.

145 fit The extent of agreement between the predictions of a model and the observed outcomes. Different indices of fit can be computed. In IRT, analysis of fit shows how well the estimated item and person parameters (e.g. difficulty and ability) predict people's scores on a test: an item's fit statistic can be seen as analogous to its discrimination index in classical test statistics.
See: item-response theory (IRT).

CA:8, DA:99, DE:248, EN:145, ES:15, FR:6, GA:268, IT:107, NE:135, PO:5.

146 floor effect A boundary effect which results from a test's being too difficult for a particular group of candidates, so that their scores all group at the bottom of the distribution.
See: boundary effects.

CA:122, DA:42, DE:61/121, EN:146, ES:128, FR:141, GA:175, IT:144, NE:49, PO:130.

147 formative assessment Testing which takes place during, rather than at the end of, a course or programme of instruction. The results may enable the teacher to give remedial help at an early stage, or change the emphasis of a course if required. Results may also help a student to identify and focus on areas of weakness.
Compare: summative assessment.
CA:32, DA:225, DE:213, EN:147, ES:184, FR:168, GA:232, IT:422, NE:137, PO:32.

148 formative evaluation Ongoing evaluation of a process, which allows for that process to be adapted and improved as it continues. It can refer to a programme of instruction.
Compare: summative evaluation.
CA:32, DA:226, DE:46, EN:148, ES:184, FR:168, GA:236, IT:414, NE:136, PO:32.

149 frequency distribution Refer to definition for distribution.
CA:113, DA:107, DE:142, EN:149, ES:114, FR:107, GA:106, IT:132, NE:138, PO:122.

150 gain score The difference between the score achieved on a test before a course of instruction and the score achieved on the same or a similar test taken at the end of the course. The gain score indicates progress during the course.
CA:352, DA:290, DE:211, EN:150, ES:32, FR:199, GA:44, IT:192, NE:434, PO:209.

151 gap-filling item Any type of item which requires the candidate to insert some written material - letters, numbers, single words, phrases, sentences or paragraphs - into spaces in a text. The response may be supplied by the candidate or selected from a set of options.
CA:223, DA:138, DE:229, EN:151, ES:241, FR:317, GA:249, IT:78, NE:192, PO:235.

152 gaussian distribution Refer to definition for normal distribution.
CA:114, DA:114, DE:129, EN:152, ES:115, FR:91, GA:105, IT:133, NE:140, PO:110.

153 G-factor In intelligence theory, a 'general factor' hypothesized to underlie all cognitive skills. This notion was popularized by John Oller during the 1970s as evidence for a unitary competence underlying language proficiency.
Further reading: Oller 1979, pp. 426–458, Bachman 1990, p. 6.
CA:176, DA:113, DE:127, EN:153, ES:194, FR:177, GA:136, IT:170, NE:139, PO:187.

154 generalizability theory A statistical model for investigating the relative effects of different sources of variance in test scores.
Further reading: Bachman 1990, p. 7; Crocker and Algina 1986, Chapter 8.
CA:400, DA:115, DE:132, EN:154, ES:393, FR:399, GA:388, IT:351, NE:152, PO:359.

155 global assessment A method of scoring which can be used in tests of writing and speaking. The assessor gives a single mark according to the general impression made by the language produced, rather than by breaking it down into a number of marks for various aspects of language use.
Compare: analytic scoring, impression marking (general impression marking).
CA:33, DA:124, DE:137, EN:155, ES:427, FR:169, GA:231, IT:186, NE:161, PO:33.

156 grade A test score may be reported to the candidate as a grade, for example on a scale of A to E, where A is the highest grade available, B is a good pass, C a pass and D and E are failing grades.
Compare: marks.
CA:275, DA:167, DE:270, EN:156, ES:288, FR:259, GA:164, IT:188, NE:426, PO:272.

157 grading The process of converting test scores or marks into grades.
CA:362, DA:168, DE:48, EN:157, ES:47, FR:52, GA:165, IT:94, NE:427, PO:277.

158 grammatical competence Within a model of communicative language ability, grammatical competence is the component which addresses knowledge of such areas of language usage as morphology, syntax, vocabulary, phonology and graphology.
Further reading: Bachman 1990, pp. 84–88.
CA:67, DA:119, DE:138, EN:158, ES:63, FR:65, GA:193, IT:65, NE:162, PO:79.

159 guessing parameter Refer to definition for C-parameter.
CA:284, DA:122, DE:319, EN:159, ES:297, FR:295, GA:277, IT:263, NE:160, PO:301.

160 guided writing task A task which involves the candidate in the production of a written text, where graphic or textual information, such as pictures, letters, postcards and instructions, is used to control

and standardize the expected response.
Compare: composition, essay question.
CA:393, DA:121, DE:130, EN:160, ES:5, FR:311, GA:377, IT:76, NE:143, PO:317.

161 halo effect A tendency of assessors involved in subjective examining to be influenced by a candidate's performance on certain test tasks and consequently to give too high or low a score for another task.
See: rater effects.
CA:117, DA:118, DE:141, EN:161, ES:127, FR:137, GA:170, IT:139, NE:164, PO:133.

162 higher-order skills Hypothesized complex abilities such as inferencing and summarizing.
Compare: lower-order skills.
CA:201, DA:130, DE:418, EN:162, ES:102, FR:45, GA:326, IT:3, NE:410, PO:53.

163 histogram A graphical representation of a frequency distribution, in which the number of cases per frequency class is shown as a vertical bar.

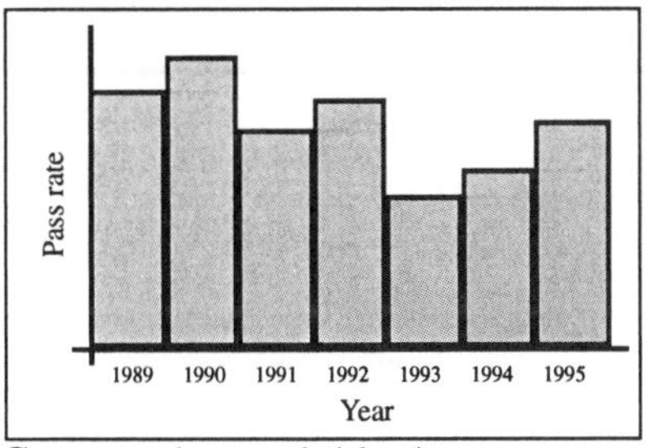

Compare: bar graph (chart).
CA:203, DA:125, DE:145, EN:163, ES:218, FR:204, GA:168, IT:207, NE:167, PO:215.

164 holistic assessment Refer to definition for global assessment.
CA:429, DA:126, DE:128, EN:164, ES:428, FR:170, GA:230, IT:187, NE:168, PO:34.

165 homogeneity A feature of a test or subtest whereby items measure the same competence, or of a group whereby individuals share the same characteristics. Degree of homogeneity is expressed by the reliability index.
CA:204, DA:127, DE:148, EN:165, ES:221, FR:205, GA:22, IT:257, NE:169, PO:216.

166 horizontal equating The process of putting the scores from two tests of approximately the same difficulty onto a single scale for the purpose of applying the same standards in both tests.
Compare: vertical equating.
CA:133, DA:128, DE:149, EN:166, ES:141, FR:37, GA:89, IT:152, NE:170, PO:44.

167 impact The effect created by a test, both in terms of influence on general educational processes, and in terms of the individuals who are affected by test results.
See: backwash, washback.
CA:205, DA:303, DE:444, EN:167, ES:222, FR:207, GA:391, IT:191, NE:171, PO:217.

168 impression marking (general impression marking) A method of scoring which can be used in tests of productive language use, i.e. writing or speaking. The assessor makes an assessment of each candidate response, without any attempt to separate the discrete features of the task.
Compare: analytic scoring, global assessment.
CA:89, DA:116, DE:133, EN:168, ES:429, FR:270, GA:220, IT:33, NE:172, PO:68.

169 independent variable In research, a variable which it is thought may relate to or influence the dependent variable. For example, scores on a test (the independent variable) may be used to predict success in the workplace (the dependent variable).
Compare: dependent variable.
See: variable.
Further reading: Hatch and Lazaraton 1991, p. 64.
CA:433, DA:420, DE:422, EN:169, ES:433, FR:426, GA:27, IT:419, NE:268, PO:425.

170 indirect test (task) A test or task which attempts to measure the abilities underlying a language skill, rather than testing performance of the skill itself. An example is testing writing ability by requiring the candidate to mark structures used incorrectly in a text.
Compare: direct test.
Further reading: Hughes 1989, pp. 14–16.
CA:329, DA:135, DE:150, EN:170, ES:337, FR:385, GA:420, IT:354, NE:173, PO:389.

171 inferential statistics Statistics which go beyond the information provided by descriptive statistics, and allow inferences to be made about how well a single data set probably represents the larger popu-

lation of which it is a sample.
Compare: descriptive statistics.
CA:166, DA:139, DE:338, EN:171, ES:173, FR:350, GA:364, IT:341, NE:175, PO:177.

172 information gap A technique of language teaching and testing which simulates real communication by setting up situations in which students do not share the same information, and thus need to communicate with each other in order to complete a task. Normally used in practising or testing the skills of speaking and writing.
CA:42, DA:140, DE:151, EN:172, ES:411, FR:213, GA:43, IT:424, NE:176, PO:223.

173 information transfer A technique of testing which involves taking information given in a certain form and presenting it in a different form. Examples of such tasks are: taking information from a text and using it to label a diagram; re-writing an informal note as a formal announcement.
Further reading: Hughes 1989, pp. 84, 124–125, 138.
CA:409, DA:141, DE:152, EN:173, ES:406, FR:402, GA:8, IT:396, NE:177, PO:404.

174 input Material provided in a test task for the candidate to use in order to produce an appropriate response. In a test of listening, for example, it may take the form of a recorded text and several accompanying written items.
CA:169, DA:142, DE:408, EN:174, ES:228, FR:147, GA:199, IT:199, NE:180, PO:254.

175 instructions General directions given to test candidates, for example on the front page of the answer paper or booklet, giving information about such things as how long the test lasts, how many tasks to attempt and where to record their responses.
Compare: rubric.
CA:211, DA:143, DE:391, EN:175, ES:230, FR:214, GA:402, IT:208, NE:181, PO:225.

176 integrative item/task Used to refer to items or tasks which require more than one skill or subskill for their completion. Examples are the items in a cloze test, an oral interview, reading a letter and writing a response to it.
Compare: discrete-point item.
CA:231, DA:144, DE:156, EN:176, ES:249, FR:316, GA:248, IT:221, NE:182, PO:245.

177 interactional authenticity A view of authenticity in language testing which sees it as a characteristic of the interaction which has to take place between the test taker and the test task in order to produce an appropriate response.
Compare: situational authenticity.
See: authenticity.
Further reading: Bachman 1990, pp. 315–323.
CA:28, DA:146, DE:157, EN:177, ES:34, FR:25, GA:116, IT:36, NE:183, PO:27.

178 interlocutor In a test of speaking, the examiner who explains the tasks, asks questions and generally interacts orally with the candidate(s). The interlocutor may also make the assessment of the candidate(s) and assign scores, or this may be done by a second examiner, who observes but does not interact with the candidate(s).
Compare: assessor.
CA:213, DA:325, DE:125, EN:178, ES:138, FR:216, GA:72, IT:201, NE:155, PO:227.

179 interlocutor frame A scripted indication of the language an interlocutor should use in conducting a test of speaking. The purpose is to standardize the language all candidates hear, thus making the test fairer and more reliable.
CA:198, DA:324, DE:438, EN:179, ES:215, FR:34, GA:151, IT:128, NE:156, PO:321.

180 internal consistency A feature of a test, represented by the degree to which candidates' scores on the individual items in a test are consistent with their total score. Estimates of internal consistency can be used as indices of test reliability; various indices can be computed, for example, KR-20, alpha.
See: alpha (alpha coefficient), Kuder-Richardson, reliability.
Further reading: Bachman 1990, p.172.
CA:77, DA:147, DE:155, EN:180, ES:74, FR:186, GA:87, IT:87, NE:186, PO:93.

181 inter-rater agreement The degree of agreement between two or more assessors on the same sample of performance. This has particular relevance to the assessment of speaking and writing skills in tests where subjective judgements by examiners are required.
CA:2, DA:31, DE:159, EN:181, ES:11, FR:2, GA:68, IT:84, NE:185, PO:2.

182 inter-rater reliability An estimate of test reliability based on the degree to

which different assessors agree in their assessment of candidates' performance.
See: inter-rater agreement, reliability.

CA:181, DA:145, DE:158, EN:182, ES:199, FR:185, GA:201, IT:8, NE:184, PO:195.

183 interval The difference between two points on a scale.

CA:214, DA:148, DE:160, EN:183, ES:232, FR:218, GA:131, IT:203, NE:187, PO:228.

184 interval scale A scale of measurement on which the distance between any two adjacent units of measurement is the same, but in which there is no absolute zero point.
Compare: categorical scale, nominal scale, ordinal scale, ratio scale.
Further reading: Crocker and Algina 1986, p.48.

CA:148, DA:149, DE:161, EN:184, ES:158, FR:126, GA:315, IT:315, NE:188, PO:162.

185 intra-rater agreement The degree of agreement between two assessments of the same sample of performance made at different times by the same assessor. This has particular relevance to the assessment of speaking and writing skills in tests where subjective judgements by examiners are required.

CA:3, DA:33, DE:163, EN:185, ES:12, FR:3, GA:69, IT:90, NE:190, PO:3.

186 intra-rater reliability An estimate of the reliability of assessment, based on the degree to which the same assessor scores the same performance similarly on different occasions.
See: intra-rater agreement, reliability.

CA:182, DA:151, DE:162, EN:186, ES:200, FR:187, GA:202, IT:89, NE:189, PO:196.

187 invariance In IRT, the important assumption that item difficulty and discrimination measures are inherent features that do not depend on the ability of candidates, and likewise that ability measures do not depend on the particular items used.

CA:216, DA:152, DE:164, EN:187, ES:234, FR:220, GA:120, IT:205, NE:191, PO:230.

188 IRT Refer to definition for item response theory.

CA:412, DA:153, DE:165, EN:188, ES:408, FR:401, GA:392, IT:352, NE:194, PO:402.

189 item Each testing point in a test which is given a separate mark or marks. Examples are: one gap in a cloze test; one multiple choice question with three or four options; one sentence for grammatical transformation; one question to which a sentence-length response is expected.
Compare: task.

CA:217, DA:154, DE:166, EN:189, ES:235, FR:221, GA:240, IT:209, NE:195, PO:231.

190 item analysis A description of the performance of individual test items, usually employing classical statistical indices such as facility and discrimination. Software such as MicroCAT Iteman is used for this analysis.
See: discrimination, facility index.

CA:13, DA:161, DE:167, EN:190, ES:25, FR:17, GA:13, IT:12, NE:198, PO:16.

191 item banking An approach to the management of test items which entails storing information about items so that tests of known content and difficulty can be constructed. Normally, the approach makes use of a computer database, and is based on latent trait theory, which means that items can be related to each other by means of a common difficulty scale.
Further reading: Henning 1987, Chapter 9.

CA:36, DA:155, DE:28, EN:191, ES:37, FR:28, GA:40, IT:111, NE:199, PO:37.

192 item characteristic curve (ICC) In Item Response Theory, an ICC shows how the probability of responding correctly to an item relates to the latent ability trait underlying performance on the items in the test.
Further reading: Crocker and Algina 1986, pp. 340–342.

CA:79, DA:157, DE:168, EN:192, ES:95, FR:90, GA:94, IT:115, NE:196, PO:109.

193 item information function In IRT, an index of how much information an item or test provides about a person of given ability level; it depends on the item's discrimination, and on how well matched it is to the level.
Compare: test information function.

CA:192, DA:156, DE:169, EN:193, ES:212, FR:190, GA:138, IT:184, NE:197, PO:206.

194 item response function In item response theory, a mathematical function that relates the probability of success on an item to ability in the trait measured by the item. Also known as the item characteristic function.

CA:193, DA:158, DE:172, EN:194, ES:210, FR:189, GA:140, IT:183, NE:200, PO:205.

195 item-response theory (IRT) A group of mathematical models for relating an individual's test performance to that individual's level of ability. These models are based on the fundamental theory that an individual's expected performance on a particular test question, or item, is a function of both the level of difficulty of the item and the individual's level of ability.
Further reading: Henning 1987, Chapter 8; Crocker and Algina 1986, Chapter 15.

CA:401, DA:159, DE:173/296, EN:195, ES:394, FR:400, GA:389, IT:352, NE:201, PO:360.

196 item score In item analysis, the sum of the correct responses to a particular item.

CA:345, DA:160, DE:171, EN:196, ES:346, FR:267, GA:336, IT:281, NE:202, PO:60.

197 item type Test items are referred to by names which tend to be descriptive of the form they take. Some examples are: multiple choice, sentence transformation, short answer, open cloze.

CA:406, DA:162, DE:174, EN:197 ES:403, FR:405, GA:58, IT:392, NE:203, PO:399.

198 key response a) The correct option in a multiple choice item.

b) More generally, a set of all correct or acceptable responses to test items.
Compare: distractor, mark scheme.
See: multiple choice item.

CA:51/52, DA:256, DE:339, EN:198, ES:54, FR:329, GA:133, DE:339, IT:53, NE:342, PO:335.

199 KR-20 (Kuder-Richardson formula 20) Refer to definition for Kuder-Richardson.

CA:234, DA:201, DE:194, EN:199, ES:252, FR:233, GA:205, IT:222, NE:210, PO:246.

200 KR-21 (Kuder-Richardson formula 21) Refer to definition for Kuder-Richardson.

CA:235, DA:202, DE:195, EN:200 ES:253, FR:234, GA:206, IT:223, NE:211, PO:247.

201 Kuder-Richardson Two measures of internal consistency developed by Kuder and Richardson and used to estimate test reliability. KR-21 requires less information and is easier to compute, but generally yields a lower estimate than KR-20.
Compare: alpha (alpha coefficient).
See: internal consistency.
Further reading: Henning 1987, p.84.

CA:236, DA:206, DE:200, EN:201, ES:254, FR:235, GA:207, IT:224, NE:212, PO:248.

202 kurtosis An indication of the extent to which a distribution is more peaked or flatter than the normal curve. Data spread out in a flat curve shows a platykurtic distribution, while data forming a sharply peaked curve shows leptokurtic distribution.

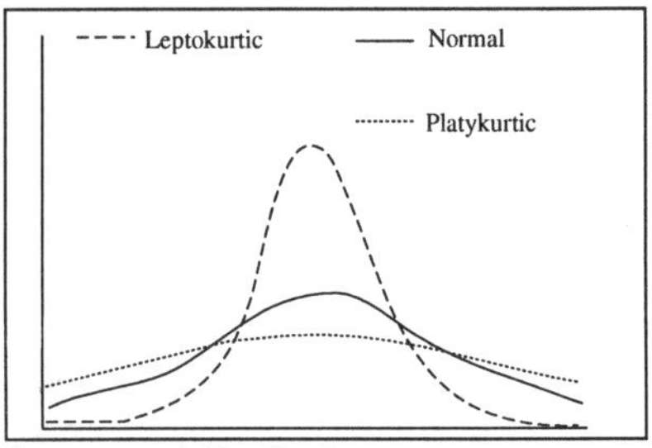

See: normal distribution.

CA:95, DA:412, DE:108, EN:202, ES:94, FR:428, GA:100, IT:114, NE:213, PO:108.

203 language ability The competencies which together define an individual's capacity to use language for a variety of communicative purposes.
Further reading: Bachman 1990, pp. 3–4.

CA:47, DA:354, DE:368, EN:203, ES:50, FR:43, GA:97, IT:4, NE:379, PO:50.

204 language acquisition The process by which ability in a first or second language is acquired. In the case of a second language, a distinction is sometimes drawn between acquisition (i.e. by natural exposure) and learning (i.e. through conscious study).

CA:7, DA:356, DE:367, EN:204, ES:14, FR:5, GA:349, IT:22, NE:380, PO:24.

205 language for specific purposes (LSP) Language teaching or testing which focuses on the area of language used for a particular activity or profession; for example, English for Air Traffic Control, Spanish for Commerce.

CA:238, DA:95, DE:111, EN:205, ES:256, FR:236, GA:385, IT:227, NE:378, PO:251.

206 language proficiency Knowledge of a language. The term is often used synonymously with 'language ability'.
Further reading: Bachman 1990, p. 16.

CA:297, DA:355, DE:365, EN:206, ES:121, FR:66, GA:267, IT:66, NE:215, PO:81.

207 latent trait theory Refer to definition for item-response theory (IRT).

CA:402, DA:211, DE:206, EN:207, ES:395, FR:398, GA:390, IT:350, NE:216, PO:358.

208 learning objective The aim or desired result of an educational activity.

CA:277, DA:136, DE:215, EN:208, ES:290, FR:289, GA:360, IT:255, NE:217, PO:292.

209 level The degree of proficiency required for a student to be in a certain class or represented by a particular test is often referred to in terms of a series of levels. These are commonly given names such as 'elementary', 'intermediate', 'advanced', etc.

CA:270, DA:247, DE:260, EN:209, ES:283, FR:259, GA:210, IT:229, NE:258, PO:272.

210 lexis A term used to refer to vocabulary.

CA:237, DA:212, DE:221, EN:210, ES:257, FR:238, GA:213, IT:225, NE:227, PO:250.

211 likert scale A type of scale used in questionnaires for measuring attitudes or opinions. People are asked to repond to a series of statements by choosing one out of approximately five possible responses such as 'strongly agree', 'agree', 'don't know', 'disagree', 'strongly disagree'.

CA:152, DA:214, DE:222, EN:211, ES:163, FR:129, GA:317, IT:325, NE:228, PO:163.

212 linear equating An approach to equating in which a score on one test is equated to a score on a second test. The equivalent scores on the two tests are the same number of standard deviations above or below the mean score of the test in which they appear.
See: regression.
Further reading: Crocker and Algina 1986, pp. 457–461.

CA:134, DA:216, DE:17, EN:212, ES:142, FR:38, GA:91, IT:151, NE:229, PO:45.

213 linear regression A regression technique that assumes a linear relationship between the dependent and independent variables.

CA:370, DA:215, DE:223, EN:213, ES:366, FR:325, GA:5, IT:299, NE:230, PO:329.

214 linguistic competence Refer to definition for competence.

CA:68, DA:217, DE:224, EN:214, ES:64, FR:67, GA:198, IT:66, NE:231, PO:80.

215 link item Refer to definition for anchor item.

CA:221, DA:218, DE:432, EN:215, ES:239, FR:231, GA:250, IT:214, NE:232, PO:244.

216 listening comprehension test A test of understanding of spoken language normally administered using tape recorder or video.

CA:315, DA:221, DE:147, EN:216, ES:324, FR:372, GA:411, IT:361, NE:235, PO:373.

217 live test (item) A test which is currently available for use, and which must for that reason be kept secure.

CA:341, DA:101, DE:225, EN:217, ES:344, FR:360, GA:407, IT:355, NE:233, PO:362.

218 logit In item-response theory (IRT), a unit of measurement, derived from the natural logarithm of the ratio of chance of success to chance of failure, i.e. log odds. The difference in logits between a person's ability and an item's difficulty is the person's log odds of succeeding on the item.
Further reading: Henning 1987, pp. 118–126.

CA:241, DA:220, DE:227, EN:218, ES:259, FR:240, GA:216, IT:232, NE:234, PO:253.

219 lower-order skills Hypothesized less complex abilities, such as word or letter recognition, required of candidates in language tests.
Compare: higher-order skills.

CA:200, DA:27, DE:424, EN:219, ES:101, FR:44, GA:327, IT:2, NE:409, PO:52.

220 many-facet Rasch model An extension of the Rasch model, which allows response probabilities to be modelled on the basis of an additive combination of facets. For example, performance on a writing task can be modelled to reflect task difficulty plus the severity of the rater. The many-facet Rasch model has been implemented, for example, by the FACETS program.
See: Rasch model.
Further reading: Linacre J.M., 1989, Many-Facet Rasch Measurement, Chicago, MESA Press.

CA:260, DA:235, DE:289, EN:220, ES:276, FR:254, GA:300, IT:249, NE:236, PO:268.

221 marker Someone who assigns a score to a candidate's responses to a written test. This may involve the use of expert judgement, or, in the case of a clerical marker, the relatively unskilled application of a mark scheme.
See: assessor.

CA:90, DA:288, DE:39, EN:221, ES:83, FR:81, GA:225, IT:102, NE:80, PO:182.

222 marking Assigning a mark to a candidate's responses to a test. This may involve professional judgement, or the application of a mark scheme which lists all acceptable responses.

CA:80, DA:289, DE:40, EN:222, ES:47, FR:265, GA:218, IT:29, NE:83, PO:57.

223 mark scheme A list of all the acceptable responses to the items in a test. A mark scheme makes it possible for a marker to assign a score to a test accurately.

CA:52/256, DA:319, DE:228, EN:223, ES:301, FR:29, GA:324, IT:329, NE:79, PO:172.

224 marks The total number of points available for an item, subtest or test, or the number of points awarded for a candidate's response to an item, subtest or test.

CA:342, DA:287, DE:313, EN:224, ES:44, FR:287, GA:224, IT:292, NE:60, PO:105.

225 mastery test A test designed to establish whether a student has mastered a well-defined domain of skills or knowledge.

CA:338, DA:227, DE:204, EN:225, ES:327, FR:376, GA:425, IT:366, NE:237, PO:376.

226 matching task A test task type which involves bringing together elements from two separate lists. One kind of matching test consists of selecting the correct phrase to complete each of a number of unfinished sentences. A type used in tests of reading comprehension involves choosing from a list something like a holiday or a book to suit a person whose particular requirements are described.

CA:397, DA:322, DE:452, EN:226, ES:7, FR:21, GA:375, IT:73, NE:238, PO:353.

227 mean A measure of central tendency often referred to as the average. The mean score in an administration of a test is arrived at by adding together all the scores and dividing by the total number of scores.
Compare: median, mode.
See: central tendency (measure of).
Further reading: Hatch and Lazaraton 1991, pp.161–163.

CA:250, DA:231, DE:244, EN:227, ES:261, FR:257, GA:226, IT:234, NE:151, PO:255.

228 mean item difficulty index (mean p) This is the average proportion correct across all items on a scale of dichotomously scored items. For example a mean p of 0.5 shows that the mean facility index for the test is 0.5.
See: dichotomous scoring.

CA:208, DA:132, DE:246, EN:228, ES:227, FR:212, GA:190, IT:195 NE:150, PO:222.

229 mean square What the variance is called in an analysis of variance (ANOVA).
See: ANOVA.

CA:251, DA:230, DE:245, EN:229, ES:262, FR:47, GA:227, IT:295, NE:149, PO:319.

230 measurement Generally, the process of finding the amount of something by comparison with a fixed unit, e.g. using a ruler to measure length. In the social sciences, measurement often refers to the quantification of characteristics of persons, such as language proficiency.
Further reading: Bachmann 1990 Chapter 2.

CA:245, DA:242, DE:241, EN:230, ES:264, FR:243, GA:395, IT:238, NE:245, PO:257.

231 measurement error Refer to definition for error.

CA:138, DA:241, DE:240, EN:231, ES:146, FR:153, GA:123, IT:159, NE:242, PO:149.

232 median The score at the centre of the distribution in a set of ranked scores. Half the scores are above the median and half below it.
See: central tendency (measure of).
Compare: mean, mode.
Further reading: Hatch and Lazaraton 1991, p. 161.

CA:244, DA:228, DE:232, EN:232, ES:263, FR:242, GA:3, IT:235, NE:239, PO:256.

233 method effect An effect on test scores produced by the method of testing used rather than by the ability of the candidate.

CA:121, DA:229, DE:242, EN:233, ES:126, FR:139, GA:171, IT:142, NE:244, PO:134.

234 minimum competency testing An approach to testing which sets out specific requirements for a minimum level of competency in a particular domain of language use. A candidate who can demonstrate this level of competency passes the test.

CA:312, DA:398, DE:304, EN:234, ES:183, FR:167, GA:378, IT:388, NE:246, PO:31.

235 mode The point in the distribution of a set of scores at which scores occur most frequently; the highest point of the distribution curve.

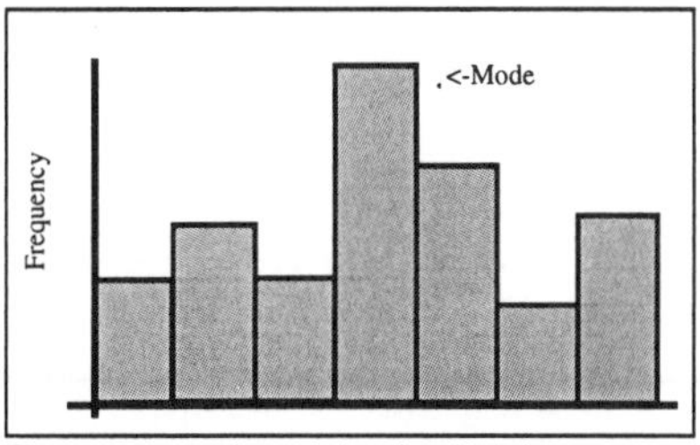

Compare: bimodal distribution, mean, median.
See: central tendency (measure of).
Further reading: Hatch and Lazaraton 1991, pp. 160–161.

CA:252, DA:232, DE:247, EN:235, ES:268, FR:247, GA:255, IT:240, NE:248, PO:261.

236 model answer A good example of the expected response to an open-ended task which is provided by the item writer, and can be used in the development of a mark scheme to guide markers.

CA:261, DA:233, DE:253, EN:236, ES:376, FR:333, GA:156, IT:245, NE:21, PO:340.

237 moderation a) Part of the process of preparing items or tasks for use in a test. At this stage the materials are examined critically by a number of experts (such as test writers and teachers) who decide whether they will eventually be acceptable for use (possibly with some editing or re-writing).

b) In the assessment process, the adjustment by a moderator of marks already assigned by an assessor.
Compare: vetting.

CA:263, DA:410, DE:31, EN:237, ES:277, FR:256, GA:260, IT:250, NE:247, PO:270.

238 multiple choice item A type of test item which consists of a question or incomplete sentence (stem), with a choice of answers or ways of completing the sentence (options). The candidate's task is to choose the correct option (key) from a set of three, four or five possibilities, and no production of language is involved. For this reason, multiple choice items are normally used in tests of reading and listening. They may be discrete or text-based.
See: discrete item, text-based item.

CA:220, DA:236, DE:249/234, EN:238, ES:244, FR:222, GA:247, IT:211, NE:252, PO:236.

239 multiple choice gap filling A type of test item in which the candidate's task is to select from a set of options the correct word or phrase to insert into a space in a text.
See: gap-filling item.

CA:224, DA:237, DE:250, EN:239, ES:242, FR:386, GA:215, IT:79, NE:251, PO:390.

240 multiple marking A method of improving the reliability of assessment of tests of extended writing, which is necessarily to some degree subjective, by ensuring that each candidate response is marked independently by more than one assessor.
Further reading: Weir 1988, pp. 65–66.

CA:87, DA:274, DE:233, EN:240, ES:45, FR:271, GA:183, IT:105, NE:241, PO:63.

241 multiple-matching task A test task in which a number of questions or sentence completion items, generally based on a reading text, are set. The responses are provided in the form of a bank of words or phrases, each of which can be used an unlimited number of times. The advantage is that options are not removed as the candidate works through the items (as with other forms of matching) so that the task does not become progressively easier.
See: matching task.

CA:396, DA:100, DE:235, EN:241, ES:8, FR:355, GA:372, IT:72, NE:253, PO:354.

242 multiple regression A statistical technique used for establishing the linear effects of several independent variables on a single dependent variable. For example, with task difficulty as the dependent variable, the effects of task type, lexical difficulty, etc. could be investigated.
See: independent variable, regression.
Further reading: Hatch and Lazaraton

1991, pp. 480–486.
CA:371, DA:117, DE:251, EN:242, ES:367, FR:326, GA:182, IT:300, NE:240, PO:330.

243 multitrait-multimethod design An experimental design used in construct validation, whereby a set of supposedly distinct traits are measured by each of a supposedly distinct set of methods. Analysis should show, for example, that measures of listening ability obtained by different methods correlate more highly with each other than measures of different skills obtained by the same test method.
Further reading: Bachman 1990, pp. 263–265.
CA:108, DA:238, DE:252, EN:243, ES:109, FR:299, GA:111, IT:277, NE:254, PO:305.

244 *N, n* Number. Upper case *N* is often used to mean the number of cases in a study or individuals in a population, while lower case *n* often means the number in a sample or subgroup. For example: 'The test was taken by graduate engineers ($N = 600$) of whom 10% were female ($n = 60$)'.
CA:269, DA:248, DE:256, EN:244, ES:282, FR:258, GA:261, IT:251, NE:259, PO:271.

245 native speaker A speaker of a language which was acquired as a first language.
CA:286, DA:234, DE:255, EN:245, ES:216, FR:217, GA:47, IT:265, NE:255, PO:190.

246 needs analysis A way of determining the language needs (in terms of skills, tasks, vocabulary, etc.) of a particular group of learners prior to devising a course of instruction for them.
CA:16, DA:35, DE:45, EN:246, ES:21, FR:11, GA:19, IT:13, NE:31, PO:17.

247 net D Refer to definition for d-index.
CA:206, DA:246, DE:257, EN:247, ES:97, FR:115, GA:102, IT:194, NE:256, PO:111.

248 nominal scale A scale used with categorical variables such as sex or first language. Such variables are either present or not present, and interest in them is focused on frequency of occurrence. Also known as a categorical scale.
Compare: interval scale, ordinal scale, ratio scale.
Further reading: Hatch and Lazaraton 1991, pp. 55–56.
CA:156, DA:249, DE:262, EN:248, ES:164, FR:133, GA:309, IT:326, NE:260, PO:166.

249 non-parametric procedures Statistical procedures that do not assume that the data comes from any particular type of distribution, or where the data is not based on an interval scale. Chi-square is a familiar example of this.
Compare: parametric procedures.
Further reading: Hatch and Lazaraton 1991, pp. 237–239.
CA:294, DA:131, DE:259, EN:249, ES:308, FR:309, GA:258, IT:274, NE:257, PO:315.

250 norm A standard of performance. In a standardized test the norm is determined by recording the scores of a large group. The norm or standards based on the performance of that group are used in assessing the performance of subsequent groups of candidates of a similar type.
See: norm group, norm-referenced test.
CA:273, DA:250, DE:263, EN:250, ES:286, FR:264, GA:262, IT:252, NE:261, PO:278.

251 norm group Typically, a large group of individuals representative of the people for whom a test is designed. The performance of the norm group is used in the interpretation of a norm-referenced test. Also referred to as a reference group.
See: norm-referenced test.
CA:197, DA:254, DE:266, EN:251, ES:214, FR:203, GA:264, IT:190, NE:265, PO:213.

252 normal distribution A mathematical distribution which is the fundamental assumption for several statistical procedures. The distribution is a symmetrical bell shape, and the mean, median and mode all occur at the same point. A whole family of distributions exists, depending on the values of the mean, standard deviation and the number of observations. Also known as Gaussian distribution.
Compare: bimodal distribution.
Further reading: Hatch and Lazaraton 1991, p. 164.
CA:115, DA:252, DE:265, EN:252, ES:116, FR:108, GA:107, IT:134, NE:262, PO:123.

253 normalization The changing of scores in such a way as to transform the distribution into a normal distribution. Typically this will involve the use of equipercentile scaling.

Compare: standard score.

CA:274, DA:253, DE:264, EN:253, ES:287, FR:263, GA:263, IT:253, NE:263, PO:279.

254 norm-referenced test A test where scores are interpreted with reference to the performance of a given group, consisting of people comparable to the individuals taking the test. The term tends to be used of tests whose interpretation focuses on ranking individuals relative to the norm group or to each other.
Compare: criterion-referenced test.

CA:336, DA:251, DE:268, EN:254, ES:340, FR:388, GA:426, IT:381, NE:264, PO:391.

255 null hypothesis A hypothesis that states that two or more variables are not related. For example, the supposition that there is no difference in test performance between members of two distinct first language groups is a null hypothesis.
Further reading: Hatch and Lazaraton 1991, p. 24; Guilford and Fruchter 1981, pp. 146–147.

CA:202, DA:255, DE:271, EN:255, ES:217, FR:206, GA:167, IT:206, NE:266, PO:214.

256 objectives The knowledge, competence and attitudes which are the stated aims of an educational course of any kind.

CA:278, DA:244, DE:216, EN:256, ES:291, FR:288, GA:359, IT:254, NE:112, PO:293.

257 objective test A test which can be scored by applying a mark scheme, without the need to bring expert opinion or subjective judgement to the task.

CA:331, DA:257, DE:272, EN:257, ES:341, FR:389, GA:427, IT:377, NE:267, PO:392.

258 observed score The score obtained by a candidate. Classical test theory considers this to be made up of the true score and error.
See: error, true score.

CA:353, DA:183, DE:49, EN:258, ES:352, FR:279, GA:331, IT:283, NE:429, PO:285.

259 one-parameter model In item-response theory (IRT), a model which operates with a single scale representing difficulty (of tasks) and ability (of persons), and does not consider variable item discrimination or guessing.
Compare: Rasch model.

CA:255, DA:92, DE:99, EN:259, ES:273, FR:249, GA:296, IT:242, NE:118, PO:265.

260 open-ended question A type of item or task in a written test which requires the candidate to supply, as opposed to select, a response. The purpose of this kind of item is to elicit a relatively unconstrained response, which may vary in length from a few words to an extended essay. The mark scheme therefore allows for a range of acceptable answers.

CA:292, DA:444, DE:273, EN:260, ES:305, FR:318, GA:56, IT:137, NE:273, PO:324.

261 optical mark reader (OMR) An electronic device used for scanning information directly from mark sheets or answer sheets. Candidates or examiners can mark item responses or tasks on a mark sheet and this information can be directly read into the computer. Also referred to as a scanner.

CA:242, DA:268, DE:274, EN:261, ES:255, FR:237, GA:214, IT:226, NE:274, PO:249.

262 options The range of possibilities in a multiple choice item or matching task from which the correct one must be selected.

CA:279, DA:425, DE:38, EN:262, ES:292, FR:290, GA:293, IT:258, NE:14, PO:294.

263 oral interview Speaking skills are often tested by means of an oral interview, which may vary from a completely free conversation between candidate(s) and assessor(s) to a tightly-structured series of spoken tasks.

CA:131, DA:150, DE:305, EN:263, ES:136, FR:148, GA:1, IT:92, NE:355, PO:143.

264 oral proficiency Competence in speaking a language.

CA:298, DA:239, DE:370, EN:264, ES:65, FR:68, GA:266, IT:67, NE:354, PO:82.

265 ordinal scale A kind of measurement scale which ranks candidates, without indicating the relative distance between them.
Compare: categorical scale, interval scale, nominal scale, ratio scale.
Further reading: Hatch and Lazaraton 1991, pp. 56–57.

CA:157, DA:271, DE:275, EN:265, ES:165, FR:134, GA:318, IT:327, NE:275, PO:167.

266 *p*-value Refer to definition for facility index.

CA:427, DA:273, DE:276, EN:266,

ES:424, FR:411, GA:269, IT:412, NE:277, PO:420.

267 paper A way of referring to a test component, e.g. Reading Paper, Listening Paper.

CA:385, DA:393, DE:277, EN:267, ES:381, FR:182, GA:270, IT:168, NE:278, PO:87.

268 parallel forms Refer to definition for equivalent forms.

CA:188, DA:275, DE:278, EN:268, ES:206, FR:196, GA:144, IT:179, NE:279, PO:202.

269 parameter A characteristic of a population, e.g. the standard deviation of a population.
Compare: statistic.

CA:280, DA:276, DE:279, EN:269, ES:293, FR:291, GA:272, IT:259, NE:280, PO:296.

270 parametric procedures Statistical procedures which assume data are normally distributed and are measured on interval or ratio scales. In practice, parametric procedures are used when there are enough cases for the data to approximate the normal distribution.
Compare: non-parametric procedures.
Further reading: Hatch and Lazaraton 1991, pp. 237–238.

CA:295, DA:277, DE:280, EN:270, ES:309, FR:310, GA:259, IT:275, NE:281, PO:316.

271 part-whole overlap An effect which is present, for example, when scores on a subtest are correlated with scores on the whole test. Because the subtest scores are included in the whole test scores, the correlation is exaggerated. Techniques exist to correct for part-whole overlap.
Further reading: Henning 1987, p. 69.

CA:63, DA:62, DE:282, EN:271, ES:387, FR:51, GA:283, IT:146, NE:276, PO:331.

272 partial credit model In item-response theory (IRT), a model for dealing with scalar data. This would be an appropriate model to use for analysing responses to sentence completion items, which use a scale, e.g. 1, 2 or 3, to score items, or an oral interview which uses several scales to rate performance.
Compare: many-facet Rasch model, rating scale model.
See: Rasch model.
Further reading: Wright and Masters 1982 pp. 40–48.

CA:257, DA:278, DE:281, EN:272, ES:270, FR:253, GA:301, IT:244, NE:282, PO:267.

273 pass mark The minimum score a candidate has to achieve in order to pass a test or examination.
Compare: cut-off score.

CA:23, DA:36, DE:52, EN:273, ES:30, FR:277, GA:278, IT:288 NE:341, PO:282.

274 Pearson's product-moment correlation (Pearson's *r*) A correlation coefficient appropriately used with variables measured on interval or ratio scales.
See: correlation coefficient.
Further reading: Hatch and Lazaraton 1991, pp. 427–431; Guilford and Fruchter 1981, p. 81.

CA:59, DA:279, DE:298, EN:274, ES:90, FR:87, GA:84, IT:98, NE:283, PO:104.

275 percentile The 99 scale points which divide a frequency distribution into 100 groups of equal size. The fiftieth percentile (P50) is called the median. Quartiles divide the distribution into four equal groups.
Further reading: Hatch and Lazaraton 1991, pp. 187–188.

CA:287, DA:280, DE:285, EN:275, ES:299, FR:49, GA:279, IT:266, NE:284, PO:302.

276 percentile rank A number or score which indicates rank by showing the percentage which fell below that score. If a candidate in a test has a percentile rank of 60 it means that 60% of all candidates achieved a score which was the same or lower than this.

CA:363, DA:281, DE:299, EN:276, ES:359, FR:53, GA:284, IT:55, NE:285, PO:276.

277 performance The act of producing language by speaking or writing. Performance, in terms of the language actually produced by people, is often contrasted with competence, which is the underlying knowledge of a language.
Compare: competence.
See: performance test.
Further reading: Bachman 1990, pp. 52, 108.

CA:5, DA:282, DE:283, EN:277, ES:9, FR:297, GA:141, IT:267, NE:286, PO:304.

278 performance test A test procedure which requires the candidate to produce a sample of language, either in writing or speech (e.g. essays and oral interviews). Such procedures are often designed to replicate language performance in non-test

contexts.
Further reading: Bachman 1990, pp. 304–305.
CA:306, DA:283, DE:284, EN:278, ES:318, FR:380, GA:416, IT:367, NE:287, PO:381.

279 phi coefficient A correlation coefficient used to show the strength of relationship between two binary variables, for example, scores on two test items scored as right or wrong.
See: correlation coefficient.
Further reading: Guilford and Fruchter 1981, pp. 316–318; Crocker and Algina 1986, pp. 92–94.
CA:62, DA:284, DE:286, EN:279, ES:59, FR:58, GA:76, IT:61, NE:288, PO:75.

280 phi correlation Refer to definition for phi coefficient.
CA:92, DA:285, DE:287, EN:280, ES:88, FR:88, GA:81, IT:101, NE:289, PO:103.

281 pilot study A preliminary study through which researchers or test developers try out their ideas on a limited number of subjects in order to locate problems before launching a full-scale trial, programme or product.
See: pretesting, trialling.
CA:170, DA:286, DE:288, EN:281, ES:179, FR:163, GA:361, IT:344, NE:290, PO:180.

282 placement test A test administered in order to place students in a group or class at a level appropriate to their degree of knowledge and ability.
CA:311, DA:137, DE:101, EN:282, ES:323, FR:377, GA:434, IT:365, NE:291, PO:372.

283 point biserial correlation An index of item discrimination for dichotomous items, written r_{pbi}; the correlation between a criterion (usually total test score) and the response to the item. An advantage of r_{pbi} over the biserial correlation (r_{bis}) is that it can be used appropriately when the underlying ability is not normally distributed.
Compare: biserial correlation.
CA:57, DA:41, DE:311, EN:283, ES:86, FR:57, GA:80, IT:97, NE:309, PO:102.

284 polytomous scoring Scoring an item using a scale of at least three points. For example, the answer to a question can be assigned 0, 1 or 2 marks, three distinctions. Open-ended questions are often scored polytomously. Also referred to as scalar, or polychotomous scoring.
Compare: dichotomous scoring.
CA:351, DA:291, DE:237, EN:284, ES:353, FR:89, GA:342, IT:34, NE:293, PO:64.

285 population A complete set of values, i.e. all possible candidates taking an examination. In statistics, also known as the universe of scores.
Compare: sample.
CA:289, DA:292, DE:290, EN:285, ES:302, FR:303, GA:280, IT:269, NE:294, PO:308.

286 portfolio assessment An assessment technique in which a candidate collects examples of his or her work over a period, and presents them as evidence of ability.
CA:386, DA:293, DE:291, EN:286, ES:185, FR:304, GA:237, IT:270, NE:37, PO:309.

287 post-test A test or other form of measurement administered at the end of a course. Contrasting the results with the results of a test administered at the beginning of the course provides evidence of the effectiveness of the course.
Compare: pre-test.
CA:327, DA:345, DE:5, EN:287, ES:336, FR:305, GA:179, IT:271, NE:295, PO:310.

288 power test A test which allows sufficient time for almost all candidates to finish it, but contains some tasks or items of a degree of difficulty which makes it unlikely that the majority of candidates will get every item correct.
Compare: speeded test.
CA:310, DA:299, DE:261/293, EN:288, ES:329, FR:379, GA:413, IT:360, NE:296, PO:371.

289 practice effect The effect on test scores of candidates' being familiar with the task types or actual items used in a test.
CA:119, DA:443, DE:419, EN:289, ES:123, FR:138, GA:169, IT:140, NE:298, PO:131.

290 pragmatic competence A possible category in a model of communicative language ability: it includes the ability to perform speech acts, and knowledge of sociolinguistic conventions.
Further reading: Bachman 1990, p.42.
CA:69, DA:294, DE:295, EN:290, ES:66, FR:69, GA:194, IT:68, NE:297, PO:83.

291 predictive validity An indication of how well a test predicts future performance in the relevant skill.

Compare: criterion-related validity.
Further reading: Guilford and Fruchter 1987, pp. 437–438.

CA:425, DA:298, DE:294/439, EN:291, ES:422, FR:422, GA:38, IT:410, NE:300, PO:418.

292 pre-test A test administered before the start of a course of instruction. The results of the pre-test can be contrasted with results obtained from another test at the end of the course of instruction in order to evaluate the effectiveness of the course.
Compare: post-test.

CA:333, DA:104, DE:440, EN:292, ES:338, FR:306, GA:290, IT:272, NE:299, PO:312.

293 pretesting A stage in the development of test materials at which items are tried out with representative samples from the target population in order to determine their difficulty. Following statistical analysis, those items that are considered satisfactory can be used in live tests.
Compare: trialling.

CA:174, DA:105, DE:436, EN:293, ES:191, FR:307, GA:289, IT:273, NE:302, PO:311.

294 probabilistic model A model in which causal relationships (such as that of item difficulty and candidate ability on test performance) are explained in terms of degree of probability. The Rasch model is an example of a probabilistic model.

CA:262, DA:295, DE:297, EN:294, ES:274, FR:255, GA:299, IT:247, NE:430, PO:269.

295 proficiency Knowledge of a language, and degree of skill in using it.
Compare: ability, competence.
Further reading: Bachman 1990, p.16.

CA:296, DA:296, DE:47, EN:295, ES:120, FR:260, GA:265, IT:62, NE:305, PO:273.

296 proficiency test A test which measures general ability or skill, without reference to any specific course of study or set of materials.

CA:319, DA:112, DE:120, EN:296, ES:326, FR:378, GA:428, IT:363, NE:306, PO:379.

297 profiling A way of presenting test results broken down into the various test components, so that the candidate or other users of the test can identify areas of relative strength and weakness.

CA:288, DA:297, DE:404, EN:297, ES:300, FR:312, GA:282, IT:395, NE:307, PO:303.

298 progress test A test administered part of the way through a course of instruction, in order to assess learning up to that point.

CA:320, DA:108, DE:214, EN:298, ES:330, FR:381, GA:418, IT:369, NE:422, PO:382.

299 prompt In tests of speaking or writing, graphic materials or texts designed to elicit a response from the candidate.

CA:390, DA:316, DE:437 EN:299, ES:178, FR:95, GA:358, IT:343, NE:321, PO:179.

300 proof reading task A test task which involves checking a text for errors of a specified type, e.g. spelling or structure. Part of the task may also consist of marking errors and supplying correct forms.

CA:395, DA:195, DE:189, EN:300, ES:4, FR:84, GA:374, IT:75, NE:304, PO:97.

301 psychometric test A test of psychological traits such as personality, intelligence, aptitude and language proficiency, which makes specific assumptions about the nature of the ability tested, e.g. that it is unidimensional and normally distributed.
Further reading: Bachman 1990, pp. 73–74.

CA:334, DA:302, DE:310, EN:301, ES:397, FR:390, GA:433, IT:379, NE:308, PO:394.

302 qualification An award after a recognised course of training or a test that qualifies a person to carry out a particular activity or job. A certificate of language proficiency can be considered a qualification for certain purposes.
Compare: certificate, diploma.

CA:360, DA:209, DE:314, EN:302, ES:405, FR:313, GA:46, IT:294, NE:214, PO:322.

303 question Sometimes used to refer to a test task or item.
See: item, task.

CA:291, DA:357, DE:122, EN:303, ES:304, FR:315, GA:55, IT:136, NE:423, PO:323.

304 question paper/booklet Sometimes used to refer to a sheet or booklet in which a test is presented.

CA:239, DA:263, DE:123, EN:304, ES:220, FR:180, GA:271, IT:169, NE:425, PO:145.

305 question type Refer to definition for: item type, task type.

CA:407, DA:358, DE:124, EN:305, ES:404, FR:406, GA:57, IT:394, NE:424, PO:400.

306 random error Refer to definition for error.

CA:137, DA:408, DE:449, EN:306, ES:145, FR:152, GA:128, IT:156, NE:310, PO:147.

307 random sample A collection of elements taken randomly from a population under investigation, such that every element in the population has an equal chance of being selected for the investigation.
See: sample.
Further reading: Crocker and Algina 1986, pp. 433–438; Guilford and Fruchter 1981, p.120.

CA:265, DA:409, DE:451, EN:307, ES:279, FR:117, GA:305, IT:47, NE:120, PO:9.

308 range A measure of the dispersion of observations. The range is the distance between the highest and lowest scores.
Further reading: Hatch and Lazaraton 1991, pp. 169–170.

CA:12, DA:431, DE:431, EN:308, ES:260, FR:241, GA:285, IT:233, NE:311, PO:12.

309 rank order correlation A correlation based not on the absolute values of the variables, but on the relative rank ordering.
Further reading: Guilford and Fruchter 1981, pp. 294–296.

CA:60, DA:304, DE:315, EN:309, ES:89, FR:59, GA:82, IT:100, NE:312, PO:72.

310 Rasch model A mathematical model, also known as the simple logistic model, which posits a relationship between the probability of a person completing a task and the difference between the ability of the person and the difficulty of the task. Mathematically equivalent to the one-parameter model in item-response theory (IRT). The Rasch model has been extended in various ways, e.g. to handle scalar responses, or multiple facets accounting for the 'difficulty' of a task.
See: item-response theory (IRT), many-facet Rasch model, partial credit model, rating scale model.
Further reading: Henning 1987, pp. 117–125.

CA:259, DA:305, DE:316, EN:310, ES:275 FR:252, GA:302, IT:248, NE:313, PO:266.

311 rater Refer to definition for assessor.

CA:361, DA:306, DE:100, EN:311, ES:187, FR:164, GA:287, IT:102, NE:34, PO:182.

312 rater agreement Refer to definitions for inter-rater agreement and intra-rater agreement.

CA:1, DA:307, DE:56, EN:312, ES:10, FR:1, GA:70, IT:84, NE:36, PO:1.

313 rater effects A source of error in assessment, the result of certain tendencies of assessors such as harshness or leniency, or a prejudice in favour of a certain type of candidate, which affect the scores given to test candidates. Examples are contamination effect, halo effect and sequence effect.

CA:124, DA:34, DE:425, EN:313, ES:130, FR:144, GA:176, IT:143, NE:35, PO:138.

314 rating a) The process of assigning a score to performance in a test through the exercise of judgement.

b) The score awarded as the result of the rating process.

CA:428, DA:171, DE:57, EN:314, ES:425, FR:265, GA:286, IT:54, NE:38, PO:57.

315 rating scale A scale consisting of several ranked categories used for making subjective judgements. In language testing, rating scales for assessing performance are typically accompanied by band descriptors which make their interpretation clear.
Compare: likert scale.
See: descriptor.

CA:154, DA:172, DE:58, EN:315, ES:161, FR:130, GA:319, IT:323, NE:40, PO:160.

316 rating scale model An extension of the simple Rasch model for dealing with scalar data, as derived from, for example, ratings on oral performance.
Compare: Rasch model.
See: partial credit model.
Further reading: Wright, B.D and Masters G.N., 1982, Rating Scale Analysis Chicago, MESA Press.

CA:254, DA:173, DE:236, EN:316, ES:272, FR:251, GA:303, IT:246, NE:41, PO:263.

317 ratio scale A scale on which there is a true zero and the distance between two adjacent points is the same for the whole scale. For example, height: a person who is 2 m tall is twice as tall as someone who is 1 m tall.
Compare: categorical scale, interval scale, ordinal scale.
Further reading: Crocker and Algina 1986, pp. 48–49.

CA:153, DA:210, DE:433, EN:317, ES:160, FR:131, GA:312, IT:324, NE:314, PO:164.

318 rational cloze Refer to definition for cloze test.

CA:314, DA:308, DE:230, EN:318, ES:316, FR:371, GA:60, IT:56, NE:315,

PO:367.

319 raw score A test score that has not been statistically manipulated by any transformation, weighting or re-scaling.
See: score.

CA:348, DA:321, DE:328, EN:319, ES:348, FR:276, GA:329, IT:282, NE:324, PO:281.

320 readability index A measure of grammatical and lexical complexity that is used to assess the extent to which readers will find a text comprehensible. Examples of readability indices are Gunning's Fog index and the Flesch readability scale.

CA:210, DA:222, DE:219, EN:320, ES:226, FR:211, GA:189, IT:198, NE:223, PO:221.

321 reading comprehension task A task type which generally consists of a reading text or texts and items of the following types: multiple choice, short answer questions, cloze/gap-filling, information transfer, etc.

CA:394, DA:223, DE:220, EN:321, ES:3, FR:357, GA:373, IT:74, NE:224, PO:351.

322 real life approach In language testing, a view that tests should include task types which resemble real life activities as closely as possible. For example, in a real life approach, the content of a test designed to assess whether candidates can cope with an academic course in a foreign language would be based on a needs analysis of the language and language activities typically found on that course.
See: authenticity.
Further reading: Bachman 1990, pp. 301–328.

CA:129, DA:433, DE:320, EN:322, ES:134, FR:345, GA:98, IT:23, NE:226, PO:349.

323 recognition The formal acceptance by an institution of a particular qualification for a specific purpose, e.g. admission to a postgraduate course of study.

CA:365, DA:15, DE:269, EN:323, ES:361, FR:321, GA:9, IT:303, NE:123, PO:325.

324 reference group A reference group is a sample from a clearly-defined population of candidates by which a test is normed.
See: norm.

CA:196, DA:309, DE:267, EN:324, ES:213, FR:202, GA:166, IT:189, NE:316, PO:212.

325 register A distinct variety of speech or writing characteristic of a particular activity or a particular degree of formality.

CA:368, DA:310, DE:366, EN:325, ES:364, FR:323, GA:291, IT:297, NE:317, PO:327.

326 regression A technique for predicting the most likely value of one variable (the dependent variable) from known values of one or more other variables (independent variables).
Further reading: Hatch and Lazaraton 1991, pp. 467–480; Guilford and Fruchter 1981, pp. 346–361.

CA:369, DA:311, DE:321, EN:326, ES:365, FR:324, GA:4, IT:298, NE:318, PO:328.

327 reliability The consistency or stability of the measures from a test. The more reliable a test is, the less random error it contains. A test which contains systematic error, e.g. bias against a certain group, may be reliable, but not valid.
Compare: validity.
See: KR-20 (Kuder-Richardson formula 20), alpha (alpha coefficient), split-half reliability, test-retest reliability.
Further reading: Bachman 1990, p. 24; Crocker and Algina 1986, Chapter 6.

CA:180, DA:312, DE:322/453, EN:327, ES:198, FR:183, GA:200, IT:6, NE:43, PO:193.

328 reliability coefficient A measure of reliability, in the range 0 to 1. Reliability estimates can be based on repeated administrations of a test (which should produce similar results) or where this is not practicable, on some form of internal consistency measure. Sometimes known as reliability index.
See: internal consistency, reliability, test-retest reliability.

CA:61, DA:313, DE:323, EN:328, ES:58, FR:61, GA:77, IT:59, NE:44, PO:74.

329 replicability The possibility of repeating the findings of a piece of research on more than one occasion, thus increasing confidence in the results.

CA:373, DA:189, DE:324, EN:329, ES:370, FR:335, GA:185, IT:301, NE:165, PO:333.

330 re-scaling Refer to definition for scaling.

CA:367, DA:314, DE:258, EN:330, ES:389, FR:320, GA:29, IT:304, NE:166, PO:326.

331 response The candidate behaviour

elicited by the input of a test. For example, the answer given to a multiple choice item or the work produced in a test of writing.
Compare: input, prompt.
CA:374, DA:315, DE:21, EN:331, ES:371, FR:327, GA:153, IT:305, NE:319, PO:334.

332 result The outcome of a test, as reported to a test taker or test user.
CA:380, DA:317, DE:103, EN:332, ES:378, FR:336, GA:397, IT:312, NE:322, PO:342.

333 right answer The response that is counted as correct in scoring a test.
CA:375, DA:190, DE:327, EN:333, ES:373, FR:331, GA:155, IT:307, NE:204, PO:337.

334 role play A task type which is sometimes used in speaking tests in which candidates have to imagine themselves in a specific situation or adopt specific roles.
CA:233, DA:320, DE:329, EN:334, ES:251, FR:232, GA:294, IT:202, NE:323, PO:345.

335 rounding The process of reducing the precision of a number by reducing the number of significant figures. For example, 564.8 could be rounded up to 565 or down to 560. The scale of rounding depends on the precision required.
CA:24, DA:245, DE:331, EN:335, ES:363, FR:22, GA:354, IT:24, NE:11, PO:25.

336 rubric The instructions given to candidates to guide their responses to a particular test task.
Compare: instructions.
CA:384, DA:264, DE:23, EN:336, ES:229, FR:78, GA:295, IT:193, NE:219, PO:92.

337 sample A selection of a sub-set of elements from a population. Various kinds of sample can be distinguished, e.g. random sample, stratified sample, etc.
Further reading: Crocker and Algina 1986, pp. 432–438; Guilford and Fruchter 1981, pp. 44–45.
CA:264, DA:371, DE:380, EN:337, ES:278, FR:116, GA:304, IT:46, NE:369, PO:8.

338 sample scripts A sample of candidate responses which represent a range of ability. These are used in the standardization of assessors.
CA:268, DA:370, DE:254, EN:338, ES:132, FR:118, GA:344, IT:330, NE:420, PO:10.

339 sample-free measurement In research, an interpretation of findings which is not dependent on the sample which was used in a particular investigation.
See: sample.
CA:247, DA:373, DE:382, EN:339, ES:265, FR:244, GA:396, IT:239, NE:371, PO:258.

340 sampling Selection of a sample.
See: sample.
CA:267, DA:374, DE:384, EN:340, ES:281, FR:120, GA:307, IT:45, NE:368, PO:313.

341 sampling error In research, the error introduced into a statistical analysis caused by the selection of the specific sample which was used in the study (e.g. where the sample is not representative of the population).
See: population.
CA:139, DA:372, DE:381, EN:341, ES:147, FR:158, GA:129, IT:155, NE:370, PO:148.

342 scalar item An item which is scored using a scale.
See: polytomous scoring.
CA:222, DA:342, DE:27, EN:342, ES:248, FR:230, GA:252, IT:220, NE:328, PO:242.

343 scale A set of numbers or categories for measuring something. Four types of measurement scale are distinguished - nominal, ordinal, interval and ratio.
Further reading: Crocker and Algina 1986, pp. 46–49.
CA:144, DA:337, DE:352, EN:343, ES:152, FR:121, GA:308, IT:314, NE:326, PO:154.

344 scale descriptor Refer to definition for descriptor.
CA:98, DA:338, DE:353, EN:344, ES:99, FR:96, GA:438, IT:119, NE:327, PO:112.

345 scaled score A score produced as a result of scaling.
See: scaling.
CA:349, DA:340, DE:354, EN:345, ES:349, FR:278, GA:337, IT:286, NE:153, PO:283.

346 scaling The process of producing scales for measurement. In language testing, this entails associating numbers with the performance of candidates in order to reflect increasing levels of knowledge or ability. Scaling may involve modifying a set of scores in order to produce a scale for a given purpose, for example, to report test results in a standardised way, or to equate one version of a test with another.
See: scale, ability scale, centile scale, common scale, interval scale, nominal scale, ordinal scale, rating scale, ratio scale,

equated forms, linear equating.
CA:159, DA:341, DE:355, EN:346, ES:167, FR:135, GA:321, IT:109, NE:329, PO:169.

347 scanner Refer to definition for optical mark reader (OMR).
CA:160, DA:327, DE:336, EN:347, ES:168, FR:342, GA:322, IT:226, NE:325, PO:346.

348 score a) The total number of points someone achieves in a test, either before scaling (raw score) or after (scaled score).

b) To assign numerical values to observed performances.
Compare: measurement.
CA:342, DA:328, DE:312, EN:348, ES:345, FR:275, GA:328, IT:278, NE:331, PO:280.

349 screening test A test, usually short and simple to administer, used to identify those candidates who can be admitted to a course or as candidates for an examination.
Compare: placement test.
CA:316, DA:424, DE:98, EN:349, ES:332, FR:375, GA:432, IT:370, NE:332, PO:375.

350 script The paper containing a candidate's responses to a test, used particularly of open-ended task types.
CA:191, DA:261, DE:341, EN:350, ES:219, FR:343, GA:343, IT:175, NE:218, PO:170.

351 security The area of test administration concerned with preventing disclosure of the content of test materials during the period of their live use.
CA:387, DA:335, DE:348, EN:351, ES:382, FR:344, GA:353, IT:333, NE:142, PO:347.

352 selected response A form of response to a test item that involves choosing from a number of alternatives, rather than supplying an answer.
Compare: constructed response.
See: response.
CA:379, DA:422, DE:37, EN:352, ES:377, FR:334, GA:158, IT:310, NE:154, PO:341.

353 selection test Refer to definition for entrance test.
CA:323, DA:330, DE:36, EN:353, ES:332, FR:382, GA:430, IT:370, NE:333, PO:383.

354 self-assessment The process by which a student assesses his/her own level of ability, either by taking a test which can be self-administered, or by means of some other device such as a questionnaire or checklist.
CA:30, DA:331, DE:345, EN:354, ES:36, FR:27, GA:142, IT:38, NE:334, PO:29.

355 semi-authentic text A text taken from a real life source that has been edited for use in a test, e.g. to adapt the vocabulary and/or grammar to the level of the candidates.
See: authentic text.
CA:405, DA:123, DE:140, EN:355, ES:400, FR:112, GA:383, IT:391, NE:335, PO:128.

356 semi-direct test A test which attempts to assess language performance by substituting some aspect of human involvement, e.g. a test of speaking using a tape recording to provide the input rather than a human interviewer. An example of a semi-direct tet is the SOPI (Semi-direct Oral Proficiency Interview).
Compare: direct test.
CA:339, DA:332, DE:347, EN:356, ES:343, FR:392, GA:423, IT:383, NE:336, PO:396.

357 sentence completion An item type in which only half of a sentence is given. The candidate's task is to complete the sentence, either by supplying suitable words (possibly based on the reading of a text), or by choosing them from various options given.
CA:72, DA:382, DE:332, EN:357, ES:69, FR:298, GA:93, IT:80, NE:442, PO:86.

358 sentence expansion An item type in which a prompt in the form of a string of content words is given, but prepositions, auxiliary verbs, articles, etc. are absent. The candidate's task is to add the missing words, thus expanding the prompt into a complete grammatical sentence.
CA:99, DA:380, DE:333, EN:358, ES:18, FR:175, GA:148, IT:166, NE:441, PO:184.

359 sentence transformation An item type in which a complete sentence is given as a prompt, followed by the first one or two words of a second sentence which expresses the content of the first in a different grammatical form. For example, the first sentence may be active, and the candidate's task is to present the identical content in passive form.
CA:410, DA:381, DE:334, EN:359, ES:407, FR:404, GA:61, IT:397, NE:440, PO:405.

360 sequence effect A rater effect created by the order in which assessments

are made.
See: rater effects.

CA:120, DA:329, DE:292, EN:360, ES:125, FR:142, GA:172, IT:148, NE:337, PO:136.

361 setter A person who writes and constructs a test.

CA:127, DA:392, DE:400, EN:361, ES:92, FR:145, GA:121, IT:149, NE:391, PO:141.

362 short answer item An open-ended item for which the candidate is required to formulate a written answer using a word or a phrase.

CA:228, DA:198, DE:205, EN:362, ES:243, FR:224, GA:246, IT:311, NE:209, PO:238.

363 significance A statistical concept relating to whether or not a finding is the result of chance.
See: null hypothesis, type 1 error, type 2 error.
Further reading: Guilford and Fruchter 1981, pp. 208–210.

CA:388, DA:333, DE:349, EN:363, ES:386, FR:76, GA:366, IT:334, NE:338, PO:348.

364 significance test A test for statistical significance.
See: significance.

CA:324, DA:334, DE:350, EN:364, ES:333, FR:373, GA:435, IT:371, NE:339, PO:384.

365 situational authenticity The extent to which a test can be considered authentic in relation to real world, non-test situations of language use.
Compare: interactional authenticity, real-life approach.
See: authenticity.
Further reading: Bachman 1990, Chapter 8.

CA:29, DA:336, DE:351, EN:365, ES:35, FR:26, GA:117, IT:37, NE:340, PO:28.

366 skew A feature of a distribution where the peak of the curve lies either to the right of centre (negative skew) or to the left of centre (positive skew).

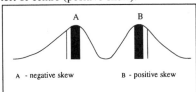

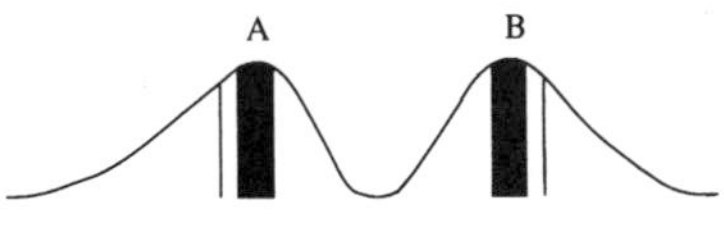

See: normal distribution.

Further reading: Hatch and Lazaraton 1991, p. 165.

CA:25, DA:343, DE:337, EN:366, ES:31, FR:109, GA:323, IT:25, NE:330, PO:120.

367 skill Ability to do something. In language testing the four skills of reading, writing, speaking and listening are often distinguished.
See: competence.

CA:199, DA:111, DE:119, EN:367, ES:100, FR:340, GA:325, IT:1B, NE:413, PO:51.

368 sociocultural knowledge Knowledge of the world that is related to how society within a particular culture operates. This is relevant to appropriate behaviour and use of language in specific cultural contexts.
Compare: sociolinguistic competence.

CA:76, DA:346, DE:357, EN:368, ES:72, FR:341, GA:135, IT:86, NE:344, PO:90.

369 sociolinguistic competence A category in models of communicative language ability: it includes the ability to adapt speech to particular settings and situations in accordance with social norms.
Further reading: Bachman 1990, p.42.

CA:70, DA:347, DE:358, EN:369, ES:67, FR:70, GA:197, IT:69, NE:345, PO:84.

370 SOPI (Semi-direct/Simulated Oral Proficiency Interview) A test of oral proficiency where the input is provided by a tape recording and the candidate's response is recorded to be rated at a later date.
See: semi-direct test.

CA:130, DA:348, DE:356, EN:370, ES:137, FR:392, GA:356, IT:93, NE:346, PO:144.

371 Spearman-Brown Prophecy formula A statistical means of estimating the reliability of a test in the event of the test being lengthened or shortened by adding or removing items. It may be used to predict the number of items required to meet a specified reliability.
Further reading: Crocker and Algina 1986, pp. 118–119.

CA:83, DA:349, DE:359, EN:371, ES:207, FR:197, GA:147, IT:180, NE:350, PO:203.

372 Spearman-Brown split-half estimate Refer to definition for split-half reliability.

CA:168, DA:350, DE:360, EN:372, ES:177, FR:161, GA:228, IT:342, NE:349, PO:178.

373 Spearman's rank-difference correlation A form of rank order correlation used for small samples, i.e. samples of less than 30.
See: rank order correlation.

CA:58, DA:351, DE:361, EN:373, ES:87, FR:60, GA:83, IT:99, NE:347, PO:73.

374 Spearman's rho Refer to definition for Spearman's rank-difference correlation.

CA:383, DA:352, DE:362, EN:374, ES:380, FR:339, GA:292, IT:302, NE:348, PO:344.

375 specific purpose test A test designed to measure a candidate's ability to operate in a specific professional or academic context. The content of the test is designed accordingly, on the basis of an analysis of the language tasks candidates will need to deal with in the target language use situation.

CA:318, DA:243, DE:112, EN:375, ES:328, FR:393, GA:431, IT:378, NE:351, PO:393.

376 speeded test A test with a time limit for completion. Slower candidates achieve a lower score because they do not reach the final questions. Normally in a speeded test the difficulty of questions is such that candidates would generally respond correctly, were it not for the time constraint. Also known as a speed test.
Compare: power test.

CA:321, DA:129, DE:340/363, EN:376, ES:334, FR:363, GA:424, IT:372, NE:352, PO:385.

377 split-half reliability An internal consistency measure of reliability. The estimate is based on a correlation between the scores of two half tests which are regarded as two alternate tests. The division into two halves can be made in a number of ways, e.g. first half, second half, or by placing even-numbered items in one half and odd-numbered items in the other.
See: reliability.
Further reading: Ebel and Frisbie 1991, pp. 82–83; Crocker and Algina 1986, pp. 136–138.

CA:183, DA:259, DE:364/398, EN:377, ES:201, FR:184, GA:203, IT:7, NE:353, PO:194.

378 stability An aspect of reliability where the estimate is based on the test-retest approach. It relates to how stable test scores are over time.
See: reliability, test-retest reliability.

CA:162, DA:359, DE:371, EN:378, ES:170, FR:79, GA:65, IT:337, NE:358, PO:173.

379 standard deviation A measure of the dispersion of a set of observations about the arithmetic mean. It is equal to the square root of the variance. In a normal distribution 68% of the sample is within one standard deviation of the mean and 95% is within two standard deviations of the mean.

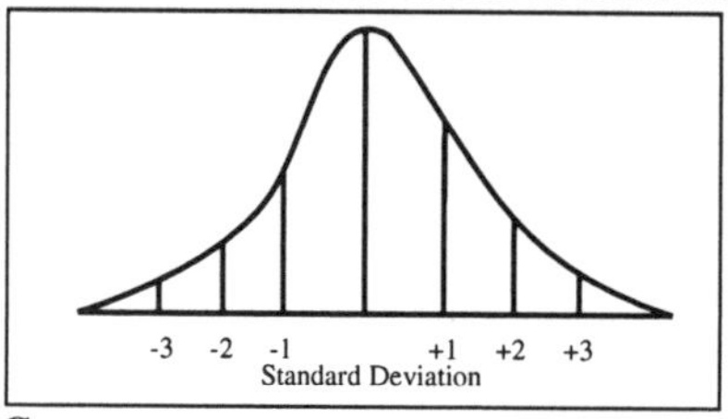

Compare: range.
See: variance.
Further reading: Ebel and Frisbie 1991, pp. 61–62; Crocker and Algina 1986, pp. 21–22.

CA:101, DA:362, DE:372, EN:379, ES:103, FR:98, GA:113, IT:122, NE:360, PO:114.

380 standard error of estimate A measure of the accuracy of predicting one variable from another, for example in linear regression. It provides confidence intervals for criterion scores.
See: confidence interval.
Further reading: Hatch and Lazaraton 1991, pp. 477–479.

CA:142, DA:361, DE:375, EN:380, ES:148, FR:156, GA:124, IT:163, NE:363, PO:152.

381 standard error of measurement In classical true score test theory, the standard error of measurement (*Se*) is an indication of the imprecision of a measurement. The size of the standard error of measurement depends on the reliability (*r*) and the standard deviation of the test scores (*Sx*). The formula for calculating *Se* is:

$$Se=Sx\sqrt{(1-r)}$$

For example, if a candidate with a true score of T on a test and a standard error of measurement of *Se* repeatedly sits the test, then 68% of the time the observed score will be in the range T±*Se*, and 95% of the time in the range T±2*Se*.
Further reading: Crocker and Algina 1986, pp. 122–124.

CA:143, DA:364, DE:374, EN:381,

ES:149, FR:157, GA:125, IT:12, NE:362, PO:153.

382 standard score A linearly transformed score from a group of scores. The mean and standard deviation are set to whatever values the user requires. Examples of standard scores are *z* and *t* scores.
Compare: stanine score, *t* score, *z* score.
Further reading: Ebel and Frisbie 1991, pp. 67–68.

CA:350, DA:365, DE:376, EN:382, ES:350, FR:281, GA:333, IT:287, NE:364, PO:291.

383 standardization The process of ensuring that assessors adhere to an agreed procedure and apply rating scales in an appropriate way.
See: assessor.

CA:167, DA:363, DE:373, EN:383, ES:175, NE:361, FR:162, GA:45, IT:338, PO:295.

384 stanine score A procedure for grouping test scores into nine groups based on the normal distribution. In both the top and bottom groups there is 4% of the candidature. The percentage of candidates in each of the groups is illustrated in the graph below.

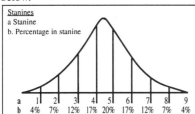

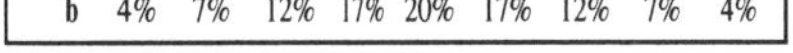

Further reading: Crocker and Algina 1986, pp. 446–447.

CA:344, DA:367, DE:377, EN:384, ES:176, FR:282, GA:332, IT:279, NE:365, PO:284.

385 statistic A quantity containing information expressed in numerical form. Strictly, a statistic is a property of a sample group, in contrast to a parameter, which is a property of a population. Statistics are generally written with Roman characters, and parameters with Greek. For example, the standard deviation of a sample is written s or SD, while for a population it is written σ (sigma).
Compare: parameter.
See: population, sample.

CA:163, DA:368, DE:379, EN:385, ES:174, FR:348, GA:363, IT:117, NE:367, PO:174.

386 statistics The science of manipulating and interpreting numerical data.

CA:164, DA:369, DE:378, EN:386, ES:171, FR:348, GA:362, IT:339, NE:366, PO:175.

387 stem Part of a written prompt, usually an incomplete sentence for which the completion has to be supplied or selected from options.
Compare: key, options.
See: multiple choice item.

CA:276, DA:360, DE:29, EN:387, ES:139, FR:10, GA:160, IT:346, NE:359, PO:224.

388 stratified sample A sample of a population under investigation which is first sub-divided into a number of sub-populations (layers, ranks, strata) from each of which a sample is then taken.
See: sample.
Further reading: Guilford and Fruchter 1981, pp. 122–123.

CA:266, DA:375, DE:134, EN:388, ES:280, FR:119, GA:306, IT:48, NE:157, PO:11.

389 subtest Refer to definition for component.

CA:389, DA:377, DE:386, EN:389, ES:388, FR:346, GA:150, IT:345, NE:373, PO:350.

390 summative assessment Testing which takes place at the end of a course or programme of instruction.
Compare: formative assessment.

CA:34, DA:267, DE:4, EN:390, ES:186, FR:172, GA:233, IT:423, NE:375, PO:36.

391 summative evaluation Evaluation of a process which takes place after it has been completed. It can refer to a programme of instruction.
Compare: formative evaluation.

CA:34, DA:266, DE:3, EN:391, ES:186, FR:172, GA:238, IT:415, NE:374, PO:36.

392 syllabus A detailed document which lists all the areas covered in a particular programme of study, and the order in which content is presented.
Compare: curriculum.

CA:299, DA:224, DE:207, EN:392, ES:310, FR:352, GA:352, IT:335, NE:225, PO:318.

393 task A combination of rubric, input and response. For example, a reading text with several multiple choice items, all of which can be responded to by referring to a

single rubric.
CA:391, DA:260, DE:26, EN:393, ES:2, FR:354, GA:371, IT:71, NE:270, PO:352.

394 task type Tasks are referred to by names which tend to be descriptive of what they are testing and the form they take, e.g. multiple choice reading comprehension, guided writing, etc.
CA:408, DA:265, DE:30, EN:394, ES:402, FR:407, GA:59, IT:393, NE:271, PO:401.

395 test A procedure for testing specific aspects of proficiency or knowledge.

a) a set of components which together constitute an assessment procedure, often used to mean the same as examination.

b) a single task or component for assessing an area of skill or knowledge, e.g. speaking or writing. In this sense a test may also form part of a complete examination as a component (e.g. the speaking test) or as a single task (e.g. cloze test).

c) an assessment procedure which is relatively short and easy to administer often devised and administered within an institution (e.g. a progress test) or used as part of a research programme or for validation purposes (e.g. anchor test).
Compare: examination.
See: cloze test, progress test, anchor test.
Further reading: Bachman, 1990, p.50.
CA:300, DA:300, DE:389, EN:395, ES:311, FR:359, GA:403, IT:353, NE:388, PO:361.

396 test analysis Analysis of tests after they have been used with candidates, often employing statistical and computerized methods. The aim may be to investigate the performance of the candidates or of the test itself.
CA:15, DA:389, DE:390, EN:396, ES:22, FR:16, GA:14, IT:17, NE:389, PO:18.

397 test battery Refer to definition for battery.
CA:39, DA:390, DE:406, EN:397, ES:41, FR:31, GA:63, IT:42, NE:390, PO:39.

398 test construction The process of selecting items or tasks and putting them into a test. This process is often preceded by the pretesting or trialling of materials. Items and tasks for test construction may be selected from a bank of materials.
CA:126, DA:394, DE:397, EN:398, ES:75, FR:146, GA:393, IT:110, NE:392, PO:140.

399 test developer Someone engaged in the process of developing a new test.
CA:109, DA:405, DE:395, EN:399, ES:133, FR:145, GA:149, IT:149, NE:399, PO:141.

400 test information function In IRT, an index of how much information a test provides about a person of a given ability level. It is the sum of the item information functions.
Compare: item information function.
Further reading: Crocker and Algina 1986, pp. 369–371.
CA:194, DA:388, DE:399, EN:400, ES:211, FR:191, GA:139, IT:185, NE:394, PO:207.

401 test method Language ability can be tested using a variety of methods such as multiple choice, cloze, composition, oral interview, etc. Test method has been observed to interact with ability in the measurement of performance.
See: test method characteristics.
Further reading: Bachman 1990, p. 77.
CA:248, DA:395, DE:401, EN:401, ES:266, FR:245, GA:257, IT:236, NE:396, PO:259.

402 test method characteristics The defining characteristics of different test methods. These may include environment, rubric, language of instructions, format, etc.
Further reading: Bachman 1990, Chapter 5.
CA:48, DA:397, DE:403, EN:402, ES:51, FR:46, GA:401, IT:50, NE:398, PO:54.

403 test method facets Refer to definition for test method characteristics.
CA:175, DA:396, DE:402, EN:403, ES:193, FR:176, GA:163, IT:50, NE:397, PO:186.

404 test specifications A detailed set of documentation normally drawn up during the process of designing a new test or revising an existing one. The specifications give details of the design, content, level, task and item types used, target population, use of the test, etc., and specimen materials are often included.
CA:161, DA:401, DE:394, EN:404, ES:169, FR:346, GA:355, IT:120, NE:400, PO:171.

405 test tailoring Adapting existing tests to meet the requirements of a particular group of test users or takers.
CA:301, DA:404, DE:410, EN:405, ES:13, FR:395, GA:370, IT:5, NE:382, PO:4.

406 test taker Refer to definition for

candidate.
CA:100, DA:402, DE:407, EN:406, ES:190, FR:351, GA:110, IT:49, NE:395, PO:183.

407 test user The person or institution (e.g. a teacher or employer) using the results of a test in order to make a decision concerning the test taker.
CA:414, DA:391, DE:392, EN:407, ES:410, FR:409, GA:440, IT:399, NE:393, PO:407.

408 test wiseness Familiarity with the format of a test or experience of test taking which enables candidates to perform above their true ability level.
CA:179, DA:406, DE:396, EN:408, ES:197, FR:314, GA:161, IT:167, NE:401, PO:191.

409 testing point The focus of an item: the particular point on which an item attempts to elicit knowledge.
CA:128, DA:399, DE:309, EN:409, ES:289, FR:300, GA:281, IT:293, NE:384, PO:307.

410 test-retest reliability An estimate of reliability obtained by administering the same test to the same candidates in the same conditions, and correlating the scores on the two sittings. It is concerned with the stability of scores over time, and is also appropriately used where estimates of internal consistency are not possible.
Compare: internal consistency.
See: reliability, stability.
CA:184, DA:318, DE:409/325, EN:410, ES:202, FR:188, GA:204, IT:9, NE:383, PO:197.

411 text A piece of connected discourse, written or spoken, used as the basis for a set of test items.
CA:403, DA:386, DE:411, EN:411, ES:399, FR:396, GA:381, IT:389, NE:381, PO:398.

412 text-based item An item based on a piece of connected discourse, e.g. multiple choice items based on a reading comprehension text.
CA:219, DA:387, DE:412, EN:412, ES:236, FR:226, GA:254, IT:213, NE:269, PO:233.

413 theta scale Refers to ability scale.
CA:158, DA:407, DE:413, EN:413, ES:166, FR:128, GA:320, IT:328, NE:385, PO:168.

414 Threshold level An influential specification in functional terms of a basic level of foreign language competence, published by the Council of Europe in 1976 for English and updated in 1990. Versions have since been produced for a number of European languages.
CA:272, DA:419, DE:414, EN:414, ES:285, FR:262, GA:212, IT:230, NE:386, PO:275.

415 trait A physical or psychological characteristic of a person, (such as language ability) or the measurement scale constructed to describe this.
CA:411, DA:416, DE:95, EN:415, ES:360, FR:23, GA:400, IT:26, NE:403, PO:403.

416 transformation item Refer to definition for sentence transformation.
CA:229, DA:413, DE:420, EN:416, ES:245, FR:403, GA:242, IT:217, NE:402, PO:239.

417 transformed score A raw score which has been transformed mathematically. This might be for the purposes of scaling or weighting.
Further reading: Ebel and Frisbie 1991, pp. 64–70.
CA:356, DA:414, DE:415, EN:417, ES:356, FR:284, GA:334, IT:290, NE:158, PO:288.

418 trialling A stage in the development of test tasks aimed at ascertaining whether the test functions as expected. Often used with subjectively marked tasks such as essay questions, which are administered to a limited population.
Compare: pretesting.
CA:26, DA:301, DE:104, EN:418, ES:135, FR:160, GA:436, IT:336, NE:303, PO:185.

419 true/false item A type of selected response item where the candidate has to indicate whether a series of statements are true or false in relation to a text.
CA:232, DA:326, DE:326, EN:419, ES:250, FR:429, GA:245, IT:218, NE:426, PO:243.

420 true score The score a candidate would obtain if no error in measurement were present at the time of testing or scoring. A fundamental concept in classical test theory.
CA:357, DA:415, DE:441, EN:420, ES:357, FR:285, GA:335, IT:285, NE:431, PO:289.

421 truncated distribution A type of frequency distribution characteristic of a sample which has a narrower range than the population it is taken from because high-scoring or low-scoring students are not present in the sample. Such a sample would be a group of students admitted to a course after passing an entrance test.

CA:116, DA:376, DE:1, EN:421, ES:117, FR:110, GA:108, IT:135, NE:343, PO:124.

422 *t* score An extension of the *z* score. It removes decimal places and negative signs. The *t* score is equal to ten times the *z* score plus 50. The distribution has a mean of 50 and a standard deviation of 10.
See: *z* score.
Further reading: Ebel and Frisbie 1991, p.68.

CA:355, DA:384, DE:388, EN:422, ES:355, FR:283, GA:367, IT:289, NE:376, PO:287.

423 t-test A statistical test used for determining if any significant difference exists between the means of two samples.

CA:340, DA:385, DE:387, EN:423, ES:398, FR:150, GA:368, IT:385, NE:377, PO:397.

424 two-parameter model In item-response theory (IRT), a model which takes into account an item discrimination parameter in addition to the ability/difficulty parameter.
Compare: one-parameter model, Rasch model.
See: item-response theory (IRT).

CA:258, DA:411, DE:454, EN:424, ES:271, FR:248, GA:298, IT:241, NE:404, PO:264.

425 type 1 error In statistics, the error of rejecting the null hypothesis, when in fact it is true.
Compare: type 2 error.
See: null hypothesis.
Further reading: Hatch and Lazaraton 1991, p. 224.

CA:140, DA:417, DE:9/117, EN:425, ES:150, FR:154, GA:126, IT:157, NE:405, PO:150.

426 type 2 error In statistics, the error of accepting the null hypothesis, when in fact it is false.
Compare: type 1 error.
See: null hypothesis.
Further reading: Hatch and Lazaraton 1991, p. 224.

CA:141, DA:418, DE:118, EN:426, ES:151, FR:155, GA:127, IT:158, NE:406, PO:151.

427 unidimensionality The notion of a single dimension, which is a necessary assumption for constructing a scale to measure psychological traits, e.g. using current item response models. Unidimensionality is a property of the measurement instrument, not of the underlying psychological processes.
Further reading: Crocker and Algina 1986, pp. 343.

CA:413, DA:90, DE:97, EN:427, ES:409, FR:408, GA:23, IT:398, NE:119, PO:406.

428 unitary competence A theory of language, promoted notably by Oller, which posited the existence of a single competence underlying all language skills.

CA:71, DA:91, DE:423, EN:428, ES:68, FR:71, GA:192, IT:70, NE:408, PO:85.

429 validation The process of gathering evidence to support the inferences made from test scores. It is the inferences regarding specific uses of a test which are validated, not the test itself.
See: validity.

CA:415, DA:426, DE:426, EN:429, ES:412, FR:412, GA:39, IT:400, NE:414, PO:408.

430 validity The extent to which scores on a test enable inferences to be made which are appropriate, meaningful and useful, given the purpose of the test. Different aspects of validity are identified, such as content, criterion and construct validity; these provide different kinds of evidence for judging the overall validity of a test for a given purpose.
See: concurrent validity, construct validity, criterion-related validity, content validity, convergent validity, discriminant validity, face validity, predictive validity.
Further reading: Bachman 1990, pp. 25, 236–237.

CA:416, DA:427, DE:427, EN:430, ES:413, FR:413, GA:30, IT:401, NE:415, PO:409.

431 variable a) The name given to a series of observations on one item, where the item could be a test item, gender, age or test score.

b) An element, in an experimental design or statistical analysis, which can take a series of values. For example, variables of interest in a language testing context include difficulty of test items, gender and age of test takers, etc.

CA:430, DA:428, DE:428, EN:431, ES:430, FR:423, GA:25, IT:416, NE:416, PO:422.

432 variance A measure of the dispersion of a set of scores. The larger the variance, the further individual scores are from the mean.

CA:434, DA:429, DE:429, EN:432, ES:434, FR:427, GA:24, IT:420, NE:417, PO:421.

433 vetting A stage in the cycle of test production at which the test developers assess materials commissioned from item writers and decide which should be rejected as not fulfilling the specifications of the test, and which can go forward to the editing stage.
Compare: moderation.

CA:382, DA:400, DE:405, EN:433 ES:383, FR:338, GA:184, IT:91, NE:115, PO:343.

434 vertical equating The process of placing the scores for two tests of different degrees of difficulty on the same scale.
Further reading: Crocker and Algina 1986 pp. 473–477.

CA:135, DA:432, DE:435, EN:434, ES:143, FR:39, GA:90, IT:153, NE:419, PO:46.

435 washback Refer to definition for backwash.

CA:372, DA:436, DE:442, EN:435, ES:124, FR:322, GA:95, IT:147, NE:432, PO:135.

436 Waystage level A specification of an elementary level of foreign language competence first published by the Council of Europe in 1977 for English and revised in 1990. It provides a less demanding objective than Threshold, being estimated to have approximately half the Threshold learning load.
Compare: Threshold level.

CA:271, DA:437, DE:443, EN:436, ES:284, FR:261, GA:211, IT:231, NE:433, PO:274.

437 weighted test score The score which a candidate is awarded in a test after weighting has been applied.
See: weighting.

CA:354, DA:434, DE:135, EN:437, ES:354, FR:280, GA:339, IT:284, NE:159, PO:286.

438 weighting The assignment of a different number of maximum points to a test item, task or component in order to change its relative contribution in relation to other parts of the same test. For example, if double marks are given to all the items in Task One of a test, Task One will account for a greater proportion of the total score than other tasks.
Further reading: Ebel and Frisbie 1991, pp. 214–216.

CA:290, DA:435, DE:136, EN:438, ES:303, FR:302, GA:439, IT:268, NE:434, PO:306.

439 word formation item An item type where the candidate has to produce a form of a word based on another form of the same word which is given as input. Example: This kind of work requires an .... of technical vocabulary. (understand)

CA:227, DA:269, DE:445, EN:439, ES:240, FR:227, GA:244, IT:216, NE:437, PO:237.

440 word frequency count A count of how frequently particular words or word-types occur in a text. In language testing, this may be useful when producing tests according to a particular lexical specification.

CA:190, DA:270, DE:143, EN:440, ES:362, FR:75, GA:67, IT:256, NE:436, PO:95.

441 y-intercept In linear regression, the point at which the regression line crosses the Y (vertical) axis.
See: linear regression.

CA:212, DA:438, DE:146, EN:441, ES:231, FR:215, GA:181, IT:200, NE:438, PO:226.

442 *z* score A commonly occurring standard score with a mean of 0 and a standard deviation of 1. The formula for calculating *z* scores is:

$$z = (X - \bar{X}) \div Sx$$

Where:

z = z score

X = test score

$\bar{X}$ = mean test score

Sx= standard deviation of test scores.

Compare: *t* score.
See: standard score.
Further reading: Ebel and Frisbie, 1991, p. 68.

CA:358, DA:439, DE:446, EN:442, ES:358, FR:286, GA:441, IT:291, NE:439, PO:290.

5 Español: Glosario multilingüe de términos de evaluación lingüística

1 acreditación Reconocimiento de un examen, normalmente por una institución oficial (entidad gubernamental, tribunal de exámenes, etc.).
CA:4, DA:10, DE:8, EN:5, ES:1, FR:4, GA:92, IT:303, NE:3, PO:325.

2 actividad Combinación de instrucciones, input y respuesta. Por ejemplo, un texto de lectura con varios items de selección múltiple que pueden ser contestados según una misma instrucción.
CA:391, DA:260, DE:26, EN:393, ES:2, FR:354, GA:371, IT:71, NE:270, PO:352.

3 actividad de comprensión de lectura Tipo de actividad que normalmente consiste en un texto o textos de lectura e items de los siguientes tipos: selección múltiple, preguntas de respuesta corta, cloze test/rellenar huecos, transferencia de información, etc.
CA:394, DA:223, DE:220, EN:321, ES:3, FR:357, GA:373, IT:74, NE:224, PO:351.

4 actividad de detección de errores Actividad de examen en la que hay que comprobar un texto buscando errores de un tipo específico, por ejemplo, faltas de ortografía o de estructura. Parte de esta actividad puede consistir en señalar los errores y aportar la foma correcta.
CA:395, DA:195, DE:189, EN:300, ES:4, FR:84, GA:374, IT:75, NE:304, PO:97.

5 actividad de expresión escrita guiada Actividad mediante la cual el candidato debe producir un texto escrito en el cual se emplea información gráfica o textual, como dibujos, cartas, postales e instrucciones, para controlar y estandarizar la respuesta esperada.
Compárese: expresión escrita, pregunta de redacción.
CA:393, DA:121, DE:130, EN:160, ES:5, FR:311, GA:377, IT:76, NE:143, PO:317.

6 actividad de expresión escrita dirigida Véase la definición de actividad de expresión escrita guiada.
CA:392, DA:43, DE:15, EN:105, ES:6, FR:356, GA:376, IT:77, NE:144, PO:355.

7 actividad de relacionar Tipo de actividad de examen que implica casar elementos de dos listas separadas. Un tipo de actividad de relacionar consiste en seleccionar la expresión correcta para completar una serie de oraciones incompletas. En las pruebas de comprensión escrita consiste, por ejemplo, en escoger de una lista algún elemento como unas vacaciones o un libro que sería adecuado para los intereses de una persona a quien se ha descrito.
CA:397, DA:322, DE:452, EN:226, ES:7, FR:21, GA:375, IT:73, NE:238, PO:353.

8 actividad de relación múltiple Actividad de examen en la cual varias preguntas o items de completar frases, basados generalmente en un texto de lectura, están fijados. Las respuestas se proporcionan en forma de un banco de palabras o locuciones, cada una de las cuales puede ser utilizada un número ilimitado de veces. La ventaja que presenta es que no se eliminan opciones durante la actividad (como ocurre en otras formas de emparejamiento) de forma que la actividad no se vuelve progresivamente más fácil.
Véase: actividad de relacionar.
CA:396, DA:100, DE:235, EN:241, ES:8, FR:355, GA:372, IT:72, NE:253, PO:354.

9 actuación Acto de producir lenguaje al hablar o escribir. La actuación lingüística, en términos del lenguaje realmente producido por las personas, es a menudo contrastada con la competencia, que es el conocimiento subyacente de una lengua.
Compárese: competencia.
Véase: prueba de actuación lingüística.
Bibliografía adicional: Bachman, 1990, pp. 52 y 108.
CA:5, DA:282, DE:283, EN:277, ES:9, FR:297, GA:141, IT:267, NE:286, PO:304.

10 acuerdo evaluador Véanse las

definiciones de acuerdo inter-evaluador y acuerdo intra-evaluador.

CA:1, DA:307, DE:56, EN:312, ES:10, FR:1, GA:70, IT:84, NE:36, PO:1.

11 acuerdo inter-evaluador Nivel de acuerdo entre dos o más calificadores acerca de la misma muestra de producción lingüística. Es especialmente relevante para la valoración de las destrezas de expresión oral y escrita en pruebas en las cuales se requiere la opinión subjetiva del examinador.

CA:2, DA:31, DE:159, EN:181, ES:11, FR:2, GA:68, IT:84, NE:185, PO:2.

12 acuerdo intra-evaluador El nivel de acuerdo entre dos valoraciones de la misma muestra de rendimiento realizadas en distintas ocasiones por el mismo calificador. Tiene que ver especialmente con la valoración de las destrezas de expresión escrita y oral en pruebas en las cuales se requiere la opinión subjetiva del examinador.

CA:3, DA:33, DE:163, EN:185, ES:12, FR:3, GA:69, IT:90, NE:190, PO:3.

13 adaptación de pruebas Adecuación de pruebas ya existentes para satisfacer las necesidades de un determinado grupo de usuarios o de examinandos.

CA:301, DA:404, DE:410, EN:405, ES:13, FR:395, GA:370, IT:5, NE:382, PO:4.

14 adquisición de la lengua Proceso mediante el cual se adquiere la capacidad en una primera o segunda lengua. En el caso de una segunda lengua, a veces se hace una distinción entre adquisición (es decir, mediante exposición natural) y aprendizaje (es decir, mediante el estudio consciente).

CA:7, DA:356, DE:367, EN:204, ES:14, FR:5, GA:349, IT:22, NE:380, PO:24.

15 ajuste Nivel de acuerdo entre los pronósticos de un modelo y los resultados observados. Pueden computarse distintos índices de ajuste. En TRI (teoría de respuesta al ítem) el análisis de ajuste muestra la medida en que el ítem estimado y los parámetros de cada persona (por ej. dificultad y capacidad) pronostican la puntuación de la persona en una prueba: la estadística de ajuste de un ítem puede considerarse como análoga a su índice de discriminación en la teoría clásica de examen.
Véase: teoría de respuesta al ítem.

CA:8, DA:99, DE:248, EN:145, ES:15, FR:6, GA:268, IT:107, NE:135, PO:5.

16 alfa (coeficiente alfa) Estimación de la fiabilidad por medio de la coherencia interna de la prueba. Toma valores entre 0 y 1. Utilizado frecuentemente en pruebas de respuesta múltiple a diferencia de pruebas con items dicótomos, aunque puede utilizarse para ambas. También denominado coeficiente alfa.
Compárese: Kuder-Richardson.
Véase: consistencia interna.
Bibliografía adicional: Henning, 1987, p. 84.

CA:9, DA:11, DE:10, EN:10, ES:16, FR:8, GA:10, IT:10, NE:12, PO:6.

17 alfa de Cronbach Véase la definición de alfa (coeficiente alfa).

CA:10, DA:54, DE:70, EN:84, ES:17, FR:9, GA:11, IT:11, NE:89, PO:7.

18 ampliación de frases Tipo de ítem en el cual se da un estímulo en forma de cadena de palabras con contenido pero en la cual faltan las preposiciones, los verbos auxiliares, los artículos, etc. El candidato debe añadir las palabras que faltan, ampliando así el estímulo para formar una frase gramatical completa.

CA:99, DA:380, DE:333, EN:358, ES:18, FR:175, GA:148, IT:166, NE:441, PO:184.

19 análisis de contenido Forma de describir y analizar el contenido del material de una prueba. Este análisis es necesario para asegurar que el contenido de la prueba cumple con su especificación. Es imprescindible para establecer la validez del contenido y del constructo.

CA:18, DA:133, DE:153, EN:72, ES:19, FR:12, GA:12, IT:15, NE:178, PO:15.

20 análisis de covarianza Véase la definición de ANCOVA.

CA:14, DA:200, DE:193, EN:12, ES:20, FR:14, GA:16, IT:18, NE:85, PO:13.

21 análisis de necesidades Manera de determinar las necesidades lingüísticas (en términos de destrezas, actividades, vocabulario, etc.) de un grupo particular de estudiantes antes de diseñar un curso de aprendizaje para ellos.

CA:16, DA:35, DE:45, EN:246, ES:21, FR:11, GA:19, IT:13, NE:31, PO:17.

22 análisis de prueba Análisis de las pruebas después de utilizarlas con candidatos, en los que se emplean a menudo métodos estadísticos y computerizados. El objetivo puede ser el de investigar el rendimiento de los candidatos o de la misma prueba.

CA:15, DA:389, DE:390, EN:396, ES:22,

FR:16, GA:14, IT:17, NE:389, PO:18.

23 análisis de varianza Véase la definición de ANOVA.
CA:17, DA:430, DE:430, EN:13, ES:23, FR:15, GA:15, IT:19, NE:418, PO:14.

24 análisis del discurso Este tipo de análisis se centra en la estructura y función de varios tipos de texto escrito o hablado.
CA:19, DA:76, DE:86, EN:107, ES:24, FR:13, GA:17, IT:16, NE: 104, PO:19.

25 análisis del ítem Descripción de la realización de items individuales en una prueba empleando, por lo general, índices estadísticos clásicos como la facilidad y la discriminación. Para este análisis se utiliza software como el MicroCAT Iteman.
Véase: discriminación, índice de facilidad.
CA:13, DA:161, DE:167, EN:190, ES:25 FR:17, GA:13, IT:12, NE:198, PO:16.

26 análisis factorial Técnica estadística que permite al investigador reducir un gran número de variables a un número menor mediante el hallazgo de modelos (esquemas comunes) en las variaciones de los valores de varias variables. Un grupo de variables altamente intercorrelacionadas componen un factor. El investigador puede utilizar el análisis factorial de modo exploratorio, con el fin de formular hipótesis, o de modo confirmatorio, mediante la exploración de hipótesis específicas.
Bibliografía adicional: Bachman, 1990, p. 262; Crocker y Algina, 1986, p. 232.
CA:20, DA:96, DE:115, EN:142, ES:26, FR:18, GA:18, IT:14, NE:133, PO:20.

27 ANCOVA Tipo de análisis de varianza que permite controlar el efecto de las variables de confusión relacionadas con la variable estudiada para aislar el efecto debido a ésta.
Véase: ANOVA.
Bibliografía adicional: Hatch y Lazaraton, 1991, p. 387.
CA:21, DA:14, DE:13, EN:17, ES:27, FR:19, GA:20, IT:20, NE:16, PO:21.

28 ANOVA Técnica estadística utilizada para comprobar la hipótesis nula de que varias medias de población son iguales. Se examina tanto la variabilidad de las observaciones en cada grupo como la variabilidad entre las medias de los grupos.
Bibliografía adicional: Hatch y Lazaraton, 1991, p. 308–312.
CA:22, DA:19, DE:20, EN:18, ES:28, FR:20, GA:21, IT:21, NE:19, PO:22.

29 apartado Parte de un examen, frecuentemente presentada como una prueba independiente con sus propias instrucciones y límite de tiempo. Los apartados se basan frecuentemente en las destrezas, y poseen denominaciones tales como Comprensión Auditiva o Expresión Escrita.
Compárese: subprueba.
CA:73, DA:181, DE:306, EN:61, ES:29, FR:72, GA:85, IT:81, NE:128, PO:87.

30 aprobado La puntuación mínima que tiene que lograr el candidato para aprobar una prueba o examen.
Compárese: puntuación límite.
CA:23, DA:36, DE:52, EN:273, ES:30, FR:277, GA:278, IT:288 NE:341, PO:282.

31 asimetría Característica de una distribución en la cual el pico de la curva se sitúa o a la derecha (asimetría negativa) o a la izquierda (asimetría positiva) del centro.

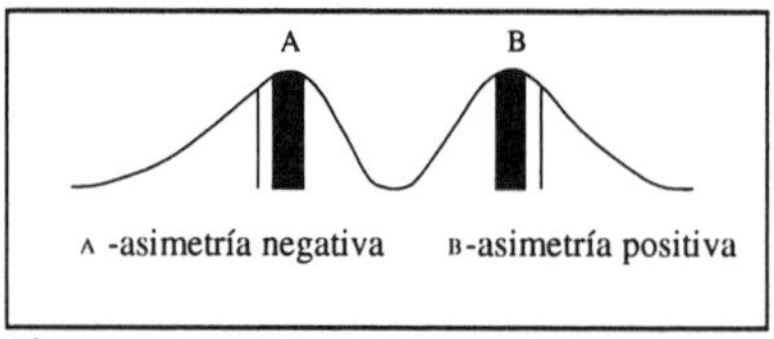

Véase: distribución normal.
Bibliografía adicional: Hatch y Lazaraton, 1991, p. 165.
CA:25, DA:343, DE:337, EN:366, ES:31, FR:109, GA:323, IT:25, NE:330, PO:120.

32 aumento de la puntuación Diferencia entre la puntuación obtenida en una prueba antes de recibir un curso de enseñanza y la puntuación obtenida en la misma prueba o en una prueba similar realizada al final del curso. El aumento de la puntuación indica el progreso durante el curso.
CA:352, DA:290, DE:211, EN:150, ES:32, FR:199, GA:44, IT:192, NE:434, PO:209.

33 autenticidad Como característica de una prueba, se refiere a la medida en que las actividades de dicha prueba reflejan el uso del lenguaje en una situación que no sea de examen.
Bibliografía adicional: Bachman, 1990, pp. 300–303.
CA:27, DA:21, DE:42, EN:24, ES:33, FR:24, GA:115, IT:35, NE:23, PO:26.

34 autenticidad interactiva Perspectiva de la autenticidad en la evaluación de lenguas mediante la cual ésta se considera una característica de la interacción que debe existir entre el examinando y la actividad de la prueba para que la respuesta produci-

da sea adecuada.
Compárese: autenticidad situacional.
Véase: autenticidad.
Bibliografía adicional: Bachman, 1990, pp. 315–323.
CA:28, DA:146, DE:157, EN:177, ES:34, FR:25, GA:116, IT:36, NE:183, PO:27.

35 autenticidad situacional La medida en que una prueba puede ser considerada auténtica en relación con el mundo real, con situaciones de uso lingüístico que no son propias de examen.
Compárese: autenticidad interactiva, enfoque de comunicación real.
Véase: autenticidad.
Bibliografía adicional: Bachman 1990, cap. 8.
CA:29, DA:336, DE:351, EN:365, ES:35, FR:26, GA:117, IT:37, NE:340, PO:28.

36 auto-evaluación Proceso por el cual un estudiante evalúa su propio nivel de capacidad, bien por medio de un examen administrado por él mismo, o bien por otros medios tales como un cuestionario o una lista de corroboración.
CA:30, DA:331, DE:345, EN:354, ES:36, FR:27, GA:142, IT:38, NE:334, PO:29.

37 banco de items Planteamiento de la gestión de items de examen que implica el almacenamiento de información acerca de los items con el fin de poder construir pruebas de contenido y dificultad conocidos. Normalmente, dicho planteamiento utiliza una base de datos informatizada y se basa en la teoría del rasgo latente, que significa que los items pueden relacionarse mediante una escala de dificultad común.
Bibliografía adicional: Henning, 1987, cap. 9.
CA:36, DA:155, DE:28, EN:191, ES:37, FR:28, GA:40, IT:111, NE:199, PO:37.

38 banda En su sentido más amplio, parte de una escala. En una prueba basada en items, este término cubre una gama de puntuaciones que pueden verse reflejadas como una calificación o una banda de puntuaciones. En una escala de calificación diseñada para evaluar una característica o capacidad específica, por ejemplo la expresión oral o la expresión escrita, una banda representa normalmente un nivel determinado.
CA:37, DA:339, DE:44, EN:29, ES:38, FR:200, GA:41, IT:39 NE:28, PO:210.

39 banda de puntuaciones Parte de una escala; se refiere a un campo específico de capacidad.
CA:346, DA:258, DE:210, EN:30, ES:39, FR:269, GA:330, IT:40, NE:29, PO:65.

40 batería Conjunto de pruebas o subpruebas relacionadas entre sí que aportan datos independientes (por ejemplo, al examinar diferentes destrezas) pero que pueden combinarse para producir una puntuación total.
CA:38, DA:28, DE:393, EN:32, ES:40, FR:30, GA:64, IT:41, NE:30, PO:38.

41 batería de pruebas Véase la definición de batería.
CA:39, DA:390, DE:406, EN:397, ES:41, FR:31, GA:63, IT:42, NE:390, PO:39.

42 calibración Proceso de determinación de la escala de una prueba o pruebas. La calibración puede implicar el anclaje de los items de diferentes pruebas en una escala común de dificultad (la escala zeta). Cuando una prueba se construye con items calibrados, las puntuaciones en la prueba indican la capacidad del candidato, es decir, su situación en la escala zeta.
CA:44, DA:164, DE:94, EN:40, ES:42, FR:35, GA:49, IT:44, NE:205, PO:42.

43 calibrar En la teoría de respuesta al ítem, calcular la dificultad de un conjunto de items para una prueba.
Véase: escala zeta.
CA:43, DA:163, DE:93, EN:39, ES:43, FR:40, GA:48, IT:43, NE:206, PO:47.

44 calificación El número total de puntos posibles para un ítem, subprueba o prueba, o el número de puntos otorgados a la respuesta del candidato a un ítem, subprueba o prueba.
CA:342, DA:287, DE:313, EN:224, ES:44, FR:287, GA:224, IT:292, NE:60, PO:105.

45 calificación múltiple Método para mejorar la fiabilidad de la valoración de las pruebas de expresión escrita extensa (valoración hasta cierto punto subjetiva), al asegurar que cada respuesta del candidato es calificada independientemente por más de un evaluador.
Bibliografía adicional: Weir 1988, pp. 65–66.
CA:87, DA:274, DE:233, EN:240, ES:45, FR:271, GA:183, IT:105, NE:241, PO:63.

46 calificador Persona que asigna una puntuación al rendimiento del candidato en una prueba, mediante un juicio subjetivo. Los calificadores normalmente están cualificados en el área pertinente, y deben someterse a un proceso de formación y estandarización. En las pruebas orales a veces se

diferencian los papeles de calificador y entrevistador. También denominado examinador.
Compárese: entrevistador, corrector.
CA:35, DA:32, DE:55, EN:22, ES:46, FR:174, GA:234, IT:165, NE:33, PO:182.

47 calificar a) Asignar una calificación a las respuestas de un candidato en una prueba. Puede implicar un juicio profesional, o la aplicación de una plantilla de corrección que detalle todas las respuestas aceptables.
CA:80, DA:289, DE:40, EN:222, ES:47, FR:265, GA:218, IT:29, NE:83, PO:57.

b)Proceso de convertir la puntuación o calificación de la prueba en nota.
CA:362, DA:168, DE:48, EN:157, ES:47, FR:52, GA:165, IT:94, NE:427, PO:277.

48 candidato Persona que se examina. También denominado examinando.
CA:45, DA:165, DE:302, EN:41, ES:48, FR:41, GA:178, IT:49, NE:207, PO:48.

49 capacidad Característica mental, habilidad o potencial para hacer algo.
Compárese: competencia, dominio.
Bibliografía adicional: Bachman, 1990, p. 16, p. 19.
CA:46, DA:2, DE:113, EN:2, ES:49, FR:42, GA:96, IT:1A, NE:411, PO:49.

50 capacidad lingüística Conjunto de competencias que define la capacidad de un individuo de emplear el lenguaje para diversos fines comunicativos.
Bibliografía adicional: Bachman, 1990, pp. 3–4.
CA:47, DA:354, DE:368, EN:203, ES:50, FR:43, GA:97, IT:4, NE:379, PO:50.

51 características de métodos de examen Las características propias de los diferentes métodos de examen. Pueden incluir el contexto, el enunciado, el lenguaje de las instrucciones, el formato, etc.
Bibliografía adicional: Bachman, 1990, cap. 5.
CA:48, DA:397, DE:403, EN:402, ES:51, FR:46, GA:401, IT:50, NE:398, PO:54.

52 categoría a) Elemento o clase de la escala categorial, por ejemplo las categorías en lo que concierne al sexo son masculina y femenina.

b) En evaluación, se dice que una escala de puntuación con, por ejemplo, cinco puntos posee cinco categorías de respuesta.
CA:49, DA:169, DE:176, EN:43, ES:52, FR:48, GA:50, IT:51, NE:52, PO:55.

53 certificado Documento que acredita que la persona en él aludida ha realizado un examen o un apartado de un examen y ha logrado cierta calificación, normalmente un aprobado como mínimo.
Compárese: diploma.
CA:50, DA:38, DE:448, EN:47, ES:53, FR:50, GA:386, IT:52, NE:56, PO:56.

54 clave de respuesta a) Opción correcta en un ítem de selección múltiple.

b) En general, conjunto de todas las respuestas correctas o aceptables a los items de una prueba.
Compárese: distractor, plantilla de corrección.
Véase: ítem de selección múltiple.
CA:51/52, DA:256, DE:339, EN:198, ES:54, FR:329, GA:133, DE:339, IT:53, NE:342, PO:335.

55 coeficiente Indice numérico utilizado para medir una propiedad o característica.
Véase: alfa (coeficiente alfa), coeficiente de correlación.
CA:53, DA:175, DE:178, EN:53, ES:55, FR:54, GA:73, IT:57, NE:62, PO:69.

56 coeficiente alfa Véase la definición de alfa (coeficiente alfa).
CA:54, DA:176, DE:179, EN:54, ES:56, FR:55, GA:74, IT:58, NE:63, PO:70.

57 coeficiente de correlación Indice que demuestra la medida en que dos o más variables se correlacionan. Varía entre -1 y +1. Las variables altamente correlacionadas son representadas por un coeficiente de correlación próximo a +1.
Bibliografía adicional: Guilford y Fruchter, 1981, pp. 86–88.
CA:55, DA:197, DE:191, EN:79, ES:57, FR:56, GA:75, IT:60, NE:82, PO:71.

58 coeficiente de fiabilidad Medida de la fiabilidad en una escala de 0 a 1. Las estimaciones de fiabilidad pueden establecerse suministrando repetidamente una prueba (que debería producir resultados similares) o, cuando ello no sea practicable, a partir de alguna forma de medida de consistencia interna. A veces conocido como índice de fiabilidad.
Véase: consistencia interna, fiabilidad, fiabilidad test-retest.
CA:61, DA:313, DE:323, EN:328, ES:58, FR:61, GA:77, IT:59, NE:44, PO:74.

59 coeficiente phi Coeficiente de correlación que se utiliza para mostrar la

fuerza de la relación entre dos variables binarias, como por ejemplo las puntuaciones en dos items de pruebas puntuados como correcto o incorrecto.
Véase: coeficiente de correlación.
Bibliografía adicional: Guilford y Fruchter, 1981, pp. 316–318; Crocker y Algina, 1986, pp. 92–94.
CA:62, DA:284, DE:286, EN:279, ES:59, FR:58, GA:76, IT:61, NE:288, PO:75.

60 competencia Conocimiento o capacidad para hacer algo. Utilizado en lingüística para referirse a una capacidad subyacente frente a la actuación, que es la manifestación de la competencia como lenguaje en uso. Esta distinción se origina en la obra de Chomsky.
Compárese: actuación.
Bibliografía adicional: Bachman, 1990, pp. 52 y 108.
CA:64, DA:180, DE:183, EN:59, ES:60, FR:62, GA:191, IT:62, NE:67, PO:76.

61 competencia comunicativa Capacidad de utilizar adecuadamente el lenguaje en diversas situaciones y entornos.
Bibliografía adicional: Bachman, 1990, p. 16, p. 68.
CA:65, DA:179, DE:182, EN:58, ES:61, FR:63, GA:195, IT:63, NE:66, PO:77.

62 competencia discursiva Capacidad de entender y producir un discurso. En algunos modelos de competencia lingüística, la competencia discursiva se diferencia como un componente.
Bibliografía adicional: Bachman, 1990, capítulo 4.
CA:66, DA:78, DE:87, EN:108, ES:62, FR:64, GA:196, IT:64, NE:105, PO:78.

63 competencia gramatical En un modelo de capacidad lingüística comunicativa, la competencia gramatical es el componente que trata los conocimientos sobre áreas de uso del lenguaje como la morfología, la sintaxis, el vocabulario, la fonología y la grafía.
Bibliografía adicional: Bachman, 1990, pp. 84–88.
CA:67, DA:119, DE:138, EN:158, ES:63, FR:65, GA:193, IT:65, NE:162, PO:79.

64 competencia lingüística Véase la definición de competencia.
CA:68, DA:217, DE:224, EN:214, ES:64, FR:67, GA:198, IT:66, NE:231, PO:80.

65 competencia oral Habilidad para hablar una lengua.
CA:298, DA:239, DE:370, EN:264, ES:65, FR:68, GA:266, IT:67, NE:354, PO:82.

66 competencia pragmática Posible categoría dentro de un modelo de capacidad lingüística comunicativa: incluye la capacidad de llevar a cabo actos de habla así como conocimientos de las convenciones sociolingüísticas.
Bibliografía adicional: Bachman, 1990, p. 42.
CA:69, DA:294, DE:295, EN:290, ES:66, FR:69, GA:194, IT:68, NE:297, PO:83.

67 competencia sociolingüística Categoría de los modelos de capacidad lingüística comunicativa: incluye la capacidad de adaptar el habla a contextos y situaciones específicos de acuerdo con las normas sociales.
Bibliografía adicional: Bachmann, 1990, p. 42.
CA:70, DA:347, DE:358, EN:369, ES:67, FR:70, GA:197, IT:69, NE:345, PO:84.

68 competencia unitaria Teoría del lenguaje, promocionada notablemente por Oller, que planteó la existencia de una única competencia que subyace a todas las destrezas lingüísticas.
CA:71, DA:91, DE:423, EN:428, ES:68, FR:71, GA:192, IT:70, NE:408, PO:85.

69 completar frases Tipo de ítem en el cual sólo se proporciona la mitad de una frase. El candidato debe completar la frase, ya sea proporcionando las palabras adecuadas (posiblemente basadas en la lectura de un texto) ya sea escogiendo entre varias opciones dadas.
CA:72, DA:382, DE:332, EN:357, ES:69, FR:298, GA:93, IT:80, NE:442, PO:86.

70 composición discursiva Actividad de expresión escrita en la cual el candidato ha de exponer un tema que admite diversos puntos de vista, o ha de argumentar para defender sus opiniones personales.
Véase: expresión escrita.
CA:74, DA:77, DE:342, EN:113, ES:70, FR:74, GA:52, IT:83, NE:42, PO:89.

71 cómputo de los distractores Frecuencia con que se escoge cada distractor en un ítem de selección múltiple. El cómputo revela la popularidad de cada distractor.
CA:243, DA:80, DE:89, EN:116, ES:71, FR:301, GA:384, IT:88, NE:9, PO:96.

72 conocimiento socio-cultural Conocimiento del mundo relacionado con la forma en que funciona una sociedad dentro de una cultura en particular. Es importante

para el comportamiento apropiado y el uso del lenguaje en contextos culturales específicos.
Compárese: competencia sociolingüística
CA:76, DA:346, DE:357, EN:368, ES:72, FR:341, GA:135, IT:86, NE:344, PO:90.

73 conocimientos previos Conocimientos que el candidato posee sobre un tema o sobre determinados aspectos culturales presentes en una prueba y que pueden afectar a la manera en que se trata el input. Es especialmente relevante en pruebas de Lengua para Fines Específicos.
Bibliografía adicional: Bachman, 1990, p. 273.
CA:75, DA:26, DE:144, EN:27, ES:73, FR:77, GA:134, IT:85, NE:4, PO:91.

74 consistencia interna Rasgo de una prueba, representado por la medida en que las puntuaciones de los candidatos en los items individuales de la prueba son coherentes con su puntuación total. Los cálculos de consistencia interna pueden ser utilizados como índices de fiabilidad de la prueba, pueden computarse diversos índices, por ejemplo, KR-20, alfa.
Véase: alfa (coeficiente alfa), Kuder-Richardson, fiabilidad.
Bibliografía adicional: Bachman, 1990, p. 172.
CA:77, DA:147, DE:155, EN:180, ES:74, FR:186, GA:87, IT:87, NE:186, PO:93.

75 construcción de la prueba Proceso de seleccionar items o actividades y colocarlos en una prueba. Este proceso suele ir precedido de una experimentación de los materiales. Los items y actividades para la construcción de la prueba pueden ser seleccionados de un banco de materiales.
CA:126, DA:394, DE:397, EN:398, ES:75, FR:146, GA:393, IT:110, NE:392, PO:140.

76 constructo Capacidad o característica mental hipotetizada que no siempre puede ser observada o medida de forma directa, por ejemplo, en las pruebas de lenguas la capacidad para la comprensión auditiva. Las pruebas pretenden medir los distintos constructos subyacentes a la capacidad lingüística. Además de la misma capacidad lingüística, son constructos pertinentes la motivación, la actitud y la aculturación.
Bibliografía adicional: Hatch y Lazaraton, 1991, p. 15
CA:78, DA:184, DE:185, EN:68, ES:76, FR:80, GA:394, IT:108, NE:72, PO:94.

77 convocatoria Fecha o período durante el cual el examen tiene lugar. Muchos exámenes tienen establecidas varias fechas de convocatoria al año, mientras que otros pueden convocarse según la demanda existente.
CA:6, DA:403, DE:308, EN:8, ES:77, FR:7, GA:288, IT:331, NE:10, PO:23.

78 corrección automática Método de corrección para el cual no se requiere de los correctores ni una formación específica ni realizar un juicio subjetivo. Las correcciones se realizan de acuerdo con un sistema de corrección que especifica todas las respuestas aceptables para cada ítem de la prueba.
Compárese: correción por examinador.
CA:86, DA:23, DE:231, EN:51, ES:78, FR:274, GA:219, IT:31, NE:25, PO:62.

79 corrección de la atenuación Método de cálculo de la correlación entre dos o más variables cuando no existe ninguna diferencia de fiabilidad entre las variables.
Bibliografía adicional: Guilford y Fruchter, 1981, pp. 450–453; Hatch y Lazaraton, 1990, pp. 444–445.
CA:88, DA:194, DE:243, EN:76, ES:79, FR:82, GA:53, IT:106, NE:78, PO:99.

80 corrección del acierto casual Manera de contrarrestar el alza de la puntuación que resulta de haber acertado por casualidad la respuesta correcta en pruebas compuestas de items objetivos.
Bibliografía adicional: Ebel y Frisbie, 1986, pp. 215–218.
CA:82, DA:193, DE:317/450, EN:77, ES:80, FR:83, GA:54, IT:103, NE:77, PO:98.

81 corrección por examinador Método de corrección realizado por correctores que necesitan poseer algún nivel de experiencia y formación especial para poder realizar un juicio subjetivo. Normalmente las pruebas de conversación y redacción extensa se corrigen de esta forma.
Compárese: corrección automática.
CA:81, DA:29, DE:107, EN:136, ES:81, FR:272, GA:223, IT:30, NE:131, PO:67.

82 corrección por ordenador (puntuación) Existen diversas formas de utilizar la informática para reducir el error al corregir pruebas objetivas. Se puede, por ejemplo, extraer información de la hoja de respuestas del candidato utilizando una lectora óptica, se consiguen así datos que pueden utilizarse para aportar puntuaciones o análisis.

CA:85, DA:53, DE:69, EN:65, ES:82, FR:273, GA:222, IT:28, NE:69, PO:66.

83 corrector Persona que asigna una puntuación a las respuestas de un candidato en una prueba escrita. Puede implicar el uso de un juicio experto, o, en el caso de la corrección automática, la aplicación relativamente no cualificada de una plantilla de corrección.
Véase: calificador

CA:90, DA:288, DE:39, EN:221, ES:83, FR:81, GA:225, IT:102, NE:80, PO:182.

84 correlación Relación existente entre dos o más mediciones, con respecto a la medida en que tienden a variar de modo idéntico. Cuando, por ejemplo, los candidatos tienden a lograr una clasificación similar en dos pruebas distintas, existe una correlación positiva entre las dos series de puntuaciones.
Compárese: covarianza.
Véase: correlación por rangos, correlación producto-momento de Pearson.
Bibliografía adicional: Guilford y Fruchter, 1981, cap. 6; Bachman, 1990, pp. 259–260.

CA:91, DA:196, DE:190, EN:78, ES:84, FR:85, GA:78, IT:95, NE:81, PO:100.

85 correlación biserial Indice de discriminación de items para items dicótomos, escrito r_b ; es la correlación entre un criterio (normalmente la puntuación total de la prueba) y la capacidad que subyace a la respuesta correcta-incorrecta al ítem. El valor de r_b es al menos 25% superior al de la correlación biserial puntual (r_{pbi}). Una ventaja de r_b es que resulta bastante estable a través de muestras de distintos niveles de capacidad.
Compárese: correlación biserial puntual.
Véase: discriminación.
Bibliografía adicional: Crocker y Algina, 1986, pp. 317–318; Guilford y Fruchter 1981, pp. 304–311.

CA:56, DA:40, DE:60, EN:35, ES:85, FR:86, GA:79, IT:96, NE:48, PO:101.

86 correlación biserial puntual Indice de discriminación de items para items dicotómicos, expresado r_{pb} ; la correlación entre un criterio (normalmente la puntuación en la prueba) y la respuesta al ítem. Una ventaja de la r_{pb} frente a la correlación biserial (r_b) es que se puede utilizar cuando la capacidad subyacente no está distribuida normalmente.
Compárese: correlación biserial.

CA:57, DA:41, DE:311, EN:283, ES:86, FR:57, GA:80, IT:97, NE:309, PO:102.

87 correlación de rangos de Spearman Forma de correlación de jerarquía utilizada para muestras pequeñas, por ejemplo, muestras de menos de 30.
Véase: Correlación por rangos.

CA:58, DA:351, DE:361, EN:373, ES:87, FR:60, GA:83, IT:99, NE:347, PO:73.

88 correlación phi Véase la definición de coeficiente phi.

CA:92, DA:285, DE:287, EN:280, ES:88, FR:88, GA:81, IT:101, NE:289, PO:103.

89 correlación por rangos Correlación basada no en los valores absolutos de las variables, sino en la jerarquía relativa.
Bibliografía adicional: Guilford y Fruchter, 1981, pp. 294–296.

CA:60, DA:304, DE:315, EN:309, ES:89, FR:59, GA:82, IT:100, NE:312, PO:72.

90 correlación producto-momento de Pearson Coeficiente de correlación utilizado con variables medidas en escalas de intervalos o de razón.
Véase: coeficiente de correlación.
Bibliografía adicional: Hatch y Lazaraton, 1991, pp. 427–431; Guilford y Fruchter, 1981, p. 81.

CA:59, DA:279, DE:298, EN:274, ES:90, FR:87, GA:84, IT:98, NE:283, PO:104.

91 covarianza Varianza conjunta de dos o más variables. Por ejemplo, la longitud de la frase y la dificultad del léxico son características del texto de comprensión de lectura que tienden a ser relacionadas, es decir, covarían. La covarianza debe ser tenida en cuenta al pronosticar una variable a partir de otras, por ejemplo, al pronosticar la dificultad de un texto de lectura a partir de la longitud de sus frases y de la dificultad del léxico.
Véase: varianza.

CA:93, DA:199, DE:192, EN:80, ES:91, FR:92, GA:71, IT:112, NE:84, PO:106.

92 creador Persona que redacta y configura una prueba.

CA:127, DA:392, DE:400, EN:361, ES:92, FR:145, GA:121, IT:149, NE:391, PO:141.

93 curriculum Descripción global de los objetivos, contenido, organización, métodos y evaluación de un curso educativo.
Compárese: programa de estudios (syllabus).
CA:94, DA:55, DE:71, EN:87, ES:93, FR:93, GA:99, IT:113, NE:220, PO:107.

94 curtosis Indicación del grado en que una distribución se desvía (o en forma de pico o más plana) de la curva normal. Los datos distribuidos en una curva plana muestran una distribución platicúrtica, mientras que los datos que forman una curva con un pico pronunciado muestran una distribución leptocúrtica.

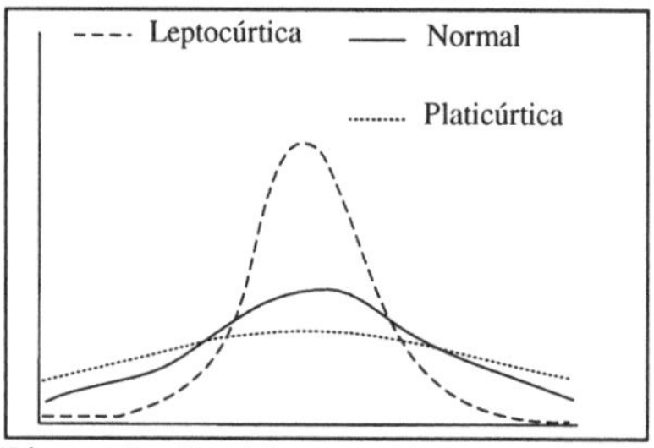

Véase: distribución normal.

CA:95, DA:412, DE:108, EN:202, ES:94, FR:428, GA:100, IT:114, NE:213, PO:108.

95 curva característica del ítem (CCI) En la teoría de respuesta al ítem, la CCI muestra cómo la probabilidad de contestar correctamente a un ítem se relaciona con la capacidad latente subyacente a la produción lingüística en los items de la prueba.
Bibliografía adicional: Crocker y Algina, 1986, pp. 340–342.

CA:79, DA:157, DE:168, EN:192, ES:95, FR:90, GA:94, IT:115, NE:196, PO:109.

96 d de Ebel Véase la definición de índice D.

CA:96, DA:85, DE:92, EN:122, ES:96, FR:94, GA:101, IT:116, NE:117, PO:111.

97 d neto Véase a la definición del índice D

CA:206, DA:246, DE:257, EN:247, ES:97, FR:115, GA:102, IT:194, NE:256, PO:111.

98 descriptor Descripción breve que acompaña a una banda en una escala de evaluación; resume el grado de dominio o tipo de rendimiento esperado para que el candidato logre una puntuación determinada.

CA:97, DA:64, DE:76, EN:96, ES:98, FR:97, GA:437, IT:118, NE:96, PO:113.

99 descriptor escalar Véase la definición de descriptor.

CA:98, DA:338, DE:353, EN:344, ES:99, FR:96, GA:438, IT:119, NE:327, PO:112.

100 destreza Capacidad para hacer algo. En la evaluación de lenguas se distinguen a menudo las destrezas de comprensión de lectura, expresión escrita, comprensión auditiva y expresión oral.
Véase: competencia.

CA:199, DA:111, DE:119, EN:367, ES:100, FR:340, GA:325, IT:1B, NE:413, PO:51.

101 destrezas de orden inferior Las capacidades hipotetizadas menos complejas exigidas a los candidatos en una prueba lingüística, por ejemplo el reconocimiento de una palabra o letra.
Compárese: destrezas de orden superior.

CA:200, DA:27, DE:424, EN:219, ES:101, FR:44, GA:327, IT:2, NE:409, PO:52.

102 destrezas de orden superior Capacidades hipotetizadas complejas como por ejemplo inferir o resumir.
Compárese: destrezas de orden inferior.

CA:201, DA:130, DE:418, EN:162, ES:102, FR:45, GA:326, IT:3, NE:410, PO:53.

103 desviación estándar Medida de la dispersión de un conjunto de observaciones sobre la media aritmética. Igual a la raíz cuadrada de la varianza. En la distribución normal, el 68% de la muestra cae dentro de una desviación estándar de la media y el 95% cae dentro de dos desviaciones estándar de la media.

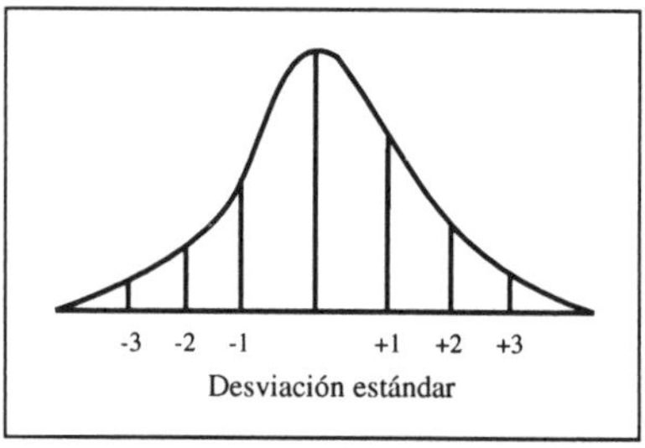

Compárese: margen de variación.
Véase: varianza.
Bibliografía adicional: Ebel y Frisbie, 1991 pp. 61–62; Crocker y Algina, 1986, pp. 21–22.

CA:101, DA:362, DE:372, EN:379, ES:103, FR:98, GA:113, IT:122, NE:360, PO:114.

104 diagrama de barras (tabla) Forma gráfica de mostrar las distribuciones de frecuencia de las variables.

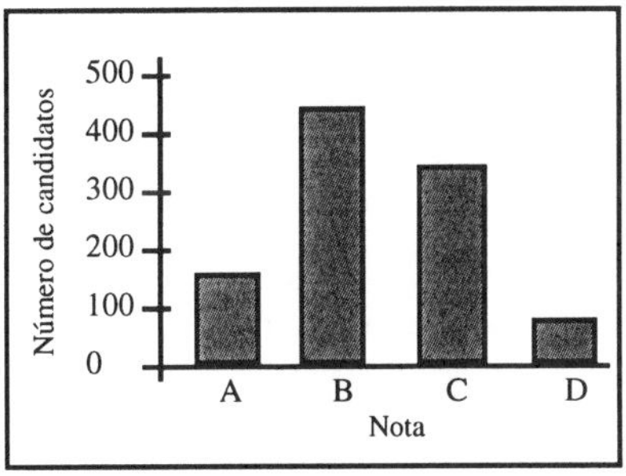

Compárese: histograma.
Bibliografía adicional: Hatch and Lazaraton, 1991, p. 147.
CA:102, DA:383, DE:335, EN:31, ES:104, FR:201, GA:42, IT:123, NE:357, PO:211.

105 dictado Tipo de actividad de examen en la cual el candidato ha de escuchar un texto y escribir las palabras escuchadas. Los criterios para la evaluación de un dictado varían según el propósito de la prueba; pueden incluir la ortografía y la puntuación.
CA:103, DA:68, DE:79, EN:99, ES:105, FR:99, GA:109, IT:121, NE:99, PO:125.

106 diploma Documento que constata que la persona designada ha hecho un examen o una sección de un examen logrando una calificación específica, normalmente el aprobado como mínimo. Frecuentemente se interpreta como una cualificación de más alto nivel que el certificado.
Compárese: certificado.
CA:104, DA:69, DE:80, EN:103, ES:106, FR:100, GA:118, IT:124, NE:101, PO:115.

107 discriminación Capacidad de un ítem de discriminar entre buenos y malos candidatos. Se utilizan diversos índices de discriminación. Algunos (por ej. punto biserial, biserial) se basan en una correlación entre la puntuación en el ítem y un criterio, como puede ser la puntuación total en la prueba o alguna medida externa de dominio. Otros se basan en la diferencia de la dificultad del ítem para grupos de alta o baja capacidad . En la teoría de respuesta al ítem los modelos de los parámetros 2 y 3 calculan la discriminación del ítem como parámetro A.
Véase: correlación biserial, correlación biserial puntual, teoría de respuesta al ítem (TRI).
Bibliografía adicional: Crocker y Algina, 1986, p. 313–320; Ebel y Frisbie, 1991, pp. 231–232.
CA:105, DA:74, DE:416, EN:112, ES:107, FR:102, GA:180, IT:126, NE:109, PO:116.

108 discurso Texto hablado o escrito, considerado como un acto de lenguaje comunicativo.
CA:106, DA:75, DE:85, EN:106, ES:108, FR:101, GA:119, IT:125, NE:103, PO:117.

109 diseño multirrasgo-multimétodo Diseño experimental utilizado en la validación de constructos, en el cual un conjunto de rasgos supuestamente distintos son medidos por un conjunto de métodos supuestamente distintos. El análisis debería mostrar, por ejemplo, que las medidas de capacidad de comprensión auditiva obtenidas por métodos diferentes se correlacionan más entre sí que las medidas de destrezas diferentes obtenidas por el mismo método de examen.
Bibliografía adicional: Bachman, 1990, pp. 263–265.
CA:108, DA:238, DE:252, EN:243, ES:109, FR:299, GA:111, IT:277, NE:254, PO:305.

110 dispersión Grado de variación o extensión en un conjunto de puntuaciones de los candidatos. Si la dispersión es amplia, las puntuaciones se encuentran muy separadas, y si la dispersión es pequeña, se encuentran agrupadas.
Véase: desviación estándar, varianza, margen de variación.
CA:107, DA:353, DE:385, EN:114, ES:110, FR:103, GA:357, IT:127, NE:356, PO:118.

111 distractor Toda opción incorrecta en un ítem de selección múltiple.
Compárese: clave de respuesta.
Véase: ítem de selección múltiple.
Bibliografía adicional: Ebel y Frisbie, 1986, pp. 176–185.
CA:110, DA:79, DE:88, EN:115, ES:111, FR:104, GA:348, IT:129, NE:8, PO:126.

112 distribución En los datos de la prueba, el número de veces que aparece cada puntuación obtenida por los candidatos. Frecuentemente se muestra en forma de histograma.

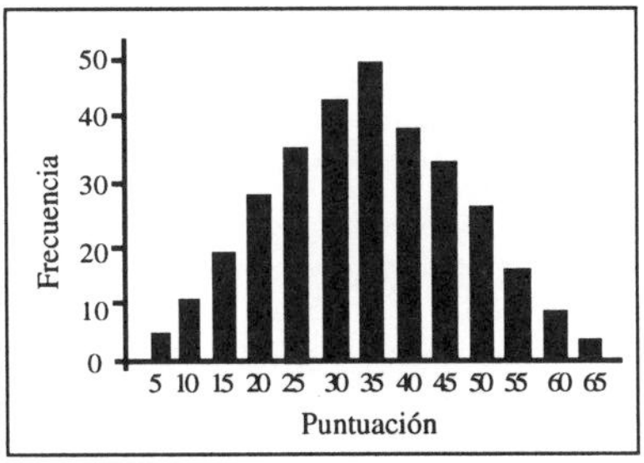

Véase: distribución normal, asimetría.
Bibliografía adicional: Hatch y Lazaraton, 1991, pp. 159–178.
CA:111, DA:103, DE:434, EN:117, ES:112, FR:105, GA:103, IT:130, NE:110, PO:119.

113 distribución bimodal Distribución con dos modos o picos que pueden sugerir la existencia de dos grupos diferentes dentro de la misma muestra.

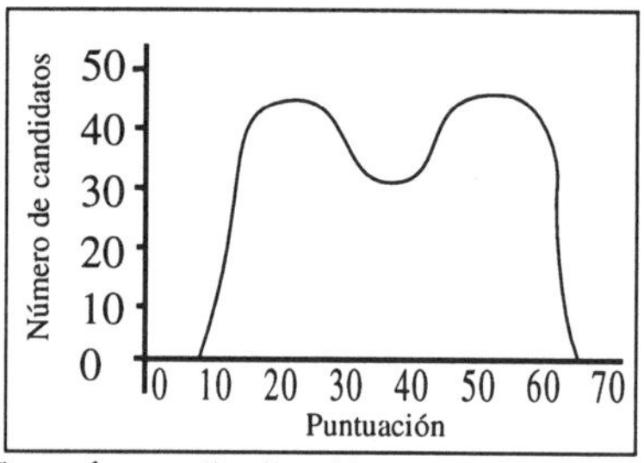

Compárese: distribución normal.
Véase: moda.
Bibliografía adicional: Hatch y Lazaraton, 1991, pp. 165–166.
CA:112, DA:39, DE:59, EN:34, ES:113, FR:106, GA:104, IT:131, NE:47, PO:121.

114 distribución de frecuencia Véase la definición de distribución.
CA:113, DA:107, DE:142, EN:149, ES:114, FR:107, GA:106, IT:132, NE:138, PO:122.

115 distribución gaussiana Véase la definición de distribución normal.
CA:114, DA:114, DE:129, EN:152, ES:115, FR:91, GA:105, IT:133, NE:140, PO:110.

116 distribución normal Distribución matemática que es el supuesto fundamental para varios procedimientos estadísticos. La distribución toma la forma de una campana simétrica, y la media, la mediana y la moda se situan en el mismo punto. Existe toda una famila de distribución, dependiendo de los valores de la media, la desviación estándar y el número de observaciones. También conocida como distribución Gaussiana.
Compárese: distribución bimodal.
Bibliografía adicional: Hatch y Lazaraton, 1991, p. 164
CA:115, DA:252, DE:265, EN:252, ES:116, FR:108, GA:107, IT:134, NE:262, PO:123.

117 distribución truncada Tipo de distribución de frecuencia característica de una muestra que tiene una amplitud más limitada que la población de donde procede porque no están presentes en la muestra o los de alta puntuación o los de baja puntuación. Una muestra de este tipo sería un grupo de alumnos admitidos en un curso después de aprobar una prueba de acceso.
CA:116, DA:376, DE:1, EN:421, ES:117, FR:110, GA:108, IT:135, NE:343, PO:124.

118 doble corrección Método para evaluar el rendimiento por el cual dos personas evalúan por separado el rendimiento del candidato en una prueba.
Véase: calificación múltiple.
CA:84, DA:82, DE:91, EN:121, ES:118, FR:114, GA:221, IT:104, NE:116, PO:61.

119 dominio Area definida del contenido y/o capacidad que se examina mediante una actividad o componente específico de un examen.
Bibliografía adicional: Bachman, 1990, pp. 244–246.
CA:11, DA:83, DE:238, EN:119, ES:119, FR:113, GA:137, IT:332, NE:113, PO:129.

120 dominio Conocimiento de un idioma y grado de destreza en su utilización.
Compárese: capacidad, competencia.
Bibliografía adicional: Bachman, 1990, p. 16.
CA:296, DA:296, DE:47, EN:295, ES:120, FR:260, GA:265, IT:62, NE:305, PO:273.

121 dominio lingüístico Conocimiento de una lengua. Frecuentemente el término se emplea como sinónimo de "capacidad lingüística".
Bibliografía adicional: Bachman, 1990, p. 16.
CA:297, DA:355, DE:365, EN:206, ES:121, FR:66, GA:267, IT:66, NE:215, PO:81.

122 efecto de contaminación Efecto producido por un evaluador cuando éste asigna una puntuación en función de un factor que no es el factor examinado. Un ejemplo sería el aumento de la puntuación del candidato en una prueba de expresión escrita debido a la claridad de su caligrafía.
Véase: efectos evaluadores.
CA:118, DA:9, DE:226, EN:71, ES:122, FR:136, GA:174, IT:141, NE:74, PO:132.

123 efecto de la práctica Efecto en las puntuaciones de pruebas causado por la familiaridad del candidato con los tipos de actividades o con los items de una prueba.
CA:119, DA:443, DE:419, EN:289, ES:123, FR:138, GA:169, IT:140, NE:298, PO:131.

124 efecto de rebote (washback) Véase la definición de repercusión.
CA:372, DA:436, DE:442, EN:435, ES:124, FR:322, GA:95, IT:147, NE:432, PO:135.

125 efecto de secuencia Efecto provocado por el evaluador y originado por el orden en que se llevan a cabo las evaluaciones.
Véase: efectos evaluadores.
CA:120, DA:329, DE:292, EN:360, ES:125, FR:142, GA:172, IT:148, NE:337, PO:136.

126 efecto del método Efecto causado en las puntuaciones por el método utilizado para examinar en vez de por la capacidad del candidato objeto de la medida.
CA:121, DA:229, DE:242, EN:233, ES:126, FR:139, GA:171, IT:142, NE:244, PO:134.

127 efecto halo Tendencia de los calificadores de pruebas subjetivas a dejarse influir por el rendimiento del candidato en ciertas actividades de la prueba y otorgar una puntuación o demasiado alta o demasiado baja en otra actividad.
Véase: efectos evaluadores.
CA:117, DA:118, DE:141, EN:161, ES:127, FR:137, GA:170, IT:139, NE:164, PO:133.

128 efecto suelo Efecto limítrofe resultante de una prueba que es demasiado difícil para cierto grupo de candidatos, por lo tanto todas las puntuaciones se agrupan en el límite inferior de la distribución.
Véase: efectos limítrofes.
CA:122, DA:42, DE:61/121, EN:146, ES:128, FR:141, GA:175, IT:144, NE:49, PO:130.

129 efecto techo Efecto limítrofe que resulta del hecho de que una prueba sea demasiado fácil para cierto grupo de candidatos, y por lo tanto sus puntuaciones se agrupen en la parte superior de la distribución.
Véase: efectos limítrofes.
CA:123, DA:219, DE:63/73, EN:44, ES:129, FR:140, GA:173, IT:145, NE:292, PO:137.

130 efectos evaluadores Fuente de errores en la valoración, resultado de ciertas tendencias de los evaluadores que afectan las puntuaciones que se dan a los candidatos de las pruebas. Por ejemplo, el efecto de contaminación, el efecto halo y el efecto de secuencia.
CA:124, DA:34, DE:425, EN:313, ES:130, FR:144, GA:176, IT:143, NE:35, PO:138.

131 efectos limítrofes Efectos que resultan del hecho de que una prueba sea o bien demasiado fácil o bien demasiado difícil para cierto grupo de candidatos. La puntuación tiende a acumularse en la parte superior de la distribución (efecto techo) o en la parte inferior (efecto suelo).
Véase: efecto techo, efecto suelo.
CA:125, DA:120, DE:139, EN:36, ES:131, FR:143, GA:177, IT:138, NE:163, PO:139.

132 ejemplares modelo Muestra de las respuestas de los candidatos que representan una determinada gama de capacidad. Se utilizan en la estandarización de los correctores.
CA:268, DA:370, DE:254, EN:338, ES:132, FR:118, GA:344, IT:330, NE:420, PO:10.

133 elaborador de pruebas Persona involucrada en el proceso de desarrollar y poner en marcha una prueba nueva.
CA:109, DA:405, DE:395, EN:399, ES:133, FR:145, GA:149, IT:149, NE:399, PO:141.

134 enfoque de comunicación real En la evaluación de lenguas, planteamiento por el que una prueba debe incluir tipos de actividades que se asemejen todo lo posible a la comunicación real. Por ejemplo, en un enfoque de vida real, el contenido de una prueba diseñada para evaluar la capacidad de los candidatos para seguir un curso académico en una lengua extranjera se basaría en un análisis de las necesidades del lenguaje y de las actividades lingüísticas que se desarollan normalmente en ese curso.
Véase: autenticidad.
Bibliografía adicional: Bachman, 1990, pp. 301–328.
CA:129, DA:433, DE:320, EN:322, ES:134, FR:345, GA:98, IT:23, NE:226, PO:349.

135 ensayo Etapa en la elaboración de actividades de prueba cuyo objetivo es averiguar si la prueba funciona tal como se esperaba. Se utiliza a menudo con actividades calificadas de manera subjetiva, como por ejemplo preguntas que implican redacción, y se administran a una población limitada.
Compárese: experimentación.
CA:26, DA:301, DE:104, EN:418, ES:135, FR:160, GA:436, IT:336, NE:303, PO:185.

136 entrevista oral La competencia

oral de un candidato se evalúa a menudo a través de la entrevista oral que puede variar desde una conversación totalmente libre entre el/los candidato/s y el/los examinador/es hasta una serie altamente estructurada de actividades orales.

CA:131, DA:150, DE:305, EN:263, ES:136, FR:148, GA:1, IT:92, NE:355, PO:143.

137 entrevista semi-directa/ simulada de dominio oral Prueba de dominio oral en la cual se proporciona el input por medio de una grabación en cinta y se graba la respuesta del candidato para su posterior evaluación.
Véase: prueba semi-directa.

CA:130, DA:348, DE:356, EN:370, ES:137, FR:392, GA:356, IT:93, NE:346, PO:144.

138 entrevistador En una prueba de expresión oral, es el examinador que explica la actividad, hace las preguntas y en general interactúa oralmente con el(los) candidato(s). El entrevistador puede asimismo valorar al (a los) candidato(s) y asignar la puntuación, o bien esto lo puede hacer un segundo examinador que sólo observa y no interactúa con el(los) candidato(s).
Compárese: calificador.

CA:213, DA:325, DE:125, EN:178, ES:138, FR:216, GA:72, IT:201, NE:155, PO:227.

139 enunciado de partida Estímulo escrito, normalmente una frase incompleta cuyo final el candidato tiene que proporcionar o seleccionar de entre varias opciones.
Compárese: clave de respuesta, opciones.
Véase: ítem de selección múltiple.

CA:276, DA:360, DE:29, EN:387, ES:139, FR:10, GA:160, IT:346, NE:359, PO:224.

140 equiparación equipercentil Método para equiparar las puntuaciones brutas de las pruebas por el cual las puntuaciones se consideran equiparadas si corresponden al mismo rango percentil en un grupo de candidatos.

CA:132, DA:440, DE:24, EN:127, ES:140, FR:36, GA:88, IT:150, NE:121, PO:43.

141 equiparación horizontal Proceso de situar las puntuaciones de dos pruebas de aproximadamente la misma dificultad en una sola escala con el fin de aplicar las mismas normas en ambas pruebas.
Compárese: equiparación vertical.
Véase: equiparación.

CA:133, DA:128, DE:149, EN:166, ES:141, FR:37, GA:89, IT:152, NE:170, PO:44.

142 equiparación lineal Planteamiento de equiparación por el cual la puntuación de una prueba es igualada a la puntuación de otra prueba. Las puntuaciones equivalentes en las pruebas son el mismo número de desviaciones estándar por encima o por debajo de la puntuación media de la prueba en que aparecen.
Bibliografía adicional: Crocker y Algina, 1986, pp. 457–461

CA:134, DA:216, DE:17, EN:212, ES:142, FR:38, GA:91, IT:151, NE:229, PO:45.

143 equiparación vertical Proceso de colocar las puntuaciones de dos pruebas de diferentes grados de dificultad en la misma escala.
Bibliografía adicional: Crocker y Algina, 1986, pp. 473–477.

CA:135, DA:432, DE:435, EN:434, ES:143, FR:39, GA:90, IT:153, NE:419, PO:46.

144 error En la teoría clásica de medición de puntuación real, la puntuación observada en una prueba consta de dos componentes: una puntuación real que refleja la capacidad de la persona, y una puntuación errónea que refleja el efecto de todos los demás factores no relacionados con la capacidad examinada. Es esperable que el error se produzca al azar, es decir de forma no sistemática. Adicionalmente puede haber factores en una prueba que afecten regularmente a la actuación de algunos individuos, causando errores sistemáticos o sesgos en el examen.
Compárese: sesgo.
Bibliografía adicional: Bachman, 1990, p. 167.

CA:136, DA:98, DE:116, EN:129, ES:144, FR:151, GA:122, IT:154, NE:124, PO:146.

145 error aleatorio Véase la definición de error.

CA:137, DA:408, DE:449, EN:306, ES:145, FR:152, GA:128, IT:156, NE:310, PO:147,

146 error de medida Véase la definición de error estándar de medida.

CA:138, DA:240/241, DE:239/240, EN:130/231, ES:146, FR:153, GA:123/130, IT:159, NE:242/243, PO:149.

147 error de muestreo En una investigación, el error introducido en el análisis estadístico causado por la selección de la muestra específica utilizada en el estudio (por ejemplo, cuando la muestra no es

representativa de la población).
Véase: población.
CA:139, DA:372, DE:381, EN:341, ES:147, FR:158, GA:129, IT:155, NE:370, PO:148.

148 error estándar de estimación Medida de la precisión existente al predecir una variable a partir de otra, por ejemplo en la regresión lineal. Proporciona intervalos de confianza para puntuaciones de criterio.
Véase: intervalo de confianza.
Bibliografía adicional: Hatch y Lazaraton, 1991, pp. 477–479.
CA:142, DA:361, DE:375, EN:380, ES:148, FR:156, GA:124, IT:163, NE:363, PO:152.

149 error estándar de medida En la teoría clásica de puntuación verdadera de pruebas, el error típico de medida (*Se*) es una indicación de la imprecisión de la medida. El tamaño del error típico de medida depende de la fiabilidad (r_{xx}) y de la desviación típica de las puntuaciones de la prueba (*Sx*) . La fórmula para calcular *Se* es:

$$Se = Sx \sqrt{(1-r)}.$$

Por ejemplo, un candidato que tiene una puntuación verdadera de T en una prueba con un error típico de medida de *Se*. Si el candidato hace repetidamente la prueba, el 68% de las veces la puntuación observada estará en el margen de variación T±*Se*, y el 95% de las veces estará en el margen de variación T±2*Se*.
Bibliografía adicional: Crocker y Algina, 1986, pp. 122–124.
CA:143, DA:364, DE:374, EN:381, ES:149, FR:157, GA:125, IT:12, NE:362, PO:153.

150 error tipo 1 En estadística, error de rechazar la hipótesis nula cuando de hecho es verdadera.
Compárese: error tipo 2.
Véase: hipótesis nula.
Bibliografía adicional: Hatch y Lazaraton, 1991, p. 224.
CA:140, DA:417, DE:9/117, EN:425, ES:150, FR:154, GA:126, IT:157, NE:405, PO:150.

151 error tipo 2 En estadística, error de aceptar la hipótesis nula, cuando de hecho es falsa.
Compárese: error tipo 1.
Véase: hipótesis nula.
Bibliografía adicional: Hatch y Lazaraton, 1991, p. 224.
CA:141, DA:418, DE:118, EN:426, ES:151, FR:155, GA:127, IT:158, NE:406, PO:151.

152 escala Conjunto de números o categorías para medir algo. Se distinguen cuatro tipos de escalas de medida: nominal, ordinal, de intervalo y de razón.
Bibliografía adicional: Crocker y Algina, 1986, pp. 46–49.
CA:144, DA:337, DE:352, EN:343, ES:152, FR:121, GA:308, IT:314, NE:326, PO:154.

153 escala absoluta Escala con un punto cero real, por ejemplo, una escala para medir la longitud. El punto cero absoluto no puede ser definido en la evaluación de lenguas, por lo tanto este tipo de escala no es aplicable.
Compárese: escala de intervalos, escala nominal, escala ordinal.
CA:145, DA:4, DE:433, EN:4, ES:153, FR:122, GA:112, IT:317, NE:2, PO:155.

154 escala categorial Escala utilizada para variables categoriales como sexo, lengua materna, profesión.
Compárese: escala de intervalos, escala nominal, escala ordinal, escala de razón.
CA:146, DA:170, DE:175, EN:42, ES:154, FR:123, GA:310, IT:318, NE:53, PO:156.

155 escala centil Escala ordinal, que se divide en 100 unidades o centiles. Si a alguien se le concede un valor centil de 95 significa que en una muestra típica de 100, dicha persona estaría por encima de otras 95. También denominada escala percentil.
Bibliografía adicional: Crocker y Algina, 1986, pp. 439–442; Guilford y Fruchter, 1981, pp. 38–41.
CA:151, DA:46, DE:300, EN:46, ES:155, FR:124, GA:311, IT:319, NE:54, PO:157.

156 escala común Manera de expresar las puntuaciones de dos o más pruebas en una escala común para permitir un contraste directo de los resultados de las mismas. Las puntuaciones de dos o más pruebas pueden ser expresadas en una escala común si las puntuaciones brutas han sido transformadas mediante un proceso estadístico, por ejemplo el de la equiparación de pruebas.
Bibliografía adicional: Bachman, 1990, pp. 340–344.
CA:147, DA:110, DE:131, EN:57, ES:156, FR:125, GA:86, IT:320, NE:148, PO:158.

157 escala de capacidad En la teoría de ítem-respuesta, escala de intervalos iguales en la que pueden situarse la capacidad de las personas y la dificultad de las

actividades de la prueba. También denominada escala zeta.
Bibliografía adicional: Bachman, 1990, p. 345.

CA:150, DA:3, DE:114, EN:3, ES:157, FR:128, GA:313, IT:322, NE:413, PO:159.

158 escala de intervalos Escala de medición en la cual la distancia entre dos unidades adyacentes de medida es la misma, pero en la que no existe ningún punto cero absoluto.
Compárese: escala categorial, escala nominal, escala ordinal, escala de razón.
Bibliografía adicional: Crocker y Algina, 1986, p. 48.

CA:148, DA:149, DE:161, EN:184, ES:158, FR:126, GA:315, IT:315, NE:188, PO:162.

159 escala de intervalos iguales Véase la definición de escala de intervalos.

CA:149, DA:213, DE:161, EN:125, ES:159, FR:127, GA:316, IT:316, NE:145, PO:161.

160 escala de razón Escala en la cual existe el cero verdadero y la distancia entre dos puntos adyacentes es la misma para toda la escala. Por ejemplo, altura: una persona que mide 2 m de alto es el doble de alta que una persona que mide1 m.
Compárese: escala categorial, escala de intervalos, escala ordinal.
Bibliografía adicional: Crocker y Algina, 1986, pp. 48–49.

CA:153, DA:210, DE:433, EN:317, ES:160, FR:131, GA:312, IT:324, NE:314, PO:164.

161 escala de valoración Escala consistente en varias categorías jerárquicamente ordenadas y utilizadas para efectuar juicios subjetivos. En la evaluación de lenguas, las escalas de valoración para evaluar la producción lingüística vienen normalmente acompañadas por descriptores de banda que aclaran su interpretación.
Compárese: escala likert.
Véase: descriptor.

CA:154, DA:172, DE:58, EN:315, ES:161, FR:130, GA:319, IT:323, NE:40, PO:160.

162 escala delta Escala normalizada con una media de 13 y una desviación estándar de 4.

CA:155, DA:60, DE:75, EN:93, ES:162, FR:132, GA:314, IT:321, NE:94, PO:165.

163 escala likert Tipo de escala utilizada en cuestionarios para medir actitudes o opiniones. Los encuestados deben responder a una serie de enunciados, deben escoger una de entre las aproximadamente cinco posibles respuestas de tipo 'totalmente de acuerdo', 'de acuerdo', 'no sé', 'en desacuerdo', totalmente en desacuerdo', etc.

CA:152, DA:214, DE:222, EN:211, ES:163, FR:129, GA:317, IT:325, NE:228, PO:163.

164 escala nominal Escala utilizada con variables categoriales, como el sexo o la primera lengua. Dichas variables o están presentes o no lo están, y su interés reside en su frecuencia. También es conocida como escala categorial.
Compárese: escala de intervalos, escala ordinal, escala de razón.
Bibliografía adicional: Hatch y Lazaraton, 1991, pp 55–56.

CA:156, DA:249, DE:262, EN:248, ES:164, FR:133, GA:309, IT:326, NE:260, PO:166.

165 escala ordinal Tipo de escala de medidas que ordena a los candidatos sin indicar la distancia relativa entre cada uno.
Compárese: escala categorial, escala de intervalos, escala nominal, escala de razón.
Bibliografía adicional: Hatch y Lazaraton, 1991, pp. 56–57.

CA:157, DA:271, DE:275, EN:265, ES:165, FR:134, GA:318, IT:327, NE:275, PO:167.

166 escala zeta Véase la definición de escala de capacidad.

CA:158, DA:407, DE:413, EN:413, ES:166, FR:128, GA:320, IT:328, NE:385, PO:168.

167 escalonamiento Proceso de elaboración de escalas para la medición. En la evaluación de lenguas, implica asociar números a la actuación de los candidatos, para así reflejar los niveles crecientes de conocimiento o capacidad. El escalonamiento puede suponer la modificación de un grupo de puntuaciones para producir una escala siguiendo un propósito determinado, por ejemplo, informar de los resultados de una prueba de forma estandarizada, o equiparar una versión de una prueba con otra.
Véase: escala, escala de capacidad, escala centil, escala común, escala de intervalos, escala nominal, escala ordinal, escala de valoración, escala de razón, formas equiparadas, equiparación lineal.

CA:159, DA:341, DE:355, EN:346,

ES:167, FR:135, GA:321, IT:109, NE:329, PO:169.

168 escáner Véase la definición de lectora óptica.

CA:160, DA:327, DE:336, EN:347, ES:168, FR:342, GA:322, IT:226, NE:325, PO:346.

169 especificaciones de examen Documentación detallada elaborada normalmente en el transcurso del proceso de diseñar una prueba o de revisar una prueba ya existente. Las especificaciones incluyen detalles sobre el diseño, contenido, nivel, tipos de items y actividades empleados, población a quien está dirigida, el uso que se hará de la prueba, etc. A menudo incluye también modelos de materiales.

CA:161, DA:401, DE:394, EN:404, ES:169, FR:346, GA:355, IT:120, NE:400, PO:171.

170 estabilidad Aspecto de la fiabilidad por el cual la estimación se basa en el enfoque test-retest. Está relacionada con la estabilidad de las puntuaciones de pruebas a lo largo del tiempo.
Véase: fiabilidad, fiabilidad test-retest.

CA:162, DA:359, DE:371, EN:378, ES:170, FR:79, GA:65, IT:337, NE:358, PO:173.

171 estadística Ciencia que trata sobre el manejo e interpretación de datos numéricos.

CA:164, DA:369, DE:378, EN:386, ES:171, FR:348, GA:362, IT:339, NE:366, PO:175.

172 estadística descriptiva Estadística empleada para la descripción de un conjunto de datos en términos de cantidades, distribución, valores medios, correlaciones con otros datos, etc. Se hace una distinción entre la estadística descriptiva y la estadística muestral o inferencial.
Compárese: estadística inferencial.

CA:165, DA:63, DE:51, EN:95, ES:172, FR:349, GA:365, IT:340, NE:95, PO:176.

173 estadística inferencial Estadística que va más allá de la información aportada por la estadística descriptiva y permite deducir la medida en que un conjunto individual de datos puede representar a una población más extensa de la cual es muestra.
Compárese: estadística descriptiva.

CA:166, DA:139, DE:338, EN:171, ES:173, FR:350, GA:364, IT:341, NE:175, PO:177.

174 estadístico Cantidad que contiene información expresada de forma numérica. En sentido estricto, un estadístico es una propiedad de un grupo de muestra, en contraste con un parámetro, que es una propiedad de una población. Normalmente, los estadísticos se designan con letras romanas y los parámetros con letras griegas. Por ejemplo, la desviación típica de una muestra se escribe s o SD, mientras que la de una población se escribe σ (sigma).
Compárese: parámetro.
Véase: población, muestra.

CA:163, DA:368, DE:379, EN:385, ES:174, FR:348, GA:363, IT:117, NE:367, PO:174.

175 estandarización Proceso para asegurar que los calificadores se atienen a un procedimiento acordado y aplican las escalas de valoración de forma apropiada.
Véase: calificador.

CA:167, DA:363, DE:373, EN:383, ES:175, NE:361, FR:162, GA:45, IT:338, PO:295.

176 estaninas Procedimiento para agrupar puntuaciones en nueve grupos basados en una distribución normal. Tanto en el grupo superior como en el grupo inferior se sitúa el 4% de los candidatos. El porcentaje de candidatos en cada grupo aparece ilustrado en el siguiente gràfico:

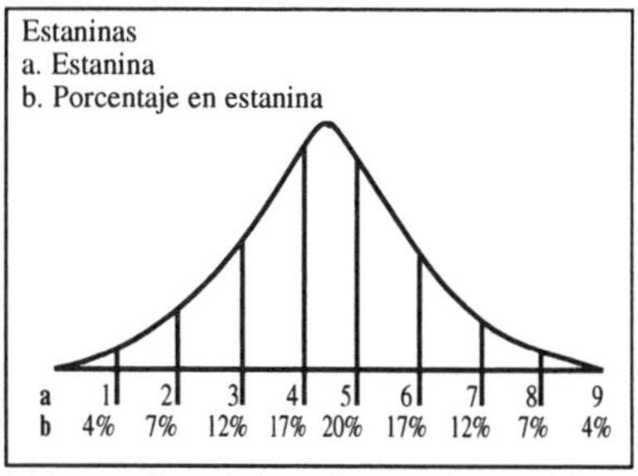

Bibliografía adicional: Crocker y Algina, 1986, pp. 446–447.

CA:344, DA:367, DE:377, EN:384, ES:176, FR:282, GA:332, IT:279, NE:365, PO:284.

177 estimación de fiabilidad por mitades de Spearman-Brown Véase la definición de fiabilidad por mitades.

CA:168, DA:350, DE:360, EN:372, ES:177, FR:161, GA:228, IT:342, NE:349, PO:178.

178 estímulo En pruebas de expresión escrita u oral, son los materiales gráficos o los textos que están diseñados para provocar una prespuesta del candidato.

CA:390, DA:316, DE:437 EN:299, ES:178, FR:95, GA:358, IT:343, NE:321, PO:179.

179 estudio piloto Estudio preliminar a través del cual los investigadores o elaboradores de exámenes ponen a prueba sus ideas en un número limitado de sujetos para poder localizar posibles problemas antes de entrar a fondo en una experimentación a gran escala, un programa, o un producto.
Véase: experimentación, ensayo.

CA:170, DA:286, DE:288, EN:281, ES:179, FR:163, GA:361, IT:344, NE:290, PO:180.

180 evaluación a)Recogida sistemática de datos con el propósito de utilizarlos como base para la toma de decisiones. En los exámenes de lenguas, la evaluación puede centrarse en la eficacia o impacto de un programa de enseñanza, de un examen o de un proyecto.

b)En la evaluación de lenguas, la medición de uno o de más aspectos de dominio lingüístico, mediante algún tipo de prueba o procedimiento.
Bibliografía adicional: Bachman, 1990, p.50.

CA:31, DA:30/93, DE:54/106, EN:21/132, ES:180, FR:165, GA:229/235, IT:413/421, NE:39/126, PO:30.

181 evaluación adaptativa informatizada Método de evaluación con base informatizada en el cual el nivel de dificultad de los items presentados al candidato puede ser adaptado a la capacidad del candidato, en función de las respuestas dadas.
Véase: evaluación con base informatizada.

CA:303, DA:51, DE:67, EN:63, ES:181, FR:362, GA:379, IT:386, NE:68, PO:364.

182 evaluación con base informatizada Método de evaluación en el cual los items son presentados al candidato en ordenador. También las respuestas pueden efectuarse por medio de ordenador.

CA:332, DA:52, DE:68, EN:64, ES:182, FR:171, GA:380, IT:387, NE:70, PO:35.

183 evaluación de competencia mínima Enfoque de la evaluación en el que se plantean requisitos específicos para un nivel mínimo de competencia en un campo particular del uso de una lengua. Un candidato que puede demostrar este nivel de competencia aprueba el examen.

CA:312, DA:398, DE:304, EN:234, ES:183, FR:167, GA:378, IT:388, NE:246, PO:31.

184 evaluación formativa a) Prueba que casi siempre tiene lugar a lo largo de un curso o programa de enseñanza en vez de al final del mismo. Los resultados pueden permitirle al profesor aportar una ayuda correctiva en una etapa temprana o cambiar el enfoque del curso si es necesario.

b) Evaluación continua de un proceso que permite la adaptación y mejora de dicho proceso a medida que continúe. Puede referirse a un programa de enseñanza.
Compárese: evaluación sumativa.

CA:32, DA:225/226, DE:46/213, EN:147/148, ES:184, FR:168, GA:232/236, IT:414/422, NE:136/137, PO:32.

185 evaluación por carpeta de trabajo Técnica de evaluación en la cual un candidato recoge muestras de su trabajo a lo largo de un periodo y las presenta como pruebas de su capacidad.

CA:386, DA:293, DE:291, EN:286, ES:185, FR:304, GA:237, IT:270, NE:37, PO:309.

186 evaluación sumativa a) Evaluación de un proceso que tiene lugar después de que éste se haya completado. Puede referirse a un programa de instrucción.

b) Examen que tiene lugar al final de un curso o programa de instrucción.
Compárese: evaluación formativa.

CA:34, DA:266/267, DE:3/4, EN:391/390, ES:186, FR:172, GA:233/238, IT:415/423, NE:374/375, PO:36.

187 evaluador Véase la definición de calificador.

CA:361, DA:306, DE:100, EN:311, ES:187, FR:164, GA:287, IT:102, NE:34, PO:182.

188 examen Procedimiento para comprobar el dominio o conocimientos de los individuos mediante actividades orales y/o escritas. La obtención de una cualificación (por ej. un certificado), la admisión a una institución educativa o programa de estudios, etc. pueden depender del resultado.
Compárese: prueba.
Bibliografía adicional: Bachman, 1990, p. 50.

CA:171, DA:86, DE:303, EN:133, ES:188, FR:173, GA:347, IT:164, NE:127, PO:181.

189 examinador Véase la definición de calificador.

CA:172, DA:89, DE:301, EN:135, ES:189, FR:174, GA:346, IT:165, NE:130, PO:182.

190 examinando Véase la definición de candidato.

CA:100, DA:87/402, DE:307/407, EN:134/406, ES:190, FR:351, GA:110/345, IT:49, NE:129/395, PO:183.

191 experimentación Etapa del desarrollo de materiales de examen en la cual se experimentan los items con muestras representativas de la población meta para determinar su dificultad. Después del análisis estadístico, aquellos items considerados satisfactorios pueden ser utilizados en pruebas vivas.
Compárese: ensayo.

CA:174, DA:105, DE:436, EN:293, ES:191, FR:307, GA:289, IT:273, NE:302, PO:311.

192 expresión escrita Actividad que requiere que el candidato elabore un texto escrito de cierta extensión. El texto puede ser de tipo narrativo, descriptivo o argumentativo. Pueden incluirse asimismo informes, cartas formales e informales. Se denomina también redacción.

CA:366, DA:109, DE:32, EN:62, ES:192, FR:73, GA:51, IT:82, NE:372, PO:88.

193 facetas de métodos de examen Véase la definición de características de métodos de examen.

CA:175, DA:396, DE:402, EN:403, ES:193, FR:176, GA:163, IT:50, NE:397, PO:186.

194 factor G En la teoría de la inteligencia, se trata de un "factor general" que en las hipótesis subyace a todas las capacidades cognitivas. Esta noción fue popularizada por John Oller durante los años 70 como testimonio de una competencia unitaria subyacente al dominio del lenguaje.
Bibliografía adicional: Oller, 1979, pp. 426–458; Bachman, 1990, p. 6.

CA:176, DA:113, DE:127, EN:153, ES:194, FR:177, GA:136, IT:170, NE:139, PO:187.

195 factores afectivos Factores de tipo no cognitivo relacionados con las variables emotivas, preferencias y actitudes de los candidatos.
Compárese: factores cognitivos.
Bibliografía adicional: Ebel y Frisbie, 1991, p. 52.

CA:177, DA:6, DE:7, EN:9, ES:195, FR:178, GA:399, IT:172, NE:6, PO:188.

196 factores cognitivos En el proceso de aprendizaje o de evaluación, factores relacionados con los esquemas y modelos de conocimiento del estudiante.
Compárese: factores afectivos.
Bibliografía adicional: Ebel y Frisbie, 1991, p. 52.

CA:178, DA:177, DE:180, EN:55, ES:196, FR:179, GA:398, IT:171, NE:65, PO:189.

197 familiaridad con el formato de la prueba Conocimiento previo del formato de una prueba o experiencia en hacer pruebas que permite a los candidatos a rendir por encima de su verdadero nivel de capacidad.

CA:179, DA:406, DE:396, EN:408, ES:197, FR:314, GA:161, IT:167, NE:401, PO:191.

198 fiabilidad La consistencia o estabilidad de las medidas de una prueba. Cuanto más fiable es una prueba, menos errores aleatorios contiene. Una prueba que contiene errores sistemáticos, por ej, un sesgo en contra de cierto grupo, puede que sea fiable, pero no válida.
Compárese: validez.
Véase: KR-20 (Fórmula 20 de Kuder-Richardson), alfa (coeficiente alfa), fiabilidad por mitades, fiabilidad test-retest.
Bibliografía adicional: Bachman, 1990, p. 24; Crocker y Algina, 1986, cap. 6.

CA:180, DA:312, DE:322/453, EN:327, ES:198, FR:183, GA:200, IT:6, NE:43, PO:193.

199 fiabilidad inter-evaluador Estimación de la fiabilidad de una prueba basada en el nivel de acuerdo de los distintos evaluadores en sus valoraciones del rendimiento del candidato.
Véase: acuerdo inter-evaluador, fiabilidad.

CA:181, DA:145, DE:158, EN:182, ES:199, FR:185, GA:201, IT:8, NE:184, PO:195.

200 fiabilidad intra-evaluador Estimación de la fiabilidad de una valoración basada en la medida en que el mismo evaluador puntúa el mismo rendimiento de forma similar en distintas ocasiones.
Véase: acuerdo intra-evaluador, fiabilidad.

CA:182, DA:151, DE:162, EN:186, ES:200, FR:187, GA:202, IT:89, NE:189, PO:196.

201 fiabilidad por mitades Medida de consistencia interna de la fiabilidad. La estimación se basa en la correlación entre las puntuaciones de las dos mitades de una prueba, consideradas como dos pruebas distintas. La división en dos mitades puede

realizarse de varias maneras: por ejemplo, la parte de arriba, la parte de abajo o al colocar los items de números pares en una mitad y los items de números impares en la otra mitad.
Véase: fiabilidad.
Bibliografía adicional: Ebel y Frisbie, 1991, pp. 82–83; Crocker y Algina, 1986, pp. 136–138.
CA:183, DA:259, DE:364/398, EN:377, ES:201, FR:184, GA:203, IT:7, NE:353, PO:194.

202 fiabilidad test-retest Estimación de la fiabilidad obtenida al pasar la misma prueba a los mismos candidatos en las mismas condiciones y al correlacionar las puntuaciones de las dos convocatorias. Se relaciona con la estabilidad de las puntuaciones a lo largo del tiempo; también se utiliza apropiadamente cuando no son posibles las estimaciones de consistencia interna.
Compárese: consistencia interna
Véase: fiabilidad, estabilidad.
CA:184, DA:318, DE:409/325, EN:410, ES:202, FR:188, GA:204, IT:9, NE:383, PO:197.

203 formas alternativas Véase la definición de formas equivalentes.
CA:185, DA:12, DE:11, EN:11, ES:203, NE:13, FR:193, GA:146, IT:176, PO:199.

204 formas equiparadas Diferentes formas de una prueba cuyas distribuciones de puntuación han sido transformadas para poder ser utilizadas de forma intercambiable.
Bibliografía adicional: Crocker y Algina, 1986, cap. 20.
CA:186, DA:442, DE:16/14, EN:126, ES:204, FR:194, GA:145, IT:177 NE:141, PO:200.

205 formas equivalentes Distintas versiones de la misma prueba consideradas equivalentes ya que se basan en las mismas especificaciones y miden la misma competencia. Para cumplir con los requisitos estrictos de la equivalencia en la teoría clásica de examen, las distintas formas de una prueba deben tener la misma dificultad media, varianza y covarianza cuando se administra a las mismas personas. En la práctica es muy difícil lograr la equivalencia. También denominadas formas alternativas o formas paralelas.
Compárese: formas equiparadas.
Bibliografía adicional: Crocker y Algina, 1986, p. 132.
CA:187, DA:441, DE:25, EN:128 ES:205, FR:195, GA:143, IT:178, NE:122, PO:201.

206 formas paralelas Véase la definición de formas equivalentes.
CA:188, DA:275, DE:278, EN:268, ES:206, FR:196, GA:144, IT:179, NE:279, PO:202.

207 fórmula predictora de Spearman-Brown Medio estadístico para estimar la fiabilidad de una prueba cuando ésta es ampliada o reducida al añadir o al eliminar items. Se puede utilizar para predecir el número de items necesarios para alcanzar una fiabilidad específica.
Bibliografía adicional: Crocker y Algina 1986, pp. 118–119.
CA:83, DA:349, DE:359, EN:371, ES:207, FR:197, GA:147, IT:180, NE:350, PO:203.

208 frecuencia acumulada Manera de presentar la distribución de los candidatos mediante el recuento, en cada categoría de puntuación, del número de candidatos que han obtenido una puntuación en dicha categoría y en todas las categorías inferiores.
Bibliografía adicional: Guilford y Fruchter, 1981, pp. 35–36.
CA:189, DA:208, DE:202, EN:86, ES:208, FR:198, GA:239, IT:181, NE:91, PO:204.

209 funcionamiento del ítem diferencial El hecho de que la dificultad relativa de un ítem dependa de alguna característica del grupo al cual ha sido administrado, tal como la lengua materna o el sexo.
Véase: sesgo.
CA:195, DA:66, DE:78, EN:100, ES:209, FR:192, GA:114, IT:182, NE:100, PO:208.

210 función de respuesta al ítem En la teoría ítem-respuesta, es una función matemática que relaciona la probabilidad de contestar correctamente a un ítem con la capacidad en el rasgo medido por dicho ítem. Se denomina también función característica del ítem.
CA:193, DA:158, DE:172, EN:194, ES:210, FR:189, GA:140, IT:183, NE:200, PO:205.

211 función informativa de prueba En TRI, índice de cuánta información proporciona una prueba sobre una persona de un nivel de capacidad dado. Es la suma de las funciones informativas de items.
Compárese: función informativa de ítem.
Bibliografía adicional: Crocker y Algina, 1986, pp. 369–371.
CA:194, DA:388, DE:399, EN:400, ES:211, FR:191, GA:139, IT:185, NE:394, PO:207.

212 función informativa del ítem

En la TRI (teoría de respuesta al ítem) es un índice de la cantidad de información que un ítem o prueba aporta acerca de una persona con un nivel determinado de capacidad; depende de la discriminación del ítem, y de su equiparación al nivel.
Compárese: función informativa de prueba.
CA:192, DA:156, DE:169, EN:193, ES:212, FR:190, GA:138, IT:184, NE:197, PO:206.

213 grupo de referencia Muestra extraída a partir de una población claramente definida de candidatos, que sirve para normalizar un examen.
Véase: norma.
CA:196, DA:309, DE:267, EN:324, ES:213, FR:202, GA:166, IT:189, NE:316, PO:212.

214 grupo normativo Normalmente un grupo grande de individuos representativo de las personas para quienes se está diseñando una prueba. El rendimiento del grupo normativo se utiliza en la interpretación de una prueba referida a una norma. También conocido como grupo de referencia.
Véase: prueba normativa.
CA:197, DA:254, DE:266, EN:251, ES:214, FR:203, GA:264, IT:190, NE:265, PO:213.

215 guión del entrevistador Indicaciones sobre el lenguaje que el entrevistador debe utilizar al dirigir una prueba de expresión oral. El propósito es estandarizar el lenguaje escuchado por todos los candidatos, haciendo así que la prueba sea más justa y fiable.
CA:198, DA:324, DE:438, EN:179, ES:215, FR:34, GA:151, IT:128, NE:156, PO:321.

216 hablante nativo Hablante de una lengua adquirida como primera lengua.
CA:286, DA:234, DE:255, EN:245, ES:216, FR:217, GA:47, IT:265, NE:255, PO:190.

217 hipótesis nula Hipótesis que afirma que dos o más variables no están relacionadas entre sí. Por ejemplo, la suposición de que en una prueba no hay diferencias entre el rendimiento de miembros de dos grupos de lengua materna diferente es una hipótesis nula. La hipótesis nula no puede ser aceptada; puede ser rechazada o no rechazada.
Bibliografía adicional: Hatch y Lazaraton, 1991, p. 24; Guilford y Fruchter, 1981, pp. 146–147.
CA:202, DA:255, DE:271, EN:255, ES:217, FR:206, GA:167, IT:206, NE:266, PO:214.

218 histograma Representación gráfica de una distribución de frecuencia en la cual el número de casos por clase de frecuencia se muestra en forma de barra vertical.

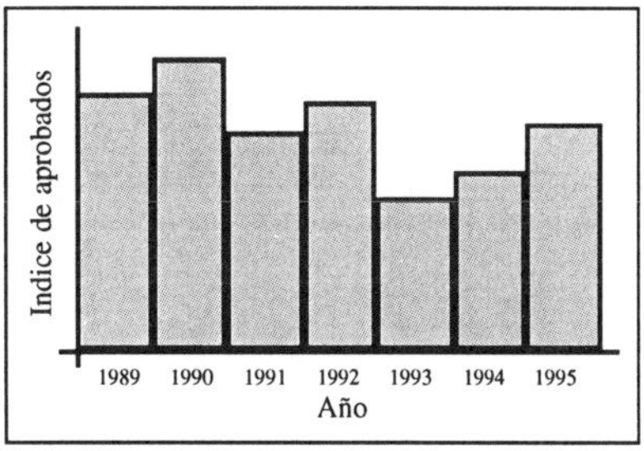

Compárese: diagrama de barras (tabla).
CA:203, DA:125, DE:145, EN:163, ES:218, FR:204, GA:168, IT:207, NE:167, PO:215.

219 hoja de respuestas a)Papel en el cual el candidato anota sus respuestas.

b) Papel en el que el candidato responde a lo solicitado en una pregunta abierta.
Compárese: lectora óptica.
CA:191, DA:37261/, DE:22/341, EN:19/350, ES:219, FR:181/343, GA:152/343, IT:174/175, NE:20/218, PO:170/198.

220 hoja/cuadernillo de preguntas Se utiliza a veces para referirse a una hoja o un cuadernillo en el que se presenta una prueba.
CA:239, DA:263, DE:123, EN:304, ES:220, FR:180, GA:271, IT:169, NE:425, PO:145.

221 homogeneidad Rasgo de una prueba o subprueba por el cual los items miden la misma competencia, o rasgo de un grupo por el cual los individuos comparten las mismas características. El nivel de homogeneidad se expresa mediante el índice de fiabilidad.
CA:204, DA:127, DE:148, EN:165, ES:221, FR:205, GA:22, IT:257, NE:169, PO:216.

222 impacto Efecto creado por un examen, referido a su influencia tanto sobre los procesos educativos generales como sobre las personas afectadas por los resultados del examen.

Véase: repercusión (backwash), efecto de rebote (washback).
CA:205, DA:303, DE:444, EN:167, ES:222, FR:207, GA:391, IT:191, NE:171, PO:217.

223 índice D Indice de discriminación para los items de una prueba. A menudo se utiliza en pruebas a pequeña escala en la clase, puesto que se puede calcular a mano. Basándose en la puntuación total de la prueba se selecciona un grupo superior y un grupo inferior de manera que cada grupo comprenda entre el 10% y el 33% de los examinandos. Para puntuaciones de distribución normal lo óptimo es utilizar el 27% en cada grupo. Las respuestas a cada ítem por parte de los examinandos de cada grupo se cuentan, y en el caso de un ítem que discrimina bien, el grupo superior puntuará más alto que el grupo inferior. La fórmula siguiente refleja el índice de discriminación de ítem:

$$D = P_s - P_i$$

donde P_s es la fracción del grupo de puntuación superior que ha contestado correctamente y donde P_i es la fracción del grupo de puntuación inferior que ha contestado correctamente. En general, los items con un índice igual o superior a 0,3 se consideran buenos discriminantes.
CA:206, DA:59, DE:72, EN:91, ES:223, FR:208, GA:186, IT:194, NE:92, PO:218.

224 índice de dificultad En la teoría clásica de examen, la dificultad de un ítem es la proporción (p) de candidatos que lo contestan de forma correcta. Esto significa que el índice de dificultad del ítem depende de la muestra, y varía según el nivel de capacidad de los candidatos.
Compárese: índice de facilidad, valor-*p*.
CA:207, DA:378, DE:343, EN:101, ES:224, FR:209, GA:187, IT:196, NE:249, PO:219.

225 índice de facilidad Proporción de respuestas correctas a un ítem, expresada en una escala de 0 a 1. A veces se expresa también como porcentaje. También denominado valor de facilidad o valor-*p*.
Compárese: índice de dificultad.
CA:209, DA:191, DE:208, EN:141, ES:225, FR:210, GA:188, IT:197, NE:146, PO:220.

226 índice de legibilidad Medida de la complejidad gramatical y léxica que se utiliza para evaluar hasta qué punto los lectores consideran que un texto es comprensible. Ejemplos de índices de legibilidad son el índice de Gunning y la escala de legibilidad de Flesch.
CA:210, DA:222, DE:219, EN:320, ES:226, FR:211, GA:189, IT:198, NE:223, PO:221.

227 índice medio de dificultad de un ítem (p media) Proporción media correcta para todos los items en una escala de items puntuados dicotómicamente. Por ejemplo, una puntuación media de 0,5 significa que el índice medio de facilidad de la prueba es de 0,5.
Véase: puntuación dicotómica.
CA:208, DA:132, DE:246, EN:228, ES:227, FR:212, GA:190, IT:195 NE:150, PO:222.

228 input Material aportado en una actividad de examen para que el candidato lo utilice en la producción de una respuesta adecuada. En una prueba de comprensión oral, por ejemplo, puede ser un texto grabado y varios items escritos asociados.
CA:169, DA:142, DE:408, EN:174, ES:228, FR:147, GA:199, IT:199, NE:180, PO:254.

229 instrucciones específicas Las instrucciones que se dan a los candidatos para guiar sus respuestas en una actividad de la prueba en particular.
Compárese: instrucciones generales.
CA:384, DA:264, DE:23, EN:336, ES:229, FR:78, GA:295, IT:193, NE:219, PO:92.

230 instrucciones generales Directrices generales que se proporcionan a los candidatos, por ejemplo, en la primera página de la hoja de respuestas o del cuadernillo de examen, con información acerca de la duración del examen, del número de actividades, de dónde debe escribir las respuestas, etc.
Compárese: norma.
CA:211, DA:143, DE:391, EN:175, ES:230, FR:214, GA:402, IT:208, NE:181, PO:225.

231 intercepción-Y En la regresión lineal, el punto en que la línea de regresión atraviesa el eje vertical (Y).
Véase: regresión lineal.
CA:212, DA:438, DE:146, EN:441, ES:231, FR:215, GA:181, IT:200, NE:438, PO:226.

232 intervalo La diferencia entre dos puntos en una escala.
CA:214, DA:148, DE:160, EN:183, ES:232, FR:218, GA:131, IT:203, NE:187, PO:228.

233 intervalo de confianza Area correspondiente a un valor estimado dentro de la cual probablemente se encontrará el valor real. El grado de probabilidad se define generalmente en niveles de confianza de 95% ó 99%.

CA:215, DA:182, DE:184, EN:67, ES:233, FR:219, GA:132, IT:204, NE:45, PO:229.

234 invariancia En TRI (teoría de respuesta al ítem), la presuposición importante de que la dificultad del ítem y las medidas de discriminación son rasgos inherentes que no dependen de la habilidad de los candidatos, al igula que las medidas de capacidad no dependen de los items concretos utilizados.

CA:216, DA:152, DE:164, EN:187, ES:234, FR:220, GA:120, IT:205, NE:191, PO:230.

235 ítem Todo elemento evaluado en una prueba que se puntúa por separado. Por ejemplo: un hueco en un "cloze test"; una pregunta de selección múltiple con tres o cuatro opciones; una oración para su transformación gramatical; una pregunta para la cual se espera una respuesta en forma de oración.
Compárese: actividad.

CA:217, DA:154, DE:166, EN:189, ES:235, FR:221, GA:240, IT:209, NE:195, PO:231.

236 ítem basado en un texto ítem basado en un fragmento de discurso con sentido completo, por ejemplo, items de selección múltiple basados en un texto de lectura.
Véase: ítem discreto.

CA:219, DA:387, DE:412, EN:412, ES:236, FR:226, GA:254, IT:213, NE:269, PO:233.

237 ítem de anclaje ítem incluido en dos o más pruebas. Los items de anclaje tienen características conocidas y forman parte de una nueva versión de un examen con el fin de proporcionar información sobre este examen y sobre los candidatos que lo han realizado; por ejemplo, para calibrar un nuevo examen en una escala de medición.

CA:218, DA:16, DE:18, EN:15, ES:237, FR:225, GA:241, IT:212, NE:17, PO:232.

238 ítem de completar Tipo de ítem en el cual el candidato debe completar una oración o un sintagma, normalmente mediante la inserción de varias palabras o la aportación de detalles, tales como horas o números de teléfono.

CA:226, DA:421, DE:102, EN:60, ES:238, FR:223, GA:243, IT:215, NE:193, PO:234.

239 ítem de enlace Véase la defininción de ítem de anclaje.

CA:221, DA:218, DE:432, EN:215, ES:239, FR:231, GA:250, IT:214, NE:232, PO:244.

240 ítem de formación de palabras Tipo de ítem en el cual el candidato tiene que producir una forma de una palabra basada en otra forma de la misma palabra que se le da como input. Ejemplo: "Este tipo de trabajo requiere un/una . . . . del vocabulario técnico. (comprender)".

CA:227, DA:269, DE:445, EN:439, ES:240, FR:227, GA:244, IT:216, NE:437, PO:237 .

241 ítem de rellenar huecos Cualquier tipo de ítem en el que el candidato debe insertar material escrito – letras, cifras, palabras aisladas, frases, oraciones o párrafos – en huecos en un texto. La respuesta puede ser aportada por el candidato o elegida a partir de un conjunto de opciones.

CA:223, DA:138, DE:229, EN:151, ES:241, FR:317, GA:249, IT:78, NE:192, PO:235.

242 ítem de rellenar huecos de selección múltiple Tipo de ítem de prueba en el cual la tarea del candidato consiste en seleccionar de un conjunto de opciones la palabra o locución correcta para insertar en el hueco de un texto.

CA:224, DA:237, DE:250, EN:239, ES:242, FR:386, GA:215, IT:79, NE:251, PO:390.

243 ítem de respuesta corta ítem abierto que requiere que el candidato formule una respuesta escrita de una palabra o frase.

CA:228, DA:198, DE:205, EN:362, ES:243, FR:224, GA:246, IT:311, NE:209, PO:238.

244 ítem de selección múltiple Tipo de ítem de examen que consiste en una pregunta o frase incompleta (enunciado de partida) junto con una serie de alternativas para responder o completar la frase (opciones). La tarea del candidato consiste en elegir la opción correcta (clave) de un conjunto de tres, cuatro o cinco posibilidades y no implica ninguna producción lingüística. Por eso, los items de selección múltiple se utilizan normalmente en pruebas de comprensión auditiva y escrita. Pueden ser discretos o basados en textos.
Véase: ítem discreto, ítem basado en un

texto.
CA:220, DA:236, DE:249/234, EN:238, ES:244, FR:222, GA:247, IT:211, NE:252, PO:236.

245 ítem de transformación Véase la definición de transformación de frases.
CA:229, DA:413, DE:420, EN:416, ES:245, FR:403, GA:242, IT:217, NE:402, PO:239.

246 ítem discreto ítem auto-contenido. No se vincula a ningún texto, ni a otro ítem o material suplementario. Un ejemplo de un tipo de ítem utilizado de este modo es el de selección múltiple.
Compárese: ítem basado en un texto.
CA:230, DA:71, DE:421, EN:109, ES:246, FR:228, GA:253, IT:219, NE:106, PO:241.

247 ítem discreto específico ítem discreto que examina un aspecto específico de, por ej. estructura o vocabulario, y que no se vincula a ningún otro ítem. Las pruebas lingüísticas de puntos discretos se hicieron populares en los años 60, gracias sobre todo a Robert Lado.
Compárese: ítem integrador/ actividad integradora.
Véase: ítem discreto.
CA:225, DA:72, DE:82, EN:110, ES:247 FR:229, GA:251, IT:210, NE:107, PO:240.

248 ítem escalar Véase la definición de puntuación politómica.
CA:222, DA:342, DE:27, EN:342, ES:248, FR:230, GA:252, IT:220, NE:328, PO:242.

249 ítem integrador/ actividad integradora Utilizado para denominar items o actividades que requieren más de una destreza o sub-destreza para su realización. Por ejemplo: los items de un "cloze test", una entrevista oral, la lectura de una carta y la redacción de una contestación a dicha carta.
Compárese: ítem discreto específico.
CA:231, DA:144, DE:156, EN:176, ES:249, FR:316, GA:248, IT:221, NE:182, PO:245.

250 ítem Verdadero/Falso Tipo de ítem de respuesta seleccionada en el cual el candidato tiene que indicar si una serie de afirmaciones son verdaderas o falsas en relación a un texto.
CA:232, DA:326, DE:326, EN:419, ES:250, FR:429, GA:245, IT:218, NE:426, PO:243.

251 juego de simulación (role play) Tipo de actividad utilizada a veces en las pruebas de expresión oral en la que los candidatos tienen que imaginar que están en una determinada situación comunicativa o tienen que desempeñar un papel específico.
CA:233, DA:320, DE:329, EN:334, ES:251, FR:232, GA:294, IT:202, NE:323, PO:345.

252 KR-20 (Fórmula 20 de Kuder-Richardson) Véase la definición de Kuder-Richardson.
CA:234, DA:201, DE:194, EN:199, ES:252, FR:233, GA:205, IT:222, NE:210, PO:246.

253 KR-21 (Fórmula 21 de Kuder-Richardson) Véase la definición de Kuder-Richardson.
CA:235, DA:202, DE:195, EN:200 ES:253, FR:234, GA:206, IT:223, NE:211, PO:247.

254 Kuder-Richardson Dos índices de consistencia interna elaborados por Kuder y Richardson y utilizados para estimar la fiabilidad de la prueba. KR-21 requiere menos información y es más fácil de computar, pero en general produce un cálculo inferior a la KR-20.
Compárese: alfa (coeficiente alfa).
Véase: consistencia interna.
Bibliografía adicional: Henning, 1987, p. 84.
CA:236, DA:206, DE:200, EN:201, ES:254, FR:235, GA:207, IT:224, NE:212, PO:248.

255 lectora óptica Aparato electrónico que se utiliza para extraer información directamente de las hojas de respuesta o de calificaciones. Los candidatos o los examinadores pueden marcar las respuestas al ítem o a las actividades en una hoja de respuestas y esta información puede ser leída directamente por el ordenador. También conocido como escáner.
CA:242, DA:268, DE:274, EN:261, ES:255, FR:237, GA:214, IT:226, NE:274, PO:249.

256 lengua para fines específicos (LSP) Enseñanza o evaluación de lenguas que se centra en un área de la lengua empleada para una actividad o profesión determinados; por ejemplo, inglés para el control del tráfico aéreo, español comercial, etc.
CA:238, DA:95, DE:111, EN:205, ES:256, FR:236, GA:385, IT:227, NE:378, PO:251.

257 léxico Término utilizado para referirse al vocabulario.
CA:237, DA:212, DE:221, EN:210,

ES:257, FR:238, GA:213, IT:225, NE:227, PO:250.

258 lista de corroboración Lista de preguntas o puntos que han de ser contestados o analizados. Se utiliza a menudo en la evaluación de lenguas como instrumento de observación o análisis.

CA:240, DA:48, DE:64, EN:48, ES:258, FR:239, GA:351, IT:228, NE:58, PO:252.

259 logit En la teoría de respuesta al ítem, unidad de medida derivada del logaritmo natural de la relación entre la posibilidad de éxito y la posibilidad de fracaso, es decir, la probabilidad logarítmica. La diferencia en logits entre la capacidad de una persona y la dificultad de un ítem es la probabilidad logarítmica de esa persona de tener éxito con el ítem.
Bibliografía adicional: Henning 1987, pp. 118–126.

CA:241, DA:220, DE:227, EN:218, ES:259, FR:240, GA:216, IT:232, NE:234, PO:253.

260 margen de variación Medida de la dispersión de observaciones. El margen es la distancia entre la puntuación más alta y más baja.
Bibliografía adicional: Hatch y Lazaraton, 1991, pp. 169–170.

CA:12, DA:431, DE:431, EN:308, ES:260, FR:241, GA:285, IT:233, NE:311, PO:12.

261 media Medida de la tendencia central tambien conocida como promedio. La puntuación media en una convocatoria de examen se calcula al sumar todas las puntuaciones y dividirlas por el número total de puntuaciones.
Compárese: mediana, moda.
Véase: tendencia central (medida de).
Bibliografía adicional: Hatch y Lazaraton, 1991, pp. 161–163.

CA:250, DA:231, DE:244, EN:227, ES:261, FR:257, GA:226, IT:234, NE:151, PO:255.

262 media cuadrática Nombre dado a la varianza en el análisis de varianza (ANOVA).
Véase: ANOVA.

CA:251, DA:230, DE:245, EN:229, ES:262, FR:47, GA:227, IT:295, NE:149, PO:319.

263 mediana Puntuación en el centro de la distribución en un conjunto de puntuaciones ordenadas de menor a mayor. La mitad de las puntuaciones cae por encima de la mediana y la otra mitad cae por debajo.
Véase: tendencia central (medida de).
Compárese: media, moda.
Bibliografía adicional: Hatch y Lazaraton, 1991, p. 161.

CA:244, DA:228, DE:232, EN:232, ES:263, FR:242, GA:3, IT:235, NE:239, PO:256.

264 medida En general, proceso por el cual se encuentra la cantidad de algo al compararlo con una unidad fija, por ejemplo, usar una regla para medir la longitud. En ciencias sociales, la medida se refiere a menudo a la cuantificación de las características de los individuos, como por ejemplo el dominio lingüístico.
Bibliografía adicional: Bachman 1990, cap. 2.

CA:245, DA:242, DE:241, EN:230, ES:264, FR:243, GA:395, IT:238, NE:245, PO:257.

265 medida libre de muestra En una investigación, interpretación de los resultados que no depende de la muestra utilizada en un trabajo de investigación en particular.
Véase: muestra.

CA:247, DA:373, DE:382, EN:339, ES:265, FR:244, GA:396, IT:239, NE:371, PO:258.

266 método de examen La capacidad lingüística puede evaluarse usando diferentes métodos, como pueden ser: selección múltiple, cloze, composición, entrevista oral, etc. Puede observarse que existe una interacción entre el método de examen y la capacidad en la medida de la actuación lingüística.
Véase: características de métodos de examen.
Bibliografía adicional: Bachman, 1990, p. 77.

CA:248, DA:395, DE:401, EN:401, ES:266, FR:245, GA:257, IT:236, NE:396, PO:259.

267 método de representación delta Manera de considerar el funcionamiento del ítem diferencial. Se emplea para la identificación de items que aumentan o minimizan las diferencias de rendimiento del grupo, y se basa en las dificultades clásicas del ítem (valores-*p*). Los valores-*p* se convierten en puntuaciones *z* normalizadas y estos valores se representan en parejas en un gráfico con el fin de demostrar la dificultad relativa de los items para los dos grupos en cuestión.
Véase: funcionamiento del ítem diferencial (FID).
Bibliografía adicional: Crocker y Algina,

1986, pp. 388–390.
CA:249, DA:61, DE:74, EN:92, ES:267, FR:246, GA:256, IT:237, NE:93, PO:260.

268 moda Punto en la distribución de un conjunto de puntuaciones en el cual las puntuaciones aparecen con más frecuencia; el punto más alto de la curva de distribución.

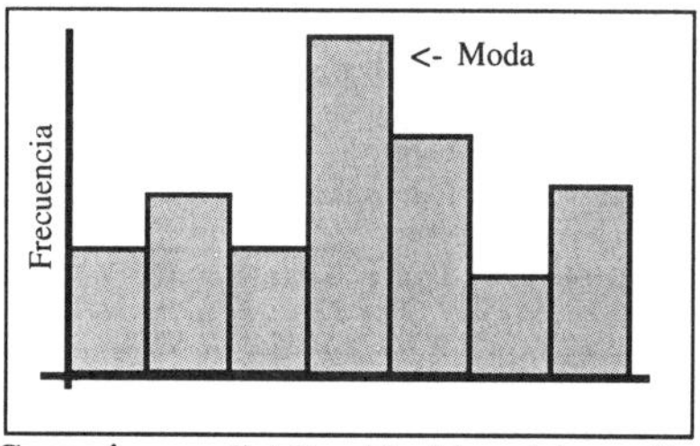

Compárese: distribución bimodal, media, mediana.
Véase: tendencia central (medida de).
Bibliografía adicional: Hatch y Lazaraton, 1991, pp. 160–161.
CA:252, DA:232, DE:247, EN:235, ES:268, FR:247, GA:255, IT:240, NE:248, PO:261.

269 modelo cognitivo Enfoque o teoría que tiene en cuenta la manera en que se estructura el conocimiento de una persona, tanto en lo que se refiere a los conceptos como a los procesos. Es importante en la evaluación de lenguas dado que esta teoría puede afectar a la elección del método o del contenido de la prueba.
CA:253, DA:178, DE:181, EN:56, ES:269, FR:250, GA:297, IT:243, NE:64, PO:262.

270 modelo de crédito parcial En la teoría de respuesta al ítem, modelo para tratar los datos escalares. Este sería un modelo apropiado para utilizar, por ejemplo, en el análisis de las respuestas a un número de items de completar frases que utilizan una escala; por ejemplo, 1,2 ó 3, para puntuar los items, o una entrevista oral que utiliza varias escalas para valorar la actuación.
Compárese: modelo de escala de valoración, modelo Rasch de facetas múltiples.
Véase: modelo Rasch.
Bibliografía adicional: Wright y Masters 1982, p. 40–48.
CA:257, DA:278, DE:281, EN:272, ES:270, FR:253, GA:301, IT:244, NE:282, PO:267.

271 modelo de dos parámetros En la teoría de respuesta al ítem, modelo que tiene en cuenta un parámetro de discriminación de ítem además del parámetro capacidad/dificultad.
Compárese: modelo de un parámetro, modelo Rasch.
Véase: teoría de respuesta al ítem (TRI).
CA:258, DA:411, DE:454, EN:424, ES:271, FR:248, GA:298, IT:241, NE:404, PO:264.

272 modelo de escala de valoración Extensión del modelo Rasch simple para tratar datos escalares, como los que se derivan, por ejemplo, de las evaluaciones de la producción oral.
Compárese: modelo Rasch.
Véase: modelo de crédito parcial.
Bibliografía adicional: Wright, B. D. y Masters, G. N, 1982, Rating Scale Analysis, Chicago, MESA Press.
CA:254, DA:173, DE:236, EN:316, ES:272, FR:251, GA:303, IT:246, NE:41, PO:263.

273 modelo de un parámetro En la teoría de respuesta al ítem, un modelo que opera con una única escala que representa la dificultad (de las actividades) y la capacidad (de las personas) y no tiene en cuenta ni la discriminación de items variables ni los aciertos por adivinación.
Compárese: modelo Rasch.
CA:255, DA:92, DE:99, EN:259, ES:273, FR:249, GA:296, IT:242, NE:118, PO:265.

274 modelo probabilístico Modelo en el cual las relaciones causales (por ejemplo, entre la dificultad del ítem y la capacidad del candidato para realizar el examen) son explicados en términos de grados de probabilidad. El modelo Rasch es un ejemplo de este tipo de modelo.
CA:262, DA:295, DE:297, EN:294, ES:274, FR:255, GA:299, IT:247, NE:430, PO:269.

275 modelo Rasch Modelo matemático, también conocido como modelo logístico sencillo, que plantea una relación entre la probabilidad de que una persona complete una actividad y la diferencia entre la capacidad de la persona y la dificultad de la actividad. Es el equivalente matemático del modelo de un parámetro en la teoría de ítem-respuesta. La utilización del modelo Rasch se ha extendido de varias maneras, por ej, para manejar las respuestas escalares, o las facetas múltiples que dan cuenta de la 'dificultad' de una actividad.
Véase: teoría de respuesta al ítem (TRI), modelo de crédito parcial, modelo de escala de valoración, modelo Rasch de facetas múltiples.

Bibliografía adicional: Henning, 1987 pp. 117–125.

CA:259, DA:305, DE:316, EN:310, ES:275, FR:252, GA:302, IT:248, NE:313, PO:266.

276 modelo Rasch de facetas múltiples Extensión del modelo Rasch que permite que se modelen las probabilidades de repuesta según una combinación aditiva de facetas. Por ejemplo, la producción lingüística en una actividad de redacción puede ser modelada para reflejar la dificultad de la actividad junto con la severidad del evaluador. El programa FACETS, por ejemplo, ha utilizado el modelo Rasch de facetas multiples
Véase: Modelo Rasch.
Bibliografía adicional: Linacre, J. M, 1989, Many-Facet Rasch Measurement, Chicago, MESA Press.

CA:260, DA:235, DE:289, EN:220, ES:276, FR:254, GA:300, IT:249, NE:236, PO:268.

277 moderación a) Parte del proceso de preparación de items o de actividades para su uso en una prueba. En esta etapa los materiales son examinados de forma crítica por varios expertos (creadores de pruebas y professores), que deciden si se aceptan (con posibles cambios o reformulaciones) o no.

b) En el proceso de evaluación, ajuste que hace un supervisor de las calificaciones otorgadas previamente por un calificador.
Compárese: selección.

CA:263, DA:410, DE:31, EN:237, ES:277, FR:256, GA:260, IT:250, NE:247, PO:270.

278 muestra Selección de un subconjunto de elementos de una población. Se pueden distinguir varios tipos de muestras, por ej, la muestra aleatoria, la muestra estratificada, etc.
Bibliografía adicional: Crocker y Algina, 1986, pp. 432–438; Guilford y Fruchter, 1981, pp. 44–45.

CA:264, DA:371, DE:380, EN:337, ES:278, FR:116, GA:304, IT:46, NE:369, PO:8.

279 muestra aleatoria Conjunto de elementos extraídos de manera no-selectiva de una población objeto de investigación de forma que todos los elementos de la población tengan las mismas oportunidades de ser seleccionado para la investigación.
Véase: muestra.
Bibliografía adicional: Crocker y Algina, 1986, pp. 433–438; Guilford y Fruchter, 1981, p. 120.

CA:265, DA:409, DE:451, EN:307, ES:279, FR:117, GA:305, IT:47, NE:120, PO:9.

280 muestra estratificada Muestra de una población investigada que primero es dividida en varias sub-poblaciones (capas, rangos, estratos), de cada una de las cuales se extrae después una muestra.
Véase: muestra.
Bibliografía adicional: Guilford y Fruchter, 1981, pp. 122–123.

CA:266, DA:375, DE:134, EN:388, ES:280, FR:119, GA:306, IT:48, NE:157, PO:11.

281 muestreo Selección de una muestra.
Véase: muestra.

CA:267, DA:374, DE:384, EN:340, ES:281, FR:120, GA:307, IT:45, NE:368, PO:313.

282 *N, n* Número. La *N* mayúscula se utiliza a menudo para designar el número de casos en un estudio o los individuos de una población, mientras que la *n* minúscula significa por lo general el número de una muestra o subgrupo. Por ejemplo: 'La prueba fue administrada a ingenieros de postgrado ($N = 600$) de los cuales el 10% eran mujeres ($n = 60$)'.

CA:269, DA:248, DE:256, EN:244, ES:282, FR:258, GA:261, IT:251, NE:259, PO:271.

283 nivel El grado de dominio exigido para que un alumno/a acceda a una clase determinada o el grado que representa un examen determinado a menudo se expresa mediante una serie de niveles. Por lo general se les designa con nombres como "elemental", 'intermedio', 'avanzado', etc.

CA:270, DA:247, DE:260, EN:209, ES:283, FR:259, GA:210, IT:229, NE:258, PO:272.

284 nivel Supervivencia Especificaciones sobre un nivel elemental de aptitud en lengua extranjera publicadas por primera vez por el Consejo de Europa en 1977 para la lengua inglesa y revisada en 1990. Aporta un objetivo menos exigente que el nivel Umbral (Threshold); se estima que tiene aproximadamente la mitad de carga de aprendizaje del nivel Umbral.
Compárese: nivel Umbral.

CA:271, DA:437, DE:443, EN:436, ES:284, FR:261, GA:211, IT:231, NE:433, PO:274.

285 nivel Umbral Importante especificación, en términos funcionales, de un nivel básico de competencia en una lengua extranjera. Fue publicado por el Consejo de Europa en 1976 para el inglés y puesto al día en 1990. Desde entonces se han producido versiones para varias lenguas europeas.

CA:272, DA:419, DE:414, EN:414, ES:285, FR:262, GA:212, IT:230, NE:386, PO:275.

286 norma Estándar de actuación lingüística. En una prueba estandarizada se determina la norma a partir de las puntuaciones obtenidas por un grupo grande. Se utilizan las normas o estándares basados en la actuación de ese grupo para evaluar la actuación de posteriores grupos de candidatos similares.
Véase: grupo normativo, prueba normativa.

CA:273, DA:250, DE:263, EN:250, ES:286, FR:264, GA:262, IT:252, NE:261, PO:278.

287 normalización Cambio de las puntuaciones de manera que se transforma la distribución en una distribución normal. En general, esto implica el uso de escalas equipercentiles.
Compárese: puntuación estándar.

CA:274, DA:253, DE:264, EN:253, ES:287, FR:263, GA:263, IT:253, NE:263, PO:279.

288 nota La puntuación en una prueba puede ser comunicada al candidato como una nota, por ejemplo utilizando una escala de A a E, donde A es la nota más alta posible, B es más que aprobado, C un aprobado, y D y E son suspensos.
Compárese: calificación.

CA:275, DA:167, DE:270, EN:156, ES:288, FR:259, GA:164, IT:188, NE:426, PO:272.

289 objetivo de evaluación del ítem Enfoque de un ítem: aspecto concreto sobre el cual un ítem intenta suscitar conocimientos.

CA:128, DA:399, DE:309, EN:409, ES:289, FR:300, GA:281, IT:293, NE:384, PO:307.

290 objetivo del aprendizaje Finalidad o resultado deseado de una actividad educativa.

CA:277, DA:136, DE:215, EN:208, ES:290, FR:289, GA:360, IT:255, NE:217, PO:292.

291 objetivos Conocimientos, competencia y actitudes que constituyen la finalidad declarada de cualquier tipo de curso educativo .

CA:278, DA:244, DE:216, EN:256, ES:291, FR:288, GA:359, IT:254, NE:112, PO:293.

292 opciones Gama de posibilidades en un ítem de selección múltiple o actividad de relacionar entre las cuales debe elegirse la correcta.

CA:279, DA:425, DE:38, EN:262, ES:292, FR:290, GA:293, IT:258, NE:14, PO:294.

293 parámetro Característica de una población, por ej, la desviación estándar de una población.
Compárese: estadística.

CA:280, DA:276, DE:279, EN:269, ES:293, FR:291, GA:272, IT:259, NE:280, PO:296.

294 parámetro A Parámetro de la teoría de respuesta al ítem relacionado con la discriminación de un ítem.
Véase: teoría de respuesta al ítem (TRI).
Bibliografía adicional: Bachman, 1990, p. 204.

CA:281, DA:1, DE:84, EN:1, ES:294, FR:292, GA:273, IT:260, NE:1, PO:297.

295 parámetro B Parámetro tomado de la teoría de respuesta al ítem que se relaciona con el grado de dificultad de un ítem.
Véase: teoría de respuesta al ítem (TRI).
Bibliografía adicional: Bachman, 1990, p. 204.

CA:282, DA:24, DE:170, EN:26, ES:295, FR:293, GA:274, IT:261, NE:26, PO:298.

296 parámetro C Parámetro de la teoría de respuesta al ítem relacionada con la posibilidad de acierto casual.
Véase: teoría de respuesta al ítem (TRI).
Bibliografía adicional: Bachman, 1990, p. 204.

CA:283, DA:44, DE:318, EN:37, ES:296, FR:294, GA:275, IT:262, NE:50, PO:299.

297 parámetro de acierto casual Véase la definición de parámetro C.

CA:284, DA:122, DE:319, EN:159, ES:297, FR:295, GA:277, IT:263, NE:160, PO:301.

298 parámetro de dificultad Véase la definición de parámetro B.

CA:285, DA:379, DE:344, EN:102, ES:298, FR:296, GA:276, IT:264, NE:250, PO:300.

299 percentil Los 99 puntos de escala que dividen una distribución de frecuencia en 100 grupos de igual tamaño. El percentil 50 (P50) se llama mediana. Los cuartiles

dividen la distribución en cuatro grupos iguales.
Bibliografía adicional: Hatch y Lazaraton, 1991, pp. 187–188.
CA:287, DA:280, DE:285, EN:275, ES:299, FR:49, GA:279, IT:266, NE:284, PO:302.

300 perfil Manera de presentar los resultados de una prueba desglosados en los varios apartados de la prueba, de forma que el candidato u otros usuarios de la prueba puedan identificar las areas de relativa fuerza y debilidad.
CA:288, DA:297, DE:404, EN:297, ES:300, FR:312, GA:282, IT:395, NE:307, PO:303.

301 plantilla de corrección Lista de todas las respuestas aceptables a los items de una prueba. La plantilla de corrección hace posible que un calificador asigne con precisión la puntuación a una prueba.
CA: 52/256, DA:319, DE:228, EN:223, ES:301, FR:29, GA:324, IT:329, NE:79, PO:172.

302 población El conjunto completo de valores, es decir, todos los candidatos posibles que hacen una prueba. En la estadística también se llama universo de puntuaciones.
Compárese: muestra.
CA:289, DA:292, DE:290, EN:285, ES:302, FR:303, GA:280, IT:269, NE:294, PO:308.

303 ponderación La asignación de un número diferente de puntos máximos a un ítem, actividad o componente de prueba para poder cambiar su contribución relativa con respecto a otras partes de la misma prueba. Por ejemplo, si se da una puntuación doble a todos los items en la Actividad Nº 1 de una prueba, la Actividad Nº 1 tendrá una mayor proporción de la puntuación total que las actividades restantes.
Bibliografía adicional: Ebel y Frisbie, 1991, pp. 214–216.
CA:290, DA:435, DE:136, EN:438, ES:303, FR:302, GA:439, IT:268, NE:434, PO:306.

304 pregunta Término que se utiliza a veces para designar una actividad o ítem en una prueba.
Véase: ítem, actividad.
CA:291, DA:357, DE:122, EN:303, ES:304, FR:315, GA:55, IT:136, NE:423, PO:323.

305 pregunta abierta Tipo de ítem o actividad en una prueba escrita que requiere que el candidato proporcione, no que elija, una respuesta. La finalidad de este tipo de ítem es solicitar una respuesta relativamente espontánea, que puede variar desde una palabra hasta una redacción extensa. El esquema de calificación permite, por consiguiente, una gama de respuestas aceptables.
CA:292, DA:444, DE:273, EN:260, ES:305, FR:318, GA:56, IT:137, NE:273, PO:324.

306 pregunta de redacción Véase la definición de composición.
CA:366, DA:262, DE:33, EN:131, ES:306, FR:159, GA:7, IT:313, NE:125, PO:142.

307 procedimientos de incitación Técnica para obtener una respuesta de un candidato en una prueba. Normalmente se utiliza en el contexto de una respuesta oral en una prueba de lengua hablada.
Bibliografía adicional: Hughes, 1989, pp. 104–110.
CA:293, DA:8, DE:212, EN:123, ES:307, FR:308, GA:162, IT:276, NE:320, PO:314.

308 procedimientos no-paramétricos Procedimientos estadísticos que suponen que los datos no proceden de ningún tipo particular de distribución, o que los datos no están basados en una escala de intervalos. El Chi-cuadrado es un buen ejemplo de esto.
Compárese: procedimientos paramétricos
Bibliografía adicional: Hatch y Lazaraton, 1991, pp. 237–239.
CA:294, DA:131, DE:259, EN:249, ES:308, FR:309, GA:258, IT:274, NE:257, PO:315.

309 procedimientos paramétricos Procedimientos estadísticos que suponen que los datos tienen una distribución normal y se miden en escalas de intervalo o de ratio. En realidad, se utilizan los procedimientos paramétricos cuando hay casos suficientes como para que los datos se aproximen a la distribución normal.
Compárese: procedimientos no-paramétricos
Bibliografía adicional: Hatch y Lazaraton, 1991, pp. 237–238.
CA:295, DA:277, DE:280, EN:270, ES:309, FR:310, GA:259, IT:275, NE:281, PO:316.

310 programa de estudios (syllabus) Documento detallado que enumera todas las áreas cubiertas en un programa de estudios determinado, y el orden en el que se presenta el contenido

Compárese: curriculum.

CA:299, DA:224, DE:207, EN:392, ES:310, FR:352, GA:352, IT:335, NE:225, PO:318.

311 prueba Procedimiento para evaluar aspectos específicos de dominio o conocimiento.

a) Conjunto de apartados que constituye un procedimiento de evaluación, frecuentemente utilizado con el mismo sentido que examen.

b) Actividad concreta o apartado para evaluar un área específica de destreza o conocimiento, por ejemplo la expresión oral o la expresión escrita. En este sentido, una prueba puede también constituir un apartado (ej. prueba de expresión oral) o una actividad individual (ej. prueba cloze) dentro de un examen completo.

c) Procedimiento de evaluación relativamente corto y fácil de administrar, que puede ser elaborado y utilizado en una determinada institución (ej. prueba de progreso) o formar parte de un programa de investigación o de validación (ej. una prueba de anclaje).
Compárese: examen.
Véase: prueba cloze (cloze test), prueba de progreso, prueba de anclaje.
Bibliografía adicional: Bachman, 1990, p. 50.

CA:300, DA:300, DE:389, EN:395, ES:311, FR:359, GA:403, IT:353, NE:388, PO:361.

312 prueba adaptativa Modalidad de prueba en la cual los items son seleccionados durante el desarrollo de la misma en función de su dificultad, como respuesta a la estimación de la capacidad del candidato. Frecuentemente este término se emplea para referirse a una prueba administrada por ordenador, aunque una entrevista oral puede ser también una prueba adaptativa.
Véase: evaluación adaptativa informatizada.
Bibliografía adicional: Bachman, 1990, p. 151; Henning, 1987, p. 136.

CA:302, DA:102, DE:6, EN:7, ES:312, FR:361, GA:429, IT:356, NE:5, PO:363.

313 prueba basada en el curriculum Prueba estrechamente vinculada a un programa específico de estudios y que desempeña un papel específico en los procesos educativos.
Compárese: prueba no basada en el curriculum.
Véase: prueba de aprovechamiento.

CA:325, DA:56, DE:217, EN:88, ES:313, FR:365, GA:406, IT:374, NE:221, PO:380.

314 prueba C Actividad del tipo "rellenar huecos" consistente en completar algunas palabras en las que la segunda mitad ha sido suprimida. La frecuencia de dicha supresión puede llegar a ser de una de cada dos palabras. La tarea del candidato es la de completar las palabras parcialmente suprimidas.
Compárese: prueba cloze (cloze test).
Bibliografía adicional: Weir 1990, p. 49.

CA:304, DA:45, DE:62, EN:38, ES:314, FR:394, GA:408, IT:384, NE:51, PO:366.

315 prueba cloze (cloze test) Tipo de actividad que consiste en rellenar huecos en un texto en el cual han sido suprimidas palabras enteras. En una prueba cloze tradicional la supresión se produce de forma fija cada x palabras. También se denominan así actividades de rellenar huecos en las que se suprimen frases cortas en un texto o en las que las palabras son eliminadas siguiendo un determinado criterio ("cloze racional"). La prueba cloze puede ser "abierta", el candidato ha de aportar las palabras omitidas, o "cerrada", ha de escoger entre diferentes opciones. La corrección de una prueba cloze abierta puede ser o bien por "palabra exacta" (se considera como respuesta correcta únicamente la palabra suprimida del texto original), o bien por "palabra aceptable" (se proporciona a los correctores una lista de respuestas aceptables).
Compárese: prueba C, ítem de rellenar huecos.
Bibliografía adicional: Weir, 1990, p. 46–48; Oller, 1979, cap. 12.

CA:313, DA:50, DE:66, EN:52, ES:315, FR:370, GA:410, IT:362, NE:61, PO:378.

316 prueba cloze racional Véase la definición de prueba cloze (cloze test).

CA:314, DA:308, DE:230, EN:318, ES:316, FR:371, GA:60, IT:56, NE:315, PO:367.

317 prueba criterial Prueba en la cual el rendimiento del candidato es interpretado con relación a criterios predeterminados. Se da más importancia al logro de los objetivos que a la puntuación del candidato como reflejo de su clasificación en el grupo.
Compárese: prueba normativa, prueba referida a un dominio.

CA:337, DA:203, DE:196, EN:81, ES:317, FR:364, GA:412, IT:380, NE:86, PO:369.

318 prueba de actuación lingüísti-

ca Prueba que requiere que los candidatos produzcan una muestra de lengua, escrita o hablada (por ej, redacciones y entrevistas orales). Éstos procedimientos están frecuentemente diseñados para reproducir la actuación tal como se produce en contextos reales de comunicación.
Bibliografía adicional: Bachman 1990, pp. 304–305.
CA:306, DA:283, DE:284, EN:278, ES:318, FR:380, GA:416, IT:367, NE:287, PO:381.

319 prueba de admisión Prueba utilizada para determinar si se acepta o no a un candidato en cierta institución o curso de estudios.
Compárese: prueba de clasificación.
CA:305, DA:5, DE:346, EN:124, ES:319, FR:369, GA:422, IT:364, NE:387, PO:377.

320 prueba de anclaje Prueba con características de medida conocidas que se administra junto con otra prueba. Los resultados obtenidos en la prueba de anclaje proporcionan información sobre la otra prueba y sobre los candidatos que han realizado ambas.
CA:307, DA:17, DE:19, EN:16, ES:320, FR:367, GA:404, IT:357, NE:18, PO:365.

321 prueba de aprovechamiento Tipo de prueba elaborada para determinar el grado de conocimiento alcanzado por un candidato con respecto a un curso específico, a un libro de texto, etc, es decir, una prueba en función del programa. También denominada prueba de rendimiento.
CA:309, DA:366, DE:369, EN:6, ES:321, FR:374, GA:419, IT:368, NE:301, PO:374.

322 prueba de aptitud Prueba diseñada para la predicción o medición del potencial de éxito del candidato en un área específica de aprendizaje, por ejemplo, el aprendizaje de una lengua extranjera.
Bibliografía adicional: Henning, 1987, p. 6; Ebel y Frisbie, 1991, p. 339.
CA:308, DA:18, DE:96, EN:20, ES:322, FR:368, GA:421, IT:358, NE:22, PO:370.

323 prueba de clasificación Una prueba administrada para colocar a los alumnos en un grupo o clase que tenga un nivel apropiado según sus conocimientos y capacidades.
CA:311, DA:137, DE:101, EN:282, ES:323, FR:377, GA:434, IT:365, NE:291, PO:372.

324 prueba de comprensión auditiva Prueba que evalúa la comprensión del lenguaje oral y en la que normalmente se utiliza un casete o un vídeo.
CA:315, DA:221, DE:147, EN:216, ES:324, FR:372, GA:411, IT:361, NE:235, PO:373.

325 prueba de diagnóstico Prueba empleada con el fin de descubrir los puntos fuertes y los puntos débiles del estudiante. Los resultados pueden ser utilizados para la toma de decisiones con respecto a su formación futura, aprendizaje o enseñanza.
CA:317, DA:65, DE:77, EN:97, ES:325, FR:383, GA:414, IT:373, NE:97, PO:386.

326 prueba de dominio Prueba que mide la capacidad o destreza general, sin referirse a ningún curso o conjunto de materias en particular.
CA:319, DA:112, DE:120, EN:296, ES:326, FR:378, GA:428, IT:363, NE:306, PO:379.

327 prueba de dominio específico Prueba diseñada para establecer si un alumno ha llegado a dominar un campo bien definido de destrezas o conocimiento.
CA:338, DA:227, DE:204, EN:225, ES:327, FR:376, GA:425, IT:366, NE:237, PO:376.

328 prueba de fines específicos Prueba diseñada para medir la capacidad de un candidato de operar en un contexto profesional o académico específico. El contenido de la prueba se diseña de acuerdo con un análisis de las actividades lingüísticas que los candidatos necesitarán llevar a cabo en la situación concreta de uso.
CA:318, DA:243, DE:112, EN:375, ES:328, FR:393, GA:431, IT:378, NE:351, PO:393.

329 prueba de potencial Prueba cuya duración permite que casi todos los candidatos puedan terminarla, pero que contiene algunas actividades o items con un grado de dificultad que hace poco probable que la mayoría de los candidatos responda correctamente a cada ítem .
Compárese: prueba de velocidad.
CA:310, DA:299, DE:261/293, EN:288, ES:329, FR:379, GA:413, IT:360, NE:296, PO:371.

330 prueba de progreso Prueba administrada a lo largo de un curso de aprendizaje para poder evaluar el aprendizaje logrado hasta ese momento.
CA:320, DA:108, DE:214, EN:298, ES:330, FR:381, GA:418, IT:369, NE:422, PO:382.

331 prueba de rendimiento Véase la

definición de prueba de aprovechamiento

CA:322, DA:20, DE:203, EN:23, ES:331, FR:366, GA:419, IT:368, NE:421, PO:374.

332 prueba de selección Prueba, normalmente breve y fácil de administrar, que se utiliza para identificar a aquellos candidatos que pueden ser admitidos en un curso o como candidatos a un examen.
Compárese: prueba de clasificación.
Véase: prueba de admisión.

CA:316/323, DA:330/424, DE:36/98, EN:349/353, ES:332, FR:375/382, GA:430/432, IT:370, NE:332/333, PO:375/383.

333 prueba de significación Prueba de significación estadística.
Véase: significación.

CA:324, DA:334, DE:350, EN:364, ES:333, FR:373, GA:435, IT:371, NE:339, PO:384.

334 prueba de velocidad Prueba de tiempo limitado para su realización. Los candidatos más lentos reciben una puntuación más baja porque no llegan a resolver las últimas preguntas. Generalmente en este tipo de prueba la dificultad de las preguntas es tal que normalmente un candidato respondería de forma correcta, si no fuera por la limitación del tiempo.
Compárese: prueba de potencial.

CA:321, DA:129, DE:340/363, EN:376, ES:334, FR:363, GA:424, IT:372, NE:352, PO:385.

335 prueba directa Prueba que mide las destrezas productivas de expresión oral o escrita, y mediante la cual se mide de forma directa la realización de la propia destreza. Un ejemplo es el de examinar la capacidad de expresión escrita pidiendo al candidato que escriba una carta.
Compárese: prueba indirecta/actividad indirecta.
Bibliografía adicional: Hughes, 1989, pp. 14–16.

CA:326, DA:70, DE:81, EN:104, ES:335, FR:384, GA:415, IT:375, NE:102, PO:387.

336 prueba final Prueba u otra forma de evaluación administrada al final de un curso. Si se contrastan sus resultados con los resultados de una prueba administrada a principios del curso, proporciona evidencias de la eficacia del curso.
Compárese: prueba inicial.

CA:327, DA:345, DE:5, EN:287, ES:336, FR:305, GA:179, IT:271, NE:295, PO:310.

337 prueba indirecta/ actividad indirecta Prueba o actividad que intenta medir las capacidades subyacentes en una destreza lingüística en vez de comprobar la realización de la propia destreza. Un ejemplo puede ser comprobar la capacidad de expresión escrita haciendo que el candidato señale estructuras empleadas de forma incorrecta en un texto.
Compárese: prueba directa.
Bibliografía adicional: Hughes, 1989, pp. 14–16.

CA:329, DA:135, DE:150, EN:170, ES:337, FR:385, GA:420, IT:354, NE:173, PO:389.

338 prueba inicial Prueba administrada antes del comienzo de un curso de aprendizaje. Los resultados de la prueba preliminar pueden ser contrastados con los resultados obtenidos en otro examen al final del curso de aprendizaje para poder evaluar la eficacia del curso.
Compárese: prueba final.

CA:333, DA:104, DE:440, EN:292, ES:338, FR:306, GA:290, IT:272, NE:299, PO:312.

339 prueba no basada en el curriculum Prueba no vinculada a ningún programa concreto de estudios ni a ningún curso específico.
Compárese: prueba basada en el curriculum.
Véase: prueba de dominio.

CA:328, DA:57, DE:218, EN:89, ES:339, FR:387, GA:405, IT:376, NE:222, PO:388.

340 prueba normativa Prueba en la cual las puntuaciones se interpretan con respecto al rendimiento de un grupo determinado que incluye personas comparables a las que hacen la prueba. El término suele usarse al referirse a pruebas cuya interpretación se centra en ordenar (de mayor a menor) a los individuos en relación al grupo normativo o los unos respecto a los otros.
Compárese: prueba criterial.

CA:336, DA:251, DE:268, EN:254, ES:340, FR:388, GA:426, IT:381, NE:264, PO:391.

341 prueba objetiva Prueba que puede puntuarse por medio de un esquema de calificación, sin tener que aportar ni opiniones expertas ni juicios subjetivos.

CA:331, DA:257, DE:272, EN:257, ES:341, FR:389, GA:427, IT:377, NE:267, PO:392.

342 prueba referida a un dominio Prueba en la cual los resultados se interpretan con respecto a un campo específico de

contenido o capacidad.
Compárese: prueba criterial, prueba normativa.

CA:335, DA:84, DE:50, EN:120, ES:342, FR:391, GA:417, IT:382, NE:114, PO:368.

343 prueba semi-directa Prueba que intenta evaluar la producción lingüística sustituyendo algún aspecto de implicación humana, por ejemplo, una prueba de producción oral que utiliza una grabación en vez de un entrevistador humano para proporcionar el input. Un ejemplo de la prueba semi-directa es la SOPI (Entrevista semidirecta de dominio oral).
Compárese: prueba directa.

CA:339, DA:332, DE:347, EN:356, ES:343, FR:392, GA:423, IT:383, NE:336, PO:396.

344 prueba viva/ ítem vivo Prueba susceptible de ser utilizada y que, por tanto, debe ser guardada bajo medidas de seguridad.

CA:341, DA:101, DE:225, EN:217, ES:344, FR:360, GA:407, IT:355, NE:233, PO:362.

345 puntuación a) Número total de puntos logrados por el candidato en una prueba, bien antes del escalonamiento (puntuación en bruto), bien después (puntuación escalada).

b) Asignar valores numéricos a una producción lingüística observada.
Compárese: medida.

CA:342, DA:328, DE:312, EN:348, ES:345, FR:275, GA:328, IT:278, NE:331, PO:280.

346 puntuación del ítem En el análisis del ítem es la suma de las respuestas correctas a un ítem determinado.

CA:345, DA:160, DE:171, EN:196, ES:346, FR:267, GA:336, IT:281, NE:202, PO:60.

347 puntuación dicotómica Puntuación basada en dos categorías, por ej. correcto/incorrecto, aprobado/suspenso, sí/no.

CA:347, DA:67, DE:455, EN:98, ES:347, FR:268, GA:341, IT:32, NE:98, PO:59.

348 puntuación en bruto Puntuación de examen que no ha sido manipulada estadísticamente por ninguna transformación, ponderación, ni sustitución de escalas.
Véase: puntuación.

CA:348, DA:321, DE:328, EN:319, ES:348, FR:276, GA:329, IT:282, NE:324, PO:281.

349 puntuación escalar Puntuación producida como resultado del escalonamiento.
Véase: escalonamiento.

CA:349, DA:340, DE:354, EN:345, ES:349, FR:278, GA:337, IT:286, NE:153, PO:283.

350 puntuación estándar Puntuación transformada linealmente de un grupo de puntuaciones. Se fija la desviación media y la típica al valor que el usuario requiera. Ejemplos de puntuaciones estándares son las puntuaciones *z* y *t*.
Compárese: puntuación *t*, puntuación *z*, estaninas.
Bibliografía adicional: Ebel y Frisbie, 1991, pp. 67–68.

CA:350, DA:365, DE:376, EN:382, ES:350, FR:281, GA:333, IT:287, NE:364, PO:291.

351 puntuación límite Puntuación mínima que un candidato debe lograr para obtener una calificación determinada en una prueba o examen. En las pruebas de dominio, es la puntuación exigida para que se considere que el candidato posee una competencia mínima o un nivel de "dominio".
Véase: prueba de dominio específico, evaluación de competencia mínima.
Compárese: aprobado.
Bibliografía adicional: Bachman, 1990, pp. 214–215; Crocker y Algina, pp. 421–428.

CA:359, DA:58, DE:199, EN:90, ES:351, FR:277, GA:338, IT:280, NE:57, PO:282.

352 puntuación observada La puntuación obtenida por un candidato. La teoría clásica de examen considera que ésta consta de la puntuación verdadera y el error.
Véase: error, puntuación verdadera.

CA:353, DA:183, DE:49, EN:258, ES:352, FR:279, GA:331, IT:283, NE:429, PO:285.

353 puntuación politómica Puntuación de un ítem que utiliza una escala de, al menos, 3 puntos. Por ejemplo, se puede asignar a la respuesta de una pregunta 0, 1 ó 2 notas, tres distinciones. Las preguntas abiertas a menudo se puntúan de manera politómica. También conocida como puntuación escalar o policotómica.
Compárese: puntuación dicotómica.

CA:351, DA:291, DE:237, EN:284, ES:353, FR:89, GA:342, IT:34, NE:293, PO:64.

354 puntuación ponderada de

prueba Puntuación otorgada a un candidato en una prueba después de aplicar la ponderación.
Véase: ponderación.
CA:354, DA:434, DE:135, EN:437, ES:354, FR:280, GA:339, IT:284, NE:159, PO:286.

355 puntuación *t* Ampliación de la puntuación *z*. Elimina los decimales y signos negativos. La puntuación *t* equivale a 10 veces la puntuación *z* más 50. La distribución tiene una media de 50 y una desviación típica de 10.
Véase: puntuación *z*.
Bibliografía adicional: Ebel y Frisbie, 1991, p. 68.
CA:355, DA:384, DE:388, EN:422, ES:355, FR:283, GA:367, IT:289, NE:376, PO:287.

356 puntuación transformada Puntuación que ha sido manipulada matemáticamente, por ejemplo, para escalonar o ponderar.
Bibliografía adicional: Ebel y Frisbie 1991, pp. 64–70.
CA:356, DA:414, DE:415, EN:417, ES:356, FR:284, GA:334, IT:290, NE:158, PO:288.

357 puntuación verdadera La puntuación verdadera que obtendría un candidato si no hubiera ningún error de medida en el momento de examinar o puntuar. Un concepto fundamental en la teoría clásica de los tests.
CA:357, DA:415, DE:441, EN:420, ES:357, FR:285, GA:335, IT:285, NE:431, PO:289.

358 puntuación *z* Puntuación estándar que ocurre generalmente y que tiene una media de 0 y una desviación típica de 1. La fórmula para calcular las puntuaciones *z* es la siguiente:

$$z = (X - \bar{X}) \div Sx$$

Donde:
z – puntuación *z*
X – puntuación de la prueba
$\bar{X}$ – puntuación media de la prueba
Sx – desviación típica de las puntuaciones de la prueba
Compárese: puntuación *t*.
Véase: puntuación estándar.
Bibliografía adicional: Ebel y Frisbie, 1991, p. 68.
CA:358, DA:439, DE:446, EN:442, ES:358, FR:286, GA:441, IT:291, NE:439, PO:290.

359 rango percentil Número o puntuación que indica rango al mostrar el porcentaje que cae por debajo de dicha puntuación. Si en una prueba un candidato tiene un rango percentil de 60 significa que el 60 % de los cadidatos puntuaron de manera igual o inferior a él.
CA:363, DA:281, DE:299, EN:276, ES:359, FR:53, GA:284, IT:55, NE:285, PO:276.

360 rasgo Característica física o psicológica de una persona (como la capacidad lingüística) o la escala de medida construida para describirla.
CA:411, DA:416, DE:95, EN:415, ES:360, FR:23, GA:400, IT:26, NE:403, PO:403.

361 reconocimiento La aprobación formal por parte de una institución de un título en particular para un propósito específico, por ej, admisión a un curso de estudio de post-grado.
CA:365, DA:15, DE:269, EN:323, ES:361 FR:321, GA:9, IT:303, NE:123, PO:325.

362 recuento de frecuencia de palabras Recuento de la frecuencia con que aparecen ciertas palabras o tipos de palabras en un texto. En la evaluación de lenguas puede ser útil en la producción de pruebas según una especificación léxica en particular.
CA:190, DA:270, DE:143, EN:440, ES:362, FR:75, GA:67, IT:256, NE:436, PO:95.

363 redondeo Proceso de reducir la precisión de una cifra al reducir el número de cifras significativas. Por ejemplo, la cifra 564. 8 puede ser redondeada a 565 o a 560. La escala de redondeo depende de la precisión requerida.
CA:24, DA:245, DE:331, EN:335, ES:363, FR:22, GA:354, IT:24, NE:11, PO:25.

364 registro Diferente variedad de lengua hablada o escrita característica de una actividad en particular o de un determinado grado de formalidad.
CA:368, DA:310, DE:366, EN:325, ES:364, FR:323, GA:291, IT:297, NE:317, PO:327.

365 regresión Técnica para predecir el valor más problable de una variable (la variable dependiente) a partir de valores conocidos de una o más variables (variables independientes).
Bibliografía adicional: Hatch y Lazaraton, 1991, pp. 467–480; Guilford y Fruchter, 1981, pp. 346–361.

CA:369, DA:311, DE:321, EN:326, ES:365, FR:324, GA:4, IT:298, NE:318, PO:328.

366 regresión lineal Técnica de regresión que supone una relación lineal entre las variables dependiente e independiente.
CA:370, DA:215, DE:223, EN:213, ES:366, FR:325, GA:5, IT:299, NE:230, PO:329.

367 regresión múltiple Técnica estadística que se usa para establecer los efectos lineales de varias variables independientes sobre una única variable dependiente. Por ejemplo, si la dificultad de la actividad es la variable dependiente, se podrían investigar los efectos del tipo de actividad, dificultad léxica, etc.
Véase: variable independiente, regresión.
Bibliografía adicional: Hatch y Lazaraton, 1991, pp. 480–486.
CA:371, DA:117, DE:251, EN:242, ES:367, FR:326, GA:182, IT:300, NE:240, PO:330.

368 relación F En el análisis de varianza, es la relación computada que indica si las diferencias entre las medias de los grupos son estadísticamente significativas o no; por ejemplo, si el rendimiento de un grupo ha resultado ser mejor, de modo significativo, que el de otro en una prueba de lengua.
Véase: formas alternativas.
Bibliografía adicional: Hatch y Lazaraton, 1991, pp. 315–317
CA:364, DA:94, DE:109, EN:139, ES:368, FR:319, GA:66, IT:296, NE:132, PO:332.

369 repercusión (backwash) Impacto de un examen en la enseñanza. El hecho de que los alumnos tengan que realizar una determinada prueba puede influir en que los profesores tengan que adaptar la metodología y los contenidos de su clase para responder a las exigencias de la prueba. El resultado puede ser positivo o negativo. También denominada efecto de rebote (washback).
Véase: impacto.
CA:372, DA:25, DE:43, EN:28, ES:369, FR:322, GA:95, IT:147, NE:27, PO:135.

370 replicabilidad La posibilidad de repetir los resultados de un trabajo de investigación en más de una ocasión, con el consiguiente incremento de confianza en los resultados.
CA:373, DA:189, DE:324, EN:329, ES:370, FR:335, GA:185, IT:301, NE:165, PO:333.

371 respuesta Comportamiento del candidato provocado por el 'input' de la prueba. Por ejemplo, la respuesta que se da a un ítem de selección múltiple o el trabajo producido en una prueba de expresión escrita.
Compárese: input, estímulo.
CA:374, DA:315, DE:21, EN:331, ES:371, FR:327, GA:153, IT:305, NE:319, PO:334.

372 respuesta construida Forma de respuesta escrita a un ítem de examen que implica la producción activa en vez de la simple selección entre varias opciones.
Compárese: respuesta seleccionada.
Véase: respuesta.
CA:376, DA:185, DE:126, EN:70, ES:372, FR:330, GA:154, IT:309, NE:272, PO:336.

373 respuesta correcta La contestación que es considerada como correcta al puntuar una prueba.
CA:375, DA:190, DE:327, EN:333, ES:373, FR:331, GA:155, IT:307, NE:204, PO:337.

374 respuesta esperada Respuesta o respuestas que el redactor de un ítem o actividad pretende obtener.
CA:377, DA:106, DE:105, EN:137, ES:374, FR:328, GA:157, IT:306, NE:32, PO:338.

375 respuesta extensa Forma de respuesta a un ítem o actividad en la cual se espera que el candidato produzca (y no escoja) una respuesta de más de una o dos oraciones.
Compárese: ítem de respuesta corta.
CA:378, DA:423, DE:35, EN:138, ES:375, FR:332, GA:159, IT:308, NE:407, PO:339.

376 respuesta modelo Respuesta esperada a una pregunta abierta, proporcionada por el creador del ítem y que puede ser empleada en la elaboración de una plantilla de corrección para guiar a los calificadores.
CA:261, DA:233, DE:253, EN:236, ES:376, FR:333, GA:156, IT:245, NE:21, PO:340.

377 respuesta seleccionada Forma de respuesta a un ítem de examen que requiere que el candidato escoja una respuesta entre varias alternativas en vez de proporcionar una respuesta.
Compárese: respuesta construida.
Véase: respuesta.
CA:379, DA:422, DE:37, EN:352, ES:377, FR:334, GA:158, IT:310, NE:154, PO:341.

378 resultado Los resultados de una

prueba, tal como se le comunican al candidato o al usuario de la prueba.

CA:380, DA:317, DE:103, EN:332, ES:378, FR:336, GA:397, IT:312, NE:322, PO:342.

379 retroalimentación (feedback) Comentarios de las personas implicadas en el proceso de la prueba (examinandos, administradores de la prueba, etc.) que aportan una base para la evaluación de dicho proceso. El 'feedback' puede obtenerse de manera informal o mediante el uso de cuestionarios diseñados específicamente para tal fin.

CA:381, DA:97, DE:330, EN:144, ES:379, FR:337, GA:6, IT:173, NE:134, PO:192.

380 rho de Spearman Véase la definición de correlación de rangos de Spearman.

CA:383, DA:352, DE:362, EN:374, ES:380, FR:339, GA:292, IT:302, NE:348, PO:344.

381 sección Una manera de designar los apartados de un examen, por ej, sección de comprensión de lectura, sección de comprensión auditiva, etc.

CA:385, DA:393, DE:277, EN:267, ES:381, FR:182, GA:270, IT:168, NE:278, PO:87.

382 seguridad Ambito de la administración de pruebas que se encarga de prevenir la revelación del contenido de los materiales de las pruebas durante su periodo de de vigencia.

CA:387, DA:335, DE:348, EN:351, ES:382, FR:344, GA:353, IT:333, NE:142, PO:347.

383 selección Etapa en el ciclo de elaboración de pruebas en la cual los elaboradores de pruebas evalúan los materiales encargados a los creadores de items y deciden sobre cuáles deben ser rechazados porque no cumplen las especificaciones de la prueba, y cuáles pueden pasar a la fase de edición.

Compárese: moderación.

CA:382, DA:400, DE:405, EN:433 ES:383, FR:338, GA:184, IT:91, NE:115, PO:343.

384 sesgo Una prueba o ítem puede considerarse sesgada si un grupo determinado de la población de candidatos resulta favorecido o perjudicado a causa de una característica de la prueba o de un ítem que no sea pertinente para lo que se pretende medir. El origen del sesgo puede estar vinculado al sexo, la edad, la cultura etc.

Bibliografía adicional: Bachman, 1990, pp. 271–279; Crocker y Algina, 1986, caps. 12 y 16.

CA:40, DA:344, DE:383, EN:33, ES:384, FR:32, GA:208, IT:160, NE:46, PO:40.

385 sesgo cultural Una prueba con un sesgo cultural puede favorecer o perjudicar a los candidatos de ciertos origenes culturales.

Véase: sesgo.

CA:41, DA:207, DE:201, EN:85, ES:385, FR:33, GA:209, IT:161, NE:90, PO:41.

386 significación Concepto estadístico referido a si un resultado es o no debido al azar.

Véase: error tipo 1, error tipo 2, hipótesis nula.

Bibliografía adicional: Guilford y Fruchter, 1981, p. 208–210.

CA:388, DA:333, DE:349, EN:363, ES:386, FR:76, GA:366, IT:334, NE:338, PO:348.

387 solapamiento parte-totalidad Efecto que está presente, por ejemplo, cuando las puntuaciones en una subprueba están correlacionadas con las puntuaciones de la prueba entera. Puesto que las puntuaciones de la subprueba están incluidas en las puntuaciones de la prueba en su totalidad, la correlación es exagerada. Existen técnicas para corregir este solapamiento parte-totalidad.

Bibliografía adicional: Henning 1987, p. 69.

CA:63, DA:62, DE:282, EN:271, ES:387, FR:51, GA:283, IT:146, NE:276, PO:331.

388 subprueba Véase la definición de apartado.

CA:389, DA:377, DE:386, EN:389, ES:388, FR:346, GA:150, IT:345, NE:373, PO:350.

389 sustitución de escala Véase la definición de escalonamiento.

CA:367, DA:314, DE:258, EN:330, ES:389, FR:320, GA:29, IT:304, NE:166, PO:326.

390 tabla de contingencia Tabla de frecuencias clasificadas según dos o más conjuntos de valores de variables categoriales.

	Dominio	No dominio
Método A	35	5
Método B	20	20

Véase: test chi-cuadrado

CA:398, DA:187, DE:187, EN:74, ES:390,

FR:353, GA:369, IT:347, NE:75, PO:320.

391 tendencia central (medida de) Manera de localizar el punto medio o la media estadística de una distribución. Las tres medidas generalmente empleadas de tendencia central son la media, la mediana y la moda.
Bibliografía adicional: Henning, 1987, pp. 39–40; Guilford y Fruchter, 1981, cap. 4; Hatch y Lazaraton, 1991, pp. 159–164.
CA:246, DA:47, DE:447, EN:45, ES:391, FR:358, GA:62, IT:348, NE:55, PO:356.

392 teoría clásica de examen Teoría de medición que consiste en un conjunto de suposiciones acerca de las relaciones existentes entre las puntuaciones reales u observadas de una prueba y los factores que afectan a dichas puntuaciones, generalmente denominados error. Se denomina también teoría de puntuación real.
Compárese: teoría de respuesta al ítem (TRI).
Bibliografía adicional: Bachman, 1990, pp. 166–187.
CA:399, DA:174, DE:177, EN:50, ES:392, FR:397, GA:387, IT:349, NE:208, PO:357.

393 teoría de generalizabilidad Modelo estadístico para investigar los efectos relativos de distintas fuentes de varianza en las puntuaciones de una prueba.
Bibliografía adicional: Bachman, 1990, p. 7; Crocker y Algina, 1986, cap. 8.
CA:400, DA:115, DE:132, EN:154, ES:393, FR:399, GA:388, IT:351, NE:152, PO:359.

394 teoría de respuesta al ítem (TRI) Grupo de modelos matemáticos que permiten relacionar la actuación de un candidato en un examen con su nivel de capacidad. Estos modelos se basan en la teoría fundamental de que la actuación esperada de un candidato en una pregunta específica de una prueba, o ítem, se halla en función tanto del nivel de dificultad del ítem como del nivel de capacidad de la persona.
Bibliografía adicional: Henning, 1987, cap. 8; Crocker y Algina, 1986, cap. 15.
CA:401, DA:159, DE:173/296, EN:195, ES:394, FR:400, GA:389, IT:352, NE:201, PO:360.

395 teoría del rasgo latente Véase la definición de teoría de respuesta al ítem (TRI).
CA:402, DA:211, DE:206, EN:207, ES:395, FR:398, GA:390, IT:350, NE:216, PO:358.

396 test chi-cuadrado Proceso estadístico que compara los valores de las respuestas observadas y las respuestas esperadas con el fin de indicar si la diferencia entre ellas es estadísticamente significativa. Es un procedimiento o técnica no paramétrico.
Véase: procedimientos no-paramétricos.
Bibliografía adicional: Hatch y Lazaraton, 1991, pp. 393–415.
CA:330, DA:49, DE:65, EN:49, ES:396, FR:149, GA:409, IT:359, NE:59, PO:395.

397 test psicométrico Test de rasgos psicológicos tales como personalidad, inteligencia, aptitud y dominio lingüístico que establece presuposiciones específicas sobre la naturaleza de la capacidad evaluada, por ejemplo, que es unidimensional y que tiene una distribución normal.
Bibliografía adicional: Bachman, 1990, p. 73–74.
CA:334, DA:302, DE:310, EN:301, ES:397, FR:390, GA:433, IT:379, NE:308, PO:394.

398 test t Test estadístico utilizado para determinar si existe o no una diferencia significativa entre las medias de dos muestras.
CA:340, DA:385, DE:387, EN:423, ES:398, FR:150, GA:368, IT:385, NE:377, PO:397.

399 texto Fragmento de discurso con sentido completo , escrito o hablado, utilizado como base de un conjunto de items de examen.
CA:403, DA:386, DE:411, EN:411, ES:399, FR:396, GA:381, IT:389, NE:381, PO:398.

400 texto adaptado Texto tomado de una fuente real y preparado para su uso en una prueba; por ejemplo, se ha adaptado el vocabulario y/o la gramática al nivel de los candidatos.
Véase: texto auténtico.
CA:405, DA:123, DE:140, EN:355, ES:400, FR:112, GA:383, IT:391, NE:335, PO:128.

401 texto auténtico Texto utilizado en una prueba que incluye material originalmente producido para fines distintos a los del examen, y no especialmente para dicha prueba.
Compárese: texto adaptado.
CA:404, DA:22, DE:41, EN:25, ES:401, FR:111, GA:382, IT:390, NE:24, PO:127.

402 tipo de actividad Las actividades tienen nombres que tienden a ser descriptivos de lo que se pretende examinar y de la forma que tienen, por ejemplo, compren-

sión de lectura de selección múltiple, expresión escrita guiada, etc.
CA:408, DA:265, DE:30, EN:394, ES:402, FR:407, GA:59, IT:393, NE:271, PO:401.

403 tipo de ítem Los items de las pruebas se conocen por denominaciones que tienden a describir su forma. Algunos ejemplos son: selección múltiple, transformación de oraciones, respuesta corta, "cloze" abierto.
CA:406, DA:162, DE:174, EN:197 ES:403, FR:405, GA:58, IT:392, NE:203, PO:399.

404 tipo de pregunta Véase la definición de tipo de ítem, tipo de actividad.
CA:407, DA:358, DE:124, EN:305, ES:404, FR:406, GA:57, IT:394, NE:424, PO:400.

405 título Reconocimiento que se ofrece al terminar un curso de formación o un examen y que cualifica a la persona para llevar a cabo una actividad o trabajo específico. Un certificado de dominio lingüístico puede ser considerado como un título para ciertos propósitos.
Compárese: certificado, diploma.
CA:360, DA:209, DE:314, EN:302, ES:405, FR:313, GA:46, IT:294, NE:214, PO:322.

406 transferencia de información Técnica de evaluación que implica la obtención de información aportada de una forma determinada y su presentación de otra forma. Ejemplos de esta actividad son: extraer información de un texto y utilizarla para completar un diagrama; redactar de nuevo una nota informal para convertirla en un anuncio formal.
Bibliografía adicional: Hughes, 1989, pp. 84, 124–125, 138.
CA:409, DA:141, DE:152, EN:173, ES:406, FR:402, GA:8, IT:396, NE:177, PO:404.

407 transformación de frases Tipo de ítem en el cual al candidato se le proporciona una frase completa como estímulo, seguida de la primera o de las dos primeras palabras de una segunda frase que debe completar y cuyo contenido es igual al de la primera frase pero representado bajo una forma gramatical diferente. Por ejemplo, la primera frase está en voz activa y el candidato tiene que presentar el mismo contenido en voz pasiva.
CA:410, DA:381, DE:334, EN:359, ES:407, FR:404, GA:61, IT:397, NE:440, PO:405.

408 TRI Véase la definición de teoría de respuesta al ítem (TRI).
CA:412, DA:153, DE:165, EN:188, ES:408, FR:401, GA:392, IT:352, NE:194, PO:402.

409 unidimensionalidad Noción de una única dimensión, la cual es un supuesto necesario para construir una escala que mida rasgos psicológicos, utilizando, por ejemplo, modelos actuales de respuesta al ítem. La unidimensionalidad es una propiedad del instrumento de medida, y no de los procesos psicológicos subyacentes.
Bibliografía adicional: Crocker y Algina, 1986, p. 343.
CA:413, DA:90, DE:97, EN:427, ES:409, FR:409, GA:23, IT:398, NE:119, PO:406.

410 usuario de pruebas Persona o institución (por ej, un profesor o empresa) que utiliza los resultados de una prueba para poder tomar una decisión en cuanto al examinando.
CA:414, DA:391, DE:392, EN:407, ES:410, FR:409, GA:440, IT:399, NE:393, PO:407.

411 vacío de información Técnica de la enseñanza y la evaluación de lenguas que simula la comunicación real mediante la creación de situaciones en las cuales los estudiantes no comparten la misma información, y por lo tanto necesitan comunicarse para poder realizar la actividad. Normalmente se utiliza en la práctica o en la evaluación de las destrezas de expresión oral y escrita.
CA:42, DA:140, DE:151, EN:172, ES:411, FR:213, GA:43, IT:424, NE:176, PO:223.

412 validación Proceso por el cual se recogen datos que apoyen las conclusiones extraídas a partir de las puntuaciones obtenidas en una prueba. Lo que se valida son las conclusiones relacionadas con los usos específicos de una prueba, y no la prueba en sí.
Véase: validez.
CA:415, DA:426, DE:426, EN:429, ES:412, FR:412, GA:39, IT:400, NE:414, PO:408.

413 validez Medida en que las puntuaciones de una prueba permiten extraer conclusiones apropiadas, significativas y útiles dada la finalidad de la prueba. Se identifican diferentes aspectos de la validez, como la validez de contenido, criterio y constructo; éstos proporcionan diferentes tipos de información para juzgar la validez global de una prueba para un fin específico.
Véase: validez concurrente, validez de

constructo, validez criterial, validez de contenido, validez convergente, validez discriminatoria, validez aparente, validez predictiva.
Bibliografía adicional: Bachman, 1990, pp. 25, 236–237.
CA:416, DA:427, DE:427, EN:430, ES:413, FR:413, GA:30, IT:401, NE:415, PO:409.

414 validez aparente Medida en que una prueba parece ser, en opinión de los candidatos o de los que la seleccionan para éstos, una determinación aceptable de la capacidad que se desea medir. Se trata de una opinión más bien subjetiva, al no basarse en un análisis objetivo de la prueba, y con frecuencia la validez aparente no es considerada una forma auténtica de validez. A veces se denomina "atractivo de la prueba".
Bibliografía adicional: Bachman, 1990, p. 285–289.
CA:417, DA:272, DE:110/34, EN:140, ES:414, FR:414 GA:2, IT:402, NE:174, PO:410.

415 validez concurrente Se considera que una prueba posee validez concurrente cuando las puntuaciones que aporta se correlacionan en gran medida con un criterio externo reconocido que mide la misma área de conocimiento o capacidad.
Véase: validez criterial.
Bibliografía adicional: Bachman, 1990, pp. 248–250.
CA:418, DA:323, DE:417, EN:66, ES:415, FR:415, GA:33, IT:403, NE:71, PO:411.

416 validez convergente Se dice que una prueba posee validez convergente cuando existe una alta correlación entre las puntuaciones obtenidas en ella y las obtenidas en una prueba diferente que mide el mismo constructo (independientemente del método). Se puede considerar un aspecto de la validez de constructo.
Compárese: validez discriminatória.
Véase: validez de constructo.
Bibliografía adicional: Guilford y Fruchter, 1981, pp. 436–437.
CA:419, DA:188, DE:188, EN:75, ES:416, FR:416, GA:32, IT:404, NE:76, PO:412.

417 validez criterial Se dice que una prueba posee validez criterial cuando puede demostrarse la relación entre la puntuación de la prueba y algún criterio externo que se cree que mide la misma capacidad. La información sobre la validez criterial se utiliza además para determinar la medida en que una prueba pronostica el comportamiento futuro.
Véase: validez concurrente, validez predictiva.
Bibliografía adicional: Bachman, 1990, pp. 248–250.
CA:421, DA:204, DE:197, EN:82, ES:417, FR:417, GA:34, IT:407, NE:87, PO:413.

418 validez de constructo Se dice que una prueba posee validez de constructo cuando se puede demostrar que las puntuaciones reflejan una teoría sobre la naturaleza de un constructo o su relación con otros constructos. Se podría predecir, por ejemplo, que dos pruebas válidas de comprensión auditiva clasificarían a los estudiantes de la misma manera, pero que cada una tendría una relación más débil con las puntuaciones obtenidas en una prueba de competencia gramatical.
Véase: validez, especificaciones de examen.
Bibliografía adicional: Ebel y Frisbie, 1991, p. 108; Hatch y Lazaraton, 1991, pp. 37–38.
CA:420, DA:186, DE:186, EN:69, ES:418, FR:418, GA:37, IT:406, NE:73, PO:414.

419 validez de contenido Se dice que una prueba posee validez de contenido cuando los items o actividades que la componen constituyen una muestra representativa de items o actividades del área de conocimiento o competencia que se examina. Estos items o actividades suelen estar relacionados con un syllabus o un curso.
Véase: validez, especificaciones de examen.
Bibliografía adicional: Bachman, 1990, pp. 244–247.
CA:422, DA:134, DE:154, EN:73, ES:419, FR:419, GA:31, IT:405, NE:179, PO:415.

420 validez discriminatoria Se dice que una prueba posee validez discriminatoria cuando su correlación con pruebas de distintas características es inferior a la correlación con pruebas de las mismas características, independientemente del método de prueba. Puede considerarse un aspecto de la validez del constructo.
Véase: validez de constructo.
Compárese: validez convergente.
Bibliografía adicional: Crocker y Algina, 1986, p. 23; Guilford y Fruchter, 1981, pp. 436–437.
CA:423, DA:73, DE:83, EN:111, ES:420, FR:420, GA:36, IT:408, NE:108, PO:416.

421 validez divergente Véase la definición de validez discriminatoria.
CA:424, DA:81, DE:90, EN:118, ES:421, FR:421, GA:35, IT:409, NE:111, PO:417.

422 validez predictiva Indicación de la exactitud con que una prueba predice la producción lingüística futura en una destreza concreta.
Compárese: validez criterial.
Bibliografía adicional: Guilford y Fruchter, 1987, pp. 437–438.

CA:425, DA:298, DE:294/439, EN:291, ES:422, FR:422, GA:38, IT:410, NE:300, PO:418.

423 valor de facilidad Véase la definición de índice de facilidad.

CA:426, DA:192, DE:209, EN:143, ES:423, FR:410, GA:217, IT:411, NE:147, PO:419.

424 valor-*p* Véase la definición de índice de facilidad.

CA:427, DA:273, DE:276, EN:266, ES:424, FR:411, GA:269, IT:412, NE:277, PO:420.

425 valoración a) Proceso consistente en asignar una puntuación a la producción de una prueba, mediante un juicio.

b) Puntuación obtenida como resultado del proceso de valoración.
Bibliografía adicional: Bachman, 1990, p. 50.

CA:428, DA:171, DE:57, EN:314, ES:425, FR:265, GA:286, IT:54, NE:38, PO:57.

426 valoración analítica Método de puntuación que puede ser utilizado en las pruebas de uso productivo de lenguaje, como las de expresión oral y expresión escrita. El evaluador realiza una valoración con la ayuda de una lista de puntos específicos. Por ejemplo, en una prueba de expresión escrita la escala analítica puede centrarse en la gramática, en el vocabulario, en el uso de conectores, etc.
Compárese: valoración global,valoración por impresión recibida (valoración por impresión general).
Bibliografía adicional: Ebel y Frisbie, 1991. p. 195.

CA:343, DA:13, DE:12, EN:14, ES:426, FR:266, GA:340, IT:27, NE:15, PO:58.

427 valoración global Método de puntuación que puede utilizarse en pruebas de expresión oral y escrita. El evaluador pone una sola nota según la impresión general que recibe de la producción del candidato, en vez de descomponerla en diversos aspectos del uso de la lengua.
Compárese: valoración analítica, valoración por impresión recibida (valoración por impresión general).

CA:33, DA:124, DE:137, EN:155, ES:427, FR:169, GA:231, IT:186, NE:161, PO:33.

428 valoración holística Véase la definición de valoración global.

CA:429, DA:126, DE:128, EN:164, ES:428, FR:170, GA:230, IT:187, NE:168, PO:34.

429 valoración por impresión recibida (valoración por impresión general) Método de puntuación que puede utilizarse en pruebas de uso productivo de la lengua, es decir, expresión escrita o expresión oral. El evaluador valora todas las respuestas de cada candidato, sin intentar separar las características individuales de la actividad.
Compárese: valoración analítica, valoración global.

CA:89, DA:116, DE:133, EN:168, ES:429, FR:270, GA:220, IT:33, NE:172, PO:68.

430 variable a) Nombre dado a una serie de observaciones sobre un ítem, donde el ítem podría ser un ítem de prueba, el sexo, la edad o la puntuación de la prueba.

b) Elemento, en un diseño experimental o análisis estadístico, que puede tomar una serie de valores. Por ejemplo, en el contexto de la evaluación de lenguas, serían variables de interés: la dificultad de los items de prueba, el género y la edad de los examinandos, etc.

CA:430, DA:428, DE:428, EN:431, ES:430, FR:423, GA:25, IT:416, NE:416, PO:422.

431 variable criterial En el campo de la investigación, es otro término para la variable dependiente.
Véase: variable dependiente.

CA:431, DA:205, DE:198, EN:83, ES:431, FR:424, GA:26, IT:417, NE:88, PO:423.

432 variable dependiente Variable investigada en un trabajo de investigación. Por ejemplo, las puntuaciones en una prueba (variable independiente) pueden ser utilizadas para pronosticar el éxito en el lugar de trabajo (variable dependiente).
Compárese: variable independiente.
Véase: variable.

CA:432, DA:7, DE:2, EN:94, ES:432, FR:425, GA:28, IT:418, NE:7, PO:424.

433 variable independiente En la investigación, se trata de una variable que se considera posiblemente relacionada con la variable dependiente o que puede afectarla. Por ejemplo, las puntuaciones en una prueba (variable independiente) pueden ser utilizadas para prognosticar el éxito en el

lugar de trabajo (variable dependiente).
Compárese: variable dependiente.
Véase: variable.
Bibliografía adicional: Hatch y Lazaraton, 1991, p. 64.
CA:433, DA:420, DE:422, EN:169, ES:433, FR:426, GA:27, IT:419, NE:268, PO:425.

434 varianza Medida de la dispersión de un conjunto de puntuaciones. Cuánto mayor es la varianza más lejos de la media están las puntuaciones individuales.
CA:434, DA:429, DE:429, EN:432, ES:434, FR:427, GA:24, IT:420, NE:417, PO:421.

6 Français: Un dictionnaire vérificateur multilingue

1 accord individuel Se réfère à la définition de l'accord inter-individuel et intra-individuel.

CA:1, DA:307, DE:56, EN:312, ES:10, FR:1, GA:70, IT:84, NE:36, PO:1.

2 accord inter-individuel Degré d'accord entre deux ou plusieurs évaluations portant sur le même type de performance faites par des examinateurs différents. Particulièrement pertinent dans l'évaluation des capacités orales et écrites dans des tests où l'examinateur doit exercer un jugement subjectif.

CA:2, DA:31, DE:159, EN:181, ES:11, FR:2, GA:68, IT:84, NE:185, PO:2.

3 accord intra-individuel Degré d'accord entre deux ou plusieurs évaluations du même type de performance, faites à des moments différents, par le même examinateur. Particulièrement pertinent dans l'évaluation des capacités orales et écrites dans des tests où l'examinateur doit exercer un jugement subjectif.

CA:3, DA:33, DE:163, EN:185, ES:12, FR:3, GA:69, IT:90, NE:190, PO:3.

4 accréditation Reconnaissance officielle du succès à un examen, fournie généralement par une entité officielle, un gouvernement, un centre d'examen, etc.

CA:4, DA:10, DE:8, EN:5, ES:1, FR:4, GA:92, IT:303, NE:3, PO:325.

5 acquisition de la langue Processus par lequel un individu acquiert une capacité dans une première ou une seconde langue. Dans le cas d'une seconde langue, on fait parfois la distinction entre acquisition (naturelle) et apprentissage (par le biais d'études conscientes).

CA:7, DA:356, DE:367, EN:204, ES:14, FR:5, GA:349, IT:22, NE:380, PO:24.

6 adéquation Mesure de la concordance entre les prédictions d'un modèle et les résultats observés. Il est possible de calculer différents indices d'adéquation. Dans la théorie item-réponse, l'analyse de l'adéquation montre comment l'item estimé et les paramètres afférents aux individus (la difficulté et le niveau de capacité), prédisent les notes qui vont être obtenues à un test: l'adéquation statistique d'un item peut être considérée comme analogue à son indice de difficulté dans les statistiques classiques de tests.

Voir: théorie de l'item-réponse TIR.

CA:8, DA:99, DE:248, EN:145, ES:15, FR:6, GA:268, IT:107, NE:135, PO:5.

7 administration Date ou période durant laquelle un examen a lieu. Certains examens sont administrés à dates fixes plusieurs fois par an, d'autres ont lieu à la demande.

CA:6, DA:403, DE:308, EN:8, ES:77, FR:7, GA:288, IT:331, NE:10, PO:23.

8 alpha (coefficient alpha) Appréciation de fidélité, qui mesure la cohérence interne d'un test. Le classement s'effectue en valeurs de 0 à 1. Souvent utilisé pour des tests comportant des échelles de notation, opposés ainsi aux tests composés d'items dichotomiques, bien qu'il puisse être utilisé pour les deux types de tests.

Cf.: Kuder-Richardson.

Voir: fidélité interne.

Lire: Henning, 1987, pp. 83–84.

CA:9, DA:11, DE:10, EN:10, ES:16, FR:8, GA:10, IT:10, NE:12, PO:6.

9 alpha de Cronbach Se réfère à la définition de alpha (coefficient alpha).

CA:10, DA:54, DE:70, EN:84, ES:17, FR:9, GA:11, IT:11, NE:89, PO:7.

10 amorce (d'un item) syn.: souche. Partie écrite d'un item, généralement sous la forme d'une phrase incomplète et dont la partie manquante doit être fournie ou sélectionnée parmi différentes options.

Cf.: options.

Voir: item à choix multiple.

CA:276, DA:360, DE:29, EN:387, ES:139, FR:10, GA:160, IT:346, NE:359, PO:224.

11 analyse de besoins Moyen permettant de déterminer les besoins langagiers (en termes d'aptitudes, de tâches, de vocabulaire, etc.) d'un groupe particulier d'apprenants. Cette analyse est préalable à l'élaboration d'un cours répondant spécifiquement à leurs besoins.

CA:16, DA:35, DE:45, EN:246, ES:21, FR:11, GA:19, IT:13, NE:31, PO:17.

12 analyse de contenu Moyen permettant de décrire et d'analyser le contenu du matériel d'un test. L'objet de cette analyse est de s'assurer que le contenu du test est pertinent par rapport à ses spécifications. Elle est essentielle dans l'établissement de la validité de contenus et de la validité de construct.

CA:18, DA:133, DE:153, EN:72, ES:19, FR:12, GA:12, IT:15, NE:178, PO:15.

13 analyse de discours Ce type d'analyse s'intéresse à la structure et à la fonction de différents types de textes oraux ou écrits.

CA:19, DA:76, DE:86, EN:107, ES:24, FR:13, GA:17, IT:16, NE: 104, PO:19.

14 analyse de la covariance Se réfère à la définition de l'ANCOVA.

CA:14, DA:200, DE:193, EN:12, ES:20, FR:14, GA:16, IT:18, NE:85, PO:13.

15 analyse de la variance Se réfère à la définition de l'ANOVA.

CA:17, DA:430, DE:430, EN:13, ES:23, FR:15, GA:15, IT:19, NE:418, PO:14.

16 analyse de test Analyse d'épreuves après leur utilisation par des candidats, souvent effectuée à l'aide de méthodes statistiques et informatisées. L'objectif peut être soit de rechercher la performance du candidat, soit celle de l'épreuve elle-même.

CA:15, DA:389, DE:390, EN:396, ES:22, FR:16, GA:14, IT:17, NE:389, PO:18.

17 analyse d'items Description de la performance des items de tests individuels, employant généralement des indices statistiques classiques tels que la facilité ou la discrimination. On utilise pour cette analyse des logiciels tels que MicroCAT Iteman.
Voir: discrimination, indice de facilité.

CA:13, DA:161, DE:167, EN:190, ES:25, FR:17, GA:13, IT:12, NE:198, PO:16.

18 analyse factorielle Technique statistique qui permet à un chercheur de réduire un grand nombre de variables à un petit nombre, en déterminant des facteurs parmi les variations des valeurs de plusieurs variables. Un ensemble de variables en intercorrélation élevée forme un facteur. Un chercheur peut commencer une analyse factorielle en mode exploratoire, afin de formuler des hypothèses, ou en mode de confirmation, en examinant des hypothèses spécifiques.
Lire: Bachman, 1990, p. 262; Croker et Algina, 1986, p. 232.

CA:20, DA:96, DE:115, EN:142, ES:26, FR:18, GA:18, IT:14, NE:133, PO:20.

19 ANCOVA Type d'analyse de la variance, qui permet de combiner plusieurs variables à vérifier (en particulier celles qui peuvent changer avec la variable d'intérêt).
Voir: ANOVA.
Lire: Hatch et Lazaraton, 1991, p. 387.

CA:21, DA:14, DE:13, EN:17, ES:27, FR:19, GA:20, IT:20, NE:16, PO:21.

20 ANOVA Technique statistique qui permet de tester l'hypothèse nulle selon laquelle plusieurs populations moyennes sont équivalentes. On examine la variabilité des observations dans chaque groupe, ainsi que la variabilité entre les groupes moyens.
Lire: Hatch et Lazaraton, 1991, pp. 308–312.

CA:22, DA:19, DE:20, EN:18, ES:28, FR:20, GA:21, IT:21, NE:19, PO:22.

21 appariement Type d'épreuve où le candidat doit relier entre eux des éléments apparaissant dans deux listes séparées. Une épreuve d'appariement consiste à sélectionner la phrase correcte qui complétera chacune des phrases tronquées proposées. Lors des épreuves de compréhension écrite, on peut par exemple faire choisir dans une liste le type de vacances ou de livres correspondant à la description des goûts ou des besoins d'un personnage précis.

CA:397, DA:322, DE:452, EN:226, ES:7, FR:21, GA:375, IT:73, NE:238, PO:353.

22 arrondir Processus qui permet de réduire la précision d'un chiffre, en réduisant le nombre de cas particuliers. Par exemple, 564,8 peut être élevé à 565 ou abaissé à 560. Le degré d'arrondissement dépend de la précision requise.

CA:24, DA:245, DE:331, EN:335, ES:363, FR:22, GA:354, IT:24, NE:11, PO:25.

23 attribut Caractéristique physique ou psychologique d'un individu (comme par exemple la capacité langagière), ou échelle de mesure servant à décrire cette caractéristique.

CA:411, DA:416, DE:95, EN:415, ES:360, FR:23, GA:400, IT:26, NE:403, PO:403.

24 authenticité Caractéristique d'un test qui rend compte du fait que les tâches à

réaliser par le candidat correspondent à des tâches qui n'ont pas été spécifiquement conçues pour une situation d'évaluation.
Lire: Bachman, 1990, pp. 300–303.
CA:27, DA:21, DE:42, EN:24, ES:33, FR:24, GA:115, IT:35, NE:23, PO:26.

25 authenticité interactionnelle Point de vue des tenants de l'authenticité dans les tests de langue qui la voient comme une caractéristique de l'interaction qui doit avoir lieu entre le sujet testé et la tâche d'évaluation afin de produire une réponse appropriée.
Cf.: authenticité situationnelle.
Voir: authenticité.
Lire: Bachman, 1990, pp. 315–323.
CA:28, DA:146, DE:157, EN:177, ES:34, FR:25, GA:116, IT:36, NE:183, PO:27.

26 authenticité situationnelle Degré auquel un test peut être considéré comme authentique, par rapport au le monde réel et aux situations dans lesquelles la langue n'est pas utilisée en situation d'évaluation.
Cf.: authenticité interactionnelle, situation de communication réelle.
Voir: authenticité.
Lire: Bachman, 1990, chapitre 8.
CA:29, DA:336, DE:351, EN:365, ES:35, FR:26, GA:117, IT:37, NE:340, PO:28.

27 auto-évaluation Processus par lequel un étudiant évalue son propre niveau de capacité, soit en s'administrant lui-même un test, soit par un autre moyen comme par exemple un questionnaire ou une liste de contrôle.
CA:30, DA:331, DE:345, EN:354, ES:36, FR:27, GA:142, IT:38, NE:334, PO:29.

28 banque d'items syn: Itemothèque. Gestion des items qui permet de stocker des informations afin de pouvoir élaborer des tests aux contenus et difficultés connus. Une base de données informatisée est généralement utilisée pour cela. Elle met en oeuvre la théorie de l'attribut latent, ce qui signifie que les items peuvent être mis en relation les uns avec les autres au moyen d'une échelle de difficulté commune.
Lire: Henning, 1987, chapitre 9.
CA:36, DA:155, DE:28, EN:191, ES:37, FR:28, GA:40, IT:111, NE:199, PO:37.

29 barème de notation Liste de toutes les réponses acceptables aux items d'un test. Le barème permet au correcteur d'assigner la note appropriée.
CA: 52/256, DA:319, DE:228, EN:223, ES:301, FR:29, GA:324, IT:329, NE:79, PO:172.

30 batterie Ensemble cohérent de tests ou de sous-tests, portant par exemple sur des capacités différentes, et qui peuvent donner lieu à une notation séparée, mais qui peuvent également être combinés afin d'obtenir une note totale.
CA:38, DA:28, DE:393, EN:32, ES:40, FR:30, GA:64, IT:41, NE:30, PO:38.

31 batterie de test Se réfère à la définition de batterie.
CA:39, DA:390, DE:406, EN:397, ES:41, FR:31, GA:63, IT:42, NE:390, PO:39.

32 biais syn: erreur systématique. Un test ou un item peuvent être considérés comme biaisés, si un de leurs attributs se révèle non pertinent par rapport à ce qu'ils sont censés tester et qu'ils avantagent ou désavantagent une partie des candidats. Le biais est principalement lié au sexe, à l'âge, à la culture, etc. des candidats.
Lire: Bachman, 1990, pp. 271–279; Croker et Algina, 1986, chapitres 12 et 16.
CA:40, DA:344, DE:383, EN:33, ES:384, FR:32, GA:208, IT:160, NE:46, PO:40.

33 biais culturel Un test comportant un biais culturel avantage ou désavantage un candidat appartenant à un contexte culturel spécifique.
Voir: biais.
CA:41, DA:207, DE:201, EN:85, ES:385, FR:33, GA:209, IT:161, NE:90, PO:41.

34 cadre de l'interlocuteur Instructions écrites concernant le langage qu'un examinateur doit utiliser pendant les tests de production orale de façon que ce que chaque candidat entend, soit standardisé, rendant ainsi le test plus juste et plus fiable.
CA:198, DA:324, DE:438, EN:179, ES:215, FR:34, GA:151, IT:128, NE:156, PO:321.

35 calibrage Détermination de l'échelle pour un ou plusieurs tests. Le calibrage peut impliquer des items d'ancrage de différents tests sur une échelle de difficulté commune (échelle theta). Quand un test est élaboré à partir d'items calibrés, les notes, en fonction de leur localisation sur l'échelle theta, indiquent la capacité du candidat.
CA:44, DA:164, DE:94, EN:40, ES:42, FR:35, GA:49, IT:44, NE:205, PO:42.

36 calibrage équicentile Méthode de calibrage des notes brutes obtenues aux tests, où l'on considère que les notes sont calibrées si elles correspondent au même rang centile dans un groupe de candidats.
CA:132, DA:440, DE:24, EN:127, ES:140, FR:36, GA:88, IT:150, NE:121, PO:43.

37 calibrage horizontal Action de reporter les notes obtenues à deux tests de difficulté similaire sur la même échelle afin d'appliquer les mêmes standards aux deux tests.
Cf.: calibrage vertical.
Voir: calibrage.
CA:133, DA:128, DE:149, EN:166, ES:141, FR:37, GA:89, IT:152, NE:170, PO:44.

38 calibrage linéaire Dans ce type de calibrage, la note obtenue à un test est calibrée par rapport à la note obtenue à un second test. Les notes équivalentes obtenues aux deux tests sont d'une déviation standard égale, au-dessus ou en dessous de la note moyenne du test dans lequel elles apparaissent.
Voir: calibrage, régression.
Lire: Croker et Algina, 1986, pp. 457–461.
CA:134, DA:216, DE:17, EN:212, ES:142, FR:38, GA:91, IT:151, NE:229, PO:45.

39 calibrage vertical Action de reporter les notes obtenues à deux tests de degré de difficulté différent, sur la même échelle.
Lire: Crocker et Algina, 1986, pp. 473–477.
CA:135, DA:432, DE:435, EN:434, ES:143, FR:39, GA:90, IT:153, NE:419, PO:46.

40 calibrer Dans la théorie item-réponse: estimer la difficulté d'un ensemble de questions.
Voir: échelle delta.
CA:43, DA:163, DE:93, EN:39, ES:43, FR:40, GA:48, IT:43, NE:206, PO:47.

41 candidat Individu qui prend part à un examen ou à un test. Appelé aussi sujet.
CA:45, DA:165, DE:302, EN:41, ES:48, FR:41, GA:178, IT:49, NE:207, PO:48.

42 capacité syn: savoir-faire. Capacité intellectuelle ou pouvoir d'accomplir un acte, de produire un comportement.
Cf.: compétence, niveau de capacité.
Lire: Bachman, 1990, p. 16, p. 19.
CA:46, DA:2, DE:113, EN:2, ES:49, FR:42, GA:96, IT:1A, NE:411, PO:49.

43 capacité langagière Ensemble de compétences qui définissent la capacité d'un individu à utiliser la langue dans des buts communicatifs variés.
Lire: Bachman, 1990, pp. 3–4.
CA:47, DA:354, DE:368, EN:203, ES:50, FR:43, GA:97, IT:4, NE:379, PO:50.

44 capacités intellectuelles inférieures Capacités hypothétiques peu complexes sollicitées des candidats lors d'un test, comme par exemple savoir reconnaître un mot ou une lettre.
Cf.: capacités intellectuelles supérieures.
CA:200, DA:27, DE:424, EN:219, ES:101, FR:44, GA:327, IT:2, NE:409, PO:52.

45 capacités intellectuelles supérieures Capacités hypothétiques complexes telles qu'être capable d'inférer ou de résumer.
Cf.: capacités intellectuelles inférieures.
CA:201, DA:130, DE:418, EN:162, ES:102, FR:45, GA:326, IT:3, NE:410, PO:53.

46 caractéristiques des modes d'évaluation Caractéristiques précises des différents modes d'évaluation. Elles peuvent inclure l'environnement, la consigne, la langue dans laquelle sont données les instructions, le format, etc.
Lire: Bachman, 1990,chapitre 5.
CA:48, DA:397, DE:403, EN:402, ES:51, FR:46, GA:401, IT:50, NE:398, PO:54.

47 carré moyen Nom donné à la variance dans une analyse de variance (ANOVA).
Voir: ANOVA.
CA:251, DA:230, DE:245, EN:229, ES:262, FR:47, GA:227, IT:295, NE:149, PO:319.

48 catégorie a) Section d'une échelle catégorique: le genre par exemple, comprend les catégories mâle et femelle. b) En évaluation, une échelle de notation qui comprend par exemple cinq points, est dite échelle à cinq catégories de réponses.
CA:49, DA:169, DE:176, EN:43, ES:52, FR:48, GA:50, IT:51, NE:52, PO:55.

49 centile syn: percentile. Echelle à 99 points qui divise une fréquence de distribution en 100 groupes de taille équivalente. La médiane correspond au cinquantième centile (P 50). La distribution est divisée en 4 groupes égaux, les quartiles.
Lire: Hatch et Lazaraton, 1991, pp. 187–188.
CA:287, DA:280, DE:285, EN:275, ES:299, FR:49, GA:279, IT:266, NE:284, PO:302.

50 certificat Document statuant nominalement qu'un individu a réussi un examen ou une partie d'un examen et a obtenu un niveau particulier, généralement au moins passable.
Cf.: diplôme.
CA:50, DA:38, DE:448, EN:47, ES:53, FR:50, GA:386, IT:52, NE:56, PO:56.

51 chevauchement de la partie à l'ensemble Effet présent lorsque par exemple, les notes obtenues à un sous-test sont mises en relation avec les notes obtenues à l'ensemble du test. Le rapport est exagéré puisque les notes du sous-test sont comprises dans celles de l'ensemble du test. Il existe des techniques qui permettent de corriger ce chevauchement de la partie à l'ensemble.
Lire: Henning, 1987, p. 69.
CA:63, DA:62, DE:282, EN:271, ES:387, FR:51, GA:283, IT:146, NE:276, PO:331.

52 classement Convertion des notes obtenues en niveaux.
CA:360, DA:, DE:48, EN:157, ES:47, FR:52, GA:161, IT:88, NE:426, PO:275.

53 classement centile Nombre ou note qui indique le classement en montrant le pourcentage existant en dessous de cette note. Si un candidat est classé au centile 60, cela signifie que 60% de tous les candidats ont obtenu une note équivalente ou inférieure.
CA:363, DA:281, DE:299, EN:276, ES:359, FR:53, GA:284, IT:55, NE:285, PO:276.

54 coefficient Indice numérique utilisé comme mesure d'une propriété ou d'une caractéristique.
Voir: alpha (coefficient alpha), coefficient de corrélation.
CA:53, DA:175, DE:178, EN:53, ES:55, FR:54, GA:73, IT:57, NE:62, PO:69.

55 coefficient alpha Se réfère à la définition de alpha (coefficient alpha).
CA:54, DA:176, DE:179, EN:54, ES:56, FR:55, GA:74, IT:58, NE:63, PO:70.

56 coefficient de corrélation Indice montrant l'ampleur de la corrélation entre deux ou plusieurs variables. Il varie de -1 à +1. Les variables à corrélation élevée sont représentées par un coefficient de corrélation proche de +1.
Lire: Guilford et Fruchter, 1981, pp. 86–88.
CA:55, DA:197, DE:191, EN:79, ES:57, FR:56, GA:75, IT:60, NE:82, PO:71.

57 coefficient de corrélation bisériale de point Indice de discrimination pour des items dichotomiques, écrit r_{pbi}. Corrélation entre un critère, (généralement la note totale du test), et la réponse à l'item. Un avantage de r_{pbi} sur la corrélation bisériale (r_{bis}) est qu'il peut être utilisé de façon appropriée lorsque la capacité sous-jacente n'est pas distribuée normalement.
Cf.: corrélation bisériale.
CA:57, DA:41, DE:311, EN:283, ES:86, FR:57, GA:80, IT:97, NE:309, PO:102.

58 coefficient de corrélation phi Coefficient de corrélation qui permet de montrer la force de la relation entre deux variables binaires, par exemple les notes obtenues à deux items vrai/faux.
Voir: coefficient de corrélation.
Lire: Guilford et Fruchter, 1981, pp.316–318; Crocker et Algina, 1986, pp. 92–94.
CA:62, DA:284, DE:286, EN:279, ES:59, FR:58, GA:76, IT:61, NE:288, PO:75.

59 coefficient de corrélation de rangs syn: coefficient de coordination. Coefficient de corrélation non basé sur les valeurs absolues des variables mais sur l'ordre relatif des rangs.
Lire: Guilford et Fruchter, 1981, pp. 294–296.
CA:60, DA:304, DE:315, EN:309, ES:89, FR:59, GA:82, IT:100, NE:312, PO:72.

60 coefficient de corrélation de Spearman Forme de coefficient de corrélation de rangs utilisé sur de petits échantillons, c'est à dire de moins de 30 éléments.
Voir: coefficient de corrélation de rangs.
CA:58, DA:351, DE:361, EN:373, ES:87, FR:60, GA:83, IT:99, NE:347, PO:73.

61 coefficient de fidélité Mesure de la fidélité, calculée de 0 à 1. Les estimations de fidélité peuvent se baser sur l'administration répétée d'un test (il devrait alors produire des résultats similaires), ou, si cela s'avère impossible, sur une mesure de fidélité (cohérence) interne. Egalement appelée indice de fidélité.
Voir: fidélité interne, fidélité, fidélité test-retest.
CA:61, DA:313, DE:323, EN:328, ES:58, FR:61, GA:77, IT:59, NE:44, PO:74.

62 compétence Aptitude reconnue à pouvoir (savoir-faire) produire telle ou telle conduite. En linguistique le terme se réfère à une capacité sous-jacente, opposée à la performance, qui est la manifestation langagière de la compétence. Cette dis-tinction est apparue dans les travaux de Chomsky.
Cf.: performance.
Lire: Bachman, 1990, pp. 52 et 108.
CA:64, DA:180, DE:183, EN:59, ES:60, FR:62, GA:191, IT:62, NE:67, PO:76.

63 compétence communicative Capacité d'utiliser un langage approprié dans des situations et des dispositifs de communication variés.

Lire: Bachman, 1990, p. 16, p. 68.
CA:65, DA:179, DE:182, EN:58, ES:61, FR:63, GA:195, IT:63, NE:66, PO:77.

64 compétence discursive Capacité à comprendre et à produire un discours. La compétence discursive est parfois considérée comme une composante de la compétence langagière.
Lire: Bachman, 1990, chapitre 4.
CA:66, DA:78, DE:87, EN:108, ES:62, FR:64, GA:196, IT:64, NE:105, PO:78.

65 compétence grammaticale Dans un modèle de compétence langagière, la compétence grammaticale est la composante qui se réfère aux domaines de connaissances morphologiques, syntaxiques, lexicales, phonologiques et graphologiques.
Lire: Bachman, 1990, pp. 84–88.
CA:67, DA:119, DE:138, EN:158, ES:63, FR:65, GA:193, IT:65, NE:162, PO:79.

66 compétence langagière Connaissance de la langue. Le terme est souvent utilisé comme synonyme de "capacité langagière".
Lire: Bachman, 1990, p. 16.
CA:297, DA:355, DE:365, EN:206, ES:121, FR:66, GA:267, IT:66, NE:215, PO:81.

67 compétence linguistique Se réfère à la définition de compétence.
CA:68, DA:217, DE:224, EN:214, ES:64, FR:67, GA:198, IT:66, NE:231, PO:80.

68 compétence orale Capacité à parler une langue.
CA:298, DA:239, DE:370, EN:264, ES:65, FR:68, GA:266, IT:67, NE:354, PO:82.

69 compétence pragmatique Catégorie possible dans un modèle de capacité langagière communicative: elle inclut la capacité à produire des actes de langage, ainsi que les connaissances des conventions sociolinguistiques.
Lire: Bachman, 1990, p. 42.
CA:69, DA:294, DE:295, EN:290, ES:66, FR:69, GA:194, IT:68, NE:297, PO:83.

70 compétence sociolinguistique Catégorie dans un modèle de capacité langagière communicative: elle inclut la capacité à adapter son discours à des situations particulières en accord avec les normes sociales.
Lire: Bachman, 1990, p. 42.
CA:70, DA:347, DE:358, EN:369, ES:67, FR:70, GA:197, IT:69, NE:345, PO:84.

71 compétence unitaire Théorie du langage, promue notamment par Oller, qui postule l'existence d'une compétence unique, à la base de toutes les capacités langagières.
CA:71, DA:91, DE:423, EN:428, ES:68, FR:71, GA:192, IT:70, NE:408, PO:85.

72 composante Partie d'un examen, souvent présentée comme un test à part entière, comportant un livret de consignes et une limite de temps. Les composantes sont souvent des épreuves basées sur les aptitudes langagières telles que la compréhension ou la production orale. Egalement appelée sous-test.
CA:73, DA:181, DE:306, EN:61, ES:29, FR:72, GA:85, IT:81, NE:128, PO:87.

73 composition Tâche dans laquelle le candidat doit produire un texte écrit relativement long. Les textes types demandés dans ce genre de production peuvent inclure les narrations d'événements, les prises de position sur un sujet, les reportages et la rédaction de lettres formelles et informelles. Egalement appelé essai ou production écrite.
CA:366, DA:109, DE:32, EN:62, ES:192, FR:73, GA:51, IT:82, NE:372, PO:88.

74 composition discursive Tâche écrite, dans laquelle le candidat doit soit produire un discours à propos d'un sujet sur lequel il peut y avoir différentes prises de position, soit argumenter pour défendre son propre point de vue.
Voir: composition.
CA:74, DA:77, DE:342, EN:113, ES:70, FR:74, GA:52, IT:83, NE:42, PO:89.

75 comptage des occurences Comptage de la fréquence d'apparition de mots particuliers dans un texte. Cela peut être utile en évaluation lorsqu'on élabore des tests en fonction d'une spécification lexicale précise.
CA:190, DA:270, DE:143, EN:440, ES:362, FR:75, GA:67, IT:256, NE:436, PO:95.

76 confiance Concept statistique qui traite le fait que la réponse est ou non due au hasard.
Voir: erreur de type 1, erreur de type 2, hypothèse nulle.
Lire: Guilford et Fruchter, 1981, p. 208–210.
CA:388, DA:333, DE:349, EN:363, ES:386, FR:76, GA:366, IT:334, NE:338, PO:348.

77 connaissances antérieures du candidat syn: Antécédents expérientiels. Connaissances du candidat sur un sujet ou sur un contenu culturel présents dans un test donné et qui peuvent affecter la façon dont les entrées sont traitées. Visible notamment dans les tests de langue sur objectifs spéci-

fiques.
Lire: Bachman, 1990, p. 273.
CA:75, DA:26, DE:144, EN:27, ES:73, FR:77, GA:134, IT:85, NE:4, PO:91.

78 consigne Instructions données aux candidats afin de guider leurs réponses à une tâche précise.
Cf.: instructions.
CA:384, DA:264, DE:23, EN:336, ES:229, FR:78, GA:295, IT:193, NE:219, PO:92.

79 constance Aspect de la fidélité où l'estimation est basée sur une approche test-retest. Se réfère à la constance des notes obtenues aux tests dans le temps.
Voir: fidélité, fidélité test-retest.
CA:162, DA:359, DE:371, EN:378, ES:170, FR:79, GA:65, IT:337, NE:358, PO:173.

80 construct syn: concept hypothétique. Attribut hypothétique des individus ou opération mentale qui ne peut être directement ni mesurée ni observée (par exemple, en évaluation des langues, la capacité de compréhension orale). Les tests de langue essaient de mesurer les différents constructs qui sous-tendent les capacités langagières. En dehors de la capacité langagière, la motivation, l'attitude et l'acculturation constituent des constructs pertinents.
Lire: Hatch et Lazararaton, 1991, p. 15.
CA:78, DA:184, DE:185, EN:68, ES:76, FR:80, GA:394, IT:108, NE:72, PO:94.

81 correcteur Personne qui attribue une note aux réponses d'un candidat à un test écrit. Cette activité peut demander un jugement expert, ou, dans le cas d'une notation mécanique, la simple application d'un barème de notation.
Voir: examinateur, évaluateur.
CA:90, DA:288, DE:39, EN:221, ES:83, FR:81, GA:225, IT:102, NE:80, PO:182.

82 correction d'atténuation Méthode d'estimation de la corrélation entre deux ou plusieurs variables à condition qu'il n'y ait pas de différence de fidélité entre elles.
Lire: Guilford et Fruchter, 1981, pp.450–453; Hatch et Lazaraton, 1990, pp.444–445.
CA:88, DA:194, DE:243, EN:76, ES:79, FR:82, GA:53, IT:106, NE:78, PO:99.

83 correction d'élucidation Méthode visant à réduire le gain de points lorsque le candidat devine la réponse correcte dans des tests comportant des questions objectives.
Lire: Ebel et Fribie, 1986, pp. 215–218.
CA:82, DA:193, DE:317/450, EN:77, ES:80, FR:83, GA:54, IT:103, NE:77, PO:98.

84 correction sur épreuve Tâche où le candidat doit relire un texte en cherchant des erreurs spécifiques, par exemple d'orthographe ou de structures. On peut également lui demander de noter les erreurs et de fournir les formes correctes.
CA:395, DA:195, DE:189, EN:300, ES:4, FR:84, GA:374, IT:75, NE:304, PO:97.

85 corrélation Rapport entre deux ou plusieurs mesures, en fonction de leur variation dans la même direction. Si par exemple différents candidats obtiennent le même niveau à deux tests différents, il existe une corrélation positive entre les deux ensembles de notes.
Cf.: covariance.
Voir: coefficient de corrélation de rangs, corrélation de covariance de Pearson.
Lire: Guilford et Fruchter, 1981, chapître 6; Bachman, 1990, pp. 259–260.
CA:91, DA:196, DE:190, EN:78, ES:84, FR:85, GA:78, IT:95, NE:81, PO:100.

86 corrélation bisériale Indice de discrimination d'item concernant les items dichotomiques, qui s'écrit r_{bis}. Corrélation entre un critère (généralement la note totale du test) et la capacité à la base de la réponse vrai-faux à cet item. La valeur de r_{bis} est d'au moins 25% plus élevée que pour le point bisérial (r_{pbi}). L'avantage de r_{bis} est d'être relativement stable selon les échantillons de population de niveaux de capacités différents.
Cf.: coefficient de corrélation bisériale de point
Voir: discrimination.
Lire: Croker et Algina, 1986, pp. 317–318; Guilford et Fruchter, pp. 304–311; Linn, 1989, p. 359.
CA:56, DA:40, DE:60, EN:35, ES:85, FR:86, GA:79, IT:96, NE:48, PO:101.

87 corrélation de covariance de Pearson Coefficient de corrélation approprié qui utilise des variables mesurées sur des échelles d'intervalles ou de rapports.
Voir: coefficient de corrélation.
Lire: Hatch et Lazaraton, 1991, pp. 427–431; Guilford et Fruchter, 1981, p. 81.
CA:59, DA:279, DE:298, EN:274, ES:90, FR:87, GA:84, IT:98, NE:283, PO:104.

88 corrélation phi Se réfère à la définition du coefficient de corrélation phi.
CA:92, DA:285, DE:287, EN:280, ES:88, FR:88, GA:81, IT:101, NE:289, PO:103.

89 cotation (classification) polytomique La cotation polytomique (parfois appelée 'polychotomique'), consiste à coter un item sur une échelle comportant au moins trois points. On peut par exemple assigner 0, 1 ou 2 points à une question, c'est à dire trois points distincts.

Les questions ouvertes sont souvent notées de façon polytomique. Egalement appelée notation échelonnée.
Cf.: notation dichotomique.
CA:351, DA:291, DE:237, EN:284, ES:353, FR:89, GA:342, IT:34, NE:293, PO:64.

90 courbe caractéristique de l'item (CCI) Dans la théorie item-réponse , la CCI montre comment la probabilité de bonne réponse à un item est liée à une capacité latente, à la base de la performance réalisée sur les items du test.
Lire: Crooker et Algina, 1986, pp. 340–342.
CA:79, DA:157, DE:168, EN:192, ES:95, FR:90, GA:94, IT:115, NE:196, PO:109.

91 courbe de Gauss Se réfère à la définition de la fréquence normale.
CA:114, DA:114, DE:129, EN:152, ES:115, FR:91, GA:105, IT:133, NE:140, PO:110.

92 covariance Point de jonction d'une variance entre deux ou plusieurs variables. La longueur d'une phrase et la difficulté lexicale sont par exemple des traits qui, dans la lecture, tendent à être mis en relation, c'est à dire à covarier. La covariance doit être prise en compte lorsqu'on infère une variable à partir d'autres, lorsque par exemple on infère la difficulté d'un texte à partir de la longueur des phrases et de la difficulté grammaticale.
Voir: variance.
CA:93, DA:199, DE:192, EN:80, ES:91, FR:92, GA:71, IT:112, NE:84, PO:106.

93 curriculum Description exhaustive des buts, des contenus, de l'organisation, des méthodes et de l'évaluation d'un programme d'études.
Cf.: syllabus.
CA:94, DA:55, DE:71, EN:87, ES:93, FR:93, GA:99, IT:113, NE:220, PO:107.

94 d de Ebel Se réfère à la définition de l'indice-D (D pour discrimination).
CA:96, DA:85, DE:92, EN:122, ES:96, FR:94, GA:101, IT:116, NE:117, PO:111.

95 déclencheur Support graphique ou écrit qui permet d'obtenir une réponse du candidat dans les tests d'expression orale ou écrite.
CA:390, DA:316, DE:437 EN:299, ES:178, FR:95, GA:358, IT:343, NE:321, PO:179.

96 descripteur d'échelle Se réfère à la définition de descripteur.
CA:98, DA:338, DE:353, EN:344, ES:99, FR:96, GA:438, IT:119, NE:327, PO:112.

97 descripteur Brève description accompagnant un graphique en bande sur une échelle de notation. Elle résume le degré de compétence ou le type de performance attendu pour qu'un candidat atteigne une note précise.
CA:97, DA:64, DE:76, EN:96, ES:98, FR:97, GA:437, IT:118, NE:96, PO:113.

98 déviation standard Mesure de la dispertion d'un ensemble d'observations au sujet de la moyenne arithmétique. Egale à la racine carré de la variance. Dans une fréquence normale, 68% de l'échantillon est dans une déviation standard de la moyenne et 95% est dans deux déviations standard de la moyenne.

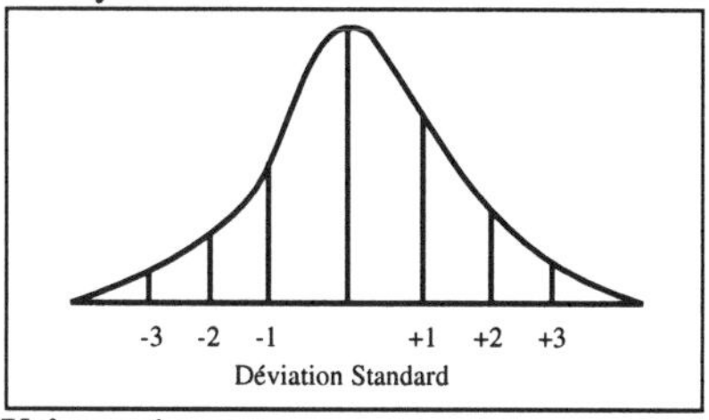

Voir: variance.
Lire: Ebel et Frisbie, 1991, pp. 61–62; Crocker et Algina, 1986, pp. 21–22.
CA:101, DA:362, DE:372, EN:379, ES:103, FR:98, GA:113, IT:122, NE:360, PO:114.

99 dictée Tâche dans laquelle le candidat doit écouter un texte et écrire les mots entendus. Les critères de notation des dictées varient selon l'objectif du test; ils peuvent inclure l'orthographe et la ponctuation.
CA:103, DA:68, DE:79, EN:99, ES:105, FR:99, GA:109, IT:121, NE:99, PO:125.

100 diplôme Document statuant nominalement qu'un individu a réussi un examen ou une partie d'un examen et a obtenu un niveau particulier, généralement passable. On considère souvent qu'il est d'un niveau supérieur au certificat.
Cf.: certificat.
CA:104, DA:69, DE:80, EN:103, ES:106, FR:100, GA:118, IT:124, NE:101, PO:115.

101 discours Texte oral ou écrit, considéré comme un acte de langage communicatif.
CA:106, DA:75, DE:85, EN:106, ES:108, FR:101, GA:119, IT:125, NE:103, PO:117.

102 discrimination Le fait qu'un item puisse établir une distinction entre des candidats en les classant selon un degré allant de plus faibles à plus forts. On utilise plusieurs indices de discrimination. Certains (comme le point bisérial) sont basés sur la corrélation entre la note obtenue à un item

et un critère. Celui-ci peut être la note totale obtenue à ce test ou une autre mesure externe de niveau de capacité. D'autres critères sont basés sur la différence de difficulté de l'item pour des groupes de capacité faible et haute. Dans la théorie item-réponse, les modèles de paramètre 2 et 3 désignent l'item de dicrimination comme le paramètre-A.
Voir: corrélation bisériale, coefficient de corrélation bisériale de point, théorie de l'item-réponse TIR.
Lire: Croker et Algina, 1986, pp. 313–320; Ebel et Frisbie, 1991, PP; 231–232.

CA:105, DA:74, DE:416, EN:112, ES:107, FR:102, GA:180, IT:126, NE:109, PO:116.

103 dispersion Taux de variation ou d'étalement des notes d'un groupe de candidats. Si la dispertion est grande, les notes sont largement éparpillées. Si elle est faible, les notes sont fortement regroupées.
Voir: déviation standard, variance.

CA:107, DA:353, DE:385, EN:114, ES:110, FR:103, GA:357, IT:127, NE:356, PO:118.

104 distracteur Dans un item à choix multiple, option autre que la réponse correcte.
Cf.: réponse clé.
Voir: item à choix multiple.
Lire: Ebel et Frisbie, 1986, pp. 176–185.

CA:110, DA:79, DE:88, EN:115, ES:111, FR:104, GA:348, IT:129, NE:8, PO:126.

105 distribution (fréquence) Dans les données apportées par le test, nombre des occurences de chaque note obtenue par les candidats. Elle est souvent représentée sous forme d'histogramme.

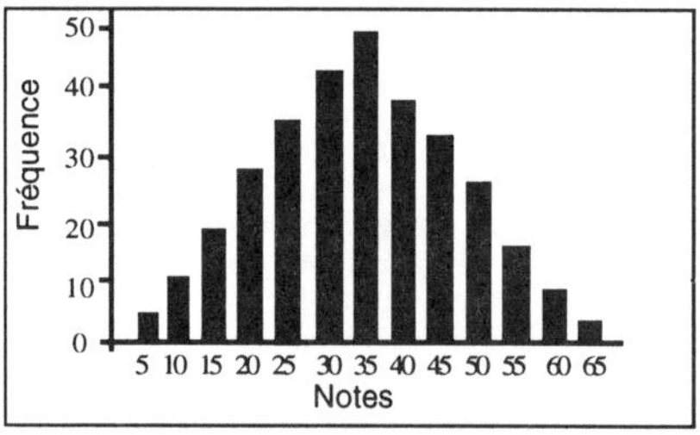

Voir: distribution (fréquence) normale, distribution symétrique.
Lire: Hatch et Lazaraton, 1991, pp. 159–178.P.18

CA:111, DA:103, DE:434, EN:117, ES:112, FR:105, GA:103, IT:130, NE:110, PO:119.

106 distribution bimodale Type de distribution à deux modes ou sommets, qui suggère que l'échantillon est constitué de deux groupes différents.

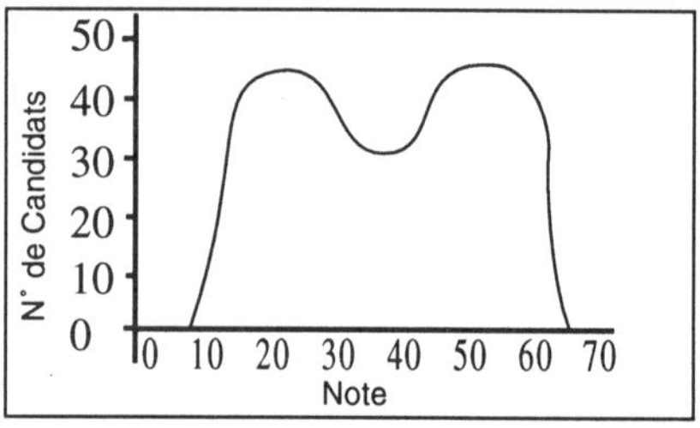

Cf.: distribution (fréquence) normale.
Voir: mode.
Lire: Hatch et Lazaraton, 1991, p. 166.

CA:112, DA:39, DE:59, EN:34, ES:113, FR:106, GA:104, IT:131, NE:47, PO:121.

107 distribution de fréquences Se réfère à la définition de distribution (fréquence).

CA:113, DA:107, DE:142, EN:149, ES:114, FR:107, GA:106, IT:132, NE:138, PO:122.

108 distribution (fréquence) normale Distribution mathématique à la base de différentes procédures statistiques. Distribution symétrique de notes qui est représentée graphiquement sous la forme d'une courbe en cloche, et où la moyenne, la médiane et le mode occupent le même point. Il existe toute une famille de distributions qui dépendent de la valeur de la moyenne, des déviations standards et du nombre d'observations. Elle est également appelée courbe de Gauss.
Cf.: distribution bimodale.
Lire: Hatch et Lazaraton, 1991, p. 164.

CA:115, DA:252, DE:265, EN:252, ES:116, FR:108, GA:107, IT:134, NE:262, PO:123.

109 distribution symétrique Caractéristique d'une distribution, lorsque le sommet de la courbe se trouve soit à droite du centre (symétrie négative), soit à gauche (symétrie positive).

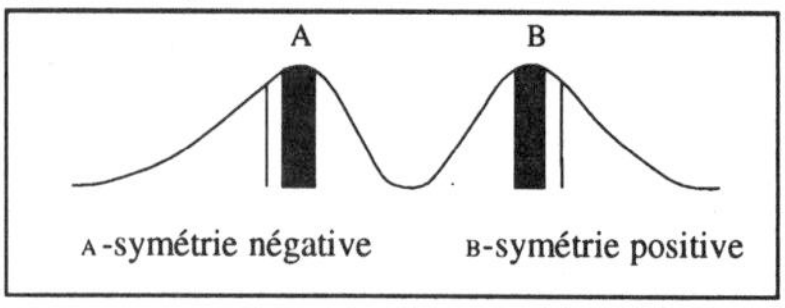

Voir: distribution (fréquence) normale.
Lire: Hatch et Lazaraton, 1991, p. 165.

CA:25, DA:343, DE:337, EN:366, ES:31, FR:109, GA:323, IT:25, NE:330, PO:120.

110 distribution tronquée Type de distribution de fréquence, caractéristique d'un échantillon de rangs plus étroits que la population d'où il est tiré, les étudiants aux notes élevées ou aux notes basses n'y étant pas représentés. Un tel échantillon serait par exemple un groupe d'étudiants admis à suivre un cours après avoir réussi l'examen d'entrée.

CA:116, DA:376, DE:1, EN:421, ES:117, FR:110, GA:108, IT:135, NE:343, PO:124.

111 document authentique Texte ou document utilisé dans un test et qui n'a pas été conçu à des fins pédagogiques ou à des situations d'évaluation. [NB: On peut l'utiliser dans des tests en y apportant quelques modifications].
Voir: document semi-authentique.

CA:404, DA:22, DE:41, EN:25, ES:401, FR:111, GA:382, IT:390, NE:24, PO:127.

112 document semi-authentique Texte authentique dont le vocabulaire ou la grammaire a été adapté au niveau des candidats pour les besoins de l'évaluation.
Voir: document authentique.

CA:405, DA:123, DE:140, EN:355, ES:400, FR:112, GA:383, IT:391, NE:335, PO:128.

113 domaine Ensemble défini de contenus et/ou de niveaux de capacacité que l'on va tester à l'aide d'une tâche spécifique ou de l'une des composantes d'un examen.
Lire: Bachman, 1990, pp. 244–246.

CA:11, DA:83, DE:238, EN:119, ES:119, FR:113, GA:137, IT:332, NE:113, PO:129.

114 double notation Méthode d'évaluation où la performance du candidat est validée de façon indépendante par deux correcteurs.
Voir: notation multiple.

CA:84, DA:82, DE:91, EN:121, ES:118, FR:114, GA:221, IT:104, NE:116, PO:61.

115 écart D Se réfère à la définition de l'indice-D.

CA:206, DA:246, DE:257, EN:247, ES:97, FR:115, GA:102, IT:194, NE:256, PO:111.

116 échantillon Sélection d'un sous-ensemble d'éléments dans une population. On peut distinguer plusieurs sortes d'échantillons, par exemple l'échantillon aléatoire, l'échantillon stratifié, etc.
Lire: Crocker et Algina, 1986, pp. 432–438; Guilford et Fruchter, 1981, pp. 44–45.

CA:264, DA:371, DE:380, EN:337, ES:278, FR:116, GA:304, IT:46, NE:369, PO:8.

117 échantillon aléatoire Echantillon choisi au hasard, tous les individus de la population ayant les mêmes chances d'être choisis pour la recherche.
Voir: échantillon.
Lire: Crocker et Algina, 1986, pp. 433–438; Guilford et Fruchter, 1981, p. 120.

CA:265, DA:409, DE:451, EN:307, ES:279, FR:117, GA:305, IT:47, NE:120, PO:9.

118 échantillon d'écrits Echantillon de réponses de candidats représentatifs d'un niveau de capacité. Utilisés dans la standardisation des examinateurs.

CA:268, DA:370, DE:254, EN:338, ES:132, FR:118, GA:344, IT:330, NE:420, PO:10.

119 échantillon stratifié Echantillon d'une population soumise à une recherche, qui est tout d'abord subdivisé en un certain nombre de sous-population (couches, rangs, strates) et dont un échantillon est extrait.
Voir: échantillon.
Lire: Guilford et Fruchter, 1981, pp. 122–123.

CA:266, DA:375, DE:134, EN:388, ES:280, FR:119, GA:306, IT:48, NE:157, PO:11.

120 échantillonage Sélection d'un échantillon.
Voir: échantillon.

CA:267, DA:374, DE:384, EN:340, ES:281, FR:120, GA:307, IT:45, NE:368, PO:313.

121 échelle Ensemble de catégories destinées à mesurer quelque chose. On en distingue quatre sortes: échelle nominale, ordinale, d'intervalle et de rapport.
Lire: Crocker et Algina, 1986, pp. 46–49.

CA:144, DA:337, DE:352, EN:343, ES:152, FR:121, GA:308, IT:314, NE:326, PO:154.

122 échelle absolue Echelle comportant un véritable point zéro, comme, par exemple, dans une échelle pour mesurer la longueur. Le zéro absolu ne pouvant être défini dans les tests de langue, cette échelle ne peut leur être appliquée.
Cf.: échelle d'intervalle, échelle nominale, échelle ordinale.

CA:145, DA:4, DE:433, EN:4, ES:153, FR:122, GA:112, IT:317, NE:2, PO:155.

123 échelle catégorique syn: échelle qualitative. Echelle utilisée pour des variables catégoriques telles que le genre, la langue maternelle, la profession.

Cf: échelle d'intervalle, échelle nominale, échelle ordinale, échelle de rapport.

CA:146, DA:170, DE:175, EN:42, ES:154, FR:123, GA:310, IT:318, NE:53, PO:156.

124 échelle centile syn: échelle percentile. Echelle ordinaire, divisée en 100 unités ou centiles. Un sujet classé au quatre-vingt-quinzième centile est supérieur à 95 sujets dans un échantillon de 100.
Lire: Croker et Algina, 1986, pp. 439–442; Guilford et Fruchter, 1981, pp. 38–41.

CA:151, DA:46, DE:300, EN:46, ES:155, FR:124, GA:311, IT:319, NE:54, PO:157.

125 échelle commune Façon de reporter les notes obtenues à deux ou plusieurs tests sur une échelle commune, permettant une comparaison directe des résultats. Cela est faisable si les notes brutes ont été au préalable transformées par une procédure statistique, comme par exemple le calibrage.
Lire: Bachman, 1990, pp. 340–344.

CA:147, DA:110, DE:131, EN:57, ES:156, FR:125, GA:86, IT:320, NE:148, PO:158.

126 échelle d'intervalle Echelle de mesure sur laquelle la distance entre deux unités de mesure adjacentes est la même, mais sur laquelle il n'existe pas de point zéro significatif.
Cf.: échelle catégorique, échelle nominale, échelle ordinale, échelle de rapport.
Lire: Crocker et Algina, 1986, p. 48.

CA:148, DA:149, DE:161, EN:184, ES:158, FR:126, GA:315, IT:315, NE:188, PO:162.

127 échelle d'intervalle égal syn: équipartition. Se réfère à la definition de l'échelle d'intervalle.

CA:149, DA:213, DE:161, EN:125, ES:159, FR:127, GA:316, IT:316, NE:145, PO:161.

128 échelle de capacité Dans la théorie de l'item-réponse TIR, échelle graduée à intervalles égaux, sur laquelle il est possible de situer à la fois les capacités d'un individu et le niveau de difficulté des tâches demandées. Egalement appelée échelle theta.
Lire: Bachman, 1990, p. 345.

CA:150/158, DA:3/407, DE:114/413, EN:3/413, ES:157/166, FR:128, GA:313/320, IT:322/328, NE:385/413, PO:159/168.

129 échelle de likert Type d'échelle utilisée dans les questionnaires pour mesurer les attitudes ou les opinions. On demande aux sujets de se définir par rapport à une série d'affirmations en choisissant l'une des cinq possibilités suivantes: "approuve totalement", "approuve", "ne sait pas", "désapprouve", "désapprouve fortement".

CA:152, DA:214, DE:222, EN:211, ES:163, FR:129, GA:317, IT:325, NE:228, PO:163.

130 échelle de notation syn: échelle d'évaluation. Echelle composée de plusieurs catégories qui permettent d'exercer un jugement subjectif. Ce type d'échelle est fréquemment accompagné de descripteurs qui permettent d'interprêter les catégories.
Cf.: échelle de likert.
Voir: descripteur.

CA:154, DA:172, DE:58, EN:315, ES:161, FR:130, GA:319, IT:323, NE:40, PO:160.

131 échelle de rapport Echelle comportant un vrai zéro et sur laquelle la distance entre deux points adjacents est la même. Pour la taille, par exemple, une personne mesurant deux mètres est deux fois plus grande que celle qui mesure un mètre de haut.
Cf.: échelle catégorique, échelle d'intervalle, échelle ordinale.
Lire: Crocker et Algina, 1986, pp. 48–49.

CA:153, DA:210, DE:433, EN:317, ES:160, FR:131, GA:312, IT:324, NE:314, PO:164.

132 échelle delta Echelle normalisée, avec une moyenne de 13 et une déviation standart de 4.

CA:155, DA:60, DE:75, EN:93, ES:162, FR:132, GA:314, IT:321, NE:94, PO:165.

133 échelle nominale Echelle comportant des variables catégoriques telles que le genre ou la première langue. De telles variables peuvent être présentes ou absentes, l'intérêt résidant en la fréquence de leur occurence. Egalement appelée échelle catégorique.
Cf.: échelle d'intervalle, échelle ordinale, échelle de rapport.
Lire: Hatch et Lazaraton, 1991, pp. 55–56.

CA:156, DA:249, DE:262, EN:248, ES:164, FR:133, GA:309, IT:326, NE:260, PO:166.

134 échelle ordinale Type d'échelle de mesure qui permet de classer les candidats sans indiquer l'écart relatif qui existe entre chacun d'eux.
Cf.: échelle catégorique, échelle d'intervalle, échelle nominale, échelle de rapport.
Lire: hatch et Lazaraton, 1991, pp. 56–57.

CA:157, DA:271, DE:275, EN:265, ES:165, FR:134, GA:318, IT:327, NE:275,

PO:167.

135 échelonnage Elaboration des échelles de mesure. En évaluation, cela signifie que des chiffres sont associés aux performances des candidats, afin de refléter l'évolution des niveaux de connaissance ou de capacité. L'échelonnage peut impliquer une modification d'un ensemble de notes afin de produire une échelle à but spécifique, par exemple pour reporter les résultats de façon standardisée, ou pour apparier une version d'un test avec une autre.
Voir: échelle, échelle de capacité, échelle centile, échelle commune, échelle d'intervalle, échelle nominale, échelle ordinale, échelle de rapport, échelle de notation, formes calibrées, calibrage linéaire.

CA:159, DA:341, DE:355, EN:346, ES:167, FR:135, GA:321, IT:109, NE:329, PO:169.

136 effet de contamination Effet qui se manifeste lorsqu'un évaluateur note en fonction d'un facteur différent de celui qui est testé. Il peut par exemple augmenter la note d'un candidat dans un test d'expression écrite si ce dernier possède une belle écriture.
Voir: effets parasites de la correction.

CA:118, DA:9, DE:226, EN:71, ES:122, FR:136, GA:174, IT:141, NE:74, PO:132.

137 effet de halo Tendance qu'ont les examinateurs, lors d'un examen qui leur demande une notation subjective, à être influencés par la performance d'un candidat à une tâche donnée et à lui donner de ce fait une note trop élevée ou trop faible lors de la réalisation d'une tâche différente.
Voir: effets parasites de la correction.

CA:117, DA:118, DE:141, EN:161, ES:127, FR:137, GA:170, IT:139, NE:164, PO:133.

138 effet de la pratique Effet sur les notes, venant de l'habitude que le candidat possède du type de tâche ou d'items proposés dans le test.

CA:119, DA:443, DE:419, EN:289, ES:123, FR:138, GA:169, IT:140, NE:298, PO:131.

139 effet de méthode Effet produit sur les notes des tests venant plus de la méthode d'évaluation utilisée que de la capacité du candidat.

CA:121, DA:229, DE:242, EN:233, ES:126, FR:139, GA:171, IT:142, NE:244, PO:134.

140 effet de plafonnement Effet limite qui résulte de la trop grande facilité d'un test par rapport à un groupe donné de candidats. Toutes les notes obtenues se regroupent alors au sommet de la distribution.
Voir: effets limite.

CA:123, DA:219, DE:63/73, EN:44, ES:129, FR:140, GA:173, IT:145, NE:292, PO:137.

141 effet de plancher Effet limite qui résulte de la trop grande difficulté d'un test pour un groupe donné de candidats. Toutes les notes obtenues se regroupent alors au bas de la distribution.
Voir: effets limite.

CA:122, DA:42, DE:61/121, EN:146, ES:128, FR:141, GA:175, IT:144, NE:49, PO:130.

142 effet séquentiel Effet parasite de l'évaluation produit par l'ordre dans lequel les tests sont corrigés.
Voir: effets parasites de la correction.

CA:120, DA:329, DE:292, EN:360, ES:125, FR:142, GA:172, IT:148, NE:337, PO:136.

143 effets limite Effets provenant de la trop grande facilité ou difficulté d'un test pour un groupe donné de candidats. Les notes tendent alors à se regrouper au sommet de la distribution (effet de plafonnement), ou au bas (effet de plancher).
Voir: effet de plancher, effet de plafonnement.

CA:125, DA:120, DE:139, EN:36, ES:131, FR:143, GA:177, IT:138, NE:163, PO:139.

144 effets parasites de la correction Source d'erreur dans l'évaluation, résultant de certaines tendances des correcteurs à noter avec sévérité ou avec indulgence, ou bien à valoriser un certain type de candidats, affectant ainsi les notes données au test. Quelques exemples sont l'effet de contamination, l'effet de halo ou l'effet séquentiel.

CA:124, DA:34, DE:425, EN:313, ES:130, FR:144, GA:176, IT:143, NE:35, PO:138.

145 élaborateur Personne qui écrit et construit un test.

CA:109/127, DA:392/405, DE:395/400, EN:361/399, ES:92/133, FR:145, GA:121/149, IT:149, NE:391/399, PO:141.

146 élaboration de test Action de sélectionner des items ou des tâches en vue de la constitution d'un test. Souvent précédé par le prétestage ou l'essai du matériel. Les items ou les tâches pour l'élaboration de tests peuvent être sélectionnés dans une banque de matériel.

CA:126, DA:394, DE:397, EN:398, ES:75, FR:146, GA:393, IT:110, NE:392, PO:140.

147 entrée Matériel donné dans un test afin que le candidat produise une réponse appropriée. Dans une épreuve de compréhension orale, par exemple, le texte peut être enregistré et accompagné d'un questionnaire écrit.

CA:169, DA:142, DE:408, EN:174, ES:228, FR:147, GA:199, IT:199, NE:180, PO:254.

148 entretien oral Les aptitudes d'expression orale sont souvent évaluées lors d'un entretien. Celui-ci peut prendre la forme d'une conversation libre entre le candidat et l'examinateur ou présenter un ensemble structuré de tâches orales à réaliser.

CA:131, DA:150, DE:305, EN:263, ES:136, FR:148, GA:1, IT:92, NE:355, PO:143.

149 épreuve du khi deux Procédure statistique qui compare les valeurs des réponses observées et celles des reponses attendues, afin d'indiquer si la différence est statistiquement significative, les réponses attendues étant données. Il s'agit d'une procédure non-paramétrique.
Voir: procédures non-paramétriques.
Lire: Hatch et Lazaraton, 1991, pp. 393–415.

CA:330, DA:49, DE:65, EN:49, ES:396, FR:149, GA:409, IT:359, NE:59, PO:395.

150 épreuve du *t* Test statistique utilisé pour déterminer s'il existe une différence significative entre les moyennes de deux échantillons.

CA:340, DA:385, DE:387, EN:423, ES:398, FR:150, GA:368, IT:385, NE:377, PO:397.

151 erreur Dans la théorie classique de la mesure de la note vraie, la note obtenue à un test possède deux composantes: une note vraie qui reflète le niveau de capacité de la personne et une note erronée qui reflète l'influence de tous les autres facteurs non liés à la capacité testée. L'erreur est censée être due au hasard, c'est-à-dire non systématique. De plus, d'autres facteurs peuvent affecter la performance de certains individus, provocant des erreurs systématiques ou des biais.
Cf.: biais.
Lire: Bachman, 1990, p. 167.

CA:136, DA:98, DE:116, EN:129, ES:144, FR:151, GA:122, IT:154, NE:124, PO:146.

152 erreur accidentelle Se réfère à la définition de l'erreur.

CA:137, DA:408, DE:449, EN:306, ES:145, FR:152, GA:128, IT:156, NE:310, PO:147,

153 erreur de mesure Se réfère à la définition de l'erreur standard de mesure.

CA:138, DA:240/241, DE:239/240, EN:130/231, ES:146, FR:153, GA:123/130, IT:159, NE:242/243, PO:149.

154 erreur de type 1 Syn: erreur de première espèce. En statistiques, erreur due au rejet de l'hypothèse nulle, quand en réalité elle est exacte.
Cf.: erreur de type 2.
Voir: hypothèse nulle.
Lire: Hatch et Lazaraton, 1991, p. 224.

CA:140, DA:417, DE:9/117, EN:425, ES:150, FR:154, GA:126, IT:157, NE:405, PO:150.

155 erreur de type 2 En statistiques, erreur due à l'acceptation de l'hypothèse nulle, quand en réalité elle est fausse.
Cf.: erreur de type 1.
Voir: hypothèse nulle.
Lire: Hatch et Lazaraton, 1991, p. 224.

CA:141, DA:418, DE:118, EN:426, ES:151, FR:155, GA:127, IT:158, NE:406, PO:151.

156 erreur standard d'estimation syn: écart type résiduel, erreur standard sur la mesure. Mesure de la précision de la prédiction d'une variable à partir d'une autre, par exemple, dans une régression linéaire. elle donne les intervalles de confiance pour des notes criteriées.
Voir: intervalle de confiance (d'une mesure).
Lire: Hatch et lazaraton, 1991, pp. 477–479.

CA:142, DA:361, DE:375, EN:380, ES:148, FR:156, GA:124, IT:163, NE:363, PO:152.

157 erreur standard de mesure Dans la théorie de la note vraie, l'erreur standard de mesure (*Se*), indique l'imprécision de la mesure. La grandeur de l'erreur standard de mesure dépend de la fidélité (*r*) et de la déviation standard des notes (*Sx*). Pour calculer *Se* la formule est:

$$Se = Sx\sqrt{(1-r)}\ .$$

Si par exemple un candidat obtient une note vraie T et si une déviation standard de mesure de *Se*, revient fréquemment dans le test, cela signifie que 68% des fois, la note

observée sera dans le rang T ± *Se*; et que 95% du temps elle sera dans le rang T ± 2*Se*.
Lire: Crocker et Algina, 1986, pp. 122–124.
CA:143, DA:364, DE:374, EN:381, ES:149, FR:157, GA:125, IT:12, NE:362, PO:153.

158 erreur sur l'échantillonage Erreur introduite dans une analyse statistique et due à la sélection de l'échantillon particulier qui a été utilisé dans l'étude (par exemple, échantillon non représentatif de la population).
Voir: population.
CA:139, DA:372, DE:381, EN:341, ES:147, FR:158, GA:129, IT:155, NE:370, PO:148.

159 essai Se réfère à la définition de la composition.
CA:366, DA:262, DE:33, EN:131, ES:306, FR:159, GA:7, IT:313, NE:125, PO:142.

160 essai Etape du développement de la tâche d'un test servant à savoir si le test fonctionne de la façon espérée. Souvent utilisé dans le cas de tâches à notation subjective telles que l'essai, administré à une population limitée.
Cf.: pré-test.
CA:26, DA:301, DE:104, EN:418, ES:135, FR:160, GA:436, IT:336, NE:303, PO:185.

161 estimation de la bipartition de Spearman-Brown Se réfère à la définition de la fidélité de bipartition.
CA:168, DA:350, DE:360, EN:372, ES:177, FR:161, GA:228, IT:342, NE:349, PO:178.

162 étalonnage syn: standardisation. Processus par lequel on s'assure que les examinateurs sont d'accord avec une procédure donnée et appliquent correctement les échelles de notation.
Voir: examinateur.
CA:167, DA:363, DE:373, EN:383, ES:175, NE:361, FR:162, GA:45, IT:338, PO:295.

163 étude pilote Etude exploratoire pendant laquelle les chercheurs ou les élaborateurs de tests éprouvent leurs idées sur un petit nombre de sujets de façon à localiser les problèmes avant de se lancer dans un essai à grande échelle, un programme ou un produit.
Voir: essai, pré-test.
CA:170, DA:286, DE:288, EN:281, ES:179, FR:163, GA:361, IT:344, NE:290, PO:180.

164 évaluateur Se réfère à la définition de l'examinateur.
CA:361, DA:306, DE:100, EN:311, ES:187, FR:164, GA:287, IT:102, NE:34, PO:182.

165 évaluation Dans l'évaluation en langue, mesure d'un ou de plusieurs aspects du niveau de capacité, au moyen d'un test ou d'un autre type de procédure.
Lire: Bachman, 1990, p. 50.
CA:31, DA:30, DE:54, EN:21, ES:180, FR:165, GA:229, IT:421, NE:39, PO:30.

166 évaluation Recueil systématique d'informations dans le but de prendre une décision (Weiss, 1972). Dans les tests de langue, l'évaluation peut être centrée sur l'efficacité ou bien l'impact d'un programme d'enseignement, d'un examen ou d'un projet.
CA:31, DA:93, DE:106, EN:132, ES:180, FR:166, GA:235, IT:413, NE:126, PO:30.

167 évaluation de la compétence minimale Evaluation qui présente des exigences spécifiques pour un niveau minimal de compétence dans un domaine particulier de l'utilisation de la langue. Un candidat qui peut démontrer ce niveau de compétence réussit le test.
CA:312, DA:398, DE:304, EN:234, ES:183, FR:167, GA:378, IT:388, NE:246, PO:31.

168 évaluation formative a) Evaluation qui prend place pendant l'apprentissage plutôt qu'à la fin. Les résultats peuvent permettre à l'enseignant de pratiquer dès le début une remédiation ou de changer si besoin est le déroulement de son enseignement.

b) Evaluation continue d'un processus, qui permet de l'adapter et de l'améliorer en permanence. Peut se référer à un programme éducatif.
Cf.: évaluation sommative.
CA:32, DA:225/226, DE:213/46, EN:147/148, ES:184, FR:168, GA:232/236, IT:414/422, NE:136/137, PO:32.

169 évaluation globale Méthode de notation qui peut être utilisée dans les tests de production écrite et orale. L'examinateur donne une note unique en fonction de l'impression générale donnée par la production, au lieu de répartir en plusieurs notes les différents aspects du langage utilisé.
Cf.: notation analytique, notation liée à l'impression générale.
CA:33, DA:124, DE:137, EN:155, ES:427, FR:169, GA:231, IT:186, NE:161, PO:33.

170 évaluation holistique ou globaliste Se réfère à la définition de l'évaluation globale.

CA:429, DA:126, DE:128, EN:164, ES:428, FR:170, GA:230, IT:187, NE:168, PO:34.

171 évaluation par ordinateur Méthode d'évaluation où les questions sont présentées par ordinateur. Les candidats peuvent y répondre directement sur l'ordinateur.

CA:332, DA:52, DE:68, EN:64, ES:182, FR:171, GA:380, IT:387, NE:70, PO:35.

172 évaluation sommative Evaluation qui prend place à la fin d'un processus. Peut se référer à un programme éducatif.
Cf.: évaluation formative.

CA:34, DA:266/267, DE:3/4, EN:390/391, ES:186, FR:172, GA:233/238, IT:415/423, NE:374/375, PO:36.

173 examen Procédure servant à évaluer le niveau de compétence ou de connaissance d'un individu par l'administration de tests oraux et/ou écrits. La réussite à une qualification (par exemple l'obtention d'un certificat), l'entrée dans un établissement éducatif ou l'accès à un programme d'études, etc. peuvent dépendre du résultat de l'examen.
Cf.: test.
Lire: Bachman, 1990, p. 50.

CA:171, DA:86, DE:303, EN:133, ES:188, FR:173, GA:347, IT:164, NE:127, PO:181.

174 examinateur syn: évaluateur. Personne chargée de noter, de façon subjective, la performance du candidat à un test donné. Les évaluateurs sont généralement qualifiés dans leur domaine. On attend d'eux qu'ils se soumettent à un processus de formation et de standardisation. A l'oral, on distingue parfois les rôles d'examinateur et d'interlocuteur.
Cf.: interlocuteur, correcteur.

CA:35/172, DA:32/89, DE:55/301, EN:22/135, ES:46/189, FR:174, GA:234/346, IT:165, NE:33/130, PO:182.

175 expansion de phrases Type d'item dans lequel une amorce de phrase, comportant des mots convenables est donnée, mais d'où les prépositions, les verbes auxiliaires, les articles, etc. sont absents. La tâche du candidat consiste à ajouter les mots manquants, complétant ainsi l'amorce pour en faire une phrase grammaticalement correcte.

CA:99, DA:380, DE:333, EN:358, ES:18, FR:175, GA:148, IT:166, NE:441, PO:184.

176 facettes des méthodes de test Se réfère à la définition des caractéristiques de la méthode de test.

CA:175, DA:396, DE:402, EN:403, ES:193, FR:176, GA:163, IT:50, NE:397, PO:186.

177 facteur-G Dans la théorie de l'intelligence, "facteur général" hypothétique sous-jacent à toutes les aptitudes cognitives. Notion vulgarisée par John Oller dans les années 70 comme marque d'une compétence unique à la base des capacités langagières.
Lire: Oller, 1979, pp. 426–458; Bachman, 1990, p. 6.

CA:176, DA:113, DE:127, EN:153, ES:194, FR:177, GA:136, IT:170, NE:139, PO:187.

178 facteurs affectifs Facteurs de nature non cognitive liés aux variables émotionnelles, aux préférences et aux comportements des sujets.
Cf.: facteurs cognitifs.
Lire: Ebel et Frisbie, 1991, p. 52.

CA:177, DA:6, DE:7, EN:9, ES:195, FR:178, GA:399, IT:172, NE:6, PO:188.

179 facteurs cognitifs Facteurs concernant l'apprentissage ou le processus d'évaluation et qui mettent en rapport les schémas et les modèles de connaissances de l'apprenant.
Cf.: facteurs affectifs.
Lire: Ebel et Frisbie, 1991, p. 52.

CA:178, DA:177, DE:180, EN:55, ES:196, FR:179, GA:398, IT:171, NE:65, PO:189.

180 feuille(s) de question Parfois utilisé pour désigner la ou les feuilles sur lesquelles le test est présenté.

CA:239, DA:263, DE:123, EN:304, ES:220, FR:180, GA:271, IT:169, NE:425, PO:145.

181 feuille de réponses Feuille sur laquelle le candidat répond aux questions.
Cf.: lecteur optique.

CA:191, DA:37, DE:22, EN:19, ES:219, FR:181, GA:152, IT:174, NE:20, PO:198.

182 feuille d'épreuves Façon de se référer à une des composantes d'un test, par exemple, feuille de compréhension de lecture, feuille de compréhension orale.

CA:385, DA:393, DE:277, EN:267, ES:381, FR:182, GA:270, IT:168, NE:278, PO:87.

183 fidélité Uniformité, constance ou stabilité des mesures dans un test. Plus un test est fidèle, moins il contient d'erreurs

accidentelles. Un test présentant une erreur systématique, par exemple un biais vis à vis de certains groupes, peut être fidèle, mais pas valide.
Cf.: validité.
Voir: KR-20 (formule 20 de Kuder-Richardson), alpha (coefficient alpha), fidélité de bi-partition, fidélité test-retest.
Lire: Bachman, 1990, p. 24; Crocker et Algina, 1986, chapitre 6.
CA:180, DA:312, DE:322/453, EN:327, ES:198, FR:183, GA:200, IT:6, NE:43, PO:193.

184 fidélité de bi-partition Mesure de cohérence interne de la fidélité. L'estimation est basée sur la corrélation entre les notes de deux demi tests considérés comme deux tests alternés. La division en deux moitiés peut être faite de différentes façons: première et seconde moitié, ou bien en regroupant les items pairs dans la première moitié et les impairs dans la seconde.
Voir: fidélité.
Lire: Ebel et Frisbie, 1991, pp. 82–83; Crocker et Algina, 1986, pp. 136–138.
CA:183, DA:259, DE:364/398, EN:377, ES:201, FR:184, GA:203, IT:7, NE:353, PO:194.

185 fidélité inter-individuelle Estimation de la fidélité d'un test basée sur le degré d'accord obtenu par différents examinateurs au sujet de la performance d'un candidat.
Voir: accord inter-individuel, fidélité.
CA:181, DA:145, DE:158, EN:182, ES:199, FR:185, GA:201, IT:8, NE:184, PO:195.

186 fidélité interne Caractéristique d'un test, représentée par le degré auquel les notes obtenues par un candidat aux questions individuelles d'un test, est en harmonie avec la note totale. Les estimations de fidélité interne peuvent être utilisées comme indice de la fidélité d'un test; plusieurs indices peuvent être calculés, par exemple KR20, alpha.
Voir: Kuder-Richardson, fidélité.
Lire: Bachman, 1990, p. 172.
CA:77, DA:147, DE:155, EN:180, ES:74, FR:186, GA:87, IT:87, NE:186, PO:93.

187 fidélité intra-individuelle Estimation de la fidélité de l'évaluation, basée sur le degré de similitude de notation d'une même performance effectuée à différentes occasions.
Voir: accord inter-individuel.
CA:182, DA:151, DE:162, EN:186, ES:200, FR:187, GA:202, IT:89, NE:189, PO:196.

188 fidélité test-retest Estimation de la fidélité obtenue en administrant deux fois le même test aux mêmes candidats, dans les mêmes conditions, et en mettant en relation les notes obtenues. Ce processus concerne la stabilité dans le temps des notes obtenues et est également utilisé lorsqu'on ne peut obtenir d'estimations de fidélité interne.
Cf.: fidélité interne.
Voir: fidélité, constance.
CA:184, DA:318, DE:409/325, EN:410, ES:202, FR:188, GA:204, IT:9, NE:383, PO:197.

189 fonction de l'item-réponse Dans la théorie de l'item-réponse TIR, fonction mathématique qui met en relation la probabilité de succès à un item avec la capacité mesurée par l'item. Connu également comme fonction caractéristique de l'item.
CA:193, DA:158, DE:172, EN:194, ES:210, FR:189, GA:140, IT:183, NE:200, PO:205.

190 fonction informative de l'item Indice de la somme d'information qu'un item ou un test peut apporter sur un sujet d'un niveau de capacité donné. Dépend du niveau de discrimination de l'item et de son adéquation au niveau de capacité (théorie IR).
Cf.: fonction informative du test.
CA:192, DA:156, DE:169, EN:193, ES:212, FR:190, GA:138, IT:184, NE:197, PO:206.

191 fonction informative du test Dans la théorie de l'item réponse, indice montrant la somme d'information apportée sur une personne ayant un niveau de capacité donné. Il s'agit de la somme des fonctions d'information de l'item.
Cf.: fonction informative de l'item.
Lire: Crocker et Algina, 1986, pp. 369–371.
CA:194, DA:388, DE:399, EN:400, ES:211, FR:191, GA:139, IT:185, NE:394, PO:207.

192 fonctionnement de l'item différentiel La difficulté relative d'un item dépend des caractéristiques du groupe à qui il est administré. Cela peut être par exemple la langue maternelle ou le sexe du sujet.
Voir: biais.
CA:195, DA:66, DE:78, EN:100, ES:209, FR:192, GA:114, IT:182, NE:100, PO:208.

193 formes alternées Se refère à la

définition des formes équivalentes.
CA:185, DA:12, DE:11, EN:11, ES:203, NE:13, FR:193, GA:146, IT:176, PO:199.

194 formes calibrées Différentes formes d'un test dont la distribution des notes a été transformée de façon à ce qu'elles puissent être utilisées de façon interchangeable.
Lire: Croker et Algnina, 1986, chapitre 20.
CA:186, DA:442, DE:16/14, EN:126, ES:204, FR:194, GA:145, IT:177 NE:141, PO:200.

195 formes équivalentes syn: formes parallèles, formes alternées. Différentes versions du même test considérées comme équivalentes car basées sur les mêmes spécifications et mesurant la même compétence. Dans la théorie classique du test, pour répondre aux exigences d'une véritable équivalence, les différentes formes du test doivent avoir le même type de difficulté, la même variance, la même covariance et avoir un critère concordant lorsqu'ils sont administrés aux mêmes personnes. Dans la pratique l'équivalence est très difficile à atteindre.
Cf.: formes calibrées.
Lire: Croker et Algina, 1986, p. 132.
CA:187, DA:441, DE:25, EN:128 ES:205, FR:195, GA:143, IT:178, NE:122, PO:201.

196 formes parallèles Se réfère à la définition des formes équivalentes.
CA:188, DA:275, DE:278, EN:268, ES:206, FR:196, GA:144, IT:179, NE:279, PO:202.

197 formule de Spearman-Brown Moyen statistique permettant d'estimer la fidélité d'un test, ralongé ou raccourci par l'ajout ou la suppression d'items. Peut être utilisé pour prédire le nombre d'items nécessaires à l'obtention de la fidelité.
Lire: Crocker et Algina, 1986, pp. 118–119.
CA:83, DA:349, DE:359, EN:371, ES:207, FR:197, GA:147, IT:180, NE:350, PO:203.

198 fréquences cumulées Façon de présenter la répartition des candidats en comptant pour chaque classe de notes, le nombre de candidats qui a obtenu une note dans cette classe et dans toutes les classes inférieures.
CA:189, DA:208, DE:202, EN:86, ES:208, FR:198, GA:239, IT:181, NE:91, PO:204.

199 gain de points Différence entre la note obtenue à un test avant l'administration d'un programme d'études, et celle obtenue au même test ou à un test similaire à la fin du cours. Le gain de points est un indicateur des progrès accomplis.
CA:352, DA:290, DE:211, EN:150, ES:32, FR:199, GA:44, IT:192, NE:434, PO:209.

200 graphique en bandes Au sens le plus large: partie d'une échelle. Dans un test basé sur des items, ce terme se réfère à une série de résultats qui peuvent être transcrits en niveaux ou en bandes. Dans une échelle de notation conçue pour valider un attribut ou une capacité spécifique, la bande représente habituellement un niveau précis.
CA:37, DA:339, DE:44, EN:29, ES:38, FR:200, GA:41, IT:39 NE:28, PO:210.

201 graphique en barres Graphique permettant de visualiser la fréquence de distribution des variables.

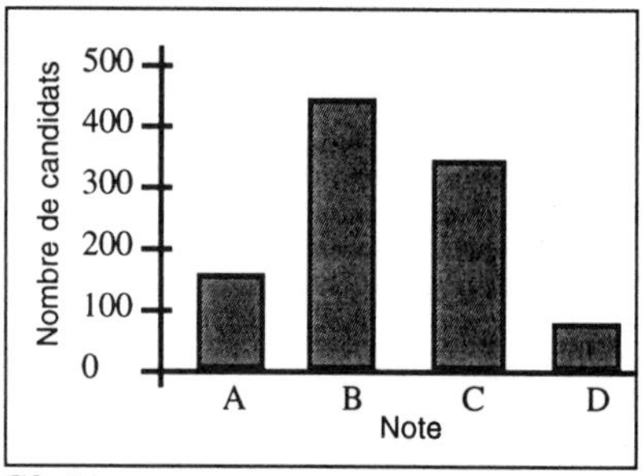

Cf.: histogramme.
Lire: Hatch et Lazaraton, 1991, p. 147.
CA:102, DA:383, DE:335, EN:31, ES:104, FR:201, GA:42, IT:123, NE:357, PO:211.

202 groupe de référence Echantillon d'une population bien définie de candidats et sur lequel on se base pour normer un test.
Voir: norme.
CA:196, DA:309, DE:267, EN:324, ES:213, FR:202, GA:166, IT:189, NE:316, PO:212.

203 groupe normé Grand groupe d'individus représentatifs de la population pour laquelle un test a été élaboré. On utilise la performance du groupe de référence pour interpréter un test normatif.
Voir: test normatif.
CA:197, DA:254, DE:266, EN:251, ES:214, FR:203, GA:264, IT:190, NE:265, PO:213.

204 histogramme Représentation graphique d'une fréquence de distribution, où le nombre de cas par classe de fréquence est montré par une barre verticale.

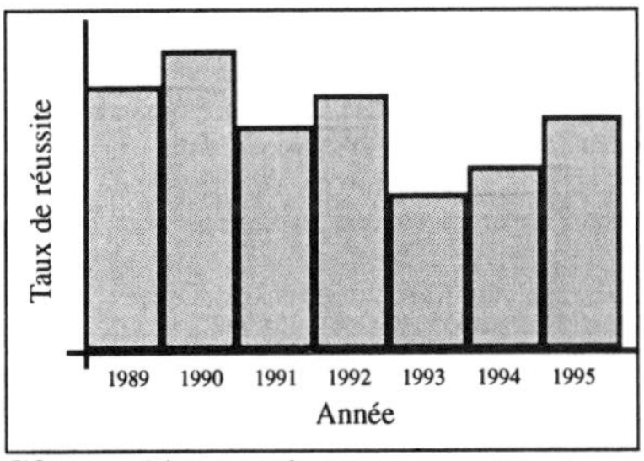

Cf.: graphique en barres.
CA:203, DA:125, DE:145, EN:163, ES:218, FR:204, GA:168, IT:207, NE:167, PO:215.

205 homogénéité Attribut d'un test ou d'un sous-test où les items mesurent la même compétence, ou d'un groupe dont les individus partagent les mêmes caractéristiques. Le degré d'homogénéité est exprimé par l'indice de fidélité.
CA:204, DA:127, DE:148, EN:165, ES:221, FR:205, GA:22, IT:257, NE:169, PO:216.

206 hypothèse nulle Hypothèse qui établit que deux ou plus de deux variables n'ont aucune relation. Exemple: supposer qu'il n'y a pas de différence de performance entre les membres de deux groupes ayant une première langue différente est une hypothèse nulle.
Lire: Hatch et Lazaraton, 1991, p. 24; Guilford et Fruchter, 1981, pp. 146–147.
CA:202, DA:255, DE:271, EN:255, ES:217, FR:206, GA:167, IT:206, NE:266, PO:214.

207 impact Effet produit par un examen, à la fois en terme d'influence sur le processus éducatif général et pour les individus intéressés par les résulats de cet examen.
Voir: reflux (effect de).
CA:205, DA:303, DE:444, EN:167, ES:222, FR:207, GA:391, IT:191, NE:171, PO:217.

208 indice-D (D pour discrimination) Indice de discrimination des items. Souvent utilisé pour des tests de classe, à petite échelle, car il peut être calculé manuellement. Deux groupes sont sélectionnés, un supérieur et un inférieur, d'après les résultats totaux au test, de telle sorte que de 10 à 33 % des testés soient présents dans chaque groupe. 27 % représente le chiffre optimal si les notes sont normalement distribuées. Dans chaque groupe, un comptage des réponses à chaque item est effectué. Pour les items à fort pouvoir de discrimination, les notes du groupe supérieur seront plus élevées que celles du groupe inférieur. L'indice de discrimination est donné par la formule suivante:

$$D = p_U - p_L$$

p_U représente la fraction du groupe supérieur qui a obtenu l'item correct et p_L la fraction du groupe inférieur qui a obtenu l'item correct.
CA:206, DA:59, DE:72, EN:91, ES:223, FR:208, GA:186, IT:194, NE:92, PO:218.

209 indice de difficulté Dans la théorie classique du test , la difficulté d'un item est fonction de la proportion (p) de candidats qui y a répondu correctement. L'indice de difficulté est lié à la population considérée et varie selon le niveau d'habileté des candidats.
Cf.: indice de facilité, valeur-*p*.
CA:207, DA:378, DE:343, EN:101, ES:224, FR:209, GA:187, IT:196, NE:249, PO:219.

210 indice de facilité Proportion de réponses correctes à un item, transcrite sur une échelle de 0 à 1. Egalement appelée valeur-*p*.
Cf.: indice de difficulté.
CA:209, DA:191, DE:208, EN:141, ES:225, FR:210, GA:188, IT:197, NE:146, PO:220.

211 indice de lisibilité Mesure de la complexité grammaticale et lexicale utilisée pour évaluer à quel point un texte est ou non compréhensible. L'indice Fog de Gunning et l'échelle de lisibilité de Flesch donnent des exemples d'indicateurs de lisibilité.
CA:210, DA:222, DE:219, EN:320, ES:226, FR:211, GA:189, IT:198, NE:223, PO:221.

212 indice moyen de difficulté à un item (moyenne p) Il s'agit du pourcentage moyen relevé dans tous les items sur une échelle d'items notés de façon dichotomique. Par exemple une moyenne p de 0.5 indique que l'indice moyen de facilité de l'item est de 0.5.
Voir: notation dichotomique.
CA:208, DA:132, DE:246, EN:228, ES:227, FR:212, GA:190, IT:195 NE:150, PO:222.

213 information lacunaire Technique d'enseignement et d'évaluation des langues où la communication réelle est simulée. L'enseignant propose des situations dans lesquelles les apprenants ne reçoivent pas tous les mêmes informations; afin qu'ils puissent réaliser la tâche donnée, ils doivent communiquer les uns avec les autres. Utilisée généralement comme activité de classe ou comme évaluation de la production orale et écrite.

CA:42, DA:140, DE:151, EN:172, ES:411, FR:213, GA:43, IT:424, NE:176, PO:223.

214 instructions Indications générales données au candidat, habituellement sur la première page de la feuille de réponse. Elles l'informent sur la durée du test, sur le nombre de tâches à réaliser et sur l'endroit où il doit consigner ses réponses.

CA:211, DA:143, DE:391, EN:175, ES:230, FR:214, GA:402, IT:208, NE:181, PO:225.

215 interception-Y En régression linéaire, point auquel la régression croise l'axe du Y (vertical).
Voir: régression linéaire.

CA:212, DA:438, DE:146, EN:441, ES:231, FR:215, GA:181, IT:200, NE:438, PO:226.

216 interlocuteur Dans un test de production orale, l'examinateur explique la tâche à réaliser, pose des questions et interagit ainsi oralement avec le(s) candidat(s). L'interlocuteur peut également évaluer le candidat et lui mettre une note. Cette seconde fonction peut être remplie par un second examinateur, qui observe mais ne prend pas part à l'interaction.
Cf.: examinateur, évaluateur.

CA:213, DA:325, DE:125, EN:178, ES:138, FR:216, GA:72, IT:201, NE:155, PO:227.

217 interlocuteur natif Interlocuteur parlant une langue acquise en tant que première langue.

CA:286, DA:234, DE:255, EN:245, ES:216, FR:217, GA:47, IT:265, NE:255, PO:190.

218 intervalle Différence entre deux degrés d'une échelle.

CA:214, DA:148, DE:160, EN:183, ES:232, FR:218, GA:131, IT:203, NE:187, PO:228.

219 intervalle de confiance (d'une mesure) Intervalle de part et d'autre d'une valeur observée et à l'intérieur duquel la valeur vraie se situe vraisemblablement. Ce degré de vraisemblance est généralement défini comme étant de 95 à 99 chances sur 100.

CA:215, DA:182, DE:184, EN:67, ES:233, FR:219, GA:132, IT:204, NE:45, PO:229.

220 invariance Dans la théorie de l'item-réponse TIR, affirmation importante qui stipule que la difficulté d'un item et la discrimination des mesures sont des caractéristiques inhérentes qui ne dépendent pas de l'habileté des candidats et que de même, les mesures de l'habileté ne dépendent pas des questions particulières posées.

CA:216, DA:152, DE:164, EN:187, ES:234, FR:220, GA:120, IT:205, NE:191, PO:230.

221 item syn: question. Chaque point particulier d'un test auquel on attribue une ou plusieurs notes séparées. Exemples: un 'blanc' dans un test de closure, une des questions dans un questionnaire à choix multiple à quatre options, une phrase donnée pour une transformation grammaticale, une question à réponse en mots limités.
Cf.: tâche.

CA:217, DA:154, DE:166, EN:189, ES:235, FR:221, GA:240, IT:209, NE:195, PO:231.

222 item à choix multiple Type d'item qui consiste en une question ou une phrase incomplète (stem), accompagnée d'un choix de réponses ou de propositions pour compléter la phrase (options). Le candidat devra choisir l'option correcte (clé) parmi trois, quatre ou cinq possibilités. Aucune production langagière ne lui est demandée. C'est pour cette raison qu'on utilise habituellement les items à choix multiple dans les tests de compréhension écrite et orale. Ils peuvent être discrets ou basés sur du texte.
Voir: item discret, item basé sur du texte.

CA:220, DA:236, DE:249/234, EN:238, ES:244, FR:222, GA:247, IT:211, NE:252, PO:236.

223 item à compléter syn: complètement de phrases. La tâche du candidat est de compléter une phrase, en écrivant généralement plusieurs mots ou en fournissant des détails tels que des dates ou des numéros de téléphone.

CA:226, DA:421, DE:102, EN:60, ES:238, FR:223, GA:243, IT:215, NE:193, PO:234.

224 item à réponse courte Item ouvert pour lequel on demande au candidat de formuler une réponse en un mot ou une phrase.

CA:228, DA:198, DE:205, EN:362, ES:243, FR:224, GA:246, IT:311, NE:209, PO:238.

225 item d'ancrage Item intégré à deux ou plusieurs tests et permettant d'estimer soit la différence du degré de difficulté entre les tests, soit la différence de performance entre les différents groupes de candidats.

CA:218, DA:16, DE:18, EN:15, ES:237, FR:225, GA:241, IT:212, NE:17, PO:232.

226 item basé sur du texte Item basé sur du discours suivi, par exemple items à choix multiple basés sur une compréhension de texte.

CA:219, DA:387, DE:412, EN:412, ES:236, FR:226, GA:254, IT:213, NE:269, PO:233.

227 item de construction de mots Type d'item dans lequel le candidat doit produire une forme d'un mot à partir d'une autre forme du même mot qui lui est donnée comme entrée. Exemple: Ce type de travail demande une .... du vocabulaire technique. (comprendre)

CA:227, DA:269, DE:445, EN:439, ES:231, FR:227, GA:244, IT:216, NE:437, PO:237 .

228 item discret Item contenant en lui-même tous les éléments de la question. Il n'est lié ni à un texte, ni à d'autres items, ni à un quelconque matériel complémentaire. Le choix multiple est un exemple de ce type d'item.
Cf.: item basé sur du texte.

CA:230, DA:71, DE:421, EN:109, ES:246, FR:228, GA:253, IT:219, NE:106, PO:241.

229 item discret spécifique Item discret évaluant un point spécifique par exemple une structure ou du lexique, et n'ayant aucune relation avec d'autres items. La vulgarisation de ce type d'item dans les tests de langue est due à Robert Lado dans les années 60.
Cf.: tâche.
Voir: item discret.

CA:225, DA:72, DE:82, EN:110, ES:247 FR:229, GA:251, IT:210, NE:107, PO:240.

230 item échelonné Item noté à l'aide d'une échelle.
Voir: cotation (classification) polytomique.

CA:222, DA:342, DE:27, EN:342, ES:248, FR:230, GA:252, IT:220, NE:328, PO:242.

231 item liaison Se réfère à la définition d'item d'ancrage.

CA:221, DA:218, DE:432, EN:215, ES:239, FR:231, GA:250, IT:214, NE:232, PO:244.

232 jeu de rôle Type de tâche parfois utilisée dans les tests d'expression orale et dans laquelle les candidats doivent se projeter dans une situation de communication précise ou jouer un rôle particulier.

CA:233, DA:320, DE:329, EN:334, ES:251, FR:232, GA:294, IT:202, NE:323, PO:345.

233 KR-20 (formule 20 de Kuder-Richardson) Se réfère à la définition de Kuder-Richardson.

CA:234, DA:201, DE:194, EN:199, ES:252, FR:233, GA:205, IT:222, NE:210, PO:246.

234 KR-21 (formule 21 de Kuder-Richardson) Se réfère à la définition de Kuder-Richardson.

CA:235, DA:202, DE:195, EN:200 ES:253, FR:234, GA:206, IT:223, NE:211, PO:247.

235 Kuder-Richardson Deux mesures de cohérence interne développées par Kuder et Richardson et utilisées pour estimer la fidélité d'un test. KR-21 nécessite moins d'informations et est plus facile à calculer, mais présente généralement une estimation plus faible que KR-20.
Cf.: alpha (coefficient alpha).
Voir: fidélité interne.
Lire: Henning, 1987, p. 84.

CA:236, DA:206, DE:200, EN:201, ES:254, FR:235, GA:207, IT:224, NE:212, PO:248.

236 langue sur objectifs spécifiques Enseignement ou évaluation de la langue utilisé dans des activités professionelles ou un domaine particuliers; par exemple, Anglais des Contrôleurs Aériens, Espagnol du Commerce.

CA:238, DA:95, DE:111, EN:205, ES:256, FR:236, GA:385, IT:227, NE:378, PO:251.

237 lecteur optique syn: scanner. Appareil électronique utilisé pour scanner l'information directement à partir des feuilles de notes ou des feuilles de réponses. Les candidats ou les examinateurs marquent les réponses aux items sur une feuille de notes et cette information est automatiquement lue par l'ordinateur.

CA:242, DA:268, DE:274, EN:261, ES:255, FR:237, GA:214, IT:226, NE:274, PO:249.

238 lexique Terme utilisé pour désigner le vocabulaire.

CA:237, DA:212, DE:221, EN:210, ES:257, FR:238, GA:213, IT:225, NE:227, PO:250.

239 liste de contrôle Liste de questions ou de points qui doivent être traités.

Souvent utilisé dans les tests de langue comme outil d'observation ou d'analyse.
CA:240, DA:48, DE:64, EN:48, ES:258, FR:239, GA:351, IT:228, NE:58, PO:252.

240 logit Unité de mesure dérivée du logarithme naturel du taux de possibilité d'échec ou de succès, c'est-à-dire des chances. La différence de logits entre les capacités d'un individu et la difficulté de l'item vient des chances qu'a cet individu de réussir à l'item.
Lire: Henning, 1987, pp. 118–126.
CA:241, DA:220, DE:227, EN:218, ES:259, FR:240, GA:216, IT:232, NE:234, PO:253.

241 marge de variation Mesure de la dispersion des observations. La marge est la distance entre les notes les plus élevées et les plus basses.
Lire: Hatch et Lazaraton, 1991, pp. 169–170.
CA:12, DA:431, DE:431, EN:308, ES:260, FR:241, GA:285, IT:233, NE:311, PO:12.

242 médiane ou Médian (Md) Note placée au centre de la distribution dans un ensemble de notes classées. La moitié des notes sont au-dessus de la médiane, l'autre moitié en dessous.
Voir: tendance centrale (mesure de la).
Cf.: moyenne, mode.
Lire: Hatch et Lazaraton, 1991, p. 161.
CA:244, DA:228, DE:232, EN:232, ES:263, FR:242, GA:3, IT:235, NE:239, PO:256.

243 mesure D'une façon générale, il s'agit du processus qui permet de trouver la somme de quelque chose par comparaison avec une unité fixe, comme lorsqu'on utilise une règle pour mesurer la longueur. En sciences sociales, la mesure se réfère souvent à la quantification des caractéristiques des individus, comme par exemple la compétence langagière.
Lire: Bachman, 1990, chapitre 2.
CA:245, DA:242, DE:241, EN:230, ES:264, FR:243, GA:395, IT:238, NE:245, PO:257.

244 mesure indépendante de l'échantillon Terme utilisé dans la rercherche, signifiant l'interprétation des résultats indépendamment de l'échantillon utilisé pour une recherche particulière.
Voir: échantillon.
CA:247, DA:373, DE:382, EN:339, ES:265, FR:244, GA:396, IT:239, NE:371, PO:258.

245 méthode de test La capacité langagière peut être testée de différentes façons, telles que le choix multiple, le test de closure, la composition, l'entretien oral, etc. On constate que la méthode de test interagit avec la capacité dans la mesure de la performance.
Voir: caractéristiques des modes d'évaluation.
Lire: Bachman, 1990, p. 77.
CA:248, DA:395, DE:401, EN:401, ES:266, FR:245, GA:257, IT:236, NE:396, PO:259.

246 méthode du graphique delta Se réfère au fonctionnement des items différentiels. Utilisée pour identifier les items qui exagèrent ou minimalisent les différences de performances dans les groupes. Basée sur la difficulté classique des items (valeurs-*p*). Les valeurs-*p* sont converties afin de normaliser les notes-*z* et sont rapportées par paires sur un graphique pour montrer la difficulté relative des items pour les deux groupes en question.
Voir: fonctionnement de l'item différentiel.
Lire: Crocker et Algina, 1986, pp. 388–390.
CA:249, DA:61, DE:74, EN:92, ES:267, FR:246, GA:256, IT:237, NE:93, PO:260.

247 mode syn: valeur dominante. Valeur la plus fréquemment observée dans une distribution de notes; point le plus haut de la courbe de distribution.

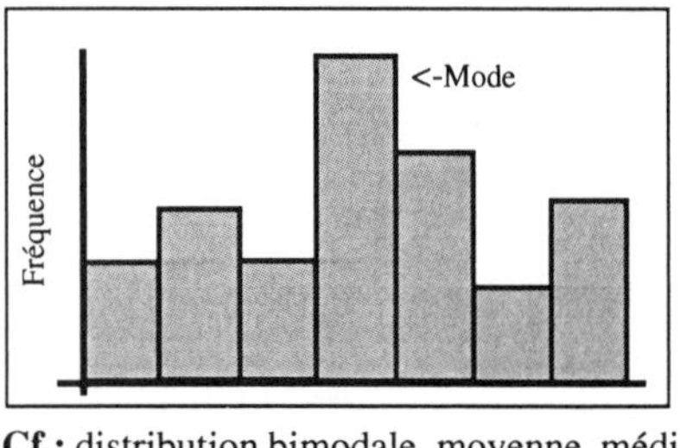

Cf.: distribution bimodale, moyenne, médiane ou médian (MD).
Voir: tendance centrale (mesure de la).
Lire: Hatch et Lazaraton, 1991, pp. 160–161.
CA:252, DA:232, DE:247, EN:235, ES:268, FR:247, GA:255, IT:240, NE:248, PO:261.

248 modèle à deux paramètres Dans la théorie item réponse, modèle qui prend en compte un paramètre de discrimination d'item en plus du paramètre capacité/difficulté.
Cf.: modèle à paramètre unique, modèle de

Rasch.
Voir: théorie de l'item-réponse TIR.
CA:258, DA:411, DE:454, EN:424, ES:271, FR:248, GA:298, IT:241, NE:404, PO:264.

249 modèle à paramètre unique Modèle qui fonctionne avec une échelle unique représentant la difficulté (des tâches) et la capacité (des individus). Elle ne prend en compte ni la discrimination ni l'élucidation.
Cf.: modèle de Rasch.
CA:255, DA:92, DE:99, EN:259, ES:273, FR:249, GA:296, IT:242, NE:118, PO:265.

250 modèle cognitif Théorie concernant la façon dont les connaissances d'un individu sont structurées (au sens large de concepts et de processus). Importante dans le domaine des tests de langue, car elle peut avoir un effet sur le choix de la méthode ou du contenu des tests.
CA:253, DA:178, DE:181, EN:56, ES:269, FR:250, GA:297, IT:243, NE:64, PO:262.

251 modèle de l'échelle de notation Extension du modèle de Rasch, qui permet de traiter les données échelonnées, dérivant, par exemple, des évaluations de la performance orale.
Cf.: modèle de Rasch.
Voir: modèle du crédit partiel.
Lire: Wright, B.D. et Masters G.N., 1982, Analyse de l'échelle de notation, Chicago, MESA Press.
CA:254, DA:173, DE:236, EN:316, ES:272, FR:251, GA:303, IT:246, NE:41, PO:263.

252 modèle de Rasch Modèle mathématique, connu également comme le modèle de la logistique simple, qui postule qu'il existe une relation entre la probabilité qu'un individu réalise une tâche et la différence entre la capacité de l'individu et la difficulté de la tâche. Equivalent mathématiquement au modèle à paramètre unique dans la théorie de l'item réponse. Le modèle de Rasch a été appliqué de différentes façons, par exemple pour manier les réponses échelonnées ou pour prendre en compte les différentes facettes pour la 'difficulté' d'une tâche.
Voir: théorie de l'item-réponse TIR, modèle du crédit partiel, modèle de l'échelle de notation, modèle multi-facettes de Rasch.
Lire: Henning, 1987,pp. 117–125.
CA:259, DA:305, DE:316, EN:310, ES:275, FR:252, GA:302, IT:248, NE:313, PO:266.

253 modèle du crédit partiel Dans la théorie de l'item réponse, modèle qui permet de traiter les données apportées par les échelles. Eventuellement approprié pour analyser les réponses aux items de phrases à compléter qui utilisent une échelle de notation, comme par exemple 1, 2 ou 3, ou pour un entretien oral qui utilise plusieurs échelles d'évaluation de la performance.
Cf.: modèle de l'échelle de notation, modèle multi-facettes de Rasch.
Voir: modèle de Rasch.
Lire: Wright et Masters, 1982, pp. 40–48.
CA:257, DA:278, DE:281, EN:272, ES:270, FR:253, GA:301, IT:244, NE:282, PO:267.

254 modèle multi-facettes de Rasch Extension du modèle de Rasch, qui permet de modeler les probabilités de réponses sur la base d'une combinaison additive de facettes. La performance demandée lors d'une tâche écrite peut par exemple être modulée pour refléter à la fois la difficulté de la tâche et la sévérité du correcteur. Le modèle multi-facettes de Rasch a été mis en oeuvre par le programme FACETS.
Voir: modèle de Rasch.
Lire: Linacre, J.M., 1989, Many-facet Rasch meeasurement, Chicago, MESA Press.
CA:260, DA:235, DE:289, EN:220, ES:276, FR:254, GA:300, IT:249, NE:236, PO:268.

255 modèle des probabilités Modèle dans lequel les relations causales (telles que la difficulté de l'item et la capacité du candidat à réaliser le test), sont expliquées en termes de degré de probabilité. Le modèle de Rasch en est un exemple.
CA:262, DA:295, DE:297, EN:294, ES:274, FR:255, GA:299, IT:247, NE:430, PO:269.

256 modération a) Partie du processus d'élaboration des items ou des tâches d'un test. Etape pendant laquelle le matériel produit est examiné par des experts (élaborateurs confirmés et enseignants) qui décideront si ce matériel est pertinent (éventuellement en demandant certaines modifications).

b) Ajustement des notes, fait par le modérateur désigné par l'évaluateur.
Cf.: révision.
CA:263, DA:410, DE:31, EN:237, ES:277, FR:256, GA:260, IT:250, NE:247, PO:270.

257 moyenne La moyenne est la mesure de la tendance centrale. On obtient la note moyenne à un test en additionant toutes les notes obtenues et en divisant ce total par le nombre de candidats.
Cf.: médiane ou médian (MD), mode.

Voir: tendance centrale (mesure de la).
Lire: Hatch et Lazaraton, 1991, pp. 151–163.

CA:250, DA:231, DE:244, EN:227, ES:261, FR:257, GA:226, IT:234, NE:151, PO:255.

258 *N, n* Nombre. *N* est souvent utilisé pour indiquer le nombre de cas dans une étude ou d'individus dans une population. *n* indique souvent le nombre dans un échantillon ou dans un sous-groupe. Exemple: 'Le test a été administré à des ingénieurs diplômés (*N* = 600) dont 10% étaient des femmes (*n* = 60)'.

CA:269, DA:248, DE:256, EN:244, ES:282, FR:258, GA:261, IT:251, NE:259, PO:271.

259 niveau a) La note obtenue à un test peut être communiquée au candidat sous forme de niveau, par exemple sur une échelle de A à E, où A représente le niveau maximum, B un bon niveau, C un niveau passable, et D et E des niveaux insuffisants.

b) On fait souvent référence à une série de niveaux pour désigner le degré de capacité requis pour qu'un étudiant soit classé dans tel ou tel groupe ou lorsqu'il a réussi à un test donné. Les termes les plus utilisés pour désigner ces niveaux sont "élémentaire", intermédiaire", "avancé", etc.
Cf.: notes.

CA:270/275, DA:167/247, DE:260/270, EN:156/209, ES:283/288, FR:259, GA:164/210, IT:188/229, NE:258/426, PO:272.

260 niveau de capacité Connaissance d'une langue et degré d'habileté à l'utiliser.
Cf.: capacité, compétence.
Lire: Bachman, 1990, p. 16.

CA:296, DA:296, DE:47, EN:295, ES:120, FR:260, GA:265, IT:62, NE:305, PO:273.

261 niveau de survie Référentiel d'un niveau élémentaire de compétence en langue étrangère, publié pour l'anglais en 1977 par le Conseil de l'Europe et revu en 1990.Il est moins exigeant que le Niveau Seuil, ne couvrant qu'environ la moitié des apprentissages définis par ce dernier.
Voir: niveau seuil.

CA:271, DA:437, DE:443, EN:436, ES:284, FR:261, GA:211, IT:231, NE:433, PO:274.

262 niveau seuil Référentiel fonctionnel définissant les compétences de base en langue étrangère. Publié en 1976 pour l'anglais par le Conseil de l'Europe, il a été remis à jour en 1990. Différentes versions ont été produites pour les langues européennes.

CA:272, DA:419, DE:414, EN:414, ES:285, FR:262, GA:212, IT:230, NE:386, PO:275.

263 normalisation Etalonnage des notes de façon à obtenir une distribution normale. Cela implique l'utilisation d'une échelle d'équicentilage.
Cf.: note standard.

CA:274, DA:253, DE:264, EN:253, ES:287, FR:263, GA:263, IT:253, NE:263, PO:279.

264 norme Standard de performance. Dans un test standardisé, on détermine la norme en enregistrant les notes d'un grand groupe. La norme ou les standards basés sur la performance de ce groupe sont utilisés pour évaluer la performance de groupes suivants composés de candidats du même type.
Voir: groupe de référence, test normatif.

CA:273, DA:250, DE:263, EN:250, ES:286, FR:264, GA:262, IT:252, NE:261, PO:278.

265 notation a) Attribution d'une note aux réponses d'un candidat à un test. Cette activité peut demander un jugement professionnel ou l'application d'un barème où sont indiquées toutes les réponses acceptables.

b) Note accordée et qui représente le résultat du processus d'évaluation.

CA:80/428, DA:171/289, DE:40/57, EN:222/314, ES:47/425, FR:265, GA:218/286, IT:29/54, NE:38/83, PO:57.

266 notation analytique Méthode de notation qui peut être utilisée dans les tests de production langagière comme ceux d'expression écrite et orale. L'examinateur évalue à partir d'une liste de points spécifiques. Dans un test de production écrite, par exemple, l'échelle analytique peut inclure des critères de grammaire, de vocabulaire, d'utilisation des articulateurs.
Cf.: évaluation globale, notation liée à l'impression générale.
Lire: Ebel et Frisbie, 1991, p. 195; Weir, 1990, p. 63.

CA:343, DA:13, DE:12, EN:14, ES:426, FR:266, GA:340, IT:27, NE:15, PO:58.

267 notation d'un item Dans l'analyse d'items, somme des réponses correctes à un item particulier.

CA:345, DA:160, DE:171, EN:196, ES:346, FR:267, GA:336, IT:281, NE:202, PO:60.

268 notation dichotomique Notation basée sur deux catégories, par exemple vrai/faux, réussi/échoué, oui/non.

CA:347, DA:67, DE:455, EN:98, ES:347, FR:268, GA:341, IT:32, NE:98, PO:59.

269 notation en bandes Partie d'une échelle qui se réfère à une série particulière de capacités.

CA:346, DA:258, DE:210, EN:30, ES:39, FR:269, GA:330, IT:40, NE:29, PO:65.

270 notation liée à l'impression générale Méthode de notation qui peut être utilisée dans les tests de production écrite et orale. L'examinateur évalue les réponses de chaque candidat sans séparer les traits distinctifs de la tâche à réaliser.
Cf.: notation analytique, évaluation globale.

CA:89, DA:116, DE:133, EN:168, ES:429, FR:270, GA:220, IT:33, NE:172, PO:68.

271 notation multiple Méthode pour améliorer la fidélité de l'évaluation de l'expression écrite lors de productions longues. Cette évaluation présente nécessairement un degré de subjectivité que l'on peut réduire si chaque candidat est corrigé par plus d'un correcteur.
Lire: Weir: 1988, pp. 65–66.

CA:87, DA:274, DE:233, EN:240, ES:45, FR:271, GA:183, IT:105, NE:241, PO:63.

272 notation par l'examinateur Méthode de notation qui demande à l'évaluateur d'avoir un certain degré de professionnalisme et de formation de façon à pouvoir exercer un jugement subjectif. Les tests de production orale et les écrits d'une certaine longueur sont habituellement notés de cette manière.
Voir: notation standardisée (mécanique).

CA:81, DA:29, DE:107, EN:136, ES:81, FR:272, GA:223, IT:30, NE:131, PO:67.

273 notation par ordinateur Différentes méthodes utilisent l'informatique afin de minimiser les erreurs dans les notations des tests objectifs. On peut par exemple scanner les feuilles de notes des candidats à l'aide d'un lecteur optique afin d'analyser les données.

CA:85, DA:53, DE:69, EN:65, ES:82, FR:273, GA:222, IT:28, NE:69, PO:66.

274 notation standardisée (mécanique) Méthode de notation dans laquelle on n'attend pas des évaluateurs qu'ils exercent quelque compétence ou jugement subjectif que ce soit. La note est établie d'après un relevé de toutes les réponses acceptables pour chaque question du test.
Cf.: notation par l'examinateur.

CA:86, DA:23, DE:231, EN:51, ES:78, FR:274, GA:219, IT:31, NE:25, PO:62.

275 note a) Nombre total de points obtenus à un test, soit avant échelonnage (note brute) soit après (note échelonnée).

b) Action d'assigner des valeurs numériques aux performances observées.
Cf.: mesure.

CA:342, DA:328, DE:312, EN:348, ES:345, FR:275, GA:328, IT:278, NE:331, PO:280.

276 note brute Note qui n'a subi aucune transformation statistique, comme la pondération ou le ré-échelonnage.
Voir: note.

CA:348, DA:321, DE:328, EN:319, ES:348, FR:276, GA:329, IT:282, NE:324, PO:281.

277 note de césure. syn: point de coupure. a) Note en dessous de laquelle un candidat échoue à un test ou à un examen.

b) Dans les tests de maîtrise, note considérée comme donnant un niveau de compétence minimale ou un niveau de 'maîtrise'.
Voir: test de maîtrise, évaluation de la compétence minimale.
Cf.: moyenne.
Lire: Bachman, 1990, pp. 214–215.

CA:23/359, DA:36/58, DE:52/199, EN:90/273, ES:30/351, FR:277, GA:278/338, IT:280/288, NE:57/341, PO:282.

278 note graduée Note résultant d'un échelonnage.
Voir: échelonnage.

CA:349, DA:340, DE:354, EN:345, ES:349, FR:278, GA:337, IT:286, NE:153, PO:283.

279 note observée Note obtenue par un candidat. Dans la théorie du test classique on considère que cette note est un mélange de la note vraie et de l'erreur.
Voir: erreur, note vraie .

CA:353, DA:183, DE:49, EN:258, ES:352, FR:279, GA:331, IT:283, NE:429, PO:285.

280 note pondérée Note attribuée au candidat après pondération.
Voir: pondération.

CA:354, DA:434, DE:135, EN:437, ES:354, FR:280, GA:339, IT:284, NE:159, PO:286.

281 note standard Note transformée linéairement à partir d'un groupe de notes. Les déviations moyenne et standard sont ajustées à la valeur que demande l'utilisateur. Des exemples de notes standard sont les notes *z* et *t*.
Cf.: note *t*, note z, note stanine.
Lire: Ebel et Frisbie, 1991, pp. 67–68.

CA:350, DA:365, DE:376, EN:382,

ES:350, FR:281, GA:333, IT:287, NE:364, PO:291.

282 note stanine Procédure permettant de grouper les notes en neuf classes basées sur la fréquence normale. Dans chacun des groupes supérieurs et inférieurs apparaissent 4% des candidats. Le pourcentage de candidats dans chaque groupe est représenté sur le schéma suivant.

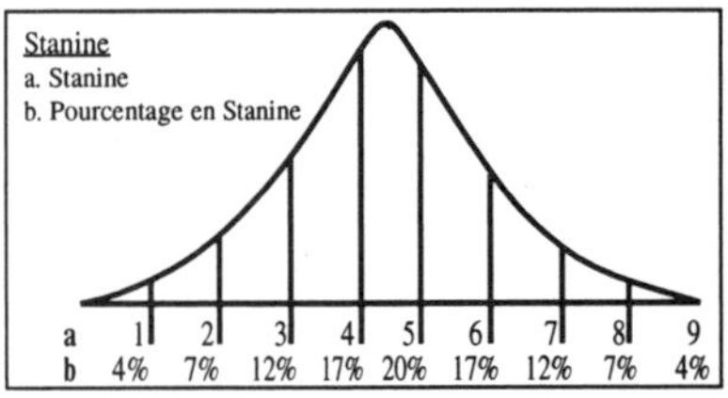

Lire: Crocker et Algina, 1986, pp. 446–447.
CA:344, DA:367, DE:377, EN:384, ES:176, FR:282, GA:332, IT:279, NE:365, PO:284.

283 note *t* Extension de la note *z*. Change les décimales et les signes négatifs de place. La note *t* est égale à dix fois la note *z* plus 50. La distribution a une moyenne de 50 et une déviation standard de 10.
Voir: note *z*.
Lire: Ebel et Frisbie, 1991, p. 68.
CA:355, DA:384, DE:388, EN:422, ES:355, FR:283, GA:367, IT:289, NE:376, PO:287.

284 note transformée Note brute qui a subi une transformation mathématique dans le but d'un échelonnage ou d'une pondération.
Lire: Ebel et Frisbie, 1991, pp. 64–70.
CA:356, DA:414, DE:415, EN:417, ES:356, FR:284, GA:334, IT:290, NE:158, PO:288.

285 note vraie Note qu'un candidat obtiendrait en l'absence d'erreur de mesure lors de l'évaluation ou de la notation. Concept fondamental dans la théorie du test classique.
CA:357, DA:415, DE:441, EN:420, ES:357, FR:285, GA:335, IT:285, NE:431, PO:289.

286 note *z* Note standard fréquente, avec une moyenne de 0 et une déviation standard de 1. La formule servant à la calculer est:

$$z = (X - \overline{X}) \div S_x$$

où:

z = note z

X = note obtenue au test

$\overline{X}$ = moyenne des notes obtenues

S_x = déviation standard des notes obtenues

Cf.: note *t*.
Voir: note.
Lire: Ebel et Frisbie, 1991, p. 68.
CA:358, DA:439, DE:446, EN:442, ES:358, FR:286, GA:441, IT:291, NE:439, PO:290.

287 notes Nombre total des points sur lesquels est noté un item, un sous-test ou un test, ou bien, nombre de points accordés à la réponse d'un candidat à un item, un sous-test ou un test.
CA:342, DA:287, DE:313, EN:224, ES:44, FR:287, GA:224, IT:292, NE:60, PO:105.

288 objectifs Buts déclarés de tous types de cours éducatifs, tels que l'acquisition de savoirs, de compétences, d'attitudes.
CA:278, DA:244, DE:216, EN:256, ES:291, FR:288, GA:359, IT:254, NE:112, PO:293.

289 objectif d'apprentissage But ou résultat souhaité d'une activité éducative.
CA:277, DA:136, DE:215, EN:208, ES:290, FR:289, GA:360, IT:255, NE:217, PO:292.

290 options Différentes possibilités parmi lesquelles le choix correct doit être sélectionné dans un item à choix multiple ou dans un exercice d'appariement.
CA:279, DA:425, DE:38, EN:262, ES:292, FR:290, GA:293, IT:258, NE:14, PO:294.

291 paramètre Caractéristique d'une population, par exemple la déviation standard.
Cf.: statistiques.
CA:280, DA:276, DE:279, EN:269, ES:293, FR:291, GA:272, IT:259, NE:280, PO:296.

292 paramètre-A Un des paramètres de la théorie de l'item-réponse TIR. Il se réfère à la discrimination d'un item.
Voir: théorie de l'item-réponse TIR.
Lire: Bachman, 1990, p. 204.
CA:281, DA:1, DE:84, EN:1, ES:294, FR:292, GA:273, IT:260, NE:1, PO:297.

293 paramètre-B Un des paramètres de la théorie de l'item-réponse TIR. Il se réfè-

re au degré de difficulté d'un item.
Voir: théorie de l'item-réponse TIR.
Lire: Bachman, 1990, p. 204.
CA:282, DA:24, DE:170, EN:26, ES:295, FR:293, GA:274, IT:261, NE:26, PO:298.

294 paramètre-C Un des paramètres de la théorie de l'item-réponse TIR. Il se réfère à l'action de deviner.
Voir: théorie de l'item-réponse TIR.
Lire: Bachman, 1990, p. 204.
CA:283, DA:44, DE:318, EN:37, ES:296, FR:294, GA:275, IT:262, NE:50, PO:299.

295 paramètre d'élucidation Se réfère à la définition du paramètre-C.
CA:284, DA:122, DE:319, EN:159, ES:297, FR:295, GA:277, IT:263, NE:160, PO:301.

296 paramètre de difficulté Se réfère à la définition du paramètre-B.
CA:285, DA:379, DE:344, EN:102, ES:298, FR:296, GA:276, IT:264, NE:250, PO:300.

297 performance Action de produire du langage en parlant ou en écrivant. La performance, en termes de langage réellement produit, est souvent opposée à la compétence sous-jacente à la connaissance de la langue.
Cf.: compétence.
Voir: test de performance.
Lire: Bachman, 1990, pp. 52 et 108.
CA:5, DA:282, DE:283, EN:277, ES:9, FR:297, GA:141, IT:267, NE:286, PO:304.

298 phrases à compléter Type d'item dans lequel seule une moitié de la phrase est donnée. La tâche du candidat consiste à compléter la phrase, soit en fournissant les mots convenables (éventuellement d'après un texte), soit en choisissant ces mots parmi différentes possibilités.
CA:72, DA:382, DE:332, EN:357, ES:69, FR:298, GA:93, IT:80, NE:442, PO:86.

299 plan multiattribut-multiméthode Plan expérimental utilisé dans la validation de construct, où un ensemble d'attributs présumés distinctifs sont mesurés à l'aide d'un ensemble de méthodes présumées distinctives. L'analyse devrait par exemple montrer que les mesures de la capacité de compréhension orale, obtenues à l'aide de différentes méthodes, sont en plus grande corrélation que les mesures de différentes aptitudes obtenues à l'aide d'une seule et même méthode d'évaluation.
Lire: Bachman, 1990, pp. 263–265.
CA:108, DA:238, DE:252, EN:243, ES:109, FR:299, GA:111, IT:277, NE:254, PO:305.

300 point clé du test Point particulier sur lequel un item révèle les connaissances du candidat.
CA:128, DA:399, DE:309, EN:409, ES:289, FR:300, GA:281, IT:293, NE:384, PO:307.

301 pointage du distracteur Fréquence à laquelle s'effectue le choix de chaque distracteur dans un questionnaire à choix multiple. Le pointage est significatif de l'attrait du distracteur.
CA:243, DA:80, DE:89, EN:116, ES:71, FR:301, GA:384, IT:88, NE:9, PO:96.

302 pondération Action d'assigner un nombre différent maximal de points à un item, une tâche ou une composante, afin de changer sa contribution relative à l'ensemble des points, en fonction des autres parties du test. Si, par exemple, on attribue une note double à tous les items de la tâche n°1 d'un test, la tâche n°1 sera proportionnellement plus importante que les autres tâches dans le total des points obtenus.
Lire: Ebel et Frisbie, 1991, pp. 214–216.
CA:290, DA:435, DE:136, EN:438, ES:303, FR:302, GA:439, IT:268, NE:434, PO:306.

303 population Ensemble complet de valeurs, par exemple ensemble de tous les candidats participant à un examen. Connu en statistiques sous le nom de 'univers de notes'.
Cf.: échantillon.
CA:289, DA:292, DE:290, EN:285, ES:302, FR:303, GA:280, IT:269, NE:294, PO:308.

304 porte-feuille d'évaluation Technique d'évaluation dans laquelle le candidat collectionne pendant une période donnée des exemples de ses travaux, et les présente comme preuve de ses capacités.
CA:386, DA:293, DE:291, EN:286, ES:185, FR:304, GA:237, IT:270, NE:37, PO:309.

305 post-test Test ou autre forme de mesure administré à la fin d'une formation. Les résultats comparés avec le même test administré en début de formation démontrent l'efficacité de la formation.
Cf.: pré-test.
CA:327, DA:345, DE:5, EN:287, ES:336, FR:305, GA:179, IT:271, NE:295, PO:310.

306 pré-test Test administré avant le début d'une formation. Les résultats du pré-test sont comparés avec ceux d'un autre test

administré à la fin de la formation afin d'évaluer l'efficacité de la formation.
Cf.: post-test.
CA:333, DA:104, DE:440, EN:292, ES:338, FR:306, GA:290, IT:272, NE:299, PO:312.

307 prétesting syn: prétestage. Etape de la conception du matériel des tests pendant laquelle on essaye les items sur des échantillons représentatifs de la population cible afin de déterminer leur degré de difficulté. Suivant une analyse statistique, les items considérés comme satisfaisants pourront être utilisés dans des tests réels.
Cf.: essai.
CA:174, DA:105, DE:436, EN:293, ES:191, FR:307, GA:289, IT:273, NE:302, PO:311.

308 procédures de déduction Technique qui permet au candidat de produire une réponse à une question. Utilisée habituellement dans les tests de production orale.
Lire: Hughes, 1989, pp. 104–110.
CA:293, DA:8, DE:212, EN:123, ES:307, FR:308, GA:162, IT:276, NE:320, PO:314.

309 procédures non-paramétriques Procédures statistiques qui ne garantissent pas que les données viennent d'un type particulier de distribution, ou dont les données ne sont pas basées sur une échelle d'intervalle. Le Khi deux en est un exemple connu.
Cf.: procédures paramétriques.
Lire: Hatch et Lazaraton,pp. 237–239.
CA:294, DA:131, DE:259, EN:249, ES:308, FR:309, GA:258, IT:274, NE:257, PO:315.

310 procédures paramétriques Procédures statistiques qui supposent que les données sont distribuées normalement et sont mesurées à l'aide d'échelles d'intervalles ou de rapports. En pratique, les procédures paramétriques sont utilisées si l'on dispose d'un nombre de cas suffisant pour que les données s'approchent d'une distribution normale.
Cf.: procédures non-paramétriques.
Lire: Hatch et Lazaraton, 1991, pp. 237–238.
CA:295, DA:277, DE:280, EN:270, ES:309, FR:310, GA:259, IT:275, NE:281, PO:316.

311 production écrite guidée Le candidat doit produire un texte écrit, dans lequel des informations graphiques ou textuelles, telles que des images, des lettres, des cartes postales ou des modes d'emplois, sont utilisées pour contrôler et standardiser la réponse attendue.
Cf.: composition, essai.
CA:393, DA:121, DE:130, EN:160, ES:5, FR:311, GA:377, IT:76, NE:143, PO:317.

312 profilage Moyen de présentation des résultats des tests, qui sépare ses différentes composantes afin que le candidat ou d'autres utilisateurs puissent identifier les points forts et les points faibles.
CA:288, DA:297, DE:404, EN:297, ES:300, FR:312, GA:282, IT:395, NE:307, PO:303.

313 qualification Mention donnée après une formation reconnue ou un test, et qui certifie qu'un individu est apte à exercer une activité ou une profession particulière. Un certificat de niveau de compétence en langue peut être considéré comme une qualification.
Cf.: certificat, diplôme.
CA:360, DA:209, DE:314, EN:302, ES:405, FR:313, GA:46, IT:294, NE:214, PO:322.

314 qualité d'être aguerri aux tests . Familiarité avec le type de test ou expérience du testing qui permet au candidat de réaliser une performance supérieure à son niveau réel.
CA:179, DA:406, DE:396, EN:408, ES:197, FR:314, GA:161, IT:167, NE:401, PO:191.

315 question Parfois utilisé pour désigner une tâche ou un item dans un test.
Voir: item, tâche.
CA:291, DA:357, DE:122, EN:303, ES:304, FR:315, GA:55, IT:136, NE:423, PO:323.

316 question intégrée Se réfère à des questions ou des tâches à réaliser qui mettent en jeu plus d'une habileté ou sous-habileté. Exemples: compléter un test de closure, participer à un entretien oral, lire une lettre et y répondre.
Cf.: item discret spécifique.
CA:231, DA:144, DE:156, EN:176, ES:249, FR:316, GA:248, IT:221, NE:182, PO:245.

317 question lacunaire Tout type d'item qui demande au candidat d'insérer du matériel écrit — des lettres, des chiffres, un mot isolé, plusieurs mots, des phrases ou des paragraphes — dans des espaces blancs aménagés dans un texte. La réponse peut être produite par le candidat ou bien sélectionnée dans une liste.
CA:223, DA:138, DE:229, EN:151,

ES:241, FR:317, GA:249, IT:78, NE:192, PO:235.

318 question ouverte syn: question à réponse construite, question à réponse libre. Type d'item ou de tâche dans un test écrit qui demande au candidat de produire une réponse (et non de la sélectionner). L'objectif de ce type d'item est de faire produire une réponse relativement libre et dont la longueur peut aller de quelques mots à un grand nombre de phrases. Le barème proposera alors tout un choix de réponses acceptables.

CA:292, DA:444, DE:273, EN:260, ES:305, FR:318, GA:56, IT:137, NE:273, PO:324.

319 rapport-F Dans l'analyse de variance, rapport estimé qui indique si les différences entre les moyennes des groupes sont statistiquement significatives; par exemple si un groupe a significativement mieux réussi qu'un autre à un test de langue.
Voir: formes alternées.
Lire: Hatch et Lazaraton, 91, pp. 313–317.

CA:364, DA:94, DE:109, EN:139, ES:368, FR:319, GA:66, IT:296, NE:132, PO:332.

320 ré-échelonnage Se réfère à la définition de l'échelonnage.

CA:367, DA:314, DE:258, EN:330, ES:389, FR:320, GA:29, IT:304, NE:166, PO:326.

321 reconnaissance Acceptation formelle de la part d'une institution d'une qualification obtenue dans un but spécifique, par exemple pour l'admission à un cours supérieur.

CA:365, DA:15, DE:269, EN:323, ES:361, FR:321, GA:9, IT:303, NE:123, PO:325.

322 reflux (effet de) Impact du test sur les pratiques de classe. Sachant que leurs élèves vont présenter un certain type de tests, les enseignants peuvent être influencés par la nature de ce test et adapter en conséquence leur méthodologie et le contenu de leurs cours de façon à les y préparer. Les résultats peuvent être positifs ou négatifs.
Voir: impact.

CA:372, DA:25/436, DE:43/442, EN:28/435, ES:124/369, FR:322, GA:95, IT:147, NE:27/432, PO:135.

323 registre Différentes variétés de discours, correspondant à des activités particulières ou à un certain degré de formalisme.

CA:368, DA:310, DE:366, EN:325, ES:364, FR:323, GA:291, IT:297, NE:317, PO:327.

324 régression Technique permettant d'estimer la valeur la plus appropriée d'une variable (la variable dépendante), à partir des valeurs connues d'une ou de plusieurs autres variables (les variables indépendantes).
Lire: Hatch et Lazaraton, 1991, pp. 467–480; Guilford et Fruchter, 1981, pp. 346–361.

CA:369, DA:311, DE:321, EN:326, ES:365, FR:324, GA:4, IT:298, NE:318, PO:328.

325 régression linéaire Technique de régression qui suppose une relation linéaire entre les variables dépendantes et indépendantes.

CA:370, DA:215, DE:223, EN:213, ES:366, FR:325, GA:5, IT:299, NE:230, PO:329.

326 regression multiple Technique statistique utilisée pour montrer les effets linéaires de plusieurs variables indépendantes sur une variable dépendante isolée. Si on prend par exemple la difficulté de la tâche comme variable dépendante, il est alors possible de rechercher les effets produits par le type de tâche, la difficulté lexicale, etc.
Voir: variable indépendante, régression.
Lire: Hatch et Lazaraton, 1991, pp. 480–486.

CA:371, DA:117, DE:251, EN:242, ES:367, FR:326, GA:182, IT:300, NE:240, PO:330.

327 réponse Comportement du candidat manifesté par les entrées données dans un test. Par exemple, la réponse donnée à un item à choix multiple, ou le travail produit dans un test d'expression écrite.
Cf.: entrée, déclencheur.

CA:374, DA:315, DE:21, EN:331, ES:371, FR:327, GA:153, IT:305, NE:319, PO:334.

328 réponse attendue La ou les réponses que l'élaborateur d'un test ou d'un item attend de la part du candidat à la question posée.

CA:377, DA:106, DE:105, EN:137, ES:374, FR:328, GA:157, IT:306, NE:32, PO:338.

329 réponse clé a) Choix correct dans un item à choix multiples.
Cf.: distracteur.
Voir: item à choix multiple.

b) Plus généralement, un ensemble de réponses correctes ou acceptables.
Cf.: barème de notation.

CA:51/52, DA:256, DE:339, EN:198, ES:54, FR:329, GA:133, DE:339, IT:53, NE:342, PO:335.

330 réponse construite Réponse écrite à un item. Cette réponse implique une production active et non un simple choix parmi différentes propositions.
Cf.: réponse sélectionnée.
Voir: réponse.
CA:376, DA:185, DE:126, EN:70, ES:372, FR:330, GA:154, IT:309, NE:272, PO:336.

331 réponse correcte Réponse considérée comme exacte lors de la notation.
CA:375, DA:190, DE:327, EN:333, ES:373, FR:331, GA:155, IT:307, NE:204, PO:337.

332 réponse longue Forme de réponse à un item ou à une tâche dans laquelle on attend du candidat qu'il produise (et non qu'il sélectionne) une réponse supérieure à une ou deux phrases.
CA:378, DA:423, DE:35, EN:138, ES:375, FR:332, GA:159, IT:308, NE:407, PO:339.

333 réponse modèle Exemple, rédigé par le concepteur de l'item, de la réponse attendue à une question ouverte. Cette réponse peut être utilisée pour construire le barème de notation qui guidera les correcteurs.
CA:261, DA:233, DE:253, EN:236, ES:376, FR:333, GA:156, IT:245, NE:21, PO:340.

334 réponse sélectionnée Forme de réponse à un item qui implique un choix entre différentes possibilités et non la production d'une réponse.
Voir: réponse.
CA:379, DA:422, DE:37, EN:352, ES:377, FR:334, GA:158, IT:310, NE:154, PO:341.

335 reproduction Possibilité de répéter de nombreuses fois les résultats d'une recherche, en augmentant ainsi la confiance accordée aux résultats.
CA:373, DA:189, DE:324, EN:329, ES:370, FR:335, GA:185, IT:301, NE:165, PO:333.

336 résultat Résultat obtenu à un test, en relation avec le sujet testé.
CA:380, DA:317, DE:103, EN:332, ES:378, FR:336, GA:397, IT:312, NE:322, PO:342.

337 rétroaction Information en retour venant des personnes impliquées dans le processus d'évaluation (sujets, examinateurs, etc.) et qui fournit une base permettant d'évaluer ce processus. Elle peut être recueillie de façon informelle ou à l'aide de questionnaires spécifiques.
CA:381, DA:97, DE:330, EN:144, ES:379, FR:337, GA:6, IT:173, NE:134, PO:192.

338 révision Etape de l'élaboration d'un test pendant laquelle les élaborateurs évaluent le matériel produit et décident de rejeter ce qui ne convient pas aux spécifications du test et de publier ce qui convient.
Cf.: modération.
CA:382, DA:400, DE:405, EN:433 ES:383, FR:338, GA:184, IT:91, NE:115, PO:343.

339 rho de Spearman Se réfère à la définition du coefficient de corrélation de Spearman.
CA:383, DA:352, DE:362, EN:374, ES:380, FR:339, GA:292, IT:302, NE:348, PO:344.

340 savoir-faire syn: aptitude. Capacité à faire quelque chose. En évaluation, on distingue souvent les quatre capacités d'expression et de compréhension orales et écrites.
Voir: compétence.
CA:199, DA:111, DE:119, EN:367, ES:100, FR:340, GA:325, IT:1B, NE:413, PO:51.

341 savoirs socioculturels Connaissance du monde liée au fonctionnement de la société d'une culture particulière. Se rapporte à un comportement et un usage pertinents de la langue dans des contextes culturels spécifiques.
Cf.: compétence sociolinguistique.
CA:76, DA:346, DE:357, EN:368, ES:72, FR:341, GA:135, IT:86, NE:344, PO:90.

342 scanner Se réfère à la définition du lecteur optique.
CA:160, DA:327, DE:336, EN:347, ES:168, FR:342, GA:322, IT:226, NE:325, PO:346.

343 script Feuille contenant les réponses du candidat à un test, dans les tâches de type réponse ouverte.
CA:191, DA:261, DE:341, EN:350, ES:219, FR:343, GA:343, IT:175, NE:218, PO:170.

344 sécurité Domaine de l'administration des tests qui consiste à éviter la divulgation des contenus pendant la période où ils sont utilisés.
CA:387, DA:335, DE:348, EN:351, ES:382, FR:344, GA:353, IT:333, NE:142, PO:347.

345 situation de communication réelle Point de vue selon lequel les tests

devraient inclure des tâches ressemblant le plus possible à des activités réelles. Le contenu d'un test évaluant si un candidat est capable de suivre un cours de langue étrangère, devrait par exemple, être basé sur une analyse de la langue et des activités langagières particulières à ce cours.
Voir: authenticité.
Lire: Bachman, 1990, pp. 301–328.

CA:129, DA:433, DE:320, EN:322, ES:134, FR:345, GA:98, IT:23, NE:226, PO:349.

346 sous-test Se réfère à la définition d'une composante.

CA:389, DA:377, DE:386, EN:389, ES:388, FR:346, GA:150, IT:345, NE:373, PO:350.

347 spécifications d'un test Ensemble détaillé de la documentation élaborée pendant la conception d'un test nouveau, ou pendant l'adaptation d'un ancien test. Les spécifications donnent les détails du projet, du contenu, du niveau, de la tâche et du type d'item utilisé, de la population cible, de l'usage du test, etc. Des spécimen de matériel y sont souvent joints.

CA:161, DA:401, DE:394, EN:404, ES:169, FR:347, GA:355, IT:120, NE:400, PO:171.

348 statistiques Ensemble d'informations exprimé sous forme numérique. Au sens strict, une statistique est une propriété d'un échantillon, contrairement à un paramètre, qui est une propriété d'une population. Les statistiques sont généralement transcrites en caractères romains, et les paramètres en grec. Par exemple, la déviation standard d'un échantillon s'écrit S ou SD, alors que dans le cas d'une population on l'écrira σ (sigma).
Cf.: paramètre.
Voir: population, échantillon.

CA:163/164, DA:368/369, DE:378/379, EN:385/386, ES:171/174, FR:348, GA:362/363, IT:117/339, NE:366/367, PO:174/175.

349 statistiques descriptives Statistiques utilisées pour décrire un ensemble de données en termes de quantité, de dispersion, de valeurs moyennes, de corrélation avec d'autres données, etc. On distingue les statistiques descriptives des statistiques inférentielles (ou d'échantillonnage).
Cf.: statistiques inférentielles.

CA:165, DA:63, DE:51, EN:95, ES:172, FR:349, GA:365, IT:340, NE:95, PO:176.

350 statistiques inférentielles Statistiques qui vont au-delà des informations données par les statistiques descriptives. Elles permettent d'inférer comment un ensemble unique de données représente probablement une population plus grande que celle de l'échantillon concerné.
Cf.: statistiques descriptives.

CA:166, DA:139, DE:338, EN:171, ES:173, FR:350, GA:364, IT:341, NE:175, PO:177.

351 sujet Se réfère à la définition du candidat.

CA:100, DA:87/402, DE:307/407, EN:134/406, ES:190, FR:351, GA:110/345, IT:49, NE:129/395, PO:183.

352 syllabus Document détaillé où sont listés tous les domaines d'un programme d'études particulier dont le contenu est présenté.
Cf.: curriculum.

CA:299, DA:224, DE:207, EN:392, ES:310, FR:352, GA:352, IT:335, NE:225, PO:318.

353 tableau de contingence Tableau de fréquences classées selon deux ou plusieurs ensembles de valeurs de variables catégoriques, exemple:

	Maîtrise	Aucune Maîtrise
Méthode A	35	5
Méthode B	20	20

Voir: épreuve du khi deux.

CA:398, DA:187, DE:187, EN:74, ES:390, FR:353, GA:369, IT:347, NE:75, PO:320.

354 tâche Combinaison de consignes, d'entrées et de réponses. Exemple: texte à lire, accompagné d'items à choix multiple, auxquels il est possible de répondre en se référant à la consigne.

CA:391, DA:260, DE:26, EN:393, ES:2, FR:354, GA:371, IT:71, NE:270, PO:352.

355 tâche d'appariement multiple On propose au candidat un certain nombre d'items à compléter sous forme de questions ou de phrases, généralement à partir d'un texte écrit. Les réponses sont fournies dans une banque de mots ou de phrases qui peuvent être utilisés plusieurs fois. L'avantage de cette présentation est que les options ne disparaissent pas au fur et à mesure que le candidat progresse dans le test (comme dans d'autre formes d'appariement), l'exercice ne devient donc pas de plus en plus facile.
Voir: appariement.

CA:396, DA:100, DE:235, EN:241, ES:8, FR:355, GA:372, IT:72, NE:253, PO:354.

356 tâche d'écriture dirigée Se réfère à la définition de production écrite guidée.

CA:392, DA:43, DE:15, EN:105, ES:6, FR:356, GA:376, IT:77, NE:144, PO:355.

357 tâche de compréhension écrite Type de tâche qui consiste généralement en la lecture d'un ou de plusieurs textes auxquels sont appliqués les items suivants: choix multiple, questions à réponses courtes, transfert d'information, etc.

CA:394, DA:223, DE:220, EN:321, ES:3, FR:357, GA:373, IT:74, NE:224, PO:351.

358 tendance centrale (mesure de la) Façon de localiser le point central ou la moyenne statistique d'une distribution. Les trois mesures de la tendance centrale que l'on utilise le plus souvent sont la moyenne, la médiane et le mode.
Lire: Henning, 1987,pp. 39–40; Guilford et Fruchter, 1981, chapitre 4; Hatch et Lazaraton, 1991, pp. 159–164.

CA:246, DA:47, DE:447, EN:45, ES:391, FR:358, GA:62, IT:348, NE:55, PO:356.

359 test Procédure servant à évaluer le niveau de comptétence ou de connaissance d'un individu.

a) une série d'éléments dont l'ensemble constitue une procédure d'évaluation souvent équivalent à examen.

b) une tâche ou un élément unique servant à évaluer un domaine spécifique de compétence ou de connaissance: productions orale et écrite. Dans ce cas, le test ne sera qu'une des composantes (exemple: test de production orale) ou une des tâches (exemple: test de closure) d'un examen complet.

c) une procédure d'évaluation simple et de passation facile, souvent conçue et administrée au sein d'un établissement (exemple: test de progrès). Elle peut également être utilisée dans le cadre d'un programme de recherche ou à des fins d'évaluation (exemple: test d'ancrage).
Cf.: examen.
Voir: test de closure, test de progrès, test d'ancrage.
Lire: Bachman 1990, p.50.

CA:300, DA:300, DE:389, EN:395, ES:311, FR:359, GA:403, IT:353, NE:388, PO:361.

360 test (item) courant Se dit d'un test communément disponible à être administré et qui doit pour cela être tenu en lieu sûr.

CA:341, DA:101, DE:225, EN:217, ES:344, FR:360, GA:407, IT:355, NE:233, PO:362.

361 test adaptatif syn: test sur mesure. Méthode d'évaluation dans laquelle le niveau de difficulté des questions est choisi pendant la passation du test, en fonction de l'estimation de la capacité du candidat. Souvent utilisé dans les tests par ordinateur.
Voir: test adaptatif par ordinateur.
Lire: Bachman, 1990, p. 151; Henning, 1987, p. 136.

CA:302, DA:102, DE:6, EN:7, ES:312, FR:361, GA:429, IT:356, NE:5, PO:363.

362 test adaptatif par ordinateur syn: test sur mesure par ordinateur. Méthode d'évaluation par ordinateur dans laquelle il est possible d'adapter à la capacité du candidat le niveau de difficulté des items présentés, en fonction des réponses données.
Voir: évaluation par ordinateur.

CA:303, DA:51, DE:67, EN:63, ES:181, FR:362, GA:379, IT:386, NE:68, PO:364.

363 test chronométré syn: test de vitesse. Test à durée limitée. Les candidats les plus lents obtiendront une note inférieure car ils ne pourront achever le test. Dans un test chronométré, le niveau de difficulté des questions doit être tel qu'il permette aux candidats d'y répondre correctement s'il n'y avait pas de contrainte de temps.
Cf.: test de niveau, test de puissance intellectuelle.

CA:321, DA:129, DE:340/363, EN:376, ES:334, FR:363, GA:424, IT:372, NE:352, PO:385.

364 test critériel syn: test centré sur les objectifs. Test dans lequel la performance du candidat est interprétée en fonction de critères prédéterminés. L'accent est mis davantage sur la maîtrise d'objectifs que sur le classement que la note du candidat lui impose dans un groupe.
Cf.: test normatif, test référé à un domaine.

CA:337, DA:203, DE:196, EN:81, ES:317, FR:364, GA:412, IT:380, NE:86, PO:369.

365 test curriculaire Test lié à un syllabus donné. Il joue un rôle particulier dans le processus éducatif.
Cf.: test non lié à un curriculum.
Voir: test de connaissances, test d'acquisition.

CA:325, DA:56, DE:217, EN:88, ES:313, FR:365, GA:406, IT:374, NE:221, PO:380.

366 test d'acquisition Se réfère à la définition du test de connaissances.

CA:322, DA:20, DE:203, EN:23, ES:331, FR:366, GA:419, IT:368, NE:421, PO:374.

367 test d'ancrage Composé d'un

groupe d'items de référence, ce test peut être administré en association avec un autre test. Cela permet d'estimer soit les différences de niveau de difficulté entre plusieurs versions du test, soit les différences de performances entre plusieurs groupes de candidats.
CA:307, DA:17, DE:19, EN:16, ES:320, FR:367, GA:404, IT:357, NE:18, PO:365.

368 test d'aptitude Test conçu pour évaluer les probabilités de succès d'un candidat dans un domaine donné, par exemple dans l'apprentissage d'une langue étrangère, ou dans des études spécifiques.
Lire: Henning, 1987, p.6; Ebel et Frisbie, 1991, p. 339.
CA:308, DA:18, DE:96, EN:20, ES:322, FR:368, GA:421, IT:358, NE:22, PO:370.

369 test d'entrée Test utilisé pour déterminer si un candidat peut ou non être admis à étudier dans un établissement donné ou à suivre un programme d'études.
Cf.: test de niveau.
CA:305, DA:5, DE:346, EN:124, ES:319, FR:369, GA:422, IT:364, NE:387, PO:377.

370 test de closure Type de tâche lacunaire dans laquelle des mots entiers sont supprimés d'un texte. Dans un test de closure traditionnel, on supprime un mot tous les x mots. On appelle également test de closure l'exercice dans lequel des phrases courtes sont supprimées d'un texte, ou lorsque l'élaborateur choisit les mots qui seront supprimés, comme c'est le cas dans le test de closure sélectif. Les candidats devront fournir les mots manquants (test ouvert), ou les choisir dans une liste (choix multiple ou test de closure à lacunes sélectives). Le corrigé d'un test ouvert peut comporter soit le mot exact (le mot supprimé du texte original étant seul accepté comme réponse correcte), soit les mots acceptables (dans ce cas, une liste de mots acceptables est donnée au correcteur).
Cf.: test-c, item à compléter.
CA:313, DA:50, DE:66, EN:52, ES:315, FR:370, GA:410, IT:362, NE:61, PO:378.

371 test de closure sélectif Se réfère à la définition du test de closure.
CA:314, DA:308, DE:230, EN:318, ES:316, FR:371, GA:60, IT:56, NE:315, PO:367.

372 test de compréhension orale Test de compréhension du langage oral. Il est généralement administré à l'aide d'un magnétophone ou d'un magnétoscope.
CA:315, DA:221, DE:147, EN:216, ES:324, FR:372, GA:411, IT:361, NE:235, PO:373.

373 test de confiance Test pour la confiance statistique.
Voir: confiance.
CA:324, DA:334, DE:350, EN:364, ES:333, FR:373, GA:435, IT:371, NE:339, PO:384.

374 test de connaissances syn: test d'acquisition. Test destiné à mesurer les connaissances acquises par un candidat dans un domaine donné, un manuel, etc. , donc lié à un curriculum.
CA:309, DA:366, DE:369, EN:6, ES:321, FR:374, GA:419, IT:368, NE:301, PO:374.

375 test de dépistage Test habituellement court et simple à administrer, utilisé pour identifier ceux des candidats qui peuvent être admis à un cours ou qui peuvent être candidats à un examen.
Voir: test de niveau.
CA:316, DA:424, DE:98, EN:349, ES:332, FR:375, GA:432, IT:370, NE:332, PO:375.

376 test de maîtrise Test dont l'objectif est d'établir si un étudiant maîtrise un domaine bien défini de savoir-faire ou de savoirs.
CA:338, DA:227, DE:204, EN:225, ES:327, FR:376, GA:425, IT:366, NE:237, PO:376.

377 test de niveau syn: test de placement. Test administré afin de placer les étudiants dans un groupe ou une classe au niveau qui correspond à leur degré de connaissances et de capacités.
CA:311, DA:137, DE:101, EN:282, ES:323, FR:377, GA:434, IT:365, NE:291, PO:372.

378 test de niveau de capacité Test qui mesure la capacité ou l'aptitude générale, sans référence à quelque formation spécifique ou ensemble de matériel que ce soit.
CA:319, DA:112, DE:120, EN:296, ES:326, FR:378, GA:428, IT:363, NE:306, PO:379.

379 test de puissance intellectuelle Test dont la durée est suffisante pour que tous les candidats puissent le terminer, mais qui contient des tâches ou des items d'un degré de difficulté qui rend peu probable que la majorité des candidats répondent à tous correctement.
Cf.: test chronométré.
CA:310, DA:299, DE:261/293, EN:288, ES:329, FR:379, GA:413, IT:360, NE:296,

PO:371.

380 test de performance Procédure d'évaluation dans laquelle on demande au candidat une production écrite ou orale (écrits longs ou entretiens oraux). De telles procédures sont souvent conçues de façon à faire simuler une performance langagière telle qu'on pourrait la trouver dans des contextes hors évaluation.
Lire: Bachman, 1990, pp. 304–305.
CA:306, DA:283, DE:284, EN:278, ES:318, FR:380, GA:416, IT:367, NE:287, PO:381.

381 test de progrès Test administré au cours de la formation et dont l'objectif est de valider l'apprentissage réalisé jusqu'à la date du test.
CA:320, DA:108, DE:214, EN:298, ES:330, FR:381, GA:418, IT:369, NE:422, PO:382.

382 test de sélection Se réfère à la définition du test d'entrée.
CA:323, DA:330, DE:36, EN:353, ES:332, FR:382, GA:430, IT:370, NE:333, PO:383.

383 test diagnostique Utilisé pour découvrir les points forts et les lacunes d'un apprenant. Les résultats peuvent servir à des prises de décision concernant la formation future, l'apprentissage ou l'enseignement.
CA:317, DA:65, DE:77, EN:97, ES:325, FR:383, GA:414, IT:373, NE:97, PO:386.

384 test direct Test qui mesure la capacité de production orale ou écrite, et où la performance est directement mesurée. Par exemple lors de l'évaluation de la production écrite lorsque la tâche du candidat est d'écrire une lettre.
Cf.: test indirect (tâche).
Lire: Hughes, 1989, pp. 14–16.
CA:326, DA:70, DE:81, EN:104, ES:335, FR:384, GA:415, IT:375, NE:102, PO:387.

385 test indirect (tâche) Test ou tâche à réaliser qui tente de mesurer les capacités sous-jacentes à une aptitude langagière, plutôt que de tester la performance au test lui-même. Un exemple est de tester la capacité de production écrite en demandant au candidat de noter dans un texte les structures incorrectes.
Cf.: test direct.
Lire: Hughes, 1989, pp. 14–16.
CA:329, DA:135, DE:150, EN:170, ES:337, FR:385, GA:420, IT:354, NE:173, PO:389.

386 test lacunaire à choix multiple Type d'item d'un test pour lequel le candidat doit choisir parmi plusieurs options le mot ou la phrase correcte à insérer dans une lacune du texte.
Voir: item à compléter.
CA:224, DA:237, DE:250, EN:239, ES:242, FR:386, GA:215, IT:79, NE:251, PO:390.

387 test non lié à un curriculum Test non lié à un programme d'études donné.
Cf.: test curriculaire.
Voir: test de niveau de capacité.
CA:328, DA:57, DE:218, EN:89, ES:339, FR:387, GA:405, IT:376, NE:222, PO:388.

388 test normatif Test dans lequel les notes sont interprétées par rapport à la performance d'un groupe donné composé de personnes comparables aux individus auxquels le test est administré. On tend à utiliser ce terme pour des tests dont l'objectif est de classer les individus en fonction du groupe de référence ou les uns par rapport aux autres.
Cf.: test critériel.
CA:336, DA:251, DE:268, EN:254, ES:340, FR:388, GA:426, IT:381, NE:264, PO:391.

389 test objectif Test auquel on peut appliquer un barème de notation et qui ne fait pas appel à une opinion d'expert ou à un jugement subjectif.
CA:331, DA:257, DE:272, EN:257, ES:341, FR:389, GA:427, IT:377, NE:267, PO:392.

390 test psychométrique Test portant sur des attributs psychologiques tels que la personnalité, l'intelligence, les capacités et le niveau de compétence en langue, et qui fait des hypothèses sur la nature de la capacité testée. Il est unidimensionnel et distribué normalement.
Lire: Bachman, 1990, p. 73–74.
CA:334, DA:302, DE:310, EN:301, ES:397, FR:390, GA:433, IT:379, NE:308, PO:394.

391 test référé à un domaine Test dont les résultats sont interprétés en fonction d'un domaine spécifique de contenus ou de niveaux de capacités.
Cf.: test critériel, test normatif.
CA:335, DA:84, DE:50, EN:120, ES:342, FR:391, GA:417, IT:382, NE:114, PO:368.

392 test semi-direct Test qui tente d'évaluer les performances langagières sans l'intervention et hors de la présence d'un examinateur. Par exemple un test d'expression orale administré à l'aide d'un

magnétophone et où les déclencheurs ont été préalablement enregistrés. Le SOPI (Semi-direct oral proficiency Interview: Entretien de capacité orale semi-direct) en est un exemple.
Cf.: test direct.

CA:130/339, DA:332/348, DE:347/356, EN:356/370, ES:137/343, FR:392, GA:356/423, IT:93/383, NE:336/346, PO:144/396.

393 test sur objectif spécifique Test conçu pour mesurer la capacité d'un candidat à travailler dans un contexte professionnel ou académique spécifique. Les contenus du test ont été élaborés en fonction d'une analyse des tâches langagières que le candidat aura à traiter dans les situations requises par la langue cible.

CA:318, DA:243, DE:112, EN:375, ES:328, FR:393, GA:431, IT:378, NE:351, PO:393.

394 test-c Type de tâche lacunaire dans laquelle la seconde partie de certains mots est supprimée. La fréquence de la suppression peut atteindre un mot sur deux. La tâche à réaliser par le candidat est de compléter la partie manquante de ces mots.
Cf.: test de closure.

CA:304, DA:45, DE:62, EN:38, ES:314, FR:394, GA:408, IT:384, NE:51, PO:366.

395 testing sur mesure Action d'adapter un test existant aux demandes d'un groupe particulier de sujets.

CA:301, DA:404, DE:410, EN:405, ES:13, FR:395, GA:370, IT:5, NE:382, PO:4.

396 texte Discours suivi, écrit ou oral utilisé pour élaborer un ensemble d'items dans un test.

CA:403, DA:386, DE:411, EN:411, ES:399, FR:396, GA:381, IT:389, NE:381, PO:398.

397 théorie classique du test Théorie de mesure qui consiste en un ensemble de suppositions au sujet des rapports entre les notes réelles ou observées et les facteurs qui peuvent les affecter. On rattache généralement ces facteurs à l'erreur. Théorie également appelée théorie de la note 'vraie'.
Cf.: théorie de l'item-réponse TIR.
Lire: Bachman, 1990, pp. 166–187.

CA:399, DA:174, DE:177, EN:50, ES:392, FR:397, GA:387, IT:349, NE:208, PO:357.

398 théorie de l'attribut latent Se réfère à la définition de la théorie de l'item-réponse TIR.

CA:402, DA:211, DE:206, EN:207, ES:395, FR:398, GA:390, IT:350, NE:216, PO:358.

399 théorie de la généralisabilité Modèle statistique de recherche des effets relatifs de différentes sources de variance dans les notes obtenues aux tests.
Lire: Bachman, 1990, p. 7; Croker et Algina, 1986, chapitre 8.

CA:400, DA:115, DE:132, EN:154, ES:393, FR:399, GA:388, IT:351, NE:152, PO:359.

400 théorie de l'item-réponse TIR Groupe de modèles mathématiques permettant de mettre en rapport la performance d'un individu à un test avec le niveau de capacité de cet individu. Ces modèles se basent sur la théorie fondamentale qui spécifie que la performance attendue d'un individu à une question particulière d'un test est fonction à la fois du niveau de difficulté de la question et du niveau de capacité de l'individu.
Lire: Henning, 1987, chapitre 8.

CA:401, DA:159, DE:173/296, EN:195, ES:394, FR:400, GA:389, IT:352, NE:201, PO:360.

401 TIR Se réfère à la définition de la théorie de l'item-réponse TIR.

CA:412, DA:153, DE:165, EN:188, ES:408, FR:401, GA:392, IT:352, NE:194, PO:402.

402 transfert d'information Technique d'évaluation qui implique qu'une information donnée sous une certaine forme soit présentée d'une façon différente. Par exemple: nommer les différentes parties d'un diagramme d'après des informations écrites; transformer une note informelle en annonce formelle.
Lire: Hughes, 1989, pp. 84, 124–125, 138.

CA:409, DA:141, DE:152, EN:173, ES:406, FR:402, GA:8, IT:396, NE:177, PO:404.

403 transformation Se réfère à la définition de la transformation de phrase.

CA:229, DA:413, DE:420, EN:416, ES:245, FR:403, GA:242, IT:217, NE:402, PO:239.

404 transformation de phrases Type d'item dans lequel l'amorce donnée est une phrase complète, suivie par le premier ou les deux premiers mots d'une seconde phrase qui reprend le contenu de la première mais sous une forme grammaticale différente. La première phrase peut être par exemple à la forme active et le candidat devra la présenter à la forme passive.

CA:410, DA:381, DE:334, EN:359, ES:407, FR:404, GA:61, IT:397, NE:440, PO:405.

405 type d'item On se réfère aux items des tests par des noms qui décrivent leur forme. Exemples: questionnaire à choix multiple, transformation de phrases, réponse courte, test de closure ouvert.

CA:406, DA:162, DE:174, EN:197 ES:405, FR:405, GA:58, IT:392, NE:203, PO:399.

406 type de question Se réfère à la définition de type d'item ou de type de tâche.

CA:407, DA:358, DE:124, EN:305, ES:404, FR:406, GA:57, IT:394, NE:424, PO:400.

407 type de tâche On se réfère aux tâches par des noms qui décrivent ce qu'elles testent et la forme qu'elles prennent, par exemple: compréhension écrite à choix multiple, production écrite guidée, etc.

CA:408, DA:265, DE:30, EN:394, ES:402, FR:407, GA:59, IT:393, NE:271, PO:401.

408 unidimensionnalité Dimension unique, qui est une supposition nécessaire pour construire une échelle permettant de mesurer des attributs psychologiques, c'est-à-dire en utilisant des modèles d'item-réponse d'usage courant. Propriété de l'instrument de mesure et non du processus psychologique sous-jacent.
Lire: Crocker et Algina, 1986, p. 343.

CA:413, DA:90, DE:97, EN:427, ES:409, FR:408, GA:23, IT:398, NE:119, PO:406.

409 utilisateur Personne ou institution (enseignant ou employeur) qui utilise les résultats d'un test afin de prendre une décision concernant le sujet.

CA:414, DA:391, DE:392, EN:407, ES:410, FR:409, GA:440, IT:399, NE:393, PO:407.

410 valeur de facilité Se réfère à la définition de l'indice de facilité.

CA:426, DA:192, DE:209, EN:143, ES:423, FR:410, GA:217, IT:411, NE:147, PO:419.

411 valeur-*p* Se réfère à la définition de l'indice de facilité.

CA:427, DA:273, DE:276, EN:266, ES:424, FR:411, GA:269, IT:412, NE:277, PO:420.

412 validation Processus par lequel on rassemble des preuves pour étayer les conclusions données par les notes des tests. Ce sont les conclusions au sujet des utilisations spécifiques d'un test qui sont validées et non pas le test lui-même.
Voir: validité.

CA:415, DA:426, DE:426, EN:429, ES:412, FR:412, GA:39, IT:400, NE:414, PO:408.

413 validité Degré auquel les notes d'un test permettent de tirer des conclusions appropriées, significatives et utiles, en relation avec l'objectif du test. On distingue différents aspects de la validité, tels que la validité de contenu, la validité critérielle et la validité de construct; elles donnent différentes sortes de preuves permettant de juger la validité globale d'un test en fonction de ses objectifs.
Voir: validité concourante, validité de construct, validité critérielle, validité de contenu, validité convergente, validité discriminante, validité prédictive.
Lire: Bachman, 1990, pp. 25, 236–237.

CA:416, DA:427, DE:427, EN:430, ES:413, FR:413, GA:30, IT:401, NE:415, PO:409.

414 validité apparente Qualité d'un test ou de toute autre mesure qui semble correcte et adéquate à l'objet mesuré. Il s'agit là d'un jugement subjectif plus que d'un jugement basé sur une analyse objective du test. La validité apparente est souvent considérée comme une fausse forme de validité. On l'appelle également attrait d'un test (*test appeal*).
Lire: Bachman, 1990, pp. 285–289.

CA:417, DA:272, DE:110/34, EN:140, ES:414, FR:414 GA:2, IT:402, NE:174, PO:410.

415 validité concourante On dit d'un test qu'il a une validité concourante si les notes obtenues sont en corrélation élevée avec un critère externe reconnu qui mesure le même domaine de connaissance ou de capacité.
Voir: validité critérielle, validité prédictive.
Lire: Bachman, 1990, pp. 248–250.

CA:418, DA:323, DE:417, EN:66, ES:415, FR:415, GA:33, IT:403, NE:71, PO:411.

416 validité convergente On dit d'un test qu'il a une validité convergente lorsqu'il y a une corrélation élevée entre les notes obtenues à ce test et celles obtenues à un autre test mesurant le même construct (indépendamment de la méthode). Il s'agit là d'un autre aspect de la validité de construct.
Cf.: validité discriminante.
Voir: validité de construct.
Lire: Guilford et Fruchter, 1981, pp.

436–437.
CA:419, DA:188, DE:188, EN:75, ES:416, FR:416, GA:32, IT:404, NE:76, PO:412.

417 validité critérielle On dit d'un test qu'il a une validité critérielle si on peut démontrer le rapport entre les notes obtenues et un critère externe qui est censé mesurer la même capacité. Lors de l'absence de critère, l'information fournie indique jusqu'à quel point le test peut prédire le comportement futur.
Voir: validité concourante, validité prédictive.
Lire: Bachman, 1990, pp. 248–250.
CA:421, DA:204, DE:197, EN:82, ES:417, FR:417, GA:34, IT:407, NE:87, PO:413.

418 validité de construct syn: validité hypothético-déductive; validité conceptuelle. On dit d'un test qu'il a une validité de construct si les notes obtenues peuvent être interprétées comme une théorie sur la nature d'un construct ou sur le rapport de ce construct avec d'autres. On pourrait prédire, par exemple, que deux tests valides de compréhension orale classent les apprenants de la même façon, mais chacun d'entre eux aurait un rapport plus éloigné avec les notes obtenues à un test de compétence grammaticale.
Voir: validité, spécifications d'un test.
Lire: Ebel et Frisbie, 1991, p. 108; Hacht et Lazaraton, 1991, pp. 37–38.
CA:420, DA:186, DE:186, EN:69, ES:418, FR:418, GA:37, IT:406, NE:73, PO:414.

419 validité de contenu On dit d'un test qu'il a une validité de contenu si les items ou les tâches dont il est composé constituent un échantillon représentatif des items ou des tâches pour une capacité ou un domaine de connaissances précis.
Voir: validité, spécifications d'un test.
Lire: Bachman, 1990, pp. 244–247.
CA:422, DA:134, DE:154, EN:73, ES:419, FR:419, GA:31, IT:405, NE:179, PO:415.

420 validité discriminante On dit d'un test qu'il a une validité discriminante si la corrélation qu'il entretient avec des tests évaluant différents attributs est plus faible que celle qu'il a avec des tests évaluant le même attribut, sans tenir compte de la méthode d'évaluation. Cela peut être considéré comme un aspect de la validité de construct.
Voir: validité de construct.
Cf.: validité convergente.
Lire: Croker et Algina, 1986, p. 23; Guilford et Fruchter, 1981, pp. 436–437.
CA:423, DA:73, DE:83, EN:111, ES:420, FR:420, GA:36, IT:408, NE:108, PO:416.

421 validité divergente Se réfère à la définition de la validité discriminante.
CA:424, DA:81, DE:90, EN:118, ES:421, FR:421, GA:35, IT:409, NE:111, PO:417.

422 validité prédictive Indique la façon dont un test peut prédire la future performance dans une aptitude donnée.
Cf.: validité critérielle.
Lire: Guilford et Fruchter, 1987, pp. 437–438.
CA:425, DA:298, DE:294/439, EN:291, ES:422, FR:422, GA:38, IT:410, NE:300, PO:418.

423 variable a) Nom donné à une série d'observations portant sur un item, qui peut être un item de test, ou bien le genre, l'âge ou la note obtenue.

b) Elément, dans un projet expérimental ou dans une analyse statistique, qui peut prendre une série de valeurs. Par exemple, les variables d'intérêt, en évaluation, contiennent la difficulté des items, le genre et l'âge des sujets, etc.
CA:430, DA:428, DE:428, EN:431, ES:430, FR:423, GA:25, IT:416, NE:416, PO:422.

424 variable critère Terme utilisé dans la recherche, équivalent de variable dépendante.
Voir: variable dépendante.
CA:431, DA:205, DE:198, EN:83, ES:431, FR:424, GA:26, IT:417, NE:88, PO:423.

425 variable dépendante Variable qui indique le phénomène que le chercheur cherche à expliquer. Les notes obtenues à un test (variable indépendante) peuvent par exemple être utilisées pour prédire la réussite professionnelle (variable dépendante).
Cf.: variable indépendante.
Lire: Hatch et Lazaraton, p. 63
CA:432, DA:7, DE:2, EN:94, ES:432, FR:425, GA:28, IT:418, NE:7, PO:424.

426 variable indépendante Pour le chercheur, une variable qui, pense-t'on, peut avoir un rapport avec la variable dépendante ou l'influencer. Par exemple, les notes obtenues à un test (variable indépendante) peuvent être utilisées pour prédire un succès professionnel (variable dépendante).
Cf.: variable dépendante.
Lire: Hatch et Lazaraton, p. 64.
CA:433, DA:420, DE:422, EN:169, ES:433, FR:426, GA:27, IT:419, NE:268, PO:425.

427 variance Mesure de la dispertion d'une série de notes; plus elle sera grande, plus les notes individuelles seront loin de la moyenne.
CA:434, DA:429, DE:429, EN:432, ES:434, FR:427, GA:24, IT:420, NE:417, PO:421.

428 voussure Caractère d'une courbe plus ou moins aplatie que la courbe normale de même écart type. Des données représentées sur une courbe aplatie présentent une fréquence platykurtique, alors que des données formant une courbe moins aplatie présentent une fréquence leptokurtique.

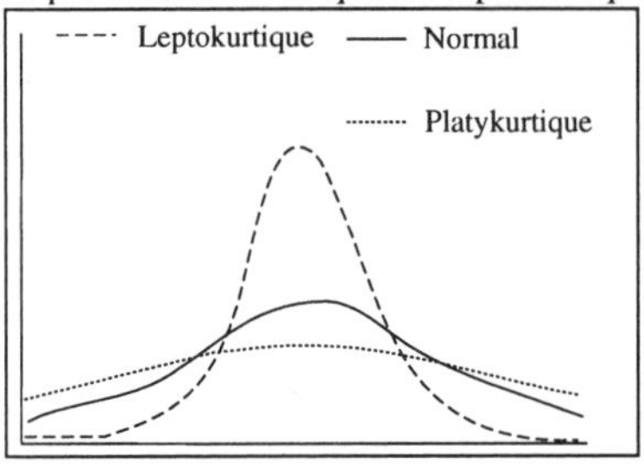

Voir: distribution (fréquence) normale.

CA:95, DA:412, DE:108, EN:202, ES:94, FR:428, GA:100, IT:114, NE:213, PO:108.

429 vrai/faux Type de réponse à choix multiple où le candidat doit indiquer si une série d'affirmations sur un texte sont vraies ou fausses.

CA:232, DA:326, DE:326, EN:419, ES:250, FR:429, GA:245, IT:218, NE:426, PO:243.

7 Gaeilge: Gluais ilteangach de théarmaí tástála teanga

1 agallamh Úsáidtear agallamh go minic chun scileanna labhartha a thástáil. Uaireanta ní bhíonn i gceist ach saorchomhrá idir na hiarrthóirí agus na measúnóirí, agus uaireanta eile is sraith dhlúthstruchtúrtha de thascanna labhartha a bhíonn ann.

CA:131, DA:150, DE:305, EN:263, ES:136, FR:148, GA:1, IT:92, NE:355, PO:143.

2 aghaidhbhailíocht Cé chomh mór is a dhealraíonn sé do na hiarrthóirí, nó dóibh siúd a roghnaigh an triail atá le cur orthu, gur tomhas inghlactha atá inti ar an gcumas is mian leo a thomhas. Is breithiúnas suibiachtúil é seo. Níl sé bunaithe ar aon anailís oibiachtúil ar an triail, agus go minic ní ghlactar leis gur foirm fhírinneach bhailíochta í an aghaidhbhailíocht. Uaireanta tagraítear di mar "thaitneamhacht trialach".

Léitheoireacht bhreise: Bachman 1990, lgh. 285–289.

CA:417, DA:272, DE:110/34, EN:140, ES:414, FR:414 GA:2, IT:402, NE:174, PO:410.

3 airmheán An scór ag lár an dáilte i gcnuasach de scóir rangaithe. Tá a leath de na scóir os cionn an airmheáin agus a leath faoina bhun.

Féach: claonadh lárnach.

Cuir i gcomparáid le: meán, mód.

Léitheoireacht bhreise: Hatch & Lazaraton 1991, lch. 161.

CA:244, DA:228, DE:232, EN:232, ES:263, FR:242, GA:3, IT:235, NE:239, PO:256.

4 aischéimniú Teicníocht chun an luach is dóichí a bheith ag athróg amháin (an athróg spleách) a thuar ó na luachanna atá ar eolas d'athróg amháin eile nó níos mó (na hathróga neamhspleácha).

Léitheoireacht bhreise: Hatch & Lazaraton 1991, lgh. 467–80; Guilford & Fruchter 1981, lgh. 346–361.

CA:369, DA:311, DE:321, EN:326, ES:365, FR:324, GA:4, IT:298, NE:318, PO:328.

5 aischéimniú líneach Teicníocht aischéimnithe ina nglactar leis go bhfuil gaol líneach idir na hathróga spleácha agus na hathróga neamhspléacha.

CA:370, DA:215, DE:223, EN:213, ES:366, FR:325, GA:5, IT:299, NE:230, PO:329.

6 aiseolas Tuairimí daoine atá bainteach leis an bpróiséas tástála (iarrthóirí, riarthóirí, srl.) arbh fhéidir a úsáid mar bhonn chun measúnú a dhéanamh ar an bpróiseas. Is féidir aiseolas a bhailiú go neamhfhoirmiúil, nó trí ceistneoirí a chur le chéile d'aon ghnó chuige seo.

CA:381, DA:97, DE:330, EN:144, ES:379, FR:337, GA:6, IT:173, NE:134, PO:192.

7 aiste Ceadaigh an sainmhíniú ar cheapadóireacht.

CA:366, DA:262, DE:33, EN:131, ES:306, FR:159, GA:7, IT:313, NE:125, PO:142.

8 aistriú eolais Teicníocht tástála ina ndéantar eolas a thugtar i bhfoirm amháin a chur in iúl i bhfoirm eile. Samplaí de thascanna dá leithéid is ea eolas a thógaint as téacs chun lipéadú a dhéanamh ar léaráid; nóta neamhfhoirmiúil a athscríobh mar fhógra foirmiúil.

Léitheoireacht bhreise: Hughes 1989, lgh. 84, 124–125, 138.

CA:409, DA:141, DE:152, EN:173, ES:406, FR:402, GA:8, IT:396, NE:177, PO:404.

9 aitheantas Insitiúid a bheith ag glacadh go foirmiúil le cáilíocht áirithe i gcomhair cuspóra ar leith, e.g. áit ar chúrsa staidéir iarchéime.

CA:365, DA:15, DE:269, EN:323, ES:361 FR:321, GA:9, IT:303, NE:123, PO:325.

10 alfa (comhéifeacht alfa) Meastachán iontaofachta a thomhasann comhsheasmhacht inmheánach trialach. Bíonn raon luachanna idir 0 agus 1 aige. Baintear leas as go minic i gcomhair trialacha a scóráltar ar scálaí rátála, murab ionann agus trialacha i bhfoirm míreanna déscartha, cé gur féidir é a úsáid sa dá chás. Tagraítear dó freisin mar comhéifeacht alfa.

Cuir i gcomparáid le: Kuder is

Richardson.
Féach: Comhsheasmhacht inmheánach.
Léitheoireacht bhreise: Henning 1987, lch. 84.

CA:9, DA:11, DE:10, EN:10, ES:16, FR:8, GA:10, IT:10, NE:12, PO:6.

11 alfa Cronbach Ceadaigh an sainmhíniú ar alfa (comhéifeacht alfa).

CA:10, DA:54, DE:70, EN:84, ES:17, FR:9, GA:11, IT:11, NE:89, PO:7.

12 anailís ábhair Slí chun cur síos agus anailís a dhéanamh ar an ábhar a bhíonn i dtriail. Is gá an anailís seo chun a dheimhniú go dtagann ábhar na trialach leis an tsonraíocht. Tá sé riachtanach chun bailíocht ábhair agus bailíocht tógán a mheas.

CA:18, DA:133, DE:153, EN:72, ES:19, FR:12, GA:12, IT:15, NE:178, PO:15.

13 anailís ar mhíreanna Cur síos ar conas a d'fheidhmigh na míreanna éagsúla i dtriail. De ghnáth úsáidtear innéacsanna clasaiceacha na staitistice, éascacht agus cumhacht idirdhealaithe, mar shampla, chuige seo. Baintear leas as bogearraí mar MicroCAT Iteman san anailís seo.
Féach: idirdhealú, innéacs éascachta.

CA:13, DA:161, DE:167, EN:190, ES:25 FR:17, GA:13, IT:12, NE:198, PO:16.

14 anailís ar thriail Anailís a dhéantar ar thrialacha tar éis iad a chur ar na hiarrthóirí. Déantar an anailís ar an ríomhaire go minic, agus baintear leas as modhanna staitistiúla. Dhéanfaí a leithéid chun imscrúdú a dhéanamh ar fheidhmiú na n-iarrthóirí, abair, nó ar fheidhmiú na trialach í féin.

CA:15, DA:389, DE:390, EN:396, ES:22, FR:16, GA:14, IT:17, NE:389, PO:18.

15 anailís athraithis Ceadaigh an sainmhíniú ar ANOVA.

CA:17, DA:430, DE:430, EN:13, ES:23, FR:15, GA:15, IT:19, NE:418, PO:14.

16 anailís chomhaithris Ceadaigh an sainmhíniú ar ANCOVA.

CA:14, DA:200, DE:193, EN:12, ES:20, FR:14, GA:16, IT:18, NE:85, PO:13.

17 anailís dioscúrsa Díríonn an cineál seo anailíse ar an struchtúr agus ar an bhfeidhm a bhíonn ag saghsanna éagsúla téacsanna labhartha nó scríofa.

CA:19, DA:76, DE:86, EN:107, ES:24, FR:13, GA:17, IT:16, NE: 104, PO:19.

18 anailís fachtóirí Teicníocht staitistice a chuireann ar chumas an taighdeora líon beag athróga a dhéanamh de líon mór athróg, trí phatrúin a aimsiú sa chaoi go mbíonn na luachanna a bhíonn ag cuid mhaith acu ag athrú. Déanann braisle d'athróga a bhfuil idirghaolmhaireacht láidir eatarthu fachtór. Is féidir leis an taighdeoir tosú ar an anailís fachtóirí ar mhodh taiscéalaíoch, d'fhonn hipitéisí a chumadh, nó ar mhodh dearbhaithe, chun iniúchadh á dhéanamh ar hipitéisí ar leith.
Léitheoireacht bhreise: Bachman 1990,lch. 262; Crocker & Algina 1986, lch. 232.

CA:20, DA:96, DE:115, EN:142, ES:26, FR:18, GA:18, IT:14, NE:133, PO:20.

19 anailís riachtanas Slí leis na riachtanais teanga (maidir le scileanna, tascanna, stór focal srl.) a bhíonn ag grúpa ar leith foghlaimeoirí a chinntiú sula leagtar amach cúrsa teagaisc dóibh.

CA:16, DA:35, DE:45, EN:246, ES:21, FR:11, GA:19, IT:13, NE:31, PO:17.

20 ANCOVA Cineál anailíse athraithe inar féidir iarmhairt na n-athróg mearaithe (is é sin na hathróga a d'fhéadfadh athrú de réir mar a athraíonn athróg na spéise) a choinneáil faoi riail.
Féach: ANOVA.
Léitheoireacht bhreise: Hatch & Lazaraton 1991, lch. 387.

CA:21, DA:14, DE:13, EN:17, ES:27, FR:19, GA:20, IT:20, NE:16, PO:21.

21 ANOVA Teicníocht staitistiúil chun an hipitéis nialasach, gurb ionann le chéile iad na meáin a bhreathnaítear i bpobail éagsúla, a thástáil. Déantar iniúchadh ar athraitheacht na mbreathnaithe laistigh de gach grúpa, chomh maith leis an athraitheacht idir mheáin na ngrúpaí.
Léitheoireacht bhreise: Hatch & Lazaraton 1991, lch. 387.

CA:22, DA:19, DE:20, EN:18, ES:28, FR:20, GA:21, IT:21, NE:19, PO:22.

22 aonchineálacht Gné de thriail nó d'fhothriail a bhfuil míreanna inti a thomhasann aon inniúlacht amháin, nó gné de ghrúpa ina bhfuil na tréithe céanna go comónta idir na baill. Cuirtear an chéim aonchineálachta in iúl leis an innéacs iontaofachta.

CA:204, DA:127, DE:148, EN:165, ES:221, FR:205, GA:22, IT:257, NE:169, PO:216.

23 aontoiseacht Nuair a bhíonn scála á chur le chéile chun tréithe síceolaíochta a thomhas e.g. le samhailteacha mírfhreagartha na linne seo, ní mór glacadh leis gur aon toise amháin atá i gceist. Baineann an aontoiseacht leis an uirlis thomhais agus ní leis an mbunphróiseas síceolaíoch.
Léitheoireacht bhreise: Crocker & Algina

1986, lch. 343.

CA:413, DA:90, DE:97, EN:427, ES:409, FR:409, GA:23, IT:398, NE:119, PO:406.

24 athraitheas Tomhas ar spré grúpa scór. Dá mhéad é an t-athraitheas is ea is faide a bhíonn na scóir aonair ón meán.

CA:434, DA:429, DE:429, EN:432, ES:434, FR:427, GA:24, IT:420, NE:417, PO:421.

25 athróg a) An t-ainm a chuirtear ar shraith de bhreathnuithe ar mhír amháin, mír trialach, mar shampla, nó inscne, aois, nó scór i dtriail.

b) Comhbhall, i ndearadh turgnamhach nó in anailís staitistiúil, ar féidir leis sraith de luachanna a ghlacadh. Mar shampla, i measc na n-athróg a gcuirtear spéis iontu i gcomhthéacs na tástála teanga, tá deacracht míreanna trialach, inscne agus aois na n-iarrthóirí, srl.

CA:430, DA:428, DE:428, EN:431, ES:430, FR:423, GA:25, IT:416, NE:416, PO:422.

26 athróg chritéir I ndearadh taighde, téarma eile ar athróg spleách.
Féach: athróg spleách.

CA:431, DA:205, DE:198, EN:83, ES:431, FR:424, GA:26, IT:417, NE:88, PO:423.

27 athróg neamhspleách Sa taighde, athróg a meastar faoi go bhfuil gaol aici le hathróg spleách nó go bhféadfadh sí dul i bhfeidhm uirthi. Mar shampla, d'fhéadfaí leas a bhaint as scóir i dtriail (an athróg neamhspleách) chun réamhaithris a dhéanamh ar dhul chun cinn ar an láthair oibre (an athróg spleách).
Cuir i gcomparáid le: athróg spleách.
Féach: athróg.
Léitheoireacht bhreise: Hatch & Lazaraton 1991, lch. 64.

CA:433, DA:420, DE:422, EN:169, ES:433, FR:426, GA:27, IT:419, NE:268, PO:425.

28 athróg spleách An athróg atá faoi scrúdú ag an taighdeoir. Mar shampla, d'fhéadfaí leas a bhaint as na scóir i dtriail (an athróg neamhspleách) chun réamhaithris a dhéanamh ar rath ar an láthair oibre (an athróg spleách).
Cuir i gcomparáid le: athróg neamhspleách.
Féach: athróg.
Léitheoireacht bhreise: Hatch & Lazaraton 1991, lch. 63.

CA:432, DA:7, DE:2, EN:94, ES:432, FR:425, GA:28, IT:418, NE:7, PO:424.

29 athscálú Ceadaigh an sainmhíniú ar scálú.

CA:367, DA:314, DE:258, EN:330, ES:389, FR:320, GA:29, IT:304, NE:166, PO:326.

30 bailíocht An méid a chuireann scóir i dtriail ar chumas daoine tátail a bhaint astu a bhfuil brí leo agus atá oiriúnach agus úsáideach, ag cur san áireamh cuspóir na trialach. Aithnítear gnéithe éagsúla den bhailíocht a bheith ann, mar atá bailíocht ábhair, bailíocht critéir agus bailíocht tógán; cuireann siad sin cineálacha éagsúla fianaise ar fáil agus breithiúnas á thabhairt ar bhailíocht trialach san iomlán, chun críche áirithe.
Féach: bailíocht chomhreathach, bailíocht tógán, bailíocht chritéarghaolmhar, bailíocht ábhair, bailíocht choinbhéirseach, bailíocht idirdhealaitheach, aghaidhbhailíocht, bailíocht tuartha.
Léitheoireacht bhreise: Bachman 1990, lgh. 25, 236–237.

CA:416, DA:427, DE:427, EN:430, ES:413, FR:413, GA:30, IT:401, NE:415, PO:409.

31 bailíocht ábhair Deirtear go bhfuil bailíocht ábhair ag triail más sampla ionadaíoch iad na míreanna agus na tascanna atá inti de mhíreanna agus de thascanna i gcomhair an réimse eolais nó cumais atá le tástáil. Baineann siad seo le curaclam nó le cúrsa go minic.
Féach: bailíocht, sonraíocht trialach.
Léitheoireacht bhreise: Bachman 1990, lgh. 244–247.

CA:422, DA:134, DE:154, EN:73, ES:419, FR:419, GA:31, IT:405, NE:179, PO:415.

32 bailíocht choinbhéirseach Deirtear go bhfuil bailíocht choinbhéirseach ag triail nuair a bhíonn comhghaolmhaireacht láidir idir na scóir a ghnóthaítear inti agus na scóir a ghnóthaítear i dtriail dhifriúil a thomhasann an tógán céanna (gan bheann ar an modh). Is féidir féachaint air seo mar ghné den bhailíocht thógánach.
Cuir i gcomparáid le: bailíocht idirdhealaitheach.
Féach: bailíocht tógán.
Léitheoireacht bhreise: Guilford & Fruchter 1981, lgh. 436–437.

CA:419, DA:188, DE:188, EN:75, ES:416, FR:416, GA:32, IT:404, NE:76, PO:412.

33 bailíocht chomhreathach Deirtear go bhfuil bailíocht chomhreathach ag triail má bhíonn comhghaol láidir idir na scóir a chuireann sí ar fáil agus critéar seachtrach aitheanta a thomhasann an réimse céanna eolais nó cumais.
Féach: bailíocht chritéarghaolmhar.
Léitheoireacht bhreise: Bachman 1990, lgh. 248–250.

CA:418, DA:323, DE:417, EN:66, ES:415,

FR:415, GA:33, IT:403, NE:71, PO:411.

34 bailíocht chritéarghaolmhar Deirtear go bhfuil bailíocht chritéarghaolmhar ag triail más féidir a thaispeáint go bhfuil gaolmhaireacht idir scóir sa triail agus critéar seachtrach éigin a shíltear a bheith ina thomhas ar an gcumas. Baintear leas as eolas ar chritéarghaolmhaireacht chun a dhéanamh amach cé chomh maith is a dhéanann triail iompraíocht san am atá le teacht a réamhaithris.
Féach: bailíocht chomhreathach, bailíocht tuartha.
Léitheoireacht bhreise: Bachman 1990, lgh. 248–250.
CA:421, DA:204, DE:197, EN:82, ES:417, FR:417, GA:34, IT:407, NE:87, PO:413.

35 bailíocht dhibhéirseach Ceadaigh an sainmhíniú ar bhailíocht idirdhealaitheach.
CA:424, DA:81, DE:90, EN:118, ES:421, FR:421, GA:35, IT:409, NE:111, PO:417.

36 bailíocht idirdhealaitheach Deirtear go bhfuil bailíocht idirdhealaithe ag triail má tá an chomhghaolmhaireacht atá aici le trialacha ar thréith dhifriúil níos laige ná an chomhghaolmhaireacht atá aici le trialacha ar an tréith chéanna, gan bheann ar an modh tástála. Is féidir féachaint uirthi seo mar ghné den bhailíocht thógánach.
Féach: bailíocht tógán.
Cuir i gcomparáid le: bailíocht choinbhéirseach.
Léitheoireacht bhreise: Crocker & Algina, 1986, p. 23; Guilford & Fruchter, 1981, pp. 436–437.
CA:423, DA:73, DE:83, EN:111, ES:420, FR:420, GA:36, IT:408, NE:108, PO:416.

37 bailíocht tógán Deirtear go bhfuil bailíocht tógán ag triail más féidir a thaispeáint go bhfuil na scóir ag teacht le teoiric faoi nádúr an tógáin nó faoin ngaol atá idir é agus tógáin eile. D'fhéadfaí a thuar, mar shampla, go mbeadh scóir na bhfoghlaimeoirí san ord céanna tar éis dóibh dhá thriail bhailí ar an gcluastuiscint a dhéanamh, ach gur gaol níos laige a bheadh ag an dá shraith scór seo le scóir ar thriail ar inniúlacht ghramadaí.
Féach: bailíocht, sonraíochtaí trialach.
Léitheoireacht bhreise: Ebel & Frisbie 1991, lch. 108; Hatch & Lazaraton 1991, lgh. 37–38.
CA:420, DA:186, DE:186, EN:69, ES:418, FR:418, GA:37, IT:406, NE:73, PO:414.

38 bailíocht tuartha Léiriú ar cé chomh maith is a dhéanann triail tuar ar fheidhmiú amach anseo sa scil atá i gceist.
Cuir i gcomparáid le: bailíocht chritéarghaolmhar.
Léitheoireacht bhreise: Guilford & Fruchter 1987, lgh. 437–438.
CA:425, DA:298, DE:294/439, EN:291, ES:422, FR:422, GA:38, IT:410, NE:300, PO:418.

39 bailmheas An próiseas trína mbailítear fianaise chun tacú leis na tátail a bhaintear as na scóir a bhaineann iarthóirí amach i dtriail. Ní ar an triail féin a dhéantar an bailmheas ach ar na tátail a bhaintear aisti agus í á húsáid chun críche ar leith.
Féach: bailíocht.
CA:415, DA:426, DE:426, EN:429, ES:412, FR:412, GA:39, IT:400, NE:414, PO:408.

40 bancáil míreanna Bealach chun bainistiú a dhéanamh ar na míreanna a úsáidtear i dtrialacha. Stóráltar eolas mar gheall orthu ionas gur féidir trialacha eile a chur le chéile agus a fhios a bheith againn roimh ré cén t-ábhar a bheidh iontu agus cé chomh deacair agus a bheidh siad. Is ar ríomhaire a choinnítear an banc de ghnáth, agus tá an cur chuige bunaithe ar theoiric na tréithe folaigh, rud a fhágann gur féidir na míreanna a chur i gcomórtas le chéile ar aon scála deacrachta amháin.
Léitheoireacht bhreise: Henning 1987, Caibidil 9.
CA:36, DA:155, DE:28, EN:191, ES:37, FR:28, GA:40, IT:111, NE:199, PO:37.

41 banda Sa chiall is leithne, cuid de scála. I dtriail a bhfuil míreanna inti, beidh raon scór laistigh den bhanda, ar féidir cur síos air mar ghrád nó mar scór banda. Ar scála rátála a dearadh chun tréith nó cumas ar leith a mheasúnú, labhairt nó scríobh mar shampla, tagraíonn banda, de ghnáth, do leibhéal áirithe.
CA:37, DA:339, DE:44, EN:29, ES:38, FR:200, GA:41, IT:39 NE:28, PO:210.

42 barraghraf (barrachairt) Slí chun dáiltí minicíochta na n-athróg a léiriú i bhfoirm ghrafach.

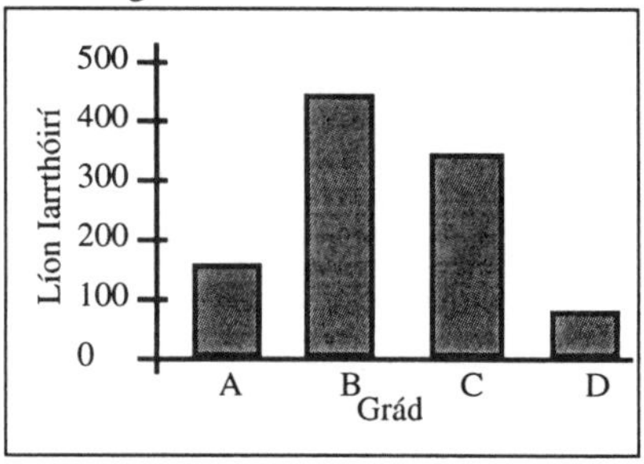

Cuir i gcomparáid le: histeagram.
Léitheoireacht bhreise: Hatch & Lazaraton 1991, lch. 147.

CA:102, DA:383, DE:335, EN:31, ES:104, FR:201, GA:42, IT:123, NE:357, PO:211.

43 bearna eolais Teicníocht mhúinte agus tástála teanga ina ndéantar insamhladh ar an a gcumarsáid réadúil. Féachtar chuige nach mbíonn an t-eolas céanna ag gach aon mhac léinn, agus, dá bhrí sin, go mbíonn orthu cumarsáid a dhéanamh le chéile chun an tasc a chur i gcrích. Baintear leas as de ghnáth i gcleachtadh nó tástáil ar na scileanna labhartha agus scríbhneoireachta.

CA:42, DA:140, DE:151, EN:172, ES:411, FR:213, GA:43, IT:424, NE:176, PO:223.

44 breis-scór An difríocht idir an scór a ghnóthaítear i dtriail roimh chúrsa teagaisc agus an scór a ghnóthaítear ar an triail chéanna nó ceann cosúil léi i ndeireadh an chúrsa. Léiríonn an breis-scór an dul chun cinn a rinneadh le linn an chúrsa.

CA:352, DA:290, DE:211, EN:150, ES:32, FR:199, GA:44, IT:192, NE:434, PO:209.

45 caighdeánú An próiseas trína ndeimhnítear go gcloíonn measúnóirí le nós imeachta comhaontaithe agus go gcuireann siad na scálaí rátála i bhfeidhm ar an tslí chóir.
Féach: measúnóir.

CA:167, DA:363, DE:373, EN:383, ES:175, NE:361, FR:162, GA:45, IT:338, PO:295.

46 cáilíocht Gradam a bhronntar ar dhaoine tar éis dóibh cúrsa aitheanta oiliúna a chríochnú nó dul faoi thriail, agus arbh ionann é agus cáilíocht chun gníomhaíocht nó jab ar leith a dhéanamh. Is féidir féachaint ar theastas oilteachta teanga mar cháilíocht i leith cuspóirí áirithe.
Cuir i gcomparáid le: teastas, dioplóma.

CA:360, DA:209, DE:314, EN:302, ES:405, FR:313, GA:46, IT:294, NE:214, PO:322.

47 cainteoir dúchais Cainteoir teanga a sealbhaíodh mar chéad teanga.

CA:286, DA:234, DE:255, EN:245, ES:216, FR:217, GA:47, IT:265, NE:255, PO:190.

48 calabraigh I dteoiric na mírfhreagartha, an deacracht a bhaineann le sraith de mhíreanna trialach a mheas.
Féach: scála téite.

CA:43, DA:163, DE:93, EN:39, ES:43, FR:40, GA:48, IT:43, NE:206, PO:47.

49 calabrú An próiseas chun teacht ar scála trialach nó trialacha. Uaireanta déantar an calabrú trí mhíreanna as trialacha difriúla a chur ar ancaireacht ar chomhscála deacrachta (an scála téite). Nuair is míreanna calabraithe amháin atá i dtriail, léiríonn scóir sa triail sin cumas na n-iarrthóirí, i.e. a suíomh ar an scála téite.

CA:44, DA:164, DE:94, EN:40, ES:42, FR:35, GA:49, IT:44, NE:205, PO:42.

50 catagóir a)Roinn de scála catagóireach, m.sh. tá dhá chatagóir ag inscne, fireannach agus baineannach.

b) Sa tástáil, mar shampla, má tá cúig phointe ar scála rátála, deirtear go bhfuil cúig chatagóir freagartha air.

CA:49, DA:169, DE:176, EN:43, ES:52, FR:48, GA:50, IT:51, NE:52, PO:55.

51 ceapadóireacht Tasc ina dtáirgíonn an t-iarrthóir téacs fada scríofa. I measc na gcineálacha téacs a bhíonn le táirgeadh i dtascanna ceapadóireachta tá, cur síos a dhéanamh ar eachtra éigin, agus plé a dhéanamh ar thopaicí ar féidir tuairimí éagsúla a bheith ag daoine fúthu. D'fhéadfadh tuarascálacha agus litreacha, foirmiúla agus neamhfhoirmiúla, a bheith san áireamh freisin. Tagraítear dó freisin mar aiste nó ceist aiste.

CA:366, DA:109, DE:32, EN:62, ES:192, FR:73, GA:51, IT:82, NE:372, PO:88.

52 ceapadóireacht dhioscúrsach Tasc scríbhneoireachta ina mbíonn ar an iarrthóir plé a dhéanamh ar thopaic ar féidir tuairimí éagsúla a bheith ag daoine fúthu, nó argóint a dhéanamh ar son tuairimí pearsanta.

CA:74, DA:77, DE:342, EN:113, ES:70, FR:74, GA:52, IT:83, NE:42, PO:89.

53 ceartú tanúcháin Modh chun an chomhghaolmhaireacht idir dhá athróg nó níos mó a mheas sa chás nach bhfuil aon difríocht idir iontaofacht na n-athróg.
Léitheoireacht bhreise: Guilford & Fruchter 1981, lgh. 450–453; Hatch & Lazaraton 1990, lgh. 444–445.

CA:88, DA:194, DE:243, EN:76, ES:79, FR:82, GA:53, IT:106, NE:78, PO:99.

54 ceartú tomhais Modh chun gearradh siar ar na marcanna a ghnóthaítear trí fhreagraí chearta a thabhairt de sheans i dtrialacha ina bhfuil míreanna oibiachtúla.
Léitheoireacht bhreise: Ebel & Frisbie 1986, lgh. 215–218.

CA:82, DA:193, DE:317/450, EN:77, ES:80, FR:83, GA:54, IT:103, NE:77, PO:98.

55 ceist Baintear leas as uaireanta chun tagairt do thasc nó do mhír i dtriail.

Féach: mír, tasc.

CA:291, DA:357, DE:122, EN:303, ES:304, FR:315, GA:55, IT:136, NE:423, PO:323.

56 ceist oscailte I gcás na míreanna nó na tascanna seo, bíonn ar an iarrthóir freagra a chumadh, seachas freagra a roghnú. Is é an cuspóir atá leis an gcineál seo míre ná freagra atá measartha saor ar shrianta a éileamh, cúpla focal i gcásanna áirithe, aiste fhada i gcásanna eile. Beidh raon freagraí cearta sa scéim mharcála mar sin.

CA:292, DA:444, DE:273, EN:260, ES:305, FR:318, GA:56, IT:137, NE:273, PO:324.

57 cineál ceiste Ceadaigh an sainmhíniú ar: cineál míre, cineál taisc.

CA:407, DA:358, DE:124, EN:305, ES:404, FR:406, GA:57, IT:394, NE:424, PO:400.

58 cineál míre Tagraítear do mhíreanna trialach le hainmneacha ar cur síos iad, de ghnáth, ar fhoirm na míre. Samplaí is ea: ceist ilroghnach, claochlú abairte, freagra gairid, clabhsúr oscailte.

CA:406, DA:162, DE:174, EN:197 ES:403, FR:405, GA:58, IT:392, NE:203, PO:399.

59 cineál taisc Tagraítear do thascanna le hainmneacha ina mbíonn iarracht de chur síos ar an ní atá á thástáil acu agus ar an leagan amach atá orthu, e.g. tuiscint léitheoireachta, ilroghnach, scríbhneoireacht threoraithe, srl.

CA:408, DA:265, DE:30, EN:394, ES:402, FR:407, GA:59, IT:393, NE:271, PO:401.

60 clabhsúr réasúnach Ceadaigh an sainmhíniú ar thriail chlabhsúir.

CA:314, DA:308, DE:230, EN:318, ES:316, FR:371, GA:60, IT:56, NE:315, PO:367.

61 claochlú abairte Cineál míre ina dtugtar abairt iomlán mar spreagthach, agus ina dhiaidh sin focal nó dhó d'abairt eile a chuireann ábhar na chéad abairte in iúl i bhfoirm ghramadaí eile. Mar shampla, d'fhéadfadh an chéad abairt a bheith san fhaí ghníomhach agus is é tasc an iarrthóra é an t-ábhar ceannann céanna a chur in iúl san fhaí chéasta.

CA:410, DA:381, DE:334, EN:359, ES:407, FR:404, GA:61, IT:397, NE:440, PO:405.

62 claonadh lárnach (tomhas ar) Slí le lárphointe nó meán staitistiúil dáilte a aimsiú. Tá trí thomhas ar chlaonadh lárnach ann a mbaintear leas astu go coitianta, is iad sin an meán, an t-airmheán agus an mód.

Léitheoireacht bhreise: Henning 1987, lgh. 39–40; Guilford & Fruchter 1981, Caibidil 4; Hatch & Lazaraton, 1991, lgh. 159–164.

CA:246, DA:47, DE:447, EN:45, ES:391, FR:358, GA:62, IT:348, NE:55, PO:356.

63 cnuasach Ceadaigh an sainmhíniú ar chnuasach trialacha.

CA:39, DA:390, DE:406, EN:397, ES:41, FR:31, GA:63, IT:42, NE:390, PO:39.

64 cnuasach trialacha Sraith de thrialacha nó de fhothrialacha gaolmhara a chuireann torthaí ar fáil neamhspleách ar a chéile (m. sh. trí scileanna difriúla a thástáil) ach ar féidir iad a chur le chéile leis chun scór iomlán a thabhairt.

CA:38, DA:28, DE:393, EN:32, ES:40, FR:30, GA:64, IT:41, NE:30, PO:38.

65 cobhsaíocht Gné d'iontaofacht nuair a bhunaítear an meastachán ar an gcur chuige triail-athriail. Baineann sé le cé chomh cobhsaí is a bhíonn scóir i dtriail le himeacht ama.

Féach: iontaofacht, iontaofacht triail-athriail.

CA:162, DA:359, DE:371, EN:378, ES:170, FR:79, GA:65, IT:337, NE:358, PO:173.

66 cóimheas F San anailís ar athraitheas, an cóimheas a ríomhtar chun a léiriú cé acu an bhfuil na difríochtaí a bhreathnaítear idir mheáin ghrúpaí suntasach ó thaobh na staitistice de, nó nach bhfuil; mar shampla, cé acu ar chruthaigh grúpa amháin níos fearr ná grúpa eile i dtriail theanga, agus an difríocht sin a bheith suntasach.

Féach: foirmeacha malartacha.

Léitheoireacht bhreise: Hatch & Lazaraton 1991, lgh. 315–17.

CA:364, DA:94, DE:109, EN:139, ES:368, FR:319, GA:66, IT:296, NE:132, PO:332.

67 comhaireamh minicíochta focal Áireamh ar a mhinice is a bhíonn focal ar leith nó cineálacha ar leith focal i dtéacs. Sa tástáil teanga d'fhéadfadh sé sin a bheith úsáideach agus trialacha á gcumadh de réir sonraíochta ó thaobh stór focal de.

CA:190, DA:270, DE:143, EN:440, ES:362, FR:75, GA:67, IT:256, NE:436, PO:95.

68 comhaontú idir-rátálaíoch An méid is atá dhá mheasúnacht nó níos mó a rinne measúnóirí difriúla ar an sampla céanna d'feidhmiúchán teanga ag teacht le chéile. Tá tábhacht ar leith leis seo i gcás measúnachta ar scileanna scríbhneoireachta agus labhartha i dtrialacha inar ghá do na scrúdaitheoirí breithiúnais shuibiachtúla a thabhairt.

CA:2, DA:31, DE:159, EN:181, ES:11, FR:2, GA:68, IT:84, NE:185, PO:2.

69 comhaontú intra-rátálaí An méid is atá dhá mheasúnacht ar an sampla céanna d'feidhmiúchán teanga a dhéanann an measúnóir céanna ag amanna difriúla ag teacht le chéile. Tá tábhacht ar leith leis seo i gcás measúnachta ar scileanna scríbhneoireachta agus labhartha i dtrialacha inar ghá do na scrúdaitheoirí breithiúnais shuibiachtúla a thabhairt.

CA:3, DA:33, DE:163, EN:185, ES:12, FR:3, GA:69, IT:90, NE:190, PO:3.

70 comhaontú rátálaithe Ceadaigh na sainmhínithe ar comhaontú idir-rátálaíoch agus comhaontú intra-rátálaí.

CA:1, DA:307, DE:56, EN:312, ES:10, FR:1, GA:70, IT:84, NE:36, PO:1.

71 comhathraitheas An t-athraitheas atá comónta idir dhá athróg nó níos mó. I gcás téacs léitheoireachta, mar shampla, is minic go mbíonn fad abairte gaolta le deacracht leicseach, i.e. bíonn siad ag comhathrú. Is gá an comhathraitheas a chur san áireamh nuair a bhíonn athróg amháin á thuar ó athróga eile, mar shampla, nuair a dhéantar tuar ar dheacracht téacs léitheoireachta trí fhad abairte agus deacracht leicseach a mheas.
Féach: athraitheas.

CA:93, DA:199, DE:192, EN:80, ES:91, FR:92, GA:71, IT:112, NE:84, PO:106.

72 comhchainteoir I dtriail labhartha, an scrúdaitheoir a mhíníonn an tasc do na hiarrthóirí, a chuireann na ceisteanna orthu agus a bhíonn i mbun an chomhrá ar fad a bhíonn eatarthu. Uaireanta deineann an comhchainteoir measúnacht ar na hiarrthóirí freisin, agus tugann scóir dóibh, agus uaireanta deineann scrúdaitheoir eile é sin, duine a bhíonn ag éisteacht leis an gcomhrá gan páirt a ghlacadh ann.
Cuir i gcomparáid le: measúnóir.

CA:213, DA:325, DE:125, EN:178, ES:138, FR:216, GA:72, IT:201, NE:155, PO:227.

73 comhéifeacht Séan (innéacs) uimhriúil a mbaintear leas as mar thomhas ar airí nó tréith.
Féach: alfa (comhéifeacht alfa), comhéifeacht chomhghaolúcháin.

CA:53, DA:175, DE:178, EN:53, ES:55, FR:54, GA:73, IT:57, NE:62, PO:69.

74 comhéifeacht alfa Ceadaigh an sainmhíniú ar alfa (comhéifeacht alfa).

CA:54, DA:176, DE:179, EN:54, ES:56, FR:55, GA:74, IT:58, NE:63, PO:70.

75 comhéifeacht chomhghaolúcháin Séan (innéacs) a léiríonn cé chomh láidir is atá an comhghaol idir dhá athróg nó níos mó. Gabhann sé ó -1 go +1. Athróga a bhfuil comhghaol láidir eatarthu, beidh comhéifeacht chomhghaolúcháin eatarthu atá i ngar do + nó -1.
Léitheoireacht bhreise: Guilford & Fruchter 1981, lgh. 86–88.

CA:55, DA:197, DE:191, EN:79, ES:57, FR:56, GA:75, IT:60, NE:82, PO:71.

76 comhéifeacht fí Comhéifeacht comhghaoil a mbaintear leas as chun treise an ghaoil idir dhá athróg dhénártha a léiriú, mar shampla, na scóir ar dhá mhír i dtriail a scóráiltear ceart nó mícheart.
Féach: comhéifeacht chomhghaolúcháin.
Léitheoireacht bhreise: Guilford and Fruchter 1981, lgh. 316–318; Crocker & Algina 1986, lgh. 92–94.

CA:62, DA:284, DE:286, EN:279, ES:59, FR:58, GA:76, IT:61, NE:288, PO:75.

77 comhéifeacht iontaofachta Tomhas ar iontaofacht, sa raon 0 go dtí 1. Is féidir iontaofacht a mheas trí thriail a chur an dara uair (ar an tuiscint go mbeidh na scóir cosúil lena chéile) nó, sa chás nach bhfuil sé seo praiticiúil, trí fhoirm éigin den tomhas ar chomhsheasmhacht inmheánach a ríomhadh. Tugtar séan (innéacs) iontaofachta air uaireanta.
Féach: comhsheasmhacht inmheánach, iontaofacht, iontaofacht triail-athriail.

CA:61, DA:313, DE:323, EN:328, ES:58, FR:61, GA:77, IT:59, NE:44, PO:74.

78 comhghaol An gaol idir dhá thomhas nó níos mó, chomh fada is a bhaineann sé leis an méid a athraíonn siad ar an tslí chéanna. Má bhíonn scóir na n-iarrthóirí ar dhá thriail mórán san ord céanna, beidh comhghaol deimhneach idir an dá ghrúpa de scóir.
Cuir i gcomparáid le: comhathraitheas.
Féach: comhghaol toradh-móiminte Pearson (r Pearson), comhghaol ord ranga.
Léitheoireacht bhreise: Guilford & Fruchter 1981, Caibidil 6; Bachman 1990, lgh. 259–260.

CA:91, DA:196, DE:190, EN:78, ES:84, FR:85, GA:78, IT:95, NE:81, PO:100.

79 comhghaol déshraitheach Séan (innéacs) ar chumhacht idirdhealaithe míreanna i gcomhair míreanna déscartha, a scríobhtar mar r_{bis}; an comhghaol idir critéar éigin (an scór iomlán i dtriail, de ghnáth) agus bunchumas an iarrthóra freagra ceart a thabhairt ar an mír. Bíonn luach r_{bis} 25% níos airde, ar a laghad, ná luach an phointe dhéshraithigh (r_{pbi}). Buntáiste a bhaineann le r_{bis} ná go mbíonn sé cuibheasach cobhsaí thar shamplaí a bhfuil leibhéil dhifriúla cumais iontu.
Cuir i gcomparáid le: comhghaol déshraitheach pointe.

Féach: idirdhealú.
Léitheoireacht bhreise: Crocker & Algina 1986, lgh. 317–318; Guilford & Fruchter 1981, lgh. 304–311.
CA:56, DA:40, DE:60, EN:35, ES:85, FR:86, GA:79, IT:96, NE:48, PO:101.

80 comhghaol déshraitheach pointe Séan ar chumhacht idirdhealaithe míreanna i gcomhair míreanna déscartha, a scríobhtar mar r_{pbi}; an comhghaol idir critéar (an scór iomlán i dtriail, de ghnáth) agus an freagra ar an mír. Buntáiste amháin a bhaineann le r_{pbi} thar an gcomhghaol déshraitheach (r_{bis}) ná gur féidir leas cuí a bhaint as nuair nach bhfuil dáileadh normalach ar an mbunchumas.
Cuir i gcomparáid le: comhghaol déshraitheach.
CA:57, DA:41, DE:311, EN:283, ES:86, FR:57, GA:80, IT:97, NE:309, PO:102.

81 comhghaol fí Ceadaigh an sainmhíniú ar comhéifeacht fí.
CA:92, DA:285, DE:287, EN:280, ES:88, FR:88, GA:81, IT:101, NE:289, PO:103.

82 comhghaol ord ranga Comhghaol atá bunaithe ar ord na n-athróg i gcomórtas lena chéile agus ní ar a ndearbhluachanna.
Léitheoireacht bhreise: Guilford & Fruchter 1981, lgh. 294–296.
CA:60, DA:304, DE:315, EN:309, ES:89, FR:59, GA:82, IT:100, NE:312, PO:72.

83 comhghaol rang-difríochtaí Spearman Leagan den chomhghaol ord ranga a mbaintear leas as i gcás samplaí beaga, i.e. samplaí níos lú ná 30.
Féach: comhghaol ord ranga.
CA:58, DA:351, DE:361, EN:373, ES:87, FR:60, GA:83, IT:99, NE:347, PO:73.

84 comhghaol toradh-móiminte Pearson (r Pearson) Comhéifeacht comhghaolúcháin is féidir a úsáid le hathróga a dhéantar a thomhas ar scálaí eatramh nó ar scálaí cóimheasa.
Féach: comhéifeacht chomhghaolúcháin
Léitheoireacht bhreise: Hatch & Lazaraton 1991, lgh. 427–431; Guilford & Fruchter 1981, lch. 81.
CA:59, DA:279, DE:298, EN:274, ES:90, FR:87, GA:84, IT:98, NE:283, PO:104.

85 comhpháirt Cuid de scrúdú, a mbíonn leabhrán treoracha agus teorainn ama dá cuid féin ag gabháil léi go minic, agus a chuirtear ar iarrthóirí mar thriail ar leith. Bíonn comhpháirteanna bunaithe ar scileanna go minic agus teidil orthu mar Cluastuiscint nó Ceapadóireacht. Tagraítear dóibh mar fhothrialacha chomh maith.
CA:73, DA:181, DE:306, EN:61, ES:29, FR:72, GA:85, IT:81, NE:128, PO:87.

86 comhscála Slí chun na scóir ó dhá thriail nó níos mó a chur ar aon scála amháin, d'fhonn is gur féidir comparáid dhíreach a dhéanamh idir thorthaí na dtrialacha sin. Is féidir na scóir ó dhá thriail nó níos mó a chur ar chomhscála má dhéantar claochlú staitistiúil ar na scóir amha, m. sh. cothromú trialacha.
Léitheoireacht bhreise: Bachman 1990, lgh. 340–344.
CA:147, DA:110, DE:131, EN:57, ES:156, FR:125, GA:86, IT:320, NE:148, PO:158.

87 comhsheasmhacht inmheánach Gné de thriail a fheictear sa chomhsheasmhacht idir scóir na n-iarrthóirí ar mhíreanna ar leith agus an scór a fhaigheann siad sa triail ina iomláine. Is féidir leas a bhaint as meastacháin ar chomhsheasmhacht inmheánach mar innéacsanna ar iontaofacht trialach; is féidir innéacsanna éagsúla a ríomh, mar shampla, KR20, alfa.
Féach: alfa (comhéifeacht alfa), Kuder is Richardson, iontaofacht.
Léitheoireacht bhreise: Bachman 1990, lch. 172.
CA:77, DA:147, DE:155, EN:180, ES:74, FR:186, GA:87, IT:87, NE:186, PO:93.

88 cothromú comhpheircintílí Modh chun na scóir amha i dtrialacha a chothromú. Meastar scóir a bheith ionann lena chéile más ionann an rang peircintíle a bhíonn acu i ngrúpa iarrthóirí.
CA:132, DA:440, DE:24, EN:127, ES:140, FR:36, GA:88, IT:150, NE:121, PO:43.

89 cothromú cothrománach An próiseas trína gcuirtear na scóir ar dhá thriail atá mórán ar aon deacracht le chéile ar aon scála amháin d'fhonn gur féidir na caighdeáin chéanna a chur i bhfeidhm sa dá thriail.
Cuir i gcomparáid le: cothromú ingearach.
CA:133, DA:128, DE:149, EN:166, ES:141, FR:37, GA:89, IT:152, NE:170, PO:44.

90 cothromú ingearach An próiseas trína gcuirtear na scóir ar dhá thriail a mbaineann leibhéil éagsúla deacrachta leo ar aon scála amháin.
Léitheoireacht bhreise: Crocker & Algina 1986, lgh. 473-477.
CA:135, DA:432, DE:435, EN:434, ES:143, FR:39, GA:90, IT:153, NE:419, PO:46.

91 cothromú líneach Slí chun scór i dtriail amháin a chothromú le scór i dtriail eile. Tá an dá scór an oiread céanna diallas caighdeánach os cionn nó faoi bhun meán-

scór na trialach lena mbaineann siad.
Féach: aischéimniú.
Léitheoireacht bhreise: Crocker & Algine 1986, lgh. 457–461.
CA:134, DA:216, DE:17, EN:212, ES:142, FR:38, GA:91, IT:151, NE:229, PO:45.

92 creidiúnú Aitheantas a bhronntar ar scrúdú, de ghnáth ag eagras oifigiúil mar eagras rialtais, bord scrúdaithe, srl.
CA:4, DA:10, DE:8, EN:5, ES:1, FR:4, GA:92, IT:303, NE:3, PO:325.

93 críochnú abairte Leathabairt a chuirtear faoi bhráid na n-iarrthóirí sa chineál seo míre. Bíonn orthu an abairt a chríochnú trí fhocail oiriúnacha a sholáthar (tar éis dóibh téacs a léamh, b'fhéidir), nó trí rogha a dhéanamh idir fhocail a thugtar dóibh.
CA:72, DA:382, DE:332, EN:357, ES:69, FR:298, GA:93, IT:80, NE:442, PO:86.

94 cuar tréithe na míre (CTM) I dTeoiric na Mírfhreagartha, tugann an CTM an dóchúlacht go bhfreagrófar mír áirithe i gceart ar bhonn tréith folaigh cumais an iarrthóra, mar atá sé le feiceáil i bhfreagairt míreanna uilig na trialach.
Léitheoireacht bhreise: Crocker & Algina 1986, lgh. 340–342.
CA:79, DA:157, DE:168, EN:192, ES:95, FR:90, GA:94, IT:115, NE:196, PO:109.

95 cúliarmhairt An tionchar a imríonn triail ar an múinteoireacht sa rang. Má thuigeann múinteoirí, cuirim i gcás, go bhfuil na mic léinn ag beartú tabhairt faoi thriail áirithe a dhéanamh, d'fhéadfaidís modhanna teagaisc agus ábhar na gceachtanna a chur in oiriúint do riachtanais na trialach. D'fhéadfadh toradh fónta nó drochthoradh a bheith air seo.
Féach: tionchar.
CA:372, DA:25/436, DE:43/442, EN:28/435, ES:124/369, FR:322, GA:95, IT:147, NE:27/432, PO:135.

96 cumas Tréith intinne, nó acmhainn nó cumhacht chun rud éigin a dhéanamh.
Cuir i gcomparáid le: inniúlacht, oilteacht.
Léitheoireacht bhreise: Bachman 1990, lgh. 16, 19.
CA:46, DA:2, DE:113, EN:2, ES:49, FR:42, GA:96, IT:1A, NE:411, PO:49.

97 cumas teanga Na hinniúlachtaí ar fad arbh ionann iad ar fad agus acmhainn duine chun teanga a úsáid ar mhaithe le cuspóirí éagsúla cumarsáide.
Léitheoireacht bhreise: Bachmann 1990, lgh. 3–4.
CA:47, DA:354, DE:368, EN:203, ES:50, FR:43, GA:97, IT:4, NE:379, PO:50.

98 cur chuige an tsaoil mhóir An tuairim gur cheart na cineálacha tasc a thugtar d'iarrthóirí i dtriail teanga a bheith ar aon dul, chomh fada agus is féidir, le rudaí a bheidh le déanamh acu leis an teanga sa saol mór. Mar shampla, i gcur chuige an tsaoil mhóir, i gcás trialach arb é an cuspóir atá léi ná a mheas an féidir le hiarrthóirí déileáil le cúrsa acadúil a mhúintear trí theanga iasachta, dhéanfaí anailís riachtanas i dtús báire ar an teanga agus ar na gníomhaíochtaí teanga a fhaightear go hiondúil ar an gcúrsa sin, agus is as seo a thiocfadh ábhar na trialach.
Féach: dílseacht.
Léitheoireacht bhreise: Bachman 1990, lgh 301–328.
CA:129, DA:433, DE:320, EN:322, ES:134, FR:345, GA:98, IT:23, NE:226, PO:349.

99 curaclam Cur síos foriomlán ar na haidhmeanna, an t-ábhar, an t-éagrú, na modhanna agus an mheasúnacht a bhaineann le cúrsa oideachais.
Cuir i gcomparáid le: siollabas.
CA:94, DA:55, DE:71, EN:87, ES:93, FR:93, GA:99, IT:113, NE:220, PO:107.

100 curtóis Léiriú ar an méid atá dáileadh níos buaicí nó níos comhréidhe ná cuar normalach. Léiríonn sonraí atá leata amach i gcuar comhréidh dáileadh platacurtach agus léiríonn sonraí a dhéanann buaic ghéar dáileadh leipteacurtach.

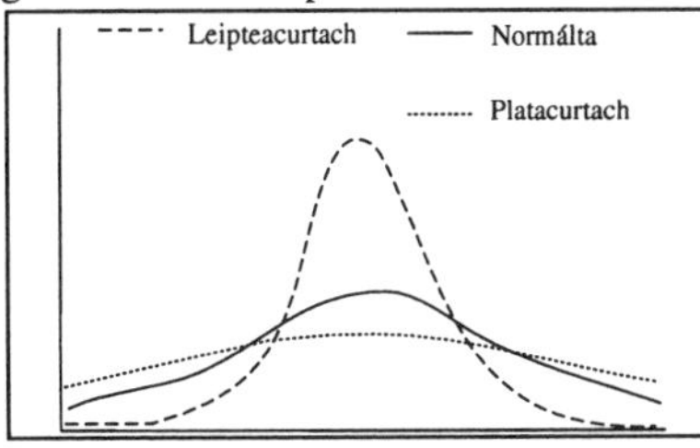

Féach: dáileadh normálta.
CA:95, DA:412, DE:108, EN:202, ES:94, FR:428, GA:100, IT:114, NE:213, PO:108.

101 d Ebel Ceadaigh an sainmhíniú ar Innéacs d.
CA:96, DA:85, DE:92, EN:122, ES:96, FR:94, GA:101, IT:116, NE:117, PO:111.

102 d glan Ceadaigh an sainmhíniú ar innéacs d.
CA:206, DA:246, DE:257, EN:247, ES:97, FR:115, GA:102, IT:194, NE:256, PO:111.

103 dáileadh I sonraí trialach, an méid

uaireanta a gnóthaíodh gach scór. Léirítear é go minic i bhfoirm histeagraim.

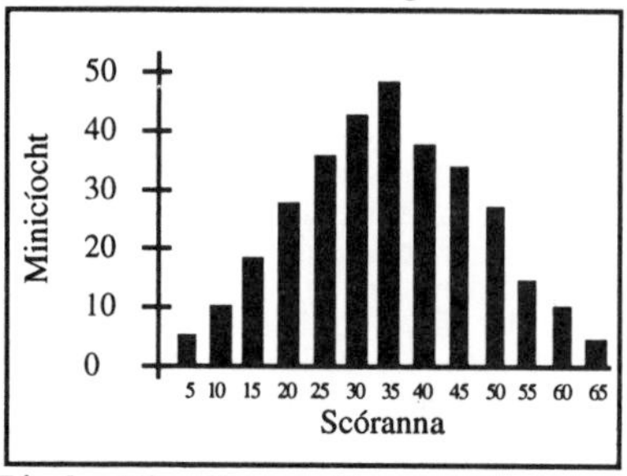

Féach: dáileadh normálta, sceabha.
Léitheoireacht bhreise: Hatch & Lazaraton 1991, lgh 159–178.

CA:111, DA:103, DE:434, EN:117, ES:112, FR:105, GA:103, IT:130, NE:110, PO:119.

104 dáileadh démhódúil Dáileadh a bhfuil dhá mhód nó dhá bhuaic ann, rud a chuirfeadh i gcéill, b'fhéidir, go bhfuil dhá ghrúpa dhifriúla laistigh den sampla céanna.

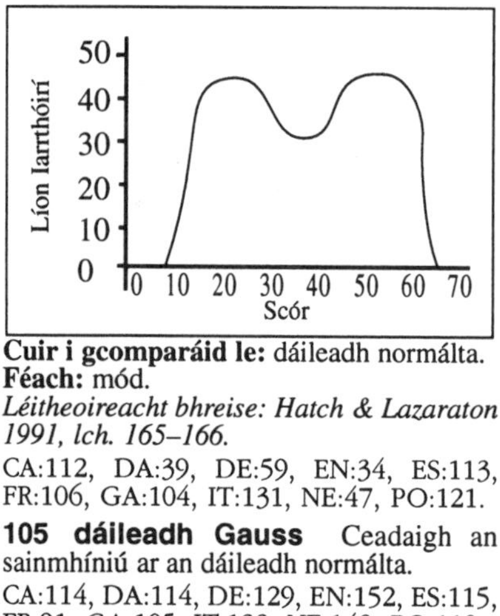

Cuir i gcomparáid le: dáileadh normálta.
Féach: mód.
Léitheoireacht bhreise: Hatch & Lazaraton 1991, lch. 165–166.

CA:112, DA:39, DE:59, EN:34, ES:113, FR:106, GA:104, IT:131, NE:47, PO:121.

105 dáileadh Gauss Ceadaigh an sainmhíniú ar an dáileadh normálta.

CA:114, DA:114, DE:129, EN:152, ES:115, FR:91, GA:105, IT:133, NE:140, PO:110.

106 dáileadh minicíochta Ceadaigh an sainmhíniú ar dháileadh.

CA:113, DA:107, DE:142, EN:149, ES:114, FR:107, GA:106, IT:132, NE:138, PO:122.

107 dáileadh normálta Dáileadh matamaiticiúil a bhfuil cuid mhaith modhanna staitistiúla bunaithe air. Tá cuma shiméadrach an chloig ar an dáileadh agus titeann an meán, an t-airmheán agus an mód ar an bpointe céanna. Is iomaí cruth dáilte atá i gceist anseo, ag brath ar luach an mheáin, an diallta chaighdeánaigh agus líon na mbrathnuithe. Tugtar dáileadh Gauss air freisin.
Cuir i gcomparáid le: dáileadh démhódúil.
Léitheoireacht bhreise: Hatch & Lazaraton 1991, lch. 164.

CA:115, DA:252, DE:265, EN:252, ES:116, FR:108, GA:107, IT:134, NE:262, PO:123.

108 dáileadh teasctha Dáileadh minicíochta a fheictear go minic i sampla a bhfuil raon níos cúinge aige ná mar atá ag an daonra as ar baineadh é, de bhrí nach bhfaightear mic léinn a scórálann go hard ná go híseal sa sampla. Bheadh grúpa de mhic léinn a scaoiltear isteach ar chúrsa tar éis dóibh pas a fháil i dtriail iontrála ina shampla den chineál sin.

CA:116, DA:376, DE:1, EN:421, ES:117, FR:110, GA:108, IT:135, NE:343, PO:124.

109 deachtú Cineál triailtaisc ina gcaitheann an t-iarrthóir éisteacht le téacs agus na focail a chloistear a scríobh síos. Athraíonn critéir mharcála trialacha deachtaithe de réir chuspóir na trialach; d'fhéadfadh litriú agus poncaíocht a bheith ina measc.

CA:103, DA:68, DE:79, EN:99, ES:105, FR:99, GA:109, IT:121, NE:99, PO:125.

110 déantóir trialach Féach an sainmhíniú ar iarrthóir.

CA:100, DA:402, DE:407, EN:406, ES:190, FR:351, GA:110, IT:49, NE:395, PO:183.

111 dearadh ilmhodh-iltréith Dearadh turgnamhach a mbaintear leas as i mbailmheas tógán ina ndéantar cnuasach de thréithe a mheastar a bheith éagsúil lena chéile a thomhas le gach ceann de chnuasach de mhodhanna a mheastar a bheith éagsúil lena chéile. Ba cheart go léireodh an anailís go mbíonn, mar shampla, comhghaolmhaireacht níos láidre idir thomhais ar chumas éisteachta a fhaightear ar mhodhanna éagsúla ná mar a bheadh idir thomhais ar scileanna éagsúla a fhaightear ar an modh céanna tástála.
Léitheoireacht bhreise: Bachman, 1990, lgh 263–265.

CA:108, DA:238, DE:252, EN:243, ES:109, FR:299, GA:111, IT:277, NE:254, PO:305.

112 dearbhscála Scála a bhfuil nialasphointe fírinneach air, m.sh. scála chun fad ruda a thomhas. Ní bhaintear aon úsáid as an gcineál seo scála i dtástáil teanga, de bharr nach féidir sainmhíniú a thabhairt ar an dearbh-nialasphointe i gcumas teanga.
Cuir i gcomparáid le: scála eatraimh, scála ainme, scála oird.

CA:145, DA:4, DE:433, EN:4, ES:153,

FR:122, GA:112, IT:317, NE:2, PO:155.

113 diall caighdeánach Tomhas ar spré tacair de bhreathnuithe timpeall ar an meán uimhríochta. Tá sé cothrom le fréamh chearnach an athraithis. I ndáileadh normalach, bíonn 68% den sampla i bhfoisceacht diall caighdeánach amháin den mheán agus bíonn 98% i bhfoisceacht dhá dhiall chaighdéanacha den mheán.

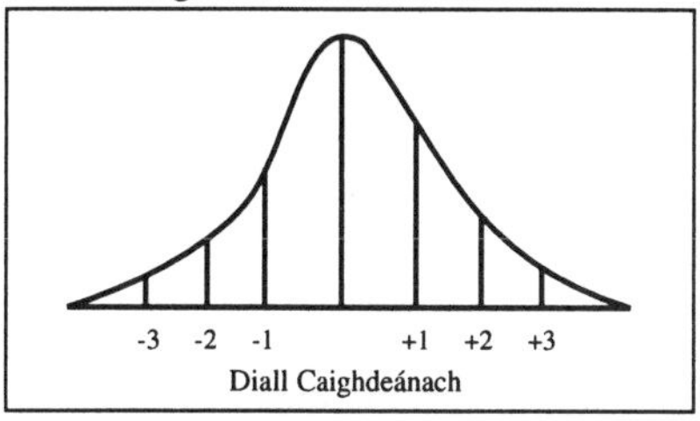

Cuir i gcomparáid le: raon.
Féach: athraitheas.
Léitheoireacht bhreise: Ebel agus Frisbie 1991, lgh. 612; Crocker & Algina 1986, lgh. 21–22.

CA:101, DA:362, DE:372, EN:379, ES:103, FR:98, GA:113, IT:122, NE:360, PO:114.

114 difríochtaí i bhFeidhmiú Míreanna (DFM) An tslí ina mbraitheann deacracht míreanna difriúla i dtriail ar thréith éigin de chuid an ghrúpa iarrthóirí ar a ndearnadh é a riar, m.sh. a gcéad theanga nó a n-inscne.
Féach: laofacht.

CA:195, DA:66, DE:78, EN:100, ES:209, FR:192, GA:114, IT:182, NE:100, PO:208.

115 dílseacht Mar shaintréith de thriail, a chóngaraí is a fhreagraíonn tascanna na trialach d'úsáid na teanga ar ócáid nach mbaineann le trialacha.
Léitheoireacht bhreise: Bachman 1990, lch. 300–303.

CA:27, DA:21, DE:42, EN:24, ES:33, FR:24, GA:115, IT:35, NE:23, PO:26.

116 dílseacht idirghníomhach Uaireanta breathnaítear ar dhílseacht trialach mar thréith den idirghníomhú is gá idir an t-iarrthóir agus an tasc trialach chun freagra oiriúnach a sholáthar.
Cuir i gcomparáid le: dílseacht ócáide.
Féach: dílseacht.
Léitheoireacht bhreise: Bachman 1990, lgh. 315–323.

CA:28, DA:146, DE:157, EN:177, ES:34, FR:25, GA:116, IT:36, NE:183, PO:27.

117 dílseacht ócáide A dhílse agus is féidir a rá go bhfuil triail i gcomórtas le hócáidí úsáide teanga sa ghnáthshaol lasmuigh de chúrsaí trialach.
Féach: dílseacht.
Léitheoireacht bhreise: Bachman 1990, Caibidil 8.

CA:29, DA:336, DE:351, EN:365, ES:35, FR:26, GA:117, IT:37, NE:340, PO:28.

118 dioplóma Doiciméad a dhearbhaíonn go ndeachaigh an té atá ainmnithe air faoi scrúdú nó faoi chomhchuid de scrúdú agus gur ghnóthaigh grád ar leith, pas ar a laghad, de ghnáth. Glactar leis go minic gur cáilíocht ar leibhéal níos airde é ná teastas.
Cuir i gcomparáid le: teastas.

CA:104, DA:69, DE:80, EN:103, ES:106, FR:100, GA:118, IT:124, NE:101, PO:115.

119 dioscúrsa Téacs scríofa nó labhartha, a bhféachtar air mar ghníomh cumarsáideach teanga.

CA:106, DA:75, DE:85, EN:106, ES:108, FR:101, GA:119, IT:125, NE:103, PO:117.

120 do-athraitheas I TMF, an bhunaicsím thábhachtach gur rudaí iontu féin is ea deacracht agus cumhacht idirdhealaithe na míreanna agus nach bhfuil siad ag brath ar chumas na n-iarrthóirí agus, ar aon dul leis sin, nach bhfuil an tomhas a dhéantar ar chumas na n-iarrthóirí ag brath ar na míreanna a úsáideadh chuige seo.

CA:216, DA:152, DE:164, EN:187, ES:234, FR:220, GA:120, IT:205, NE:191, PO:230.

121 dréachtóir Duine a scríobhann agus a chuireann le chéile triail.

CA:127, DA:392, DE:400, EN:361, ES:92, FR:145, GA:121, IT:149, NE:391, PO:141.

122 earráid Sa teoiric chlasaiceach ar thomhas fíorscóir, is cumasc é an scór a fhaigheann iarrthóir i dtriail de dhá chomhchuid, fíorscór atá ag teacht le cumas an iarrthóra agus scór earráide a léiríonn tionchar na dtosca eile go léir ar an scór nach bhfuil aon bhaint acu leis an gcumas atá á thástáil. Glactar leis go bhfuil earráid randamach, i.e. neamhchórasach. Ach bíonn tionchar seasta chomh maith ag trialacha ar na freagraí a thugann iarrthóirí áirithe, is é sin earráid chórasach nó laofacht trialach.
Cuir i gcomparáid le: laofacht.
Léitheoireacht bhreise: Bachman 1990, lch. 167.

CA:136, DA:98, DE:116, EN:129, ES:144, FR:151, GA:122, IT:154, NE:124, PO:146.

123 earráid tomhais Ceadaigh an sainmhíniú ar earráid chaighdeánach tomhais.

CA:138, DA:241, DE:240, EN:231, ES:146, FR:153, GA:123, IT:159, NE:242, PO:149.

124 earráid chaighdeánach mheastacháin Tomhas ar a chruinne agus is féidir athróg amháin a thuar ó athróg eile, mar shampla, san aischéimniú líneach. Cuireann sé eatraimh mhuiníne ar fáil i gcomhair scór critéir.
Féach: eatramh muiníne.
Léitheoireacht bhreise: Hatch & Lazaraton 1991, lgh. 477–479.

CA:142, DA:361, DE:375, EN:380, ES:148, FR:156, GA:124, IT:163, NE:363, PO:152.

125 earráid chaighdeánach tomhais De réir na teoirice clasaicí faoi thástáil fíorscóir, is léiriú é an earráid chaighdeánach tomhais ar neamhchruinneas tomhais. Braitheann méid na hearráide caighdeánaí tomhais (*Se*) ar an iontaofacht (*r*) agus ar dhiall caighdeánach na scór sa triail (*Sx*). Seo an fhoirmle chun *Se* a ríomh:

$$Se = Sx \sqrt{(1-r)}$$

Mar shampla, iarrthóirí a bhfuil fíorscór de T acu i dtriail áirithe agus earráid chaighdeánach tomhais de *Se*, má dhéanann siad an triail arís agus arís eile, 68% den am beidh an scór a bhreathnaítear sa raon T±*Se*, agus 95% den am beidh sé sa raon T±2*Se*.
Léitheoireacht bhreise: Crocker & Algina 1986, lgh. 122–124.

CA:143, DA:364, DE:374, EN:381, ES:149, FR:157, GA:125, IT:162, NE:362, PO:153.

126 earráid de chineál 1 Dearmad a dhéantar sa staidreamh, nuair nach ngéilltear don hipitéis nialasach cé go bhfuil sí fíor i ndáiríre.
Cuir i gcomparáid le: earráid de chineál 2.
Féach: hipitéis nialasach.
Léitheoireacht bhreise: Hatch & Lazaraton 1991, lch. 224.

CA:140, DA:417, DE:9/117, EN:425, ES:150, FR:154, GA:126, IT:157, NE:405, PO:150.

127 earráid de chineál 2 Dearmad a dhéantar sa staidreamh nuair a ghéilltear don hipitéis nialasach, cé go bhfuil sí bréagach i ndáiríre.
Cuir i gcomparáid le: earráid de chineál 1.
Féach: hipitéis nialasach.
Léitheoireacht bhreise: Hatch & Lazaraton 1991, lch. 224.

CA:141, DA:418, DE:118, EN:426, ES:151, FR:155, GA:127, IT:158, NE:406, PO:151.

128 earráid randamach Ceadaigh an sainmhíniú ar earráid.

CA:137, DA:408, DE:449, EN:306, ES:145, FR:152, GA:128, IT:156, NE:310, PO:147,

129 earráid samplála An earráid a thugtar isteach in anailís staitistiúil de bharr gur roghnaigh an taighdeoir sampla áirithe (m.sh. nuair nach bhfuil an sampla ionadaíoch ar an bpobal).
Féach: pobal.

CA:139, DA:372, DE:381, EN:341, ES:147, FR:158, GA:129, IT:155, NE:370, PO:148.

130 earráid tomhais Ceadaigh an sainmhíniú ar earráid.

CA:138, DA:240, DE:239, EN:130, ES:146, FR:153, GA:130, IT:159, NE:243, PO:149.

131 eatramh An difríocht idir dhá phointe ar scála.

CA:214, DA:148, DE:160, EN:183, ES:232, FR:218, GA:131, IT:203, NE:187, PO:228.

132 eatramh muiníne An raon timpeall ar an meastachán ar luach ar dócha go dtiteann an fíorluach laistigh dó. Sainítear an chéim dhóchúlachta, de ghnáth, ar leibhéil mhuiníne de 95% nó 99%.

CA:215, DA:182, DE:184, EN:67, ES:233, FR:219, GA:132, IT:204, NE:45, PO:229.

133 eochairfhreagra a) An rogha cheart i mír ilroghnach.
Cuir i gcomparáid le: seachrántóir
Féach: mír ilroghnach.

b) Ar bhonn níos ginearálta, tacar de na freagraí go léir le míreanna trialach atá ceart nó inghlactha.
Cuir i gcomparáid le: scéim mharcanna.

CA:51/52, DA:256, DE:339, EN:198, ES:54, FR:329, GA:133, IT:53, NE:342, PO:335.

134 eolas cúlra An t-eolas a bhíonn ag iarrthóirí faoi thopaic nó faoi ábhar cultúrtha ar leith a bhíonn i dtriail, rud a d'fhéadfadh dul i bhfeidhm ar an tslí a láimhsíonn siad ábhar na trialach. Tá tábhacht ar leith leis seo i dtrialacha ar Theanga do Shainchuspóirí.
Léitheoireacht bhreise: Bachman 1990, lch. 273.

CA:75, DA:26, DE:144, EN:27, ES:73, FR:77, GA:134, IT:85, NE:4, PO:91.

135 eolas sochchultúrtha Eolas ar an saol agus ar an tslí go n-iompraíonn daoine iad féin i gcultúr áirithe. Go mór mór, eolas ar an glacadh a bheadh le hiompraíocht agus le húsáid áirithe teanga i gcomhthéacsanna cultúrtha ar leith.
Cuir i gcomparáid le: inniúlacht shochtheangeolaíoch.

CA:76, DA:346, DE:357, EN:368, ES:72, FR:341, GA:135, IT:86, NE:344, PO:90.

136 fachtóir G I dteoiric na hintleachta, "fachtóir ginearálta" atá go hipitéiseach mar bhonnsraith faoi na scileanna cognaíocha go léir. Chuir John Oller an tuairim seo chun cinn go mór sna 1970í mar fhianaise ar inniúlacht aontaitheach atá mar bhonnsraith faoi oilteacht teanga.
Léitheoireacht bhreise: Oller 1979, lgh. 426–458; Bachman 1990, lch. 6.
CA:176, DA:113, DE:127, EN:153, ES:194, FR:177, GA:136, IT:170, NE:139, PO:187.

137 fearann An réimse ábhair agus/nó cumais a leagtar amach chun tástáil a dhéanamh air le tasc éigin nó le chomhchuid de scrúdú.
Léitheoireacht bhreise: Bachman 1990, lgh. 244–246.
CA:11, DA:83, DE:238, EN:119, ES:119, FR:113, GA:137, IT:332, NE:113, PO:129.

138 feidhm eolais na míre In TMF, innéacs a léiríonn an méid eolais a chuireann mír nó triail ar fáil mar gheall ar iarrthóir ar leibhéal áirithe cumais; braitheann sé ar cumhacht idirdhealaithe na míre, agus cé chomh oiriúnach is atá sé do leibhéal cumais an iarrthóra.
Cuir i gcomparáid le: feidhm eolais na trialach.
CA:192, DA:156, DE:169, EN:193, ES:212, FR:190, GA:138, IT:184, NE:197, PO:206.

139 feidhm eolais na trialach I dteoiric na mírfhreagartha, séan a léiríonn an méid eolais a chuireann triail ar fáil faoi iarrthóir ar leibhéal áirithe cumais. Is é atá inti ná suim fheidhmeanna eolais na míreanna.
Cuir i gcomparáid le: feidhm eolais na míre.
Léitheoireacht bhreise: Crocker & Algina 1986, lgh. 369–371.
CA:194, DA:388, DE:399, EN:400, ES:211, FR:191, GA:139, IT:185, NE:394, PO:207.

140 feidhm fhreagartha na míre I dteoiric na mírfhreagartha, feidhm mhatamaiticiúil a thugann an dóchúlacht go n-éireoidh leis na hiarrthóirí i gcás míre ar leith, bunaithe ar a gcumas sa tréith a thomhasann an mhír sin. Tugtar feidhm shaintréithe na míre uirthi freisin.
CA:193, DA:158, DE:172, EN:194, ES:210, FR:189, GA:140, IT:183, NE:200, PO:205.

141 feidhmiú(chán) An gníomh cainte nó scríbhneoireachta lena gcuirtear táirge teanga ar fáil. Déantar comórtas go minic idir fheidhmiú(chán), is é sin an friotal féin a tháirgeann daoine, agus inniúlacht, is é sin an t-eolas ar an teanga atá mar bhun leis an bhfeidhmiú(chán).
Cuir i gcomparáid le: inniúlacht.
Féach: Triail feidhmiúcháin.
Léitheoireacht bhreise: Bachman 1990, lgh. 52 agus 108.
CA:5, DA:282, DE:283, EN:277, ES:9, FR:297, GA:141, IT:267, NE:286, PO:304.

142 féinmheasúnú An próiseas trína ndéanann mic léinn measúnú ar a leibhéal cumais féin, trí thriail ar féidir leo a riar iad féin a dhéanamh, nó ar shlí eile, m. sh. trí cheistneoir nó seicliosta a líonadh amach.
CA:30, DA:331, DE:345, EN:354, ES:36, FR:27, GA:142, IT:38, NE:334, PO:29.

143 foirmeacha comhionanna Leaganacha difriúla den triail chéanna, a mheastar a bheith comhionann le chéile sa mhéid go bhfuil siad bunaithe ar na sonraíochtaí céanna agus go dtomhasann siad an inniúlacht chéanna. Le go mbeidís ag teacht le riachtanais dhiana an chomhionannais de réir na triailteoirice clasaicí, caithfidh foirmeacha difriúla de thriail an mheándeacracht, an t-athraitheas agus an comhathraitheas céanna a bheith acu nuair a chuirtear ar na daoine céanna iad. Tá sé thar a bheith deacair comhionannas a bhaint amach go praiticiúil. Tugtar foirmeacha malartacha nó comhthreomhara orthu freisin.
Cuir i gcomparáid le: foirmeacha cothromaithe.
Léitheoireacht bhreise: Crocker & Algina 1986, lch. 132.
CA:187, DA:441, DE:25, EN:128 ES:205, FR:195, GA:143, IT:178, NE:122, PO:201.

144 foirmeacha comhthreomhara Ceadaigh an sainmhíniú ar fhoirmeacha comhionanna.
CA:188, DA:275, DE:278, EN:268, ES:206, FR:196, GA:144, IT:179, NE:279, PO:202.

145 foirmeacha cothromaithe Foirmeacha difriúla de thriail a ndearnadh claochló ar an dáileadh scóir a bhainean le gach ceann acu ionas gur féidir leas a bhaint astu in áit a chéile.
Léitheoireacht bhreise: Crocker & Algina 1986, Caibidil 20.
CA:186, DA:442, DE:16/14, EN:126, ES:204, FR:194, GA:145, IT:177 NE:141, PO:200.

146 foirmeacha malartacha Ceadaigh an sainmhíniú ar fhoirmeacha comhionanna.
CA:185, DA:12, DE:11, EN:11, ES:203, NE:13, FR:193, GA:146, IT:176, PO:199.

147 foirmle Fáistine Spearman is Brown Bealach staitistiúil chun iontaofacht trialach a mheas, tar éis don taighdeoir fad na trialach a athrú, trí mhíreanna a chur léi nó a bhaint di. Is féidir leas a bhaint aisti chun tuar a dhéanamh ar an líon míreanna is gá chun iontaofacht áirithe a bhaint amach. *Léitheoireacht bhreise: Crocker & Algina 1986, lgh. 118–119.*

CA:83, DA:349, DE:359, EN:371, ES:207, FR:197, GA:147, IT:180, NE:350, PO:203.

148 forbairt abairte Cineál míre a bhfuil spreagthach ann i bhfoirm sraith d'ábharfhocail ach go bhfuil réamhfhocail, briathra cúnta, ailt srl. fágtha ar lár aisti. Is é tasc an iarrthóra é na focail atá ar iarraidh a chur leis an abairt agus ar an tslí sin an spreagthach a fhorbairt agus abairt iomlán gramadúil a dhéanamh di.

CA:99, DA:380, DE:333, EN:358, ES:18, FR:175, GA:148, IT:166, NE:441, PO:184.

149 forbróir trialach Duine atá i mbun triail nua a fhorbairt.

CA:109, DA:405, DE:395, EN:399, ES:133, FR:145, GA:149, IT:149, NE:399, PO:141.

150 fothriail Ceadaigh an sainmhíniú ar chomhpháirt.

CA:389, DA:377, DE:386, EN:389, ES:388, FR:346, GA:150, IT:345, NE:373, PO:350.

151 fráma comhchainte Léiriú i bhfoirm scripte ar an friotal is ceart don chomhchainteoir a úsáid agus é i mbun triail labhartha a riar. Is é an chúis atá leis ná chun an friotal a chloiseann na hiarrthóirí go léir a chaighdeánú i dtreo is go mbeidh an triail níos cothroime agus níos iontaofa.

CA:198, DA:324, DE:438, EN:179, ES:215, FR:34, GA:151, IT:128, NE:156, PO:321.

152 freagarbhileog An páipéar ar a scríobhann iarrthóir na freagraí.
Cuir i gcomparáid le: léitheoir optúil marcanna.

CA:191, DA:37, DE:22, EN:19, ES:219, FR:181, GA:152, IT:174, NE:20, PO:198.

153 freagra An t-iompar de chuid an iarrthóra a éilíonn ionchur trialach. Mar shampla, an freagra a thugtar ar mhír ilroghnach nó an saothar a tháirgtear i dtriail scríbhneoireachta.
Cuir i gcomparáid le: ionchur, spreagthach.

CA:374, DA:315, DE:21, EN:331, ES:371, FR:327, GA:153, IT:305, NE:319, PO:334.

154 freagra ceaptha Freagra scríofa ar mhír trialach a bhfuil táirgeadh gníomhach ag teastáil chuige, seachas rogha a dhéanamh idir freagraí éagsúla a thugtar don iarrthóir.
Cuir i gcomparáid le: freagra roghnaithe.
Féach: freagra.

CA:376, DA:185, DE:126, EN:70, ES:372, FR:330, GA:154, IT:309, NE:272, PO:336.

155 freagra ceart Freagra a áirítear mar fhreagra ceart nuair a bhíonn an triail á scóráil.

CA:375, DA:190, DE:327, EN:333, ES:373, FR:331, GA:155, IT:307, NE:204, PO:337.

156 freagra eiseamlárach Sampla maith den chineál freagra a mbítear ag súil leis ar thasc ceannoscailte, agus a chuireann scríbhneoir míre ar fáil agus ar féidir é a úsáid i bhforbairt scéime marcanna mar threoir do mharcóirí.

CA:261, DA:233, DE:253, EN:236, ES:376, FR:333, GA:156, IT:245, NE:21, PO:340.

157 freagra ionchais An freagra nó na freagraí a bhíonn ag teastáil ag scríbhneoir míre nó taisc.

CA:377, DA:106, DE:105, EN:137, ES:374, FR:328, GA:157, IT:306, NE:32, PO:338.

158 freagra roghnaithe Freagra a chuireann iarrthóirí ar fáil trí rogha a dhéanamh idir fhreagraí éagsúla a chuirtear faoina mbráid, seachas freagra dá gcuid féin a sholáthar.
Cuir i gcomparáid le: freagra ceaptha.
Féach: freagra.

CA:379, DA:422, DE:37, EN:352, ES:377, FR:334, GA:158, IT:310, NE:154, PO:341.

159 freagra sínte Freagra níos faide ná abairt nó dhó a éilíonn mír nó tasc, agus a mbíonn ar na hiarrthóirí é a sholáthar (in áit a roghnú).
Cuir i gcomparáid le: mír ghearrfhreagra.

CA:378, DA:423, DE:35, EN:138, ES:375, FR:332, GA:159, IT:308, NE:407, PO:339.

160 fréamh Cuid de spreagthach scríofa, abairt neamhchríochnaithe, de ghnáth, ar gá deireadh a chumadh di nó a roghnú as roghanna.
Cuir i gcomparáid le: eochairfhreagra, roghanna.
Féach: mír ilroghnach.

CA:276, DA:360, DE:29, EN:387, ES:139, FR:10, GA:160, IT:346, NE:359, PO:224.

161 gaois thrialach Cur amach ar fhormáid trialach nó taithí ar thrialacha a dhéanamh, rud a chuireann ar chumas iarrthóirí feidhmiú os cionn an fhíorleibhéil chumais atá acu.

CA:179, DA:406, DE:396, EN:408, ES:197, FR:314, GA:161, IT:167, NE:401, PO:191.

162 gnásanna éiliúcháin Teicníocht le freagra a fháil ó iarrthóir i dtriail. Úsáidtear an frása, de ghnáth, i gcomhthéacs freagra ó bhéal i dtriail ar an teanga labhartha.

Léitheoireacht bhreise: Hughes 1989, lgh. 104–110.

CA:293, DA:8, DE:212, EN:123, ES:307, FR:308, GA:162, IT:276, NE:320, PO:314.

163 gnéithe mhodh trialach Ceadaigh an sainmhíniú ar thréithe modh trialach.

CA:175, DA:396, DE:402, EN:403, ES:193, FR:176, GA:163, IT:50, NE:397, PO:186.

164 grád Cuirtear scór trialach in iúl don iarrthóir i bhfoirm ghráid go minic, mar shampla ar scála ó A go E, áit arb é A an grád is airde ar féidir a fháil, ar pas maith é B, ar pas é C agus ar gráid teipthe iad D agus E.
Cuir i gcomparáid le: marcanna.

CA:275, DA:167, DE:270, EN:156, ES:288, FR:259, GA:164, IT:188, NE:426, PO:272.

165 grádú An próiseas trína dtiontaítear scóir nó marcanna i dtriail ina ngráid.

CA:362, DA:168, DE:48, EN:157, ES:47, FR:52, GA:165, IT:94, NE:427, PO:277.

166 grúpa tagartha Is é atá i ngrúpa tagartha ná sampla a roghnaítear as pobal cinnte iarrthóirí chun triail a normú.
Féach: norm.

CA:196, DA:309, DE:267, EN:324, ES:213, FR:202, GA:166, IT:189, NE:316, PO:212.

167 hipitéis nialasach Hipitéis nach bhfuil gaol idir dhá athróg nó níos mó. Mar shampla, má cheaptar nach bhfeidhmeoidh na baill de dhá ghrúpa ar leith, a bhfuil chéad teanga éagsúla acu, ar bhealach difriúil i dtriail teanga, is hipitéis nialasach í sin.
Léitheoireacht bhreise: Hatch & Lazaraton 1991, lch. 24; Guilford & Fruchter 1981, lgh. 146–147.

CA:202, DA:255, DE:271, EN:255, ES:217, FR:206, GA:167, IT:206, NE:266, PO:214.

168 histeagram Léiriú grafach ar dháileadh minicíochta ina léirítear an líon cásanna in aghaidh an ranga minicíochta mar bharra ingearach.

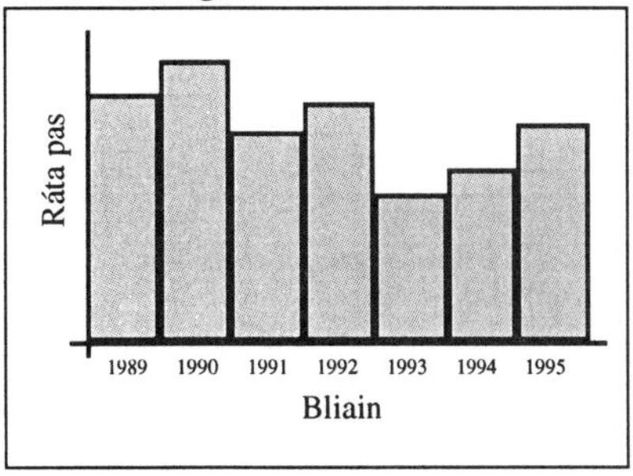

Cuir i gcomparáid le: barraghraf.

CA:203, DA:125, DE:145, EN:163, ES:218, FR:204, GA:168, IT:207, NE:167, PO:215.

169 iarmhairt an chleachtaidh An iarmhairt a fhágtar ar scóir i dtriail nuair a bhíonn cur amach ag na hiarrthóirí ar na cineálacha taisc nó ar chuid de na míreanna féin a mbaintear leas astu sa triail.

CA:119, DA:443, DE:419, EN:289, ES:123, FR:138, GA:169, IT:140, NE:298, PO:131.

170 iarmhairt luain An claonadh atá ann i measc measúnóirí marcanna atá ró-ard nó ró-íseal a thabhairt do iarrthóirí ar thascanna áirithe mar gheall ar an gcaoi a chruthaigh siad ar thascanna eile.
Féach: iarmhairtí rátálaí.

CA:117, DA:118, DE:141, EN:161, ES:127, FR:137, GA:170, IT:139, NE:164, PO:133.

171 iarmhairt mhodha Iarmhairt a bhíonn ag an modh tástála ar scóir na n-iarrthóirí, neamhspleách ar a gcumas.

CA:121, DA:229, DE:242, EN:233, ES:126, FR:139, GA:171, IT:142, NE:244, PO:134.

172 iarmhairt sheichimh Iarmhairt rátálaí arb é an t-ord ina ndéantar na measúnaithe is siocair leis.
Féach: iarmhairtí rátálaí.

CA:120, DA:329, DE:292, EN:360, ES:125, FR:142, GA:172, IT:148, NE:337, PO:136.

173 iarmhairt síleála Iarmhairt fóireach a eascraíonn as triail a bheith ró-éasca do ghrúpa ar leith iarrthóirí, ionas go mbailíonn na scóir acu go léir ag barr an dáilte.
Féach: iarmhairtí teorann.

CA:123, DA:219, DE:63/73, EN:44, ES:129, FR:140, GA:173, IT:145, NE:292, PO:137.

174 iarmhairt thruaillmheasctha Iarmhairt rátálaí a tharlaíonn nuair a thugann rátálaí scór ar chúis eile seachas an cumas áirithe de chuid an iarrthóra atá á thástáil. Mar shampla, scóir iarrthóra ar thriail scríbhneoireachta a ardú de bhrí go bhfuil lámh néata acu.
Féach: iarmhairtí rátálaí.

CA:118, DA:9, DE:226, EN:71, ES:122, FR:136, GA:174, IT:141, NE:74, PO:132.

175 iarmhairt urláir Iarmhairt teorann atá mar thoradh ar thriail a bheith ródheacair do ghrúpa áirithe iarrthóirí, ionas go mbailíonn na scóir go léir ina ngrúpa ag bun an dáilte.
Féach: iarmhairtí teorann.

CA:122, DA:42, DE:61/121, EN:146, ES:128, FR:141, GA:175, IT:144, NE:49,

PO:130.

176 iarmhairtí rátálaí Foinse earraidí sa mheasúnacht arbh é is cúis leis, rátálaithe áirithe a bheith ródhian nó róbhog, nó róthógtha le cineálacha áirithe iarrthóirí, sa chaoi is go dtéann an scóráil amú. Samplaí di is ea iarmhairt thruaillmheasctha, iarmhairt luain agus iarmhairt sheicimh.

CA:124, DA:34, DE:425, EN:313, ES:130, FR:144, GA:176, IT:143, NE:35, PO:138.

177 iarmhairtí teorann Na hiarmhairtí a leanann de scrúdú a bheith ró-éasca nó ró-dheacair do ghrúpa áirithe iarrthóirí. Bailíonn na scóir le chéile i dtreo bharr an dáilte (iarmhairt síleála) nó i dtreo bhun an dáilte (iarmhairt urláir).
Féach: iarmhairt urláir, iarmhairt síleála.

CA:125, DA:120, DE:139, EN:36, ES:131, FR:143, GA:177, IT:138, NE:163, PO:139.

178 iarrthóir Duine a théann faoi scrúdú/thriail. Tagraítear dó freisin mar scrúdaí.

CA:45, DA:165, DE:302, EN:41, ES:48, FR:41, GA:178, IT:49, NE:207, PO:48.

179 iarthriail Triail nó saghas eile tomhais a dhéantar i ndeireadh cúrsa. Má chuirtear na torthaí i gcomórtas le torthaí trialach a riaradh i dtosach an chúrsa faightear léiriú ar éifeachtúlacht an chúrsa.
Cuir i gcomparáid le: réamhthriail.

CA:327, DA:345, DE:5, EN:287, ES:336, FR:305, GA:179, IT:271, NE:295, PO:310.

180 idirdhealú An chumhacht atá i mír trialach idirdhealú idir na hiarrthóirí laga agus na hiarrthóirí láidre. Tá innéacsanna éagsúla idirdhealaithe in úsáid. Tá cuid acu (m.sh. déshrathach pointe, déshrathach) bunaithe ar chomhghaolmhaireacht idir an scór ar mhír agus critéar mar an scór iomlán sa triail nó tomhas seachtrach éigin ar oilteachta. Tá cinn eile bunaithe ar an difríocht idir dheacracht míre do ghrúpaí ardchumais agus do ghrúpaí ísealchumais.
I dteoiric na mírfhreagartha, i gcás na samhlacha 2 agus 3 pharaiméadar, déantar meastachán ar chumas idirdhealaithe mír leis an Paraiméadar A.
Féach: comhghaol déshraitheach, teoiric na mírfhreagartha, comhghaol déshraitheach pointe.
Léitheoireacht bhreise: Crocker & Algina 1986, lgh. 313–320; Ebel & Frisbie 1991, lgh. 231–232.

CA:105, DA:74, DE:416, EN:112, ES:107, FR:102, GA:180, IT:126, NE:109, PO:116.

181 idirlíne y San aischéimniú líneach, an pointe ag a dtrasnaíonn an líne aischéimnithe an Y-ais (ingearach).
Féach: aischéimniú líneach.

CA:212, DA:438, DE:146, EN:441, ES:231, FR:215, GA:181, IT:200, NE:438, PO:226.

182 il-aischéimniú Teicníocht staitistiúil a mbaintear leas as chun teacht ar na hiarmhairtí líneacha a bhíonn ag athróga neamhspleácha éagsúla ar athróg spleách amháin. Mar shampla, agus deacracht taisc ina athróg spleách, d'fhéadfadh an taighdeoir iniúchadh a dhéanamh ar na hiarmhairtí a leanann de chineál taisc, deacracht leicseach, srl.
Féach: athróg neamhspleách, aischéimniú.
Léitheoireacht bhreise: Hatch & Lazaraton 1991, lgh. 480–486.

CA:371, DA:117, DE:251, EN:242, ES:367, FR:326, GA:182, IT:300, NE:240, PO:330.

183 ilmharcáil Bealach chun iontafacht mharcáil trialacha sínte scríbhneoireachta a fheabhasú, rud a bhíonn suibiachtúil go pointe áirithe i gcónaí, trí féachaint chuige go dtugann breis agus aon mheasúnóir amháin breithiúnas neamhspleách ar gach freagra a scríobhann na hiarrthóirí.
Léitheoireacht bhreise: Weir 1988, lch. 65–66.

CA:87, DA:274, DE:233, EN:240, ES:45, FR:271, GA:183, IT:105, NE:241, PO:63.

184 iniúchóireacht Céim i dtáirgeadh trialach ina ndéanann lucht forbartha na trialach measúnú ar ábhair a coimisiúnaíodh ó scríbhneoirí míreanna agus ina ndéanann siad cinneadh faoi na míreanna nach nglacfar leo de bhrí nach gcloíonn siad le sonraíochtaí na trialach, agus faoi na cinn a thabharfar ar aghaidh go céim na heagarthóireachta.
Cuir i gcomparáid le: modhnóireacht.

CA:382, DA:400, DE:405, EN:433 ES:383, FR:338, GA:184, IT:91, NE:115, PO:343.

185 inmhacasamhlaitheacht A indéanta is atá sé píosa taighde a dhéanamh an dara huair agus na torthaí céanna a fháil, rud a chuirfeadh leis an muinín is féidir a chur iontu.

CA:373, DA:189, DE:324, EN:329, ES:370, FR:335, GA:185, IT:301, NE:165, PO:333.

186 innéacs d Innéacs idirdhealaithe do mhíreanna trialach. Úsáidtear go minic é le miontrialacha don seomra ranga de bharr gur féidir é a ríomhadh de láimh. Roghnaítear uasghrúpa agus íosghrúpa ar bhonn scórann don triail san iomlán, sa chaoi is go mbíonn idir 10% agus 33% de na hiarrthóirí i ngach ceann acu. I gcás scóir a bhfuil dáileadh normálta orthu, 27% i ngach grúpa an méid optamach. Comhraítear freagraí na n-iarrthóirí ar gach mír, agus bíonn an t-uasghrúpa chun tosaigh ar an íosghrúpa i gcás míreann a bhfuil comhacht idirdhealaithe iontu. Tugtar innéacs idirdhealaithe na míre leis an bhfoirmle:

$$D = p_u - p_f$$

nuair is p_u codán na n-iarrthóirí san uasghrúpa a bhfuil an mír freagartha i gceart acu, agus p_f codán na n-iarrthóirí san íosghrúpa a bhfuil an mhír freagartha i gceart acu. Meastar, i gcoitinne, go bhfuil cumas maith idirdhealaithe ag míreann a bhfuil innéacs 0.3 nó níos mó leo.

CA:206, DA:59, DE:72, EN:91, ES:223, FR:208, GA:186, IT:194, NE:92, PO:218.

187 innéacs deacrachta Sa teoiric trialach chlasaiceach, is é atá i ndeacracht míre ná an páirtlíon (p) de na hiarrthóirí a fhreagraíonn i gceart í. Ciallaíonn sé sin go mbraitheann séan deacrachta míre ar an sampla agus go n-athraíonn sé de réir leibhéal cumais na n-iarrthóirí.
Cuir i gcomparáid le: innéacs éascachta, p-luach.

CA:207, DA:378, DE:343, EN:101, ES:224, FR:209, GA:187, IT:196, NE:249, PO:219.

188 innéacs éascachta I gcás aon mhíre, líon na bhfreagraí cearta mar chodán de líon na bhfreagraí ar fad, curtha in iúl ar scála ó 0 go dtí 1. Tugtar mar chéatadán é in amanna. Tagraítear dó freisin mar luach éascachta nó luach p .
Cuir i gcomparáid le: innéacs deacrachta.

CA:209, DA:191, DE:208, EN:141, ES:225, FR:210, GA:188, IT:197, NE:146, PO:220.

189 innéacs inléiteachta Tomhas ar chastacht ghramatúil agus leicseach a mbaintear leas as chun meas a dhéanamh ar a intuigthe is a bheidh téacs ag na léitheoirí. Samplaí de shéin inléiteachta is ea innéacs Fog Gunning agus scála inléiteachta Flesh.

CA:210, DA:222, DE:219, EN:320, ES:226, FR:211, GA:189, IT:198, NE:223, PO:221.

190 innéacs meándeacrachta míreanna (meán P) Is é seo meánchodán na n-iarrthóirí ar éirigh leo thar na míreanna go léir ar scála de mhíreanna déscartha. Mar shampla, léiríonn meán P de 0.5 gurb é 0.5 an t-innéacs meán-éascaíochta don triail.
Féach: scóráil dhéscartha.

CA:208, DA:132, DE:246, EN:228, ES:227, FR:212, GA:190, IT:195 NE:150, PO:222.

191 inniúlacht An t-eolas nó an cumas is gá chun rud éigin a dhéanamh. Úsáidtear é sa teangeolaíocht chun tagairt do bhunchumas, murab ionann agus feidhmiú, is é sin léiriú ar inniúlacht trí úsáid na teanga. Eascraíonn an t-idirdhealú seo as saothar Chomsky.
Cuir i gcomparáid le: feidhmiú(chán).
Léitheoireacht bhreise: Bachman, 1990, lch. 52 agus 108.

CA:64, DA:180, DE:183, EN:59, ES:60, FR:62, GA:191, IT:62, NE:67, PO:76.

192 inniúlacht aonadach Teoiric teanga, a chuir Oller chun cinn go háirithe, a chuir i gcéill go bhfuil inniúlacht amháin ann atá mar dhúshraith faoi na scileanna teanga go léir.

CA:71, DA:91, DE:423, EN:428, ES:68, FR:71, GA:192, IT:70, NE:408, PO:85.

193 inniúlacht ghramadaí I samhail de chumas teanga cumarsáidí, is é atá in inniúlacht ghramadaí ná an chomhchuid a bhaineann le heolas ar réimsí d'úsáid teanga ar nós moirfeolaíocht, comhréir, stór focal, fóineolaíocht agus graifeolaíocht.
Léitheoireacht bhreise: Bachman 1990, lch. 84–88.

CA:67, DA:119, DE:138, EN:158, ES:63, FR:65, GA:193, IT:65, NE:162, PO:79.

194 inniúlacht phragmatach Catagóir a d'fhéadfadh a bheith i samhail de chumas cumarsáideach teanga; tá an cumas chun gníomhartha cainte a thabhairt i gcrích agus eolas ar ghnásanna soch-theangeolaíocha san áireamh ann.
Léitheoireacht bhreise: Bachmann 1990, lch. 42.

CA:69, DA:294, DE:295, EN:290, ES:66, FR:69, GA:194, IT:68, NE:297, PO:83.

195 inniúlacht sa chumarsáid An cumas chun teanga a úsáid go iomchuí in éagsúlacht d'ócáidí agus de shuímh.
Léitheoireacht bhreise: Bachman 1990, lch. 16, lch. 68.

CA:65, DA:179, DE:182, EN:58, ES:61, FR:63, GA:195, IT:63, NE:66, PO:77.

196 inniúlacht sa dioscúrsa An cumas chun dioscúrsa a tháirgeadh agus a thuiscint. I samhlacha áirithe d'inniúlacht teanga déantar inniúlacht sa dioscúrsa a shainiú mar inniúlacht ar leith.
Léitheoireacht bhreise: Bachman 1990, Caibidil 4.

CA:66, DA:78, DE:87, EN:108, ES:62, FR:64, GA:196, IT:64, NE:105, PO:78.

197 inniúlacht shochtheangeolaíoch Catagóir i samhlacha de chumas cumarsaídeach teanga: tá an cumas chun an chaint a chur in oiriúint do shuímh agus

d'ócáidí áirithe de réir norm sóisialta san áireamh inti.
Léitheoireacht bhreise: Bachmann 1990, lch 42.
CA:70, DA:347, DE:358, EN:369, ES:67, FR:70, GA:197, IT:69, NE:345, PO:84.

198 inniúlacht theangeolaíoch Ceadaigh an sainmhíniú ar inniúlacht.
CA:68, DA:217, DE:224, EN:214, ES:64, FR:67, GA:198, IT:66, NE:231, PO:80.

199 ionchur Ábhar a chuirtear ar fáil i dtasc trialach chun freagra oiriúnach a bhaint as an iarrthóir. Téacs ar théip, abair, i gcás dtriail chluastuisceana, agus roinnt míreanna scríofa ag gabháil leis.
CA:169, DA:142, DE:408, EN:174, ES:228, FR:147, GA:199, IT:199, NE:180, PO:254.

200 iontaofacht Comhsheasmhacht nó cobhsaíocht na dtomhas a fhaightear ó thriail. Dá iontaofacht í an triail is ea is lú earráidí randamacha a bhíonn inti. D'fhéadfadh triail a bhfuil earráid chórasach inti, e.g. laofacht i gcoinne grúpa áirithe, a bheith iontaofa ach ní fhéadfadh sí a bheith bailí.
Cuir i gcomparáid le: bailíocht.
Féach: KR-20 (Foirmle 20 Kuder is Richardson), alfa (comhéifeacht alfa), iontaofacht leath-is-leath, iontaofacht triail-athriail.
Léitheoireacht bhreise: Bachman 1990, lch 24; Crocker & Algina 1986, Caibidil 6.
CA:180, DA:312, DE:322/453, EN:327, ES:198, FR:183, GA:200, IT:6, NE:43, PO:193.

201 iontaofacht idir-rátálaí Meastachán ar iontaofacht trialach atá bunaithe ar an méid atá measúnóirí ag teacht lena chéile sa mheasúnacht a dhéanann siad ar fheidhmiú na n-iarrthóirí.
Féach: comhaontú idir-rátálaíoch, iontaofacht.
CA:181, DA:145, DE:158, EN:182, ES:199, FR:185, GA:201, IT:8, NE:184, PO:195.

202 iontaofacht intra-rátálaí Meastachán ar iontaofacht measúnachta atá bunaithe ar cé chomh cosúil is atá na scóir a thugann an measúnóir céanna ar an bhfeidhmiú céanna ar ócáidí éagsúla.
Féach: comhaontú intra-rátálaí, iontaofacht.
CA:182, DA:151, DE:162, EN:186, ES:200, FR:187, GA:202, IT:89, NE:189, PO:196.

203 iontaofacht leath-is-leath Tomhas ar iontaofacht atá bunaithe ar chomhsheasmhacht inmheánach. Bunaítear an meastachán ar chomhghaol idir na scóir ar dhá leath-thriail, a bhféachtar orthu mar dhá thrial mhalartacha. Is féidir an triail a roinnt ina dhá leath ar chúpla bealach m.sh. an chéad leath, an dara leath, nó trí mhíreanna a bhfuil ré-uimhir leo a chur i leath amháin agus míreanna a bhfuil uimhir chorr leo a chur sa leath eile.
Féach: iontaofacht.
Léitheoireacht bhreise: Ebel agus Frisbie, 1991, lgh 82–83; Crocker agus Algina, 1986, lch 136–138.
CA:183, DA:259, DE:364/398, EN:377, ES:201, FR:184, GA:203, IT:7, NE:353, PO:194.

204 iontaofacht triail-athriail Meastachán ar iontaofacht a fhaightear tríd an triail chéanna a chur ar na hiarrthóirí céanna faoi na dálaí céanna agus comhghaolú a dhéanamh idir scóir an dá iarrachta. Baineann sí le cobhsaíocht scór thar am, agus tá sí feiliúnach nuair nach féidir meastacháin a dhéanamh ar comhsheasmhacht inmheánach.
Cuir i gcomparáid le: comhsheasmhacht inmheánach.
Féach: iontaofacht, cobhsaíocht.
CA:184, DA:318, DE:409/325, EN:410, ES:202, FR:188, GA:204, IT:9, NE:383, PO:197.

205 KR-20 (Foirmle 20 Kuder is Richardson) Ceadaigh an sainmhíniú ar Kuder is Richardson.
CA:234, DA:201, DE:194, EN:199, ES:252, FR:233, GA:205, IT:222, NE:210, PO:246.

206 KR-21 (Foirmle 21 Kuder is Richardson) Ceadaigh an sainmhíniú ar Kuder is Richardson.
CA:235, DA:202, DE:195, EN:200 ES:253, FR:234, GA:206, IT:223, NE:211, PO:247.

207 Kuder is Richardson Dhá thomhas ar chomhsheasmhacht inmheánach a d'fhorbair Kuder agus Richardson agus a mbaintear leas astu le meastachán a dhéanamh ar iontaofacht trialach. Bíonn níos lú eolais de dhíth i gcomhair KR-21 agus tá sé níos éasca é a ríomh ach de ghnáth cuireann sé meastachán níos ísle ar fáil ná KR-20.
Cuir i gcomparáid le: alfa (comhéifeacht alfa).
Féach: comhsheasmhacht inmheánach.
Léitheoireacht bhreise: Henning 1987, lch. 84.
CA:236, DA:206, DE:200, EN:201, ES:254, FR:235, GA:207, IT:224, NE:212, PO:248.

208 laofacht Is féidir a rá go bhfuil triail nó mír laofa má bhíonn cuid den phobal

iarrthóirí faoi bhuntáiste nó faoi mhíbhuntáiste de bharr gné éigin den triail nó de mhír nach bhfuil aon bhaint aige leis an gcumas atá á thomhas. D'fhéadfadh nithe a bhaineann le cúrsaí inscne, aoise nó cultúir a bheith ina n-údair laofachta.
Léitheoireacht bhreise: Bachman 1990, lgh. 271–279; Crocker & Algina 1986, Caibidilí 12 agus 16.
CA:40, DA:344, DE:383, EN:33, ES:384, FR:32, GA:208, IT:160, NE:46, PO:40.

209 laofacht chultúrtha Cuireann triail a bhfuil laofacht chultúrtha inti iarrthóirí ó chúlra cultúrtha ar leith faoi bhuntáiste nó faoi mhíbhuntáiste.
Féach: laofacht.
CA:41, DA:207, DE:201, EN:85, ES:385, FR:33, GA:209, IT:161, NE:90, PO:41.

210 leibhéal Tagraítear go minic don chéim oilteachta is gá do mhic léinn le go mbeidís i rang áirithe, nó an chéim a léiríonn triail ar leith, mar shraith de leibhéil. De ghnáth, cuirtear ainmneacha mar "bunleibhéal", "meánleibhéal", "ardleibhéal" srl. orthu sin.
CA:270, DA:247, DE:260, EN:209, ES:283, FR:259, GA:210, IT:229, NE:258, PO:272.

211 leibhéal Leathbhealaigh Sonraíocht ar bhunleibhéal inniúlachta teanga iasachta ar fhoilsigh Comhairle na hEorpa leagan di i gcomhair an Bhéarla i dtosach i 1977 agus a ndearnadh athbhreithniú uirthi i 1990. Tá an sprioc níos ísle ná an leibhéal Tairsí, agus meastar go bhfuil tuairim is a leath den ualach foghlama i gceist léi is atá i gcás an leibhéil Tairsí.
Cuir i gcomparáid le: leibhéal Tairsí.
CA:271, DA:437, DE:443, EN:436, ES:284, FR:261, GA:211, IT:231, NE:433, PO:274.

212 leibhéal Tairsí Sonraíocht i dtéarmaí feidhmeacha ar bhunleibhéal inniúlachta i dteanga iasachta a bhfuil an-tionchar aici, ar fhoilsigh Comhairle na hEorpa leagan an Bhéarla di i 1976 agus a ndearnadh nuashonrú uirthi i 1990. Cuireadh leaganacha ar fáil i gcomhair roinnt teangacha Eorpacha ó shin.
CA:272, DA:419, DE:414, EN:414, ES:285, FR:262, GA:212, IT:230, NE:386, PO:275.

213 léicsis Téarma a mbaintear leas as chun tagairt don stór focal.
CA:237, DA:212, DE:221, EN:210, ES:257, FR:238, GA:213, IT:225, NE:227, PO:250.

214 léitheoir optúil marcanna Feiste leictreonach a mbaintear leas as chun eolas a scanadh go díreach ó bhileoga marcanna nó ó fhreagarbhileoga. Is féidir le hiarrthóirí nó le scrúdaitheoirí freagraí ar mhíreanna nó ar thascanna a mharcáil ar bhileog mharcanna agus is féidir an t-eolas a léamh go díreach isteach i ríomhaire. Tagraítear dó freisin mar scanóir.
CA:242, DA:268, DE:274, EN:261, ES:255, FR:237, GA:214, IT:226, NE:274, PO:249.

215 líonadh bearnaí ilroghnach Cineál míre i dtriail inarb é tasc an iarrthóra an focal nó an frása ceart a roghnú as cnuasach de roghanna le cur isteach i spás i dtéacs.
Féach: mír líonta bearnaí.
CA:224, DA:237, DE:250, EN:239, ES:242, FR:386, GA:215, IT:79, NE:251, PO:390.

216 loigit I dteoiric na mírfhreagartha, aonad tomhais, a dhíorthaítear ó logartam nádúrtha an cóimheasa idir an seans ar rath agus an seans ar mhírath, i.e. an corrlach logartaim. An difríocht i loigití idir chumas duine agus deacracht míre, is ionann é agus an corrlach logartaim go n-éireoidh leis an duine ar an mír.
Léitheoireacht bhreise: Henning 1987, lgh. 118–126.
CA:241, DA:220, DE:227, EN:218, ES:259, FR:240, GA:216, IT:232, NE:234, PO:253.

217 luach éascachta Ceadaigh an sainmhíniú ar innéacs (séan) éascachta.
CA:426, DA:192, DE:209, EN:143, ES:423, FR:410, GA:217, IT:411, NE:147, PO:419.

218 marcáil Marc a thabhairt do fhreagraí iarrthóra i dtriail. D'fhéadfadh breithiúnas proifisiúnta a bheith i gceist, nó scéim mharcanna a chur i bhfeidhm ina liostaítear gach freagra atá inghlactha.
CA:80, DA:289, DE:40, EN:222, ES:47, FR:265, GA:218, IT:29, NE:83, PO:57.

219 marcáil chléiriúil Modh marcála a fhágann nach gá do na marcálaithe aon saineolas ar leith a úsáid ná aon bhreithiúnas suibiachtúil a dhéanamh agus iad i mbun marcála. Déanann siad an mharcáil trí scéim marcanna a leanúint ina shainítear na freagraí go léir atá inghlactha le haghaidh gach míre den triail.
Cuir i gcomparáid le: marcáil scrúdaitheora.
CA:86, DA:23, DE:231, EN:51, ES:78, FR:274, GA:219, IT:31, NE:25, PO:62.

220 marcáil de réir barúla (ginearálta) Modh scórála ar féidir leas a bhaint as i dtrialacha ar úsáid tháirgeach teanga i.e. scríobh agus labhairt. Déanann an measúnóir measúnacht ar fhreagra gach iarrthóra, gan iarracht a dhéanamh ar ghnéithe scoite an taisc a dheighilt ó chéile.

Cuir i gcomparáid le: scóráil anailíseach, measúnacht iltaobhach.

CA:89, DA:116, DE:133, EN:168, ES:429, FR:270, GA:220, IT:33, NE:172, PO:68.

221 marcáil dhúbailte Slí le feidhmiú a mheas ina ndéanann beirt mharcálaithe feidhmiú iarrthóra i dtriail a mheas go neamhspleách ar a chéile.
Féach: ilmharcáil.

CA:84, DA:82, DE:91, EN:121, ES:118, FR:114, GA:221, IT:104, NE:116, PO:61.

222 marcáil (scóráil) ríomhairithe Bealaí éagsúla le leas a bhaint as ríomhairí d'fhonn líon na n-earráidí sa mharcáil ar thrialacha oibiachtúla a laghdú. Mar shampla, is féidir sin a dhéanamh trí eolas ó bhileog mharcála an iarrthóra a scanadh le léitheoir optúil marcanna, agus sonraí a tháirgeadh ar féidir leas a bhaint astu chun scóir agus anailís a chur ar fáil.

CA:85, DA:53, DE:69, EN:65, ES:82, FR:273, GA:222, IT:28, NE:69, PO:66.

223 marcáil scrúdaitheora Modh marcála gur ghá marcálaithe chuige a bhfuil saineolas acu agus oiliúint éigin orthu chun gur féidir leo breithiúnas suibiachtúil a thabhairt. Déantar trialacha fada labhartha agus scríbhneoireachta a mharcáil ar an tslí seo de ghnáth.
Cuir i gcomparáid le: marcáil chléiriúil

CA:81, DA:29, DE:107, EN:136, ES:81, FR:272, GA:223, IT:30, NE:131, PO:67.

224 marcanna An t-iomlán de phointí atá ar fáil do mhír, do fhothriail nó do thriail, nó an líon pointí a thugtar do fhreagra iarrthóra ar mhír, ar fhothriail nó ar thriail.

CA:342, DA:287, DE:313, EN:224, ES:44, FR:287, GA:224, IT:292, NE:60, PO:105.

225 marcóir Duine a thugann scór do fhreagraí iarrthóra i dtriail scríofa. Bíonn gá le breithiúnas saineolaí chuige sin i gcásanna áirithe, ach i gcás marcóra cléirigh, níl i gceist ach scéim mharcanna a chur i bhfeidhm, ní nár ghá mórán scile chuige.
Féach: measúnóir.

CA:90, DA:288, DE:39, EN:221, ES:83, FR:81, GA:225, IT:102, NE:80, PO:182.

226 meán Tomhas ar chlaonadh lárnach. Ríomhtar ar an meánscór i riaradh den triail trí na scóir ar fad a shuimiú agus a roinnt ar líon iomlán na scór.
Cuir i gcomparáid le: airmheán, mód.
Féach: claonadh lárnach
Léitheoireacht bhreise: Hatch agus Lazaraton 1991, lgh. 161–163.

CA:250, DA:231, DE:244, EN:227, ES:261, FR:257, GA:226, IT:234, NE:151, PO:255.

227 meán na gcearnóg Seo a thugtar ar an athraitheas in anailís athraithis.
Féach: anailís athraithis

CA:251, DA:230, DE:245, EN:229, ES:262, FR:47, GA:227, IT:295, NE:149, PO:319.

228 meastachán leath-is-leath Spearman is Brown Ceadaigh an sainmhíniú ar iontaofacht leath-is-leath.

CA:168, DA:350, DE:360, EN:372, ES:177, FR:161, GA:228, IT:342, NE:349, PO:178.

229 measúnacht I dtástáil teanga, tomhas ar ghné amháin nó níos mó d'oilteacht theanga trí leagan éigin de thriail a chur ar dhaoine nó nós áirithe imeachta a leanacht leo.
Léitheoireacht bhreise: Bachman 1990, lch. 50.

CA:31, DA:30, DE:54, EN:21, ES:180, FR:165, GA:229, IT:421, NE:39, PO:30.

230 measúnacht holaisteach Ceadaigh an sainmhíniú ar mheasúnacht iltaobhach.

CA:429, DA:126, DE:128, EN:164, ES:428, FR:170, GA:230, IT:187, NE:168, PO:34.

231 measúnacht iltaobhach Modh scórála ar féidir leas a bhaint as i dtrialacha scríbhneoireachta agus labhartha. Aon mharc amháin a bhronann an measúnóir de réir an imprisean ginearálta a fhaightear ón teanga a táirgeadh, seachas marcanna difriúla le haghaidh ghnéithe éagsúla d'úsáid teanga.
Cuir i gcomparáid le: scóráil anailíseach, marcáil de réir barúla.

CA:33, DA:124, DE:137, EN:155, ES:427, FR:169, GA:231, IT:186, NE:161, PO:33.

232 measúnacht mhúnlaitheach Tástáil a dhéantar le linn cúrsa nó cláir theagaisc seachas ina dheireadh. D'fhéadfadh múinteoir na torthaí a úsáid chun cúnamh feabhais a thabhairt d'fhoghlaimeoirí áirithe go luath sa chúrsa, nó chun béim an chúrsa a athrú. D'fhéadfadh foghlaimeoirí iad a úsáid chun teacht ar na deacrachtaí is mó atá acu, agus chun díriú orthu.
Cuir i gcomparáid le: measúnú suimitheach.

CA:32, DA:225, DE:213, EN:147, ES:184, FR:168, GA:232, IT:422, NE:137, PO:32.

233 measúnacht shuimitheach Tástáil a dhéantar ag deireadh cúrsa nó clár teagaisc.
Cuir i gcomparáid le: measúnacht mhúnlaitheach.

CA:34, DA:266, DE:3, EN:390, ES:186, FR:172, GA:233, IT:415, NE:374, PO:36.

234 measúnóir An té a thugann scór d'fheidhmiú iarrthóra i dtriail de réir a bhreithiúnas suibiachtúil féin. De ghnáth, bíonn cáilíocht ag measúnóirí sa réimse atá i gceist agus bíonn orthu gabháil trí phróiseas oiliúna agus caighdeánaithe. Sa bhéaltriail déantar idirdhealú uaireanta idir an measúnóir agus an comhchainteoir. Tagraítear dó freisin mar scrúdaitheoir nó rátálaí.
Cuir i gcomparáid le: comhchainteoir, marcóir.
CA:35, DA:32, DE:55, EN:22, ES:46, FR:174, GA:234, IT:165, NE:33, PO:182.

235 measúnú Bailiú eolais ar mhaithe le cinní a dhéanamh. I dtástáil teanga, dírítear an measúnú go minic ar an éifeacht nó ar an toradh a bhíonn ar chlár teagaisc, ar scrúdaithe, nó ar thionscadail.
CA:31, DA:93, DE:106, EN:132, ES:180, FR:166, GA:235, IT:413, NE:126, PO:30.

236 measúnú múnlaitheach Measúnú leantach ar phróiseas (m.sh. clár teagaisc), sa chaoi is gur féidir an próiseas a oiriúnú agus a fheabhsú de réir mar a théann sé ar aghaidh.
Cuir i gcomparáid le: measúnú suimitheach.
CA:32, DA:226, DE:46, EN:148, ES:184, FR:168, GA:236, IT:414, NE:136, PO:32.

237 measúnú punainne Teicníocht mheasúnaithe ina mbailíonn na hiarrthóirí samplaí dá gcuid oibre thar thréimhse ama, agus cuireann ar fáil iad mar fhianaise ar a gcumas.
CA:386, DA:293, DE:291, EN:286, ES:185, FR:304, GA:237, IT:270, NE:37, PO:309.

238 measúnú suimitheach Measúnú ar phróiseas (m. sh. clár teagaisc) a dhéantar nuair a bhíonn sé thart
Cuir i gcomparáid le: measúnú múnlaitheach.
CA:34, DA:267, DE:4, EN:391, ES:186, FR:172, GA:233, IT:423, NE:375, PO:36.

239 minicíocht charnach Slí le dáileadh na n-iarrthóirí a léiriú tríd an líon iarrthóirí a ghnóthaigh scór i ngach aicme scórála ar leith, nó in aicme níos ísle ná é, a chomhaireamh.
Léitheoireacht bhreise: Guilford & Fruchter, 1981, lgh. 35–36.
CA:189, DA:208, DE:202, EN:86, ES:208, FR:198, GA:239, IT:181, NE:91, PO:204.

240 mír Gach pointe tástála i dtriail a dtugtar marc nó marcanna ar leith dó. Samplaí is ea: bearna amháin i dtriail chlabhsúir; ceist ilroghnach amháin a bhfuil trí nó ceithre rogha ag gabháil léi; abairt amháin a bhfuil claochlú gramadaí le déanamh uirthi; ceist amháin a bhfuil súil le freagra ar fhad abairte uirthi.
CA:217, DA:154, DE:166, EN:189, ES:235, FR:221, GA:240, IT:209, NE:195, PO:231.

241 mír ancaireachta Mír a chuirtear in dhá thriail nó níos mó. Bíonn tréithe aitheanta ag míreanna ancaireachta, agus cuirtear i gcuid de thriail nua iad chun eolas a fháil mar gheall ar an triail agus ar na hiarrthóirí, m.sh. d'fhonn triail nua a chalabrú ar scála tomhais.
Cuir i gcomparáid le: triail ancaireachta
Féach: calabrú.
CA:218, DA:16, DE:18, EN:15, ES:237, FR:225, GA:241, IT:212, NE:17, PO:232.

242 mír chlaochlaithe Ceadaigh an sainmhíniú ar chlaochlú abairte
CA:229, DA:413, DE:420, EN:416, ES:245, FR:403, GA:242, IT:217, NE:402, PO:239.

243 mír chríochnúcháin Mír ina gcaitheann an t-iarrthóir abairt nó frása a chríochnú, de ghnáth, trí roinnt focal a scríobh nó trí shonraí mar amanna agus uimhreacha guthháin a sholáthar.
CA:226, DA:421, DE:102, EN:60, ES:238, FR:223, GA:243, IT:215, NE:193, PO:234.

244 mír dhéanta focal Cineál míre ina gcaitheann an t-iarrthóir foirm d'fhocal a chur ar fáil bunaithe ar fhoirm eile den fhocal céanna a thugtar mar ionchur. Sampla: Tá gá le ...... ar théarmaí teicniúla i gcomhair an chineáil seo oibre (Tuigeann)
CA:227, DA:269, DE:445, EN:439, ES:240, FR:227, GA:244, IT:216, NE:437, PO:237

245 mír fíor/bréagach Cineál mhír roghnaithe inar gá don iarrthóir a chur in iúl cé acu a bhfuil sraith de ráitis fíor nó bréagach de réir mar atá ráite i dtéacs áirithe.
CA:232, DA:326, DE:326, EN:419, ES:250, FR:429, GA:245, IT:218, NE:426, PO:243.

246 mír ghearrfhreagra Mír cheannoscailte ar gá don iarrthóir freagra scríofa a chur uirthi, ag bain úsaide as focal nó as frása.
CA:228, DA:198, DE:205, EN:362, ES:243, FR:224, GA:246, IT:311, NE:209, PO:238.

247 mír ilroghnach Cineál míre i dtriail ina bhfuil ceist nó abairt neamhiomlán (an fhréamh) agus rogha de fhreagraí nó bealaí chun an abairt a chríochnú (roghanna). Is é tasc an iarrthóra é, an rogha cheart (an eochair) a roghnú as an gcnuasach de thrí nó ceithre nó cúig fhéidearthachtaí, agus ní bhíonn aon táirgeadh teanga i

gceist. Ar an ábhar sin, baintear leas de ghnáth as míreanna ilroghnacha i dtrialacha léitheoireachta agus éisteachta. Is féidir leo a bheith ina míreanna scoite nó bunaithe ar théacs.
Féach: mír scoite, mír théacsbhunaithe.
CA:220, DA:236, DE:249/234, EN:238, ES:244, FR:222, GA:247, IT:211, NE:252, PO:236.

248 mír (tasc) imeasctha Úsáidtear seo ag tagairt do mhíreanna nó tascanna ar gá níos mó ná scil nó fo-scil amháin chun iad a chur i gcrích. Samplaí is ea na míreanna i dtriail chlabhsúir, agallamh béil, litir a léamh agus freagra a scríobh uirthi.
Cuir i gcomparáid le: mír phointe scoite.
CA:231, DA:144, DE:156, EN:176, ES:249, FR:316, GA:248, IT:221, NE:182, PO:245.

249 mír líonta bearnaí Aon chineál míre a thugann ar na hiarrthóirí ábhar scríofa éigin – litreacha, uimhreacha, focail aonair, frásaí, abairtí nó ailt – a chur isteach i mbéarnaí a dhéantar i dtéacs. Soláthraíonn na hiarrthóirí féin an freagra uaireanta, nó roghnaíonn siad é as grúpa de roghanna.
CA:223, DA:138, DE:229, EN:151, ES:241, FR:317, GA:249, IT:78, NE:192, PO:235.

250 mír naisc Ceadaigh an sainmhíniú ar mhír ancaireachta.
CA:221, DA:218, DE:432, EN:215, ES:239, FR:231, GA:250, IT:214, NE:232, PO:244.

251 mír phointe scoite Mír scoite a thástálann pointe sainiúil amháin m.sh. struchtúr nó stór focal, agus nach bhfuil naiscthe le haon mhíreanna eile. Rinne Robert Lado tástáil teanga míre scoite a chur chun cinn sna 1960í.
Cuir i gcomparáid le: mír/tasc imeasctha.
Féach: mír scoite.
CA:225, DA:72, DE:82, EN:110, ES:247 FR:229, GA:251, IT:210, NE:107, PO:240.

252 mír scálach Mír a scóráiltear trí leas a bhaint as scála.
Féach: scóráil ilscartha.
CA:222, DA:342, DE:27, EN:342, ES:248, FR:230, GA:252, IT:220, NE:328, PO:242.

253 mír scoite Mír atá slán inti féin. Níl sí naiscthe le téacs, le míreanna eile ná le haon ábhar breise. Sampla de chineál míre a mbaintear leas aisti ar an tslí seo is ea an cheist ilroghnach.
Cuir i gcomparáid le: mír théacsbhunaithe.
CA:230, DA:71, DE:421, EN:109, ES:246, FR:228, GA:253, IT:219, NE:106, PO:241.

254 mír théacsbhunaithe Mír atá bunaithe ar phíosa comhleanúnach dioscúrsa, e.g. míreanna ilroghnacha atá bunaithe ar théacs léamhtuisceana.
CA:219, DA:387, DE:412, EN:412, ES:236, FR:226, GA:254, IT:213, NE:269, PO:233.

255 mód An pointe sa dáileadh ar chnuasach scóir ag a dtarlaíonn scóir níos minicí ná aon áit eile, an pointe is airde ar chuar dáilte.

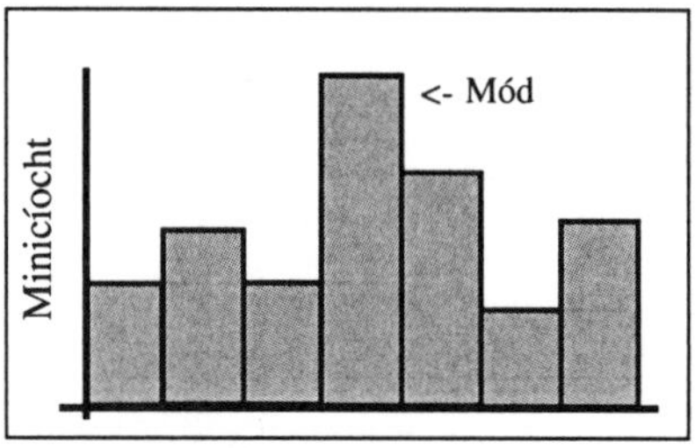

Cuir i gcomparáid le: dáileadh démhódúil, meán, airmheán.
Féach: claonadh lárnach.
Léitheoireacht bhreise: Hatch agus Lazaraton 1991, lgh. 160–161.
CA:252, DA:232, DE:247, EN:235, ES:268, FR:247, GA:255, IT:240, NE:248, PO:261.

256 modh an phlota deilte Slí le féachaint ar an gcaoi go bhfeidhmíonn míreanna éagsúla ar bhealaí éagsúla. Baintear leas as chun teacht ar mhíreanna a mhéadódh nó a laghdódh difríochtaí idir grúpaí iarrthóirí, agus tá sé bunaithe ar mhír-dheacrachtaí clasaiceacha (luachanna *p*). Tiontaítear na luachanna *p* ina *z*-scóir normalaithe agus breactar na luachanna sin ina bpéirí ar ghraf d'fhonn difríochtaí i ndeacracht na míreanna don dá ghrúpa atá i gceist a thaispeáint.
Féach: Difríochtaí i bFeidhmiú Míreanna (DFM).
Léitheoireacht bhreise: Crocker & Algina 1986, lgh. 388–390.
CA:249, DA:61, DE:74, EN:92, ES:267, FR:246, GA:256, IT:237, NE:93, PO:260.

257 modh trialach Is féidir cumas teanga a thástáil trí leas a bhaint as modhanna éagsúla mar cheisteanna ilroghnacha, clabhsúr, aiste, agallamh, srl. Tá sé tugtha faoi deara go n-imríonn modh tástála agus cumas an iarrthóra tionchar ar a chéile nuair a thomhastar feidhmiú teanga.
Féach: tréithe mhodh trialach.
Léitheoireacht bhreise: Bachmann, 1990, lch 77.
CA:248, DA:395, DE:401, EN:401, ES:266, FR:245, GA:257, IT:236, NE:396, PO:259.

258 modhanna neamhpharaiméadracha Modhanna staitistiúla is féidir a úsáid gan glacadh go dtagann na sonraí ó aon dáileadh ar leith, nó nuair nach bhfuil na sonraí bunaithe ar scála eatramh. Is sampla aithnidiúil é an chí-chearnóg de seo.

CA:294, DA:131, DE:259, EN:249, ES:308, FR:309, GA:258, IT:274, NE:257, PO:315.

259 modhanna paraiméadracha Modhanna staitistiúla ina nglactar leis go bhfuil sonraí dáilte go normalach agus go bhfuil siad á dtomhas ar scálaí eatramh nó cóimheasa. De ghnáth, baintear leas as modhanna paraiméadracha nuair atá go leor cásanna ann chun go mbeidh na sonraí gar go leor do dháileadh normalach.
Cuir i gcomparáid le: modhanna neamhpharaiméadracha.
Léitheoireacht bhreise: Hatch & Lazaraton 1991, lgh. 237–238.

CA:295, DA:277, DE:280, EN:270, ES:309, FR:310, GA:259, IT:275, NE:281, PO:316.

260 modhnóireacht a) Gné amháin den phróiseas lena gcuirtear míreanna nó tascanna in oiriúint do thriail. Sa chéim seo déanann roinnt saineolaithe (scríbhneoirí trialacha nó múinteoirí) an t-ábhar a iniúchadh go criticiúil agus deimhníonn siad cé acu an mbeidh sé inghlactha ar deireadh (tar éis roinnt eagarthóireachta nó athscríbhneoireachta más gá).

b) Sa phróiseas measúnachta, an coigeartú a dhéanann modhnóir ar na marcanna a thug measúnóir don iarrthóir.
Cuir i gcomparáid le: iniúchóireacht.

CA:263, DA:410, DE:31, EN:237, ES:277, FR:256, GA:260, IT:250, NE:247, PO:270.

261 *N, n* Líon. Baintear leas as *N* mar cheannlitir go minic chun an líon de chásanna i staidéar nó de bhaill aonair i bpobal a chiallú agus go minic ciallaíonn *n* beag an líon i sampla nó i bhfoghrúpa. Mar shampla: Rinne céimithe innealtóireachta ($N = 600$) an triail agus bhí 10% díobh sin baineann ($n = 60$).

CA:269, DA:248, DE:256, EN:244, ES:282, FR:258, GA:261, IT:251, NE:259, PO:271.

262 norm Caighdeán feidhmiúcháin. I gcás triail chaighdeánaithe, aimsítear an norm trí thaifead a dhéanamh de na scóir a fhaigheann grúpa mór iarrthóirí. Ansin is féidir na scóir a fhaigheann grúpaí eile iarrthóirí a chur i gcomórtas le norm nó le caighdeán an ghrúpa mhóir.
Féach: normghrúpa, triail normthagartha.

CA:273, DA:250, DE:263, EN:250, ES:286, FR:264, GA:262, IT:252, NE:261, PO:278.

263 normalú Athrú a dhéanamh ar scóir chun go ndéanfar dáileadh normalach de dháileadh. De ghnáth, bainfear leas as scálú comhpheircintíleach.
Cuir i gcomparáid le: scór caighdeánach.

CA:274, DA:253, DE:264, EN:253, ES:287, FR:263, GA:263, IT:253, NE:263, PO:279.

264 normghrúpa Grúpa mór iarrthóirí aonair, de ghnáth, ar sampla ionadaíoch iad de na daoine ar dearadh an triail faoina gcomhair. Baintear leas as torthaí an normghrúpa chun torthaí trialacha normthagartha a mheas. Tagraítear dó freisin mar ghrúpa tagartha.
Féach: triail normthagartha.

CA:197, DA:254, DE:266, EN:251, ES:214, FR:203, GA:264, IT:190, NE:265, PO:213.

265 oilteacht Eolas ar theanga, agus leibhéal scile ina húsáid.
Cuir i gcomparáid le: cumas, inniúlacht.
Léitheoireacht bhreise: Bachman 1990, lch. 16.

CA:296, DA:296, DE:47, EN:295, ES:120, FR:260, GA:265, IT:62, NE:305, PO:273.

266 oilteacht béil Inniúlacht i labhairt teanga.

CA:298, DA:239, DE:370, EN:264, ES:65, FR:68, GA:266, IT:67, NE:354, PO:82.

267 oilteacht teanga Eolas ar theanga. Baintear leas as go minic mar théarma atá comhchiallach le "cumas teanga".
Léitheoireacht bhreise: Bachmann, 1990, lch. 16.

CA:297, DA:355, DE:365, EN:206, ES:121, FR:66, GA:267, IT:66, NE:215, PO:81.

268 oiriúint An méid a bhíonn na torthaí a fhaightear ar thriail éigin ag teacht leis na torthaí a rabhthas ag súil leo, ar bhonn samhla éigin. Is féidir innéacsanna éagsúla oiriúna a ríomh. I dteoiric na mírfhreagartha, léiríonn an anailís ar an oiriúint cé chomh maith is a dhéanann paraiméadair na míre agus an duine (i.e. deacracht agus cumas) scóir daoine i dtriail a réamhaithris: is féidir a rá go bhfuil staitistic oiriúna míre ar aon dul lena hinnéacs idirdhealaithe i staitistic chlasaiceach na trialach.
Féach: teoiric na mírfhreagartha.

CA:8, DA:99, DE:248, EN:145, ES:15, FR:6, GA:268, IT:107, NE:135, PO:5.

269 *p*-luach Ceadaigh an sainmhíniú ar innéacs éascachta.

CA:427, DA:273, DE:276, EN:266, ES:424, FR:411, GA:269, IT:412, NE:277, PO:420.

270 páipéar Slí ina dtagraítear do chomhpháirt de thriail e.g. Páipéar Léitheoireachta,

Páipéar Éisteachta.
CA:385, DA:393, DE:277, EN:267, ES:381, FR:182, GA:270, IT:168, NE:278, PO:87.

271 paipéar/leabhrán ceisteanna Baintear leas as uaireanta chun tagairt don bhileog nó don leabhrán ina gcuirtear an triail i láthair.
CA:239, DA:263, DE:123, EN:304, ES:220, FR:180, GA:271, IT:169, NE:425, PO:145.

272 paraiméadar Tréith de chuid pobail m.sh. diall caighdeánach pobail.
Cuir i gcomparáid le: staitistic.
CA:280, DA:276, DE:279, EN:269, ES:293, FR:291, GA:272, IT:259, NE:280, PO:296.

273 paraiméadar a An paraiméadar, i dteoiric na mírfhreagartha, a bhaineann le cumhacht idirdhealaithe na míre.
Féach: Teoiric na mírfhreagartha.
Léitheoireacht bhreise: Bachman 1990, lch. 204.
CA:281, DA:1, DE:84, EN:1, ES:294, FR:292, GA:273, IT:260, NE:1, PO:297.

274 paraiméadar b An paraiméadar i dteoiric na mírfhreagartha a bhaineann le deacracht na míre.
Féach: teoiric na mírfhreagartha.
Léitheoireacht bhreise: Bachman 1990, lch. 204.
CA:282, DA:24, DE:170, EN:26, ES:295, FR:293, GA:274, IT:261, NE:26, PO:298.

275 paraiméadar c An paraiméadar i dteoiric na mír-fhreagartha a bhaineann le freagraí a bheith á dtomhas ag na hiarrthóirí.
Féach: teoiric na mírfhreagartha.
Léitheoireacht bhreise: Bachman 1990, lch. 204.
CA:283, DA:44, DE:318, EN:37, ES:296, FR:294, GA:275, IT:262, NE:50, PO:299.

276 paraiméadar deacrachta Ceadaigh an sainmhíniú ar paraiméadar b.
CA:285, DA:379, DE:344, EN:102, ES:298, FR:296, GA:276, IT:264, NE:250, PO:300.

277 paraiméadar tomhais Ceadaigh an sainmhíniú ar paraiméadar c.
CA:284, DA:122, DE:319, EN:159, ES:297, FR:295, GA:277, IT:263, NE:160, PO:301.

278 pasmharc An scór is ísle is gá d'iarrthóir a ghnóthú chun go dtabharfaí pas dó/di i dtriail nó i scrúdú.
Cuir i gcomparáid le: scór scoite.
CA:23, DA:36, DE:52, EN:273, ES:30, FR:277, GA:278, IT:288 NE:341, PO:282.

279 peircintíl An 99 pointe scála a roinneann dáileadh minicíochta ina 100 grúpa de mhéid cothrom. Tugtar an t-airmheán ar an gcaogadú peircintíl (P50). Roinneann ceathairíleacha an dáileadh ina cheithre ghrúpa cothroma.
Léitheoireacht bhreise: Hatch & Lazaraton 1991, lgh. 187–188.
CA:287, DA:280, DE:285, EN:275, ES:299, FR:49, GA:279, IT:266, NE:284, PO:302.

280 pobal Cnuasach iomlán de luachanna m.sh. na hiarrthóirí go léir a théann faoi scrúdú. Sa staitistic, tugtar cruinne na scór air freisin.
Cuir i gcomparáid le: sampla.
CA:289, DA:292, DE:290, EN:285, ES:302, FR:303, GA:280, IT:269, NE:294, PO:308.

281 pointe tástála Fócas míre, an pointe ar leith a bhféachann an mhír le heolas a éileamh faoi.
CA:128, DA:399, DE:309, EN:409, ES:289, FR:300, GA:281, IT:293, NE:384, PO:307.

282 próifíliú Slí le torthaí a chur i láthair agus iad briste síos de réir na gcomhbhall éagsúil den triail i dtreo is gur féidir leis na hiarrthóirí nó le húsáideoirí eile na trialach réimsí cumais agus éagumais na n-iarrthóirí a aithint.
CA:288, DA:297, DE:404, EN:297, ES:300, FR:312, GA:282, IT:395, NE:307, PO:303.

283 rádal páirte is iomláin Iarmhairt a fheictear, mar shampla, nuair a dhéantar scóir na n-iarrthóirí ar fhothriail a chomhghaolú leis na scóir a fuair siad ar an triail iomlán. De bhrí go bhfuil scóir na fothrialach san áireamh sa scór iomlán, bíonn an comhghaol ró-ard. Tá teicníochtaí ann a dhéanann rádal páirte is iomláin a cheartú.
Léitheoireacht bhreise: Henning 1987, lch. 69.
CA:63, DA:62, DE:282, EN:271, ES:387, FR:51, GA:283, IT:146, NE:276, PO:331.

284 rang peircintíle Uimhir nó scór a léiríonn ord nó rang na n-iarrthóirí i bhfoirm céatadán na n-iarrthóirí a fuair scór níos ísle ná iad. Má tá rang peircintíle de 60 ag iarrthóir i dtriail, ciallaíonn sé sin gur ghnóthaigh 60% de na hiarrthóirí go léir scór a bhí cothrom leis nó níos ísle ná é.
CA:363, DA:281, DE:299, EN:276, ES:359, FR:53, GA:284, IT:55, NE:285, PO:276.

285 raon Tomhas ar spré na mbreathnuithe. Is é atá sa raon ná an fad idir an scór is airde agus an scór is ísle.
Léitheoireacht bhreise: Hatch & Lazaraton 1991, lgh. 169–170.
CA:12, DA:431, DE:431, EN:308, ES:260,

FR:241, GA:285, IT:233, NE:311, PO:12.

286 rátáil a) An próiseas trína dtugtar scór trí bhreithiúnas a dhéanamh ar fheidhmiú an iarrthóra i dtriail.

b) An scór a thugtar mar thoradh ar an bpróiseas rátála.

CA:428, DA:171, DE:57, EN:314, ES:425, FR:265, GA:286, IT:54, NE:38, PO:57.

287 rátálaí Ceadaigh an sainmhíniú ar mheasúnóir.

CA:361, DA:306, DE:100, EN:311, ES:187, FR:164, GA:287, IT:164, NE:34, PO:182.

288 reáchtáil An dáta nó an tréimhse a ndéantar scrúdú a chur. Tá dátaí cinnte reáchtála ag mórchuid scrúdaithe méid áirithe uaireanta sa bhliain, agus reáchtáltar scrúduithe eile de réir an éilimh.

CA:6, DA:403, DE:308, EN:8, ES:77, FR:7, GA:288, IT:331, NE:10, PO:23.

289 réamhthástáil Céim i bhforbairt ábhar le haghaidh trialach ina ndéantar tástáil ar mhíreanna le samplaí ionadaíocha iarrthóirí ón spriocphobal féachaint cé chomh deacair is atá siad. Is féidir na míreanna a mheastar a bheith sásúil, ar bhonn anailís staitistiúil, a úsáid i dtrialacha beo.
Cuir i gcomparáid le: triailiú

CA:174, DA:105, DE:436, EN:293, ES:191, FR:307, GA:289, IT:273, NE:302, PO:311.

290 réamhthriail Triail a riartar sula dtosaíonn cúrsa teagaisc. Is féidir torthaí na réamhthrialach a chur i gcomórtas leis na torthaí a fhaightear ó thriail eile i ndeireadh an chúrsa teagaisc d'fhonn éifeachtúlacht an chúrsa a mheas.
Cuir i gcomparáid le: iarthriail.

CA:333, DA:104, DE:440, EN:292, ES:338, FR:306, GA:290, IT:272, NE:299, PO:312.

291 réim Cineál áirithe cainte nó scríbhneoireachta a bhaineann le gníomhaíocht ar leith nó le leibhéal ar leith foirmiúlachta.

CA:368, DA:310, DE:366, EN:325, ES:364, FR:323, GA:291, IT:297, NE:317, PO:327.

292 ró Spearman Ceadaigh an sainmhíniú ar chomhghaol rang-difríochtaí Spearman.

CA:383, DA:352, DE:362, EN:374, ES:380, FR:339, GA:292, IT:302, NE:348, PO:344.

293 roghanna An raon d'fhéidearthachtaí i mír ilroghnach nó i dtasc comhoiriúnúcháin a gcaithfear an ceann ceart a roghnú astu.

CA:279, DA:425, DE:38, EN:262, ES:292, FR:290, GA:293, IT:258, NE:14, PO:294.

294 rólaisteoireacht Cineál taisc a mbaintear leas as uaireanta i dtrialach béil ina gcaitheann na hiarrthóirí iad féin a shamhlú i suíomh áirithe nó a ligean orthu féin go bhfuil rólanna áirithe acu.

CA:233, DA:320, DE:329, EN:334, ES:251, FR:232, GA:294, IT:202, NE:323, PO:345.

295 rúibric Na treoracha a thugtar d'iarrthóirí maidir leis an tslí ba chóir dóibh tabhairt faoi thasc ar leith i dtriail.
Cuir i gcomparáid le: treoracha.

CA:384, DA:264, DE:23, EN:336, ES:229, FR:78, GA:295, IT:193, NE:219, PO:92.

296 samhail aon pharaiméadair I dteoiric na mírfhreagartha, samhail a fheidhmíonn le haon scála amháin a sheasann do dheacracht (tascanna) agus cumas (daoine), gan difríochtaí i gcumas idirdhealaithe na míreanna a chur san áireamh ná líon na bhfreagraí cearta atá dá dtomhas.
Cuir i gcomparáid le: samhail Rasch.

CA:255, DA:92, DE:99, EN:259, ES:273, FR:249, GA:296, IT:242, NE:118, PO:265.

297 samhail chognaíoch Tuiscint áirithe ar an gcaoi a leagann daoine amach an t-eolas a bhíonn acu, idir coincheapa agus próisis. Nuair a bhíonn rogha le déanamh idir cineálacha éagsúla trialacha agus ábhair chun cumas teanga a thástáil, d'fhéadfadh an tuiscint seo ról tábhachtach a imirt.

CA:253, DA:178, DE:181, EN:56, ES:269, FR:250, GA:297, IT:243, NE:64, PO:262.

298 samhail dhá pharaiméadar I dteoiric na mírfhreagartha, samhail a chuireann paraiméadar idirdhealaithe na míreanna san áireamh chomh maith leis an bparaiméadar cumais/deacrachta.
Cuir i gcomparáid le: samhail aon pharaiméadair, samhail Rasch.
Féach: teoiric na mírfhreagartha.

CA:258, DA:411, DE:454, EN:424, ES:271, FR:248, GA:298, IT:241, NE:404, PO:264.

299 samhail dhóchúlaíoch Samhail ina mhínítear i dtéarmaí céime dochúlachta an éifeacht a bhíonn ag rudaí ar a chéile (m.sh. deacracht míre agus cumas iarrthóra, i gcás triail feidhmiúlachta). Sampla de shamhail dhóchúlach is ea samhail Rasch.

CA:262, DA:295, DE:297, EN:294, ES:274, FR:255, GA:299, IT:247, NE:430, PO:269.

300 samhail ilghnéitheach Rasch Síneadh ar shamhail Rasch, trínar féidir dóchúlachtaí freagraí a shamhaltú mar chumasc suimitheach de ghnéithe. Mar shampla, is féidir saothar i dtriail scríbhneoireachta a shamhaltú ionas go léireofar deacracht an taisc agus déine an rátálaí

araon. Tá an tsamhail ilghnéitheach Rasch curtha i bhfeidhm sa ríomhchlár FACETS, mar shampla.
Féach: samhail Rasch
Léitheoireacht bhreise: Linacre, J.M. 1989, Many-Facet Rasch Measurement, Chicago, MESA Press.
CA:260, DA:235, DE:289, EN:220, ES:276, FR:254, GA:300, IT:249, NE:236, PO:268.

301 samhail na páirtchreidiúna I dteoiric na mírfhreagartha, samhail chun déileáil le sonraí scálacha. Ba shamhail oiriúnach é seo chun anailís a dhéanamh ar fhreagraí ar mhíreanna ina mbíonn ar an iarrthóir abairt a chríochnú agus ina ndéantar scóráil ar scála, m.sh. 1, 2 nó 3, nó in agallamh béil ina mbaintear leas as roinnt scálaí difriúla chun saothar a rátáil.
Cuir i gcomparáid le: samhail scála rátála, samhail ilghnéitheach Rasch.
Léitheoireacht bhreise: Wright & Masters 1982, lgh 40–48.
CA:257, DA:278, DE:281, EN:272, ES:270, FR:253, GA:301, IT:244, NE:282, PO:267.

302 samhail Rasch Samhail mhatamaiticiúil, a dtugtar an tsamhail loighisticiúil shimplí uirthi freisin, bunaithe ar an ngaol a shamhlaítear idir an dóchúlacht atá ann go gcríochnóidh duine tasc agus an difríocht idir chumas an duine agus deacracht an taisc. Is ionann é, ó thaobh na matamaitice de, agus samhail an aon pharaiméadair i dteoiric na mírfhreagartha. Rinneadh síneadh ar shamhail Rasch ar shlite éagsúla m.sh. chun déileáil le freagraí scálacha nó le gnéithe éagsúla de "dheacracht" taisc.
Féach: teoiric na mírfhreagrachta, samhail ilghnéitheach Rasch, samhail na páirtchreidiúna, samhail scála rátála.
Léitheoireacht bhreise: Henning 1987, lgh. 117–125.
CA:259, DA:305, DE:316, EN:310, ES:275, FR:252, GA:302, IT:248, NE:313, PO:266.

303 samhail scála rátála Síneadh ar an tsamhail Rasch shimplí chun déileáil le sonraí scálacha, mar a dhíorthaítear iad ó rátálaithe ar shaothar labhartha, mar shampla.
Cuir i gcomparáid le: samhail Rasch.
Féach: samhail na páirtchreidiúna.
Léitheoireacht bhreise: Wright, B.D & Masters G.N., 1982, Rating Scale Analysis Chicago, MESA Press.
CA:254, DA:173, DE:236, EN:316, ES:272, FR:251, GA:303, IT:246, NE:41, PO:263.

304 sampla Roghnú fo-thacair de na baill de phobal. Tá cineálacha éagsúla samplaí ann, e.g sampla randamach, sampla srathaithe.
Léitheoireacht bhreise: Crocker & Algina 1986, lgh. 432–438; Guilford & Fruchter 1981, lgh. 44–45.
CA:264, DA:371, DE:380, EN:337, ES:278, FR:116, GA:304, IT:46, NE:369, PO:8.

305 sampla randamach Bailiúchán de bhaill a thógtar go randamach ón bpobal atá faoi imscrúdú, ionas go bhfuil an seans céanna ag gach ball sa phobal go roghnófar é.
Féach: sampla.
Léitheoiracht bhreise: Crocker & Algina 1986, lgh. 433–438; Guilford & Fruchter 1981, lch. 120.
CA:265, DA:409, DE:451, EN:307, ES:279, FR:117, GA:305, IT:47, NE:120, PO:9.

306 sampla srathaithe Sampla de phobal atá faoi imscrúdú a dhéantar tríd an bpobal a roinnt i dtús báire ina fhophobail (cisil, ranganna, sraitheanna) agus sampla a bhaint as gach ceann acu.
Féach: sampla.
Léitheoireacht bhreise: Guilford & Fruchter 1981, lgh. 122–123.
CA:266, DA:375, DE:134, EN:388, ES:280, FR:119, GA:306, IT:48, NE:157, PO:11.

307 sampláil Roghnú sampla.
Féach: sampla.
CA:267, DA:374, DE:384, EN:340, ES:281, FR:120, GA:307, IT:45, NE:368, PO:313.

308 scála Cnuasach d'uimhreacha nó de chatagóirí chun ní éigin a thomhas. Aithnítear ceithre chineál scála – scála ainm, scála oird, scála eatramh agus scála cóimheasa.
Léitheoireacht bhreise: Crocker & Algina 1986, lgh. 46–49.
CA:144, DA:337, DE:352, EN:343, ES:152, FR:121, GA:308, IT:314, NE:326, PO:154.

309 scála ainme Scála le haghaigh athróga catagóire, mar ghnéas nó céad theanga. Tagrann athróga den chineál sin do rudaí ar ann iad nó as, agus cuirtear spéis iontu ó thaobh a mhinicí is a tharlaíonn siad. Tagraítear dó freisin mar scála catagóire.
Cuir i gcomparáid le: scála eatraimh, scála oird, scála cóimheasa.
Léitheoireacht bhreise: Hatch & Lazaraton 1991, lgh. 55–56.
CA:156, DA:249, DE:262, EN:248, ES:164, FR:133, GA:309, IT:326, NE:260, PO:166.

310 scála catagóire Scála a mbaintear leas as i gcomhair athróga catagóire mar inscne,an chéad teanga, gairm.

Cuir i gcomparáid le: scála eatraimh, scála ainme, scála oird, scála cóimheasa.

CA:146, DA:170, DE:175, EN:42, ES:154, FR:123, GA:310, IT:318, NE:53, PO:156.

311 scála ceintíle Scála orduimhriúil atá roinnte ina 100 aonad nó ceintílí. Má thugtar luach ceintíleach de 95 do dhuine is ionann sin is a rá go rangófaí an duine sin os cionn 94 duine eile i sampla tipiciúil de 100 duine. Tagraítear dó freisin mar scála peircintíleach.
Léitheoireacht bhreise: Crocker & Algina 1986, lgh. 439–442; Guilford & Fruchter 1981, lgh. 38–41.

CA:151, DA:46, DE:300, EN:46, ES:155, FR:124, GA:311, IT:319, NE:54, PO:157.

312 scála cóimheasa Scála a bhfuil nialas fírinneach air agus a bhfuil an fad idir gach dhá phointe atá in aice a chéile mar an gcéanna thar an scála iomlán. Mar shampla, airde: tá duine atá 2m ar airde dhá oiread níos airde ná duine atá 1m ar airde.
Cuir i gcomparáid le: scála catagóire, scála eatraimh, scála oird.
Léitheoireacht bhreise: Crocker & Algina 1986, lgh. 48–49.

CA:153, DA:210, DE:433, EN:317, ES:160, FR:131, GA:312, IT:324, NE:314, PO:164.

313 scála cumais Scála eatramh cothrom, i dteoiric na mírfhreagartha, ar féidir cumas daoine agus deacracht míreanna araon a bhreacadh air. Tagraítear dó leis mar scála téite.
Léitheoireacht bhreise: Bachman 1990, lch. 345.

CA:150, DA:3, DE:114, EN:3, ES:157, FR:128, GA:313, IT:322, NE:413, PO:159.

314 scála deilte Scála normalaithe a bhfuil meán de 13 aige agus diallas caighdeánach de 4.

CA:155, DA:60, DE:75, EN:93, ES:162, FR:132, GA:314, IT:321, NE:94, PO:165.

315 scála eatraimh Scála tomhais ar a bhfuil an fad idir aon dá aonad tomhais atá in aice a chéile mar an gcéanna, ach nach bhfuil aon nialasphointe a bhfuil brí leis air.
Cuir i gcomparáid le: scála catagóire, scála ainme, scála oird, scála cóimheasa.
Léitheoireacht bhreise: Crocker & Algina 1986, lch. 48

CA:148, DA:149, DE:161, EN:184, ES:158, FR:126, GA:315, IT:315, NE:188, PO:162.

316 scála eatramh cothrom Ceadaigh an sainmhíniú ar scála eatraimh.

CA:149, DA:213, DE:161, EN:125, ES:159, FR:127, GA:316, IT:316, NE:145, PO:161.

317 scála likert Baintear leas as an gcineál seo scála i gceistneoirí chun an dearcadh nó na tuairimí a bhíonn ag daoine faoi rudaí a thomhas. Iarrtar orthu freagraí a thabhairt ar shraith de ráitis trí cheann amháin as timpeall is cúig cinn de fhreagraí ceadaithe a roghnú, freagraí mar "aontaím go hiomlán", "aontaím", "níl fhios agam", "ní aontaím", "ní aontaím in aon chor".

CA:152, DA:214, DE:222, EN:211, ES:163, FR:129, GA:317, IT:325, NE:228, PO:163.

318 scála oird Cuirtear iarrthóirí in ord cumais ar an gcineál seo scála tomhais, gan a thabhairt le fios cén bhearna atá eatarthu.
Cuir i gcomparáid le: scála catagóire, scala eatraimh, scála ainme, scála cóimheasa.
Léitheoireacht bhreise: Hatch & Lazaraton 1991, lgh. 56–57.

CA:157, DA:271, DE:275, EN:265, ES:165, FR:134, GA:318, IT:327, NE:275, PO:167.

319 scála rátála Roinnt catagóirí in ord feabhais a bhíonn sa scála seo, agus baintear leas as chun breithiúnais shuibiachtúla a thabhairt. De ghnáth bíonn tuaraiscíní banda ag gabháil leis na scálaí nuair is cumas teanga atá á mheas, chun na catagóirí a dhéanamh níos soiléire.
Cuir i gcomparáid le: scála likert.
Féach: tuairiscín.

CA:154, DA:172, DE:58, EN:315, ES:161, FR:130, GA:319, IT:323, NE:40, PO:160.

320 scála téite Tagraíonn do scála cumais.

CA:158, DA:407, DE:413, EN:413, ES:166, FR:128, GA:320, IT:328, NE:385, PO:168.

321 scálú Táirgeadh scálaí tomhais. I gcás tástáil teanga, is é atá i gceist ná

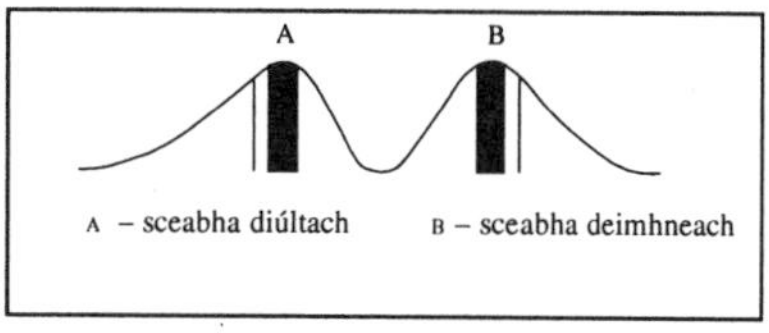

uimhreacha a cheangal le saothar na n-iarrthóirí d'fhonn leibhéil éagsúla cumais a chur in ord a chéile. Nó, athruithe a dhéanamh ar chnuasach de scóir chun scála a chruthú ar mhaithe le cuspóir ar leith, mar shampla, chun torthaí scrúdaithe a thuairisciú ar shlí chaighdeánach, nó chun leagan amháin de thriail a chothromú le leagan eile.
Féach: scála, scála cumais, scála ceintíle, comhscála, scála eatraimh, scála ainme,

scála oird, scála cóimheasa, scála rátála, foirmeacha cothromaithe, cothromú líneach.

CA:159, DA:341, DE:355, EN:346, ES:167, FR:135, GA:321, IT:109, NE:329, PO:169.

322 scanóir Ceadaigh an sainmhíniú ar léitheoir optúil marcanna.

CA:160, DA:327, DE:336, EN:347, ES:168, FR:342, GA:322, IT:226, NE:325, PO:346.

323 sceabha Dáileadh a bheith sa riocht go bhfuil buaic an chuair ar thaobh na láimhe deise den lár (sceabha diúltach) nó ar thaobh na láimhe clé (sceabha dearfach).
Féach: dáileadh normálta.
Léitheoireacht bhreise: Hatch & Lazaraton 1991, lch. 165.

CA:25, DA:343, DE:337, EN:366, ES:31, FR:109, GA:323, IT:25, NE:330, PO:120.

324 scéim mharcanna Liosta de na freagraí go léir a bhfuil glacaint leo mar fhreagraí cearta ar mhíreanna na trialach. Cuireann scéim mharcanna ar chumas an mharcóra an triail a scóráil go beacht.

CA: 52/256, DA:319, DE:228, EN:223, ES:301, FR:29, GA:324, IT:329, NE:79, PO:172.

325 scil Cumas chun ní éigin a dhéanamh. Sa tástáil teanga is minic a dhéantar dealú idir na ceithre scileanna, léamh, scríobh, labhairt agus éisteacht.
Féach: inniúlacht.

CA:199, DA:111, DE:119, EN:367, ES:100, FR:340, GA:325, IT:1B, NE:413, PO:51.

326 scileanna ard-oird Scileanna casta hipitéiseacha, mar infeiriú agus achoimriú.
Cuir i gcomparáid le: scileanna íseal-oird.

CA:201, DA:130, DE:418, EN:162, ES:102, FR:45, GA:326, IT:3, NE:410, PO:53.

327 scileanna íseal-oird Cumais hipitéiseacha nach bhfuil chomh casta sin, aithint focal nó litreacha, a bhíonn de dhíth ar iarrthóirí i dtrialacha teanga.
Cuir i gcomparáid le: scileanna ard-oird.

CA:200, DA:27, DE:424, EN:219, ES:101, FR:44, GA:327, IT:2, NE:409, PO:52.

328 scór a) Scór: Iomlán na bpointí a ghnóthaíonn duine i dtriail, bíodh sin roimh scálú (amhscór) nó ina dhiaidh (scór scálaithe).

b) Scóráil: Luachanna uimhriúla a bhronnadh ar an saothar teanga atá á bhreathnú.
Cuir i gcomparáid le: tomhas.

CA:342, DA:328, DE:312, EN:348, ES:345, FR:275, GA:328, IT:278, NE:331, PO:280.

329 scór amh Scór trialach nach ndearnadh láimhseáil staitistiúil air trí aon chlaochlú, ualú ná athscalú a dhéanamh air.
Féach: scór.

CA:348, DA:321, DE:328, EN:319, ES:348, FR:276, GA:329, IT:282, NE:324, PO:281.

330 scór banda Cuid de scála a thagraíonn do raon áirithe cumais.

CA:346, DA:258, DE:210, EN:30, ES:39, FR:269, GA:330, IT:40, NE:29, PO:65.

331 scór breathnaithe An scór a fhaigheann iarrthóir. Tá dhá chuid ann, de réir teoiric chlasaiceach na trialach, an scór fírinneach agus an earráid.
Féach: earráid, scór fírinneach.

CA:353, DA:183, DE:49, EN:258, ES:352, FR:279, GA:331, IT:283, NE:429, PO:285.

332 scór caghnaonach Nós imeachta chun scóir i dtriail a ghrúpáil ina naoi ngrúpa atá bunaithe ar dháileadh normalach. Bíonn 4% de na hiarrthóirí sa ghrúpa ag an mbarr agus sa ghrúpa ag an mbun araon. Léirítear an céatadán de na hiarrthóirí atá i ngach grúpa ar leith sa ghraf seo thíos.

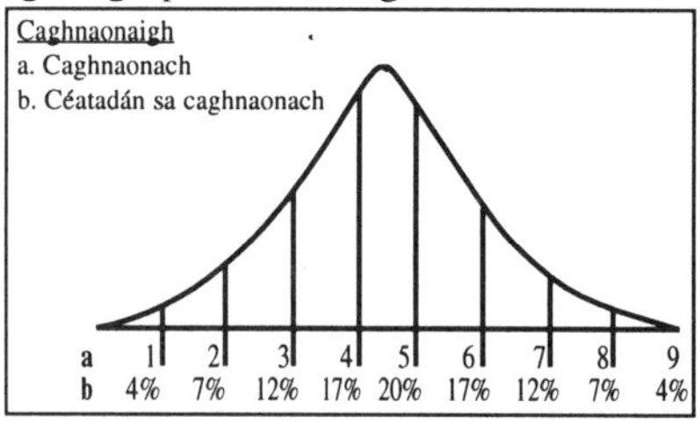

Léitheoireacht bhreise: Crocker & Algina, 1986, lgh 446–447.

CA:344, DA:367, DE:377, EN:384, ES:176, FR:282, GA:332, IT:279, NE:365, PO:284.

333 scór caighdeánach Scór a ghintear le trasfhoirmiú líneach ar ghrúpa scór. Socraítear an meán agus an diall caighdeánach ag cibé luachanna a theastaíonn ón úsáideoir. Samplaí de scóir chaighdeánacha is ea *t*-scór agus *z*-scór.
Cuir i gcomparáid le: scór caghnaonach, *t*-scór, *z*-scór.
Léitheoireacht bhreise: Ebel & Frisbie 1991, lgh. 67–68.

CA:350, DA:365, DE:376, EN:382, ES:350, FR:281, GA:333, IT:287, NE:364, PO:291.

334 scór claochlaithe Amhscór a ndearnadh claochlú matamaiticiúil air. Dhéanfaí é sin ar mhaithe le scálú nó ualú.
Léitheoireacht bhreise: Ebel & Frisbie 1991, lgh. 64–70.

CA:356, DA:414, DE:415, EN:417, ES:356,

FR:284, GA:334, IT:290, NE:158, PO:288.

335 scór fírinneach An scór a ghnóthódh iarrthóir mura mbeadh aon earráid tomhais ann ag an am a dhéantar an triail nó an scóráil. Coincheap bunúsach i dteoiric chlasaiceach na trialach.

CA:357, DA:415, DE:441, EN:420, ES:357, FR:285, GA:335, IT:285, NE:431, PO:289.

336 scór míre In anailís ar mhíreanna, suim na bhfreagraí cearta ar mhír áirithe.

CA:345, DA:160, DE:171, EN:196, ES:346, FR:267, GA:336, IT:281, NE:202, PO:60.

337 scór scálaithe Scór a tháirgtear mar thoradh ar scálú.
Féach: scálú.

CA:349, DA:340, DE:354, EN:345, ES:349, FR:278, GA:337, IT:286, NE:153, PO:283.

338 scór scoite An scór is lú is gá don iarrthóir chun grád áirithe a bhaint amach i dtriail nó i scrúdú. I dtástáil máistreachta, an scór i dtriail a mheastar a bheith ar an leibhéal is gá chun go measfaí go bhfuil íosinniúlacht ag duine nó go bhfuil sé/sí ar an leibhéal "máistreachta".
Féach: triail mháistreachta, tástáil íosinniúlachta.
Cuir i gcomparáid le: pasmharc.
Léitheoireacht bhreise: Bachman, 1990, lgh. 214–215. Crocker & Algina, lgh. 421–428.

CA:359, DA:58, DE:199, EN:90, ES:351, FR:277, GA:338, IT:280, NE:57, PO:282.

339 scór ualaithe trialach An scór a thugtar d'iarrthóir i dtriail tar éis ualú a dhéanamh air.
Féach: ualú.

CA:354, DA:434, DE:135, EN:437, ES:354, FR:280, GA:339, IT:284, NE:159, PO:286.

340 scóráil anailíseach Modh scórála ar féidir leas a bhaint as i dtrialacha ar úsáid chruthaitheach teanga mar labhairt agus scríobh. Déanann an measúnóir measúnacht le cúnamh liosta de phointí sainiúla. I dtriail ar an scríobh, mar shampla, d'fhéadfadh fócas ar ghramadach, ar stór focal agus ar an úsáid a bhaintear as seifteanna nascála a bheith san áireamh sa scála anailíseach.
Cuir i gcomparáid le: measúnacht iltaobhach, marcáil de réir barúla.
Léitheoireacht bhreise: Ebel & Frisbie, 1991 lch. 195.

CA:343, DA:13, DE:12, EN:14, ES:426, FR:266, GA:340, IT:27, NE:15, PO:58.

341 scóráil dhéscartha Scóráil atá bunaithe ar dhá chatagóir m.sh. ceart /mícheart, pas/teip, tá/níl, is ea/ní hea.

CA:347, DA:67, DE:455, EN:98, ES:347, FR:268, GA:341, IT:32, NE:98, PO:59.

342 scóráil ilscartha Scóráil míre ar scála trí phointe nó níos mó. Mar shampla, 0, 1 nó 2 a thabhairt ar fhreagra ar cheist, i.e. idirdhealú a dhéanamh idir trí rud. Déantar scóráil ilscartha ar cheisteanna ceannoscailte go minic. Tagraítear di freisin mar scóráil scálach.
Cuir i gcomparáid le: scóráil dhéscartha.

CA:351, DA:291, DE:237, EN:284, ES:353, FR:89, GA:342, IT:34, NE:293, PO:64.

343 script An páipéar ar a bhfuil na freagraí a thug an t-iarrthóir le linn na trialach, go mór mór más tascanna ceannoscailte atá i gceist.

CA:191, DA:261, DE:341, EN:350, ES:219, FR:343, GA:343, IT:175, NE:218, PO:170.

344 scripteanna samplacha Sampla de fhreagraí iarrthóirí a léiríonn leibhéil éagsúla cumais. Baintear leas astu seo chun caighdeánú a dhéanamh ar mheasúnóirí.

CA:268, DA:370, DE:254, EN:338, ES:132, FR:118, GA:344, IT:330, NE:420, PO:10.

345 scrúdaí Ceadaigh an sainmhíniú ar iarrthóir.

CA:173, DA:87, DE:307, EN:134, ES:190, FR:351, GA:345, IT:49, NE:129, PO:183.

346 scrúdaitheoir Ceadaigh an sainmhíniú ar mheasúnóir.

CA:172, DA:89, DE:301, EN:135, ES:189, FR:174, GA:346, IT:165, NE:130, PO:182.

347 scrúdú Gnás chun oilteacht nó eolas daoine aonair a thástáil trí thascanna scríofa agus/nó ó bhéal a thabhairt le déanamh dóibh. Uaireanta bíonn gnóthachtáil cáilíochta (teastas, mar shampla), ionad in institiúid oideachais nó ar chlár staidéir srl. ag brath ar an toradh.
Cuir i gcomparáid le: triail.
Léitheoireacht bhreise: Bachman 1990, lch. 50.

CA:171, DA:86, DE:303, EN:133, ES:188, FR:173, GA:347, IT:164, NE:127, PO:181.

348 seachrántóir Gach rogha mhícheart i mír ilroghnach.
Cuir i gcomparáid le: eochairfhreagra.
Féach: mír ilroghnach.
Léitheoireacht bhreise: Ebel & Frisbie 1986, lgh. 176–185.

CA:110, DA:79, DE:88, EN:115, ES:111, FR:104, GA:348, IT:129, NE:8, PO:126.

349 sealbhú teanga An próiseas trína sealbhaítear cumas sa chéad nó sa dara teanga. Maidir le dara teanga, déantar idirdhealú uaireanta idir shealbhú (i.e. trí theagmháil nádúrtha) agus foghlaim (i.e. trí

staidéar comhfhiosach).
CA:7, DA:356, DE:367, EN:204, ES:14, FR:5, GA:349, IT:22, NE:380, PO:24.

350 séan = innéacs

351 seicliosta Liosta de cheisteanna nó pointí atá le freagairt nó le clúdach. Baintear leas as go minic i dtástáil teanga mar uirlis bhreathnadóireachta nó anailíse.
CA:240, DA:48, DE:64, EN:48, ES:258, FR:239, GA:351, IT:228, NE:58, PO:252.

352 siollabas Doiciméad mionchruinn ina liostaítear na réimsí go léir a chlúdaítear i gclár staidéir agus an t-ord ina gcuirtear an t-ábhar i láthair.
Cuir i gcomparáid le: curaclam.
CA:299, DA:224, DE:207, EN:392, ES:310, FR:352, GA:352, IT:335, NE:225, PO:318.

353 slándáil An iarracht a dhéantar i riaradh trialacha féachaint chuige nach scaoiltear eolas do na hiarrthóirí ar a bhfuil sna trialacha fad is atá siad beo agus in úsáid.
CA:387, DA:335, DE:348, EN:351, ES:382, FR:344, GA:353, IT:333, NE:142, PO:347.

354 slánú An próiseas trína laghdaítear ar bheachtas uimhreach tríd an líon figiúirí suntasacha a laghdú. Mar shampla, d'fhéadfaí 564.8 a shlánú suas go dtí 565 nó a shlánú síos go dtí 560. Braitheann déine an tslánaithe ar an mbeachtas atá de dhíth.
CA:24, DA:245, DE:331, EN:335, ES:363, FR:22, GA:354, IT:24, NE:11, PO:25.

355 sonraíochtaí trialacha Sraith de dhoiciméid mhionchruinne a dhréachtar, de ghnáth, le linn do thriail nua a bheith á dearadh nó seantriail á leasú. Tugann na sonraíochtaí cuntas ar dhearadh, ar ábhar, ar leibhéal, ar na cineálacha taisc agus míreanna a úsáidtear, ar an spriocphobal, ar úsáid na trialach srl. agus tugtar ábhar samplach go minic freisin.
CA:161, DA:401, DE:394, EN:404, ES:169, FR:346, GA:355, IT:120, NE:400, PO:171.

356 SOPI Triail ar oilteacht béil ina mbaintear leas as téipthaifeadadh mar ionchur agus ina ndéantar freagraí an iarrthóra a thaifeadadh chun gur féidir iad a rátáil ar lá níos faide anonn.
Féach: triail leathdhíreach.
CA:130, DA:348, DE:356, EN:370, ES:137, FR:392, GA:356, IT:93, NE:346, PO:144.

357 spré An méid aithraithis nó an leathadh atá ar scóir iarrthóirí. Nuair a bhíonn an spré mór, bíonn na scóir scaipthe go forleathan agus nuair a bhíonn sé beag, bíonn siad bailithe le chéile.
Féach: diall caighdeánach, athraitheas, raon.
CA:107, DA:353, DE:385, EN:114, ES:110, FR:103, GA:357, IT:127, NE:356, PO:118.

358 spreagthach Ábhair ghrafacha nó téacsanna a chuirtear le chéile chun freagra a éileamh ar an iarrthóir i dtrialacha labhartha nó scríbhneoireachta.
CA:390, DA:316, DE:437 EN:299, ES:178, FR:95, GA:358, IT:343, NE:321, PO:179.

359 spriocanna An t-eolas, an inniúlacht agus an dearcadh a mhaítear a bheith mar aidhmeanna le cúrsa oideachais de chineál ar bith.
CA:278, DA:244, DE:216, EN:256, ES:291, FR:288, GA:359, IT:254, NE:112, PO:293.

360 sprioc foghlama An aidhm nó an toradh inmhianaithe atá le gníomhaíocht oideachais.
CA:277, DA:136, DE:215, EN:208, ES:290, FR:289, GA:360, IT:255, NE:217, PO:292.

361 staidéar píolótach Réamhstaidéar trína ndéanann lucht taighde agus lucht forbartha trialacha a gcuid smaointe a thriail ar líon teoranta suibiachtaí chun fadhbanna a aimsiú sula ndéantar tástáil, clár nó táirge a sheoladh go forleathan.
Féach: réamhthástáil, triailiú.
CA:170, DA:286, DE:288, EN:281, ES:179, FR:163, GA:361, IT:344, NE:290, PO:180.

362 staidreamh An eolaíocht a bhaineann le sonraí uimhriúla a ionramháil agus ciall a bhaint astu. Tugtar staitistic air freisin.
CA:164, DA:369, DE:378, EN:386, ES:171, FR:348, GA:362, IT:339, NE:366, PO:175.

363 staitistic Cainníocht i bhfoirm uimhriúil a bhfuil eolas le baint aisti. Is airí de chuid grúpa samplach í an staitistic ó cheart, murab ionann agus paraiméadar, ar airí é de chuid pobail. De ghnáth, scríobhtar staitisticí i gcarachtair Rómhánacha, agus scríobhtar paraiméadair i gcarachtair Ghréagacha. Mar shampla, scríobhtar an diall caighdeánach de shampla mar s nó SD, agus scríobhtar mar s (sigme) i gcás pobail.
Cuir i gcomparáid le: paraiméadar.
Féach: pobal, sampla.
CA:163, DA:368, DE:379, EN:385, ES:174, FR:348, GA:363, IT:117, NE:367, PO:174.

364 staitisticí infeireacha Staitisticí a chuireann níos mó eolais ar fáil ná mar a dhéanann staitisticí tuarascálach, sa mhéid is gur féidir infeiris dhóchúla a bhunú orthu mar gheall ar cé chomh ionadaíoch is atá

bailiúchán áirithe sonraí i leith an phobail as a baineadh iad.
Cuir i gcomparáid le: staitistic thuarascálach.
CA:166, DA:139, DE:338, EN:171, ES:173, FR:350, GA:364, IT:341, NE:175, PO:177.

365 staitistic thuarascálach An staitistic a mbaintear leas aisti d'fhonn cur síos a dhéanamh ar shonraí i dtéarmaí cainníochtaí, spré, meánluachanna, comhghaolmhaireachtaí le sonraí eile srl. Déantar idirdhealú idir staitistic thuarascálach agus staitistic infeireach nó shamplála.
Cuir i gcomparáid le: staitistic infeireach.
CA:165, DA:63, DE:51, EN:95, ES:172, FR:349, GA:365, IT:340, NE:95, PO:176.

366 suntasacht Coincheap staitistiúil ag tagairt do thoradh a bheith faighte de sheans, nó gan a bheith.
Féach: earráid de chineál 1, earráid de chineál 2, hipitéis nialasach.
Léitheoireacht bhreise: Guilford & Fruchter 1981, lch 208–210.
CA:388, DA:333, DE:349, EN:363, ES:386, FR:76, GA:366, IT:334, NE:338, PO:348.

367 *t*-scór Síneadh ar an *z*-scór. Baintear amach ionaid dhéachúlacha agus síneacha mínis. Tá an *t*-scór cothrom leis an *z*-scór faoina deich, móide 50. Tá meán de 50 agus diall caighdeánach de 10 ag an dáileadh.
Féach: *z*-scór.
Léitheoireach bhreise: Ebel & Frisbie 1991, lch. 68.
CA:355, DA:384, DE:388, EN:422, ES:355, FR:283, GA:367, IT:289, NE:376, PO:287.

368 *t*-thriail Triail staitistiúil a mbaintear leas as chun a fháil amach an bhfuil aon difríocht shuntasach idir na meáin de dhá shampla.
CA:340, DA:385, DE:387, EN:423, ES:398, FR:150, GA:368, IT:385, NE:377, PO:397.

369 tábla teagmhasachta Tábla minicíochtaí rangaithe de réir dhá ghrúpa nó níos mó de luachanna ar athróga catagóireacha, m.sh.

	Pas	Teip
Modh A	35	5
Modh B	20	20

Féach: triail chí cearnaithe.
CA:398, DA:187, DE:187, EN:74, ES:390, FR:353, GA:369, IT:347, NE:75, PO:320.

370 táiliúracht thrialach Seantrialacha a chur in oiriúint do riachtanais ghrúpa ar leith d'úsáideoirí trialach nó de dhaoine a ghabhfaidh faoi thriail.
CA:301, DA:404, DE:410, EN:405, ES:13, FR:395, GA:370, IT:5, NE:382, PO:4.

371 tasc Cumasc de rúibric, ionchur agus freagra. Mar shampla, téacs léitheoireachta a bhfuil roinnt míreanna ilroghnacha ag gabháil leis ar féidir iad a fhreagairt trí thagairt a dhéanamh do rúibric amháin.
CA:391, DA:260, DE:26, EN:393, ES:2, FR:354, GA:371, IT:71, NE:270, PO:352.

372 tasc ilmheaitseála Tasc trialach ina gcuirtear roinnt ceisteanna nó míreanna críochnaithe abairtí ar an iarrthóir, bunaithe de ghnáth ar théacs léitheoireachta. Cuirtear na freagraí ar fáil i bhfoirm bainc d'fhocail nó de fhrásaí, agus is féidir leis na hiarrthóirí leas a bhaint as gach ceann acu oiread uaireanta agus is mian leo. An buntáiste a bhaineann leis, nach bhfaightear réidh le roghanna de réir mar a théann an t-iarrthóir tríd na míreanna (faoi mar a tharlaíonn i gcás foirmeacha eile meaitseála) agus ar an tslí sin ní éiríonn an tasc níos éasca de réir a chéile.
Féach: tasc meaitseála.
CA:396, DA:100, DE:235, EN:241, ES:8, FR:355, GA:372, IT:72, NE:253, PO:354.

373 tasc léamhthuisceana Cineál taisc a bhíonn comhdhéanta, de ghnáth, de théacs nó de théacsanna léitheoireachta agus míreanna mar na cineálacha seo a leanas: ceisteanna ilroghnacha, ceisteanna gearrfhreagraí, clabhsúr/líonadh bearnaí, aistriú eolais, srl.
CA:394, DA:223, DE:220, EN:321, ES:3, FR:357, GA:373, IT:74, NE:224, PO:351.

374 tasc léite profaí Tasc i dtriail inar ghá earráidí de chineál áirithe a lorg i dtéacs, m.sh. litriú nó struchtúr mícheart. Uaireanta bíonn ar an iarrthóir na hearráidí a mharcáil agus foirmeacha cearta a sholáthar.
CA:395, DA:195, DE:189, EN:300, ES:4, FR:84, GA:374, IT:75, NE:304, PO:97.

375 tasc meaitseála Tasc trialach ina mbíonn ar an iarrthóir eilimintí as dhá liosta a chur le chéile, m.sh. na frásaí cearta a roghnú chun liosta d'abairtí a chríochnú, nó, i dtrialacha léamhthuisceana, ní éigin ar nós laethanta saoire nó leabhar a roghnú as liosta i gcomhair daoine a bhfuil cur síos déanta ar a gcuid riachtanas.
CA:397, DA:322, DE:452, EN:226, ES:7, FR:21, GA:375, IT:73, NE:238, PO:353.

376 tasc scríbhneoireachta dírithe Ceadaigh an sainmhíniú ar thasc scríbhneoireacht treoraithe.

CA:392, DA:43, DE:15, EN:105, ES:6, FR:356, GA:376, IT:77, NE:144, PO:355.

377 tasc scríbhneoireachta treoraithe Tasc ina gcaitheann an t-iarrthóir téacs scríofa a sholáthar agus ina mbaintar leas as eolas grafach agus téacsúil, mar phictiúir, litreacha, cártaí poist agus treoracha, chun an freagra ceart a choinneáil faoi riail agus a chaighdeánú.
Cuir i gcomparáid le: ceapadóireacht, aiste.

CA:393, DA:121, DE:130, EN:160, ES:5, FR:311, GA:377, IT:76, NE:143, PO:317.

378 tástáil íos-inniúlachta Cur chuige sa tástáil ina leagtar amach sainriachtanais i gcomhair íosleibhéil inniúlachta i bhfearann ar leith den úsáid teanga. Iarrthóirí ar féidir leo an leibhéal sin inniúlachta a léiriú, tugtar pas dóibh.

CA:312, DA:398, DE:304, EN:234, ES:183, FR:167, GA:378, IT:388, NE:246, PO:31.

379 tástáil ríomhoiriúnaitheach Modh tástála ar ríomhairí inar féidir leibhéal deacrachta na míreanna a cuirtear faoi bhráid na n-iarrthóirí a chur in oiriúint don chumas a léirigh siad sna freagraí a thug siad roimhe sin.
Féach: tástáil (measúnacht) ríomhbhunaithe.

CA:303, DA:51, DE:67, EN:63, ES:181, FR:362, GA:379, IT:386, NE:68, PO:364.

380 tástáil (measúnacht) ríomhbhunaithe Modh tástála ina dtugtar míreanna le déanamh d'iarrthóirí ar ríomhaire. Is féidir freagraí a thabhairt ar an ríomhaire chomh maith.

CA:332, DA:52, DE:68, EN:64, ES:182, FR:171, GA:380, IT:387, NE:70, PO:35.

381 téacs Píosa comhleanúnach dioscúrsa, scríofa nó labhartha, a mbaintear leas as mar bhonn le sraith de mhíreanna trialach.

CA:403, DA:386, DE:411, EN:411, ES:399, FR:396, GA:381, IT:389, NE:381, PO:398.

382 téacs dílis Téacs a mbaintear leas as i dtriail agus arb é atá ann ná ábhair a cruthaíodh i dtús báire ar chúiseanna nach mbaineann le tástáil teanga agus nár cruthaíodh d'aon ghnó don triail.
Cuir i gcomparáid le: téacs leathdhílis.

CA:404, DA:22, DE:41, EN:25, ES:401, FR:111, GA:382, IT:390, NE:24, PO:127.

383 téacs leathdhílis Téacs a baineadh as foinse ón ngnáthshaol agus a ndearnadh eagarthóireacht air chun é a úsáid i dtriail, m.sh. chun an stór focal agus/nó an ghramadach a chur in oiriúint do leibhéal cumais na n-iarrthóirí.
Féach: téacs dílis.

CA:405, DA:123, DE:140, EN:355, ES:400, FR:112, GA:383, IT:391, NE:335, PO:128.

384 teailí seachrántóirí An mhinicíocht lena roghnaítear gach seachránóir i mír ilroghnach. Léiríonn an teailí cé chomh coitianta is atá gach seachrántóir.

CA:243, DA:80, DE:89, EN:116, ES:71, FR:301, GA:384, IT:88, NE:9, PO:96.

385 teanga do shainchuspóirí (TSC) Múineadh nó tástáil teanga a dhíríonn ar réimse teanga a úsáidtear i ngníomhaíocht nó gairm ar leith, mar shampla, Béarla do Rialú Tráchta Aeir, Spáinnis don Tráchtáil.

CA:238, DA:95, DE:111, EN:205, ES:256, FR:236, GA:385, IT:227, NE:378, PO:251.

386 teastas Doiciméad a dheimhníonn go ndeachaigh an té a ainmnítear air faoi scrúdú nó comhpháirt de scrúdú agus gur ghnóthaigh sé/sí grád ar leith, pas ar a laghad, de ghnáth.

Cuir i gcomparáid le: dioplóma.

CA:50, DA:38, DE:448, EN:47, ES:53, FR:50, GA:386, IT:52, NE:56, PO:56.

387 teoiric chlasaiceach na trialach Teoiric thomhais bunaithe ar thuiscintí áirithe maidir leis na scóir a fhaightear nó a bhreathnaítear agus na tosca a théann i bhfeidhm ar na scóir sin, agus a dtagraítear dóibh, de ghnáth, mar earráidí. Tagraítear di freisin mar theoiric an fhíorscóir.
Cuir i gcomparáid le: teoiric na mírfhreagartha.
Léitheoireacht bhreise: Bachman 1990, lgh. 166–187.

CA:399, DA:174, DE:177, EN:50, ES:392, FR:397, GA:387, IT:349, NE:208, PO:357.

388 teoiric na hinghinearálaitheachta Samhail staitistice chun imscrúdú a dhéanamh ar na foinsí éagsúla athraithis a léirítear i scóir i dtriail, agus ar na hiarmhairtí éagsúla a bhíonn acu.
Léitheoireacht bhreise: Bachman 1990, lch. 7; Crocker & Algina 1986, Caibidil 8.

CA:400, DA:115, DE:132, EN:154, ES:393, FR:399, GA:388, IT:351, NE:152, PO:359.

389 teoiric na mírfhreagartha Grúpa de shamhlacha matamaiticiúla a mbaintear leas astu chun gaol a aimsiú idir an chaoi go bhfeidhmíonn duine i dtriail agus an leibhéal cumais atá ag an duine sin. Tá na samhlacha seo bunaithe ar an dteoiric bhunúsach gur feidhm (mhatamaiticiúil) is ea an iompar is féidir a bheith ag súil leis

ón iarrthóir, ar cheist trialach nó ar mhír áirithe, de leibhéal deacrachta na míre agus de leibhéal cumais an duine araon.
Léitheoireacht bhreise: Henning, 1987, Caibidil 8; Crocker & Algina 1986, Caibidil 15.

CA:401, DA:159, DE:173/296, EN:195, ES:394, FR:400, GA:389, IT:352, NE:201, PO:360.

390 teoiric na tréithe folaigh Ceadaigh an sainmhíniú ar theoiric na mírfhreagartha.

CA:402, DA:211, DE:206, EN:207, ES:395, FR:398, GA:390, IT:350, NE:216, PO:358.

391 tionchar An iarmhairt a fhágann scrúdú, ó thaobh dul i bhfeidhm ar na próisis ghinearálta oideachais agus, ina theannta sin, ó thaobh na ndaoine go léir a mbaineann torthaí scrúdaithe leo ar shlí éigin.
Féach: cúliarmhairt.

CA:205, DA:303, DE:444, EN:167, ES:222, FR:207, GA:391, IT:191, NE:171, PO:217.

392 TMF Ceadaigh an sainmhíniú ar theoiric na mírfhreagartha.

CA:412, DA:153, DE:165, EN:188, ES:408, FR:401, GA:392, IT:350, NE:194, PO:402.

393 tógáil trialach An próiseas trína roghnaítear míreanna nó tascanna agus a gcuirtear iad i dtriail. Go minic, roimh an bpróiseas seo, déantar réamhthástáil agus triailiú ábhar. Uaireanta roghnaítear na míreanna agus tascanna chun triail a thógáil as banc ábhar.

CA:126, DA:394, DE:397, EN:398, ES:75, FR:146, GA:393, IT:110, NE:392, PO:140.

394 tógán Cumas nó tréith intinne hipitéiseach nach gá gur féidir breathnadóireacht dhíreach a dhéanamh air ná a thomhas, mar shampla, i dtástáil teanga, cumas éisteachta. Iarracht is ea triail theanga chun na tógáin dhifriúla atá mar dhúshraith faoi chumas teanga a thomhas. Tógáin eile a bhaineann le hábhar, seachas cumas teanga ann féin, is ea inspreagadh, dearcadh agus athchultúrú.
Léitheoireacht bhreise: Hatch & Lazaraton 1991, lch. 15.

CA:78, DA:184, DE:185, EN:68, ES:76, FR:80, GA:394, IT:108, NE:72, PO:94.

395 tomhas Go ginearálta, an próiseas trína bhfaightear an méid de ní atá ann i gcomparáid le haonad socraithe e.g. leas a bhaint as rialóir chun fad a thomhas. Sna heolaíochtaí sóisialta, tagraíonn tomhas go minic do chainníochtú tréithe daoine, mar oilteacht teanga.
Léitheoireacht bhreise: Bachmann 1990, caibidil 2.

CA:245, DA:242, DE:241, EN:230, ES:264, FR:243, GA:395, IT:238, NE:245, PO:257.

396 tomhas saor ó shampla Sa taighde, léirléamh ar thorthaí nach bhfuil spleách ar an sampla ar baineadh leas as in imscrúdú ar leith.
Féach: sampla.

CA:247, DA:373, DE:382, EN:339, ES:265, FR:244, GA:396, IT:239, NE:371, PO:258.

397 toradh Iarmhairt trialach mar a thuairiscítear é don té a dhéanann triail nó a úsáideann triail.

CA:380, DA:317, DE:103, EN:332, ES:378, FR:336, GA:397, IT:312, NE:322, PO:342.

398 tosca cognaíocha Tosca sa phróiseas foghlamtha nó tástála a bhaineann le scéimrí agus patrúin eolais an fhoghlaimeora.
Cuir i gcomparáid le: tosca mothachtála.
Léitheoireacht bhreise: Ebel & Frisbie 1991, lch. 52.

CA:178, DA:177, DE:180, EN:55, ES:196, FR:179, GA:398, IT:171, NE:65, PO:189.

399 tosca mothachtála Tosca neamhchognaíocha a bhaineann le hathróga mothúchánacha, le tosaíochtaí agus le dearcadh lucht glactha trialacha.
Cuir i gcomparáid le: tosca cognaíocha
Léitheoireacht bhreise: Ebel & Frisbie 1991, lch. 52.

CA:177, DA:6, DE:7, EN:9, ES:195, FR:178, GA:399, IT:172, NE:6, PO:188.

400 tréith Cáilíocht fhisiceach nó shíceolaíoch a bhíonn ag duine (mar chumas teanga) nó an scála tomhais a cheaptar chun cur síos air.

CA:411, DA:416, DE:95, EN:415, ES:360, FR:23, GA:400, IT:26, NE:403, PO:403.

401 tréithe mhodh trialach Na tréithe a bhaineann go sonrach le cineálacha éagsúla modhanna trialach. D'fhéadfadh nithe mar thimpeallacht, rúibric, teanga teagaisc, formáid srl. a bheith ina measc.
Léitheoireacht bhreise: Bachman 1990, Caibidil 5.

CA:48, DA:397, DE:403, EN:402, ES:51, FR:46, GA:401, IT:50, NE:398, PO:54.

402 treoracha Treoir ghinearálta a thugtar do na hiarrthóirí, mar shampla, ar an leathanach tosaigh den fhreagarbhileog nó den fhreagarleabhar, mar gheall ar fhad na trialach, cé mhéad tasc is ceart tabhairt fúthu, cá háit is ceart na freagraí a scríobh, agus a leithéid.

Cuir i gcomparáid le: rúibric.
CA:211, DA:143, DE:391, EN:175, ES:230, FR:214, GA:402, IT:208, NE:181, PO:225.

403 triail Slí chun gnéithe de oilteacht daoine nó den eolas atá acu a thástáil;

(a) bailiúchán comhpháirteanna arbh ionann é agus modh measúnachta nó scrúdú;

(b) tasc nó comhpháirt aonair chun measúnacht a dhéanamh ar scil nó ar eolas ar leith, m.sh. labhairt nó scríobh teanga;

(c) modh measúnachta atá réasúnta sciobtha agus éasca lena eagrú, agus a chuirtear le chéile lena úsáid laistigh de eagras éigin (m.sh. triail chun an dul chun cinn atá déanta ag daoine a mheas), nó mar chuid de chlár taighde, nó chun bailíocht trialach a léiriú (m.sh. triail ancaireachta).
Cuir i gcomparáid le: scrúdú.
Féach: triail chlabhsúir, triail fhoráis, triail ancaireachta.
Léitheoireacht bhreise: Bachman 1990, lch. 50
CA:300, DA:300, DE:389, EN:395, ES:311, FR:359, GA:403, IT:353, NE:388, PO:361.

404 triail ancaireachta Triail a bhfuil tréithe tomhais aitheanta aici agus a gcuirtear ar iarrthóirí i dtaca le triail eile. Cuireann na torthaí a bhaintear amach ar an triail ancaireachta eolas ar fáil faoin triail eile agus faoi na hiarrthóirí.
Cuir i gcomparáid le: mír ancaireachta.
CA:307, DA:17, DE:19, EN:16, ES:320, FR:367, GA:404, IT:357, NE:18, PO:365.

405 triail atá neamhspleách ar churaclam Triail nach bhfuil nasctha le haon siollabas ná cúrsa staidéir ar leith.
Cuir i gcomparáid le: triail atá spleách ar churaclam.
Féach: triail oilteachta.
CA:325, DA:56, DE:217, EN:89, ES:313, FR:365, GA:405, IT:374, NE:221, PO:380.

406 triail atá spleách ar churaclam Triail atá nasctha go dlúth le siollabas ar leith agus a bhfuil ról ar leith aici i bpróisis an oideachais.
Cuir i gcomparáid le: triail atá neamhspleách ar churaclam.
Féach: triail ghnóthachtála.
CA:328, DA:57, DE:218, EN:88, ES:339, FR:387, GA:406, IT:376, NE:222, PO:388.

407 triail (mír) bheo Triail atá ar fáil chun a húsáide faoi láthair agus a chaithfear a choimeád i dtaisce dá bhrí sin.
CA:341, DA:101, DE:225, EN:217, ES:344, FR:360, GA:407, IT:355, NE:233, PO:362.

408 triail c Tasc líonta bearnaí ina bhfuil an dara leath d'fhocail ar leith scriosta. D'fhéadfadh minicíocht an scriosta a bheith chomh hard le gach dara focal. Is é tasc an iarrthóra é na focail a páirtscriosadh a chomhlánú.
Cuir i gcomparáid le: triail chlabhsúir.
Léitheoireacht bhreise: Weir 1990, lch. 49.
CA:304, DA:45, DE:62, EN:38, ES:314, FR:394, GA:408, IT:384, NE:51, PO:366.

409 triail chí cearnaithe Gnás staitistiúil chun freagairtí a bhreathnaítear a chur i gcomparáid leis na freagairtí a mbeifí ag súil leo ar bhonn teoirice, féachaint an bhfuil an difríocht atá eatarthu suntasach ó thaobh na staitistice de. Is gnás neamhpharaiméadrach é.
Féach: modhanna neamhpharaiméadracha.
Léitheoireacht bhreise: Hatch & Lazaraton 1991, lgh. 393–415.
CA:330, DA:49, DE:65, EN:49, ES:396, FR:149, GA:409, IT:359, NE:59, PO:395.

410 triail chlabhsúir Tasc líonta bearnaí ina bhfuil focail iomlána scriosta den téacs. Scriostar gach n-ú focal sa triail chlabhsúir thraidisiúnta. Trialacha clabhsúir chomh maith is ea tascanna líonta bearnaí de chineálacha eile, nuair a scriostar frásaí gairide den téacs, nó nuair a roghnaíonn scríbhneoir na míre na focail atá le scrios, "clabhsúr réasúnach" mar shampla. Uaireanta bíonn ar na hiarrthóirí na focail a fágadh ar lár a sholáthar (clabhsúr oscailte) nó roghnú as sraith de roghanna (clabhsúr ilroghnach nó clabhsúr bainc). Is féidir chlabhsúr oscailte a mharcáil de réir "an focal cruinn" (glactar leis an bhfocal a scriosadh den bhuntéacs mar fhreagra agus leis sin amháin) nó de réir "focal inghlactha" (tugtar liosta d'fhocail a bhfuil glacaint leo do na marcálaithe).
Cuir i gcomparáid le: triail c, mír líonta bearnaí.
Léitheoireacht bhreise: Weir 1990, lgh. 46–48; Oller 1979, Caibidil 12.
CA:313, DA:50, DE:66, EN:52, ES:315, FR:370, GA:410, IT:362, NE:61, PO:378.

411 triail chluastuisceana Triail tuisceana ar an teanga labhartha a riartar de ghnáth trí leas a bhaint as téipthaifeadán nó físeán.
CA:315, DA:221, DE:147, EN:216, ES:324, FR:372, GA:411, IT:361, NE:235, PO:373.

412 triail chritéarthagartha Triail ina gcuirtear feidhmiú an iarrthóra i gcomórtas le critéir a socraíodh roimh ré. Leagtar an bhéim ar spriocanna a bheith bainte amach, agus ní ar sheasamh an iarrthóra i gcomór-

tas le daoine eile sa ghrúpa.
Cuir i gcomparáid le: triail fhearanntagartha, triail normthagartha,

CA:337, DA:203, DE:196, EN:81, ES:317, FR:364, GA:412, IT:380, NE:86, PO:369.

413 triail chumhachta Triail ina dtugtar dóthain ama don chuid is mó de na hiarrthóirí, ach go bhfuil roinnt tascanna nó míreanna atá inti chomh deacair sin nach dócha go bhfreagróidh formhór na n-iarrthóirí gach mír i gceart.
Cuir i gcomparáid le: triail luais.

CA:310, DA:299, DE:261/293, EN:288, ES:329, FR:379, GA:413, IT:360, NE:296, PO:371.

414 triail dhiagnóiseach Triail a úsáidtear chun teacht ar na buanna nó ar laigí ar leith a bhíonn ag foghlaimeoirí. Is féidir na torthaí a úsáid chun cinní á ndéanamh mar gheall ar an oiliúint, an fhoghlaim nó an teagasc a bheidh ag teastáil as sin amach.

CA:317, DA:65, DE:77, EN:97, ES:325, FR:383, GA:414, IT:373, NE:97, PO:386.

415 triail dhíreach Triail a thomhasann scileanna táirgiúla na labhartha is na scríbhneoireachta, ina dtomhastar go díreach feidhmiú na scile féin. Sampla de is ea cumas scríbhneoireachta a thástáil trí thabhairt ar an iarrthóir litir a scríobh.
Cuir i gcomparáid le: triail (tasc) indíreach.
Léitheoireacht bhreise: Hughes 1989, lgh. 14–16.

CA:326, DA:70, DE:81, EN:104, ES:335, FR:384, GA:415, IT:375, NE:102, PO:387.

416 triail feidhmiúcháin I dtriail den chineál seo, bíonn ar an iarrthóir sampla den teanga a tháirgeadh, píosa scríbhneoireachta, abair, nó píosa cainte (m.sh. aistí nó agallaimh bhéil). Go minic is chun macsamhlú a dhéanamh ar úsáid na teanga lasmuigh de chomhthéacs na trialach a dhéantar amhlaidh.
Léitheoireacht bhreise: Bachmann 1990, lgh. 304–305.

CA:306, DA:283, DE:284, EN:278, ES:318, FR:380, GA:416, IT:367, NE:287, PO:381.

417 triail fhearanntagartha Déantar torthaí na trialach seo a mheas i gcomhthéacs fearann áirithe ábhair nó cumais.
Cuir i gcomparáid le: triail chritéarthagartha, triail normthagartha.

CA:335, DA:84, DE:50, EN:120, ES:342, FR:391, GA:417, IT:382, NE:114, PO:368.

418 triail fhoráis Triail a riartar cuid den tslí trí chúrsa teagaisc, chun meas a dhéanamh ar an bhfoghlaim go nuige sin.

CA:320, DA:108, DE:214, EN:298, ES:330, FR:381, GA:418, IT:369, NE:422, PO:382.

419 triail ghnóthachtála Triail a chuirtear le chéile chun a fháil amach cé mhéad de chúrsa áirithe teagaisc, de théacsleabhar, srl, atá foghlamtha ag an iarrthóir. i.e. triail atá spleách ar churaclam.

CA:309/322, DA:20/366, DE:203/369, EN:6/23, ES:321/331, FR:366/374, GA:419, IT:364/368, NE:301/421, PO:374.

420 triail (tasc) indíreach Triail nó tasc ina ndéantar iarracht ar na cumais atá mar bhun le scil teanga a thomhas seachas feidhmiú na scile féin a thástáil. Sampla de is ea cumas scríbhneoireachta a thástáil trí tabhairt ar an iarrthóir marc a chur ar struchtúir a úsáidtear go mícheart i dtéacs.
Cuir i gcomparáid le: triail dhíreach.
Léitheoireacht bhreise: Hughes 1989, lch. 14–16.

CA:329, DA:135, DE:150, EN:170, ES:337, FR:385, GA:420, IT:354, NE:173, PO:389.

421 triail infheidhmeachta Triail a leagadh amach chun réamhaithris nó meas a dhéanamh ar an acmhainneacht chun ratha atá in iarrthóir maidir le réimse ar leith léinn m.sh. teanga iasachta a fhoghlaim, nó maidir le cúrsa áirithe staidéir
Léitheoireacht bhreise: Henning 1987, lch. 6; Ebel & Frisbie 1991, lch. 339.

CA:308, DA:18, DE:96, EN:20, ES:322, FR:368, GA:421, IT:358, NE:22, PO:370.

422 triail iontrála Triail a mbaintear leas as chun a dhéanamh amach cé acu an bhfaighidh iarrthóir ionad in institiúid nó ar chúrsa staidéir ar leith nó nach bhfaighidh.
Cuir i gcomparáid le: triail socrúcháin.

CA:305, DA:5, DE:346, EN:124, ES:319, FR:369, GA:422, IT:364, NE:387, PO:377.

423 triail leathdhíreach Triail ina dhéantar iarracht ar fheidhmiú teanga a mheas trí rud neamhdhaonna a chur in áit an duine, e.g. triail chainte ina mbaintear leas as téipthaifeadadh mar ionchur seachas agallóir daonna. Sampla de thriail leathdhíreach is ea SOPI (Semi-Direct Oral Proficiency Interview)
Cuir i gcomparáid le: triail dhíreach.

CA:339, DA:332, DE:347, EN:356, ES:343, FR:392, GA:423, IT:383, NE:336, PO:396.

424 triail luais Triail a bhfuil teorainn ama ann chun í a chríochnú. Faigheann iarrthóirí atá níos moille scór níos ísle de bhrí nach mbaineann siad na ceisteanna deireanacha amach. De ghnáth i dtriail luais níl na ceisteanna chomh deacair sin nach bhf-

reagródh na hiarrthóirí i gceart iad go hiondúil murach an teorainn ama.
Cuir i gcomparáid le: triail chumhachta.

CA:321, DA:129, DE:340/363, EN:376, ES:334, FR:363, GA:424, IT:372, NE:352, PO:385.

425 triail mháistreachta Triail chun a dheimhniú gur éirigh le mac léinn máistreacht a bhaint amach ar réimse cinnte scileanna nó eolais.

CA:338, DA:227, DE:204, EN:225, ES:327, FR:376, GA:425, IT:366, NE:237, PO:376.

426 triail normthagartha Triail ina ndéantar meas ar scóir trí thagairt do fheidhmiú grúpa ar leith ina bhfuil daoine atá inchurtha leis na daoine a dhéanann an triail. Baintear leas go coitianta as an téarma ag tagairt do thrialacha a ndéantar meas orthu go príomha trí bhaill aonair a rangú i gcoibhneas le normghrúpa nó lena chéile.
Cuir i gcomparáid le: triail chritéarthagartha.

CA:336, DA:251, DE:268, EN:254, ES:340, FR:388, GA:426, IT:381, NE:264, PO:391.

427 triail oibiachtúil Triail ar féidir í a mharcáil trí scéim mharcanna a chur i bhfeidhm, agus nach gá tuairim atá bunaithe ar shaineolas ná breithiúnas suibiachtúil a chur i bhfeidhm ar an tasc.

CA:331, DA:257, DE:272, EN:257, ES:341, FR:389, GA:427, IT:377, NE:267, PO:392.

428 triail oilteachta Triail a thomhasann cumas ginearálta nó scil, gan tagairt a dhéanamh d'aon chúrsa staidéir ná d'ábhair staidéir ar leith.

CA:319, DA:112, DE:120, EN:296, ES:326, FR:378, GA:428, IT:363, NE:306, PO:379.

429 triail oiriúnaitheach Modh tástála ina roghnaítear na míreanna, ar bhonn deacrachta, de réir mar a bhíonn an triail féin ag dul ar aghaidh agus meastacháin á ndéanamh ar chumas an iarrthóra. Trialacha a reáchtáltar ar ríomhaire a bhíonn i gceist go minic, cé gur féidir béaltriail a áireamh mar thriail oiriúnaitheach freisin.
Féach: tástáil ríomhoiriúnaitheach.
Léitheoireacht bhreise: Bachman 1990, lch. 151; Henning 1987, lch. 136.

CA:302, DA:102, DE:6, EN:7, ES:312, FR:361, GA:429, IT:356, NE:5, PO:363.

430 triail roghnúcháin Ceadaigh an sainmhíniú ar thriail iontrála.

CA:323, DA:330, DE:36, EN:353, ES:332, FR:382, GA:430, IT:370, NE:333, PO:383.

431 triail sainchuspóra Triail a dearadh chun cumas iarrthóra chun feidhmiú i gcomhthéacs proifisiúnta nó acadúil ar leith a thomhas. Déantar ábhar na trialach a dhearadh, dá réir sin, ar bhonn anailíse ar na tascanna teanga a mbeidh ar na hiarrthóirí déileáil leo sa spriocréimse úsáide teanga.

CA:318, DA:243, DE:112, EN:375, ES:328, FR:393, GA:431, IT:378, NE:351, PO:393.

432 triail scagtha Triail, ceann gairid de ghnáth, ar féidir í a riaradh go héasca, a mbaintear leas as chun na hiarrthóirí sin a aithint ar féidir ionad a thabhairt dóibh ar chúrsa nó mar iarrthóir le haghaidh scrúdaithe.
Cuir i gcomparáid le: triail socrúcháin.

CA:316, DA:424, DE:98, EN:349, ES:332, FR:375, GA:432, IT:370, NE:332, PO:375.

433 triail shíciméadrach Triail ar thréithe síceolaíocha mar phearsantacht, éirim aigne, infheidhmeacht, agus oilteacht teanga, ina nglactar le nithe áirithe faoi nádúr an chumais atá á thriail, m.sh. go bhfuil sé aontoiseach agus go bhfuil dáileadh normálta air.
Léitheoireacht bhreise: Bachman 1990, lch. 73–74.

CA:334, DA:302, DE:310, EN:301, ES:397, FR:390, GA:433, IT:379, NE:308, PO:394.

434 triail socrúcháin Triail a riartar d'fhonn mic léinn a shocrú i ngrúpa nó i rang ar leibhéal atá oiriúnach don eolas nó don chumas atá acu.

CA:311, DA:137, DE:101, EN:282, ES:323, FR:377, GA:434, IT:365, NE:291, PO:372.

435 triail suntasachta Triail chun suntasacht staitistiúil a dheimhniú.
Féach: suntasacht.

CA:324, DA:334, DE:350, EN:364, ES:333, FR:373, GA:435, IT:371, NE:339, PO:384.

436 triailiú Céim i bhforbairt tascanna trialach arb é is aidhm léi ná a fháil amach an bhfeidhmíonn an triail faoi mar atáthar ag súil leis. Baintear leas as go minic i gcás tascanna a mharcáiltear go suibiachtúil, mar aistí, a chuirtear ar phobal teoranta.
Cuir i gcomparáid le: réamhthástáil.

CA:26, DA:301, DE:104, EN:418, ES:135, FR:160, GA:436, IT:336, NE:303, PO:185.

437 tuairiscín Cur síos gairid a ghabhann le banda ar scála rátála agus a dhéanann achoimre ar an gcéim oilteachta nó ar an gcineál feidhmiúcháin a bhfuiltear ag súil leis chun an scór sin a ghnóthachtáil.

CA:97, DA:64, DE:76, EN:96, ES:98, FR:97, GA:437, IT:118, NE:96, PO:113.

438 tuairiscín scála Ceadaigh an sainmhíniú ar thuairiscín.

CA:98, DA:338, DE:353, EN:344, ES:99, FR:96, GA:438, IT:119, NE:327, PO:112.

439 ualú Athrú ar an uasmhéid pointí is féidir a bhaint amach ar mhír nó ar thasc nó ar chomhpháirt de thriail, d'fhonn an tábhacht a bhaineann leo i gcomórtas le codanna eile den triail chéanna a athrú. Mar shampla, má thugtar marcanna dúbailte do na míreanna go léir i dTasc a hAon i dtriail, bainfidh codán níos mó den scór iomlán le Tasc a hAon ná mar a bhainfidh le haon tasc eile.

Léitheoireacht bhreise: Ebel agus Frisbie, 1991, lgh 214–216.

CA:290, DA:435, DE:136, EN:438, ES:303, FR:302, GA:439, IT:268, NE:434, PO:306.

440 úsáideoir trialach An duine nó an institiúid (m.sh. múinteoir nó fostóir) a bhaineann leas as torthaí i dtriail d'fhonn cinneadh a dhéanamh i dtaobh duine a rinne an triail.

CA:414, DA:391, DE:392, EN:407, ES:410, FR:409, GA:440, IT:399, NE:393, PO:407.

441 *z*-scór Scór caighdeánach coitianta a bhfuil meán de 0 aige agus diall caighdeánach de 1. Is í an fhoirmle atá ann chun *z*-scór a ríomh ná:

$$z = (X-\overline{X}) \div Sx$$

Áit a bhfuil:

z = z-scór

X = scór i dtriail

$\overline{X}$ = meán na scór i dtriail

Sx = diall caighdeánach na scór i dtriail.

Cuir i gcomparáid le: *t*-scór.
Féach: scór caighdeánach.

Léitheoireacht bhreise: Ebel & Frisbie 1991, lch. 68.

CA:358, DA:439, DE:446, EN:442, ES:358, FR:286, GA:441, IT:291, NE:439, PO:290.

8 Italiano: Glossario terminologico del testing linguistico

1 abilità (a) Una capacità acquisita tramite l'esercizio della volontà al fine di esercitare determinate facoltà e di eseguire determinate operazioni.
cfr.: competenza.
Per approfondire: Bachman, 1990. p.16, p. 19.
CA:46, DA:2, DE:113, EN:2, ES:49, FR:42, GA:96, IT:1A, NE:411, PO:49.
(b) La capacità di fare qualcosa. Nel testing linguistico vengono abitualmente distinte quattro abilità: comprensione della lettura, produzione scritta e orale ed ascolto.
V.: competenza.
CA:199, DA:111, DE:119, EN:367, ES:100, FR:340, GA:325, IT:1B, NE:413, PO:51.

2 abilità di ordine inferiore Abilità ipotizzate di tipo meno complesso, quali ad esempio la capacità di riconoscere lettere o parole in test linguistici.
cfr.: abilità di ordine superiore.
CA:200, DA:27, DE:424, EN:219, ES:101, FR:44, GA:327, IT:2, NE:409, PO:52.

3 abilità di ordine superiore Abilità ipotizzate di tipo più complesso quali ad esempio la capacità di compiere inferenze o di riassumere.
cfr.: abilità di ordine inferiore.
CA:201, DA:130, DE:418, EN:162, ES:102, FR:45, GA:326, IT:3, NE:410, PO:53.

4 abilità linguistica L'insieme delle competenze che definisce la capacità di un individuo di usare la lingua per una varietà di scopi comunicativi.
Per approfondire: Bachman 1990, pp. 3–4.
CA:47, DA:354, DE:368, EN:203, ES:50, FR:43, GA:97, IT:4, NE:379, PO:50.

5 adeguamento di test Adattare test già esistenti in modo tale da soddisfare le richieste di un particolare gruppo di candidati o di chi dovrà prendere delle decisioni sulla base dei risultati.
CA:301, DA:404, DE:410, EN:405, ES:13, FR:395, GA:370, IT:5, NE:382, PO:4.

6 affidabilità La stabilità delle misure ottenute da un test. Più un test è affidabile, meno errori casuali contiene. Un test che contenga errori sistematici, ad esempio nei confronti di un determinato gruppo, può essere affidabile, ma non valido.
cfr.: validità.
V.: KR-20 (formula 20 di Kuder-Richardson), alfa (coefficiente alfa), affidabilità di bipartizione, affidabilità test-ritest.
Per approfondire: Bachman 1990, p.24; Crocker e Algina 1986, Capitolo 6.
CA:180, DA:312, DE:322/453, EN:327, ES:198, FR:183, GA:200, IT:6, NE:43, PO:193.

7 affidabilità di bipartizione Una misura della consistenza interna dell'affidabilità. La stima si basa sulla correlazione fra i punteggi di due metà di un medesimo test che vengono però considerate come due test diversi. La divisione a metà puo essere fatta in modi diversi, ad esempio si può dividere la prima parte del test dalla seconda, o dividere gli item con numeri pari da quelli con numeri dispari.
V.: affidabilità.
Per approfondire: Ebel e Frisbie 1991, pp. 82–83; Crocker e Algina 1986, pp. 136–138.
CA:183, DA:259, DE:364/398, EN:377, ES:201, FR:184, GA:203, IT:7, NE:353, PO:194.

8 affidabilità di giudizio Una stima dell'affidabilità di un test relativa alla concordanza del giudizio espresso da esaminatori diversi sulla prestazione fornita dai candidati.
V.: concordanza di giudizio, affidabilità.
CA:181, DA:145, DE:158, EN:182, ES:199, FR:185, GA:201, IT:8, NE:184, PO:195.

9 affidabilità test-ritest Una stima dell'affidabilità ottenuta somministrando lo stesso test agli stessi candidati nelle stesse condizioni e correlando i punteggi ottenuti nelle due situazioni. É relativa alla stabilità dei punteggi nel tempo. Viene

anche usata in modo appropriato qualora non sia possibile calcolare i valori della consistenza interna.
cfr.: consistenza interna.
V.: affidabilità, stabilità.
CA:184, DA:318, DE:409/325, EN:410, ES:202, FR:188, GA:204, IT:9, NE:383, PO:197.

10 alfa (coefficiente alfa) Una stima dell'affidabilità di un test; ne misura infatti la coerenza interna. Può oscillare da 0 a 1. E' spesso usato per test corredati da scale per l'attribuzione dei punteggi, l'opposto cioè di test con item dicotomici. Può tuttavia essere utilizzato per entrambi. Viene anche chiamato coefficiente alfa.
cfr.: Kuder-Richardson.
V.: consistenza interna.
Per approfondire: Henning 1987, p.84.
CA:9, DA:11, DE:10, EN:10, ES:16, FR:8, GA:10, IT:10, NE:12, PO:6.

11 alfa di Cronbach Si rimanda alla definizione di alfa (coefficiente alfa).
CA:10, DA:54, DE:70, EN:84, ES:17, FR:9, GA:11, IT:11, NE:89, PO:7.

12 analisi degli item Una descrizione della prestazione fornita dai candidati nei singoli item del test. La descrizione viene abitualmente fatta ricorrendo ad indici propri della statistica classica quali l'indice di facilità o l'indice di discriminazione. Per condurre tale analisi vengono usati dei software quali MicroCAT Iteman.
V.: discriminazione, indice di facilità.
CA:13, DA:161, DE:167, EN:190, ES:25 FR:17, GA:13, IT:12, NE:198, PO:16.

13 analisi dei bisogni Un modo per definire i bisogni linguistici (in termini di abilità, compiti, vocabolario, ecc.) di un determinato gruppo di discenti. Scopo prioritario di tale analisi è l'elaborazione di un corso d'insegnamento adeguato ai bisogni dei discenti stessi.
CA:16, DA:35, DE:45, EN:246, ES:21, FR:11, GA:19, IT:13, NE:31, PO:17.

14 analisi dei fattori Una tecnica statistica che consente di ridurre il numero delle variabili, individuando per molte di esse schemi di variazione dei valori. Un insieme di variabili fortemente correlate fra loro costituisce un fattore. Un'analisi dei fattori può essere di tipo esplorativo, al fine di formulare delle ipotesi, o di tipo confermativo, partendo da delle ipotesi specifiche.
Per approfondire: Bachman, 1990, p.262; Crocker e Algina, 1986, p.232.
CA:20, DA:96, DE:115, EN:142, ES:26, FR:18, GA:18, IT:14, NE:133, PO:20.

15 analisi del contenuto Un modo per descrivere ed analizzare il contenuto dei materiali di un test. Un tale tipo di analisi risulta necessario ai fini di garantire che il contenuto del test rispetti effettivamente la descrizione che ne è stata data. E' inoltre essenziale per stabilire sia la validità di contenuto sia la validità di costrutto.
CA:18, DA:133, DE:153, EN:72, ES:19, FR:12, GA:12, IT:15, NE:178, PO:15.

16 analisi del discorso Tipo di analisi rivolta alla struttura e alla funzione dei vari tipi di testi scritti o parlati.
CA:19, DA:76, DE:86, EN:107, ES:24, FR:13, GA:17, IT:16, NE: 104, PO:19.

17 analisi del test Un'analisi condotta su un test, di solito con metodi statistici e tramite elaboratori elettronici, dopo che questo è stato sottoposto ai candidati. Il fine dell'analisi può essere quello di studiare la prestazione fornita dai candidati o il funzionamento del test stesso.
CA:15, DA:389, DE:390, EN:396, ES:22, FR:16, GA:14, IT:17, NE:389, PO:18.

18 analisi della covarianza Si rimanda alla definizione di ANCOVA.
CA:14, DA:200, DE:193, EN:12, ES:20, FR:14, GA:16, IT:18, NE:85, PO:13.

19 analisi della varianza Si rimanda alla definizione di ANOVA.
CA:17, DA:430, DE:430, EN:13, ES:23, FR:15, GA:15, IT:19, NE:418, PO:14.

20 ANCOVA Un tipo di analisi della varianza che permette di mettere insieme più variabili da verificare (in particolare quelle il cui cambiamento può essere legato a quello della variabile presa in esame).
V.: ANOVA.
Per approfondire: Hatch e Lazaraton, 1991, p.387.
CA:21, DA:14, DE:13, EN:17, ES:27, FR:19, GA:20, IT:20, NE:16, PO:21.

21 ANOVA Una tecnica statistica che consente di verificare l'ipotesi nulla secondo cui le medie di gruppi diversi sono uguali. Si esamina la variazione delle osservazioni all'interno di ciascun gruppo e fra le medie dei gruppi.
Per approfondire: Hatch e Lazaraton 1991, pp. 308–312.
CA:22, DA:19, DE:20, EN:18, ES:28, FR:20, GA:21, IT:21, NE:19, PO:22.

22 apprendimento linguistico Il processo attraverso il quale è possibile acquisire quella che abitualmente chiamiamo abilità linguistica nella lingua 1 o nella lingua 2. Nel caso di una lingua seconda viene fatta a volte la distinzione fra un apprendimento di tipo spontaneo (ad esempio per una esposizione naturale alla lingua) ed un apprendimento di tipo consapevole (ad esempio attraverso lo studio).

CA:7, DA:356, DE:367, EN:204, ES:14, FR:5, GA:349, IT:22, NE:380, PO:24.

23 approccio realistico Nell'ambito del testing linguistico, un approccio in base al quale andrebbero inseriti nei test compiti che rispecchino il più possibile attività tipiche della vita reale. Ad esempio, in base a tale approccio, il contenuto di un test il cui scopo sia quello di valutare se i candidati siano in grado di affrontare un corso universitario in una lingua straniera, dovrebbe essere basato su un'analisi sia dei contenuti linguistici specifici di quella data lingua, sia delle attività che caratterizzeranno il corso stesso.

V.: autenticità.

Per approfondire: Bachman 1990, pp. 301–328.

CA:129, DA:433, DE:320, EN:322, ES:134, FR:345, GA:98, IT:23, NE:226, PO:349.

24 arrotondamento Il processo in base al quale viene ridotta la precisione di un numero, tramite sostituzione con un numero più semplice, ottenuto diminuendo il numero delle cifre di partenza. Ad esempio 564.8 può essere portato a 565 o a 560. La scala di arrotondamento dipende dal livello di precisione richiesto.

CA:24, DA:245, DE:331, EN:335, ES:363, FR:22, GA:354, IT:24, NE:11, PO:25.

25 asimmetria Caratteristica di una distribuzione in cui il picco della curva si trova sia alla destra del centro (asimmetria negativa), sia alla sinistra del centro (asimmetria positiva).

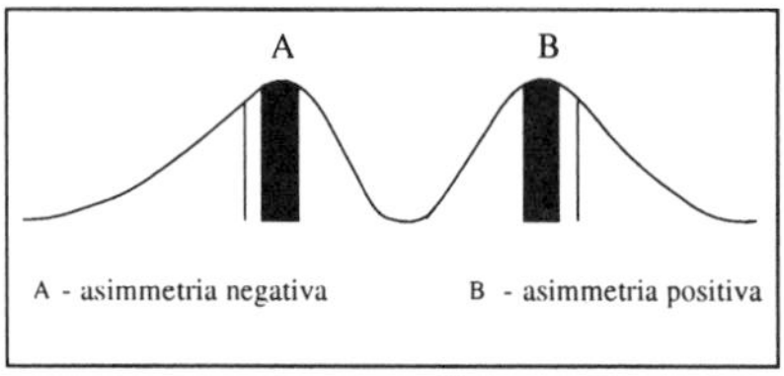

V.: distribuzione normale.

Per approfondire: Hatch e Lazaraton 1991,p.165.

CA:25, DA:343, DE:337, EN:366, ES:31, FR:109, GA:323, IT:25, NE:330, PO:120.

26 attributo/carattere Caratteristica fisica o psicologica di un individuo (quale ad esempio l'abilità linguistica), o scala di misurazione per descrivere tale caratteristica.

CA:411, DA:416, DE:95, EN:415, ES:360, FR:23, GA:400, IT:26, NE:403, PO:403.

27 attribuzione analitica del punteggio Un metodo per l' attribuzione del punteggio che può essere usato per test linguistici di tipo produttivo, quali, per l'appunto, quelli di produzione scritta e orale. Chi attribuisce il punteggio fa abitualmente riferimento ad una serie di punti specifici. Ad esempio, in un test di produzione scritta, una scala di tipo analitico può essere costituita da una serie di punti quali la grammatica, il vocabolario, l'uso dei connettivi.

Per approfondire: Ebel e Frisbie, 1991, p. 195; Weir, 1990, p.63.

CA:343, DA:13, DE:12, EN:14, ES:426, FR:266,.GA:340, IT:27, NE:15, PO:58.

28 attribuzione computerizzata del punteggio Sono diversi i modi di impiego del computer per ridurre al minimo la possibilità di errore nella correzione e nella conseguente attribuzione del punteggio nei test oggettivi. Un modo può essere ad esempio quello di controllare il foglio delle risposte del candidato tramite un lettore ottico ed elaborare poi dei dati che possano essere usati per attribuire punteggi o per altri tipi di analisi.

CA:85, DA:53, DE:69, EN:65, ES:82, FR:273, GA:222, IT:28, NE:69, PO:66.

29 attribuzione del punteggio L'operazione di attribuire un punteggio alle risposte di un candidato in un test. Tale operazione può comportare di dover dare un giudizio di tipo professionale o quanto meno di dover applicare uno schema che includa tutte le risposte accettabili.

CA:80, DA:289, DE:40, EN:222, ES:47, FR:265, GA:218, IT:29, NE:83, PO:57.

30 attribuzione del punteggio da parte di esaminatori Un metodo di correzione ed attribuzione del punteggio in base al quale chi viene adibito a ciò deve avere un certo grado di esperienza e preparazione per poter esprimere dei giudizi soggettivi. I test di produzione orale e scritta vengono di solito corretti con questo metodo.

cfr.: attribuzione del punteggio da parte di personale non specializzato.

CA:81, DA:29, DE:107, EN:136, ES:81, FR:272, GA:223, IT:30, NE:131, PO:67.

31 attribuzione del punteggio da parte di personale non specializzato Un metodo per attribuire il punteggio, che non richiede del personale specializzato,

non comportando giudizi soggettivi. L'attribuzione del punteggio avviene infatti seguendo un apposito schema che indica tutte le possibili risposte per ogni item del test.
cfr.: attribuzione del punteggio da parte di esaminatori.
CA:86, DA:23, DE:231, EN:51, ES:78, FR:274, GA:219, IT:31, NE:25, PO:62.

32 attribuzione dicotomica del punteggio L'operazione di attribuire il punteggio facendo riferimento a due categorie, ad esempio giusto/sbagliato, superato/non superato, si/no.
CA:347, DA:67, DE:455, EN:98, ES:347, FR:268, GA:341, IT:32, NE:98, PO:59.

33 attribuzione globale del punteggio Un metodo per l'attribuzione del punteggio che può essere usato in test linguistici di tipo produttivo, ad esempio test di produzione scritta o orale. L'esaminatore verifica la risposta di ciascun candidato, senza cercare di distinguere ed isolare le caratteristiche 'discrete' del compito assegnato.
cfr.: attribuzione analitica del punteggio, giudizio globale.
CA:89, DA:116, DE:133, EN:168, ES:429, FR:270, GA:220, IT:33, NE:172, PO:68.

34 attribuzione politomica del punteggio L'operazione di attribuire un punteggio ad un item facendo riferimento ad una scala di almeno tre punti. Ad esempio alla risposta ad una domanda possono essere assegnati: 0 punti, 1 punto o 2 punti. Questo sistema viene abitualmente usato per attribuire il punteggio alle domande aperte. Viene anche detta attribuzione scalare del punteggio.
cfr.: attribuzione dicotomica del punteggio.
CA:351, DA:291, DE:237, EN:284, ES:353, FR:89, GA:342, IT:34, NE:293, PO:64.

35 autenticità Caratteristica di un test i cui compiti riflettano l'uso della lingua in situazioni reali.
Per approfondire: Bachman, 1990, pp. 300–303.
CA:27, DA:21, DE:42, EN:24, ES:33, FR:24, GA:115, IT:35, NE:23, PO:26.

36 autenticità d'interazione L'autenticità vista, nell'ambito del testing linguistico, come una caratteristica di quella 'interazione' che si deve realizzare fra candidato e compito del test, onde poter fornire una risposta appropriata.
cfr.: autenticità situazionale.
V.: autenticità.
Per approfondire: Bachman 1990, pp. 315–323.
CA:28, DA:146, DE:157, EN:177, ES:34, FR:25, GA:116, IT:36, NE:183, PO:27.

37 autenticità situazionale La misura in cui un test può essere considerato autentico in relazione al mondo reale e a quelle situazioni in cui la lingua non viene utilizzata al fine di una sua verifica.
cfr.: autenticità d'interazione.
V.: autenticità.
Per approfondire: Bachman 1990, Capitolo 8.
CA:29, DA:336, DE:351, EN:365, ES:35, FR:26, GA:117, IT:37, NE:340, PO:28.

38 autovalutazione Il processo in base al quale uno studente valuta il proprio livello di abilità, sia sottoponendosi ad un test autonomamente, sia servendosi di altri mezzi quali questionari o liste di controllo.
CA:30, DA:331, DE:345, EN:354, ES:36, FR:27, GA:142, IT:38, NE:334, PO:29.

39 banda In senso lato, parte di una scala. In un test basato su item, il termine si riferisce ad una serie di punteggi, che possono essere riportati come gradi o, appunto, bande. In una scala costruita per misurare una caratteristica o abilità specifica, una banda corrisponde normalmente ad un livello specifico.
CA:37, DA:339, DE:44, EN:29, ES:38, FR:200, GA:41, IT:39, NE:28, PO:210.

40 banda di punteggi Parte di una scala che si riferisce ad un determinato livello di abilità.
CA:346, DA:258, DE:210, EN:30, ES:39, FR:269, GA:330, IT:40, NE:29, PO:65.

41 batteria Un insieme coerente di test o subtest, che pur verificando abilità diverse e avendo punteggi diversi, possono essere messi insieme per ottenere un punteggio totale.
CA:38, DA:28, DE:393, EN:32, ES:40, FR:30, GA:64, IT:41, NE:30, PO:38.

42 batteria di test Si rimanda alla definizione di batteria.
CA:39, DA:390, DE:406, EN:397, ES:41, FR:31, GA:63, IT:42, NE:390, PO:39.

43 calibrare Nella teoria della risposta agli item la valutazione della difficoltà di un gruppo di item in un test.
V.: scala teta.
CA:43, DA:163, DE:93, EN:39, ES:43, FR:40, GA:48, IT:43, NE:206, PO:47.

44 calibratura Il processo in base al quale viene creata un'unica scala per uno o più test. Tale processo implica ancorare item tratti da test diversi ad una scala comune di difficoltà (la scala teta). Quando un test risulta costituito da item così calibrati, i punteggi ottenuti nel test indicano l'abilità dei candidati, vale a dire la loro collocazione nella scala teta.

CA:44, DA:164, DE:94, EN:40, ES:42, FR:35, GA:49, IT:44, NE:205, PO:42.

45 campionamento Selezione di un campione.
V.: campione.

CA:267, DA:374, DE:384, EN:340, ES:281, FR:120, GA:307, IT:45, NE:368, PO:313.

46 campione Selezione di un sotto-insieme di elementi all'interno di una popolazione. Si possono distinguere vari tipi di campioni quali, ad esempio, campione casuale, campione stratificato, ecc.
Per approfondire: Crocker e Algina 1986, pp. 432–438; Guilford e Fruchter 1981,pp. 44–45.

CA:264, DA:371, DE:380, EN:337, ES:278, FR:116, GA:304, IT:46, NE:369, PO:8.

47 campione casuale Una serie di elementi presi a caso da una popolazione oggetto di studio, in modo tale che ciascun elemento riferentesi a tale popolazione abbia una uguale probabilità di essere studiato.
V.: campione.
Per approfondire: Crocker e Algina 1986, pp. 433–438; Guilford e Fruchter 1981, p.120.

CA:265, DA:409, DE:451, EN:307, ES:279, FR:117, GA:305, IT:47, NE:120, PO:9.

48 campione stratificato Un campione di una popolazione oggetto di studio. Quest'ultima viene prima suddivisa in un certo numero di gruppi (strati, classi) da ciascuno dei quali viene quindi preso un campione.
V.: campione.
Per approfondire: Guilford e Fruchter 1981, pp. 122–123.

CA:266, DA:375, DE:134, EN:388, ES:280, FR:119, GA:306, IT:48, NE:157, PO:11.

49 candidato Chi si sottopone ad un test.

CA:45/100, DA:165/402, DE:302/407, EN:41/406, ES:48/190, FR:41/351, GA:163/110, IT:49, NE:207/395, PO:48/183.

50 caratteristiche del metodo del test Le caratteristiche che distinguono metodi di test diversi. Queste possono comprendere: l'ambiente in cui viene somministrato il test, le indicazioni dei compiti, la lingua delle istruzioni per i candidati, il formato, ecc. Noto anche come: aspetti del metodo del test.
Per approfondire: Bachman 1990, Capitolo 5.

CA:48/175, DA:396/397, DE:402/403, EN:402/403, ES:51/193, FR:46/176, GA:/163401, IT:50, NE:397/398, PO:54/186.

51 categoria (a) Una suddivisione all'interno di una scala categoriale. Ad esempio il sesso si suddivide in due categorie: maschile e femminile.

b) Nel testing si dice che una scala di misurazione ad esempio con cinque punti, ha cinque categorie di risposta.

CA:49, DA:169, DE:176, EN:43, ES:52, FR:48, GA:50, IT:51, NE:52, PO:55.

52 certificato Un documento che attesta che una persona si è sottoposta ad un esame o a parte di esso, conseguendo un grado corrispondente almeno alla sufficienza.
cfr.: diploma.

CA:50, DA:38, DE:448, EN:47, ES:53, FR:50, GA:386, IT:52, NE:56, PO:56.

53 chiave/i a) La opzione corretta in un item a scelta multipla.

b) Più in generale, la serie di tutte le risposte corrette o accettabili agli item di un test.
cfr.: distraente, schema per la correzione e l'attribuzione del punteggio.
V.: item a scelta multipla.

CA:51/52, DA:256, DE:339, EN:198, ES:54, FR:329, GA:133, DE:339, IT:53, NE:342, PO:335.

54 classificare/classificazione a) Assegnare un punteggio di merito alla prestazione fornita da un candidato sulla base di un giudizio soggettivo.

b) Il punteggio di merito ottenuto dal candidato.

CA:428, DA:171, DE:57, EN:314, ES:425, FR:265, GA:286, IT:54, NE:38, PO:57.

55 classificazione percentuale Un numero o punteggio che permette di classificare indicando la percentuale che si situa al di sotto di tale punteggio. Se ad esempio un candidato ha raggiunto il grado percentuale di 60, questo significa che il 60% dei candidati ha ottenuto lo stesso punteggio o un punteggio più basso.

CA:363, DA:281, DE:299, EN:276, ES:359, FR:53, GA:284, IT:55, NE:285, PO:276.

56 cloze razionale Si rimanda alla definizione di test di cloze.

CA:314, DA:308, DE:230, EN:318, ES:316, FR:371, GA:60, IT:56, NE:315, PO:367.

57 coefficiente Un indice numerico per misurare una proprietà o caratteristica.
V.: alfa (coefficiente alfa), coefficiente di correlazione.

CA:53, DA:175, DE:178, EN:53, ES:55, FR:54, GA:73, IT:57, NE:62, PO:69.

58 coefficiente alfa Si rimanda alla definizione di alfa (coefficiente alfa).

CA:54, DA:176, DE:179, EN:54, ES:56, FR:55, GA:74, IT:58, NE:63, PO:70.

59 coefficiente di affidabilità Una misura dell'affidabilità compresa fra 0 e 1. Stime di affidabilità possono basarsi o su somministrazioni multiple di un test (che dovrebbero produrre risultati simili) o, qualora questo non sia possibile, su una qualche forma di misura della consistenza interna. A volte detto anche indice di affidabilità.

V.: consistenza interna, affidabilità, affidabilità test-ritest.

CA:61, DA:313, DE:323, EN:328, ES:58, FR:61, GA:77, IT:59, NE:44, PO:74.

60 coefficiente di correlazione Un indice rivelatore del grado di correlazione fra due o più variabili. Varia da –1 a +1. Le variabili a correlazione più elavata sono rappresentate da un indice di correlazione che si avvicina a +1.

Per approfondire: Guilford e Fruchter, 1981, pp. 86–88.

CA:55, DA:197, DE:191, EN:79, ES:57, FR:56, GA:75, IT:60, NE:82, PO:71.

61 coefficiente phi Un coefficiente di correlazione usato per dimostrare la forza del rapporto tra due variabili binarie. Ad esempio i punteggi relativi agli item di un test attribuiti secondo il metodo giusto/sbagliato.

V.: coefficiente di correlazione.

Per approfondire: Guilford e Fruchter 1981, pp. 316–318; Crocker e Algina 1986,pp. 92–94.

CA:62, DA:284, DE:286, EN:279, ES:59, FR:58, GA:76, IT:61, NE:288, PO:75.

62 competenza La conoscenza o abilità che permette di 'fare' qualcosa. In linguistica il termine viene usato per indicare una abilità sottesa, contrapposta a esecuzione o performance, termine che indica invece la manifestazione della competenza. Tale distinzione risale a Chomsky.

cfr.: performance/esecuzione.

Per approfondire: Bachman, 1990, pp 52 e 108.

CA:64/296, DA:180/296, DE:47/183, EN:59/295, ES:60/120, FR:62/260, GA:191/265, IT:62, NE:67/305, PO:76/273.

63 competenza comunicativa La abilità di usare la lingua in modo appropriato in una varietà di situazioni.

Per approfondire: Bachman, 1990, p. 16, p. 68.

CA:65, DA:179, DE:182, EN:58, ES:61, FR:63, GA:195, IT:63, NE:66, PO:77.

64 competenza di discorso La capacità di capire e produrre discorsi. All'interno di alcuni modelli di competenza, la competenza di discorso rappresenta una delle componenti che costituiscono la più generica competenza comunicativa.

Per approfondire: Bachman,1990, capitolo 4.

CA:66, DA:78, DE:87, EN:108, ES:62, FR:64, GA:196, IT:64, NE:105, PO:78.

65 competenza grammaticale All'interno di un modello di competenza comunicativa, la competenza grammaticale rappresenta una componente relativa alla conoscenza strutturale.

Per approfondire: Bachman 1990, pp. 84–88.

CA:67, DA:119, DE:138, EN:158, ES:63, FR:65, GA:193, IT:65, NE:162, PO:79.

66 competenza linguistica La conoscenza di una lingua. Spesso il termine è usato come sinonimo di abilità linguistica.

Per approfondire: Bachman 1990, p.16.

CA:68/297, DA:217/355, DE:224/365, EN:206/214, ES:64/121, FR:66/67, GA:198/267, IT:66, NE:215/231, PO:80/81.

67 competenza orale La competenza nel saper parlare una lingua.

CA:298, DA:239, DE:370, EN:264, ES:65, FR:68, GA:266, IT:67, NE:354, PO:82.

68 competenza pragmatica Una componente all'interno di un modello di competenza comunicativa; comprende l'abilità di capire e produrre atti di parola e la conoscenza di convenzioni di tipo sociolinguistico.

Per approfondire: Bachman 1990, p. 42.

CA:69, DA:294, DE:295, EN:290, ES:66, FR:69, GA:194, IT:68, NE:297, PO:83.

69 competenza sociolinguistica Una componente all'interno di modelli di competenza comunicativa: comprende l'abilità di adattare la lingua a determinate situazioni in sintonia con norme di tipo socioculturale.

Per approfondire: Bachman 1990, p.42.

CA:70, DA:347, DE:358, EN:369, ES:67, FR:70, GA:197, IT:69, NE:345, PO:84.

70 competenza unitaria Teoria linguistica, sostenuta in particolare da Oller, che afferma l'esistenza di un'unica competenza alla base delle abilità linguistiche.

CA:71, DA:91, DE:423, EN:428, ES:68, FR:71, GA:192, IT:70, NE:408, PO:85.

71 compito L'insieme costituito dalle indicazioni relative alla modalità di esecuzione, dall'input e dalla risposta. Ad esempio: un testo di comprensione della lettura seguito da diversi item a scelta multipla ai quali si può rispondere seguendo le indicazioni fornite.

CA:391, DA:260, DE:26, EN:393, ES:2, FR:354, GA:371, IT:71, NE:270, PO:352.

72 compito di abbinamento multiplo Un compito di un test in cui vengono inserite una serie di domande a cui rispondere o di frasi da completare. Le risposte vengono fornite sotto forma di un elenco di parole o frasi, ciascuna delle quali può essere impiegata più volte. Il vantaggio di un tale tipo di compito è che le opzioni non vengono eliminate man mano che il candidato le seleziona (come invece avviene in altri tipi di abbinamenti) e di conseguenza il compito non diventa progressivamente sempre più facile.
V.: compito di abbinamento.

CA:396, DA:100, DE:235, EN:241, ES:8, FR:355, GA:372, IT:72, NE:253, PO:354.

73 compito di abbinamento Un compito all'interno di un test che richiede di ricomporre insieme elementi tratti da due liste diverse. Un tipo di compito di abbinamento consiste anche nello scegliere il modo corretto per completare un certo numero di frasi non completate. Un altro tipo di compito di abbinamento, usato in test di comprensione della lettura, comporta lo scegliere da una lista elementi quali una vacanza o un libro che si possano ben adattare ad una persona di cui siano già state indicate le esigenze.

CA:397, DA:322, DE:452, EN:226, ES:7, FR:21, GA:375, IT:73, NE:238, PO:353.

74 compito di comprensione della lettura Un tipo di compito generalmente costituito da uno o più testi da leggere o da testi e item del tipo: scelte multiple, risposte brevi, cloze/completamenti, trasferimenti di informazioni.

CA:394, DA:223, DE:220, EN:321, ES:3, FR:357, GA:373, IT:74, NE:224, PO:351.

75 compito di correzione di errori Un compito all'interno di un test che implica la ricerca in un testo di errori di un determinato tipo, ad esempio errori di ortografia o errori di struttura. Parte del compito può consistere nel segnalare gli errori contenuti nel testo e fornire le forme corrette.

CA:395, DA:195, DE:189, EN:300, ES:4, FR:84, GA:374, IT:75, NE:304, PO:97.

76 compito scritto guidato Un tipo di compito che richiede al candidato di produrre un testo scritto. Al fine di controllare e standardizzare la risposta attesa si ricorre all'uso di informazioni di tipo grafico o testuale quali ad esempio: fotografie, lettere, cartoline, istruzioni di vario genere.
cfr.: composizione, saggio.

CA:393, DA:121, DE:130, EN:160, ES:5, FR:311, GA:377, IT:76, NE:143, PO:317.

77 compito scritto orientato Si rimanda alla definizione di compito scritto guidato.

CA:392, DA:43, DE:15, EN:105, ES:6, FR:356, GA:376, IT:77, NE:144, PO:355.

78 completamenti Qualsiasi tipo di item che richieda al candidato di inserire del materiale scritto – lettere, numeri, singole parole, frasi semplici o complesse – in spazi lasciati vuoti all'interno di un testo. La risposta può essere prodotta dal candidato o semplicemente scelta fra una serie di opzioni.

CA:223, DA:138, DE:229, EN:151, ES:241, FR:317, GA:249, IT:78, NE:192, PO:235.

79 completamenti a scelta multipla Un tipo di item in un test in cui il candidato deve scegliere da una serie di opzioni la parola o frase corretta da inserire in uno spazio lasciato vuoto all'interno di un testo.
V.: completamenti.

CA:224, DA:237, DE:250, EN:239, ES:242, FR:386, GA:215, IT:79, NE:251, PO:390.

80 completamento di frasi Un tipo di item in cui viene fornita soltanto la metà di una frase. Compito del candidato è quello di completare la frase con le parole opportune, possibilmente sulla base di un testo letto, oppure scegliendole fra una serie di opzioni.

CA:72, DA:382, DE:332, EN:357, ES:69, FR:298, GA:93, IT:80, NE:442, PO:86.

81 componente Parte di un esame. Spesso si presenta come singolo test, con proprie istruzioni e limiti di tempo. Le componenti (ascolto, produzione scritta, ecc.) vengono abitualmente distinte in base alle abilità linguistiche da cui prendono il nome. Può essere anche chiamata subtest.

CA:73, DA:181, DE:306, EN:61, ES:29, FR:72, GA:85, IT:81, NE:128, PO:87.

82 composizione Un compito per eseguire il quale il candidato deve produrre un testo articolato scritto. I tipi di testi richiesti possono essere narrazioni di fatti, riflessioni ed espressioni di punti di vista su temi di attualità, nonché resoconti, lettere formali o informali. Può anche essere chiamata saggio.

CA:366, DA:109, DE:32, EN:62, ES:192, FR:73, GA:51, IT:82, NE:372, PO:88.

83 composizione di tipo argomentativo

Un compito scritto in cui il candidato deve affrontare un argomento su cui si possono esprimere diversi punti di vista, spiegando e sostenendo le proprie opinioni.
V.: composizione.

CA:74, DA:77, DE:342, EN:113, ES:70, FR:74, GA:52, IT:83, NE:42, PO:89.

84 concordanza di giudizio La corrispondenza fra i giudizi espressi da due o più esaminatori sullo stesso campione di prestazione. Di particolare importanza nella verifica di abilità produttive scritte o orali in test di tipo soggettivo, dove è richiesto l'intervento di esaminatori.

CA:1/2, DA:31/307, DE:56/159, EN:181/312, ES:10/11, FR:1/2, GA:68/70, IT:84, NE:36/185, PO:1/2.

85 conoscenze di sfondo Le conoscenze che un candidato ha di un certo argomento o contenuto utilizzato in un test. Tali conoscenze possono risultare determinanti nel rispondere all'input. Il verificarsi di una simile possibilità va tenuto particolarmente presente nei test di lingua per scopi specifici.

CA:75, DA:26, DE:144, EN:27, ES:73, FR:77, GA:134, IT:85, NE:4, PO:91.

86 conoscenze socioculturali Le conoscenze relative al modo di operare della società nell'ambito di una particolare cultura. Di particolare rilevanza per poter adattare comportamenti ed usi linguistici a contesti culturali specifici.
cfr.: competenza sociolinguistica.

CA:76, DA:346, DE:357, EN:368, ES:72, FR:341, GA:135, IT:86, NE:344, PO:90.

87 consistenza interna Quella caratteristica di un test, rappresentata dal grado di corrispondenza fra i punteggi ottenuti dai candidati nei singoli item del test e il punteggio complessivo. Stime della consistenza interna possono essere usate come indici dell'affidabilità di un test. Sono diversi gli indici che possono essere calcolati in questo modo, ad esempio KR-20, alpha.
V.: affidabilità, alfa (coefficiente alfa), Kuder-Richardson.
Per approfondire: Bachman 1990, p.172.

CA:77, DA:147, DE:155, EN:180, ES:74, FR:186, GA:87, IT:87, NE:186, PO:93.

88 conteggio dei distraenti La frequenza con la quale viene scelto ciascun distraente in un item a scelta multipla. Il conteggio indica il numero di preferenze di ciascun distraente.

CA:243, DA:80, DE:89, EN:116, ES:71, FR:301, GA:384, IT:88, NE:9, PO:96.

89 continuità d'affidabilità Una stima dell'affidabilità del giudizio relativa alla misura in cui lo stesso esaminatore riesce ad attribuire punteggi simili alla stessa prestazione in momenti diversi.
V.: affidabilità, continuità di giudizio.

CA:182, DA:151, DE:162, EN:186, ES:200, FR:187, GA:202, IT:89, NE:189, PO:196.

90 continuità di giudizio La corrispondenza fra i giudizi espressi in momenti diversi dallo stesso esaminatore sullo stesso campione di prestazione. Di particolare rilevanza nella verifica di abilità produttive scritte o orali in test di tipo soggettivo dove è richiesto l'intervento di esaminatori.

CA:3, DA:33, DE:163, EN:185, ES:12, FR:3, GA:69, IT:90, NE:190, PO:3.

91 controllo La fase all'interno del ciclo di produzione di un test, durante la quale chi si occupa dell'elaborazione e dello sviluppo del test stesso valuta i materiali prodotti da chi è adibito alla preparazione degli item e decide quali debbano essere scartati, in quanto non rispondenti alle descrizioni del test, e quali invece possano passare alla fase di revisione e correzione.
cfr.: moderazione.

CA:382, DA:400, DE:405, EN:433 ES:383, FR:338, GA:184, IT:91, NE:115, PO:343.

92 conversazione orale Le abilità di produzione orale vengono spesso verificate tramite una conversazione. Quest'ultima può andare da una conversazione completamente libera fra candidato/i e esaminatore/i ad una serie di compiti orali più o meno rigidamente strutturata.

CA:131, DA:150, DE:305, EN:263, ES:136, FR:148, GA:1, IT:92, NE:355, PO:143.

93 conversazione semidiretta/ simulata per la verifica della competenza orale (In letteratura nota come SOPI sigla di: Semi-Direct/Simulated Oral Proficiency Interview) Un test di competenza orale dove l'input è fornito da un nastro registrato e dove la risposta del candidato viene ugualmente registrata per essere poi giudicata successivamente.
V.: test semidiretto.

CA:130, DA:348, DE:356, EN:370, ES:137, FR:392, GA:356, IT:93, NE:346, PO:144.

94 conversione in gradi Il processo in base al quale è possibile convertire il punteggio ottenuto in un test in gradi.

CA:362, DA:168, DE:48, EN:157, ES:47, FR:52, GA:165, IT:94, NE:427, PO:277.

95 correlazione Il rapporto tra due o più misure in base al fatto che le stesse tendono

a variare nel medesimo modo. Se ad esempio dei candidati tendono ad avere punteggi simili in due test diversi, vi è evidentemente una correlazione positiva fra i due gruppi di punteggi.
cfr.: covarianza.
V.: correlazione di Pearson prodotto-momento (r di Pearson), correlazione per 'ranghi'.
Per approfondire: Guilford e Fruchter, 1981, capitolo 6; Bachman, 1990, pp. 259–260.
CA:91, DA:196, DE:190, EN:78, ES:84, FR:85, GA:78, IT:95, NE:81, PO:100.

96 correlazione biseriale Un indice di discriminazione in particolare per item dicotomici, riportato come r_{bis}. Indica la correlazione fra un criterio (di solito il punteggio totale del test) e l'abilità alla base della risposta, corretta o sbagliata, all'item stesso. Il valore di r_{bis} è come minimo il 25% più alto del biseriale di punto (r_{pbi}) Un vantaggio del r_{bis} è che rimane sostanzialmente stabile anche con campioni di diverso livello di abilità.
cfr.: correlazione biseriale di punto.
V.: discriminazione.
Per approfondire: Crocker e Algina, 1986, pp. 317–318; Guilford e Fruchter, 1981, pp. 304–311.
CA:56, DA:40, DE:60, EN:35, ES:85, FR:86, GA:79, IT:96, NE:48, PO:101.

97 correlazione biseriale di punto L'indice di discriminazione di un item, riferito a item di tipo dicotomico, riportato come r_{pbi}. La correlazione è fra un criterio (di solito il punteggio totale del test) e la risposta all'item. Un vantaggio di r_{pbi} rispetto a r_{bis} è quello di poter essere usato appropriatamente quando l'abilità sottesa non ha una distribuzione normale.
cfr.: correlazione biseriale.
CA:57, DA:41, DE:311, EN:283, ES:86, FR:57, GA:80, IT:97, NE:309, PO:102.

98 correlazione di Pearson prodotto-momento (r di Pearson) Un coefficiente di correlazione usato appropriatamente con variabili misurate su scale a intervalli o di rapporti.
V.: coefficiente di correlazione.
Per approfondire: Hatch e Lazaraton 1991, pp. 427–431; Guilford e Fruchter 1981, p. 81.
CA:59, DA:279, DE:298, EN:274, ES:90, FR:87, GA:84, IT:98, NE:283, PO:104.

99 correlazione per 'ranghi' di Spearman Una forma di correlazione per 'ranghi' usata su campioni piccoli, inferiori, ad esempio, ai 30 soggetti.
V.: correlazione per 'ranghi'.
CA:58, DA:351, DE:361, EN:373, ES:87, FR:60, GA:83, IT:99, NE:347, PO:73.

100 correlazione per 'ranghi' Una correlazione basata non sul valore assoluto delle variabili, ma sull' ordine relativo di classificazione.
Per approfondire: Guilford e Fruchter 1981, pp. 294–296.
CA:60, DA:304, DE:315, EN:309, ES:89, FR:59, GA:82, IT:100, NE:312, PO:72.

101 correlazione phi Si rimanda alla definizione di coefficiente phi.
CA:92, DA:285, DE:287, EN:280, ES:88, FR:88, GA:81, IT:101, NE:289, PO:103.

102 correttore Chi attribuisce un punteggio alle risposte di un candidato ad un test scritto. Tale operazione richiede che il correttore sia in grado di formulare un giudizio basato sull'esperienza o, nel caso di correttori non specializzati, la relativamente passiva applicazione di uno schema per la correzione e l'attribuzione del punteggio.
V.: esaminatore.
CA:90, DA:288, DE:39, EN:221, ES:83, FR:81, GA:225, IT:102, NE:80, PO:182.

103 correzione del fattore casualità Un modo per ridurre la possibilità di ottenere un punteggio maggiore semplicemente tirando ad indovinare la risposta corretta in test costituiti da item oggettivi.
Per approfondire: Ebel e Frisbie, 1986, pp. 215–218.
CA:82, DA:193, DE:317/450, EN:77, ES:80, FR:83, GA:54, IT:103, NE:77, PO:98.

104 correzione doppia Un metodo in base al quale due persone vengono incaricate di giudicare separatamente la prestazione fornita dai candidati in un test.
V.: correzione multipla.
CA:84, DA:82, DE:91, EN:121, ES:118, FR:114, GA:221, IT:104, NE:116, PO:61.

105 correzione multipla Un metodo per migliorare l'affidabilità del giudizio espresso su test di produzione scritta estesa, giudizio che è necessariamente in larga misura soggettivo, garantendo che la risposta di ciascun candidato venga corretta indipendentemente da più di un esaminatore.
Per approfondire: Weir 1988, pp. 65–66.
CA:87, DA:274, DE:233, EN:240, ES:45, FR:271, GA:183, IT:105, NE:241, PO:63.

106 correzione per attenuazione Un

metodo per valutare la correlazione fra due o più variabili qualora non vi sia differenza di affidabilità fra le variabili stesse.
Per approfondire: Guilford e Fruchter, 1981, pp. 450–453; Hatch e Lazaraton, 1990, pp. 444–445.
CA:88, DA:194, DE:243, EN:76, ES:79, FR:82, GA:53, IT:106, NE:78, PO:99.

107 corrispondenza La misura in cui vi è corrispondenza fra le previsioni di un modello e i risultati osservati. Possono essere calcolati diversi indici di corrispondenza. Nella teoria della risposta agli item l'analisi della corrispondenza mostra come la stima dell'item e i parametri relativi alle persone (vale a dire la difficoltà e il livello di abilità) danno una previsione dei risultati che saranno ottenuti nel test; la corrispondenza statistica di un item può essere considerata analoga al suo indice di difficoltà nella statistica classica.
V.: teoria della risposta agli item.
CA:8, DA:99, DE:248, EN:145, ES:15, FR:6, GA:268, IT:107, NE:135, PO:5.

108 costrutto Facoltà ipotetica di un individuo o caratteristica mentale che non può essere direttamente osservata o misurata. Per esempio, nel testing linguistico, l'abilità di ascolto. I test linguistici si propongono di misurare i diversi costrutti che sono alla base della abilità linguistica. Oltre l'abilità linguistica vera e propria anche la motivazione, l'attitudine e la formazione culturale costituiscono dei costrutti rilevanti.
Per approfondire: Hatch e Lazaraton, 1991, p.15.
CA:78, DA:184, DE:185, EN:68, ES:76, FR:80, GA:394, IT:108, NE:72, PO:94.

109 costruzione di scale Il processo in base al quale vengono costruite scale di misurazione. Nel testing linguistico questo comporta associare a dei numeri la prestazione fornita dai candidati per poter dimostrare il progressivo aumento della loro conoscenza o abilità. Tale processo può comportare la necessità di modificare una serie di punteggi per poter costruire una scala per scopi specifici, ad esempio per riportare i risultati di un test in modo standardizzato o per equiparare una versione di un test con un'altra.
V.: scala, scala di abilità, scala centile, scala comune, scala a intervalli, scala nominale, scala ordinale, scala di classificazione, scala di rapporti, forme equiparate, equiparazione lineare.
CA:159, DA:341, DE:355, EN:346, ES:167, FR:135, GA:321, IT:109, NE:329, PO:169.

110 costruzione di un test Il processo di selezione degli item (o compiti) e il loro inserimento nel test. Tale processo è spesso preceduto da una fase di pretesting o sperimentazione dei materiali. Item (e compiti) con cui costruire un test possono essere selezionati direttamente da una banca di materiali.
CA:126, DA:394, DE:397, EN:398, ES:75, FR:146, GA:393, IT:110, NE:392, PO:140.

111 costruzione di una banca di item Un approccio per la gestione degli item che comporta raccogliere informazioni sugli item in modo da poter costruire test di cui siano noti il contenuto e la difficoltà. Abitualmente la realizzazione di tale approccio comporta l'uso di un database e fa riferimento alla cosiddetta teoria della caratteristica latente in virtù della quale gli item possono essere messi in relazione l'uno con l'altro per mezzo di una scala comune di difficoltà.
Per approfondire: Henning 1987, Capitolo 9.
CA:36, DA:155, DE:28, EN:191, ES:37, FR:28, GA:40, IT:111, NE:199, PO:37.

112 covarianza La varianza congiunta di due o più variabili. Ad esempio la lunghezza delle frasi e la difficoltà lessicale sono caratteristiche di un test di comprensione della lettura che tendono ad essere messe in relazione l'una con l'altra, cioè a variare insieme o a covariare. La covarianza va tenuta in considerazione quando è possibile predire una variabile da altre; ad esempio quando si deduce la difficoltà di un testo di lettura dalla lunghezza delle frasi e dalla difficoltà lessicale.
V.: varianza.
CA:93, DA:199, DE:192, EN:80, ES:91, FR:92, GA:71, IT:112, NE:84, PO:106.

113 curricolo Una descrizione complessiva degli obiettivi, dei contenuti, dell'organizzazione, del metodo e della valutazione in un programma di studio.
cfr.: sillabo.
CA:94, DA:55, DE:71, EN:87, ES:93, FR:93, GA:99, IT:113, NE:220, PO:107.

114 curtosi Un' indicazione di quanto una distribuzione assuma una forma più a picco o più piatta rispetto ad una curva normale. I dati che si dipongono in una curva piatta mostrano una distribuzione platicurtica o iponormale, mentre i dati che vanno a formare una curva a picco, mostrano una distribuzione leptocurtica o ipernormale.

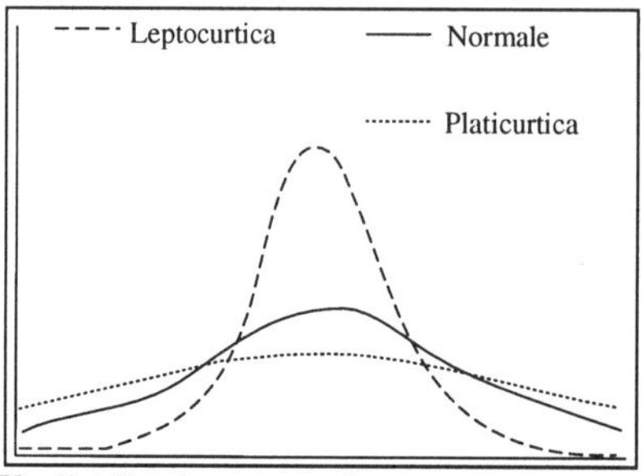

V.: distribuzione normale.

CA:95, DA:412, DE:108, EN:202, ES:94, FR:428, GA:100, IT:114, NE:213, PO:108.

115 curva caratteristica degli item (in letteratura noto come ICC, sigla di: Item Characteristic Curve) Nella teoria della risposta agli item tale curva mostra come la probabilità di risposta corretta ad un item sia relativa all'abilità latente che è alla base della prestazione fornita dai candidati negli item di un test.

Per approfondire: Crocker e Algina 1986, pp. 340–342.

CA:79, DA:157, DE:168, EN:192, ES:95, FR:90, GA:94, IT:115, NE:196, PO:109.

116 D di Ebel Si rimanda alla definizione di indice D.

CA:96, DA:85, DE:92, EN:122, ES:96, FR:94, GA:101, IT:116, NE:117, PO:111.

117 dato statistico/statistica Una quantità che contiene un'informazione espressa in forma numerica. Un dato statistico fa riferimento ad un gruppo campione, mentre un parametro fa riferimento ad una popolazione. I dati statistici vengono generalmente riportati con lettere dell'alfabeto latino, mentre i parametri con lettere dell'alfabeto greco. Ad esempio la deviazione standard di un campione viene indicata con s o con DS, mentre la deviazione standard calcolata su una popolazione viene indicata con σ (sigma).

cfr.: parametro.

V.: campione, popolazione.

CA:163, DA:368, DE:379, EN:385, ES:174, FR:348, GA:363, IT:117, NE:367, PO:174.

118 descrittore Una breve descrizione che accompagna una banda o una scala di classificazione e che descrive sommariamente il grado di competenza o il tipo di prestazione richiesti ad un candidato per raggiungere un determinato punteggio.

CA:97, DA:64, DE:76, EN:96, ES:98, FR:97, GA:437, IT:118, NE:96, PO:113.

119 descrittore di scala Si rimanda alla definizione di descrittore.

CA:98, DA:338, DE:353, EN:344, ES:99, FR:96, GA:438, IT:119, NE:327, PO:112.

120 descrizione del test Una documentazione dettagliata messa a punto abitualmente durante il processo di elaborazione di un nuovo test o di revisione di un test già esistente. La descrizione deve fornire precise indicazioni sul progetto, contenuto, livello, tipologia di item e compiti, popolazione cui il test è destinato, uso del test, ecc. Spesso alla descrizione viene allegato del materiale, come modello del test stesso.

CA:161, DA:401, DE:394, EN:404, ES:169, FR:346, GA:355, IT:120, NE:400, PO:171.

121 dettato Un tipo di compito all'interno di un test in cui si richiede al candidato di ascoltare un testo e di scrivere ciò che sente. I criteri per la correzione del dettato variano a seconda dello scopo del test; possono comprendere anche l'ortografia e la punteggiatura.

CA:103, DA:68, DE:79, EN:99, ES:105, FR:99, GA:109, IT:121, NE:99, PO:125.

122 deviazione standard Una misura della dispersione di una serie di osservazioni rispetto alla media aritmetica. Corrisponde alla radice quadrata della varianza. In una distribuzione normale il 68% del campione si colloca all'interno di una deviazione standard dalla media, mentre il 95% si colloca all'interno di due deviazioni standard dalla media.

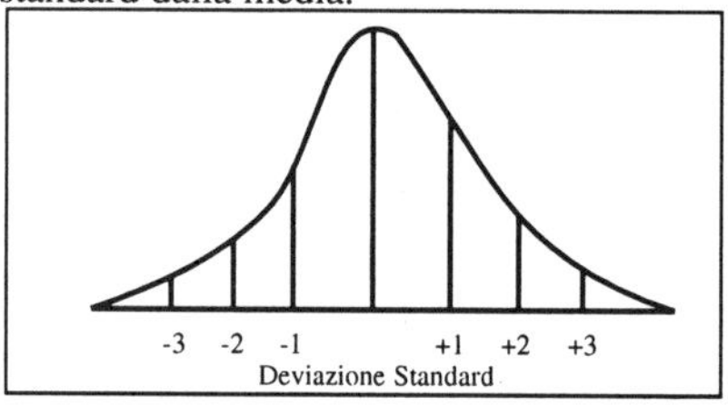

cfr.: margine di oscillazione.

V.: varianza.

Per approfondire: Ebel e Frisbie 1991, pp. 61–62; Crocker e Algina 1986, pp. 21–22.

CA:101, DA:362, DE:372, EN:379, ES:103, FR:98, GA:113, IT:122, NE:360, PO:114.

123 diagramma a colonne Un grafico che permette di visualizzare la frequenza di distribuzione delle variabili.

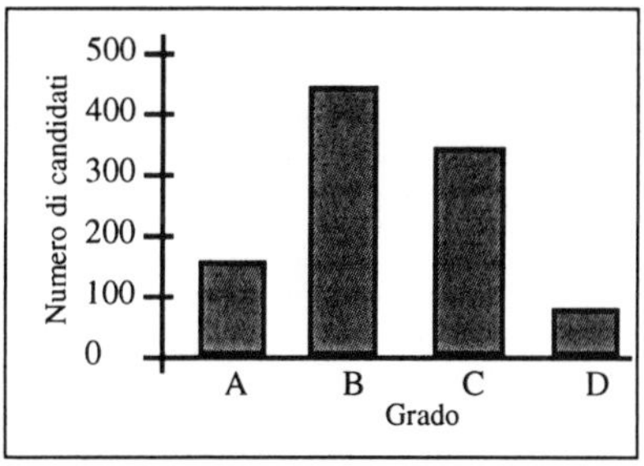

cfr.: istogramma.
Per approfondire: Hatch e Lazaraton, 1991, p. 147.
CA:102, DA:241, DE:240, EN:31, ES:104, FR:201, GA:42, IT:123, NE:357, PO:211.

124 diploma Un documento attestante che una certa persona ha superato un esame o una componente di un esame raggiungendo un punteggio corrispondente almeno alla sufficienza. Spesso viene inteso come una forma di qualificazione superiore ad un certificato.
CA:104, DA:69, DE:80, EN:103, ES:106, FR:100, GA:118, IT:124, NE:101, PO:115.

125 discorso Testo scritto o parlato visto come atto di comunicazione linguistica.
CA:106, DA:75, DE:85, EN:106, ES:108, FR:101, GA:119, IT:125, NE:103, PO:117.

126 discriminazione Il potere che ha un item di distinguere i candidati più bravi dai candidati meno bravi. Vengono usati vari indici di discriminazione. Alcuni (ad esempio il biseriale di punto, o il biseriale) si basano sulla correlazione fra il punteggio di un item ed un criterio quale il punteggio totale del test o altre misure esterne della competenza. Altri si basano invece sulla differenza di difficoltà di un item a seconda che i candidati siano più bravi o meno bravi. Nella teoria della risposta agli item, i modelli a 2 o 3 parametri indicano la capacità di discriminazione dell'item come parametro *a*.
V.: correlazione biseriale, correlazione biseriale di punto, teoria della risposta agli item.
Per approfondire: Crocker e Algina, 1986, pp. 313–320; Ebel e Frisbie, 1991,pp. 231–232.
CA:105, DA:74, DE:416, EN:112, ES:107, FR:102, GA:180, IT:126, NE:109, PO:116.

127 dispersione L' entità della variazione o della dispersione nei punteggi di un gruppo di candidati. Se la dispersione è ampia, i punteggi risultano notevolmente sparpagliati, se la dispersione è contenuta i punteggi risultano raggruppati.
V.: deviazione standard, varianza, margine di oscillazione.
CA:107, DA:353, DE:385, EN:114, ES:110, FR:103, GA:357, IT:127, NE:356, PO:118.

128 disposizioni per l'interlocutore Indicazioni scritte su come l'interlocutore deve condurre una prova di produzione orale. Loro scopo è quello di standardizzare, per quanto possibile, sia la prova in generale, sia il tipo di lingua a cui saranno sottoposti tutti i candidati, rendendo in questo modo il test più equanime ed affidabile.
CA:198, DA:324, DE:438, EN:179, ES:215, FR:34, GA:151, IT:128, NE:156, PO:321.

129 distraente Ciascuna opzione non corretta in un item a scelta multipla.
cfr.: chiave/i.
V.: item a scelta multipla.
Per approfondire: Ebel e Frisbie, 1986, pp. 176-185.
CA:110, DA:79, DE:88, EN:115, ES:111, FR:104, GA:348, IT:129, NE:8, PO:126.

130 distribuzione Nei dati relativi ad un test, quante volte compare ciascun punteggio ottenuto dai candidati. La distribuzione viene rappresentata spesso sotto forma di istogramma.

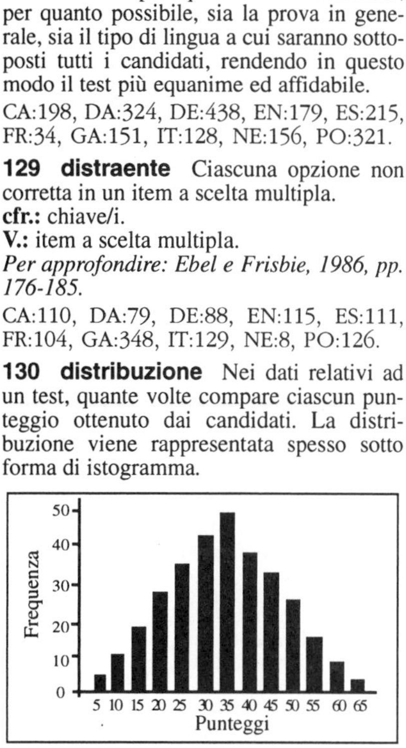

V.: distribuzione normale, asimmetria.
Per approfondire: Hatch e Lazaraton, 1991, pp. 159–178.
CA:111, DA:103, DE:434, EN:117, ES:112, FR:105, GA:103, IT:130, NE:110, PO:119.

131 distribuzione bimodale Un tipo di distribuzione con due moda o picchi, per indicare la presenza di due gruppi diversi all'interno del gruppo campione.

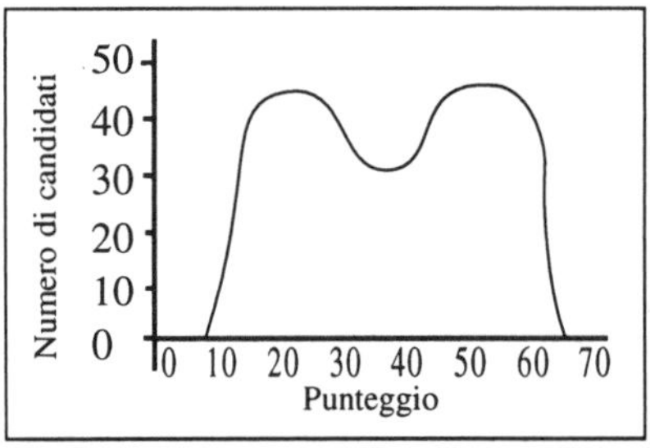

cfr.: distribuzione normale.
V.: moda.
Per approfondire: Hatch e Lazaraton, 1991,pp. 165–166.

CA:112, DA:39, DE:59, EN:34, ES:113, FR:106, GA:104, IT:131, NE:47, PO:121.

132 distribuzione della frequenza Si rimanda alla definizione di distribuzione.

CA:113, DA:107, DE:142, EN:149, ES:114, FR:107, GA:106, IT:132, NE:138, PO:122.

133 distribuzione gaussiana Si rimanda alla definizione di distribuzione normale.

CA:114, DA:114, DE:129, EN:152, ES:115, FR:91, GA:105, IT:133, NE:140, PO:110.

134 distribuzione normale Una distribuzione matematica, presupposto essenziale di diverse procedure statistiche. La distribuzione ha la forma di una campana simmetrica; inoltre la media, la mediana e la moda coincidono. Esiste un' intera famiglia di distribuzioni a seconda dei valori della media, della deviazione standard e del numero delle osservazioni. Nota anche come distribuzione gaussiana.
cfr.: distribuzione bimodale.
Per approfondire: Hatch e Lazaraton 1991, p.164.

CA:115, DA:252, DE:265, EN:252, ES:116, FR:108, GA:107, IT:134, NE:262, PO:123.

135 distribuzione troncata Un tipo di distribuzione della frequenza caratteristico di un campione che ha un intervallo più stretto rispetto alla popolazione da cui proviene, in quanto gli studenti con punteggio alto o basso non sono compresi nel campione. Un tale campione potrebbe corrispondere a un gruppo di studenti ammessi a frequentare un corso dopo essersi sottoposti ad un test di ingresso.

CA:116, DA:376, DE:1, EN:421, ES:117, FR:110, GA:108, IT:135, NE:343, PO:124.

136 domanda Termine a volte usato per riferirsi ad un tipo di item o di compito.
V.: compito, item.

CA:291, DA:357, DE:122, EN:303, ES:304, FR:315, GA:55, IT:136, NE:423, PO:323.

137 domande aperte (domande a risposta libera, domande a risposta costruita) Un tipo di item o compito, in un test di produzione scritta, che richiede al candidato di produrre e non puramente di scegliere una risposta. Lo scopo di un tale tipo di item è quello di provocare una risposta relativamente libera, che può variare, per quanto riguarda la lunghezza, da poche parole ad un breve saggio. Lo schema di correzione dovrebbe fornire una serie di risposte da considerare accettabili.

CA:292, DA:444, DE:273, EN:260, ES:305, FR:318, GA:56, IT:137, NE:273, PO:324.

138 effetti limite Le conseguenze provocate da un test che risulti troppo facile o troppo difficile per un determinato gruppo di candidati. I punteggi tendono in questo caso ad accumularsi o verso l'alto (effetto limite superiore) o verso il basso (effetto limite inferiore) della distribuzione.
V.: effetto limite inferiore, effetto limite superiore.

CA:125, DA:120, DE:139, EN:36, ES:131, FR:143, GA:177, IT:138, NE:163, PO:139.

139 effetto alone La tendenza da parte degli esaminatori, in prove d'esame di tipo soggettivo, ad essere influenzati dalla prestazione fornita dai candidati in alcuni compiti del test, attribuendo su questa base un punteggio o troppo alto o troppo basso anche ad altri compiti.
V.: effetto di squilibrio nel giudizio.

CA:117, DA:118, DE:141, EN:161, ES:127, FR:137, GA:170, IT:139, NE:164, PO:133.

140 effetto d'uso L'effetto, riscontrabile nei punteggi ottenuti in un test, dovuto alla familiarità dei candidati con i tipi di compiti o di item usati nel test stesso.

CA:119, DA:443, DE:419, EN:289, ES:123, FR:138, GA:169, IT:140, NE:298, PO:131.

141 effetto di contaminazione Effetto che si verifica quando il punteggio viene attribuito in base a fattori diversi da quelli che dovrebbero essere oggetto della verifica. Un esempio potrebbe essere quello di attribuire ad un candidato in un test di produzione scritta un punteggio più alto semplicemente perché ha una bella calligrafia.
V.: effetti di squilibrio nel giudizio.

CA:118, DA:9, DE:226, EN:71, ES:122, FR:136, GA:174, IT:141, NE:74, PO:132.

142 effetto di metodo L'effetto, riscontrabile nei punteggi ottenuti in un test,

dovuto più al metodo di testing usato che all'abilità dei candidati.
CA:121, DA:229, DE:242, EN:233, ES:126, FR:139, GA:171, IT:142, NE:244, PO:134.

143 effetto di squilibrio nel giudizio Una possibile fonte di errore nel giudizio. Può dipendere dalla tendenza dell'esaminatore alla severità o alla disponibilità o può essere determinato da una disposizione favorevole nei confronti di un certo tipo di candidati; in ogni caso può influenzare il punteggio. Esempi possono essere l'effetto di contaminazione, l'effetto alone e l'effetto sequenza.
CA:124, DA:34, DE:425, EN:313, ES:130, FR:144, GA:176, IT:143, NE:35, PO:138.

144 effetto limite inferiore Un effetto limite dovuto alla eccessiva difficoltà di un test per un particolare gruppo di candidati; ne risulta che i punteggi ottenuti risultano tutti raggruppati nella parte bassa della distribuzione.
V.: effetti limite.
CA:122, DA:42, DE:61/121, EN:146, ES:128, FR:141, GA:175, IT:144, NE:49, PO:130.

145 effetto limite superiore Un effetto limite provocato dall'eccessiva facilità di un test per un particolare gruppo di candidati, così che i punteggi ottenuti risultano tutti raggruppati nella parte alta della distribuzione.
V.:effetti limite.
CA:123, DA:219, DE:63/73, EN:44, ES:129, FR:140, GA:173, IT:145, NE:292, PO:137.

146 effetto prevaricante di una parte sull'insieme L' effetto che si verifica quando, ad esempio, i punteggi riportati in un subtest vengono messi in relazione con il punteggio dell'intero test. Dal momento che i punteggi del subtest sono compresi nel punteggio complessivo, la correlazione risulta esagerata. Esistono delle tecniche per correggere tale effetto prevaricante.
Per approfondire: Henning 1987, p.69.
CA:63, DA:62, DE:282, EN:271, ES:387, FR:51, GA:283, IT:146, NE:276, PO:331.

147 effetto retroattivo L'impatto di un test sull'insegnamento. Il fatto di sapere che gli studenti intendano sottoporsi ad un certo test può infatti spingere gli insegnanti ad adattare il proprio metodo nonché i contenuti dell'insegnamento a quanto il test richiede, con conseguenze che possono rivelarsi sia positive, sia negative.
V.: impatto.
CA:372, DA:25/436, DE:43/442, EN:28/435, ES:124/369, FR:322, GA:95, IT:147, NE:27/432, PO:135.

148 effetto sequenza Un effetto nell'attribuzione del giudizio determinato dall'ordine in cui è stata condotta la verifica.
V.: effetto di squilibrio nel giudizio.
CA:120, DA:329, DE:292, EN:360, ES:125, FR:142, GA:172, IT:148, NE:337, PO:136.

149 elaboratore di test Chi elabora e prepara un test.
CA:109, DA:392/405, DE:400/395, EN:361/399, ES:92/133, FR:145, GA:121/149, IT:149, NE:391/399, PO:141.

150 equiparazione equipercentile Un metodo per equiparare il punteggio grezzo di test per cui i punteggi si considerano equiparati solo qualora corrispondano alla stessa classificazione percentile in un gruppo di candidati.
CA:132, DA:440, DE:24, EN:127, ES:140, FR:36, GA:88, IT:150, NE:121, PO:43.

151 equiparazione lineare Un tipo di approccio al processo di equiparazione in cui il punteggio ottenuto in un test è equiparato al punteggio ottenuto in un altro test. I punteggi equivalenti nei due test hanno lo stesso valore di deviazione standard sopra o sotto la media del punteggio complessivo del test di cui fanno parte.
V.: regressione.
Per approfondire: Crocker e Algina 1986, pp. 457–461.
CA:134, DA:216, DE:17, EN:212, ES:142, FR:38, GA:91, IT:151, NE:229, PO:45.

152 equiparazione orizzontale Il processo in base al quale i punteggi di due test, approssimativamente dello stesso grado di difficoltà, vengono inseriti in un'unica scala, allo scopo di applicare gli stessi 'standards' ad entrambi.
cfr.: equiparazione verticale.
CA:133, DA:128, DE:149, EN:166, ES:141, FR:37, GA:89, IT:152, NE:170, PO:44.

153 equiparazione verticale Il processo in base al quale i punteggi di due test di diverso grado di difficoltà vengono collocati sulla medesima scala.
cfr.: equiparazione orizzontale.
Per approfondire: Crocker e Algina 1986, pp. 473–477.
CA:135, DA:432, DE:435, EN:434, ES:143, FR:39, GA:90, IT:153, NE:419, PO:46.

154 errore Nella teoria classica della misurazione del punteggio reale, un punteg-

gio osservato in un test è costituito da due componenti: un punteggio reale che riflette l'abilità della persona, ed un punteggio erroneo, influenzato cioè da vari fattori che niente hanno a che vedere con l'abilità che si intende verificare. Tale tipo di errore viene considerato casuale, vale a dire non sistematico. In aggiunta a ciò vi possono essere altri fattori all'interno di un test che possono invece influenzare regolarmente la prestazione fornita da alcuni candidati, causando quelli che vengono chiamati errori sistematici.
cfr.: errore sistematico (bias).
Per approfondire: Bachman,1990, p.167.
CA:136, DA:98, DE:116, EN:129, ES:144, FR:151, GA:122, IT:154, NE:124, PO:146.

155 errore campione In un'analisi statistica l'errore determinato dalla selezione dello specifico campione usato nello studio (ad esempio quando il campione prescelto non è rappresentativo della popolazione).
V.: popolazione.
CA:139, DA:372, DE:381, EN:341, ES:147, FR:158, GA:129, IT:155, NE:370, PO:148.

156 errore casuale Si rimanda alla definizione di errore.
CA:137, DA:408, DE:449, EN:306, ES:145, FR:152, GA:128, IT:156, NE:310, PO:147,

157 errore di 1ª specie In statistica, l'errore di respingere l'ipotesi nulla, quando è vera.
cfr.: errore di 2ª specie.
V.: ipotesi nulla.
Per approfondire: Hatch e Lazaraton 1991, p.224.
CA:140, DA:417, DE:9/117, EN:425, ES:150, FR:154, GA:126, IT:157, NE:405, PO:150.

158 errore di 2ª specie In statistica, l'errore di accettare l'ipotesi nulla, quando non è vera.
cfr.: errore di 1ª specie.
V.: ipotesi nulla.
Per approfondire: Hatch e Lazaraton 1991, p.224.
CA:141, DA:418, DE:118, EN:426, ES:151, FR:155, GA:127, IT:158, NE:406, PO:151.

159 errore di misurazione Si rimanda alla definizione di errore e di errore standard di misurazione.
CA:138, DA:240/241, DE:239/240, EN:130/231, ES:146, FR:153, GA:123/130, IT:159, NE:242/243, PO:149.

160 errore sistematico (bias) Un test o un item può essere considerato errato, se parte della propria utenza risulta avvantaggiata o svantaggiata da una qualche caratteristica del test o dell'item, non rilevante ai fini della verifica. Cause di tale errata impostazione possono essere connesse con il sesso, l'età, la formazione culturale dei candidati.
Per approfondire: Bachman,1990, pp. 271–279; Crocker e Algina, 1986, capitoli 12 e 16.
CA:40, DA:344, DE:383, EN:33, ES:384, FR:32, GA:208, IT:160, NE:46, PO:40.

161 errore sistematico di carattere culturale Un test che contenga un errore sistematico di carattere culturale si trova ad avvantaggiare o a danneggiare candidati con un determinato retroterra culturale.
V.: errore sistematico (bias).
CA:41, DA:207, DE:201, EN:85, ES:385, FR:33, GA:209, IT:161, NE:90, PO:41.

162 errore standard di misurazione Nella teoria classica del punteggio reale di un test , l'errore standard di misurazione (*Se*) è l'indicazione di un'imprecisione nella misurazione. La portata dell'errore standard di misurazione dipende dall'affidabilità (*r*) e dalla deviazione standard dei punteggi del test (*Sx*). La formula per calcolare *Se* è la seguente:

$$Se = Sx \sqrt{(1-r)}.$$

Ad esempio, se un candidato con un punteggio reale in un test di T ed un errore standard di misurazione di *Se*, ripete più volte il test, avremo che il 68% delle volte il punteggio osservato sarà nel 'range' T±*Se* e il 95% delle volte nel range T±2*Se*.
Per approfondire: Crocker e Algina 1986, pp. 122–124.
CA:143, DA:364, DE:374, EN:381, ES:149, FR:157, GA:125, IT:162, NE:362, PO:153.

163 errore standard di stima Una misura dell'accuratezza nel predire una variabile da un'altra, ad esempio nella regressione lineare. Indica gli intervalli di confidenza per punteggi basati su dei criteri.
V.: intervallo di confidenza (di una misura).
Per approfondire: Hatch e Lazaraton 1991, pp. 477–479.
CA:142, DA:361, DE:375, EN:380, ES:148, FR:156, GA:124, IT:163, NE:363, PO:152.

164 esame Una procedura per verificare le competenze o le conoscenze dei candidati tramite dei compiti orali e/o scritti. Dal risultato può dipendere il conseguimento di una qualifica (per esempio di un certificato), la possibilità di essere ammessi in una istituzione scolastica o universitaria o di accedere ad un determinato corso di studi.

cfr.: test.
Per approfondire: Bachman,1990, p.50.
CA:171/361, DA:86/306, DE:100/303, EN:133, ES:187/188, FR:164/173, GA:287/347, IT:164, NE:34/127, PO:181/182.

165 esaminatore Chi attribuisce un punteggio alla prestazione fornita da un candidato in un test, ricorrendo ad un giudizio soggettivo. Gli esaminatori sono in genere persone professionalmente qualificate, che hanno dovuto seguire uno specifico corso di preparazione e standardizzazione. Nei test di produzione orale i ruoli dell'esaminatore e dell'interlocutore vengono a volte distinti.
cfr.: interlocutore, correttore.
CA:35/172, DA:32/89, DE:55/301, EN:22/135, ES:46/189, FR:174, GA:234/346, IT:165, NE:33/130, PO:182.

166 espansione di frasi Un tipo di item in cui viene fornita come stimolo una sequenza di parole in cui è già possibile rintracciare un significato anche se mancano parole grammaticali quali: preposizioni, verbi ausiliari, articoli, ecc. Il candidato deve espandere la traccia fornitagli inserendo le parole mancanti e ricreando una frase grammaticalmente completa.
CA:99, DA:380, DE:333, EN:358, ES:18, FR:175, GA:148, IT:166, NE:441, PO:184.

167 familiarità con il test Una consuetudine con il formato del test o comunque un'esperienza in questo settore, che permettano ad un candidato di fornire una prestazione al di sopra del proprio reale livello di abilità.
CA:179, DA:406, DE:396, EN:408, ES:197, FR:314, GA:161, IT:167, NE:401, PO:191.

168 fascicolo Un modo per indicare una componente di un test. Ad esempio fascicolo della prova di comprensione della lettura, fascicolo della prova di ascolto.
CA:385, DA:393, DE:277, EN:267, ES:381, FR:182, GA:270, IT:168, NE:278, PO:87.

169 fascicolo/foglio delle domande Termine usato a volte per fare riferimento ad un foglio o ad un fascicolo che contiene il test.
CA:239, DA:263, DE:123, EN:304, ES:220, FR:180, GA:271, IT:169, NE:425, PO:145.

170 fattore-G Nella teoria dell'intelligenza si tratta di un 'fattore generale' che si ipotizza essere alla base di qualsiasi abilità di tipo cognitivo. Tale nozione si può far risalire a John Oller (1970) che la usa per dimostrare che una competenza di tipo unitario è alla base della competenza linguistica.
Per approfondire: Oller 1979, pp. 426–458, Bachman 1990, p.6.
CA:176, DA:113, DE:127, EN:153, ES:195, FR:177, GA:136, IT:170, NE:139, PO:187.

171 fattori cognitivi Fattori interni ad un processo di apprendimento o ad un processo di testing, relativi a schemi e modelli cognitivi del discente.
cfr.: fattori emozionali.
Per approfondire: Ebel e Frisbie, 1991, p. 52.
CA:178, DA:177, DE:180, EN:55, ES:196, FR:179, GA:398, IT:171, NE:65, PO:189.

172 fattori emozionali Fattori di natura non cognitiva che si riferiscono a fenomeni di tipo emotivo, o a preferenze e attitudini di chi si sottopone al test.
cfr.: fattori cognitivi.
Per approfondire: Ebel e Frisbie, 1991, p. 52.
CA:177, DA:6, DE:7, EN:9, ES:195, FR:178, GA:399, IT:172, NE:6, PO:188.

173 feedback/retroazione Reazioni e commenti delle persone coinvolte in un processo di testing (candidati, amministratori, ecc.), al fine di fornire delle basi per la valutazione del processo stesso. La raccolta delle informazioni può essere fatta in modo informale o attraverso appositi questionari.
CA:381, DA:97, DE:330, EN:144, ES:379, FR:337, GA:6, IT:173, NE:134, PO:192.

174 foglio delle risposte Il foglio su cui il candidato scrive/trascrive le sue risposte.
cfr.: lettore ottico.
CA:191, DA:37, DE:22, EN:19, ES:219, FR:181, GA:152, IT:174, NE:20, PO:198.

175 foglio/i con la produzione scritta del candidato Il/I foglio/i contenente/i le risposte di un candidato ad un test. Il termine si riferisce, in particolare, a forme di produzione scritta estesa.
CA:191, DA:261, DE:341, EN:350, ES:219, FR:343, GA:343, IT:175, NE:218, PO:170.

176 forme alternate Si rimanda alla definizione di forme equivalenti.
CA:185, DA:12, DE:11, EN:11, ES:203, NE:13, FR:193, GA:146, IT:176, PO:199.

177 forme equiparate Forme diverse della distribuzione del punteggio di un test o forme che sono state, a loro volta, trasformate in modo da poter essere usate in modo intercambiabile.
Per approfondire: Crocker e Algina 1986, Capitolo 20.

CA:186, DA:442, DE:16/14, EN:126, ES:204, FR:194, GA:145, IT:177 NE:141, PO:200.

178 forme equivalenti Diverse versioni delle stesso test. Tali versioni vengono considerate equivalenti l'una all'altra in quanto sono basate sulle stesse specificazioni e misurano la medesima competenza. Per rispondere ai rigidi requisiti dell'equivalenza nella teoria classica del testing, forme diverse dello stesso test devono avere la stessa media di difficoltà, la stessa varianza e covarianza, quando somministrate agli stessi candidati. In pratica è molto difficile arrivare ad una reale equivalenza. Vengono anche chiamate forme alternate o parallele.
cfr.: forme equiparate.
Per approfondire: Crocker e Algina 1986, p. 132.

CA:187, DA:441, DE:25, EN:128 ES:205, FR:195, GA:143, IT:178, NE:122, PO:201.

179 forme parallele Si rimanda alla definizione di forme equivalenti.

CA:188, DA:275, DE:278, EN:268, ES:206, FR:196, GA:144, IT:179, NE:279, PO:202.

180 formula predittiva di Spearman-Brown Uno strumento statistico per stimare l'affidabilità di un test nel caso in cui venga allungato o accorciato, aggiungendo o togliendo degli item. Può essere usata per predire il numero degli item necessari per raggiungere una determinata affidabilità.
Per approfondire: Crocker e Algina 1986, pp. 118–119.

CA:83, DA:349, DE:359, EN:371, ES:207, FR:197, GA:147, IT:180, NE:350, PO:203.

181 frequenza cumulativa Un modo di presentare la distribuzione dei candidati contando, per ciascuna classe di punteggi, il numero dei candidati che hanno ottenuto un punteggio compreso in tale classe e in tutte le classi inferiori.
Per approfondire: Guilford e Fruchter, 1981, pp. 35–36.

CA:189, DA:208, DE:202, EN:86, ES:208, FR:198, GA:239, IT:181, NE:91, PO:204.

182 funzionamento differenziale degli item La difficoltà relativa di un item dipende da certe caratteristiche del gruppo cui viene somministrato, quali lingua madre, sesso di appartenenza.
V.: errore sistematico (bias).

CA:195, DA:66, DE:78, EN:100, ES:209, FR:192, GA:114, IT:182, NE:100, PO:208.

183 funzione della risposta agli item Nell'ambito della teoria della risposta agli item, una funzione matematica che mette in relazione la probabilità di risposta corretta ad un item con l'abilità misurata dall'item stesso. Anche nota come funzione caratteristica dell'item.

CA:193, DA:158, DE:172, EN:194, ES:210, FR:189, GA:140, IT:183, NE:200, PO:205.

184 funzione informativa di un item Nell'ambito della teoria della risposta agli item, un indice di quante informazioni un item o un test forniscono su un candidato di un dato livello di abilità. Dipende dalla capacità discriminatoria dell'item e da quanto quest'ultimo è ben calibrato sul livello.
cfr.: funzione informativa di un test.

CA:192, DA:156, DE:169, EN:193, ES:212, FR:190, GA:138, IT:184, NE:197, PO:206.

185 funzione informativa di un test Nell'ambito della teoria della risposta agli item, un indice di quante informazioni un test fornisce su un candidato di un dato livello di abilità. E' costituito dalla somma delle funzioni informative dei vari item.
cfr.: funzione informativa di un item.
Per approfondire: Crocker e Algina 1986, pp. 369–371.

CA:194, DA:388, DE:399, EN:400, ES:211, FR:191, GA:139, IT:185, NE:394, PO:207.

186 giudizio globale Un metodo per l'attribuzione del punteggio che può essere usato in test di produzione scritta e orale. L'esaminatore da un punteggio unico sulla base dell'impressione generale che ha avuto della lingua prodotta, senza suddividerlo in punteggi diversi, ciascuno relativo ad un particolare aspetto dell'uso linguistico.
cfr.: attribuzione analitica del punteggio, attribuzione globale del punteggio.

CA:33, DA:124, DE:137, EN:155, ES:427, FR:169, GA:231, IT:186, NE:161, PO:33.

187 giudizio olistico Si rimanda alla definizione di giudizio globale.

CA:429, DA:126, DE:128, EN:164, ES:428, FR:170, GA:230, IT:187, NE:168, PO:34.

188 grado Il punteggio conseguito in un test può essere riportato in gradi, ad esempio in una scala da A ad E, dove A rappresenta il grado più alto, B una buona sufficienza, C la sufficienza, mentre D ed E rappresentano gradi negativi, vale a dire indicano il non superamento del test.
cfr.: punti.

CA:275, DA:167, DE:270, EN:156, ES:288, FR:259, GA:164, IT:188, NE:426, PO:272.

189 gruppo di riferimento Un gruppo di riferimento è un campione di una ben

definita popolazione di candidati sulla quale un test è modellato.
V.: norma.

CA:196, DA:309, DE:267, EN:324, ES:213, FR:202, GA:166, IT:189, NE:316, PO:212.

190 gruppo-norma Un vasto gruppo di individui rappresentativi del tipo di pubblico per cui un test viene progettato. La prestazione fornita dal gruppo norma è usata per interpretare i risultati di un test relativo a tale gruppo. Viene anche chiamato gruppo di riferimento.
V.: test relativo ad un gruppo-norma.

CA:197, DA:254, DE:266, EN:251, ES:214, FR:203, GA:264, IT:190, NE:265, PO:213.

191 impatto L'effetto determinato da un test, sia nel senso di una sua influenza su un più generico processo educativo, sia nel senso delle conseguenze che esso produce per chi vi si è sottoposto.
V.: effetto retroattivo.

CA:205, DA:303, DE:444, EN:167, ES:222, FR:207, GA:391, IT:191, NE:171, PO:217.

192 incremento di punteggio La differenza fra il punteggio ottenuto da un candidato in un test prima di seguire un determinato corso e il punteggio ottenuto dallo stesso candidato nello stesso test o in un test simile alla fine del corso. L'incremento del punteggio è indicativo dei progressi fatti durante il corso.

CA:352, DA:290, DE:211, EN:150, ES:32, FR:199, GA:44, IT:192, NE:434, PO:209.

193 indicazioni del compito Le istruzioni che vengono date ai candidati per guidarne le risposte ad un compito specifico all'interno di un test.
cfr.: istruzioni.

CA:384, DA:264, DE:23, EN:336, ES:229, FR:78, GA:295, IT:193, NE:219, PO:92.

194 indice D (In letteratura, noto anche come net D). Un indice di discriminazione relativo agli item di un test. Viene spesso usato per test su piccola scala in un contesto di classe e può essere calcolato manualmente. In base al punteggio totale del test, viene individuato il gruppo con punteggio più alto e il gruppo con punteggio più basso. Ciascun gruppo risulterà costi-tuito da un numero di candidati compreso fra il 10% e il 33% del numero complessivo. Il 27% rappresenta la percentuale ideale, nel caso di punteggi con distribuzione normale. Per ciascun gruppo vengono calcolate le risposte dei candidati a ciascun item e, relativamente agli item con maggiore capacità discriminante, risulterà che il gruppo dei candidati più bravi avrà un punteggio più alto rispetto al gruppo dei candidati meno bravi. La formula seguente permette di calcolare l'indice di discriminazione:

$$D = p_U - p_L ,$$

dove p_U (u=upper) è la frazione del gruppo con punteggio più alto che ha risposto correttamente all'item, mentre p_L (l=lower) è la frazione del gruppo con punteggio più basso che ha risposto correttamente all'item. Di solito si ritiene che gli item con un indice di discriminazione dello 0.3 o superiore allo 0.3 abbiano una buona capacità discriminante.

CA:206, DA:59/246, DE:72/257, EN:91/247, ES:97/223, FR:115/208, GA:102/186, IT:194, NE:92/256, PO:111/218.

195 indice della media della difficoltà degli item (mean p) E' rappresentato dalla media delle risposte corrette a tutti gli item dicotomici di un test. Ad esempio un indice di 0.5 indica che l'indice di facilità media relativo allo stesso test è di 0.5.
V.: attribuzione dicotomica del punteggio.

CA:208, DA:132, DE:246, EN:228, ES:227, FR:212, GA:190, IT:195 NE:150, PO:222.

196 indice di difficoltà Nella teoria classica del testing, la difficoltà di un item è data dalla proporzione (p) dei candidati che rispondono correttamente. Questo significa che l'indice di difficoltà dell'item è dipendente dal campione preso in esame e varia a seconda del livello di abilità dei candidati.
cfr.: indice di facilità, valore *p*.

CA:207, DA:378, DE:343, EN:101, ES:224, FR:209, GA:187, IT:196, NE:249, PO:219.

197 indice di facilità La proporzione di risposte corrette ad un item, trascritta in una scala da 0 ad 1. Si può anche esprimere in percentuale. Viene anche chiamato valore di facilità o valore *p*.
cfr.: indice di difficoltà.

CA:209, DA:191, DE:208, EN:141, ES:225, FR:210, GA:188, IT:197, NE:146, PO:220.

198 indice di leggibilità Una misura della complessità grammaticale e lessicale utilizzata per giudicare in quale misura i lettori potranno trovare un testo comprensibile. Esempi di indici di leggibilità sono l'indice di Gunning Fog e la scala di leggibilità di Flesch.

CA:210, DA:222, DE:219, EN:320, ES:226, FR:211, GA:189, IT:198, NE:223, PO:221.

199 input Materiale fornito al candidato in un compito di un test per poter produrre una risposta appropriata. Ad esempio in un test di ascolto può essere costituito da un testo registrato accompagnato da alcuni item scritti.

CA:169, DA:142, DE:408, EN:174, ES:228, FR:147, GA:199, IT:199, NE:180, PO:254.

200 intercetta delle y Nella regressione lineare il punto in cui la linea di regressione attraversa l'asse (verticale) y.
V.: regressione lineare.

CA:212, DA:438, DE:146, EN:441, ES:231, FR:215, GA:181, IT:200, NE:438, PO:226.

201 interlocutore In un test di produzione orale l'esaminatore che illustra il compito, pone le domande e più generalmente interagisce oralmente con il/i candidato/i. L'interlocutore può anche fungere da esaminatore, assegnando un punteggio ai candidati, oppure questo può essere compito di un secondo esaminatore, che è presente alla prova, ma non interagisce con il/i candidato/i.
cfr.: esaminatore.

CA:213, DA:325, DE:125, EN:178, ES:138, FR:216, GA:72, IT:201, NE:155, PO:227.

202 interpretazione di ruoli Un tipo di compito cui si ricorre a volte nei test di produzione orale. I candidati devono immaginare se stessi come attori in una determinata situazione e dunque assumere ruoli specifici.

CA:233, DA:320, DE:329, EN:334, ES:251, FR:232, GA:294, IT:202, NE:323, PO:345.

203 intervallo La differenza fra due punti della medesima scala.

CA:214, DA:148, DE:160, EN:183, ES:232, FR:218, GA:131, IT:203, NE:187, PO:228.

204 intervallo di confidenza (di una misura) Il campo di oscillazione di un valore osservato all'interno del quale con molta probabilità si colloca il vero valore. Il grado di probabilità viene definito generalmente in livelli di confidenza del 95% o 99%.

CA:215, DA:182, DE:184, EN:67, ES:233, FR:219, GA:132, IT:204, NE:45, PO:229.

205 invarianza Nella teoria della risposta agli item, l'importante presupposto per cui la difficoltà degli item e gli indici di discriminazione sono caratteristiche intrinseche e non dipendono dalla abilità dei candidati, così come la misura della abilità non dipende dagli item usati.

CA:216, DA:152, DE:164, EN:187, ES:234, FR:220, GA:120, IT:205, NE:191, PO:230.

206 ipotesi nulla Un'ipotesi che sostiene che due o più variabili non sono in relazione fra loro. Ad esempio, l'ipotesi che non vi sia differenza nella prestazione di due gruppi di candidati di lingua madre diversa, relativamente allo stesso test, è un' ipotesi nulla.
Per approfondire: Hatch e Lazaraton 1991, p. 24; Guilford e Fruchter 1981, pp. 146–147.

CA:202, DA:255, DE:271, EN:255, ES:217, FR:206, GA:167, IT:206, NE:266, PO:214.

207 istogramma Una rappresentazione grafica di una distribuzione della frequenza in cui il numero di casi per ciascuna frequenza è indicato da una colonna verticale.

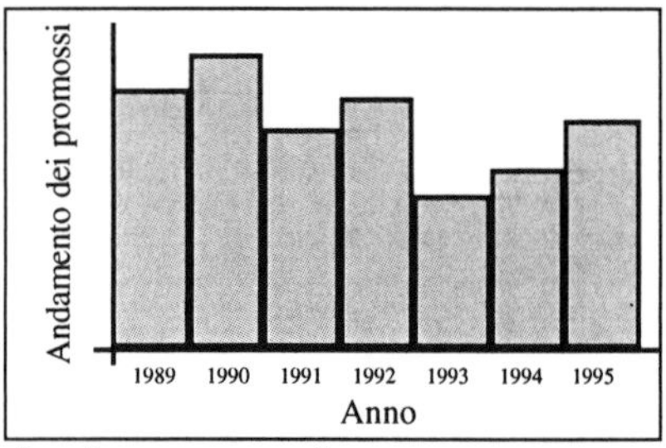

cfr.: diagramma a colonne.

CA:203, DA:125, DE:145, EN:163, ES:218, FR:204, GA:168, IT:207, NE:167, PO:215.

208 istruzioni Indicazioni generali fornite in un test o esame nella prima pagina del foglio delle risposte o di uno dei fascicoli. Loro scopo è quello di informare i candidati ad esempio sul tempo a loro disposizione per completare il test, sul numero dei compiti, o su dove trascrivere le risposte.

CA:211, DA:143, DE:391, EN:175, ES:230, FR:214, GA:402, IT:208, NE:181, PO:225.

209 item Ciascun elemento di un test a cui venga assegnato un punteggio. Ad esempio uno spazio da riempire in un cloze, una domanda a scelta multipla a tre o quattro opzioni, una frase su cui operare una trasformazione grammaticale, una domanda a cui rispondere con un prefissato numero di parole.
cfr.: compito.

CA:217, DA:154, DE:166, EN:189, ES:235, FR:221, GA:240, IT:209, NE:195, PO:231.

210 item a punti discreti Un item che verifica ad esempio un elemento specifico della struttura o del vocabolario e non è collegato ad altri item. Il testing a punti discreti è diventato popolare negli anni '60, soprattutto grazie a R. Lado.
cfr.: item/compito integrativo.
V.: item discreto.

CA:225, DA:72, DE:82, EN:110, ES:247 FR:229, GA:251, IT:210, NE:107, PO:240.

211 item a scelta multipla Un tipo di item di un test costituito da una domanda o da una affermazione incompleta accompagnate da una serie di alternative per rispondere alla domanda o completare la affermazione (opzioni). Compito del candidato è quello di scegliere l'opzione corretta (chiave) fra tre, quattro o cinque possibilità. Non viene dunque richiesto di produrre lingua. Per questo motivo gli item a scelta multipla vengono abitualmente impiegati in test di comprensione della lettura o di ascolto. Possono essere sia item discreti, sia basati su un testo.
V.: item discreto, item basato su testo.
CA:220, DA:236, DE:249/234, EN:238, ES:244, FR:222, GA:247, IT:211, NE:252, PO:236.

212 item àncora Un item incluso in due o più test. Gli item àncora, il cui formato deve essere familiare ai candidati e le cui caratteristiche devono essere ben determinate, vanno a costituire una sezione di una nuova versione di un test. Loro scopo è quello di fornire informazioni sia sul test sia sui candidati che al test si sono sottoposti, ad esempio permettendo di calibrare il test su una scala di misurazione.
cfr.: test àncora.
V.: calibratura.
CA:218, DA:16, DE:18, EN:15, ES:237, FR:225, GA:241, IT:212, NE:17, PO:232.

213 item basato su testo Un item basato su un testo; ad esempio gli item a scelta multipla riferiti ad un testo di comprensione della lettura.
CA:219, DA:387, DE:412, EN:412, ES:236/285, FR:226, GA:254, IT:213, NE:269, PO:233.

214 item di collegamento Si rimanda alla definizione di item àncora.
CA:221, DA:218, DE:432, EN:215, ES:239, FR:231, GA:250, IT:214, NE:232, PO:244.

215 item di completamento Un tipo di item in cui il candidato deve completare una frase o un testo inserendo, ad esempio, alcune parole o fornendo dettagli quali ad esempio orari o numeri telefonici.
CA:226, DA:421, DE:102, EN:60, ES:238, FR:223, GA:243, IT:215, NE:193, PO:234.

216 item di formazione di parole Un tipo di item in cui il candidato deve produrre una parola formandola da un'altra, data come input e appartenente etimologicamente alla stessa famiglia. Esempio: Questo tipo di lavoro richiede una buona........... di un lessico specialistico. (*comprendere*).
CA:227, DA:269, DE:445, EN:439, ES:231, FR:227, GA:244, IT:216, NE:437, PO:237 .

217 item di trasformazione Si rimanda alla definizione di trasformazione di frasi.
CA:229, DA:413, DE:420, EN:416, ES:245, FR:403, GA:242, IT:217, NE:402, PO:239.

218 item di vero/falso Un tipo di item selettivo, dove il candidato deve indicare se una serie di affermazioni siano vere o false in relazione ad un testo.
CA:232, DA:326, DE:326, EN:419, ES:250, FR:429, GA:245, IT:218, NE:426, PO:243.

219 item discreto Un item indipendente o isolato. Non è collegato ad un testo, ad altri item o ad altri materiali supplementari. Un esempio di un tipo di item che può essere usato in questo modo è la scelta multipla.
cfr.: item basato su testo.
CA:230, DA:71, DE:421, EN:109, ES:246, FR:228, GA:253, IT:219, NE:106, PO:241.

220 item scalare Un item il cui punteggio viene attribuito facendo riferimento ad una scala di punteggi.
V.: attribuzione politomica del punteggio.
CA:222, DA:342, DE:27, EN:342, ES:248, FR:230, GA:252, IT:220, NE:328, PO:242.

221 item/compito integrativo Termine usato per indicare item o compiti per completare i quali sono necessarie più di una abilità o sotto-abilità. Ad esempio gli item di un test di cloze, una conversazione orale, o saper leggere una lettera e produrre una risposta appropriata.
cfr.: item a punti discreti.
CA:231, DA:144, DE:156, EN:176, ES:249, FR:316, GA:248, IT:221, NE:182, PO:245.

222 KR-20 (formula 20 di Kuder-Richardson) Si rimanda alla definizione di Kuder-Richardson.
CA:234, DA:201, DE:194, EN:199, ES:252, FR:233, GA:205, IT:222, NE:210, PO:246.

223 KR-21 (formula 21 di Kuder-Richardson) Si rimanda alla definizione di Kuder-Richardson.
CA:235, DA:202, DE:195, EN:200 ES:253, FR:234, GA:206, IT:223, NE:211, PO:247.

224 Kuder-Richardson Due misure della consistenza interna introdotte da Kuder e Richardson ed usate per stimare la affidabilità di un test. KR-21 richiede meno informazioni ed è più facile da calcolare, anche se generalmente dà una stima più bassa rispetto a KR-20.
cfr.: alpha (coefficiente alfa).

V.: consistenza interna.
Per approfondire: Henning 1987, p.84.
CA:236, DA:206, DE:200, EN:201, ES:254, FR:235, GA:207, IT:224, NE:212, PO:248.

225 lessico Termine usato per vocabolario.
CA:237, DA:212, DE:221, EN:210, ES:257, FR:238, GA:213, IT:225, NE:227, PO:250.

226 lettore ottico Uno strumento elettronico usato per leggere meccanicamente le informazioni direttamente dal foglio delle risposte. I candidati o gli esaminatori possono segnare le risposte agli item o ai compiti direttamente nel foglio delle risposte e tali informazioni possono essere lette direttamente nel computer. Viene anche chiamato scanner.
CA:160/242, DA:268/327, DE:274/336, EN:261/347, ES:168/255, FR:237/342, GA:214/322, IT:226, NE:274/325, PO:249/346.

227 lingua per scopi specifici Un tipo di insegnamento o di testing che si focalizza sulla lingua usata a scopo professionale o per specifiche attività lavorative. Ad esempio l'inglese usato come lingua comune per il controllo del traffico aereo, o l'italiano per scopi commerciali.
CA:238, DA:95, DE:111, EN:205, ES:256, FR:236, GA:385, IT:227, NE:378, PO:251.

228 lista di controllo Una lista di domande cui rispondere o di punti da trattare. Spesso viene usata nel testing linguistico come strumento di riflessione e di analisi.
CA:240, DA:48, DE:64, EN:48, ES:258, FR:239, GA:351, IT:228, NE:58, PO:252.

229 livello Il livello di competenza che si richiede ad uno studente per poter essere inserito in una certa classe o il livello rappresentato da un determinato test. In quest'ultimo caso si parla spesso di più livelli, comunemente e genericamente definiti: 'elementare', 'intermedio', 'avanzato', ecc.
CA:270, DA:247, DE:260, EN:209, ES:283, FR:259, GA:210, IT:229, NE:258, PO:272.

230 livello 'Treshold' Una descrizione 'cardine' in termini funzionali della competenza linguistica in una lingua straniera ad un livello elementare, pubblicata dal Consiglio d'Europa nel 1976 per la lingua inglese, ed aggiornata nel 1990. Esistono diverse versioni per le varie lingue europee, la versione italiana denominata Livello Soglia è stata pubblicata, sempre dal Consiglio d'Europa, nel 1981.
CA:272, DA:419, DE:414, EN:414, ES:285, FR:262, GA:212, IT:230, NE:386, PO:275.

231 livello 'Waystage' Una descrizione dettagliata di un livello elementare di competenza in una lingua straniera, pubblicata per la prima volta dal Consiglio d'Europa nel 1977 per la lingua inglese e aggiornata nel 1990. Fornisce degli obiettivi meno impegnativi di quelli indicati nel livello 'Treshold' e può corrispondere alla metà della preparazione richiesta dal livello 'Treshold'.
cfr.: livello 'Treshold'.
CA:271, DA:437, DE:443, EN:436, ES:284, FR:261, GA:211, IT:231, NE:433, PO:274.

232 logit Nella teoria della risposta agli item corrisponde ad un' unità di misura, ed è derivato dal logaritmo naturale del rapporto fra la probabilità di risposta corretta e la probabilità di risposta errata, vale a dire un logaritmo della probabilità. La differenza in logit fra l'abilità di un candidato e la difficoltà dell'item è il logaritmo che indica la probabilità che ha un candidato di rispondere correttamente all'item.
Per approfondire: Henning 1987, pp. 118–126.
CA:241, DA:220, DE:227, EN:218, ES:259, FR:240, GA:216, IT:232, NE:234, PO:253.

233 margine di oscillazione Una misura della dispersione delle osservazioni. Corrisponde alla distanza fra i punteggi più alti e quelli più bassi.
Per approfondire: Hatch e Lazaraton 1991, pp. 169–170.
CA:12, DA:431, DE:431, EN:308, ES:260, FR:241, GA:285, IT:233, NE:311, PO:12.

234 media Una misura della tendenza centrale. La media del punteggio relativa ad una 'amministrazione' di un test è ottenuta sommando tutti i punteggi ottenuti e dividendo quindi per il numero complessivo dei punteggi.
cfr.: mediana, moda.
V.: tendenza centrale (misura della tendenza centrale).
Per approfondire: Hatch e Lazaraton 1991, pp. 161–163.
CA:250, DA:231, DE:244, EN:227, ES:261, FR:257, GA:226, IT:234, NE:151, PO:255.

235 mediana Il punteggio al centro della distribuzione in un gruppo di punteggi già preordinati. Metà dei punteggi risultano sopra la mediana l'altra metà sotto.
V.: tendenza centrale (misura della tendenza centrale).
cfr.: media, moda.
Per approfondire: Hatch e Lazaraton 1991, p. 161.
CA:244, DA:228, DE:232, EN:232, ES:263, FR:242, GA:3, IT:235, NE:239, PO:256.

236 metodo del test L'abilità linguistica può essere verificata usando una

varietà di metodi quali: scelta multipla, cloze, composizione, conversazione, ecc. E' stato osservato che il metodo interagisce con l'abilità, nella misurazione della prestazione fornita dai candidati.
V.: caratteristiche del metodo del test.
Per approfondire: Bachman 1990, p. 77.
CA:248, DA:395, DE:401, EN:401, ES:266, FR:245, GA:257, IT:236, NE:396, PO:259.

237 metodo di rappresentazione delta Un metodo per osservare il diverso funzionamento degli item. Viene usato per identificare gli item che amplificano o riducono al minimo le differenze di prestazione all'interno di un gruppo. Si basa sulla difficoltà classica degli item (valori-*p*). I valori-*p* sono convertiti per normalizzare i punteggi *z* e vengono riportati in coppia in un grafico per mostrare la difficoltà relativa degli item per i due gruppi in questione.
V.: funzionamento differenziale degli item.
Per approfondire: Crocker e Algina, 1986, pp. 388–390.
CA:249, DA:61, DE:74, EN:92, ES:267, FR:246, GA:256, IT:237, NE:93, PO:260.

238 misurazione In generale il processo in base al quale è possibile misurare qualcosa per mezzo di un'unità fissa di misurazione. Ad esempio un metro consente di misurare la lunghezza. Nelle scienze sociali, la misurazione fa spesso riferimento alla quantificazione delle caratteristiche degli individui, caratteristiche quali, ad esempio, la competenza linguistica.
Per approfondire: Bachman 1990, Capitolo 2.
CA:245, DA:242, DE:241, EN:230, ES:264, FR:243, GA:395, IT:238, NE:245, PO:257.

239 misurazione indipendente da un campione In ricerca, un'interpretazione dei risultati non dipendente dal campione usato.
V.: campione.
CA:247, DA:373, DE:382, EN:339, ES:265, FR:244, GA:396, IT:239, NE:371, PO:258.

240 moda Il punto nella distribuzione di una serie di punteggi in cui si concentra il maggior numero di punteggi: il punto più alto di una curva di distribuzione.

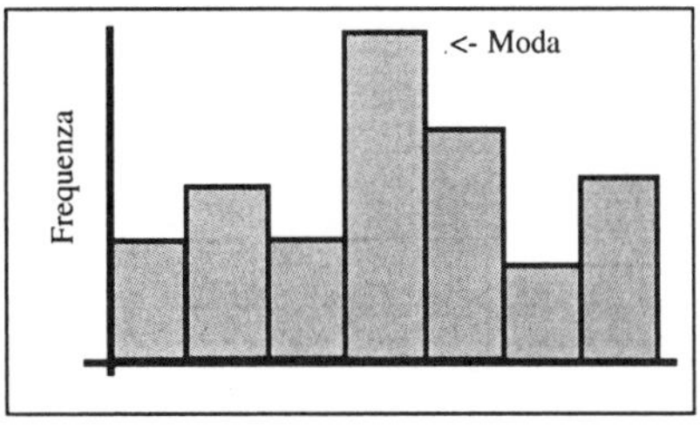

cfr.: distribuzione bimodale, media, mediana.
V.: tendenza centrale (misura della tendenza centrale).
Per approfondire: Hatch e Lazaraton 1991, pp. 160–161.
CA:252, DA:232, DE:247, EN:235, ES:268, FR:247, GA:255, IT:240, NE:248, PO:261.

241 modello a due parametri Nella teoria della risposta agli item, un modello che tiene conto di un parametro di discriminazione degli item oltre che del parametro abilità/difficoltà.
cfr.: modello ad un parametro, modello Rasch.
V.: teoria della risposta agli item.
CA:258, DA:411, DE:454, EN:424, ES:271, FR:248, GA:298, IT:241, NE:404, PO:264.

242 modello ad un parametro Nell' ambito della teoria della risposta agli item, un modello operante su una scala singola, che rappresenta sia la difficoltà (del compito) sia l'abilità (del candidato). Tale modello non prende in considerazione variabili quali la capacità discriminatoria di in item o il fattore casualità.
cfr.: modello Rasch.
CA:255, DA:92, DE:99, EN:259, ES:273, FR:249, GA:296, IT:242, NE:118, PO:265.

243 modello cognitivo La teoria relativa al modo in cui si acquisisce una conoscenza sia concettualmente sia come processo di apprendimento. L'importanza di tale teoria nel testing linguistico è dovuta alla sua influenza sulla scelta del metodo di testing nonché dei contenuti del test in elaborazione.
CA:253, DA:178, DE:181, EN:56, ES:269, FR:250, GA:297, IT:243, NE:64, PO:262.

244 modello di credito parziale Nella teoria della risposta agli item un modello per trattare dati di tipo scalare. Un modello appropriato dunque per analizzare le risposte date ad item di completamento di frasi, item cioè che ricorrono, per assegnare il punteggio, ad una scala ad esempio dall'1 al 3, ma utilizzabile anche per una conversazione orale, dove vengono usate scale di punteggi diverse, per giudicare la prestazione fornita dai candidati.
cfr.: modello Rasch ad aspetti multipli, modello di scala di classificazione.
V.: modello Rasch.
Per approfondire: Wright e Masters 1982, pp. 40–48.
CA:257, DA:278, DE:281, EN:272, ES:270, FR:253, GA:301, IT:244, NE:282, PO:267.

245 modello di risposta Un esempio

del tipo di risposta che si richiede per un compito aperto. L'esempio viene fornito dalla stessa persona che ha preparato il compito. Può essere inserito all'interno di uno schema per la correzione e l'attribuzione del punteggio come modello per i correttori.

CA:261, DA:233, DE:253, EN:236, ES:376, FR:333, GA:156, IT:245, NE:21, PO:340.

246 modello di scala di classificazione Un'estensione del modello Rasch per poter trattare anche dati di tipo scalare, quali, ad esempio, quelli che si possono ottenere assegnando un punteggio di merito alla prestazione fornita dai candidati in una prova di produzione orale.
cfr.: modello Rasch.
V.: modello di credito parziale.
Per approfondire: Wright B.D. e Masters G.N., 1982, rating Scale Analysis Chigago, MESA Press.

CA:254, DA:173, DE:236, EN:316, ES:272, FR:251, GA:303, IT:246, NE:41, PO:263.

247 modello probabilistico Un modello in cui rapporti di causa-effetto (quali la difficoltà degli item e l'abilità dei candidati nella prestazione fornita in un test) vengono spiegati in termini di grado di probabilità. Il modello Rasch è un esempio di modello probabilistico.

CA:262, DA:295, DE:297, EN:294, ES:274, FR:255, GA:299, IT:247, NE:430, PO:269.

248 modello Rasch Un modello matematico, noto anche come modello logistico semplice, che mette in relazione la probabilità che ha un candidato di completare un compito e la differenza fra l'abilità dello stesso candidato e la difficoltà del compito. Equivalente da un punto di vista matematico al modello ad un solo parametro nella teoria della risposta agli item. Il modello Rasch è stato esteso in vari modi, ad esempio per verificare risposte di tipo scalare, o per spiegazioni dei molteplici aspetti relativi alla difficoltà di un compito.
V.: teoria della risposta agli item, modello Rasch ad aspetti multipli, modello di credito parziale, modello di scala di classificazione.
Per approfondire: Henning 1987, pp. 117–125.

CA:259, DA:305, DE:316, EN:310, ES:275, FR:252, GA:302, IT:248, NE:313, PO:266.

249 modello Rasch ad aspetti multipli Una estensione del modello Rasch, che consente di modellare le probabilità di risposta sulla base di una aggiuntiva combinazione di aspetti diversi. Ad esempio, la prestazione fornita da un candidato in un compito di produzione scritta può essere modellata per poter riflettere non solo la difficoltà del compito ma anche la severità dell'esaminatore. Tale estensione del modello Rasch è stata adattata a programmi di computer, ad esempio il programma FACETS.
V.: modello Rasch.
Per approfondire: Linacre J. M. 1989, Many Facets Rasch Measurement, Chicago, MESA Press.

CA:260, DA:235, DE:289, EN:220, ES:276, FR:254, GA:300, IT:249, NE:236, PO:268.

250 moderazione a) Fase del processo di sviluppo di item o compiti da inserire in un test. In tale fase i materiali vengono esaminati criticamente da una serie di esperti (quali ad esempio insegnanti o chi prepara test) che decidono quali accettare, magari apportando delle modifiche.

b) Nell' espressione del giudizio, intervento di un moderatore per rettificare il punteggio assegnato da un esaminatore.
cfr.: controllo.

CA:263, DA:410, DE:31, EN:237, ES:277, FR:256, GA:260, IT:250, NE:247, PO:270.

251 *N, n* Numero. La lettera maiuscola *N* è spesso usata per indicare il numero dei casi in uno studio o di individui in una popolazione, mentre la lettera minuscola *n* spesso è usata per indicare il numero in un campione o sottogruppo. Ad esempio:'Al test si sono sottoposti dei laureati in ingegneria (*N*= 600). Il 10% erano donne (*n*= 60)'.

CA:269, DA:248, DE:256, EN:244, ES:282, FR:258, GA:261, IT:251, NE:259, PO:271.

252 norma Uno standard di performance. In un test standardizzato la norma è determinata dalla documentazione sui punteggi di un vasto gruppo di candidati. La norma o gli standard basati sulla performance di questo gruppo vengono poi usati per valutare le performance di altri gruppi di candidati dello stesso o simile tipo.
V.: gruppo-norma, test relativo ad un gruppo-norma.

CA:273, DA:250, DE:263, EN:250, ES:286, FR:264, GA:262, IT:252, NE:261, PO:278.

253 normalizzazione Cambiamenti apportati al punteggio in modo tale da trasformare la distribuzione in una distribuzione normale. Ciò comporta l'uso di una gradazione equipercentile.
cfr.: punteggio standard.

CA:274, DA:253, DE:264, EN:253, ES:287, FR:263, GA:263, IT:253, NE:263, PO:279.

254 obiettivi Le conoscenze, le competenze e le attitudini che un corso o program-

ma educativo si è prefissato di raggiungere.
CA:278, DA:244, DE:216, EN:256, ES:291, FR:288, GA:359, IT:254, NE:112, PO:293.

255 obiettivo dell'apprendimento Lo scopo o il risultato che si desidera raggiungere tramite una attività di apprendimento.
CA:277, DA:136, DE:215, EN:208, ES:290, FR:289, GA:360, IT:255, NE:217, PO:292.

256 occorrenze Un conteggio di quante volte una data parola o un dato tipo di parola ricorre in un testo. Nel testing linguistico il calcolo delle occorrenze può risultare particolarmente utile qualora sia necessario produrre o reperire testi sulla base di particolari indicazioni lessicali.
CA:190, DA:270, DE:143, EN:440, ES:362, FR:75, GA:67, IT:256, NE:436, PO:95.

257 omogeneità La caratteristica di un test o subtest in base alla quale si suppone che gli item misurino la stessa competenza. Può essere anche intesa come la caratteristica di un gruppo di persone che condividano le medesime caratteristiche. Il grado di omogeneità è espresso dall'indice di affidabilità.
CA:204, DA:127, DE:148, EN:165, ES:221, FR:205, GA:22, IT:257, NE:169, PO:216.

258 opzioni La serie delle possibilità di risposta fra cui va scelta la risposta corretta, in un item a scelta multipla o in un compito di abbinamento.
CA:279, DA:425, DE:38, EN:262, ES:292, FR:290, GA:293, IT:258, NE:14, PO:294.

259 parametro Una caratteristica di una popolazione; ad esempio la deviazione standard di una popolazione.
cfr.:dato statistico/statistica.
CA:280, DA:276, DE:279, EN:269, ES:293, FR:291, GA:272, IT:259, NE:280, PO:296.

260 parametro A Il parametro, nella teoria della risposta agli item, relativo alla capacità discriminatoria di un item.
V.: teoria della risposta agli item.
Per approfondire: Bachman, 1990, p. 204.
CA:281, DA:1, DE:84, EN:1, ES:294, FR:292, GA:273, IT:260, NE:1, PO:297.

261 parametro B Il parametro, nella teoria della risposta agli item, che si riferisce al grado di difficoltà di un item.
V.: teoria della risposta agli item.
Per approfondire: Bachman, 1990, p.204.
CA:282, DA:24, DE:170, EN:26, ES:295, FR:293, GA:274, IT:261, NE:26, PO:298.

262 parametro C Uno dei parametri della teoria della risposta agli item relativo al fattore casualità.
V.: teoria della risposta agli item.
Per approfondire: Bachman, 1990, p.204.
CA:283, DA:44, DE:318, EN:37, ES:296, FR:294, GA:275, IT:262, NE:50, PO:299.

263 parametro della casualità Si rimanda alla definizione di parametro C.
CA:284, DA:122, DE:319, EN:159, ES:297, FR:295, GA:277, IT:263, NE:160, PO:301.

264 parametro della difficoltà Si rimanda alla definizione di parametro B.
CA:285, DA:379, DE:344, EN:102, ES:298, FR:296, GA:276, IT:264, NE:250, PO:300.

265 parlante nativo Chi ha acquisito la lingua come lingua madre.
CA:286, DA:234, DE:255, EN:245, ES:216, FR:217, GA:47, IT:265, NE:255, PO:190.

266 percentile I 99 punti di una scala che dividono una distribuzione di frequenza in 100 gruppi di uguale dimensione. Il cinquantesimo percentile (P50) è detto mediana. I quartili dividono la distribuzione in quattro gruppi uguali.
Per approfondire: Hatch e Lazaraton 1991, pp. 187–188.
CA:287, DA:280, DE:285, EN:275, ES:299, FR:49, GA:279, IT:266, NE:284, PO:302.

267 performance/esecuzione L'azione di produrre lingua parlando o scrivendo. Il termine 'performance', nel senso di lingua realmente prodotta dalla gente, è spesso contrapposto al termine competenza, che invece sta ad indicare ciò che è alla base della conoscenza di una lingua.
cfr.: competenza.
V.: test di performance/esecuzione.
Per approfondire: Bachman 1990, pp. 52 e 108.
CA:5, DA:282, DE:283, EN:277, ES:9, FR:297, GA:141, IT:267, NE:286, PO:304.

268 ponderazione Attribuzione di un diverso punteggio massimo ad un item di un test, o ad un suo compito, o ad una sua componente per variarne il contributo relativo rispetto ad altre parti del medesimo test. Ad esempio se a tutti gli item del compito n° 1 di un test è stato attribuito un punteggio doppio, ne risulterà che il compito n° 1 avrà sul punteggio totale un peso maggiore rispetto agli altri compiti.
Per approfondire: Ebel e Frisbie 1991, pp. 214–216.
CA:290, DA:435, DE:136, EN:438, ES:303, FR:302, GA:439, IT:268, NE:434, PO:306.

269 popolazione Un insieme completo di valori. Ad esempio tutti i possibili candi-

dati ad un esame. In statistica viene anche chiamato universo di punteggi.
cfr.: campione.

CA:289, DA:292, DE:290, EN:285, ES:302, FR:303, GA:280, IT:269, NE:294, PO:308.

270 portfolio di valutazioni Una tecnica di valutazione per cui un candidato raccoglie esempi del proprio lavoro attraverso un certo arco di tempo, per presentarli come manifestazioni della propria abilità.

CA:386, DA:293, DE:291, EN:286, ES:185, FR:304, GA:237, IT:270, NE:37, PO:309.

271 post-test Un test o altre forme di misurazione somministrate alla fine di un corso. Il raffronto con i risultati di un test somministrato all'inizio del corso dovrebbe dimostrare l'efficacia del corso stesso.
cfr.: pre-test.

CA:327, DA:345, DE:5, EN:287, ES:336, FR:305, GA:179, IT:271, NE:295, PO:310.

272 pre-test Un test somministrato prima dell'inizio di un corso. I risultati del pre-test potranno essere confrontati con i risultati ottenuti in un altro test somministrato alla fine del corso per poter valutare l'efficacia del corso stesso.
cfr.: post-test.

CA:333, DA:104, DE:440, EN:292, ES:338, FR:306, GA:290, IT:272, NE:299, PO:312.

273 pretesting Una fase nel processo di sviluppo dei materiali di un test in cui gli item vengono sperimentati su un campione rappresentativo della popolazione finale, onde determinarne la difficoltà. Analisi statistiche consentiranno di selezionare gli item più adeguati che potranno essere poi inseriti negli esami effettivi.
cfr.: sperimentazione.

CA:174, DA:105, DE:436, EN:293, ES:191, FR:307, GA:289, IT:273, NE:302, PO:311.

274 procedure non parametriche Procedure di tipo statistico che non presuppongono che i dati derivino da un particolare tipo di distribuzione, o che siano basati su una scala a intervalli. Il 'chi-quadrato' ne è un tipico esempio.
cfr.: procedure parametriche.
Per approfondire: Hatch e Lazaraton 1991, pp. 237–239.

CA:294, DA:131, DE:259, EN:249, ES:308, FR:309, GA:258, IT:274, NE:257, PO:315.

275 procedure parametriche Procedure di tipo statistico che presuppongono che i dati siano distribuiti normalmente e vengano misurati su scale a intervalli o scale di rapporto. In pratica le procedure parametriche vengono usate quando i dati forniscono casi sufficienti per arrivare ad una distribuzione normale.
cfr.: procedure non parametriche.
Per approfondire: Hatch e Lazaraton 1991, pp. 237–238.

CA:295, DA:277, DE:280, EN:270, ES:309, FR:310, GA:259, IT:275, NE:281, PO:316.

276 procedure per provocare risposte Una tecnica per portare il candidato a produrre una risposta. Viene abitualmente usata in un contesto di risposta orale all'interno di un test di produzione orale.
Per approfondire: Hughes, 1989, pp. 104–110.

CA:293, DA:8, DE:212, EN:123, ES:307, FR:308, GA:162, IT:276, NE:320, PO:314.

277 progetto di un metodo multiplo per tratti caratteristici distinti Un progetto sperimentale usato nella validazione di costrutto, in base al quale una serie di presunti tratti caratteristici distinti vengono misurati con metodi diversi. L'analisi dovrebbe dimostrare, ad esempio, che misure dell'abilità di ascolto, ottenute con metodi diversi, sono maggiormente correlate fra loro rispetto a misure di abilità diverse ottenute con lo stesso metodo di test.
Per approfondire: Bachman 1990, pp. 263–265.

CA:108, DA:238, DE:252, EN:243, ES:109, FR:299, GA:111, IT:277, NE:254, PO:305.

278 punteggio a) Il numero complessivo dei punti che un candidato raggiunge in un test, sia prima che vengano trasferiti su scala (punteggio grezzo), sia dopo (punteggio scalare).

b) Valori numerici attribuiti a 'performance' dei candidati, nel rispondere a dei compiti.
cfr.: misurazione.

CA:342, DA:328, DE:312, , EN:348, ES:345, FR:275, GA:328, IT:278, NE:331, PO:280.

279 punteggio 'stanine' Una procedura per raggruppare i punteggi di un test in nove gruppi sulla base di una distribuzione normale. Sia nel gruppo con punteggio più alto che nel gruppo con punteggio più basso è compreso il 4% dei candidati. La percentuale dei candidati per ogni gruppo è illustrata nel grafico.

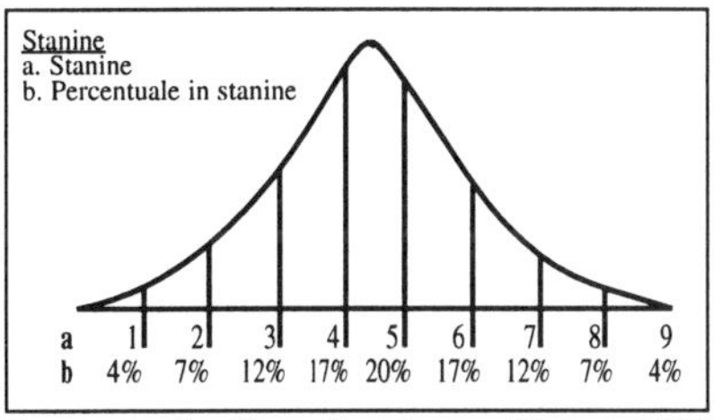

Per approfondire: Crocker e Algina 1986, pp. 446–447.

CA:344, DA:367, DE:377, EN:384, ES:176, FR:282, GA:332, IT:279, NE:365, PO:284.

280 punteggio di taglio Il punteggio minimo che un candidato deve raggiungere per poter ottenere un certo grado in un test o in un esame. In un test di padronanza è il punteggio che indica il livello minimo di padronanza richiesta.
V.: test di padronanza, testing di competenza minima.
cfr.: punteggio sufficiente/sufficienza.
Per approfondire: Bachman, 1990, pp. 214–215; Crocker e Algina, pp. 421–428. .

CA:359, DA:58, DE:199, EN:90, ES:351, FR:277, GA:338, IT:280, NE:57, PO:282.

281 punteggio di un item Nell'analisi degli item è la somma delle risposte corrette date ad un item.

CA:345, DA:160, DE:171, EN:196, ES:346, FR:267, GA:336, IT:281, NE:202, PO:60.

282 punteggio grezzo Il punteggio di un test che non ha subito manipolazioni statistiche del tipo: trasformazioni, ponderazioni, trasferimenti su scale di misurazione.
V.: punteggio.

CA:348, DA:321, DE:328, EN:319, ES:348, FR:276, GA:329, IT:282, NE:324, PO:281.

283 punteggio osservato Il punteggio ottenuto da un candidato. Nell'ambito della teoria classica del testing lo si considera costituito dal punteggio reale più eventuali errori di misurazione.
V.: errore, punteggio reale.

CA:353, DA:183, DE:49, EN:258, ES:352, FR:279, GA:331, IT:283, NE:429, PO:285.

284 punteggio ponderato di un test Il punteggio assegnato ad un candidato in un test dopo che è stato ponderato.

CA:354, DA:434, DE:135, EN:437, ES:354, FR:280, GA:339, IT:284, NE:159, PO:286.

285 punteggio reale Il punteggio che il candidato otterrebbe se non vi fossero stati errori al momento della verifica o dell'attribuzione del punteggio. Un concetto fondamentale nella teoria classica del testing.

CA:357, DA:415, DE:441, EN:420, ES:357, FR:285, GA:335, IT:285, NE:431, PO:289.

286 punteggio scalare Un punteggio ottenuto tramite la costruzione di una scala.
V.: costruzione di scale.

CA:349, DA:340, DE:354, EN:345, ES:349, FR:278, GA:337, IT:286, NE:153, PO:283.

287 punteggio standard Un punteggio trasformato linearmente da un gruppo di punteggi. La media e la deviazione standard vengono fissate al valore richiesto da chi deve fare uso dei punteggi. Esempi di punteggi standard sono i punteggi *z* e *t*.
cfr.: punteggio 'stanine', punteggio *t*, punteggio *z*.
Per approfondire: Ebel e Frisbie 1991, pp. 67–68.

CA:350, DA:365, DE:376, EN:382, ES:350, FR:281, GA:333, IT:287, NE:364, PO:291.

288 punteggio sufficiente/sufficienza Il punteggio minimo che un candidato deve raggiungere per poter superare un test o un esame.
cfr.: punteggio di taglio.

CA:23, DA:36, DE:52, EN:273, ES:30, FR:277, GA:278, IT:288 NE:341, PO:282.

289 punteggio *t* Un'estensione del punteggio *z*. Non tiene conto dei decimali e dei segni negativi. Il punteggio *t* corrisponde a dieci volte il punteggio $z + 50$. La distribuzione ha una media di 50 e una deviazione standard di 10.
V.: punteggio *z*.
Per approfondire: Ebel e Frisbie 1991, p.68.

CA:355, DA:384, DE:388, EN:422, ES:355, FR:283, GA:367, IT:289, NE:376, PO:287.

290 punteggio trasformato Un punteggio grezzo che ha subito una trasformazione matematica, o ai fini di una trasposizione su scala o ai fini di una ponderazione.
Per approfondire: Ebel e Frisbie 1991, pp. 64–70.

CA:356, DA:414, DE:415, EN:417, ES:356, FR:284, GA:334, IT:290, NE:158, PO:288.

291 punteggio *z* Un punteggio standard molto frequente con una media di 0 e una deviazione standard di 1. La formula per calcolare i punteggi *z* è la seguente:

$$z = (X - \overline{X}) \div S_x.$$

Dove:
z = punteggio *z*.

$\underline{X}$ = punteggio del test.
X = media del punteggio del test.
S_x = deviazione standard dei punteggi del test.
cfr.: punteggio *t*.
V.: punteggio standard.
Per approfondire: Ebel e Frisbie, 1991, p.68.

CA:358, DA:439, DE:446, EN:442, ES:358, FR:286, GA:441, IT:291, NE:439, PO:290.

292 punti Il numero complessivo dei punti disponibili per ciascun item, subtest o test, o il numero dei punti disponibili per ciascuna risposta ad un item, subtest o test.

CA:342, DA:287, DE:313, EN:224, ES:44, FR:287, GA:224, IT:292, NE:60, PO:105.

293 punto chiave della verifica L'elemento centrale di un item: come attraverso l'item, si cerca di far emergere la conoscenza.

CA:128, DA:399, DE:309, EN:409, ES:289, FR:300, GA:281, IT:293, NE:384, PO:307.

294 qualificazione Un riconoscimento a seguito di un corso o tirocinio oppure di un test che qualifichi una persona a svolgere una determinata attività o lavoro. Un certificato di competenza linguistica può essere considerato una forma di qualificazione per determinate finalità.
cfr.: certificato, diploma.

CA:360, DA:209, DE:314, EN:302, ES:405, FR:313, GA:46, IT:294, NE:214, PO:322.

295 radice quadrata della media Viene comunemente indicata come varianza, nell'analisi della varianza (ANOVA). **V.:** ANOVA.

CA:251, DA:230, DE:245, EN:229, ES:262, FR:47, GA:227, IT:295, NE:149, PO:319.

296 rapporto F Nell'analisi della varianza, il rapporto stimato che indica se le differenze fra le medie dei gruppi sono significative statisticamente; per esempio se un gruppo è riuscito meglio di un altro in un test di lingua.
V.: forme alternate.
Per approfondire: Hatch e Lazaraton, 1991, pp. 315–317.

CA:364, DA:94, DE:109, EN:139, ES:368, FR:319, GA:66, IT:296, NE:132, PO:332.

297 registro Una ben definità varietà di lingua orale o scritta, caratteristica di una particolare attività o di un particolare grado di formalità.

CA:368, DA:310, DE:366, EN:325, ES:364, FR:323, GA:291, IT:297, NE:317, PO:327.

298 regressione Una tecnica per predire il valore più probabile di una variabile (la variabile dipendente) sulla base dei valori noti di un'altra o di altre variabili (variabili indipendenti).
Per approfondire: Hatch e Lazaraton 1991, pp. 467–480; Guilford e Fruchter 1981, pp. 346–361.

CA:369, DA:311, DE:321, EN:326, ES:365, FR:324, GA:4, IT:298, NE:318, PO:328.

299 regressione lineare Una regressione tecnica che presuppone una relazione lineare fra la variabile dipendente e la variabile indipendente.

CA:370, DA:215, DE:223, EN:213, ES:366, FR:325, GA:5, IT:299, NE:230, PO:329.

300 regressione multipla Una tecnica statistica per stabilire gli effetti lineari di alcune variabili indipendenti su una singola variabile dipendente. Ad esempio se prendiamo come variabile dipendente la difficoltà del compito, possono essere studiati gli effetti del tipo di compito, la difficoltà lessicale, ecc.
V.: variabile indipendente, regressione.
Per approfondire: Hatch e Lazaraton 1991, pp. 480–486.

CA:371, DA:117, DE:251, EN:242, ES:367, FR:326, GA:182, IT:300, NE:240, PO:330.

301 replicabilità La possibilità di replicare i dati emersi da una specifica ricerca in più di una occasione, con lo scopo di avvalorare ulteriormente l'affidabilità dei risultati.

CA:373, DA:189, DE:324, EN:329, ES:370, FR:335, GA:185, IT:301, NE:165, PO:333.

302 rho di Spearman Si rimanda alla definizione di correlazione per 'ranghi' di Spearman.

CA:383, DA:352, DE:362, EN:374, ES:380, FR:339, GA:292, IT:302, NE:348, PO:344.

303 riconoscimento (a) La concessione, da parte di istituzioni ufficiali, quali ministeri, università o altre, di un riconoscimento ufficiale ad un test.

CA:4, DA:10, DE:8, EN:5, ES:1, FR:4, GA:92, IT:303, NE:3, PO:325.

(b) L'atto che un' istituzione fa nell' accettare formalmente un titolo di studio o di specializzazione per uno scopo specifico; ad esempio, l'ammissione ad un corso di studio post-laurea.

CA:365, DA:15, DE:269, EN:323, ES:361 FR:321, GA:9, IT:303, NE:123, PO:325.

304 ricostruzione di scale Si rimanda alla definizione di costruzione di scale.

CA:367, DA:314, DE:258, EN:330, ES:389, FR:320, GA:29, IT:304, NE:166, PO:326.

305 risposta Il comportamento del candidato provocato dall'input di un test. Ad

esempio la risposta data ad un item a scelta multipla o quanto prodotto in un test di produzione scritta.
cfr.: input, stimolo.
CA:374, DA:315, DE:21, EN:331, ES:371, FR:327, GA:153, IT:305, NE:319, PO:334.

306 risposta attesa La risposta o le risposte che chi ha elaborato l'item intendeva provocare.
CA:377, DA:106, DE:105, EN:137, ES:374, FR:328, GA:157, IT:306, NE:32, PO:338.

307 risposta corretta La risposta considerata corretta al momento di assegnare il punteggio ad un test.
CA:375, DA:190, DE:327, EN:333, ES:373, FR:331, GA:155, IT:307, NE:204, PO:337.

308 risposta estesa Un tipo di risposta ad un item o ad un compito in cui il candidato deve produrre (non semplicemente scegliere) una risposta che non sia più lunga di una o due frasi.
cfr.: risposte brevi.
CA:378, DA:423, DE:35, EN:138, ES:375, FR:332, GA:159, IT:308, NE:407, PO:339.

309 risposta produttiva Un tipo di risposta scritta ad un item di un test, che implichi una produzione e non semplicemente una scelta fra un certo numero di opzioni.
cfr.: risposta selettiva.
V.: risposta.
CA:376, DA:185, DE:126, EN:70, ES:372, FR:330, GA:154, IT:309, NE:272, PO:336.

310 risposta selettiva Una forma di risposta ad un item di un test, che implichi scegliere fra un certo numero di alternative senza dover produrre una risposta.
cfr.: risposta produttiva.
V.: risposta.
CA:379, DA:422, DE:37, EN:352, ES:377, FR:334, GA:158, IT:310, NE:154, PO:341.

311 risposte brevi Un item a risposta aperta in cui si richiede al candidato di formulare una risposta scritta usando soltanto una parola o una frase.
CA:228, DA:198, DE:205, EN:362, ES:243, FR:224, GA:246, IT:311, NE:209, PO:238.

312 risultato Il risultato conseguito da un candidato in un test, così come viene riferito allo stesso candidato o a chi, di tale risultato, debba fare uso.
CA:380, DA:317, DE:103, EN:332, ES:378, FR:336, GA:397, IT:312, NE:322, PO:342.

313 saggio Si rimanda alla definizione di composizione.
CA:366, DA:262, DE:33, EN:131, ES:306, FR:159, GA:7, IT:313, NE:125, PO:142.

314 scala Una serie di numeri o categorie per misurare qualcosa. Vengono distinti quattro tipi di scale di misurazione: nominale, ordinale, a intervalli, di rapporti.
Per approfondire: Crocker e Algina 1986, pp. 46–9.
CA:144, DA:337, DE:352, EN:343, ES:152, FR:121, GA:308, IT:314, NE:326, PO:154.

315 scala a intervalli Una scala di misurazione in cui la distanza fra due unità adiacenti di misurazione è la medesima, ma in cui non esiste un punto zero assoluto.
cfr.: scala categoriale, scala nominale, scala ordinale, scala di rapporti.
Per approfondire: Crocker e Algina 1986, p.48.
CA:148, DA:149, DE:161, EN:184, ES:158, FR:126, GA:315, IT:315, NE:188, PO:162.

316 scala a intervalli regolari Si rimanda alla definizione di scala a intervalli.
CA:149, DA:213, DE:161, EN:125, ES:159, FR:127, GA:316, IT:316, NE:145, PO:161.

317 scala assoluta Una scala con un punto zero non arbitrario; ad esempio una scala per misurare la lunghezza. Dal momento che risulta impossibile nel testing linguistico definire il punto zero, risulta parimenti impossibile utilizzare tale scala.
cfr.: scala a intervalli, scala nominale, scala ordinale.
CA:145, DA:4, DE:433, EN:4, ES:153, FR:122, GA:112, IT:317, NE:2, PO:155.

318 scala categoriale Una scala usata per variabili di tipo categoriale, quali: sesso, lingua madre, occupazione.
cfr.: scala a intervalli, scala nominale, scala di rapporti.
CA:146, DA:170, DE:175, EN:42, ES:154, FR:123, GA:310, IT:318, NE:53, PO:156.

319 scala centile Una scala ordinale, che è divisa in 100 unità distinte da 99 valori centili. Per esempio, se a un candidato è dato un valore centile di 95 all'interno di un campione di 100 candidati, lo stesso sarà classificato sopra gli altri 95. Viene chiamata anche scala percentile.
Per approfondire: Crocker e Algina 1986, pp. 439–442, Guilford e Fruchter, 1981 pp. 38–41.
CA:151, DA:46, DE:300, EN:46, ES:155, FR:124, GA:311, IT:319, NE:54, PO:157.

320 scala comune Un modo per riportare i punteggi di due o più test su una scala comune onde permetterne il confron-

to. I punteggi di due o più test possono essere riportati su scala comune, qualora i punteggi grezzi siano stati trasformati attraverso procedure di tipo statistico, quale ad esempio quella della equiparazione degli item.
Per approfondire: Bachman, 1990, pp. 340–344.
CA:147, DA:110, DE:131, EN:57, ES:156, FR:125, GA:86, IT:320, NE:148, PO:158.

321 scala delta Una scala normalizzata con una media di 13 e una deviazione standard di 4.
CA:155, DA:60, DE:75, EN:93, ES:162, FR:132, GA:314, IT:321, NE:94, PO:165.

322 scala di abilità All'interno della teoria della risposta agli item, una scala a intervalli regolari dove collocare sia l'abilità dei candidati sia la difficoltà dei compiti di un test. Viene anche chiamata scala teta.
V.: scala teta.
Per approfondire: Bachman 1990, p. 345.
CA:150, DA:3, DE:114, EN:3, ES:157, FR:128, GA:313, IT:322, NE:413, PO:159.

323 scala di classificazione Una scala costituita da diverse categorie ordinate gerarchicamente ed usata come supporto a giudizi soggettivi. Nel testing linguistico tali scale, usate per giudicare la prestazione fornita dai candidati, sono abitualmente accompagnate da relative descrizioni, che hanno lo scopo di renderle più chiare.
cfr.: scala likert.
V.: descrittore.
CA:154, DA:172, DE:58, EN:315, ES:161, FR:130, GA:319, IT:323, NE:40, PO:160.

324 scala di rapporti Una scala con un punto zero non arbitrario in cui la distanza fra due punti adiacenti rimane la stessa per tutta la scala. Ad esempio, parlando di statura: una persona alta 2 metri è alta due volte una persona alta un metro.
cfr.: scala categoriale, scala a intervalli, scala ordinale.
Per approfondire: Crocker e Algina 1986, pp. 48–49.
CA:153, DA:210, DE:433, EN:317, ES:160, FR:131, GA:312, IT:324, NE:314, PO:164.

325 scala likert Un tipo di scala usata nei questionari per misurare attitudini o opinioni. A chi si sottopone al questionario viene chiesto di rispondere ad una serie di affermazioni scegliendo una risposta fra cinque proposte del tipo: 'sono assolutamente d'accordo', 'sono d'accordo', 'non so', 'non sono d'accordo', 'sono completamente in disaccordo'.
CA:152, DA:214, DE:222, EN:211, ES:163, FR:129, GA:317, IT:325, NE:228, PO:163.

326 scala nominale Una scala usata per variabili categoriali, quali il sesso o la lingua madre. Tali variabili sono presenti o non presenti, quello che interessa è la frequenza con la quale si verificano. Viene anche detta scala categoriale.
cfr.: scala a intervalli, scala ordinale, scala di rapporti.
Per approfondire: Hatch e Lazaraton 1991, pp. 55–56.
CA:156, DA:249, DE:262, EN:248, ES:164, FR:133, GA:309, IT:326, NE:260, PO:166.

327 scala ordinale Un tipo di scala di misurazione che classifica i candidati, senza indicare la distanza relativa fra l'uno e l'altro.
cfr.: scala categoriale, scala a intervalli, scala nominale, scala di rapporti.
Per approfondire: Hatch e Lazaraton 1991, pp. 56–57.
CA:157, DA:271, DE:275, EN:265, ES:165, FR:134, GA:318, IT:327, NE:275, PO:167.

328 scala teta Si rimanda alla definizione di scala di abilità.
CA:158, DA:407, DE:413, EN:413, ES:166, FR:128, GA:320, IT:328, NE:385, PO:168.

329 schema per la correzione e l'attribuzione del punteggio Una lista di tutte le risposte agli item di un test da considerare accettabili. Uno schema di correzione permette ad un correttore di attribuire il punteggio in modo accurato.
CA: 52/256, DA:319, DE:228, EN:223, ES:301, FR:29, GA:324, IT:329, NE:79, PO:172.

330 scritti campione Un campione delle risposte date dai candidati che sia rappresentativo di un livello di abilità. Vengono usati per standardizzare i giudizi degli esaminatori.
CA:268, DA:370, DE:254, EN:338, ES:132, FR:118, GA:344, IT:330, NE:420, PO:10.

331 sessione La data o il periodo durante il quale si svolge un esame. Diversi esami hanno una data o delle date fisse, mentre altri possono essere effettuati su richiesta.
CA:6, DA:403, DE:308, EN:8, ES:77, FR:7, GA:288, IT:331, NE:10, PO:23.

332 settore Area definita di contenuto e/o abilità che deve essere verificata da un compito specifico o da una componente di un esame.
Per approfondire: Bachman,1990, pp.

244–246.
CA:11, DA:83, DE:238, EN:119, ES:119, FR:113, GA:137, IT:332, NE:113, PO:129.

333 sicurezza Il settore, nell'amministrazione di un test, che si occupa di evitare che i materiali vengano divulgati prima o durante il periodo della somministrazione effettiva del test.

CA:387, DA:335, DE:348, EN:351, ES:382, FR:344, GA:353, IT:333, NE:142, PO:347.

334 significatività Un concetto statistico che si riferisce alla possibilità che un risultato sia o meno frutto della casualità.
V.: ipotesi nulla, errore di 1ª specie, errore di 2ª specie.
Per approfondire: Guilford e Fruchter 1981, p.208–210.

CA:388, DA:333, DE:349, EN:363, ES:386, FR:76, GA:366, IT:334, NE:338, PO:348.

335 sillabo Un documento dettagliato che elenca tutti gli aspetti affrontati in un particolare programma di studio e l'ordine in cui verranno presentati.
cfr.: curricolo.

CA:299, DA:224, DE:207, EN:392, ES:310, FR:352, GA:352, IT:335, NE:225, PO:318.

336 sperimentazione Una fase nel processo di sviluppo dei compiti di un test, che mira ad accertare che il test funzioni come previsto. Può risultare estremamente utile per compiti di tipo soggettivo quali brevi saggi, somministrati ad una popolazione limitata.
cfr.: pretesting.

CA:26, DA:301, DE:104, EN:418, ES:135, FR:160, GA:436, IT:336, NE:303, PO:185.

337 stabilità Un aspetto dell'affidabilità la cui stima è basata sull'approccio test-ritest. Si riferisce a quanto costanti rimangano nel tempo i punteggi di un test.
V.: affidabilità, affidabilità test-ritest.

CA:162, DA:359, DE:371, EN:378, ES:170, FR:79, GA:65, IT:337, NE:358, PO:173.

338 standardizzazione Il processo che può garantire che gli esaminatori si adeguino alle procedure stabilite e applichino le scale per l'attribuzione dei giudizi in modo appropriato.
V.: esaminatore.

CA:167, DA:363, DE:373, EN:383, ES:175, NE:361, FR:162, GA:45, IT:338, PO:295.

339 statistica La scienza della manipolazione e della interpretazione dei dati numerici.

CA:164, DA:369, DE:378, EN:386, ES:171, FR:348, GA:362, IT:339, NE:366, PO:175.

340 statistica descrittiva La statistica usata per descrivere un insieme di dati in termini di quantità, dispersione, media, valori, correlazioni con altri dati, ecc. Si distingue dalla statistica inferenziale o di campionamento.
cfr.: statistica inferenziale.

CA:165, DA:63, DE:51, EN:95, ES:172, FR:349, GA:365, IT:340, NE:95, PO:176.

341 statistica inferenziale La statistica che va oltre l'informazione fornita dalla statistica descrittiva e consente di fare inferenze su quanto un singolo gruppo di dati sia rappresentativo della popolazione di cui rappresenta un campione.
cfr.: statistica descrittiva.

CA:166, DA:139, DE:338, EN:171, ES:173, FR:350, GA:364, IT:341, NE:175, PO:177.

342 stima dell'affidabilità di bipartizione di Spearman-Brown Si rimanda alla definizione di affidabilità di bipartizione.

CA:168, DA:350, DE:360, EN:372, ES:177, FR:161, GA:228, IT:342, NE:349, PO:178.

343 stimolo Nei test di produzione orale o scritta, materiale illustrato o testi che servano per sollecitare risposte da parte dei candidati.

CA:390, DA:316, DE:437 EN:299, ES:178, FR:95, GA:358, IT:343, NE:321, PO:179.

344 studio pilota Uno studio preliminare, condotto su un numero limitato di soggetti, in cui studiosi e ricercatori o chi deve elaborare test sperimentano il proprio progetto onde individuarne eventuali punti critici, prima di iniziare una sperimentazione su più vasta scala di un programma o di un prodotto.
V.: pretesting, sperimentazione.

CA:170, DA:286, DE:288, EN:281, ES:179, FR:163, GA:361, IT:344, NE:290, PO:180.

345 subtest Si rimanda alla definizione di componente.

CA:389, DA:377, DE:386, EN:389, ES:388, FR:346, GA:150, IT:345, NE:373, PO:350.

346 supporto di un item Parte del materiale scritto, usato come stimolo. Di solito è costituito da una frase incompletta da completare liberamente o scegliendo fra opzioni diverse.
cfr.: chiave/i, opzioni.
V.: item a scelta multipla.

CA:276, DA:360, DE:29, EN:387, ES:139, FR:10, GA:160, IT:346, NE:359, PO:224.

347 tavola di contingenza Una tavola di frequenze classificate secondo due o più serie di valori di variabili categoriali.

	Padronanza	Non Padronanza
Metodo A	35	5
Metodo B	20	20

V.: test chi-quadrato.
CA:398, DA:187, DE:187, EN:74, ES:390, FR:353, GA:369, IT:347, NE:75, PO:320.

348 tendenza centrale (misura della tendenza centrale) Un modo per localizzare il punto centrale o la media statistica di una distribuzione. Le misure di tendenza centrale comunemente usate sono tre: la media, la mediana e la moda.
Per approfondire: Henning, 1987, pp. 39–40, Guilford e Fruchter, 1981, Capitolo. 4, Hatch e Lazaraton, 1991, pp. 159–164.
CA:246, DA:47, DE:447, EN:45, ES:391, FR:358, GA:62, IT:348, NE:55, PO:356.

349 teoria classica del testing Una teoria di misurazione che consiste in una serie di supposizioni sulle relazioni fra i punteggi reali e i fattori che possono averli influenzati, chiamati comunemente errori. Viene anche chiamata teoria del punteggio reale.
cfr.: teoria della risposta agli item.
Per approfondire: Bachman, 1990, pp. 166–187.
CA:399, DA:174, DE:177, EN:50, ES:392, FR:397, GA:387, IT:349, NE:208, PO:357.

350 teoria della caratteristica/ attributo latente Si rimanda alla definizione di teoria della risposta agli item.
CA:402/412, DA:153,/211 DE:165/206, EN:207, ES:395/408, FR:398/401, GA:390/392, IT:350, NE:194/216, PO:358/402.

351 teoria della generalizzabilità Un modello statistico per ricercare gli effetti relativi di fonti diverse della varianza nei punteggi di un test.
Per approfondire: Bachman 1990, p.7; Crocker e Algina 1986, Capitolo 8.
CA:400, DA:115, DE:132, EN:154, ES:393, FR:399, GA:388, IT:351, NE:152, PO:359.

352 teoria della risposta agli item (in letteratura noto come IRT, sigla di: Item Response Theory) Una serie di modelli matematici che consentono di mettere in relazione la prestazione fornita da un individuo in un determinato test con il suo livello di abilità. Tali modelli si basano sulla teoria fondamentale per cui la risposta che ci si attende da un individuo ad una domanda o ad un item di un test è una funzione sia del livello di difficoltà dell'item sia del livello di abilità dell'individuo.
Per approfondire: Henning 1987, Capitolo 8; Crocker e Algina 1986, Capitolo15.
CA:401, DA:159, DE:173/296, EN:188/195, ES:394, FR:400, GA:389, IT:352, NE:201, PO:360.

353 test Una procedura per verificare aspetti specifici della competenza. a) Una serie di componenti che combinate insieme costituiscono una procedura per la verifica e la valutazione. In questa accezione è spesso usato per indicare un esame.

b) Un singolo compito o una singola componente per la verifica di un settore specifico della competenza, quale ad esempio la produzione scritta o orale. In questa accezione un test può anche costituire una parte di un esame, sia come singola componente (ad esempio la produzione orale), sia come singolo compito (ad esempio un test di cloze).
CA:300, DA:300, DE:389, EN:395, ES:311, FR:359, GA:403, IT:353, NE:388, PO:361.

354 test (compito) indiretto Test o compito che si propone di misurare le capacità che sono alla base di una determinata abilità linguistica, piuttosto che verificare la performance in quella stessa abilità. Ad esempio per verificare l'abilità di produzione scritta si può richiedere al candidato di individuare e correggere le strutture usate in modo non corretto all'interno di un testo.
cfr.: test diretto.
Per approfondire: Hughes 1989, pp. 14–16.
CA:329, DA:135, DE:150, EN:170, ES:337, FR:385, GA:420, IT:354, NE:173, PO:389.

355 test (item) effettivo Un test o un item pronto per la somministrazione e per il quale devono essere garantite le necessarie misure di segretezza.
CA:341, DA:101, DE:225, EN:217, ES:344, FR:360, GA:407, IT:355, NE:233, PO:362.

356 test adattabile Un tipo di testing in cui il livello di difficoltà degli item si seleziona automaticamente, man mano che il candidato svolge i compiti del test. La selezione avviene sulla base della stima delle capacità del candidato stesso. Spesso il termine viene usato per fare riferimento ad un test somministrato direttamente tramite computer.
V.: testing adattabile computerizzato.
Per approfondire: Bachman 1990, p.151; Henning 1987, p.136.
CA:302, DA:102, DE:6, EN:7, ES:312,

FR:361, GA:429, IT:356, NE:5, PO:363.

357 test àncora Un test costruito con determinate tecniche di misurazione e distribuito insieme ad un altro test. La prestazione fornita nel test àncora fornisce informazioni sia sull'altro test, distribuito in contemporanea, sia sui candidati che si sono sottoposti ad entrambi i test.
cfr.: item àncora.
CA:307, DA:17, DE:19, EN:16, ES:320, FR:367, GA:404, IT:357, NE:18, PO:365.

358 test attitudinale Un test elaborato per prevedere o misurare le potenzialità di successo di un candidato in una particolare area di apprendimento; ad esempio lo studio delle lingue straniere, o in un altro specifico corso di studio.
Per approfondire: Henning, 1987, p. 6: Ebel e Frisbie, 1991, p. 339.
CA:308, DA:18, DE:96, EN:20, ES:322, FR:368, GA:421, IT:358, NE:22, PO:370.

359 test chi-quadrato Una procedura di tipo statistico che mette a confronto i valori delle risposte effettive con quelli delle risposte attese per indicare se la differenza fra loro sia statisticamente significativa.
V.: procedure non parametriche.
Per approfondire: Hatch e Lazaraton,1991, pp. 393–415.
CA:330, DA:49, DE:65, EN:49, ES:396, FR:149, GA:409, IT:359, NE:59, PO:395.

360 test di abilità Un test che potrebbe essere completato da quasi tutti i candidati nel tempo a disposizione, ma che contiene alcuni item o compiti di tale difficoltà da rendere improbabile che la maggioranza riesca a rispondere correttamente a tutti.
cfr.: test di velocità.
CA:310, DA:299, DE:261/293, EN:288, ES:329, FR:379, GA:413, IT:360, NE:296, PO:371.

361 test di ascolto Un test di comprensione della lingua parlata, somministrato di solito attraverso un registratore o un video.
CA:315, DA:221, DE:147, EN:216, ES:324, FR:372, GA:411, IT:361, NE:235, PO:373.

362 test di cloze Un tipo di test di completamento in cui, da un testo, vengono tolte intere parole. In un cloze tradizionale si stabilisce ogni quante parole eliminarne una e si rispetta tale scansione. Vengono comunemente chiamati cloze o cloze razionali anche altri tipi di completamenti dove da un testo vengono tolte intere frasi o dove, chi elabora gli item, sceglie le parole da eliminare. I candidati devono completare il testo con le parole mancanti (cloze aperti) o scegliere la parola mancante da una serie di opzioni (cloze a scelta multipla o banked cloze). La correzione e attribuzione del punteggio di un cloze aperto può avvenire sia in base alla 'parola esatta' (nel senso che viene accettata come risposta solo la parola tolta dal testo originale) sia in base alla 'parola accettabile' (nel senso che viene fornita a chi corregge e attribuisce il punteggio una lista delle risposte da considerare accettabili).
cfr.: test-c, item di completamento.
CA:313, DA:50, DE:66, EN:52, ES:315, FR:370, GA:410, IT:362, NE:61, PO:378.

363 test di competenza Un test che misura competenze ed abilità, senza fare riferimento ad un determinato corso o programma di studio o ad una serie di materiali.
CA:319, DA:112, DE:120, EN:296, ES:326, FR:378, GA:428, IT:363, NE:306, PO:379.

364 test di ingresso Un test usato per stabilire se un candidato può essere ammesso o meno ad un determinato corso di studi o può essere assunto in una determinata istituzione pubblica o privata.
cfr.: test di livello.
CA:305/322, DA:5/20, DE:203/346, EN:124, ES:319/331, FR:366/369, GA:419/422, IT:364, NE:387/421, PO:374/377.

365 test di livello Un test somministrato al fine di inserire studenti in un gruppo o in una classe di livello appropriato al loro grado di conoscenza o abilità.
CA:311, DA:137, DE:101, EN:282, ES:323, FR:377, GA:434, IT:365, NE:291, PO:372.

366 test di padronanza Un test elaborato per stabilire se uno studente abbia sufficiente padronanza di un determinato settore della competenza o di una determinata abilità.
CA:338, DA:227, DE:204, EN:225, ES:327, FR:376, GA:425, IT:366, NE:237, PO:376.

367 test di performance/esecuzione Una procedura di testing che richiede al candidato la produzione di un campione di lingua, scritta o orale (ad esempio i saggi o le conversazioni orali). Si ricorre spesso a tali procedure per riprodurre l'uso linguistico in contesti diversi da quello del test.
Per approfondire: Bachman 1990, pp. 304–305.
CA:306, DA:283, DE:284, EN:278, ES:318, FR:380, GA:416, IT:367, NE:287, PO:381.

368 test di profitto Un test elaborato

per misurare il livello di apprendimento di un candidato relativamente ad un particolare corso di insegnamento, libro di testo, ecc.; ad esempio un test dipendente da un determinato curricolo.

CA:309, DA:366, DE:369, EN:6/23, ES:321, FR:374, GA:419, IT:368, NE:301, PO:374.

369 test di progresso Un test somministrato durante un corso per verificare quanto appreso dagli studenti fino a quel punto.

CA:320, DA:108, DE:214, EN:298, ES:330, FR:381, GA:418, IT:369, NE:422, PO:382.

370 test di selezione Un test, di solito breve e semplice da somministrare, il cui fine è quello di identificare i candidati che possono essere ammessi ad un corso o che possono accedere ad un esame.
cfr.: test di livello.

CA:316/323, DA:330/424, DE:36/98, EN:349/353, ES:332, FR:375/382, GA:430/432, IT:370, NE:332/333, PO:375/383.

371 test di significatività Un test di significatività statistica.
V.: significatività.

CA:324, DA:334, DE:350, EN:364, ES:333, FR:373, GA:435, IT:371, NE:339, PO:384.

372 test di velocità Un test con un limite di tempo per il suo completamento. I candidati più lenti acquisiranno un punteggio inferiore perché non riusciranno a completare il test. Di solito la facilità delle domande è tale che tutti i candidati potrebbero rispondere correttamente se non vi fossero limiti di tempo.
cfr.: test di abilità.

CA:321, DA:129, DE:340/363, EN:376, ES:334, FR:363, GA:424, IT:372, NE:352, PO:385.

373 test diagnostico Un test usato per individuare quanto appreso da un discente o le sue eventuali lacune. I risultati di tale verifica possono essere usati per prendere delle decisioni su come colmare tali lacune, su come sostenere il discente nell'apprendimento o su come procedere nell'insegnamento.

CA:317, DA:65, DE:77, EN:97, ES:325, FR:383, GA:414, IT:373, NE:97, PO:386.

374 test dipendente da un curricolo Un test che è strettamente legato ad un determinato sillabo e che ha un significato particolare all'interno di un processo educativo.
cfr.: test non dipendente da un curricolo.
V.: test di profitto.

CA:325, DA:56, DE:217, EN:88, ES:313, FR:365, GA:406, IT:374, NE:221, PO:380.

375 test diretto Un test che misura le abilità di produzione scritta e orale e che permette una misurazione diretta della prestazione fornita dal candidato nelle suddette abilità. Ad esempio si richiede al candidato di scrivere una lettera per verificare l' abilità di produzione scritta.
cfr.: test (compito) indiretto.
Per approfondire: Hughes, 1989,pp. 14–16.

CA:326, DA:70, DE:81, EN:104, ES:335, FR:384, GA:415, IT:375, NE:102, PO:387.

376 test non dipendente da un curricolo Un test non collegato a nessun particolare sillabo o corso.
cfr.: test dipendente da un curricolo.
V.: test di competenza.

CA:328, DA:57, DE:218, EN:89, ES:339, FR:387, GA:405, IT:376, NE:222, PO:388.

377 test oggettivo Un test che può essere corretto seguendo una griglia di correzione e che quindi non necessita di un giudizio soggettivo o dell'opinione di un esperto.

CA:331, DA:257, DE:272, EN:257, ES:341, FR:389, GA:427, IT:377, NE:267, PO:392.

378 test per scopi specifici Un test progettato per misurare l'abilità di un candidato ad operare linguisticamente in uno specifico contesto accademico o professionale. Il contenuto del test viene definito in base ad un'analisi dei compiti che il candidato dovrà affrontare nelle varie situazioni in cui si troverà ad interagire.

CA:318, DA:243, DE:112, EN:375, ES:328, FR:393, GA:431, IT:378, NE:351, PO:393.

379 test psicometrico Un test relativo a caratteristiche psicologiche quali la personalità, l'intelligenza, le attitudini, la competenza linguistica. Il test parte da presupposti specifici; ad esempio l'unidimensionalità e una distribuzione normale.
Per approfondire: Bachman 1990, p.73–74.

CA:334, DA:302, DE:310, EN:301, ES:397, FR:390, GA:433, IT:379, NE:308, PO:394.

380 test relativo ad un criterio Un test in cui la prestazione fornita dal candidato viene interpretata in base a criteri predeterminati. Viene data particolare importanza, in questo tipo di test, al raggiungimento degli obiettivi piuttosto che al punteggio ottenuto dai candidati come semplice riflesso della loro posizione nella classifica del gruppo.
cfr.: test relativo ad un gruppo-norma, test relativo ad un settore specifico.

CA:337, DA:203, DE:196, EN:81, ES:317, FR:364, GA:412, IT:380, NE:86, PO:369.

381 test relativo ad un gruppo-norma Un test in cui i punteggi vengono interpretati sulla base della prestazione di un determinato gruppo, costituito da persone con caratteristiche simili a quelle dei candidati che si sono sottoposti al test oggetto di analisi. Tale denominazione viene usata in particolare per quei test, l'interpretazione dei risultati dei quali mira soprattutto a classificare i candidati mettendoli appunto in relazione con il gruppo-norma o fra loro.
cfr.: test relativo ad un criterio.

CA:336, DA:251, DE:268, EN:254, ES:340, FR:388, GA:426, IT:381, NE:264, PO:391.

382 test relativo ad un settore specifico Un test i cui risultati vengono interpretati sulla base di un contenuto specifico o di una abilità specifica.
cfr.: test relativo ad un criterio, test relativo ad un gruppo-norma.

CA:335, DA:84, DE:50, EN:120, ES:342, FR:391, GA:417, IT:382, NE:114, PO:368.

383 test semidiretto Un test che si propone di verificare la prestazione linguistica sostituendo per certi aspetti l'elemento umano. Ad esempio in un test di produzione orale un nastro registrato che si sostituisce all'intervistatore. In letteratura un esempio di test semidiretto è la cosiddetta SOPI (Semi-Direct Oral Proficiency Interview).
cfr.: test diretto.

CA:339, DA:332, DE:347, EN:356, ES:343, FR:392, GA:423, IT:383, NE:336, PO:396.

384 test-c Un tipo di test di completamento in cui si elimina la seconda metà di alcune parole. Si può arrivare alla frequenza di un completamento ogni due parole. Il compito del candidato è quello di completare la parola della parte mancante.
cfr.: test di cloze.
Per approfondire: Weir 1990, p.49.

CA:304, DA:45, DE:62, EN:38, ES:314, FR:394, GA:408, IT:384, NE:51, PO:366.

385 test *t* Un test statistico usato per determinare ogni differenza significativa fra le medie di due campioni.

CA:340, DA:385, DE:387, EN:423, ES:398, FR:150, GA:368, IT:385, NE:377, PO:397.

386 testing adattabile computerizzato Un metodo di testing basato sull'uso del computer, in cui è possibile adattare il livello di difficoltà dell'item all'abilità del candidato, sulla base delle risposte che il candidato stesso man mano fornisce.
V.: testing computerizzato (verifica computerizzata).

CA:303, DA:51, DE:67, EN:63, ES:181, FR:362, GA:379, IT:386, NE:68, PO:364.

387 testing computerizzato (verifica computerizzata) Un metodo di testing in cui gli item vengono presentati ai candidati direttamente nel computer. Anche le risposte di conseguenza devono essere date tramite il computer.

CA:332, DA:52, DE:68, EN:64, ES:182, FR:171, GA:380, IT:387, NE:70, PO:35.

388 testing di competenza minima Un approccio al testing che individua gli specifici requisiti per un livello minimo di competenza in un particolare settore dell'uso linguistico. Supera il test il candidato che dimostri tale livello minimo di competenza richiesta.

CA:312, DA:398, DE:304, EN:234, ES:183, FR:167, GA:378, IT:388, NE:246, PO:31.

389 testo Una unità coerente di discorso scritto o parlato, usata come base di riferimento per una serie di item di un test.

CA:403, DA:386, DE:411, EN:411, ES:399, FR:396, GA:381, IT:389, NE:381, PO:398.

390 testo autentico Un testo di un test, originariamente destinato ad altro utilizzo e quindi non creato appositamente.
cfr.: testo semiautentico.

CA:404, DA:22, DE:41, EN:25, ES:401, FR:111, GA:382, IT:390, NE:24, PO:127.

391 testo semiautentico Un testo tratto da una fonte reale, ma sottoposto a delle modifiche per poterlo inserire in un test; ad esempio adattattando il lessico e/o la grammatica al livello dei candidati.
V.: testo autentico.

CA:405, DA:123, DE:140, EN:355, ES:400, FR:112, GA:383, IT:391, NE:335, PO:128.

392 tipologia degli item Gli item di un test vengono indicati con termini che tendono a descriverne il formato. Ad esempio, scelta multipla, trasformazione di frasi, risposte brevi, cloze aperto.

CA:406, DA:162, DE:174, EN:197 ES:403, FR:405, GA:58, IT:392, NE:203, PO:399.

393 tipologia dei compiti I compiti vengono indicati con dei termini che già di per sé descrivono ciò che si intende verificare e sotto quale forma. Ad esempio scelte multiple nella comprensione della lettura, compiti scritti guidati, ecc.

CA:408, DA:265, DE:30, EN:394, ES:402, FR:407, GA:59, IT:393, NE:271, PO:401.

394 tipologia delle domande Si

rimanda alla definizione di tipologia degli item e di tipologia dei compiti.

CA:407, DA:358, DE:124, EN:305, ES:404, FR:406, GA:57, IT:394, NE:424, PO:400.

395 tracciare un profilo Un modo di presentare i risultati di un test riportando i risultati conseguiti in ciascuna delle componenti che costituiscono il test stesso, in modo da poter agilmente identificare aree di relativa debolezza o di relativa bravura.

CA:288, DA:297, DE:404, EN:297, ES:300, FR:312, GA:282, IT:395, NE:307, PO:303.

396 trasferimento di informazioni Una tecnica di verifica che comporta l'acquisizione di certe informazioni tramite un determinato canale e la loro presentazione tramite un canale diverso. Esempi di tale tipo di compito possono essere: acquisire informazioni da un testo ed inserirle in una tabella o diagramma o riscrivere alcuni appunti informali sotto forma di comunicazione di tipo formale.

Per approfondire: Hughes 1989,pp. 84, 124–125, 138.

CA:409, DA:141, DE:152, EN:173, ES:406, FR:402, GA:8, IT:396, NE:177, PO:404.

397 trasformazione di frasi Un tipo di item in cui viene fornita come stimolo una frase completa, seguita dalla prima o dalle prime due parole di una seconda frase che deve esprimere un contenuto analogo in una forma grammaticalmente diversa. Ad esempio la prima frase può essere attiva e compito del candidato è quello di trasformarla in forma passiva.

CA:410, DA:381, DE:334, EN:359, ES:407, FR:404, GA:61, IT:397, NE:440, PO:405.

398 unidimensionalità La nozione di un' unica dimensione, presupposto fondamentale alla costruzione di una scala per misurare caratteristiche psicologiche, usando i modelli di risposta agli item suggeriti dalla letteratura. L'unidimensionalità è una proprietà dello strumento di misurazione, non del processo psicologico sotteso.

Per approfondire: Crocker e Algina 1986, p.343.

CA:413, DA:90, DE:97, EN:427, ES:410, FR:409, GA:23, IT:398, NE:119, PO:406.

399 utente del test La persona o l'istituzione (ad esempio un insegnante o una banca) che può utilizzare i risultati conseguiti da un candidato in un test, per prendere delle decisioni a suo riguardo.

CA:414, DA:391, DE:392, EN:407, ES:410, FR:409, GA:440, IT:399, NE:393, PO:407.

400 validazione La raccolta di prove a sostegno dell'inferenza fatta sui punteggi di un test. L'inferenza riguarda gli usi specifici del test che vengono sottoposti a validazione e non il test stesso.

V.: validità.

CA:415, DA:426, DE:426, EN:429, ES:412, FR:412, GA:39, IT:400, NE:414, PO:408.

401 validità La misura in cui i punteggi di un test rendono possibili delle inferenze appropriate, significative ed utili, in base allo scopo del test stesso. Vengono identificati diversi aspetti della validità, quali la validità di contenuto, di criterio e di costrutto, che a loro volta contribuiscono a fornire elementi per giudicare la validità complessiva di un test relativamente allo scopo per cui è stato costruito.

V.: validità concorrente, validità convergente, validità di criterio, validità apparente, validità di contenuto, validità di costrutto, validità discriminante, validità divergente, validità predittiva.

Per approfondire: Bachman 1990, pp. 25, 236–237.

CA:416, DA:427, DE:427, EN:430, ES:413, FR:413, GA:30, IT:401, NE:415, PO:409.

402 validità apparente La capacità che un test ha di apparire ai candidati, o a chi deve scegliere il test per loro conto, come un accettabile strumento di verifica della abilità che si intende misurare. Si tratta ovviamente di un giudizio soggettivo, non basato su un'analisi obiettiva del test stesso; proprio per questo la validità d'aspetto o apparente viene spesso considerata una falsa forma di validità. Può anche essere chiamata: l' attrattiva del test (test appeal).

V.: validità.

Per approfondire: Bachman, 1990, pp. 285–289.

CA:417, DA:272, DE:110/34, EN:140, ES:414, FR:414 GA:2, IT:402, NE:174, PO:410.

403 validità concorrente Si può parlare di validità concorrente di un test se i punteggi che fornisce sono strettamente correlati con un criterio esterno riconosciuto, che misuri la stessa area di conoscenza o abilità.

V.: validità di criterio.

Per approfondire: Bachman, 1990, pp. 248–250.

CA:418, DA:323, DE:417, EN:66, ES:415, FR:415, GA:33, IT:403, NE:71, PO:411.

404 validità convergente Si dice che un test è dotato di validità convergente quando vi è una correlazione molto alta tra i

punteggi ottenuti nel test e quelli ottenuti in un altro test che misuri però il medesimo costrutto (indipendentemente dal metodo). Si tratta quindi di un altro aspetto della validità di costrutto.
cfr.: validità discriminante.
V.: validità di costrutto.
Per approfondire: Guilford e Fruchter, 1981, pp. 436–437.
CA:419, DA:188, DE:188, EN:75, ES:416, FR:416, GA:32, IT:404, NE:76, PO:412.

405 validità di contenuto Si dice che un test ha validità di contenuto se gli item o i compiti da cui risulta costituito rappresentano un campione significativo del tipo di item o di compito idoneo a verificare determinate aree di conoscenza o abilità. Considerazioni di questo tipo fanno spesso riferimento ad un preciso sillabo o corso.
V.: validità, descrizione del test.
Per approfondire: Bachman, 1990, pp. 244–247.
CA:422, DA:134, DE:154, EN:73, ES:419, FR:419, GA:31, IT:405, NE:179, PO:415.

406 validità di costrutto Si dice che un test ha una validità di costrutto se i punteggi ottenuti possono essere interpretati come espressioni di una teoria sulla natura di tale costrutto o sui rapporti intercorrenti fra tale costrutto ed altri. Si potrebbe ad esempio prevedere che due test di ascolto dotati di tale validità, classifichino i discenti allo stesso modo, mentre ciascuno dei due test sarebbe meno rapportabile ai punteggi ottenuti ad esempio in un test di competenza grammaticale.
V.: validità, descrizione del test.
Per approfondire: Ebel e Frisbie, 1991, p. 10; Hatch e Lazaraton, 1991, pp. 37–38.
CA:420, DA:186, DE:186, EN:69, ES:418, FR:418, GA:37, IT:406, NE:73, PO:414.

407 validità di criterio Si dice che un test è dotato di tale tipo di validità se è possibile dimostrare il rapporto tra i punteggi in esso conseguiti ed un criterio esterno che si suppone misuri la stessa abilità. L'informazione sul criterio preso a riferimento può essere utile anche per predire futuri comportamenti.
V.: validità concorrente, validità predittiva.
Per approfondire: Bachman, 1990, pp. 248–250.
CA:421, DA:204, DE:197, EN:82, ES:417, FR:417, GA:34, IT:407, NE:87, PO:413.

408 validità discriminante Si dice che un test ha validità discriminante se la sua correlazione con altri test che verificano aspetti diversi è inferiore a quella con altri test che verificano lo stesso aspetto, a prescindere dal metodo di testing impiegato. Si può considerare come un aspetto della validità di costrutto.
V.: validità di costrutto.
cfr.: validità convergente.
Per approfondire: Crocker e Algina, 1986, p.23; Guilford e Fruchter, 1981, pp. 436–437.
CA:423, DA:73, DE:83, EN:111, ES:420, FR:420, GA:36, IT:408, NE:108, PO:416.

409 validità divergente Si rimanda alla definizione di validità discriminante.
CA:424, DA:81, DE:90, EN:118, ES:421, FR:421, GA:35, IT:409, NE:111, PO:417.

410 validità predittiva Un'indicazione della capacità di un test di predire la performance futura nell'abilità presa in esame.
cfr.: validità di criterio.
Per approfondire: Guilford e Fruchter 1987, pp. 437–438.
CA:425, DA:298, DE:294/439, EN:291, ES:422, FR:422, GA:38, IT:410, NE:300, PO:418.

411 valore di facilità Si rimanda alla definizione di indice di facilità.
CA:426, DA:192, DE:209, EN:143, ES:423, FR:410, GA:217, IT:411, NE:147, PO:419.

412 valore *p* Si rimanda alla definizione di indice di facilità.
CA:427, DA:273, DE:276, EN:266, ES:424, FR:411, GA:269, IT:412, NE:277, PO:420.

413 valutazione Raccolta di informazioni al fine di prendere delle decisioni. Nel testing linguistico la valutazione può focalizzarsi sull'efficacia o sull'impatto di un certo programma di studi, di un esame o di un progetto.
CA:31, DA:93, DE:106, EN:132, ES:180, FR:166, GA:235, IT:413, NE:126, PO:30.

414 valutazione formativa Valutazione continua di un processo, che ne permette un miglioramento ed adeguamento continuo. Può riferirsi ad uno specifico programma di istruzione.
cfr.: valutazione sommativa.
CA:32, DA:226, DE:46, EN:148, ES:184, FR:168, GA:236, IT:414, NE:136, PO:32.

415 valutazione sommativa La valutazione di un processo giunto al suo compimento. Può fare riferimento a un determinato programma di studi.
cfr.: valutazione formativa.
CA:34, DA:266, DE:3, EN:391, ES:186, FR:172, GA:238, IT:415, NE:374, PO:36.

416 variabile a) Termine in uso per indicare una serie di osservazioni su un item, dove per item si può intendere sia un item di un test, sia età, sesso del candidato o punteggio ottenuto nel test.

b) Un elemento in uno studio sperimentale o in un'analisi statistica che può prendere valori diversi. Ad esempio, variabili di interesse nel testing linguistico possono essere la difficoltà degli item di un test, l'età e il sesso dei candidati, ecc.

CA:430, DA:428, DE:428, EN:431, ES:430, FR:423, GA:25, IT:416, NE:416, PO:422.

417 variabile di criterio Termine utilizzato in ricerca con significato equivalente a variabile dipendente.
V.: variabile dipendente.

CA:431, DA:205, DE:198, EN:83, ES:431, FR:424, GA:26, IT:417, NE:88, PO:423.

418 variabile dipendente Una variabile oggetto di studio in un lavoro di ricerca. Ad esempio il punteggio ottenuto da un candidato in un test (variabile indipendente) può essere utilizzato per predire il probabile successo dello stesso candidato nel posto di lavoro (variabile dipendente).
cfr.: variabile indipendente.
V.: variabile.
Per approfondire: Hatch e Lazaraton p.63.

CA:432, DA:7, DE:2, EN:94, ES:432, FR:425, GA:28, IT:418, NE:7, PO:424.

419 variabile indipendente In ricerca si indica con questo termine una variabile che si pensa possa riferirsi o influenzare la variabile dipendente. Ad esempio, i punteggi ottenuti in un test (variabile indipendente) possono essere usati per prevedere un eventuale successo nell' ambiente di lavoro (variabile dipendente).
cfr.: variabile dipendente.
V.: variabile.
Per approfondire: Hatch e Lazaraton 1991, p.64.

CA:433, DA:420, DE:422, EN:169, ES:433, FR:426, GA:27, IT:419, NE:268, PO:425.

420 varianza Misura della dispersione di una serie di punteggi. Più grande è la varianza, più lontani risultano i singoli punteggi dalla media.

CA:434, DA:429, DE:429, EN:432, ES:434, FR:427, GA:24, IT:420, NE:417, PO:421.

421 verifica Nel testing linguistico, la misurazione di uno o più aspetti della competenza linguistica, tramite determinati tipi di test, o altri tipi di procedure.
Per approfondire: Bachman, 1990, p. 50.

CA:31, DA:30, DE:54, EN:21, ES:180, FR:165, GA:229, IT:421, NE:39, PO:30.

422 verifica formativa Un tipo di verifica che avviene durante un corso o programma di istruzione invece che alla fine. I risultati possono permettere sia all'insegnante di colmare in tempo eventuali lacune o, se necessario, di rivedere l'impostazione del corso, sia allo studente di identificare le proprie lacune.
cfr.: verifica sommativa.

CA:32, DA:225, DE:213, EN:147, ES:184, FR:168, GA:232, IT:422, NE:137, PO:32.

423 verifica sommativa Un tipo di verifica che avviene alla fine di un corso o di un programma di studi.

CA:34, DA:267, DE:4, EN:390, ES:186, FR:172, GA:233, IT:423, NE:375, PO:36.

424 vuoto di informazione Una tecnica nell'insegnamento o nel testing linguistico che simula la comunicazione reale creando delle situazioni su cui gli studenti non hanno le stesse informazioni, per cui devono necessariamente comunicare l'uno con l'altro per poter ricostruire la situazione. Viene di solito usata per esercitare gli studenti o per verificare la loro competenza in abilità produttive scritte o orali.

CA:42, DA:140, DE:151, EN:172, ES:411, FR:213, GA:43, IT:424, NE:176, PO:223.

9 Nederlands: Een meertalig glossarium van taaltestterminologie

1 a-parameter De parameter uit de itemresponsetheorie die betrekking heeft op het discriminerend vermogen van een item.
Zie: itemresponsetheorie (IRT) .
Meer informatie: Bachman, 1990, p. 204.
CA:281, DA:1, DE:84, EN:1, ES:294, FR:292, GA:273, IT:260, NE:1, PO:297.

2 absolute schaal Een schaal met een waar nulpunt, bijvoorbeeld een schaal voor het meten van lengte. Aangezien in taaltoetsen het absolute nulpunt niet valt aan te geven, wordt deze schaal niet gebruikt.
Vergelijk: intervalschaal, nominale schaal, ordinale schaal.
CA:145, DA:4, DE:433, EN:4, ES:153, FR:122, GA:112, IT:317, NE:2, PO:155.

3 accreditatie Erkenning van een examen, meestal door een officieel orgaan, bijvoorbeeld een ministerie, een examen-instantie, etc.
CA:4, DA:10, DE:8, EN:5, ES:1, FR:4, GA:92, IT:303, NE:3, PO:325.

4 achtergrondkennis De kennis van een kandidaat over een onderwerp of de culturele inhoud van een bepaalde toets die van invloed kan zijn op de manier waarop de input verwerkt wordt. Deze kennis is met name van belang bij beroepsgerichte taaltoetsen.
Meer informatie: Bachman, 1990, p. 273.
CA:75, DA:26, DE:144, EN:27, ES:73, FR:77, GA:134, IT:85, NE:4, PO:91.

5 adaptieve toets Een vorm van toetsing waarin tijdens de toets items worden geselecteerd op moeilijkheidsgraad, als reactie op een schatting van de vaardigheid van de kandidaat. Heeft dikwijls betrekking op een gecomputeriseerde toets, al kan een geleid gesprek ook een adaptieve toets zijn.
Zie: computer-adaptieve toetsing.
Meer informatie: Bachman, 1990, p. 151; Henning, 1987. p. 136.
CA:302, DA:102, DE:6, EN:7, ES:312, FR:361, GA:429, IT:356, NE:5, PO:363.

6 affectieve factoren Factoren van non-cognitieve aard die te maken hebben met de emotionele variabelen, voorkeuren en attitudes van toetskandidaten.
Vergelijk: cognitieve factoren.
Meer informatie: Ebel en Frisbie, 1991, p. 52.
CA:177, DA:6, DE:7, EN:9, ES:195, FR:178, GA:399, IT:172, NE:6, PO:188.

7 afhankelijke variabele De variabele waarop het onderzoek zich richt. Zo kunnen bijvoorbeeld scores op een toets (de onafhankelijke variabele) gebruikt worden om succes op de werkplek (de afhankelijke variabele) te voorspellen.
Vergelijk: onafhankelijke variabele.
Zie: variabele.
Meer informatie: Hatch en Lazaraton p. 63.
CA:432, DA:7, DE:2, EN:94, ES:432, FR:425, GA:28, IT:418, NE:7, PO:424.

8 afleider Het niet-juiste antwoord in een multiple-choice item.
Vergelijk: juiste antwoord.
Zie: multiple-choice item
Meer informatie: Ebel en Frisbie, 1986, pp. 176–185.
CA:110, DA:79, DE:88, EN:115, ES:111, FR:104, GA:348, IT:129, NE:8, PO:126.

9 afleiderwaarde (of a-waarde) De frequentie waarmee een afleider in een multiple-choice item wordt gekozen. Uit deze waarde blijkt hoe populair zo'n afleider is.
CA:243, DA:80, DE:89, EN:116, ES:71, FR:301, GA:384, IT:88, NE:9, PO:96.

10 afname Datum waarop of periode waarin een examen plaatsvindt. Veel examens worden meerdere malen per jaar op een vaste datum afgenomen, andere kunnen op verzoek worden afgenomen.
CA:6, DA:403, DE:308, EN:8, ES:77, FR:7, GA:288, IT:331, NE:10, PO:23.

11 afronden De precisie van een getal

verminderen door het aantal significante cijfers terug te dringen. Zo kan bijvoorbeeld 564.8 naar boven worden afgerond op 565 of naar beneden op 560. De afrondingsschaal hangt af van de vereiste precisie.
CA:24, DA:245, DE:331, EN:335, ES:363, FR:22, GA:354, IT:24, NE:11, PO:25.

12 alpha (alpha-coëfficiënt) Een betrouwbaarheidsschatting waarmee de interne consistentie van een toets wordt gemeten. De waarde ligt tussen de 0 en 1. Wordt vaak gebruikt voor toetsen met score-schalen, in tegenstelling tot toetsen met dichotome items, al kan deze methode voor beide soorten toetsen worden gebruikt.
Wordt ook wel coëfficiënt alpha genoemd.
Vergelijk: Kuder-Richardson.
Zie: interne consistentie.
Meer informatie: Henning, 1987, pp. 83–84.
CA:9, DA:11, DE:10, EN:10, ES:16, FR:8, GA:10, IT:10, NE:12, PO:6.

13 alternatieve vormen Zie voor definitie: equivalente vormen.
CA:185, DA:12, DE:11, EN:11, ES:203, FR:193, GA:146, IT:176, NE:13, PO:199.

14 alternatieven De mogelijkheden in een multiple-choice item of matching-opdracht waaruit de juiste moet worden gekozen.
CA:279, DA:425, DE:38, EN:262, ES:292, FR:290, GA:293, IT:258, NE:14, PO:294.

15 analytische scoring Een scoringsmethode die kan worden gebruikt in produktief-taalgebruiktoetsen, zoals spreek- en schrijftoetsen. De beoordelaar geeft een evaluatie met behulp van een lijst met specifieke punten. In een schrijftoets zou de analytische schaal bijvoorbeeld kunnen bestaan uit een grammatica-component, een vocabulaire-component, een verbindingswoorden-component.
Vergelijk: globale beoordeling, impressie-correctie (algemeneimpressiecorrectie).
Meer informatie: Ebel en Frisbie, 1991, p. 195.
CA:343, DA:13, DE:12, EN:14, ES:426, FR:266, GA:340, IT:27, NE:15, PO:58.

16 ANCOVA (Co-variantie-analyse) Een soort variantie-analyse waarin het effect van variabelen die ruis veroorzaken (de variabelen die met de variabele waarin men geïnteresseerd is mee kunnen veranderen) onder controle wordt gehouden.
Zie: ANOVA
Meer informatie: Hatch en Lazaraton, 1991, p. 387.
CA:21, DA:14, DE:13, EN:17, ES:27, FR:19, GA:20, IT:20, NE:16, PO:21.

17 anker-item Een item dat in twee of meer toetsen voorkomt. Ankeritems waarvan de kenmerken altijd bekend zijn, maken samen onderdeel uit van een nieuwe versie van een toets en worden gebruikt om informatie te krijgen over deze toets en de kandidaten die de toets hebben afgelegd, dat wil zeggen om een nieuwe toets op een meetschaal te kunnen kalibreren.
Vergelijk: ankertoets.
Zie: kalibratie.
CA:218, DA:16, DE:18, EN:15, ES:237, FR:225, GA:241, IT:212, NE:17, PO:232.

18 ankertoets Een toets met bekende meetkenmerken, die wordt afgenomen met een andere toets. Performance op de ankertoets geeft informatie over de andere toets en over de kandidaten die beide toetsen hebben afgelegd.
Vergelijk: anker-item.
CA:307, DA:17, DE:19, EN:16, ES:320, FR:367, GA:404, IT:357, NE:18, PO:365.

19 ANOVA (variantie-analyse) Een statistische techniek voor het toetsen van de nul-hypothese dat verschillende populatie-gemiddelden gelijk zijn. Zowel de variabiliteit van de observaties binnen de groepen als de variabiliteit tussen de groepsgemiddelden wordt onderzocht.
Meer informatie: Hatch en Lazaraton, 1991, pp. 308–312.
CA:22, DA:19, DE:20, EN:18, ES:28, FR:20, GA:21, IT:21, NE:19, PO:22.

20 antwoorblad Het blad waarop een kandidaat zijn/haar antwoorden geeft.
Vergelijk: optische lezer.
CA:191, DA:37, DE:22, EN:19, ES:219, FR:181, GA:152, IT:174, NE:20, PO:198.

21 antwoordmodel De itemschrijver maakt een inventarisatie van de antwoorden die men bij een opdracht met open vragen kan verwachten. Dit antwoordmodel kan gebruikt worden bij de ontwikkeling van een correctieschema, als leidraad voor de correctoren.
CA:261, DA:233, DE:253, EN:236, ES:376, FR:333, GA:156, IT:245, NE:21, PO:340.

22 aptitude-toets Een toets voor het voorspellen of meten van de kans op succes bij een kandidaat op een bepaald terrein van leren, bijvoorbeeld bij het leren van een vreemde taal, of bij het volgen van een bepaalde studie.

Meer informatie: Henning, 1987, p. 6; Ebel en Frisbie, 1991, p. 339.
CA:308, DA:18, DE:96, EN:20, ES:322, FR:368, GA:421, IT:358, NE:22, PO:370.

23 authenticiteit Een toetskenmerk; geeft aan in hoeverre toetsopdrachten een afspiegeling zijn van taalgebruik in een niet-toetsgebonden situatie.
Meer informatie: Bachman, 1990, pp. 300–303.
CA:27, DA:21, DE:42, EN:24, ES:33, FR:24, GA:115, IT:35, NE:23, PO:26.

24 authentieke tekst Tekst in een toets die bestaat uit materiaal dat oorspronkelijk niet voor taaltoetsing werd gemaakt en niet speciaal voor de toets in kwestie werd samengesteld.
NB Het materiaal kan enigszins worden geredigeerd om het geschikt te maken voor gebruik in de toets.
Vergelijk: semi-authentieke tekst.
CA:404, DA:22, DE:41, EN:25, ES:401, FR:111, GA:382, IT:390, NE:24, PO:127.

25 automatische correctie Een corrigeermethode waarbij de correctoren geen speciale expertise nodig hebben en geen eigen oordeel hoeven te geven. Ze corrigeren aan de hand van een correctieschema waarin alle acceptabele antwoorden op een toetsitem staan weergegeven.
Vergelijk: examinator-correctie.
CA:86, DA:23, DE:231, EN:51, ES:78, FR:274, GA:219, IT:31, NE:25, PO:62.

26 b-parameter De parameter uit de itemresponsetheorie die betrekking heeft op de moeilijkheidsgraad van een item.
Zie: itemresponsetheorie (IRT) .
Meer informatie: Bachman, 1990, p. 204.
CA:282, DA:24, DE:170, EN:26, ES:295, FR:293, GA:274, IT:261, NE:26, PO:298.

27 backwash De impact van een toets op de lespraktijk. Docenten kunnen worden beïnvoed door de wetenschap dat hun leerlingen aan een bepaalde toets gaan meedoen en hun methodologie en lesinhoud afstemmen op wat er in de toets zal worden gevraagd. Het resultaat kan positief of negatief zijn.
Wordt ook wel washback genoemd.
Zie: impact.
CA:372, DA:25, DE:43, EN:28, ES:369, FR:322, GA:95, IT:147, NE:27, PO:135.

28 band In de meest ruime zin: onderdeel van een schaal. In een toets met items staat de band voor een reeks scores (de cijfer- of bandscore). Bij een beoordelingsschaal waarmee een bepaalde eigenschap of vaardigheid wordt gemeten (bijv. spreken of schrijven), staat de band meestal voor een bepaald niveau.
CA:37, DA:339, DE:44, EN:29, ES:38, FR:200, GA:41, IT:39 NE:28, PO:210.

29 bandscore Deel van een schaal, die betrekking heeft op een specifiek vaardigheidsbereik.
CA:346, DA:258, DE:210, EN:30, ES:39, FR:269, GA:330, IT:40, NE:29, PO:65.

30 batterij Een set verwante toetsen of subtoetsen die ieder op zich een bepaalde bijdrage leveren (ze toetsen bijvoorbeeld verschillende vaardigheden) maar in combinatie een totaalscore opleveren.
CA:38, DA:28, DE:393, EN:32, ES:40, FR:30, GA:64, IT:41, NE:30, PO:38.

31 behoeftenanalyse Een manier om de taalbehoeften (in termen van vaardigheden, taken, vocabulaire, etc.) te bepalen van een bepaalde groep lerenden, voordat er voor hen een cursus wordt ontworpen.
CA:16, DA:35, DE:45, EN:246, ES:21, FR:11, GA:19, IT:13, NE:31, PO:17.

32 beoogde response De response of responsen die de bedenker van een item of opdracht wil oproepen.
CA:377, DA:106, DE:105, EN:137, ES:374, FR:328, GA:157, IT:306, NE:32, PO:338.

33 beoordelaar Iemand die een score toekent aan de performance van een kandidaat op een toets en daarbij een subjectieve beoordeling hanteert. Beoordelaars zijn meestal vakdocenten die extra instructie krijgen (bijvoorbeeld in het normeren). Bij mondelinge toetsing wordt soms verschil gemaakt tussen degene die het gesprek leidt en degene die beoordeelt. Wordt ook wel examinator genoemd.
Vergelijk: gespreksleider, corrector.
CA:35, DA:32, DE:55, EN:22, ES:46, FR:174, GA:234, IT:165, NE:33, PO:182.

34 beoordelaar Zie voor definitie: assessor.
CA:361, DA:306, DE:100, EN:311, ES:187, FR:164, GA:287, IT:102, NE:34, PO:182.

35 beoordelaarseffecten Een bron van fouten bij de beoordeling, het resultaat van een bepaalde houding bij beoordelaars (bijvoorbeeld te streng of te mild zijn) of een positief beeld van een bepaald soort kandidaat, factoren die de score van toetskandidaten kunnen beïnvloeden. Voorbeelden: contaminatie-effect, halo-effect en sequentie-

effect.
CA:124, DA:34, DE:425, EN:313, ES:130, FR:144, GA:176, IT:143, NE:35, PO:138.

36 beoordelaarsovereenstemming Zie voor definitie: interbeoordelaarsovereenstemming en intra-beoordelaarsovereenstemming
CA:1, DA:307, DE:56, EN:312, ES:10, FR:1, GA:70, IT:84, NE:36, PO:1.

37 beoordeling van map met werk van de kandidaat Een beoordelingstechniek waarbij een kandidaat, gedurende een x periode een map met voorbeelden van zijn/haar werk aanlegt en deze map vervolgens presenteert als bewijs van zijn/haar vaardigheid.
CA:386, DA:293, DE:291, EN:286, ES:185, FR:304, GA:237, IT:270, NE:37, PO:309.

38 beoordeling a) Het toekennen van een score aan toetsperformance door het geven van een beoordeling.
b) De score die wordt toegekend op basis van de beoordeling.
CA:428, DA:171, DE:57, EN:314, ES:425, FR:265, GA:286, IT:54, NE:38, PO:57.

39 beoordeling Bij taaltoetsing: het meten van een of meer aspecten van taalvaardigheid via een bepaalde toetsvorm of procedure.
Meer informatie: Bachman, 1990, p. 50.
CA:31, DA:30, DE:54, EN:21, ES:180, FR:165, GA:229, IT:421, NE:39, PO:30.

40 beoordelingsschaal Een schaal bestaande uit een aantal geordende categorieën voor het geven van een subjectieve beoordeling. In de taaltoetsing gaan de beoordelingsschalen voor het evalueren van performance meestal gepaard met band-descriptoren die aangeven hoe deze schalen moeten worden geïnterpreteerd.
Vergelijk: likert-schaal.
Zie: descriptor.
CA:154, DA:172, DE:58, EN:315, ES:161, FR:130, GA:319, IT:323, NE:40, PO:160.

41 beoordelingsschaalmodel Een uitbreiding van het simpele Rasch-model voor het omgaan met schaalgegevens, bijvoorbeeld schaalgegevens ontleend aan een spreekvaardigheidsbeoordeling.
Vergelijk: Rasch-model.
Zie: partial-creditmodel.
Meer informatie: Wright, B.D. en Masters G.N., 1982, Rating Scale Analysis Chicago, MESA Press.
CA:254, DA:173, DE:236, EN:316, ES:272, FR:251, GA:303, IT:246, NE:41, PO:263.

42 betogende stelopdracht Een schrijfopdracht waarbij de kandidaat een onderwerp moet bespreken waarover verschil van mening mogelijk is of zijn eigen mening moet beargumenteren.
Zie: stelopdracht.
CA:74, DA:77, DE:342, EN:113, ES:70, FR:74, GA:52, IT:83, NE:42, PO:89.

43 betrouwbaarheid De consistentie of stabiliteit van de maten die een toets heeft voortgebracht. Hoe betrouwbaarder de toets, hoe minder 'random error' deze bevat. Een toets met systematische 'error', bijvoorbeeld 'bias' ten opzichte van een bepaalde groep, kan wel betrouwbaar zijn, maar is niet valide.
Vergelijk: validiteit.
Zie: KR-20 (Kuder-Richardson formule 20), split-halfbetrouwbaarheid, test-retestbetrouwbaarheid.
Meer informatie: Bachman, 1990, p. 24; Crocker en Algina, 1986, hoofdstuk 6.
CA:180, DA:312, DE:322/453, EN:327, ES:198, FR:183, GA:200, IT:6, NE:43, PO:193.

44 betrouwbaarheids-coëfficiënt Een betrouwbaarheidsmaat, in de range van 0 tot 1. Betrouwbaarheidsschattingen kunnen gebaseerd zijn op herhaalde afnames van een toets (dergelijke afnames dienen een vergelijkbaar resultaat te laten zien) of als dit praktisch niet haalbaar is, op een of andere vorm van interne-consistentiemaat. Ook wel bekend onder de naam betrouwbaarheidsindex.
Zie: interne consistentie, betrouwbaarheid, test-retestbetrouwbaarheid.
CA:61, DA:313, DE:323, EN:328, ES:58, FR:61, GA:77, IT:59, NE:44, PO:74.

45 betrouwbaarheidsinterval Het gebied rond de schatting van de waarde waarin de ware waarde waarschijnlijk zal vallen. De mate van waarschijnlijkheid ligt meestal op een betrouwbaarheidsniveau van 95 of 99%.
CA:215, DA:182, DE:184, EN:67, ES:233, FR:219, GA:132, IT:204, NE:45, PO:229.

46 bias Bij een toets of item is sprake van 'bias' als een bepaald deel van de kandidatenpopulatie voor- of nadeel heeft van een bepaald kenmerk van de toets of het item dat niet relevant is voor wat er wordt gemeten. Bias kan te maken hebben met verschil in sekse, leeftijd, cultuur, etc.
Meer informatie: Bachman, 1990, pp.

271–279; Crocker en Algina, 1986, hoofdstuk 12 en 16.

CA:40, DA:344, DE:383, EN:33, ES:384, FR:32, GA:208, IT:160, NE:46, PO:40.

47 bimodale distributie/verdeling Een verdeling met daarin twee 'modi' of pieken die erop kan wijzen dat er binnen dezelfde steekproef sprake is van twee verschillende groepen.

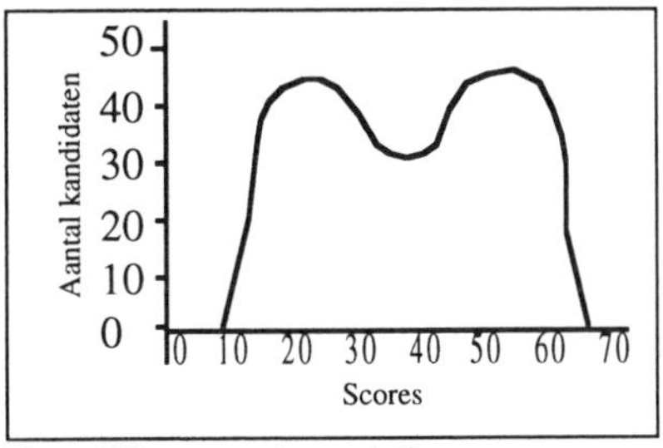

Vergelijk: normale verdeling.
Zie: modus.
Meer informatie: Hatch en Lazaraton, 1991, pp. 165–166.

CA:112, DA:39, DE:59, EN:34, ES:113, FR:106, GA:104, IT:131, NE:47, PO:121.

48 biseriële correlatie Een item-discriminatie-index voor dichotome items weergegeven als r_{bis}; de correlatie tussen een criterium (meestal de score van de totale toets) en de vaardigheid die ten grondslag ligt aan het goed-fout-antwoord op het item. De waarde van r_{bis} ligt minstens 25% hoger dan bij de punt-biseriële correlatie (r_{pbi}). r_{bis} heeft als voordeel dat deze correlatie redelijk stabiel is over steekproeven van verschillend vaardigheidsniveau.
Vergelijk: punt-biseriële correlatie
Zie: discriminatie
Meer informatie: Crocker en Algina, 1986, pp. 317–318; Guilford en Fruchter pp. 304–311.

CA:56, DA:40, DE:60, EN:35, ES:85, FR:86, GA:79, IT:96, NE:48, PO:101.

49 bodemeffect Een grenseffect als gevolg van het feit dat een toets te moeilijk is voor een bepaalde groep kandidaten, zodat hun scores allemaal onderaan de verdelingsschaal samenklonteren.
Zie: grenseffect.

CA:122, DA:42, DE:61/121, EN:146, ES:128, FR:141, GA:175, IT:144, NE:49, PO:130.

50 c-parameter (gisparameter) De parameter uit de itemresponsetheorie die betrekking heeft op raden.
Zie: itemresponsetheorie (IRT).
Meer informatie: Bachman, 1990, p. 204.

CA:283, DA:44, DE:318, EN:37, ES:296, FR:294, GA:275, IT:262, NE:50, PO:299.

51 c-toets Een soort invulopdracht waarbij de tweede helft van bepaalde woorden wordt weggelaten. De gaten kunnen om het woord worden geplaatst. Het is aan de kandidaten om de woorden aan te vullen.
Vergelijk: cloze-toets.
Meer informatie: Weir, 1990, p. 49.

CA:304, DA:45, DE:62, EN:38, ES:314, FR:394, GA:408, IT:384, NE:51, PO:366.

52 categorie a) Een verdeling op een categorische schaal; zo is bijvoorbeeld 'sekse' onderverdeeld in de categorie 'man' en 'vrouw'.

b) In de toetspraktijk heeft een vijfpuntsbeoordelingsschaal bijvoorbeeld vijf responsecategorieën.

CA:49, DA:169, DE:176, EN:43, ES:52, FR:48, GA:50, IT:51, NE:52, PO:55.

53 categorische schaal Een schaal voor categorische variabelen, zoals sekse, moedertaal, beroep.
Vergelijk: intervalschaal, nominale schaal, ordinale schaal, ratio-schaal.

CA:146, DA:170, DE:175, EN:42, ES:154, FR:123, GA:310, IT:318, NE:53, PO:156.

54 centiel-schaal Een ordinale schaal verdeeld in 100 eenheden of centielen. Als iemand een centielscore van 95 heeft, betekent dat in een typische steekproef van 100 dat deze persoon 94 anderen onder zich zou hebben.
Vergelijk: percentielscore.
Meer informatie: Crocker en Algina, pp. 439–442; Guilford en Fruchter, 1981, pp. 38–41.

CA:151, DA:46, DE:300, EN:46, ES:155, FR:124, GA:311, IT:319, NE:54, PO:157.

55 centrale tendentie (meting van) Een manier om het midden of het statische gemiddelde van een verdeling te bepalen. Drie veelgebruikte maten voor centrale tendentie zijn het gemiddelde, de mediaan en de modus.
Meer informatie: Henning, 1987, pp. 39–40, Guilford en Fruchter, 1981, hoofdstuk 4, Hatch en Lazaraton, 1991, pp. 159–164.

CA:246, DA:47, DE:447, EN:45, ES:391, FR:358, GA:62, IT:348, NE:55, PO:356.

56 certificaat Een document dat aan-

geeft dat de persoon die op het document vermeld wordt een examen of deel van een examen heeft afgelegd en een bepaald cijfer heeft behaald, meestal minstens een voldoende.
Vergelijk: diploma.

CA:50, DA:38, DE:448, EN:47, ES:53, FR:50, GA:386, IT:52, NE:56, PO:56.

57 cesuur De minimumscore die een kandidaat moet hebben om een bepaald cijfer voor een toets of examen te behalen. Bij beheersingsgerichte toetsen de toetsscore op het niveau dat mimimaal gehaald moet worden om competent of tot beheersing in staat geacht te worden.
Zie: mastery-toets, minimale-competentietoetsing.
Vergelijk: slaagcijfer.
Meer informatie: Bachman, 1990, pp. 214–215.

CA:359, DA:58, DE:199, EN:90, ES:351, FR:277, GA:338, IT:280, NE:57, PO:282.

58 checklist Een lijst met vragen of punten die moeten worden beantwoord/afgehandeld. In taaltoetsen vaak gebruikt als observatie- of analysemiddel.

CA:240, DA:48, DE:64, EN:48, ES:258, FR:239, GA:351, IT:228, NE:58, PO:252.

59 chi-kwadraattoets Een statistische methode waarbij de waarden van de response zoals die wordt waargenomen en de response zoals die werd ingeschat worden vergeleken om te zien of het verschil tussen de twee waarden statistisch significant is. Het is een niet-parametrische methode.
Zie: niet-parametrische procedures.
Meer informatie: Hatch en Lazaraton, 1991, pp. 393–415.

CA:330, DA:49, DE:65, EN:49, ES:396, FR:149, GA:409, IT:359, NE:59, PO:395.

60 cijfer Het totaal aantal punten dat een kandidaat kan behalen voor een item, toetsonderdeel of toets, of het aantal punten dat wordt toegekend aan het antwoord van een kandidaat op een item, toetsonderdeel of toets.

CA:342, DA:287, DE:313, EN:224, ES:44, FR:287, GA:224, IT:292, NE:60, PO:105.

61 cloze-toets Een soort invultoets waarbij hele woorden worden weggelaten in een toets. In een traditionele cloze wordt om de zoveel woorden een woord weggelaten. Andere invultoetsen waarbij korte zinnen/stukken van zinnen worden weggelaten, of waarbij de itemschrijver zelf bepaalt welke woorden komen te vervallen, wordt meestal een 'rationele cloze-toets' genoemd. De kandidaten moeten de ontbrekende woorden zelf aanvullen (open cloze) of kiezen uit een aantal mogelijkheden (multiple-choice cloze). Bij de open cloze kan de correctie gebeuren op basis van 'exacte woorden' (er is maar één woord dat op de lege plek past) of op basis van 'acceptabele woorden' (de correctoren krijgen een lijst met acceptabele antwoorden).
Vergelijk: c-toets,invulitem.
Meer informatie: Weir, 1990, p. 46–48; Oller, 1979, hoofdstuk 12.

CA:313, DA:50, DE:66, EN:52, ES:315, FR:370, GA:410, IT:362, NE:61, PO:378.

62 coëfficiënt Een numerieke index om een eigenschap of kenmerk mee te meten.
Zie: alpha (alpha-coëfficiënt), correlatiecoëfficiënt.

CA:53, DA:175, DE:178, EN:53, ES:55, FR:54, GA:73, IT:57, NE:62, PO:69.

63 coëfficiënt alpha Zie onder alpha (alpha-coëfficiënt).

CA:54, DA:176, DE:179, EN:54, ES:56, FR:55, GA:74, IT:58, NE:63, PO:70.

64 cognitief model Een theorie over de manier waarop iemands kennis, dat wil zeggen zowel kennis-noties als kennis-processen, is gestructureerd. Vooral belangrijk in de taaltoetsing, omdat een dergelijke theorie effect kan hebben op de keuze van de toetsmethode of toetsinhoud.

CA:253, DA:178, DE:181, EN:56, ES:269, FR:250, GA:297, IT:243, NE:64, PO:262.

65 cognitieve factoren Factoren in het leer- of toetsproces die te maken hebben met de kennis-schemata en -patronen van een leerling.
Vergelijk: affectieve factoren.
Meer informatie: Ebel en Frisbie, 1991, p. 52.

CA:178, DA:177, DE:180, EN:55, ES:196, FR:179, GA:398, IT:171, NE:65, PO:189.

66 communicatieve competentie Het vermogen om taal op de juiste manier te gebruiken in een verscheidenheid aan situaties en contexten.
Meer informatie: Bachman, 1990, p. 16, p. 68.

CA:65, DA:179, DE:182, EN:58, ES:61, FR:63, GA:195, IT:63, NE:66, PO:77.

67 competentie De kennis of het vermogen om iets te doen. In de taalkunde wordt de term gebruikt voor een onderliggend vermogen, dit in tegenstelling tot performance. Performance is de manier waarop de competentie zich manifesteert als taalgebruik.

Het onderscheid is afkomstig uit het werk van Chomsky.
Vergelijk: performance.
Meer informatie: Bachman, 1990, pp. 52 en 108.
CA:64, DA:180, DE:183, EN:59, ES:60, FR:62, GA:191, IT:62, NE:67, PO:76.

68 computer-adaptieve toetsing Een computer-toetsmethode waarbij de moeilijkheidsgraad van de aan de kandidaten voor te leggen items kan worden aangepast aan de vaardigheid van de leerling, op basis van de reeds gegeven antwoorden.
Zie: computer-toetsing (-evaluatie).
CA:303, DA:51, DE:67, EN:63, ES:181, FR:362, GA:379, IT:386, NE:68, PO:364.

69 computer-correctie (-scoring) Diverse manieren om computersystemen te gebruiken om fouten bij het corrigeren van objectieve toetsen tot een minimum te beperken. Dit kan bijvoorbeeld worden gedaan door het werk van de kandidaten met een optische lezer door te lopen en gegevens te produceren die in scores kunnen worden omgezet of voor analyse-doeleinden kunnen worden gebruikt.
CA:85, DA:53, DE:69, EN:65, ES:82, FR:273, GA:222, IT:28, NE:69, PO:66.

70 computer-toetsing (-evaluatie) Een toetsmethode waarbij de items per computer aan de kandidaten worden voorgelegd. Ook de antwoorden kunnen per computer worden gegeven.
CA:332, DA:52, DE:68, EN:64, ES:182, FR:171, GA:380, IT:387, NE:70, PO:35.

71 concurrente validiteit Bij een toets is sprake van concurrente validiteit, als de scores van de toets een hoge correlatie vertonen met een algemeen erkend extern criterium dat hetzelfde kennis- of vaardigheidsterrein meet.
Zie: criterium validiteit.
Meer informatie: Bachman, 1990, pp. 248–250.
CA:418, DA:323, DE:417, EN:66, ES:415, FR:415, GA:33, IT:403, NE:71, PO:411.

72 construct/begrip Een hypothetisch vermogen of mentale eigenschap/trek die zich niet makkelijk direct laat observeren of meten, bijvoorbeeld in een taaltoets luistervaardigheid. In taaltoetsen wordt een poging gedaan de verschillende constructen(begrippen) die aan de taalvaardigheid ten grondslag liggen te meten. Andere relevante constructen, naast taalvaardigheid, zijn bijvoorbeeld: motivatie, attitude en acculturatie.
Meer informatie: Hatch en Lazaraton, 1991, p. 15.
CA:78, DA:184, DE:185, EN:68, ES:76, FR:80, GA:394, IT:108, NE:72, PO:94.

73 construct-validiteit (begripsvaliditeit) Een toets is construct-valide als de scores een aantoonbare afspiegeling zijn van voorspellingen over de aard van een construct of de relatie van het construct met andere constructen. Zo zou men bijvoorbeeld kunnen voorspellen dat bij twee valide luistertoetsen leerlingen op dezelfde manier worden ingeschaald, maar dat beide toetsen een zwakkere relatie vertonen met scores op een grammaticale-competentietoets.
Zie: validiteit, toetsspecificaties.
Meer informatie: Ebel en Frisbie, 1991, p. 108; Hatch en Lazaraton, 1991, pp. 37.
CA:420, DA:186, DE:186, EN:69, ES:418, FR:418, GA:37, IT:406, NE:73, PO:414.

74 contaminatie-effect Een beoordelaarseffect dat optreedt wanneer een beoordelaar een score toekent op basis van een factor die niet wordt getoetst. Een voorbeeld: de schrijftoets-score van een kandidaat verhogen, omdat hij of zij een keurig handschrift heeft.
Zie: beoordelaarseffecten.
CA:118, DA:9, DE:226, EN:71, ES:122, FR:136, GA:174, IT:141, NE:74, PO:132.

75 contingentie-tabel Een tabel met frequenties geklassificeerd volgens twee of meer sets waarden van categorische variabelen, bijv.:

	Beheersing	Geen beheersing
Methode A	35	5
Methode B	20	20

Zie: chi-kwadraattoets.
CA:398, DA:187, DE:187, EN:74, ES:390, FR:353, GA:369, IT:347, NE:75, PO:320.

76 convergente validiteit Bij een toets is sprake van convergente validiteit, als er een hoge correlatie is tussen scores op deze toets en de scores uit een andere toets waarin hetzelfde construct wordt gemeten (los van de gebruikte methode). Kan worden gezien als onderdeel van constructvaliditeit.
Vergelijk: discriminante validiteit.
Zie: construct-validiteit (begripsvaliditeit).
Meer informatie: Guilford en Fruchter, 1981, pp. 436–437.
CA:419, DA:188, DE:188, EN:75, ES:416, FR:416, GA:32, IT:404, NE:76, PO:412.

77 correctie voor raden Een manier om de puntenwinst ongedaan te maken. Het gaat hier om een puntenwinst ontstaan door het raden van het juiste antwoord in een toets met objectieve items.
Meer informatie: Ebel en Frisbie, 1986, pp. 215–218.
CA:82, DA:193, DE:317/450, EN:77, ES:80, FR:83, GA:54, IT:103, NE:77, PO:98.

78 correctie voor attenuatie Een methode om de correlatie tussen twee of meer variabelen te schatten als er geen verschil in betrouwbaarheid is tussen de variabelen.
Meer informatie: Guilford en Fruchter, 1981, pp. 450–453 Hatch en Lazaraton, 1990. pp. 444–445.
CA:88, DA:194, DE:243, EN:76, ES:79, FR:82, GA:53, IT:106, NE:78, PO:99.

79 correctieschema Een lijst met alle acceptabele antwoorden op de items in een toets. Met een correctieschema is een corrector in staat een toets heel precies na te kijken.
CA: 52/256, DA:319, DE:228, EN:223, ES:301, FR:29, GA:324, IT:329, NE:79, PO:172.

80 corrector Iemand die de schriftelijke toets van een kandidaat nakijkt. Het kan hierbij gaan om iemand met kennis van zaken, of bij automatische correctie om het, zonder specifieke kennis van zaken, toepassen van een correctieschema.
Zie: beoordelaar.
CA:90, DA:288, DE:39, EN:221, ES:83, FR:81, GA:225, IT:102, NE:80, PO:182.

81 correlatie De relatie tussen twee of meer metingen: in hoeverre zijn ze op dezelfde manier gespreid? Als kandidaten bijvoorbeeld op twee verschillende toetsen op vergelijkbare manier worden geordend, dan is er sprake van positieve correlatie tussen de twee score-sets.
Vergelijk: covariantie.
Zie: rangorde-correlatie, Pearsons produktmoment correlatie (Pearson's *r*).
Meer informatie: Guilford en Fruchter, 1981, hoofdstuk 6; Bachman, 1990, pp. 259–260.
CA:91, DA:196, DE:190, EN:78, ES:84, FR:85, GA:78, IT:95, NE:81, PO:100.

82 correlatie-coëfficiënt Een index die de mate van correlatie tussen twee of meer variabelen aangeeft. Kan variëren van -1 tot +1. Variabelen met een hoge correlatie worden weergegeven met een correlatiecoëfficiënt van tegen de +1.
Meer informatie: Guilford en Fruchter, 1981, pp. 86–88.
CA:55, DA:197, DE:191, EN:79, ES:57, FR:56, GA:75, IT:60, NE:82, PO:71.

83 corrigeren Het nakijken van de schriftelijke toets van een kandidaat. Het kan hierbij gaan om een beoordeling door experts, of om de toepassing van een correctieschema met daarin alle acceptabele antwoorden.
CA:80, DA:289, DE:40, EN:222, ES:47, FR:265, GA:218, IT:29, NE:83, PO:57.

84 covariantie De gezamenlijke variantie van twee of meer variabelen. Zo zijn bijvoorbeeld zinslengte en lexicale moeilijkheidsgraad kenmerken van een leestekst waarvan men redelijkerwijs mag verwachten dat ze aan elkaar gerelateerd zijn, dat wil zeggen het zijn kenmerken die covariëren.
Met covariantie moet rekening worden gehouden, wanneer men variabelen los van elkaar wil inschatten, bijvoorbeld wanneer men voorspellingen wil doen over de moeilijkheidsgraad van een leestekst op basis van zinslengte en lexicale moeilijkheidsgraad.
Zie: variantie.
CA:93, DA:199, DE:192, EN:80, ES:91, FR:92, GA:71, IT:112, NE:84, PO:106.

85 covariantie-analyse Zie voor definitie: ANCOVA
CA:14, DA:200, DE:193, EN:12, ES:20, FR:14, GA:16, IT:18, NE:85, PO:13.

86 criterium-gerichte toets Een toets waarin de performance van een kandidaat wordt afgezet tegen van tevoren bepaalde criteria. De nadruk ligt op het behalen van bepaalde doelen en niet zozeer op de scores van de kandidaten in termen van hun positie binnen de groep.
Vergelijk: normgerichte toets, domeingerichte toets.
CA:337, DA:203, DE:196, EN:81, ES:317, FR:364, GA:412, IT:380, NE:86, PO:369.

87 criterium-validiteit Een toets is criterium-valide, als er een relatie kan worden aangetoond tussen de toetsscores en een extern criterium dat geacht wordt dezelfde vaardigheid te meten. Informatie over al dan niet voldoen aan een criterium wordt ook gebruikt om te bepalen hoe goed een toets toekomstig gedrag voorspelt.
Zie: concurrente validiteit, predictieve validiteit.
Meer informatie: Bachman, 1990, pp.

248–250.
CA:421, DA:204, DE:197, EN:82, ES:417, FR:417, GA:34, IT:407, NE:87, PO:413.

88 criterium-variabele In de onderzoekstheorie een andere term voor afhankelijke variabele.
Zie: afhankelijke variabele.
CA:431, DA:205, DE:198, EN:83, ES:431, FR:424, GA:26, IT:417, NE:88, PO:423.

89 Cronbachs alpha Zie voor definitie: alpha (alpha-coëfficiënt).
CA:10, DA:54, DE:70, EN:84, ES:17, FR:9, GA:11, IT:11, NE:89, PO:7.

90 culturele bias Een toets met culturele bias werkt bij kandidaten met een bepaalde culturele achtergrond nadelig, of levert hun juist voordeel op.
Zie: bias.
CA:41, DA:207, DE:201, EN:85, ES:385, FR:33, GA:209, IT:161, NE:90, PO:41.

91 cumulatieve frequentie Een manier om de distributie van kandidaten weer te geven door voor iedere scorecategorie het aantal kandidaten te tellen die een score in die categorie en alle categoriëen daaronder hebben behaald.
Meer informatie: Guilford en Fruchter, 1981, pp. 35–36.
CA:189, DA:208, DE:202, EN:86, ES:208, FR:198, GA:239, IT:181, NE:91, PO:204.

92 d-index Een discriminatie index voor toetsitems.Vaak gebruikt voor kleinschalige toetsen die in de klas afgenomen worden, aangezien hij met de hand berekend kan worden. Uitgaande van de totale score op de toets worden zodanig een hoogstscorende en een laagstscorende groep gekozen dat tussen de 10% en 33% procent van de totale toetspopulatie in elk van beide groepen opgenomen is. Voor een normaalverdeling van de scores is het het beste om 27% in elke groep op te nemen. De itemresponsen van alle kandidaten in elk van beide groepen worden opgeteld voor elk item afzonderlijk. Op items die goed discrimineren, zal de hoogstscorende groep beter scoren dan de laagste scorende groep. De volgende formule geeft de item discriminatie index:

$$d=p_u-p_l$$

waarin p_u het deel is van de hoogstscorende groep die het item correct heefb en waarin p_l het deel van de laagstscorende groep is die het item goed heefb. In het algemeen worden items met een index van 0.3 of meer geacht goed te discrimineren.
CA:206, DA:59, DE:72, EN:91, ES:223, FR:208, GA:186, IT:194, NE:92, PO:218.

93 delta plot methode Een manier om te kijken naar Differential Item Functioning. Wordt gebruikt om items te identificeren die verschillen in groepsprestaties 'aandikken' of minimaliseren. Gebaseerd op klassieke-item-moeilijkheidsgraden (*p*-waarden). De *p*-waarden worden omgezet in genormaliseerde *z*-scores en deze waarden worden twee aan twee op een grafiek uitgezet om de relatieve moeilijkheidsgraad van items voor de twee groepen in kwestie te laten zien.
Zie: differential item functioning (DIF).
Meer informatie: Crocker en Algina, 1986, pp. 388–390.
CA:249, DA:61, DE:74, EN:92, ES:267, FR:246, GA:256, IT:237, NE:93, PO:260.

94 deltaschaal Een genormaliseerde schaal met een gemiddelde van 13 en een standaarddeviatie van 4.
CA:155, DA:60, DE:75, EN:93, ES:162, FR:132, GA:314, IT:321, NE:94, PO:165.

95 descriptieve statistiek De statistische methode die gebruikt wordt om een set gegevens te beschrijven in termen van hoeveelheid, spreiding, gemiddelde waarden, correlaties met andere gegevens, etc. Er wordt een onderscheid gemaakt tussen descriptieve statistiek en inferentiële statistiek.
Vergelijk: inferentiële statistiek.
CA:165, DA:63, DE:51, EN:95, ES:172, FR:349, GA:365, IT:340, NE:95, PO:176.

96 descriptor Een korte beschrijving bij een band op een beoordelingsschaal; een korte aanduiding van de mate van proficiency of het soort performance dat voor een kandidaat bij die score verwacht wordt.
CA:97, DA:64, DE:76, EN:96, ES:98, FR:97, GA:437, IT:118, NE:96, PO:113.

97 diagnostische toets Een toets die wordt gebruikt om de sterke en zwakke punten in een leerling te ontdekken. De resultaten kunnen worden gebruikt voor het nemen van beslissingen over toekomstige opleiding of scholing.
CA:317, DA:65, DE:77, EN:97, ES:325, FR:383, GA:414, IT:373, NE:97, PO:386.

98 dichotome scoring Scoring op basis van twee categorieën, namelijk goed/fout, voldoende/onvoldoende, ja/nee.
CA:347, DA:67, DE:455, EN:98, ES:347, FR:268, GA:341, IT:32, NE:98, PO:59.

99 dictee Een soort toets waarbij de kandidaat gevraagd wordt te luisteren naar een tekst en vervolgens moet opschrijven wat hij hoort. Criteria voor correctie van dictees variëren afhankelijk van het doel van de toets; het kan daarbij bijvoorbeeld ook gaan om spelling en interpunctie.

CA:103, DA:68, DE:79, EN:99, ES:105, FR:99, GA:109, IT:121, NE:99, PO:125.

100 differential item functioning (DIF) Het feit dat de relatieve moeilijkheidsgraad van een item afhankelijk is van een kenmerk van de groep die de toets heeft gemaakt, bijvoorbeeld moedertaal of sekse.
Zie: bias.

CA:195, DA:66, DE:78, EN:100, ES:209, FR:192, GA:114, IT:182, NE:100, PO:208.

101 diploma Een document waarop staat vermeld dat de persoon die in het document wordt genoemd een examen of een deel van een examen heeft afgelegd en een bepaald cijfer heeft behaald, meestal minstens een voldoende. Heeft vaak meer aanzien dan een certificaat.
Vergelijk: certificaat.

CA:104, DA:69, DE:80, EN:103, ES:106, FR:100, GA:118, IT:124, NE:101, PO:115.

102 directe toets Een toets die een productieve vaardigheid meet (lezen of schrijven) en waarin de beheersing van die vaardigheid zelf direct wordt gemeten. Een voorbeeld: schrijfvaardigheid toetsen door een kandidaat een brief te laten schrijven.
Vergelijk: indirecte toets (opdracht).
Meer informatie: Hughes, 1989, pp. 14–16.

CA:326, DA:70, DE:81, EN:104, ES:335, FR:384, GA:415, IT:375, NE:102, PO:387.

103 discourse Gesproken of geschreven tekst, als communicatieve taalhandeling.

CA:106, DA:75, DE:85, EN:106, ES:108, FR:101, GA:119, IT:125, NE:103, PO:117.

104 discourse-analyse In dit soort analyse staat de structuur en functie van verschillende soorten gesproken of geschreven tekst centraal.

CA:19, DA:76, DE:86, EN:107, ES:24, FR:13, GA:17, IT:16, NE: 104, PO:19.

105 discourse-competentie Het vermogen om discourse te begrijpen en te produceren. In sommige taalcompetentiemodellen is discourse-competentie soms een apart onderdeel.
Meer informatie: Bachman, 1990, hoofdstuk 4.

CA:66, DA:78, DE:87, EN:108, ES:62, FR:64, GA:196, IT:64, NE:105, PO:78.

106 discrete item Een op zichzelf staand item. Hoort niet bij een tekst, bij andere items of bij aanvullend materiaal. Een voorbeeld van een itemtype dat op deze manier wordt gebruikt, is een multiple choice item.
Vergelijk: op tekst gebaseerd item.

CA:230, DA:71, DE:421, EN:109, ES:246, FR:228, GA:253, IT:219, NE:106, PO:241.

107 discrete-point item Een 'discrete item' dat een bepaald aspect toetst, bijvoorbeeld structuur of vocabulaire, en losstaat van andere items. De discrete-point-taaltoetsing werd in de jaren zestig heel populair, onder andere door toedoen van Robert Lado.
Vergelijk: integratief item/integratieve opdracht.
Zie: discrete item.

CA:225, DA:72, DE:82, EN:110, ES:247 FR:229, GA:251, IT:210, NE:107, PO:240.

108 discriminante validiteit Een toets is discriminant valide als de correlatie van de toets met toetsen die een ander kenmerk meten, lager is dan de correlatie met toetsen die hetzelfde kenmerk meten, ongeacht de toetsmethode. Kan worden gezien als onderdeel van constructvaliditeit.
Zie: constructvaliditeit (begripsvaliditeit).
Vergelijk: convergente validiteit.
Meer informatie: Crocker en Algina, 1986, p. 23; Guilford en Fruchter, 1981, pp. 436–437.

CA:423, DA:73, DE:83, EN:111, ES:420, FR:420, GA:36, IT:408, NE:108, PO:416.

109 discriminatie Het vermogen van een item om te discrimineren tussen zwakkere en sterkere kandidaten. Er worden verschillende discriminatie-indexen gebruikt. Een aantal daarvan (bijvoorbeeld puntbiserieel, biserieel) is gebaseerd op een correlatie tusen de score op een item en een criterium, zoals totaalscore op de toets of een of andere externe proficiency-maat. Andere zijn gebaseerd op het verschil in de moeilijkheidsgraad van het item voor groepen met lage en hoge vaardigheidsniveaus. In de itemresponsetheorie vinden we in het 2 en 3-parametermodel de itemdiscriminatie terug als a-parameter.
Zie: biseriële correlatie, punt-biseriële correlatie, itemresponsetheorie (IRT) .
Meer informatie: Crocker en Algina, 1986, pp. 313–320; Ebel en Frisbie, 1991, pp. 231–232.

CA:105, DA:74, DE:416, EN:112, ES:107, FR:102, GA:180, IT:126, NE:109, PO:116.

110 distributie In toetsgegevens het aantal malen dat een kandidatenscore voorkomt. Dit wordt vaak aangegeven in een histogram.

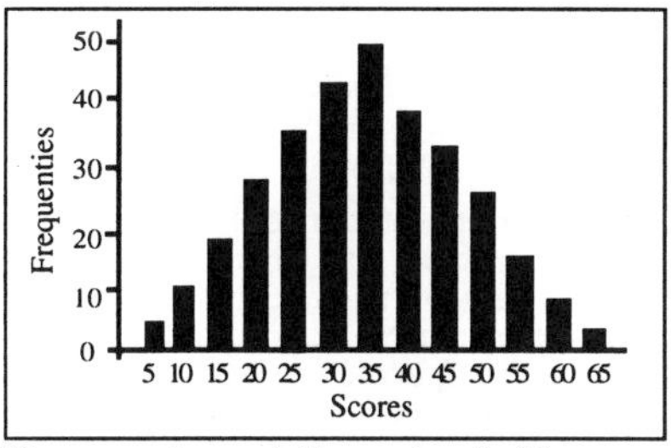

Zie: normale verdeling, scheefheid.
Meer informatie: Hatch en Lazaraton, 1991, pp. 159–178.

CA:111, DA:103, DE:434, EN:117, ES:112, FR:105, GA:103, IT:130, NE:110, PO:119.

111 divergente validiteit Zie ook: discriminante validiteit

CA:424, DA:81, DE:90, EN:118, ES:421, FR:421, GA:35, IT:409, NE:111, PO:417.

112 doelen De kennis, competentie en attitudes die vastgelegd worden als doelstelling van een onderwijskundig proces.

CA:278, DA:244, DE:216, EN:256, ES:291, FR:288, GA:359, IT:254, NE:112, PO:293.

113 domein Precieze afbakening van inhoud en/of vaardigheid die moet worden getoetst via een specifieke opdracht of onderdeel van een examen.
Meer informatie: Bachman, 1990, pp. 244–246.

CA:11, DA:83, DE:238, EN:119, ES:119, FR:113, GA:137, IT:332, NE:113, PO:129.

114 domein-gerichte toets Een toets waarin de resultaten worden geïnterpreteerd op basis van een specifiek inhouds- of vaardigheidsdomein.
Vergelijk: criterium-gerichte toets, normgerichte toets.

CA:335, DA:84, DE:50, EN:120, ES:342, FR:391, GA:417, IT:382, NE:114, PO:368.

115 doorlichten Een stadium in het toetsproductieproces waarbij de toetsontwikkelaars materiaal van itemschrijvers beoordelen en bepalen welke items moeten worden afgewezen, omdat ze niet voldoen aan de toetsspecificaties en welke door kunnen naar het redigeerstadium.
Vergelijk: moderation.

CA:382, DA:400, DE:405, EN:433 ES:383, FR:338, GA:184, IT:91, NE:115, PO:343.

116 dubbele correctie Een methode voor het evalueren van performance waarbij twee personen onafhankelijk van elkaar de performance van een kandidaat op een toets beoordelen.
Zie: meervoudige correctie.

CA:84, DA:82, DE:91, EN:121, ES:118, FR:114, GA:221, IT:104, NE:116, PO:61.

117 Ebel's d Zie voor definitie: d-index.

CA:96, DA:85, DE:92, EN:122, ES:96, FR:94, GA:101, IT:116, NE:117, PO:111.

118 een-parametermodel In de itemresponsetheorie een model dat werkt met een enkele schaal waarop moeilijkheidsgraad (van opdrachten) en vaardigheid (van personen) worden uitgezet en waarin geen rekening wordt gehouden met variabele itemdiscriminatie of met raden.
Vergelijk: Rasch-model.

CA:255, DA:92, DE:99, EN:259, ES:273, FR:249, GA:296, IT:242, NE:118, PO:265.

119 eendimensionaliteit Uitgaan van één enkele dimensie, een noodzakelijke voorwaarde voor het construeren van een schaal voor het meten van psychologische trekken, bijvoorbeeld door gebruikmaking van moderne itemresponsemodellen. Eendimensionaliteit is een kenmerk van het meetinstrument, niet van de onderliggende psychologische processen.
Meer informatie: Crocker en Algina, 1986, p. 343.

CA:413, DA:90, DE:97, EN:427, ES:410, FR:408, GA:23, IT:398, NE:119, PO:406.

120 enkelvoudige steekproef Een verzameling elementen die aselect worden 'getrokken' uit de populatie die men onderzoekt, zodat elk element uit de populatie evenveel kans heeft om in het onderzoek te worden betrokken.
Zie: steekproef.
Meer informatie: Crocker en Algina, 1986, pp. 433–438; Guilford en Fruchter, 1981, p. 120.

CA:265, DA:409, DE:451, EN:307, ES:279, FR:117, GA:305, IT:47, NE:120, PO:9.

121 equipercentiele equivalering Een methode voor het equivaleren van ruwe scores van toetsen, waarbij scores als geëquivaleerd worden beschouwd, als ze in een groep kandidaten betrekking hebben op dezelfde percentielrang.

CA:132, DA:440, DE:24, EN:127, ES:140, FR:36, GA:88, IT:150, NE:121, PO:43.

122 equivalente vormen Worden ook wel parallelle of alternatieve vormen genoemd. Verschillende versies van dezelfde toets die als equivalent worden gezien, omdat ze dezelfde specificaties als basis hebben en dezelfde competentie meten. Om binnen de klassieke toetstheorie aan de strenge equivalentie-eisen te kunnen voldoen, moeten verschillende vormen van een toets dezelfde gemiddelde moeilijkheidsgraad, variantie en covariantie met een concurrent criterium vertonen, wanneer ze aan dezelfde personen worden voorgelegd. Equivalentie is in de praktijk moeilijk te verwezenlijken.
Worden ook wel parallelle vormen genoemd.
Vergelijk: geëquivaleerde vormen.
Meer informatie: Crocker en Algina, 1986, p. 132.
CA:187, DA:441, DE:25, EN:128 ES:205, FR:195, GA:143, IT:178, NE:122, PO:201.

123 erkenning De officiële acceptatie van een instelling van een bepaalde kwalificatie (bewijs van geschiktheid) voor een bepaald doel, bijvoorbeeld toelating tot een tertiaire opleiding.
CA:365, DA:15, DE:269, EN:323, ES:361, FR:321, GA:9, IT:303, NE:123, PO:325.

124 error In de klassieke theorie voor het meten van de ware score bestaat een waargenomen score op een toets uit twee delen: een ware score die iemands vaardigheid weergeeft en een error-score die het effect weergeeft van alle andere factoren die niets de met getoetste vaardigheid te maken hebben.
Vergelijk: bias.
Meer informatie: Bachman, 1990, p. 167.
CA:136, DA:98, DE:116, EN:129, ES:144, FR:151, GA:122, IT:154, NE:124, PO:146.

125 essay-vraag Zie voor definitie: stelopdracht.
CA:366, DA:262, DE:33, EN:131, ES:306, FR:159, GA:7, IT:313, NE:125, PO:142.

126 evaluatie Het verzamelen van informatie die als basis moet dienen voor het nemen van beslissingen. In de taaltoetsing kan evaluatie zich richten op de effectiviteit of impact van een lesprogramma, een examen of project.
CA:31, DA:93, DE:106, EN:132, ES:180, FR:166, GA:235, IT:413, NE:126, PO:30.

127 examen/examinering Een procedure voor het toetsen van iemands proficiency of kennis door het voorleggen van mondelinge en/of schriftelijke opdrachten. Het behalen van een bepaalde kwalificatie (bijvoorbeeld een certificaat), toegang tot een onderwijsinstituut of cursus etc. kan afhankelijk zijn van de resultaten van een examen.
Vergelijk: toets.
Meer informatie: Bachman, 1990, p. 50.
CA:171, DA:86, DE:303, EN:133, ES:188, FR:173, GA:347, IT:164, NE:127, PO:181.

128 examen-onderdeel Deel van een examen, meestal aangeboden als aparte toets, met eigen instructieboekje en tijdslimiet. Examenonderdelen zijn vaak gebaseerd op een specifieke vaardigheid. Zo is er bijvoorbeeld een onderdeel als Luistervaardigheid of Stelopdracht.
Vergelijk: subtoets.
CA:73, DA:181, DE:306, EN:61, ES:29, FR:72, GA:85, IT:81, NE:128, PO:87.

129 examenkandidaat Zie voor definitie: kandidaat.
CA:173, DA:87, DE:307, EN:134, ES:190, FR:351, GA:345, IT:49, NE:129, PO:183.

130 examinator Zie voor definitie: beoordelaar.
CA:172, DA:89, DE:301, EN:135, ES:189, FR:174, GA:346, IT:165, NE:130, PO:182.

131 examinator-correctie Een methode van correctie door correctoren die extra moeten worden geïnstrueerd om subjectieve evaluaties te kunnen geven. Spreektoetsen en langere schrijftoetsen worden meestal op deze manier gecorrigeerd.
Vergelijk: automatische correctie.
CA:81, DA:29, DE:107, EN:136, ES:81, FR:272, GA:223, IT:30, NE:131, PO:67.

132 F-ratio In de variantie-analyse de berekende ratio die aangeeft of verschillen tussen de gemiddelden van groepen statistisch significant zijn; bijvoorbeeld of de ene groep het op een taaltoets beter heeft gedaan dan de andere.
Zie: alternatieve vormen.
Meer informatie: Hatch en Lazaraton, 1991, pp. 315–317.
CA:364, DA:94, DE:109, EN:139, ES:368, FR:319, GA:66, IT:296, NE:132, PO:332.

133 factor-analyse Een statistische methode waarbij de onderzoeker het aantal variabelen kan reduceren door patronen te zoeken in de waarde-variaties van verschillende variabelen. Een aantal variabelen met een hoge intercorrelatie vormen samen een factor. De onderzoeker kan een verkennende factoranalyse uitvoeren om een hypothese op te stellen of een bevestigende fac-

toranalyse doen om bepaalde hypotheses te onderzoeken.
Meer informatie: Bachman, 1990, p. 262; Crocker en Algina, 1986, p. 232.
CA:20, DA:96, DE:115, EN:142, ES:26, FR:18, GA:18, IT:14, NE:133, PO:20.

134 feedback Commentaar van mensen die betrokken zijn bij het toetsproces (examenkandidaten, personen/ instanties die het examen afnemen, etc.), een basis vormt voor het evalueren van dit toetsproces. Feedback kan informeel worden verkregen of met behulp van speciaal ontworpen vragenformulieren.
CA:381, DA:97, DE:330, EN:144, ES:379, FR:337, GA:6, IT:173, NE:134, PO:192.

135 fit De mate van overeenstemming tussen de voorspellingen van een model en de waargenomen uitkomsten. Er kunnen verschillende fit-indices worden berekend. In de itemresponsetheorie laat de fit-analyse zien hoe goed de ingeschatte item- en persoonsparameters (bijvoorbeeld moeilijkheidsgraad en vaardigheid) iemands scores op een toets voorspellen: de fitgegevens van een item zijn vergelijkbaar met de discriminatie-index uit de klassieke-toetsstatistiek.
Zie: itemresponsetheorie (IRT) .
CA:8, DA:99, DE:248, EN:145, ES:15, FR:6, GA:268, IT:107, NE:135, PO:5.

136 formatieve evaluatie Continue evaluatie van een proces waardoor dit proces 'onderweg' kan worden aangepast en verbeterd. Kan betrekking hebben op een lesprogramma.
Vergelijk: summatieve evaluatie.
CA:32, DA:226, DE:46, EN:148, ES:184, FR:168, GA:236, IT:414, NE:136, PO:32.

137 formatieve beoordeling Toetsing die plaatsvindt tijdens en niet zozeer aan het einde van een cursus of lesprogramma. Met behulp van de resultaten kan de docent in een vroeg stadium remediale hulp geven of het accent binnen een cursus, indien nodig, verleggen.
Vergelijk: summatieve beoordeling.
CA:32, DA:225, DE:213, EN:147, ES:184, FR:168, GA:232, IT:422, NE:137, PO:32.

138 frequentie-distributie Zie voor definitie: distributie.
CA:113, DA:107, DE:142, EN:149, ES:114, FR:107, GA:106, IT:132, NE:138, PO:122.

139 G-factor In de intelligentie-theorie, een 'general factor', die als basis voor alle cognitieve vaardigheden geldt. Deze notie werd in de jaren zeventig gepromoot door John Oller en gaat uit van één competentie als basis voor taal-proficiency.
Meer informatie: Oller, 1979, pp. 426–458, Bachman, 1990, p. 6.
CA:176, DA:113, DE:127, EN:153, ES:195, FR:177, GA:136, IT:170, NE:139, PO:187.

140 gaussverdeling Zie voor definitie: normale verdeling.
CA:114, DA:114, DE:129, EN:152, ES:115, FR:91, GA:105, IT:133, NE:140, PO:110.

141 geëquivaleerde vormen Verschillende vormen van een toets waarvan de score-distributies zijn omgezet, zodat ze onderling kunnen worden uitgewisseld.
Meer informatie: Crocker en Algina, 1986, hoofdstuk 20.
CA:186, DA:442, DE:16/14, EN:126, ES:204, FR:194, GA:145, IT:177 NE:141, PO:200.

142 geheimhouding Ervoor zorgen dat er voor en tijdens toetsafnames geen toetsmateriaal 'uitlekt'.
CA:387, DA:335, DE:348, EN:351, ES:382, FR:344, GA:353, IT:333, NE:142, PO:347.

143 geleide schrijfopdracht Een opdracht waarbij de kandidaat een geschreven tekst moet produceren en waarbij grafische of tekstuele informatie, zoals plaatjes, brieven, kaarten en instructies, wordt gebruikt om de response te sturen en te standaardiseren.
CA:393, DA:121, DE:130, EN:160, ES:5, FR:311, GA:377, IT:76, NE:143, PO:317.

144 geleide/gestuurde schrijftoets Een opdracht waarbij de kandidaat een tekst moet schrijven en waarbij visuele of tekstuele informatie, bijvoorbeeld plaatjes, brieven, kaarten en instructies, wordt gebruikt om de te verwachten response in bepaalde banen te leiden en te standaardiseren.
Vergelijk: stelopdracht, essay-vraag.
CA:392, DA:43, DE:15, EN:105, ES:6, FR:356, GA:376, IT:77, NE:144, PO:355.

145 gelijke-intervalschaal Zie voor definitie: intervalschaal
CA:149, DA:213, DE:161, EN:125, ES:159, FR:127, GA:316, IT:316, NE:145, PO:161.

146 gemakkelijkheidsindex De proportie juiste antwoorden op een item, neergezet op een schaal van 0 tot 1. Wordt soms

ook weergegeven als percentage. Wordt ook wel gemakkelijkheidswaarde of *p*-waarde genoemd.
Vergelijk: moeilijkheidsindex.
CA:209, DA:191, DE:208, EN:141, ES:225, FR:210, GA:188, IT:197, NE:146, PO:220.

147 gemakkelijkheidswaarde Zie voor definitie: gemakkelijkheidsindex
CA:426, DA:192, DE:209, EN:143, ES:423, FR:410, GA:217, IT:411, NE:147, PO:419.

148 gemeenschappelijke schaal Een manier om scores van twee of meer toetsen op een gezamenlijke schaal te zetten, zodat de resultaten van deze toetsen rechtstreeks met elkaar kunnen worden vergeleken. De scores van twee of meer toetsen kunnen op een gemeenschappelijke schaal worden gezet, als de ruwe scores via een statistische procedure zijn getransformeerd, bijvoorbeeld toets-equivalering.
Meer informatie: Bachman, 1990, pp. 340–344.
CA:147, DA:110, DE:131, EN:57, ES:156, FR:125, GA:86, IT:320, NE:148, PO:158.

149 gemiddelde kwadraat Naam van de variantie in een variantie-analyse (ANOVA)
Zie: ANOVA.
CA:251, DA:230, DE:245, EN:229, ES:262, FR:47, GA:227, IT:295, NE:149, PO:319.

150 gemiddelde moeilijkheidsgraad van items (gemiddelde *p*-waarde) Het gemiddelde aantal goede antwoorden op alle items uitgezet op een schaal van dichotoom-gescoorde items. Een gemiddele *p*-waarde van 0.5 betekent dat de gemiddelde moeilijkheidsgraad van de toets 0.5 is.
Zie: dichotome scoring.
CA:208, DA:132, DE:246, EN:228, ES:227, FR:212, GA:190, IT:195 NE:150, PO:222.

151 gemiddelde Centrale-tendentiemaat. Een gemiddelde toetsscore berekent men door alle scores op deze toets op te tellen en de som te delen door het aantal scores.
Vergelijk: mediaan, modus.
Zie: centrale tendentie (meting van).
Meer informatie: Hatch en Lazaraton, 1991, pp. 161–163.
CA:250, DA:231, DE:244, EN:227, ES:261, FR:257, GA:226, IT:234, NE:151, PO:255.

152 generaliseerbaarheidstheorie Een statistisch model voor het onderzoeken van de relatieve effecten van verschillende variantie-bronnen in toetsscores.
Meer informatie: Bachman, 1990, p. 7; Crocker en Algina, 1986, hoofdstuk 8.
CA:400, DA:115, DE:132, EN:154, ES:393, FR:399, GA:388, IT:351, NE:152, PO:359.

153 geschaalde score Een score die via schaling tot stand is gekomen.
Zie: schaling.
CA:349, DA:340, DE:354, EN:345, ES:349, FR:278, GA:337, IT:286, NE:153, PO:283.

154 geselecteerde response Een soort response op een toetsitem waarbij uit een aantal alternatieven moet worden gekozen en het antwoord niet door de kandidaten zelf wordt bedacht.
Vergelijk: open antwoord.
Zie: response.
CA:379, DA:422, DE:37, EN:352, ES:377, FR:334, GA:158, IT:310, NE:154, PO:341.

155 gespreksleider In een spreektoets de examinator die de opdrachten uitlegt, de vragen stelt en in het algemeen met de kandidaat (kandidaten) communiceert. De gespreksleider kan ook degene zijn die de kandidaat (kandidaten) beoordeelt en de scores toekent. Dit kan ook door een tweede examinator worden gedaan die observeert, maar niet met de kandidaat (kandidaten) communiceert.
Vergelijk: beoordelaar.
CA:213, DA:325, DE:125, EN:178, ES:138, FR:216, GA:72, IT:201, NE:155, PO:227.

156 gespreksleiderskader Een script voor de taal waarvan een gespreksleider zich tijdens een spreektoets moet bedienen. Het doel is de standaardisatie van de taal die alle kandidaten te horen krijgen, zodat de toets er eerlijker en betrouwbaarder door wordt.
CA:198, DA:324, DE:438, EN:179, ES:215, FR:34, GA:151, IT:128, NE:156, PO:321.

157 gestratificeerde (gelaagde/gelede) steekproef Een steekproef uit een populatie die men aan het onderzoeken is en die eerst wordt onderverdeeld in een aantal deelpopulaties (lagen, geledingen, strata). Uit elke deelpopulatie wordt vervolgens een steekproef genomen.
Zie: steekproef.
Meer informatie: Guilford en Fruchter, 1981, pp. 122–123.

CA:266, DA:375, DE:134, EN:388, ES:280, FR:119, GA:306, IT:48, NE:157, PO:11.

158 getransformeerde (omgezette) score Een ruwe score die mathematisch is omgezet, bijvoorbeeld voor schalings- of wegingsdoeleinden.
Meer informatie: Ebel en Frisbie, 1991, pp. 64–70.

CA:356, DA:414, DE:415, EN:417, ES:356, FR:284, GA:334, IT:290, NE:158, PO:288.

159 gewogen toetsscore De score die een kandidaat bij een toets krijgt toebedeeld na weging.
Zie: weging.

CA:354, DA:434, DE:135, EN:437, ES:354, FR:280, GA:339, IT:284, NE:159, PO:286.

160 gisparameter Zie voor definitie: c-parameter (gisparameter).

CA:284, DA:122, DE:319, EN:159, ES:297, FR:295, GA:277, IT:263, NE:160, PO:301.

161 globale beoordeling Een scoringsmethode die kan worden gebruikt bij schrijf- en spreektoetsen. De beoordelaar geeft slechts één cijfer naar aanleiding van de algemene indruk van het taalgebruik in plaats van een aantal cijfers voor verschillende aspecten van taalgebruik.
Vergelijk: analytische scoring, impressiecorrectie (algemeneimpressiecorrectie).

CA:33, DA:124, DE:137, EN:155, ES:427, FR:169, GA:231, IT:186, NE:161, PO:33.

162 grammaticale competentie Binnen een communicatief taalvaardigheidsmodel, is grammaticale competentie de component die betrekking heeft op kennis van taalgebruik-gebieden als morfologie, syntaxis, vocabulaire, fonologie en orthografie.
Meer informatie: Bachman, 1990, pp. 84–88.

CA:67, DA:119, DE:138, EN:158, ES:63, FR:65, GA:193, IT:65, NE:162, PO:79.

163 grenseffect Het effect dat ontstaat, wanneer een toets te makkelijk of te moeilijk is voor een bepaalde groep kandidaten. Scores hebben de neiging bovenaan de verdelingsschaal (plafond-effect) of onderaan de schaal (bodemeffect) samen te klonteren.
Zie: bodemeffect, plafond-effect.

CA:125, DA:120, DE:139, EN:36, ES:131, FR:143, GA:177, IT:138, NE:163, PO:139.

164 halo-effect Een neiging van beoordelaars om zich bij subjectieve examinering te laten beïnvloeden door de performance van een kandidaat op bepaalde toetsopdrachten en vervolgens een te hoge of te lage score voor een andere opdracht te geven.
Zie: beoordelaarseffecten.

CA:117, DA:118, DE:141, EN:161, ES:127, FR:137, GA:170, IT:139, NE:164, PO:133.

165 herhaalbaarheid De mogelijkheid tot meervoudige herhaling van onderzoeksbevindingen teneinde het vertrouwen in de resultaten te vergroten.

CA:373, DA:189, DE:324, EN:329, ES:370, FR:335, GA:185, IT:301, NE:165, PO:333.

166 herschaling Zie voor definitie: schaling.

CA:367, DA:314, DE:258, EN:330, ES:389, FR:320, GA:29, IT:304, NE:166, PO:326.

167 histogram Een grafische weergave van een frequentie-distributie waarbij het aantal gevallen per frequentie-klasse wordt weergegeven als een verticale kolom.

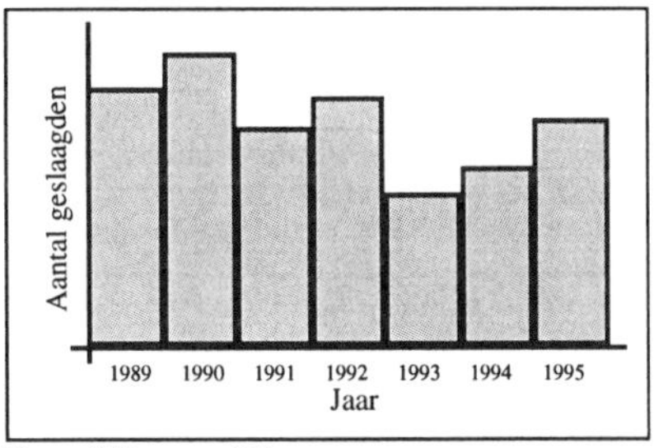

Vergelijk: staafdiagram.

CA:203, DA:125, DE:145, EN:163, ES:218, FR:204, GA:168, IT:207, NE:167, PO:215.

168 holistische beoordeling Zie voor definitie: globale beoordeling.

CA:429, DA:126, DE:128, EN:164, ES:428, FR:170, GA:230, IT:187, NE:168, PO:34.

169 homogeniteit Een kenmerk van een toets of subtoets waarbij items dezelfde competentie meten, of van een groep waarbij individuen dezelfde kenmerken hebben. De mate van homogeniteit wordt uitgedrukt via de betrouwbaarheidsindex.

CA:204, DA:127, DE:148, EN:165, ES:221, FR:205, GA:22, IT:257, NE:169, PO:216.

170 horizontale equivalering Het proces waarbij de scores van twee toetsen van ongeveer gelijke moeilijkheidsgraad op eenzelfde schaal worden uitgezet om bij beide toetsen dezelfde normen te kunnen hanteren.
Vergelijk: verticale equivalering.
CA:133, DA:128, DE:149, EN:166, ES:141, FR:37, GA:89, IT:152, NE:170, PO:44.

171 impact Het effect van een examen zowel op algemeen educatieve processen als op de individuen die worden beïnvloed door de examenresultaten.
Zie: backwash, washback.
CA:205, DA:303, DE:444, EN:167, ES:222, FR:207, GA:391, IT:191, NE:171, PO:217.

172 impressie-correctie (algemene-impressiecorrectie) Een scoringsmethode die in productief-taalgebruiktoetsen kan worden gebruikt, dat wil zeggen in schrijf- of spreektoetsen. De beoordelaar geeft een beoordeling van iedere response van een kandidaat zonder daarbij onderscheid aan te brengen in de verschillende kenmerken van de opdracht.
Vergelijk: analytische scoring, globale beoordeling.
CA:89, DA:116, DE:133, EN:168, ES:429, FR:270, GA:220, IT:33, NE:172, PO:68.

173 indirecte toets (opdracht) Een toets of opdracht die de vaardigheden probeert te meten die ten grondslag liggen aan een bepaalde taalvaardigheid en niet zozeer uit is op het toetsen van de manier waarop die vaardigheid in de praktijk wordt gehanteerd (niet gericht op performance). Een voorbeeld: het toetsen van schrijfvaardigheid door de kandidaat te vragen een streep te zetten onder structuren die in een tekst niet juist worden gebruikt.
Vergelijk: directe toets.
Meer informatie: Hughes, 1989, pp. 14–16.
CA:329, DA:135, DE:150, EN:170, ES:337, FR:385, GA:420, IT:354, NE:173, PO:389.

174 indruksvaliditeit De mate waarin een toets op kandidaten of degenen die de toets namens de kandidaten uitkiezen, de indruk maakt dat er op een acceptabele manier wordt gemeten wat er moet worden gemeten. Dit is een subjectief oordeel en niet zozeer een oordeel op basis van een objectieve analyse van de toets. Indruksvaliditeit wordt dikwijls niet als echte validiteit gezien. Het wordt soms ook wel 'test appeal' genoemd.
Meer informatie: Bachman, 1990, pp. 285–289.
CA:417, DA:272, DE:110/34, EN:140, ES:414, FR:414 GA:2, IT:402, NE:174, PO:410.

175 inferentiële statistiek Statistische methode die verder gaat dan de informatie zoals die gegeven wordt in de descriptieve tegenhanger. Er kunnen conclusies worden getrokken over de mate waarin een enkele set gegevens een adequate afspiegeling zou kunnen zijn van de grotere populatie waarvan dit slechts een steekproef is.
Vergelijk: descriptieve statistiek.
CA:166, DA:139, DE:338, EN:171, ES:173, FR:350, GA:364, IT:341, NE:175, PO:177.

176 informatiekloof Een taalonderwijs- en taaltoetstechniek waarin de echte communicatie wordt gesimuleerd door situaties te creëren waarin leerlingen niet allemaal over dezelfde informatie beschikken en dus met elkaar moeten communiceren om een opdracht te kunnen doen. Wordt meestal gebruikt bij het oefenen of toetsen van spreek- en schrijfvaardigheid.
CA:42, DA:140, DE:151, EN:172, ES:411, FR:213, GA:43, IT:424, NE:176, PO:223.

177 informatietransfer Een toetstechniek waarbij de informatie op een bepaalde manier binnenkomt en op een andere manier wordt weergegeven. Voorbeelden van dit soort opdrachten: informatie uit een tekst halen en er tekst voor bij een diagram van maken; een informele aantekening herschrijven en er een formele mededeling van maken.
Meer informatie: Hughes, 1989, pp. 84, 124–125, 138.
CA:409, DA:141, DE:152, EN:173, ES:406, FR:402, GA:8, IT:396, NE:177, PO:404.

178 inhoudsanalyse Een manier om de inhoud van toetsmateriaal te beschrijven en analyseren. Deze analyse is nodig om er zeker van te kunnen zijn dat de inhoud van de toets aan de toetsspecificatie voldoet. Essentieel voor het vaststellen van de inhouds- en constructvaliditeit.
CA:18, DA:133, DE:153, EN:72, ES:19, FR:12, GA:12, IT:15, NE:178, PO:15.

179 inhoudsvaliditeit Een toets is inhoudsvalide als de items of opdrachten waaruit de toets bestaat representatief zijn voor het kennis- of vaardigheidsgebied dat wordt getoetst. Deze hebben vaak betrek-

king op een lesprogramma of cursus.
Zie: validiteit, toetsspecificatie.
Meer informatie: Bachman, 1990, pp. 244–247.
CA:422, DA:134, DE:154, EN:73, ES:419, FR:419, GA:31, IT:405, NE:179, PO:415.

180 input Materiaal in een toetsopdracht dat een kandidaat kan gebruiken om de juiste response te leveren. In een luistertoets kan dit bijvoorbeeld een tekst op de band zijn met een aantal schriftelijke items.
CA:169, DA:142, DE:408, EN:174, ES:228, FR:147, GA:199, IT:199, NE:180, PO:254.

181 instructies Algemene aanwijzingen aan toetskandidaten, bijvoorbeeld op de voorkant van het antwoordblad of boekje. De informatie kan bijvoorbeeld gaan over de lengte van de toets, het aantal opdrachten en de plaats waar de antwoorden moeten worden gegeven.
Vergelijk: leerlinginstructie.
CA:211, DA:143, DE:391, EN:175, ES:230, FR:214, GA:402, IT:208, NE:181, PO:225.

182 integratief item/ integratieve opdracht Wordt gebruikt voor items of opdrachten waarvoor het gebruik van meer dan één vaardigheid of subvaardigheid nodig is. Voorbeelden: de items in een cloze-toets, het voeren van een gesprekje, het lezen van een brief en daar een antwoord op schrijven.
Vergelijk: discrete-point item.
CA:231, DA:144, DE:156, EN:176, ES:249, FR:316, GA:248, IT:221, NE:182, PO:245.

183 interactionele authenticiteit Een visie in de taaltoetsing waarbij authenticiteit wordt gezien als kenmerkend voor de interactie die moet plaatsvinden tussen degene die de toets aflegt en de toetsopdracht om een passende response te kunnen geven.
Vergelijk: situationele authenticiteit.
Zie: authenticiteit.
Meer informatie: Bachman, 1990, pp. 315–323.
CA:28, DA:146, DE:157, EN:177, ES:34, FR:25, GA:116, IT:36, NE:183, PO:27.

184 interbeoordelaarsbetrouwbaarheid Een schatting van de betrouwbaarheid van een toets gebaseerd op de mate waarin verschillende beoordelaars het met elkaar eens zijn in hun beoordeling van de performance van een kandidaat.
Zie: interbeoordelaarsovereenstemming, betrouwbaarheid.
CA:181, DA:145, DE:158, EN:182, ES:199, FR:185, GA:201, IT:8, NE:184, PO:195.

185 interbeoordelaarsovereenstemming De mate van overeenstemming tussen twee of meer beoordelaars betreffende dezelfde performance. Dit geldt met name voor de beoordeling van spreek- en schrijfvaardigheid in toetsen waarin van de beoordelaars subjectieve beoordeling wordt gevraagd.
CA:2, DA:31, DE:159, EN:181, ES:11, FR:2, GA:68, IT:84, NE:185, PO:2.

186 interne consistentie Een kenmerk van een toets aangeduid via de mate waarin de kandidatenscores op de individuele items stroken met de totaalscore. Interne-consistentieschattingen kunnen worden gebruikt als toetsbetrouwbaarheids-index; er kunnen verschillende van dit soort indices worden berekend, bijvoorbeeld KR-20, alpha (alpha-coëfficiënt).
Zie: alpha (alpha-coëfficiënt), Kuder-Richardson, betrouwbaarheid.
Meer informatie: Bachman, 1990, p. 172.
CA:77, DA:147, DE:155, EN:180, ES:74, FR:186, GA:87, IT:87, NE:186, PO:93.

187 interval Het verschil tussen twee punten op een schaal.
CA:214, DA:148, DE:160, EN:183, ES:232, FR:218, GA:131, IT:203, NE:187, PO:228.

188 intervalschaal Een meetschaal waarop de afstand tussen twee aan elkaar grenzende meeteenheden gelijk is, maar een zinnig nulpunt ontbreekt (Vogt).
Vergelijk: categorische schaal, nominale schaal, ordinale schaal, ratio-schaal.
Meer informatie: Crocker en Algina, 1986. p. 48.
CA:148, DA:149, DE:161, EN:184, ES:158, FR:126, GA:315, IT:315, NE:188, PO:162.

189 intrabeoordelaarsbetrouwbaarheid Een schatting van de betrouwbaarheid van een toets gebaseerd op de mate waarin dezelfde beoordelaar op verschillende momenten eenzelfde score toekent aan dezelfde prestatie.
Zie: intrabeoordelaarsovereenstemming, betrouwbaarheid.
CA:182, DA:151, DE:162, EN:186, ES:200, FR:187, GA:202, IT:89, NE:189, PO:196.

190 intrabeoordelaarsovereenstemming De mate van overeenstemming tussen twee beoordelingen van dezelfde performance die dezelfde beoordelaar op verschillende momenten geeft. Dit geldt met name voor de beoordeling van spreek- en schrijfvaardigheid in toetsen waarin van de beoordelaars subjectieve beoordeling wordt gevraagd.

CA:3, DA:33, DE:163, EN:185, ES:12, FR:3, GA:69, IT:90, NE:190, PO:3.

191 invariantie In de itemresponsetheorie, de belangrijke aanname dat de moeilijkheidsgraad van een item en de discriminatie-mate inherente eigenschappen zijn die niet afhankelijk zijn van de vaardigheid van kandidaten en evenzo dat de gemeten vaardigheid niet afhankelijk is van de specifieke items die worden gebruikt.

CA:216, DA:152, DE:164, EN:187, ES:234, FR:220, GA:120, IT:205, NE:191, PO:230.

192 invulitem Alle soorten items waarbij een kandidaat geschreven materiaal moet invullen – letters, getallen, losse woorden, stukken zin, zinnen of alinea's – in bepaalde ruimtes in een tekst. De response kan of door de kandidaat zelf worden gegeven of hij of zij kan kiezen uit een aantal opties.

CA:223, DA:138, DE:229, EN:151, ES:241, FR:317, GA:249, IT:78, NE:192, PO:235.

193 invulitem Een type item waarbij de kandidaat een zin of deel van een zin moet aanvullen, meestal met een paar woorden of met details zoals bijvoorbeeld tijden en telefoonnummers.

CA:226, DA:421, DE:102, EN:60, ES:238, FR:223, GA:243, IT:215, NE:193, PO:234.

194 IRT Zie voor definitie: itemresponsetheorie (IRT) .

CA:412, DA:153, DE:165, EN:188, ES:408, FR:401, GA:392, IT:352, NE:194, PO:402.

195 item Een onderdeel van een toets waaraan een apart cijfer/aparte cijfers wordt/worden gegeven. Voorbeelden: een gat in een cloze-toets; een multiplechoicevraag met drie of vier keuzemogelijkheden; een zin die grammaticaal moet worden omgezet; een vraag waarop met een zin moet worden geantwoord.
Vergelijk: opdracht.

CA:217, DA:154, DE:166, EN:189, ES:235, FR:221, GA:240, IT:209, NE:195, PO:231.

196 item characteristic curve (ICC) In de itemresponsetheorie geeft de ICC de relatie weer tussen de waarschijnlijkheid waarmee het juiste antwoord op een item wordt gekozen en de latente vaardigheidstrek die ten grondslag ligt aan de performance op de items in de toets.
Meer informatie: Crocker en Algina, 1986, pp. 340–342.

CA:79, DA:157, DE:168, EN:192, ES:95, FR:90, GA:94, IT:115, NE:196, PO:109.

197 item-informatie-functie In de itemresponsetheorie een index die aangeeft hoeveel informatie een item geeft over een persoon van een bepaald vaardigheidsniveau; is afhankelijk van de item-discriminatie en de mate van niveau-afstemming.
Vergelijk: toetsinformatiefunctie.

CA:192, DA:156, DE:169, EN:193, ES:212, FR:190, GA:138, IT:184, NE:197, PO:206.

198 itemanalyse Een beschrijving van het functioneren van individuele toetsitems, meestal met gebruikmaking van klassieke statistische indices zoals makkelijkheidsgraad en discriminatie. Bij deze analyse wordt gebruik gemaakt van software zoals bijvoorbeeld MicroCAT Iteman.
Zie: discriminatie, gemakkelijkheidsindex.

CA:13, DA:161, DE:167, EN:190, ES:25, FR:17, GA:13, IT:12, NE:198, PO:16.

199 itembank Een methode voor het beheren van toetsitems, dat wil zeggen het opslaan van informatie over items zodat er toetsen met een van tevoren bekende inhoud en moeilijkheidsgraad kunnen worden opgesteld. Normaal gesproken wordt hierbij gebruik gemaakt van een computer - database waarbij wordt uitgegaan van de latente-trektheorie, dat wil zeggen dat items aan elkaar kunnen worden gerelateerd via een gemeenschappelijke moeilijkheidsschaal.
Meer informatie: Henning, 1987, hoofdstuk 9.

CA:36, DA:155, DE:28, EN:191, ES:37, FR:28, GA:40, IT:111, NE:199, PO:37.

200 itemresponsefunctie In de itemresponsetheorie een mathematische functie die de kans op het goed beantwoorden van een item relateert aan de vaardigheid van een kandidaat wat betreft de trek die door het item wordt gemeten. Wordt ook wel de itemkarakteristiekfunctie genoemd.

CA:193, DA:158, DE:172, EN:194, ES:210, FR:189, GA:140, IT:183, NE:200, PO:205.

201 itemresponsetheorie (IRT) Een groep mathematische modellen voor het

leggen van verbanden tussen iemands prestatie op een toets en het vaardigheidsniveau van deze persoon. De modellen gaan uit van de theorie dat de te verwachten prestatie op een bepaalde toetsvraag of item te maken heeft met zowel de moeilijkheidsgraad van het item als het vaardigheidsniveau van de kandidaat.
Meer informatie: Henning, 1987, hoofdstuk. 8; Crocker en Algina, 1986, hoofdstuk 15.
CA:401, DA:159, DE:173/296, EN:195, ES:394, FR:400, GA:389, IT:352, NE:201, PO:360.

202 itemscore In de itemanalyse het totaal aantal goede antwoorden op een bepaald item.
CA:345, DA:160, DE:171, EN:196, ES:346, FR:267, GA:336, IT:281, NE:202, PO:60.

203 itemtype Toetsitems hebben namen die betrekking hebben op de vorm. Enkele voorbeelden: multiple-choice-items, zinstransformatie-items, kort-antwoorditems, open-cloze-items.
CA:406, DA:162, DE:174, EN:197 ES:405, FR:405, GA:58, IT:392, NE:203, PO:399.

204 juiste antwoord De response die bij het scoren van een toets als correct wordt aangemerkt.
CA:375, DA:190, DE:327, EN:333, ES:373, FR:331, GA:155, IT:307, NE:204, PO:337.

205 kalibratie Het bepalen van de schaal van een of meerdere toetsen. Tijdens een kalibratie kunnen items uit verschillende toetsen worden geankerd op een gemeenschappellijke moeilijkheidsschaal (de theta-schaal). Als een toets bestaat uit gekalibreerde items, dan geven de toetsscores een indicatie van de vaardigheid van een kandidaat, dat wil zeggen de plaats op de theta-schaal.
CA:44, DA:164, DE:94, EN:40, ES:42, FR:35, GA:49, IT:44, NE:205, PO:42.

206 kalibreren In de itemresponsetheorie, het inschatten van de moeilijkheidsgraad van een set toetsitems.
Zie: theta-schaal.
CA:43, DA:163, DE:93, EN:39, ES:43, FR:40, GA:48, IT:43, NE:206, PO:47.

207 kandidaat Iemand die een toets/examen aflegt.
Vergelijk: examenkandidat.
CA:45, DA:165, DE:302, EN:41, ES:48, FR:41, GA:178, IT:49, NE:207, PO:48.

208 klassieke toetstheorie Een meettheorie die bestaat uit een serie aannames over de relaties tussen werkelijke en waargenomen toetsscores en de factoren die deze scores beïnvloeden, die meestal met de term 'error' worden aangeduid. Deze theorie wordt ook wel 'ware-score'-theorie genoemd.
Vergelijk: itemresponsetheorie (IRT) .
Meer informatie: Bachman, 1990, pp. 166–187.
CA:399, DA:174, DE:177, EN:50, ES:392, FR:397, GA:387, IT:349, NE:208, PO:357.

209 kort-antwoorditem Een 'open' item waarbij de kandidaat zelf het antwoord moet opschrijven. Het antwoord bestaat uit een enkel woord of een paar woorden.
CA:228, DA:198, DE:205, EN:362, ES:243, FR:224, GA:246, IT:311, NE:209, PO:238.

210 KR-20 (Kuder-Richardson formule 20) Zie voor definitie: Kuder Richardson
CA:234, DA:201, DE:194, EN:199, ES:252, FR:233, GA:205, IT:222, NE:210, PO:246.

211 KR-21 (Kuder-Richardson formule 21) Zie voor definitie: Kuder-Richardson.
CA:235, DA:202, DE:195, EN:200 ES:253, FR:234, GA:206, IT:223, NE:211, PO:247.

212 Kuder-Richardson Twee interne-consistentiematen ontwikkeld door Kuder en Richardson gebruikt om de betrouwbaarheid van een toets in te schatten. Voor de KR-21 is minder informatie nodig en bovendien is hij makkelijker te berekenen. De KR-21 geeft over het algemeen wel een lagere schatting dan de KR-20.
Vergelijk: alpha (alpha-coëfficiënt).
Zie: interne consistentie.
Meer informatie: Henning, 1987, p. 84.
CA:236, DA:206, DE:200, EN:201, ES:254, FR:235, GA:207, IT:224, NE:212, PO:248.

213 kurtosis Een aanwijzing voor de mate waarin een distributie/verdeling meer piek of vlakte vertoont dan de normale curve. Gegevens in een platte curve vertonen een platykurtische distributie, gegevens in een scherpe piek vertonen een leptokurtische distributie.

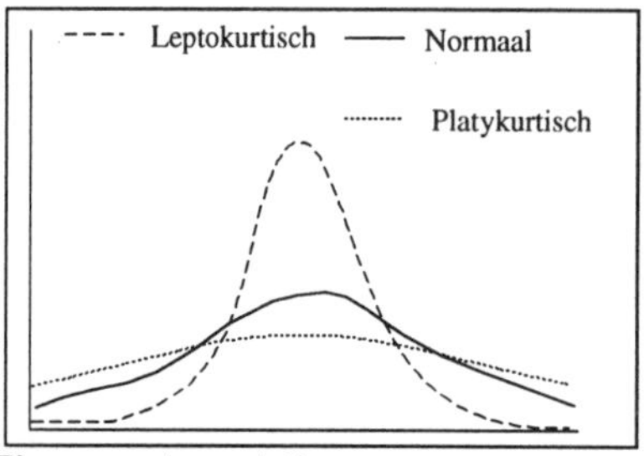

Zie: normale verdeling.

CA:95, DA:412, DE:108, EN:202, ES:94, FR:428, GA:100, IT:114, NE:213, PO:108.

214 kwalificatie (bewijs van geschiktheid) Een bewijs van geschiktheid voor een bepaalde activiteit of bepaald beroep dat wordt toegekend na het volgen van een erkende cursus of het afleggen van een toets. Een taalvaardigheids certificaat kan bijvoorbeeld voor bepaalde doeleinden gelden als bewijs van geschiktheid.
Vergelijk: certificaat, diploma.

CA:360, DA:209, DE:314, EN:302, ES:405, FR:313, GA:46, IT:294, NE:214, PO:322.

215 (Language) Proficiency Kennis van/bedrevenheid in een taal. De term is vaak synoniem aan'taalvaardigheid'.
Meer informatie: Bachman, 1990, p. 16.

CA:297, DA:355, DE:365, EN:206, ES:121, FR:66, GA:267, IT:66, NE:215, PO:81.

216 latente-trektheorie Zie voor definitie: itemresponsetheorie (IRT).

CA:402, DA:211, DE:206, EN:207, ES:395, FR:398, GA:390, IT:350, NE:216, PO:358.

217 leerdoel Het doel of gewenste resultaat van een onderwijskundige activiteit.

CA:277, DA:136, DE:215, EN:208, ES:290, FR:289, GA:360, IT:255, NE:217, PO:292.

218 leerlingenwerk De geschreven antwoorden van leerlingen op een toets, met name op een toets met open vragen.

CA:191, DA:261, DE:341, EN:350, ES:219, FR:343, GA:343, IT:175, NE:218, PO:170.

219 leerlinginstructie De instructies die kandidaten krijgen om hun response op een toetsopdracht in bepaalde banen te leiden.
Vergelijk: instructies.

CA:384, DA:264, DE:23, EN:336, ES:229, FR:78, GA:295, IT:193, NE:219, PO:92.

220 leerplan Een algemene beschrijving van de doelstellingen, inhoud, opzet, methodes en evaluatie van een leergang.
Vergelijk: lesprogramma.

CA:94, DA:55, DE:71, EN:87, ES:93, FR:93, GA:99, IT:113, NE:220, PO:107.

221 leerplanafhankelijke toets Een toets die hoort bij een bepaalde syllabus en een bepaalde rol speelt in de onderwijskundige processen.
Vergelijk: leerplanonafhankelijke toets.
Zie: prestatietoets.

CA:325, DA:56, DE:217, EN:88, ES:313, FR:365, GA:406, IT:374, NE:221, PO:380.

222 leerplanonafhankelijke toets Een toets die niet te maken heeft met een bepaalde syllabus of leergang.
Vergelijk: leerplanafhankelijke toets.
Zie: proficiency-toets.

CA:328, DA:57, DE:218, EN:89, ES:339, FR:387, GA:405, IT:376, NE:222, PO:388.

223 leesbaarheidsindex Een maat voor grammaticale en lexicale complexiteit die gebruikt wordt om te bepalen in welke mate lezers een tekst begrijpelijk zullen vinden. Voorbeelden van leesbaarheidsindices: Gunnin's Fog index en de Flesch leesbaarheidsschaal.

CA:210, DA:222, DE:219, EN:320, ES:226, FR:211, GA:189, IT:198, NE:223, PO:221.

224 leesvaardigheids- / tekstbegripopdracht Een soort opdracht die meestal bestaat uit een leestekst of leesteksten en items van de volgende soort: multiple-choice, vragen met korte antwoorden, cloze/invultoets, informatie-transfer, etc.

CA:394, DA:223, DE:220, EN:321, ES:3, FR:357, GA:373, IT:74, NE:224, PO:351.

225 lesprogramma Een gedetailleerd document dat alle gebieden uit een bepaald studieprogramma opsomt en aangeeft in welke volgorde de inhoud wordt gepresenteerd.
Vergelijk: leerplan.

CA:299, DA:224, DE:207, EN:392, ES:310, FR:352, GA:352, IT:335, NE:225, PO:318.

226 levensechte benadering In de taaltoetsing de opvatting dat toetsen opdrachten dienen te bevatten die zo veel mogelijk gelijkenis vertonen met activiteiten zoals men die in het dagelijks leven verricht. In een levensechte benadering zou bijvoorbeeld de inhoud van een toets om te

bepalen of kandidaten een academische opleiding in een vreemde taal aan kunnen, gebaseerd zijn op een behoeftenanalyse van de taal/taalactiviteiten die horen bij dit soort opleiding.
Zie: authenticiteit.
Meer informatie: Bachman, 1990, pp. 301–328.
CA:129, DA:433, DE:320, EN:322, ES:134, FR:345, GA:98, IT:23, NE:226, PO:349.

227 lexis Een andere term voor vocabulaire.
CA:237, DA:212, DE:221, EN:210, ES:257, FR:238, GA:213, IT:225, NE:227, PO:250.

228 likert-schaal Een soort schaal die in vragenformulieren wordt gebruikt voor het meten van een houding of mening. Degenen die de vragenformulieren krijgen voorgelegd, moeten bij een serie beweringen kiezen uit een stuk of vijf mogelijke reacties, zoals 'helemaal mee eens', 'mee eens', 'weet niet', 'niet mee eens', 'helemaal niet mee eens'.
CA:152, DA:214, DE:222, EN:211, ES:163, FR:129, GA:317, IT:325, NE:228, PO:163.

229 lineair equivaleren Een equivaleringsmethode waarbij de score op de ene toets zodanig wordt geëquivaleerd met de score op de andere toets, dat de equivalente scores op de twee toetsen op een even groot aantal standaarddeviaties liggen boven of onder de gemiddelde score van de toets waarin ze voorkomen.
Zie: regressie.
Meer informatie: Crocker en Algina, 1986, pp. 457–461.
CA:134, DA:216, DE:17, EN:212, ES:142, FR:38, GA:91, IT:151, NE:229, PO:45.

230 lineaire regressie Een regressietechniek die uitgaat van een lineaire relatie tussen de afhankelijke en onafhankelijke variabelen.
CA:370, DA:215, DE:223, EN:213, ES:366, FR:325, GA:5, IT:299, NE:230, PO:329.

231 linguistische competentie Zie voor definitie: competentie.
CA:68, DA:217, DE:224, EN:214, ES:64, FR:67, GA:198, IT:66, NE:231, PO:80.

232 link-item Zie voor definitie: ankeritem
CA:221, DA:218, DE:432, EN:215, ES:239, FR:231, GA:250, IT:214, NE:232, PO:244.

233 live toets (item) Een toets die afgenomen gaat worden en die om die reden geheim moet blijven.
CA:341, DA:101, DE:225, EN:217, ES:344, FR:360, GA:407, IT:355, NE:233, PO:362.

234 logit In de itemresponsetheorie een maateenheid, afgeleid van de natuurlijke logaritme betreffende de verhouding tussen de kans op een goed of fout antwoord, dat wil zeggen de 'log odds'. Het verschil in logits tussen iemands vaardigheid en de moeilijkheid van een item bepaalt of iemand een item goed of fout beantwoordt.
Meer informatie: Henning, 1987, pp. 118–126.
CA:241, DA:220, DE:227, EN:218, ES:259, FR:240, GA:216, IT:232, NE:234, PO:253.

235 luistervaardigheidstoets Een toets van het begrip van gesproken taal; wordt meestal afgenomen met behulp van een cassetterecorder of video.
CA:315, DA:221, DE:147, EN:216, ES:324, FR:372, GA:411, IT:361, NE:235, PO:373.

236 many-facet Rasch-model Een uitbreiding van het Raschmodel, waarbij response-opties kunnen worden ingedeeld volgens een extra combinatie van facetten. Zo kan de performance bij een schrijftoets zo worden ingericht dat deze de moeilijkheidsgraad van de opdracht plus de strengheid van de beoordelaar weergeeft. Van dit model wordt bijvoorbeeld gebruikt gemaakt in het computerprogramma 'FACETS'.
Zie: Rasch-model.
Meer informatie: Linacre, J.M., 1989, Many-Facet Rasch Measurement, Chicago, MESA Press.
CA:260, DA:235, DE:289, EN:220, ES:276, FR:254, GA:300, IT:249, NE:236, PO:268.

237 mastery-toets Een toets die bepaalt of een kandidaat een afgebakend vaardigheids- of kennisdomein beheerst.
CA:338, DA:227, DE:204, EN:225, ES:327, FR:376, GA:425, IT:366, NE:237, PO:376.

238 matching-opdracht Een soort toetsopdracht waarbij elementen uit twee verschillende lijsten moeten worden gecombineerd. Een voorbeeld van een matching-toets is een lijst met zinnen die niet af zijn. Uit een tweede lijst moeten vervolgens de zinsdelen worden gekozen waarmee de zinnen kunnen worden aangevuld. In leesvaardigheidstoetsen wordt bijvoorbeeld een beschrijving van een persoon gegeven en moet in een lijst worden opgezocht welke vakantie of welk boek bij deze persoon past.

CA:397, DA:322, DE:452, EN:226, ES:7, FR:21, GA:375, IT:73, NE:238, PO:353.

239 mediaan De score in het midden van de verdeling in een lijst met scores. De ene helft van de scores bevindt zich boven de mediaan, de andere onder de mediaan.
Zie: centrale tendentie (meting van).
Vergelijk: gemiddelde, modus.
Meer informatie: Hatch en Lazaraton, 1991, p. 161.

CA:244, DA:228, DE:232, EN:232, ES:263, FR:242, GA:3, IT:235, NE:239, PO:256.

240 meervoudige regressie Een statistische techniek voor het vaststellen van de lineaire effecten van een aantal onafhankelijke variabelen op een enkele afhankelijke variabele. Zo zou men bijvoorbeeld de moeilijkheidsgraad van een toets als afhankelijke variabele kunnen nemen en kunnen nagaan wat de effecten zijn van het soort opdracht, de lexicale moeilijkheidsgraad, etc.
Zie: onafhankelijke variabele, regressie.
Meer informatie: Hatch en Lazaraton, 1991, pp. 480–486.

CA:371, DA:117, DE:251, EN:242, ES:367, FR:326, GA:182, IT:300, NE:240, PO:330.

241 meervoudige correctie Een manier om de betrouwbaarheid van de beoordeling van langere schrijftoetsen die altijd enigszins subjectief is, te vergroten door ervoor te zorgen dat de antwoorden van iedere kandidaat worden nagekeken door meerdere beoordelaars die onafhankelijk van elkaar werken.
Meer informatie: Weir, 1988, pp. 65–66.

CA:87, DA:274, DE:233, EN:240, ES:45, FR:271, GA:183, IT:105, NE:241, PO:63.

242 meetfout Zie voor definitie: error.

CA:138, DA:241, DE:240, EN:231, ES:146, FR:153, GA:123, IT:159, NE:242, PO:149.

243 meetfout Zie voor definitie: standaardmeetfout.

CA:138, DA:240, DE:239, EN:130, ES:146, FR:153, GA:130, IT:159, NE:243, PO:149.

244 methode-effect Een effect op de toetsscore, dat te maken heeft met de manier van toetsen en niet zozeer met de vaardigheid van de kandidaat.

CA:121, DA:229, DE:242, EN:233, ES:126, FR:139, GA:171, IT:142, NE:244, PO:134.

245 meting In het algemeen: de hoeveelheid van iets bepalen door het te vergelijken met een vaste eenheid, bijvoorbeeld een liniaal gebruiken om lengte te meten. In de sociale wetenschappen wordt meting vaak gebruikt als term voor het kwantificeren van bepaalde eigenschappen van personen, bijvoorbeeld (language) proficiency.
Meer informatie: Bachman 1990, hoofdstuk 2.

CA:245, DA:242, DE:241, EN:230, ES:264, FR:243, GA:395, IT:238, NE:245, PO:257.

246 minimale-competentietoetsing Een toetsbenadering waarbij specifieke eisen worden neergelegd voor een minimaal competentieniveau op een bepaald taalgebruik-domein. Een kandidaat die dit vereiste competentieniveau aan de dag legt, slaagt voor de bewuste toets.

CA:312, DA:398, DE:304, EN:234, ES:183, FR:167, GA:378, IT:388, NE:246, PO:31.

247 moderation a) Onderdeel van het gereedmaken van items of opdrachten voor gebruik in een toets. In dit stadium worden de materialen kritisch onderzocht door een aantal experts (bijvoorbeeld toetsenmakers en docenten) die beslissen of de materialen uiteindelijk in de toets gebruikt zullen gaan worden (eventueel na redigeren/herschrijven).

b) Als onderdeel van het beoordelingsproces, de aanpassing door een 'moderator' van punten die al toegekend zijn door een beoordelaar.
Vergelijk: doorlichten.

CA:263, DA:410, DE:31, EN:237, ES:277, FR:256, GA:260, IT:250, NE:247, PO:270.

248 modus Het punt in de verdeling van een aantal scores met de hoogste scorefrequentie; het hoogste punt in een verdelings-curve.

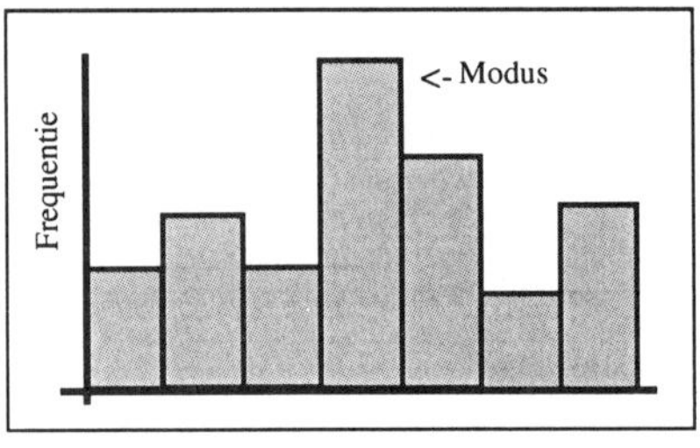

Vergelijk: bimodale distributie, gemiddelde, mediaan.
Zie: centrale tendentie (meting van).
Meer informatie: Hatch en Lazaraton, 1991, pp. 160–161.
CA:252, DA:232, DE:247, EN:235, ES:268, FR:247, GA:255, IT:240, NE:248, PO:261.

249 moeilijkheidsindex In de klassieke toetstheorie is de moeilijkheidsgraad van een item de proportie kandidaten (p) die het item goed heeft beantwoord. Dit betekent dat de moeilijkheidsgraad van een item steekproef-afhankelijk is en verandert met het vaardigheidsniveau van de kandidaten.
Vergelijk: gemakkelijkheidsindex, *p*-waarde.
CA:207, DA:378, DE:343, EN:101, ES:224, FR:209, GA:187, IT:196, NE:249, PO:219.

250 moeilijkheidsparameter Zie voor definitie: b-parameter
CA:285, DA:379, DE:344, EN:102, ES:298, FR:296, GA:276, IT:264, NE:250, PO:300.

251 multiple-choice invul-item Een soort toetsitem waarbij de kandidaat uit een aantal keuzemogelijkheden het juiste woord/zinsdeel moet kiezen en dat vervolgens in de open ruimte in een tekst moet invullen.
Zie: invulitem.
CA:224, DA:237, DE:250, EN:239, ES:242, FR:386, GA:215, IT:79, NE:251, PO:390.

252 multiple-choice item Een soort toetsitem bestaande uit een vraag of zin die moet worden afgemaakt (de stam) waarbij kan worden gekozen uit een aantal antwoorden of manieren om de zin af te maken (alternatieven). Het is aan de kandidaat om het juiste antwoord te kiezen uit drie, vier of vijf keuzemogelijkheden. Hierbij wordt van de kandidaat zelf geen productief taalgebruik verwacht. Om die reden worden multiple-choice items doorgaans in lees- en luistertoetsen gebruikt. Het kan gaan om 'discrete-items' of op tekst gebaseerde items.
Zie: discrete item, op tekst gebaseerde items.
CA:220, DA:236, DE:249/234, EN:238, ES:244, FR:222, GA:247, IT:211, NE:252, PO:236.

253 multiple-matching-opdracht Een toetsopdracht bestaande uit een aantal vragen of zin-aanvulitems, meestal met een leestekst als basis. De antwoorden worden geboden in de vorm van een lijstje met woorden of zinnen, die elk meerdere malen kunnen worden gebruikt. Het voordeel hiervan is dat de keuzemogelijkheden niet kunnen worden weggestreept tijdens het maken van de opdracht (hetgeen bij andere soorten match-opdrachten wel het geval is) zodat de opdracht niet gaandeweg steeds makkelijker wordt.
Zie: matching-opdracht.
CA:396, DA:100, DE:235, EN:241, ES:8, FR:355, GA:372, IT:72, NE:253, PO:354.

254 multitrek-multimethode strategie Een experimentele strategie, die gebruikt wordt in de constructvalidatie, waarbij een aantal trekken waarvan men aanneemt dat ze van elkaar verschillen, wordt gemeten met behulp van meerdere, eveneens hypothetisch van elkaar verschillende, methodes. Uit een analyse moet bijvoorbeeld blijken dat de luistervaardigheidsmaten die via verschillende methodes zijn gevonden, onderling meer correlatie vertonen dan de uitkomsten uit metingen van verschillende vaardigheden waarbij een en dezelfde toetsmethode wordt gehanteerd.
Meer informatie: Bachman, 1990, pp. 263–265.
CA:108, DA:238, DE:252, EN:243, ES:109, FR:299, GA:111, IT:277, NE:254, PO:305.

255 native speaker Een spreker van een taal die als moedertaal werd verworven.
CA:286, DA:234, DE:255, EN:245, ES:216, FR:217, GA:47, IT:265, NE:255, PO:190.

256 netto D Zie voor definitie: d-index.
CA:206, DA:246, DE:257, EN:247, ES:97, FR:115, GA:102, IT:194, NE:256, PO:111.

257 niet-parametrische procedures Statistische procedures waarbij er niet vanuit wordt gegaan dat de gegevens afkomstig zijn van een specifiek soort verdeling, of waarbij de gegevens niet gebaseerd zijn op een intervalschaal. Chi-kwadraat is hiervan een bekend voorbeeld.
Vergelijk: parametrische procedures.
Meer informatie: Hatch en Lazaraton, pp. 237–239.
CA:294, DA:131, DE:259, EN:249, ES:308, FR:309, GA:258, IT:274, NE:257, PO:315.

258 niveau De mate van proficiency

die een leerling/student moet hebben om tot een bepaalde klas te worden toegelaten of de mate van proficiency die in een bepaalde toets wordt gemeten, wordt vaak aangeduid in termen van een serie niveaus, met bekende namen als 'elementair', 'gevorderd', 'vergevorderd', etc.
CA:270, DA:247, DE:260, EN:209, ES:283, FR:259, GA:210, IT:229, NE:258, PO:272.

259 *N, n* *N* staat voor 'number'. De cursieve hoofdletter *N* wordt vaak gebruikt voor het aantal 'cases' in een studie of personen in een populatie. De cursieve kleine letter *n* wordt vaak gebruikt voor het aantal in een steekproef of subgroep. Bijvoorbeeld: De toets werd gemaakt door afgestudeerde ingenieurs (*N*=600) van wie 10% vrouwen (*n*=60)'.
CA:269, DA:248, DE:256, EN:244, ES:282, FR:258, GA:261, IT:251, NE:259, PO:271.

260 nominale schaal Een schaal die wordt gebruikt bij categorische variabelen zoals sekse of moedertaal. Dergelijke variabelen zijn aan- of afwezig en de interesse richt zich daarbij op de frequentie van voorkomen. Ook bekend onder de naam categorische schaal.
Vergelijk: intervalschaal, ordinale schaal, ratio-schaal.
Meer informatie: Hatch en Lazaraton, 1991, pp. 55–56.
CA:156, DA:249, DE:262, EN:248, ES:164, FR:133, GA:309, IT:326, NE:260, PO:166.

261 norm Een performance-standaard. In een gestandaardiseerde toets wordt de norm bepaald door notering van de scores van een grote groep. De norm of standaarden die gelden voor de performance van die groep worden gebruikt bij het bepalen van de performance van volgende groepen kandidaten van eenzelfde type.
Zie: normgroep, normgerichte toets.
CA:273, DA:250, DE:263, EN:250, ES:286, FR:264, GA:262, IT:252, NE:261, PO:278.

262 normale verdeling Een mathematische verdeling die als hypothese aan verscheidene statistische procedures ten grondslag ligt. De verdeling ziet eruit als een symmetrische klokvorm, waarin het gemiddelde, de mediaan en de modus samenvallen. Er bestaat een heel complex aan verdelingen, afhankelijk van de waarde van het gemiddelde, de standaarddeviatie en het aantal waarnemingen. Ook bekend onder de naam Gaussverdeling.
Vergelijk: bimodale distributie/verdeling.
Meer informatie: Hatch en Lazaraton, 1991, p. 164.
CA:115, DA:252, DE:265, EN:252, ES:116, FR:108, GA:107, IT:134, NE:262, PO:123.

263 normalisatie Het zodanig veranderen van de scores dat de verdeling een normale verdeling wordt. Kenmerkend voor dit proces is het gebruik van equipercentielschalen.
Vergelijk: standaardscore.
CA:274, DA:253, DE:264, EN:253, ES:287, FR:263, GA:263, IT:253, NE:263, PO:279.

264 normgerichte toets Een toets waarin bij de interpretatie van de scores wordt verwezen naar de performance van een gegeven groep die bestaat uit personen die vergelijkbaar zijn met de personen die de toets afleggen. De term wordt meestal gebruikt voor toetsen waarbij in de interpretatie personen worden afgezet tegen de normgroep of tegen elkaar.
Vergelijk: criterium-gerichte toets.
CA:336, DA:251, DE:268, EN:254, ES:340, FR:388, GA:426, IT:381, NE:264, PO:391.

265 normgroep Een grote groep individuen die representatief is voor de mensen voor wie een toets wordt ontworpen. De performance van de normgroep wordt gebruikt bij de interpretatie van een normgerichte toets.Wordt ook wel referentiegroep genoemd.
Zie: normgerichte toets.
CA:197, DA:254, DE:266, EN:251, ES:214, FR:203, GA:264, IT:190, NE:265, PO:213.

266 nulhypothese Een hypothese die stelt dat twee of meer variabelen niet aan elkaar gerelateerd zijn. Bijvoorbeeld de veronderstelling dat er geen verschil in toets-performance is tussen leden van twee verschillende moedertaalgroepen.
Meer informatie: Hatch en Lazaraton, 1991, p. 24; Guilford en Fruchter, 1981, pp. 146–147.
CA:202, DA:255, DE:271, EN:255, ES:217, FR:206, GA:167, IT:206, NE:266, PO:214.

267 objectieve toets Een toets waarvan de scores kunnen worden vastgesteld met behulp van een correctieschema zonder tussenkomst van een expert of zonder een subjectief oordeel.

CA:331, DA:257, DE:272, EN:257, ES:341, FR:389, GA:427, IT:377, NE:267, PO:392.

268 onafhankelijke variabele In een onderzoekssituatie een variabele waarvan men aanneemt dat deze gerelateerd kan zijn aan de afhankelijke variabele of deze kan beïnvloeden. Zo kunnen toetsscores (de onafhankelijke variabele) bijvoorbeeld worden gebruikt om het succes op de werkplek (de afhankelijke variabele) te voorspellen.
Vergelijk: afhankelijke variabele.
Zie: variabele.
Meer informatie: Hatch en Lazaraton, p. 64.

CA:433, DA:420, DE:422, EN:169, ES:433, FR:426, GA:27, IT:419, NE:268, PO:425.

269 op tekst gebaseerd item Een item gebaseerd op een lopende tekst, bijvoorbeeld multiple-choice items gebaseerd op een leesvaardigheidstekst.

CA:219, DA:387, DE:412, EN:412, ES:236, FR:226, GA:254, IT:213, NE:269, PO:233.

270 opdracht Een combinatie van leerlinginstructie, input en response. Bijvoorbeeld een leestekst met een aantal multiple-choice items, die allemaal kunnen worden beantwoord met behulp van één enkele leerlinginstructie.

CA:391, DA:260, DE:26, EN:393, ES:2, FR:354, GA:371, IT:71, NE:270, PO:352.

271 opdracht-type Voor opdrachten worden namen gebruikt die meestal beschrijven wat er getoetst wordt en in welke vorm dat gebeurt, bijvoorbeeld multiple-choice leesvaardigheid, geleid schrijven, etc.

CA:408, DA:265, DE:30, EN:394, ES:402, FR:407, GA:59, IT:393, NE:271, PO:401.

272 open antwoord Een vorm van schriftelijke respons op een toetsvraag waarbij sprake is van actieve productie en waarbij niet gekozen kan worden uit een aantal mogelijke antwoorden.

CA:376, DA:185, DE:126, EN:70, ES:372, FR:330, GA:154, IT:309, NE:272, PO:336.

273 open vraag Een soort item of opdracht in een schriftelijke toets waarbij de kandidaat zelf het antwoord moet geven in plaats van kiezen. Het doel van dit soort item is de kandidaat aan te zetten tot een betrekkelijk ongedwongen antwoord dat in lengte kan variëren van een paar woorden tot een uitgebreid essay. Het correctieschema geeft dan ook een scala aan mogelijke antwoorden.

CA:292, DA:444, DE:273, EN:260, ES:305, FR:318, GA:56, IT:137, NE:273, PO:324.

274 optische lezer Een elektronisch apparaat voor het scannen van antwoordbladen. Kandidaten of examinatoren kunnen de juiste antwoorden op een antwoordblad aangeven. Deze informatie wordt vervolgens door de computer gelezen.
Wordt ook wel scanner genoemd.

CA:242, DA:268, DE:274, EN:261, ES:255, FR:237, GA:214, IT:226, NE:274, PO:249.

275 ordinale schaal Een soort meetschaal die kandidaten indeelt zonder de relatieve afstand tussen die kandidaten aan te geven.
Vergelijk: categorische schaal, intervalschaal, nominale schaal, ratio-schaal.
Meer informatie: Hatch en Lazaraton, 1991, pp. 56–57.

CA:157, DA:271, DE:275, EN:265, ES:165, FR:134, GA:318, IT:327, NE:275, PO:167.

276 overlapping van deel en geheel Een effect dat zich bijvoorbeeld voordoet als scores op een subtoets worden gecorreleerd aan scores op de hele toets. Omdat de subtoetsscores deel uitmaken van de scores op de hele toets, is de correlatie overtrokken. Er bestaan technieken om deze overlapping van deel en geheel te corrigeren.
Meer informatie: Henning, 1987, p. 69.

CA:63, DA:62, DE:282, EN:271, ES:387, FR:51, GA:283, IT:146, NE:276, PO:331.

277 *p*-waarde Zie voor definitie: gemakkelijkheidsindex.

CA:427, DA:273, DE:276, EN:266, ES:424, FR:411, GA:269, IT:412, NE:277, PO:420.

278 paper Engelse benaming voor een toetsonderdeel, bijvoorbeeld Reading Paper (toestonderdeel waarin de leesvaardigheid centraal staat), Listening Paper (toetsonderdeel waarin het gaat om luistervaardigheid).

CA:385, DA:393, DE:277, EN:267, ES:381, FR:182, GA:270, IT:168, NE:278, PO:87.

279 parallelle vormen Zie voor definitie: equivalente vormen.

CA:188, DA:275, DE:278, EN:268, ES:206, FR:196, GA:144, IT:179, NE:279, PO:202.

280 parameter Een kenmerk van een

populatie, bijvoorbeeld de standaarddeviatie van een populatie.
Vergelijk: statistisch gegeven.
CA:280, DA:276, DE:279, EN:269, ES:293, FR:291, GA:272, IT:259, NE:280, PO:296.

281 parametrische procedures Statistische procedures die uitgaan van een normale verdeling van gegevens en uitzetting op een interval- of ratio-schaal. In de praktijk worden parametrische procedures gebruikt als er voldoende materiaal is om een normale verdeling van gegevens te realiseren.
Vergelijk: niet-parametrische procedures.
Meer informatie: Hatch en Lazaraton, 1991, pp. 237–238.
CA:295, DA:277, DE:280, EN:270, ES:309, FR:310, GA:259, IT:275, NE:281, PO:316.

282 partial-creditmodel In de itemresponse-theorie een model voor het omgaan met schaalgegevens. Dit zou een goed model zijn voor het analyseren van antwoorden op zin-aanvulitems waarbij een schaal, bijv. 1, 2 of 3, wordt gebruikt voor het scoren van items of voor een spreekvaardigheidstoets waarbij verschillende performance-schalen worden gebruikt.
Vergelijk: beoordelingsschaalmodel, manyfacet Rasch-model.
Zie: Rasch-model.
Meer informatie: Wright en Masters, 1982, pp. 40–48.
CA:257, DA:278, DE:281, EN:272, ES:270, FR:253, GA:301, IT:244, NE:282, PO:267.

283 Pearsons product-moment correlatie (Pearsons *r*) Een correlatie-coëfficiënt die goed te gebruiken is bij variabelen gemeten op een interval- of ratioschaal.
Zie: correlatie-coëfficiënt.
Meer informatie: Hatch en Lazaraton, 1991, pp. 427–431; Guilford en Fruchter, 1981, p. 81.
CA:59, DA:279, DE:298, EN:274, ES:90, FR:87, GA:84, IT:98, NE:283, PO:104.

284 percentiel De 99 schaalwaarden die een frequentieverdeling verdelen in 100 groepen van gelijke grootte. Het vijftigste percentiel (P50) wordt de mediaan genoemd. Kwartielen splitsen de verdeling in vier gelijke groepen.
Meer informatie: Hatch en Lazaraton, 1991, pp. 187–188.
CA:287, DA:280, DE:285, EN:275, ES:299, FR:49, GA:279, IT:266, NE:284, PO:302.

285 percentielscore Een getal of score dat positie aangeeft door het percentage lager dan deze score te vermelden. Als een kandidaat in een toets een percentielscore van 60 heeft, betekent dit dat 60% van alle kandidaten de genoemde score of een lagere heeft behaald.
CA:363, DA:281, DE:299, EN:276, ES:359, FR:53, GA:284, IT:55, NE:285, PO:276.

286 performance Het produceren van taal via spreken of schrijven. Performance als taal die geproduceerd wordt, wordt vaak gecontrasteerd met competentie, de onderliggende kennis van een taal.
Vergelijk: competentie.
Zie: performance-toets.
Meer informatie: Bachman, 1990, pp. 52 en 108.
CA:5, DA:282, DE:283, EN:277, ES:9, FR:297, GA:141, IT:267, NE:286, PO:304.

287 performance-toets Een toetsprocedure waarin de kandidaat gevraagd wordt om een schriftelijke of mondelinge ‘proeve van taalgebruik’ (bijv. essays, een gesprek). Een dergelijke procedure is vaak een afspiegeling van de performance in een niet-toetsgebonden context.
Meer informatie: Bachman, 1990, pp. 304–305.
CA:306, DA:283, DE:284, EN:278, ES:318, FR:380, GA:416, IT:367, NE:287, PO:381.

288 phi-coëfficiënt Een correlatiecoëfficiënt om de sterkte van de relatie tussen twee binaire variabelen mee aan te geven, bijvoorbeeld, scores op twee toetsitems die als ‘fout’ of ‘goed’ worden gescoord.
Zie: correlatie-coëfficiënt.
Meer informatie: Guilford en Fruchter, 1981, pp. 316–318; Crocker en Algina, 1986, pp. 92–94.
CA:62, DA:284, DE:286, EN:279, ES:59, FR:58, GA:76, IT:61, NE:288, PO:75.

289 phi-correlatie Zie voor definitie: phi-coëfficiënt.
CA:92, DA:285, DE:287, EN:280, ES:88, FR:88, GA:81, IT:101, NE:289, PO:103.

290 pilot-studie Een studie vooraf, waarin onderzoekers of toetsontwikkelaars hun ideeën op een beperkt aantal personen uitproberen om problemen te kunnen lokaliseren, voordat er een grootschalige proefafname plaatsvindt of een kant-en-klaar programma of product wordt gelanceerd.
Zie: proefafnames houden, pretesten.

CA:170, DA:286, DE:288, EN:281, ES:179, FR:163, GA:361, IT:344, NE:290, PO:180.

291 plaatsingstoets Een toets om leerlingen/studenten in een groep of klas te plaatsen op een niveau dat past bij hun mate van kennis en vaardigheid.

CA:311, DA:137, DE:101, EN:282, ES:323, FR:377, GA:434, IT:365, NE:291, PO:372.

292 plafond-effect Een grenseffect, veroorzaakt, doordat een toets te makkelijk is voor een bepaalde groep kandidaten, zodat hun scores allemaal bovenaan de verdelingsschaal te vinden zijn.
Zie: grenseffect.

CA:123, DA:219, DE:63/73, EN:44, ES:129, FR:140, GA:173, IT:145, NE:292, PO:137.

293 polytome scoring Polytome scoring (soms ook wel 'polychotome scoring' genoemd) is het scoren van een item met een schaal van tenminste drie punten. Zo kan het antwoord op een vraag bijvoorbeeld verschillend worden beloond: met 0, 1 of 2 punten. Open vragen worden vaak polytoom gescoord. Wordt ook wel schaalscoring genoemd.
Vergelijk: dichotome scoring.

CA:351, DA:291, DE:237, EN:284, ES:353, FR:89, GA:342, IT:34, NE:293, PO:64.

294 populatie Een complete set waarden, dat wil zeggen alle mogelijke kandidaten die aan een examen deelnemen. In de statistiek ook wel 'score-universum' genoemd.
Vergelijk: steekproef.

CA:289, DA:292, DE:290, EN:285, ES:302, FR:303, GA:280, IT:269, NE:294, PO:308.

295 post-test Een toets of andere vorm van meting die plaatsvindt aan het einde van een leerroute. Het vergelijken van de resultaten met de resultaten van een toets die aan het begin van de leerroute werd afgenomen geeft informatie over de effectiviteit van deze route.
Vergelijk: pre-test.

CA:327, DA:345, DE:5, EN:287, ES:336, FR:305, GA:179, IT:271, NE:295, PO:310.

296 power-test Een toets die vrijwel alle kandidaten binnen de gestelde tijd kunnen maken, maar die een aantal opdrachten of items bevat van een moeilijkheidsgraad die het onwaarschijnlijk maakt dat de meerderheid van de kandidaten alle items goed hebben.
Vergelijk: speeded test.

CA:310, DA:299, DE:261/293, EN:288, ES:329, FR:379, GA:413, IT:360, NE:296, PO:371.

297 pragmatische competentie Een mogelijke categorie in een model voor communicatieve taalvaardigheid: het omvat het vermogen tot het verrichten van spreekhandelingen en kennis van sociolinguïstische conventies.
Meer informatie: Bachman, 1990, p. 42.

CA:69, DA:294, DE:295, EN:290, ES:66, FR:69, GA:194, IT:68, NE:297, PO:83.

298 praktijkeffect Het effect op toetsscores van het feit dat kandidaten vertrouwd zijn met de soorten opdrachten of met de items zoals die in een toets gebruikt worden.

CA:119, DA:443, DE:419, EN:289, ES:123, FR:138, GA:169, IT:140, NE:298, PO:131.

299 pre-test Een toets die wordt afgenomen voor de aanvang van een leerroute. De resultaten van de pre-test kunnen worden vergeleken met de resultaten van een tweede toets aan het einde van de leerroute om de effectiviteit van deze route te evalueren
Vergelijk: post-test.

CA:333, DA:104, DE:440, EN:292, ES:338, FR:306, GA:290, IT:272, NE:299, PO:312.

300 predictieve validiteit Een indicatie over de mate van succes waarmee een toets toekomstige performance op het gebied van een bepaalde vaardigheid voorspelt.
Vergelijk: criterium validiteit.
Meer informatie: Guilford en Fruchter, 1987, pp. 437–438.

CA:425, DA:298, DE:294/439, EN:291, ES:422, FR:422, GA:38, IT:410, NE:300, PO:418.

301 prestatietoets Een toets om te meten hoeveel een kandidaat geleerd heeft van bepaalde lessen, boeken, etc.; het gaat hier om een leerplan-afhankelijke toets. Wordt ook wel voortgangstoets genoemd.

CA:309, DA:366, DE:369, EN:6, ES:321, FR:374, GA:419, IT:368, NE:301, PO:374.

302 pretesten Een stadium in de ontwikkeling van toetsmaterialen waarin de items worden uitgeprobeerd bij representatieve steekproeven van de doelpopulatie om de moeilijkheidsgraad van deze items te bepalen. Na statistische analyse kunnen de

items die goed zijn bevonden door naar de uiteindelijke toets.
Vergelijk: proefafname houden.
CA:174, DA:105, DE:436, EN:293, ES:191, FR:307, GA:289, IT:273, NE:302, PO:311.

303 proefafnames houden Een stadium in de ontwikkeling van toetsopdrachten dat tot doel heeft te bepalen of de toets naar verwachting functioneert. Gaat vaak gepaard met subjectief te beoordelen opdrachten, bijvoorbeeld essay-vragen die aan een beperkte populatie worden voorgelegd.
Vergelijk: pretesten.
CA:26, DA:301, DE:104, EN:418, ES:135, FR:160, GA:436, IT:336, NE:303, PO:185.

304 proeflees-opdracht Een toetsopdracht waarbij een tekst moet worden nagekeken op een bepaald type fouten, bijvoorbeeld spelling of structuur. Het verbeteren van de fouten kan ook onderdeel van de opdracht zijn.
CA:395, DA:195, DE:189, EN:300, ES:4, FR:84, GA:374, IT:75, NE:304, PO:97.

305 proficiency Kennis van een taal en bedrevenheid in het gebruik van die taal.
Vergelijk: vaardigheid, competentie.
Meer informatie: Bachman, 1990, p. 16.
CA:296, DA:296, DE:47, EN:295, ES:120, FR:260, GA:265, IT:62, NE:305, PO:273.

306 proficiency-toets Een toets die algemene vaardigheid of bedrevenheid meet zonder te verwijzen naar een specifieke leerroute of materialenset.
CA:319, DA:112, DE:120, EN:296, ES:326, FR:378, GA:428, IT:363, NE:306, PO:379.

307 profileren Een manier om toetsresultaten te presenteren, dat wil zeggen opgesplitst in de verschillende toetscomponenten, zodat de kandidaat of andere toetsgebruikers kunnen zien wat de relatief sterke en zwakke gebieden zijn.
CA:288, DA:297, DE:404, EN:297, ES:300, FR:312, GA:282, IT:395, NE:307, PO:303.

308 psychometrische toets Een toets van psychologische 'trekken', zoals persoonlijkheid, intelligentie, aptitude en language proficiency, met specifieke aannames over de aard van de vaardigheid die wordt getoetst, bijvoorbeeld dat deze eendimensionaal is en een normale verdeling vertoont.
Meer informatie: Bachman, 1990, p. 73–74.
CA:334, DA:302, DE:310, EN:301, ES:397, FR:390, GA:433, IT:379, NE:308, PO:394.

309 punt-biseriële correlatie Een item-discriminatie-index voor dichotome items, aangeduid als r_{pbi}; de correlatie tussen een criterium (meestal de toetsscore) en de itemresponse. Een voordeel van de *rpbi* op de biseriële correlatie (*rbis*) is dat de eerstgenoemde goed te gebruiken is, als de onderliggende vaardigheid geen normale verdeling vertoont.
Vergelijk: biseriële correlatie.
CA:57, DA:41, DE:311, EN:283, ES:86, FR:57, GA:80, IT:97, NE:309, PO:102.

310 random error Zie voordefinitie: error
CA:137, DA:408, DE:449, EN:306, ES:145, FR:152, GA:128, IT:156, NE:310, PO:147,

311 range Een maat voor de spreiding van waarnemingen. De range is de afstand tussen de hoogste en de laagste score.
Meer informatie: Hatch en Lazaraton, 1991, pp. 169–170.
CA:12, DA:431, DE:431, EN:308, ES:260, FR:241, GA:285, IT:233, NE:311, PO:12.

312 rangorde-correlatie Een correlatie die niet gebaseerd is op de absolute waarden van de variabelen maar op de relatieve rangorde.
Meer informatie: Guilford en Fruchter, 1981, pp. 294–296.
CA:60, DA:304, DE:315, EN:309, ES:89, FR:59, GA:82, IT:100, NE:312, PO:72.

313 Rasch-model Een mathematisch model, ook bekend als 'simple logistic model'. Het Rasch-model gaat uit van een relatie tussen de mate van waarschijnlijkheid waarmee iemand een opdracht tot een succesvol einde zal brengen en het verschil tussen de vaardigheid van de persoon in kwestie en de moeilijkheidsgraad van de opdracht. Het is de wiskundige equivalent van het een-parametermodel in de itemresponsetheorie. Het Rasch-model is in verschillende richtingen uitgebreid, bijvoorbeeld met mogelijkheden voor geschaalde antwoorden of met 'multiple facets' om de 'moeilijkheidsgraad' van een opdracht te kunnen verklaren.
Zie: itemresponsetheorie (IRT) , partialcreditmodel, beoordelingsschaalmodel, many-facet Rasch-model.
Meer informatie: Henning, 1987, pp. 117–125.
CA:259, DA:305, DE:316, EN:310,

ES:275, FR:252, GA:302, IT:248, NE:313, PO:266.

314 ratio-schaal Een schaal met een zuiver nulpunt waarbij de afstand tussen twee opeenvolgende punten de hele schaal door gelijk is. Bijvoorbeeld bij lengte: iemand die 2 meter lang is, is twee keer zo lang als iemand die 1 meter lang is.
Vergelijk: categorische schaal, intervalschaal, ordinale schaal.
Meer informatie: Crocker en Algina, 1986, pp. 48–49.

CA:153, DA:210, DE:433, EN:317, ES:160, FR:131, GA:312, IT:324, NE:314, PO:164.

315 rationele cloze Zie voor definitie: cloze-toets.

CA:314, DA:308, DE:230, EN:318, ES:316, FR:371, GA:60, IT:56, NE:315, PO:367.

316 referentiegroep Een referentiegroep is een steekproef uit een duidelijk afgebakende kandidatenpopulatie die gebruikt wordt om een toets te ijken.
Zie: norm.

CA:196, DA:309, DE:267, EN:324, ES:213, FR:202, GA:166, IT:189, NE:316, PO:212.

317 register Een specifieke manier van spreken of schrijven die karakteristiek is voor een bepaalde activiteit of een bepaalde mate van formaliteit.

CA:368, DA:310, DE:366, EN:325, ES:364, FR:323, GA:291, IT:297, NE:317, PO:327.

318 regressie Een techniek voor het voorspellen van de meest waarschijnlijke waarde van een variabele (de afhankelijke variabele) op basis van bekende waarden van een of meer andere variabelen (onafhankelijke variabelen).
Meer informatie:Hatch en Lazaraton, 1991, pp. 467–480; Guilford en Fruchter, 1981, pp. 346–361.

CA:369, DA:311, DE:321, EN:326, ES:365, FR:324, GA:4, IT:298, NE:318, PO:328.

319 response Het gedrag van een kandidaat opgeroepen door de toetsinput. Bijvoorbeeld het antwoord op een multiple-choicevraag of het werk dat door een kandidaat wordt geproduceerd in een schrijftoets.
Vergelijk: input, response-stimulus.

CA:374, DA:315, DE:21, EN:331, ES:371, FR:327, GA:153, IT:305, NE:319, PO:334.

320 response-stimuleringsprocedures Een techniek voor het oproepen van een response bij een kandidaat tijdens een toets. Wordt meestal gebruikt voor een mondelinge response in een gesproken-taaltoets.
Meer informatie: Hughes, 1989, pp. 104–110.

CA:293, DA:8, DE:212, EN:123, ES:307, FR:308, GA:162, IT:276, NE:320, PO:314.

321 response-stimulus Bij spreek- of schrijftoetsen grafisch materiaal of teksten ontworpen om een bepaalde response van de kandidaat uit te lokken.

CA:390, DA:316, DE:437 EN:299, ES:178, FR:95, GA:358, IT:343, NE:321, PO:179.

322 resultaat De uitkomst van een toets zoals die aan de toetskandidaat of toetsgebruiker wordt medegedeeld.

CA:380, DA:317, DE:103, EN:332, ES:378, FR:336, GA:397, IT:312, NE:322, PO:342.

323 rollenspel Een soort opdracht die soms in spreektoetsen wordt gebruikt waarbij de kandidaten zich in een bepaalde situatie moeten verplaatsen of een specifieke rol moeten aannemen.

CA:233, DA:320, DE:329, EN:334, ES:251, FR:232, GA:294, IT:202, NE:323, PO:345.

324 ruwe score Een toets die niet statistisch is gemanipuleerd door transformatie, weging of herschaling.
Zie: score.

CA:348, DA:321, DE:328, EN:319, ES:348, FR:276, GA:329, IT:282, NE:324, PO:281.

325 scanner Zie voor definitie: optische lezer.

CA:160, DA:327, DE:336, EN:347, ES:168, FR:342, GA:322, IT:226, NE:325, PO:346.

326 schaal Een aantal getallen of categorieën waarmee iets kan worden gemeten. Er worden vier soorten meetschaal onderscheiden – nominale schaal, ordinale schaal, intervalschaal en ratio-schaal.
Meer informatie: Crocker en Algina, 1986, pp. 46–49.

CA:144, DA:337, DE:352, EN:343, ES:152, FR:121, GA:308, IT:314, NE:326, PO:154.

327 schaal-descriptor Zie voor definitie: descriptor.

CA:98, DA:338, DE:353, EN:344, ES:99, FR:96, GA:438, IT:119, NE:327, PO:112.

328 schaal-item Een item dat wordt gescoord met behulp van een schaal.
Zie: polytome scoring.
CA:222, DA:342, DE:27, EN:342, ES:248, FR:230, GA:252, IT:220, NE:328, PO:242.

329 schaling Het creëren van meetschalen. In de taaltoetsing betekent dit: de performance van kandidaten omzetten in getallen om kennis- of vaardigheidsniveaus mee aan te geven. Als onderdeel van de schaling kunnen score-sets worden gewijzigd om een schaal met een bepaald doel te kunnen creëren, bijvoorbeeld om de toetsresultaten op een gestandaardiseerde manier te kunnen weergeven of toetsversies te kunnen equivaleren.
Zie: schaal, vaardigheidsschaal, centielschaal, gemeenschappelijke schaal, intervalschaal, nominale schaal, ordinale schaal, ratio-schaal, beoordelingsschaal, geëquivaleerde vormen, lineaire equivalering.
CA:159, DA:341, DE:355, EN:346, ES:167, FR:135, GA:321, IT:109, NE:329, PO:169.

330 scheefheid Een distributiekenmerk waarbij de piek van de curve ofwel rechts van het midden (negatieve scheefheid) ofwel links van het midden (positieve scheefheid) ligt.

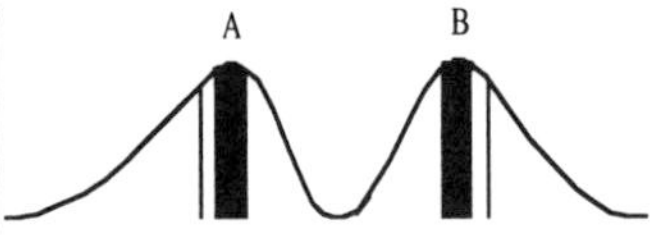

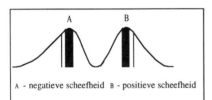

A - negatieve scheefheid B - positieve scheefheid

Zie: normale verdeling.
Meer informatie: Hatch en Lazaraton, 1991, p. 165.
CA:25, DA:343, DE:337, EN:366, ES:31, FR:109, GA:323, IT:25, NE:330, PO:120.

331 score Het totale aantal punten dat iemand in een toets behaalt, hetzij van het midden (negatieve scheefheid) ofwel links van het midden.
Vergelijk: meting.
CA:342, DA:328, DE:312, , EN:348, ES:345, FR:275, GA:328, IT:278, NE:331, PO:280.

332 screeningtoets Een meestal korte, makkelijk af te nemen toets om te bepalen welke kandidaten tot een bepaalde opleiding/bepaald examen kunnen worden toegelaten.
Vergelijk: plaatsingstoets.
CA:316, DA:424, DE:98, EN:349, ES:332, FR:375, GA:432, IT:370, NE:332, PO:375.

333 selectietoets Zie voor definitie: toelatingstoets.
CA:323, DA:330, DE:36, EN:353, ES:332, FR:382, GA:430, IT:370, NE:333, PO:383.

334 self-assessment (zelfbeoordeling) Het proces waarin studenten/leerlingen hun eigen vaardigheidsniveau bepalen, ofwel door bij zichzelf een toets af te nemen, ofwel met behulp van bijvoorbeeld een enquêteformulier of een checklist.
CA:30, DA:331, DE:345, EN:354, ES:36, FR:27, GA:142, IT:38, NE:334, PO:29.

335 semi-authentieke tekst Een authentieke tekst die voor gebruik in een toets is geredigeerd en waarin bijvoorbeeld het vocabulaire en/of de grammatica is aangepast aan het niveau van de kandidaten.
Zie: authentieke tekst.
CA:405, DA:123, DE:140, EN:355, ES:400, FR:112, GA:383, IT:391, NE:335, PO:128.

336 semi-directe toets Een toets waarin de performance op taalkundig gebied wordt vastgesteld door bepaalde aspecten van menselijke inmenging uit te schakelen. Voorbeeld: een spreektoets, waarbij een bandje in plaats van een menselijke gespreksleider wordt gebruikt. Een voorbeeld van een semi-directe toets is de SOPI-toets. (SOPI-Semi-Direct Oral Proficiency Interview).
Vergelijk: directe toets.
CA:339, DA:332, DE:347, EN:356, ES:343, FR:392, GA:423, IT:383, NE:336, PO:396.

337 sequentie-effect Een beoordelaarseffect dat optreedt door de volgorde waarin beoordelingen plaatsvinden.
Zie: beoordelaarseffecten.
CA:120, DA:329, DE:292, EN:360, ES:125, FR:142, GA:172, IT:148, NE:337, PO:136.

338 significantie Een begrip uit de statistiek dat betrekking heeft op de vraag of een bevinding al dan niet het resultaat is van 'kans'.
Zie: type-1-fout, type-2-fout, nulhypothese.
Meer informatie: Guilford en Fruchter, 1981, p. 208–210.
CA:388, DA:333, DE:349, EN:363, ES:386, FR:76, GA:366, IT:334, NE:338, PO:348.

339 significantietoets Een toets voor

het bepalen van statistische significantie.
Zie: significantie.
CA:324, DA:334, DE:350, EN:364, ES:333, FR:373, GA:435, IT:371, NE:339, PO:384.

340 situationele authenticiteit De mate waarin een toets als authentiek kan worden gezien vergeleken met echte, niet toetsgebonden taalgebruikssituaties.
Vergelijk: interactionele authenticiteit, levensechte benadering.
Zie: authenticiteit.
Meer informatie: Bachman, 1990, hoofdstuk 8.
CA:29, DA:336, DE:351, EN:365, ES:35, FR:26, GA:117, IT:37, NE:340, PO:28.

341 slaagcijfer De minimumscore die een kandidaat moet behalen om te slagen voor een toets of examen.
Vergelijk: cesuur.
CA:23, DA:36, DE:52, EN:273, ES:30, FR:277, GA:278, IT:288 NE:341, PO:282.

342 sleutel Alle correcte of acceptabele antwoorden op toetsitems samen.
Vergelijk: correctieschema.
CA:51/52, DA:256, DE:339, EN:198, ES:54, FR:329, GA:133, DE:339, IT:53, NE:342, PO:335.

343 smalle distributie Een frequentiedistributie die kenmerkend is voor een steekproef met een smallere 'range' dan de populatie waaruit de steekproef is getrokken, omdat leerlingen/studenten met een hoge of lage score in de steekproef ontbreken. Voorbeeld van een dergelijke steekproef: een groep studenten/leerlingen die tot een opleiding/cursus worden toegelaten na het slagen voor een toelatingstoets.
CA:116, DA:376, DE:1, EN:421, ES:117, FR:110, GA:108, IT:135, NE:343, PO:124.

344 socioculturele kennis Kennis van de wereld, namelijk over de manier waarop de maatschappij binnen een bepaalde cultuur funtioneert. Dit is relevant voor het juiste gedrag en het juiste taalgebruik in bepaalde culturele contexten.
Vergelijk: socioculturele competentie.
CA:76, DA:346, DE:357, EN:368, ES:72, FR:341, GA:135, IT:86, NE:344, PO:90.

345 sociolinguistische competentie Een model dat iemands communicatieve taalvaardigheid aangeeft: het omvat het vermogen om de taal, in overeenstemming met de sociale normen, aan te passen aan bepaalde contexten en omstandigheden.
Meer informatie: Bachman 1990, p. 42.
CA:70, DA:347, DE:358, EN:369, ES:67, FR:70, GA:197, IT:69, NE:345, PO:84.

346 SOPI (Semi-Direct/Simulated Oral Proficiency Interview) Een spreektoets waarbij de input op de band staat en het antwoord van de kandidaat op de band wordt opgenomen om op een later tijdstip te worden beoordeeld.
Zie: semi-directe toets.
CA:130, DA:348, DE:356, EN:370, ES:137, FR:392, GA:356, IT:93, NE:346, PO:144.

347 Spearman's rank-difference correlatie Een soort rangorde-correlatie die gebruikt wordt voor kleine steekproeven, bijvoorbeeld steekproeven van minder dan 30.
Zie: rangorde-correlatie.
CA:58, DA:351, DE:361, EN:373, ES:87, FR:60, GA:83, IT:99, NE:347, PO:73.

348 Spearman's rho Zie voor definitie: Spearman's rank-difference correlatie.
CA:383, DA:352, DE:362, EN:374, ES:380, FR:339, GA:292, IT:302, NE:348, PO:344.

349 Spearman-Brown split-half-schatting Zie voor definitie: split-halfbetrouwbaarheid
CA:168, DA:350, DE:360, EN:372, ES:177, FR:161, GA:228, IT:342, NE:349, PO:178.

350 Spearman-Brownformule Een statistische methode om de betrouwbaarheid van een toets te schatten in het geval de toets zou worden verlengd of verkort, door een aantal items toe te voegen, respectievelijk weg te laten. Kan worden gebruikt om te voorspellen hoeveel items er nodig zijn om een bepaalde betrouwbaarheid te kunnen halen.
Meer informatie: Crocker en Algina, 1986, pp. 118–119.
CA:83, DA:349, DE:359, EN:371, ES:207, FR:197, GA:147, IT:180, NE:350, PO:203.

351 specifieke-doeleindentoets Een toets ontwikkeld voor het meten van het vermogen van een kandidaat tot functioneren in een specifiek beroep of specifieke opleiding. De inhoud van de toets wordt hierop afgestemd en is gebaseerd op een analyse van de taalopdrachten die de kandidaten moeten kunnen vervullen in de beoogde taalgebruikssituatie.
CA:318, DA:243, DE:112, EN:375, ES:328, FR:393, GA:431, IT:378, NE:351, PO:393.

352 speeded test Een toets die binnen een bepaalde tijd moet worden voltooid.

Langzamere kandidaten krijgen een lagere score, omdat ze niet aan de laatste vragen toekomen. Normaal gesproken is in een 'speeded test' de moeilijkheidsgraad van de vragen van dien aard dat de kandidaten over het algemeen - onder tijdslimiet - wel het goede antwoord zouden kunnen geven. Ook bekend onder de naam 'speed test'.
Vergelijk: power-test.
CA:321, DA:129, DE:340/363, EN:376, ES:334, FR:363, GA:424, IT:372, NE:352, PO:385.

353 split-halfbetrouwbaarheid Een betrouwbaarheidsmaat voor het bepalen van interne consistentie. De schatting is gebaseerd op een correlatie tussen de scores van twee toetshelften die als twee parallelle toetsen worden gezien. De tweedeling kan op een aantal manieren worden gerealiseerd, bijvoorbeeld eerste helft, tweede helft, of door de even-genummerde items in de ene helft en de oneven-genummerde items in de andere helft te plaatsen.
Zie: betrouwbaarheid.
Meer informatie: Ebel en Frisbie, 1991, pp. 82–83; Crocker en Algina, 1986, pp. 136–138.
CA:183, DA:259, DE:364/398, EN:377, ES:201, FR:184, GA:203, IT:7, NE:353, PO:194.

354 spreekvaardigheid Competentie in het spreken van een taal.
CA:298, DA:239, DE:370, EN:264, ES:65, FR:68, GA:266, IT:67, NE:354, PO:82.

355 spreekvaardigheidstoetsing Voor het toetsen van spreekvaardigheid wordt vaak een vorm gebruikt die kan variëren van een volledig vrij gesprek tussen een kandidaat/meerdere kandidaten en een beoordelaar/beoordelaars tot een strakgestructureerde serie spreekopdrachten.
CA:131, DA:150, DE:305, EN:263, ES:136, FR:148, GA:1, IT:92, NE:355, PO:143.

356 spreiding De mate van variatie in de scores van een groep kandidaten. Als de spreiding groot is liggen de scores ver uiteen, als de spreiding klein is liggen ze dicht bij elkaar.
Zie: standaarddeviatie, variantie, range.
CA:107, DA:353, DE:385, EN:114, ES:110, FR:103, GA:357, IT:127, NE:356, PO:118.

357 staafdiagram Grafische representatie van frequentie-verdeling van variabelen

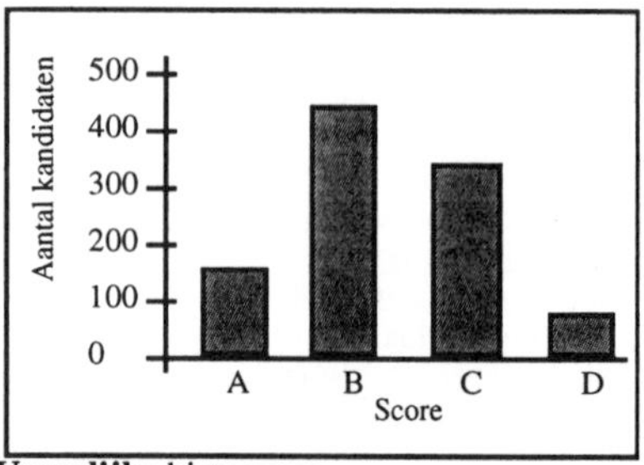

Vergelijk: histogram.
Meer informatie: Hatch en Lazaraton, 1991, p.147.
CA:102, DA:383, DE:335, EN:31, ES:104, FR:201, GA:42, IT:123, NE:357, PO:211.

358 stabiliteit Een betrouwbaarheidsaspect waarbij de schatting is gebaseerd op de test-retest-benadering. Het geeft aan hoe stabiel de toetsscores door de tijd heen zijn.
Zie: betrouwbaarheid, test-retest-betrouwbaarheid.
CA:162, DA:359, DE:371, EN:378, ES:170, FR:79, GA:65, IT:337, NE:358, PO:173.

359 stam Deel van een schriftelijke response-stimulus, meestal een niet volledige zin die door de kandidaat zelf moet worden aangevuld of waarvoor de kandidaat kan kiezen uit een aantal kant-en-klare alternatieven.
Vergelijk: juiste antwoord, alternatieven.
Zie: multiple-choice item.
CA:276, DA:360, DE:29, EN:387, ES:139, FR:10, GA:160, IT:346, NE:359, PO:224.

360 standaarddeviatie Een maat voor de spreiding van een aantal waarnemingen rond het rekenkundig gemiddelde. Het is gelijk aan de vierkantswortel van de variantie. In een normale verdeling bevindt 68% van de steekproef zich binnen één standaarddeviatie van het gemiddelde en 95% binnen twee standaarddeviaties van het gemiddelde.

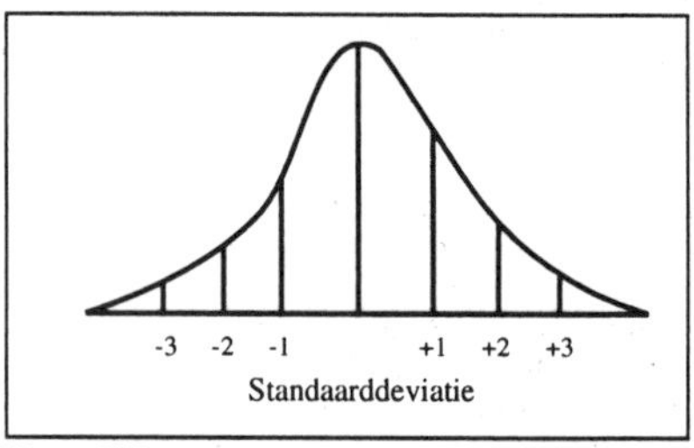

Vergelijk: range.

Zie: variantie.
Meer informatie: Ebel en Frisbie, 1991, pp. 61–62; Crocker en Algina, 1986, pp. 21–22.

CA:101, DA:362, DE:372, EN:379, ES:103, FR:98, GA:113, IT:122, NE:360, PO:114.

361 standaardisering Erop toezien dat beoordelaars zich houden aan een afgesproken procedure en beoordelingsschalen op de juiste wijze toepassen.
Zie: beoordelaar.

CA:167, DA:363, DE:373, EN:383, ES:175, FR:162, GA:45, IT:338, NE:361, PO:295.

362 standaardmeetfout In de klassieke ware-score-toetstheorie is de standaardmeetfout (*Se*) een indicatie voor de onnauwkeurigheid van een meting. De grootte van de standaardmeetfout hangt af van de betrouwbaarheid (*r*) en de standaarddeviatie van de toetsscores (*Sx*). De formule voor het berekenen van de *Se* is:

$$Se = Sx\sqrt{(1-r)}$$

Als een kandidaat met een ware score van T op een toets en een standaardmeetfout van *Se* de toets meermalen aflegt, dan zal de waargenomen score zich 68% van de tijd in de T±*Se* range bevinden en 95% van de tijd in de T±2*Se* range.
Meer informatie: Crocker en Algina, 1986, pp. 122–124.

CA:143, DA:364, DE:374, EN:381, ES:149, FR:157, GA:125, IT:12, NE:362, PO:153.

363 standaardschattingsfout De mate van precisie waarmee de ene variabele uit de andere kan worden voorspeld, bijvoorbeeld bij lineaire regressie. Het levert de betrouwbaarheidsintervallen voor de criteriumscores.
Zie: betrouwbaarheidsinterval.
Meer informatie: Hatch en Lazaraton, 1991, pp. 477–479.

CA:142, DA:361, DE:375, EN:380, ES:148, FR:156, GA:124, IT:163, NE:363, PO:152.

364 standaardscore Een score die lineair is omgezet uit een aantal scores. Het gemiddelde en de standaarddeviatie worden aangepast aan de waarden die de gebruiker hanteert. Voorbeelden van standaardscores: de *z*- en de *t*-score.
Vergelijk: *t*-score, *z*-score, stanine score.
Meer informatie: Ebel en Frisbie, 1991, pp. 67–68.

CA:350, DA:365, DE:376, EN:382, ES:350, FR:281, GA:333, IT:287, NE:364, PO:291.

365 stanine score Een methode om toetsscores, op basis van de normale distributie in negen groepen in te delen. 4% van de kandidaten bevind zich in de hoogste en 4% van de kandidaten bevind zich in de laagste groep. Het percentage kandidaten per groep staat in de grafiek hieronder.

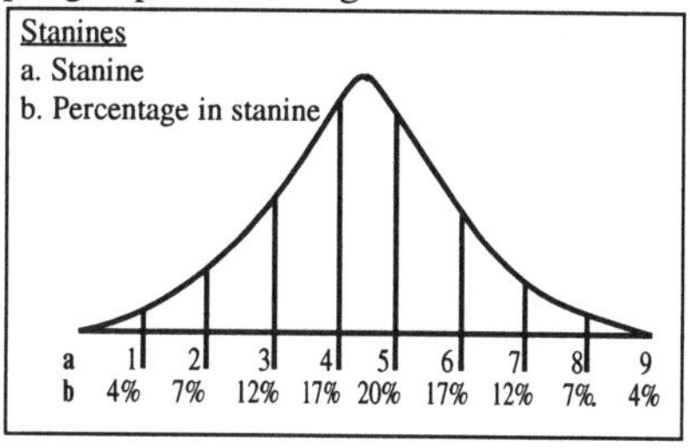

Meer informatie: Crocker en Algina, 1986, pp. 446–447.

CA:344, DA:367, DE:377, EN:384, ES:176, FR:282, GA:332, IT:279, NE:365, PO:284.

366 statistiek De wetenschap die zich bezighoudt met het manipuleren en interpreteren van numerieke gegevens.

CA:164, DA:369, DE:378, EN:386, ES:171, FR:348, GA:362, IT:339, NE:366, PO:175.

367 statistisch gegeven Een informatie-grootheid weergegeven in numerieke vorm. Strikt genomen vertelt een statistisch gegeven iets over een steekproefgroep in tegenstelling tot een parameter. Een parameter geeft informatie over een populatie. Statistische gegevens worden meestal met Romeinse letters weergegeven, parameters met Griekse. Zo wordt bijvoorbeeld de standaarddeviatie van een steekproef aangeduid met *s* of *Sd*; de standaarddeviatie van een populatie duiden we aan met σ (sigma).
Vergelijk: parameter.
Zie: populatie, steekproef.

CA:163, DA:368, DE:379, EN:385, ES:174, FR:348, GA:363, IT:117, NE:367, PO:174.

368 steekproef trekken Het nemen van een steekproef.
Zie: steekproef.

CA:267, DA:374, DE:384, EN:340, ES:281, FR:120, GA:307, IT:45, NE:368, PO:313.

369 steekproef Een keuze van een aantal elementen uit een populatie. Er kunnen verschillende soorten steekproeven worden onderscheiden, bijvoorbeeld enkelvoudige steekproef, gestratificeerde/ gelede/gelaagde

steekproef, etc.
Meer informatie: Crocker en Algina 1986, pp. 432–438; Guilford en Fruchter, 1981, pp. 44–45.
CA:264, DA:371, DE:380, EN:337, ES:278, FR:116, GA:304, IT:46, NE:369, PO:8.

370 steekproeffout In de researchcontext de fout in een statistische analyse die veroorzaakt wordt door de keuze van een bepaalde steekproef in het onderzoek (bijvoorbeeld als de steekproef niet representatief is voor de populatie).
Zie: populatie.
CA:139, DA:372, DE:381, EN:341, ES:147, FR:158, GA:129, IT:155, NE:370, PO:148.

371 steekproefvrije meting In de research-context, een interpretatie van bevindingen die niet afhankelijk is van de steekproef die in een bepaald onderzoek werd gehanteerd.
CA:247, DA:373, DE:382, EN:339, ES:265, FR:244, GA:396, IT:239, NE:371, PO:258.

372 stelopdracht Een opdracht waarbij de kandidaat een langere tekst moet schrijven. Daarbij kan het gaan om een verslag van gebeurtenissen of een bespreking van een onderwerp waarover verschillende meningen mogelijk zijn. Een stelopdracht kan ook het schrijven van een rapport of van een informele/formele brief zijn.
Vergelijk: essay-vraag.
CA:366, DA:109, DE:32, EN:62, ES:192, FR:73, GA:51, IT:82, NE:372, PO:88.

373 subtoets Zie voor definitie: examen-onderdeel.
CA:389, DA:377, DE:386, EN:389, ES:388, FR:346, GA:150, IT:345, NE:373, PO:350.

374 summatieve evaluatie Evaluatie die plaatsvindt na afloop van een proces. De term kan verwijzen naar een lesprogramma.
Vergelijk: formatieve evaluatie.
CA:34, DA:266, DE:3, EN:391, ES:186, FR:172, GA:238, IT:415, NE:374, PO:36.

375 summatieve beoordeling Toetsing die plaatsvindt aan het einde van een opleiding/lesprogramma.
Vergelijk: formatieve beoordeling.
CA:34, DA:267, DE:4, EN:390, ES:186, FR:172, GA:233, IT:423, NE:375, PO:36.

376 *t*-score Een uitbreiding van de *z*-score. Deze score kent geen decimaal en negatieve scores. De *t*-score is gelijk aan tienmaal de *z*-score plus 50. De distributie heeft een gemiddelde van 50 en een standaarddeviatie van 10.
Zie: *z*-score.
Meer informatie: Ebel en Frisbie, 1991, p. 68.
CA:355, DA:384, DE:388, EN:422, ES:355, FR:283, GA:367, IT:289, NE:376, PO:287.

377 *t*-test Een statistische test om te bepalen of er significante verschillen zijn tussen de gemiddelden van twee steekproeven.
CA:340, DA:385, DE:387, EN:423, ES:398, FR:150, GA:368, IT:385, NE:377, PO:397.

378 taalgebruik voor Specifieke Doeleinden Taalonderricht of -toetsing, gericht op het taalgebruik dat hoort bij een bepaalde activiteit of bepaald beroep; bijv. Engels voor luchtverkeersleiders, Spaans voor de handel.
CA:238, DA:95, DE:111, EN:205, ES:256, FR:236, GA:385, IT:227, NE:378, PO:251.

379 taalvaardigheid De vaardigheden die samen het vermogen bepalen waarmee een individu in staat is taal voor een verscheidenheid aan communicatieve doeleinden te gebruiken.
Meer informatie: Bachman, 1990, pp. 3–4.
CA:47, DA:354, DE:368, EN:203, ES:50, FR:43, GA:97, IT:4, NE:379, PO:50.

380 taalverwerving Het proces waarmee vaardigheid in een eerste of tweede taal wordt verworven. Bij tweede talen wordt soms een onderscheid gemaakt tussen verwerving (dat wil zeggen door natuurlijke blootstelling aan de taal) en leren (d.w.z. door bewust bestuderen van de taal).
CA:7, DA:356, DE:367, EN:204, ES:14, FR:5, GA:349, IT:22, NE:380, PO:24.

381 tekst Een lopend geheel van geschreven of gesproken taaluitingen als basis voor een set toetsitems.
CA:403, DA:386, DE:411, EN:411, ES:399, FR:396, GA:381, IT:389, NE:381, PO:398.

382 test tailoring (het pasklaar maken van toetsen) Het aanpassen van bestaande toetsen om tegemoet te kunnen komen aan de eisen van een bepaalde groep van toetsgebruikers of toetskandidaten.
CA:301, DA:404, DE:410, EN:405, ES:13, FR:395, GA:370, IT:5, NE:382, PO:4.

383 test-retestbetrouwbaarheid Een

betrouwbaarheidsschatting die wordt gerealiseerd door dezelfde toets onder dezelfde omstandigheden aan dezelfde kandidaten voor te leggen en de score van de twee zittingen de correleren. Heeft te maken met de stabiliteit van de scores door de tijd heen en kan ook heel goed worden gebruikt, wanneer interne-consistentieschattingen niet mogelijk zijn.
Vergelijk: interne consistentie.
Zie: betrouwbaarheid, stabiliteit.

CA:184, DA:318, DE:409/325, EN:410, ES:202, FR:188, GA:204, IT:9, NE:383, PO:197.

384 testing point Het doel van een item: het specifieke aspect waarop een item kennis aan het licht probeert te brengen.

CA:128, DA:399, DE:309, EN:409, ES:289, FR:300, GA:281, IT:293, NE:384, PO:307.

385 theta schaal De wetenschappelijke term voor vaardigheidsschaal.

CA:158, DA:407, DE:413, EN:413, ES:166, FR:128, GA:320, IT:328, NE:385, PO:168.

386 Threshold level Een invloedrijke specificatie in functionele termen gesteld, van een elementair niveau van beheersing van een vreemde taal. De specificatie werd in 1976 door de Raad van Europa gepubliceerd voor het Engels en bijgewerkt in 1990. Sindsdien hebben verschillende versies voor een aantal andere Europese talen het licht gezien.

CA:272, DA:419, DE:414, EN:414, ES:285, FR:262, GA:212, IT:230, NE:386, PO:275.

387 toelatingstoets Een toets om te bepalen of een kandidaat al of niet toegang krijgt tot een bepaald instituut of bepaalde cursus.
Vergelijk: plaatsingstoets.

CA:305, DA:5, DE:346, EN:124, ES:319, FR:369, GA:422, IT:364, NE:387, PO:377.

388 toets Een procedure voor het beoordelen van bepaalde aspecten van een vaardigheid of van kennis.

a) een beoordelingsprocedure die bestaat uit een aantal onderdelen, vaak synoniem met examen.

b) een enkel (toets) onderdeel ter beoordeling van een vaardigheids - of kennisdomein, b.v. spreken of schrijven. In deze betekenis kan een toets ook deel uitmaken van een volledig examen (b.v. de spreektoets of een cloze-toe ts).

c) een relatief korte en gemakkelijk af te nemen beoordelingsprocedure die vaak binnen een instelling wordt gebruikt (b.v. een voortgangstoets).

d) een relatief korte en gemakkelijk af te nemen beoordelingsprocedure die deel uitmaakt van een onderzoeksprogramma ter validering (b.v. een ankertoets).

CA:300, DA:300, DE:389, EN:395, ES:311, FR:359, GA:403, IT:353, NE:388, PO:361.

389 toetsanalyse Analyse van toetsen, nadat deze bij kandidaten zijn afgenomen. De analyse vindt dikwijls plaats met behulp van statistische en gecomputeriseerde methoden. Het doel kan zijn na te gaan hoe de kandidaten hebben gefunctioneerd of hoe de toets zelf heeft gefunctioneerd.

CA:15, DA:389, DE:390, EN:396, ES:22, FR:16, GA:14, IT:17, NE:389, PO:18.

390 toetsbatterij Zie voor definitie: batterij.

CA:39, DA:390, DE:406, EN:397, ES:41, FR:31, GA:63, IT:42, NE:390, PO:39.

391 toetsconstructeur Iemand die een toets schrijft en construeert.

CA:127, DA:392, DE:400, EN:361, ES:92, FR:145, GA:121, IT:149, NE:391, PO:141.

392 toetsconstructie Het uitkiezen van items of opdrachten en er een toets van maken. Dit proces wordt dikwijls voorafgegaan door een stadium waarin materialen worden gepretest of aan een proefafname onderworpen. Items en opdrachten voor een toets kunnen ook uit een materialenbank worden gehaald.

CA:126, DA:394, DE:397, EN:398, ES:75, FR:146, GA:393, IT:110, NE:392, PO:140.

393 toetsgebruiker De persoon of het instituut (bijvoorbeeld een leerkracht of werkgever) die de resultaten van een toets gebruikt om een beslissing omtrent de toetskandidaat te nemen.

CA:414, DA:391, DE:392, EN:407, ES:410, FR:409, GA:440, IT:399, NE:393, PO:407.

394 toetsinformatiefunctie In de IRT een index die aangeeft hoeveel informatie een toets geeft over een persoon van een bepaald vaardigheidsniveau. Het is de som van de iteminformatiefuncties.
Vergelijk: item-informatie-functie.
Meer informatie: Crocker en Algina, 1986, pp. 369–371.

CA:194, DA:388, DE:399, EN:400, ES:211, FR:191, GA:139, IT:185, NE:394,

PO:207.

395 toetskandidaat Zie voor definitie: kandidaat.

CA:100, DA:402, DE:407, EN:406, ES:190, FR:351, GA:110, IT:49, NE:395, PO:183.

396 toetsmethode Taalvaardigheid kan worden getoetst aan de hand van een verscheidenheid aan methodes, zoals multiple choice, cloze, stelopdracht, gesprek, etc. Uit waarnemingen is gebleken dat de toetsmethode, bij meting van performance, interactie met de vaardigheid kan vertonen.
Zie: toetsmethode-kenmerken
Meer informatie: Bachman, 1990, p. 77.

CA:248, DA:395, DE:401, EN:401, ES:266, FR:245, GA:257, IT:236, NE:396, PO:259.

397 toetsmethode-facetten Zie voor definitie: toetstmethode-kenmerken.

CA:175, DA:396, DE:402, EN:403, ES:193, FR:176, GA:163, IT:50, NE:397, PO:186.

398 toetsmethode-kenmerken De karakteristieke kenmerken van verschillende toetsmethoden. Dit kunnen onder andere zijn: context, de taal die in de instructie wordt gehanteerd, structuur/uiterlijk, etc.
Meer informatie: Bachman, 1990, hoofdstuk 5.

CA:48, DA:397, DE:403, EN:402, ES:51, FR:46, GA:401, IT:50, NE:398, PO:54.

399 toetsontwikkelaar Iemand die zich bezighoudt met het ontwikkelen van een nieuwe toets.

CA:109, DA:405, DE:395, EN:399, ES:133, FR:145, GA:149, IT:149, NE:399, PO:141.

400 toetsspecificaties Een lijst met gedetailleerde informatie die meestal tijdens het ontwerpen van een nieuwe toets of het herzien van een bestaande toets wordt aangelegd. De specificaties bevatten details omtrent ontwerp, inhoud, niveau, gebruikte opdracht- en itemsoorten, doelpopulatie, gebruik van de toets, etc. In de lijst is ook dikwijls voorbeeldmateriaal opgenomen.

CA:161, DA:401, DE:394, EN:404, ES:169, FR:346, GA:355, IT:120, NE:400, PO:171.

401 toetsvertrouwdheid Bekendheid met de structuur van een toets of ervaring met het afleggen van een toets waardoor kandidaten boven hun reële vaardigheidsniveau kunnen presteren.

CA:179, DA:406, DE:396, EN:408, ES:197, FR:314, GA:161, IT:167, NE:401, PO:191.

402 transformatie-item Zie voor definitie: zinnen transformeren.

CA:229, DA:413, DE:420, EN:416, ES:245, FR:403, GA:242, IT:217, NE:402, PO:239.

403 trek Een fysiek of psychologisch kenmerk van een persoon (bijvoorbeeld taalvaardigheid) of de meetschaal om een dergelijk kenmerk te beschrijven.

CA:411, DA:416, DE:95, EN:415, ES:360, FR:23, GA:400, IT:26, NE:403, PO:403.

404 twee-parametermodel In de itemresponsetheorie een model waarin, naast de vaardigheids/moeilijkheidsparameter rekening wordt gehouden met een itemdiscriminatieparameter.
Vergelijk: een-parametermodel, Raschmodel.
Zie: itemresponsetheorie (IRT) .

CA:258, DA:411, DE:454, EN:424, ES:271, FR:248, GA:298, IT:241, NE:404, PO:264.

405 type-1-fout In de statistiek de fout dat de nulhypothese wordt verworpen, terwijl die in feite juist is.
Vergelijk: type-2-fout.
Zie: nulhypothese.
Meer informatie: Hatch en Lazaraton, 1991, p. 224.

CA:140, DA:417, DE:9/117, EN:425, ES:150, FR:154, GA:126, IT:157, NE:405, PO:150.

406 type-2-fout In de statistiek de fout dat de nulhypothese wordt aangenomen, terwijl die in feite niet juist is.
Vergelijk: type-1-fout.
Zie: nulhypothese.
Meer informatie: Hatch en Lazaraton, 1991, p. 224.

CA:141, DA:418, DE:118, EN:426, ES:151, FR:155, GA:127, IT:158, NE:406, PO:151.

407 uitgebreide response Een vorm van response op een item of opdracht waarbij de kandidaat zelf een response moet produceren (en niet zelf kan kiezen uit een aantal antwoorden). Deze response dient langer dan één of twee zinnen te zijn.
Vergelijk: kort-antwoorditem.

CA:378, DA:423, DE:35, EN:138, ES:375, FR:332, GA:159, IT:308, NE:407, PO:339.

408 unitary competence (een-competentie-theorie) Een taaltheorie waarvoor met name Oller zich sterk maakte. De theorie gaat uit van één enkele competentie als basis voor alle taalvaardigheden.

CA:71, DA:91, DE:423, EN:428, ES:68, FR:71, GA:192, IT:70, NE:408, PO:85.

409 vaardigheden van een lagere orde Vaardigheden waarover kandidaten bij taaltoetsen moeten beschikken en waarvan men aanneemt dat ze minder complex zijn zoals woord- of letterherkenning.
Vergelijk: vaardigheden van een hogere orde.

CA:200, DA:27, DE:424, EN:219, ES:101, FR:44, GA:327, IT:2, NE:409, PO:52.

410 vaardigheden van een hogere orde Verondersteld complexe vaardigheden zoals conclusies trekken en samenvatten.
Vergelijk: vaardigheden van een lagere orde.

CA:201, DA:130, DE:418, EN:162, ES:102, FR:45, GA:326, IT:3, NE:410, PO:53.

411 vaardigheid Een mentale eigenschap of het vermogen tot het verrichten van handelingen.
Vergelijk: competentie, proficiency.
Meer informatie: Bachman, 1990, p. 16, p. 19.

CA:46, DA:2, DE:113, EN:2, ES:49, FR:42, GA:96, IT:1A, NE:411, PO:49.

412 vaardigheid Vermogen om iets te doen. In de taaltoetsing maakt men vaak onderscheid tussen de vier vaardigheden lezen, schrijven, spreken, en luisteren.
Zie: competentie.

CA:199, DA:111, DE:119, EN:367, ES:100, FR:340, GA:325, IT:1B, NE:412, PO:51.

413 vaardigheidsschaal In de itemresponsetheorie, een schaal met gelijke intervallen waarop de vaardigheid van personen en de moeilijkheidsgraad van toetsopdrachten kan worden uitgezet.
Wordt ook wel de theta-schaal genoemd.
Meer informatie: Bachman 1990, p. 345.

CA:150, DA:3, DE:114, EN:3, ES:157, FR:128, GA:313, IT:322, NE:413, PO:159.

414 validering Het verzamelen van bewijsmateriaal ter ondersteuning van de conclusies uit toetsscores. De conclusies betreffende de specifieke gebruiksdoeleinden van een toets worden gevalideerd, niet de toets zelf.
Zie: validiteit.

CA:415, DA:426, DE:426, EN:429, ES:412, FR:412, GA:39, IT:400, NE:414, PO:408.

415 validiteit De mate waarin op basis van toetsscores conclusies kunnen worden getrokken die juist, zinvol en nuttig zijn, gegeven het doel van de toets. Er kunnen verschillende soorten validiteit worden onderscheiden, bijvoorbeeld inhouds-, criterium- en constructvaliditeit; deze leveren verschillende soorten bewijsmateriaal, om te kunnen beoordelen of een toets voor een bepaald doel 'algeheel valide' is.
Zie: concurrente validiteit, constructvaliditeit (begrigsvaliditeit), criteriumvaliditeit, inhoudsvaliditeit, convergente validiteit, discriminante validiteit, indruksvaliditeit, predictieve validiteit.
Meer informatie: Bachman, 1990, pp. 25, 236–237.

CA:416, DA:427, DE:427, EN:430, ES:413, FR:413, GA:30, IT:401, NE:415, PO:409.

416 variabele a) De naam voor een serie waarnemingen op één aspect, bijvoorbeeld een toetsitem, sekse, leeftijd of toetsscore.

b) Een grootheid in een experimenteel ontwerp of een statistische analyse, die een serie waarden kan aannemen. Belangrijke variabelen in de taaltoetsing zijn bijvoorbeeld: moeilijkheidsgraad van toetsitems, sekse en leeftijd van toetskandidaten, etc.

CA:430, DA:428, DE:428, EN:431, ES:430, FR:423, GA:25, IT:416, NE:416, PO:422.

417 variantie Een mate voor de spreiding van een set scores. Hoe groter de variantie, hoe verder de individuele scores van het gemiddelde af liggen.

CA:434, DA:429, DE:429, EN:432, ES:434, FR:427, GA:24, IT:420, NE:417, PO:421.

418 variantie–analyse Zie voor definitie: ANOVA

CA:17, DA:430, DE:430, EN:13, ES:23, FR:15, GA:15, IT:19, NE:418, PO:14.

419 verticale equivalering De scores van twee toetsen van verschillende moeilijkheidsgraad op dezelfde schaal zetten.
Meer informatie: Crocker en Algina, 1986, pp. 473–477.

CA:135, DA:432, DE:435, EN:434, ES:143, FR:39, GA:90, IT:153, NE:419, PO:46.

420 voorbeeldwerk Een keuze uit het werk van kandidaten, die een scala aan vaardigheden weergeeft. Voorbeeldwerk

wordt gebruikt bij de standaardisering van de beoordelingsprocedure.
CA:268, DA:370, DE:254, EN:338, ES:132, FR:118, GA:344, IT:330, NE:420, PO:10.

421 voortgangstoets Zie voor definitie: prestatietoets
CA:322, DA:20, DE:203, EN:23, ES:331, FR:366, GA:419, IT:368, NE:421, PO:374.

422 vorderingentoets Een toets die tijdens een leerroute wordt afgenomen om te zien wat de leerlingen/studenten tot dan toe hebben geleerd.
CA:320, DA:108, DE:214, EN:298, ES:330, FR:381, GA:418, IT:369, NE:422, PO:382.

423 vraag Wordt soms gebruikt in plaats van 'toetsopdracht' of 'item'.
Zie: item, opdracht.
CA:291, DA:357, DE:122, EN:303, ES:304, FR:315, GA:55, IT:136, NE:423, PO:323.

424 vraagtype Zie voor definitie: itemtype, opdracht-type.
CA:407, DA:358, DE:124, EN:305, ES:404, FR:406, GA:57, IT:394, NE:424, PO:400.

425 vragenblad/vragenboekje Wordt soms gebruikt voor 'toetsblad' of 'toetsboekje'.Een soort geselecteerde-response-item, waarbij de kandidaat voor een serie beweringen die betrekking hebben op een tekst moet aangeven of ze waar of niet waar zijn.
CA:239, DA:263, DE:123, EN:304, ES:220, FR:180, GA:271, IT:169, NE:425, PO:145.

426 waar/ niet waar-item Een sort geselecteerde-response-item waarbij de kandidaat voor een serie beweringen die betrekking hebben op een tekst moet aangeven of ze waar of niet waar zijn.
CA:232, DA:326, DE:326, EN:419, ES:250, FR:429, GA:245, IT:218, NE:426, PO:243.

427 waardering Een toetsscore kan aan de kandidaat worden meegedeeld in de vorm van een waardering, bijvoorbeeld op een schaal van A tot E, waarbij A staat voor 'zeer goed', B voor 'goed', C voor 'voldoende' en D en E voor 'onvoldoende'.
Vergelijk: cijfer.
CA:275, DA:167, DE:270, EN:156, ES:288, FR:259, GA:164, IT:188, NE:426, PO:272.

428 waardering toekennen Het proces waarbij toetsscores of cijfers in een waarderingsschaal worden vertaald.
CA:362, DA:168, DE:48, EN:157, ES:47, FR:52, GA:165, IT:94, NE:427, PO:277.

429 waargenomen score De score die een kandidaat behaalt. In de klassieke toetstheorie bestaat de waargenomen score uit 'ware score' en 'error'.
Zie: error, ware score.
CA:353, DA:183, DE:49, EN:258, ES:352, FR:279, GA:331, IT:283, NE:429, PO:285.

430 waarschijnlijkheidsmodel Een model waarbij causale relaties (zoals die tussen moeilijkheidsgraad en vaardigheid van een kandidaat aan de ene en toetsperformance aan de andere kant) worden verklaard in termen van 'mate van waarschijnlijkheid'. Het Rasch-model is een voorbeeld van een waarschijnlijkheidsmodel.
CA:262, DA:295, DE:297, EN:294, ES:274, FR:255, GA:299, IT:247, NE:430, PO:269.

431 ware score De score die een kandidaat zou behalen, als er tijdens het toetsen of scoren geen meetfout zou optreden. Een elementaire notie in de klassieke toetstheorie.
CA:357, DA:415, DE:441, EN:420, ES:357, FR:285, GA:335, IT:285, NE:431, PO:289.

432 washback Zie voor definitie: backwash.
CA:372, DA:436, DE:442, EN:435, ES:124, FR:322, GA:95, IT:147, NE:432, PO:135.

433 Waystage level Een specificatie van een elementair niveau van beheersing van een vreemde taal. Dit level werd voor het Engels in 1977 gepubliceerd door de Raad van Europa en in 1990 herzien. De doelstelling ligt minder hoog dan bij het Threshold level (naar schatting ongeveer de helft van de Threshold-leerinhoud).
Vergelijk: Threshold level.
CA:271, DA:437, DE:443, EN:436, ES:284, FR:261, GA:211, IT:231, NE:433, PO:274.

434 weging De toekenning van een verschillend aantal maximumpunten aan een toetsitem, -opdracht of -onderdeel om de relatieve bijdrage van een dergelijk onderdeel ten opzichte van andere onderdelen van diezelfde toets te wijzigen. Als er bijvoorbeeld dubbele punten worden toegekend aan alle items in opdracht 1 van een toets, dan zal opdracht 1 meer van de

totaalscore voor zijn rekening nemen dan de andere opdrachten.
Meer informatie: Ebel en Frisbie, 1991, pp. 214–216.
CA:290, DA:435, DE:136, EN:438, ES:303, FR:302, GA:439, IT:268, NE:434, PO:306.

435 winstscore Het verschil tussen de score op een toets vóór een lesprogramma en de score op dezelfde of een soortgelijke toets, afgelegd aan het eind van het programma. De wintscore geeft de vorderingen tijdens een lesprogramma aan.
CA:352, DA:290, DE:211, EN:150, ES:32, FR:199, GA:44, IT:192, NE:435,PO:209.

436 woordfrequentietelling Een telling van het aantal malen dat bepaalde woorden of typen woorden in een tekst voorkomen. In de taaltoetsing kan dit nuttig zijn, wanneer toetsen in overeenstemming moeten zijn met een bepaalde lexicale specificatie.
CA:190, DA:270, DE:143, EN:440, ES:362, FR:75, GA:67, IT:256, NE:436, PO:95.

437 woordvormingsitem Een soort item waarbij de kandidaat een vorm van een woord moet produceren op basis van een andere vorm van hetzelfde woord dat als input dient. Voorbeeld: Dit soort werk vraagt om .... van technisch vocabulaire. (begrijpen)
CA:227, DA:269, DE:445, EN:439, ES:240, FR:227, GA:244, IT:216, NE:437, PO:237 .

438 y-snijpunt In de lineaire regressie het punt waarop de regressielijn de Y-as (de verticale as) snijdt.
Zie: lineaire regressie.
CA:212, DA:438, DE:146, EN:441, ES:231, FR:215, GA:181, IT:200, NE:438, PO:226.

439 *z*-score Een veelgebruikte standaardscore met een gemiddelde van 0 en een standaarddeviatie van 1.

De formule voor het berekenen van *z*-scores luidt:

$$z = (X - \bar{X}) \div Sx$$

Hierin staat:

z voor *z*-score
$\underline{X}$ voor toetsscore
X voor gemiddelde toetsscore
Sx voor standaarddeviatie van toetsscores

Vergelijk: *t*-score.
Zie: standaardscore.
Meer informatie: Ebel en Frisbie, 1991, p. 68.
CA:358, DA:439, DE:446, EN:442, ES:358, FR:286, GA:441, IT:291, NE:439, PO:290.

440 zinnen transformeren Een itemtype waarbij een complete zin wordt gegeven als response-stimulus gevolgd door de eerste één of twee woorden van een tweede zin, waarin de inhoud van de eerste zin in een andere grammaticale vorm wordt uitgedrukt. Zo kan bijvoorbeeld zin 1 een actieve zin zijn en moet de kandidaat dezelfde inhoud in zin 2 in de lijdende vorm gieten.
CA:410, DA:381, DE:334, EN:359, ES:407, FR:404, GA:61, IT:397, NE:440, PO:405.

441 zinnen uitbreiden Een itemtype waarbij de response-stimulus bestaat uit een serie inhoudelijke woorden, maar waarbij voorzetsels, hulpwerkwoorden, lidwoorden, etc. ontbreken. Het is aan de kandidaten om de ontbrekende woorden in te vullen en dus van de stimulus een volledige grammaticaal juiste zin te maken.
CA:99, DA:380, DE:333, EN:358, ES:18, FR:175, GA:148, IT:166, NE:441, PO:184.

442 zinnen aanvullen Een itemtype waarin de zin slechts voor de helft wordt gegeven. Het is aan de kandidaten om de zin af te maken, hetzij door passende woorden te leveren (bijvoorbeeld via het lezen van een tekst) hetzij door deze woorden te kiezen uit een lijst.
CA:72, DA:382, DE:332, EN:357, ES:69, FR:298, GA:93, IT:80, NE:442, PO:86.

10 Português: Glossário multilingue de termos de avaliação de línguas

1 acordo individual Refere-se à definição de acordo inter-individual e de acordo intra-individual.

CA:1, DA:307, DE:56, EN:312, ES:10, FR:1, GA:70, IT:84, NE:36, PO:1.

2 acordo inter-individual Grau de acordo entre dois ou mais avaliadores sobre a mesma performance (na totalidade ou parcialmente) de um examinando. É particularmente pertinente na avaliação das capacidades orais e escritas em testes em que os examinadores exercem um juízo subjectivo.

CA:2, DA:31, DE:159, EN:181, ES:11, FR:2, GA:68, IT:84, NE:185, PO:2.

3 acordo intra-individual Grau de acordo entre duas avaliações da mesma performance (na totalidade ou parcialmente) de um examinando feitas em alturas diferentes pelo mesmo avaliador. É particularmente pertinente na avaliação das capacidades orais e escritas em testes em que os examinadores exercem um juízo subjectivo.

CA:3, DA:33, DE:163, EN:185, ES:12, FR:3, GA:69, IT:90, NE:190, PO:3.

4 adaptação de teste Acção de adaptar um teste existente aos requisitos de um grupo determinado de utilizadores de testes ou de examinandos.

CA:301, DA:404, DE:410, EN:405, ES:13, FR:395, GA:370, IT:5, NE:382, PO:4.

5 adequação Relação entre as previsões dum modelo e os resultados observados. Podem ser calculados diferentes índices de adequação. Na teoria item-resposta, a análise da adequação mostra como o item estimado e os parâmetros dos candidatos (a dificuldade e o nível de capacidade) predizem as notas que vão ser obtidas num teste: a adequação estatística dum item pode ser considerada análoga ao seu índice de discriminação na estatística clássica aplicada a testes.
Ver: teoria item-resposta (TIR).

CA:8, DA:99, DE:248, EN:145, ES:15, FR:6, GA:268, IT:107, NE:135, PO:5.

6 alfa (coeficiente alfa) Apreciação de fiabilidade que mede a consistência interna dum teste. A apreciação faz-se em valores de 0 a 1. Utilizado muitas vezes em testes com escalas de classificação, por oposição aos testes de itens dicotómicos, se bem que possa ser utilizado nos dois tipos de testes.
Cf: Kuder-Richardson.
Ver: consistência interna.
Ler: Henning, 1987, p.84.

CA:9, DA:11, DE:10, EN:10, ES:16, FR:8, GA:10, IT:10, NE:12, PO:6.

7 alfa de Cronbach Refere-se à definição de alfa (coeficiente alfa).

CA:10, DA:54, DE:70, EN:84, ES:17, FR:9, GA:11, IT:11, NE:89, PO:7.

8 amostra Selecção de um sub-conjunto de elementos duma dada população. Podemos distinguir vários tipos de amostras, por exemplo, a amostra aleatória, a amostra estratificada, etc.
Ler: Crocker e Algina, 1986, pp. 432–438; Guilford e Fruchter, 1981, pp. 44–45.

CA:264, DA:371, DE:380, EN:337, ES:278, FR:116, GA:304, IT:46, NE:369, PO:8.

9 amostra aleatória Amostra escolhida ao acaso, tendo todos os indivíduos da população as mesmas possibilidades de ser escolhidos para a pesquisa.
Ver: amostra.
Ler: Crocker e Algina, 1986, pp.433–438; Guilford e Fruchter, 1981, p.120.

CA:265, DA:409, DE:451, EN:307, ES:279, FR:117, GA:305, IT:47, NE:120, PO:9.

10 amostra de escritos Amostra de respostas de candidatos representativas dum nível de capacidade. Usados na padronização dos examinadores.

CA:268, DA:370, DE:254, EN:338, ES:132, FR:118, GA:344, IT:330, NE:420, PO:10.

11 amostra estratificada Amostra de uma população submetida a uma pesquisa, que é subdividida num certo número de sub-populações de cada uma das quais é extraída uma amostra.
Ver: amostra.
Ler: Guilford e Fruchter, 1981, pp. 122–123.
CA:266, DA:375, DE:134, EN:388, ES:280, FR:119, GA:306, IT:48, NE:157, PO:11.

12 amplitude de variação Medida da dispersão das observações. A amplitude é a distância entre as notas mais altas e as mais baixas.
Ler: Hatch e Lazaraton, 1991, pp.169–170.
CA:12, DA:431, DE:431, EN:308, ES:260, FR:241, GA:285, IT:233, NE:311, PO:12.

13 análise da covariância Refere-se à definição de ANCOVA.
CA:14, DA:200, DE:193, EN:12, ES:20, FR:14, GA:16, IT:18, NE:85, PO:13.

14 análise da variância Refere-se à definição de ANOVA.
CA:17, DA:430, DE:430, EN:13, ES:23, FR:15, GA:15, IT:19, NE:418, PO:14.

15 análise de conteúdo Meio que permite descrever e analisar o conteúdo do material dum teste. O objecto desta análise consiste em assegurar que o conteúdo do teste é pertinente em relação às suas especificações. É essencial na determinação da validade de conteúdo e da validade de elaboração.
CA:18, DA:133, DE:153, EN:72, ES:19, FR:12, GA:12, IT:15, NE:178, PO:15.

16 análise de itens Descrição da performance dos itens (na totalidade ou parcialmente) dos testes usando, normalmente, índices estatísticos clássicos como a facilidade ou a discriminação. Neste tipo de análise usam-se pacotes informáticos como MicroCat e Iteman.
Ver: discriminação, índice de facilidade.
CA:13, DA:161, DE:167, EN:190, ES:25 FR:17, GA:13, IT:12, NE:198, PO:16.

17 análise de necessidades Meio que permite determinar as necessidades linguístico-comunicativas (em termos de capacidades, tarefas, vocabulário, etc.) de um dado grupo de aprendentes. Esta análise pré-existe à elaboração dum curso, e deve responder especificamente às necessidades do grupo-alvo.
CA:16, DA:35, DE:45, EN:246, ES:21, FR:11, GA:19, IT:13, NE:31, PO:17.

18 análise de teste Análise de testes feitos pelos candidatos, muitas vezes efectuada com recurso a métodos estatísticos e informatizados. O objectivo pode ser a investigação sobre a performance do candidato ou sobre o teste propriamente dito.
CA:15, DA:389, DE:390, EN:396, ES:22, FR:16, GA:14, IT:17, NE:389, PO:18.

19 análise do discurso Este tipo de análise está relacionada com a estrutura e a função de diferentes tipos de textos orais ou escritos.
CA:19, DA:76, DE:86, EN:107, ES:24, FR:13, GA:17, IT:16, NE: 104, PO:19.

20 análise factorial Técnica estatística que permite a um investigador reduzir um grande número de variáveis a um pequeno número, determinando os factores entre as variações dos valores de várias variáveis. Um conjunto de variáveis em intercorrelação elevada forma um factor. Um investigador pode começar uma análise factorial de modo exploratório, com o objectivo de explorar hipóteses, ou de modo confirmatório, examinando as hipóteses específicas.
Ler: Bachman, 1990, p.262; Crocker e Algina, 1986, p.232.
CA:20, DA:96, DE:115, EN:142, ES:26, FR:18, GA:18, IT:14, NE:133, PO:20.

21 ANCOVA Tipo de análise da variância, que permite combinar várias variáveis a verificar (em particular aquelas que podem mudar com a variável de interesse).
Ver: ANOVA.
Ler: Hatch e Lazaraton, 1991, p.387.
CA:21, DA:14, DE:13, EN:17, ES:27, FR:19, GA:20, IT:20, NE:16, PO:21.

22 ANOVA Técnica estatística que permite testar a hipótese nula segundo a qual várias populações médias são equivalentes. Examina-se a variabilidade das observações em cada grupo, assim como a variabilidade entre os grupos médios.
Ler: Hatch e Lazaraton, 1991, pp.308–312.
CA:22, DA:19, DE:20, EN:18, ES:28, FR:20, GA:21, IT:21, NE:19, PO:22.

23 aplicação sin: época. Data ou período durante o qual se realiza um exame. Certos exames são aplicados em datas fixas mais de uma vez por ano, outros realizam-se a pedido do(s) candidato(s).
CA:6, DA:403, DE:308, EN:8, ES:77, FR:7, GA:288, IT:331, NE:10, PO:23.

24 aquisição da língua Processo pelo qual um indivíduo adquire uma capacidade numa primeira ou numa segunda língua. No caso duma segunda língua, faz-se, às vezes, a distinção entre aquisição (natural) e aprendizagem (através de estudos conscientes).

CA:7, DA:356, DE:367, EN:204, ES:14, FR:5, GA:349, IT:22, NE:380, PO:24.

25 arredondamento Processo que permite reduzir a precisão de um número. Por exemplo, 564,8 pode ser arredondado para 565 ou 560. O grau de arredondamento depende da precisão requerida.

CA:24, DA:245, DE:331, EN:335, ES:363, FR:22, GA:354, IT:24, NE:11, PO:25.

26 autenticidade Como característica dos testes, é a forma como os itens dos testes reflectem o uso da língua fora da situação de avaliação.
Ler: Bachman, 1990, pp.300–303.

CA:27, DA:21, DE:42, EN:24, ES:33, FR:24, GA:115, IT:35, NE:23, PO:26.

27 autenticidade interaccional Em avaliação de línguas, é uma perspectiva da autenticidade, encarada como uma característica da interacção entre o examinando e a tarefa avaliativa de modo a produzir uma reacção apropriada.
Cf: autenticidade situacional.
Ver: autenticidade.
Ler: Bachman, 1990, pp.315–323.

CA:28, DA:146, DE:157, EN:177, ES:34, FR:25, GA:116, IT:36, NE:183, PO:27.

28 autenticidade situacional Característica de um teste, tendo em consideração a sua relação com o mundo real e com as situações em que a língua não é usada em situação de avaliação.
Cf: autenticidade interaccional, situação de comunicação real.
Ver: autenticidade.
Ler: Bachman, 1990, capítulo 8.

CA:29, DA:336, DE:351, EN:365, ES:35, FR:26, GA:117, IT:37, NE:340, PO:28.

29 auto-avaliação Processo pelo qual um estudante avalia o seu próprio nível de capacidade, quer aplicando a si próprio um teste quer por um outro meio como, por exemplo, através de um questionário ou de uma lista de controle.

CA:30, DA:331, DE:345, EN:354, ES:36, FR:27, GA:142, IT:38, NE:334, PO:29.

30 avaliação (a) Recolha de informações com o objectivo de poder tomar uma decisão.

(b) Em avaliação de línguas, a avaliação pode incidir na eficácia ou no impacto de um programa de ensino, de um exame ou de um projecto.

(c) Em avaliação de línguas, é a medição de um ou vários aspectos do nível de capacidade, através de um teste ou de outro tipo de procedimento.
Ler: Bachman, 1990, p.50.

CA:31, DA:30/93, DE:54/106, EN:21/132, ES:180, FR:165/166, GA:229/235, IT:413/421, NE:39/126, PO:30.

31 avaliação da competência mínma Uma abordagem da avaliação que estipula requisitos específicos para um nível mínimo de competência num dado domínio de uso da língua. Um candidato que possua este nível de competência passa no teste.

CA:312, DA:398, DE:304, EN:234, ES:183, FR:167, GA:378, IT:388, NE:246, PO:31.

32 avaliação formativa (a) Avaliação que se realiza durante a aprendizagem. Os resultados fornecem ao ensinante indicações que lhe permitem continuar ou introduzir modificações no processo de ensino-aprendizagem. Os resultados também podem ajudar o aprendente a identificar áreas de maior dificuldade durante a aprendizagem.

(b) Avaliação contínua dum processo que permite a sua adaptação e o seu melhoramento à medida que se vai realizando.
Cf: avaliação somativa.

CA:32, DA:225/226, DE:46/213, EN:147/148, ES:184, FR:168, GA:232/236, IT:414/422, NE:136/137, PO:32.

33 avaliação global Método de classificação que pode ser usado nos testes de produção escrita e oral. O examinador dá uma nota única em função da impressão geral fornecida pela produção, em vez de dividir em várias notas os diferentes aspectos da língua usados.
Cf: classificação analítica, classificação por impressão geral.

CA:33, DA:124, DE:137, EN:155, ES:427, FR:169, GA:231, IT:186, NE:161, PO:33.

34 avaliação holística Refere-se à definição de avaliação global.

CA:429, DA:126, DE:128, EN:164, ES:428, FR:170, GA:230, IT:187, NE:168, PO:34.

35 avaliação por computador Método de avaliação no qual as questões são apresentadas por computador. Os candidatos podem responder directamente no computador.

CA:332, DA:52, DE:68, EN:64, ES:182,

FR:171, GA:380, IT:387, NE:70, PO:35.

36 avaliação somativa Avaliação que se realiza no fim de um processo de ensino-aprendizagem ou de um programa educacional.
Cf: avaliação formativa.
CA:34, DA:266/267, DE:3/4, EN:390/391, ES:186, FR:172, GA:233/238, IT:415/423, NE:374/375, PO:36.

37 banco de itens Gestão de itens permitindo o armazenamento de informações a fim de se poder elaborar testes com conteúdos e graus de dificuldade conhecidos (por terem sido previamente testados). Esta abordagem socorre-se de uma base de dados informatizada e baseia-se na teoria do atributo latente, o que significa que os itens podem ser relacionados uns com os outros através de uma escala de dificuldade comum.
Ler: Henning, 1987, capítulo 9.
CA:36, DA:155, DE:28, EN:191, ES:37, FR:28, GA:40, IT:111, NE:199, PO:37.

38 bateria Conjunto coerente de testes ou de sub-testes, com contribuições independentes (por exemplo, por testarem diferentes capacidades), mas combináveis entre si de modo a produzirem um resultado global.
CA:38, DA:28, DE:393, EN:32, ES:40, FR:30, GA:64, IT:41, NE:30, PO:38.

39 bateria de teste Refere-se à definição de bateria.
CA:39, DA:390, DE:406, EN:397, ES:41, FR:31, GA:63, IT:42, NE:390, PO:39.

40 bias Pode considerar-se que um teste ou item de teste tem um bias, se uma parte dos candidatos estiver em vantagem ou em desvantagem devido a uma característica do teste ou de um item que não é relevante para o que está a ser avaliado. As origens do bias podem estar relacionadas com questões como a idade, a cultura, etc.
Ler: Bachman, 1990, pp.271–279; Crocker e Algina, 1986, capítulo 12 e 16.
CA:40, DA:344, DE:383, EN:33, ES:384, FR:32, GA:208, IT:160, NE:46, PO:40.

41 bias cultural Um teste com um bias cultural constitui uma vantagem ou desvantagem para um candidato que pertença a um contexto cultural específico.
Ver: bias.
CA:41, DA:207, DE:201, EN:85, ES:385, FR:33, GA:209, IT:161, NE:90, PO:41.

42 calibração Processo para determinar a escala de um ou mais testes. A calibração pode implicar itens-âncora de diferentes testes sobre uma escala de dificuldade comum (escala teta). Quando um teste é elaborado a partir de itens calibrados, as notas, em função da sua localização na escala teta, indicam a capacidade do candidato.
CA:44, DA:164, DE:94, EN:40, ES:42, FR:35, GA:49, IT:44, NE:205, PO:42.

43 calibração equipercentil Método de calibração das notas brutas obtidas nos testes. As notas são consideradas calibradas se corresponderem ao mesmo nível percentil num grupo de candidatos.
CA:132, DA:440, DE:24, EN:127, ES:140, FR:36, GA:88, IT:150, NE:121, PO:43.

44 calibração horizontal Acção de relacionar as notas de dois testes de dificuldade semelhante na mesma escala a fim de aplicar os mesmos padrões aos dois testes.
Cf: calibração vertical.
Ver: calibração.
CA:133, DA:128, DE:149, EN:166, ES:141, FR:37, GA:89, IT:152, NE:170, PO:44.

45 calibração linear Neste tipo de calibração, a nota obtida num teste é calibrada com a nota obtida num segundo teste. As notas equivalentes obtidas nos dois testes correspondem ao mesmo número de desvios-padrão acima ou baixo da nota média do teste em que elas aparecem.
Ver: calibração, regressão.
Ler: Crocker e Algina, 1986, pp.457–461.
CA:134, DA:216, DE:17, EN:212, ES:142, FR:38, GA:91, IT:151, NE:229, PO:45.

46 calibração vertical Acção de relacionar as notas obtidas em dois testes de grau de dificuldade diferente na mesma escala.
Ler: Crocker e Algina, 1986, pp.473–477.
CA:135, DA:432, DE:435, EN:434, ES:143, FR:39, GA:90, IT:153, NE:419, PO:46.

47 calibrar Na teoria item-resposta, consiste em determinar a dificuldade dum conjunto de itens de teste.
Ver: escala teta.
CA:43, DA:163, DE:93, EN:39, ES:43, FR:40, GA:48, IT:43, NE:206, PO:47.

48 candidato Pessoa que faz um teste ou um exame. Também designado examinando.
CA:45, DA:165, DE:302, EN:41, ES:48, FR:41, GA:178, IT:49, NE:207, PO:48.

49 capacidade Capacidade intelectual

para realizar um acto.
Cf: competência, nível de capacidade.
Ler: Bachman, 1990, p.16, p.19.
CA:46, DA:2, DE:113, EN:2, ES:49, FR:42, GA:96, IT:1A, NE:411, PO:49.

50 capacidade numa língua Conjunto de competências que definem a capacidade de um indivíduo para usar uma língua com fins comunicativos variados.
Ler: Bachman, 1990, pp.3–4.
CA:47, DA:354, DE:368, EN:203, ES:50, FR:43, GA:97, IT:4, NE:379, PO:50.

51 capacidades Em avaliação de línguas, distinguem-se muitas vezes as quatro capacidades: compreensão e expressão orais e escritas.
Ver: competência.
CA:199, DA:111, DE:119, EN:367, ES:100, FR:340, GA:325, IT:1B, NE:413, PO:51.

52 capacidades intelectuais inferiores Capacidades pouco complexas solicitadas aos candidatos durante um teste, como por exemplo, saber reconhecer uma palavra ou uma letra.
Cf: capacidades intelectuais superiores.
CA:200, DA:27, DE:424, EN:219, ES:101, FR:44, GA:327, IT:2, NE:409, PO:52.

53 capacidades intelectuais superiores Capacidades complexas como, por exemplo, ser capaz de inferir ou de resumir.
Cf: capacidades intelectuais inferiores.
CA:201, DA:130, DE:418, EN:162, ES:102, FR:45, GA:326, IT:3, NE:410, PO:53.

54 características dos métodos de teste Características definidoras dos diferentes métodos de teste, as quais podem incluir o ambiente, as instruções, a língua em que são dadas as instruções, o formato do teste, etc.
Ler: Bachman, 1990, capítulo 5.
CA:48, DA:397, DE:403, EN:402, ES:51, FR:46, GA:401, IT:50, NE:398, PO:54.

55 categoria (a) Divisão de uma escala categórica: o género, por exemplo, compreende as categorias masculino e feminino;

(b) Em avaliação, uma escala de avaliação que compreende, por exemplo, cinco pontos, chama-se uma escala com cinco categorias de respostas.
CA:49, DA:169, DE:176, EN:43, ES:52, FR:48, GA:50, IT:51, NE:52, PO:55.

56 certificado (a) Documento nominal que atesta que um indivíduo passou num exame ou numa parte dum exame e obteve uma determinada nota.

(b) Documento nominal que atesta a participação num curso; normalmente menciona o curso, o local de realização e a duração.
Cf: diploma.
CA:50, DA:38, DE:448, EN:47, ES:53, FR:50, GA:386, IT:52, NE:56, PO:56.

57 classificação (a) Atribuição duma nota às respostas dum candidato a um teste. Esta actividade pode exigir um juízo profissional ou a aplicação dum esquema de classificação no qual estão indicadas todas as respostas aceitáveis.

(b) Nota atribuída e que representa o resultado do processo de avaliação.
CA:80/428, DA:171/289, DE:40/57, EN:222/314, ES:47/425, FR:265, GA:218/286, IT:29/54, NE:38/83, PO:57.

58 classificação analítica Método de classificação que pode ser utilizado nos testes de produção oral ou escrita. O examinador avalia a partir duma lista de pontos específicos. Num teste de produção escrita, por exemplo, a escala analítica pode incidir na gramática, no vocabulário, no uso de conectores, etc.
CA:343, DA:13, DE:12, EN:14, ES:426, FR:266, GA:340, IT:27, NE:15, PO:58.

59 classificação dicotómica Classificação baseada em duas categorias, por exemplo verdadeiro/falso, sim/não.
CA:347, DA:67, DE:455, EN:98, ES:347, FR:268, GA:341, IT:32, NE:98, PO:59.

60 classificação dum item Na análise de itens, é a soma das respostas correctas a um determinado item.
CA:345, DA:160, DE:171, EN:196, ES:346, FR:267, GA:336, IT:281, NE:202, PO:60.

61 classificação dupla Método de avaliação através do qual a performance do candidato é avaliada de forma independente por duas pessoas.
Ver: classificação múltipla.
CA:84, DA:82, DE:91, EN:121, ES:118, FR:114, GA:221, IT:104, NE:116, PO:61.

62 classificação mecânica Método de classificação em que os avaliadores não precisam de exercer nenhum tipo de juízo subjectivo nem precisam de ter nenhuma formação específica. Seguem um esquema de classificação que especifica todas as respostas aceitáveis a cada item do teste.
Cf: classificação por examinador.

CA:86, DA:23, DE:231, EN:51, ES:78, FR:274, GA:219, IT:31, NE:25, PO:62.

63 classificação múltipla Método para melhorar a fiabilidade da avaliação da expressão escrita no caso de produções longas. Esta avaliação apresenta necessariamente um grau de subjectividade que pode ser reduzido se a performance de cada candidato for classificada por mais de um avaliador.
Ler: Weir, 1988, pp.65–66.
CA:87, DA:274, DE:233, EN:240, ES:45, FR:271, GA:183, IT:105, NE:241, PO:63.

64 classificação politómica A classificação politómica (por vezes também "policotómica") consiste em classificar um item numa escala com pelo menos três pontos. Pode atribuir-se, por exemplo, 0, 1 ou 2 pontos a uma questão, isto é, três pontos diferentes. As questões abertas são muitas vezes classificadas de forma politómica. Também se lhe pode chamar classificação escalonada.
Cf: classificação dicotómica.
CA:351, DA:291, DE:237, EN:284, ES:353, FR:89, GA:342, IT:34, NE:293, PO:64.

65 classificação por bandas Parte duma escala que se refere a uma área específica da capacidade.
CA:346, DA:258, DE:210, EN:30, ES:39, FR:269, GA:330, IT:40, NE:29, PO:65.

66 classificação por computador A informática socorre-se de diferentes métodos para minimizar os erros nas classificações dos testes objectivos. Pode-se, por exemplo, ler as folhas de notas dos candidatos com um leitor óptico e obter dados que podem ser usados para fornecer notas ou análises.
CA:85, DA:53, DE:69, EN:65, ES:82, FR:273, GA:222, IT:28, NE:69, PO:66.

67 classificação por examinador Método de classificação que exige que o avaliador tenha um certo grau de profissionalismo e de formação de modo a poder fazer um juízo subjectivo. Os testes de produção oral e escrita com uma extensão relativamente longa são habitualmente classificados desta forma.
Cf: classificação mecânica.
CA:81, DA:29, DE:107, EN:136, ES:81, FR:272, GA:223, IT:30, NE:131, PO:67.

68 classificação por impressão geral Método de classificação que pode ser usado nos testes de produção escrita e oral. O examinador avalia as respostas de cada candidato não separando os traços distintivos da tarefa a realizar.
Cf: classificação analítica, avaliação global.
CA:89, DA:116, DE:133, EN:168, ES:429, FR:270, GA:220, IT:33, NE:172, PO:68.

69 coeficiente Índice numérico usado como medida de uma propriedade ou de uma característica.
Ver: alfa (coeficiente alfa), coeficiente de correlação.
CA:53, DA:175, DE:178, EN:53, ES:55, FR:54, GA:73, IT:57, NE:62, PO:69.

70 coeficiente alfa Refere-se à definição de alfa (coeficiente alfa).
CA:54, DA:176, DE:179, EN:54, ES:56, FR:55, GA:74, IT:58, NE:63, PO:70.

71 coeficiente de correlação Índice que mostra a amplitude da correlação entre duas ou mais variáveis. Varia de +1 a -1. As variáveis de correlação elevada são representadas por um coeficiente de correlação próximo de ±1.
Ler: Guilford e Fruchter, 1981, pp.86–88.
CA:55, DA:197, DE:191, EN:79, ES:57, FR:56, GA:75, IT:60, NE:82, PO:71.

72 coeficiente de correlação de níveis Coeficiente de correlação baseado na ordem relativa dos níveis e não nos valores absolutos das variáveis.
Ler: Guilford e Fruchter, 1981, pp.294-296.
CA:60, DA:304, DE:315, EN:309, ES:89, FR:59, GA:82, IT:100, NE:312, PO:72.

73 coeficiente de correlação de Spearman Forma de coeficiente de correlação de níveis usado em pequenas amostragens, isto é, menos de trinta elementos.
Ver: coeficiente de correlação de níveis.
CA:58, DA:351, DE:361, EN:373, ES:87, FR:60, GA:83, IT:99, NE:347, PO:73.

74 coeficiente de fiabilidade Medida de fiabilidade calculada de 0 a 1. As estimativas de fiabilidade podem basear-se na aplicação repetida de um teste (o que deveria produzir resultados semelhantes) ou, se tal for impossível, numa medida de consistência interna. Também designado índice de fiabilidade.
Ver: consistência interna, fiabilidade, fiabilidade teste-reteste.
CA:61, DA:313, DE:323, EN:328, ES:58, FR:61, GA:77, IT:59, NE:44, PO:74.

75 coeficiente phi Coeficiente de correlação que permite mostrar a força da relação entre duas variáveis binárias, por

exemplo, as notas obtidas em dois itens verdadeiro/falso.
Ver: coeficiente de correlação.
Ler: Guilford e Fruchter, 1981, pp. 316–318; Crocker e Algina, 1986, pp.92–94.
CA:62, DA:284, DE:286, EN:279, ES:59, FR:58, GA:76, IT:61, NE:288, PO:75.

76 competência Conhecimento ou capacidade para poder fazer algo. Em linguística, o termo refere-se a uma capacidade subjacente, oposta à performance que consiste na manifestação linguística da competência. Esta distinção aparece nos trabalhos de Chomsky.
Cf: performance.
Ler: Bachman, 1990, pp.52 e 108.
CA:64, DA:180, DE:183, EN:59, ES:60, FR:62, GA:191, IT:62, NE:67, PO:76.

77 competência comunicativa Capacidade para usar uma língua adequadamente em diferentes situações de comunicação.
Ler: Bachman, 1990, p.16, p.68.
CA:65, DA:179, DE:182, EN:58, ES:61, FR:63, GA:195, IT:63, NE:66, PO:77.

78 competência discursiva Capacidade para compreender e produzir um discurso. A competência discursiva é, por vezes, considerada como uma componente da competência comunicativa.
Ler: Bachman, 1990, capítulo 4.
CA:66, DA:78, DE:87, EN:108, ES:62, FR:64, GA:196, IT:64, NE:105, PO:78.

79 competência gramatical Num modelo de competência comunicativa, a competência gramatical é a componente que se refere à morfologia, à sintaxe, ao léxico, à fonologia e à ortografia.
Ler: Bachman, 1990, pp.84–88.
CA:67, DA:119, DE:138, EN:158, ES:63, FR:65, GA:193, IT:65, NE:162, PO:79.

80 competência linguística Refere-se à definição de competência.
CA:68, DA:217, DE:224, EN:214, ES:64, FR:67, GA:198, IT:66, NE:231, PO:80.

81 competência numa língua Conhecimento de uma língua. O termo é muitas vezes usado como sinónimo de "capacidade numa língua".
Ler: Bachman, 1990, p.16.
CA:297, DA:355, DE:365, EN:206, ES:121, FR:66, GA:267, IT:66, NE:215, PO:81.

82 competência oral Competência para falar uma língua.
CA:298, DA:239, DE:370, EN:264, ES:65, FR:68, GA:266, IT:67, NE:354, PO:82.

83 competência pragmática Categoria possível num modelo de competência comunicativa: inclui a capacidade de produzir actos de fala adequados às situações de comunicação e conhecimento das convenções sociolinguísticas.
CA:69, DA:294, DE:295, EN:290, ES:66, FR:69, GA:194, IT:68, NE:297, PO:83.

84 competência sociolinguística Categoria num modelo de competência comunicativa: inclui a capacidade para adaptar a produção de textos orais e escritos às situações de comunicação, tendo em consideração as características do interlocutor (como por exemplo a idade, o sexo, estatutos sócio-económico e profissional), o espaço de comunicação e as normas sociais.
Ler: Bachman, 1990, p.42.
CA:70, DA:347, DE:358, EN:369, ES:67, FR:70, GA:197, IT:69, NE:345, PO:84.

85 competência unitária Teoria da linguagem, divulgada por Oller, que postula a existência de uma competência única na base de todas as capacidades da linguagem.
CA:71, DA:91, DE:423, EN:428, ES:68, FR:71, GA:192, IT:70, NE:408, PO:85.

86 completamento de frases Tipo de item no qual só metade da frase é dada. A tarefa do candidato consiste em completar a frase, fornecendo as palavras convenientes (eventualmente de acordo com um texto) ou escolhendo-as duma lista de possibilidades.
CA:72, DA:382, DE:332, EN:357, ES:69, FR:298, GA:93, IT:80, NE:442, PO:86.

87 componente Parte de um exame apresentada muitas vezes como um teste separado com instruções e duração próprias. As componentes correspondem normalmente a capacidades numa língua como, por exemplo, compreensão oral, expressão escrita, etc.
CA:73/385, DA:181/393, DE:306/277, EN:61/267, ES:29/381, FR:72/182, GA:85/270, IT:81/168, NE:128/278, PO:87.

88 composição Produção de um texto escrito de acordo com as instruções dadas, nomeadamente respeitantes à extensão. Os textos-tipo solicitados neste tipo de expressão escrita podem incluir a narração de acontecimentos, tomada de posição sobre um determinado assunto, cartas formais e informais. Também designado expressão escrita.

CA:366, DA:109, DE:32, EN:62, ES:192, FR:73, GA:51, IT:82, NE:372, PO:88.

89 composição discursiva Produção de texto discursivo sobre um determinado assunto relativamente ao qual pode haver diferentes tomadas de posição ou produção de texto argumentativo com apresentação e defesa de pontos de vista.
Ver: composição.
CA:74, DA:77, DE:342, EN:113, ES:70, FR:74, GA:52, IT:83, NE:42, PO:89.

90 conhecimento sociocultural Conhecimento do mundo ligado ao funcionamento da sociedade duma cultura específica. Está relacionado com um comportamento e um uso pertinentes da língua em contextos culturais específicos.
Cf: competência sociolinguística.
CA:76, DA:346, DE:357, EN:368, ES:72, FR:341, GA:135, IT:86, NE:344, PO:90.

91 conhecimentos anteriores sin: background do candidato. Conhecimentos do candidato sobre um assunto ou sobre um conteúdo cultural presente num teste e que pode afectar a forma como esse assunto ou conteúdo é tratado. Adquire uma importância maior nos testes de língua para fins específicos.
Ler: Bachman, 1990, p.273.
CA:75, DA:26, DE:144, EN:27, ES:73, FR:77, GA:134, IT:85, NE:4, PO:91.

92 conselhos Instruções dadas aos candidatos com o objectivo de orientar as respostas de uma determinada tarefa.
Cf: instruções.
CA:384, DA:264, DE:23, EN:336, ES:229, FR:78, GA:295, IT:193, NE:219, PO:92.

93 consistência interna Característica dum teste representada pela consistência entre as notas obtidas por um candidato em cada questão do teste e a nota total. As estimativas da consistência interna podem ser usadas como índice de fiabilidade de um teste; podem ser calculados vários índices, por exemplo, KR-20, alfa.
Ver: Kuder-Richardson, fiabilidade.
Ler: Bachman, 1990, p.172.
CA:77, DA:147, DE:155, EN:180, ES:74, FR:186, GA:87, IT:87, NE:186, PO:93.

94 constructo sin: conceito hipotético. Capacidade hipotética dos indivíduos ou traço mental que não pode ser directamente medido ou observado (por exemplo, em avaliação de línguas, a compreensão oral). Os testes de língua tentam medir os diferentes constructos que subjazem às capacidades da linguagem. Para além da capacidade numa lingua, a motivação, as atitudes e a aculturação constituem constructos pertinentes.
Ler: Hatch e Lazaraton, 1991, p.15.
CA:78, DA:184, DE:185, EN:68, ES:76, FR:80, GA:394, IT:108, NE:72, PO:94.

95 contagem de ocorrências Contagem da frequência de determinadas palavras num texto. Este procedimento pode ser útil em avaliação sobretudo quando se elaboram testes em função de uma especificação lexical precisa.
CA:190, DA:270, DE:143, EN:440, ES:362, FR:75, GA:67, IT:256, NE:436, PO:95.

96 contagem do diversor Frequência com que se efectua a escolha de cada diversor num questionário de escolha múltipla. A contagem revela o modo de funcionamento de cada diversor.
CA:243, DA:80, DE:89, EN:116, ES:71, FR:301, GA:384, IT:88, NE:9, PO:96.

97 correcção de texto Tarefa em que o candidato tem de reler um texto procurando erros específicos, por exemplo, de ortografia ou de estruturas. Pode também ser solicitado ao candidato que assinale os erros e forneça as formas correctas.
CA:395, DA:195, DE:189, EN:300, ES:4, FR:84, GA:374, IT:75, NE:304, PO:97.

98 correcção por adivinhação Método que visa reduzir o ganho de pontos quando o candidato adivinha a resposta correcta em testes com itens objectivos.
Ler: Ebel e Frisbie, 1986, pp.215–218.
CA:82, DA:193, DE:317/450, EN:77, ES:80, FR:83, GA:54, IT:103, NE:77, PO:98.

99 correcção por atenuação Método de estimativa da correlação entre duas ou mais variáveis desde que não haja diferença na fiabilidade entre elas.
Ler: Guilford e Fruchter, 1981, pp.450–453; Hatch e Lazaraton, 1990, pp.444–445.
CA:88, DA:194, DE:243, EN:76, ES:79, FR:82, GA:53, IT:106, NE:78, PO:99.

100 correlação Relação entre duas ou mais medidas em função da sua variação na mesma direcção. Se, por exemplo, candidatos diferentes obtêm o mesmo nível em dois testes diferentes, existe uma correlação positiva entre os dois conjuntos de notas.
Cf: covariância.
Ver: coeficiente de correlação de níveis, correlação produto-momento de Pearson (*r* de Pearson).
Ler: Guilford e Fruchter, 1981, capítulo 6;

Bachman, 1990, pp. 259–260.
CA:91, DA:196, DE:190, EN:78, ES:84, FR:85, GA:78, IT:95, NE:81, PO:100.

101 correlação biserial Índice de discriminação de um item, para itens dicotómicos, cuja fórmla é r_{bis}. Correlação entre um critério (geralmente a nota total do teste) e a capacidade subjacente à resposta verdadadeiro-falso a esse item. O valor de r_{bis} é pelo menos 25% mais alto do que o ponto biserial (r_{pbi}). Uma vantagem do r_{bis} consiste em ser relativamente estável em amostragens de nível de capacidade diferente.
Cf: correlação biserial de ponto.
Ver: discriminação.
Ler: Crocker e Algina, 1986, pp. 317–318; Guilford e Fruchter, pp.304–311
CA:56, DA:40, DE:60, EN:35, ES:85, FR:86, GA:79, IT:96, NE:48, PO:101.

102 correlação biserial de ponto Índice de discriminação para itens dicotómicos, cuja fórmula é r_{pbi}; a correlação entre um critério (geralmente a nota total do teste) e a resposta a um item. Uma vantagem do r_{pbi} em relação à correlação biserial (r_{bis}) reside no facto de poder ser usada de forma adequada quando a capacidade subjacente não está distribuída normalmente.
Cf: correlação biserial.
CA:57, DA:41, DE:311, EN:283, ES:86, FR:57, GA:80, IT:97, NE:309, PO:102.

103 correlação phi Refere-se à definição de coeficiente phi.
CA:92, DA:285, DE:287, EN:280, ES:88, FR:88, GA:81, IT:101, NE:289, PO:103.

104 correlação produto-momento de Pearson (r de Pearson) Coeficiente de correlação usado apropriadamente com variáveis, medidas a partir de escalas de intervalo ou escalas de relação.
Ver: coeficiente de correlação.
Ler: Hatch e Lazaraton, 1991, pp.427–431; Guilford e Fruchter, 1981, p.81
CA:59, DA:279, DE:298, EN:274, ES:90, FR:87, GA:84, IT:98, NE:283, PO:104.

105 cotação Número total de pontos atribuídos a um item, a um sub-teste ou a um teste. Por vezes também designada pontuação.
CA:342, DA:287, DE:313, EN:224, ES:44, FR:287, GA:224, IT:292, NE:60, PO:105.

106 covariância Variância conjunta de duas ou mais variáveis. A extensão de uma frase e a dificuldade lexical são, por exemplo, características que, na leitura, tendem a ser relacionadas, isto é, a covariar. A covariância deve ser tomada em conta quando se infere uma variável a partir de outras, quando, por exemplo, se infere a dificuldade de um texto a partir da extensão das frases e da dificuldade gramatical.
Ver: variância.
CA:93, DA:199, DE:192, EN:80, ES:91, FR:92, GA:71, IT:112, NE:84, PO:106.

107 curriculum Descrição geral de objectivos, conteúdos, organização, métodos e avaliação de um programa de estudos.
Cf: programa.
CA:94, DA:55, DE:71, EN:87, ES:93, FR:93, GA:99, IT:113, NE:220, PO:107.

108 curtose Carácter duma curva ser mais ou menos plana do que a curva normal. Os dados representados numa curva plana apresentam uma distribuição platicúrtica, enquanto os dados que formam uma curva menos plana apresentam uma distribuição leptocúrtica.

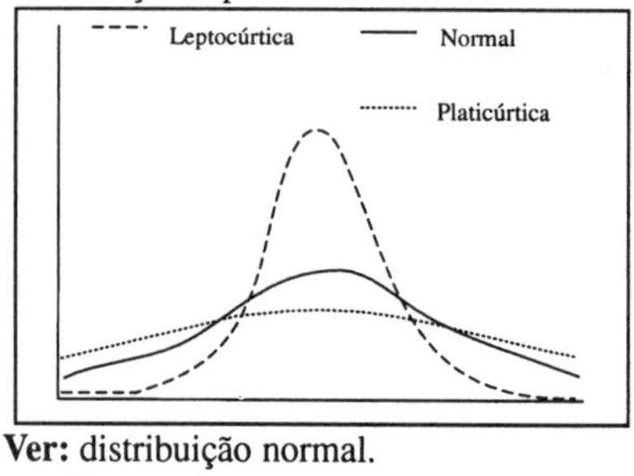

Ver: distribuição normal.
CA:95, DA:412, DE:108, EN:202, ES:94, FR:428, GA:100, IT:114, NE:213, PO:108.

109 curva característica de um item (CCI) Na teoria item-resposta, a CCI mostra como a probabilidade de responder correctamente a um item está ligada à capacidade latente que subjaz à performance nos itens do teste.
Ler: Crocker e Algina, 1986, pp.340–342.
CA:79, DA:157, DE:168, EN:192, ES:95, FR:90, GA:94, IT:115, NE:196, PO:109.

110 curva de Gauss Refere-se à definição de distribuição normal.
CA:114, DA:114, DE:129, EN:152, ES:115, FR:91, GA:105, IT:133, NE:140, PO:110.

111 D de Ebel Refere-se à definição de índice-D.
CA:96/206, DA:85/246, DE:92/257, EN:122/247, ES:96/97, FR:94/115,

GA:101/102, IT:116/194, NE:117/256, PO:111.

112 descritor de escalas Refere-se à definição de descritor.

CA:98, DA:338, DE:353, EN:344, ES:99, FR:96, GA:438, IT:119, NE:327, PO:112.

113 descritor Breve descrição que acompanha um gráfico de bandas numa escala de classificação e que resume o grau de competência ou o tipo de performance esperada de modo a que o candidato obtenha uma dada nota.

CA:97, DA:64, DE:76, EN:96, ES:98, FR:97, GA:437, IT:118, NE:96, PO:113.

114 desvio-padrão Medida da dispersão de um conjunto de observações sobre a média aritmética. É igual à raíz quadrada da variância. Numa distribuição normal, 68% da amostragem está num desvio-padrão da média e 95% está a dois desvios-padrão da média.

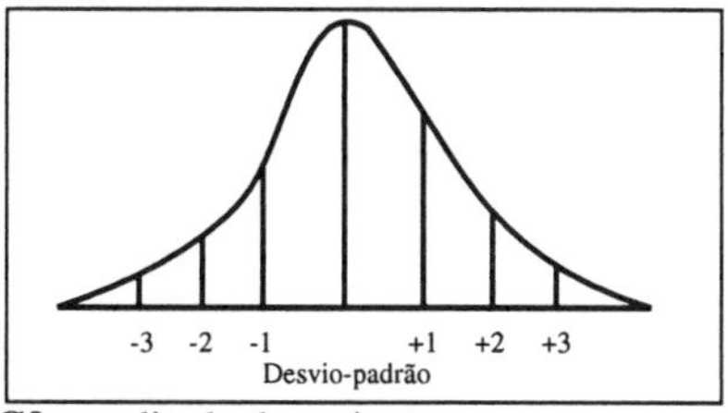

Cf: amplitude de variação.
Ver: variância.
Ler: Ebel e Frisbie, 1991, pp.61–62; Crocker e Algina, 1986, pp. 21–22.

CA:101, DA:362, DE:372, EN:379, ES:103, FR:98, GA:113, IT:122, NE:360, PO:114.

115 diploma Documento nominal que atesta que um indivíduo passou num exame ou numa parte de um exame e obteve um determinado nível. Considera-se normalmente que o diploma é de nível superior ao certificado.
Cf: certificado.

CA:104, DA:69, DE:80, EN:103, ES:106, FR:100, GA:118, IT:124, NE:101, PO:115.

116 discriminação Consiste no facto de um item poder estabelecer uma distinção entre candidatos classificando-os em graus que vão de mais fraco a mais forte. Utilizam-se vários índices de discriminação. Alguns (como o ponto biserial e biserial) baseiam-se na correlação entre a nota obtida num item e um critério. Este pode ser a nota total obtida no teste ou uma outra medida externa de nível de capacidade. Os outros critérios baseiam-se na diferença de dificuldade do item para grupos de capacidade baixa e alta. Na teoria item-resposta, os modelos de parâmetro 2 e 3 designam o item de discriminação como o parâmetro-A.
Ver: correlação biserial, correlação biserial de ponto, teoria item-resposta (TIR).
Ler: Crocker e Algina, 1986, pp.313–320; Ebel e Frisbie, 1991, pp.231–232.

CA:105, DA:74, DE:416, EN:112, ES:107, FR:102, GA:180, IT:126, NE:109, PO:116.

117 discurso Texto oral ou escrito, considerado um acto de fala.

CA:106, DA:75, DE:85, EN:106, ES:108, FR:101, GA:119, IT:125, NE:103, PO:117.

118 dispersão Taxa de variação ou dispersão das notas de um grupo de candidatos. Se a dispersão é grande, as notas são bastante dispersas. Se é fraca, as notas são bastante agrupadas.
Ver: desvio-padrão, variância, amplitude de variação.

CA:107, DA:353, DE:385, EN:114, ES:110, FR:103, GA:357, IT:127, NE:356, PO:118.

119 distribuição É o número de ocorrências de cada nota obtida pelos candidatos. A distribuição é muitas vezes representada sob a forma de histograma.

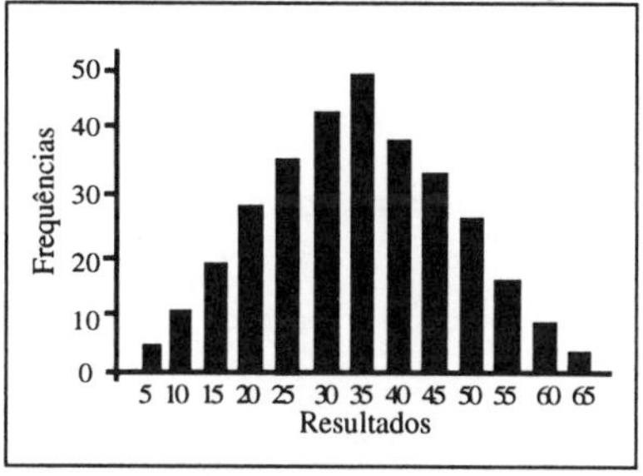

Ver: distribuição normal, distribuição assimétrica.
Ler: Hatch e Lazaraton, 1991, pp.159-178.

CA:111, DA:103, DE:434, EN:117, ES:112, FR:105, GA:103, IT:130, NE:110, PO:119.

120 distribuição assimétrica Tipo de distribuição na qual o cimo da curva se encontra à direita do centro (simetria negativa) ou à esquerda do centro (simetria positiva).

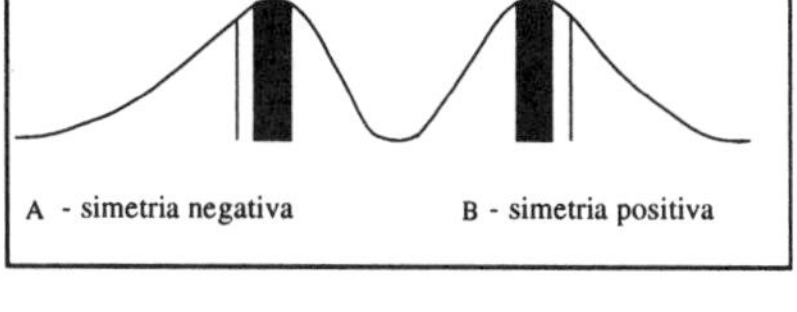

Ver: distribuição normal.
Ler: Hatch e Lazaraton, 1991, p. 165.
CA:25, DA:343, DE:337, EN:366, ES:31, FR:109, GA:323, IT:25, NE:330, PO:120.

121 distribuição bimodal Tipo de distribuição com duas modas ou cimos, que sugere que a amostragem é constituída por dois grupos diferentes.

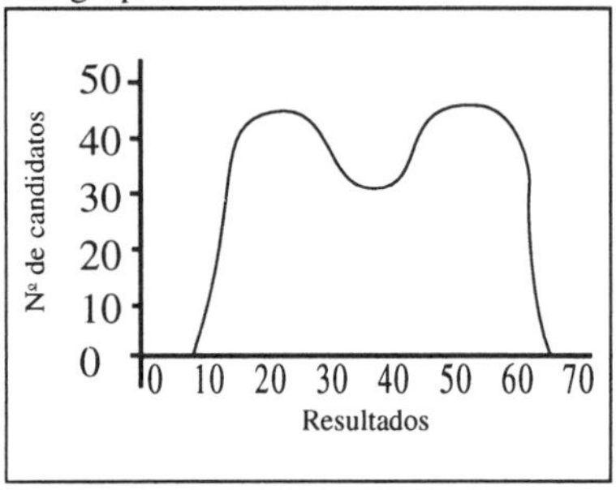

Cf: distribuição normal.
Ver: moda.
Ler: Hatch e Lazaraton, 1991, p.165–166.
CA:112, DA:39, DE:59, EN:34, ES:113, FR:106, GA:104, IT:131, NE:47, PO:121.

122 distribuição de frequências Refere-se à definição de distribuição.
CA:113, DA:107, DE:142, EN:149, ES:114, FR:107, GA:106, IT:132, NE:138, PO:122.

123 distribuição normal Distribuição matemática considerada a suposição fundamental para vários procedimentos estatísticos. Distribuição simétrica de notas representada graficamente sob a forma de curva em sino e na qual a média, a mediana e a moda ocupam o mesmo ponto. Existe toda uma série de distribuições que dependem do valor da mediana, dos desvios-padrão e do número de observações. Também se chama curva de Gauss.
Cf: distribuição bimodal.
Ler: Hatch e Lazaraton, 1991, p.164.
CA:115, DA:252, DE:265, EN:252, ES:116, FR:108, GA:107, IT:134, NE:262, PO:123.

124 distribuição truncada Tipo de distribuição de frequência característica duma amostragem com uma amplitude mais estreita do que a população de onde é retirada, porque não estão representadas nela nem os estudantes com as notas mais altas nem os que tiveram as mais baixas. Uma amostragem deste tipo seria por exemplo um grupo de estudantes admitidos num curso depois de terem passado no exame de admissão.
CA:116, DA:376, DE:1, EN:421, ES:117, FR:110, GA:108, IT:135, NE:343, PO:124.

125 ditado Tarefa em que o candidato deve ouvir um texto e escrever as palavras ouvidas. Os critérios de classificação dos ditados variam segundo os objectivos do teste; podem incluir a ortografia e a pontuação.
CA:103, DA:68, DE:79, EN:99, ES:105, FR:99, GA:109, IT:121, NE:99, PO:125.

126 diversor Num item de escolha múltipla, o diversor é aquele que não é a resposta correcta.
Cf: resposta-chave.
Ver: item de escolha múltipla.
Ler: Ebel e Frisbie, 1986, pp.176–185.
CA:110, DA:79, DE:88, EN:115, ES:111, FR:104, GA:348, IT:129, NE:8, PO:126.

127 documento autêntico sin: texto autêntico. Texto ou documento utilizado num teste e que não foi elaborado nem para fins pedagógicos nem para situações de avaliação.
Ver: documento semi-autêntico.
CA:404, DA:22, DE:41, EN:25, ES:401, FR:111, GA:382, IT:390, NE:24, PO:127.

128 documento semi-autêntico sin: texto semi-autêntico. Texto autêntico no qual houve adaptação lexical ou gramatical ao nível dos candidatos por razões de avaliação.
Ver: documento autêntico.
CA:405, DA:123, DE:140, EN:355, ES:400, FR:112, GA:383, IT:391, NE:335, PO:128.

129 domínio Conjunto definido de conteúdos e/ou de níveis de capacidade a testar com o auxílio duma tarefa específica ou de uma das componentes dum exame.
Ler: Bachman, 1990, pp. 244–246.
CA:11, DA:83, DE:238, EN:119, ES:119, FR:113, GA:137, IT:332, NE:113, PO:129.

130 efeito-chão Efeito-limite resultante da excessiva dificuldade dum teste para um dado grupo de candidatos. Todas as notas obtidas se agrupam na base da distribuição.
Ver: efeitos-limite.
CA:122, DA:42, DE:61/121, EN:146, ES:128, FR:141, GA:175, IT:144, NE:49, PO:130.

131 efeito da prática Efeito sobre os resultados dos testes devido ao facto de o candidato estar familiarizado com o tipo de tarefa ou de itens propostos no teste.
CA:119, DA:443, DE:419, EN:289,

ES:123, FR:138, GA:169, IT:140, NE:298, PO:131.

132 efeito de contaminação Efeito que se manifesta quando um avaliador classifica em função de um factor diferente do que é testado. Pode, por exemplo, aumentar a nota dum candidato num teste de expressão escrita se o candidato tiver uma boa caligrafia.
Ver: efeitos da classificação.

CA:118, DA:9, DE:226, EN:71, ES:122, FR:136, GA:174, IT:141, NE:74, PO:132.

133 efeito de halo Tendência que os examinadores têm, quando um exame lhes pede uma classificação subjectiva, para serem influenciados pela performance dum candidato em algumas tarefas e a dar-lhe consequentemente uma nota muito alta ou muito baixa numa outra tarefa.
Ver: efeitos da classificação.

CA:117, DA:118, DE:141, EN:161, ES:127, FR:137, GA:170, IT:139, NE:164, PO:133.

134 efeito de método Efeito produzido nas notas dos testes influenciado mais pelo método de avaliação do que pela capacidade do candidato.

CA:121, DA:229, DE:242, EN:233, ES:126, FR:139, GA:171, IT:142, NE:244, PO:134.

135 efeito de refluxo Impacto do teste na prática lectiva. Ao saberem que os aprendentes vão ser submetidos a um determinado tipo de teste, os ensinantes podem ser influenciados pela natureza do teste e adaptar consequentemente a sua metodologia e os conteúdos do curso de forma a preparar os aprendentes para esse tipo de teste. Os resultados podem ser positivos ou negativos.
Ver: impacto.

CA:372, DA:25/436, DE:43/442, EN:28/435, ES:124/369, FR:322, GA:95, IT:147, NE:27/432, PO:135.

136 efeito sequencial Efeito da avaliação produzido pela ordem de classificação dos testes.
Ver: efeitos da classificação.

CA:120, DA:329, DE:292, EN:360, ES:125, FR:142, GA:172, IT:148, NE:337, PO:136.

137 efeito-tecto Efeito-limite resultante da excessiva facilidade dum teste para um dado grupo de candidatos. Todas as notas obtidas se agrupam no cimo da distribuição.
Ver: efeitos-limite.

CA:123, DA:219, DE:63/73, EN:44, ES:129, FR:140, GA:173, IT:145, NE:292, PO:137.

138 efeitos da classificação Fonte de erro em avaliação resultante de certas tendências dos avaliadores para classificarem com severidade ou indulgência ou para valorizarem um determinado tipo de candidatos, afectando assim as notas dadas ao teste. Alguns exemplos são o efeito de contaminação, o efeito de halo e o efeito sequencial.

CA:124, DA:34, DE:425, EN:313, ES:130, FR:144, GA:176, IT:143, NE:35, PO:138.

139 efeitos-limite Efeitos oriundos da excessiva dificuldade ou facilidade dum teste para um dado grupo de candidatos. As notas tendem a agrupar-se ou no cimo (efeito-tecto) ou na base (efeito-chão) da distribuição.
Ver: efeito-chão, efeito-tecto.

CA:125, DA:120, DE:139, EN:36, ES:131, FR:143, GA:177, IT:138, NE:163, PO:139.

140 elaboração de testes Acção de seleccionar itens ou tarefas com o objectivo de elaborar um teste, muitas vezes precedida por pretestagem ou experimentação do material. Os itens ou as tarefas para a elaboração de testes podem ser seleccionados a partir de um banco de dados.

CA:126, DA:394, DE:397, EN:398, ES:75, FR:146, GA:393, IT:110, NE:392, PO:140.

141 elaborador de testes Pessoa que elabora um teste.

CA:109/127, DA:405/392, DE:395/400, EN:399/361, ES:92/133, FR:145, GA:121/149, IT:149, NE:391/399, PO:141.

142 ensaio Refere-se à definição de composição.

CA:366, DA:262, DE:33, EN:131, ES:306, FR:159, GA:7, IT:313, NE:125, PO:142.

143 entrevista A expressão oral é muitas vezes avaliada através de uma entrevista, a qual pode ser uma conversa livre entre o candidato e o examinador ou ter uma estrutura exigindo do candidato um número de tarefas orais.

CA:131, DA:150, DE:305, EN:263, ES:136, FR:148, GA:1, IT:92, NE:355, PO:143.

144 entrevista semi-directa Teste de competência oral no qual o material-estímulo é fornecido por um gravador e as respostas do candidato são gravadas para classificação posterior.
Ver: teste semi-directo.

CA:130, DA:348, DE:356, EN:370, ES:137, FR:392, GA:356, IT:93, NE:346, PO:144.

145 enunciado Designa a(s) folha(s) em que as questões do teste são apresentadas.

CA:239, DA:263, DE:123, EN:304, ES:220, FR:180, GA:271, IT:169, NE:425, PO:145.

146 erro Na teoria clássica da determinação da nota real, a nota obtida num teste possui duas componentes: uma nota real que reflecte o nível de capacidade da pessoa e uma nota errónea que reflecte a influência de todos os outros factores não ligados à capacidade testada. O erro é devido ao acaso, isto é, não sistemático. Além disso, outros factores podem afectar a performance de alguns indivíduos, provocando erros sistemáticos ou bias.
Cf: bias.
Ler: Bachman, 1990, p.167.

CA:136, DA:98, DE:116, EN:129, ES:144, FR:151, GA:122, IT:154, NE:124, PO:146.

147 erro acidental Refere-se à definição de erro.

CA:137, DA:408, DE:449, EN:306, ES:145, FR:152, GA:128, IT:156, NE:310, PO:147,

148 erro de amostragem Erro introduzido numa análise estatística devido à selecção da amostragem específica usada no estudo (por exemplo, uma amostragem não representativa da população).
Ver: população.

CA:139, DA:372, DE:381, EN:341, ES:147, FR:158, GA:129, IT:155, NE:370, PO:148.

149 erro de medição Refere-se à definição de erro-padrão de medição.

CA:138, DA:240/241, DE:239/240 EN:130/231, ES:146, FR:153, GA:123/130, IT:159, NE:242/243, PO:149.

150 erro de tipo 1 sin: erro de primeira espécie. Em estatística é o erro devido à rejeição da hipótese nula, quando, na realidade, ela é exacta.
Cf: erro de tipo 2.
Ver: hipótese nula.
Ler: Hatch e Lazaraton, 1991, p.224.

CA:140, DA:417, DE:9/117, EN:425, ES:150, FR:154, GA:126, IT:157, NE:405, PO:150.

151 erro de tipo 2 Em estatística é o erro devido à aceitação da hipótese nula, quando, na realidade, ela é falsa.
Cf: erro de tipo 1.
Ver: hipótese nula.
Ler: Hatch e Lazaraton, 1991, p.224.

CA:141, DA:418, DE:118, EN:426, ES:151, FR:155, GA:127, IT:158, NE:406, PO:151.

152 erro-padrão de estimativa Medida da precisão da predição duma variável a partir de outra, por exemplo, numa regressão linear. Dá os intervalos de confiança para as notas baseadas em critérios.
Ver: intervalo de confiança.
Ler: Hatch e Lazaraton, 1991, pp.477–479.

CA:142, DA:361, DE:375, EN:380, ES:148, FR:156, GA:124, IT:163, NE:363, PO:152.

153 erro-padrão de medição Na teoria clássica da nota verdadeira, o erro-padrão de medição (*Se*) indica a imprecisão da medição. A grandeza do erro-padrão de medição depende da fiabilidade (*r*) e do desvio-padrão das notas (*Sx*). A fórmula para calcular o *Se* é:

$$Se=Sx\sqrt{(1-r)}$$

Se, por exemplo, um candidato obtiver uma nota verdadeira T e se um desvio-padrão de medição de *Se* aparece repetidamente no teste, tal significa que 68% das vezes a nota observada está no nível T±*Se* e que 95% das vezes está no nível T±2*Se*.
Ler: Crocker e Algina, 1986, pp. 122–124.

CA:143, DA:364, DE:374, EN:381, ES:149, FR:157, GA:125, IT:12, NE:362, PO:153.

154 escala Conjunto de números ou categorias destinadas a medir qualquer coisa. Podem distinguir-se quatro tipos: escala nominal, ordinal, de intervalo e de relação.
Ler: Crocker e Algina, 1986, pp.46–49.

CA:144, DA:337, DE:352, EN:343, ES:152, FR:121, GA:308, IT:314, NE:326, PO:154.

155 escala absoluta Escala com um verdadeiro ponto zero como, por exemplo, uma escala para medir o comprimento. Dado que o zero absoluto não pode ser definido nos testes de língua, esta escala não se lhes pode aplicar.
Cf: escala de intervalo, escala nominal, escala ordinal.

CA:145, DA:4, DE:433, EN:4, ES:153, FR:122, GA:112, IT:317, NE:2, PO:155.

156 escala categórica sin: escala qualitativa. Escala usada para variáveis categóricas tais como o género, a língua

materna, a profissão.
Cf: escala de intervalo, escala nominal, escala ordinal, escala de relação.
CA:146, DA:170, DE:175, EN:42, ES:154, FR:123, GA:310, IT:318, NE:53, PO:156.

157 escala centil sin: escala percentil Escala comum, dividida em 100 unidades ou centis. Se alguém tem um centil de 95, tal significa que numa amostragem de 100, essa pessoa estaria à frente de 95.
Ler: Crocker e Algina, 1986, pp. 439–442; Guilford e Fruchter, 1981, pp.38–41
CA:151, DA:46, DE:300, EN:46, ES:155, FR:124, GA:311, IT:319, NE:54, PO:157.

158 escala comum Forma de relacionar as notas obtidas em dois ou mais testes numa escala comum, permitindo uma comparação directa dos resultados. Tal pode ser feito se as notas brutas tiverem sido transformadas através de procedimento estatístico como, por exemplo, a calibração.
Ler: Bachman, 1990, pp.340–344.
CA:147, DA:110, DE:131, EN:57, ES:156, FR:125, GA:86, IT:320, NE:148, PO:158.

159 escala de capacidade Na teoria item-resposta, é a escala graduada em intervalos iguais, na qual é possível situar as capacidades de um indíviduo e o nível de dificuldade das tarefas pedidas. Também designada escala teta.
Ler: Bachman, 1990, p.345.
CA:150, DA:3, DE:114, EN:3, ES:157, FR:128, GA:313, IT:322, NE:413, PO:159.

160 escala de classificação sin: escala de avaliação. Escala composta por várias categorias niveladas que permitem exercer um juízo subjectivo. Este tipo de escala é frequentemente acompanhado de descritores que permitem tornar a interpretação das categorias mais fácil.
Cf: escala de likert.
Ver: descritor.
CA:154, DA:172, DE:58, EN:315, ES:161, FR:130, GA:319, IT:323, NE:40, PO:160.

161 escala de intervalo igual sin: equipartição. Refere-se à definição de escala de intervalo.
CA:149, DA:213, DE:161, EN:125, ES:159, FR:127, GA:316, IT:316, NE:145, PO:161.

162 escala de intervalo Escala de medida na qual a distância entre duas unidades de medida adjacentes é a mesma, mas na qual não existe ponto zero absoluto.
Cf: escala categórica, escala nominal, escala ordinal, escala de relação.
Ler: Crocker e Algina, 1986, p.48.
CA:148, DA:149, DE:161, EN:184, ES:158, FR:126, GA:315, IT:315, NE:188, PO:162.

163 escala de likert Tipo de escala usada nos questionários para medir as atitudes ou as opiniões. São dadas várias possibilidades (cerca de cinco) e os inquiridos optam por uma, como por exemplo, "concordo completamente", "concordo", "não sei", "discordo", "discordo completamente".
CA:152, DA:214, DE:222, EN:211, ES:163, FR:129, GA:317, IT:325, NE:228, PO:163.

164 escala de relação Escala que contém um zero real e na qual a distância entre dois pontos adjacentes é a mesma em toda a escala. Em altura, por exemplo, uma pessoa que meça dois metros é duas vezes maior do que uma que meça um metro.
Cf: escala categórica, escala de intervalo, escala ordinal.
Ler: Crocker e Algina, 1986, pp.48–49.
CA:153, DA:210, DE:433, EN:317, ES:160, FR:131, GA:312, IT:324, NE:314, PO:164.

165 escala delta Escala normalizada com uma média de 13 e um desvio-padrão de 4.
CA:155, DA:60, DE:75, EN:93, ES:162, FR:132, GA:314, IT:321, NE:94, PO:165.

166 escala nominal Escala com variáveis categóricas como o género ou a primeira língua. O seu interesse reside na frequência da ocorrência de tais variáveis.
Cf: escala de intervalo, escala ordinal, escala de relação.
Ler: Hatch e Lazaraton, 1991, pp.55–56.
CA:156, DA:249, DE:262, EN:248, ES:164, FR:133, GA:309, IT:326, NE:260, PO:166.

167 escala ordinal Tipo de escala de medida que permite nivelar os candidatos sem indicar a distância relativa que existe entre cada um deles.
Cf: escala categórica, escala de intervalo, escala nominal, escala de relação.
Ler: Hatch e Lazaraton, 1991, pp.56–57.
CA:157, DA:271, DE:275, EN:265, ES:165, FR:134, GA:318, IT:327, NE:275, PO:167.

168 escala teta Refere-se a escala de capacidade.
CA:158, DA:407, DE:413, EN:413, ES:166, FR:128, GA:320, IT:328, NE:385,

PO:168.

169 escalamento Elaboração de escalas de medida. Em avaliação, isto significa associar números às performances dos candidatos, com o objectivo de reflectir a evolução dos níveis de conhecimento ou de capacidade. O escalamento pode implicar uma modificação de um conjunto de notas a fim de produzir uma escala com um objectivo específico, por exemplo, para apresentar os resultados de forma padronizada ou para calibrar uma versão de um teste com outra.
Ver: escala, escala de capacidade, escala centil, escala comum, escala de intervalo, escala nominal, escala ordinal, escala de relação, escala de classificação, formas calibradas, calibração linear.

CA:159, DA:341, DE:355, EN:346, ES:167, FR:135, GA:321, IT:109, NE:329, PO:169.

170 escrito Folha contendo as respostas do candidato a um teste, nas tarefas de resposta aberta.

CA:191, DA:261, DE:341, EN:350, ES:219, FR:343, GA:343, IT:175, NE:218, PO:170.

171 especificações dum teste Conjunto detalhado da documentação elaborada durante a concepção dum teste novo ou durante a adaptação dum antigo. As especificações fornecem informação detalhada relativamente ao projecto, ao conteúdo, ao nível, à tarefa e ao tipo de item usado, à população-alvo, etc. Junta-se, muitas vezes, às especificações dum teste amostras de material que funcionam como exemplos.

CA:161, DA:401, DE:394, EN:404, ES:169, FR:346, GA:355, IT:120, NE:400, PO:171.

172 esquema de classificação Lista de todas as respostas aceitáveis para um item de um teste. O esquema de classificação permite ao avaliador atribuir a nota apropriada.

CA: 52/256, DA:319, DE:228, EN:223, ES:301, FR:29, GA:324, IT:329, NE:79, PO:172.

173 estabilidade Aspecto da fiabilidade em que a estimativa se baseia numa abordagem teste-reteste. Refere-se à estabilidade das notas obtidas nos testes ao longo do tempo.
Ver: fiabilidade, fiabilidade teste-reteste.

CA:162, DA:359, DE:371, EN:378, ES:170, FR:79, GA:65, IT:337, NE:358, PO:173.

174 estatística Conjunto de informações expressas sob forma numérica. Em sentido restrito, uma estatística é uma propriedade dum grupo-amostra, contrariamente a um parâmetro, que é uma propriedade duma população. As estatísticas são geralmente transcritas em caracteres romanos e os parâmetros em caracteres gregos. Por exemplo, o desvio-padrão duma amostra escreve-se S ou SD, enquanto no caso duma população se escreve σ (sigma).
Cf: parâmetro.
Ver: população, amostra.

CA:163, DA:368, DE:379, EN:385, ES:174, FR:348, GA:363, IT:117, NE:367, PO:174.

175 estatística Ciência que manipula e interpreta informação numérica.

CA:164, DA:369, DE:378, EN:386, ES:171, FR:348, GA:362, IT:339, NE:366, PO:175.

176 estatística descritiva Estatística usada para descrever um conjunto de dados em termos de quantidade, de dispersão, de valores médios, de correlação com outros dados, etc. Distingue-se estatística descritiva de amostragem ou estatística inferencial.
Cf: estatística inferencial.

CA:165, DA:63, DE:51, EN:95, ES:172, FR:349, GA:365, IT:340, NE:95, PO:176.

177 estatística inferencial Estatísticas que vão além das informações dadas pelas estatísticas descritivas. Permitem inferir como um conjunto único de dados representa provavelmente uma população maior que a da amostragem em causa.
Cf: estatística descritiva.

CA:166, DA:139, DE:338, EN:171, ES:173, FR:350, GA:364, IT:341, NE:175, PO:177.

178 estimativa da bipartição de Spearman-Brown Refere-se à definição de fiabilidade da bipartição.

CA:168, DA:350, DE:360, EN:372, ES:177, FR:161, GA:228, IT:342, NE:349, PO:178.

179 estímulo Suporte gráfico ou escrito que permite obter uma resposta do candidato nos testes de expressão oral ou escrita.

CA:390, DA:316, DE:437 EN:299, ES:178, FR:95, GA:358, IT:343, NE:321, PO:179.

180 estudo-piloto Estudo preliminar durante o qual os investigadores ou os elaboradores de testes testam as suas ideias num pequeno número de pessoas de forma

a localizar problemas antes de o fazerem em grande escala ou antes de concluirem um programa ou um produto.
Ver: experimentação, pré-testagem.
CA:170, DA:286, DE:288, EN:281, ES:179, FR:163, GA:361, IT:344, NE:290, PO:180.

181 exame Procedimento que visa avaliar o nível de competência ou de conhecimento de um indivíduo através da aplicação de testes orais e/ou escritos. A obtenção de uma qualificação, a entrada numa instituição de ensino ou o acesso a um programa de estudos podem depender do resultado de um exame.
Cf: teste.
Ler: Bachman, 1990, p.50.
CA:171, DA:86, DE:303, EN:133, ES:188, FR:173, GA:347, IT:164, NE:127, PO:181.

182 examinador sin: avaliador. Pessoa que classifica, de forma subjectiva, ou no caso de uma atribuição de pontos mecânica (objectiva), a simples aplicação de um esquema de classificação, a performance do candidato num teste ou numa componente dum teste. Os avaliadores possuem normalmente uma qualificação obtida depois dum processo de formação e de padronização. Na parte oral, por vezes, coexistem um examinador e um interlocutor.
Cf: interlocutor.
CA:35/90/172/361, DA:32/89/288/306, DE:39/55/100/301, EN:22/135/221/311, ES:46/83/187/189, FR:81/164/174, GA:225/234/287/346, IT:102/165, NE:33/34/80/130, PO:182.

183 examinando Refere-se à definição de candidato.
CA:100, DA:87/402, DE:307/407, EN:134/406, ES:190, FR:351, GA:110/345, IT:49, NE:129/395, PO:183.

184 expansão de frases Tipo de item no qual são dadas as palavras lexicais e omitidas as palavras gramaticais (preposições, artigos, etc.). A tarefa do candidato consiste em introduzir as palavras que faltam, tornando a frase gramaticalmente completa.
CA:99, DA:380, DE:333, EN:358, ES:18, FR:175, GA:148, IT:166, NE:441, PO:184.

185 experimentação Etapa no desenvolvimento de tarefas dum teste que consiste em saber se o teste funciona da forma esperada. Muitas vezes usado no caso das tarefas de classificação subjectiva como a composição. É aplicada a uma pequena população.
Cf: pré-testagem.
CA:26, DA:301, DE:104, EN:418, ES:135, FR:160, GA:436, IT:336, NE:303, PO:185.

186 facetas dos métodos de teste Refere-se à definição das características dos métodos de teste.
CA:175, DA:396, DE:402, EN:403, ES:193, FR:176, GA:163, IT:50, NE:397, PO:186.

187 factor-G Na teoria da inteligência, é um "factor geral" hipotético subjacente a todas as aptidões cognitivas. Noção divulgada por Oller nos anos setenta como marca duma competência única na base das capacidades de linguagem.
Ler: Oller, 1979, pp.426–458; Bachman, 1990, p.6.
CA:176, DA:113, DE:127, EN:154, ES:195, FR:177, GA:136, IT:170, NE:139, PO:187.

188 factores afectivos Factores de natureza não-cognitiva ligados às variáveis emocionais, às preferências e às atitudes dos examinandos.
Cf: factores cognitivos.
Ler: Ebel e Frisbie, 1991, p.52.
CA:177, DA:6, DE:7, EN:9, ES:195, FR:178, GA:399, IT:172, NE:6, PO:188.

189 factores cognitivos Factores que dizem respeito à aprendizagem ou ao processo de avaliação e que se relacionam com os esquemas e os modelos de conhecimento do aprendente.
Cf: factores afectivos.
Ler: Ebel e Frisbie, 1991, p.52.
CA:178, DA:177, DE:180, EN:55, ES:196, FR:179, GA:398, IT:171, NE:65, PO:189.

190 falante nativo sin: interlocutor nativo. Falante de uma língua adquirida como primeira língua.
CA:286, DA:234, DE:255, EN:245, ES:216, FR:217, GA:47, IT:265, NE:255, PO:190.

191 familiaridade com os testes Familiaridade com o tipo de teste ou experiência a resolver testes que permitem ao candidato ter uma performance superior ao seu verdadeiro nível.
CA:179, DA:406, DE:396, EN:408, ES:197, FR:314, GA:161, IT:167, NE:401, PO:191.

192 feedback sin: Retroacção. Informação de pessoas implicadas no processo de avaliação (examinandos, examinadores, etc.) com o objectivo de avaliar o mesmo processo. Esta informação pode ser obtida de maneira informal ou através de questionários especialmente elaborados para este fim.

CA:381, DA:97, DE:330, EN:144, ES:379, FR:337, GA:6, IT:173, NE:134, PO:192.

193 fiabilidade Consistência ou estabilidade das medidas dum teste. Quanto mais fiável for um teste, menos erros acidentais conterá. Um teste que apresente um erro sistemático, por exemplo, um bias para alguns grupos, pode ser fiável, mas não é válido.
Cf: validade.
Ver: KR-20 (fórmula 20 de Kuder-Richardson), alfa (coeficiente alfa), fiabilidade da bipartição, fiabilidade teste-reteste.
Ler: Bachman, 1990, p.24; Crocker e Algina, 1986, capítulo 6.

CA:180, DA:312, DE:322/453, EN:327, ES:198, FR:183, GA:200, IT:6, NE:43, PO:193.

194 fiabilidade da bipartição Medida de consistência interna da fiabilidade. A estimativa baseia-se na correlação entre as notas de duas metades de teste consideradas como dois testes alternados. A divisão em duas metades pode ser feita de formas diferentes: primeira e segunda metades, ou reagrupando os itens pares numa metade e os ímpares na outra.
Ver: fiabilidade.
Ler: Ebel e Frisbie, 1991, pp. 82–83; Crocker e Algina, 1986, pp. 136–138.

CA:183, DA:259, DE:364/398, EN:377, ES:201, FR:184, GA:203, IT:7, NE:353, PO:194.

195 fiabilidade inter-individual Estimativa da fiabilidade dum teste baseada no grau de concordância obtida entre diferentes examinadores relativamente à avaliação da performance dos candidatos.
Ver: acordo inter-individual, fiabilidade.

CA:181, DA:145, DE:158, EN:182, ES:199, FR:185, GA:201, IT:8, NE:184, PO:195.

196 fiabilidade intra-individual Estimativa da fiabilidade da avaliação baseada no grau de fiabilidade com que o avaliador classifica a mesma performance realizada em diferentes ocasiões.
Ver: acordo inter-individual, fiabilidade.

CA:182, DA:151, DE:162, EN:186, ES:200, FR:187, GA:202, IT:89, NE:189, PO:196.

197 fiabilidade teste-reteste Estimativa da fiabilidade obtida através da aplicação dupla do mesmo teste aos mesmos candidatos, nas mesmas condições e relacionando as notas obtidas. Este processo diz respeito à estabilidade no tempo das notas obtidas e é igualmente usado quando não se pode obter estimativas de consistência interna.
Cf: consistência interna.
Ver: fiabilidade, estabilidade.

CA:184, DA:318, DE:409/325, EN:410, ES:202, FR:188, GA:204, IT:9, NE:383, PO:197.

198 folha de respostas Folha(s) em que o candidato responde às questões.
Cf: leitor óptico.

CA:191, DA:37, DE:22, EN:19, ES:219, FR:181, GA:152, IT:174, NE:20, PO:198.

199 formas alternadas Refere-se à definição de formas equivalentes.

CA:185, DA:12, DE:11, EN:11, ES:203, NE:13, FR:193, GA:146, IT:176, PO:199.

200 formas calibradas Diferentes formas dum teste cuja distribuição das notas foi transformada de modo a serem usadas alternadamente.

CA:186, DA:442, DE:16/14, EN:126, ES:204, FR:194, GA:145, IT:177 NE:141, PO:200.

201 formas equivalentes Diferentes versões do mesmo teste consideradas equivalentes por serem baseadas nas mesmas especificações e avaliarem a mesma competência. Para ir ao encontro dos requisitos da equivalência na teoria clássica do teste, as diferentes formas do teste devem ter o mesmo tipo de dificuldade, a mesma variância e a mesma covariância quando são aplicados às mesmas pessoas. Na prática, é muito difícil alcançar a equivalência. Também designadas formas paralelas ou formas alternadas.
Cf: formas calibradas.
Ler: Crocker e Algina, 1986, p.132.

CA:187, DA:441, DE:25, EN:128 ES:205, FR:195, GA:143, IT:178, NE:122, PO:201.

202 formas paralelas Refere-se à definição de formas equivalentes.

CA:188, DA:275, DE:278, EN:268, ES:206, FR:196, GA:144, IT:179, NE:279, PO:202.

203 fórmula de Spearman-Brown Meio estatístico que permite estimar a fiabilidade de um teste, no caso de ser aumentado ou encurtado pela junção ou supressão de itens. Pode ser utilizado para predizer o número de itens necessários à obtenção de uma fiabilidade específica.
Ler: Crocker e Algina, 1986, pp. 118–119.

CA:83, DA:349, DE:359, EN:371, ES:207, FR:197, GA:147, IT:180, NE:350, PO:203.

204 frequências acumuladas Forma de apresentar a distribuição dos candidatos, contando para cada classe de notas o número de candidatos que obteve uma nota numa classe e em todas as classes inferiores.

CA:189, DA:208, DE:202, EN:86, ES:208, FR:198, GA:239, IT:181, NE:91, PO:204.

205 função do item-resposta Na teoria item-resposta, é a função matemática que relaciona a probabilidade de sucesso num item com a capacidade medida pelo item. Também designada função característica do item.

CA:193, DA:158, DE:172, EN:194, ES:210, FR:189, GA:140, IT:183, NE:200, PO:205.

206 função informativa do item Na teoria item-resposta, é o índice que mostra a quantidade de informação fornecida por um item ou teste relativamente a uma pessoa de um deteminado nível de capacidade. Depende do item de discriminação e da sua adequação ao nível de capacidade.

CA:192, DA:156, DE:169, EN:193, ES:212, FR:190, GA:138, IT:184, NE:197, PO:206.

207 função informativa do teste Na teoria item-resposta, é um índice da quantidade de informação fornecida por um teste sobre uma pessoa de um determinado nível de capacidade. É a soma das funções informativas do item.

CA:194, DA:388, DE:399, EN:400, ES:211, FR:191, GA:139, IT:185, NE:394, PO:207.

208 funcionamento do item diferencial A dificuldade relativa dum item depende das características do grupo a que é aplicado, por exemplo a língua materna.
Ver: bias.

CA:195, DA:66, DE:78, EN:100, ES:209, FR:192, GA:114, IT:182, NE:100, PO:208.

209 ganho de pontos Diferença entre a nota obtida num teste antes dum curso e a nota obtida no mesmo teste ou num teste semelhante no fim do curso. O ganho de pontos é um indicador dos progressos alcançados durante o curso.

CA:352, DA:290, DE:211, EN:150, ES:32, FR:199, GA:44, IT:192, NE:434, PO:209.

210 gráfico em bandas No sentido mais lato é uma parte duma escala. Num teste de itens refere-se a uma série de resultados que podem ser transmitidos em níveis ou em bandas. Numa escala de classificação concebida para avaliar uma capacidade específica (como a expressão oral ou a expressão escrita) uma banda representa normalmente um determinado nível.

CA:37, DA:339, DE:44, EN:29, ES:38, FR:200, GA:41, IT:39 NE:28, PO:210.

211 gráfico de barras Gráfico que permite visualizar as distribuições de frequência das variáveis.

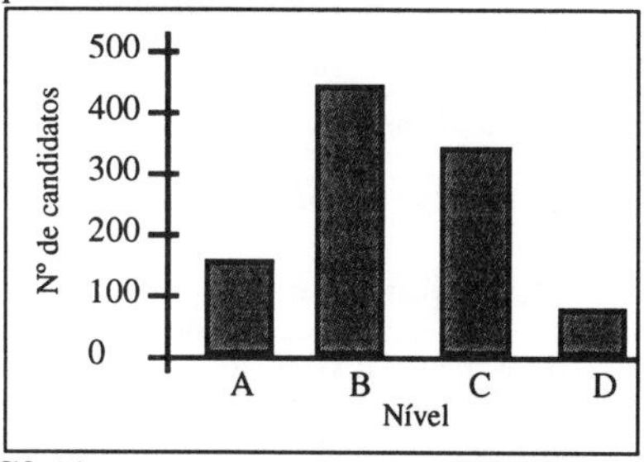

Cf: histograma.
Ler: Hatch e Lazaraton, 1991, p.147.

CA:102, DA:383, DE:335, EN:31, ES:104, FR:201, GA:42, IT:123, NE:357, PO:211.

212 grupo de referência Amostra duma população de candidatos bem definida sobre a qual é feita a normalização de um teste.
Ver: norma.

CA:196, DA:309, DE:267, EN:324, ES:213, FR:202, GA:166, IT:189, NE:316, PO:212.

213 grupo-norma Grande grupo de indivíduos representativos da população para a qual é elaborado um teste. Usa-se a performance do grupo-norma para interpretar um teste normativo. Também designado grupo de referência.

CA:197, DA:254, DE:266, EN:251, ES:214, FR:203, GA:264, IT:190, NE:265, PO:213.

214 hipótese nula Hipótese que estabelece que duas ou mais variáveis não têm nenhuma relação. Exemplo: não haver diferença de performance entre os membros de dois grupos com uma língua primeira diferente.
Ler: Hatch e Lazaraton, 1991, p.24; Guilford e Fruchter, 1981, pp. 146–147.

CA:202, DA:255, DE:271, EN:255, ES:217, FR:206, GA:167, IT:206, NE:266, PO:214.

215 histograma Representação gráfica duma frequência de distribuição, na qual o número de casos por classe de frequência é mostrado através duma barra vertical.

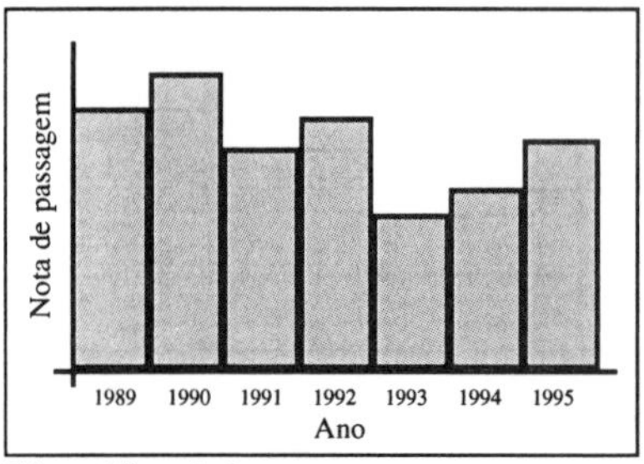

Cf: gráfico de barras.

CA:203, DA:125, DE:145, EN:163, ES:218, FR:204, GA:168, IT:207, NE:167, PO:215.

216 homogeneidade Atributo dum teste ou dum sub-teste no qual os itens medem a mesma competência ou dum grupo cujos elementos têm as mesmas características. O grau de homogeneidade exprime-se pelo índice de fiabilidade.

CA:204, DA:127, DE:148, EN:165, ES:221, FR:205, GA:22, IT:257, NE:169, PO:216.

217 impacto Efeito produzido por um teste em termos de influência nos processos educacionais gerais e nas pessoas afectadas pelos resultados dos testes.
Ver: efeito de refluxo.

CA:205, DA:303, DE:444, EN:167, ES:222, FR:207, GA:391, IT:191, NE:171, PO:217.

218 índice-D Índice de discriminação dos itens. Muitas vezes usado em testes durante o processo de ensino-aprendizagem, em pequena escala, dado que pode ser calculado manualmente. São seleccionados dois grupos, um superior e um inferior, de acordo com os resultados totais num teste, de modo a que 10 a 33% dos examinados esteja em cada um dos grupos. Se as notas estiverem distribuídas normalmente, 27% representa o número ideal em cada grupo. Efectua-se uma contagem das respostas a cada item. Para os itens com grande poder de discriminação, as notas do grupo superior serão mais altas do que as do grupo inferior. O índice de discriminação é dado pela seguinte fórmula:

$$D=p_U-p_L$$

em que p_U representa a fracção do grupo superior que obteve o item correcto e p_L a fracção do grupo inferior que obteve o item correcto. Considera-se que itens com um índice de 0.3 ou acima discriminam bem.

CA:206, DA:59, DE:72, EN:91, ES:223, FR:208, GA:186, IT:194, NE:92, PO:218.

219 índice de dificuldade Na teoria clássica do teste, a dificuldade dum item é a proporção (p) de candidatos que responde correctamente. Isto significa que o índice de dificuldade dum item está ligado à população considerada e varia segundo o nível de capacidade dos candidatos.
Cf: índice de facilidade, valor-*p*.

CA:207, DA:378, DE:343, EN:101, ES:224, FR:209, GA:187, IT:196, NE:249, PO:219.

220 índice de facilidade Proporção de respostas correctas a um item, expressa numa escala de 0 a 1 ou percentualmente. Também designado valor-*p* ou valor de facilidade.
Cf: índice de dificuldade.

CA:209, DA:191, DE:208, EN:141, ES:225, FR:210, GA:188, IT:197, NE:146, PO:220.

221 índice de leitura Medida da complexidade gramatical e lexical usada para avaliar a que ponto um texto é ou não compreensível. O índice Fog de Gunning e a escala de leitura de Flesch são exemplos de índices de leitura.

CA:210, DA:222, DE:219, EN:320, ES:226, FR:211, GA:189, IT:198, NE:223, PO:221.

222 índice médio de dificuldade dum item (Média p) É a proporção média correcta em todos os itens numa escala de itens classificados de forma dicotómica. Por exemplo, uma média p de 0.5 indica que o índice médio de facilidade do teste é de 0.5.
Ver: classificação dicotómica.

CA:208, DA:132, DE:246, EN:228, ES:227, FR:212, GA:190, IT:195 NE:150, PO:222.

223 informação lacunar Técnica de ensino e de avaliação de línguas na qual a comunicação real é simulada. O ensinante propõe situações em que nem todos os aprendentes recebem as mesmas informações; para poderem realizar a tarefa proposta, devem comunicar uns com os outros. É normalmente usado como actividade na sala de aula ou para avaliação da produção oral e escrita.

CA:42, DA:140, DE:151, EN:172, ES:411, FR:213, GA:43, IT:424, NE:176, PO:223.

224 início (dum item) Parte escrita dum item, geralmente sob a forma de frase

incompleta a qual deve ser completada com uma frase do examinando ou a partir de diferentes opções.
Cf: resposta-chave, opções.
Ver: item de escolha múltipla.
CA:276, DA:360, DE:29, EN:387, ES:139, FR:10, GA:160, IT:346, NE:359, PO:224.

225 instruções Indicações gerais dadas aos candidatos, por exemplo na primeira página da folha de respostas. Contêm informação sobre a duração do teste, o número de tarefas a realizar e o espaço em que as respostas devem ser dadas.
CA:211, DA:143, DE:391, EN:175, ES:230, FR:214, GA:402, IT:208, NE:181, PO:225.

226 intercepção-Y Em regressão linear, ponto em que a linha de regressão cruza o eixo das ordenadas (vertical).
Ver: regressão linear.
CA:212, DA:438, DE:146, EN:441, ES:231, FR:215, GA:181, IT:200, NE:438, PO:226.

227 interlocutor Num teste de produção oral, o examinador explica a tarefa a realizar, coloca questões e interage oralmente com o(s) candidato(s). O interlocutor pode também avaliar o candidato e dar-lhe uma nota. Esta segunda função pode ser desempenhada por um segundo examinador que observa, mas não participa na interacção com o(s) candidato(s).
Cf: examinador.
CA:213, DA:325, DE:125, EN:178, ES:138, FR:216, GA:72, IT:201, NE:155, PO:227.

228 intervalo Diferença entre dois pontos numa escala.
CA:214, DA:148, DE:160, EN:183, ES:232, FR:218, GA:131, IT:203, NE:187, PO:228.

229 intervalo de confiança Amplitude sobre uma estimativa dum valor dentro do qual pode estar o valor verdadeiro. Esse grau de possibilidade é definido normalmente em níveis de confiança de 95% ou 99%.
CA:215, DA:182, DE:184, EN:67, ES:233, FR:219, GA:132, IT:204, NE:45, PO:229.

230 invariância Na teoria item-resposta, conceito que estipula que a dificuldade dum item e a medida de discriminação são características inerentes que não dependem da capacidade dos candidatos e que, da mesma forma, as medidas de capacidade não dependem dos itens usados.
CA:216, DA:152, DE:164, EN:187, ES:234, FR:220, GA:120, IT:205, NE:191, PO:230.

231 item sin: questão. Cada ponto dum teste ao qual é atribuído uma cotação. Exemplos: uma lacuna ou espaço em branco num teste de estruturação perceptiva ("teste cloze"), uma das questões num questionário com questões de escolha múltipla com três ou quatro opções, uma frase para transformação gramatical, uma questão que exige uma resposta com um determinado número de palavras.
CA:217, DA:154, DE:166, EN:189, ES:235, FR:221, GA:240, IT:209, NE:195, PO:231.

232 item-âncora Item integrado em dois ou mais testes que permite determinar a diferença do grau de dificuldade entre os testes ou a diferença de performance entre os diferentes grupos de candidatos. Os itens-âncora constituem uma parte da versão nova dum teste de modo a fornecerem informação sobre o teste e os candidatos que o fizeram, por exemplo, para calibrar um novo teste com uma escala de medição.
Cf: teste-âncora.
Ver: calibração.
CA:218, DA:16, DE:18, EN:15, ES:237, FR:225, GA:241, IT:212, NE:17, PO:232.

233 item baseado em texto Item baseado num texto. Exemplo: itens de escolha múltipla para compreensão de um texto escrito.
CA:219, DA:387, DE:412, EN:412, ES:236, FR:226, GA:254, IT:213, NE:269, PO:233.

234 item de completamento Consiste, geralmente, em completar uma frase, usando várias palavras ou fornecendo dados como números de telefone ou datas.
CA:226, DA:421, DE:102, EN:60, ES:238, FR:223, GA:243, IT:215, NE:193, PO:234.

235 item de completamento sin: item de espaços ou lacunas. Todo o tipo de item que exige do candidato a inserção de material escrito – letras, números, uma palavra isolada, várias palavras, frases, parágrafos – em espaços brancos ao longo dum texto. A resposta pode ser produzida pelo candidato ou seleccionada a partir de uma lista.
CA:223, DA:138, DE:229, EN:151, ES:241, FR:317, GA:249, IT:78, NE:192, PO:235.

236 item de escolha múltipla Tipo de item que consiste numa questão ou numa

frase incompleta (estímulo), acompanhado duma escolha de respostas ou de proposições para completar a frase (opções). O candidato deve escolher a opção correcta (chave) entre três, quatro ou cinco possibilidades. Não é exigida a produção de texto escrito. É por esta razão que se utiliza normalmente os itens de escolha múltipla nos testes de compreensão escrita e oral. Estes itens podem ser discretivos ou baseados em texto.
Cf: item discretivo, item baseado em texto.
CA:220, DA:236, DE:249/234, EN:238, ES:244, FR:222, GA:247, IT:211, NE:252, PO:236.

237 item de formação de palavras Tipo de item no qual o candidato deve produzir uma forma duma palavra a partir de outra forma da mesma palavra que lhe é dada. Exemplo: Este tipo de trabalho exige uma ______________ do vocabulário técnico. (compreender)
CA:227/354, DA:269/434, DE:135/445, EN:437/439, ES:231/354, FR:227/280, GA:244/339, IT:216/284, NE:159/437, PO:237.

238 item de resposta curta Item aberto que exige do candidato a formulação de uma resposta com uma palavra ou uma frase.
CA:228, DA:198, DE:205, EN:362, ES:243, FR:224, GA:246, IT:311, NE:209, PO:238.

239 item de transformação Refere-se à definição de transformação de frases.
CA:229, DA:413, DE:420, EN:416, ES:245, FR:403, GA:242, IT:217, NE:402, PO:239.

240 item discretivo específico Item discretivo que avalia um ponto específico, por exemplo uma estrutura ou léxico, e que não tem nenhuma relação com outros itens. A vulgarização deste item nos testes de língua deve-se a Robert Lado nos anos sessenta.
Cf: item/tarefa integrativo/a.
Ver: item discretivo.
CA:225, DA:72, DE:82, EN:110, ES:247 FR:229, GA:251, IT:210, NE:107, PO:240.

241 item discretivo Item que contém todos os elementos da questão. Não está ligado ao texto nem a outros itens nem a qualquer material complementar. A escolha múltipla é um exemplo deste tipo de item.
Cf: item baseado em texto.
CA:230, DA:71, DE:421, EN:109, ES:246, FR:228, GA:253, IT:219, NE:106, PO:241.

242 item escalado Item classificado com a ajuda duma escala.
CA:222, DA:342, DE:27, EN:342, ES:248, FR:230, GA:252, IT:220, NE:328, PO:242.

243 item verdadeiro/falso Tipo de resposta de escolha múltipla na qual o candidato deve indicar se uma série de afirmações sobre um texto são verdadeiras ou falsas.
CA:232, DA:326, DE:326, EN:419, ES:250, FR:429, GA:245, IT:218, NE:426, PO:243.

244 item-ligação Refere-se à definição de item-âncora.
CA:221, DA:218, DE:432, EN:215, ES:239, FR:231, GA:250, IT:214, NE:232, PO:244.

245 item/tarefa integrativo/a Refere-se às questões ou tarefas cuja resolução depende de mais do que uma capacidade. Exemplos: completar um teste de estruturação perceptiva, participar numa entrevista, ler uma carta e dar a resposta.
Cf: item discretivo específico.
CA:231, DA:144, DE:156, EN:176, ES:249, FR:316, GA:248, IT:221, NE:182, PO:245.

246 KR-20 (fórmula 20 de Kuder-Richardson) Refere-se à definição de Kuder-Richardson.
CA:234, DA:201, DE:194, EN:199, ES:252, FR:233, GA:205, IT:222, NE:210, PO:246.

247 KR-21 (fórmula 21 de Kuder-Richardson) Refere-se à definição de Kuder-Richardson.
CA:235, DA:202, DE:195, EN:200 ES:253, FR:234, GA:206, IT:223, NE:211, PO:247.

248 Kuder-Richardson Duas medidas de consistência interna desenvolvidas por Kuder e Richardson e usadas na determinação da fiabilidade dum teste. KR-21 necessita de menos informações e é mais fácil de calcular, apresentando, no entanto, uma estimativa mais fraca do que KR-20.
Cf: alfa (coeficiente alfa).
Ver: consistência interna.
Ler: Henning, 1987, p. 84.
CA:236, DA:206, DE:200, EN:201, ES:254, FR:235, GA:207, IT:224, NE:212, PO:248.

249 leitor óptico sin: scanner. Aparelho electrónico usado para ler a informação directamente a partir das folhas de resposta ou de notas. Os candidatos ou os examinadores marcam as respostas aos

itens numa folha de notas e esta informação é automaticamente lida pelo computador.
Ler: Bachman, 1990, p.42.
CA:242, DA:268, DE:274, EN:261, ES:255, FR:237, GA:214, IT:226, NE:274, PO:249.

250 léxico Termo utilizado para designar o vocabulário.
CA:237, DA:212, DE:221, EN:210, ES:257, FR:238, GA:213, IT:225, NE:227, PO:250.

251 língua para fins específicos Ensino ou avaliação da língua centrado num domínio especifico da língua usado nas actividades ou profissões correspondentes; por exemplo, Português Comercial, Inglês para Controladores Aéreos, etc.
CA:238, DA:95, DE:111, EN:205, ES:256, FR:236, GA:385, IT:227, NE:378, PO:251.

252 lista de controle Lista de questões ou de pontos que devem ser tratados. Usado muitas vezes nos testes de língua como instrumento de observação ou de análise.
CA:240, DA:48, DE:64, EN:48, ES:258, FR:239, GA:351, IT:228, NE:58, PO:252.

253 logit Na teoria item-resposta, é uma unidade de medição derivada do logaritmo natural da taxa de possibilidade de sucesso à de reprovação, isto é das possibilidades. A diferença de logit entre as capacidades dum indivíduo e a dificuldade do item deriva das possibilidades que o indivíduo tem de acertar o item.
Ler: Henning, 1987, pp. 118–126.
CA:241, DA:220, DE:227, EN:218, ES:259, FR:240, GA:216, IT:232, NE:234, PO:253.

254 material-estímulo Material dado num teste com o objectivo de o candidato produzir uma resposta adequada. Num teste de compreensão oral, por exemplo, o texto pode ser gravado e acompanhado por um conjunto de itens escritos.
CA:169, DA:142, DE:408, EN:174, ES:228, FR:147, GA:199, IT:199, NE:180, PO:254.

255 média A média é a medida da tendência central. Obtém-se a nota média dum teste adicionando todas as notas obtidas e dividindo o resultado pelo número de candidatos.
Cf: mediana, moda.
Ver: tendência central.
Ler: Hatch e Lazaraton, 1991, pp.151–163.
CA:250, DA:231, DE:244, EN:227, ES:261, FR:257, GA:226, IT:234, NE:151, PO:255.

256 mediana Nota colocada no centro da distribuição num conjunto de notas niveladas. Metade das notas está abaixo da mediana e outra metade está acima.
Cf: média, moda.
Ver: tendência central (medida da).
Ler: Hatch e Lazaraton, 1991, p.161
CA:244, DA:228, DE:232, EN:232, ES:263, FR:242, GA:3, IT:235, NE:239, PO:256.

257 medição De uma forma geral trata-se do processo que permite encontrar a soma de qualquer coisa por comparação com uma unidade fixa, como por exemplo, quando se usa uma régua para medir o comprimento. Em ciências sociais, a medida refere-se muitas vezes à quantificação das características dos indivíduos, como por exemplo a competência numa língua.
Ler: Bachman, 1990, capítulo 2.
CA:245, DA:242, DE:241, EN:230, ES:264, FR:243, GA:395, IT:238, NE:245, PO:257.

258 medição independente da amostra Termo usado na interpretação dos resultados independentemente da amostra usada numa determinada investigação.
Ver: amostra.
CA:247, DA:373, DE:382, EN:339, ES:265, FR:244, GA:396, IT:239, NE:371, PO:258.

259 método de teste O uso de uma língua pode ser testado de maneiras diferentes, como a escolha múltipla, o teste de estruturação perceptiva, a composição, a expressão oral, etc. Constata-se que o método de teste interage com a capacidade na medição da performance.
Cf: características dos métodos de teste.
Ler: Bachman, 1990, p.77.
CA:248, DA:395, DE:401, EN:401, ES:266, FR:245, GA:257, IT:236, NE:396, PO:259.

260 método do gráfico delta Refere-se ao funcionamento dos itens diferenciais. Usado na identificação dos itens que exageram ou minimizam as diferenças de performance dos grupos. Baseado na dificuldade clássica dos itens (valores-*p*). Os valores-*p* são convertidos com o objectivo de normalizar as notas-*z* e são registados aos pares num gráfico para mostrar a dificuldade relativa dos itens para os dois grupos em questão.

Ver: funcionamento do item diferencial.
Ler: Crocker e Algina, 1986, pp. 388–390.
CA:249, DA:61, DE:74, EN:92, ES:267, FR:246, GA:256, IT:237, NE:93, PO:260.

261 moda sin: valor dominante. É o valor mais frequentemente observado numa distribuição de notas; ponto mais alto da curva de distribuição.

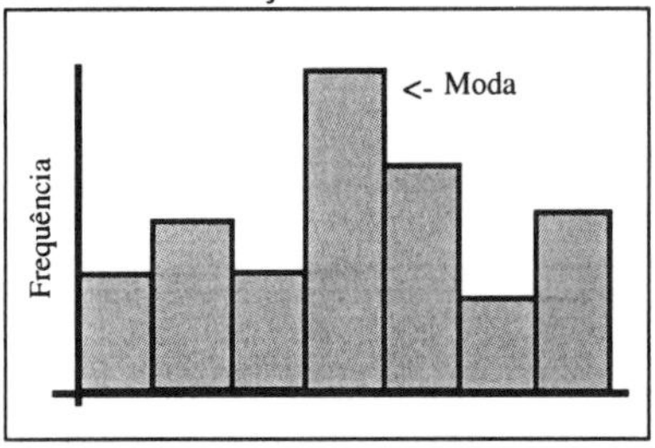

Cf: distribuição bimodal, média, mediana.
Ver: tendência central (medida da).
Ler: Hatch e Lazaraton, 1991, pp. 160–161
CA:252, DA:232, DE:247, EN:235, ES:268, FR:247, GA:255, IT:240, NE:248, PO:261.

262 modelo cognitivo Teoria sobre a maneira como os conhecimentos dum indivíduo (no sentido de conceitos e de processos) são estruturados. Importante no domínio dos testes de língua, dado que pode ter um efeito sobre a escolha do método ou do conteúdo dos testes.
CA:253, DA:178, DE:181, EN:56, ES:269, FR:250, GA:297, IT:243, NE:64, PO:262.

263 modelo da escala de classificação Extensão do modelo de Rasch que permite tratar os dados escalados, derivados, por exemplo, das classificações da performance oral.
Cf: modelo de Rasch.
Ver: modelo do crédito parcial.
Ler: Wright, B.D. e Masters G.N., 1982, Rating Scale Analysis, Chicago, MESA Press.
CA:254, DA:173, DE:236, EN:316, ES:272, FR:251, GA:303, IT:246, NE:41, PO:263.

264 modelo de dois parâmetros Na teoria item-resposta, é o modelo constituído pelo parâmetro de discriminação do item e o parâmetro capacidade/dificuldade.
Cf: modelo de parâmetro único, modelo de Rasch.
Ver: teoria item-resposta (TIR).
CA:258, DA:411, DE:454, EN:424, ES:271, FR:248, GA:298, IT:241, NE:404, PO:264.

265 modelo de parâmetro único Modelo que funciona com uma escala única representando a dificuldade (das tarefas) e a capacidade (dos indivíduos). Não considera nem a discriminação nem a adivinhação.
Cf: modelo de Rasch.
CA:255, DA:92, DE:99, EN:259, ES:273, FR:249, GA:296, IT:242, NE:118, PO:265.

266 modelo de Rasch Modelo matemático, conhecido igualmente como modelo da logística simples, que postula a existência duma relação entre a capacidade do indivíduo e a dificuldade da tarefa. Equivale, matematicamente, ao modelo de parâmetro único na teoria do item-resposta. O modelo de Rasch tem sido alargado de várias formas, por exemplo, para tratar as respostas escaladas ou as multi-facetas dando conta da "dificuldade" duma tarefa.
Ver: teoria item-resposta, modelo do crédito parcial, modelo da escala de classificação, modelo multi-facetas de Rasch.
Ler: Henning, 1987, pp. 117–125.
CA:259, DA:305, DE:316, EN:310, ES:275, FR:252, GA:302, IT:248, NE:313, PO:266.

267 modelo do crédito parcial Na teoria do item-resposta é o modelo que permite tratar os dados fornecidos pelas escalas. Pode também ser usado para analisar as respostas aos itens de frases para completar que utilizam uma escala de classificação, como, por exemplo, 1, 2 ou 3 ou numa entrevista que usa várias escalas de avaliação da performance.
Cf: modelo da escala de classificação, modelo multi-facetas de Rasch.
Ver: modelo de Rasch.
Ler: Wright e Masters, 1982, pp.40–48.
CA:257, DA:278, DE:281, EN:272, ES:270, FR:253, GA:301, IT:244, NE:282, PO:267.

268 modelo multi-facetas de Rasch Extensão do modelo de Rasch o qual permite modelar as probabilidades de resposta na base duma combinação aditiva de facetas. A performance exigida numa tarefa escrita, pode, por exemplo, ser modelada para reflectir a dificuldade da tarefa e a severidade do avaliador. O modelo multi-facetas de Rasch foi desenvolvido, por exemplo, pelo programa FACETS.
Ver: modelo de Rasch.
Ler: Linacre, J.M., 1989, Many-facet Rasch measurement, Chicago, MESA Press.
CA:260, DA:235, DE:289, EN:220, ES:276, FR:254, GA:300, IT:249, NE:236,

PO:268.

269 modelo probalilístico Modelo no qual as relações causais (como a dificuldade do item e a capacidade do candidato para fazer o teste) são explicadas em termos de grau de probabilidade. O modelo de Rasch é um exemplo dum modelo probabilístico.

CA:262, DA:295, DE:297, EN:294, ES:274, FR:255, GA:299, IT:247, NE:430, PO:269.

270 moderação a) Parte do processo de elaboração de itens ou de tarefas dum teste. Etapa durante a qual o material produzido é examinado por especialistas (elaboradores qualificados e ensinantes) que decidem se o material é pertinente (solicitando, eventualmente, algumas modificações).

b) No processo de avaliação, é o ajustamento, feito pelo moderador das notas, designado pelo avaliador.
Cf: revisão.

CA:263, DA:410, DE:31, EN:237, ES:277, FR:256, GA:260, IT:250, NE:247, PO:270.

271 *N,n* Número. *N* é muitas vezes usado para indicar o número de casos num estudo ou de indivíduos numa população enquanto *n* indica o número numa amostra ou num sub-grupo. Exemplo: O teste foi aplicado a engenheiros(*N*=600) dos quais 10% eram mulheres (*n*=60).

CA:269, DA:248, DE:256, EN:244, ES:282, FR:258, GA:261, IT:251, NE:259, PO:271.

272 nível (a) A nota obtida num teste pode ser comunicada ao candidato sob a forma de nível, por exemplo numa escala de A a E na qual A representa o nível máximo, B um nível bom, C um nível suficiente, D e E níveis insuficientes.

(b) Faz-se muitas vezes referência a uma série de níveis para designar o grau de capacidade necessário a um estudante para ser integrado num dado grupo ou depois de ter passado num exame. Os termos mais utilizados para designar estes níveis são 'elementar', 'intermédio', 'avançado', etc.
Cf: nota.

CA:270/275, DA:167/247, DE:260/270, EN:156/209, ES:283/288, FR:259, GA:164/210, IT:188/229, NE:258/426, PO:272.

273 nível de capacidade sin: Nível de proficiência. Conhecimento duma língua e grau de capacidade para a utilizar.
Cf: capacidade, competência.
Ler: Bachman, 1990, p.16.

CA:296, DA:296, DE:47, EN:295, ES:120, FR:260, GA:265, IT:62, NE:305, PO:273.

274 nível de iniciação Referencial dum nível elementar de competência em língua estrangeira, publicado para o inglês em 1977 pelo Conselho da Europa e revisto em 1990. É menos vasto que o Nível Limiar, abarcando cerca de metade dos conteúdos deste último.
Ver: nível limiar.

CA:271, DA:437, DE:443, EN:436, ES:284, FR:261, GA:211, IT:231, NE:433, PO:274.

275 nível limiar Referencial funcional que define as competências de base em língua estrangeira necessárias para comunicar nas situações de comunicação do quotidiano. Publicado em 1976 para o inglês pelo Conselho da Europa, foi revisto em 1990. Foram produzidas diferentes versões para as línguas europeias, tendo a portuguesa sido publicada em 1988.

CA:272, DA:419, DE:414, EN:414, ES:285, FR:262, GA:212, IT:230, NE:386, PO:275.

276 nivelamento percentil Número ou nota que indica o nivelamento, mostrando a percentagem existente abaixo dessa nota. Se a um candidato é atribuído o nível percentil 60, isso significa que 60% dos candidatos obtiveram uma nota equivalente ou inferior.

CA:363, DA:281, DE:299, EN:276, ES:359, FR:53, GA:284, IT:55, NE:285, PO:276.

277 nivelamento Conversão das notas obtidas em níveis.

CA:362, DA:168, DE:48, EN:157, ES:47, FR:52, GA:165, IT:94, NE:427, PO:277.

278 norma Padrão de performance. Num teste padronizado, determina-se a norma registando as notas dum grupo grande. A norma ou os padrões baseados nas performances deste grupo são usadas para avaliar a performance de outros grupos constituídos por candidatos do mesmo tipo.
Ver: grupo de referência, teste normativo.

CA:273, DA:250, DE:263, EN:250, ES:286, FR:264, GA:262, IT:252, NE:261, PO:278.

279 normalização Alteração das notas de modo a obter uma distribuição normal o que implica a utilização duma escala de equicentilagem.
Cf: nota-padrão.

CA:274, DA:253, DE:264, EN:253, ES:287, FR:263, GA:263, IT:253, NE:263, PO:279.

280 nota sin: classificação. (a) Número total de pontos atribuídos à resposta dum candidato a um item, um sub-teste ou a um teste;

(b) Número total de pontos obtidos num teste quer antes do escalamento (nota bruta) quer depois (nota escalada);

(c) Acção de atribuir valores numéricos às performances observadas.
Cf: medição.

CA:342, DA:328, DE:312, EN:348, ES:345, FR:275, GA:328, IT:278, NE:331, PO:280.

281 nota bruta Nota que não sofreu nenhuma manipulação estatística por transformação, ponderação ou reescalamento.

CA:348, DA:321, DE:328, EN:319, ES:348, FR:276, GA:329, IT:282, NE:324, PO:281.

282 nota de passagem a) Nota mínima que um candidato tem de obter para passar num teste ou num exame.

b) Nos testes de domínio, nota considerada o nível necessário para ter um nível mínimo de competência ou um nível de 'domínios'.
Ver: teste de domínio, avaliação da competência mínima.
Ler: Bachman, 1990, pp.214–215; Crocker e Algina, pp.421–428.

CA:23/359, DA:36/58, DE:52/199, EN:90/273, ES:30/351, FR:277, GA:278/338, IT:280/288, NE:57/341, PO:282.

283 nota escalada Nota resultante dum escalamento.
Ver: escalamento.

CA:349, DA:340, DE:354, EN:345, ES:349, FR:278, GA:337, IT:286, NE:153, PO:283.

284 nota-estanino Procedimento que permite agrupar as notas em nove classes baseadas na frequência normal. Em cada um dos grupos superior e inferior aparecem 4% dos candidatos. A percentagem de candidatos em cada grupo é representada pelo esquema seguinte.

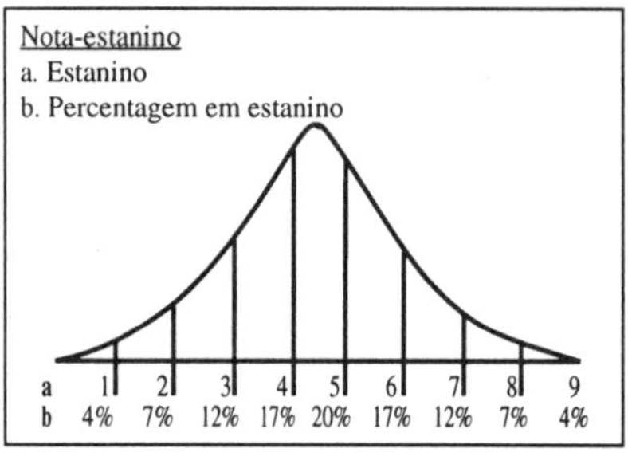

Ler: Crocker e Algina, 1986, pp. 446–447.

CA:344, DA:367, DE:377, EN:384, ES:176, FR:282, GA:332, IT:279, NE:365, PO:284.

285 nota observada Nota obtida por um candidato. Na teoria do teste clássico considera-se que esta nota é uma mistura da nota verdadeira e do erro.
Cf: erro, nota verdadeira.

CA:353, DA:183, DE:49, EN:258, ES:352, FR:279, GA:331, IT:283, NE:429, PO:285.

286 nota ponderada Nota atribuída ao candidato após ponderação.
Ver: ponderação.

CA:354, DA:434, DE:135, EN:437, ES:354, FR:280, GA:339, IT:284, NE:159, PO:286.

287 nota *t* Extensão da nota *z*. Elimina os espaços decimais e os sinais negativos. A nota *t* é igual a 10 vezes a nota *z* mais 50. A distribuição tem uma média de 50 e um desvio-padrão de 10.
Ver: nota *z*.
Ler: Ebel e Frisbie, 1991, p.68.

CA:355, DA:384, DE:388, EN:422, ES:355, FR:283, GA:367, IT:289, NE:376, PO:287.

288 nota transformada Nota bruta que sofreu uma transformação matemática com o objectivo de se proceder a um escalamento ou a uma ponderação.
Ler: Ebel e Frisbie, 1991, pp.64–70.

CA:356, DA:414, DE:415, EN:417, ES:356, FR:284, GA:334, IT:290, NE:158, PO:288.

289 nota verdadeira Nota que um candidato obteria se não houvesse nenhum erro de medição no momento da avaliação ou da classificação. É um conceito fundamental na teoria clássica do teste.

CA:357, DA:415, DE:441, EN:420, ES:357, FR:285, GA:335, IT:285, NE:431, PO:289.

290 nota *z* Nota-padrão frequente, com uma média de 0 e um desvio-padrão de 1. A fórmula para calcular a nota *z* é a seguinte:

$$z=(X-\overline{X}) \div Sx$$

em que

z = nota *z*
X = nota do teste
$\overline{X}$ = nota média do teste
Sx = desvio-padrão das notas do teste

Cf: nota *t*.

Ver: nota-padrão.
Ler: Ebel e Frisbie, 1991, p.68.
CA:358, DA:439, DE:446, EN:442, ES:358, FR:286, GA:441, IT:291, NE:439, PO:290.

291 nota-padrão Nota transformada linearmente a partir dum grupo de notas. Os desvios médio e padrão são ajustados ao valor que exige o utilizador. Exemplos de notas-padrão são as notas z e t.
Cf: nota *t*, nota *z*, nota estanino.
Ler: Ebel e Frisbie, 1991, pp. 67–68.
CA:350, DA:365, DE:376, EN:382, ES:350, FR:281, GA:333, IT:287, NE:364, PO:291.

292 objectivo de aprendizagem Fim ou resultado desejado duma actividade educativa.
CA:277, DA:136, DE:215, EN:208, ES:290, FR:289, GA:360, IT:255, NE:217, PO:292.

293 objectivos Objectivos dos cursos e programas educacionais envolvendo conhecimentos, competências e atitudes.
CA:278, DA:244, DE:216, EN:256, ES:291, FR:288, GA:359, IT:254, NE:112, PO:293.

294 opções Diferentes possibilidades a partir das quais a escolha correcta deve ser seleccionada num item de escolha múltipla ou de correspondência.
CA:279, DA:425, DE:38, EN:262, ES:292, FR:290, GA:293, IT:258, NE:14, PO:294.

295 padronização Processo pelo qual se assegura que os examinadores concordam com um determinado procedimento e aplicam correctamente as escalas de classificação.
Ver: examinador.
CA:167, DA:363, DE:373, EN:383, ES:175, NE:361, FR:162, GA:45, IT:338, PO:295.

296 parâmetro Característica duma população, por exemplo, o desvio-padrão.
Cf: estatística.
CA:280, DA:276, DE:279, EN:269, ES:293, FR:291, GA:272, IT:259, NE:280, PO:296.

297 parâmetro-A Um dos parâmetros da teoria item-resposta. Refere-se à discriminação dum item.
Ver: teoria item-resposta (TIR).
Ler: Bachman, 1990, p.204.
CA:281, DA:1, DE:84, EN:1, ES:294, FR:292, GA:273, IT:260, NE:1, PO:297.

298 parâmetro-B Um dos parâmetros da teoria item-resposta. Refere-se ao grau de dificuldade dum item.
Ver: teoria item-resposta (TIR).
Ler: Bachaman, 1990, p.204.
CA:282, DA:24, DE:170, EN:26, ES:295, FR:293, GA:274, IT:261, NE:26, PO:298.

299 parâmetro-C Um dos parâmetros da teoria item-resposta. Refere-se à acção de adivinhar.
Ver: teoria item-resposta (TIR).
Ler: Bachman, 1990, p.204.
CA:283, DA:44, DE:318, EN:37, ES:296, FR:294, GA:275, IT:262, NE:50, PO:299.

300 parâmetro de dificuldade Refere-se à definição de parâmetro-B.
CA:285, DA:379, DE:344, EN:102, ES:298, FR:296, GA:276, IT:264, NE:250, PO:300.

301 parâmetro por adivinhação Refere-se à definição de parâmetro-C.
CA:284, DA:122, DE:319, EN:159, ES:297, FR:295, GA:277, IT:263, NE:160, PO:301.

302 percentil Escala com 99 pontos que divide uma frequência de distribuição em 100 grupos de grandeza equivalente. A média corresponde ao quinquagésimo percentil (P50). A distribuição é dividida em quatro grupos iguais designados quartis.
Ler: Hatch e Lazaraton, 1991, pp. 187–188.
CA:287, DA:280, DE:285, EN:275, ES:299, FR:49, GA:279, IT:266, NE:284, PO:302.

303 perfilar Meio de apresentação dos resultados dos testes, que separa as diferentes componentes a fim de que o candidato ou outros utilizadores possam identificar os pontos fortes e os pontos fracos.
CA:288, DA:297, DE:404, EN:297, ES:300, FR:312, GA:282, IT:395, NE:307, PO:303.

304 performance sin: actuação. Uso de uma língua pela produção de textos orais ou escritos. A performance, na acepção de uso da língua, é muitas vezes oposta à competência subjacente ao conhecimento da língua.
Cf: competência.
Ver: teste de performance.
Ler: Bachman, 1990, pp.52 e 108.
CA:5, DA:282, DE:283, EN:277, ES:9, FR:297, GA:141, IT:267, NE:286, PO:304.

305 plano multiatributo-multimétodo Plano experimental utilizado na validação de constructos na qual um conjunto de

atributos supostamente distintos são medidos por cada um de um conjunto de métodos supostamente distintos. A análise deveria, por exemplo, mostrar que as medidas da capacidade de compreensão oral, obtidas com ajuda de diferentes métodos, estão em maior correlação umas com as outras do que as medidas de diferentes capacidades obtidas com a ajuda dum único método de avaliação.
Ler: Bachman, 1990, pp.263–265.
CA:108, DA:238, DE:252, EN:243, ES:109, FR:299, GA:111, IT:277, NE:254, PO:305.

306 ponderação Acção de atribuir um número diferente de pontos máximos a um item de teste, uma tarefa ou uma composição, com o objectivo de mudar a sua contribuição relativa para o conjunto dos pontos, em função das outras partes do teste. Se, por exemplo, se atribui uma nota dupla a todos os itens da tarefa nº1 dum teste, a tarefa nº1 é proporcionalmente mais importante que as outras tarefas no total de pontos obtidos.
Ler: Ebel e Frisbie, 1991, pp. 214–216.
CA:290, DA:435, DE:136, EN:438, ES:303, FR:302, GA:439, IT:268, NE:434, PO:306.

307 ponto testável Foco dum item: ponto específico com o qual se tenta obter produção de conhecimento.
CA:128, DA:399, DE:309, EN:409, ES:289, FR:300, GA:281, IT:293, NE:384, PO:307.

308 população Conjunto completo de valores, por exemplo o conjunto de todos os candidatos que participam num teste. Conhecido em estatística com o nome 'universo de notas'.
Cf: amostra.
CA:289, DA:292, DE:290, EN:285, ES:302, FR:303, GA:280, IT:269, NE:294, PO:308.

309 portefólio de avaliação Técnica de avaliação pela qual o candidato guarda, durante um determinado período, exemplos dos seus trabalhos e apresenta-os como prova das suas capacidades.
CA:386, DA:293, DE:291, EN:286, ES:185, FR:304, GA:237, IT:270, NE:37, PO:309.

310 pós-teste Teste ou outra forma de medição aplicada no fim duma formação. Os resultados comparados com o mesmo teste aplicado no início da formação determinam a eficácia da formação.
Cf: pré-teste.
CA:327, DA:345, DE:5, EN:287, ES:336, FR:305, GA:179, IT:271, NE:295, PO:310.

311 pré-testagem Etapa da concepção do material dos testes durante a qual se testam os itens em amostras representativas da população-alvo com o objectivo de determinar o seu grau de dificuldade. Depois de analisados estatisticamente, os itens considerados satisfatórios podem ser usados nos testes reais.
Cf: experimentação.
CA:174, DA:105, DE:436, EN:293, ES:191, FR:307, GA:289, IT:273, NE:302, PO:311.

312 pré-teste Teste aplicado antes do início duma formação. Os resultados do pré-teste são comparados com os do teste aplicado no fim da formação com o objectivo de avaliar a eficácia da formação.
Cf: pós-teste.
CA:333, DA:104, DE:440, EN:292, ES:338, FR:306, GA:290, IT:272, NE:299, PO:312.

313 preparação de amostras Selecção de uma amostragem.
Ver: amostra.
CA:267, DA:374, DE:384, EN:340, ES:281, FR:120, GA:307, IT:45, NE:368, PO:313.

314 procedimentos de dedução Técnica para obter do candidato uma resposta a uma questão. Usado habitualmente nos testes de produção oral.
Ler: Hughes, 1989, pp. 104–110.
CA:293, DA:8, DE:212, EN:123, ES:307, FR:308, GA:162, IT:276, NE:320, PO:314.

315 procedimentos não-paramétricos Procedimentos estatísticos que garantem apenas que os dados vêm dum tipo determinado de distribuição ou que os dados não se baseiam numa escala de intervalo. O Qui-quadrado é um exemplo.
Cf: procedimentos paramétricos.
Ler: Hatch e Lazaraton, 1991, 237–239.
CA:294, DA:131, DE:259, EN:249, ES:308, FR:309, GA:258, IT:274, NE:257, PO:315.

316 procedimentos paramétricos Procedimentos estatísticos que pressupõem que os dados estão distribuídos normalmente e são medidos com escalas de intervalo e de relação. Na prática, os procedimentos paramétricos são usados quando se dispõe dum número de casos suficiente para que os dados se aproximem duma distribuição normal.

Cf: procedimentos não-paramétricos.
Ler: Hatch e Lazaraton, 1991, pp. 237–238.
CA:295, DA:277, DE:280, EN:270, ES:309, FR:310, GA:259, IT:275, NE:281, PO:316.

317 produção escrita guiada O candidato deve produzir um texto escrito de acordo com informação gráfica ou textual, como imagens, cartas, postais, gráficos, etc., dada com o objectivo de controlar e padronizar a resposta esperada.
Cf: composição, ensaio.
CA:393, DA:121, DE:130, EN:160, ES:5, FR:311, GA:377, IT:76, NE:143, PO:317.

318 programa Documento detalhado no qual se encontram listadas todas as áreas dum programa de estudos específico e a ordem em que o conteúdo é apresentado.
Cf: curriculum.
CA:299, DA:224, DE:207, EN:392, ES:310, FR:352, GA:352, IT:335, NE:225, PO:318.

319 quadrado da média Designação dada à variância numa análise de variância (ANOVA).
Ver: ANOVA.
CA:251, DA:230, DE:245, EN:229, ES:262, FR:47, GA:227, IT:295, NE:149, PO:319.

320 quadro de contingência Quadro de frequências classificadas segundo dois ou mais conjuntos de valores de variáveis categóricas.
Exemplo:

	Domínio	Não–Domínio
Método A	35	5
Método B	20	20

Ver: teste Qui-quadrado.
CA:398, DA:187, DE:187, EN:74, ES:390, FR:353, GA:369, IT:347, NE:75, PO:320.

321 quadro do interlocutor Instruções escritas sobre a linguagem que um examinador deve utilizar durante os testes de expressão oral de forma a que ela seja padronizada tornando assim o teste mais justo e fiável para todos os candidatos.
CA:198, DA:324, DE:438, EN:179, ES:215, FR:34, GA:151, IT:128, NE:156, PO:321.

322 qualificação Menção dada após uma formação reconhecida ou um teste, certificando que um indíviduo está apto a exercer uma actividade ou uma profissão determinada. Um certificado de nível de competência em língua pode ser considerado uma qualificação.
Cf: certificado, diploma.
CA:360, DA:209, DE:314, EN:302, ES:405, FR:313, GA:46, IT:294, NE:214, PO:322.

323 questão Usado, por vezes, para designar uma tarefa ou um item num teste.
Ver: item, tarefa.
CA:291, DA:357, DE:122, EN:303, ES:304, FR:315, GA:55, IT:136, NE:423, PO:323.

324 questão aberta sin: Questão de resposta livre. Tipo de item ou de tarefa num teste escrito que exige do candidato a produção duma resposta (e não seleccioná-la a partir de uma lista de possibilidades). O objectivo deste tipo de item consiste em levar a produzir uma resposta relativamente livre cuja extensão pode ser de algumas palavras ou de um grande número de frases. O esquema de classificação prevê todo um conjunto de respostas mais previsivelmente aceitáveis.
CA:292, DA:444, DE:273, EN:260, ES:305, FR:318, GA:56, IT:137, NE:273, PO:324.

325 reconhecimento (a) Aceitação formal por parte duma instituição duma classificação obtida para um fim específico, por exemplo para admissão num curso superior.

(b) Reconhecimento oficial de sucesso num exame, geralmente por uma entidade oficial, um governo, um centro de exames, etc.
CA:4/365, DA:10/15, DE:8/269, EN:5/323, ES:1/361, FR:4/321, GA:9/92, IT:303, NE:3/123, PO:325.

326 reescalamento Refere-se à definição de escalamento.
CA:367, DA:314, DE:258, EN:330, ES:389, FR:320, GA:29, IT:304, NE:166, PO:326.

327 registo Diferentes variedades de uma língua correspondentes a actividades específicas ou a um certo grau de formalidade.
CA:368, DA:310, DE:366, EN:325, ES:364, FR:323, GA:291, IT:297, NE:317, PO:327.

328 regressão Técnica que permite determinar o valor mais adequado duma variável (variável dependente), a partir de valores conhecidos duma ou de várias outras variáveis (variáveis independentes).
Ler: Hatch e Lazaraton, 1991, pp.

467–480; Guilford e Fruchter, 1981, pp. 346–361.
CA:369, DA:311, DE:321, EN:326, ES:365, FR:324, GA:4, IT:298, NE:318, PO:328.

329 regressão linear Técnica de regressão que pressupõe uma relação linear entre as variáveis dependentes e independentes.
CA:370, DA:215, DE:223, EN:213, ES:366, FR:325, GA:5, IT:299, NE:230, PO:329.

330 regressão múltipla Técnica estatística usada para demostrar os efeitos lineares de várias variáveis independentes sobre uma variável dependente isolada. Se se tomar, por exemplo, a dificuldade da tarefa como variável dependente, é possível investigar os efeitos produzidos por este tipo de tarefa, a dificuldade lexical, etc.
Ver: variável independente, regressão.
Ler: Hatch e Lazaraton, 1991, pp.480–486.
CA:371, DA:117, DE:251, EN:242, ES:367, FR:326, GA:182, IT:300, NE:240, PO:330.

331 relação da parte com o todo Efeito presente, quando, por exemplo, as notas obtidas num sub-teste são relacionadas com a nota obtida no conjunto do teste. A relação é exagerada, dado que as notas do sub-teste estão incluídas nas do conjunto do teste. Existem técnicas que permitem corrigir esta relação da parte para o todo.
Ler: Henning, 1987, p.69.
CA:63, DA:62, DE:282, EN:271, ES:387, FR:51, GA:283, IT:146, NE:276, PO:331.

332 relação-F Na análise da variância, é a relação estimada que indica se as diferenças entre as médias dos grupos são estatisticamente significativas; por exemplo, se um grupo conseguiu melhor média de sucesso num teste de língua do que outro.
Ver: formas alternadas.
Ler: Hatch e Lazaraton, 1991, pp.315–317.
CA:364, DA:94, DE:109, EN:139, ES:368, FR:319, GA:66, IT:296, NE:132, PO:332.

333 repetição Possibilidade de repetir várias vezes os resultados de uma pesquisa, aumentando assim a confiança nos resultados.
CA:373, DA:189, DE:324, EN:329, ES:370, FR:335, GA:185, IT:301, NE:165, PO:333.

334 resposta Reacção do candidato às questões dum teste. Por exemplo, a resposta dada a um item de escolha múltipla ou o trabalho produzido num teste de expressão escrita.
Cf: material-estímulo, estímulo.
CA:374, DA:315, DE:21, EN:331, ES:371, FR:327, GA:153, IT:305, NE:319, PO:334.

335 resposta-chave (a) Opção correcta num item de escolha múltipla.
Cf: diversor.
Ver: item de escolha múltipla.
(b) De forma mais lata, conjunto de todas as respostas correctas ou aceitáveis a itens de testes.
Cf: esquema de classificação.
CA:51/52, DA:256, DE:339, EN:198, ES:54, FR:329, GA:133, DE:339, IT:53, NE:342, PO:335.

336 resposta construída Resposta escrita a um item. Esta resposta implica uma produção activa e não uma simples escolha entre diferentes opções.
Cf: resposta seleccionada.
Ver: resposta.
CA:376, DA:185, DE:126, EN:70, ES:372, FR:330, GA:154, IT:309, NE:272, PO:336.

337 resposta correcta Resposta considerada exacta.
CA:375, DA:190, DE:327, EN:333, ES:373, FR:331, GA:155, IT:307, NE:204, PO:337.

338 resposta esperada Resposta ou respostas que o elaborador dum teste ou dum item espera do candidato numa questão.
CA:377, DA:106, DE:105, EN:137, ES:374, FR:328, GA:157, IT:306, NE:32, PO:338.

339 resposta longa Forma de resposta a um item ou a uma tarefa na qual se espera que o candidato produza (e não seleccione) uma resposta com uma extensão superior a uma ou duas frases.
Cf: item de resposta curta.
CA:378, DA:423, DE:35, EN:138, ES:375, FR:332, GA:159, IT:308, NE:407, PO:339.

340 resposta modelo Exemplo, escrito pelo elaborador do item, de resposta esperada a uma questão aberta. Esta resposta pode ser utilizada na elaboração do esquema de classificação para os avaliadores.
CA:261, DA:233, DE:253, EN:236, ES:376, FR:333, GA:156, IT:245, NE:21, PO:340.

341 resposta seleccionada Forma de resposta a um item que implica uma escolha entre diferentes possibilidades e

não a produção de uma resposta.
Cf: resposta construída.
Ver: resposta.
CA:379, DA:422, DE:37, EN:352, ES:377, FR:334, GA:158, IT:310, NE:154, PO:341.

342 resultado Resultado obtido num teste ou num exame.
CA:380, DA:317, DE:103, EN:332, ES:378, FR:336, GA:397, IT:312, NE:322, PO:342.

343 revisão Etapa na elaboração dum teste durante a qual os elaboradores avaliam o material produzido e decidem rejeitar o que não está conforme às especificações do teste e publicar o que está.
Cf: moderação.
CA:382, DA:400, DE:405, EN:433 ES:383, FR:338, GA:184, IT:91, NE:115, PO:343.

344 rho de Spearman Refere-se à definição do coeficiente de correlação de Spearman.
CA:383, DA:352, DE:362, EN:374, ES:380, FR:339, GA:292, IT:302, NE:348, PO:344.

345 role play sin: Jogo de papéis, jogo de simulações. Tipo de tarefa usada por vezes nos testes de expressão oral e na qual os candidatos devem imaginar estar numa determinada situação de comunicação ou desempenhar um papel.
CA:233, DA:320, DE:329, EN:334, ES:251, FR:232, GA:294, IT:202, NE:323, PO:345.

346 scanner Refere-se à definição de leitor óptico.
CA:160, DA:327, DE:336, EN:347, ES:168, FR:342, GA:322, IT:226, NE:325, PO:346.

347 segurança Área da aplicação dos testes que consiste em evitar a divulgação dos seus conteúdos durante o período em que são usados.
CA:387, DA:335, DE:348, EN:351, ES:382, FR:344, GA:353, IT:333, NE:142, PO:347.

348 significância Conceito estatístico que trata o facto de a resposta ser ou não devida ao acaso.
Ver: erro de tipo 1, erro do tipo 2, hipótese nula.
Ler: Guilford e Fruchter, 1981, pp.208–210.
CA:388, DA:333, DE:349, EN:363, ES:386, FR:76, GA:366, IT:334, NE:338, PO:348.

349 situação de comunicação real Ponto de vista segundo o qual os testes deveriam incluir tarefas que se assemelhassem o mais possível a actividades reais. O conteúdo dum teste para avaliar se um candidato é capaz de participar num curso de língua estrangeira deveria, por exemplo, ser baseado numa análise da língua e das actividades linguístico-comunicativas específicas desse curso.
Ver: autenticidade.
Ler: Bachman, 1990, pp.302–328.
CA:129, DA:433, DE:320, EN:322, ES:134, FR:345, GA:98, IT:23, NE:226, PO:349.

350 subteste Refere-se à definição de componente.
CA:389, DA:377, DE:386, EN:389, ES:388, FR:346, GA:150, IT:345, NE:373, PO:350.

351 tarefa de compreensão escrita Tipo de tarefa que consiste geralmente na leitura de um ou de mais textos com os quais são usados os seguintes itens: escolha múltipla, questões com respostas curtas, transferência de informação, etc.
CA:394, DA:223, DE:220, EN:321, ES:3, FR:357, GA:373, IT:74, NE:224, PO:351.

352 tarefa Combinação de instruções, material-estímulo e respostas. Exemplo: compreensão escrita (leitura de texto), acompanhada de itens de escolha múltipla, aos quais se pode responder com referência a apenas um conjunto de instruções.
CA:391, DA:260, DE:26, EN:393, ES:2, FR:354, GA:371, IT:71, NE:270, PO:352.

353 tarefa de correspondência Tipo de tarefa em que o candidato deve fazer corresponder dois elementos que aparecem em duas listas separadas. Este tipo de tarefa consiste em seleccionar a frase correcta que completa cada uma das frases incompletas propostas. Na componente compreensão escrita, pode, por exemplo, escolher-se de uma lista o tipo de férias ou de livros correspondente à descrição de gostos ou de necessidades de uma determinada personagem.
CA:397, DA:322, DE:452, EN:226, ES:7, FR:21, GA:375, IT:73, NE:238, PO:353.

354 tarefa de correspondência múltipla Propõe-se ao candidato um determinado número de itens para completar sob a forma de questões ou de frases, geralmente a partir dum texto escrito. As respostas são fornecidas por um banco de palavras ou frases que pode ser usado

várias vezes. A vantagem desta apresentação é que as opções não são retiradas à medida que o candidato progride no teste (como noutras formas de correspondência), de modo a que a tarefa não se torna progressivamente mais fácil.
Cf: tarefa de correspondência.
CA:396, DA:100, DE:235, EN:241, ES:8, FR:355, GA:372, IT:72, NE:253, PO:354.

355 tarefa de produção escrita dirigida Refere-se à definição de produção escrita guiada.
CA:392, DA:43, DE:15, EN:105, ES:6, FR:356, GA:376, IT:77, NE:144, PO:355.

356 tendência central (medida da) Maneira de localizar o ponto central ou a média estatística duma distribuição. As três medidas da tendência central mais usadas são a média, a mediana e a moda.
Ler: Henning, 1987, pp.39–40; Guilford e Fruchter, 1981, capítulo 4; Hatch e Lazaraton, 1991, pp.159–164.
CA:246, DA:47, DE:447, EN:45, ES:391, FR:358, GA:62, IT:348, NE:55, PO:356.

357 teoria clássica do teste Teoria de medição que consiste num conjunto de suposições sobre as relações entre as notas reais ou observadas e os factores que as podem afectar, comummente designados erros. Teoria também chamada teoria da nota verdadeira.
Cf: teoria item-resposta (TIR).
Ler: Bachman, 1990, pp.166–187.
CA:399, DA:174, DE:177, EN:50, ES:392, FR:397, GA:387, IT:349, NE:208, PO:357.

358 teoria do atributo latente Refere-se à definição da teoria item-resposta.
CA:402, DA:211, DE:206, EN:207, ES:395, FR:398, GA:390, IT:350, NE:216, PO:358.

359 teoria do generalizável Modelo estatístico de investigação dos efeitos relativos das diferentes fontes de variância nas notas obtidas nos testes.
Ler: Bachman, 1990, p.7; Crocker e Algina, 1986, capítulo 8.
CA:400, DA:115, DE:132, EN:154, ES:393, FR:399, GA:388, IT:351, NE:152, PO:359.

360 teoria item-resposta (TIR) Grupo de modelos matemáticos que permitem relacionar a performance dum indivíduo num teste com o nível de capacidade deste indivíduo. Esses modelos baseiam-se na teoria fundamental que especifica que a performance esperada dum indivíduo a uma determinada questão dum teste é função do nível de dificuldade da questão e do nível de capacidade do indivíduo.
Ler: Henning, 1987, capítulo 8; Crocker e Algina, 1986, capítulo 15.
CA:401, DA:159, DE:173/296, EN:195, ES:394, FR:400, GA:389, IT:352, NE:201, PO:360.

361 teste Procedimento para avaliar aspectos específicos da proficiência ou do conhecimento usado muitas vezes na mesma acepção de exame.

a) Conjunto de componentes que constituem um procedimento avaliativo.

b) Tarefa ou componente para avaliar uma capacidade ou conhecimento, como por exemplo, a expressão escrita ou oral. Neste sentido, um teste pode também fazer parte dum exame completo como componente (por exemplo, o teste de expressão oral) ou como uma única tarefa (por exemplo, o teste cloze).

c) Um procedimento avaliativo relativamente pequeno e fácil de aplicar, muitas vezes concebido e aplicado dentro de uma instituição (por exemplo um teste de progresso) ou usado no âmbito de uma investigação ou com o objectivo de validar (por exemplo, teste-âncora).
Cf: exame.
Ver: teste de estruturação perceptiva, teste de progresso, teste-âncora.
Ler: Bachman, 1990, p.50
CA:300, DA:300, DE:389, EN:395, ES:311, FR:359, GA:403, IT:353, NE:388, PO:361.

362 teste (item) activo Teste pronto para ser aplicado e que deve, por isso, ser guardado em segurança.
CA:341, DA:101, DE:225, EN:217, ES:344, FR:360, GA:407, IT:355, NE:233, PO:362.

363 teste adaptativo sin: teste a pedido. Método de avaliação no qual o nível de dificuldade das questões é escolhido durante a aplicação do teste, em função da determinação da capacidade do candidato. É muitas vezes usado nos testes por computador.
Ver: teste adaptativo por computador.
Ler: Bachman, 1990, p.151; Henning, 1987, p.136.
CA:302, DA:102, DE:6, EN:7, ES:312, FR:361, GA:429, IT:356, NE:5, PO:363.

364 teste adaptativo por computador Método de avaliação por computador no qual é possível adaptar o nível de dificuldade dos itens apresentados à capacidade

do candidato, em função das respostas dadas.
Ver: avaliação por computador.
CA:303, DA:51, DE:67, EN:63, ES:181, FR:362, GA:379, IT:386, NE:68, PO:364.

365 teste-âncora Composto por um grupo de itens-âncora, este teste, com características de medição conhecidas, é aplicado em associação com outro teste. A performance no teste-âncora dá informação sobre o outro teste e os candidatos que fi-zeram ambos os testes. Isto permite determinar quer as diferenças de nível de dificuldade entre várias versões do teste, quer as diferenças de performance entre vários grupos de candidatos.
Cf: item-âncora.
CA:307, DA:17, DE:19, EN:16, ES:320, FR:367, GA:404, IT:357, NE:18, PO:365.

366 teste-C Tipo de tarefa lacunar na qual a segunda parte de algumas palavras é suprimida. A frequência da supressão pode ir até uma palavra em cada duas. A tarefa a realizar pelo candidato consiste em completar a parte que falta a essas palavras.
Cf: teste de estruturação perceptiva.
Ler: Weir, 1990, p.49.
CA:304, DA:45, DE:62, EN:38, ES:314, FR:394, GA:408, IT:384, NE:51, PO:366.

367 teste cloze racional Refere-se à definição de teste de estruturação perceptiva ou teste cloze.
CA:314, DA:308, DE:230, EN:318, ES:316, FR:371, GA:60, IT:56, NE:315, PO:367.

368 teste com referência a um domínio Teste cujos resultados são interpretados em função dum domínio específico de conteúdos ou de níveis de capacidade.
Cf: teste criterial, teste normativo.
CA:335, DA:84, DE:50, EN:120, ES:342, FR:391, GA:417, IT:382, NE:114, PO:368.

369 teste criterial sin: teste centrado em objectivos. Teste no qual a performance do candidato é interpretada em função de critérios pré-determinados. Atingir os objectivos é mais importante do que os resultados dos candidatos.
CA:337, DA:203, DE:196, EN:81, ES:317, FR:364, GA:412, IT:380, NE:86, PO:369.

370 teste de aptidão Teste concebido para avaliar as probabilidades de sucesso dum candidato numa determinada área, por exemplo, na aprendizagem duma língua estrangeira ou em estudos específicos.
Ler: Henning, 1987, p.6; Ebel e Frisbie, 1991, p.339.
CA:308, DA:18, DE:96, EN:20, ES:322, FR:368, GA:421, IT:358, NE:22, PO:370.

371 teste de capacidade Teste com uma duração que permite que todos os candidatos o possam terminar, contendo, no entanto, tarefas ou itens com um grau de dificuldade que tornam pouco provável que a maioria dos candidatos o resolvam correctamente na totalidade.
Cf: teste de velocidade.
CA:310, DA:299, DE:261/293, EN:288, ES:329, FR:379, GA:413, IT:360, NE:296, PO:371.

372 teste de colocação sin: teste de nível. Teste aplicado com o objectivo de colocar os estudantes num grupo com o nível que corresponda ao seu grau de conhecimentos e de capacidades.
CA:311, DA:137, DE:101, EN:282, ES:323, FR:377, GA:434, IT:365, NE:291, PO:372.

373 teste de compreensão oral Teste de compreensão da linguagem oral. É aplicado normalmente com a ajuda dum gravador ou dum video.
CA:315, DA:221, DE:147, EN:216, ES:324, FR:372, GA:411, IT:361, NE:235, PO:373.

374 teste de conhecimentos Teste destinado a medir os conhecimentos adquiridos por um candidato num curso, num manual, etc., ligado, por isso, a um curriculum.
CA:309/322, DA:20/366, DE:203/369, EN:6/23, ES:321/331, FR:366/374, GA:419, IT:368, NE:301/421, PO:374.

375 teste de despistagem Teste normalmente curto e simples de aplicar, usado com o objectivo de identificar quais dos candidatos podem ser admitidos num curso ou quem pode candidatar-se a um exame.
Ver: teste de nível.
CA:316, DA:424, DE:98, EN:349, ES:332, FR:375, GA:432, IT:370, NE:332, PO:375.

376 teste de domínio Teste cujo objectivo consiste em determinar se um estudante domina bem uma dada área de conhecimento ou uma ou mais capacidades.
CA:338, DA:227, DE:204, EN:225, ES:327, FR:376, GA:425, IT:366, NE:237, PO:376.

377 teste de entrada Teste usado para determinar se um candidato pode ou não ser admitido num estabelecimento de ensino ou a seguir um programa de estudos.
Cf: teste de nível de capacidade.

CA:305, DA:5, DE:346, EN:124, ES:319, FR:369, GA:422, IT:364, NE:387, PO:377.

378 teste de estruturação perceptiva sin: teste cloze. Tipo de tarefa lacunar na qual palavras inteiras são suprimidas dum texto. Num teste de estruturação perceptiva tradicional, suprime-se uma palavra cada x palavras. Também se designa teste cloze o exercício em que frases curtas são suprimidas dum texto ou quando o elaborador escolhe as palavras que serão suprimidas, como é o caso do teste de estruturação perceptiva racional. Os candidatos devem fornecer as palavras que faltam (teste aberto) ou escolhê-las a partir de uma lista (escolha múltipla ou teste cloze de lacunas selectivas). A classificação dum teste aberto pode ser feita pelo método da palavra exacta (só é aceite a palavra do texto que foi apagada) ou pelo método das palavras aceitáveis (o que pressupõe a existência duma lista de palavras aceitáveis).
Cf: teste-C, item de completamento.
Ler: Weir, 1990, pp.46–48; Oller, 1979, capítulo 12.

CA:313, DA:50, DE:66, EN:52, ES:315, FR:370, GA:410, IT:362, NE:61, PO:378.

379 teste de nível de capacidade sin: teste de proficiência. Teste que avalia a capacidade ou aptidão geral, sem referência a nenhuma formação específica nem a qualquer conjunto de material.

CA:320, DA:112, DE:120, EN:296, ES:326, FR:378, GA:428, IT:363, NE:306, PO:379.

380 teste dependente de curriculum Teste ligado a um programa determinado. Desempenha um papel importante no processo educativo.
Cf: teste independente de curriculum.
Ver: teste de conhecimentos.

CA:325, DA:56, DE:217, EN:88, ES:313, FR:365, GA:406, IT:374, NE:221, PO:380.

381 teste de performance Procedimento de avaliação no qual se pede ao candidato uma produção oral ou escrita. Estes procedimentos são concebidos muitas vezes de modo a simular uma performance com um uso da língua semelhante ao que se encontraria em contextos reais de comunicação.
Ler: Bachman, 1990, pp.304–305.

CA:306, DA:283, DE:284, EN:278, ES:318, FR:380, GA:416, IT:367, NE:287, PO:381.

382 teste de progresso Teste aplicado durante a formação e cujo objectivo consiste em validar a aprendizagem realizada até à data do teste.

CA:320, DA:108, DE:214, EN:298, ES:330, FR:381, GA:418, IT:369, NE:422, PO:382.

383 teste de selecção Refere-se à definição de teste de entrada.

CA:323, DA:330, DE:36, EN:353, ES:332, FR:382, GA:430, IT:370, NE:333, PO:383.

384 teste de significância Teste para a significância estatística.

CA:324, DA:334, DE:350, EN:364, ES:333, FR:373, GA:435, IT:371, NE:339, PO:384.

385 teste de velocidade Teste com duração limitada. Os candidatos mais lentos têm uma nota inferior dado que não conseguem acabar o teste. Num teste de velocidade, o nível de dificuldade das questões é tal que os candidatos responderiam correctamente se não fosse a restrição de tempo.
Cf: teste de capacidade.

CA:321, DA:129, DE:340/363, EN:376, ES:334, FR:363, GA:424, IT:372, NE:352, PO:385.

386 teste diagnóstico Usado para determinar os pontos fortes e as dificuldades dum aprendente. Os resultados podem ser úteis na tomada de decisões relativamente à formação, aprendizagem ou ensino futuros.

CA:317, DA:65, DE:77, EN:97, ES:325, FR:383, GA:414, IT:373, NE:97, PO:386.

387 teste directo Teste que avalia a capacidade de produção oral ou escrita e no qual a performance é avaliada directamente. Um exemplo consiste em avaliar a produção escrita através duma carta.
Cf: teste indirecto (tarefa).
Ler: Hughes, 1989, pp.14–16.

CA:326, DA:70, DE:81, EN:104, ES:335, FR:384, GA:415, IT:375, NE:102, PO:387.

388 teste independente de curriculum Teste independente de programas de estudos.
Cf: teste dependente de curriculum.
Ver: teste de nível de capacidade.

CA:328, DA:57, DE:218, EN:89, ES:339, FR:387, GA:405, IT:376, NE:222, PO:388.

389 teste indirecto (tarefa) Teste ou tarefa cujo objectivo consiste mais em avaliar as capacidades subjacentes a uma capacidade da linguagem do que a performance na própria capacidade. Um exemplo consiste em avaliar a capacidade de pro-

dução escrita solicitando ao candidato que assinale as estruturas usadas incorrectamente num texto.
Cf: teste directo.
Ler: Hughes, 1989, pp.14–16.
CA:329, DA:135, DE:150, EN:170, ES:337, FR:385, GA:420, IT:354, NE:173, PO:389.

390 teste lacunar de escolha múltipla Tipo de item dum teste no qual o candidato deve escolher a palavra ou frase correcta, a partir de várias opções, para inserir num espaço em branco num texto.
Ver: item de completamento.
CA:224, DA:237, DE:250, EN:239, ES:242, FR:386, GA:215, IT:79, NE:251, PO:390.

391 teste normativo sin: teste centrado em normas. Teste em que as notas são interpretadas em relação à performance dum dado grupo composto por pessoas comparáveis àquelas a quem o teste foi aplicado. Tende a usar-se este termo em testes cujo objectivo consiste em nivelar os indivíduos em função do grupo de referência ou uns em relação aos outros.
Cf: teste criterial.
CA:336, DA:251, DE:268, EN:254, ES:340, FR:388, GA:426, IT:381, NE:264, PO:391.

392 teste objectivo Teste a que se pode aplicar um esquema de classificação e que dispensa a opinião de um especialista ou de um juízo subjectivo.
CA:331, DA:257, DE:272, EN:257, ES:341, FR:389, GA:427, IT:377, NE:267, PO:392.

393 teste para fins específicos Teste concebido para avaliar a capacidade dum candidato num contexto profissional ou académico específico. Os conteúdos do teste são elaborados em função duma análise das tarefas comunicativas em que o candidato se verá envolvido nas situações de comunicação da língua-alvo.
CA:318, DA:243, DE:112, EN:375, ES:328, FR:393, GA:431, IT:378, NE:351, PO:393.

394 teste psicométrico Teste que assenta em traços psicológicos como a personalidade, a inteligência, as capacidades e o nível de competência em língua e que coloca hipóteses sobre a natureza da capacidade testada, como por exemplo, que é unidimensional e distribuída normalmente.
Ler: Bachman, 1990, pp.73–74.
CA:334, DA:302, DE:310, EN:301, ES:397, FR:390, GA:433, IT:379, NE:308, PO:394.

395 teste Qui-quadrado Procedimento estatístico que compara os valores das respostas observadas e os das respostas esperadas, com o objectivo de indicar se a diferença é estatisticamente significativa, tendo em consideração as respostas esperadas. Trata-se de um procedimento não-paramétrico.
Ver: procedimentos não-paramétricos.
Ler: Hatch e Lazaraton, 1991, pp.393–415.
CA:330, DA:49, DE:65, EN:49, ES:396, FR:149, GA:409, IT:359, NE:59, PO:395.

396 teste semi-directo Teste que tenta avaliar as performances em língua sem a intervenção dum examinador, por exemplo, num teste de expressão oral, o uso de um gravador que fornece o material-estímulo em vez deste ser dado por um entrevistador. O SOPI (semi-direct proficiency interview – entrevista de capacidade oral semi-directa) é um exemplo deste tipo de teste.
Cf: teste directo.
CA:339, DA:332, DE:347, EN:356, ES:343, FR:392, GA:423, IT:383, NE:336, PO:396.

397 teste-T Teste estatístico usado para determinar se existe uma diferença significativa entre as médias de duas amostragens.
CA:340, DA:385, DE:387, EN:423, ES:398, FR:150, GA:368, IT:385, NE:377, PO:397.

398 texto Discurso articulado, escrito ou oral, usado para elaborar um conjunto de itens dum teste.
CA:403, DA:386, DE:411, EN:411, ES:399, FR:396, GA:381, IT:389, NE:381, PO:398.

399 tipo de item Os itens de testes são nomeados pelos nomes que descrevem a sua forma. Exemplos: escolha múltipla, transformação de frases, resposta curta, teste cloze aberto.
CA:406, DA:162, DE:174, EN:197 ES:403, FR:405, GA:58, IT:392, NE:203, PO:399.

400 tipo de questão Refere-se à definição de tipo de item ou de tipo de tarefa.
CA:407, DA:358, DE:124, EN:305, ES:404, FR:406, GA:57, IT:394, NE:424, PO:400.

401 tipo de tarefa Os tipos de tarefa

são nomeados pelos nomes que descrevem o que está a ser testado e a sua forma. Exemplos: compreensão escrita com escolha múltipla, produção escrita guiada, etc.

CA:408, DA:265, DE:30, EN:394, ES:402, FR:407, GA:59, IT:393, NE:271, PO:401.

402 TIR Refere-se à definição de teoria item-resposta.

CA:412, DA:153, DE:165, EN:188, ES:408, FR:401, GA:392, IT:352, NE:194, PO:402.

403 traço Característica de uma pessoa (como por exemplo a capacidade numa língua), ou escala de medida para descrever esta característica.

CA:411, DA:416, DE:95, EN:415, ES:360, FR:23, GA:400, IT:26, NE:403, PO:403.

404 transferência de informação Técnica de avaliação que implica apresentar uma informação dada sob uma determinada forma numa outra de forma diferente. Exemplo: transformar uma nota informal num anúncio formal; legendar um quadro a partir de informação dada num texto.
Ler: Hughes, 1989, pp. 84, 124–125, 138.

CA:409, DA:141, DE:152, EN:173, ES:406, FR:402, GA:8, IT:396, NE:177, PO:404.

405 transformação de frases Tipo de item no qual é dado uma frase completa, seguida pela primeira ou duas ou três primeiras palavras duma segunda frase com o mesmo conteúdo da frase completa dada, mas com uma forma gramatical diferente. A primeira frase pode estar, por exemplo, na forma activa e deve ser transformada na forma passiva, mantendo o mesmo significado.

CA:410, DA:381, DE:334, EN:359, ES:407, FR:404, GA:61, IT:397, NE:440, PO:405.

406 unidimensionalidade Dimensão única que é uma suposição necessária para elaborar uma escala que permite medir os traços psicológicos, por exemplo utilizando modelos item-resposta de uso corrente. A unidimensionalidade é a propriedade do instrumento de medição e não do processo psicológico subjacente.
Ler: Crocker e Algina, 1986, p.343.

CA:413, DA:90, DE:97, EN:427, ES:410, FR:409, GA:23, IT:398, NE:119, PO:406.

407 utilizador de teste Pessoa (por exemplo, um ensinante ou empregador) ou instituição que utiliza os resultados dum teste com o objectivo de tomar uma decisão sobre o examinando.

CA:414, DA:391, DE:392, EN:407, ES:410, FR:409, GA:440, IT:399, NE:393, PO:407.

408 validação Processo pelo qual se recolhe informação para apoiar as conclusões tiradas a partir das notas dos testes. São as conclusões respeitantes a usos específicos dum teste que são validadas e não o teste propriamente dito.
Ver: validade.

CA:415, DA:426, DE:426, EN:429, ES:412, FR:412, GA:39, IT:400, NE:414, PO:408.

409 validade Grau pelo qual as notas dum teste permitem tirar conclusões adequadas, significativas e úteis, em relação com o objectivo do teste. Há vários tipos de validade: validade de conteúdo, validade criterial e validade de constructo, as quais fornecem diferentes tipos de informação que permite avaliar a validade global dum teste em função dos seus objectivos.
Ver: validade concorrente, validade de constructo, validade criterial, validade de conteúdo, validade convergente, validade discriminante, validade predictiva.
Ler: Bachman, 1990, pp. 25, 236–237.

CA:416, DA:427, DE:427, EN:430, ES:413, FR:413, GA:30, IT:401, NE:415, PO:409.

410 validade aparente Qualidade dum teste ou de qualquer outra medida que pareça correcta e adequada ao objecto medido. Trata-se mais de um juízo subjectivo do que de um juízo baseado numa análise objectiva do teste. A validade aparente é muitas vezes considerada uma forma falsa de validade. Também se designa muitas vezes 'atracção dum teste'.
Cf: validade.
Ler: Bachman, 1990, pp.285–289.

CA:417, DA:272, DE:110/34, EN:140, ES:414, FR:414 GA:2, IT:402, NE:174, PO:410.

411 validade concorrente Diz-se que um teste tem validade concorrente se as notas obtidas estão em correlação alta com um critério reconhecido que mede a mesma área de conhecimento ou de capacidade.
Ver: validade criterial.
Ler: Bachman, 1990, pp.248–250.

CA:418, DA:323, DE:417, EN:66, ES:415, FR:415, GA:33, IT:403, NE:71, PO:411.

412 validade convergente Diz-se que um teste tem validade convergente quando há uma correlação alta entre as notas obtidas nesse teste e as notas obtidas

noutro teste que mede o mesmo constructo (independentemente do método). Tal pode ser considerado um aspecto da validade de constructo.
Cf: validade discriminante.
Ver: validade de constructo.
Ler: Guilford e Fruchter, 1981, pp.436–437.
CA:419, DA:188, DE:188, EN:75, ES:416, FR:416, GA:32, IT:404, NE:76, PO:412.

413 validade criterial Diz-se que um teste tem uma validade criterial se se puder demonstrar a relação entre as notas obtidas num teste e um critério externo que se pensa ser uma medida da mesma capacidade. Na ausência de critério, a informação fornecida indica até que ponto o teste pode predizer o comportamento futuro.
Ver: validade concorrente, validade predictiva.
Ler: Bachman, 1990, pp.248–250.
CA:421, DA:204, DE:197, EN:82, ES:417, FR:417, GA:34, IT:407, NE:87, PO:413.

414 validade de constructo sin: validade hipotético-dedutiva/validade conceptual. Diz-se que um teste tem uma validade de constructo se as notas obtidas puderem reflectir uma teoria sobre a natureza dum constructo ou sobre a relação deste constructo com outros. Poder-se-ia predizer, por exemplo, que dois testes válidos de compreensão oral nivelam os aprendentes da mesma maneira, mas cada um deles teria uma relação mais fraca com as notas obtidas num teste de competência gramatical.
Ver: validade, especificações dum teste.
Ler: Ebel e Frisbie, 1991, p.108; Hatch e Lazaraton, 1991, pp. 37–38.
CA:420, DA:186, DE:186, EN:69, ES:418, FR:418, GA:37, IT:406, NE:73, PO:414.

415 validade de conteúdo Diz-se que um teste tem uma validade de conteúdo se os itens ou as tarefas que o compõem constituem uma amostragem representativa dos itens ou das tarefas para a capacidade ou área de conhecimentos a ser testada.
Ver: validade, especificações dum teste.
Ler: Bachman, 1990, p.244–247.
CA:422, DA:134, DE:154, EN:73, ES:419, FR:419, GA:31, IT:405, NE:179, PO:415.

416 validade discriminante Diz-se que um teste tem uma validade discriminante se a correlação que estabelece com testes que avaliam diferentes traços é mais fraca do que aquela que tem com testes que avaliam o mesmo traço sem ter em conta o método de avaliação, o que pode ser considerado um aspecto da validade de constructo.
Cf: validade convergente.
Ver: validade de constructo.
Ler: Crocker e Algina, 1986, p.23; Guilford e Fruchter, 1981, pp.436–437.
CA:423, DA:73, DE:83, EN:111, ES:420, FR:420, GA:36, IT:408, NE:108, PO:416.

417 validade divergente Refere-se à definição de validade discriminante.
CA:424, DA:81, DE:90, EN:118, ES:421, FR:421, GA:35, IT:409, NE:111, PO:417.

418 validade predictiva sin: validade de previsão. Indica a maneira como um teste pode predizer a performance futura numa dada capacidade.
Cf: validade criterial.
Ler: Guilford e Fruchter, 1987, pp.437–438.
CA:425, DA:298, DE:294/439, EN:291, ES:422, FR:422, GA:38, IT:410, NE:300, PO:418.

419 valor de facilidade Refere-se à definição de índice de facilidade.
CA:426, DA:192, DE:209, EN:143, ES:423, FR:410, GA:217, IT:411, NE:147, PO:419.

420 valor-*p* Refere-se à definição de índice de facilidade.
CA:427, DA:273, DE:276, EN:266, ES:424, FR:411, GA:269, IT:412, NE:277, PO:420.

421 variância Medida da dispersão duma série de notas; quanto maior for, mais as notas individuais se afastarão da média.
CA:434, DA:429, DE:429, EN:432, ES:434, FR:427, GA:24, IT:420, NE:417, PO:421.

422 variável (a) Nome dado a uma série de observações a um item o qual pode ser um item de teste, o género, a idade ou a nota obtida.

(b) Elemento, num projecto experimental ou numa análise estatística, que pode ter uma série de valores. Por exemplo, as variáveis de interesse, em avaliação de línguas, contém a dificuldade dos itens, o género e a idade dos examinandos, etc.
CA:430, DA:428, DE:428, EN:431, ES:430, FR:423, GA:25, IT:416, NE:416, PO:422.

423 variável-critério Termo usado em investigação, equivalente a variável dependente.
Cf: variável dependente.
CA:431, DA:205, DE:198, EN:83, ES:431, FR:424, GA:26, IT:417, NE:88, PO:423.

424 variável dependente Variável que indica o fenómeno que o investigador

procura explicar. As notas obtidas num teste (variável independente) podem, por exemplo, ser usadas para predizer o sucesso profissional (variável dependente).
Cf: variável independente.
Ver: variável.
Ler: Hatch e Lazaraton, 1991, p.63.
CA:432, DA:7, DE:2, EN:94, ES:432, FR:425, GA:28, IT:418, NE:7, PO:424.

425 variável independente Para o investigador é uma variável que pode ter uma relação com uma variável dependente ou influenciá-la. Por exemplo, as notas obtidas num teste (variável independente) podem ser usadas para predizer um sucesso profissional (variável dependente).
Cf: variável dependente.
Ver: variável.
Ler: Hatch e Lazaraton, 1991, p.64.
CA:433, DA:420, DE:422, EN:169, ES:433, FR:426, GA:27, IT:419, NE:268, PO:425.

References

Bachman, L. F., 1990. *Fundamental Considerations in Language Testing*. Oxford University Press.

Bortz, J., 1984. *Leherbuch der empirischen Forschung*. Berlin:Springer.

Bortz, J., 1993. *Statistik. Für Sozialwissenschaftler (4.Aufl.)*. Berlin: Springer.

Bortz, J., Lienert, G. A., Boehne, K., 1990, *Verteilungsfreie Methoden in der Biostatistik*. Berlin:Springer.

Crocker, L. and Algina J., 1986. *Introduction to Classical and Modern Test Theory*. Harcourt Brace Jovanovich.

Ebel, R. L. and Frisbie, D. A., 1991. *Essentials of Educational Measurement*. Prentice-Hall.

Fischer, G. H., 1983, 'Neuere Testtheorie', in C. F. Graumann, T. Hermann, M. Irle, H. Thomae & F. Weinert (Hg.), *Enzyklopädie der Psychologie, 3, Messen und Testen* (S. 604–692). Göttingen: Hogrefe.

Fisseni, H.-J., 1990, *Leherbuch der psychologischen Diagnostik*. Göttingen: Hogrefe.

Gronlund, N. E., 1988. *How to Construct Achievement Tests*. Prentice-Hall.

Guilford, J. P. and Fruchter, B., 1981. *Fundamental Statistics in Psychology and Education.*, McGraw-Hill.

Hambleton, R. K., Swaminathan, H., Rogers, H. J., 1991. *Fundamentals of Item Response Theory (vol. 2)*. Sage Publications.

Hatch, E. and Lazaraton, A., 1991. *The Research Manual - design and statistics for applied linguistics*. Newbury House.

Henning, G., 1987. *A Guide to Language Testing - Development, Evaluation,*

Research. Newbury House.

Hughes, A., 1989. *Testing for Language Teachers*. Cambridge University Press.

Lienert, G. A., Raatz, U., 1994, *Testaufbau und Testanalyse*. (5. neuerbearb. und erw. Aufl.), Weinheim: Beltz, Psychologie Verlags Union.

Oller Jnr., J. W., 1979. *Language Tests at School*. Longman.

Vogt, W. P., 1993. *Dictionary of Statistics and Methodology*. Sage Publications.

Weir, C. J., 1990. *Communicative Language Testing*. Prentice-Hall.

Wright, B. D. and Masters, G. N., 1982. *Rating Scale Analysis (Rasch Measurement)*. Mesa Press, Chicago.

Appendices

Appendix 1 List of Acronyms

Appendix 2 Computer Programs

Appendix 1 List of Acronyms

ACTFL/ILR Oral Proficency The American Council on the Teaching of Foreign Languages

ASLPR Australian Second Language Proficiency Ratings

CALL Center for the Advancement of Language Learning

CALT Computer Adaptive Language Testing

CAT Computer Adaptive Testing

EAP English for Academic Purposes

EFL English as a Foreign Language

ELTS English Language Testing System

EOP English for Occupational Purposes

ESL English as a Second Language

ESP English for Specific Purposes (or: English for Special Purposes)

ETS Educational Testing Service

FSI Foreign Service Interview

IELTS International English Language Testing System

ILR Inter-Agency Language Round Table

IRT Item response theory

LSP Language for Specific Purposes (or: Language for Special Purposes)

OPI Oral Proficiency Interview

RSA Royal Society of Arts

SOPI Semi-direct/Simulated Oral Proficiency Interview

TEFL Teaching English as a Foreign Language

TESOL Teachers of English to Speakers of Other Languages

TOEFL Test Of English as a Foreign Language

UCLES University of Cambridge Local Examinations Syndicate

Appendix 2 Computer Programs

BIGSTEPS

This program performs Rasch analysis. It handles dichotomous and scalar data, and allows the user to specify a variety of analysis parameters.

ORIGIN MESA Press
University of Chicago

BILOG

This program uses Item Response Theory to analyse test data. It will estimate parameters for the 1-, 2- and 3- parameter models.

ORIGIN Scientific Software Inc.,
Mooresville, Indiana, USA

FACETS

This program performs multi-faceted Rasch analysis. An example of this is a writing test where ratings are believed to depend on the ability of the candidate, the difficulty of the task and the severity of the rater.

ORIGIN MESA Press
University of Chicago

ITEMAN

This item analysis program uses classical procedures.

ORIGIN Assessment Systems Corporation
St Paul, Minnesota

LISREL (Analysis of LI(near) S(tructural) REL(ationships) by Maximum Likelihood, Instrumental Variables, and Least Squares Methods).

This program is for investigating structural equation models - variously referred to as simultaneous equation systems, linear causal analysis, path analysis, dependence analysis, etc.

ORIGIN: Scientific Software Inc. (original program) ,
Mooresville, Indiana, USA in SPSS
SPSS Inc., Chicago, Illinois, USA

LOGIST

This program uses Item Response Theory to analyse test data. It will estimate parameters for the 1-, 2- and 3- parameter models.

ORIGIN Educational Testing Service
Princeton, New Jersey

MicroCAT

The MicroCAT Testing System is a microcomputer-based system for developing, administering, scoring and analyzing computerized tests. The components of the system are grouped into four subsystems - the Development, Examination, Assessment, and Conventional Testing Subsystems - each representing a set of related programs or functions.

ORIGIN Assessment Systems Corporation
St. Paul, Minnesota

OPLM

This program package consists of a a family of computer programs amongst which the only commercially available program that allows to take full advantage of the specific properties of the Rasch Model, i. e., statistical valid tests of fit are available. The package contains many options such as the Marginal Maximum Likelihood estimation and Conditional Maximum Likelihood estimation. The program handles dichotomous and scalar data and an option to vary the discrimination parameter. Many additional features ranging from data handling to testing bias are available to the user.

ORIGIN CITO,
Dutch National Institute for Education Measurement

QUEST

This program performs traditional and rasch test analyses. It can be used to construct and validate variables based on both dichotomous and polychotomous observations.

ORIGIN The Australian Council for Educational Research
Radford House
Frederick Street
Hawthorn
Victoria 3122
Australia

RASCAL

This item analysis program uses IRT procedures.

ORIGIN Assessment Systems Corporation
St Paul, Minnesota